Indians
JOURNAL

Year by Year & Day by Day with the Cleveland Indians Since 1901

Indians JOURNAL

JOHN SNYDER

For further information, contact the publisher at:

Clerisy Press
1700 Madison Road
Cincinnati, OH 45206
www.clerisypress.com

Library of Congress Cataloging-in-Publication Data

Snyder, John, 1951–
Indians journal : year by year & day by day with the Cleveland Indians since 1901
John Snyder.
p. cm.
ISBN-13: 978-1-57860-308-4
ISBN-10: 1-57860-308-0
1. Cleveland Indians (Baseball team)—History. I. Title. II. Title: Year by year & day by day with the Cleveland Indians since 1901.
GV875.C7S59 2008
796.357'640977132—dc22

2008001184

Distributed by Publishers Group West
Printed in the United States of America
First edition, first printing
Edited by Jack Heffron
Cover designed by Stephen Sullivan
Interior designed by Mary Barnes Clark

Front cover photo © Elsa/Getty Images
Back cover photos:
Left: Rocky Colavito (Cleveland State University Library, Special Collections)
Center: Omar Vizquel (Cleveland Indians)
Right: Jim Thome (Cleveland Indians)

Thanks to the following for permission to use photos in this book:
Greg Rhodes: 19
Dennis Goldstein: 58, 63, 69, 125, 132, 200
The Cleveland Indians: 536, 560, 578, 600, 617, 629, 644, 659, 672, 683
All other photos courtesy of The Cleveland State University Library, Special Collections.

About the Author

John Snyder has a master's degree in history from the University of Cincinnati and a passion for baseball. He had authored 16 books on baseball, soccer, tennis, football, basketball, hockey, and travel and lives in Cincinnati.

Acknowledgments

This book is part of a series that takes a look at Major League Baseball teams. The first was *Redleg Journal: Year by Year and Day by Day with the Cincinnati Reds Since 1866*, the winner of the 2001 Baseball Research Award issued by *The Sporting News* and SABR. That work was followed by *Cubs Journal: Year by Year and Day by Day with the Chicago Cubs Since 1876, Red Sox Journal: Year by Year and Day by Day with the Boston Red Sox Since 1901* and *Cardinals Journal: Year by Year and Day by Day with the St. Louis Cardinals since 1882*. Each of these books is filled with little-known items that have never been published in book form.

Greg Rhodes was my co-author on *Redleg Journal*, in addition to publishing the book under his company's name Road West Publishing. While Greg did not actively participate in the books about the Cubs, Red Sox, Cardinals, or Indians, he deserves considerable credit for the success of these books because they benefited from many of the creative concepts he initiated in *Redleg Journal*.

The idea for turning *Redleg Journal* into a series of books goes to Richard Hunt, president and publisher of Emmis Books and its successor company Clerisy Press, and editorial director Jeff Heffron. For photos I am grateful to the Cleveland Indians, to Vern Morrison of the Digital Production Unit of the Cleveland State University Library, and to Dennis Goldstein.

I would also like to thank the staff at the Public Library of Cincinnati and Hamilton County. The vast majority of the research for this book came from contemporary newspapers and magazines. The library staff was extremely helpful with patience and understanding while retrieving the materials for me, not only for this book but for all of my other endeavors as well. Dick Miller deserves thanks for providing me with material from his personal collection of baseball books. Dick was a lifelong friend of my father, who passed away in 1999, and installed in me a love of both history and baseball.

And finally, although they should be first, thanks to my wife, Judy, and sons Derek and Kevin, whose encouragement and support helped me through another book.

Contents

Part One: Indians Day by Day

Part Two: Indians by the Numbers

Day
by
Day

When Does Time Begin?

The Cleveland Indians first season as a major league franchise was in 1901. Prior to that, however, the city had a long and colorful history that includes four different franchises in four different leagues during the 19th century.

The first prominent team in Cleveland was the Forest Citys, which was formed in 1868 as a strictly amateur outfit that included some of the city's leaders of industry and politics. A year later, the club began to use paid professionals among its members. That same year, baseball's first all-professional team was conceived in Cincinnati and named the Red Stockings. The Red Stockings traveled to Cleveland on June 2, 1869, to play the Forest Citys on Case Common, an unfenced field located on present day East 38th Street between Central and Community College Avenues. A crowd of 2,000 paid 25 cents for the privilege of watching the Forest Citys lose 25–6. The Red Stockings made a return visit on August 6 and won 43–20. But the Cleveland club faired better than many of the Red Stockings' opponents. Undefeated in 1869, the Red Stockings won games by scores such as 80–5 and 103–8. The Forest Citys continued to play through the 1870 season, and on May 17 defeated the Atlantics of Brooklyn 132–1 in a contest that mercifully ended after five innings.

Cleveland's Major League Teams During The 19th Century

1871 Forest Citys (National Association)

Finish	Won	Lost	Pct.	GB
Seventh	10	19	.345	11.5

Manager

Charlie Pabor

The Forest Citys in 1871 joined the National Association, which is considered to be baseball's first organized league. The organization consisted of nine teams located as far east as Boston and as far west as Keokuk, Iowa. The Forest Citys played their games on a lot bounded by Ensign Street, East Willson Avenue (later 55th Street), Sheridan (later Grand) Avenue, and Warrensville (later Kinsman Road).

The Forest Citys participated in the first game played in the National Association, which was therefore the first major league game in history. It was played on May 4 against the Kekiongas in Fort Wayne, Indiana. The Forest Citys lost 2–0.

The most prominent player on the 1871 Forest City club was James "Deacon" White, who played in Cleveland from 1869 through 1872 at the start of a long and distinguished career. A native of Buffalo, White drew his nickname from his pious manner in a rough-and-tumble era. Being called Deacon shouldn't be mistaken for a lack of toughness, however. His primary position was catcher at a time when all players played their positions barehanded. After the Forest Citys folded at the end of the 1872 season, White played on five consecutive pennant winners in Boston and Chicago in both the National Association and National Leagues. His last major league season was in 1890 at the age of 42.

1872 Forest City (National Association)

Finish	Won	Lost	Pct.	GB
Seventh	6	16	.273	20.5

Managers

Scott Hastings (6–14) and Deacon White (0–2)

A 10–19 record in 1871 was followed by a 6–16 mark in 1872. The Forest Citys disbanded on August 19, failing to finish the season.

The National Association dissolved at the close of the 1875 campaign. Scheduling was piecemeal, contract jumping rampant, betting openly flaunted at the ballparks, and rowdiness abounded. The National League was formed in February 1876. The organization insisted on a strict schedule, drawn up by the league instead of the teams, with heavy fines imposed for any club that failed to play its games. Each club would respect the contracts of the others. Open betting was prohibited, along with the sale of alcohol at the ballparks. Cleveland, however, would not field a club in the National League until 1879.

1879 Blues (National League)

Finish	Won	Lost	Pct.	GB
Sixth	27	55	.329	31.0

Manager

Jim McCormick

Cleveland returned to major league status in 1879 with a team in the National League. The club was named the Blues because of the color of the uniforms. The Blues played on a lot bounded by Silby (later Carnegie) Avenue, Kennard (later 46th) Street, Cedar Avenue, and East 49th Street. There were trees in the outfield in 1879, and the distance to left field in 1880 and 1881 was so short that balls hit over the fence were doubles.

The Blues were managed by Jim McCormick, who was just 22 years old and was also the team's star pitcher. McCormick pitched in 62 of Cleveland's 85 games in 1879, posting a record of 20–40 despite an ERA of only 2.42.

1880 Blues (National League)

Finish	Won	Lost	Pct.	GB
Third	47	37	.560	20.0

Manager

Jim McCormick

The 1880 club showed a vast improvement, landing in third place in an eight-team league. Jim McCormick started 74 of Cleveland's 85 games, and completed 74 of them. His 45 victories and 657⅔ innings topped the National League. Second baseman Fred Dunlap led the NL in doubles with 27, and the team also featured outfielder Ned Hanlon, playing the first season of what would become a Hall-of-Fame career.

The Blues were involved in a milestone when John Lee Richmond of Worcester pitched the first perfect game in major league history against Cleveland on June 12, winning 1–0.

1881 Blues (National League)

Finish	Won	Lost	Pct.	GB
Seventh	36	48	.429	20.0

Managers

Mike McGeary (4–7) and John Clapp (32–41)

McCormick found it too difficult to pitch nearly every game and manage the club at the same time and was replaced first by Mike McGeary, and then by John Clapp. Both were player-managers. McGeary was a third baseman and Clapp a catcher. In May, a local gambler tried to bribe Clapp $5,000 to throw a game. When he reported the incident to police, Clapp earned the nickname "Honest John." Despite his honesty, the Blues compiled a losing record under his guidance.

1882 Blues (National League)

Finish	Won	Lost	Pct.	GB
Fifth	42	40	.512	12.0

Managers

Jim McCormick (0–4) and Fred Dunlap (42–36)

The Blues returned to their winning ways under new manager Fred Dunlap, who was also the club's slick-fielding second baseman. Jim McCormick was again the workhorse of the pitching staff, starting 67 of the Blues 84 games, pitching 595 2/3 innings and winning 36 times. He missed the game against the Chicago White Stockings (the present day Cubs) on July 24, however. Dave Rowe, normally an outfielder, was pressed into service and allowed 35 runs in a 35–4 loss. The 35 runs is the all-time major league record for runs allowed in a game by a single pitcher that probably will stand for all eternity.

1883 Blues (National League)

Finish	Won	Lost	Pct.	GB
Fourth	55	42	.567	7.5

Manager

Frank Bancroft

For the first time, the Blues hired an individual who was not a player to manage the team. Frank Bancroft was a 37-years-old Civil War veteran who had volunteered to serve in the Union Army at the age of 16. He had previously managed Worcester in 1880 and Detroit in 1881 and 1882 without significant success. The Blues improved under Bancroft, but he was let go at the end of the season. In 1884, Bancroft managed Providence to the National League pennant. He later served as business manager of the Cincinnati Reds from 1892 until his death in 1921. Bancroft also helped pioneer baseball in Cuba, beginning with a visit to that country in 1879. He had a lifelong fascination with Cuba, and while with the Reds he brought the first two Cuban-born players to the major leagues in 1911.

There were several important incidents involving the Blues in 1883. The club visited the White House, where they were greeted by President Chester Arthur on April 3. They were the victims of a no-hitter on July 25 when Old Hoss Radbourne, a future Hall of Famer, beat Cleveland 8–0 on July 25. Hugh "One Arm" Daily was the first Cleveland major league pitcher to throw a no-hitter, defeating the Phillies 1–0 on September 13. Like many players of his generation, Daily was a native of Ireland who came to the United States as a youngster. Before his major league career began, Daily lost his left hand in a gun accident, which required amputation at the wrist, thus earning his unusual nickname. He compensated by fashioning a pad covering his wrist. Daily fielded his position by trapping the ball between the pad and his good hand. Nothing is known of Daily's life after baseball. The date of his death is still a mystery despite diligent research.

1884 Blues (National League)

Finish	Won	Lost	Pct.	GB
Seventh	35	77	.313	49.0

Manager

Charlie Hackett

Under new manager Charlie Hackett, the Blues completely came apart at the seams in 1884, compiling a record of 35–77. The team was hampered greatly when Jim McCormick, Fred Dunlap, Jack Glassock, and One Arm Daily, Cleveland's four best players, left the Blues to sign contracts with Union Association clubs. At the end of the season, the Brooklyn franchise in the American Association (the present day Los Angeles Dodgers) bought the Blues and transferred the best players to Brooklyn. For the next two years, there would be no major league baseball in Cleveland.

1887 Spiders (American Association)

Finish	Won	Lost	Pct.	GB
Eighth	39	92	.298	54.0

Manager

Jimmy Williams

Cleveland streetcar magnate Frank DeHaas Robison and his brother Stanley brought major league ball back to Cleveland with a club in the eight-team American Association, an organization created in 1882 to compete with the National League. The Robisons owned two streetcar lines on Payne and Superior Avenues. It made good business sense to build a ballpark on one of the lines, and the brothers did so on the corner of Payne and East 39th Street. The Cleveland team also earned the nickname Spiders because of the gangly and spindly appearance of many of the players. The lack of brawn may have contributed to the Spiders finishing dead last in the league.

1888 Spiders (American Association)

Finish	Won	Lost	Pct.	GB
Sixth	50	82	.379	40.5

Managers

Jimmy Williams (20–44) and Tom Loftus (30–38)

There was improvement in 1888, but the club still compiled a record of 50–82. The most memorable game took place on June 6 when Cleveland defeated Louisville 23–19. With Sunday baseball illegal in Cuyahoga County, the Spiders played four home games on Sundays at Beyerle's Park in Geauga Lake, 20 miles southeast of the city and just across the county line.

Jersey Bakely took the mound 61 times for the team and compiled 25–33 record with a 2.97 ERA. Shortstop Ed McKean led the team in nearly every offensive category. At the end of the season, the Detroit franchise of the National League folded. Cleveland was offered a chance to join the more prestigious NL and owner Frank Robison jumped at the opportunity.

1889 Spiders (National League)

Finish	Won	Lost	Pct.	GB
Sixth	61	72	.459	25.5

Manager

Tom Loftus

Rejoining the National League under manager Tom Loftus, who took over as manager in mid-season in 1888, the Spiders continued to show improvement but not enough to get over the .500 mark. The high point came on August 17 when Cleveland scored 14 runs in the third inning, still a major league record for that frame, in a 20–6 win over Washington. Larry Twitchell achieved another milestone on August 15 by becoming the only Cleveland player during the 19th century to hit for the cycle. He collected six hits in that contest, including three triples, and scored five runs.

Twitchell, a Cleveland native, led the Spiders in triples with 11 and in RBIs with 95, but the club's best hitter that year again was little shortstop Ed McKean, who compiled a .318 average, which was seventh in the league. McKean played 12 seasons in Cleveland and from 1893 through 1896 was one of the top hitters in the game.

The Players League was formed during a tumultuous 1889–90 off-season. The new league grew out of dissatisfaction among players over their salaries and contracts. Cleveland was one of eight cities chosen to field teams in the PL. Cub Stricker, Patsy Tebeau, Jimmy McAleer, Henry Gruber, and Jersey Bakely, all regulars with the 1889 Spiders, joined the Cleveland team in the Players League.

1890 Spiders (National League)

Finish	Won	Lost	Pct.	GB
Seventh	44	88	.333	43.5

Managers

Gus Schmelz (21–55) and Bob Leadley (23–33)

The Spiders lost too much talent to the Players League to compete in the National League and sank to 44–88. The season was noteworthy, however, for the major league debut of Cy Young on August 6. He was 9–7 in 1890 as a 23-year-old rookie and would go on to a career in which he posted 511 victories, the majority of which he recorded with Cleveland teams. Young won 241 times with the Spiders from 1890 through 1898, and 29 more with the Indians from 1909 through 1911. Another future Hall of Framer also began a long career with the Spiders that year. George Davis—a hard-hitting, 19-year-old outfielder—led the team with 22 doubles and 73 RBIs. Davis would go on to play 20 years in the major leagues and was elected to the Hall of Fame in 1998.

1890 Infants (Players League)

Finish	Won	Lost	Pct.	GB
Seventh	55	75	.423	26.5

Managers

Henry Larkin (34–45) and Patsy Tebeau (21–30)

The Players League club in Cleveland in 1890 fared little better than their National League counterparts, but the team did boast some interesting characters. Outfielder Pete Browning won the PL batting title with a .373 average. Browning compiled a lifetime batting average of .341 over 13 seasons but is best remembered for starting the customized bat industry. In 1884, while playing for Louisville, Browning walked into J. F. Hillerich's wood shop and complained of a batting slump. Hillerich manufactured a bat to Browning's liking. Pete broke out of the slump and extolled the virtues of his personalized bat throughout baseball. In a short time, Hillerich's wood shop grew into Hillerich & Bradsby, the world's largest bat manufacturer and the maker of the Louisville Slugger.

Willie McGill was a 16-year-old pitcher who compiled a record of 11–9. A year later, with Cincinnati and St. Louis in the American Association, he was 20–14 to become the youngest 20-game winner in big league history. McGill had issues with sobriety, however, and finished his career in 1896 with 71 wins and 73 losses.

Outfielder Ed Delahanty was a Cleveland native who jumped to the Players League after two seasons with the Phillies. He returned to Philadelphia in 1891 and went on to become one of the greatest hitters in baseball history. Delahanty had a .346 lifetime batting average when he died under mysterious circumstances on July 2, 1903, while playing for the Washington Senators. Delahanty left the club in Detroit and boarded a train headed for New York. Drinking heavily, he was put off the train in Niagara Falls, Ontario, after brandishing a razor at some passengers. Delahanty tried to cross the bridge into the United States but fell into the river and his body was swept over Niagara Falls.

Ed was one of five Delahanty brothers to reach the majors. All were born in Cleveland. The others were Frank, Jim, Joe and Tom. Tom played 16 games for the Spiders in 1896 and Frank appeared in 15 contests for the Indians in 1907.

1891 Spiders (National League)

Finish	Won	Lost	Pct.	GB
Fifth	65	74	.468	22.5

Managers

Bob Leadley (34–34) and Patsy Tebeau (31–40)

The Players League folded at the end of the 1890 season, leaving Cleveland with one team again. Before the season started, the Spiders participated in a baseball milestone. On April 3, the club played the Pirates in St. Augustine in the first spring training game between two major league teams in Florida.

When the Spiders moved north, they played at a new ballpark known as League Park, located at Lexington Avenue and East 66th Street, which the Robison brothers built on their streetcar lines. The site would be used by the Spiders until 1899 and by the Indians from 1900 until 1946.

Patsy Tebeau, who had played third base for the Spiders in 1889 but bolted to the Players League in 1890, returned to the Spiders in 1891 and was named manager in mid-season. The move was too late to salvage the 1891 campaign, but Tebeau would lead Cleveland baseball to its first successful period. He would manage the club until 1898, and while the Spiders never finished a season in first place, the club had winning seasons seven years in a row and finished second in a 12-team league in 1892, 1895, and 1896.

The 1890s were characterized by rough, even dirty, baseball with many managers encouraging players to bend every rule and challenge every call. Brawling became commonplace. A tough and aggressive leader, Tebeau was at the forefront of these tactics.

1892 Spiders (National League)

Finish	Won	Lost	Pct.	GB
Second	93	56	.624	8.5

Manager

Patsy Tebeau

After ten years of existence, the American Association folded during the 1891–92 off-season. Four of the eight clubs in the AA were absorbed into the National League, giving the circuit 12 clubs. It was also made the NL the only major league, a situation that would exist until 1901. The 154-games schedule in 1892 was split into two halves, with the winner of each half meeting in a post-season series. With the exception of the strike-interrupted 1981 season, the 1892 campaign was the only time that a major league had two pennant races in a season.

The Spiders finished in fifth place in the first half with a 40–33 record, 11½ games behind Boston, a franchise that is the present day Atlanta Braves. Cleveland topped the league in the second half by winning 53 and losing only 23. The Spiders met Boston in the post-season competition, which was called the Temple Cup. It was a best-of-nine affair with Boston winning five with one tie and the Spiders failing to capture a single victory.

Second baseman Cupid Childs led the National League in runs (136) and on base percentage (.443). Cy Young was 36–12. His winning percentage of .750 topped the majors as did his nine shutouts and 1.93 earned run average. The team also included Hall of Famers John Clarkson, George Davis, and Jesse Burkett, who was known as "Crab" for his chronically sour disposition.

1893 Spiders (National League)

Finish	Won	Lost	Pct.	GB
Third	73	55	.570	12.5

Manager

Patsy Tebeau

Baseball changed in 1893 with the introduction of the 60 feet, six inch pitching distance. Previously pitchers stood 55 feet from home plate. As a result, the National League batting average increased from .245 in 1892 to .280 in 1893 and runs per team per game leaped from 5.1 to 6.6.

Hopes were high in Cleveland after the strong finish by the Spiders in 1892, but the club slipped back to third in 1893. Cupid Childs led the league in on base percentage for the second year in a row with a figure of .463. Ed McKean finished second in the RBI race with 133. Cy Young posted a record of 34–16.

Young was one of four players on the 1893 Spiders who would be elected to baseball's Hall of Fame. The others were Jesse Burkett, John Clarkson, and Buck Ewing.

1894 Spiders (National League)

Finish	Won	Lost	Pct.	GB
Sixth	68	61	.527	21.5

Manager

Patsy Tebeau

There has never been a season with more offense in baseball than 1894. The Spiders averaged 7.2 runs per game and had a team batting average of .303, but were in the bottom half of the NL in both categories. National League clubs averaged 7.4 runs per game and compiled a batting average of .309.

The Spiders had three players who topped .350 in batting average that year, with Cupid Childs, Ed McKean, and Jesse Burkett all exceeding that mark. With the help of a pitching staff that was second in the league in earned run average, Cleveland spent 33 days in first place early in the season, but a 9–14 June and a 9–15 August burst any hopes for a pennant. The best single-game achievement was a six-hit performance by catcher Chief Zimmer in a ten-inning, 15–10 win over Washington on July 11.

1895 Spiders (National League)

Finish	Won	Lost	Pct.	GB
Second	84	46	.646	3.0

Manager

Patsy Tebeau

The Spiders spent much of the 1895 season in a tight pennant race that was so close in July that the club leaped from sixth place to first in a span of two days. The Spiders led the National League by 2½ games at the end of July but were caught and surpassed by the Orioles in September. Baltimore, with a cast that included future Hall of Famers Willie Keeler, Joe Kelley, John McGraw, Hughie Jennings, and Wilbert Robinson, won the title by three games with the Spiders landing in second. From 1893 through 1897, the first and second place teams in the National League met in the post-season series called the Temple Cup. The second place Spiders stunned the champion Orioles four games to one to take the Cup.

Cleveland outfielder Jesse Burkett led the NL in batting average (.409) and hits (225). Cy Young led the league in victories with a 35–10 record. Ed McKean led the team in doubles (32), triples (17), and RBI (119) while compiling a .342 batting average.

1896 Spiders (National League)

Finish	Won	Lost	Pct.	GB
Second	80	48	.625	9.5

Manager

Patsy Tebeau

The Spiders were in first place in the NL for 35 days but fell out of the race with a 10–12 record in August and finished 9½ games behind the Orioles. Cleveland and Baltimore met in the Temple Cup series for the second year in a row, but the Orioles avenged their 1895 defeat by sweeping the Spiders in four straight games.

Jesse Burkett was even better in 1896. He led the National League in batting average (.410), hits (240), runs (160), and total bases (317). Cy Young was outstanding again with a 28–15 record and topped a pitching staff that led the league in earned run average. Fellow hurler "Nig" Cuppy achieved his third 20-win season in a row, finishing 25–14 with a 3.12 ERA, lowest on the team. Cupid Childs and Ed McKean once again turned in excellent seasons, continuing to be one of the most productive keystone combinations in the league.

1897 Spiders (National League)

Finish	Won	Lost	Pct.	GB
Fifth	69	62	.527	23.5

Manager

Patsy Tebeau

The Spiders began a decline in 1897, falling to fifth place. At 33 years of age, Ed McKean started to lose his skills, and several other stars were beginning to fade. There was a new star, however, in outfielder Louis Sockalexis, an American Indian from Maine. He was 25 when he reached the majors and had attended college at both Holy Cross and Notre Dame. Sockalexis was a sensation during the first half of the season and became one of the most popular players in baseball. The newspapers began calling the team the Indians instead of the Spiders. But in July, Sockalexis injured his ankle, and during a period of inactivity, began drinking heavily. He barely played during the second half of the season, and finished the campaign with a .338 batting average in 66 games.

Sockalexis appeared in only 21 games in 1898 and seven more in 1899 before the Spiders let him go. He died in 1913. Cleveland's American League baseball was given the name of Indians in January 1915 in part because of the legend of Louis Sockalexis.

1898 Spiders (National League)

Finish	Won	Lost	Pct.	GB
Fifth	81	68	.544	21.0

Manager

Patsy Tebeau

The Spiders finished fifth again in 1898 with an aging club that posted a 15–22 record after the end of August. With four starters over the age of 30, the team continued to decline. Jesse Burkett shined once again but was the only starter to hit over .300. Jack Powel, a young hurler in only his second season in the majors, teamed with 31-year-old Cy Young to give the Spiders a powerful 1–2 punch, with Powel winning 23 games and Young 25.

Despite fielding strong teams that were often in the pennant race during most of the 1890s, the Spiders never were a drawing card in Cleveland. The club played most of the last two months of the season on the road, including three "home" games in Rochester, New York. In the 12-team National League, the club ranked seventh in attendance in 1892, tenth in 1893, 11th in 1894, 1895, and 1896, last in 1897, and 11th in 1898.

1899 Spiders (National League)

Finish	Won	Lost	Pct.	GB
Twelfth	20	134	.130	84.0

Managers

Lave Cross (8–30) and Joe Quinn (12–104)

In 1899, there was no rule against an individual owning more than one team in the National League. The Spiders were headed by Frank Robison and his brother Stanley, who were concerned over the lack of attendance in Cleveland. On March 14, they bought the St. Louis club, then known mostly as the Perfectos (now the Cardinals). Every year from 1892 through 1898, the Perfectos outdrew the Spiders despite putting a vastly inferior product on the field. St. Louis was also a larger city, with a population just about 600,000, while Cleveland contained less than 400,000 people. The Robisons decided on a novel strategy. Even though they were Cleveland natives and had amassed a fortune operating streetcars in the city, the brothers would transfer the best players on the Spiders roster to St. Louis in an attempt to field a strong club in a larger market. Among those who were sent from Cleveland to St. Louis were future Hall of Famers Cy Young, Jesse Burkett, and Bobby Wallace, along with other stars such as Cupid Childs, Ed McKean, Jack Powell, Nig Cuppy, and even player-manager Patsy Tebeau.

The St. Louis team, a last-place club with a 39–111 record in 1898, leaped to 84–67 in 1899 with the infusion of new talent. The Spiders, 81–68 in 1898, became the worst team in the history of baseball in 1899, winning only 20 times while losing a major league record 134. Naturally Clevelanders, who failed to show in significant numbers with a winning club, stayed away from League Park. The Spiders played only 42 of their 154 games in Cleveland, and drew slightly more than 6,000 fans, an average of about 150 per contest. There were only eight home games after July 3, as the club played almost exclusively on the road. The demoralized and exhausted Spiders lost 55 of their last 58 games. The club was outscored 1,252 to 529.

Jim Hughey and Charlie Knepper tied for the club lead in pitching victories. Hughey had a record of 4–30 while Knepper was 4–22. The team's most productive hitter was 34-year-old second baseman Joe Quinn, who led in hits, doubles, RBI, and average.

The franchise disbanded on March 8, 1900 when the National League reduced its membership from 12 teams to eight. At about the same time, the American League was forming with designs on eventually becoming a major league to compete with the National League, then entering its 25th season. Cleveland was granted one of the American League franchises.

Cleveland's Best Players During The 19th Century

The following is an alphabetical listing of the top Cleveland players who appeared in a uniform for one of the clubs representing the city during the 19th century. Only a player's time spent in Cleveland is considered when compiling the list.

Jesse Burkett, left fielder (1891–98)

A future Hall of Famer, Burkett holds single season records for Cleveland major leaguers by hitting .410 with 160 runs and 240 hits in 1896. He also batted over .400 in 1895 with an average of .405. Overall, Burkett's average was .355 in eight seasons with the Spiders. He is one of only three players in major league history to bat over .400 in a season.

Burkett drew the nickname "Crab" or often "The Crab," because of his constant barbs and caustic complaints. He had a ferocious temper and took offense very easily. Throughout his career he insulted rivals, fans, and even teammates and would fight at the slightest provocation.

Cupid Childs, second baseman (1891–98)

Clarence "Cupid" Childs was the second baseman and lead-off hitter on the pennant-contending Spiders clubs of the 1890s. He annually ranked among the NL leaders in on-base percentage, walks, and runs. In 1893, Childs drew 120 base on balls while striking out only 12 times. A year later he batted .353.

Exactly why he received the nickname of Cupid remains a mystery. Some say it was because of his cherubic features. Others claim it was a result of a lovable personality. There is also the assertion that it was a sarcastic response to an unlovable disposition. One thing that is documented is Childs's central role in many of the vicious brawls in which the Spiders become embroiled during the 1890s.

Nig Cuppy, pitcher (1892–98)

George "Nig" Cuppy was the Spiders number-two starter behind Cy Young during much of the 1890s. He won 24 or more games in four seasons and was 139–80 during his seven years in Cleveland.

Cuppy was tagged with a nickname that would be highly offensive today. Players with dark complexions were often given racists names during the early years of professional ball.

George Davis, center fielder (1890–92)

Davis played in Cleveland at the start of a 20-year big league career. He gained a long overdue selection to baseball's Hall of Fame in 1998. Davis earned a plaque in Cooperstown based mainly on his work as a shortstop, a position he began playing with regularity with the Giants in 1897. In Cleveland, Davis was a center fielder with occasional forays at third base.

The Spiders made a huge miscalculation in 1893 by trading Davis to the Giants for Buck Ewing. Ewing was one of the greatest players of the era and would also gain admission to the Hall of Fame, but he was 11 years older than Davis and was nearly washed up at the time of the transaction. After leaving Cleveland, Davis played 17 more seasons included an appearance in the World Series in 1906 with a White Sox club, known as the "Hitless Wonders," that upset the Cubs in the only all-Chicago Fall Classic in history.

Fred Dunlap, second baseman (1880–83)

Dunlap played for the Blues during the first four years of a 12-year career. Nicknamed "Sure Shot" because of his fielding abilities, Dunlap is considered by some sources to be the best second baseman of the 1880s. With shortstop Jack Glassock, Dunlap was part of what was billed in the newspapers of the period as the "Stonewall Infield." He led the National League in doubles as a 21-year-old rookie in 1880 and in games played in both 1880 and 1882.

When the Union Association was formed during the 1883–84 off-season as a third major league to compete with the National League and the American Association. Dunlap signed with the St. Louis club of the UA for $3,400, which made him the highest-paid player in baseball. He responded by leading the UA in batting average, runs, hits, and home runs. Both the UA and the Blues folded after the 1884 season and Dunlap closed out his career with five different teams, one of them the 1887 National League champion Detroit Wolverines.

Jack Glassock, shortstop, (1879–84)

Glassock was one of baseball's premier shortstops during the 19th century. He earned the nickname "Pebbly Jack" for his habit of picking up and tossing away pebbles while at his position in the field to minimize bad hops. He played bare handed, was one of the first to use a signal to inform his catcher which middle infielder would cover second on a steal, and was one of the first to back up throws to the second baseman. Over the course of a 17-year big league career, Glassock led the NL six times in both fielding average and assists.

Glassock left Cleveland in mid-season in 1884 for the salary inducements of the Union Association. The Cincinnati club in that organization offered to increase his salary from $1,800 to $2,500. Glassock lost on the deal, however, because he had to pay a $1,000 fine to be allowed to play again in the National League after the Union Association folded at the end of the 1884 campaign. Glassock played in the majors until 1897 and although he never played on a pennant-winner, "Pebbly Jack" led the NL in hits in 1889 and 1890 and batting average in 1890.

Pete Hotaling, center field (1880, 1883–84, 1887–88)

Hotaling had three stints with Cleveland clubs as a starting center fielder. He was involved in a serious incident on May 13, 1880, in an outfield collision with teammate Al Hall. Hotaling came out of it unscathed, but Hall suffered a broken leg. At the time, injured players drew no salary, and the Blues and Cincinnati Reds played a benefit game for Hall four days later and raised $500. Hall never played in another game and died in a mental institution in 1885.

Jimmy McAleer, center fielder (1889–98)

Never a great hitter, McAleer was the Spiders starting center fielder for ten seasons because of his abilities on defense. When the American League was established in 1900, McAleer was named as the manager of the Cleveland franchise and was still on the job a year later when the AL gained major league status.

Jim McCormick, pitcher (1879–84), manager (1879–80, 1882)

Jim McCormick was born in Glasgow, Scotland, in 1856 and emigrated to the United States with his family as a youngster, though little is known about his early life. He was not only the star pitcher of the Cleveland Blues in their inaugural season of 1879, he was also the manager even though he was only 22 years old.

During McCormick's time in Cleveland, pitchers were required by rule to throw from a position below the waist. Also, pitchers stood 50 feet from home plate. The motion and the distance put less strain on a pitcher's arm than today's parameters. But even by the standards of the 1880s,

The Forest Citys meet the Cincinnati Red Stockings for a game in Cleveland on May 31, 1870.

McCormick was a workhorse. He pitched $546\frac{1}{3}$ innings in 1879, $657\frac{2}{3}$ in 1880 (to lead the National League), 526 in 1881 and $595\frac{2}{3}$ in 1882, which led the NL a second time. Those four seasons combined, McCormick started 73 percent of the Blues games. He had won-lost records of 45–28 in 1880, 36–20 in 1882 and 28–12 in 1883. McCormick's numbers would have been more incredible if he had played on clubs that won more often. The Blues never finished higher than fourth during his years with the club.

Like Fred Dunlap and Jack Glassock, McCormick succumbed to the more lucrative salary offers of the Union Association. In mid-season in 1884, McCormick signed with the Cincinnati club in the UA, where he compiled a record of 21–3.

Both the Union Association and the Blues folded at the end of the 1884 campaign. McCormick hooked up with the Chicago White Stockings (the present day Chicago Cubs), and helped that franchise to National League pennants in 1885 and 1886 with records of 20–4 and 31–11. When his days in the majors ended in 1887, McCormick had a lifetime mark of 265–214.

Ed McKean, shortstop (1887–98)

McKean joined the Spiders as a 22-year-old rookie in 1887, and played 12 years with the club. His 1,588 games with the club rank higher than all Indians players with the exception of Terry Turner (1,625) and Nap Lajoie (1,614). One of the better hitting shortstops of his generation, McKean also had more at-bats (6,621), runs (1,187) and triples (155) as a Spider than anyone who has ever played for the Indians since the franchise was established as a major league entity in 1901. Only Lajoie had more hits than McKean, and only Earl Averill drove in more runs. Overall, McKean had a batting average of .304 in Cleveland with a high of .357 in 1894.

In an era marked by brawling and umpire-baiting, McKean was one of the roughest and toughest. In 1892, he accidentally shot himself in the finger with a revolver but was playing again in less than a month. In the aftermath of a brawl in Louisville in June 1896, McKean was hauled into court along with manager Patsy Tebeau and three teammates and was fined $75 for disturbing the peace.

Bill Phillips, first baseman (1879–84)

Phillips was the starting first baseman during the entire six-year run of the Cleveland Blues in the National League. He stood an even six-feet tall and weighed 202 pounds, which was huge for the era. A native of St. John's, New Brunswick, Canada, Phillips led the NL in games played in both 1880 and 1881. When the Blues were sold to the Brooklyn franchise of the American Association during the 1884–85 off-season, Phillips went to Brooklyn (the present day Los Angeles Dodgers) for three seasons.

Patsy Tebeau, first baseman and third baseman (1889–98), manager (1891–98)

Tebeau took over as manager of the Spiders in mid-season in 1891, and he led them to seven consecutive winning seasons from 1892 through 1898. The club finished second in a 12-team league in 1892, 1895, and 1896. Tebeau was a flamboyant and aggressive leader on the field, and modest and unassuming off of it. He insisted on maximum effort from his players. "Show me a team of fighters," he once said, "and I'll show you a team with a chance."

After the Robison brothers purchased the Cardinals in 1899, Tebeau was transferred to St. Louis, his hometown, as player-manager. He was fired in mid-season in 1900. After his playing days ended, Tebeau opened a saloon in St. Louis. In 1918, he was suffering from heart disease and committed suicide, shooting himself with a revolver he had tied to his right wrist.

Bobby Wallace, third baseman (1894–98)

Wallace played in Cleveland during the first five seasons of a 25-year, Hall of Fame playing career. He debuted in 1894 as a pitcher but was moved to third base in 1897 and batted 335. Wallace was one of those sent to the Cardinals after the Robison brothers bought the club in 1899. The Cards made him a shortstop. Wallace played the last 20 seasons of his career in St. Louis, 15 of them with the Browns.

Cy Young, pitcher (1890–98)

Denton True (Cy) Young established records that will never be broken. He won 511 career games, nearly 100 more than anyone else who has taken the mound in a big league game. Walter Johnson is a distant second with 417. Young is also the record holder in innings pitched with 7,356, far ahead of second place Pud Galvin, who had 5,951⅓. Young also tops the list in games started (815) and complete games (749). Remarkable control was one of the keys to his success. Young led his league in fewest walks per nine innings 13 times.

A native of Newcomerstown, Ohio, Young made his big league debut with the Spiders in 1890. Known as a gentleman and often praised for his sportsmanship among his brawling contemporaries, Young was 241–135 with the club through 1898. He became one of the players transferred from Cleveland to St. Louis in 1899 when the Robisons brothers bought the team. After two years in St. Louis, Young jumped to the American League and the Boston Red Sox, and played there for eight seasons. Following a trade in 1909, he returned to Cleveland with the Indians and posted a 19–15 record. Young closed out his career in 1911 with the Boston Braves. When combining his years with the Spiders and Indians, Young ranks first among Cleveland major league pitchers in wins (270), complete games (430), and innings pitched (3,857). Among his victories was a no-hitter against Cincinnati on September 18, 1897.

Young died in 1955. The next year the annual award for the best pitcher in baseball was given for the first time and bore his name. Beginning in 1967, two Cy Young Awards were granted, with one pitcher honored from each league.

Chief Zimmer, catcher (1887–99)

Zimmer is the only individual to play for the Spiders in each of the 13 seasons of their existence in the middle of a 19-year big league career. The finest defensive catcher of his day, he caught 943 games in a Cleveland uniform, many of them with legendary Cy Young on the mound.

Zimmer was the first catcher to play directly behind the batter on every play. Previously, catchers would move farther back of the plate with runners on base to better guard against wild pitches. Playing forward, he was better able to better throw out base stealers and the style was quickly adapted by other receivers. Zimmer also put raw steak in his mitt to lessen the sting of fastballs.

THE STATE OF THE INDIANS

The Indians were 697–632 during the first nine seasons that the American League was recognized as a major league (1901–09). The winning percentage of .524 was the third best in the league during that period, trailing only the Chicago White Sox and Philadelphia Athletics. Although Cleveland had several pennant contenders during the decade, the club fell short of finishing the season in first place. The Indians had the best run differential (runs scored minus runs allowed) in the American League in 1904, 1906, and 1908, but it wasn't enough for a World Series berth. AL pennant winners were the White Sox (1901 and 1906), Athletics (1902, 1904 and 1905), Red Sox (1903) and Tigers (1907, 1908 and 1909).

THE BEST TEAM

The 1908 Indians were 90–64 and just missed winning Cleveland's first AL pennant, finishing just one-half game behind the Tigers.

THE WORST TEAM

The worst team was the first one in 1901, which was 54–82 and ended the season in seventh place.

THE BEST MOMENT

The best moment was the arrival of Nap Lajoie in 1902. A crowd of 10,000 turned out for Lajoie's Cleveland debut on Wednesday June 4, 1902. It was an astounding crowd for a weekday game during the period when attendance was usually under 2,000.

THE WORST MOMENT

The Indians lost an opportunity to win their first American League pennant in 1908, finishing one-half game behind the Tigers. Detroit had a record of 90–63, while the Indians were 90–64. The difference was a rained-out game between the Tigers and Senators in August. In those days, teams were not required to make-up postponed games if they occurred in the last series of the season between the two clubs, even when the contest had a bearing on the pennant race.

THE ALL-DECADE TEAM • YEARS W/INDIANS

Player	Years
Harry Bemis, c	1902–10
George Stovall, 1b	1904–11
Nap Lajoie, 2b	1902–14
Bill Bradley, 3b	1901–10
Terry Turner, ss	1904–18
Bill Hinchman, lf	1907–09
Harry Bay, cf	1902–08
Elmer Flick, rf	1902–10
Addie Joss, p	1902–10
Bob Rhoads, p	1903–09
Earl Moore, p	1901–07
Bill Bernhard, p	1902–07

Lajoie, Flick, and Joss are in the Hall of Fame. Other outstanding Indians during the decade were first baseman Charley Hickman (1902–04, 1908), center fielder Joe Birmingham (1906–14), pitcher Otto Hess (1902, 1904–08), and catcher Nig Clarke (1905–10).

THE DECADE LEADERS

Category	Player	Total
Batting Avg:	Nap Lajoie	.336
On-Base Pct:	Nap Lajoie	.381
Slugging Pct:	Nap Lajoie	.462
Home Runs:	Bill Bradley	27
RBIs:	Bill Bradley	637
Runs:	Nap Lajoie	566
Stolen Bases:	Elmer Flick	206
Wins:	Addie Joss	155
Strikeouts:	Addie Joss	871
ERA:	Addie Joss	1.87
Saves:	Addie Joss	5

THE HOME FIELD

League Park, located on a plot on East 66th Street, between Lexington and Linwood, was the site of major league baseball in Cleveland from 1891 through 1947. It was first utilized by the National League Spiders, owned by Frank and Stanley Robison, from 1891 through 1899. It was readily accessible on streetcar lines owned by the Robisons. When the Spiders ceased to exist after a dismal 1899 season in which the club posted a record of 20–134, the American League moved in and established a franchise in Cleveland. The new club was the second to occupy League Park. When the ballpark was constructed, the grandstands were all wood and consisted of a single deck behind home plate, a covered pavilion behind first base, and a small bleacher section. The distance to the left field bleachers was 375 feet, and 460 feet to dead center. The right field line was only 290 feet long because the owners of a saloon and two adjacent houses on Lexington Avenue refused to sell their property. Many fans reached the ballpark on Euclid Avenue, which was four blocks to the south and connected to downtown. By 1909, the avenue was known as "Millionaire's Row" and boasted some 250 mansions. Among those who lived on Euclid was oil magnate John D. Rockefeller. In 1910, the wooden grandstand was replaced by a double-decked ballpark built with concrete and steel.

THE GAME YOU WISH YOU HAD SEEN

In the heat of the 1908 pennant race, Addie Joss pitched a perfect game against the White Sox at League Park on October 2, winning 1–0. In one of the greatest pitching duels in history, Chicago hurler Ed Walsh fanned 15 batters.

THE WAY THE GAME WAS PLAYED

In this decade of pitching and defense, the AL set all-time lows in ERA and batting average. In 1908, the AL batting average was .239 and the earned run average was 2.39. In part, this was the result of a 1903 rule that counted all foul balls as strikes. The merits of the foul-strike rule was hotly debated for years afterward. Offense started a gradual decline that was not reversed until the introduction of the cork-center ball in 1910.

THE MANAGEMENT

The original owners of the Indians were John Kilfoyl and Charles Somers. Kilfoyl was installed as president with Somers as vice-president. After Kilfoyl retired in 1908, Somers assumed the presidency, a position he held until 1916. Somers was also a major financier of the Boston Red Sox, Philadelphia Athletics, and St. Louis Browns in the new American League. Somers, in fact, was majority owner of the Red Sox in 1901 and 1902. At the time, ownership of more than one major league club was permitted. The practice was banned in 1910. Ernest Barnard was hired as the Indians business manager in 1903 to help run the front office, and was promoted to vice-president in 1908. He was an employee of the Indians until 1927. Field managers were Jimmy McAleer (1901), Bill Armour (1902–04), Bill Bradley (1905), Nap Lajoie (1905–09), and Deacon McGuire (1909–11).

THE BEST PLAYER MOVE

The best player move was the deal that brought Nap Lajoie and Bill Bernhard from the Athletics for Ossee Schreckengost and Frank Bonner in June 1902.

THE WORST PLAYER MOVE

The worst trade sent Charlie Hemphill to the Browns on May 30, 1902, for a player to be named later. Red Donahue was received in exchange in 1903 but was not adequate compensation. The worst player move, however, was the *failure* to make a trade. During spring training in 1908, the Tigers offered to trade Ty Cobb to the Indians for Elmer Flick, but Cleveland management declined the offer.

The Birth of the Indians

The creation of the Cleveland Indians and the American League as major league entities are due to the vision, energy, and perseverance of former Cincinnati sportswriter Ban Johnson and the money of Cleveland coal baron Charles Somers. The American League had its genesis in November 1893, when a new minor league called the Western League was formed in Grand Rapids, Sioux City (Iowa), Minneapolis, Milwaukee, Kansas City, Toledo, Indianapolis, and Detroit. With the backing of Cincinnati Reds owner John Brush, who had an interest in the Indianapolis franchise, Johnson was asked to head the Western League as president, treasurer, and secretary.

At the time, the National League was baseball's only major league. It had prior competition from the American Association, which existed from 1882 through 1891, the Union Association in 1884, and from the Players League, which lasted only the 1890 season. The National League, from 1892 through 1899 was a 12-team circuit with clubs in Baltimore, Boston, Brooklyn, Chicago, Cincinnati, Cleveland, Louisville, New York, Philadelphia, Pittsburgh, St. Louis, and Washington. The Cleveland club, nicknamed the Spiders, had been in the NL since 1889.

Like many monopolies, the National League had grown arrogant during the 1890s. Tight controls were placed on the players, including a maximum salary of $2,400. Competitive balance was almost non-existent. Meanwhile Johnson's Western League had grown stronger each year as the top circuit in the minor leagues. Johnson harbored ambitions to jettison the smaller cities in the organization, place clubs in larger Eastern metropolises, and create a second major league.

The National League reduced its roster from 12 to eight in March 1900 by dropping clubs in Baltimore, Cleveland, Louisville, and Washington. This gave Johnson room to expand to achieve his aspirations. Within days after the contraction of the National League, Johnson changed the name of his organization to the American League. Teams in Grand Rapids, Sioux City, and Toledo were replaced by new ones in Chicago, Cleveland, and Buffalo. Many players were without jobs because of the reduction of four clubs in the National League, and cast their lot with the American League.

The new Cleveland club was owned by John Kilfoyl and Charles Somers, two men in their thirties. Kilfoyl owned a men's clothing store and was also involved in his family's real estate business. Somers was in the coal business with his father. Kilfoyl was installed as president-treasurer and Somers as vice-president. The club was nicknamed the Blues and played at League Park, a facility previously used by the Spiders on 66th Street between Lexington and Linwood. The manager was Jimmy McAleer, who played as an outfielder with the Spiders from 1889 through 1898.

Although the American League in 1900 was still confined to the Midwest and Great Lakes area and was considered a minor league, Johnson had plans to expand to the Eastern Seaboard. Shortly after the end of the 1900 season, Johnson announced plans for his American League to become a second major league to compete with the Nationals. The franchises in Minneapolis, Kansas City, Buffalo, and Indianapolis were eliminated in favor of those in the larger Eastern cities of Baltimore, Boston, Philadelphia, and Washington. Johnson wrote a letter in late-October 1900 to National League president Nick Young seeking peace and an arrangement in which each league would respect the contracts of the other, which would prevent player raids and escalating salaries. The National League immediately rejected the plan. The league owners had vanquished all previous opposition and had no doubt that the American League would soon follow into oblivion.

Johnson retaliated by announcing that his new American League would attempt to sign the top players in baseball away from the NL. They certainly found a receptive audience. Players were not only saddled with a maximum salary of $2,400, they had to pay for their uniforms and other basic amenities.

The task of Johnson and Somers to place a team in Cleveland was daunting. The city had been a graveyard of a succession of major league teams during the 19th century. The first was the Cleveland Forest Citys, which began playing professionally during the summer of 1869 on Putnam (now East 38th Street) between Scovill and Central (now Central Community) avenues. The Forest Citys were a part of the National Association, baseball's first league, in 1871. The Cleveland club was not a success artistically or financially and disbanded a year later. The National Association broke apart in 1875. The National League filled the void and began play with eight teams in 1876.

A young businessman named William Hollinger organized a team in Cleveland that joined the NL in 1879. This outfit was also called the Forest Citys and built a ballpark at Kennard (now East 46th Street) at Cedar Avenue. After a 35–77 record in 1884, the Forest Citys dropped out of the league.

Cleveland's third major league club was the Spiders, owned by Frank and Stanley Robison, a pair of brothers who became wealthy by building streetcar lines in Cleveland. The Spiders were a part of the American Association and played on Payne Avenue at East 39th Street. In 1889, the Spiders joined the National League. In 1890, Cleveland had two major league clubs, with the second one a part of the Players League. The PL folded after just one season, and the Spiders were again the only team in town. League Park was built by the Robisons in 1891 on one of the streetcar lines. Its location on East 66th Street would be the site of Cleveland baseball until 1947.

The Spiders never won a National League pennant but were strong contenders during most of the 1890s. Despite the success on the field, the club was usually near the bottom of the league in attendance. The Robisons despaired of ever making a profit on baseball in Cleveland.

At the time, it was legal for an individual to own more than one major league club. The Robisons bought the Cardinals and transferred most of Cleveland's best players to their new venture in St. Louis, including future Hall of Famers Cy Young, Jesse Burkett and Bobby Wallace. As a result, the Cleveland Spiders became the worst team in big league history, posting a record of 20–134. Due to sparse attendance at League Park, the Spiders played only 41 home games.

The new Cleveland franchise in the AL began play only months after the demise of the Spiders. In 1900, Cleveland was 64–73 and landed in sixth place in the eight-team league. Our story begins with the 1901 campaign, the Indians first as a major league club.

What is an Indian?

For the purposes of simplicity and consistency, Cleveland's major league baseball is called the "Indians" throughout this book. A fan of the club prior to 1915 would be thoroughly confused by the name "Indians," however, because it wasn't until that year that the nickname was coined. It came about in a meeting between club officials and sportswriters on January 16, 1915. It was one of a long line of nicknames attached to Cleveland's professional baseball teams, including:

Forest Citys (1869–75)
The Forest Citys were Cleveland's first professional team. The organization became part of the National Association (baseball's first league) in 1871. The National Association and the Forest Citys disbanded after the 1875 season.

Blues (1879–84)
Major league baseball returned to Cleveland in 1879 with a club in the National League. It was named the Blues because of the predominate color of the team's uniforms. The Blues disbanded following the 1884 season due to poor attendance.

Spiders (1888–99)
The Spiders were a member of the American Association in 1888 and 1889 and the National League from 1890 through 1899. The unusual nickname was the idea of a sportswriter who noted the "spindly appearance" of many of the players on the club. That the name "Spiders" originated in a newspaper was typical of the period. Many of the most famous nicknames in baseball, such as Cubs,

Reds, Yankees, Dodgers, Giants, Braves, Phillies, Pirates, Cardinals, Orioles, and Tigers were created not by the clubs themselves but by an enterprising sportswriter. The names eventually caught the imagination of the public and began to be used in everyday speech until it became part of the team's identity.

Indians (1897–98)

The Spiders were also named the Indians in 1897 and 1898 because of the presence of outfielder Louis Sockalexis, a Penobscot Indian from Maine. He was an immediate sensation, becoming one of baseball's top drawing cards as a rookie with his speed, strong arm, and ability to hit for both average and power. He batted .338 in 66 games before being sidelined with an ankle injury. The injury and a fondness for alcohol wrecked his career. Sockalexis played in only 28 games after 1897 and batted just .236. He died of alcoholism in 1913 at the age of 42, and his death and the tale of his tragic career was a big story in sports pages around the country.

The National League reduced its membership from 12 teams to eight in March 1900 and the Cleveland franchise was one of the four eliminated. Within days, a new team was formed in the city and became a part of the American League. This was the birth of the present day Indians franchise. It took more than a decade, however, before the 'Indians' nickname was attached to the club. Other nicknames included:

Blues/Bluebirds (1900–08)

At first, the club had no official name. The nicknames used most often in the newspapers during the early years were Blues and Bluebirds because of the blue color of the uniforms and the former National League club of 1879 through 1884.

Bronchos (1902)

The players hated the nickname Bluebirds, considering it to be unmanly. They asked the writers to use the Bronchos (pronounced BRON-kos) as a nickname for the club. Some writers used it in their stories, but the Wild West theme seemed inappropriate for Cleveland and never caught on with the fans. Bronchos also took up too much space in newspaper headlines.

Naps (1903–14)

The *Cleveland Press* announced a new contest in the spring of 1903 to decide on a new nickname for the club and invited fans to vote. Results of the balloting were announced with the following totals reported: Naps 365 votes; Buckeyes 281; Emperors 276; Metropolitans 239; Giants 223; and Cyclops 214. Trailing in order of votes were Terrors, Pashas, Dachshunds, Majestics, Mastodons, Midgets, Tip Tops, Crackerjacks, and Prospectors. The nickname Naps was in honor of star second baseman Nap Lajoie, who joined the club in June 1902. Many other Cleveland newspapers, including the *Plain Dealer*, continued to call the club Blues and Bluebirds until at least 1908.

Lajoie was sold to the Philadelphia Athletics on January 5, 1915, requiring the Cleveland club to find a new nickname. Club officials and sportswriters met eleven days later to decide on a name, and Indians was the consensus choice.

The January 18, 1915, edition of the *Plain Dealer* clarified the decision. "Many years ago there was an Indian named Sockalexis who was the star player of the Cleveland team," reported the paper. "As batter, fielder, and base runner he was a marvel. Sockalexis so far outshone his teammates that he naturally came to be regarded as the whole team. The 'fans' throughout the country began to call the Clevelanders the 'Indians.' It was an honorable name, and while it stuck the team had an excellent record. It has now been decided to revive this name. The Cleveland's of 1915 will be the 'Indians.' There will be no real red Indians on the roster, but the name will recall fine traditions. It is looking backward to a time when Cleveland had one of the most popular teams of the United States. It also serves to revive the memory of a single great player who has gathered to his fathers in the happy hunting grounds of the Abenakis." The last sentence referred to Sockalexis's death on Christmas Eve in 1913. Henry Edwards, reported in *The Sporting News* that "the choice is but temporary, however, but will be made permanent if no better cognomen is thought of before the season is over, it being the wish that the team would go out and make a name for itself."

There were likely other influences as well. Five other AL clubs (Boston Red Sox, Chicago White Sox, Philadelphia Athletics, St. Louis Browns, and Washington Senators) had nicknames that were derived from 19th century teams that pre-dated the creation of the American League. Many professional and amateur teams of the period adopted nicknames with Native Americans themes. Only three months before the Cleveland club assumed the nickname Indians, the Boston Braves won the 1914 World Series over the Philadelphia Athletics in a stunning upset. The Braves were in last place in the National League in late-July before soaring to win the pennant. This came during a season in which the Cleveland ball club posted a record of 51–102, a winning percentage of .333 that is still the worst in franchise history. According to a story in the *Cleveland News*, "One Cleveland fan, James Thayer, thinks the Indians may emulate the example of the National League counterparts, the Boston Braves, and show just as much reversal of form as the Braves did in 1914." Many Native Americans athletes were also in the news. The most prominent was Jim Thorpe, who won the decathlon and pentathlon in the 1912 Olympics. And, anyone in 1915 over the age of 30 could remember hearing and reading first-hand accounts of the "Indian Wars" in the newspapers, which ended only as recently as 1890, and many knew, or were, soldiers who had fought with the U.S. military in the wars.

With political correctness far in the future, there was no controversy over calling the club the Indians in 1915. That would come about in the 1970s when many Native Americans began to protest the use of Indian-themed nicknames for professional and amateur clubs (see January 15, 1972). While many universities and high schools have changed their nicknames due to the objections of Native Americans, owners of the Cleveland Indians have not seriously contemplated changing the name of the club.

1901

Season in a Sentence

In their first season as a major league team, the Indians are not a success, finishing seventh in an eight-team league and ranking last in attendance.

Finish • Won • Lost • Pct • GB

Finish	Won	Lost	Pct	GB
Seventh	54	82	.397	29.0

Manager

Jimmy McAleer

Stats

Stats	Indians	AL	Rank
Batting Avg:	.271	.277	6
On-Base Pct:	.313	.333	8
Slugging Pct:	.348	.371	7
Home Runs:	12		8
Stolen Bases:	125		8
ERA:	4.12	3.66	8
Fielding Avg:	.942	.938	4
Runs Scored:	667		7
Runs Allowed:	831		8

Starting Line-up

Bob Wood, c
Candy LaChance, 1b
Erve Beck, 2b
Bill Bradley, 3b
Frank Schiebeck, ss
Jack McCarthy, lf
Ollie Pickering, cf
Jack O'Brien, rf-lf
Erwin Harvey, rf-lf
George Yeager, c

Pitchers

Earl Moore, sp
Pete Dowling, sp
Bill Hart, sp
Ed Scott, rp
Jack Bracken, sp
Bill Hoffer, sp
Harry McNeal, sp

Attendance

131,380 (eighth in AL)

Club Leaders

Batting Avg:	Ollie Pickering	.309
On-Base Pct:	Ollie Pickering	.383
Slugging Pct:	Bill Bradley	.403
Home Runs:	Erve Beck	6
RBIs:	Erve Beck	79
Runs:	Ollie Pickering	102
Stolen Bases:	Ollie Pickering	36
Wins:	Earl Moore	16
Strikeouts:	Earl Moore	99
	Pete Dowling	99
ERA:	Earl Moore	2.90
Saves:	Bill Hoffer	3

April 24 The Indians play their first game as a major league club and lose 8–3 to the White Sox in Chicago. Starting pitcher Bill Hoffer put Cleveland in a hole early by allowing two runs in the first inning and five in the second. The Indians line-up in the first game consisted of Ollie Pickering, right field; Jack McCarthy, left field, Frank Genins, center field; Candy LaChance, first base; Bill Bradley, third base; Erve Beck, second base; Bill Hallman, shortstop; Bob Wood, catcher; and Hoffer, pitcher. Hallman played only five games with the Indians before being traded to the Milwaukee Brewers.

The April 24 meeting between the Indians and the White Sox is recognized as the first in the history of the American League. The first batter in AL history was Pickering, who flied out to center field on the second pitch from Chicago hurler Roy Patterson. Three other games were scheduled that day, but each was rained out.

April 25 Indians second baseman Erve Beck hits the first home run in American League history, although the Indians lose 7–3 to the White Sox in Chicago. The drive cleared the right field fence. It was Beck's first major league homer. The pitcher was John Skopec.

April 27 After losing their first two games, the Indians earn the first victory in club history by defeating the White Sox 10–4 in Chicago. Bill Hart was the winning pitcher.

Hart had a 7–11 record with the Indians in 1901, his last year in the majors. He finished the season as an American League umpire. After several seasons officiating in the minors, Hart was also a National League ump in 1914 and 1915.

April 28 Making his major league debut, Indians pitcher Bock Baker gives up a record 23 singles during a 13–1 loss to the White Sox in Chicago. On the first Sunday of the season, a total of 16,500 jammed into South Side Park, which overflowed the stands. The excess ringed the outfield. By a pre-game agreement, it was decided that any ball hit into the multitude would be a ground-rule single. All 23 Chicago hits were singles, and Baker surrendered each one while pitching a complete game.

The April 28 contest was the only one that Baker pitched in a Cleveland uniform. He appeared in only one more big league, that with the Athletics later in the 1901 season. Baker pitched 14 innings in the majors and allowed 24 runs, 12 of them earned, and 29 hits for an 0–2 record and a 7.71 ERA.

April 29 The Indians play the first regular season home game in club history, and defeat the Milwaukee Brewers 4–3 before 8,000 at League Park. Cleveland overcame a 3–1 deficit by scoring three runs in the eighth.

The Indians hit just 12 home runs in 1901, and oddly, none of them were hit in 69 home games. The pitching staff allowed 13 home runs at home and nine on the road.

May 9 Earl Moore holds the White Sox hitless for the first nine innings of a game before a crowd of only 400 at League Park but winds up losing 4–2. In the fourth inning, the White Sox put runners on second and third with an error, a walk, and a sacrifice. In an attempt to pick Fielder Jones off third, Moore threw the ball past the bag and both runners scored. The contest went into extra innings with the score 2–2 and Chicago still looking for its first hit. In a drizzling rain, Sam Mertes broke Moore's spell by leading off the tenth with a single. Mertes moved to third on another single by Fred Hartman. Frank Shugart hit a slow roller to shortstop Danny Shay, who threw to the plate. Mertes slid under the tag for the go-ahead run. Later, Hartman scored on an infield out, and the White Sox held on for the win.

MAY 17 The Indians lose their 11th game in a row by dropping a 6–4 decision to the Detroit Tigers at League Park.

The loss dropped Cleveland's record to 4–17, which dampened fan enthusiasm. The Indians finished last in the major leagues in attendance. The club's lack of success was due in large part to a failure to sign as many quality players away from the National League as most of the other American League clubs. The only regulars on the 1901 Indians who were also regulars in the NL in 1900 were Jack McCarthy, Bill Bradley, and Ed Scott. McCarthy and Bradley were lured away from the Cubs and Scott from the Reds.

MAY 23 The Indians put together a sensational rally in the ninth inning by scoring nine runs in the ninth inning after the first two batters are retired to defeat the Washington Senators 14–13 at League Park. The batting onslaught set a major league record that still stands for most runs scored in the ninth inning with two out and no one on base. Heading into the ninth, Cleveland trailed 13–5. Bill Hoffer started the inning by striking out, and Ollie Pickering grounded out. Jack McCarthy singled to right field, and Bill Bradley followed with another single. Candy LaChance, with two strikes, singled McCarthy home for the first run. Bob Wood was hit by a pitch to load the bases. Frank Schielbeck doubled in two runs and Frank Genins contributed an RBI-single to make the score 13–9. At this point, Washington manager Jimmy Manning relieved pitcher Casey Patten with Watty Lee. Truck Eagan walked, and Erve Beck, pinch-hitting for Hoffer, doubled. The score was now 13–12. Pickering tied the score with a single. Some enthusiastic fans couldn't contain themselves and ran onto the field, threatening a forfeit. After the field was cleared, Pickering went to second on a passed ball and scored on a walk-off single by McCarthy.

MAY 24 The day after winning a game by scoring nine runs in the ninth inning, the Indians blow a big lead against the Senators at League Park. Cleveland held a 5–0 advantage heading into the ninth before allowing Washington to score five times. The Indians failed to dent the plate in the bottom half, and the contest went into the books as a 5–5 tie when called due to darkness at the end of the ninth.

MAY 25 In a game at League Park that begins in a snowstorm, the Indians suffer the first shutout loss in club history with a 5–0 defeat at the hands of Red Sox pitcher Fred Lewis.

MAY 30 The Indians play two games in one day for the first time and lose twice to the Philadelphia Athletics at League Park. It was a split admission double header, with one game in the morning and one in the afternoon. In the opener, Philadelphia won 3–1. In the second tilt, called after eight inning by darkness, the Indians lost 8–2.

MAY 31 The Indians lose a 15–14 slugging match to the Athletics at League Park. Philadelphia led 10–0 in the second inning before Cleveland mounted a comeback that fell just short.

JUNE 8 The Indians wallop the Orioles 13–5 in Baltimore.

JUNE 10 The Indians rout the Orioles again, winning 13–6 in Baltimore.

JUNE 12 Earl Moore pitches the first shutout in Indians history, winning 5–0 against the Senators in Washington.

JUNE 30 Pete Dowling pitches a one-hitter to defeat the Brewers 7–0 in Milwaukee. The only hit off Dowling was an infield hit by Wid Conroy. Third baseman Bill Bradley fielded the ball cleanly, but his throw to first base was late.

Dowling started the season with the Brewers before being traded to Cleveland in May with a 1–3 record. He was 11–22 with the Indians in 1901, his last season in the majors and still holds the club record for most losses in a season. Cleveland's only other 20-game loser is Luis Tiant, who was 9–20 in 1969. The date of Dowling's birth is unknown. He died in 1905 when he was decapitated by a train while walking between the Oregon towns of Hot Lake and LaGrande.

JULY 13 The Indians lose a 19–12 slugfest against the Tigers in Detroit. Manager Jimmy McAleer pitched the eighth inning after Pete Dowling was ejected by umpire John Haskell.

JULY 16 After the Red Sox score five runs in the ninth inning to defeat the Indians 10–8 at League Park, umpire Al Manassau is pelted with cushions and bottles. It was only through the efforts of the Cleveland players, who protected Manassau, that he was not mobbed.

JULY 17 For the second day in a row, an umpire draws the wrath of the Cleveland faithful at League Park. After a 9–3 and 10–2 double-header loss to the Red Sox, Tom Connolly needed police protection to leave the ball yard.

Connolly was the only umpire on the field, a common practice during the early 1900s.

JULY 20 Open season on umpires continues as Tom Connolly once more needs police to help him safely leave League Park following a 9–7 loss to the Senators.

JULY 23 The Indians win a forfeit against the Senators at League Park. Washington manager Jimmy Manning pulled his team from the field after Cleveland's Jack O'Brien was called safe on a close play at the plate that tied the score 4–4 in the ninth inning. When the Senators refused to return to the field, umpire Tom Connolly declared the forfeit. The Washington club left the field just ahead of a howling mob.

AUGUST 2 Pete Dowling pitches a one-hitter against the Brewers in Milwaukee for the second time in 1901, winning 7–0. The lone hit off Dowling was a single by Bill Hallman.

AUGUST 3 Cleveland pitcher Ed Scott wins his own game with a tenth-inning homer to defeat the Brewers 8–7 in Milwaukee. It was the first extra-inning home run in

Indians history. After making several questionable calls in favor of Cleveland, umpire Al Manassau was escorted from the ballpark by police when threatened by fans.

The homer came in Scott's last big league at-bat. The Indians released him a few days later, and he never appeared in the majors again.

AUGUST 7 Cleveland pitcher Jack Bracken hits a two-run, walk-off double in the ninth inning to beat the Brewers 5–4 at League Park. The drive by Bracken landed just fair down the left field line. Milwaukee players disagreed, claiming the ball was foul, and rushed at umpire Al Manassau. Brewers player-manager Hugh Duffy landed a right on the umpire's jaw. Two other Milwaukee players threw punches at Manassau before order was restored.

The Brewers moved to St. Louis in 1902 and were renamed the Browns.

AUGUST 12 The Indians lose 17–2 to the White Sox at League Park.

AUGUST 13 Earl Moore pitches a one-hitter to defeat the White Sox 4–0 in the first game of a double header at League Park. In the second contest, Chicago players collected 22 hits off Harry McNeal in defeating the Indians 14–1.

AUGUST 31 The Indians score nine runs in the seventh inning and hammer the Senators 16–4 in the first game of a double header at League Park. Washington won the second game, called after five innings by darkness, 2–0.

SEPTEMBER 3 The Indians win both ends of a double header against the Red Sox at League Park with shutouts. In the opener, Earl Moore pitched a two-hitter to win 1–0. Boston pitcher Fred Lewis also threw a two-hitter. Cleveland scored in the sixth inning on two Red Sox errors. In the nightcap, Bill Cristall made his major league debut and shut out the Red Sox 4–0.

Cristall pitched only five more big league games and lost all five. He finished his brief career in the majors with a 1–5 record and a 4.84 ERA.

SEPTEMBER 15 The Indians suffer the worst shutout loss in club history with a 21–0 humiliation at the hands of the Tigers at Detroit in a contest called after seven innings to allow the Indians to catch a train. Jack Bracken pitched a complete game for Cleveland and allowed 23 hits.

SEPTEMBER 19 The Indians game against the Athletics in Philadelphia is postponed by the funeral of President William McKinley. He was shot by Leon Czolgosz at a reception in Buffalo on September 6 and died on September 14. Theodore Roosevelt became the new President.

SEPTEMBER 21 The Indians set an American League record for most errors in a double header with 16. Playing the Senators in Washington, the Indians committed seven errors in the opener and lost 18–7. Although the second encounter lasted only six innings because of darkness, Cleveland fielders found enough time to make nine errors in an 11–3 defeat. The seven first-game errors were made by seven different players. Ten players committed errors during the twin bill.

1902

Season in a Sentence

Cleveland baseball takes a dramatic turn for the better with the arrival of future Hall of Famers Nap Lajoie, Elmer Flick, and Addie Joss.

Finish • Won • Lost • Pct • GB

Finish	Won	Lost	Pct	GB
Fifth	69	67	.507	14.0

Manager

Bill Armour

Stats

Stats	Indians	AL	Rank
Batting Avg:	.289	.275	1
On-Base Pct:	.336	.331	3
Slugging Pct:	.389	.369	2
Home Runs:	33		4 (tie)
Stolen Bases:	140		4
ERA:	3.28	3.57	2
Fielding Avg:	.950	.949	5
Runs Scored:	686		5
Runs Allowed:	667		6

Starting Line-up

Harry Bemis, c
Charley Hickman, 1b
Nap Lajoie, 2b
Bill Bradley, 3b
John Gochnauer, ss
Jack McCarthy, lf
Harry Bay, cf
Elmer Flick, rf
Ollie Pickering, cf
Bob Wood, c

Pitchers

Earl Moore, sp
Addie Joss, rp
Bill Bernhard, sp
Clarence Wright, sp

Attendance

275,395 (fifth in AL)

Club Leaders

Batting Avg:	Charley Hickman	.378
On-Base Pct:	Charley Hickman	.399
Slugging Pct:	Charley Hickman	.559
Home Runs:	Bill Bradley	11
RBIs:	Charley Hickman	94
Runs:	Bill Bradley	104
Stolen Bases:	Ollie Pickering	22
	Harry Bay	22
Wins:	Three tied with	17
Strikeouts:	Addie Joss	106
ERA:	Bill Bernhard	2.20
Saves:	Three tied with	1

April 23 The Indians lose the season opener 5–2 to the Browns in St. Louis. The Browns scored all five of their runs in the third inning.

For the second straight season, the Indians were off to a bad start, losing 24 of their first 35 games. The new manager in 1902 was Bill Armour, who replaced Jimmy McAleer. Armour was 32-years-old and had never played in the majors. He served as Cleveland's manager for three seasons. McAleer later managed the St. Louis Browns from 1902 through 1909 and the Washington Senators in 1910 and 1911. He was also part-owner of the Red Sox in 1912 and 1913.

April 25 Ervin Harvey collects six singles in six at-bats during a 10–0 victory over the Browns in St. Louis. In all, Cleveland registered 21 hits.

Ervin (Zaza) Harvey played in only 76 major league games, but he hit .332 in a promising career that ended at the age of 23 by injuries. Before being acquired by the Indians from the White Sox in May 1901, Harvey pitched in 17 big league games. Gene Wright pitched the shutout in his debut with the Indians and his second appearance in the majors. The April 25 contest was Wright's only shutout in a Cleveland uniform. He was 10–20 with the club over two seasons.

April 26 In his major league debut, Addie Joss pitches a one-hitter to defeat the Browns 3–0 in St. Louis. The only hit off Joss was a controversial single by Jesse Burkett. Right fielder Ervin Harvey claimed he caught Burkett's drive three inches off the ground, but umpire Bob Caruthers disagreed and ruled it a trap.

April 28 Indians pitcher Luther (Dummy) Taylor pitches a 2–0 complete game win over the White Sox in Chicago.

Taylor was a deaf mute who jumped from the New York Giants to the Indians during the 1901–02 season. He pitched only four games in Cleveland but grew increasingly depressed because none of his teammates knew sign language. The Indians released Taylor, and he returned to the Giants to continue a big league career that lasted until 1908.

May 4 In his third big league start, Addie Joss hurls a two-hitter to beat the Tigers 2–1 in Detroit. Joss carried a no-hitter into the ninth inning before surrendering singles to Doc Casey and Dick Harley.

Had he not died at the age of 31 in 1911 from tubercular meningitis, Addie Joss might have been ranked among the greatest pitchers of all time. As it was, Joss compiled a lifetime record of 160–97 and an almost unbelievable career ERA of 1.89, which earned him admission into the Hall of Fame in 1978. His earned run average is the second best of all time. Joss's .257 opponent's on base percentage is the best of the modern era. Tall and gangly at six-foot-three and 185 pounds, Joss pitched with an exaggerated pinwheel motion that earned him the nickname "the Human Hairpin" and helped him baffle batters from the outset. He was 17–13 as a rookie. Among Indians pitchers, Joss still ranks first in ERA, first in shutouts (45), second in complete games (234), third in winning percentage (.623), sixth in wins, sixth in innings pitched (2,327), and ninth in strikeouts (920).

May 6 In the home opener, the Indians lose 6–3 to the White Sox before 11,749 at League Park.

May 7 The Indians purchase future Hall of Fame outfielder Elmer Flick from the Athletics.

Flick made his major league debut with the Philadelphia Phillies in 1898 and became an almost instant star. When the American League was formed in 1901, the Athletics tried to lure Flick to the new Philadelphia club with the promise of a higher salary, but he preferred to remain with the Phillies. The money proved to be too tempting, however, and Flick jumped to the Athletics before the start of the 1902 season. Flick played only 11 games with the A's before the Phillies secured an injunction preventing him from playing baseball in Pennsylvania for anyone but the NL club. In order to keep Flick in the American League, Athletics owner and manager Connie Mack sold him to the Indians. The sale was in part the return of a favor, because Cleveland owner Charles Somers had helped Mack financially. Flick was the first of three stars to move from the Athletics to the Indians in 1902 (see June 3, 1902). He became one of the best hitters in Indians history, batting .299 from 1902 through the end of his career in 1910.

May 13 Bob Wood hits a walk-off, two-run double in the ninth inning that defeats the Browns 4–3 at League Park.

May 17 The Indians pound the Tigers 14–0 at League Park.

May 18 The Indians lose a 19–11 slugfest to the Tigers in a contest at League Park called after seven innings by darkness.

May 22 The Indians slip past the Athletics 11–9 in Philadelphia.

May 24 The Indians explode for six runs in the 11th inning to defeat the Athletics 15–9 in Philadelphia, after the A's scored five runs in the ninth to tie the score 9–9.

A native of Cleveland, third baseman Bill Bradley hit homers in four consecutive games, each of them in a series against the Athletics in Philadelphia. It was a remarkable feat for the era. There were only 258 homers struck in 1,106 American League games in 1902. Bradley hit 11 home runs, along with a batting average of .340, 104 runs, 39 doubles, and 12 triples. He also had a 29-game hitting streak that still ranks as the third longest in club history. Bradley played for the Indians from 1901 through 1910, but an attack of typhoid fever in 1906 drastically reduced his effectiveness. He is credited with being the first third baseman to field bunts by grabbing them barehanded and throwing to first with the same motion. After his playing career ended, Bradley ran a tavern near League Park and scouted for the Indians for 25 years.

May 30 The Indians trade Candy LaChance to the Red Sox for Charley Hickman. On the same day, the Indians sent Charlie Hemphill to the Browns for a player to be named later.

Hickman had spindly legs on a five-foot-eleven, 215-pound body that earned him the nickname "Piano Legs." He proved to be an excellent acquisition, batting .378 with eight homers over the rest of the 1902 season. Despite Hickman's stellar hitting credentials, he was defensively challenged and played at eight different positions, none of them effectively. In 12 seasons, Hickman played on seven clubs, each of which failed to find a place for him on the field. The Indians received Red Donahue in exchange for Hemphill a year later. It was not adequate compensation. Donahue won 19 games for Cleveland in 1904, but it was his only good season with the club. Hemphill was a starting outfielder for the Browns and the Yankees until 1908.

June 3 The Indians trade Ossee Schreckengost and Frank Bonner to the Athletics for Nap Lajoie and Bill Bernhard.

Like the Elmer Flick deal a month earlier (see May 7, 1902), the Indians were able to obtain Lajoie and Bernhard because of litigation. Lajoie and Bernhard jumped from the Phillies to the Athletics before the 1901 season. Lajoie was the American League's best player in 1901, with a .426 batting average, 14 homers, 125 RBIs, and 145 runs. Bernhard was 17–10 for the A's. Due to an April 1902 injunction, Lajoie and Bernhard were prevented from playing for any team other than the Phillies in the state of Pennsylvania. Lajoie and Bernhard absolutely refused to rejoin the Phillies, and they risked damage suits if they played with the

Athletics, so they did neither for a month. Charles Somers approached Connie Mack and the two worked out a deal that brought Lajoie and Bernhard to Cleveland. The Phillies lawsuit against the two players was thrown out of court, though the restraining order against them appearing for any team other than the Phillies in Pennsylvania was upheld. Thus, in 1902, the Indians played games in Philadelphia without Lajoie and Bernhard.

JUNE 4 Nap Lajoie makes his debut with the Indians, a 4–3 win over the Red Sox before a crowd of 10,000 at League Park. He doubled in three at-bats.

Ranked as one of the greatest second basemen in baseball history, Napoleon (Nap) Lajoie played in the majors from 1896 through 1916. A native of Woonsocket, Rhode Island, of French-Canadian descent, he compiled a .338 batting average and collected 3,242 hits, 1,504 runs, 657 doubles, 163 triples, 82 homers, 1,599 runs-batted-in, and 380 stolen bases. Nap was a member of the Indians from 1902 through 1914 and managed the club between 1905 and 1909. In 1903, the Cleveland club was nicknamed the Naps in his honor. Among Indians batters, Lajoie is first in hits (2,046), at-bats (6,033), second in games (1,614), second in doubles (424), third in RBIs (919), third in batting average (.339), fourth in stolen bases (240), seventh in runs (865), and eighth in triples (78). In the first Hall of Fame balloting conducted by the Baseball Writers Association of America in 1936, Lajoie finished sixth. Only five (Ty Cobb, Babe Ruth, Honus Wagner, Christy Mathewson, and Walter Johnson) received the 75 percent of the vote necessary for induction, but Lajoie reached that figure in 1937.

JUNE 5 Red Sox pitcher Cy Young hits a fluke two-run homer off Addie Joss in the eighth inning to defeat the Indians 3–2 at League Park. The drive cleared the head of Charley Hickman and rolled under the left field scoreboard.

JUNE 6 Charley Hickman collects five hits, including a triple and a double, in five-bats during a 14–3 win over the Red Sox at League Park. The Indians had 21 hits in all.

JUNE 8 The Indians play a Sunday "home" game before a crowd of 4,900 at Fairview Park in Dayton, Ohio, and lose 6–2 to the Orioles in Baltimore.

Due to local laws, the Indians were not permitted to play in Cleveland on Sundays until 1911. In 1902 and 1903, the club played eight Sunday "home" games in other cities. There were three games in Canton, Ohio, two in Columbus, Ohio, two in Fort Wayne, Indiana, and one in Dayton.

JUNE 15 The Indians play a home game at Mahaffey Park in Canton, Ohio and lose 5–2 to the Red Sox.

JUNE 22 The Indians play a Sunday home game in Fort Wayne, Indiana and defeat the Senators 6–4 at a ballpark with the unusual name of Jailhouse Flats.

JUNE 24 In the sixth inning of a 12–4 win over the Browns at League Park, Nap Lajoie hits the first grand slam in Indians history. Bill Bernhard retired the first 18 batters to face him before allowing four runs and eight hits over the final three innings.

In 86 games with the Indians in 1902, Lajoie batted .379.

JUNE 30 Nap Lajoie, Charley Hickman and Bill Bradley hit consecutive homers during the sixth inning of a 12–2 win over the Browns in the first game of a double header in St. Louis. They were struck on three consecutive pitches from Jack Harper, and each drive landed in the left field bleachers. The second tilt went 15 innings before it was called by darkness with the score 3–3. Nap Lajoie appeared to hit a game-winning double in the tenth, but the umpire called it foul. Lajoie was ejected in the ensuing argument. Bill Bernhard of the Indians and Bill Reidy of the Browns each pitched complete games.

The back-to-back-to-back homers were the first by a major league club since 1894. It didn't happen again until 1922. The next time that three Indians hit homers in succession was June 25, 1939.

JULY 1 Addie Joss pitches a two-hitter to beat the Tigers 3–0 in Detroit. The only hits off Joss were singles by Doc Casey and Pop Dillon. A few disgruntled Detroit fans interrupted the contest in the eighth inning by throwing rocks at umpire Silk O'Loughlin after a call went against the Tigers.

JULY 6 Elmer Flick hits three triples during a 6–2 win over the White Sox in Chicago.

JULY 30 Earl Moore pitches the Indians to a 1–0 win over the White Sox at League Park. Elmer Flick drove in the winning run with a walk-off double in the ninth inning.

The game started over an hour late because of a train wreck on the Baltimore and Ohio line. The previous day, the Indians played in Baltimore and the White Sox in Washington. Both clubs were delayed until the accident could be cleared from the tracks.

AUGUST 3 The Indians play a Sunday home game before 4,500 in Columbus, Ohio and lose 5–2 to the Senators.

AUGUST 4 Earl Moore not only pitches a shutout, but drives in the lone run of a 1–0 win over the Senators at League Park with a walk-off single.

AUGUST 5 Two days after his major league debut, Indians pitcher Otto Hess wobbles to a ten-inning, 7–6 win over the Senators at League Park. Washington tested Hess with 14 bunts, three of which were booted by Hess for errors. Four were hits and seven were sacrifices. Shortstop John Gochnauer broke a finger in the third inning trying to flag down a line drive by Ed Delahanty but stayed in the game. Gochnauer doubled home the tying run in the eighth inning and the winning tally in the tenth.

AUGUST 14 Batting is his customary fourth spot in the batting order, Charley Hickman is the starting pitcher and takes an 8–7 loss to the Orioles in Baltimore.

Hickman, normally an outfielder, was on the mound because the Indians were in a pitching crisis in August 1902. At the time, major league teams carried only four or five pitchers on the roster. In Cleveland, those ranks were depleted by Gene Wright's sore arm, Addie Joss's wrenched knee and Bill Bernhard's sprained ankle. Cleveland manager Bill Armour was so desperate for pitching that he persuaded a sportswriter for the Cleveland Plain Dealer *to advertise for pitchers in his daily column. During August and September, the Indians tried out about a half-dozen amateur pitchers who responded to the plea.*

AUGUST 31 The Indians play a Sunday game before 3,500 at Jailhouse Flats in Ft. Wayne, Indiana, and lose 3–1 to the Red Sox in 11 innings.

SEPTEMBER 1 The Indians win a double header against the Red Sox 1–0 and 8–0 against the Red Sox at League Park. Earl Moore and Bill Bernhard pitched the shutouts.

SEPTEMBER 2 A seven-run eighth inning caps a 23–7 thrashing of the Orioles at League Park. Bill Bradley and Harry Bay both scored five runs during the afternoon, and Bay collected five of Cleveland's 23 hits with four singles and a double. John Katoll pitched a complete game for Baltimore.

Bay's swiftness on the diamond earned him the nickname "Deerfoot." He led the AL in stolen bases in both 1903 and 1904. Bay was an accomplished musician as well. Throughout his baseball career, he appeared in many concerts and vaudeville performances playing the cornet. Bay also played the piano and a number of string instruments.

SEPTEMBER 4 Some 5,000 school children are given free admission to League Park and went home happy after watching the Indians defeat the Orioles 7–5.

The Orioles moved to New York after the 1902 season, establishing the present-day Yankees franchise, though until 1913 they were more often called the Highlanders.

SEPTEMBER 10 The Indians sweep the White Sox 9–6 and 12–0 at League Park. The Indians scored seven runs in the eighth inning of the second game. Nap Lajoie collected six hits, including three doubles and a homer, in nine at-bats during the twinbill. Addie Joss pitched a two-hitter in the second tilt. The only Chicago hits were singles by Sam Mertes and Frank Isbell.

SEPTEMBER 13 Charley Hickman's walk-off homer in the tenth inning beats the Browns 2–1 in the second game of a double header at League Park. After Hickman crossed the plate, he was carried off the field by enthusiastic fans. Cleveland also won the first game 4–1.

SEPTEMBER 21 Bill Bernhard wins his 11th game in a row, defeating the Browns 4–1 in ten innings in the second game of a double header in St. Louis. The Browns won the opener 2–1 in ten innings.

After being acquired by the Indians from the Athletics in June, Bernhard was 17–5 with an ERA of 2.20.

1903

Season in a Sentence

After another poor start, the Indians recover to finish the season in third place.

Finish • Won • Lost • Pct • GB

Finish	Won	Lost	Pct	GB
Third	77	63	.550	15.0

Manager

Bill Armour

Stats

Stats	Indians	AL	Rank
Batting Avg:	.265	.255	2
On-Base Pct:	.308	.303	5
Slugging Pct:	.373	.344	2
Home Runs:	31		3
Stolen Bases:	175		2
ERA:	2.73	2.96	2
Fielding Avg:	.946	.953	8
Runs Scored:	639		2
Runs Allowed:	579		6

Starting Line-up

Harry Bemis, c
Charlie Hickman, 1b
Nap Lajoie, 2b
Bill Bradley, 3b
Jack Gochnauer, ss
Jack McCarthy, lf
Harry Bay, cf
Elmer Flick, rf
Fred Abbott, c

Pitchers

Addie Joss, sp
Earl Moore, sp
Bill Bernhard, sp
Red Donahue, sp
Gene Wright, sp
Gus Dorner, sp-rp

Attendance

224,523 (sixth in AL)

Club Leaders

Batting Avg:	Nap Lajoie	.344
On-Base Pct:	Nap Lajoie	.379
Slugging Pct:	Nap Lajoie	.518
Home Runs:	Charlie Hickman	12
RBIs:	Charlie Hickman	97
Runs:	Bill Bradley	101
Stolen Bases:	Harry Bay	45
Wins:	Earl Moore	19
Strikeouts:	Earl Moore	148
ERA:	Earl Moore	1.74
Saves:	Earl Moore	1

JANUARY 10 The National and American leagues reach a peace accord at a meeting in Cincinnati, ending the costly war and contract jumping that had driven salaries skyward. The two leagues agreed to refrain from raiding each other's rosters and set up a three-man governing body consisting of the presidents of the two organizations and Cincinnati Reds President Garry Herrmann.

APRIL 22 The Indians open the 1903 season with a 4–2 loss to the Tigers in Detroit.

Cleveland started the season with seven losses in their first nine games but edged over the .500 mark by the end of May. The club reached second place for a brief spell in August but never seriously challenged for the pennant, which was won by the Red Sox.

APRIL 28 The home opener draws 19,867, the largest ever for an Indians game up to that time. The crowd overflowed the stands, and thousands were placed in foul territory and along the outfield walls. As the game progressed, the excess crept forward toward the infield, making it impossible to continue play. The players had to grab hands and form a ring and push the fans back in order to resume the game. The Indians lost 6–3 to the Browns.

MAY 10 Playing a Sunday home game in Canton, the Indians win 6–2 over the Tigers.

May 12 Addie Joss pitches a two-hitter, defeating the Red Sox 2–1 at League Park. The only Boston hits were singles by Patsy Dougherty and Jimmy Collins.

Joss was 18–13 with an earned run average of 2.19 in 1903 but missed the final month of the season with a high fever.

May 17 Playing a Sunday home game in Columbus, Ohio, the Indians defeat the Yankees 9–2.

Ernest "Barney" Barnard joined the Indians in 1903 as business manager, which included most of the duties of a present-day general manager. He was a valued member of the front office for nearly a quarter century. Previously, Barnard had been a baseball and football coach at Otterbein College in Westerville, Ohio, and sports editor of the Columbus Dispatch. *He was also involved in the operation of the minor league American Association and the Columbus club in that organization. By 1908, Barnard was promoted to vice-president of the Indians, and in that capacity he created one of baseball's first farm systems. By 1922 he was president of the Cleveland club, a position he held until 1927 when he became president of the American League, succeeding Ban Johnson. Barnard was AL president until he died in 1931.*

May 30 The Indians sweep the White Sox 3–2 and 15–4 in a Memorial Day double header at League Park. In the opener, Earl Moore struck out 12 batters. In the second tilt, Cleveland scored 15 runs in just two innings, plating seven in the second and eight in the sixth.

Moore was 19–9 with an ERA of 1.74 in 1903 but missed the final month of the season with a sore arm.

June 4 The Indians play in New York for the first time and defeat the Yankees 6–3.

June 9 Bill Bradley collects five hits, including a home run and a double, in five at-bats during an 8–4 win over the Senators in Washington.

Bradley hit .313 with 101 runs, 168 hits, 36 doubles, 22 triples and six homers in 1903.

June 12 Addie Joss allows only two runs and six hits in 14 innings of pitching, but loses 2–1 to the Athletics in Philadelphia. Former Indian Ollie Pickering ended the game with a homer over the right field fence. Rube Waddell, who like Joss would be elected to the Hall of Famer, pitched a complete game for the A's.

June 21 The Indians play a Sunday home game in Canton, and lose 12–7 to the Red Sox.

June 24 After the Indians lose the first game of a double header 6–3 to the Yankees at League, Addie Joss pitches a shutout for a 6–0 victory in game two.

June 25 Earl Moore shuts out the Senators 4–0 at League Park.

June 26 Gus Dorner pitches the Indians to a 1–0 win over the Senators at League Park.

JUNE 27 — Bill Bernhard records the Indians fourth consecutive shutout, defeating the Senators 6–0 in the first game of a double header at League Park. Washington won the second tilt 5–2 in 11 innings.

JULY 4 — Nap Lajoie is ejected by umpire Bob Caruthers in the first inning of an Independence Day clash against the Senators in Washington, which the Indians lost 10–3. Lajoie refused to leave the field on his own accord and needed to be escorted from the premises by a park policeman. AL president Ban Johnson suspended Lajoie for two games.

Lajoie won the AL batting crown in 1903 by hitting .344. He also led the circuit in slugging percentage (.518) in addition to collecting 41 doubles and 93 RBIs.

A newspaper advertisement for the "Cleveland Base Ball Team" touts the upcoming season and new team captain Napoleon Lajoie.

JULY 6 — The Indians sweep the Senators 1–0 and 3–1 in a double header in Washington. Bill Bernhard pitched the first game shutout.

JULY 28 — Bill Bradley collects three triples and a single in four at-bats, leading the Indians to a 10–2 win over the Browns in St. Louis.

AUGUST 8 — The Indians lose a game by forfeit to the Tigers in Cleveland. With the Indians trailing 6–5 in the bottom of the tenth, Detroit catcher Fritz Buelow put an old black ball into play. When the objections of the Cleveland players to the discolored ball were ignored by umpire Tommy Connolly, Nap Lajoie threw it over the grandstand. Connolly was unamused and declared the forfeit.

AUGUST 13 — The Indians commit eight errors in the first six innings and fall behind the Yankees 5–1, before scoring three runs in the eighth inning and two in the ninth to win 6–5 at League Park.

AUGUST 17 — The Indians extend their winning streak to eight games with a 9–3 decision over the Red Sox at League Park.

AUGUST 21 — The Indians pummel the Senators 10–0 at League Park.

AUGUST 24 Indians pitcher Bob Rhoads hurls a one-hitter to beat the Athletics 3–0 at League Park. The only Philadelphia hit was a single by Topsy Hartsel.

Rhoads helped finance spring training in 1904 in a novel way. The team trained in San Antonio and the final two games were rained out. Club owner Charles Somers had counted on ticket sales to help pay the team's expenses back to Cleveland. Rhoads asked Somers how much was needed. Somers said it would take $1,600. Rhoads told him not to worry and headed for the Crystal Palace, a local casino. Rhoads hit the craps tables and piled up $1,800 in winnings. He loaned the money to Somers, allowing the team to settle its bills and leave town.

AUGUST 29 A train carrying both the Indians and Browns is involved in an accident. The two clubs were traveling from Cleveland to St. Louis when the train left the rails after running through an open switch in Napoleon, Ohio, at 12:45 a.m. while moving at 40 miles per hour. The Indians sleeper was turned upside down, but no one was seriously injured.

SEPTEMBER 3 In just his second major league game, Jesse Stovall pitches 11 innings and beats the Tigers 1–0 in Detroit. The lone run of the game scored on a single by Bill Bradley, a stolen base, and a single by Charlie Hickman.

A Spanish-American War veteran who made his big league debut at the age of 28, Stovall pitched another shutout in his next start, beating the White Sox 6–0 in Cleveland on September 8. He pitched 28 consecutive scoreless innings from August 31 through September 12. In six starts as a rookie in 1903, Stovall was 5–1 with a 2.05 ERA. He was traded to the Tigers during the following off-season, however, and pitched only one more big league season, posting a record of 3–13.

SEPTEMBER 6 Marty Glendon allows only three hits in ten innings but loses 1–0 to the White Sox in Chicago. Two errors by shortstop Jack Gochnauer and a passed ball led to the lone run of the contest.

What the Indians saw in Gochnauer is difficult to fathom. In two seasons with the club, he posted an abysmal batting average of .185 in 261 games with below average fielding percentages and range factors at shortstop. In 1903, Gochnauer committed 95 errors, which not only led AL shortstops that season but is the all-time modern major league record.

SEPTEMBER 16 The Red Sox score in all eight turns at bat and defeat the Indians 14–7 in Boston.

SEPTEMBER 24 Bill Bradley hits for the cycle during a 12–2 win over the Senators in Washington. In five at-bats, Bradley collected two doubles in addition to a homer, triple, and single.

SEPTEMBER 25 The Indians score seven runs in the fifth inning and defeat the Senators 14–5 in Washington.

OCTOBER 3 The championship of Ohio commences with a 2–1 Indians victory over the Reds in Cleveland.

The series was a best-of-eleven affair, played at the same time as baseball's first modern World Series between the Pittsburgh Pirates and Boston Red Sox. The teams appeared to be evenly matched. The Indians had a record of 77–63, while the Reds were 74–65. In addition to the contests in Cleveland and Cincinnati, the Ohio towns of Columbus and Newark also hosted games. It was the first of four "Ohio championships." The other three were held in 1910, 1911, and 1917.

October 7 The Indians score seven runs in the fifth inning and defeat the Reds 11–5 in a game in Newark, Ohio, called after 7½ innings by darkness.

October 11 Playing two games against the Reds in Cincinnati, the Indians win the Ohio championship six games to three. The Indians lost the first game 7–6 but won the second 3–1.

Prior to the game, major league players were caught on camera by moving pictures for the first time. The Cincinnati Enquirer *reported "a moving picture man took a camera shot at 'Nap' Lajoie at bat in the act of hitting the ball. (Jack) Sutthoff was at the slab for the Reds and when (Lajoie) hit through (Reds shortstop Tommy) Corcoran, Harry Bay came in from third with all the steam on. The diamond scene will be shown in theaters."*

1904

Season in a Sentence

The Indians outscore the opposition by 165 runs, a larger differential than any other American League club but finish in fourth place.

Finish • Won • Lost • Pct • GB

Finish	Won	Lost	Pct	GB
Fourth	86	65	.570	7.5

Stats

Stats	Indians	AL	Rank
Batting Avg:	.260	.244	1
On-Base Pct:	.308	.295	2
Slugging Pct:	.354	.321	1
Home Runs:	27		2 (tie)
Stolen Bases:	178		2
ERA:	2.22	2.60	2
Fielding Avg:	.959	.959	6
Runs Scored:	647		1
Runs Allowed:	482		2 (tie)

Starting Line-up

Harry Bemis, c
Charley Hickman, 1b-2b
Nap Lajoie, 2b-ss
Bill Bradley, 3b
Terry Turner, ss
Billy Lush, lf
Harry Bay, cf
Elmer Flick, rf
George Stovall, 1b

Pitchers

Bill Bernhard, sp
Red Donahue, sp
Earl Moore, sp
Addie Joss, sp
Bob Rhoads, sp
Otto Hess, sp

Attendance

264,749 (sixth in AL)

Club Leaders

Batting Avg:	Nap Lajoie	.376
On-Base Pct:	Nap Lajoie	.413
Slugging Pct:	Nap Lajoie	.546
Home Runs:	Bill Bradley	6
	Elmer Flick	6
RBIs:	Nap Lajoie	102
Runs:	Elmer Flick	97
Stolen Bases:	Elmer Flick	38
	Harry Bay	38
Wins:	Bill Bernhard	23
Strikeouts:	Earl Moore	139
ERA:	Addie Joss	1.59
Saves:	None	

April 14 — Four months after Orville and Wilbur Wright's first successful flight, the Indians defeat the White Sox 6–1 in the season opener in Chicago. Bill Bernhard was the winning pitcher.

April 18 — Nap Lajoie collects five hits, including two doubles, in five at-bats during a 10–4 win over the Browns in St. Louis.

In 1904, Lajoie led the AL in batting average (.376), on base percentage (.413), slugging percentage (.546), hits (208), doubles (49), total bases (302), and RBIs (102) in addition to scoring 92 runs. Other Cleveland batting stars during the season were Bill Bradley (.300 and 94 runs) and Elmer Flick (.306, 97 runs, 17 triples and 36 stolen bases).

April 22 — In the home opener, the Indians easily defeat the White Sox 10–2 before an overflow crowd of 17,000 at League Park.

July 5 — Charlie Hickman hits a grand slam during a 14–4 win over the Browns at League Park.

July 13 — The Indians hammer the Yankees 16–3 in New York. Nap Lajoie collected three triples and a single and Bill Bradley scored five runs.

July 14 — The day after winning by 13 runs, the Indians lose by 18 in a 21–3 trouncing at the hands of the Yankees in New York. New York scored ten runs in the eighth inning off Otto Hess.

July 19 — Center fielder Harry Bay sets a major league record (since tied) for most putouts in a game by an outfielder with 12 during a 12-inning, 3–1 win over the Red Sox in Boston.

July 21 — After taking a 14–1 lead in the top of the eighth inning, the Indians win 14–8 over the Athletics in Philadelphia.

August 2 — Four Red Sox put out a fire after a 4–1 win over the Indians at League Park.

Just after arriving at the team hotel in downtown Cleveland, Hobe Ferris, Freddie Parent, Bill Dinneen, and Norwood Gibson noticed flames bursting from a room and several employees of the tavern located in the establishment running panic-stricken about the fifth floor. The four dashed out of the elevator, and after the fire had spread from one room to another, managed to extinguish the blaze by means of a fire hose without calling the fire department.

August 4 — The Indians drub the Red Sox 11–1 at League Park.

August 7 — The Indians trade Charlie Hickman to the Tigers for Charlie Carr and Fritz Buelow.

After his playing career ended, Carr ran a successful sporting goods company called Bradley & Carr, which supplied baseballs to several minor leagues. Buelow was born in Berlin, Germany.

August 8 Cleveland police are needed to remove Yankee manager Clark Griffith and center fielder Dave Fultz from League Park after they were ejected during a wrangle with umpire Silk O'Loughlin. The Indians won the game 9–1.

August 15 Earl Moore pitches a two-hitter to defeat the Senators 1–0 at League Park. The only Washington hits were singles by Barry McCormick and opposing pitcher Jack Townsend. Bill Bradley drove in the lone run of the game with a single in the fourth inning.

August 26 Addie Joss pitches a 12-inning shutout to defeat the Senators 1–0 in Washington. Joss allowed only four hits. A double by Terry Turner drove in the lone run of the game.

A five-foot-eight-inch, 149-pound infielder, Turner was never a star but still ranks first among Indians players in games played with 1,625. (The Indians are the only one of the 16 franchises in existence in 1903 without a single player to appear in at least 1,750 career games for the club.) Turner played for Cleveland from 1904 through 1918. Turner is also third among Indians players in stolen bases (254), third in at-bats (5,783), ninth in hits (1,470) and ninth in triples (77).

August 27 For the second day in a row, the Indians defeat the Senators 1–0 in Washington, this one in the conventional nine innings with Red Donahue pitching the shutout.

Donahue was 19–14 with a 2.40 ERA in 1904. Addie Joss compiled a 14–10 record, but his 1.59 earned run average led the American League.

September 9 With the team in disarray due to disorganization and dissension, Bill Armour resigns as manager, effective at the end of the season.

The 1904 Indians scored 647 runs and allowed 482. The plus 165 run differential was the best in the American League that season. Yet the Indians finished fourth behind the Red Sox (plus 142 run differential), Yankees (plus 72), and White Sox (plus 118). Cleveland hovered around the .500 mark until late June, never seriously threatened for the pennant, and needed a nine-game winning streak in September and October to slip past the Athletics into fourth.

September 10 The Indians sweep the White Sox 5–4 and 11–6 during a double header against the White Sox at League Park. In the opener, pitcher Bill Bernhard drove in the winning run with a walk-off single. In the nightcap, Cleveland scored seven runs in the first inning.

September 27 Bob Rhoads no-hits the Red Sox at League Park until two are out in the ninth inning, when Chick Stall singles. Rhoads had to settle for a one-hit, 3–1 win. The Red Sox scored a run in the fourth inning without benefit of a hit.

October 1 The Indians run their winning streak to nine games with 4–0 and 9–2 decisions over the Senators at League Park. Cleveland scored seven runs in the eighth inning of the nightcap just before the contest was called because of darkness.

OCTOBER 7 Indians first baseman George Stovall homers off of his brother Jesse in the first inning of an 8–1 win over the Tigers in the first game of a double header at League Park. George was three years younger than Jesse. The homer was also George's first in the majors. Cleveland completed the sweep by winning the second game, called after six innings by darkness, 9–0. Bill Bernhard pitched the shutout for his 23rd win of the season.

The game in which he surrendered a home run to his brother was the last that Jesse Stovall pitched in the majors. He played for the Indians in 1903 (see September 3, 1903). Nicknamed "Firebrand" for his explosive temper, George struck manager Nap Lajoie in 1907 over the head with a heavy chair in a hotel lobby following an argument. Stovall played in Cleveland from 1904 through 1911 and managed the club for most of the 1911 season.

OCTOBER 27 A week before Theodore Roosevelt wins the Presidential election, the Indians name Nap Lajoie as manager, replacing Bill Armour, who resigned on September 9.

As the best and most popular player on the club, the choice of Lajoie pleased Cleveland fans. With the exception of 41 games in 1905 when he was hospitalized with blood poisoning, Lajoie managed the Indians through the end of the 1909 season. Armour was manager of the Tigers from 1904 through 1906.

1905

Season in a Sentence

The Indians spend 73 days in first place, but injuries ruin a promising season and the club winds up with a losing record.

Finish • Won • Lost • Pct • GB

Finish	Won	Lost	Pct	GB
Fifth	76	78	.494	19.0

Managers

Nap Lajoie (37–21), Bill Bradley (20–21) and Lajoie (19–36)

Stats

Stats	Indians	AL	Rank
Batting Avg:	.255	.241	1
On-Base Pct:	.301	.299	5
Slugging Pct:	.334	.314	2
Home Runs:	18		5
Stolen Bases:	188		5
ERA:	2.85	2.65	6
Fielding Avg:	.962	.957	2
Runs Scored:	567		5
Runs Allowed:	587		6

Starting Line-up

Fritz Buelow, c
Charlie Carr, 1b
George Stovall, 2b-1b
Bill Bradley, 3b
Terry Turner, ss
Jim Jackson, lf
Harry Bay, cf
Elmer Flick, rf
Nap Lajoie, 2b
Harry Bemis, c

Pitchers

Addie Joss, sp
Earl Moore, sp
Bob Rhoads, sp
Otto Hess, sp
Bill Bernhard, sp
Red Donahue, sp

Attendance

316,306 (fifth in AL)

Club Leaders

Batting Avg:	Elmer Flick	.306
On-Base Pct:	Elmer Flick	.382
Slugging Pct:	Elmer Flick	.462
Home Runs:	Elmer Flick	4
	Terry Turner	4
RBIs:	Terry Turner	72
Runs:	Elmer Flick	71
Stolen Bases:	Harry Bay	36
Wins:	Addie Joss	20
Strikeouts:	Addie Joss	132
ERA:	Addie Joss	2.01
Saves:	None	

April 14 A heavy Cleveland snowstorm postpones the scheduled season opener against the Tigers at League Park.

April 15 The Indians get the 1905 season underway with a 6–2 win over the Tigers before 7,544 on a bitterly cold day at League Park. Earl Moore was the winning pitcher. Nap Lajoie, in his first game as manager, was the hitting star with a triple and two singles in five at-bats.

April 26 Bob Rhoads pitches the Indians to a 1–0 win over the Tigers in Detroit. Harry Bay drove in the lone run of the game with a triple in the fifth inning.

April 27 Otto Hess pitches a two-hitter to defeat the Tigers 2–0 in Detroit. The only hits off Hess were singles by Matty McIntyre and Charley O'Leary.

April 30 The Indians trounce the Browns 11–1 in St. Louis.

May 7 Bob Rhoads pitches a two-hitter to beat the White Sox 2–0 in Chicago. The only hits against Rhoads were singles by Ed McFarland and opposing pitcher Frank Owen.

May 19 The Indians defeat a group of badly shaken Red Sox 11–4 at League Park. On the way to the game, the bus carrying the Boston club was struck by a streetcar at the corner of Euclid and Dunham. Fortunately, no one was seriously injured.

May 26 Otto Hess not only pitches a ten-inning shutout to beat the Yankees 1–0 at League Park, he drives in the lone run of the game with a walk-off single.

May 30 The Indians sweep the Browns 6–3 and 1–0 in a double header at League Park. Addie Joss pitched the second game shutout.

May 31 The Indians win their eighth game in a row with a 12–4 decision over the Browns at League Park.

The Indians closed the month of May in first place with a 22–11 record. By June 20 Cleveland was 32–14 and had a four-game lead in the pennant race.

June 19 Nap Lajoie collects five hits in six at-bats during a 12–3 win over the Yankees in New York.

June 26 The Indians pummel the Tigers 14–5 in Detroit.

June 29 Center fielder Harry Bay commits three errors in the ninth inning, leading to three Tiger runs and a 3–2 loss in the second game of a double header in Detroit. Cleveland won the first game 8–3.

June 30 Elmer Flick keys a 2–0 win over the Tigers at League Park by driving in a run with a triple in the fifth inning and scoring on Nap Lajoie's single.

Flick led the AL in batting average (.306) and triples (18) in 1905. Harry Bay hit .298 and scored 90 runs. Terry Turner batted .263 and drove in 72 runs. Bill Bradley compiled an average of .268.

July 1 The Indians collect 22 hits and defeat the Tigers 14–3 at League Park. The game was called after 7½ innings to allow the Indians to catch a train.

The win was costly because Nap Lajoie was spiked at second base. It seemed to be a minor cut, and Lajoie remained in the game, but it became infected with the blue dye in his stockings and he played in only a handful of games for the rest of the season. The infection was serious enough to keep Lajoie away from the ballpark for six weeks. Bill Bradley served as interim manager for 41 games. Lajoie returned, playing first base, in late August, but fouled a ball off his ankle, shelving him again. Lajoie's infection had one lasting effect. Players began to wear white "sanitary" socks with colored stirrups over them.

July 24 The Indians defeat the Senators 7–1 in Washington.

The victory gave Cleveland a 52–29 record and a four-game lead. Overall, the Indians spent 73 days in first place in 1905, the last on July 31. Mounting injuries wrecked a promising season. During the last week of July, Nap Lajoie, Harry Bay, George Stovall, Nick Kahl, Addie Joss, Bill Bernhard, and Bob

Rhoads were out of the line-up. As a result, the club collapsed, losing 49 of their last 73 games, including one streak of ten defeats in succession.

JULY 26 Bill Bernhard loses a shutout when opposing pitcher Barney Wolfe hits a fluke homer, but the Indians win 7–1 in the second game of a double header at League Park. Wolfe's homer rolled through a hole in the left field fence. Washington won the first game 3–2.

AUGUST 1 With the Tigers out of catchers due to injuries, the Indians "loan" Nig Clarke to the Detroit club. After playing three games for the Tigers, Clarke returned to Cleveland.

Jay (Nig) Clarke played for the Indians from 1905 through 1910. He had already made a name for himself in the minors. While with Corsicana of the Class D Texas League on June 15, 1902, Clarke hit eight home runs in one game, an organized baseball record that stands today. Because Sunday baseball was not allowed in Corsicana, the game was played in a field in Ennis, Texas, with a right field fence only 210 feet from home plate, a distance that Clarke, a left-handed pull hitter, exploited. Corsicana beat Texarkana 51–3. During his major league career, Clarke batted 1,536 times and struck only six home runs.

AUGUST 4 With injuries depleting the infield, the Indians use semi-pro third baseman Eddie Grant from nearby Lynn, Massachusetts, for a game against the Red Sox in Boston. Grant collected three hits in four at-bats in his big league debut, a 7–5 Cleveland loss.

A graduate of Harvard, Grant played only one more game for the Indians. He was left by the club in Boston as the Indians continued their road trip. Grant later returned to the majors and played with the Phillies, Reds, and Giants from 1907 through 1915. After enlisting in the Army in 1917 at the start of World War I, Grant rose to the rank of captain and led a mission in the Argonne Forest offensive to rescue the "Lost Battalion" trapped behind German lines. When he met with machine gun fire on October 5, 1918, he became the only major leaguer to be killed during the war.

AUGUST 7 The Indians lose their tenth game in a row, dropping a 4–3 decision to the Red Sox in Boston.

AUGUST 14 The Indians win a raucous 13-inning, 3–2 decision over the Senators in Washington. With two out in the bottom of the 13th, Punch Knoll of the Senators tried to steal home and was called out by umpire Tommy Connolly. The decision was questioned by some of the Washington players and the crowd surged on to the field surrounding the umpire. One fan struck Connolly before police dispersed the mob.

SEPTEMBER 5 A "crowd" of only 224 turns out for a 6–0 loss to the Browns at League Park.

SEPTEMBER 20 The Indians commit seven errors in the eighth inning helping the White Sox score eight runs in a 9–6 loss at League Park.

SEPTEMBER 29 Bob Rhoads pitches the Indians to a 1–0 win over the Yankees in New York. Just two days after his major league debut, second baseman Jap Barbeau drove in the winning run in the seventh inning with a triple.

OCTOBER 6 Addie Joss wins his 20th game of 1905 with a 5–3 decision over the Tigers at League Park.

Joss was 20–12 with a 2.01 ERA in 1905.

1906

Season in a Sentence

The Indians fail to win the pennant despite leading the league in runs scored, fielding average, earned run average, and run differential, and possessing three pitchers with at least 20 wins.

Finish • Won • Lost • Pct • GB

Finish	Won	Lost	Pct	GB
Third	89	64	.582	5.0

Manager

Nap Lajoie

Stats

Stats	Indians	AL	Rank
Batting Avg:	.279	.249	1
On-Base Pct:	.325	.303	1
Slugging Pct:	.357	.318	1
Home Runs:	12		6
Stolen Bases:	203		5
ERA:	2.09		1
Fielding Avg:	.967	.957	1
Runs Scored:	663		1
Runs Allowed:	482		2

Starting Line-up

Harry Bemis, c
George Stovall, 1b-3b
Nap Lajoie, 2b
Bill Bradley, 3b
Terry Turner, ss
Jim Jackson, lf
Elmer Flock, cf-rf
Bunk Congalton, rf
Claude Rossman, 1b
Harry Bay, cf
Nig Clarke, c

Pitchers

Otto Hess, sp
Bob Rhoads, sp
Addie Joss, sp
Bill Bernhard, sp
Jack Townsend, sp
Harry Eells, sp-rp

Attendance

325,733 (sixth in AL)

Club Leaders

Batting Avg:	Nap Lajoie	.355
On-Base Pct:	Nap Lajoie	.392
Slugging Pct:	Nap Lajoie	.465
Home Runs:	Bunk Congalton	3
RBIs:	Nap Lajoie	91
Runs:	Elmer Flick	98
Stolen Bases:	Elmer Flick	39
Wins:	Bob Rhoads	22
Strikeouts:	Otto Hess	167
ERA:	Addie Joss	1.72
Saves:	Otto Hess	3

APRIL 17 The Indians open the season with a 3–1 loss to the Browns in St. Louis. Otto Hess was the losing pitcher despite hurling a three-hitter.

APRIL 21 Half of the gate receipts from a 5–1 Indians loss to the Browns in St. Louis is donated to the San Francisco relief fund. Three days earlier, San Francisco was devastated by an earthquake and fire.

APRIL 28 Trailing 7–6 to the Tigers in Detroit, the Indians explode for eight runs in the ninth inning to win 14–7. With the bases loaded, one out, and Cleveland still trailing by a run, Indians outfielder Jim Jackson hit a bouncer back to pitcher John Eubank. It appeared to be an easy double play to end the game, but catcher Fred Payne dropped the throw, which tied the score. From there, the Indians scored seven more runs.

April 30 In the home opener at League Park, the Browns score two runs with two out in the ninth off Addie Joss to defeat the Indians 4–3.

For the second time in three years, the underachieving Indians had the best run differential in the AL, but failed to win the pennant. The Indians outscored the opposition 663 to 481, yet finished third. The plus 182-run differential easily outdistanced the pennant-winning White Sox (plus 110) and the second-place Yankees (plus 97).

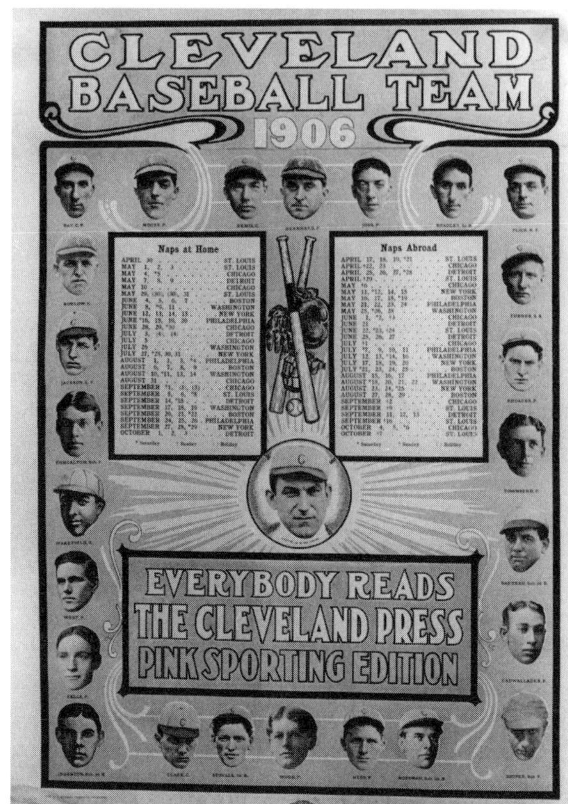

The 1906 team and schedule.

May 10 The Indians score seven runs in the sixth inning and pummel the White Sox 15–1 at League Park.

May 12 Addie Joss pitches an 11-inning shutout to beat the Yankees 2–0 in New York.

May 18 The Indians collect 21 hits and rout the Red Sox 14–1 in Boston.

May 21 Catcher Harry Bemis homers in the 13th inning to beat the Athletics 2–1 in Philadelphia. The Cleveland victory stopped the A's 11-game winning streak.

May 26 The Indians score five runs in the ninth inning to stun the Senators 6–4 in Washington.

June 14 The Indians take hold of first place with a 5–2 victory over the Yankees at League Park.

June 22 The Indians trounce the Browns 12–2 in St. Louis.

July 3 The Indians win a six-inning rain-shortened game by a 5–0 score over the Tigers at League Park. It began to rain in the top of the fifth inning, but umpire Billy Evans forced the teams to continue play despite the fact that the downpour turned the field into a sea of mud and water. Detroit second baseman Germany Schaefer went to his position wearing a raincoat, which finally convinced Evans to halt the proceedings.

July 4 Addie Joss pitches a two-hitter to defeat the Tigers 2–1 in the second game of a double header at League Park. The only two Detroit hits were singles by Matty McIntyre and opposing pitcher George Mullin. Cleveland also won the opener 3–2.

July 6 The idle Indians are knocked out of first place when the Yankees win two games from the Red Sox.

The Indians never regained first place but remained in range until late August in a four-team race with the Yankees, White Sox, and Athletics. The Indians were the first of the four to drop out of contention.

July 9 Bob Rhoads pitches a two-hitter to defeat the Athletics 6–0 in Philadelphia. The only hits off Rhoads were singles by Bris Lord and Topsy Hartsel.

July 26 The Indians score eight runs in the third inning and defeat the Senators 13–4 at League Park. Cleveland collected 21 hits, four of them by pitcher Otto Hess.

August 14 Trailing 8–0, the Indians rally to shock the Senators 9–8 at League Park. Cleveland scored a run in the sixth inning and another in the seventh before erupting for seven tallies in the eighth.

August 15 The Indians purchase Malachi Kittridge from the Senators.

August 16 Otto Hess pitches a two-hitter to defeat the Athletics 4–1 in the first game of a double header in Philadelphia. The only hits off Hess were singles by Harry Davis and Socks Seybold. The A's won the second contest 3–1.

August 21 The Indians record the first triple play in club history during a 2–0 win over the Senators in the first game of a double header in Washington. In the first inning, with runners on first and second base moving with the pitch, shortstop Terry Turner made a shoetop catch of a soft liner, stepped on second, and threw to first baseman Claude Rossman. The Senators won the second game 2–1.

September 3 The Indians sweep a Labor Day double header with 10–3 and 4–3 victories over the first-place White Sox at League Park. Nap Lajoie was ejected from the first game for throwing a handful of dirt toward umpire Jack Sheridan.

September 5 Addie Joss pitches the Indians to a 1–0 win over the Browns at League Park. Nap Lajoie drove in the lone run of the game with a single in the eighth inning.

Lajoie was the Indians top hitter in 1906. He was second in the AL in batting average (.355), on base percentage (.392), slugging percentage (.465), and runs-batted-in (91). He led the circuit in hits (214) and doubles (48). Elmer Flick batted .311, collected 194 hits, and led the league in triples (22), runs (98), and stolen bases (39). Bunk Congalton hit .320 and Terry Turner contributed an average of .291 to the American League's best offense.

September 16 Bill Bernhard hurls a shutout to beat the Browns 2–0 in St. Louis.

September 25 Otto Hess pitches a one-hitter to defeat the Athletics 5–0 at League Park. Hess had a no-hitter until the ninth inning when opposing pitcher Jack Coombs hit a pop fly that dropped between second baseman Nap Lajoie and right fielder Bunk Congalton with none out.

September 27 After the Indians beat the Yankees 10–1 in the opener of a double header in Cleveland, the two clubs play to a 2–2 tie in the nightcap, called after six innings by darkness. At the conclusion of the fifth, it was the opinion of almost everyone in the ballpark that it was too dark to continue. With the sunset and moon shining brightly, umpire Tim Hurst ordered a start to the sixth frame. Some spectators built bonfires in the stands, creating a dangerous situation in a ballpark constructed entirely of wood. Hurst finally came to his senses and the close of the sixth and ended the game.

September 28 Addie Joss records his 21st win of the year with a 2–1 decision over the Yankees at League Park.

Joss was 21–9 with nine shutouts and an earned run average of 1.72 in 1906.

October 3 Otto Hess earns victory number 20 in 1906 with a 4–3 decision over the Tigers at League Park.

Hess was 20–17 with an ERA of 1.83 in 333 2/3 innings and 33 complete games in 36 starts in 1906.

October 6 Bob Rhoads records his 22nd win of the season with a 5–3 triumph over the White Sox in Chicago.

Rhoads's final won-lost 1906 figures were 22–10. His ERA was 1.80 in 315 innings and he completed 31 games in 34 starts.

1907

Season in a Sentence

The Indians field another strong team but a team-wide batting slump results in a fourth-place finish.

Finish • Won • Lost • Pct • GB

Finish	Won	Lost	Pct	GB
Fourth	85	67	.559	8.0

Manager

Nap Lajoie

Stats

Stats	Indians	AL	Rank
Batting Avg:	.241	.247	6
On-Base Pct:	.295	.302	7
Slugging Pct:	.310	.309	5
Home Runs:	11		5 (tie)
Stolen Bases:	193		3
ERA:	2.26	2.54	2
Fielding Avg:	.960	.957	2
Runs Scored:	530		6
Runs Allowed:	525		3

Starting Line-up

Nig Clarke, c
George Stovall, 1b
Nap Lajoie, 2b
Bill Bradley, 3b
Terry Turner, ss
Bill Hinchman, lf
Joe Birmingham, cf
Elmer Flick, rf
Harry Bemis, c
Pete O'Brien, 2b-3b-ss

Pitchers

Addie Joss, sp
Glenn Liebhardt, sp
Bob Rhoads, sp
Jake Thielman, sp
Otto Hess, sp
Walter Clarkson, sp-rp
Heinie Berger, sp-rp

Attendance

382,046 (fifth in AL)

Club Leaders

Batting Avg:	Elmer Flick	.302
On-Base Pct:	Elmer Flick	.386
Slugging Pct:	Elmer Flick	.412
Home Runs:	Elmer Flick	3
	Nig Clarke	3
RBIs:	Nap Lajoie	63
Runs:	Elmer Flick	78
Stolen Bases:	Elmer Flick	41
Wins:	Addie Joss	27
Strikeouts:	Addie Joss	127
ERA:	Addie Joss	1.83
Saves:	Addie Joss	2

APRIL 11 The Indians open the season with a 2–0 loss to the Tigers in Detroit. George Mullin pitched the shutout, allowing only three hits. Making only his third big league start, Glenn Liebhardt was the pitcher for the Indians. Nap Lajoie didn't want to use any of his regular pitchers because of the cold.

Still technically a rookie, Liebhardt was 18–14 with an ERA of 2.09 in 1907. Arm trouble developed two years later, however, and he pitched his last big league game at the age of 26. His son, also named Glenn, pitched three seasons for the Athletics and Browns during the 1930s.

APRIL 13 In a game played in a snowstorm, the Indians defeat the Tigers 9–3 in Detroit.

APRIL 15 The Indians take out a $100,000 policy to insure players against railroad accidents.

APRIL 18 In the home opener, the Indians lose 2–0 to the Tigers at League Park. George Mullin pitched a three-hitter for Detroit. Mullin also pitched a three-hit shutout against Cleveland on Opening Day seven days earlier.

APRIL 20 Addie Joss pitches a one-hitter to defeat the Tigers 4–1 at League Park. Sam Crawford collected the only Detroit hit with a single in the seventh inning.

Joss was 27–11 with an ERA of 1.83 in 1907. In addition to leading the league in wins, six of them with shutouts, Joss pitched 338 2/3 innings and completed 34 of his 38 starts.

April 24 Playing in his first game with the Indians, center fielder Bill Hinchman drives in both Cleveland runs with a fifth-inning triple to beat the White Sox 2–1 at League Park. Hinchman also made a remarkable running catch to stop a Chicago rally.

May 1 Addie Joss not only shuts out the Browns 2–0 at League Park, he drives in both runs with a seventh-inning double.

May 16 The Indians trade Earl Moore to the Yankees for Walter Clarkson.

May 20 The Indians sell Bunk Congalton to the Red Sox.

May 30 Bob Rhoads pitches a ten-inning shutout to defeat the Tigers 1–0 in the first game of a double header at League Park. Detroit won the second tilt 6–0.

June 12 The Indians score seven runs in the seventh inning and beat the Red Sox 12–6 in Boston.

June 13 Trailing 5–1, the Indians stun the Athletics with five runs in the ninth inning off Rube Waddell to win 6–5 in Philadelphia. The last four runs crossed the plate when A's outfielder Rube Oldring misplayed Elmer Flick's fly ball with the bases loaded.

June 29 The Indians win the fistic battle, but lose the war in a 12–2 defeat to the Tigers in Detroit. In the second inning, Ty Cobb collided with catcher Harry Bemis at the plate. Cobb was called safe, and while he was on the ground, Cobb was punched several times by Bemis, who was ejected.

July 5 The Indians defeat the Yankees 2–1 at League Park with the help of a fluke homer from Nap Lajoie. In the eighth inning and the score 1–1, Lajoie hit a drive with such force that it became stuck in the wire netting on the center field fence. New York outfielder Danny Hoffman was unable to extract the ball, and Lajoie circled the bases.

Bothered by a re-occurrence of the blood poisoning that sidelined him for much of the 1905 season, Lajoie hit .299 in 1907. The Indians leading hitter was Elmer Flick, who batted .302 and led the league in triples with 18. Catcher Nig Clarke contributed an average of .269.

July 11 Walter Clarkson pitches a shutout and in the eighth inning scores the lone run of a 1–0 win over the Red Sox at League Park.

July 19 The Indians and Senators play 12 innings to a 0–0 tie in a contest called on account of darkness at League Park. Glenn Liebhardt pitched the Cleveland shutout.

July 23 Walter Clarkson pitches a two-hitter to defeat the Senators 3–1 at League Park. The only Washington hits were a single by John Anderson and a double by Jim Delahanty.

Jim was one of five Delahanty brothers, each of whom were born in Cleveland, to play in the big leagues. They are the only family in which five brothers reached the majors. The five were Ed (born in 1867), Tom (born in 1872), Joe (born in 1875), Jim (born in 1879), and Frank (born in 1883). Ed is the best known of the brothers. He played in the majors from 1888 until 1903, when he died from a fall off of a railroad bridge over the Niagara River while playing for the Washington Senators. Frank was the only one of the five to play for the hometown Indians. He appeared in 15 games for the club in 1907.

JULY 27 The Indians outlast the Yankees 11–10 in an 11-inning contest in New York. Cleveland had a 10–6 lead before the Yanks scored one run in the eighth and three in the ninth.

After the win, the Indians had a record of 53–35 and were just one-half game behind the first-place White Sox. Dreams of a World Series in Cleveland evaporated when the Indians split their last 64 games.

AUGUST 3 The Indians score seven runs in the third inning and pound the Yankees 15–6 at League Park.

AUGUST 29 Nap Lajoie hits a grand slam with two out in the third inning off Frank Smith to account for all four Cleveland runs in a 4–1 win over the White Sox at League Park.

SEPTEMBER 2 The ejection of Bill Bradley helps the Indians defeat the Browns 3–2 in ten innings in the first game of a double header at League Park. With the score 2–2 and one out in the tenth, Bradley was put out of the game by umpire Tommy Connolly for objecting to a called third strike. Harry Bemis replaced Bradley to complete the at-bat, and delivered a game-winning single. St. Louis won the opener 4–1.

SEPTEMBER 5 Addie Joss pitches a one-hitter to defeat the Tigers 3–0 in Detroit. The only hit off Joss was a single by opposing pitcher Ed Killian. On his 33rd birthday, Nap Lajoie was presented with a wagonload of gifts, including a live black sheep.

At the conclusion of the game, the Indians were in third place with a record of 73–57 and were 1½ games behind the first-place Athletics. The Tigers were second, one-half game out. The fourth-place White Sox were just two games from the top.

SEPTEMBER 13 The Indians and Tigers participate in a contentious double header in Detroit. Cleveland won the opener 4–1. There was a time limit of 6:00 p.m. on the second game to allow the Indians to catch a train. When the Indians fell behind early, the club tried to prevent five innings from being completed so that the contest could not be declared an official game. The Indians intentionally misjudged easy fly balls and refused to make plays on runners on the bases, which nearly incited a riot among the Detroit rooters. In the end, six innings were played with the Tigers winning 10–0.

SEPTEMBER 15 Glenn Liebhardt wins his own game with a walk-off single in the ninth inning that beats the White Sox 3–2 at League Park.

SEPTEMBER 25 Addie Joss pitches a one-hitter to defeat the Yankees 3–1 in New York. The only hit off Joss was a single by Danny Hoffman. It was Addie's 27th win of 1907.

September 26 — For the second day in a row, an Indian pitcher hurls a one-hitter as Heinie Berger stops the Yankees 6–0 in New York. Berger was three outs from a no-hitter when Kid Elberfield delivered a pinch-single in the ninth.

1908

Season in a Sentence

The Indians participate in one of the most thrilling pennant races in major league history and are bitterly disappointed after falling short of first place by the slim margin of one-half game to the Tigers.

Finish • Won • Lost • Pct • GB

Finish	Won	Lost	Pct	GB
Second	90	64	.584	0.5

Manager

Nap Lajoie

Stats

Stats	Indians	AL	Rank
Batting Avg:	.239	.239	4
On-Base Pct:	.297	.294	3
Slugging Pct:	.309	.304	4
Home Runs:	18		4
Stolen Bases:	177		3
ERA:	2.02	2.39	1
Fielding Avg:	.962	.958	3
Runs Scored:	568		2
Runs Allowed:	457		1

Starting Line-up

Nig Clarke, c
George Stovall, 1b
Nap Lajoie, 2b
Bill Bradley, 3b
George Perring, ss
Bill Hinchman, rf-lf-ss
Josh Clarke, lf
Joe Birmingham, cf
Harry Bemis, c
Terry Turner, rf-ss
Charlie Hickman, rf-1b
Wilbur Good, rf-cf

Pitchers

Addie Joss, sp
Bob Rhoads, sp
Glenn Liebhardt, sp
Heinie Berger, sp
Charlie Chech, sp

Attendance

422,262 (sixth in AL)

Club Leaders

Batting Avg:	George Stovall	.292
On-Base Pct:	Nap Lajoie	.352
Slugging Pct:	George Stovall	.380
Home Runs:	Bill Hinchman	6
RBIs:	Nap Lajoie	74
Runs:	Nap Lajoie	77
Stolen Bases:	Josh Clarke	37
Wins:	Addie Joss	24
Strikeouts:	Glenn Liebhardt	146
ERA:	Addie Joss	1.16
Saves:	Addie Joss	2
	Slim Foster	2

March 7 — Four months after Oklahoma becomes the 46th state in the Union, the train carrying the Indians is struck by two bricks, shattering windows. The act by unknown perpetrators occurred near Lexington, Kentucky. Bill Bradley and Harry Bay were struck by flying glass. The Indians were on the way from Cleveland to their spring training headquarters at Macon, Georgia.

March 17 — The Indians reject a trade that would have brought Ty Cobb to Cleveland from the Tigers in exchange for Elmer Flick.

While meeting with a group of sportswriters during spring training practice in Macon, Georgia, Indians owner Charles Somers received a call from Detroit manager Hughie Jennings. Jennings called to propose trading Cobb for Flick. In his first season as an everyday player, Cobb had hit .350 and had 49 stolen bases in 1907 on a club that won the American League pennant, while Flick had batted .302 and swiped 41 bases. Cobb was 21-years-old, and Flick was 32. Somers pondered the offer and asked why the Tigers wanted to trade Cobb, fearing a concealed injury. Jennings assured Somers that Cobb was in perfect shape but said that the temperamental outfielder "can't get along with our players, and we want him to get away. He's had two fights already this spring. We want harmony on this team, not scrapping." Somers made his decision immediately. "We'll keep Flick," he said. "Maybe he isn't as good a batter as Cobb, but he's much nicer to have on the team. We don't want any troublemakers either." It proved to be a terrible mistake. Cobb remained with the Tigers until 1926 and in the majors until 1928. From 1908 through the end of his career, he batted .371 and collected 3,829 hits. Flick, on the other hand, was beset by a mysterious stomach ailment that started during spring training in 1908. His weight dropped to 135 pounds. From 1908 through the end of his career in 1910, Flick played in only 99 big league contests and batted just .254.

April 14 In the home opener, the Indians lose 2–1 in 10 innings to the Browns in St. Louis. Cleveland tied the score 1–1 in the ninth, but Addie Joss allowed a run in the tenth for a loss.

Joss was 23–11 in 1908 and led the American League in earned run average with a microscopic mark of 1.16, which is also the Indians single-season club record. He completed 29 of his 35 starts and walked only 30 batters in 325 innings.

April 17 The Indians win 12–8 over the Tigers in 12 innings in Detroit. The Indians led 5–0 early in the contest and were still ahead 6–4 heading into the ninth. Detroit scored twice, however, to send the game into extra innings. Cleveland plated two runs in the top of the 11th, but the Tigers tied the score again in their half. The Indians finally put the contest out of reach with four tallies in the 12th.

April 21 In the home opener, the Indians win 5–1 over the White Sox at League Park.

June 9 Trailing 2–1, the Indians explode for ten runs in the fifth inning and win 15–6 over the Red Sox at League Park. Every Cleveland player in the line-up collected a hit and scored a run in the big inning.

June 13 Glenn Liebhardt pitches the Indians to a 1–0 win over the Senators at League Park. Liebhardt also scored the only run of the contest. In the ninth inning, he tripled with one out and scored on Bill Bradley's two-out single.

June 17 The Indians collect two hits but defeat the Senators 2–0 at League Park. Addie Joss pitched the shutout.

July 10 Indians owner John Kilfoyl calls Yankees owner Frank Farrell to purchase first baseman Jake Stall. Kilfoyl and Farrell had been talking about the deal for weeks before Kilfoyl finally decided to pull the trigger. Unfortunately, Farrell had also been talking to the Red Sox and agreed to send Stall to Boston about an hour prior to receiving the call from Kilfoyl. At the time, Stall was among the top first baseman in baseball and Kilfoyl's delay in phoning the Yankees may have cost Cleveland the 1908 pennant. Stall remained with in Boston until 1913 and led the Red Sox to the 1912 world championship as player-manager.

Later in the year, Kilfoyl retired as club president due to ill health.

Vice-president Charles Somers became president of the Indians and Emil Barnard was promoted from business manager to vice-president. In that capacity, Barnard put together baseball's first farm system, with the Indians controlling minor league clubs in Toledo, Ohio; Ironton, Ohio; Waterbury, Connecticut; Portland, Oregon: and New Orleans.

JULY 15 The Indians drub the Yankees 16–1 in the first game of a double header in New York, then complete the sweep with a 3–2 decision in the nightcap.

JULY 30 The Indians win 3–2 over the Yankees in 14 innings at League Park. Bill Hinchman drove in the winning run with a single. Heinie Berger pitched a complete game.

Entering the game, the Indians were 47–43 and in fourth place, nine games out of first. There seemed to be a slim chance for a pennant, but the Indians battled back with 43 wins in the last 64 games and weren't eliminated from the race until the second-to-last day of the season.

For the fourth season in a row, Addie Joss was a twenty-game winner in 1908, while posting a microscopic 1.16 ERA.

JULY 31 The Indians wallop the Yankees 16–3 at League Park.

AUGUST 4 Otis Clymer and Jim Delahanty of the Senators are ejected from a 7–5 Indians win at League Park for verbally abusing umpire Silk O'Loughlin. Delahanty, a Cleveland native, was later fined $50 and barred from the Cleveland ballpark for one year for his unbecoming conduct.

AUGUST 5 The Indians thrash the Senators 12–1 at League Park. Cleveland scored in seven of their eight turns at bat.

AUGUST 30 Although Sunday ball is illegal in Detroit, the Indians and Tigers play on the Christian Sabbath at Detroit's Bennett Field. The Indians won 6–1. Police made no attempt to interfere with the game.

In 1908, only five of the 16 big league clubs could play on Sundays due to local statutes. The five were the White Sox and Browns in the American

League and the Cubs, Cardinals, and Reds in the National League. The Tigers were allowed to play at home legally on Sundays in 1909. The Indians were permitted to do so in Cleveland for the first time in 1911. The three Pennsylvania clubs (Pirates, Phillies, and Athletics) couldn't open their ballparks at home on Sundays until 1934.

SEPTEMBER 1 Addie Joss pitches a one-hitter to beat the Tigers 1–0 in Detroit. The only hit off Joss was a single by Ty Cobb in the first inning on a pop fly that fell just beyond the infield. Joe Birmingham drove in the lone run of the game with a single in the second inning.

For the third time in five years, the Indians led the American League in run differential, but failed to win a pennant. It also happened in 1904 and 1906. During the 1908 campaign, Cleveland scored 568 runs and allowed 457 for a run differential of plus 111, a figure better than pennant-winning Detroit's plus 100.

SEPTEMBER 7 Addie Joss hurls a two-hitter to beat the White Sox 6–0 in the second game of a double header at League Park. Freddy Parent collected both Chicago hits with a pair of singles. The Indians also won the opener 5–2.

SEPTEMBER 9 The Indians edge the Browns 1–0 in ten innings at League Park. Glenn Liebhardt pitched the shutout. St. Louis hurler Rube Waddell allowed only one hit through nine innings before allowing the Cleveland run in the tenth on singles by Bill Hinchman, Nap Lajoie, and Harry Bemis.

Lajoie batted .289 and led the Indians in runs (77), RBIs (74), hits (168), and doubles (32). George Stovall topped the club in batting average (.292).

SEPTEMBER 17 Addie Joss pitches the Indians to a 1–0 win over the Red Sox at League Park. Cleveland scored the game's lone in the ninth inning on three consecutive singles by Bill Hinchman, Nap Lajoie, and George Stovall off Cy Young.

SEPTEMBER 18 Bob Rhoads pitches a no-hitter to defeat the Red Sox 2–1 at League Park. Rhoads walked two and struck out two. The win put the Indians one game behind the Tigers in the AL pennant race. Boston scored their lone run in the second inning on a walk, an error, a sacrifice and a wild pitch. Cleveland evened the score with a run in the fourth and took the lead with another in the eighth off Frank Arellanes.

Rhoads was 18–12 with an ERA of 1.77 in 1908.

SEPTEMBER 19 The Indians defeat the Red Sox 6–5 with a run in the ninth inning at League Park. The victory placed Cleveland only two percentage points behind Detroit in the pennant race. When Bill Bradley drove in the winning tally, he was carried off the field on the shoulders of some of the enthusiastic fans at the ballpark. Then, the crowd, headed by drums and horns, paraded the field for nearly half an hour, refusing to disperse.

SEPTEMBER 21 The Indians take first place with a 5–2 win over the Yankees at League Park. It was Cleveland's eighth win in a row.

September 23 The Indians record their tenth win in a row with a 9–3 decision over the Yankees at League Park. Nap Lajoie had no official at-bats in four plate appearances. He was hit by pitches three times in addition to drawing a walk.

September 24 The Indians ten-game winning streak comes to a halt with a 2–1 loss to Walter Johnson and the Senators at League Park.

September 25 The Senators score five runs in the ninth inning off Charlie Chech to beat the Indians 6–1 at League Park. Frank Robison, a Cleveland native who owned the St. Louis Cardinals, was listening on the telephone to a friend's play-by-play account of the Washington rally when Robison suffered a heart attack. He died a few hours later. Robison also owned the Cleveland Spiders with his brother Stanley from 1889 through 1899.

September 27 The idle Indians are knocked out of first place when the Tigers defeat the Athletics 5–2 in Detroit. With nine days left in the season, the Indians were one percentage point behind Detroit. The White Sox were third, one-half game out.

October 2 Addie Joss pitches a perfect game to beat the White Sox 1–0 at League Park. Chicago's Ed Walsh surrendered only four hits and fanned 15 Cleveland batters. To add to the drama, it came near the end of a nail-biting pennant race. Many historians consider this game to be the best pitching duel in history. The lone run of the game scored in the third inning. Joe Birmingham started the rally with a single. Birmingham took a large lead in an attempt at a delayed steal. Walsh fired to first baseman Frank Isbell and Birmingham took off for second. Isbell's throw to second hit Birmingham in the shoulder, and as the ball glanced into the outfield, the Cleveland runner took third. Moments later, Birmingham crossed the plate on a wild pitch. The White Sox used three pinch-hitters in the ninth in an effort to stop Joss. Doc White led off the frame and grounded out to Nap Lajoie at second. Jiggs Donahue struck out on three pitches to put Joss one out from his perfect game. With two strikes, John Anderson hit a grounder to third baseman Bill Bradley, who whipped the ball toward first. The throw was low, but first baseman George Stovall scooped it out of the dirt just in time. The victory put the Indians one-half game behind the Tigers with four days left on the schedule.

October 3 The pennant aspirations of the Indians take a hit with a 3–2 loss to the White Sox before 20,729 at League Park. The game ended when Ed Walsh, pitching in relief, struck out Nap Lajoie with the bases loaded.

October 4 The Indians and Browns play to a controversial 3–3 tie in an 11-inning game called by darkness in St. Louis. With two out in the Indians half of the ninth, Addie Joss was the base runner on third and Bill Bradley was on second. Bill Hinchman hit a bounder over the middle, which was flagged down by Browns shortstop Bobby Wallace. With Joss already across the plate, Wallace's throw to first arrived at the same time as Hinchman, and umpire Jack Egan signaled out. The Indians rushed Egan in protest, believing that Hinchman was safe and that Cleveland had a 4–3 lead, but the umpire would not reverse the call.

October 5 On the second to last day of the season, the Indians are knocked out of the pennant race with a 3–1 loss to the Browns in the first game of a double header in St. Louis.

The Browns broke a 1–1 tie with two runs in the sixth. The rally started on a throwing error by Nap Lajoie. The Indians won the meaningless nightcap 5–3.

At the end of the season, the Tigers had a record of 90–63, one-half game ahead of the Indians, who were 90–64. The White Sox, at 88–64, were third. At the time, teams were not required to make up postponements that occurred on the last home series of the season. On August 25, the Tigers were rained out in Washington in a contest that wasn't played. Under today's rules, that game would have been played, and if Detroit lost, a playoff tilt between the Tigers and Indians would have been required to determine the champion. That wasn't the case in 1908, however, and the Tigers moved on to the World Series, where they lost four games to one to the Cubs.

1909

Season in a Sentence

After narrowly missing the World Series in 1908 and having acquired Cy Young during the off-season, the Indians are heavy favorites to win the pennant, but nearly everything goes wrong in a fall to sixth place.

Finish • Won • Lost • Pct • GB

Finish	Won	Lost	Pct	GB
Sixth	71	82	.464	27.5

Managers

Nap Lajoie (57–57) and Deacon McGuire (14–25)

Stats

Stats	Indians	AL	Rank
Batting Avg:	.241	.244	5
On-Base Pct:	.288	.303	6
Slugging Pct:	.313	.309	4
Home Runs:	10		5 (tie)
Stolen Bases:	174		6
ERA:	2.40	2.47	4
Fielding Avg:	.957	.957	5
Runs Scored:	493		5
Runs Allowed:	532		4

Starting Line-up

Ted Easterly, c
George Stovall, 1b
Nap Lajoie, 2b
Bill Bradley, 3b
Neal Ball, ss
Bill Hinchman, lf-cf
Joe Birmingham, cf
Wilbur Good, rf
George Perring, 3b
Bris Lord, lf
Elmer Flick, rf
Terry Turner, 2b-ss
Nig Clarke, c

Pitchers

Cy Young, sp
Addie Joss, sp
Heinie Berger, sp
Cy Falkenberg, sp
Bob Rhoads, sp

Attendance

354,627 (sixth in AL)

Club Leaders

Batting Avg:	Nap Lajoie	.324
On-Base Pct:	Nap Lajoie	.378
Slugging Pct:	Nap Lajoie	.431
Home Runs:	George Stovall	2
	Bill Hinchman	2
RBIs:	Bill Hinchman	53
Runs:	George Stovall	60
Stolen Bases:	George Stovall	25
Wins:	Cy Young	19
Strikeouts:	Heinie Berger	162
ERA:	Addie Joss	1.71
Saves:	Heinie Berger	1
	Fred Winchell	1

February 18 Three months after Ohioan William Howard Taft wins the presidential election, the Indians send Charlie Chech, Jack Ryan, and $12,500 to the Red Sox for Cy Young.

The annual award for the best pitcher in each league is named after Cy Young because of his unparalleled accomplishments. He began his career in 1890 in Cleveland as a member of the National League Spiders. Young's stay in Cleveland ended just prior to the 1899 season when Frank and Stanley Robison, owners of the Spiders, also purchased the St. Louis Cardinals. The Robison brothers transferred all of the Spiders best players, including Young, to St. Louis. After two seasons with the Cardinals, Young jumped to the American League and pitched for the Red Sox from 1901 through 1908. Young had a 478–282 career record and was 42-years-old at the start of the 1909 season. With the Indians missing the pennant by a scant one-half game in 1908, it was believed that the trade for Young would be enough to put Cleveland into the World Series. He gave the Indians one good season, going 19–15 with an earned run average of 2.26, but the club fell out of contention. After a 7–10 record in 1910 and 3–4 in 1911, Young was released and finished out his career with the Boston Braves. In 1937, he became the eighth player elected to the Hall of Fame.

April 14 In the season opener, the Indians defeat the Browns 4–2 in St. Louis. All four Cleveland runs scored in the fourth inning. Addie Joss pitched the complete game victory.

The Indians pennant hopes for 1909 were still alive in mid-July when the club was 44–32 in third place and five games out of first. A 27–50 record over the remainder of the season, despite an eleven-game winning streak, ended dreams of a World Series in Cleveland.

April 15 In his first game with the Indians, Cy Young defeats the Browns 4–3 in St. Louis.

April 22 In the home opener, the Indians lose 6–4 to the Browns in 14 innings at League Park.

May 1 The Indians game against the White Sox at League Park is postponed by snow.

May 2 Addie Joss pitches a four-hitter to beat the Browns 1–0 at League Park. Joss held the Browns hitless until the seventh inning.

May 13 Bill Bradley ties an American League record for most putouts by a third baseman in a game with seven, but the Indians lose 8–1 to the Red Sox at League Park.

May 27 The Indians and Browns combine for 44 assists, a major league record for a nine-inning game, in an encounter won by the Indians 5–2 in St. Louis. There were 22 assists by each team. The two pitchers were Addie Joss and Barney Pelty.

June 7 The Indians play at Shibe Park in Philadelphia for the first time, and defeat the Athletics 3–1.

Shibe Park was baseball's first double-decked ballpark constructed of concrete and steel. The Athletics played there until 1954 when the club moved to Kansas City. Renamed Connie Mack Stadium in 1953, it was the home of the Phillies from 1939 through 1970.

June 8 Addie Joss pitches a one-hitter to beat the Athletics 2–0 in Philadelphia. The only hit off Joss was a double by Danny Murphy.

June 11 Pitching in Boston for the first time since his trade from the Red Sox to the Indians, Cy Young hurls a two-hitter to win 3–1. The only hits off Young were singles by Harry Niles and Harry Wolter.

Young won 19 games in 1909, just missing his 17th season of 20 wins or more. He holds the all-time record for 20-win seasons with 16. Christy Mathewson and Warren Spahn rank second on the list with 13 each.

July 4 Addie Joss pitches a two-hitter to defeat the White Sox 3–0 at League Park. The only Chicago hits were singles by Freddy Parent and Billy Purtell.

Indians fans cheered the return of star pitcher Cy Young, who even at 42 could still get batters out, though 1909 would be his final productive year.

July 7 The Indians score three runs in the ninth inning to defeat the Tigers 4–3 in Detroit. The winning run scored on a walk-off, pinch-hit single by Harry Bemis.

July 13 Addie Joss pitches ten innings to beat the Athletics 1–0 in Philadelphia. Joss surrendered only two hits. The lone run of the game scored on singles by Bill Hinchman and George Perring and a sacrifice by Neal Ball. The only hits off Joss were singles by Danny Murphy and Jack Barry.

Perring used a bat that was more than 30 years old, made from a prison scaffold. His father had used it for 20 years before bestowing the bat to his son.

July 19 Indians shortstop Neal Ball pulls off the first officially recognized unassisted triple play in major league history and hits a home run during the second inning of a 6–1 win over the Red Sox in the first game of a double header at League Park. With the Indians winning 1–0, Heinie Wagner and Jake Stall led off the second with singles off Cy Young, both on infield rollers. After failing twice to sacrifice, Amby McConnell stung a vicious liner on a 3–2 pitch toward short with both runners moving with the pitch. Ball snared it with a leaping catch, raced to second to force out Wagner, and tagged Stall as he pulled up two strides short of the base. Facing Ray Collins in the bottom of the inning, Ball hit an inside-the-park homer over the head of center fielder Tris Speaker.

Ball had been purchased from the Yankees in May to replace injured starting shortstop Terry Turner. There have been only 12 unassisted triple plays in major league history, including the one by Cleveland second baseman Bill Wambsganss in the 1920 World Series. Ball and Wambsganss are the only Indians with unassisted triple plays. The Indians have also hit into three triple plays by George Burns of the Red Sox in 1923, Johnny Neun of the Tigers in 1927, and Ron Hansen of the Senators in 1968. The home run by Ball in the July 19, 1909, game was his first in the majors. He hit only four homers in 1,613 at-bats over seven major league seasons. The other three occurred in 1911.

AUGUST 17 With the team spiraling into the second division, Nap Lajoie resigns as manager of the Indians. The resignation was effective as soon as the club could find a replacement. Lajoie remained with the Indians as the starting second baseman and continued his excellent play. In 1909, he batted .324.

AUGUST 22 The Indians name 45-year-old Deacon McGuire as manager.

McGuire previous managed the Washington Senators in 1898 and the Red Sox in 1907 and 1908. A catcher during his playing days, McGuire appeared in at least one game in 26 different seasons from 1884 through 1912, the last at the age of 48. He managed the Indians until May 1911 to a record of 91–117.

SEPTEMBER 4 Tigers outfielder Ty Cobb becomes engaged in a fight with the hotel operator and night watchman, both of them African-American, at Cleveland's Hotel Euclid at 2:00 a.m. Cobb slapped the elevator operator, at which point George Stansfield, the hotel night watchman, who was also black, intervened. Cobb and Stansfield began shouting at each other, and Stansfield struck Cobb with his nightstick. They struggled and fell to the floor, where Cobb managed to get a knife from his pocket and slashed at Stansfield. The night watchman made it to his feet, threw Cobb off, and knocked the ballplayer to his knees with another blow from his nightstick. Other hotel employees then came between the two. Cobb was fined $100 for assault and battery in a Cleveland court on November 22, 1909. The Detroit club paid Stansfield's medical expenses.

SEPTEMBER 22 The Indians lose their 11th game in a row, dropping a 3–1 decision to the Red Sox in Boston.

THE STATE OF THE INDIANS

The Indians were in a rebuilding stage at the start of the 1910s, and it wasn't until near the end of the decade that the franchise found a winning combination. The 1918 and 1919 clubs just missed winning a pennant before Cleveland finally reached the World Series for the first time in 1920. Overall, the Indians were 742–747 during the decade, a winning percentage of .498 that was the fifth best in the AL. Pennant winners were the Athletics (1910, 1911, 1913, and 1914), Red Sox (1912, 1915, 1916, and 1918), and White Sox (1917 and 1919).

THE BEST TEAM

The 1919 Indians were 84–55 and in second place 2½ games behind the White Sox. It was the first club in the history of the franchise to win at least 60 percent of its games.

THE WORST TEAM

The 1914 Indians were an abysmal 51–102 under manager Joe Birmingham. The winning percentage of .333 is the worst in club history.

THE BEST MOMENT

The best moments were individual milestones. Cy Young won his 500th game in 1910 and Nap Lajoie collected his 3,000th hit in 1914.

THE WORST MOMENT

Addie Joss collapsed on the bench during an exhibition game in Chattanooga, Tennessee, on April 3, 1911. Eleven days later, he was dead at the age of 31 from tubercular meningitis.

THE ALL-DECADE TEAM • YEARS W/INDIANS

Steve O'Neill, c	1911–23
Doc Johnston, 1b	1912–14, 1918–21
Nap Lajoie, 2b	1902–14
Terry Turner, 3b	1904–18
Ray Chapman, ss	1912–20
Jack Graney, lf	1908, 1910–22
Tris Speaker, cf	1916–26
Joe Jackson, rf	1910–15
Jim Bagby, Sr., p	1916–22
Stan Coveleski, p	1916–24
Guy Morton, p	1914–24
Vean Gregg, p	1911–14

Lajoie and Turner were also on the 1900s All-Decade Team. Turner made the 1900s All-Decade Team as a shortstop. Lajoie, Speaker, and Coveleski are all in the Hall of Fame. There is little doubt that Jackson would also be in the Hall of Fame if he wasn't permanently barred from baseball for his role in fixing the 1919 World Series while he was playing for the White Sox. Chapman was building a Hall of Fame resume when he was killed by a pitch in 1920. Other outstanding players with the Indians during the 1910s included second baseman Bill Wambsganss (1914–23), right fielder Elmer Smith (1914–17, 1919–21), right fielder Braggo Roth (1915–18), catcher Ted Easterly (1909–12), and pitchers Willie Mitchell (1909–16), Cy Falkenberg (1908–11, 1913), and Fred Blanding (1910–14).

THE DECADE LEADERS

Batting Avg:	Joe Jackson	.375
On-Base Pct:	Joe Jackson	.442
Slugging Pct:	Joe Jackson	.542
Home Runs:	Joe Jackson	24
RBIs:	Joe Jackson	353
Runs:	Jack Graney	650
Stolen Bases:	Ray Chapman	220
Wins:	Stan Coveleski	80
Strikeouts:	Willie Mitchell	767
ERA:	Vean Gregg	2.32
Saves:	Jim Bagby	21

THE HOME FIELD

The period between 1909 and 1914 was a significant one in the evolution of stadium construction as wooden ballparks were being replaced by double-decked facilities built with concrete and steel. Among them were such classic baseball venues as Shibe Park (1909), Forbes Field (1909), Comiskey Park (1910), the Polo Grounds (1912), Crosley Field (1912), Fenway Park (1912), Tiger Stadium (1912), Ebbets Field (1913), and Wrigley Field (1914). The Indians became part of this trend by tearing down wooden League Park during the 1909–10 off-season and constructing a new ball field on the same site with concrete and steel. It opened on April 21, 1910, and served the Indians until 1947. At the beginning, the park had no official name and in the local newspapers was called both League Park and Somers Park, the latter moniker after the owner of the Indians. The name of the facility was changed to Dunn Field when Charles Somers sold the Indians to James Dunn in 1916, and back to the original name of League Park in 1927 when Dunn's heirs sold the club to Alva Bradley.

THE GAME YOU WISHED YOU HAD SEEN

Although it wasn't an official league contest, the Indians played a team of American League All-Stars in a benefit for Addie Joss on July 24, 1911, at League Park. The AL All-Star team featured seven future Hall of Famers.

THE WAY THE GAME WAS PLAYED

Pitching and defense continued to dominate baseball. Offense spiked in the early years of the decade after the AL adopted the cork-centered ball in 1910, but by the mid-teens, the league batting average was back around .250. Home runs were at a premium. There were more than twice as many triples as home runs, and speedy outfielders were a necessity to cover playing fields that were much larger than those common today. AL pitchers completed 56 percent of their starts, but this was a significant drop from the 79 percent of the previous decade. During the 1910s, the strategic use of relief pitching, pinch-hitters, and platooning became an important aspect of the game for the first time.

THE MANAGEMENT

Charles Somers owned the Indians until 1916, when because of financial difficulties, he sold out to James "Sunny Jim" Dunn. Dunn would continue as owner until 1917. Emil Barnard was vice-president with the duties of a present-day general manager. Field managers were Deacon McGuire (1909–11), George Stovall (1911), Harry Davis (1912), Joe Birmingham (1912–15), Lee Fohl (1917–19), and Tris Speaker (1919–26).

THE BEST PLAYER MOVE

The best move, perhaps the best in franchise history, brought Tris Speaker from the Red Sox in April 1916 for Sad Sam Jones, Pinch Thomas, and $55,000.

THE WORST PLAYER MOVE

With the club at a low ebb, the Indians traded Joe Jackson to the White Sox for Braggo Roth, Larry Chappell, and Ed Klepfer along with a reported $31,500.

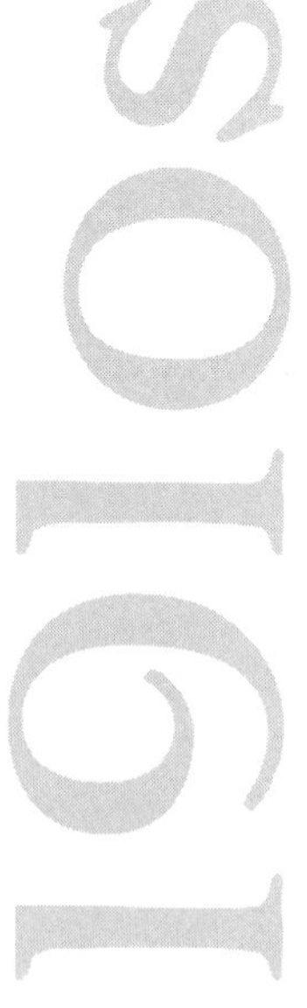

1910

Season in a Sentence

The season begins with the opening of a new ballpark and high hopes for a pennant, and ends with a fifth-place finish and a controversial batting race between Nap Lajoie and Ty Cobb.

Finish • Won • Lost • Pct • GB

Finish	Won	Lost	Pct	GB
Fifth	71	81	.467	32.0

Manager

Deacon McGuire

Stats

Stats	Indians	AL	Rank
Batting Avg:	.244	.243	5
On-Base Pct:	.297	.306	6
Slugging Pct:	.308	.313	5
Home Runs:	9		6 (tie)
Stolen Bases:	189		6
Fielding Avg:	.964	.956	2
ERA:	2.88	2.52	7
Runs Scored:	548		5
Runs Allowed:	657		7

Starting Line-up

Ted Easterly, c
George Stovall, 1b
Nap Lajoie, 2b
Bill Bradley, 3b
Terry Turner, ss-3b
Jack Graney, lf
Joe Birmingham, cf
Harry Niles, rf
Art Kruger, lf
Bris Lord, rf-lf
Harry Bemis, c

Pitchers

Cy Falkenberg, sp
Willie Mitchell, sp-rp
Specs Harkness, sp-rp
Cy Young, sp
Fred Link, sp
Addie Joss, sp
George Kahler, sp
Harry Fanwell, sp-rp
Elmer Koestner, rp-sp

Attendance

391,288 (fourth in AL)

Club Leaders

Batting Avg:	Nap Lajoie	.384
On-Base Pct:	Nap Lajoie	.445
Slugging Pct:	Nap Lajoie	.514
Home Runs:	Nap Lajoie	4
RBIs:	Nap Lajoie	76
Runs:	Nap Lajoie	94
Stolen Bases:	Terry Turner	31
Wins:	Cy Falkenberg	14
Strikeouts:	Cy Falkenberg	107
ERA:	Cy Young	2.53
Saves:	Elmer Koestner	2

April 14 In the season opener, the Indians win 9–7 in ten innings against the Tigers in Detroit. The Indians trailed 4–0 after four innings before taking a 5–4 lead. The Tigers tied the score 5–5 with a run in the ninth to send the contest into extra innings. In the tenth, Cleveland plated four runs and Detroit countered with two.

April 15 In the second game of the season, the Indians score four runs in the tenth inning for the second day in a row, winning 6–2 over the Tigers in Detroit.

April 20 Addie Joss pitches a no-hitter, beating the White Sox 1–0 in Chicago. It was his second career no-hitter, both of which came against the White Sox (see October 2, 1908). Joss helped himself with ten assists, one shy of the major league record for pitchers in a nine-inning game. Addie walked two and struck out two. The Indians scored the lone run of the contest in the sixth inning on a single by Art Kruger and a double by Terry Turner. In the ninth inning, opposing pitcher Doc White and Ed Hahn were retired on grounders hit back to Joss. The final out was recorded on a ground out by Rollie Zeider to third baseman Bill Bradley.

April 21 In the first game at new League Park, the Indians lose 5–0 to the Tigers before a crowd of 18,832. Ed Willett pitched the shutout. Prior to the start of the game, both teams, accompanied by American League president Ban Johnson and National Commission chairman Garry Herrmann, paraded to the flagpole in center field, where the Stars and Stripes were raised.

The dimensions of the new League Park were among the wackiest in baseball because of the odd configuration of the lot on which the facility was built. It was 385 feet down the left field line, 505 feet to the deepest part of the field in left-center, 420 feet to dead center, 460 feet in right-center and, officially, 290 feet down the right field line. The right field wall and screen, bordering Lexington Avenue, was 45 feet high. Balls that struck the barrier could carom in almost any direction depending upon whether it struck the 25-foot high concrete wall, the 20-foot chicken wire extension above it, or the vertical steel beams supporting the wire. Left fielders sometimes ended up fielding drives hit off the right field wall and also had to deal with a slight embankment in front of the wall. Part of the screen was torn down during the 1930s when Earl Averill and Eddie Morgan began hitting home runs with regularity. Another unusual feature were box seats down the third base line beyond the bag in which fans were able to look directly into the Indians dugout and issue comments on the club's play. The stands were double-decked and extended from foul pole to foul pole. The roof of the grandstand was 79 feet high and the uninspiring exterior, which resembled a warehouse, was red brick. A single deck of stands ran from ten feet outside the left-field foul pole to left-center. Capacity was about 21,000. The large green scoreboard was in center. A drive to the outfield could roll under the board, and occasionally a center fielder would have to crawl under it to retrieve a ball that was still in play. Despite the short distance to right field, League Park was one of the most difficult places in the American League to hit a home run because of the high wall and the large expanses of center and left fields. The press box, directly behind home plate, was considered the most dangerous in baseball because it was windowless and very close to the field. Although called League Park in present day histories of the ballpark and the club, it had no official name in 1910. It was often called Somers Park, after Indians owner Charles Somers, in contemporary newspapers from 1910 through 1915.

MAY 1 The Indians win 5–4 in 11 innings over the Browns in St. Louis. George Perring drove in the winning run with a pinch-single.

MAY 2 The Indians edge the Browns 2–1 in 11 innings in St. Louis. Bris Lord drove in the winning tally with a double.

MAY 4 Following a postponement of a game on May 3 due to cold weather, the Browns and Indians meet again and play to a 3–3 tie in a contest called after 14 innings by darkness.

President William Howard Taft attended part of the game. To avoid showing favoritism, Taft went to both the Browns-Indians contest at Sportsman's Park, and the Cardinals-Reds clash at Robison Field a few blocks away.

MAY 5 After a train trip to Cleveland, the Indians and Browns play into extra innings for the fourth straight game. The Indians won the game at League Park in ten innings. Bill Bradley drove in the winning run with a single. The Indians won three of the four games with one resulting in a tie.

May 12 Chief Bender of the Athletics faces the minimum 27 batters and pitches a no-hitter to defeat the Indians 4–0 in Philadelphia. The only Cleveland base runner was Terry Turner, who walked in the fourth inning and was thrown out stealing. The last out was recorded when pinch-hitter Elmer Flick lofted a foul pop-up to catcher Pinch Thomas.

June 21 Cy Young pitches a 12-inning complete game to defeat the White Sox 3–2 in the first game of a double header at League Park. It was Young's first victory of the 1910 season and the 498th of his career. Chicago won the second tilt 3–0 in ten innings.

Few people in team history personify the Indians more than Jack Graney, shown here during his 14-year playing career, all spent with the Tribe. In 1929 he became the first ex-major league player to become a broadcaster, calling games on radio and later on television into the 1950s.

June 22 The Indians outlast the White Sox 3–2 in 14 innings at League Park. Cleveland scored a run in the ninth to send the contest into extra innings. Bris Lord won the contest with a walk-off double. It was the third extra-inning game in two days between the two clubs.

June 30 Cy Young wins his 499th career game with a two-hitter to defeat the Browns 5–0 at League Park. The only St. Louis hits were singles by Jack Truesdale and George Stone.

Young failed in his next three starts before finally winning number 500 (see July 19, 1910).

July 19 Cy Young wins his 500th career game, defeating the Senators 5–2 in 11 innings in Washington. Young allowed only one hit through eight innings but surrendered a run and two hits in the ninth, which tied the game 2–2. Cleveland won the contest with three runs in the 11th. While pitching an 11-inning complete game at the age of 43, Young gave up only four hits. Washington won the opener 7–0.

Young entered the 1910 season with 497 career victories. Coming off of a 19-win season in 1909, it appeared as though he would reach 500 fairly quickly, but he had a won-lost record of 2–7 entering the game on July 19, 1910. Young ended his career in 1911 with 511 career wins. He is far ahead of Walter Johnson, who is second in lifetime wins with 417 in a career that lasted from 1907 through 1927. Young is also the record holder in career innings pitched with 7,356. Pud Galvin is a distant second with 5,941⅓ innings. In addition, Young is first on the career lists in games started (815), complete games (749), and seasons of 20 or more wins (16).

JULY 22 Cy Falkenberg allows one run in pitching a 15-inning complete game, but the result is a 1–1 tie when the contest against the Athletics in Philadelphia is called by darkness. The Indians won the first game 7–6.

JULY 25 The Indians trade Bris Lord to the Athletics for Joe Jackson.

The Indians pulled off one of the best trades in club history in acquiring Jackson, who played for Cleveland until August 21, 1915, when he was dealt to the White Sox in one of the worst transactions in club history. Among Indians with at least 2,000 plate appearances, Jackson ranks first in batting average (.375), second in on base percentage (.442) and fifth in slugging percentage (.542). He also holds single season records for batting average (.408 in 1911), hits (233 in 1911), and triples (26 in 1912). Jackson made his major league debut with the Athletics in 1908. He showed his batting brilliance in the minors, where he won three batting titles, but in eight games with Philadelphia, he hit just .150. A man who was illiterate and came from an impoverished family in rural South Carolina, Jackson was taunted mercilessly about his lack of education from insensitive Athletics teammates. Connie Mack had a pennant-winning club in 1910 and kept Jackson in the minors with New Orleans in the Southern League in the interests of club harmony. Close friends with Cleveland club owner Charles Somers, Mack offered Jackson to the Indians for Lord, a veteran outfielder, with the proviso that Jackson remain in New Orleans until the Southern League season ended. The hard-hitting outfielder was arrived in Cleveland in September shortly after his 21st birthday and was an immediate sensation, hitting .387 in 20 games.

AUGUST 16 Cy Falkenberg is left in the game by manager Deacon McGuire to absorb a pounding in an 18–3 loss to the Athletics at League Park. Falkenberg pitched the complete game, allowed 23 hits, and was staggering at the finish. He gave up eight runs in the eighth inning and six in the ninth.

AUGUST 30 The Indians are held hitless for the first nine innings by Yankees pitcher Tom Hughes before scoring five runs in the 11th to win 5–0 in the second game of a double header in New York. George Kahler pitched a complete game shutout for the Indians, surrendering just three hits. Through nine innings, the only Indians base runner was Terry Turner, who reached on an error by third baseman Jimmy Austin. Cleveland picked-up their first hits in the tenth on back-to-back singles by Harry Niles and Nap Lajoie with one out. In the eleventh, Hughes retired the first two batters to face him before Kahler singled to start a rally in which the Indians scored five runs on four hits. Harry Niles drove in the first two tallies with a bases loaded single.

Lajoie finished second in a controversial batting race (see October 9, 1910) with a .384 average. Nap did lead the league in hits (227), doubles (51), and total bases (304). He scored 94 runs and drove in 78. Catcher Ted Easterly was another key contributor, batting .306.

September 5 The Indians play at Comiskey Park in Chicago for the first time, and split a double header with the White Sox. The Indians won the first game 5–0 and lost the second 10–5.

The original Comiskey Park was the home of the White Sox from July 1, 1910, through the end of the 1990 season.

September 11 Indians pitcher Willie Mitchell, a 20-year-old rookie, hurls a one-hitter to beat the Browns 2–0 in the first game of a double header at Sportsman's Park. The only St. Louis hit was a single by Roy Hartzell. The Indians also won the second contest 7–5.

September 15 In his major league debut, Indians pitcher Fred Blanding pitches a shutout to defeat the Senators 3–0 at League Park. Walter Johnson was the losing pitcher. Blanding was one of five rookies in the Cleveland line-up. The others were catcher Grover Land, outfielder Dave Callahan, first baseman Eddie Hohnhorst, and shortstop Roger Peckinpaugh. It was also the big league debut for Peckinpaugh.

October 5 The Indians score five runs in the tenth inning to defeat the Tigers 8–3 in the first game of a double header in Detroit. The Tigers won the nightcap, called after five innings by darkness, 4–2.

October 9 The battle for the American League batting title is decided on the final day with Ty Cobb edging Nap Lajoie .385 to .384. Neither man could be proud of their behavior. Lajoie went eight-for-eight in a double header, against the Browns in St. Louis, accepting six "gift" hits on bunt singles on which Browns rookie third baseman Red Corriden was purposely stationed too deep to field the ball in time to throw Lajoie out at first. The St. Louis official scorer also credited Lajoie with a hit on a wild throw to first base. The Indians lost the first game 5–4 but won the second 3–0. Cobb meanwhile, sat out the last two games to protect his lead.

October 18 The Reds defeat the Indians 8–3 in Cincinnati to win the championship of Ohio before only 1,949 fans. The Reds captured the seven-game series four games to three.

The 1910 Batting Race

The 1910 American League batting race was one of the most controversial in baseball history and still hasn't been fully resolved to this day. It pitted good (Nap Lajoie) versus evil (Ty Cobb) with a glamorous, luxury automobile as the prize. The two players battled each other for the batting crown during the final weeks with both Lajoie's Indians and Cobb's Tigers out of the pennant chase. One of the most respected players in the game, Lajoie was 36 years old and in his 15th season in the majors. Cobb was an upstart, who at the age of 23 was almost universally despised, even by his own teammates. Both had won three previous batting titles. To up the ante, Hugh Chalmers, president of the Chalmers Motor Company, had announced before the season started that a new automobile would be given to the player with the highest batting average in the major leagues. While such a prize would excite few today, when players earn enough to purchase a fleet of cars, a Chalmers in 1910 was a status symbol at a time when the mere ownership of an automobile brought an individual a certain social standing and players drew relatively modest salaries.

Both hitters set a torrid batting pace down the stretch. Entering the final day of the season, Cobb had 25 hits in his last 47 at-bats. Lajoie was 30-for-54. Cobb went into the final weekend with a comfortable lead, and to protect it, sat out the last two games against the White Sox. On the final day, Sunday October 9, the Indians were scheduled to play a double header against the Browns in St. Louis. Lajoie needed a hit every trip to the plate to have a chance at the batting title. With the help of Browns manager Jack O'Connor, Lajoie did just that with eight hits in eight at-bats. Such was the animosity toward Cobb that O'Connor decided to help the Cleveland second baseman take the batting title. O'Connor instructed rookie third baseman Red Corriden, a veteran of only 24 big league games, to play back on the outfield grass whenever Lajoie came to the plate, telling the gullible Corriden that it was a precaution against injury because of Nap's propensity to strike vicious line drives.

On his first trip to the plate in the first game, Lajoie's deep drive cleared the head of center fielder Hub Northen, another rookie, for a triple. Next, Lajoie bunted toward shortstop Bobby Wallace, who fielded the ball slowly and threw too late to get Lajoie. The time after that, he bunted to third, where Corriden was so far back he had no chance for a play.

From then on, Lajoie bunted to Corriden six more times, including his final plate appearance in game one and all five in game two. On all but one, a play on which he was credited with a sacrifice in the third inning of the second game, he made easy base hits, even though at that advanced stage of his career, Lajoie was anything but lightning fast. Browns pitchers did their part by grooving pitches over the center of the plate so that Lajoie could make easy contact. Determined that Lajoie should be credited with a ninth hit, Browns coach Harry Howell first went to the press section to inquire about the scoring on the sacrifice, and then sent over the bat boy, offering official scorer E. V. Parrish a suit of clothes if he changed his ruling to a single. Parrish refused.

The next day, St. Louis sportswriters accused O'Connor of giving Lajoie hits. The Browns lamely replied that Lajoie "outguessed us. We figured he did not have the nerve to bunt every time." When the writers quizzed Corriden, the rookie third sacker said that he "wasn't going to get killed playing in on Lajoie." That afternoon, Lajoie received a congratulatory telegram from eight of Cobb's teammates.

American League president Ban Johnson had Robert McRoy, his secretary and keeper of the official statistics, hurriedly calculate the season's averages. On October 15, Johnson declared Cobb the batting champion with an average of .385 to Lajoie's .384.

Recognizing the unprecedented publicity, Chalmers gave an automobile to both Cobb and Lajoie and presented them before the opening game of the World Series between the Athletics and Cubs. National Commission chairman Garry Herrmann announced that in the future, no prizes would be given for winning a batting championship alone. The Browns fired both O'Connor and Howell and released Corriden. O'Connor, whose club was 47–107 in 1910, never worked in organized baseball again. Corriden made it back to the majors in 1912 and was active in baseball until shortly before his death in 1959 as a player, coach, scout, and manager. He managed the White Sox for part of the 1950 season.

From 1911 through 1914, Chalmers awarded an auto to the most valuable player, which was voted upon by a committee of sportswriters. It was baseball's first MVP award. Through a series of mergers, the Chalmers Company became part of the Chrysler Corporation during the 1920s.

The Sporting News reported in 1981, following an exhaustive examination of the score sheets from the 1910 season, that one of Cobb's games, in which he was two-for-four, was recorded twice. Once that game was removed, Lajoie had the better average .384 to .383. Despite the discovery, Cobb is still listed as the 1910 batting champion in most baseball encyclopedias. It was one of a major league record 11 batting titles won by Cobb.

1911

Season in a Sentence

Addie Joss dies two days after Opening Day, Deacon McGuire resigns as manager, Cy Young is released, and Nap Lajoie misses 63 games, but the Indians overcome the adversity to rise from fifth place to third.

Finish • Won • Lost • Pct • GB

Finish	Won	Lost	Pct	GB
Third	80	73	.523	20.0

Managers

Deacon McGuire (6–11) and George Stovall (74–62)

Stats

Stats	Indians	AL	Rank
Batting Avg:	.282	.273	4
On-Base Pct:	.333	.338	5
Slugging Pct:	.369	.358	3
Home Runs:	20		5 (tie)
Stolen Bases:	209		5
ERA:	3.36	3.34	4
Fielding Avg:	.954	.953	3
Runs Scored:	691		4
Runs Allowed:	712		4

Starting Line-up

Gus Fisher, c
George Stovall, 1b
Neal Ball, 2b
Terry Turner, 3b
Ivy Olson, ss
Jack Graney, lf
Joe Birmingham, cf
Joe Jackson, rf-cf
Nap Lajoie, 1b-2b
Ted Easterly, rf
Syd Smith, c

Pitchers

Vean Gregg, sp
Gene Krapp, sp
George Kahler, sp-rp
Willie Mitchell, sp
Fred Blanding, sp-rp
Cy Falkenberg, sp

Attendance

406,296 (fifth in AL)

Club Leaders

Batting Avg:	Joe Jackson	.408
On-Base Pct:	Joe Jackson	.468
Slugging Pct:	Joe Jackson	.590
Home Runs:	Joe Jackson	7
RBIs:	Joe Jackson	83
Runs:	Joe Jackson	126
Stolen Bases:	Joe Jackson	41
Wins:	Vean Gregg	23
Strikeouts:	Gene Krapp	130
ERA:	Vean Gregg	1.80
Saves:	Fred Blanding	2

APRIL 12 In the season opener, the Browns pelt the Indians 12–3 in St. Louis.

APRIL 13 Cyclonic winds and hailstones bring an end to the Indians-Browns clash in St. Louis in the top of the ninth inning. The Indians had just tied the score 2–2 and had two runners on base with no one out when the terrific storm struck Sportsman's Park. The flagpole snapped and crashed into the bleachers. Advertising signs on the outfield walls blew down. Players, umpires, writers, and fans hurriedly took refuge under the stands. There were no serious injuries, but many were badly bruised by the hailstones traveling at high speed because of the wind. The score reverted back to the close of the eighth inning, and the Browns were given a 2–1 victory.

APRIL 14 Addie Joss dies of tubercular meningitis at the age of 31.

Joss became ill and fainted on the bench during an exhibition game in Chattanooga, Tennessee, on April 3. He rejoined the team a few days later, but soon took sick again and returned to his home in Toledo, Ohio. His illness was diagnosed as tubercular meningitis, and within a week he was dead. Though he played nine seasons in the majors, one short of the number required for admission to the Hall of Fame, the Veterans Committee waived the rule for Joss and inducted him in 1978.

APRIL 17 The funeral for Addie Joss is held at the Masonic Hall in his hometown of Toledo, Ohio. Evangelist, and former major league outfielder, Billy Sunday preached at the service. Joss was buried at Woodlawn Cemetery.

The Indians were scheduled to play the Tigers that day in Detroit. The club requested that the contest be postponed so that the players could attend the funeral, but AL president Ban Johnson and Detroit management insisted that it be played as scheduled. Johnson threatened suspensions and fines if the Indians did not play, but the players said they would travel Toledo regardless. Fearing adverse public reaction, Johnson relented and postponed the game.

APRIL 20 In the home opener, the Indians lose 4–3 in ten innings to the Browns at League Park. Gene Krapp pitched eight shutout innings before allowing three runs in the ninth inning and one in the tenth.

MAY 3 The White Sox score three runs in the ninth inning to defeat the White Sox 8–7 at League Park.

The game was George Stovall's first as manager. His appointment followed the resignation of Deacon McGuire with the club holding a 6–11 record. Under Stovall's direction, Cleveland was 74–62 over the remainder of the season.

MAY 7 An inside-the-park grand slam by Joe Jackson in the 12th inning off Jack Powell beats the Browns 6–2 in St. Louis.

Jackson exploded onto the scene in his first full season in the majors. Only 22 years old, he hit .408, scored 126 runs, and collected 233 hits, 45 doubles, 19 triples, and 337 total bases. Unfortunately, he didn't lead the AL in any of those categories because Ty Cobb had an even better year, batting .420. Jackson's 1911 batting average remains the sixth highest in the modern era, and the best since 1900 of any individual who did not win a batting title. Shoeless Joe is also the only Indian in history to hit over .400 in a season.

MAY 14 The Indians play on a Sunday in Cleveland for the first time and romp to a 14–3 win over the Yankees at League Park. The Indians scored seven runs in the third inning.

MAY 18 With the score 2–2, the Indians erupt for seven runs in the sixth inning and defeat the Senators 9–6 at League Park. Ivy Olson hit a grand slam off Tom Hughes during the big inning.

The homer by Olson was the first of his career. He didn't hit another one until 1914 and collected just 13 home runs in 6,111 big league at-bats over 14 seasons.

MAY 30 All five runs in a ten-inning, 3–2 loss to the Tigers in the first game of a double header at League Park are scored on sacrifice flies. The runs were driven in by Oscar Stanage, Charley O'Leary, and Jim Delahanty of the Tigers, and George Stovall and Ted Easterly of the Indians. Detroit won the second game 6–5.

JULY 18 At League Park, the Indians win their ninth game in a row by scoring all nine runs of a 9–6 win over the Yankees in the seventh inning. Cleveland trailed 3–0 when the rally started. Nap Lajoie's two-run, pinch-single put the Indians into the lead.

JULY 24 A benefit game is held at League Park for the family of Addie Joss with the Indians losing 5–3 to a team of American League All-Stars. A crowd of 15,272 raised a total of $12,914. The All-Stars included future Hall of Famers Ty Cobb, Walter Johnson, Tris Speaker, Eddie Collins, Home Run Baker, Sam Crawford, and Bobby Wallace. The field announcer was Germany Schaefer of the Senators, who kept the crowd laughing at his antics.

AUGUST 3 The Indians edge the Yankees 11–10 in New York. Down 4–0 after four innings, the Indians rallied and broke a 7–7 tie with two runs in the seventh.

AUGUST 7 Nap Lajoie collects three doubles and a homer during an 8–3 win over the Red Sox in Boston.

AUGUST 15 The Indians release Cy Young.

Young was 44 years old and had a 3–4 record when released. Counting the 241 games he won with the Spiders from 1890 through 1898, Young had 270 victories with two Cleveland clubs. He signed with the Boston Braves and pitched ten more big league games, four of them victories, before retiring at the end of the 1911 season.

AUGUST 19 Hank Butcher's hit with two out in the ninth inning drives in two runs and lifts the Indians to a 3–2 win over the Yankees at League Park.

AUGUST 20 The Indians purchase Steve O'Neill from the Athletics.

O'Neill was a month past his 20th birthday when acquired by the Indians and played for the club for 13 seasons. He caught 1,335 games, second most in franchise history behind Jim Hegan's 1,491. O'Neill was later manager of the Indians from 1935 through 1937. He was the second youngest of four brothers from a Minooka, Pennsylvania, family to reach the majors. The other three were Jack (born in 1873), Mike (1877), and Jim (1893). Jack and Jim were born in Ireland before the O'Neills emigrated to the United States. Steve and Jim were born in Minooka.

AUGUST 22 Vean Gregg pitches the Indians to a 1–0 win over the Red Sox at League Park. Nap Lajoie drove in a double in the first inning.

AUGUST 27 Vean Gregg not only pitches the Indians to a 1–0 win over the Senators at League Park, he drives in the lone run of the game with a bases-loaded infield ground out in the eighth inning.

Sylveanus Augustus (Vean) Gregg was an immediate sensation as a 26-year-old rookie in 1911, posting a 23–7 record and a league-leading 1.80 earned run average. He followed the campaign with 20 wins in both 1912 and 1913, but a sore arm eventually reduced his effectiveness. Gregg was traded to the Red Sox in August 1914 with a won-lost ledger of 72–36 as an Indian. His winning percentage of .667 is the best among Indians pitchers with at least 100 decisions. Gregg's brother Dave had a one-game, one-inning big league career, pitching for Cleveland in 1913.

AUGUST 30 Fred Blanding allows three runs in the ninth inning, which ties the game against the Senators at League Park 3–3, but he redeems himself by starting an eleventh-inning rally with a single. Blanding scored on a sacrifice and Ivy Olson's single for a 4–3 victory.

SEPTEMBER 1 Shortstop Ivy Olson chokes off a ninth-inning White Sox rally by tagging out Felix Chouinard on a "hidden ball trick" at second base. The Indians won 2–1 in Chicago.

SEPTEMBER 3 The Indians score five runs in the 12th inning for a 7–2 win over the White Sox in the first game of a double header in Chicago. The Indians completed the sweep with a 3–1 victory in the second contest.

SEPTEMBER 9 The Indians record their tenth win in a row by building an 8–0 lead after two innings and thrashing the Browns 9–2 at League Park.

SEPTEMBER 20 U.S. Vice-President James Sherman witnesses a double header between the Indians and Yankees in New York. The Indians won the opener 12–9 but lost the second tilt, called after seven innings by darkness, 5–4.

SEPTEMBER 24 Umpire Billy Evans is attacked by thousands of fans following a 5–3 loss to the Athletics on a Sunday afternoon at League Park. The crowd objected to Evans's decision on a foul, and hooted his calls at every opportunity. With two out in the ninth, Hank Butcher was ejected with two strikes on him for objecting to the calls, further inflaming the Cleveland fans. Just as Evans started to leave the grounds, he was struck by one of the spectators. The umpire struck back, and knocked the fan out cold. The crowd then rushed at Evans, who was backed by Indians and Athletics players. Evans knocked out two more fans who attacked him, and Eddie Collins of the A's and Joe Birmingham of the Indians laid out two more. The players managed to force a hole through the crowd, allowing Evans to reach safety. Police dispersed the crowd after several other fights started.

October 15 The Reds win the championship of Ohio with a 7–0 win in Cleveland. The Reds won the series four games to two. The first game was played in Cincinnati with the remainder in Cleveland.

October 27 The Indians hire Harry Davis as manager to replace George Stovall.

Few in Cleveland were happy with the switch in managers. The Indians had played well under Stovall after he was chosen as manager in May, posting a 74–62 record over the rest of the 1911 season. Davis, who was 38-years-old, had been a first baseman with the Athletics from 1901 through 1911. During that period, he played on four AL pennant-winners. Davis failed to last a year as Cleveland manager. A strict disciplinarian, his management style hurt team morale, and he resigned in September 1912 with the club holding a 54–72 record. Stovall was traded to the Browns in February 1912. He was named manager of the club 40 games into the 1912 season, a position he held until September 1913. Stovall also managed the Kansas City club in the Federal League in 1914 and 1915.

1912

Season in a Sentence

After a change in managers from Harry Davis to Joe Birmingham, the Indians win 21 of their last 28 games but finish the season in fifth place.

Finish • Won • Lost • Pct • GB

Finish	Won	Lost	Pct	GB
Fifth	75	78	.490	30.5

Managers

Harry Davis (54–71) and
Joe Birmingham (21–7)

Stats

Stats	Indians	AL	Rank
Batting Avg:	.273	.265	3
On-Base Pct:	.333	.333	4
Slugging Pct:	.353	.348	3
Home Runs:	12		8
Stolen Bases:	194		6
ERA:	3.30	3.34	4
Fielding Avg:	.954	.952	5
Runs Scored:	677		5
Runs Allowed:	681		5

Starting Line-up

Steve O'Neill, c
Art Griggs, 1b
Nap Lajoie, 2b
Terry Turner, 3b
Ivy Olson, ss-3b
Buddy Ryan, lf-rf
Joe Birmingham, cf
Joe Jackson, rf
Roger Peckinpaugh, ss
Jack Graney, lf
Ted Easterly, c
Doc Johnston, 1b

Pitchers

Vean Gregg, sp
Fred Blanding, sp
George Kahler, sp
Bill Steen, sp-rp
Willie Mitchell, sp-rp
Jim Baskette, rp-sp

Attendance

336,844 (sixth in AL)

Club Leaders

Batting Avg:	Joe Jackson	.395
On-Base Pct:	Joe Jackson	.458
Slugging Pct:	Joe Jackson	.579
Home Runs:	Joe Jackson	3
RBIs:	Joe Jackson	90
	Nap Lajoie	90
Runs:	Joe Jackson	121
Stolen Bases:	Joe Jackson	35
Wins:	Vean Gregg	20
Strikeouts:	Vean Gregg	184
ERA:	Vean Gregg	2.59
Saves:	Vean Gregg	2

FEBRUARY 17 The Indians trade George Stovall to the Browns for Lefty George.

APRIL 12 Two months after New Mexico and Arizona become the 47th and 48th states, the Indians win the season opener 3–2 in 11 innings against the Tigers before 20,000 at League Park. Ted Easterly drove in the winning run with a double. Willie Mitchell pitched the complete game, allowing five hits. Joe Jackson collected three hits.

Jackson had another tremendous year in 1912, batting .395 with 121 runs scored, 226 hits, 44 doubles, 26 triples, and a league-leading 331 total bases.

APRIL 20 Five days after the sinking of the Titanic, the Indians take part in the first ever game at Navin Field in Detroit, losing 6–5 in 11 innings. Jack Graney was the first batter, facing George Mullin. Known later as Briggs Stadium and Tiger Stadium, the ballpark served as the home of the Tigers through the end of the 1999 season.

Graney was a man of many firsts. Not only was he the first batter in a ballpark that was used for major league baseball for 88 years, but he was the first batter to face Babe Ruth when Ruth made his debut as a pitcher 1914. Graney was also the first batter in the first game in which the Indians became the first team to wear uniforms numbers in 1916. And, he was the first ex-player to become a radio broadcaster. He played his entire 14-year playing career, which ended in 1922, as an Indian. After selling cars for a few years, Graney became the radio broadcaster for Indians games in 1932, a job he held until 1953.

MAY 10 Indians manager and longtime Athletics star Harry Davis is presented with a silver tea service before a game in Philadelphia. Davis's club then walloped the A's 11–3.

MAY 12 Rookie outfielder Buddy Ryan hits a grand slam off Jerry Akers in the sixth inning of a 6–1 win over the Senators at League Park. The game was scheduled on a Sunday in Cleveland sandwiched between Indians-Senators clashes on Saturday and Monday in Washington because sporting events on the Christian Sabbath were illegal in the nation's capital.

The homer was the only that Ryan hit during his major league career, which lasted two years, 166 games, and 571 at-bats.

MAY 21 The Indians play at Fenway Park for the first time and lose 3–1 to the Red Sox.

MAY 25 The Indians score two runs in the ninth inning and one in the tenth to beat the Browns 7–6 in the first game of a double header at Sportsman's Park. St. Louis won the second tilt 5–4.

JUNE 4 The Indians honor Nap Lajoie on the tenth anniversary of his first game with the club. Before the game against the Red Sox at League Park, he was given a horseshoe containing 1,000 silver dollars and $125 in gold. During the game, Lajoie contributed a double, a single, and a sacrifice fly in a 5–1 win.

Lajoie was limited to 117 games in 1912 due to injuries but hit .368 and drove in 90 runs.

JUNE 8 George Kahler pitches the Indians to a 1–0 win over the Yankees at League Park.

June 30 Joe Jackson collects three triples and a single during a 15–1 pounding of the Browns in the second game of a double header at Sportsman's Park. St. Louis won the opener 6–4.

July 25 Vean Gregg beats the Red Sox 1–0 in Boston.

Gregg was 20–13 with a 2.59 earned run average in 1912.

August 3 Shortstop Ivy Olson makes six errors in a double header against the Athletics at League Park. Olson committed three miscues in each game as the Indians lost 7–4 and 9–2.

August 11 Joe Jackson steals four bases, including home twice, during an 8–3 win over the Yankees at League Park. Jackson stole home in the first inning during a double steal with Art Griggs. In the seventh, Shoeless Joe singled, then swiped second and third, then stole home again on a second double steal with Griggs.

Though still only 22 years old, Joe Jackson had established himself as one of the top hitters in the game by 1912.

August 20 The Indians are the victims of a six-inning no-hitter by Carl Cashion of the Senators in the second game of a double header in Washington. The game ended with the score 2–0 in favor of the Senators to allow the Indians to catch a train to Boston. Walter Johnson beat Cleveland 4–2 in the opener for his 15th win in a row.

September 2 Harry Davis resigns as manager and is replaced by 29-year-old outfielder Joe Birmingham.

Birmingham's first move as manager was to lighten many of the strict disciplinary rules that had been in place. The Indians responded by winning 21 of their last 28 games. The improvement continued in 1913 when the club was 86–68 despite open animosity between Birmingham and star player Nap Lajoie. The Cleveland club collapsed in 1914, however, losing 102 games. Birmingham was fired in May 1915. Davis was a coach with the Athletics from 1913 through 1919. He never managed another big league club.

September 17 Reserve catcher Fred Carisch collects five hits, including a triple and a double, in five at-bats to lead the Indians to a 4–3 win in 11 innings over the Red Sox in the first game of a double header at League Park. Nap Lajoie drove in the winning run with a single. Cleveland also won the second contest, called after 4 1/2 innings by darkness.

September 19 In an unusual double header between the Indians and the Red Sox at League Park, neither game goes the required nine innings. The first contest was called at the end of the fifth inning because of rain with the Indians leading 9–3. After a wait of an hour, the second game began but was stopped on account of darkness at the end of the sixth with Cleveland ahead 6–0.

September 26 The Indians record their eighth win in a row with a 12–2 decision over the Tigers at League Park.

September 27 The Indians hammer the Tigers 16–5 at League Park for Cleveland's ninth win in a row. Tim Hendryx hit a three-run homer on a ball that rolled under the fence at the end of the left field stands. Harvey Grubb of the Indians made the only appearance of his big league career and was hit by a pitch in his only at-bat.

The homer by Hendryx was his first in the majors. He didn't hit another one until 1917 when he played for the Yankees.

September 29 Vean Gregg picks up his 20th win of the season with an 8–1 decision over the Tigers at League Park.

October 4 After playing in an exhibition game in Herrin, Illinois, the Indians board a train for the season finale in St. Louis. The train was in an accident in Southwick, Missouri, and while no players were injured, the engineer was killed.

1913

Season in a Sentence

New manager Joe Birmingham openly clashes with star player Nap Lajoie, but the Indians show improvement by winning 86 games.

Finish • Won • Lost • Pct • GB

Finish	Won	Lost	Pct	GB
Third	86	68	.566	9.5

Manager

Joe Birmingham

Stats

	Indians	AL	Club
Batting Avg:	.268	.256	2
On-Base Pct:	.331	.325	4
Slugging Pct:	.348	.336	4
Home Runs:	16		7
Stolen Bases:	151		8
ERA:	2.54	2.93	2
Fielding Avg:	.962	.959	2
Runs Scored:	633		2
Runs Allowed:	536		2

Starting Line-up

Fred Carisch, c
Doc Johnston, 1b
Nap Lajoie, 2b
Ivy Olson, 3b
Ray Chapman, ss
Jack Graney, lf
Nemo Leibold, cf
Joe Jackson, rf
Terry Turner, 3b
Buddy Ryan, cf
Steve O'Neill, c

Pitchers

Cy Falkenberg, sp
Vean Gregg, sp
Fred Blanding, sp-rp
Willie Mitchell, sp-rp
George Kahler, sp-rp
Bill Steen, sp-rp
Nick Cullop, rp-sp

Attendance

541,000 (third in AL)

Club Leaders

Batting Avg:	Joe Jackson	.373
On-Base Pct:	Joe Jackson	.460
Slugging Pct:	Joe Jackson	.571
Hone Runs:	Joe Jackson	7
RBIs:	Joe Jackson	71
Runs:	Joe Jackson	109
Stolen Bases:	Ray Chapman	29
Wins:	Cy Falkenberg	23
Strikeouts:	Cy Falkenberg	166
	Vean Gregg	166
ERA:	Willie Mitchell	1.87
Saves:	Vean Gregg	3

April 10 The scheduled opener against the White Sox in Cleveland is rained out.

April 11 The Indians get the 1913 season underway with a 3–1 victory over the White Sox before 15,000 at League Park. Vean Gregg pitched a complete game and Joe Jackson collected a triple and two singles.

Jackson hit .373 in 1913 and was the runner-up to Ty Cobb in the AL batting race for the third straight season. Jackson did lead the league in hits (197), slugging percentage (.551), and doubles (39) in addition to 109 runs, 17 triples, and seven homers.

April 12 Team secretary William Blackwood is quarantined with a slight case of smallpox. None of the players were exposed and doctors determined vaccinations were unnecessary.

There were two professional baseball teams in Cleveland from 1913 through 1915. The other one in 1913 played in the Federal League, which was organized on March 8 with eight teams. Managed by Cy Young, that Cleveland team was 63–54 and finished in second place. The club played at Luna Park. The Federal League had ambitions to become a third major league by raiding rosters of the

American and National Leagues during the 1913–14 off-season. There was no Cleveland team in the Federal League in 1914 or 1915, in part because Indians owner Charles Somers transferred the minor league Toledo, Ohio, franchise he owned in the American Association to Cleveland. The American Association club played at League Park while the Indians were on the road. Although Somers succeeded in keeping a Federal League team out of Cleveland, he couldn't prevent players like Cy Falkenberg, Grover Land, and Nick Cullop from jumping to the new circuit. The competition in Cleveland from his own minor league club and an Indians club that lost 102 games in 1914 worsened Somers's financial problems and contributed to his sale of the team to James Dunn at the end of the 1915 season. After the Federal League folded, Dunn sent Cleveland's American Association team back to Toledo in 1916.

MAY 2 Trailing 5–3, the Indians score seven runs in the sixth inning and defeat the Browns 11–8 in St. Louis.

MAY 11 Joe Jackson hits a grand slam off Al Schultz in the first inning of a 7–2 win over the Yankees at League Park. Jackson also contributed a double and two singles.

MAY 20 The Indians score three runs in the ninth inning to beat the Senators 10–9 at League Park. The tying and winning runs crossed the plate on a pinch-double by Fred Carisch.

On the same day, the Indians traded Roger Peckinpaugh to the Yankees for Bill Stumpf and Jack Lelivelt. The Indians had two tremendous young shortstops in 1913 in Roger Peckinpaugh and Ray Chapman. The club decided to trade Peckinpaugh and keep Chapman. Cleveland would have been better off finding another infield position for Peckinpaugh in order to keep them both. He grew up in the city right across the street from the home of Nap Lajoie and signed with the Indians right out of high school. After the trade to New York, Peckinpaugh appeared in 1,926 more big league games before his playing career ended in 1927. He then returned to Cleveland and was the manager of the Indians from 1928 through 1933 and again in 1941. Stumpf never played in a game for the Indians while Lelivelt was nothing more than a reserve outfielder.

JUNE 1 The Indians extend their winning streak to nine games with 6–1 and 9–3 wins over the Browns in a double header at League Park.

JUNE 3 Cy Falkenberg runs his season record to 10–0 with an 8–2 win over the Yankees in New York.

The Indians were 34–13 on June 8 and were in second place behind the Athletics, who had a record of 35–10. The Indians spent all season chasing the A's, and never caught up, finishing 9½ games out of first.

JUNE 9 Cy Falkenberg's ten-game winning streak ends with a 4–1 loss to the Red Sox in Boston. Falkenberg received some consolation when he received a dispatch from Washington informing him that his wife gave birth to a son.

After spending the entire 1912 season in the minors, Falkenberg earned his way back to the big leagues in 1913 and posted a record of 23–10 and an ERA of

2.22 at the age of 32. Unfortunately, it was his last season in Cleveland. During the following off-season, Falkenberg was among the first major leaguers to accept a lucrative contract offer to jump to the Federal League. Pitching for Indianapolis in the FL, he was 25–16, but blew out his arm pitching 377 innings and was never again an effective pitcher. Vean Gregg also won 20 games for the Indians in 1913, the third consecutive season that he reached that figure. He was 20–13 with a 2.24 ERA. Falkenberg and Gregg both missed a start during a crucial road trip in September after engaging in a friendly wrestling match on the train en route to Washington. The two star hurlers fell and suffered injuries to their pitching arms.

JUNE 11 The Indians score four runs in the 15th inning and win 9–5 over the Red Sox in Boston. Two of the four runs came on steals of home by Ivy Olson and Jack Graney. Grover Land also tried to swipe home but was tagged out.

JUNE 18 Indians players are guests of Woodrow Wilson at the White House. "Larry," the bull terrier owned by Jack Graney, trailed the players into the president's office. Later in the day, the Cleveland club defeated the Senators 4–0 at Griffith Stadium.

JUNE 21 After the Tigers score six runs in the top of the first inning at League Park, the Indians rebound with four in their half, then added three in the sixth to win 7–6.

JUNE 24 Trailing 4–2, the Indians score two runs in the ninth inning and two in the 12th to defeat the Tigers 6–4 at Detroit. The Indians won with only five hits. They lost the second tilt 6–5 when the Tigers scored five runs in the ninth.

JUNE 26 Nap Lajoie makes three errors at second base during a 7–5 loss to the White Sox in Chicago.

The next day, manager Joe Birmingham benched Lajoie. The two didn't get along and had clashed many times. Lajoie, who was batting .323 at the time of the benching, cursed Birmingham to his face and in the newspapers. Nap was restored to the line-up a week later and finished the year batting .335.

JULY 6 Willie Mitchell pitches a one-hitter to beat the White Sox 7–0 in the second game of a double header at League Park. The only Chicago hit was a single by Buck Weaver in the sixth inning. Cleveland also won the opener 6–2.

JULY 25 The Indians edge the Yankees 3–2 in 13 innings in New York. Willie Mitchell pitched a complete game, striking out 12 and walking eight.

SEPTEMBER 1 The Indians record their eighth win in a row with a 7–0 decision over the White Sox at League Park.

SEPTEMBER 5 The Indians score three runs in the ninth inning to defeat the Tigers 7–6 in Detroit. Fred Blanding, pitching in relief, drove in the winning run with a walk-off single.

Blanding left baseball after the 1914 season after receiving a large sum of money from a wealthy aunt. Later, the aunt changed her mind, and Blanding went to court to retrieve the cash, and won the case.

September 22 Cy Falkenberg wins his 23rd game of 1913 with a 5–4 decision over the Yankees in New York.

October 1 Vean Gregg picks up his 20th win of the season with a 8–1 triumph over the Tigers in Detroit.

October 6 The Indians open a best-of-seven, post-season series against the Pittsburgh Pirates with a 3–0 win at League Park behind the two-hit pitching of Cy Falkenberg.

October 13 In game six of the series against the Pirates, Vean Gregg strikes out 19 batters in pitching a 13-inning, five-hit shutout to win 1–0 at Forbes Field in Pittsburgh. Gregg also scored the winning run. In the 13th inning, her doubled and scored on a single by Nemo Leibold.

October 14 The Indians win the post-season series against the Pirates with a 4–1, game seven victory in Pittsburgh.

1914

Season in a Sentence

Just a season after winning 86 games, nearly everything goes wrong, as the Indians compile the worst winning percentage (.333) in club history in the course of losing 102 games.

Finish • Won • Lost • Pct • GB

Finish	Won	Lost	Pct	GB
Eighth	51	102	.333	48.5

Manager

Joe Birmingham

Stats

Stats	Indians	AL	Rank
Batting Avg:	.245	.248	4
On-Base Pct:	.310	.319	6
Slugging Pct:	.312	.323	6
Home Runs:	10		8
Stolen Bases:	167		7 (tie)
ERA:	3.21	2.73	8
Fielding Avg:	.953	.959	7
Runs Scored:	538		5
Runs Allowed:	709		8

Starting Line-up

Steve O'Neill, c
Doc Johnston, 1b
Nap Lajoie, 2b
Terry Turner, 3b
Ray Chapman, ss-3b
Jack Graney, lf
Nemo Leibold, cf
Joe Jackson, rf
Ivy Olson, ss-2b-3b
Jay Kirke, lf-rf-1b
Ray Wood, rf-cf-1b

Pitchers

Willie Mitchell, sp
Bill Steen, sp
Rip Hagerman, sp-rp
Vean Gregg, sp
Guy Morton, sp-rp
Fred Blanding, rp-sp
Guy Collamore, rp

Attendance

185,997 (eighth in AL)

Club Leaders

Batting Avg:	Joe Jackson	.338
On-Base Pct:	Joe Jackson	.399
Slugging Pct:	Joe Jackson	.464
Home Runs:	Joe Jackson	3
RBIs:	Joe Jackson	53
Runs:	Jack Graney	63
Stolen Bases:	Ray Chapman	24
Wins:	Willie Mitchell	12
Strikeouts:	Willie Mitchell	179
ERA:	Bill Steen	2.60
Saves:	Three tied with	1

April 14 The Indians open the season with a 5–2 loss to the White Sox in Chicago.

April 22 The Indians lose the home opener 7–0 to the White Sox at League Park. The defeat dropped Cleveland's record on the 1914 season to 0–8.

April 23 After opening the season with eight straight defeats, the Indians finally win with a 4–1 decision over the White Sox at League Park.

With the exception of June 30 and July 1, the Indians spent the entire 1914 season in last place and finished 18½ games behind the seventh-place Yankees. Cleveland's final record was 51–102. The winning percentage of .333 is the worst in club history.

April 25 Rip Hagerman pitches the Indians to a 1–0 win over the White Sox at League Park. The winning run scored on a walk-off single by Nap Lajoie in the ninth inning.

May 14 Rip Hagerman allows one run and six hits in a complete game but loses 1–0 in a grueling 13-inning duel with Eddie Plank of the Athletics in Philadelphia. The sole tally scored on a single by Wally Schang and a three-base throwing error by Hagerman on a bunt by Plank.

Hagerman's given name was Zerah Zequiel.

May 31 Joe Benz of the White Sox no-hits the Indians for a 6–1 win at Comiskey Park. The Cleveland run scored in the fourth inning on two errors and an infield out. The game ended on a double-play grounder struck by shortstop Rivington Bisland.

June 2 Terry Turner spoils the no-hit bid of Wiley Taylor of the Browns by stroking a single with none out in the ninth inning. The Indians lost 3–0 at League Park.

June 15 A two-run, walk-off triple by Terry Turner in the ninth inning beats the Senators 7–6 at League Park.

June 20 Ray Chapman commits four errors at shortstop during a 7–1 loss to the Yankees at League Park.

June 24 Entering the game as a reliever in the ninth, Guy Morton allows a run is the losing pitcher in a 5–4 Indians defeat in the first game of a double header against the Browns at Sportsman's Park. St. Louis also won the second contest 3–1.

Morton had an unusual career. He lost his first 13 major league decisions and finished his rookie season with a 1–13 record. Morton overcame the nightmarish beginning and went on to forge an 11-year big league career, all with Cleveland, and finished his sojourn in the majors with a record of 98–85.

June 27 The Indians wallop the Browns 16–4 in the first game of the double header at Sportsman's Park. St. Louis won the second tilt, called after 4½ innings to allow the Indians to catch a train, by a 4–3 score.

June 30 Two days after the assassination of Archduke Ferdinand of Austria, an event that precipitates the start of World War I in August, Terry Turner hits his first home run since 1906 during a 8–3 win against the Browns in the first game of a double header at Dunn Field. St. Louis won the nightcap 4–0.

Turner had gone 3,186 at-bats without a homer. He played in the majors until 1918, a span of 1,473 at-bats, and never hit another home run.

JULY 11 Babe Ruth makes his major league debut with a starting pitching assignment for the Red Sox against the Indians in Boston. Ruth pitched seven innings in a game won by the Red Sox 4–3. The first batter to face Ruth was Jack Graney, who singled and scored.

Vean Gregg was a consistently effective pitcher during his years with the Tribe, but trading him in 1914 turned out to be a good idea, given his lack of success after he left.

JULY 16 Rip Hagerman pitches a two-hitter and defeats the Senators 2–0 at Griffith Stadium. The only Washington hits were singles by Rip Williams and George McBride. Jack Graney led off the first inning with an inside-the-park homer.

JULY 21 Willie Mitchell strikes out 13 batters but loses 2–1 to the Athletics in the first game of a double header at Shibe Park. Philadelphia also won the nightcap 7–6.

JULY 28 Willie Mitchell holds the Red Sox hitless until the seventh inning and then holds on for a three-hitter and a 4–3 win at League Park.

On the same day, the Indians traded Vean Gregg to the Red Sox for Adam Johnson, Fritz Coumbe, and Ben Egan.

AUGUST 1 Outfielder Jay Kirke tangles with umpire Billy Evans during a 7–0 win over the Yankees in the first game of a double header at League Park. Kirke was ordered off the field by Evans for protesting a called third strike. As Kirke continued to argue, Evans pushed Kirke in the shoulder toward the bench. A fistfight was averted only by Yankees catcher Ed Sweeney who stepped between the umpire and player. New York won the second tilt 9–2.

Judson Fabian (Jay) Kirke was suspended for a week by AL president Ban Johnson. Kirke was a legendary eccentric who cared about little other than the number of base hits he could collect. He had a .301 lifetime batting average in

320 big league games during the dead ball era, but played on four clubs because his abysmal defense. Kirke picked up over 3,000 hits during a long minor league career that lasted from 1906 through 1935.

SEPTEMBER 7 Three weeks after the opening of the Panama Canal, the Indians defeat the Browns 4–3 in a 15-inning marathon in the first game of a double header at League Park. Bill Steen, who entered the game as a reliever in the tenth inning, drove in the winning run with a single. Cleveland also won the nightcap, called after five innings by darkness, 6–2.

SEPTEMBER 20 Guy Morton's career record in the majors drops to 0–13 with a 4–1 loss to the Athletics at League Park.

SEPTEMBER 27 Nap Lajoie collects his 3,000 career hit with a double off Marty McHale during a 5–3 win over the Yankees in the first game of a double header in New York. The game was stopped so the ball could be presented to Lajoie. The winning pitcher was Guy Morton, who finally achieved his first big league victory after 13 losses. The Yanks won the second game 5–2. It was the Indians 100th defeat of the season.

The hit proved to be Lajoie's last as a member of the Indians. He turned 40 on September 5, 1914, near the end of a season in which he hit just .258. In January 1915, Lajoie was sold to the Athletics, where he played two seasons before retiring.

DECEMBER 14 The Indians sell Ivy Olson to the Reds.

DECEMBER 31 The financial affairs of Charles Somers are placed in the hands of a committee of bankers from Cleveland, Elyria, and Buffalo. Somers was $1,750,000 in debt because of imprudent real estate investments and losses in his coal business. The reverses eventually reached over $2,000,000 forced Somers to sell the club (see February 16, 1916).

1915

Season in a Sentence

With club owner Charles Somers facing financial ruin, the Indians sell or trade many of their top players, including Joe Jackson and Nap Lajoie, and lose 95 games.

Finish • Won • Lost • Pct • GB

Finish	Won	Lost	Pct	GB
Seventh	57	95	.375	44.5

Managers

Joe Birmingham (12–16) and Lee Fohl (45–79)

Stats

Stats	Indians	AL	Rank
Batting Avg:	.240	.248	6
On-Base Pct:	.312	.325	7
Slugging Pct:	.317	.326	4
Home Runs:	20		4
Stolen Bases:	138		6
ERA:	3.13	2.93	7
Fielding Avg:	.957	.959	6
Runs Scored:	539		7
Runs Allowed:	670		7

Starting Line-up

Steve O'Neill, c
Jay Kirke, 1b
Bill Wambsganss, 2b-3b
Walter Barbare, 3b
Ray Chapman, ss
Jack Graney, lf
Joe Jackson, cf-lf-1b
Elmer Smith, rf
Nemo Leibold, cf
Terry Turner, 2b
Billy Southworth, cf
Braggo Roth, cf
Denney Wilie, cf-lf

Pitchers

Guy Morton, sp
Willie Mitchell, sp
Rip Hagerman, sp
Roy Walker, sp-rp
Sad Sam Jones, rp
Fritz Coumbe, rp-sp
Oscar Harstad, rp

Attendance

159,285 (sixth in AL)

Club Leaders

Batting Avg:	Ray Chapman	.270
On-Base Pct:	Jack Graney	.357
Slugging Pct:	Ray Chapman	.370
Home Runs:	Braggo Roth	4
RBIs:	Ray Chapman	67
	Elmer Smith	67
Runs:	Ray Chapman	101
Stolen Bases:	Ray Chapman	36
Wins:	Guy Morton	16
Strikeouts:	Willie Mitchell	149
ERA:	Guy Morton	2.14
Saves:	Sad Sam Jones	5

JANUARY 5 The Indians sell Nap Lajoie to the Athletics.

JANUARY 16 The nickname of Cleveland's major league baseball team is changed from Naps to Indians at a meeting of club officials and baseball writers. The name Naps became obsolete when Nap Lajoie was sold to the Athletics. The nickname was bestowed on the club in honor of Lajoie in 1903. Among the nicknames considered but discarded during the meeting were the Spiders and the Bearcats.

APRIL 14 The Indians open the season with a 5–1 win over the Tigers in Detroit. Willie Mitchell was the winning pitcher.

APRIL 23 In the home opener, the Indians lose 8–4 to the Tigers at League Park.

APRIL 29 The Indians score three runs in the ninth inning to defeat the White Sox 5–4 in Chicago.

MAY 5 Guy Morton pitches the Indians to a 1–0 triumph over the White Sox at League Park. The run scored in the ninth inning on a triple by Ray Chapman, intentional walks to Joe Jackson and Jack Graney, and a sacrifice fly by pinch-hitter Elmer Smith. An unusual situation occurred in the second inning when all four White Sox batters reached safely on a walk, two singles, and an error, but none scored. Two were thrown out at third base and one at home.

Chapman hit .270 and scored 101 runs for the Indians in 1915.

May 9 Two days after the sinking of the luxury liner *Luisitania* by a German submarine, resulting in the deaths of over 1,200, including 128 Americans, Nap Lajoie makes his first appearance in Cleveland since his sale by the Indians to the Athletics. He was 1-for-3 during a 3–0 Cleveland victory at League Park. Guy Morton pitched the shutout.

May 12 Rip Hagerman walks ten batters but allows only three hits during a 3–1 complete game win over the Yankees at League Park.

May 16 Guy Morton shuts out the Red Sox for 13 innings but gives up three runs in the 14th to lose 3–0 at League Park. Morton retired the first 22 batters to face him before Dick Hoblitzel walked with one out in the eighth. The first hit was a single by opposing pitcher Joe Wood with one out in the ninth.

May 21 With the Indians holding a record of 12–16, 44-year-old Lee Fohl replaces Joe Birmingham as manager of the Indians.

Birmingham had been manager since September 1912, a period marked by personality clashes with several players, including Nap Lajoie, Vean Gregg, Doc Johnston, and Ivy Olson. Birmingham was also released as a player. Even though he had a contract through the end of the 1916 season, the Indians cut off Birmingham's salary. He sued the club for $20,000 in lost pay in a case that was settled out of court. Birmingham never managed or played in the majors again. Fohl had been a coach with the Indians. The change in managers had no immediate effect, as the Indians were 45–79 over the rest of the 1915 season. But Fohl nearly won an AL pennant in 1918 before he was fired in July 1919.

May 23 Senators pitcher Walter Johnson becomes the first player to hit a home run over the left field wall at League Park. The blast was struck during a 4–1 Washington win over the Indians.

May 31 The Indians sweep the Browns 12–1 and 9–6 at League Park.

June 11 Guy Morton pitches a two-hitter and smacks a two-run double during a 3–0 victory over the Athletics at Shibe Park. The only Philadelphia hits were singles by Snuffy McInnis and Larry Kopf.

June 24 The Indians lose 5–4 in a 19-inning marathon against the White Sox at Comiskey Park. Cleveland took a 4–3 lead with two runs in the eighth, but Chicago knotted the contest in the ninth. There was no more scoring until the 19th when Buck Weaver singled and Eddie Collins doubled with two out. Guy Morton, in his first inning of relief, allowed the ninth-inning run that sent the contest into extra innings. Morton pitched nine consecutive scoreless innings before giving up the 19th-inning tally.

JULY 7 The Indians sell Nemo Leibold to the White Sox.

Standing five-foot-seven, Harry (Nemo) Leibold was named after a comic strip character named "Little Nemo." He was a starting outfielder for the White Sox and Red Sox from 1917 through 1921 and played in the World Series for Chicago in 1917 and 1919.

JULY 15 Right fielder Elmer Smith records an unassisted double play during a 4–3 loss to the Red Sox at League Park. Smith caught a shallow fly ball and raced to first base before the runner could return.

JULY 19 Plagued by a sore arm, Steve O'Neill allows a major league record eight stolen bases in the first inning of an 11–4 loss to the Senators at League Park.

JULY 24 The Indians sweep the Athletics 4–3 and 12–4 in a double header at League Park. The second game ended on a triple play by the Indians. With Lew Malone on second base and Wally Schang on first, Nap Lajoie hit a bullet toward left field. Third baseman Walter Barbare caught it and relayed the ball to second baseman Bill Wambsganss, who in turn, fired the horsehide to Jay Kirke at first.

Wambsganss is much better known for the unassisted triple play he pulled off during the 1920 World Series, the only one in post-season history. He played for the Indians from 1914 through 1923.

JULY 27 The Indians lose 1–0 in a brilliant pitcher's duel against the Senators in Washington. Rip Hagerman hurled a two-hitter for Cleveland while Bert Gallia tossed a one-hitter for Washington. The lone run scored on a steal of home by Clyde Milan in the first inning. The only hits off Hagerman were singles by Danny Moeller and John Henry. Terry Turner broke up Gallia's no-hit bid with a one-base hit in the eighth.

AUGUST 15 Guy Morton wins a 1–0 decision over the Browns at League Park. Morton struck out 11 batters, including three in succession in the ninth inning. The run scored in the seventh when Jay Kirke doubled, took third on an infield out, and scored on a sacrifice fly by Bill Wambsganss. The losing hurler was George Sisler, who would soon give up pitching to become one of the greatest first basemen of all-time.

AUGUST 16 Bernie Boland of the Tigers holds the Indians hitless for $8^2/_3$ innings in the second game of a double header at League Park before settling for a one-hitter and a 3–1 win. The no-hit bid was broken up by pinch-hitter Ben Paschal, who made his big league debut in the first game of that day's twinbill, which Detroit won 6–2.

The hit that broke up the no-hitter was Paschal's first in the majors and his only one in nine at-bats as a member of the Indians. Paschal didn't collect his second big league hit until 1920 when he played for the Red Sox.

AUGUST 20 The Indians send Joe Jackson to the White Sox for Braggo Roth, Larry Chappell, Ed Klepfer and $31,500.

The trade of Jackson to the White Sox was prompted by the financial problems of Charles Somers. Following the trade, Jackson hit .340 before he was suspended from the game for life near the end of the 1920 season for his role in fixing the 1919 World Series in collusion with gamblers. Fans will always wonder what might have been if the Indians had not made the deal of one of the greatest hitters of his generation for three journeymen. It's probable that Jackson would have helped Cleveland win the pennant in 1917, 1918, and 1919. Had the Indians played in the 1919 Fall Classic, the White Sox would not have been in position to throw the Series. And if Jackson had not been connected with gamblers leading to his lifetime ban there is no doubt that he would have gained admission to the Hall of Fame.

SEPTEMBER 3 A rulebook would have come in handy during a 6–5 win over the White in the first game of a double header at Comiskey Park. In the Cleveland half of the fourth inning, two Cleveland players had scored and Elmer Smith was the base runner on first. Jay Kirke swung at a wild pitch for the third strike, and Smith reached second and Kirke was safe at first. Under the rules, Kirke should have been called out because first base was already occupied, but the umpires failed to notice. Two more wild pitches and an error enabled Smith and Kirke to score. The White Sox protested to American League president Ban Johnson, who ordered that the entire contest be replayed.

1916

Season in a Sentence

The Indians are 77–77, but win 20 more games than the previous season and hold first place for 47 days following the arrival of new owner James Dunn and future Hall of Famers Tris Speaker and Stan Coveleski.

Finish	Won	Lost	Pct	GB
Sixth	77	77	.500	14.0

Manager

Lee Fohl

Stats	Indians	AL	Rank
Batting Avg:	.250	.248	3
On-Base Pct:	.324	.321	3
Slugging Pct:	.331	.324	3
Home Runs:	16		5
Stolen Bases:	160		6
ERA:	2.90	2.82	6
Fielding Avg:	.965	.965	5
Runs Scored:	630		2
Runs Allowed:	602		7

Starting Line-up

Steve O'Neill, c
Chick Gandil, 1b
Terry Turner, 2b-3b
Ray Chapman, ss-3b
Bill Wambsganss, ss
Jack Graney, lf
Tris Speaker, cf
Braggo Roth, rf
Ivan Howard, 2b
Elmer Smith, rf

Pitchers

Jim Bagby, sp-rp
Stan Coveleski, sp-rp
Guy Morton, sp-rp
Fred Beebe, sp-rp
Ed Klepfer, rp-sp
Fritz Coumbe, rp-sp
Al Gould, rp-sp

Attendance

492,106 (fourth in AL)

Club Leaders

Batting Avg:	Tris Speaker	.386
On-Base Pct:	Tris Speaker	.470
Slugging Pct:	Tris Speaker	.502
Home Runs:	Jack Graney	5
RBIs:	Tris Speaker	79
Runs:	Jack Graney	106
Stolen Bases:	Tris Speaker	35
Wins:	Jim Bagby	16
Strikeouts:	Jim Bagby	88
	Guy Morton	88
ERA:	Jim Bagby	2.61
Saves:	Jim Bagby	5

FEBRUARY 16 A group of businessmen headed by James "Sunny Jim" Dunn purchases the Indians from Charles Somers for $500,000.

Somers was forced to sell the Indians because he was $2 million in debt as a result of losses in real estate and other business ventures. The end of his reign in baseball because of financial distress was sadly ironic because he was the financial angel of the American League 15 years earlier. Somers was not only the original owner of the Indians when the club was formed in 1900 but was the founding owner the Red Sox as well, running the Boston club in 1901 and 1902. He was also a minority owner of the Athletics and loaned money on several occasions to White Sox magnate Charles Comiskey. Were it not for Somers and his large bankroll, the American League might not have survived. After he relinquished ownership of the Indians, Somers returned to the business world and recouped his fortune. When he died in 1934 at the age of 65, he left an estate valued at $3 million. Dunn was born in Marshalltown, Iowa, and was a partner in a Chicago railroad construction firm. He was also a close friend and drinking buddy of AL president Ban Johnson and a member of the Woodland Bards, a White Sox rooting organization. Dunn's offices in Chicago were across the street from the American League's headquarters. He said that he would spare no expense in building a winning team and succeeded in the endeavor. Taking over a club that won only 108 games in 1914 and 1915 combined, Dunn guided the Indians through one of the most successful periods in club history, which included the world championship in 1920. He died in 1922 at the age of 57. Dunn's heirs ran the club until 1927.

FEBRUARY 21 New owner James Dunn hires Bob McRoy as general manager.

Dunn knew little about operating a baseball team and asked Johnson for advice as to the best person to run the front office. Johnson suggested McRoy, who had been part owner of the Red Sox from 1911 through 1915, and prior to that, had been Johnson's second-in-command in the AL office. McRoy replaced Emil Barnard as general manager. It was part of Johnson's plan to discredit Barnard. Johnson had been at odds with many AL owners, who let it be known that they believed Barnard to be a fitting successor to the league presidency. When asked about the status of the popular Barnard, Dunn replied, "Barnard goes." Dunn's intention of firing Barnard so angered Cleveland's sportswriters, who knew of his baseball acumen and Johnson's vendetta, that Dunn reconsidered and kept Barnard, though in a subordinate position to McRoy. Unknown to anyone outside the Cleveland front office, Johnson also owned $55,000 in stock in the Indians in a blatant conflict of interest. The fact became public in 1919 and caused considerable embarrassment to Johnson and well as the enmity of the owners of other AL clubs. McRoy engineered the trade for Tris Speaker and laid much of the groundwork for the club that would win the 1920 World Series but became ill shortly after arriving in Cleveland and died on December 2, 1917, when he was only 35 years old. Barnard then returned to the position of general manager.

FEBRUARY 26 The Indians purchase Chick Gandil from the Senators for $7,500.

APRIL 8 The Indians send Sad Sam Jones, Fred Thomas, and $55,000 to the Red Sox for Tris Speaker.

After purchasing the Indians in February, James Dunn looked to make a splash and did so by trading for Speaker. One of the greatest center fielders in major league history, Speaker had just turned 28, and carried a .338 lifetime batting average. He played on world championship teams in Boston in both 1912 and 1915. Despite Speaker's contributions to the success of the club, Sox owner Joseph Lannin wanted to drastically cut Speaker's salary. The dispute between the Speaker and ownership dragged through spring training. Finally, four days before Opening Day, Lannin agreed to deal Speaker to Cleveland. The transaction ranks among the best in club history, although it didn't come without cost as Jones won 225 big league games after leaving Cleveland. Speaker ranks first on the Indians all-time list in doubles (488), first in on base percentage (.444), second in walks (857), second in batting average (.354), second in hits (1,965), second in triples (108), fourth in runs (1,079), fifth in RBIs (883), fifth in games (1,519), and eighth in slugging percentage (.520).

April 12 The Indians open the season with a 6–1 loss to the Browns in Cleveland. Tris Speaker made his debut with the club, and was 0-for-1 with three walks.

James Dunn changed the name of the Indians home field from League Park to Dunn Field.

April 16 The expected starting pitching match-up of two brothers fails to materialize when Harry Coveleski of the Tigers refuses to pitch against his younger brother Stan, who was scheduled to make his first appearance as a member of the Indians. George Cunningham took Harry's place, and went 12 innings for a 3–1 win over the Indians at Dunn Field. Stan Coveleski also pitched a complete game for Cleveland. Harry started against the Indians the following day, and lasted only ⅓ of an inning while allowing two runs, although Detroit won 4–3.

Harry Coveleski won 22 games for the Tigers in 1914 and 22 in 1915. Stan's only major league experience prior to 1916 consisted of six games for the Athletics in 1912. "I've made good in the big leagues and the kid has his place to make," said Harry in explaining his decision not to start against his younger sibling. "I know I would be holding him back if I went against him. I couldn't put my heart into an effort that might send him back to the bushes." (See September 4, 1916.) Harry won 21 games for the Tigers in 1916, his third straight season above the 20-win mark but developed arm trouble the following season, all but ending his career. Stan, however, became a star during a career that lasted until 1928. He pitched for the Indians from 1916 through 1924. The son of Polish immigrants, Coveleski quit school and began working 12 hours a day, six days a week, in the Pennsylvania coal mines at the age of 12. He played baseball in what little free time he had at his disposal and caught the attention of scouts. It took him awhile to establish himself as a major league pitcher; he turned 27 during his first full season in the majors. He was at his peak from 1918 through 1921, posting a record of 93–52. Among Cleveland pitchers, Coveleski's ranks fourth in wins (172), third in complete games (195), third in shutouts (31), fifth in games started (304), fifth in innings pitched (2,513⅔), and sixth in ERA (2.79). His final record in the majors was 215–142. He was elected to the Hall of Fame in 1969.

April 22 Ed Klepfer pitches a 15-inning complete game against the Browns at Sportsman's Park, but the contest ends in a 1–1 tie when called on account of darkness. St. Louis scored their lone run in the ninth inning.

Klepfer was one of the worst hitters ever to swing a bat in a major league game. Over a six-year career, he collected six hits, all singles, in 125 at-bats for an average of .048.

April 23 The Indians pound the Browns 14–2 in St. Louis.

April 25 The Indians defeat the White Sox 9–2 on "James Dunn Day" at Dunn Field. Before the game, there was an automobile parade from downtown to the ballpark. Two bands were on hand for a music presentation while Dunn was presented with a large wardrobe trunk by the Cleveland Fire Department.

The arrival of Dunn and a team that remained in contention until August brought about a huge increase in attendance. After drawing 159,285 in 1915, the Indians attracted 492,106 in 1916.

May 5 The Indians score three runs in the sixth inning for a 3–2 win over the White Sox at Comiskey Park. Jack Graney led off the sixth for Cleveland, and Chicago catcher Ray Schalk called to the umpires attention that Graney's bat was flat on one side in a blatant violation of the rules. Graney went back to the bench for a new bat, and singled, starting the game-winning rally.

May 9 The Indians lose 8–1 to the Red Sox on Tris Speaker Day in Boston. It was Speaker's first appearance in the city since being traded from the Red Sox to the Indians. Before the game, the Shriners presented Speaker with a fez and a jeweled badge. The Boston club's gift was a massive loving cup.

In his first season with the Indians, Speaker led the American League in batting average (.386), on base percentage (.470), slugging percentage (.502), hits (211), and doubles (41). In the AL batting race, Speaker beat out Ty Cobb, who batted .371. It was the only time from 1907 though 1919 that Cobb failed to finish a season leading the league in batting average.

May 11 A wind-blown pop-up scores the winning run with two out in the tenth inning to enable the Red Sox to defeat the Indians 6–5 in Boston. Jack Barry hit what appeared to be a high foul to the left of home plate, but the wind carried the ball into fair territory. Catcher Steve O'Neill was unable to make the catch, allowing Dick Hoblitzel to cross the plate with the deciding tally.

June 8 The Indians score three runs in the ninth inning to tie the score 5–5, but the game against the Senators at Dunn Field ends with that score when called by darkness after 14 innings. Washington scored all five of their runs in the first inning off starter Stan Coveleski, who lasted only ⅓ of an inning. Cleveland relievers Marty McHale and Jim Bagby did not allow a hit between the first and eleventh innings.

Jim Bagby pitched for the Indians from 1916 through 1922 and posted a record of 122–86 to rank tenth all-time in career victories with the club. He is first in victories in a season on the virtue of a 31–12 campaign in 1920. Bagby soon after developed arm trouble, however, and won only 20 more games after 1920. His son, Jim Bagby, Jr., had a ten-year big league career as a pitcher and played for the Indians from 1941 through 1945.

JUNE 10 Tris Speaker collects five hits, including a double, in five at-bats during a 10–1 win over the Senators at Dunn Field.

Tris Speaker arrived in Cleveland in 1916 and gave the team eleven excellent seasons as one of the best hitters in its history.

Speaker is not only the Indians all-time doubles leader with 488, but has more doubles than any other player in major league history. With the Red Sox, Indians, and Senators from 1907 though 1928, Speaker doubled 792 times and led the AL in the category in eight seasons. He is also sixth all-time in triples with 222.

June 11 Guy Morton strikes out 13 batters, including four in the sixth inning, during a 7–2 win over the Athletics at Dunn Field. The four strikeout victims in the sixth were Whitey Witt, Charlie Pick, Nap Lajoie, and Snuffy McInnis. Witt reached base after he swung at and missed a wild pitch.

O'Neill set a major league record for most double plays by a catcher in a season with 36 in 1916.

June 15 The Indians lose 2–1 in ten innings to the Yankees at Dunn Field despite the presence of some noisy electricians. Some 3,000 members of the Electrical League came equipped with dozens of electrical horns and gongs along with thousands of megaphones.

June 16 marked the peak of the 1916 season. The Indians were 32–19 on that date and held a 4½-gamed lead in the AL race.

June 26 The Indians become the first team in major league history to wear uniform numbers during a 2–0 win over the White Sox at Dunn Field. The numbers corresponded with information in the scorecards. Lead-off hitter Jack Graney earned the distinction of being the first player to bat wearing a number. The numbers were difficult to see from the stands, however, because they were placed on the sleeves. The club abandoned the experiment after the 1917 season. Numbers permanently affixed to the backs of uniforms were not a feature until 1929.

July 1 Stan Coveleski pitches five hitless innings of relief and starts an 11th-inning rally with a single to beat the Browns 5–4 at Dunn Field. Coveleski reached third on Ray Chapman's single and scored when Braggo Roth drove the ball into the bleachers. Roth was credited with only a single instead of a home run, however, because of the scoring rules of the day, which considered the game ended as soon as Coveleski crossed the plate. The rule was changed three years later. Beginning in 1919, players who hit the ball over the fence to end a game were given credit for a home run.

July 12 The Indians sweep the Yankees 1–0 and 6–3 in New York. Jim Bagby pitched the shutout in the opener.

July 13 The Indians are knocked out of first place with a 6–3 loss to the Yankees in New York.

Cleveland never regained first place again in 1916 but remained in contention for a little over a month. On August 10, the Indians were 60–45 and in second place, one game behind, but went 17–32 from that juncture to the end of the season.

July 27 The Indians discover that music hath no charms to soothe a grumpy umpire prior to a 7–6 loss to the Red Sox at Dunn Field. Umpire Silk O'Loughlin held up the start of the game for 15 minutes until a band ended its pre-game concert.

July 29 The Indians beat the Senators 10–0 on Terry Turner Day at Dunn Field. Turner, who had played for Cleveland since 1904, was given a variety of gifts before the game.

July 30 Umpire Silk O'Loughlin is again a source of controversy during a ten-inning, 2–1 loss to the Senators at Dunn Field. O'Loughlin called a Washington runner safe on a close play at first in the tenth, angering the Cleveland players and fans. After the game, the umpire had to leave the field with a police escort while dodging bottles thrown in his direction.

AUGUST 5 Whitey Witt of the Athletics hits a fluke homer during a 12–3 Cleveland win at Dunn Field. The drive by Witt lodged in one of the steel uprights in the right field fence.

AUGUST 12 Braggo Roth gets into a row with St. Louis fans during an 11–0 loss to the Browns. Playing right field, Roth was ridden unmercifully by bleachers fans. Unable to take anymore, Roth fired a ball full force into the stands. Some fans began throwing bottles at Roth, and he responded by throwing one back along with some obscene gestures.

AUGUST 13 A day after wrangling with St. Louis fans, Braggo Roth collects four hits, including a home run, to lead the Indians to a 4–3 win over the Browns. Roth's homer was struck in the ninth inning and broke a 3–3 tie.

Shortly after the end of the game, Roth received notice that he had been suspended for a week by AL president Ban Johnson for his altercation with fans during the August 12 contest.

AUGUST 18 The Indians trade Elmer Smith and Joe Leonard to the Senators for Joe Boehling and Danny Moeller.

The Indians made a mistake by trading Smith and rectified it by purchasing him from the Senators in August 1917.

AUGUST 25 The Indians sweep the Athletics 13–9 and 10–2 in Philadelphia. Cleveland scored in 14 of 18 turns at bat. Joe Bush started the second game for the A's and lasted only three innings, allowing five runs and six hits.

AUGUST 26 Just a day following a miserable start, Joe Bush goes to the mound again against the Indians and pitches a no-hitter and a 5–0 victory for the Athletics in Philadelphia. After Jack Graney walked leading off the first inning on a 3–1 pitch, Bush retired 27 batters in a row. Graney recorded the last out by lifting a pop fly to first baseman Snuffy McInnis.

AUGUST 31 Ollie Welf of the Indians starts and completes one of the shortest careers in big league history during a 3–1 loss to the Senators in Washington. In his lone appearance in the majors, Welf was in the game only as a pinch-runner for Bob Coleman in the ninth inning.

SEPTEMBER 4 In Detroit, the Coveleski brothers appear together in a major league game for the only time in their careers. Stan started for the Indians, but was knocked out in a five-run first inning. Harry relieved later as the Tigers won 7–5.

SEPTEMBER 24 Marty Kavanagh hits a fluke pinch-hit, grand slam off Dutch Leonard of the Red Sox during a 5–3 win at Dunn Field. The drive by Kavanagh rolled under the screen in left field.

The homer was the first pinch-hit grand slam in major league history. It was also the only one struck by Kavanagh in the 46 games he played for the Indians from 1916 through 1918.

1917

Season in a Sentence

In a season that starts less than a week after the United States enters World War I, the Indians continue to improve and post their first winning season since 1913.

Finish • Won • Lost • Pct • GB

Finish	Won	Lost	Pct	GB
Third	88	66	.571	12.0

Manager

Lee Fohl

Stats

Stats	Indians	AL	Rank
Batting Avg:	.245	.248	6
On-Base Pct:	.324	.318	3
Slugging Pct:	.322	.320	4
Home Runs:	13		7
Stolen Bases:	210		2
ERA:	2.52	2.66	3
Fielding Avg:	.964	.964	4
Runs Scored:	584		3
Runs Allowed:	545		3

Starting Line-up

Steve O'Neill, c
Joe Harris, 1b
Bill Wambsganss, 2b
Joe Evans, 3b
Ray Chapman, ss
Jack Graney, lf
Tris Speaker, cf
Braggo Roth, rf
Lou Guisto, 1b
Terry Turner, 3b-2b
Elmer Smith, rf

Pitchers

Jim Bagby, sp
Stan Coveleski, sp
Ed Klepfer, sp-rp
Guy Morton, sp-rp
Fritz Coumbe, rp
Al Gould, rp
Otis Lambeth, rp-sp

Attendance

477,298 (second in AL)

Club Leaders

Batting Avg:	Tris Speaker	.352
On-Base Pct:	Tris Speaker	.432
Slugging Pct:	Tris Speaker	.486
Home Runs:	Jack Graney	3
	Elmer Smith	3
RBIs:	Braggo Roth	72
Runs:	Ray Chapman	98
Stolen Bases:	Ray Chapman	52
Wins:	Jim Bagby	23
Strikeouts:	Jim Bagby	133
ERA:	Jim Bagby	1.81
Saves:	Jim Bagby	7

FEBRUARY 24 The Indians purchase Joe Wood from the Red Sox.

When acquired by the Indians, Wood was 27 years old and had a lifetime record of 117–56 as a major league pitcher, including a 34–5 record in 1912. He missed the entire 1916 season with an injured shoulder, however. The Indians failed in their hopes to revive Wood's arm and converted him into a capable outfielder in 1918, a position he played for five seasons.

MARCH 1 The Indians sell Chick Gandil to the White Sox.

APRIL 12 The Indians open the season with a 2–1 win over the Tigers in Detroit. Braggo Roth broke a 1–1 tie in the seventh inning on a sacrifice fly. Tris Speaker collected three hits in four at-bats. Jim Bagby was the winning pitcher.

Speaker hit .352, scored 90 runs, and collected 42 doubles in 1917.

APRIL 19 In the home opener, the Indians win a thrilling 8–7 decision over the Tigers at Dunn Field. Down 7–1, the Indians scored three runs in the fifth inning, two in the eighth, and two in the ninth. The final-inning rally consisted of singles by Milo Allison,

Bill Wambsganss, and Lou Guisto, a sacrifice by Ray Chapman, and a passed ball. Players on both clubs took part in military drills before the game under the direction of a uniformed soldier with their bats simulating rifles. The climax of the patriotic celebration came when the players of the teams, headed by a band, marched around the field in military formation.

Chapman batted .302 and scored 98 runs in 1917.

April 24 Stan Coveleski pitches a two-hitter, but loses 1–0 to the White Sox in Chicago. The run scored in the ninth inning on a triple by Swede Risberg and a sacrifice fly by Eddie Collins.

May 14 Ray Chapman steals four bases during a 7–6 win over the Red Sox at Dunn Field.

May 20 Indians pitcher Al Gould throws a one-hitter to defeat the Athletics 3–1 in the first game of a double header at Dunn Field. The only Philadelphia hit was a triple by Ray Bates in the first inning. Cleveland also won the second game 5–2. Jim Bagby was the winning pitcher and stole home in the seventh inning.

May 25 Down 5–0, the Indians stun the Yankees with six runs in the ninth inning to win 6–5 at Dunn Field. The rally started with one out and no one on base. Four singles and two doubles scored the first four runs. With two out and two strikes on Ivan Howard, Tris Speaker stole home. The next pitch from pitcher Allan Russell sailed past catcher Les Nunamaker, and Bill Wambsganss scored all the way from second base with the winning run.

May 29 Stan Coveleski pitches a ten-inning shutout to down the Tigers 1–0 in Detroit. Joe Harris, playing in his first game with the Indians and his first in the majors in three years, doubled in the lone run of the afternoon.

Coveleski led the AL in shutouts in 1917 with nine. Overall, he had a 19–14 record and a 1.81 ERA.

June 1 Guy Morton pitches a one-hitter on his 24th birthday to defeat Red Sox 3–0 at Fenway Park. The Sox went into the game with a ten-game winning streak. The only hit off Morton was a single in the eighth inning by opposing pitcher Babe Ruth. Ruth held the Indians to one hit until the ninth inning. Braggo Roth and Ray Chapman both stole home in the fourth to give Cleveland a 2–0 lead.

June 6 Indians pitcher Otis Lambeth hurls a two-hitter to defeat the Yankees 6–1 in New York. The only hits off Lambeth were singles by Les Nunamaker and Lee Magee.

Lambeth threw with an unorthodox underhand motion. He had an 11–10 record during a three-year career.

June 9 Joe Harris drives in Ray Chapman with both runs of a 2–0 triumph over the Yankees in New York. Harris hit a double in the second inning and a sacrifice fly in the seventh. Stan Coveleski pitched the shutout.

June 13 The Indians and the Senators play 16 innings to a 2–2 tie in Washington. The contest was called on account of darkness.

On the same day, the Indians purchased Elmer Smith from the Senators.

JUNE 21 Jim Bagby pitches the Indians to a 1–0 win over the White Sox at Dunn Field.

Bagby was 23–13, pitched eight shutouts, and posted a 1.99 ERA in 320⅔ innings in 1917.

JUNE 30 The Indians splatter the White Sox 11–1 at Dunn Field.

JULY 1 In the first inning, Braggo Roth triples and steals home on consecutive pitches, sparking the Indians to a 5–4 victory over the White Sox at Dunn Field.

Roth hit .285 for the Indians in 1917. He stole 51 bases, included six steals of home.

JULY 4 Jim Bagby defeats the Browns 2–0 in the first game of a double header in St. Louis. The Indians also took the second tilt 5–2.

JULY 6 The Indians score eight runs in the third inning and rout the Browns 12–6 in St. Louis.

JULY 8 Jim Bagby defeats the Red Sox 1–0 at Dunn Field. The run scored in the eighth inning on a double by Bill Wambsganss and a single by Braggo Roth.

JULY 12 Jim Bagby pitches his third consecutive shutout to defeat the Senators 7–0 at Dunn Field.

Bagby pitched 38 consecutive shutout innings over five starts from June 30 through July 16.

JULY 20 The Indians wallop the Athletics 20–6 at Dunn Field. The score was 3–0 in favor of Philadelphia before Cleveland collected eight runs in the sixth inning, three in the seventh, and six in the eighth.

JULY 26 Prior to a double header against the Senators in Washington, players of both teams participated in a "bomb throwing" exhibition under the direction of an officer in the Australian Army who was stationed in the U.S. as a military instructor. The players threw dummy bombs from the plate, using second base as a "target." Washington won the opener 5–2, while the Indians took the nightcap, called after five innings by rain, 2–1.

AUGUST 6 The Indians collect only one hit off Rube Foster of the Red Sox but win 2–0 in Boston. In the first inning, two walks and a double by Joe Harris produced the two runs.

AUGUST 8 In an unusual game for the dead ball era, all three runs of a 2–1 Cleveland win over the Yankees in New York are scored on solo homers. Elmer Smith and Jack Graney went deep for the Indians, and pitcher Ray Caldwell homered for the Yanks.

The Indians hit only 13 home runs all year in 1917. Smith and Graney were the club leaders with three apiece.

August 10 Elmer Smith homers in the 14th inning off Bob Shawkey to win 8–7 in New York. New York scored six runs in the first inning to take a 6–1 lead. Cleveland staged a comeback to forge a 7–6 advantage during the top of the seventh inning, but the Yanks deadlocked the contest in their half. There was no more scoring until Smith's homer.

August 18 During a 7–1 loss to the Red Sox at Dunn Field, a group of "pretty girls" collect over $1,000 from fans for a fund to purchase baseball equipment for American servicemen.

August 21 Jim Bagby collects four hits, including a double, in five at-bats during a 16–3 thrashing of the Athletics at Dunn Field.

Before the season, AL president Ban Johnson ordered all eight clubs in the organization to conduct military drills. A prize of $500 was offered to the best drilled team. Prior to the August 21 game, the Indians and Athletics drilled in regulation Army uniforms and toted Springfield rifles before Colonel Raymond Shelton, who was the judge of the contest. The Browns won the $500 purse. The Indians finished third in the competition.

Now known mostly as the only player ever killed on a major league field, Ray Chapman provided nifty defense and solid hitting during his career with the Indians. He batted .302 in 1917.

August 26 Jim Bagby wins his 20th game of the season with a 2–1 decision over the Senators at Dunn Field.

August 27 Braggo Roth steals four bases, including one of home at the head of a triple steal in the fifth inning, but the Indians lose 11–3 to the Senators at Dunn Field.

August 31 Stan Coveleski tosses a 1–0 shutout to defeat the Tigers at Dunn Field. Terry Turner drove in the lone run of the contest with a double in the fourth inning.

September 1 The Indians defeat the Tigers 3–2 at Dunn Field with the help of an act of kindness from Detroit manager Hughie Jennings. In attempting to steal home in the first inning, Tris Speaker was hit in the face by a ball batted by Joe Evans. Through the courtesy of Jennings, Speaker was allowed to remain out of the game for one inning while the cut was being sewed up, then returned to his position in center field, which was temporarily filled by Elmer Smith.

After his baseball career ended, Evans set up a medical practice in Gulfport, Mississippi.

SEPTEMBER 3 The Indians score eight runs in the fifth inning of a 9–3 win over the Browns in the first game of a double header at Dunn Field. Cleveland also won the second game 7–6 in 12 innings.

SEPTEMBER 9 The Indians lose a game by forfeit to the White Sox at Comiskey Park as a result of some juvenile behavior. The Clevelanders were angry about a play in the tenth inning with the score 3–3. When Jack Graney took a long lead off third, Chicago catcher Ray Schalk fired the ball to third. Graney slid back and barreled into Chicago third baseman Fred McMullin. The throw caromed away and Graney headed home, but only after wrestling free from McMullin, who grabbed Graney's belt. Umpire Brick Owens called Graney out for interfering with McMullin. The Indians argued the play for ten minutes. When they finally took the field, the players threw their gloves in the air and a couple of them rolled on the ground. After Fritz Coumbe struck out Sox pitcher Dave Danforth, catcher Steve O'Neill chucked the ball over the head of third baseman Ivan Howard. Graney, in left field, made no effort to retrieve the throw as it rolled all the way to the wall. At that point, Owens had enough and declared the forfeit.

SEPTEMBER 11 Stan Coveleski beats the Tigers 1–0 in Detroit with a three-hitter. All three hits were achieved by the first three batters in the first inning on singles by Donie Bush, Ossie Vitt, and Ty Cobb. Coveleski worked out of the jam without allowing a run and held Detroit hitless the rest of the way. In the fifth inning, Jack Graney stole home on the front end of a double steal with Braggo Roth for the lone run of the game.

SEPTEMBER 14 On the tenth anniversary of his first game in the majors, Tris Speaker is presented with a gold stickpin and a silver cigarette case by teammates before a game against the Browns in St. Louis. Speaker had a double and two singles and scored three runs during the 6–1 Cleveland victory.

SEPTEMBER 19 Stan Coveleski pitches a one-hitter to down the Yankees 2–0 at the Polo Grounds. The lone New York hit was a single by Fritz Maisel in the seventh inning.

SEPTEMBER 24 The Indians win their tenth game in a row with a 5–4 decision over the Athletics in Philadelphia.

1918

Season in a Sentence

With the nation embroiled in World War I, the federal government requests that the season end on Labor Day with the Indians only 2½ games out of first place.

Finish • Won • Lost • Pct • GB

Finish	Won	Lost	Pct	GB
Second	73	54	.575	2.5

Manager

Lee Fohl

Stats

	Indians	AL	Rank
Batting Avg:	.260	.254	1
On-Base Pct:	.344	.323	1
Slugging Pct:	.341	.322	1
Home Runs:	9		5
Stolen Bases:	165		1
ERA:	2.64	2.77	3
Fielding Avg:	.961	.964	5
Runs Scored:	504		1
Runs Allowed:	447		4

Starting Line-up

Steve O'Neill, c
Doc Johnston, 1b
Bill Wambsganss, 2b
Joe Evans, 3b
Ray Chapman, ss
Joe Wood, lf
Tris Speaker, cf
Braggo Roth, rf
Terry Turner, 3b-2b
Jack Graney, lf

Pitchers

Stan Coveleski, sp
Jim Bagby, sp-rp
Guy Morton, sp
Fritz Coumbe, sp-rp
Johnny Enzmann, sp-rp

Attendance

295,515 (first in AL)

Club Leaders

Batting Avg:	Tris Speaker	.318
On-Base Pct:	Tris Speaker	.403
Slugging Pct:	Tris Speaker	.435
Home Runs:	Joe Wood	5
RBIs:	Joe Wood	66
Runs:	Ray Chapman	84
Stolen Bases:	Braggo Roth	35
Wins:	Stan Coveleski	22
Strikeouts:	Guy Morton	123
ERA:	Stan Coveleski	1.82
Saves:	Jim Bagby	6

FEBRUARY 15 The Indians purchase Bob Groom from the Browns.

APRIL 16 The scheduled season opener against the Tigers in Cleveland is postponed by rain. The April 17 contest was also postponed.

APRIL 18 The Indians open the season with a 6–2 win over the Tigers at Dunn Field in a contest played in a constant rain. Braggo Roth hit a three-run triple during a five-run eighth inning. Stan Coveleski pitched a complete game for the win. Tris Speaker provided the highlight with an unassisted double play in the ninth inning. Speaker trapped a fly ball in shallow center, ran into the infield, and tagged Ossie Vitt, then stepped on second to force Babe Ellison.

At the start of the 1918 season, Ed Klepfer, Elmer Smith, Joe Harris, Red Torkelson, Hank DeBerry, and Louis Guisto were in military service. Before the end of the year, they were joined by Guy Morton, Bill Wambsganss, Otis Lambeth, Joe Evans, and Josh Billings. Harris served in France with the Army and suffered a debilitating poison gas attack.

APRIL 27 Ray Chapman homers in the 12th inning to defeat the Tigers 3–2 in Detroit.

The homer was the only one that Chapman hit in 1918. He batted .267 and led the AL in runs (84) and walks (84).

APRIL 29 Tris Speaker pulls off his second unassisted double play in the young season during an 8–4 loss to the White Sox at Dunn Field. With Eddie Collins on second base and Joe Jackson on first, Speaker trapped a ball in short center field, sped toward the infield to tag Collins, then stepped on second to force Jackson.

Speaker holds the all-time record for unassisted double plays by an outfielder in a career with six. He had four with the Red Sox and two with the Indians. Speaker probably played closer to home plate than any other center fielder in history. In the deadball era center fielders tended to play shallower than they do today, but Speaker was able to move in even farther because of his extraordinary ability to break backward on fly balls hit over his head.

MAY 15 Starting pitcher Stan Coveleski takes a 2–1 lead into the bottom of the 13th only to allow two runs for a 3–2 loss to the Athletics in Philadelphia.

MAY 16 In his only game as a member of the Indians, John Peters ties a major league record for most errors in a game by a catcher with four during a 6–5 loss to the Athletics in Philadelphia. Peters's nickname was "Shotgun" because of his strong arm, but he misfired on this day, making all four errors on throws. He may have made even more errors if he wasn't spiked in the sixth inning on a play at the plate, which caused his removal from the game.

Prior to May 16, 1918, Peters had appeared in only one big league game, that with the Tigers in 1915. He didn't play in the majors again for another three years. He took part in 110 contests with the Phillies in 1921 and 1922. However, he played 22 seasons of professional ball, including his long career in the minors. He died from a heart attack at the age of 38 during spring training in 1932 while playing for the Kansas City Blues of the American Association.

MAY 19 Stan Coveleski pitches into extra innings for the second start in a row and loses 1–0 in 12 innings to the Senators in Washington. It was the first major league game ever played in Washington on a Sunday.

MAY 20 Tris Speaker is hit on the top of the head by a pitch from Carl Mays of the Red Sox during the eighth inning of an 11–1 Cleveland loss in Boston.

Mays immediately apologized and said that the beaning was an accident. Speaker wasn't buying it, believing the throw was intentional. "I was on the same team with you long enough to know what you do," yelled Speaker. "If you throw at anyone else on this ball club, you might not even walk out of the park." Mays would hit another Indians player two years later with tragic consequences *(see August 16, 1920)**.*

MAY 23 Guy Morton pitches a one-hitter for a 1–0 win over the Red Sox at Fenway Park. The only Boston hit was a single by Amos Strunk into shallow center field. Braggo Roth's double drove in the lone run of the game.

Roth hit .283 in 1918.

MAY 24 The Indians outlast the Yankees 3–2 during a 19-inning marathon at the Polo Grounds. Stan Coveleski pitched all 19 innings, allowing 12 hits. It was the third consecutive start in which he pitched into extra innings. He lost the first two (see May 15 and 19, 1918). The 19th-inning run scored on a home run by Joe Wood. He also homered in the seventh inning to give Cleveland a 2–0 lead. Coveleski allowed runs in the seventh and ninth, then pitched ten straight scoreless innings.

With Wood's pitching arm beyond repair and Elmer Smith and Joe Harris in the service, the Indians converted Wood into an outfielder in 1918. Entering the season, he had a lifetime batting average of .241 and five homers in 502 at-bats. In 1918, Wood played 119 games, hit .296, and clubbed five home runs. Oddly, all five homers were struck against the Yankees in New York.

JUNE 2 Jim Bagby wins a duel with Walter Johnson to defeat the Senators 1–0 in 11 innings at Dunn Field. With two out in the Cleveland 11th inning and Al Halt as the runner on third, second baseman Ray Morgan and right fielder Burt Shotton collided going after Ray Chapman's fly ball allowing the winning run to score.

JUNE 6 Stan Coveleski pitches a three-hitter, but loses 1–0 to the Red Sox in ten innings at Dunn Field. It was the third extra-inning loss for Coveleski in a span of less than a month.

Despite the hard-luck defeats, Coveleski was 22–13 in 1918 and had a 1.82 ERA in 311 innings.

JUNE 29 The Indians explode for ten runs in the eighth inning and defeat the Tigers 13–4 at Dunn Field.

JULY 4 A double-header sweep of the Browns at Dunn Field catapults the Indians from third place into first past the Red Sox and Yankees. Cleveland won the first game 4–2 and the second 9–8.

JULY 6 The Indians drop out of first place with a 5–4 loss to the Red Sox in Boston.

The Indians were unable to recapture the top spot in the American League in 1918, but stayed in the race until the final week while chasing the Red Sox to no avail.

JULY 14 Stan Coveleski pitches the Indians to a 1–0 win over the Yankees in New York. He also scored the lone run of the game. In the third inning, Coveleski singled and came around on singles by Ray Chapman and Tris Speaker.

Speaker batted .318 and led the AL in doubles with 33 in 1918.

JULY 20 After losing the first game of a double header 10–1 to the Athletics in Philadelphia, the Indians win the second tilt by forfeit. Cleveland led 9–1 in the ninth inning when the crowd surged onto to the field. With no police on hand to clear the diamond, umpire Billy Evans declared the forfeit.

JULY 27 The Indians score two runs in the ninth inning and one in the tenth to beat the Yankees 7–6 at Dunn Field. The ninth-inning runs were driven home on triples by

Joe Evans and Ray Chapman. In the tenth, Doc Johnston doubled and Terry Turner singled for the winning tally.

AUGUST 1 The National Commission, baseball's governing body, announces that the 1918 season will end on September 1 to comply with a draft order issued by the federal government requiring all men of draft age to either enter military service or find a war-related job. The two pennant-winning teams were given an extension until September 15 to complete the World Series.

Fifteen of the 16 major league owners, unwilling to give up lucrative Labor Day double headers played on Monday, September 2, defied the government edict by playing on that date. Cleveland owner James Dunn was the lone holdout, however, believing that it was his patriotic duty to obey the letter of the law. He stated that the Indians would disband on September 1 and would not play on September 2. Dunn also said that his club would not play in the World Series if the Indians won the pennant, which dampened the enthusiasm of the players who were battling for first place (see September 2, 1918).

AUGUST 6 Jim Bagby pitches a ten-inning shutout to win 1–0 against the Senators at Dunn Field despite allowing 11 hits. Joe Wood led off the final inning with a triple and scored on a pinch-single by Joe Evans.

AUGUST 12 Guy Morton pitches a two-hitter to defeat the White Sox 11–2 at Dunn Field. The only Chicago hits were singles by Nemo Leibold and Wilbur Good.

AUGUST 27 During an 8–6 win over the Athletics in Philadelphia, Tris Speaker makes physical contact with umpire Tommy Connolly. Speaker claimed it was accidental but was suspended for the rest of the season by AL president Ban Johnson.

SEPTEMBER 2 The Indians fail to show for the final two games of the season against the Browns in St. Louis. The Browns appealed to Ban Johnson to declare the two games a forfeit, but Johnson refused to grant the request since the Cleveland club was simply obeying the government's "work or fight" order (see August 1, 1918).

NOVEMBER 11 An armistice is signed with Germany ending World War I.

When the 1918 season came to a close, it appeared that there would be no baseball in 1919 because the end of the war was nowhere in sight. But a series of victories by the Allies sped a conclusion to the war. Owners hastily made plans for the 1919 season, but due to the late start in preparing for the campaign and the anticipation of a poor year at the gate, baseball executives shortened the season to 140 games. It was a decision that officials came to regret, as attendance reached record levels in 1919.

1919

Season in a Sentence

After a change in managers from Lee Fohl to Tris Speaker, the Indians are in contention for the pennant until the final week only to finish a close second for the second year in a row.

Finish • Won • Lost • Pct • GB

Finish	Won	Lost	Pct	GB
Second	84	55	.604	3.5

Managers

Lee Fohl (44–34) and Tris Speaker (40–21)

Stats

Stats	Indians	AL	Rank
Batting Avg:	.278	.268	2
On-Base Pct:	.354	.334	1
Slugging Pct:	.381	.359	2
Home Runs:	24		6 (tie)
Stolen Bases:	113		4
ERA:	2.94	.322	2
Fielding Avg:	.965	.965	4
Runs Scored:	636		2
Runs Allowed:	537		2

Starting Line-up

Steve O'Neill, c
Doc Johnston, 1b
Bill Wambsganss, 2b
Larry Gardner, 3b
Ray Chapman, ss
Jack Graney, lf
Tris Speaker, cf
Joe Wood, rf
Joe Harris, 1b

Pitchers

Stan Coveleski, sp
Jim Bagby, sp
Guy Morton, sp
Elmer Myers, sp-rp
Hi Jasper, sp
George Uhle, rp-sp

Attendance

538,135 (fourth in AL)

Club Leaders

Batting Avg:	Ray Chapman	.300
	Larry Gardner	.300
On-Base Pct:	Tris Speaker	.395
Slugging Pct:	Tris Speaker	.433
Home Runs:	Elmer Smith	9
RBIs:	Larry Gardner	79
Runs:	Tris Speaker	83
Stolen Bases:	Doc Johnston	21
Wins:	Stan Coveleski	24
Strikeouts:	Stan Coveleski	118
ERA:	Stan Coveleski	2.52
Saves:	Stan Coveleski	4

MARCH 1 The Indians trade Braggo Roth to the Athletics for Larry Gardner, Charlie Jamieson, and Elmer Myers.

The Indians made an excellent trade, as Gardner became the club's starting third baseman for four seasons, and Jamieson played in Cleveland as an outfielder for 14 seasons. Both were key elements on the 1920 world championship club. An underrated player who deserves Hall of Fame consideration, Gardner had played on three previous world champion clubs with the Red Sox in 1912, 1915, and 1916. Jamieson played a total of 1,483 games as an Indian, ninth most in club history. He also ranks fourth in runs scored (942), fifth in hits (1,753), seventh in doubles (296), tenth in triples (74), and tenth in batting average (.316).

APRIL 23 The scheduled season opener against the Tigers in Detroit is postponed by rain. The April 24 contest was also postponed.

APRIL 25 The Indians get the 1919 season underway with a 4–2 loss to the Tigers in Detroit.

MAY 1 The Indians lose the home opener 8–1 against the Tigers at Dunn Field.

May 31 A fight between Tris Speaker and Chicago first baseman Chick Gandil highlights a 5–2 loss to the White Sox at Comiskey Park. In the eighth inning, Gandil claimed that Speaker had tried to spike him when he slid into first. The two players fought for three minutes and several healthy wallops were exchanged before they could be separated.

Speaker hit .296 for the Indians in 1919. Other offensive leaders were Ray Chapman (.300) and Steve O'Neill (.289).

June 2 An unusual triple play by the Indians is the feature of a 5–3 win over the Browns at Dunn Field. With the bases loaded in the fourth inning, Wally Gerber hit a sacrifice fly to Joe Wood in center field, scoring George Sisler. Shortstop Ray Chapman intercepted Wood's throw and Browns runners Baby Doll Jacobson and Tom Sloan were retired in rundowns between third baseman Larry Gardner and second baseman Bill Wambsganss. Doc Johnston was four-for-four with three singles and a double. Combined with two singles in the final two plate appearances against the White Sox in Chicago the previous day, Johnston had hits in six consecutive at-bats.

June 3 Doc Johnston runs his streak of hits in consecutive at-bats to nine during a double header against the Browns at Dunn Field. Johnston had two singles and two sacrifices in the opener, a 14–6 Cleveland loss. After another sacrifice in his first plate appearance in the second tilt, Johnston singled in the fourth to run his streak to nine. His streak was stopped in the sixth when he fouled to the catcher. The Indians won the game 8–5.

Prohibition began in the state of Ohio on May 26, 1919, which effectively ended the sale of alcohol at Dunn Field. Prohibition became national law in January 1920 when the 18th amendment took effect. Beer sales did not return to major league ballparks until 1933.

June 8 Guy Morton pitches a complete game and drives in the winning run with a walk-off single in the ninth to defeat the Athletics 2–1 at Dunn Field.

June 10 An umpire is attacked at the close of a 3–2 win over the Senators in Washington. For protesting a close decision in the seventh inning, Senators manager Clark Griffith was ordered off the field by umpire Dick Nallin, who later was made a target for seat cushions and bottles thrown by the fans. George McBride of the Washington club was lightly cut on the face by a piece of flying glass. After the game, Nallin was slugged by an irate fan.

June 16 Stan Coveleski pitches the Indians to a 1–0 win over the Red Sox in Boston. The lone run of the game was driven home on a first-inning single by Elmer Smith.

Coveleski was 24–12 and had a 2.61 ERA in 1919.

June 18 The Indians move into a tie for first place with the White Sox by defeating the Yankees 13–3 in New York.

June 20 The idle Indians drop out of first place when the White Sox defeat the Senators in Washington.

The 1919 Indians. First row: Joe Wood, bat boy, Bill Wambsganss. Second row: Les Nunamaker, Charlie Jamieson, Marty Fiedler, Walter McNichols, Jim Bagby, Steve O'Neill, Ray Chapman, Doc Johnston. Third row: Johnny Enzmann, Terry Turner, Fred Coumbe, Jack McCallister, Lee Fohl, Chet Thomas, Stan Coveleski, Guy Morton. Top row: Elmer Dobard, Tris Speaker, Joe Harris, Joe Engel, Jack Graney, Elmer Smith, George Uhle, Harry Lunte, Hi Jasper.

The Indians failed to regain the top spot in the AL over the remainder of the 1919 season but remained on the heels of the White Sox into September.

JUNE 30 The Indians lose 5–2 to the White Sox during a stormy afternoon at Dunn Field. Chicago manager Kid Gleason was ejected from the field in the first inning for protesting an umpiring decision. Later, the Cleveland team delayed the game for ten minutes insisting that White Sox pitcher Eddie Cicotte committed a balk. Indians outfielders threw out four runners at home plate, with two each by right fielder Elmer Smith and center fielder Tris Speaker. Smith also contributed a homer, triple, and double.

JULY 1 The Indians score seven runs in the first inning to defeat the White Sox 14–9 at Dunn Field.

JULY 3 The Indians are hammered 17–1 by the White Sox at Dunn Field. Chicago scored ten runs in the fourth inning.

JULY 18 The Red Sox score five runs in the ninth inning to defeat the Indians 8–7 at Dunn Field. Boston had the bases loaded with two out and the score 7–4 when Babe Ruth stepped to the plate with right-hander Elmer Myers on the mound. Indians manager Lee Fohl brought in lefty Fritz Coumbe to face the left-hand hitting Ruth, even though Coumbe hadn't pitched in two months. Two pitches later, Ruth drove a slow curve over the 290-foot right field wall.

Apoplectic over the loss, owner James Dunn fired Fohl as the Indians manager the next day with the club holding a record of 44–34. Tris Speaker replaced Fohl. Cleveland was 40–21 under Speaker over the rest of the 1919 season but were unable to catch the White Sox and finished second, 3½ games out of first. The following season, Speaker led the Indians to a world championship and remained in the dual role of manager and starting center fielder through the end of the 1926 season. Fohl later managed the St. Louis Browns from 1921 through 1923, coming within one game of the pennant in 1922, and the Red Sox from 1924 through 1926.

AUGUST 11 Tris Speaker scores five runs during a 15–9 victory over the Yankees in New York. The Indians broke a 6–6 tie with five runs in the seventh inning.

AUGUST 19 The Indians purchase Ray Caldwell from the Red Sox.

AUGUST 24 Ray Caldwell makes quite an impression when he is struck by lightning during a game against the Athletics at Dunn Field. With two out in the ninth inning and the Indians leading 2–1, a violent thunderstorm hit the ballpark. Caldwell was struck by a bolt of lightning and was thrown to the ground. The other Indians players also felt the effects of the lightning with their spiked shoes attracting the electricity. Ray Chapman nearly fell when one leg went numb. After about five minutes of unconsciousness, Caldwell was revived, regained his feet and composure, shook off the effects of the blow, which included a burn on his chest, and assured manager Tris Speaker that he could continue. The storm cleared up just as quickly as it arrived, and Caldwell pitched to the next batter, retiring Joe Dugan on a grounder to end the game with a victory.

Caldwell added to his legend with a no-hitter 17 days later (see September 10, 1919). He came to the Indians at the age of 31 with a 102–103 lifetime record and frustrated his previous ball clubs with his drinking problems. Caldwell won five of his six decisions with Cleveland in 1919. To counter Caldwell's love of alcohol, Tris Speaker inserted a clause into the pitcher's 1920 contract ordering him to drink, even though the country was legally dry due to the Prohibition amendment. The contract read: "After each game he pitches, Ray Caldwell must get drunk. He is not to report to the park the next day. The second day he is to report to Manager Speaker and run around the park as many times as Manager Speaker stipulates. The third day he is to pitch batting practice, and the fourth day he is to pitch in a championship game." Caldwell responded with a 20–10 record in 1920, leading the Indians to the AL pennant and a win in the World Series. It was the only time in his career that he won 20 or more games in a season. Caldwell was 6–6 in 1921, however, his last season in the majors.

AUGUST 25 The Indians wallop the Athletics 12–0 at Dunn Field. George Uhle pitched the shutout.

A native of Cleveland, Uhle made his major league debut with the Indians as a 20-year-old in 1919 and pitched for the club until 1928. Many historians credit Uhle with inventing the slider. He was 147–119 with Cleveland during a career in which he won 200 and lost 166. Uhle had records of 22–16 in 1922, 26–16 in 1923, and 27–11 in 1926. Among Indians pitchers, he is eighth in wins, ninth in games started (267), sixth in complete games (166), and eighth in innings pitched (2,200⅓).

August 31 Ray Chapman ties a major league record with four sacrifices during a 6–1 win over the White Sox at Dunn Field.

September 10 Ray Caldwell pitches a no-hitter, defeating the Yankees 3–0 in the first game of a double header in New York. Caldwell pitched for the Yanks from 1910 through 1918. The only New York base runners were Truck Hannah, who walked in the sixth inning, and Frank Baker, who reached on an error in the seventh. Caldwell struck out five batters. The Indians also won the second contest 3–2.

September 16 The Indians sweep the Athletics 8–2 and 12–8 during a double header in Philadelphia. In the first game, Ray Chapman stole four bases. In the second tilt, the Indians overcame a 5–0 deficit with eight runs in the third inning.

September 20 The Indians run their winning streak to nine games with a 6–3 and 3–1 double header sweep of the Senators in Washington.

The late-season surge put the Indians only 3½ games out of first place by the end of the season, but the club didn't pose a serious threat to the pennant aspirations of the White Sox after the first of September.

September 21 The Indians record their tenth win in a row with an 8–4 decision over the Senators in Washington.

September 25 The Indians lose 9–5 to the Tigers in Detroit.

The game would have lasting implications concerning the reputations of Tris Speaker and Ty Cobb. Seven years later, Detroit pitcher Dutch Leonard charged Speaker with deliberately losing the game in collusion with Cobb and gamblers (see November 29, 1926). Cobb and Speaker were exonerated by baseball commissioner Kenesaw Landis on January 27, 1927.

THE STATE OF THE INDIANS

The Indians won the first World Series in franchise history in 1920 and finished a close second in 1921. The only other contender during the 1920s was the 1926 club, however. Overall, the Indians were 786–749 during the 1920s, a winning percentage of .512 that was third best in the AL behind the Yankees and Senators. American League World Series participants outside of Cleveland were the Yankees (1921, 1922, 1923, 1926, 1927 and 1928), Senators (1924 and 1925) and Athletics (1929).

THE BEST TEAM

The 1920 Indians won the AL pennant with a record of 98–56, then defeated the Brooklyn Dodgers in the World Series.

THE WORST TEAM

The 1928 club sank to seventh place with a 62–92 record in Roger Peckinpaugh's first season as manager.

THE BEST MOMENT

The Indians won their first world championship in 1920 by defeating the Brooklyn Dodgers five games to two in a best-of-nine World Series.

THE WORST MOMENT

Ray Chapman was hit in the head by a pitch from Carl Mays of the Yankees on August 16, 1920. Chapman died from the beaning the following morning.

THE ALL-DECADE TEAM • YEARS W/INDIANS

Steve O'Neill, c	1912–23
George Burns, 1b	1920–21, 1924–28
Bill Wambsganss, 2b	1914–23
Larry Gardner, 3b	1919–24
Joe Sewell, ss	1920–32
Charlie Jamieson, lf	1919–32
Tris Speaker, cf	1916–26
Homer Summa, rf	1922–28
Stan Coveleski, p	1916–24
George Uhle, p	1919–28
Joe Shaute, p	1922–30
Sherry Smith, p	1922–27

Speaker, Sewell, and Coveleski are all in the Hall of Fame. O'Neill, Wambsganss, Speaker, and Coveleski were also on the Indians All-Decade Team during the 1910s. Other outstanding players during the 1920s were pitchers Jake Miller (1924–33) and Willis Hudlin (1926–40), and catchers Glenn Myatt (1923–35) and Luke Sewell (1920–30).

THE DECADE LEADERS

Batting Avg:	Tris Speaker	.363
On-Base Pct:	Tris Speaker	.455
Slugging Pct:	Tris Speaker	.552
Home Runs:	Tris Speaker	67
RBIs:	Joe Sewell	817
Runs:	Charlie Jamieson	868
Stolen Bases:	Charlie Jamieson	100
Wins:	George Uhle	137
Strikeouts:	George Uhle	708
ERA:	Stan Coveleski	3.17
Saves:	George Uhle	19

THE HOME FIELD

The only significant modifications to the Indians home field during the 1920s was a change of names. It opened as League Park in 1910, was renamed Dunn Field in 1916, then went back to being referred to as League Park in 1928.

THE GAME YOU WISH YOU HAD SEEN

The only two world championships achieved by the Indians have been in 1920 and 1948. The 1920 world title was the only one of the two clinched in Cleveland, occurring on October 12. It is hard to top watching your club win a World Series, but the contest two days earlier may have been the best day to be at the ballpark during the 1920s. Fans at Dunn Field were treated to an 8–1 win over the Dodgers that featured the only unassisted triple play in World Series history (by second baseman Bill Wambsganss), the first grand slam (by Elmer Smith), and the first home run by a pitcher (from Jim Bagby).

THE WAY THE GAME WAS PLAYED

Rule changes in 1920 and the emergence of Babe Ruth as a star transformed baseball from a low-scoring defensive affair to a high-scoring offensive carnival. AL teams went from 3.5 runs a game in 1917 to 5.1 per game in 1921 and 5.4 per game in 1930. Not surprisingly, team ERA jumped by nearly two runs. Pitchers completed fewer than half their starts in the AL in 1923, the first time that had happened, as relief pitching continued to gain importance.

THE MANAGEMENT

James Dunn, who bought the club in 1916, delivered a world championship in 1920. Dunn died in 1922, and the Indians were run by his heirs until Alva Bradley purchased the franchise in 1927. Ernest Barnard was general manager until 1927 when he was elevated to the presidency of the American League. Billy Evans succeeded Barnard in the front office. Field managers were Tris Speaker (1919–26), Jack McCallister (1927), and Roger Peckinpaugh (1928–33).

THE BEST PLAYER MOVE

The best move was the purchase of Earl Averill from the San Francisco Seals of the Pacific Coast League in 1929 for $50,000 and two players.

THE WORST PLAYER MOVE

The worst move sent Stan Coveleski to the Senators in December 1924 for Byron Speece and Carr Smith.

1920

Season in a Sentence

In a season of tragedy and triumph, Ray Chapman is killed by a pitch in August, and the Indians win the American League pennant and the World Series for the first time.

Finish • Won • Lost • Pct • GB

Finish	Won	Lost	Pct	GB
First	98	56	.636	+2.0

World Series

The Indians defeated the Brooklyn Dodgers five games to two.

Manager

Tris Speaker

Stats

Stats	Indians	AL	Rank
Batting Avg:	.303	.284	2
On-Base Pct:	.376	.347	1
Slugging Pct:	.417	.387	3
Home Runs:	35		6
Stolen Bases:	73		6
ERA:	3.41	3.79	2
Fielding Avg:	.971	.966	2
Runs Scored:	857		1
Runs Allowed:	642		2

Starting Line-up

Steve O'Neill, c
Doc Johnston, 1b
Bill Wambsganss, 2b
Larry Gardner, 3b
Ray Chapman, ss
Charlie Jamieson, lf
Tris Speaker, cf
Elmer Smith, rf
Joe Evans, lf
Joe Graney, lf
Joe Wood, rf

Pitchers

Jim Bagby, sp
Stan Coveleski, sp
Ray Caldwell, sp
Guy Morton, sp-rp
George Uhle, rp

Attendance

912,832 (second in AL)

Club Leaders

Batting Avg:	Tris Speaker	.388
On-Base Pct:	Tris Speaker	.482
Slugging Pct:	Tris Speaker	.562
Home Runs:	Elmer Smith	12
RBIs:	Larry Gardner	118
Runs:	Tris Speaker	137
Stolen Bases:	Doc Johnston	13
	Ray Chapman	13
Wins:	Jim Bagby	31
Strikeouts:	Stan Coveleski	133
ERA:	Stan Coveleski	2.49
Saves:	Stan Coveleski	2
	Dick Niehaus	2

FEBRUARY 9 Baseball's rules committee adopts new regulations that usher in the era of the lively ball. The changes were spurred in part by the owners' recognition of the positive impact of Babe Ruth upon the game. Ruth clubbed a then-record 29 home runs for the Red Sox in 1919 and helped the American League set an all-time attendance record. Baseball's rules committee adopted a more-lively ball, agreed to keep a fresh ball in play at all times, and banned pitchers from using any foreign substances to deface a ball. These included paraffin, resin, powder, emery boards, files, and saliva.

MARCH 29 The Indians purchase George Burns from the Athletics.

APRIL 14 The Indians open the season with a 5–0 win over the Browns before 19,984 at Dunn Field. Stan Coveleski pitched a five-hit shutout and added a double and a single in three at-bats. Elmer Smith collected three hits. With the temperature just above the freezing point, some fans kept warm by building bonfires made of newspapers.

The Indians drew 912,832 fans in 1920, shattering the old mark of 541,000 set in 1913. The 1920 figure stood as the club record until 1946.

APRIL 20 The Indians outlast the Tigers 11–10 at Dunn Field. Cleveland broke a 7–7 tie with four runs in the seventh inning, then weathered a three-run Detroit rally in the eighth.

MAY 22 Umpire George Hildebrand is surrounded by angry Philadelphia fans after a 4–1 Indians win at Shibe Park. After crowds swarmed the umpire at the conclusion of the game, he was escorted off the field by Cleveland players.

MAY 28 The Indians win a 13–6 slugging match over the White Sox at Dunn Field.

On the same day, the wife of Stan Coveleski died in Shamokin, Pennsylvania, following a long illness.

MAY 30 Down 6–1, the Indians score five runs in the seventh inning and two in the eighth to defeat the White Sox 8–6 at Dunn Field.

JUNE 1 Trailing 10–2, the Indians score seven runs in the sixth inning to make the game close, but lose 11–10 to the Tigers at Dunn Field.

JUNE 13 Babe Ruth hits a long home run over the right field fence at Dunn Field that clears a house on the opposite side of Lexington Avenue during a 14–0 Yankees victory over the Indians.

JUNE 22 The Indians wallop the Red Sox 13–5 at Dunn Field. Cleveland received five hits by the right fielders. Elmer Smith had four hits, including a double, in four at-bats. In the seventh inning Smith was replaced by Joe Wood, who singled in his lone plate appearance.

JUNE 23 The Indians edge the Red Sox 7–6 in 14 innings at Dunn Field. Elmer Smith drove in the winning run with a single. Both teams scored three runs in the ninth inning.

JUNE 29 Elmer Smith hits a grand slam in the fifth inning of a 9–6 win over the Browns in the first game of a double header in St. Louis. The homer off Urban Shocker gave the Indians a 6–3 lead. Cleveland completed the sweep with a 5–4 win in the second tilt.

Smith hit .316 with 12 homers and 103 RBIs in 1920.

JULY 8 After being retired in his first three plate appearances, Tris Speaker collects seven consecutive hits during a sweep of the Senators in Washington, won by scores of 4–2 and 9–6. All seven hits, five of which occurred in game two, were singles.

JULY 9 Tris Speaker is 3-for-3 to run his steak of hits in consecutive at-bats to ten during an 8–4 win over the Senators in Washington. He left the game in the seventh inning with an injured leg.

JULY 10 Tris Speaker extends his streak of hits in consecutive at-bats to eleven during a 7–2 victory over the Senators during the first game of a double header at Griffith Stadium. Washington won the second game 2–1. Speaker was 5-for-8 in the twin bill.

Speaker had 15 hits in 18 consecutive at-bats during the five-game, three-day series against the Senators on July 8, 9, and 10. He had one of the greatest seasons of any hitter in Cleveland history with a .388 batting average, 137 runs, 214 hits, 97 walks, 12 homers, and a league-leading 50 doubles.

JULY 13 The Indians win an unusual 4–3 decision over the Athletics in Philadelphia. The Indians scored three runs in the first inning off A's starter Dave Keefe, who was replaced by Eddie Rommel. Cleveland collected only one hit off Rommel in 8⅔ innings of relief, but that one hit was a homer by Ray Chapman in the sixth inning that broke a 3–3 tie.

Chapman hit .303 and scored 97 runs in 1920 before his life was cut short by a beaning on August 16.

JULY 29 Down 3–2, the Indians score seven runs in the eighth inning to beat the Red Sox 9–3 at Dunn Field.

JULY 30 The Indians mash the Red Sox 13–4 at Dunn Field.

JULY 31 Guy Morton pitches a one-hitter for a 2–1 win over the Red Sox at Dunn Field. The only Boston hit was a hard grounder by Stuffy McInnis that bounced off third baseman Larry Gardner in the second inning. After the game, thousands gathered below the press box and begged the official scorer to change the decision on McInnis's hit to an error on Gardner, which would have given Morton a no-hitter, but the ruling stood.

On August 5, the Indians had a 4½-game lead in the American League pennant race. The Yankees were in second place. The White Sox were third, five games out. Five straight Cleveland losses beginning on August 10 made it a three-team race.

The Death of Ray Chapman

Cleveland shortstop Ray Chapman stepped into the batter's box at New York's Polo Grounds against Carl Mays of the Yankees in the fifth inning of a game on August 16, 1920. A pitch barely outside the strike zone struck Chapman on the left temple and he was carried from the field on a stretcher. He died 12 hours later in a New York hospital to become the only major leaguer to die as a result of an on-field incident. Chapman was 29 years old.

The Indians were involved in a tight three-team pennant race with the Yankees and White Sox. Mays was a right-handed pitcher who threw in a submarine style and had a long-standing reputation as a head hunter. Chapman was a hitter who liked to crouch the plate. Catcher Muddy Ruel had trouble seeing the fateful pitch, which was headed straight at Chapman. One witness said Chapman seemed "hypnotized." There was an "explosive sound" and the ball hit Chapman with such force that it bounded back to Mays, who believing it hit Chapman's bat, fielded the ball and flipped it to first baseman Wally Pipp for what he thought was the inning's first out. Pipp started to toss the ball around the infield when he noticed that something was wrong with Chapman.

"We need a doctor," shouted home plate umpire Tommy Connolly. "Is there a doctor in the house?" The Indians gathered around Chapman, who at first could not speak as the Yankee team physician applied ice to his injury. After a few minutes, Chapman was able to stand, to the immense relief of everyone in the stadium. With the assistance of two teammates, Chapman began walking off the field toward the center field clubhouse. He tried to speak, but no words were forthcoming as the shock of the blow paralyzed his vocal chords. At second base, he crumpled to the ground. He was rushed to St. Lawrence Hospital, where it was learned that his skull was crushed on one side, and fractured on the other, causing an inter-cranial hemorrhage. His neck was also broken. He died at 4:00 a.m. the following day.

Mays pitched the rest of the game, losing 4–3. After learning of Chapman's death, Mays gave himself up to the district attorney in New York. Mays made his statement accompanied by Yankee business manager Charles McManus, Indians manager Tris Speaker, and Walter McNichols, secretary of the Cleveland club. Chapman's death was ruled to be accidental.

The public reaction was one of sadness mixed with shock and anger. Players on the Red Sox, Tigers, and Browns circulated a petition demanding that Mays be barred from baseball and said they would boycott any game that Mays pitched. But AL president Ban Johnson refused to act on the petition.

In response, Mays said, "It is terrible to consider the case at all, but when any man, however ignorant, illiterate, or malicious, even hints that a white man in his normal mind would stand out there on the field of sport and try to kill another, the man making the assertion is inhuman, uncivilized, bestial."

Mays shook off the death of Chapman and followed a 26–11 season in 1920 with a 27–9 mark in 1921. He pitched in the majors until 1928, finishing with a record of 208–126 and an ERA of 2.92. Mays is the only pitcher in baseball with at least 200 wins and a winning percentage of over .600 during the 20th century who is not in the Hall of Fame, a situation directly attributable to the pitch that killed Ray Chapman.

Tragedy continued to haunt the Chapman family. When Ray died, his wife Kathleen was pregnant with their first child. Rae Marie Chapman was born on February 27, 1921. Kathleen remarried two years later and moved to California. On April 21, 1928, she died suddenly after drinking a poisonous substance. Her family said it was accidental. The coroner ruled her death a suicide. Rae Marie died from the measles on April 27, 1929.

AUGUST 2 George Burns hits a two-run, pinch-single in the eighth to provide the only runs in a 2–0 win over the Senators at Dunn Field. Stan Coveleski pitched the shutout.

Coveleski was 24–14 in 1920 with a 2.49 earned run average in 315 innings. He led the league in strikeouts with 133. Coveleski wasn't the best pitcher on the club, however. That honor went to Jim Bagby who set an all-time club record for victories in a season by posting a 31–12 record and a 2.89 ERA. He led the AL in wins, winning percentage (.721), games pitched (48), complete games (30 in 36 starts), and innings pitched (339⅔). Ray Caldwell was 20–10 with an earned run average of 3.89.

AUGUST 15 In his first major league start, Bob Clark pitches a shutout to beat the Browns 5–0 with a four-hitter at Dunn Field.

Clark made only one more start during his big league career and never won another game. In two seasons in the majors, Clark pitched in 16 games, 14 of them in relief, and had a 1–2 record and a 5.44 ERA.

AUGUST 16 At the Polo Grounds in New York, Yankees pitcher Carl Mays hits Ray Chapman in the head with one of his submarine pitches in the fifth inning of a 4–3 Indians victory.

Fans gather outside the ballpark before a World Series game.

AUGUST 17 Ray Chapman dies from the effects of the beaning he suffered the previous day. He is the only fatality as the result of being hit by a pitch in the history of major league baseball.

AUGUST 20 Ray Chapman's funeral is held at St. John's Catholic Cathedral in Cleveland. Indians players were among the nearly 2,000 in attendance inside. Another 3,000 were in the streets outside. The service was presided over by 24 priests. A local newspaper collected donations from 20,000 mourners and bought a floral arrangement over nine feet long and six feet wide. Tris Speaker was so distraught that he couldn't attend the service. The game that day against the Red Sox in Boston was postponed.

AUGUST 21 The day after Ray Chapman's funeral, the grieving and listless Indians are knocked out of first place after losing a double header 12–0 and 4–0 against the Red Sox in Boston. Tris Speaker, tormented over the death of Chapman, remained in Cleveland. Joe Wood ran the club in Speaker's absence.

On the same day, the Indians purchased Duster Mails from Portland in the Pacific Coast League. With the death of Ray Chapman and the Indians involved in a tight three-way race for the franchise's first American League pennant, the purchase of Mails attracted scant notice. He was 25 years old, and his only prior big league experience consisted of 13 games with the Dodgers in 1915 and 1916 with an 0–2 record. It's unlikely the Indians would have won the world championship in 1920 if it were not for Mails, however. He had a 7–0 regular season record for Cleveland in 1920, making eight September and October starts. During the World Series against the Dodgers, he pitched 15⅔ scoreless innings in a relief appearance and a start. Mails followed with a 14–6 record in 1921 but was bothered by arm troubles in 1922 and was sent back to the minors with a 4–7 record.

AUGUST 26 On the day that women are granted the right to vote with the passage of the 19th amendment, the Indians fall 3½ games behind the first place White Sox after a 3–2 loss to the Athletics in Philadelphia.

AUGUST 27 The Indians collect 21 hits and pummel the Athletics 15–3 in Philadelphia. Jim Bagby had four hits, including a double, in five at-bats.

SEPTEMBER 1 The Indians recapture first place after a 9–5 win over the Senators in Washington.

On the same day, the White Sox lost their fifth game in a row. The Sox lost the 1919 World Series to the Reds amid accusations that eight players had conspired to throw the Series in collusion with gamblers. Seven of the eight returned to play for the White Sox in 1920. There were suspicions that some or all of the seven helped to fix the five games that Chicago lost from August 27 through September 1.

SEPTEMBER 3 The Indians play in Cleveland for the first time since the death of Ray Chapman, and lose 1–0 to the Tigers at Dunn Field. A short memorial service was held for Chapman prior to the game. A lone bugler stood at Chapman's old shortstop position and played taps. The bugler was a member of Cleveland's naval reserves, Chapman's old unit during World War I. Owner James Dunn issued a 12-page booklet honoring Chapman to each of the 15,000 fans in attendance.

SEPTEMBER 6 The Indians sweep the Browns 7–2 and 6–5 at Dunn Field. Right fielder Elmer Smith contributed an unassisted double play in the opener. Harry Lunte, who replaced Ray Chapman at shortstop, was injured in the first game. There was no one else on the roster capable of playing the position, which left the Indians to look to the minors for help.

SEPTEMBER 7 The Indians purchase Joe Sewell from New Orleans in the Southern Association.

The son of an Alabama doctor, Sewell was purchased to fill the void at shortstop left by the death of Ray Chapman and the injury to Lunte. Sewell was immediately placed in the starting line-up. Despite being only 21 years old, just four months out of the University of Alabama, replacing a player who died in a tragic accident, and playing during the stress of a pennant race, Sewell hit .329 in 22 games during the 1920 stretch drive. He remained Cleveland's starting shortstop until 1930. Among Indians players, Sewell ranks fourth in hits (1,800), fourth in doubles (375), sixth in RBIs (865), sixth in games played (1,513), seventh in at-bats (5,621), seventh in batting average (.320), seventh in on base percentage (.398), eighth in runs (857), and eighth in walks (655). From September 13, 1922 through April 30, 1930, Sewell appeared in

1,103 consecutive games, the seventh longest in major league history and the longest by a Cleveland player. He was also the most difficult batter to strike out in major league history. In 7,132 big league at-bats, Sewell fanned only 113 times. Joe's brother Luke played for the Indians from 1921 through 1932 and again in 1939. Another brother, Tommy, had a one-game big league career with the Cubs in 1927. Joe was elected to the Hall of Fame in 1977.

SEPTEMBER 9 The Yankees play in Cleveland for the first time since the death of Ray Chapman and lose 10–1 to the Indians at Dunn Field.

Carl Mays was not with the Yankees during the series in Cleveland. "We are not taking Mays to Cleveland," said Yankee owner T. L. Huston, "but not because we think there is danger of any trouble, but out of respect to the feelings of the people there. We don't want to offend them."

SEPTEMBER 14 The Indians drop out of first place behind the Yankees following an 8–0 loss to the Athletics at Dunn Field.

SEPTEMBER 15 The Indians thrash the Athletics 14–0 at Dunn Field.

SEPTEMBER 16 The Indians leap back into first place with a 1–0 triumph over the Senators at Dunn Field. Duster Mails pitched the shutout. The run scored in the eighth inning when Joe Sewell singled, moved to third on Steve O'Neill's double, and scored on a wild pitch.

O'Neill hit .321 for the Indians in 1920.

SEPTEMBER 20 Larry Gardner drives in six runs on two triples and a double during an 8–3 win over the Red Sox at Dunn Field.

Gardner hit .310 and drove in 118 runs in 1920. He played in every inning of every game.

SEPTEMBER 21 The Indians run their winning streak to seven with a 12–1 win over the Red Sox at Dunn Field. Elmer Smith collected six runs-batted-in on a homer, double, and single.

SEPTEMBER 25 The Indians lead over the White Sox in the AL pennant race is cut to one-half game with a 5–1 loss to Chicago at Dunn Field. After hitting a home run, Joe Jackson twice flipped an obscene gesture in the direction of the stands while circling the bases. In attendance were thousands of ex-soldiers attending an American Legion convention in Cleveland. Jackson was booed lustily and taunted with repeated chants of "shipyard." The chant was in reference to Jackson's avoidance of serving in the military two years earlier while the country was at war by working in a shipyard.

SEPTEMBER 26 The Indians move one step closer to the pennant with a 7–5 win over the Browns before an overflow crowd of 30,000 in St. Louis. Steve O'Neill contributed a drive that struck a mounted policeman's horse for a ground rule double.

SEPTEMBER 28 Jim Bagby wins his 30th game of the 1920 season by defeating the Browns 9–5 in St. Louis.

On the same day, eight White Sox players who were involved in throwing the 1919 World Series to the Reds were suspended by Chicago owner Charles Comiskey.

SEPTEMBER 29 Stan Coveleski wins his 24th game of the season, defeating the Browns 10–2 in St. Louis. The win gave the Indians a 1½-game lead.

OCTOBER 1 Ray Caldwell wins his 20th game of 1920 with a 10–2 decision over the Tigers in the second game of a double header in Detroit. The Tigers won the opener 5–4 in ten innings. At the end of the day, the Indians had a two-game lead with two contests left on the schedule.

OCTOBER 2 The Indians clinch the American League pennant with a 10–1 win over the Tigers in Detroit. Jim Bagby earned his 31st win of the season. Thousands of Indians fans traveled to Detroit for the pennant-clinching.

The Indians played the Brooklyn Dodgers in the World Series. Managed by Wilbert Robinson, the Dodgers were 93–61 during the regular season. The 1920 World Series was a best-of-nine affair, requiring five wins to claim the world championship.

OCTOBER 5 The Indians open the World Series with a 3–1 win over the Dodgers at Ebbets Field in Brooklyn. Stan Coveleski pitched a complete game, allowing five hits. Steve O'Neill contributed two run-scoring doubles in the second and fourth innings.

OCTOBER 6 The Dodgers even the Series with a 3–0 win in Brooklyn behind the pitching of Burleigh Grimes. Jim Bagby, who won 31 games during the regular season, took the loss.

Doc Johnston started the game at first base for the Indians while his brother Jimmy was in the Brooklyn line-up at third. They were the first siblings to play each other in a World Series.

OCTOBER 7 The Dodgers take a two-games-to-one lead with a 2–1 victory in Brooklyn. Sherry Smith hurled a three-hitter for the Dodgers. Ray Caldwell was the starting pitcher for Cleveland, but failed to finish the first inning allowing two runs. Duster Mails was brilliant in relief, surrendering no runs and three hits in 6⅔ innings.

OCTOBER 9 In the first World Series game ever played in Cleveland, the Indians win 5–1 with Stan Coveleski pitching his second five-hit complete game victory before 25,734 at Dunn Field. The Indians put the game away early with two runs in the first inning and two in the third.

OCTOBER 10 The Indians take a three-games-to-two advantage with an 8–1 runaway victory over the Dodgers in front of 26,884 at Dunn Field. The game produced a trio of significant firsts. In the first inning, Elmer Smith smacked the first grand slam in Series history. It came off Burleigh Grimes with none out after Charlie Jamieson, Bill Wambsganss, and Tris Speaker loaded the bases with singles. Jim Bagby became the first pitcher to homer in the Fall Classic with a three-run blast off Grimes into the center field stands. In the fifth, Wambsganss produced the first, and to date only, unassisted triple play in the post-season. Pete Kilduff was the Brooklyn base runner on second and Otto Miller was on first with none out. Dodger relief pitcher Clarence Mitchell lined a shot toward right field. With both runners moving with the pitch, Wambsganss leaped high from his second baseman position to spear the ball. He instantly stepped on second to force Kilduff, and then tagged the surprised Miller near second base. Mitchell also hit into a double play in the eighth. Jim Bagby allowed only one run despite being touched for 13 hits.

OCTOBER 11 The Indians move within one game of their first world championship with a 1–0 win over the Dodgers before 27,184 at Dunn Field. Duster Mails tossed a three-hit shutout. The lone run scored in the sixth. With two out, no one on base, and Sherry Smith pitching, Tris Speaker singled and scored on a double by George Burns.

Principal L. W. MacKinnon of Central High School in Akron, Ohio, had trouble with truancy during the 1920 World Series as students skipped school to follow the progress of the Indians. To combat the problem, MacKinnon had the blackboards in every room blocked off by innings. The principal relayed the score to each room, where it was posted on the boards after each half inning.

OCTOBER 12 The Indians win the World Series with a 3–0 victory over the Dodgers before 27,525 at Dunn Field. Stan Coveleski pitched the shutout for his third win of the Series. In 27 innings, he allowed two runs and 15 hits. Cleveland pitchers were brilliant throughout the Series, surrendering only eight runs in seven games.

Rube Marquard, a native of Cleveland, was scheduled to start game seven for the Dodgers but was charged with scalping tickets. Marquard claimed it was a misunderstanding, but disgusted manager Wilbert Robinson took him out of the game and pitched Burleigh Grimes instead on one day of rest. Marquard was traded to the Reds during the following off-season.

OCTOBER 13 The city of Cleveland celebrates its first world championship.

A crowd of 50,000 attended a nighttime public demonstration held at Wade Park. Streets nearby were blocked with thousands of automobiles. So great was the enthusiasm of the baseball-crazy mob that it became uncontrollable and broke through the ropes marking off the stage where city officials and Indians players sat. Chairs were smashed, and several people were pushed into a small lake.

OCTOBER 31 Two days before the election of Marion, Ohio, native Warren Harding as president, Dunn Field hosts the first National Football League game staged in Cleveland. The Cleveland Tigers defeated the Columbus Panhandles 7–0.

Dunn Field/League Park was the home of three NFL franchises. The Cleveland Tigers played there in 1920 and 1921, the Cleveland Bulldogs from 1923 through 1925, and the Cleveland Rams in 1937, 1942, 1944, and 1945. The Rams also played at Municipal Stadium from 1939 through 1941. The club disbanded in 1943 due to World War II and moved to Los Angeles in 1946, the same season the Browns began play at Municipal Stadium.

1921

Season in a Sentence

The defending world champion Indians spend 115 days in first place before losing a close pennant race with the Yankees.

Finish • Won • Lost • Pct • GB

Finish	Won	Lost	Pct	GB
Second	93	60	.610	4.5

Manager

Tris Speaker

Stats

Stats	Indians	AL	Rank
Batting Avg:	.308	.292	2
On-Base Pct:	.383	.357	2
Slugging Pct:	.430	.408	3
Home Runs:	42		5 (tie)
Stolen Bases:	51		8
ERA:	3.90	4.28	2
Fielding Avg:	.967	.965	3
Runs Scored:	925		2
Runs Allowed:	712		3

Starting Line-up

Steve O'Neill, c
Doc Johnston, 1b
Bill Wambsganss, 2b
Larry Gardner, 3b
Joe Sewell, ss
Charlie Jamieson, lf
Tris Speaker, cf
Elmer Smith, rf
George Burns, 1b
Riggs Stephenson, 2b
Joe Wood, rf
Joe Evans, lf

Pitchers

Stan Coveleski, sp
George Uhle, sp-rp
Jim Bagby, sp-rp
Duster Mails, sp
Allen Sothoron, sp
Ray Caldwell, sp-rp
Guy Morton, rp

Attendance

748,705 (second in AL)

Club Leaders

Batting Avg:	Tris Speaker	.362
On-Base Pct:	Tris Speaker	.439
Slugging Pct:	Tris Speaker	.538
Home Runs:	Elmer Smith	16
RBIs:	Larry Gardner	115
Runs:	Tris Speaker	107
Stolen Bases:	Bill Wambsganss	13
Wins:	Stan Coveleski	23
Strikeouts:	Stan Coveleski	99
ERA:	Stan Coveleski	3.36
Saves:	Ray Caldwell	4
	Jim Bagby	4

April 13 The defending world champion Indians open the 1921 season with a 4–2 loss to the Browns in St. Louis. Elmer Smith drove a pitch over the wall in the ninth inning to become the first player in Indians history to hit a home run on Opening Day.

The words "Worlds Champions" were emblazoned on the front of both the home and road shirts in 1921. The idea was borrowed from John McGraw, who did the same thing with the Giants in 1906. It was not a hit with manager Tris Speaker or the players, who believed that the jerseys were a jinx.

April 14 Trailing 9–2 after three innings of play, the Indians rally with three runs in the fourth inning, three in the fifth, two in the sixth and two in the ninth to win 12–9 against the Browns in St. Louis.

April 17 The Indians game against the Tigers in Detroit is postponed by snow.

April 19 The Indians break a 1–1 tie with nine runs in the seventh inning and beat the Tigers 12–3 in Detroit.

April 21 In the home opener, the Indians defeat the Browns 4–3 at Dunn Field. Before the contest, Tris Speaker was presented with an automobile, a saddle, and a bridle.

April 24 In the fifth inning of a 6–5 win over the Browns at Dunn Field, Joe Sewell is allowed to re-enter the contest by opposing manager Lee Fohl. Sewell was spiked in the heel by pitcher Nick Cullop during a play at first base in the fifth inning. Jack Graney replaced Sewell as a pinch-runner, and after the injury was bandaged, Fohl allowed Sewell to remain in the game at shortstop in the top of the sixth.

The brief time that Sewell was being treated was the only action he missed all year. Otherwise, Sewell played every inning of every game. In his first full season in the majors, he hit .318, scored 101 runs, and drove in 93.

April 28 The Indians collect 23 hits during an 18–5 thrashing of the Tigers at Dunn Field. Seven runs were scored in the seventh inning. George Uhle pitched a complete game and hit a grand slam and two singles to account for six runs-batted-in. The slam was struck off Dutch Leonard in the fourth inning.

May 8 The Indians explode for nine runs in the fourth inning of a 17–3 hammering of the White Sox at Dunn Field. George Burns collected five hits, including two doubles, in six at-bats.

May 11 The Indians raise the 1920 world championship flag and trounce the Senators 14–1 at Dunn Field.

May 16 Carl Mays makes his first appearance in Cleveland since throwing the pitch that killed Ray Chapman (see August 16 and 17, 1920) and hurls a complete game to lead the Yankees to a 6–3 win over the Indians.

May 20 The Indians score in seven of their eight turns at-bat and pound the Athletics 16–3 at Dunn Field.

May 29 The Indians take a 7–0 lead in the second inning and hang on for an 11–9 win over the Browns in St. Louis.

June 10 Trailing 6–3, the Indians score three runs in the ninth inning and two in the 11th to win 8–6 over the Yankees in New York. Larry Gardner broke the 6–6 tie with a home run.

Gardner hit only three homers in 1921, but drove in 120 runs, scored 101, and batted .319.

June 26 The Indians score eight runs in the fourth inning to take a 14–0 lead and wallop the Browns 15–1 at Dunn Field.

July 4 The Indians sweep the White Sox 6–4 and 11–10 at Dunn Field. Relief hurler Guy Morton was the winning pitcher in both games.

July 5 The Indians mash the White Sox 16–4 at Dunn Field.

July 10 The Indians beat the Athletics with two shutouts in a double header at Dunn Field. Duster Mails won the opener despite allowing 12 hits, two walks, and a wild pitch. Guy Morton won the second contest 1–0 and drove in the lone run with a single in the fifth inning.

The wins gave the Indians a 50–31 record and a 3½-game lead in the AL pennant race.

JULY 21 Joe Sewell collects five hits, including three doubles, in six at-bats during a 17–8 win over the Yankees at Dunn Field. There were 16 doubles by the two clubs, nine by the Indians. Cleveland scored seven runs in the third inning.

JULY 26 The Indians explode for six runs in the tenth inning to win 8–2 over the Red Sox in Boston.

JULY 30 Doc Johnston drives in seven runs with a homer, triple, and single during a 16–1 hammering of the Yankees in New York.

AUGUST 7 The Indians score three runs in the ninth inning to beat the Athletics 4–3 at Dunn Field. Tris Speaker drove in the tying and winning runs with a two-run single.

Speaker hit .362, scored 107 runs, collected 14 triples, and smacked a league-leading 52 doubles in 1921.

AUGUST 8 The Indians regain first place from the Yankees with a sweep of the Athletics in Philadelphia by scores of 4–2 and 7–6, with the second game lasting 13 innings. At the conclusion of game two, umpires Bill Dinneen and Billy Evans were bombarded with cushions, bottles, and newspapers from A's fans angered by their calls during the twin bill.

Stan Coveleski was a 20-game winner for the fourth season in a row in 1921 and is one of the great pitchers in team history.

AUGUST 17 After the Athletics score four runs in the top of the first inning, the Indians rally for five tallies in their half and move forward to win 15–8 at Dunn Field. In the first, Cleveland set a major league record (since tied) for most assists in an inning with ten.

The game was played on the first anniversary of Ray Chapman's death. The Indians marked the occasion by giving out single rosebuds to the 6,000 fans as they entered the gates. The flowers were handed out by young ladies from the local YWCA. In the second inning, A's first baseman Johnny Walker was struck in the head by a drive off the bat of Charlie Jamieson which took a wicked hop off the hard-packed infield dirt. Walker was knocked unconscious, and was on the ground ten minutes as those in attendance wondered if he would suffer the same cruel fate as Chapman a year earlier. Fortunately, Walker was not injured seriously. He was taken to the hospital and treated for a severe concussion.

AUGUST 25 The Indians take back first place from the Yankees with a 15–1 trouncing of the New York club at Dunn Field. The game was marked by a brawl in the eighth inning. Yanks pitcher Harry Harper hit Charlie Jamieson with a pitch in the ribs, Larry Gardner on the arm, and Steve O'Neill in the back. The enraged O'Neill grabbed the ball and threw it back toward Harper, missing his target. The two men squared off with their fists but were separated before either had inflicted any damage. Mounted policemen came onto the field when the game ended and protected the New York players and the umpires from molestation from infuriated fans.

The Indians and Yankees were in a heated two-team pennant race that went down to the final week of the season. There was still considerable animosity by the Indians toward the Yanks because of the death of Ray Chapman the previous August. Due a scheduling quirk, Cleveland played its last 21 games on the road.

SEPTEMBER 2 The Indians maul the Tigers 12–1 in Detroit.

SEPTEMBER 5 Elmer Smith sets a major league record with extra base hits in seven consecutive official at-bats during a double header against the Browns at Dunn Field. The previous day, Smith doubled, then homered, in his last two plate appearances during a 9–5 victory over the Tigers in Detroit. In the first game of a September 5 twin bill, Smith was 3-for-3 with homers in his first two plate appearances, followed by an intentional walk and a double in a 10–5 Cleveland win. The double missed going over the wall by a few feet. In the second tilt, Smith had a double, a homer, two walks and a sacrifice. Smith's seven extra base hits included four homers and three doubles. The streak came to an end when Smith was retired in the first plate appearance of a 2–1 win over the Browns on September 6.

SEPTEMBER 10 Bill Wambsganss scores five runs after reaching base on four walks and a single during a 10–2 win over the Browns in the second game of a double header at Sportsman's Park. St. Louis won the opener 2–0.

SEPTEMBER 15 The Indians sweep the Athletics 17–3 and 6–0 at Shibe Park. In the opener, the two clubs combined for 27 walks. Duster Mails pitched a complete game for the Indians and walked 11. Four Philadelphia pitchers issued 16 passes. Charlie Jamieson scored five runs after hitting a homer, a triple, and two singles and drawing a walk.

SEPTEMBER 16 Joe Wood's two-run triple in the eighth inning accounts for both runs in a 2–0 win over the Senators in Washington. George Uhle pitched the shutout. The victory gave the Indians a one-game lead in the AL pennant race.

SEPTEMBER 20 The Indians are ousted from first place with a 7–4 loss to the Red Sox in Boston. The Yankees took the top spot with a 4–2 win over the Tigers in New York.

SEPTEMBER 23 In the first game of a four-game pennant showdown series against the Yankees in New York, the Indians lose 4–2 to fall one game behind the Yanks.

SEPTEMBER 24 The Indians move within two percentage points of the first-place Yankees with a 9–0 win at the Polo Grounds. George Uhle pitched a shutout and drew three walks and hit a sacrifice in four plate appearances. Tris Speaker returned to the line-up after missing 13 games with an injured knee.

SEPTEMBER 25 The Yankees regain their one-game lead with a convincing 21–7 win over the Indians in New York.

SEPTEMBER 26 The Indians fall two games behind the Yankees with an 8–7 loss in New York. Babe Ruth was 3-for-3 with two homers and a double. The Indians had four games left on the schedule, and the Yanks had six contests remaining.

SEPTEMBER 29 The White Sox deal a fatal blow to the Indians pennant chances with a 5–0 win in Chicago.

SEPTEMBER 30 Stan Coveleski wins his 23rd game of the season with a 3–2 decision over the White Sox in Chicago.

Coveleski was 23–13 with a 3.37 ERA in 315 innings in 1921.

DECEMBER 24 The Indians trade George Burns, Joe Harris, and Elmer Smith for Stuffy McInnis.

The Indians made a horrible miscalculation by trading three useful players for McInnis, who was released after spending only one season in Cleveland. The Indians reacquired Burns in a trade with the Red Sox in 1924.

1922

Season in a Sentence

Injuries, a wretched first-half record, and disappointing performances by key pitchers, cause a fall to fourth place.

Finish • Won • Lost • Pct • GB

Finish	Won	Lost	Pct	GB
Fourth	78	76	.506	16.0

Manager

Tris Speaker

Stats

Stats	Indians	AL	Rank
Batting Avg:	.292	.285	3
On-Base Pct:	.364	.348	3
Slugging Pct:	.398	.398	5
Home Runs:	32		8
Stolen Bases:	90		4
ERA:	4.59	4.03	7
Runs Scored:	768		3
Runs Allowed:	817		7

Starting Line-up

Steve O'Neill, c
Stuffy McInnis, 1b
Bill Wambsganss, 2b
Larry Gardner, 3b
Joe Sewell, ss
Charlie Jamieson, lf
Tris Speaker, cf
Joe Wood, rf
Riggs Stephenson, 3b-2b

Pitchers

George Uhle, sp
Stan Coveleski, sp
Guy Morton, sp
Duster Mails, sp-rp
Jim Lindsey, rp
Jim Bagby, rp-sp
Jim Joe Edwards, rp

Attendance

528,145 (fifth in AL)

Club Leaders

Batting Avg:	Tris Speaker	.378
On-Base Pct:	Tris Speaker	.474
Slugging Pct:	Tris Speaker	.606
Home Runs:	Tris Speaker	11
RBIs:	Joe Wood	92
Runs:	Bill Wambsganss	89
Stolen Bases:	Bill Wambsganss	17
Wins:	George Uhle	22
Strikeouts:	Guy Morton	102
ERA:	Stan Coveleski	3.32
Saves:	George Uhle	3

April 12 The Indians open the season with a 7–4 win over the Tigers at Dunn Field. Guy Morton pitched a complete game on a day in which the high temperature was only 42 degrees. In his first game with the Indians, Stuffy McInnis collected a triple, double, and single in four at-bats.

April 18 The Indians score eight runs in the third inning of a 17–2 thrashing of the Browns at Dunn Field.

April 19 The day after winning by 15 runs, the Indians lose by 14, dropping a 15–1 decision to the Browns at Dunn Field.

May 8 The Indians score seven runs in the fifth inning and defeat the Athletics 14–4 in Philadelphia.

May 20 Tris Speaker hits a grand slam off Bill Piercy in the fifth inning of a 5–2 win over the Red Sox in Boston.

Speaker hit .378 and led the AL in on base percentage (.474) and doubles (48) in 1922.

June 4 The Indians score eight runs in the sixth inning and trounce the Tigers 14–6 at Dunn Field. Riggs Stephenson had a triple and a double in the big inning and was 4-for-4 on the day.

Stephenson hit .337 in 332 games over five seasons with the Indians from 1921 through 1925 but couldn't find a regular place in the line-up because of defensive deficiencies and injuries. Cleveland tried him at third base, second base, and in the outfield, but a weak shoulder, sustained as a football star at the University of Alabama, hampered his effectiveness. He played 978 games with the Cubs as an outfielder from 1926 and 1934 and closed his career with a batting average of .336.

JUNE 9 Indians owner James Dunn dies at the age of 57 after a long, lingering illness. The game that day between the Indians and Senators at Dunn Field was postponed.

Ownership of the franchise was left to Dunn's widow Edith. She was the second woman to own a major league club. The first was Helen Britton, who owned the St. Louis Cardinals from 1911 through 1917. Emil Barnard took over as club president. Edith Dunn ran the club with Barnard's help until 1927 when Alva Bradley bought it. At that time, Barnard became president of the American League following the resignation of Ban Johnson.

JUNE 11 A two-run, two-out, walk-off triple by Joe Evans beats the Athletics 9–8 at Dunn Field.

JUNE 17 The Indians outlast the Red Sox 5–4 in 14 innings at Dunn Field. Joe Sewell hit a two-run homer in the seventh inning to tie the score 4–4, then drove in the winning run with a two-out double in the 14th.

Sewell hit .299 with two home runs in 1922.

JUNE 27 Down 7–3, the Indians score six runs in the eighth inning to defeat the Browns 9–7 at League Park. Charlie Jamieson put Cleveland into the lead with a bases-loaded double.

The Indians had a record of 34–44 on July 7, won 12 in a row to elevate the club's record to 46–44, then played .500 ball the rest of the way.

JULY 9 The Indians score two runs in the ninth and two in the 13th to win 9–7 over the Yankees in New York. Stuffy McInnis tied the score with a two-out single. In the 13th, Bill Wambsganss and Tris Speaker doubled and Joe Sewell singled.

JULY 12 Joe Sewell collects five of Cleveland's 20 hits during an 11–7 win over the Red Sox in Boston.

JULY 21 The Indians record their 12th win in a row with a 1–0 decision over the Senators in Washington. Guy Morton pitched the shutout. The lone run of the game scored in the seventh inning on a triple by Joe Wood and a single from Joe Sewell.

JULY 25 Guy Morton starts both ends of a double header against the Athletics in Philadelphia. Morton pitched a complete game shutout to win the opener 4–0. In game two, he held the A's scoreless through the first three innings before allowing three runs in the fourth inning and two in the fifth. The Indians lost 11–4.

JULY 31 The Indians score in seven of eight at-bats and wallop the Senators 14–5 at Dunn Field.

August 1 — Larry Gardner collects a home run and three doubles in five at-bats during a 17–3 hammering of the Senators at Dunn Field. The Indians scored seven runs in the third inning and had 21 hits during the game.

August 16 — Trailing 9–1, against the Athletics in Philadelphia, the Indians score seven runs in the eighth inning and one in the ninth to tie the game 9–9, only to lose 10–9 when the A's plate a run in their half of the ninth. In the eighth, Larry Gardner singled as a pinch-hitter, batted once more before the inning was completed, then singled again.

August 20 — Indians pitcher Dan Boone hurls a 12-inning complete game shutout to win 2–0 against the Senators in Washington. Boone also drove in the first run of the game with a single off Walter Johnson.

August 31 — The Indians score five runs in the ninth inning to stun the Browns 7–6 at Dunn Field. Joe Connolly drove in the winning run with a double.

September 18 — The Indians purchase Sherry Smith from the Dodgers.

September 21 — In the only game of his major league career, Indians pitcher Doc Hamann faces seven batters and retires no one during a 15–5 loss to the Red Sox at Dunn Field. Entering the game in relief in the ninth inning, Hamann hit a batter and allowed three hits and three walks in addition to throwing a wild pitch. He was credited with six runs allowed, all earned.

October 1 — George Uhle records his 22nd win on the last day of the season with a 6–5 decision over the Tigers at Dunn Field.

Uhle was 22–16 in 1922 with an ERA of 4.07 and led the AL with five shutouts.

November 5 — The Indians sell Jim Bagby to the Pirates.

1923

Season in a Sentence

The Indians spend the first 15 days of the season in first place, compile a team batting average of .301, and lead the league in runs scored but end up the year in third place.

Finish • Won • Lost • Pct • GB

Finish	Won	Lost	Pct	GB
Third	82	71	.536	16.5

Manager

Tris Speaker

Stats

	Indians	AL	Rank
Batting Avg:	.301	.282	1
On-Base Pct:	.381	.351	1
Slugging Pct:	.420	.388	2
Home Runs:	59		3
Stolen Bases:	79		4 (tie)
ERA:	3.91	3.98	2
Fielding Avg:	.965	.968	6
Runs Scored:	888		1
Runs Allowed:	746		5

Starting Line-up

Steve O'Neill, c
Frank Brower, 1b
Bill Wambsganss, 2b
Rube Lutzke, 3b
Joe Sewell, ss
Charlie Jamieson, lf
Tris Speaker, cf
Homer Summa, rf
Riggs Stephenson, 2b
Glenn Myatt, c

Pitchers

George Uhle, sp
Stan Coveleski, sp
Jim Joe Edwards, sp-rp
Joe Shaute, sp-rp
Sherry Smith, sp-rp
Guy Morton, rp-sp

Attendance

558,856 (fourth in AL)

Club Leaders

Batting Avg:	Tris Speaker	.380
On-Base Pct:	Tris Speaker	.469
Slugging Pct:	Tris Speaker	.610
Home Runs:	Tris Speaker	17
RBIs:	Tris Speaker	130
Runs:	Tris Speaker	133
Stolen Bases:	Charlie Jamieson	19
Wins:	George Uhle	26
Strikeouts:	George Uhle	109
ERA:	Stan Coveleski	2.76
Saves:	George Uhle	5

JANUARY 8 The Indians trade Joe Evans to the Senators for Frank Brower.

APRIL 18 The Indians open the season with a two-run rally in the ninth inning to win 6–5 over the White Sox before 20,372 at Dunn Field. Chicago took a 5–4 lead with four runs in the eighth inning. The two ninth-inning runs scored on a double by Bill Wambsganss, a walk to Louis Guisto, and singles by Homer Summa and Joe Sewell.

The Indians swept the opening four-game series against the White Sox, then ran their record to 6–0 with a pair of victories over the Tigers in Cleveland. The Indians were 10–3 in April but weren't able to sustain the momentum.

APRIL 19 The Indians commit eight errors but defeat the White Sox 6–5 in 11 innings at Dunn Field.

APRIL 22 The Indians edge the Tigers 1–0 at Dunn Field. Stan Coveleski pitched the complete game shutout and scored the lone run of the game. With two out in the tenth inning, Coveleski was hit by a Rip Collins pitch, reached second on a walk, and crossed the plate on an error.

APRIL 27 Trailing 6–1, the Indians score five runs in the fifth inning and two in the seventh to win 8–6 over the White Sox in Chicago.

MAY 1 Indians pitcher Jim Joe Edwards is 4-for-4 at the plate, but gives up two runs in the ninth inning to lose 6–5 to the Tigers in Detroit.

MAY 15 After the Senators score two runs in the top of the tenth, the Indians rally for three in their half to win 10–9 at Dunn Field. It was the third time during the afternoon that the Indians rallied from behind. Earlier, Washington led 5–0, and after Cleveland scored six runs in the fourth, pulled ahead again 7–6. Bill Wambsganss tied a major league record for most errors by a second baseman in an inning with three in the fourth.

MAY 20 Stan Coveleski pitches a shutout and drives in the lone run for a 1–0 triumph over the Red Sox at Dunn Field. The contest was called after 7½ innings by rain. In the fifth with a runner on second and two out, Glenn Myatt was intentionally walked to get to Coveleski, who foiled the strategy with a single. Coveleski also starred with his glove, recording ten assists, one shy of the big league record.

Coveleski was 13–14 in 1923, but he led the American League in earned run average (2.76) and shutouts (five).

George Uhle was a Tribe ace through most of the 1920s winning 127 games.

JUNE 1 George Uhle collects three doubles and a single during a 17–4 mashing of the Tigers in Detroit. The three doubles tied a major league record for pitchers in a game.

Uhle had a .289 career batting average in 1,360 at-bats. During the 1923 season, he had 52 hits and a .361 average. On the mound, he was 26–16 with a 3.77 ERA and led the AL in wins, innings pitched (357 2/3), complete games (29), and games started (44). Uhle also recorded five saves in ten relief appearances.

JUNE 6 The Indians win by a 17–4 score for the second time in less than a week, thrashing the Red Sox in Boston. In the fourth inning, Joe Connolly hit a pinch-hit grand slam off George Murray while batting for Homer Summa.

June 10 The Indians play at Yankee Stadium for the first time and score seven runs in the sixth inning to win 13–3. Tris Speaker hit a grand slam off Carl Mays.

Speaker was brilliant as usual in 1923. He hit .380, led the AL in doubles with 59, smacked 17 homers, collected 218 hits, drove in 130 runs, and scored 133. Charlie Jamieson led the AL in hits with 222 in addition to batting .345 and scoring 130 runs. Joe Sewell contributed a .353 average, 41 doubles, 98 runs, and 109 RBIs.

June 19 Frank Brower hits a fluke pinch-hit home run during a 7–6 loss to the Senators in Washington. The ball caromed off the pavilion railing through an opening in the fence.

June 30 Tris Speaker hits a grand slam off Ted Blankenship in the ninth inning, but it's too late to prevent a 5–4 loss to the White Sox at Dunn Field.

July 4 A three-run, pinch-hit, walk-off homer by Glenn Myatt in the tenth inning beats the Tigers 10–7 in the first game of a double header at Dunn Field. Detroit won the second tilt 15–3.

July 5 The Indians swamp the Tigers 10–0 at Dunn Field.

July 7 The Indians set an all-time club record for runs and margin of victory with a 27–3 pounding of the Red Sox in the first game of a double header at Dunn Field. Cleveland scored in all eight turns at bat. The big inning was the sixth when the Indians scored 13 runs to take a 20–2 lead. Boston pitcher Lefty O'Doul was the unlucky hurler who allowed the 13 runs, setting a modern major league mark for most runs allowed by a pitcher in an inning. He might have gotten out of the inning without a run being scored, but center fielder Mike Menosky dropped a fly ball with the bases loaded and none out. The thirteen runs by the Indians after two were out also set a major league mark. The runs scored on two doubles (both by Riggs Stephenson), five singles, and six walks. Red Sox manager Frank Chance left O'Doul in the game because the pitcher was three hours late for curfew the previous evening. The Indians also won the nightcap 8–5.

July 9 The Indians win a 15–10 slugfest against the Red Sox at Dunn Field. The Indians trailed 5–0 before scoring seventh runs in the fifth inning and six in the sixth.

July 12 The Indians spank the Athletics 11–0 at Dunn Field.

July 13 The Indians continue to score almost at will, defeating the Athletics 16–7 at Dunn Field.

July 17 The Indians collect 20 hits and wallop the Yankees 13–0 at Dunn Field.

From July 4 through July 17, the Indians scored 139 runs in 16 games.

July 18 Guy Morton pitches a two-hitter and defeats the Senators 4–1 at Dunn Field. Morton had a no-hitter until two were out in the eighth inning when Nemo Leibold doubled and Otto Bluege tripled.

July 24 Charlie Jamieson hits a homer in the 13th inning to beat the Browns 3–2 in the second game of a double header at Sportsman's Park. Jim Joe Edwards pitched a complete game. St. Louis won the opener 3–1.

July 28 Tris Speaker collects five hits in five at-bats, but the Indians lose 10–5 to the Red Sox in Boston.

August 3 The Indians game against the Yankees in New York is postponed to observe a national day of mourning following the August 2 death of President Warren Harding, who died on a trip to San Francisco. The Indians contest against the Athletics in Philadelphia on August 10 was also postponed for Harding's funeral.

August 4 The Indians trounce the Yankees 15–7 in New York. Frank Brower hit two homers and drove in five runs.

August 7 Frank Brower collects six hits in six at-bats during a 22–2 walloping of the Senators in Washington. Brower had five singles and a double. The Indians scored eight runs in the second inning to take a 9–0 lead.

August 11 Tris Speaker's grand slam in the 11th inning beats the Athletics 9–5 in the first game of a double header in Philadelphia. Cleveland also won the second contest 10–2.

August 15 Tris Speaker collects five hits, including a homer and two doubles, in five at-bats, but the Indians lose 8–6 to the Red Sox at Dunn Field.

August 19 The Indians pummel the Athletics 16–3 at Dunn Field. George Uhle pitched a complete game, collected three singles and a double in four at-bats, and drove in five runs.

August 23 The Indians lose 20–8 to the Senators at League Park. In his only big league plate appearance, Jackie Gallagher of the Indians drove in a run with a single to finish his career with a batting average of 1.000. Gallagher entered the game as a substitute in right field for Homer Summa.

August 26 The Indians score three runs in the ninth inning and defeat the Yankees 4–3 at Dunn Field. It was George Uhle's sixth win of the 1923 season against the pennant-winning Yankees.

September 14 Red Sox first baseman George Burns completes an unassisted triple play during a 4–3 Boston win over the Indians at Fenway Park. With Riggs Stephenson on second base and Rube Lutzke on first in the second inning, Burns snared a liner off the bat of Frank Brower. Burns tagged Lutzke while Stephenson was well on his way to third. Burns raced to second base and slid into the bag ahead of Stephenson.

October 1 The Indians rout the Browns 13–5 in St. Louis.

October 3 Homer Summa hits a grand slam off Ray Kolp in the fourth innings of a 6–2 win over the Browns in St. Louis. It was George Uhle's 26th win of the season.

October 4 Tris Speaker collects five hits, including a homer and a double, during a 9–1 victory over the Browns in St. Louis.

1924

Season in a Sentence

Hampered by injuries and illnesses, the Indians score 133 fewer runs than in 1923 and suffer a losing season for the first time since 1915.

Finish • Won • Lost • Pct • GB

Finish	Won	Lost	Pct	GB
Sixth	67	86	.438	24.5

Manager

Tris Speaker

Stats

Stats	Indians	AL	Rank
Batting Avg:	.296	.290	2
On-Base Pct:	.361	.358	4
Slugging Pct:	.399	.396	4
Home Runs:	41		4 (tie)
Stolen Bases:	85		4 (tie)
ERA:	4.40	4.23	6
Fielding Avg:	.967	.969	7
Runs Scored:	755		5
Runs Allowed:	814		7

Starting Line-up

Glenn Myatt, c
George Burns, 1b
Chick Fewster, 2b
Rube Lutzke, 3b
Joe Sewell, ss
Charlie Jamieson, lf
Tris Speaker, cf
Homer Summa, rf
Pat McNulty, rf-cf
Riggs Stephenson, 2b
Luke Sewell, c

Pitchers

Joe Shaute, sp
Stan Coveleski, sp
Sherry Smith, sp-rp
George Uhle, sp
Dewey Metivier, rp

Attendance

481,905 (seventh in AL)

Club Leaders

Batting Avg:	Charlie Jamieson	.359
On-Base Pct:	Tris Speaker	.432
Slugging Pct:	Tris Speaker	.510
Home Runs:	Tris Speaker	9
RBIs:	Joe Sewell	104
Runs:	Joe Sewell	99
Stolen Bases:	Charlie Jamieson	21
Wins:	Joe Shaute	20
Strikeouts:	Joe Shaute	68
ERA:	Sherry Smith	3.02
Saves:	Dewey Metivier	3

January 7 The Indians trade Steve O'Neill, Bill Wambsganss, Dan Boone, and Joe Connolly for George Burns, Roxy Walters, and Chick Fewster.

The Indians made a mistake in trading Burns to the Red Sox during the 1921–22 off-season and rectified the move by bringing him back to Cleveland. Although 31 when re-acquired by the Indians, Burns gave the club five solid seasons, batting .325 in 629 games. The players sent to Boston weren't missed. O'Neill and Wambsganss were beginning to slip, and Boone and Connolly were marginal talents at best.

April 15 The Indians open the 1924 season with a 5–4 loss to the Tigers in Detroit. Riggs Stephenson collected a double and two singles.

April 22 The Indians win a thrilling ten-inning 6–5 decision over the Tigers at Dunn Field. Trailing 4–2, the Indians bunched four hits with two out in the ninth to tie the game 4–4. After Detroit scored in the top of the tenth, Cleveland roared back with two in their half for the victory. Tris Speaker drove in the winning run with a double.

Speaker hit .344 for the Indians in 1924. Other leading hitters on the club were Charlie Jamieson (.359, 213 hits), Joe Sewell (.316, 106 RBIs and a league-leading 45 doubles) and Glenn Myatt (.342).

April 27 In a swatfest in St. Louis, the Indians take a 7–0 lead over the Browns in the second inning, fall behind 9–7, then score a run in the eighth and two in the ninth for a 10–9 win.

May 4 The Indians trounce the White Sox 14–7 at Dunn Field.

May 23 George Burns extends his hitting streak to 22 games during a 5–1 loss to the Red Sox in Boston.

June 10 Acting as a pinch-hitter for Pat McNulty, George Uhle hits a double to key a two-run, ninth-inning rally that beats the Senators 4–3 at Dunn Field.

Uhle led the American League in pinch-hits in 1924 with 11 in 26 at-bats, an average of .423. He wasn't quite so successful on the mound, however. After a 26–16 record in 1923, Uhle was 9–15 in 1924 and his ERA jumped from 3.77 to 4.77. Over the course of a career, Uhle had 44 pinch-hits in 169 at-bats (.260).

June 14 Pat McNulty steals home with two out in the 11th inning to end a 3–2 win over the Red Sox at Dun Field. Tris Speaker hit into a triple play in the fourth inning.

A veteran of World War I, McNulty was a Cleveland native who attended Ohio State University. He played for the Indians in 1922 and from 1924 through 1927, hitting .290 in 308 games.

June 19 George Burns collects six hits in six at-bats, leading the Indians to a 16–3 win over the Tigers in the first game of a double header in Detroit. Four of Burns's six hits went for extra bases with a triple and three doubles. Cleveland scored nine runs in the fifth inning and collected 22 hits in all. The Indians lost game two 3–2.

June 20 The Indians outlast the Tigers 11–9 in Detroit.

July 13 On a hot and testy afternoon at Griffith Stadium, the Indians lose 15–11 to the Senators. In the ninth inning, Washington manager Bucky Harris was banished by umpire Ducky Holmes for protesting balls and strikes calls. When the game ended, several thousand excited fans poured onto the field and surrounded the ump. One fan struck Holmes in the face and knocked him into a wall, but fellow umpire George Moriarty, players from both teams, and police came to the rescue and further trouble was averted.

July 23 George Burns collects four extra base hits in a game for the second time in 1924 with two homers and two doubles in five at-bats during a 16–12 loss to the Red Sox in Boston.

August 2 Joe Hauser of the Athletics hits three homers during a 12–2 Philadelphia win over the Indians at Dunn Field. Hauser nearly hit a fourth homer when one of his drives hit the top of the right field wall and fell back for a double.

August 4 Down 4–1, the Indians score seven runs in the third inning and roll to a 14–5 win over the Red Sox at Dunn Field.

August 5 Stan Coveleski pitches the Indians to a 1–0 win over the Red Sox at Dunn Field.

AUGUST 8 Glenn Myatt hits a two-run, walk-off homer in the ninth inning to cap a three-run rally that beats the Yankees 10–8 at Dunn Field. Tris Speaker drove in the tying run with a double. It was his fifth hit and third double of the game.

AUGUST 16 An Old-Timers Game is played at Dunn Field for the benefit of the Cleveland Amateur and Athletic Association, which raised funds for youth teams. A combined team of former major league players beat a squad of ex-Cleveland sandlotters 5–3 in a five-inning game. Among the players in the game were future Hall of Famers Cy Young, Nap Lajoie, and Elmer Flick.

AUGUST 18 The Indians hammer the Athletics 13–3 in Philadelphia.

AUGUST 27 Stan Coveleski beats the Yankees 1–0 in the first game of a double header in New York. The run scored in the fourth inning on a sacrifice fly by George Burns. The Indians lost the second tilt 5–4.

AUGUST 30 Joe Shaute records his 20th win of the season with an 11–6 win over the White Sox at Dunn Field.

Shaute was 24 years old when the season began and had a career record of 10–8. He was a revelation in 1924, posting a record of 20–17 and a 3.75 ERA in 283 innings. Shaute struggled in 1925, however, with a 4–12 mark and an earned run average of 5.43. He never came close to winning 20 in a season again. His next best season was a 14–10 ledger in 1926. In nine seasons with Cleveland (1922–30), Shaute was 79–88.

SEPTEMBER 1 After losing in the first game of a double header in St. Louis 11–8, the Indians lace the Browns 13–2 in the nightcap. There were five Cleveland home runs in the contest. Riggs Stephenson struck two of them, with Frank Brower, Tris Speaker, and pitcher Sherry Smith accounting for the others. Speaker and Charlie Jamieson homered in the opener.

SEPTEMBER 3 Charlie Jamieson collects five hits, including a double, in six at-bats to lead the Indians to a 12–4 win over the Browns in St. Louis.

SEPTEMBER 5 The Indians suffer an excruciating double header against the Tigers in Detroit, losing 7–3 and 20–1. In the second game, Cleveland pitcher Carl Yowell made his major league debut and allowed 13 runs in five innings of relief.

SEPTEMBER 11 The Indians sweep the Browns 12–7 and 10–6 in a double header against the Browns in St. Louis. In the opener, Cleveland scored five runs in the top of the ninth to break a 7–7 tie. Frank Ellerbe hit a grand slam in the big inning. He was the first batter to face reliever Dave Danforth after he replaced Elam Vangilder.

The Indians acquired Ellerbe from the Browns on June 3, 1924. The slam on September 11 was his only home run in 46 games and 120 at-bats with Cleveland and the last of four he struck during a six-year big league career.

SEPTEMBER 27 The Indians swamp the Browns 12–1 in Cleveland.

DECEMBER 12 The Indians trade Stan Coveleski to the Senators for Byron Speece and Carr Smith.

The Indians made a blunder of major proportions in trading Coveleski. He was 35-years-old, but still had enough left to lead the AL in earned run average in 1925 and post a 20–5 record in helping Washington win a pennant. Smith never played a game for the Indians. A pitcher with an underhanded motion, Speece contributed only a 3–5 record over two seasons.

1925

Season in a Sentence

The Indians win 21–14 on Opening Day and hold first place through the first week of May, then nose dive into sixth place.

Finish • Won • Lost • Pct • GB

Finish	Won	Lost	Pct	GB
Sixth	70	84	.455	27.5

Manager

Tris Speaker

Stats

Stats	Indians	AL	Rank
Batting Avg:	.297	.292	5
On-Base Pct:	.361	.360	5
Slugging Pct:	.399	.407	6
Home Runs:	52		5
Stolen Bases:	90		4
ERA:	4.49	4.40	5
Fielding Avg:	.966	.969	6
Runs Scored:	792		6
Runs Allowed:	817		5

Starting Line-up

Glenn Myatt, c
George Burns, 1b
Chick Fewster, 2b
Freddy Spurgeon, 3b-2b
Joe Sewell, ss
Charlie Jamieson, lf
Tris Speaker, cf
Pat McNulty, rf
Rube Lutzke, 3b
Cliff Lee, rf
Homer Summa, rf-lf

Pitchers

Sherry Smith, sp
George Uhle, sp
Benn Karr, sp
Garland Buckeye, sp-rp
Jake Miller, sp-rp
Joe Shaute, sp-rp
Byron Speece, rp

Attendance

419,005 (seventh in AL)

Club Leaders

Batting Avg:	Tris Speaker	.389
On-Base Pct:	Tris Speaker	.479
Slugging Pct:	Tris Speaker	.578
Home Runs:	Tris Speaker	12
RBIs:	Joe Sewell	98
Runs:	Charlie Jamieson	109
Stolen Bases:	George Burns	16
Wins:	George Uhle	13
	Garland Buckeye	13
Strikeouts:	George Uhle	68
Saves:	Joe Shaute	4

April 14 — In the highest-scoring Opening Day game in American League history, the Indians defeat the Browns 21–14 in St. Louis. Cleveland collected 19 hits while St. Louis committed ten errors, four by first baseman George Sisler. The Indians broke open the game with 12 runs in the eighth inning to take a 21–13 lead. Charlie Jamieson, Glenn Myatt, Tris Speaker, and Pat McNulty all hit home runs.

The Indians set a modern major league record for most runs in the first game of the season. The 35 runs by the two clubs is the second highest scoring opener in major league history, one behind the record of 36, set in 1900 when the Philadelphia Phillies defeated the Boston Braves 19–17.

April 17 — Joe Shaute pitches the Indians to a 1–0 win over the Browns in St. Louis.

The Indians opened the season with three games against the Browns. After scoring 21 games on Opening Day, the Indians collected only three runs in their next two games but won both 2–1 and 1–0.

April 20 The Indians outlast the Tigers 5–4 in 15 innings in Detroit. The 15th-inning run was accomplished by four walks from Detroit pitcher Syl Johnson, the last to Chick Fewster.

The Indians started the season winning their first five games and were 12–5 and in first place on May 7. After losing 35 of their next 50, Cleveland had a 27–40 record on June 29.

April 22 In the home opener, the Indians lose 3–2 in ten innings to the Browns before 22,616 at Dunn Field.

April 23 Trailing 7–2 in the third inning, the Indians rally to defeat the Browns 14–9 at Dunn Field. Cleveland took a 9–8 lead with four runs in the fifth.

April 26 The Indians win a game over the White Sox in Chicago by forfeit. The contest at Comiskey Park was attended by 44,000, the largest ever to attend a baseball game in Chicago up to that time, with the overflow standing on the field. In the ninth inning, with the Indians leading 7–2, fans swarmed the field. Police officers were unable to clear the diamond making further play impossible, and the umpires declared a forfeit.

May 2 The Indians score three runs in the ninth inning and one in the 11th to defeat the Tigers 8–7 at Dunn Field. With two out and two on base in the ninth, Pat McNulty hit a dramatic three-run homer to tie the game 7–7. In the 11th, Tris Speaker doubled, moved to third on an infield out, and scored on a sacrifice fly by Glenn Myatt.

May 17 Tris Speaker collects his 3,000th career hit during a 2–1 loss to the Senators at League Park. He came into the contest with 2,997 hits and picked up two singles and a double. Number 3,000 was a single off Tom Zachary in the ninth inning.

At the age of 37, Speaker was limited to 117 games because of injuries but hit .389 and led the AL in on base percentage (.474).

May 20 The Indians stage an incredible six-run rally in the ninth inning to shock the Yankees 10–9 at Dunn Field. The Indians were still trailing 9–7 with two out and the bases loaded with Tris Speaker the runner on first base. Speaker sent pitcher Joe Shaute up as a pinch-hitter because the Indians had run out of position players. Shaute delivered a single. With two runs across the plate, Yankee second baseman Aaron Ward took the throw from the outfield and was stunned to see Speaker steaming around third. Ward's throw to the plate was high and Speaker scored the winning run on a thrilling dash around the bases.

May 23 The Indians lose a tension-filled 7–6 decision to the Yankees at Dunn Field on Ben Paschal's two-run homer in the ninth inning. In the seventh, Speaker and Cleveland second baseman Joe Klugman were ejected by umpire Pants Rowland on a disputed play at the plate. Bottles were thrown in Rowland's direction, and after the game, police had to escort the umpire from the field.

June 4 The Indians score three runs in the ninth inning for an exciting 11–10 win over the Browns at Dunn Field. Cleveland led 8–3 before St. Louis scored a run in the seventh inning, two in the eighth, and four in the ninth to take a 10–8 lead. In the bottom of the ninth, Browns hurler Dixie Davis loaded the bases and Joe Bush was brought in to pitch to pinch-hitter Harvey Hendrick, who hit a three-run triple to win the game.

June 5 Indians pitcher Benn Karr hits a home run in the top of the ninth inning to break a 3–3 tie, then allowed two runs in the bottom half to lose 5–4 to the Red Sox in Boston.

The home run was the second of two that Karr hit during a career that spanned 392 at-bats. The first one occurred when he played for the Red Sox in 1920.

A mainstay for the Tribe throughout the 1920s, Hall of Famer Joe Sewell remains one of the toughest men to strike out in major league history.

June 6 Indians shortstop Freddy Spurgeon makes four errors, but the Indians survive the miscues to win 8–4 over the Red Sox in Boston.

The game was one of only three that Spurgeon played at shortstop during his major league career. It came during a brief experiment in which Spurgeon was moved from second base to shortstop, and Joe Sewell from short to second. Sewell hit .336 in 1925.

June 15 The Indians are the victims of the greatest comeback in baseball history, losing 17–15 to the Athletics in Philadelphia. The Indians took a 15–3 lead in the top of the seventh inning before the A's scored what seemed to be a meaningless run in the bottom half. In the eighth, Philadelphia exploded for 13 runs off Jake Miller, Byron Speece, Carl Yowell, and George Uhle. The rally was capped by a three-run homer from Al Simmons. To add to the strangeness of the day, umpire Brick Owens had to leave the game in the second inning when Freddy Spurgeon crashed into him on a play at the plate.

The Indians played in three cities in three days from Saturday June 13 through Monday June 15. The club played the Yankees in New York on the 13th and the Athletics in Cleveland on the 14th before moving on to Philadelphia to play the A's on the 15th. The game on June 14 was staged in Cleveland because games on Sunday were illegal in Pennsylvania until 1934. After the Athletics and Indians met in Philadelphia on the 15th, 16th, and 17th, the two clubs returned to Cleveland for a game on the 18th to conclude the five-game series at Dunn Field because the Rotarians were holding a national convention in the city and a large crowd was expected at the ballpark.

JUNE 16 The Athletics score four runs in the first inning and six in the second and move on to defeat the Indians 12–7 in Philadelphia. Combined with the eighth inning debacle the previous day, the A's scored 23 runs off Cleveland pitching in three consecutive turns at bat.

JUNE 19 Goose Goslin hits three homers for the Senators in a 12-inning, 7–5 win over the Indians at Dunn Field. Goslin's third homer was struck with a man on base in the 12th.

JULY 1 The Indians score seven runs in the seventh inning and lambaste the Tigers 11–0 in the first game of a double header at Dunn Field. Detroit won the second fray 4–1.

JULY 4 The Indians score three runs in the ninth inning to win 5–4 in the second game of a double header against the White Sox at Dunn Field. Chicago won the opener 14–5.

JULY 8 Trailing 4–2, the Indians score ten runs in the fifth inning and defeat the Athletics 14–3 in the first game of a double header at Dunn Field. Philadelphia won the second tilt 7–5.

JULY 9 The Indians edge the Athletics 13–11 at Dunn Field in a game called by rain at the end of the seventh inning. Cleveland led 13–5 before the A's scored six times in the seventh.

JULY 12 The Indians hammer the Red Sox 13–2 at Dunn Field.

JULY 16 The Indians collect 20 hits and score in seven of eight turns at bat during a 17–9 win over the Yankees at Dunn Field.

JULY 18 A sixth-inning disturbance highlights a 19–6 loss to the Senators at Dunn Field. Goose Goslin thought that Indians hurler Bert Cole tried to hit him with a pitch and strode to the mound with his bat raised. Umpire Tommy Connolly pulled Goslin back. Goslin then grounded to first baseman George Burns, and Cole raced over to cover the play. As the pitcher reached the bag, Goslin jumped to put his spikes in one of Cole's legs. Cole rushed at Goslin, and the two were separated by umpire Bill Evans. Goslin was banished from the game. As he walked to the Washington bench, fans threw bottles and debris at him, striking him in the face with a bag of peanuts.

JULY 28 Four days after John Scopes in convicted and fined $100 for teaching evolution in the Scopes Monkey Trial in Dayton, Tennessee, the Indians have no problems with Red Sox pitching, piling up 24 hits for a 16–7 victory at Boston. Sherry Smith pitched a complete game and was 4-for-4 at the plate with three singles and a double.

AUGUST 7 In a game completed in just 65 minutes, the Indians lose 2–0 to the Athletics in Philadelphia in the second game of a double header. The A's also won the opener 10–4.

AUGUST 23 An odd triple play helps the Indians defeat the Athletics 4–3 at Dunn Field. In the third inning, Bing Miller of the A's was the base runner on third with Cy Perkins at first. Chick Galloway hit to second baseman Freddy Spurgeon, who tagged out Perkins on the base line and threw to catcher Luke Sewell in time to get Miller at the plate. Meanwhile, Galloway rounded first and was thrown out at second base when Luke fired the ball to his brother Joe, who was playing shortstop.

SEPTEMBER 10 Indians pitcher Garland Buckeye hits two homers and drives in five runs during a 7–2 win over the Tigers in the second game of a double header in Detroit. Cleveland lost the opener 6–1.

At six-foot tall, Buckeye weighed 260 pounds, which made him the largest player of his era. He was a guard in the National Football League from 1920 through 1924, primarily with the Chicago Cardinals. During his years in the NFL, Buckeye played semipro baseball and worked as a bank teller in Chicago.

SEPTEMBER 20 At Dunn Field, the Old-Timers clubs representing the Cubs and Indians play to a 6–6, eight-inning tie for the benefit of the Amateur and Old-Timers Baseball Association of Cleveland. Future Hall of Famers in the game included Cy Young, Nap Lajoie, and Three-Finger Brown.

SEPTEMBER 26 In his major league debut, Ray Benge of the Indians pitches a shutout to defeat the Athletics 6–0 at Philadelphia in the second game of a double header. Cleveland also won the opener 7–2.

Benge pitched only nine more games, one of them a start, as a member of the Indians. Later, he pitched for four National League clubs and finished his career in 1938 with a record of 101–130.

1926

Season in a Sentence

The Indians are surprise contenders for the American League flag, but star center fielder and manager Tris Speaker is released at the end of the season amid allegations that he helped to fix a game seven years earlier.

Finish • Won • Lost • Pct • GB

Finish	Won	Lost	Pct	GB
Second	88	66	.571	3.0

Manager

Tris Speaker

Stats

Stats	Indians	AL	Rank
Batting Avg:	.289	.281	4
On-Base Pct:	.349	.351	5
Slugging Pct:	.386	.392	6
Home Runs:	27		8
Stolen Bases:	88		3 (tie)
ERA:	3.40	4.02	2
Fielding Avg:	.972	.969	2
Runs Scored:	738		4
Runs Allowed:	612		2

Starting Line-up

Luke Sewell, c
George Burns, 1b
Freddy Spurgeon, 2b
Rube Lutzke, 3b
Joe Sewell, ss
Charlie Jamieson, lf
Tris Speaker, cf
Homer Summa, rf

Pitchers

George Uhle, sp
Dutch Levsen, sp
Joe Shaute, sp
Sherry Smith, sp
Garland Buckeye, sp-rp
Jake Miller, sp-rp
Benn Karr, rp

Attendance

627,426 (fifth in AL)

Club Leaders

Batting Avg:	George Burns	.358
On-Base Pct:	Tris Speaker	.408
Slugging Pct:	George Burns	.494
Home Runs:	Tris Speaker	7
RBIs:	George Burns	114
Runs:	Freddy Spurgeon	101
Stolen Bases:	Joe Sewell	17
Wins:	George Uhle	27
Strikeouts:	George Uhle	159
ERA:	George Uhle	2.83
Saves:	Four tied with	1

FEBRUARY 28 At Crescent City, Florida, a train carrying several Indians players derails. No one was injured.

APRIL 13 The Indians open the season with a 2–1 win over the Tigers in Detroit. George Uhle pitched the shutout.

Uhle had one of the best seasons by a pitcher in Cleveland history in 1926 by composing a 27–11 record and a 2.83 ERA. He led the AL in wins, winning percentage (.711), innings pitched (318⅓), and complete games (32 in 36 starts).

APRIL 21 In the home opener, the Indians wallop the Tigers 12–2 before 25,000 at Dunn Field.

APRIL 26 The Indians score six runs in the second inning to take a 9–0 lead and pummel the Browns 12–1 in St. Louis.

MAY 4 George Uhle helps police nab a robbery suspect in suburban Cleveland. Driving his automobile with his wife at his side, Uhle happened upon the robbery of a gas station. When the bandit's car sped away with a female companion, Uhle picked up

George Burns put together a career year in 1926, winning the American League MVP Award.

the owner of the station and started after the car. After a chase at high speed, Uhle's car caught up with the robber and forced his vehicle into a curb, which caused two of the tires to blow out. At this juncture, the male occupant of the car jumped out and fled. The young woman who served as his accomplice was arrested.

May 8 After the crowd clears Fenway Park following a 10–4 Indians win over the Red Sox, the ballpark catches fire. The bleacher section along the left field line was destroyed.

May 10 The Indians win 3–0 in Boston after being held hitless by Howard Ehmke of the Red Sox until the eighth inning. Two batters reached on errors before Tris Speaker doubled in both with Cleveland's first hit. Speaker scored on a single by Joe Sewell.

Sewell hit .324 for the Indians in 1926.

May 19 Down 5–1 to the Athletics at the end of the seventh inning in Philadelphia, the Indians rally to win 6–5. Joe Sewell hit a three-run homer in the eighth inning. Tris Speaker added a two-run double in the ninth.

After hitting .389 in 1925, Speaker dropped to .304 in 1926, but he was still a productive player at the age of 38 with 94 walks, 96 runs, and 52 doubles.

MAY 25 George Uhle pitches a complete game and hits a two-run, walk-off homer in the 11th inning to defeat the Browns 6–4 at Dunn Field. It was Uhle's only home run between 1924 and 1928.

JUNE 2 During a double header against the Tigers at Dunn Field, the Indians win the opener 13–1, but lose the second game 7–0.

JUNE 5 Garland Buckeye has a big day during a 15–3 win over the Yankees at Dunn Field. Buckeye pitched a complete game, went 4-for-4 at the plate with a home run, double, and two singles, and started a triple play. With the bases loaded in the seventh inning, Mark Koenig hit a line drive to Buckeye. The pitcher's toss to third baseman Rube Lutzke caught Mike Gazella, and Lutzke's bullet throw across the diamond to first baseman George Burns got Ben Paschal before he could get back to the bag.

JUNE 6 Tris Speaker lifts himself for pinch-hitter George Uhle during a 6–5 loss to the Yankees at Dunn Field. It was the first time that anyone had pinch-hit for Speaker since his big league career began in 1907. It happened in the seventh inning with a runner on second base, two out, and Cleveland trailing 6–5. Uhle was a right-handed batter and was brought in to replace lefty-swinging Speaker to face southpaw Garland Braxton. Uhle flied out. The game was then called by the umpires because of rain and darkness.

JUNE 12 The Indians win 1–0 in 11 innings against the Athletics at Dunn Field. Sherry Smith pitched the complete-game shutout defeating Lefty Grove. With two out in the 11th, Tris Speaker and Glen Myatt walked, and Speaker scored from second base on an infield hit by Charlie Jamieson.

JUNE 13 George Uhle pitches a two-hitter to defeat the Athletics 4–1 at Dunn Field. The only Philadelphia hits were a double by Sammy Hale in the fifth inning and a single by Bill Lamar in the ninth.

JUNE 20 Jake Miller pitches the Indians to a 1–0 win over the Red Sox at Dunn Field.

JULY 21 The Indians break open a scoreless game with six runs in the ninth inning and win 6–0 against the Athletics in Philadelphia.

AUGUST 11 Tris Speaker collects his 700th career double during a 7–2 loss to the White Sox at Dunn Field.

Speaker finished his career with an all-time record 792 doubles. Pete Rose ranks second with 746.

AUGUST 22 George Uhle wins his 20th game of the season with a 10–2 decision over the Senators in the first game of a double header in Washington. Cleveland also won the second tilt 6–0.

AUGUST 27 Relief pitcher Sherry Smith hits a home run in the 12th inning to defeat the Red Sox 5–4 in the second game of a double header in Boston. The Indians also won the opener 9–3.

AUGUST 28 Indians pitcher Dutch Levsen pitches two complete-game victories in a double header against the Red Sox in Boston. Levsen allowed four hits in each game, winning

5–1 and 6–1. The Indians also started the same nine players in each game, and made no substitutions in either. The line-ups were: Charlie Jamieson, left field; Freddy Spurgeon, second base; Tris Speaker center field; George Burns first base; Joe Sewell, shortstop; Homer Summa, right field; Luke Sewell, catcher; Rube Lutzke, third base; and Levsen.

Levsen is the last major league pitcher to throw two complete-game victories in one day. Entering the 1926 season, he had a record of 2–3. Levsen was 16–13 with a 3.41 earned run average in 1926, and then returned to obscurity. Over the remainder of his career, Levsen was 3–10 with an ERA of 5.47.

SEPTEMBER 5 During a 12-inning, 8–7 win over the Tigers in the first game of a double header at Dunn Field, George Burns hits his 60th double of the season to break the record for most two-baggers in a season, set by Tris Speaker, who hit 59 in 1923. The incident was received with fans throwing straw hats in the air, while Speaker had time called to walk to second to congratulate Burns. Detroit won the second contest 2–0. It was called after five innings to allow the Tigers to catch a train.

Burns finished the year with 64 doubles. His record was broken by Earl Webb, who hit 67 doubles for the Red Sox in 1931, but Burns's mark still ranks second all-time. He also led the AL in hits in 1926 with 215, batted .358, and drove in 114 runs.

SEPTEMBER 11 The Indians pull off a weird triple play during an 8–1 win over the Senators in the first game of a double header at Dunn Field. Joe Judge was on third base and Bucky Harris on second when Bennie Tate hit a bouncer back to George Uhle. Tate was thrown out at first. Trapped off second, Harris was retired on a toss from first baseman George Burns to shortstop Joe Sewell. Judge tried to score on the play and became the third out when Sewell fired home to his brother Luke.

SEPTEMBER 12 The Indians take an 11–0 lead after three innings and win 14–4 in a game at Dunn Field played in mud, pelted by rain, and finished in semi-darkness.

The Indians started the season with a 10–3 record, but dropped to 23–24 on June 3. Cleveland improved to 60–48 by August 6 and were in second place, but a distant 11 games behind the first-place Yankees. A Yankee slump allowed the Indians into the race. On September 15, the Indians began a six-game series against the Yankees at Dunn Field while 5½ games out of first.

SEPTEMBER 15 In the first game of the pennant-showdown series against the Yankees, the Indians lose 6–4 at Dunn Field. George Uhle had a 4–1 lead before allowing four runs in the seventh inning.

SEPTEMBER 16 The Indians cut the lead to 4½ games with a double-header sweep of the Yankees at Dunn Field. In the opener, Dutch Levsen won his own game with a walk-off single in the ninth inning. Levsen allowed only two hits, a double by Lou Gehrig and a single by Joe Dugan. In the second tilt, Garland Buckeye walked ten batters and hit another, but like Levsen, allowed only two hits to win 6–0. The only New York hits were singles by Gehrig and Bob Meusel.

SEPTEMBER 18 The Indians move to within 2½ games of first with a 3–1 victory over the Yankees at Dunn Field.

September 19 The Yankees pull 3½ games ahead of the Indians with an 8–3 win at Dunn Field. The loss effectively ended Cleveland's chance for a pennant in 1926.

November 3 Ty Cobb announces his resignation as manager of the Tigers and his retirement as a player.

November 29 In a surprise move, Tris Speaker announces his resignation as manager of the Indians and his retirement as a player.

Unbeknownst to the public, the resignations of Cobb and Speaker were linked. The two were forced out under pressure by commissioner Kenesaw Landis and AL. president Ban Johnson. The two star players were implicated by former Tiger pitcher Dutch Leonard of betting on a fixed game played on September 25, 1919. The story and testimony were released on December 21. At a secret meeting of AL directors, it was decided to let Cobb and Speaker resign with no publicity. Landis held hearings into the matter, but Leonard refused to appear. Cobb and Speaker were exonerated by Landis on January 27, 1927. Speaker signed a contract to play with the Senators on January 31, and Cobb inked a deal with the Athletics on February 3.

December 11 The Indians name 47-year-old Jack McCallister as manager.

McCallister had never played or managed in the majors prior to his appointment as manager. He had been a scout and a coach with the Indians for 12 years. McCallister managed the Indians only one season, to a record of 66–87.

The Cobb-speaker Scandal

The big news in baseball during the month of November in 1926 was the sudden retirements of Ty Cobb and Tris Speaker, two of the greatest players the game had ever known. Cobb announced the end of a 22-year career, all with the Tigers, on November 3, a month shy of his 40th birthday. He had been a player in Detroit since 1905 and player-manager since 1921. Speaker retired on November 29. He made his major league debut in 1907 with the Red Sox and joined the Indians in 1916. Speaker had been player-manager in Cleveland since July 1919.

Cobb read a statement saying that he left because "I foresaw I could not win a pennant within the next few years under existing circumstances and I want to quit while I'm still among the best." He had 3,902 career hits, and while he batted .339 in 1926, was limited to 79 games because of injuries.

Cobb's departure raised few eyebrows. The Tigers finished in sixth place during the previous season, and attendance declined for the second year in a row. His abrasive personality had alienated almost everyone associated with the club. But the resignation of Speaker came as a complete surprise. After losing seasons in 1924 and 1925, the Indians finished a close second to the Yankees in 1926, Cleveland's best season in five years. Speaker said that he considered quitting after the Indians finished sixth in 1925 but didn't want to leave a "rudderless ship." Following the dramatic improvement in 1926, Speaker explained that "I can step out now without any question of my action." He also played in 150 games that season, and hit .304. Speaker had 3,292 lifetime base hits at the time of his resignation, then the third highest figure behind Cobb and Honus Wagner. Leaving a contending ball club while still an effective player seemed to make no sense at all, and writers and fans argued for weeks about his motive.

Unknown to the public, Cobb and Speaker were forced out by American League president Ban Johnson with the backing of league owners. Johnson was in possession of letters from former major league pitcher Dutch Leonard, who accused Cobb and Speaker and Indians outfielder Joe Wood of betting on a fixed game on September 25, 1919, between the Indians and Tigers in Detroit. The letters were written by Cobb and Wood to Leonard mentioning a bet. According to Cobb, Leonard sold the letters to Johnson for $20,000. Leonard denied the claim. Johnson turned the correspondence over to commissioner Kenesaw Landis. According to Leonard, Speaker said that since the Tigers didn't have to worry about winning the game that day. The Indians had second place clinched, and a victory would help the Tigers claim third place and a share of the World Series money. Speaker said that he would help Cobb and the Tigers win to finish third, a common practice at the time. Then, according to Leonard, the four agreed to bet some money on the game. Cobb was to put up $2,000, Leonard $1,500, and Wood and Speaker $1,000 each. However, said Leonard, neither Cobb nor Speaker got his money down in time, while he and Wood won $130 on a game the Tigers won 9–5 and was completed in only 66 minutes. One sportswriter noted the "good fellowship" among the players. Speaker had three hits in five at-bats. Cobb was 1-for-5 with two stolen bases.

The startling story accusing Cobb and Speaker of betting on the September 25, 1919, game broke on December 21, 1926, and was front-page news on virtually every paper in the country, including *The New York Times*. The accusations looked damning, and it looked as though the careers of Cobb and Speaker were over.

Leonard pitched for the Red Sox from 1913 through 1918 and with the Tigers from 1919 through 1921 when he left the game with a record of 125–107. Cobb convinced Leonard to return in 1924, and he was 14–6 over two seasons, but developed arm trouble. Cobb refused to believe that Leonard was ailing and continued to send him to the mound. When his arm was dead late in the 1925 campaign, Leonard was sold by the Tigers to a club in the Pacific Coast League, and he became bent on revenge against Cobb for cutting his career short.

Cobb and Speaker professed their innocence of any wrongdoing and said they knew of no bets placed on the game. Speaker said that the bets referred to in Leonard's letters were on a horse, not on a baseball game. Leonard's story soon began to unravel. He refused to come to Landis's office in Chicago, and the commissioner had to travel to Leonard's ranch in California to take his testimony. Leonard never faced Cobb and Speaker with his accusations, although given every opportunity to do so by Landis. Meanwhile, both Cobb and Speaker lined up prominent attorneys and threatened legal action if they were barred from organized baseball.

Landis acquitted the two stars on January 27, 1927, with this simple notice: "This is the Cobb-Speaker case. These players have not been, nor are they now, found guilty of fixing a ball game. By no decent system of justice could such a finding be made. Therefore, they were not placed on the ineligible list. As they desire to rescind their withdrawal from baseball, the releases which the Detroit and Cleveland clubs granted at their requests, in the circumstances detailed above, are canceled and the players' names are restored to the reserve lists of those clubs." Speaker signed a contract on January 31 to play for the Senators. Cobb inked a deal with the Athletics on February 3. Both played two more big league seasons. Cobb and Speaker were teammates in Philadelphia in 1928. Neither ever managed another big league club.

Landis also put an end to the practice of teams "laying down" to allow the opposition to win a game, which Speaker admitted he did for his friend Cobb late in the 1919 season. After 1927, anyone who participated in such action, or gave a gift to an opposing player, would be subject to a one-year suspension.

Some historians have claimed that Cobb and Speaker were found not guilty by Landis because of their status in the game. But Landis was never one to shy from confrontation or controversy. He had banned nearly two-dozen players for life for betting on baseball, most notably the eight "Black Sox" who fixed the 1919 World Series. Landis also suspended

Babe Ruth for the first 30 days of the 1922 season for engaging in a barnstorming tour in violation of baseball rules at a time when Ruth was not only the most popular player in baseball but was the most popular individual in all of North America. Also, Cobb and Speaker were near the ends of their careers and were no longer strong gate attractions. Landis simply had no concrete evidence to support Leonard's claim that would stand up in court should the two players decide to sue.

1927

Season in a Sentence

A dismal sixth-place finish leads to the sale of the Indians and sweeping changes in the organization.

Finish • Won • Lost • Pct • GB

Finish	Won	Lost	Pct	GB
Sixth	66	87	.431	43.5

Manager

Jack McCallister

Stats

	Indians	AL	Rank
Batting Avg:	.283	.285	5
On-Base Pct:	.337	.351	7
Slugging Pct:	.379	.399	6
Home Runs:	26		8
Stolen Bases:	65		8
ERA:	4.27	4.14	6
Fielding Avg:	.968	.967	6
Runs Scored:	668		6
Runs Allowed:	766		5

Starting Line-up

Luke Sewell, c
George Burns, 1b
Lew Fonseca, 2b
Rube Lutzke, 3b
Joe Sewell, ss
Charlie Jamieson, lf
Ike Eichrodt, cf
Homer Summa, rf
Johnny Hodapp, 3b
Freddy Spurgeon, 2b

Pitchers

Willis Hudlin, sp-rp
Joe Shaute, sp-rp
Garland Buckeye, sp-rp
Jake Miller, sp-rp
George Uhle, sp
Benn Karr, rp

Attendance

373,138 (seventh in AL)

Club Leaders

Batting Avg:	Joe Sewell	.316
On-Base Pct:	Charlie Jamieson	.394
Slugging Pct:	George Burns	.435
Home Runs:	Johnny Hodapp	5
RBIs:	Joe Sewell	92
Runs:	George Burns	84
Stolen Bases:	George Burns	13
Wins:	Willis Hudlin	18
Strikeouts:	George Uhle	69
ERA:	Jake Miller	3.21
Saves:	Joe Shaute	2
	Benn Karr	2

April 12 — The Indians open the season with a 3–2 win over the White Sox at Dunn Field. George Uhle pitched a complete game and was the hitting star with two RBIs, including the game-winner with a walk-off double. Chicago left 14 runners on base.

May 7 — The Indians outlast the Athletics 11–10 in 11 innings at Dunn Field. Bernie Neis drove in the winning run with a single. Cleveland trailed 10–5 before scoring four runs in the sixth inning and one in the seventh.

May 14 — Playing in his first game in Cleveland since resigning as manager the previous November, Tris Speaker is given a $1,500 chest of silver and other gifts in ceremonies preceding a game against the Senators at Dunn Field. Speaker was hitless in four at-bats, and the Indians won 5–2.

The 1927 team was blessed with many talented infielders, who gathered on a bench for this photo. From left to right: Rube Lutzke, Lew Fonseca, Ernie Padgett, George Burns, Joe Sewell, Freddy Spurgeon, Dutch Ussat, Johnny Hodapp.

MAY 18 The Indians win 5–4 over the Yankees in 12 innings on George Burns Day at Dunn Field. Burns received an automobile and a silver bat containing $1,150 in cash.

MAY 22 The day after Charles Lindbergh arrives in Paris at the end of his historic solo flight across the Atlantic, Babe Ruth is honored by a group of Native Americans during a 7–2 Yankees win over the Indians at Dunn Field. The Native Americans were part of a rodeo performing in Cleveland and attended the game. After he flied out in the fifth inning, Ruth was beckoned to the stands along the first base line, and one of the female members of the group decorated the Babe with a headdress of feathers. Ruth wore the headdress in the outfield while the Indians batted in the bottom of the inning. Returning to his conventional baseball cap, in the sixth, Ruth hit a home run over the right field wall.

MAY 25 Trailing 4–1, the Indians score seven runs in the fifth inning and beat the Tigers 9–4 in the first game of a double header at Dunn Field. Detroit won the nightcap 7–6.

May 30 Down 7–4, the Indians score five runs in the ninth inning and hang on for a 9–8 triumph over the Tigers in the first game of a Memorial Day double header in Detroit. The Tigers won the second contest 11–3.

May 31 Detroit first baseman Johnny Neun pulls off an unassisted triple play against the Indians during a 1–0 Tiger win at Detroit. The triple play ended the tight game. Glen Myatt was the Cleveland runner on second base, Charlie Jamieson was on first, and Homer Summa was batting against Rip Collins. Summa lined to Neun with the runners moving on the pitch. Neun took the ball standing still, ran over and tagged Jamieson between first and second, and continued to second base, landing there before Myatt could return.

The unassisted triple play was the second in the majors in two days. Shortstop Johnny Cooney of the Cubs performed the feat against the Pirates a little more than 24 hours earlier. There wasn't another unassisted triple play in the majors until 1968. The Indians were the victims of that one as well (see July 30, 1968).

June 1 The Indians collect 20 hits and pound out a 14–1 win over the Tigers in Detroit. Cleveland scored seven runs in the third inning.

Joe Sewell was the Indians top hitter in 1927 with a .316 batting average, 92 RBIs, and 48 doubles.

June 12 The Indians purchase Baby Doll Jacobson from the Browns.

July 4 Dutch Levsen holds the White Sox hitless until the seventh inning and pitches a two-hitter to win 2–0 in the first game of a double header in Chicago. Cleveland completed the sweep with a 6–2 win in the second tilt.

August 5 The Indians sell Baby Doll Jacobson to the Athletics.

August 13 Willis Hudlin pitches the Indians to a 1–0 win over the White Sox at Cleveland. Ike Eichrodt drove in the lone run of the game with a double in the eighth inning.

Hudlin looked like a coming star in 1927 when he was 18–12 with a 4.01 ERA as a 21-year-old rookie in 1927. He never won as many as 18 games again, but he had five seasons of 15 wins or more and pitched in the majors as late as 1944. Hudlin played for the Indians until 1940 and had a 157–151 record with the club. He ranks seventh on the club's all-time list in wins and is fourth in games started (320), fourth in innings pitched (2,557 2/3), and seventh in complete games (154).

August 20 The Indians take down the Yankees 14–8 at Dunn Field.

September 10 The Indians score two runs in the ninth inning and two in the tenth to defeat the Senators 6–4 in Washington. George Burns broke the 4–4 tie with a two-run double.

September 29 The Indians split a double header with the Browns, winning 5–4 and losing 9–4, before only 600 fans at storm-ravaged Sportsman's Park.

Earlier in the day, a tornado ripped through St. Louis resulting in the deaths of 87 people. At Sportsman's Park, the twister flipped the pavilion roof onto Grand Avenue, bent the flagpole in center field, and scattered debris all over the ballpark.

November 2 Indians president and general manager Ernest Barnard is named president of the American League.

Barnard had been associated with the Indians since 1903. Barnard succeeded Ban Johnson as AL president. Johnson had been the head of the circuit since its founding in 1900, and resigned because of poor health. Few mourned his retirement, however, because Johnson had managed to alienate nearly everyone connected with the game due to his arrogant and autocratic manner. Barnard was a more conciliatory figure. He remained AL president until his death from a heart attack on March 27, 1931, at the age of 56. Ironically, Johnson passed away a day later.

November 15 A group headed by Alva Bradley purchases the Indians from the Dunn family.

A wealthy native Clevelander who made a fortune in downtown real estate, Bradley had a lifelong interest in sports. He headed an eight-man syndicate that paid $1 million to buy the ball club. Bradley's group spent months buying shares of the club, many of them above market value, to obtain a controlling interest. Alva and his brother Charles together owned 17.5 percent of the stock. The largest shareholder was John Sherwin, Sr., with 30 percent. Bradley was president of the Indians until 1946, a period in which the club had 13 winning seasons but never reached the World Series and were in serious contention for a pennant only in 1940.

November 28 Billy Evans is named general manager of the Indians.

Evans's previous position had been as an American League umpire for 22 seasons from 1906 through 1927. He was general manager of the Indians until 1935.

December 10 Roger Peckinpaugh is named manager of the Indians, replacing Jack McCallister.

Peckinpaugh was 38-years-old, had played on the Cleveland sandlots as a youngster, and was a shortstop in the majors from 1910 until 1927. He played for the Indians at the start of his big league career in 1910 and again in 1912 and 1913. Peckinpaugh was traded to the Yankees, where he managed the club for 20 games at the end of the 1914 season when he was only 23, thereby becoming the youngest manager in big league history. After that, he was strictly a player but was good enough to appear in 2,012 games as a major leaguer. Peckinpaugh was a starter in the World Series with the Yankees in 1921 and with the Senators in 1924 and 1925. He managed the Indians from 1928 through June 1933 to a record of 415–402.

1928

Season in a Sentence

Under new manager Roger Peckinpaugh, the Indians start well by winning 12 of their first 16 games, but a 4–20 September dooms the club to a seventh-place finish.

Finish • Won • Lost • Pct • GB

Finish	Won	Lost	Pct	GB
Seventh	62	92	.403	39.0

Manager

Roger Peckinpaugh

Stats

Stats	Indians	AL	Rank
Batting Avg:	.285	.281	3
On-Base Pct:	.336	.344	6
Slugging Pct:	.382	.397	6
Home Runs:	34		7
Stolen Bases:	50		8
ERA:	4.47	4.04	8
Fielding Avg:	.965	.969	7
Runs Scored:	674		7
Runs Allowed:	830		8

Starting Line-up

Luke Sewell, c
Lew Fonseca, 1b
Carl Lind, 2b
Johnny Hodapp, 3b
Joe Sewell, ss
Charlie Jamieson, lf
Sam Langford, cf
Homer Summa, rf
Eddie Morgan, 1b-cf
George Burns, 1b

Pitchers

Joe Shaute, sp
Willis Hudlin, sp-rp
George Uhle, sp
George Grant, sp-rp
Jake Miller, sp
Bill Bayne, rp

Attendance

375,907 (seventh in AL)

Club Leaders

Batting Avg:	Joe Sewell	.323
	Johnny Hodapp	.323
On-Base Pct:	Joe Sewell	.391
Slugging Pct:	Johnny Hodapp	.432
Home Runs:	George Burns	5
RBIs:	Johnny Hodapp	73
Runs:	Carl Lind	102
Stolen Bases:	Carl Lind	8
Wins:	Willis Hudlin	14
Strikeouts:	Joe Shaute	31
ERA:	Willie Hudlin	4.04
	Joe Shaute	4.04
Saves:	Willis Hudlin	7

MARCH 4 The Indians purchase Aaron Ward from the White Sox.

APRIL 11 In the season opener, the Indians defeat the White Sox 8–3 in Chicago. George Uhle pitched a complete game and contributed three hits including a double. Joe Sewell also had three hits. Center fielder Eddie Morgan, playing in his major league debut, wrenched his shoulder chasing a fly ball and missed three weeks.

APRIL 18 In the home opener, the Indians beat the White Sox 7–1 before a crowd of 20,000.

With the Dunn family no longer involved in the ownership of the Indians, the name of the ballpark changed from Dunn Field to League Park. It had been known previously as League Park prior to James Dunn's purchase of the Indians in 1916.

APRIL 27 The Tigers score five runs in the first inning, but the Indians bounce back to win 10–6 at Detroit.

The Indians won seven of their first eight games, were 12–4 on April 28, and had a 21–13 record on May 18, but any hopes for a successful season soon went up in smoke. The club had a record of 4–20 in September, including an 11-game losing streak.

MAY 1 Center fielder Sam Langford ties a major league record for most assists by an outfielder in a game with four during a 4–3 win over the Browns at League Park. Cleveland also tied another big league mark for most assists by an outfield in a game with five. Right fielder Homer Summa added the other one.

MAY 13 George Uhle pitches a one-hitter to defeat the Athletics 3–0 at League Park. The only Philadelphia hit was a double by Mickey Cochrane in the second inning. The game was played before an overflow crowd of 26,000 on a Sunday afternoon in between Saturday and Monday contests between the two clubs in Philadelphia. Sunday games in the City of Brotherly Love were illegal until 1934.

MAY 24 The Indians pull off an unusual triple play, but wind up losing 4–3 in ten innings to the White Sox at Comiskey Park. The triple play occurred with the score 3–3 and the bases loaded in the Chicago half of the ninth. Bud Clancy popped to Cleveland left fielder Charlie Jamieson, who threw home to catcher Luke Sewell to retire Johnny Mann trying to score. Caught in a rundown between second and third, Ray Schalk was retired on throws from Luke Sewell to shortstop Joe Sewell to third baseman Johnny Hodapp.

JUNE 9 Left fielder Charlie Jamieson starts his second triple play in less than three weeks during a 7–3 loss to the Yankees at League Park. With Ben Paschal on third base and Tony Lazzeri on first in the second inning, Jamieson came tearing in to make a fine catch on Joe Dugan's liner. Lazzeri was caught flat-footed between first and second and was retired on a throw from Jamieson to second baseman Carl Lind to first baseman Lew Fonseca. Paschal tagged up and tried to score during the rundown of Lazzeri. Paschal was out on the throw from Fonseca to catcher Luke Sewell.

Jamieson is the only outfielder in major league history to start two triple plays in a season.

JUNE 16 Eddie Morgan collects three doubles, a triple, and a walk in five plate appearances during a 9–3 victory over the Athletics at League Park.

JUNE 25 A home run by Eddie Morgan highlights a three-run tenth inning that beats the Browns 7–4 in St. Louis.

Morgan played six seasons (1928–33) for the Indians, mainly as a first baseman, in which his star rose and fell quickly. His batting average of .323 during his years in Cleveland ranks fifth all-time among Indians with at least 2,000 plate appearances. In 1930 and 1931 combined, Morgan batted .350 with 37 home runs.

JULY 7 The Indians sell Garland Buckeye to the Giants.

JULY 10 In the second game of a double header at Griffith Stadium, the Indians collect 14 hits and two walks but fail to score in a 9–0 loss to the Senators. The 14 hits tied a major league record for most hits in a shutout loss. Milt Gaston pitched a complete game for Washington. Cleveland left 14 men on base. The Senators won the opener 9–5.

July 25 The Indians sweep the Red Sox 10–2 and 15–5 at League Park.

Joe Sewell was Cleveland's leading hitter in 1928, hitting .315.

July 26 The Indians score two runs in the ninth inning to beat the Red Sox 4–3 in the second game of a double header in Cleveland. Pinch-hitter Glenn Myatt doubled in the tying run and scored on Sam Langford's triple. The Indians also won the opener 4–2.

July 29 In a reversal of roles, the Indians overpower the defending world champion Yankees 24–6 at League Park. The game was over early, as Cleveland scored eight runs in the first inning and nine in the second to take a 17–1 lead. Another run followed in the third and six more in the sixth. The Indians collected 27 hits. Luke Sewell was 5-for-6 with four singles and a triple. Johnny Hodapp also picked five hits, including a double, in seven at-bats. He had two hits in both the second and sixth innings.

Hodapp is one of only four players in major leaguer history with two hits in an inning twice in the same game. He hit .318 in eight seasons in Cleveland in 608 games from 1925 through 1932. Injuries kept him from the stardom his great talent seemed sure to achieve. In 1926, Hodapp stepped on a ball during spring training and broke an ankle that limited him to three games that season. Other ailments often kept him out of the lineup in the succeeding years until 1930, when he was able to play in 154 games and lead the league in hits (225) and doubles (51) in addition to batting .354 with 121 runs-batted-in and 111 runs scored as a 24-year-old. Hodapp was unable to build on that season, however, because of a knee injury and played his last big league game in 1933.

August 19 Reserve catcher Chick Autry hits a two-run homer in the tenth inning to give the Indians a 3–1 lead in an eventual 3–2 victory over the Yankees in the first game of a double header in New York. In the nightcap, the Yankees won 10–3.

The homer was the first of Autry's career and is only one as a member of the Indians. He hit two home runs in the majors in 277 at-bats.

September 16 The Indians lose their 11th game in a row, dropping a 7–1 decision to the Athletics at League Park.

September 27 The Red Sox score seven runs in the top of the first inning, but the Indians rally to win 14–10 in the first game of a double header in Cleveland. The comeback started with four runs in the bottom half of the first and five more in the second. Boston won the second tilt 7–4.

September 28 A "crowd" of fewer than 200 watches the Indians lose 1–0 to the Red Sox at League Park.

The Indians top rookie in 1928 was second baseman Carl Lind, who hit .294 and scored 102 runs at the age of 24. An off-season illness sapped his strength, however, and he played only two more seasons, batting .242 in 90 games.

November 6 On the same day that Herbert Hoover defeats Al Smith in the presidential election, voters in Cleveland approve a $2.5 million bond issue to build a municipal stadium, capable of holding more than 80,000 fans, near the lakefront. The vote was 112,648 for and 76,975 against.

The stadium was years in the planning. Among the advocates were Indians president Alva Bradley and AL president Ernest Barnard, who preceded Bradley as the head of the Cleveland ball club. Both realized that League Park, with a capacity of 21,414, most of them poorly situated, was inadequate. Parking was also a problem. When the ballpark was built in 1910, few in Cleveland owned automobiles and little consideration was given in planning the facility for those who drove to the game. Soon after, however, automobile ownership across the country exploded. Those who arrived by car had to find street parking or space in a small handful of vacant lots in the vicinity. The development of parking lots would be an expensive proposition as League Park was hemmed in by neighborhood structures. The site for the new stadium was on filled-in land on the lakefront about three blocks north of the Public Square. The bond issue also included roadways extending West Third and East Ninth Streets to connect the stadium to downtown. The stadium was designed for a multitude of events, not just sports, which was the reason for its oval construction. Large stadiums such as the one constructed on the Cleveland lakefront were part of a trend during the 1920s. Others included Memorial Coliseum in Los Angeles (1923), Soldier Field in Chicago (1925) and Municipal Stadium in Philadelphia (1926). At the time Cleveland's Municipal Stadium was proposed, backers were hopeful of attracting the 1932 Olympic Games to the city. The Olympics were ultimately granted to Los Angeles. To convince voters to support the bond issue, some 60 possible uses for the facility were listed, including "pageants, dramatic offerings, musical entertainment, civic gatherings and business expositions as well as athletic contests," among them "boxing and wrestling matches, gymnastics, track and field events, skating, hockey, tennis, soccer, and even cricket, in addition to football and baseball." Several obstacles, including a lawsuit filed by a taxpayer (see May 29, 1929), delayed the start of the project until June 24, 1930. It was completed on July 1,1931, at a cost of $2,986,685. The Indians did not play there for more than a year, however, as Bradley was unable to come to a lease agreement with city officials. The ball club played its first game at Municipal Stadium on July 31, 1932. With that inaugural contest, the Indians became the first major league club to play in a stadium built at taxpayer's expense. The Indians was also the first in the majors to play at a downtown location. Until the opening of Municipal Stadium, big league ballparks were privately built by the owners of the clubs, generally on land that could be bought cheaply about two to four miles from the business center.

December 11 The Indians trade George Uhle to the Tigers for Jackie Tavener and Ken Holloway.

1929

Season in a Sentence

Armed with new talent, led by rookies Earl Averill and Wes Ferrell, the Indians improve by 19 games over their 1928 record and leap from seventh place to third.

Finish • Won • Lost • Pct • GB

Finish	Won	Lost	Pct	GB
Third	81	73	.533	24.0

Manager

Roger Peckinpaugh

Stats

Stats	Indians	AL	Rank
Batting Avg:	.294	.284	4
On-Base Pct:	.353	.349	4
Slugging Pct:	.417	.404	4
Home Runs:	62		4
Stolen Bases:	75		5
ERA:	4.05	4.24	2
Fielding Avg:	.968	.969	5
Runs Scored:	717		6
Runs Allowed:	736		3

Starting Line-up

Luke Sewell, c
Lew Fonseca, 1b
Johnny Hodapp, 2b
Joe Sewell, 3b
Jackie Tavener, ss
Charlie Jamieson, lf
Earl Averill, cf
Bibb Falk, rf-lf
Eddie Morgan, rf
Ray Gardner, ss
Carl Lind, 2b
Dick Porter, rf-2b

Pitchers

Wes Ferrell, sp-rp
Willis Hudlin, sp
Jake Miller, sp
Joe Shaute, sp
Jimmy Zinn, sp-rp
Johnny Miljus, rp-sp
Ken Holloway, rp-sp

Attendance

536, 210 (fourth in AL)

Club Leaders

Batting Avg:	Lew Fonseca	.369
On-Base Pct:	Lew Fonseca	.426
Slugging Pct:	Earl Averill	.534
Home Runs:	Earl Averill	18
RBIs:	Lew Fonseca	103
Runs:	Earl Averill	110
Stolen Bases:	Lew Fonseca	19
Wins:	Wes Ferrell	21
Strikeouts:	Wes Ferrell	100
ERA:	Willis Hudlin	3.34
Saves:	Wes Ferrell	5

January 5 The Indians sell Homer Summa to the Athletics.

February 28 Two weeks after Chicago's St. Valentine's Day massacre, the Indians trade Martin Autry to the White Sox for Bibb Falk.

April 16 The Indians open the season with an 11-inning, 5–4 victory over the Tigers before 15,000 on a cold day at League Park. The high temperature in Cleveland was 42 degrees. Before the game, the two clubs marched in formation to the center field flagpole, where the American flag was raised. Fire Chief George Wallace threw out the ceremonial first pitch. In his first major league plate appearance, Indians center fielder Earl Averill hit a home run. It happened in the first inning facing Earl Whitehill. Cleveland tied the contest 4–4 in the ninth when Lew Fonseca doubled and completed the circuit on Charlie Jamieson's bunt and Luke Sewell's single. The winning run scored on a double by Carl Lind with two on and two out in the 11th.

Numbers appeared on the backs of Indians uniforms for the first time in 1929. The club tried uniform numbers worn on the shoulders in 1916 (see June 26, 1916), but abandoned the experiment a year later. The 1929 Indians and the Yankees were the first teams to place numbers on the backs of uniforms large enough to be identified from distant portions of the stands. The Indians were technically the first to wear numbers since their season opened to days ahead of the Yanks. The numbers at the start of the season were assigned to Jackie Tavener (1), Carl Lind (2), Dick Porter (3), Joe Sewell (4), Earl Averill (5), Lew Fonseca (6), Charlie Jamieson (7), Luke Sewell (8), Glenn Myatt (9), coach Howie Shanks (10), Grover Hartley (11), Joe Shaute (12), Jake Miller (14), Willis Hudlin (15), Ken Holloway (17), Johnny Miljus (18), Wes Ferrell (22), Ray Gardner (34), Mel Harder (49), Bibb Falk (51), Eddie Morgan (61), and Johnny Hodapp (71). The Indians wore the numbers only at home in 1929, however, while the Yankees wore them both at home and on the road. All major league clubs sported numbers by 1932. Also in 1929, the Indians recognized the team nickname on the uniforms with a colorful insignia featuring the head of a Native American wearing a feathered headdress on the left breast of the shirts. Previously, the club was identified on the uniforms with either a letter "C" or the word Cleveland. The "Indian head" uniforms lasted only a year, however. The word "Indians" didn't appear on a jersey until 1946.

April 17 After hitting a home run in his first big league at-bat the previous day, Earl Averill homers in his second game in the majors, a 15–3 loss to the Tigers at League Park.

Averill was acquired by the Indians from the San Francisco Seals of the Pacific Coast League in November 1928 for $40,000 and two players. Despite his small stature (five-foot nine and 172 pounds), and late start (he was nearly 27 years old when he played in his first big league game), Averill quickly established himself as a power hitter and one of the greatest hitters in Indians history. As a rookie in 1929, he hit .332 with 43 doubles, 18 home runs, and 110 RBIs. He played for Cleveland until 1939 and still leads the club's career lists in runs (1,154), triples (121), and RBIs (1,085). Averill also ranks second in at-bats (5,915), third in hits (1,904), third in doubles (377), fourth in home runs (226), fourth in walks (726), sixth in batting average (.322), sixth in on base percentage (.399), seventh in slugging percentage (.541), and eighth in games (1,510). He was elected to the Hall of Fame in 1975 and the number 3 he wore from 1930 through 1939 was retired by the Indians in 1976.

April 30 A hidden ball trick by the White Sox against the Indians ends a triple play during an 8–4 Chicago victory at Comiskey Park. With Cleveland runners Charlie Jamieson on second and Johnny Hodapp on third, Carl Lind grounded out to shortstop Bill Cissell. Both runners tried to advance, and Hodapp was thrown out by first baseman Bud Clancy to catcher Buck Crouse. Jamieson barely beat a throw from Crouse to third baseman Willie Kamm. Instead of returning the ball to the pitcher, Kamm kept it and tagged Jamieson as soon as he took a lead off the bag.

May 5 The Indians collect only two hits off Senators pitcher Ad Liska but win 1–0 at League Park. Jake Miller pitched the shutout.

May 6 Leading 1–0, the Indians allow ten runs in the fifth inning to the Senators and lose 13–5 at League Park.

May 10 Earl Averill hits a grand slam off Rube Walberg in the third inning of a 9–0 win over the Athletics at League Park.

MAY 11 Cleveland fans create a disturbance during a 4–2 loss to the Athletics at League Park. The contest was interrupted by bottles thrown at the end of the eighth inning when Lew Fonseca was called out. Umpire Red Ormsby, stationed at third base, was struck on the head and knocked unconscious. Police rushed on to the field, but were unable to quell the demonstrators. Finally Indians general manager Billy Evans, himself a former umpire, appeared and eventually restored order. Ormsby was taken from the field for medical attention, and groundskeepers and players soon cleared the empty bottles, allowing the game to proceed.

MAY 13 For the first time in major league history, both teams wear uniform numbers with the Indians defeating the Yankees 4–3 at League Park.

MAY 29 Two weeks after an explosion and poison gas kills 124 people at the Cleveland Clinic Hospital, Lew Fonseca collects two homers and two triples during an 11–1 thrashing of the White Sox in Chicago.

On the same day, Cleveland taxpayer Andrew Meyer brought suit in Cuyahoga County Common Pleas County seeking an injunction to prevent the construction of the new stadium on the lakefront from going forward. Voters had approved the project on November 6, 1928. Among his charges, Meyer claimed that the City of Cleveland held dubious title to the land. The case went all the way to the Ohio Supreme Court. On April 30, 1930, the high court declined to hear the case, and the legal battle was over. Under the direction of the Osborn Engineering Company of Cleveland, construction began on June 24, 1930. Osborn Engineering had previously been involved in the building of League Park in Cleveland (1910), Comiskey Park in Chicago (1910), Fenway Park in Boston (1912), and Yankee Stadium in New York (1923) as well as many downtown Cleveland buildings.

JUNE 7 The Indians purchase Joe Hauser from the Athletics.

JUNE 25 Lew Fonseca drives in seven runs with a homer and two singles during a 10–7 win over the Browns in the first game of a double header at Sportsman's Park. St. Louis won the second tilt 8–0.

At the age of 30, Fonseca came out of nowhere to win the American League batting title with a .369 average in 148 games in 1929. He also collected 209 hits, 44 doubles, 15 triples and 103 RBIs. It was one of only four seasons during a 12-year career with four clubs that Fonseca played in at least 100 games due in large part to a succession of injuries, some of them on the bizarre side. Fonseca was sidelined by broken shoulders (four times), a fractured wrist, a chipped bone in his ankle, a dislocated hip, a concussion, a broken leg, and a severed artery in his leg. Lew once missed several games when he was cut on the abdomen by his belt buckle. During the off-season after winning the 1929 batting crown, Fonseca contracted scarlet fever and nearly died. His greatest contribution to baseball came after his playing career ended when he became the major league director of motion picture production. Fonseca produced some 33 baseball movies, including the official World Series film from its inception in 1943 through 1965. He served as narrator on many of them.

Three-fourths of the Indians starting rotation: Walter "Jake" Miller, Willis Hudlin, and Joe Shaute.

June 27 Joe Sewell plays in his 1,000th consecutive game, a 6–3 loss to the Tigers in Detroit.

July 2 The Indians win in extra innings in both games of a double header against the White Sox at League Park. Cleveland won the opener 4–3 in ten innings with Earl Averill driving in the winning run with a walk-off double. The nightcap was a 5–4 decision in 11 innings. The contest ended when Lew Fonseca tripled and scored on an infield out.

July 3 The Indians and White Sox play their third extra-inning game in two days, with Chicago winning 6–3 in ten innings at League Park.

July 5 The Indians collect 20 hits during an 11–10 slugfest against the White Sox at League Park. Cleveland took a 10–9 lead with five runs in the seventh inning, then broke a 10–10 tie with a tally in the eighth.

July 10 Down 7–2 to the Senators at League Park, the Indians rally with two runs in the fourth inning, three in the fifth, and two in the seventh to win 9–7.

July 25 The Athletics clobber the Indians 21–3 in Philadelphia. The A's scored nine runs in the first inning and collected 25 hits during the contest. Starting pitcher Johnny Miljus gave up 14 runs in three innings.

August 2 A three-run homer by Bibb Falk highlights a four-run, ninth inning that beats the Yankees 9–8 in New York.

Before playing professional baseball, Falk was a football star at the University of Texas. Later, he returned to the school as a baseball coach and won 20 consecutive Southwest Conference championships as well as national titles in 1949 and 1950.

August 4 The Indians score nine runs with two out in the ninth inning to defeat the Yankees 14–6 in the second game of a double header in New York. With a runner on first and two out, Yankee third baseman Lyn Lary fumbled Lew Fonseca's grounder to keep the rally alive. After Bibb Falk walked to load the bases, the Yankees once again blew a chance to finish the game with a ground ball out when Mark Koenig committed an error on a bouncer off the bat of Johnny Hodapp. A run scored on the play to tie the score and the bases remained loaded. Then came four consecutive singles from Jackie Tavener, Glenn Myatt, Johnny Miljus, and Eddie Morgan. Joe Sewell finished the rally with a three-run homer. The nine runs tied a major league record for "most runs scored in the ninth inning with two out." The Yanks won the opener 12–0.

August 11 Willis Hudlin gives up Babe Ruth's 500th career home run during a 6–5 Indians win over the Yankees at League Park.

Hudlin was 17–15 with a 3.34 ERA in 1929.

August 13 A two-out, two-run, walk-off triple by Johnny Hodapp in the ninth inning beats the Yankees 3–2 at League Park.

August 14 The Indians collect 20 hits but score only three runs during a 17-inning, 5–3 loss to the Athletics at League Park. Cleveland left 23 runners on base as Lefty Grove pitched a complete game for the A's. In what would prove to be the only game of his major eague career, Dan Jessee was a pinch-runner for Grover Hartley in the eighth inning.

SEPTEMBER 1 Ken Holloway pitches a two-hitter to defeat the White Sox 5–0 at Comiskey Park. The only Chicago hits were singles by Alex Metzler and Willie Kamm.

SEPTEMBER 19 Joe Sewell strikes out for the first time since May 17, 1929. The pitcher was Milt Gaston of the Red Sox during a 3–2 Indians loss in Boston. Sewell set a major league record for most consecutive games (115) and most consecutive at-bats (437447) without striking out.

SEPTEMBER 25 Glenn Myatt hits a two-out, three-run, ninth-inning home run over the right field wall to beat the White Sox 9–7 at League Park.

SEPTEMBER 28 All American League games are postponed out of respect for Yankee manager Miller Huggins, who was buried that day in Cincinnati. Huggins died three days earlier of blood poisoning.

SEPTEMBER 29 A month to the day before the historic stock market crash, which starts the country on the road to the Great Depression, Wes Ferrell records his 20th win of the season with a two-hitter and a 4–0 defeat of the Browns at League Park. The only two St. Louis hits were singles by Red Kress and opposing pitcher George Blaeholder.

At the start of the 1929 season, Ferrell was 21-years-old and had pitched in just three big league games. He began the year in the bullpen but by June was in the starting rotation. Ferrell ended the 1929 campaign with a 21–10 record and a 3.60 ERA in addition to leading the club in saves with five. It was the first of six seasons in which he won 20 or games. Four of those came consecutively with Cleveland from 1929 through 1932 in which he posted a cumulative record of 91–48. His hot temper often got him in trouble with management, however. Ferrell was suspended for ten days in 1932 when he refused to come out of a game for a reliever. Overall, he was 102–62 as an Indian before a trade to the Red Sox in May 1934 after a protracted holdout. Ferrell's .622 winning percentage with the club ranks fifth among Indians pitchers with at least 100 decisions.

THE STATE OF THE INDIANS

Nine of the ten teams fielded in Cleveland during the 1930s had winning records. The only one that failed finished a scant one game below .500. Overall, the Indians had a record of 824–708, which was the second best in the American League. However, the winning percentage of .538 posted by the franchise during the decade, was far behind the Yankees, who were 970–554 (.636). Despite the collection of winning records, the Indians were never serious pennant contenders. The 1935 team ended the season 12 games out of first place, the closest the Indians came to the top of the league. AL champions were the Athletics (1930 and 1931), Yankees (1932, 1936, 1937, 1938 and 1939), Senators (1933) and Tigers (1934 and 1935).

THE BEST TEAM

The best club in terms of winning percentage was in 1932, when the Indians were 87–65 (.572) under Roger Peckinpaugh.

THE WORST TEAM

The worst season was a year after the best one, when the Indians were 75–76 in 1933 and Roger Peckinpaugh was replaced by Walter Johnson. The fact that just 11½ games separated the best and worst clubs during the 1930s speaks volumes about the rut the Indians found themselves in during the decade of the Great Depression.

THE BEST MOMENT

The first of five All-Star Games to be played in Cleveland occurred on July 8, 1935. The American League won 4–1 before 69,831 at Municipal Stadium.

THE WORST MOMENT

Johnny Allen pitched a game on June 7, 1938, wearing an old tattered undershirt. When the umpire ordered Allen to remove it because it was distracting the hitters, Allen refused and walked off the mound.

THE ALL-DECADE TEAM • YEARS W/INDIANS

Frankie Pytlak, c	1932–40
Hal Trosky, 1b	1933–41
Johnny Hodapp, 2b	1925–32
Odell Hale, 3b	1931, 1933–40
Billy Knickerbocker, ss	1933–36
Joe Vosmik, lf	1930–36
Earl Averill, cf	1929–39
Dick Porter, rf	1929–34
Mel Harder, p	1928–47
Wes Ferrell, p	1927–33
Willie Hudlin, p	1926–40
Bob Feller, p	1936–41, 1945–56

Feller and Averill are Hall of Famers. Harder and Ferrell also deserve plaques at Cooperstown. Other outstanding Indians of the 1930s included right fielder Bruce Campbell (1935–39), catcher Rollie Hemsley (1938–41), and pitchers Johnny Allen (1936–40), Clint Brown (1928–35, 1941–42), and Oral Hildebrand (1931–36).

THE DECADE LEADERS

Batting Avg:	Earl Averill	.321
On-Base Pct:	Earl Averill	.399
Slugging Pct:	Earl Averill	.542
Home Runs:	Earl Averill	208
RBIs:	Earl Averill	988
Runs:	Earl Averill	1,044
Stolen Bases:	Earl Averill	42
Wins:	Mel Harder	158
Strikeouts:	Mel Harder	802
ERA:	Bob Feller	3.43
Saves:	Willis Hudlin	23

THE HOME FIELD

The Indians went from playing in the second smallest ballpark in the major leagues to the largest in 1932 by moving from League Park (with a seating capacity of only 21,000) to Municipal Stadium (holding 78,189 permanent seats). The Indians first game on the lakefront was held on July 31, 1932, before 80,184. Despite the tremendous crowd at the inaugural, the expected attendance increase at the new facility failed to materialize, and the Indians pulled out of Municipal Stadium after the 1933 season and returned to League Park. For the next three years, Municipal Stadium was utilized only for the 1935 All-Star Game and one regular season contest in 1936. From 1937 through 1947, the Indians had two ballparks. Municipal Stadium was used generally for weekends, holidays, and night games with the rest of the schedule played at League Park. Night games at the stadium began in 1939 following the addition of lights on the roof.

THE GAME YOU WISH YOU HAD SEEN

Making his first major league start at the age of 17, Bob Feller struck out 15 batters during a 4–1 victory over the Browns at League Park August 23, 1936.

THE WAY THE GAME WAS PLAYED

The offensive explosion that changed baseball during the 1920s continued throughout the 1930s. Batting averages in the AL floated around .280, with a peak of .289 in 1936, when teams in the circuit averaged 5.7 runs per game. In 1930, there were more home runs than stolen bases in the American League for the first time.

THE MANAGEMENT

Alva Bradley, who became president of the Indians in November 1927, headed the franchise throughout the 1930s. General managers were Billy Evans (1927–35) and Cy Slapnicka (1935–41). Field managers were Roger Peckinpaugh (1928–33), Bibb Falk (1933), Walter Johnson (1933–35), Steve O'Neill (1935–37), and Ossie Vitt (1938–40).

THE BEST PLAYER MOVE

The best move was the signing of 17-year-old pitching phenom Bob Feller in 1936. The Indians scouting staff, under the direction of Cy Slapnicka, also signed Lou Boudreau, Bob Lemon, Ken Keltner, Hal Trosky, and Jeff Heath during the 1930s.

THE WORST PLAYER MOVE

The worst move was the trade of Wes Ferrell and Dick Porter to the Red Sox for Bob Weiland and Bob Seeds and cash on May 24, 1934.

1930

Season in a Sentence

The Indians are in first place in mid-June, but like 1929, finish the year with 81 wins and a distant third-place finish.

Finish • Won • Lost • Pct • GB

Finish	Won	Lost	Pct	GB
Third	81	73	.526	19.0

Manager

Roger Peckinpaugh

Stats

Stats	Indians	AL	Rank
Batting Avg:	.304	.288	2
On-Base Pct:	.364	.351	4
Slugging Pct:	.431	.421	3
Home Runs:	72		4
Stolen Bases:	51		7
ERA:	4.88		7
Fielding Avg:	.962	.965	7
Runs Scored:	890		4
Runs Allowed:	915		8

Starting Line-up

Luke Sewell, c
Eddie Morgan, 1b
Johnny Hodapp, 2b
Joe Sewell, 3b
Jonah Goldman, ss
Charlie Jamieson, lf
Earl Averill, cf
Dick Porter, rf
Bob Seeds, lf
Glenn Myatt, c
Bibb Falk, rf
Ed Montague, ss
Johnny Burnett, 3b-ss

Pitchers

Wes Ferrell, sp
Willis Hudlin, sp
Clint Brown, sp
Mel Harder, sp-rp
Pete Jablonowksi, rp
Jake Miller, rp-sp
Milt Shoffner, rp-sp

Attendance

528,657 (fifth in AL)

Club Leaders

Batting Avg:	Johnny Hodapp	.354
On-Base Pct:	Dick Porter	.420
Slugging Pct:	Eddie Morgan	.601
Home Runs:	Eddie Morgan	26
RBIs:	Eddie Morgan	136
Runs:	Eddie Morgan	122
Stolen Bases:	Earl Averill	10
Wins:	Wes Ferrell	25
Strikeouts:	Wes Ferrell	143
ERA:	Wes Ferrell	3.31
Saves:	Wes Ferrell	3

April 15 The scheduled season opener against the White Sox in Chicago is postponed by rain. The April 16 contest was also rained out.

April 17 The Indians get the 1930 season underway, but lose 8–7 in ten innings to the White Sox at Comiskey Park. Cleveland led 4–0 before Chicago scored six runs in the sixth inning, but the Indians rallied to send the game into extra innings. Dick Porter collected three hits, including a double, and Earl Averill drove in three runs.

Porter was 27 when he made his big league debut in 1929 and had a career year in 1930, batting .350 with 100 runs scored and 43 doubles. He earned the nicknames of "Twitchy" and "Wiggles" because of his gyrations at the plate in an attempt to relax.

April 20 A two-run, pinch-single by Johnny Burnett in the seventh inning accounts for the only runs in a 2–0 win over the Tigers in Detroit. Willis Hudlin pitched the shutout.

April 23 In the home opener, the Indians lose 4–3 to the White Sox at League Park. Despite the loss, the Indians set an American League record (since tied) for most hits by pinch-hitters in a game with four. The pinch-hits were collected by Earl Averill, Bibb Falk, Johnny Burnett, and Glenn Myatt.

Averill was out of the starting line-up that day because of a twisted ankle he suffered a few days earlier when he stepped on a ball during batting practice. By the time the season ended, he had a .339 batting average, 19 homers, 119 runs-batted-in, and 102 runs scored.

April 26 The Indians score seven runs in the first inning and defeat the Tigers 11–4 in Cleveland.

May 2 Joe Sewell's playing streak comes to an end at 1,103 games. He missed an 8–3 win over the Red Sox in Boston because of a high fever.

Sewell's streak began in September 1922. From the start of his career in 1920 through April 30, 1930, Sewell played in 1,416 of the Indians 1,419 games. The only playing streaks in major league history longer than Sewell's 1,103 are by Cal Ripken (2,632), Lou Gehrig (2,130), Everett Scott (1,307), Steve Garvey (1,207), Miguel Tejada (1,152) and Billy Williams (1,117). The only other Indian to play in at least 500 consecutive games is Earl Averill, who appeared in 673 in a row from 1930 through 1935.

May 4 Trailing 7–2, the Indians score five runs in the ninth inning and one in the tenth to stun the Red Sox 8–7 at Braves Field in Boston. Luke Sewell started the five-run ninth with a double and drove in the winning tally in the tenth by stroking a single. Charlie Jamieson provided another key blow with a three-run homer that tied the score 7–7.

Sunday games were illegal in Boston until 1929. From 1929 through 1932, the Red Sox used Braves Field, home of the Boston Braves, for Sunday contests. Because of local statutes, the Sox couldn't use Fenway Park on Sundays because the ballpark was too close to a church.

May 11 The Indians wallop the defending world champion Athletics 25–7 before an overflow crowd of 29,000 at League Park. Ground rules were necessary because several thousand fans stood along the left and center field walls. Balls hit into the crowd were doubles. There were 11 two-baggers in the game, nine of them by the Indians. The Indians scored all 25 runs in the first seven innings, seven of them in the fourth. Cleveland collected 25 hits in all. Bibb Falk was 5-for-5 with three doubles and two singles. He also drove in five runs.

The game was played in Cleveland on a Sunday in between Saturday and Monday games in Philadelphia because Sunday games in Pennsylvania were illegal until 1934. The large crowd at League Park justified the expense of sending the clubs on the round trip by train.

May 12 Indians pitcher Milt Shoffner sets a major league record (since tied) for most balks in an inning with three in the third inning of a 13–7 loss to the Athletics in Philadelphia.

May 26 Facing White Sox pitcher Pat Caraway, Joe Sewell strikes out twice during a 5–3 Cleveland win in the second game of a double header at League Park. Sewell fanned in only one other at-bat all season in 414 plate appearances. The only other time during his 14-year career that Sewell struck out twice in a game was against Cy Warmoth of the Senators in 1923.

The 1930 campaign was Sewell's last as an Indian. He was released at the end of the season to make way for a youth movement. Sewell played three more major league seasons with the Yankees and was their starting third baseman on the 1932 world championship club.

JUNE 5 The Indians score nine runs in the first inning of a 17–7 trouncing of the Red Sox at League Park. Cleveland batters collected 25 hits during the afternoon.

JUNE 6 Wes Ferrell wins his own game with a walk-off single in the ninth inning to defeat the Senators 3–2 at League Park.

JUNE 13 The Indians move into first place with a 15–2 thrashing of the Athletics at League Park. Cleveland scored seven runs in the sixth. Wes Ferrell recorded his tenth win of the season.

Following the victory, the Indians had a record of 32–19. The stay at the top of the American League standings lasted only two days, however. Beginning on June 14, the Indians had a stretch of 20 losses in 23 games to fall hopelessly out of the race.

JUNE 18 Wes Ferrell gives up consecutive homers to Al Simmons, Jimmie Foxx, and Bing Miller in the fifth inning of a 7–2 loss to the Athletics at League Park.

JUNE 19 Johnny Hodapp runs his hitting streak to 22 games during a 4–3 loss to the Athletics in Philadelphia.

JUNE 25 The Senators score ten runs in the second inning and wallop the Indians 13–5 in Washington.

On the same day, the construction of Municipal Stadium began. Though original estimates said the project would take 18 months to complete, it was open for business on July 2, 1931, six months ahead of schedule.

JULY 20 Eddie Morgan hits a two-run homer in the ninth inning to defeat the Yankees 9–8 at League Park. The ball cleared the right field wall and landed on the roof of a house across the street.

Morgan became the first Indians player to hit at least 20 homers in a season. He finished the 1930 campaign with 26 homers, 136 RBIs, 122 runs scored, 47 doubles, and a .349 batting average.

JULY 22 The Indians sweep the Yankees 6–5 and 10–8 in a double header at League Park. Down 5–0 in the opener, the Indians rallied to win with four runs in the fourth inning and two in the ninth. New York manager Bob Shawkey was honored before the game by a delegation of fans from his hometown of Brookville, Pennsylvania. In addition to watching his club lose twice, Shawkey was ejected in the second game for arguing with the umpires.

JULY 25 The Athletics pull off two triple steals during a 14–1 hammering of the Indians at League Park. It is the only time in major league history that a club had two triple steals in one game. The Cleveland battery was pitcher Pete Jablonowski and catcher Joe Sprinz.

Manager Roger Peckinpaugh shakes hand with Cleveland's young ace Wes Ferrell, who won twenty-five games for the team in 1930.

Sprinz lasted only 21 games as a major leaguer, batting .170. In 1939, while playing for the San Francisco Seals in the Pacific Coast League, Sprinz was badly injured during a publicity stunt. Sprinz tried to catch a ball dropped 1,000 feet from a blimp over Treasure Island. The ball glanced off his glove, broke his jaw, and knocked out four teeth.

July 28 A two-run, walk-off double by Dick Porter off Tiger pitcher Chief Hogsett lifts the Indians to a 7–6 win at League Park. Hogsett homered in the top of the ninth to break a 5–5 tie.

July 29 Trailing 4–0, the Indians score seven runs in the second inning and five in the third, defeating the Tigers 14–7 at League Park. Earl Averill smacked a home run and a double in the second. Eddie Morgan collected five hits, including two doubles, in five at-bats.

July 31 A two-out, two-run, walk-off home run by Eddie Morgan defeats the Tigers 5–3 at League Park.

August 9 The Indians sweep the Senators 13–7 and 4–2 in Washington.

August 10 The Senators break open a close game by piling up 11 runs in the eighth inning to defeat the Indians 18–6 in Washington. All 11 runs were scored off Pete Jablonowski on seven hits, four walks, and two wild pitches.

An accomplished pianist and college bandleader at the University of Michigan, Jablonowski played for the Indians from 1930 through 1932 during a major league career in which he played for seven clubs from 1927 until 1945. He was truly a player to be named later. From 1927 through 1933, Pete was known by his birth name of Peter William Jablonowski. After the 1933 season, he changed his name to Pete Appleton.

August 14 Wes Ferrell records his 20th win of the season with a 15–0 bashing of the Athletics in Philadelphia. The Indians collected 20 hits in the contest.

The Indians had a strange season series against the Athletics, a club in the second year of a three-year run as AL champions. Cleveland was 7–15 against the A's in 1930, yet won games by scores of 25–7, 15–2 and 15–0.

August 21 Dick Porter's inside-the-park homer in the 12th inning beats the Yankees 6–5 in New York.

August 29 Clint Brown pitches 12 shutout innings before allowing three runs in the 13th to lose 3–0 to the White Sox at League Park. Pat Caraway pitched a complete game shutout for Chicago, allowing just three hits.

Even though this game didn't count officially as a shutout, Brown tied for the AL lead in the category with three in 1930. He showed his inconsistency, however, by finishing the season with an 11–13 record and a 4.97 ERA. A native of Blackash, Pennsylvania, Brown was a finesse pitcher who could throw underhand, sidearm, or with a three-quarters motion depending upon the situation. He was 60–65 in ten seasons (1928–35 and 1941–42) in Cleveland.

August 30 The Indians score three runs in the ninth inning to defeat the White Sox 7–6 at League Park. Johnny Hodapp drove in the winning run with a single.

August 31 Trailing 6–5, the Indians score ten runs in the seventh inning and rout the Browns 17–6 in St. Louis. Johnny Hodapp and Eddie Morgan both hit a home run and a single in the inning.

September 1 The Indians celebrate Labor Day by sweeping the Browns 13–8 and 9–5 in a double header in St. Louis. Dick Porter hit a grand slam in the opener. The second game was called by darkness after eight innings. Wes Ferrell was the winning pitcher in the nightcap. It was his 24th victory of the season and his 13th in a row.

September 6 Wes Ferrell's 13-game winning streak ends with a 2–1 loss to the White Sox in the first game of a double header in Chicago. The winning pitcher was future Hall of Famer Ted Lyons. Cleveland won the second tilt 4–2.

Ferrell's winning streak is the third longest in Indians history, trailing only Johnny Allen (15 in 1937) and Gaylord Perry (15 in 1974). In 1930, Ferrell had a record of 25–13 and an ERA of 3.31 in 296⅔ innings. He completed 25 of his 35 starts and also recorded three saves in eight relief appearances.

September 17 Earl Averill has one the greatest days of any hitter in Indians history with four runs and 11 runs-batted-in during a double header against the Senators at League Park. He had three homers and eight RBIs in the opener, as the Indians overcame a 6–0 deficit to win 13–7. Averill thus became the first player in Indians history with three homers in a game. Two of his homers were struck against Bump Hadley with the third off of the delivery of Firpo Marberry. The three homers were hit in consecutive at-bats. One of them was a grand slam. Averill just missed his fourth home run of the game in his last at-bat when a long fly was foul by a few feet. He then grounded out. On his first trip to the plate in the second game, Averill hit a three-run homer off Lloyd Brown. Averill later doubled, but the Indians lost 6–4.

Averill is one of only two Cleveland players with four home runs in one day. The other was Rocky Colavito, who homered four times in a single game on June 10, 1959.

September 28 On the final day of the season, the Indians lose 11–5 and win 15–5 during a double header against the Browns at League Park.

1931

Season in a Sentence

In a year of ups and downs, the Indians lose 12 in a row and win ten in succession during a four-week period in May and June before settling two games above .500 at the end of the season.

Finish • Won • Lost • Pct • GB

Finish	Won	Lost	Pct	GB
Fourth	78	76	.506	30.0

Manager

Roger Peckinpaugh

Stats

Stats	Indians	AL	Rank
Batting Avg:	.296	.278	2
On-Base Pct:	.363	.344	2
Slugging Pct:	.419	.398	3
Home Runs:	71		4
Stolen Bases:	63		6
ERA:	4.63	4.38	6
Fielding Avg:	.963	.968	7
Runs Scored:	885		2
Runs Allowed:	833		5

Starting Line-up

Luke Sewell, c
Eddie Morgan, 1b
Johnny Hodapp, 2b
Willie Kamm, 3b
Johnny Burnett, ss-2b
Joe Vosmik, lf
Earl Averill, cf
Dick Porter, rf
Ed Montague, ss
Glenn Myatt, c
Bibb Falk, rf

Pitchers

Wes Ferrell, sp
Willis Hudlin, sp
Clint Brown, sp-rp
Mel Harder, sp
Sarge Connolly, sp-rp
Pete Jablonowski, rp

Attendance

483,027 (fourth in AL)

Club Leaders

Batting Avg:	Eddie Morgan	.351
On-Base Pct:	Eddie Morgan	.451
Slugging Pct:	Earl Averill	.576
Home Runs:	Earl Averill	32
RBIs:	Earl Averill	143
Runs:	Earl Averill	140
Stolen Bases:	Willie Kamm	13
Wins:	Wes Ferrell	22
Strikeouts:	Wes Ferrell	123
ERA:	Wes Ferrell	3.75
Saves:	Willie Hudlin	4

March 25 Three weeks after Congress adopts "The Star-Spangled Banner" as the National Anthem, Alva Bradley gives controversial Louisiana governor Huey Long one share of Indians stock. The Indians held spring training in New Orleans from 1916 through 1920 and again from 1928 through 1939. The New Orleans team in the Southern Association was also a Cleveland farm club.

April 14 The Indians open the season with a 5–4 win over the White Sox before 25,162 at League Park. The Indians scored twice in the eighth inning to take the lead. Wes Ferrell pitched a complete game and drove in two runs with a pair of singles. Lew Fonseca collected three hits.

April 18 Two weeks after celebrating his 21st birthday, rookie left fielder Joe Vosmik collects a triple, three doubles, and a single in five at-bats during an 11–2 trouncing of the White Sox at League Park.

A native of Cleveland and a favorite of the club's female fans with his blond hair and strikingly good looks, Vosmik debuted in 1930, playing nine games in September. He started the 1931 season with 14 hits, including a home run, two triples and five doubles, in his first 22 at-bats. Vosmik finished the season with a .320 average and 117 RBIs. He played for Cleveland for seven seasons, and compiled a batting average of .313.

APRIL 28 The Indians win an odd 10–9 decision in ten innings over the Browns at League Park. Cleveland led 6–1 before St. Louis exploded for eight runs in the top of the ninth inning to take a 9–6 advantage. The Indians rebounded with three runs in the bottom of the ninth and one in the tenth for the victory. Pinch-hitter Glenn Myatt drove in the winning run with a walk-off single.

APRIL 29 Wes Ferrell pitches a no-hitter, defeating the Browns 9–0 at League Park. Ferrell also drove in four runs with a home run in the second inning, a single in the fourth and a two-run double in the eighth. The home run was struck with Ferrell's brother Rick, the St. Louis catcher, calling the pitch from Browns hurler Dolly Gray. Rick was hitless in three at-bats but reached base in the eighth on an error by shortstop Bill Hunnefield, who made a great stop in the hole but threw wildly to first. Wes fanned eight batters and walked three. In the ninth, Jack Burns grounded out to second baseman Johnny Hodapp. Goose Goslin walked, and Red Kress struck out. The final out was recorded when Frank Schulte hit a grounder to Hodapp.

Ferrell was 22–12 in 1931 with a 3.75 earned run average in 276⅓ innings. He led the league in complete games with 27 in 35 starts.

MAY 17 The Indians trade Lew Fonseca to the White Sox for Willie Kamm.

Kamm made his major league debut with the White Sox in 1923, and was the club's regular third baseman until his trade to Cleveland. He continued in the role with the Indians until 1935. Although barely adequate as a hitter, Kamm kept a starting job as one of the best defensive players of his generation. He led AL third baseman eight times in fielding average, eight times in total chances per games, seven in putouts, four in assists and three in double plays.

MAY 21 The Indians lose their twelfth game in a row, dropping a 7–6 decision to the Yankees at League Park.

The last 11 losses of the 12-game streak were at home. The 12-game losing streak is a club record.

MAY 23 The 12-game losing streak comes to an end with a 10–5 win over the White Sox at League Park. Earl Averill starred with three doubles and a home run in four at-bats.

Averill hit .333 for the Indians in 1931 in addition to collecting 140 runs, 209 hits, 36 doubles, ten triples, 32 home runs, and 143 RBIs. He was the first player in franchise history to hit at least 30 home runs in a season.

MAY 26 The Indians sweep the Browns 12–0 and 4–2 at League Park.

MAY 27 The Indians score four runs in the ninth inning to win 5–4 against the Browns at League Park. Johnny Burnett drove in the winning run with a single.

MAY 29 Willie Kamm steals four bases during a 9–2 win over the Tigers in Detroit.

JUNE 2 The Indians survive a five-run Red Sox rally in the ninth inning to win 12–11 in Boston. Cleveland broke a 3–3 tie with eight runs in the sixth inning. It was the club's eighth win in a row.

JUNE 3 Joe Vosmik hits a home run in the 11th inning to beat the Red Sox 5–4 at Boston.

JUNE 4 The Indians record their tenth win in a row with a 10–2 decision over the Red Sox in Boston.

JUNE 8 Held to one hit through eight innings by Red Ruffing, the Indians explode for four runs in the ninth inning to defeat the Yankees 4–1 in New York. The rally consisted of a single by Johnny Hodapp, triples from Dick Porter and Glenn Myatt, and Earl Averill's home run.

JUNE 23 The Indians shut down the Red Sox 13–0 and 10–0 at League Park. The sweep set a club record for most runs scored in a double-header shutout. Clint Brown pitched the shutout in the opener. The Indians scored eight runs in the seventh inning. In the second tilt, Willis Hudlin tossed a one-hitter. The lone Boston hit was a single by Earl Webb. Earl Averill collected seven hits, including two doubles, in ten at-bats during the twin bill.

JUNE 29 The Indians sweep the Yankees 15–6 and 4–2 during a double header at League Park. Cleveland scored eight runs in the fifth inning of the first game.

JULY 2 The Indians score seven runs in the sixth inning of a 12–4 victory over the Athletics at League Park.

On the same day, Municipal Stadium opened to the public. Clevelanders were invited for free tours, beginning at noon. Formal dedication of the facility took place at 8:00 p.m. City officials anticipated a crowd of 75,000 would come to the opening festivities, but only 8,000 showed up.

JULY 3 The first sporting event takes place at Municipal Stadium with a boxing match between Max Schmeling and Young Stripling for the heavyweight championship of the world. Schmeling retained his title with a technical knockout in the 15th round. With seats placed on the field around the ring, capacity for the event was 110,000, but the crowd was only 36,936. Ticket prices were $25, $12.50, and $5.49.

JULY 6 The Indians score eight runs in the sixth inning of a 13–4 win over the Tigers at League Park. It was expected that this would be the last game played at League Park. The Indians were expected to play at Municipal Stadium beginning on July 26 following a long road trip, but that plan failed to occur (see July 13, 1931).

JULY 8 The Indians score five runs in the 11th inning and defeat the White Sox 10–6 in Chicago. Relief pitcher Willis Hudlin broke the 5–5 tie with an RBI-single.

JULY 11 Earl Averill hits two home runs, the second in the 11th inning, to lead the Indians to a 7–4 victory over the White Sox in Chicago.

JULY 13 The Indians announce that they will not be playing in Municipal Stadium in 1931. Plans to play the defending world champion Philadelphia Athletics at the stadium on July 26 were spiked when City Council voted against the lease drawn up between Indians management and City Manager Daniel Morgan. Problems developed over the amount for rent, cleaning, and maintenance the ball club would pay. Indians president Alva Bradley said that the club had submitted its final offer and would make no more concessions. Bradley further intimated the club might build a ballpark of its own. The Indians would not play in the new stadium until July 31, 1932.

JULY 14 Going from one extreme to the other, the Indians lose 19–2 and win 5–1 during a double header against the Yankees in New York.

JULY 26 The Indians wallop the Athletics 13–2 at League Park. The A's entered the game with a 13-game winning streak. Johnny Burnett collected five hits, including a double, in six at-bats. Earl Averill contributed a homer, triple, and double.

JULY 29 Wes Ferrell allows ten hits and walks five, but defeats the Senators 6–0 at Griffith Stadium. Washington stranded 15 runners.

AUGUST 2 The Indians sweep the Browns 9–4 and 11–9 in St. Louis.

AUGUST 12 In a reversal of fortune, the Indians lose 18–1 to the Yankees in the first game of a double header at League Park, but win the second tilt 17–7. Cleveland scored eight runs in the seventh inning of the nightcap.

AUGUST 14 The Indians wallop the Yankees 12–7 and 9–1 during a double header at League Park. Earl Averill hit a grand slam off Red Ruffing in the fourth inning of the first game.

AUGUST 19 The Indians win two games from the Senators by scores of 10–5 and 10–8 at League Park.

AUGUST 20 The Indians score ten runs for the third game in a row, defeating the Senators 10–8 at League Park.

AUGUST 28 Eddie Morgan scores five runs during a 12–1 triumph over the Browns at League Park.

Morgan hit .351 with 11 homers for the Indians in 1931.

AUGUST 31 Wes Ferrell clubs two homers during a 15–5 win over the White Sox in Chicago. Ferrell also contributed a single, drove in five runs, and scored four.

Ferrell was one of the best hitting pitchers of all-time. He finished his career with 38 home runs. Of those, one was as a pinch-hitter. The remaining 37 came while in the game as pitcher, which gave him the major league record for the position. Ferrell also posted a batting average of .280 and a slugging percentage of .448 in 1,176 big league at-bats. He clubbed nine homers in 1931, a record for pitchers in a single season. Ferrell doesn't hold the Indians record for career homers by a pitcher, however. He hit 21 for the club from 1927 through 1933. The Indians record is held by Bob Lemon, who had 35 home runs as a pitcher and two as a pinch-hitter.

September 6 The Indians down the Browns 7–5 and 12–2 in a double header in St. Louis.

September 7 The Indians take two from the White Sox 6–2 and 5–2 at League Park.

September 8 The Indians sweep their third double header in three days and extend their winning streak to eight games, beating the White Sox 8–7 and 6–3 at League Park.

September 14 The Indians and Athletics combine for an American League record 12 double plays during a double header in Philadelphia. The A's completed nine of the double plays. The Indians won the first game 6–2, but lost the second 9–7.

September 26 Wes Ferrell records his 22nd win of 1931 with a 7–5 decision over the Tigers at League Park.

1932

Season in a Sentence

The Indians play their first game at Municipal Stadium and draw over 80,000 to the event, but with the country in the depths of the Great Depression, the season attendance figures drop despite the team's posting the best winning percentage in 11 years.

Finish • Won • Lost • Pct • GB

Finish	Won	Lost	Pct	GB
Fourth	87	65	.572	19.0

Manager

Roger Peckinpaugh

Stats

Stats	Indians	AL	Rank
Batting Avg:	.285	.277	3
On-Base Pct:	.356	.346	3
Slugging Pct:	.413	.404	3
Home Runs	78		5
Stolen Bases:	52		6
ERA:	4.12	4.48	2
Fielding Avg:	.969	.969	5
Runs Scored:	845		3
Runs Allowed:	747		3

Starting Line-up

Luke Sewell, c
Eddie Morgan, 1b
Bill Cissell, 2b
Willie Kamm, 3b
Johnny Burnett, ss
Joe Vosmik, lf
Earl Averill, cf
Dick Porter, rf
Glenn Myatt, c
Ed Montague, ss

Pitchers

Wes Ferrell, sp
Clint Brown, sp
Mel Harder, sp
Willis Hudlin, sp-rp
Oral Hildebrand, sp-rp
Jack Russell, sp-rp
Sarge Connally, rp

Attendance

468,953 (second in AL)

Club Leaders

Batting Avg:	Bill Cissell	.314
On-Base Pct:	Eddie Morgan	.402
Slugging Pct:	Earl Averill	.569
Home Runs:	Earl Averill	32
RBIs:	Earl Averill	124
Runs:	Earl Averill	116
Stolen Bases:	Bill Cissell	18
Wins:	Wes Ferrell	23
Strikeouts:	Wes Ferrell	105
ERA:	Wes Ferrell	3.66
Saves:	Sarge Connally	3

April 12 — Six weeks after the kidnapping of the Lindbergh baby, the Indians season opener against the Tigers in Detroit is postponed by cold weather.

April 13 — In the season opener, the Indians defeat the Tigers 6–5 in 11 innings in Detroit. Wes Ferrell pitched a complete game. Earl Averill drove in the winning run with a single, scoring Dick Porter.

April 20 — In the home opener, the Indians lose 2–1 to the Tigers before 22,995 at League Park.

April 24 — Earl Averill drives in seven runs with two homers and a double during a 14–3 runaway victory over the Browns at St. Louis.

On the same day, the Indians traded Johnny Hodapp and Bob Seeds to the White Sox for Bill Cissell and Jim Moore. Cissell was purchased by the White Sox from Portland of the Pacific Coast League in 1928 for $123,000, then a record price for a minor leaguer. He never panned out in Chicago, however. Cissell gave the Indians one good season, batting .320, before descending back into mediocrity and was sent packing after batting .230 in 1933. Alcoholism was a cause for Cissell's failure to live up to expectations. He was destitute and suffering from malnutrition when he died in 1949 of a heart attack at the age of 45 in a Chicago rooming house.

April 30 — After spotting the White Sox a 5–0 lead, the Indians roar back to win 10–7 at League Park. A bases-loaded double by Eddie Morgan in the eighth inning broke a 7–7 tie.

Averill hit .314 with 32 homers, 124 RBIs, 116 runs scored, and 198 hits in 1932.

May 1 — The Indians score seven runs in the eighth inning and defeat the White Sox 11–1 at League Park. It was Cleveland's eighth win in a row.

May 2 — The Indians record their ninth win in a row with a 6–5 decision over the Browns at League Park.

May 20 — The Indians break a 2–2 tie with seven runs in the fourth inning and defeat the Browns 11–7 at League Park.

May 30 — The Indians wallop the White Sox 12–6 and 12–11 in a double header at League Park. In the second game, Cleveland trailed 11–5 before scoring two runs in the seventh inning, one in the eighth, and four in the ninth.

The White Sox had been jawing with umpire George Moriarty all day. After the second game, Moriarty offered to fight the Sox one by one, and twice punched Milt Gaston. In turn, Gaston, fellow players Charlie Berry and Frank Grube and manager Lew Fonseca set upon Moriarty and pummeled him. The umpire was hospitalized with a broken hand (from punching Gaston), bruises, and spike wounds.

June 10 — The Indians trade Pete Jablonowski to the Red Sox for Jack Russell.

June 15 Joe Vosmik drives in six runs with a triple, double, and two singles during a 9–3 victory over the Red Sox at League Park.

July 9 In his only major league appearance, Indians pitcher Leo Moon allows seven earned runs in 5⅔ innings of relief during a 14–4 loss to the Senators in the second game of a double header in Washington. Cleveland won the opener 4–1.

Moon was the only left-hander to pitch for the Indians in 1932. Cleveland southpaws accounted for only 81⅓ innings in 1931, 5⅔ innings in 1932, and 17⅓ innings in 1933.

July 10 Johnny Burnett collects nine hits and Jimmie Foxx of the Athletics clouts three homers into the distant left-field bleachers among his six base hits, as Philadelphia defeats the Indians 18–17 in 18 innings at League Park. It was one of the strangest games in big league history. With Sunday baseball illegal in Philadelphia, the Indians interrupted a swing through the East, and the Athletics a long home stand, to travel to Cleveland to take advantage of what figured to be a large gate. The previous day, the Indians played a double header in Washington. To cut down on train fare, A's manager Connie Mack brought only 15 players, two of them pitchers, to Cleveland, and also left starting catcher Mickey Cochrane behind for a rest. The Indians scored three runs in the first inning to take a 2–2 lead, and Mack lifted starting pitcher Lew Krausse for Eddie Rommel, which meant that Rommel had to stay on the mound for the remainder of the game with the rest of the staff back in Philadelphia. To make matters worse, Rommel pitched batting practice as well. As events unfolded, he had to pitch 17 innings. The A's scored seven runs in the top of the seventh to take a 12–8 advantage, but Cleveland came back with six in the bottom half to move ahead 14–13. Philadelphia took the lead again with two in the ninth, but the Indians tied it 15–15 with a tally in their half. Both teams scored twice in the 16th. The Athletics finally won the game with the run in the 18th on a single by Foxx and a double by Eric McNair that took a freak hop over the head of left fielder Joe Vosmik. Wes Ferrell, who pitched 11⅓ innings of relief, was the losing pitcher. The game was completed in four hours and five minutes. It was a record-setting day. Burnett's nine hits set a mark for most hits in a game. The Indians had 33 hits in all, a modern (post-1900) record for a team. Cleveland also tied a record for most players with five or more hits with three. Earl Averill was 5-for-9 and Joe Vosmik 5-for-11. The 29 hits allowed by Rommel is a modern record for a pitcher in a game, along with surrendering 14 runs, yet emerged as the winning pitcher. Jimmie Foxx had six hits and Al Simmons five to mark the only time that five or more players have had at least five hits in a contest. The 58 hits by the two clubs is also a big league mark. The combined 85 total bases (45 by Cleveland) is an American League record. The Indians left 24 men on base, one short of the present-day record.

Burnett etched his name into the record books with nine hits on seven singles and two doubles in 11 at-bats. No one in big league history has collected more than seven hits in a contest. Otherwise, Burnett had a nondescript career. He hit .284 and had 521 base hits over nine seasons with the Indians and Browns. The victory was the last of Rommel's career. He finished with a record of 171–119. From 1938 through 1959, Rommel was an American League umpire.

July 11 In Philadelphia, Earl Averill hits three homers and three singles in ten at-bats during a 9–8 and 12–7 double header sweep of the Athletics.

Over a three-day span, the Indians played 54 innings in five games in three different cities with a double header in Washington on July 9, the 18-inning contest versus the Athletics on July 10 in Cleveland, and the twin bill facing the A's on July 11 in Philadelphia.

JULY 27 The Indians sweep the Yankees 2–1 and 12–10 during a double header at League Park. Cleveland trailed 9–4 in the third inning of the nightcap before mounting a comeback. The club broke a 10–10 tie with two runs in the eighth. The second game win was accomplished despite being out hit 21–9. Yankee pitchers walked 14 batters.

The two wins placed the Indians in second place 7½ games behind the Yankees, giving fans a brief flicker of hope for a pennant. Cleveland failed to pull any closer to the top, however.

JULY 30 In what was anticipated to be the last game at League Park, the Indians lose 9–2 to the Athletics before 10,000.

The Indians wanted to move into Municipal Stadium as soon as the facility opened, but negotiations between Indians president Alva Bradley and the city of Cleveland over a lease agreement dragged on for a year (see July 13, 1931) before an agreement was finally reached.

JULY 31 The Indians play their first game at Municipal Stadium, and lose 1–0 to the Athletics as Lefty Grove outduels Mel Harder. Harder was moved up a day in the rotation because Wes Ferrell reported to the park with a sore arm. The crowd was 80,184 (76,979 paid), which at the time was the largest ever to see a major league game. The lone run scored on a walk to Max Bishop, a sacrifice, and a single from Mickey Cochrane. Among those in attendance was baseball commissioner Kenesaw Landis, AL president Will Harridge, NL president John Heydler, Ohio governor George White, who threw out the ceremonial first pitch, and Cleveland mayor Ray Miller, who caught it. Before the game, Indians radio announcer Jack Graney introduced stars of Cleveland's past, including Cy Young, Nap Lajoie, Tris Speaker, Bill Bradley, Lee Fohl, Elmer Flick, Elmer Smith, and Bill Wambsganss.

The Indians power hitters were not happy with the deep fences at Municipal Stadium. It was only 322 feet to the foul lines, but the power alleys were 463 feet from home plate, and it was 470 feet to dead center.

AUGUST 1 The second game at Municipal Stadium is another 1–0 Philadelphia Athletics victory with Rube Walberg besting Wes Ferrell. The run scored in the ninth inning. The crowd was 12,000 on a Monday afternoon.

Municipal Stadium was the only new ball park introduced to the majors between 1923, when Yankee Stadium opened, and 1953, a year in which the Boston Braves moved to Milwaukee and began playing at County Stadium.

AUGUST 4 In the third and fourth games at Municipal Stadium, the Indians finally win at the new ball park sweeping a double header 8–2 and 8–7 against the Red Sox. The second game went 13 innings. Both teams scored in the 11th. Cleveland collected five triples in the opener from Joe Vosmik, Eddie Morgan, Dick Porter, Johnny Burnett and Earl Averill.

August 6 Wes Ferrell pitches a one-hitter to defeat the Red Sox 2–0 before a crowd of 2,000 on a Saturday afternoon at Municipal Stadium. The lone hit by Dale Alexander in the fourth inning was the result of a difficult decision by the official scorer. The ball left Alexander's bat in a line over the pitcher's mound. Second baseman Bill Cissell raced over for it, reaching the ball about four feet from second base. He got his glove on it, but the ball escaped his grasp, with Alexander reaching first safely.

When Municipal Stadium, Alva Bradley predicted: "We'll fill the place often, every Sunday." His prophecy was proved to be completely inaccurate as there were many more crowds in the neighborhood of 2,000 like the one on August 6 than the 80,000 that attending the first game six days earlier. Inside the massive stadium, crowds of 2,000 looked more like 200. Despite moving into the larger facility, the Indians attendance figure dropped from 483,027 in 1931 to 468,953 in 1932. The Great Depression had much to do with the decrease. Attendance in the American League declined by 19.3 per cent from 1931 to 1932. Attendance in major league baseball fell from 10,132,262 in 1930 to 6,089,031 in 1933. The Indians ranked second in the AL in attendance in 1932, trailing only the Yankees.

August 7 Johnny Burnett collects the first home run at Municipal Stadium during a 7–4 victory over the Senators in the first game of a double header. It came in the seventh game at the facility. The pitcher was Tommy Thomas. The Indians completed the sweep with a 6–2 triumph in the nightcap.

August 21 Wes Ferrell wins his 20th game of the season with an 11–5 decision over the Senators in Washington.

Ferrell was 22–13 with a 3.66 ERA in 287⅓ innings in 1932. He completed 26 of his 34 starts.

August 28 The Indians score seven runs in the first inning of a 10–1 win over the Red Sox in the first game of a double header at Fenway Park. Boston won the second encounter 4–3 in 11 innings.

On the original schedule, August 28 was to be the first of four single games in a series against the Red Sox. But astronomers were calling for a total eclipse of the sun on the afternoon of August 31, and the game was moved up to create a double header on the 28th.

August 31 Wes Ferrell is suspended ten days for insubordination after refusing to leave a game for a relief pitcher during a 6–2 loss to the Red Sox in Boston. Ferrell recorded only one out during Boston's five-run first inning. When Roger Peckinpaugh called for a relief pitcher, Ferrell refused to give the Cleveland manager the ball, kicked up dust, and wouldn't leave the mound.

September 18 Willie Kamm hits a grand slam off Firpo Marberry in the third inning of a 7–3 over the Senators in the first game of a double header at Municipal Stadium. Washington won the second contest 7–3.

September 23 The Indians trounce the White Sox 12–6 at Municipal Stadium.

September 24 Trailing 4–0, the Indians score seven runs in the fifth inning, but wind up losing 8–7 to the White Sox at Municipal Stadium.

December 15 Six weeks after Franklin Roosevelt defeats Herbert Hoover in the Presidential election, the Indians trade Jack Russell and Bruce Connaster to the Senators for Harley Boss.

The Indians made a mistake in trading Russell. The Senators converted him into one of baseball's first relief specialists, and he played in the World Series in 1933 and was named to the All-Star team in 1934. After retiring, Russell settled in Clearwater, Florida, and became the city commissioner. While in office, he helped put through the construction of a new spring training stadium for the Phillies, which was named Jack Russell Stadium.

1933

Season in a Sentence

The Indians spend an entire season at spacious Municipal Stadium, but attendance drops as well as the club's offensive statistics and win total.

Finish • Won • Lost • Pct • GB

Finish	Won	Lost	Pct	GB
Fourth	75	76	.497	23.5

Managers

Roger Peckinpaugh (26–25), Bibb Falk (1–0) and Walter Johnson (48–51).

Stats

Stats	Indians	AL	Rank
Batting Avg:	.261	.273	7
On-Base Pct:	.321	.342	8
Slugging Pct:	.360	.390	6
Home Runs:	50		6 (tie)
Stolen Bases:	36		7
ERA:	3.71	4.28	1
Fielding Avg:	.974	.972	3
Runs Scored:	654		8
Runs Allowed:	669		2

Starting Line-up

Roy Spencer, c
Harley Boss, 1b
Bill Cissell, 2b-ss
Willie Kamm, 3b
Bill Knickerbocker, ss
Joe Vosmik, lf
Earl Averill, cf
Dick Porter, rf
Odell Hale, 2b
Johnny Burnett, ss
Frankie Pytlak, c
Milt Galatzer, rf-lf

Pitchers

Mel Harder, sp
Oral Hildebrand, sp
Wes Ferrell, sp
Clint Brown, sp
Willis Hudlin, sp-rp
Monte Pearson, sp
Sarge Connally, rp

Attendance

387,936 (fourth in AL)

Club Leaders

Batting Avg:	Earl Averill	.301
On-Base Pct:	Earl Averill	.363
Slugging Pct:	Earl Averill	.474
Home Runs:	Earl Averill	11
RBIs:	Earl Averill	92
Runs:	Earl Averill	83
Stolen Bases:	Willie Kamm	7
Wins:	Oral Hildebrand	16
Strikeouts:	Oral Hildebrand	90
ERA:	Mel Harder	2.95
Saves:	Mel Harder	4

January 7 The Indians trade Luke Sewell to the Senators for Roy Spencer.

Spencer was a flop, batting .201 in 80 games with the Indians, while Sewell was a starting catcher with the Senators and White Sox for five more seasons.

April 12 The Indians open with a 13-inning, 4–1 victory over the Tigers in Detroit. Tiger hurler Tommy Bridges surrendered only four hits over the first 12 innings, but in the 13th, put two runners on base before allowing two-out singles to Willie Kamm, Roy Spencer, and Clint Brown. Brown also pitched a complete game for Cleveland.

Before the season started, club owner Alva Bradley announced a ban on radio broadcasting of Indians games in the belief that play-by-play accounts hurt attendance.

April 13 Trailing 4–1, the Indians explode for six runs in the ninth inning to defeat the Tigers 7–4 in Detroit.

April 20 In the home opener, the Indians win 2–1 over the Tigers before 25,000 at Municipal Stadium.

With the end of Prohibition, beer was sold at major league ballparks in 1933 for the first time since 1919.

April 26 Oral Hildebrand pitches a one-hitter for a 2–0 victory over the Browns in near freezing temperatures at Municipal Stadium. Art Scharein provided the lone St. Louis hit with a single in the third inning.

Hildebrand led the AL in shutouts in 1933 with six while posting a 16–11 record and a 3.76 ERA.

May 6 Earl Averill collects eight hits during a double header split with the Yankees before 55,000 at Municipal Stadium. In the opener, Averill was 4-for-5 during a 7–6 win. He was also 4-for-5 in the second tilt, won by New York 8–4. All eight hits were singles.

May 11 The Indians take sole possession of first place with a 4–1 win over the Red Sox at Municipal Stadium.

May 16 The Indians are knocked out of first place with an 11–10 loss to the Senators in 12 innings in Washington. Cleveland fought back from a 7–1 deficit to take a 10–8 lead in the eighth inning, only to lose.

The club sank quickly in the American League standings. By June 9, manager Roger Peckinpaugh was out of a job.

May 30 The Indians collect 23 hits and defeat the White Sox 15–8 in the first game of a double header at Comiskey Park. Chicago won the opener 7–2.

June 2 The Indians sweep the Browns 2–1 and 1–0 in St. Louis. Mel Harder pitched the shutout. The run scored in the first inning on doubles by Dick Porter and Johnny Burnett off Bump Hadley.

Harder was a mainstay of the Indians pitching staff from 1928 through 1947, posting a record of 222–186. He is the only individual in club history to play for 20 seasons. Only one of those clubs was in pennant contention in September, however, and none reached the post-season. Had he played in a World Series or two, it is likely that Harder would be in the Hall of Fame. Both Joe DiMaggio and Ted Williams ranked Harder the toughest pitcher they ever faced. Among Indians pitchers all-time, he ranks second in wins, first in games pitched (582), second in innings pitched (3,426⅓), second in games started (433), fifth in complete games (181), sixth in shutouts (25) and sixth in strikeouts (1,161). After retiring as an active player, Harder served as a pitching coach for the club from 1948 through 1963. During that period, the Indians had some of the best staffs ever assembled, led by such stalwarts as Bob Feller, Bob Lemon, Early Wynn, Mike Garcia, Herb Score, and Dick Donovan, each of whom won 20 or more games in a season at least once. Harder's number 18 is among those retired by the Indians.

JUNE 9 Walter Johnson replaces Roger Peckinpaugh as manager. Coach Bibb Falk served as interim manager for one game until Johnson could arrive. The club had a record of 26–25 and had lost 16 of their last 25 games.

Firing Peckinpaugh, who had been manager since 1928, was not a popular move with the media or the fans. Alva Bradley said his decision was based upon the fact that the Indians "lacked pep" and "played loosely." Peckinpaugh was later hired by Bradley to manage the Indians again in 1941. Johnson was one of the greatest pitchers in baseball history, winning 417 games, the second highest figure of all-time, while pitching for the Senators from 1907 through 1927. He was one of the five original players inducted into the Hall of Fame in 1936, along with Ty Cobb, Babe Ruth, Honus Wagner, and Christy Mathewson. Johnson previously managed the Senators from 1929 through 1932 in which the club finished fifth, second, and third twice. Like many former star players, Johnson expected his players to have the same abilities and dedication that he possessed and became impatient with his charges. Although the Senators were 92–61 in 1932, owner Clark Griffith fired Johnson and replaced him with Joe Cronin. In Cronin's first season, Washington won the 1933 AL pennant. Johnson managed the Indians until August 1935 to a 179–168 record amid constant complaints from players and the press that he didn't know how to handle a team. By the time Johnson was fired, players were on the verge of insurrection.

JUNE 11 In his first game as manager, Walter Johnson throws out the ceremonial first pitch, then watches the Indians win 1–0 in ten innings against the Browns at Municipal Stadium. Mel Harder started but was relieved by Oral Hildebrand in the tenth with one out and the bases loaded. Hildebrand worked out of the jam, then hit a single with two out in the bottom of the inning to drive in the lone run. Bump Hadley was the losing pitcher. It was the second time that he lost 1–0 to Cleveland in a span of ten days.

JUNE 13 Walter Johnson is 2–0 as Indians manager with a pair of 1–0 victories after the Indians edge the Tigers by that score in Detroit. Oral Hildebrand was the winning pitcher in both contests, first as a reliever on June 11, then with a two-hit, complete game two days later. The only hits off Hildebrand were singles by Charlie Gehringer and Gee Walker. The lone run scored in the ninth inning on a triple by Joe Vosmik and a single by Frankie Pytlak.

JUNE 18 The Indians sweep the Red Sox 7–0 and 4–0 during a double header at Municipal Stadium behind the pitching of Oral Hildebrand and Mel Harder.

The wins gave the Indians a 5–1 record under Walter Johnson with four shutouts. Over the remainder of the season, the club was 42–50.

JUNE 21 The Indians belt the Athletics 11–1 at Municipal Stadium.

JUNE 25 In his major league debut, right fielder Milt Galatzer walks four times in four plate appearances, but the Indians lose 9–0 in the first game of a double header against the Senators at Municipal Stadium. Washington also won the second tilt 10–1.

Galatzer played four seasons with the Indians, in which he batted .270 with one home run in 712 at-bats.

JUNE 30 Trailing 9–2 early in the game, the Indians stage an amazing comeback climaxed by a four-run rally in the ninth inning to take an exhilarating 12–12 decision from the Yankees at Municipal Stadium. All four runs in the ninth scored before a man was retired. Milt Galatzer drove in the winning run with a single.

JULY 6 Earl Averill participates in the first All-Star Game, won by the American League 4–2 at Comiskey Park in Chicago. In the sixth inning, Averill delivered a pinch-single that drove in a run. Wes Ferrell and Oral Hildebrand were also on the team, but did not play.

Ferrell made the All-Star Game based on a strong first half but slumped badly after the break. He finished the year with an 11–12 record and a 4.21 ERA after winning 91 games over the previous four seasons. In September, Ferrell played 13 games in left field while the Indians contemplated turning him into an outfielder. In 140 at-bats in 1933, Ferrell hit .271 with seven home runs.

JULY 8 In his first appearance in Washington in an opposing uniform, Walter Johnson is presented with a huge bouquet of flowers in pre-game ceremonies. Pleasantries went out the window once play started, as the Senators won both games of the double header 6–2 and 5–4.

JULY 16 Willis Hudlin pitches a 14-inning complete game and allows just five hits to defeat the Red Sox 2–1 in Boston. Billy Knickerbocker drove in the winning run with a sacrifice fly.

JULY 19 Both Wes Ferrell and his brother Rick, who was catching for the Red Sox, hit home runs during a 13-inning, 8–7 Indians win at Fenway Park. Wes connected first in the top of the fourth off Hank Johnson, with Rick calling the pitch behind the plate. In the bottom half, Rick countered with a round-tripper off Wes. Both clouts traveled over the left field wall.

Rick was elected to the Hall of Fame in 1984 based mostly on his defensive abilities as a catcher. He had a batting average of .281 in 6,028 at-bats but was almost devoid of power with just 28 career homers. Wes, who was 28 months younger than Rick, clubbed 38 home runs in 1,176 at-bats in addition to a .280 batting average and his prodigious pitching prowess. Wes was 192–128 with six seasons of 20 or more wins but has never been seriously considered for the Hall of Fame.

JULY 29 Clint Brown not only pitches a shutout, but scampers home in the seventh inning with the winning run of a 1–0 victory over the Tigers at Municipal Stadium. The run was driven in by Johnny Oulibber.

JULY 31 Oral Hildebrand and Walter Johnson clash during a 12–8 loss to the Browns in St. Louis. Johnson took Hildebrand out of the game after he walked three batters in a row in the eighth inning. Hildebrand slammed the resin bag to the turf and demanded to be left in the game. Johnson responded by suspending Hildebrand for three days.

AUGUST 2 The Indians break an 8–8 tie with eight runs in the ninth inning to win 16–8 over the Browns in St. Louis.

AUGUST 5 The Indians erupt for nine runs in the 13th inning and beat the Tigers 15–6 in the first game of a double header in Detroit. Odell Hale hit a three-run homer in the ninth inning to tie the contest 6–6. Detroit won the second tilt 7–1.

AUGUST 14 Athletics slugger Jimmie Foxx hits for the cycle and drives in nine runs during an 11–5 Philadelphia win at Municipal Stadium.

AUGUST 17 Earl Averill hits for the cycle during a 15–4 victory over the Athletics at Municipal Stadium. The Indians scored seven runs in the fifth inning.

AUGUST 20 Trailing 6–4, the Indians erupt with a ten-run attack in the sixth inning to win 14–6 over the Red Sox in the first game of a double header at Municipal Stadium. Cleveland completed the sweep with a 9–4 triumph in the second contest. In the fifth inning of the nightcap, Red Sox manager Marty McManus took a swing at Cleveland coach Patsy Gharrity during an argument over an umpire's decision.

AUGUST 21 The Indians score eight runs in the eighth inning of a 10–1 win over the Red Sox at Municipal Stadium. Roy Spencer cracked two doubles during the inning.

AUGUST 27 The Indians commit nine errors during a 14–1 loss to the Senators in the first game of a double header at Municipal Stadium. The Indians didn't make an error in the second tilt, winning 6–3 with all six runs scoring in the third inning.

AUGUST 29 Monte Pearson pitches a two-hitter to defeat the Senators 7–2 in the second game of a double header at Municipal Stadium. Pearson took a no-hitter into the ninth inning before allowing a single to Otto Bluege and a triple by Heinie Manush. Washington won the opener 2–1 in ten innings.

A rookie in 1933, Pearson was 10–5 and his 2.33 earned run average led the American League. Mel Harder was 15–17, but despite the losing record was second in the AL in ERA with a 2.95 mark.

SEPTEMBER 3 The Indians drub the White Sox 14–3 in Chicago.

SEPTEMBER 18 Oral Hildebrand pitches a two-hitter to defeat the Red Sox 9–0 at Fenway Park. The only Boston hits were a single by Dusty Cooke in the fourth inning and a double by George Stumpf in the seventh.

SEPTEMBER 30 In his second major league start, Indians pitcher Thornton Lee holds the Tigers hitless for seven innings before allowing four consecutive singles and three runs to lose 2–0 in Detroit.

As a result of large financial losses in 1933, Alva Bradley asked general manager Billy Evans to take a pay cut from $30,000 to $12,500. Evans resisted but finally agreed to accept the $12,500 as a base salary when Bradley consented to pay him a $5,000 bonus if the team made a profit of $100,000 in 1934.

OCTOBER 12 The Indians trade Bill Cissell to the Red Sox for Lloyd Brown.

OCTOBER 14 The Indians break their lease with the city of Cleveland and announce they will abandon Municipal Stadium to return to League Park in 1934.

Attendance at Indians games dropped from 468,953 in 1932 to 387,936 in 1933. Bradley said that the club simply couldn't afford to pay rent at the stadium with such a small return at the box office. From 1934 through 1936, the Indians played exclusively at League Park, with the exception of one game in 1936. The 1935 All-Star Game was also played at Municipal Stadium. Bradley was severely criticized for the move by city officials, as the massive and expensive multi-purpose stadium was rarely utilized.

1934

Season in a Sentence

The Indians are in first place in early June but end the year in third, a slight improvement after finishing in fourth place four consecutive seasons from 1930 through 1933.

Finish • Won • Lost • Pct • GB

Finish	Won	Lost	Pct	GB
Third	85	69	.552	16.0

Manager

Walter Johnson

Stats

Stats	Indians	AL	Rank
Batting Avg:	.287	.279	2
On-Base Pct:	.353	.351	3
Slugging Pct:	.423	.399	3
Home Runs:	100		3
Stolen Bases:	52		5
ERA:	4.28	4.50	3
Fielding Avg:	.972	.970	4
Runs Scored:	814		4
Runs Allowed:	763		3

Starting Line-up

Frankie Pytlak, c
Hal Trosky, 1b
Odell Hale, 2b
Willie Kamm, 3b
Billy Knickerbocker, ss
Joe Vosmik, lf
Earl Averill, cf
Sam Rice, rf
Johnny Burnett, 3b
Milt Galatzer, rf
Bob Seeds, lf-rf

Pitchers

Mel Harder, sp
Monte Pearson, sp
Willis Hudlin, sp
Oral Hildebrand, sp
Lloyd Brown, rp-sp
Thornton Lee, rp
Ralph Winegarner, rp

Attendance

391,388 (fourth in AL)

Club Leaders

Batting Avg:	Earl Averill	.341
On-Base Pct:	Earl Averill	.414
Slugging Pct:	Hal Trosky	.598
Home Runs:	Hal Trosky	35
RBIs:	Hal Trosky	142
Runs:	Earl Averill	128
Stolen Bases:	Frankie Pytlak	11
Wins:	Mel Harder	20
Strikeouts:	Monte Pearson	140
ERA:	Mel Harder	2.61
Saves:	Lloyd Brown	6

April 17 — The Indians open the season with a 5–2 win over the Browns before 21,000 at League Park. Earl Averill paced the attack with a home run and a double.

April 24 — The Indians hammer the Browns 15–2 in St. Louis. Hal Trosky drove in six runs with two homers and two singles.

Born Harold Troyavesky in Norway, Iowa, Trosky became an immediate star as a 21-year-old rookie first baseman in 1934. He hit .330 with 35 homers, 142 runs-batted-in, 117 runs scored, 206 hits and 45 doubles. From 1934 through 1940, he hit .314 in 1,024 games and averaged 101 runs, 29 homers and 122 RBIs per season. Trosky was well on the way to a potential Hall of Fame career when beset with migraine headaches. He missed the entire 1942, 1943 and 1945 seasons because of the illness, and last played in the majors in 1946 when he was only 33. Despite the short career, Trosky ranks fourth all-time among Indians batters in slugging percentage (.551), fourth in RBIs (911), fifth in home runs (216), sixth in total bases (2,406), and ninth in doubles (287).

April 30 — The Indians lose 20–10 to the White Sox in Chicago.

MAY 1 The day after a 20–10 loss, the Indians thrash the White Sox 12–1 in Chicago. Billy Knickerbocker hit a grand slam in the sixth inning off Milt Gaston.

Knickerbocker hit .317 for the Indians in 1934.

MAY 10 After spotting the Red Sox a 6–0 lead in the first inning, the Indians rally to win 11–10 in Boston. A three-run homer by Joe Vosmik in the eighth inning gave Cleveland an 11–9 lead.

MAY 12 The Indians score six runs in the ninth inning to defeat the Red Sox 7–2 in Boston. Roy Spencer drove in the tying and winning runs with a pinch-double.

MAY 17 The Indians score seven runs in the seventh inning of a 14–6 win over the Senators at League Park.

After playing 19 years with the Senators, Sam Rice appeared in 97 games for the Indians as a right fielder in 1934 at the age of 44. He retired at the end of the season with 2,987 career hits. No one else has gotten as close to the 3,000-hit level without reaching the coveted figure. Rice was elected to the Hall of Fame in 1963.

MAY 21 Earl Averill hits two homers and drive in five runs during a 9–5 win over the Yankees at League Park.

Averill hit .313 with 31 homers, 113 RBIs, 128 runs scored and 48 doubles in 1934.

MAY 25 The Indians score seven runs in the fifth inning of an 8–3 win over the Red Sox at League Park.

On the same day, the Indians sent Wes Ferrell and Dick Porter to the Red Sox for Bob Weiland, Bob Seeds, and $25,000. Ferrell was a holdout after posting an 11–12 record in 1933, and hadn't pitched a game in 1934 when the trade was completed. It proved to be a horrible deal. Ferrell was 59–34 over the next three seasons in Boston, where his brother Rick was a catcher. Neither Seeds nor Weiland made any contribution to the future success of the Indians and were sent packing before the start of the 1935 campaign.

MAY 27 The Indians take over first place with a 7–6 record over the Athletics at League Park.

MAY 30 Hal Trosky hits three homers during a 5–4 win over the White Sox in the second game of a double header at League Park. All three traveled over the right field wall. Trosky connected with a man on base in the fourth inning and a solo shot off Les Tietje in the sixth to help the Indians to a 4–0 lead. The White Sox tied the contest 4–4 in the seventh, but Trosky broke the deadlock with a homer against Phil Gallivan in the eighth. Chicago won the opener 8–7 in 12 innings.

At the end of the day, the Indians had a 21–13 record and a one-half game lead over the Yankees.

June 3 The Indians are knocked out of first place with a 12–8 loss to the Browns in St. Louis.

The Indians were still just 5½ games out of first place at the end of July, but the Tigers ran away with the pennant by putting together a 14-game winning streak in early August. During that month, the Indians were 10–17. As the summer progressed manager Walter Johnson continued to have conflicts with his players and received severe criticism from the local media. Ed Bang, sports editor of the Cleveland News *wrote in July that Johnson had "showed anything but mental alertness and managerial ability. Truth be told, he fell so far short of what a wide-awake manager should do that the fans who were wont to cheer him in the days gone by as a great pitcher, groaned in despair and booed him." There were constant rumors that Johnson would be fired, but Indians management announced late in the season that he would return in 1935.*

June 5 The Indians win the second game of a double header against the Tigers in Detroit with a ninth-inning rally following a trouncing in the first game. In the opener, the Indians lost 20–3. In the nightcap, Cleveland scored three in the ninth for a 5–4 victory. The last two runs scored on a triple by Billy Knickerbocker.

June 15 Hal Trosky drives in six runs on a two-run homer and a grand slam during an 11–7 win over the Athletics in Philadelphia. The slam was struck in the ninth inning off Bob Kline.

June 29 The Indians win an odd 11-inning 5–2 decision over the White Sox at Comiskey Park. All seven runs scored in the final inning. Mel Harder and Chicago pitcher Les Tietje each pitched ten shutout innings before tiring. Neither retired a batter in the 11th before being lifted for relievers.

July 10 Earl Averill and Mel Harder contribute to a 9–7 American League victory in the All-Star Game, played at the Polo Grounds in New York. Averill drove in a run with a pinch-hit triple in the fourth inning, stayed in the game as a center fielder, and smacked a two-run double in the fifth that broke a 4–4 tie. Harder pitched five shutout innings from the fifth through the ninth, allowing only one hit.

Harder appeared in four consecutive All-Star Games from 1934 through 1937 and pitched 13 shutout innings, surrendering nine hits and a walk.

July 15 The Indians defeat the Senators by duplicate 10–8 scores during a double header at League Park. Odell Hale hit a grand slam off Tommy Thomas in the first inning of the second game.

Hale hit .304 with 44 doubles, 13 homers, and 101 RBIs in 1934.

July 17 The Indians wallop the Yankees 12–5 at League Park.

July 18 The Indians score three runs in the ninth inning to win a wild 15–14 slugfest at League Park. The Yanks scored five runs in the top of the ninth to take a 14–12 lead. During the Cleveland half of the inning, Willie Kamm doubled, Frankie Pytlak tripled, pinch-hitter Dutch Holland smacked a double, and Earl Averill singled in the winning tally.

JULY 19 The Indians strike in the ninth inning for the second day in a row, scoring five times to defeat the Red Sox 6–5 at League Park. The runs scored on a two-run single by Earl Averill, an RBI-single by Joe Vosmik, and a two-run triple from Hal Trosky.

AUGUST 1 A week after John Dillinger is shot by the FBI outside of a Chicago theater, the Indians sign free agent catcher Moe Berg following his release by the Senators.

Berg played in the majors from 1923 through 1939 with various clubs. He may have been the most intelligent man ever to play professional baseball. Berg read and spoke 12 languages, including Sanskrit. He held degrees from Princeton University, Columbia Law School, and the Sorbonne. Berg enthralled newsmen with discourses on such diverse topics as ancient Greek history and astronomy. He appeared on the popular radio program Information Please, *correctly answering questions on Roman Mythology, French impressionism, spatial geometry, and the infield fly rule. Berg was never more than a reserve catcher, but he stayed in the majors because of his intelligence and defensive abilities. He was reportedly the subject of Mike Gonzalez's legendary scouting report: "Good field, no hit." White Sox pitcher Ted Lyons once quipped, "Berg can speak 12 languages but can't hit in any of them." Few knew that Berg was also working as a spy for the United States government during his playing career. At the end of the 1934 season, Berg was added at the last minute to a team of All-Stars, which included Babe Ruth, on a goodwill trip to Japan. Organizers cited Berg's fluent Japanese as the reason for including him on the roster of stars. However, instead of playing, Berg spent much of his time taking photographs. By order of the State Department, Berg was to photograph key Japanese military installations and other potential targets from the roof of a Tokyo hospital. In April 1942, Major General Jimmy Doolittle used these photos in making the first American air attack on Japan during World War II. Once the war started, Berg joined the Office of Strategic Services (OSS), the forerunner of the CIA. His primary objective was to determine Germany's nuclear potential. Berg undertook several dangerous missions behind enemy lines to keep track of German scientists. Some of these missions were rumored to have involved assassinations. His gift for languages served him well, and he always returned home safely.*

AUGUST 18 Earl Averill reached base in nine consecutive plate appearances during a double header in Philadelphia. In the opener, he walked four times during a 2–1 loss. In the second tilt, he contributed a triple, three doubles, and a single in five at-bats as the Indians won 10–0.

AUGUST 21 Trailing 11–3, the Indians stun the Athletics with nine runs in the ninth inning to win 12–11 in Philadelphia. The nine-run rally was achieved with four hits, six walks, and an error.

SEPTEMBER 2 Mel Harder pitches a two-hitter to win 1–0 over the Tigers at League Park. He also contributed to the lone run of the game. In the fifth inning, Willie Kamm walked and scored on singles by Harder and Milt Galatzer. The only Detroit hits were singles by Hank Greenberg and Charlie Gehringer.

SEPTEMBER 5 Hal Trosky drives in six runs on a grand slam and a two-run single during an 11–2 win over the Red Sox at League Park. The slam was struck off Lefty Grove in the fourth inning.

SEPTEMBER 10 Down 5–0, the Indians score a run in the fourth inning, three in the eighth, one in the ninth, and one in the tenth to defeat the Athletics 6–5 in the second game of a double header at League Park. Earl Averill's home run tied the score 5–5. Johnny Burnett followed with a walk-off homer in the tenth.

SEPTEMBER 16 The Indians sweep the Senators 5–4 and 9–6 at League Park. The opener went 12 innings with a triple by Milt Galatzer and a single by Earl Averill providing the winning run. Cleveland overcame a 5–0 deficit to win the second tilt.

SEPTEMBER 29 Mel Harder notches his 20th win of the season with a 4–0 decision over the White Sox at League Park.

Harder had a record of 20–12 with six shutouts and a 2.61 earned run average in 1934. He also recorded four saves while making 29 starts and 15 relief appearances. Monte Pearson was 18–13 with an ERA of 4.52.

NOVEMBER 20 The Indians send Johnny Burnett, Bob Weiland, and cash to the Browns for Bruce Campbell.

Campbell was stricken with meningitis in August 1935 and was given a 50–50 chance to live. He survived and was a solid starting outfielder with the club until 1939. Weiland didn't win a game for the Browns but gave the Cardinals three good seasons as a starting pitcher beginning in 1937.

1935

Season in a Sentence

Walter Johnson's testy relationship with his players reaches the boiling point, leading to his dismissal in August and the hiring of Steve O'Neill as manager.

Finish • Won • Lost • Pct • GB

Finish	Won	Lost	Pct	GB
Third	82	71	.536	12.0

Managers

Walter Johnson (46–48) and Steve O'Neill (36–23)

Stats

Stats	Indians	AL	Rank
Batting Avg:	.284	.280	3
On-Base Pct:	.341	.351	6
Slugging Pct:	.421	.402	2
Home Runs:	93		4
Stolen Bases:	63		4
ERA:	4.15	4.46	4
Fielding Avg:	.972	.972	5
Runs Scored:	776		4
Runs Allowed:	739		4

Starting Line-up

Eddie Phillips, c
Hal Trosky, 1b
Boze Berger, 2b
Odell Hale, 3b
Billy Knickerbocker, ss
Joe Vosmik, lf
Earl Averill, cf
Bruce Campbell, rf
Milt Galatzer, rf
Roy Hughes, ss-2b
Ab Wright, rf

Pitchers

Mel Harder, sp
Willis Hudlin, sp
Oral Hildebrand, sp
Monte Pearson, sp
Thornton Lee, sp-rp
Lloyd Brown, rp
Lefty Stewart, rp-sp

Attendance

397,615 (fifth in AL)

Club Leaders

Batting Avg:	Earl Averill	.348
On-Base Pct:	Earl Averill	.408
Slugging Pct:	Earl Averill	.537
Home Runs:	Hal Trosky	26
RBIs:	Hal Trosky	113
Runs:	Earl Averill	109
Stolen Bases:	Odell Hale	15
Wins:	Mel Harder	22
Strikeouts:	Mel Harder	95
ERA:	Mel Harder	3.29
Saves:	Willis Hudlin	5
	Oral Hildebrand	5

April 16 — The Indians win the season opener 2–1 in 14 innings against the Browns in St. Louis. Mel Harder pitched a complete game. A double by Glenn Myatt drove in the winning run.

> *Hopes were high in Cleveland after a national poll of sports writers conducted by the Associated Press during spring training picked the Indians to win the AL pennant. The club started the season with eight wins in their first nine games, and it looked as though the pennant predictions might come true. The Indians were still going strong in late June with a record of 37–25 despite discord between the players and manager Walter Johnson (see May 23, 1935). A seven-game losing streak during the first week of July sent the Indians into a tailspin, however, and by August, Johnson was replaced as manager.*

April 20 — Playing the Tigers in Detroit after three days of postponements due to inclement weather in St. Louis, the Indians win 2–1 in 14-innings for the second game in a row. Oral Hildebrand pitched a complete game. Earl Averill drove in the winning run with a single.

April 21 — The Indians play their third consecutive extra-inning game, losing 3–2 to the Tigers in Detroit. Monte Pearson pitched a complete game.

The Indians opened the season playing 41 innings in three games using only three pitchers.

April 23 — In the home opener, the Indians score two runs in the ninth inning to defeat the Browns 7–6 before 23,000 at League Park.

April 27 — Hal Trosky hits two homers and drives in five runs during a 9–2 win over the Tigers at League Park.

Trosky hit .271, clubbed 26 homers, and drove in 113 runs in 1935.

May 14 — The Indians trade Belve Bean to the Senators for Lefty Stewart.

May 19 — In his first start with the Indians, Lefty Stewart pitches an 11-inning, complete game shutout to defeat the Yankees 1–0 in New York. Pinch-hitter Bruce Campbell drove in the winning run with a sacrifice fly off Red Ruffing.

The shutout was the only one that Stewart pitched as a member of the Indians. He was 6–9 with a 5.44 ERA with the club.

May 23 — Walter Johnson suspends Willie Kamm and releases Glenn Myatt.

With the Indians in Philadelphia, the manager told reporters that he had discovered an "anti-Johnson" bloc among the players headed by Kamm and Myatt. Both were former regulars who seldom played early in the 1935 season. Johnson said that the young players on the team were complaining that Kamm and Myatt were cramping their style of play. "Those men are influencing the young players on the team," charged Johnson. "Why not more than five players know who's the manager of the club. For the good of the team, I'm dismissing Kamm and Wyatt." Cleveland fans exploded in anger and blamed Johnson for the lack of harmony on the club. Petitions demanding the manager's removal were circulated. Kamm demanded a chance to clear his name, and with the help of club owner Alva Bradley, received a hearing before commissioner Kenesaw Landis on May 31. After listening to both sides for two hours, Landis said: "They (Johnson and Kamm) are both nice boys of excellent character and reputation, but they just can't get along. It's too bad, but I can't do anything about it." Bradley stood by his manager and refused to reinstate Kamm and Myatt to the active roster, and neither played another game for Cleveland, although the Indians owner did give Kamm a job as a scout on June 3. Myatt signed a contract with the New York Giants (see June 6, 1935).

May 24 — The Indians score in seven of nine innings and defeat the Athletics 12–2 in Philadelphia.

June 3 — The Indians score seven runs in the 14th inning and beat the Browns 11–4 in St. Louis. Bruce Campbell's grand slam off Bob Weiland completed the rout.

June 6 — An advertisement appears in all three Cleveland papers, the *Plain Dealer, Press*, and *News*, denying that dissension exists among the Indians following the release of Willie Kamm and Glenn Myatt (see May 23, 1935).

The ad was headed, "Some Inside Stuff Direct from the Camp of the Indians." It stated in part: "We, the members of the Cleveland Baseball Club, want the fans to know that we are not a team split wide open by dissension, arrayed against our manager." It continued for 12 inches of space in carefully worded prose in which Johnson's virtues were not extolled, but neither was he criticized. At the bottom were the facsimile signatures of 21 players. The only player on the roster at the time whose name didn't appear in the ad was catcher Eddie Phillips who appeared in 70 games in 1935. It was his only season with the club.

June 8 — In the first home game since the release of Willie Kamm and Glenn Myatt, extra police are on hand for a 3–2 win over the Browns at League Park. The precaution was taken because fans had threatened to picket the ballpark in protest of the dismissal of Kamm and Myatt. For the first time, liquid refreshment was not sold in bottles. Fans were served drinks in paper containers. No trouble erupted.

June 16 — Mel Harder pitches a one-hitter to defeat the Red Sox 4–0 in the second game of a double header at League Park. The only Boston hit was a second-inning single by Bing Miller that rolled between third baseman Odell Hale and shortstop Billy Knickerbocker. The Indians also won the opener 9–3.

June 20 — Acting as a pinch-hitter, pitcher Ralph Winegarner hits a home run in the eighth inning to tie the score 6–6 against the Senators at League Park. The Indians added two more runs in the eighth to win 8–6.

A former minor league third baseman, Winegarner had an 8–6 career record with a 5.33 ERA over five seasons in the majors as a pitcher and hit .275 with five homers in 185 at-bats as a hitter. He played for the Indians from 1933 through 1936, and after a 13-year interval, pitched nine games with the Browns in 1949 while serving as a coach with the club.

June 25 — The Indians score two runs in the ninth inning to defeat the Yankees 5–4 at League Park. Hal Trosky drove in the tying run with a triple, and after two intentional walks, Pat Malone delivered an unintentional walk on five pitches to Eddie Phillips.

June 26 — Earl Averill's playing streak of 673 consecutive games, dating back to 1931, comes to an end in a bizarre manner from an injury suffered at a park in the Cleveland suburb of Orange. Averill, his wife, and their four sons were picnicking with three teammates and their families when a firecracker exploded in his hand after he lit it, dropped it, then picked it up thinking the fuse had gone out. The force of the explosion seared the flesh off Averill's fingers and the palm of his right hand and inflicted severe burns on his forehead and chest. It was initially feared that his fingers might have to be amputated. However, Averill's hand healed, and he missed only 14 games.

July 8 — The American League wins the All-Star Game before 69,812 at Municipal Stadium. Jimmie Foxx hit a two-run homer in the first inning to give the AL a 2–0 lead and singled in the last run of the game in the fifth. Mel Harder closed out the contest with three shutout innings.

The 1935 contest was the first of four All-Star Games played at Municipal Stadium. The others were in 1954, 1963, and 1981. It was also the only professional baseball game played at Cleveland's lakefront stadium in 1935. The Indians played all of their home games that season at League Park. Future Hall of Famers on the rosters of the two clubs at the 1935 game included Earl Averill, Mickey Cochrane, Joe Cronin, Dizzy Dean, Frankie Frisch, Rick Ferrell, Jimmie Foxx, Lou Gehrig, Charlie Gehringer, Lefty Gomez, Lefty Grove, Gabby Hartnett, Billy Herman, Carl Hubbell, Joe Medwick, Mel Ott, Al Simmons, Bill Terry, Arky Vaughan, and Paul Waner.

JULY 20 The Indians score eight runs in the first inning and defeat the Athletics 15–3 in Philadelphia. Cleveland batters collected 21 hits during the contest, five by Bruce Campbell.

JULY 24 The Indians sweep the Senators 10–6 and 13–8 over the Senators in Washington. Big ninth-inning rallies helped win both games. In the opener, the Indians scored four in the ninth to break a 6–6 deadlock. During the second tilt, Cleveland trailed 7–0 before scoring 13 runs in the final five innings. Five runs in the ninth broke an 8–8 tie.

Outfielder Joe Vosmik put together the best year of an outstanding career in 1935, leading the team in most offensive categories.

JULY 31 Mel Harder hits two home runs, but the Indians lose 6–4 to the White Sox at League Park. Harder's homers in the fifth and seventh innings gave Cleveland a 4–2 lead, but Chicago rallied for four runs in the eighth.

The two home runs by Harder on July 31, 1935, were the only two he struck in the majors between 1933 and 1939. He hit just four homers in 1,203 career at-bats.

August 3 Bruce Campbell is stricken with a form of spinal meningitis during a 12-inning, 5–4 loss against the Tigers in the first game of a double header in Detroit.

Midway through the tenth inning, Campbell walked in from his position in right field and slumped down on the bench in the Indians dugout. He told manager Walter Johnson he was too sick to continue and that he could hardly see the ball. Campbell was removed from the game and returned to the team hotel. When he awoke the next day in a delirium, his roommate Lloyd Brown, frantically called Johnson and trainer Lefty Weisman. Campbell was rushed to Harper Hospital, where he was diagnosed with spinal meningitis. When his condition worsened in the days that followed, he was given a 50–50 chance to survive. He beat the odds and lived to the ripe old age of 85 but not without a few more bumps in the road. Campbell was hospitalized with the disease twice more—October 1935 and May 1936 (see May 1, 1936).

August 4 Walter Johnson resigns as manager and is replaced by Steve O'Neill, who was serving as one of Johnson's coaches.

With the club sporting a record of 46–48, and 23 losses in their previous 32 games, the players and the public were arrayed against Johnson. The personality of the easygoing O'Neill was the polar opposite of the prickly and demanding Johnson. O'Neill played with the Indians as a catcher from 1911 through 1923. The Indians were 37–23 under O'Neill over the remainder of the 1935 season. After records of 80–74 in 1936 and 83–71 in 1937, O'Neill was fired and replaced by Ossie Vitt. Johnson never managed another big league club.

August 8 The Indians win 14–8 and lose 9–5 during a double header against the Browns in St. Louis.

August 14 A two-out, two-run, bases-loaded, walk-off double by Odell Hale beats the Yankees 7–6 at League Park.

Hale batted .304 with 16 homers and 101 RBIs in 1935.

August 19 The Indians score six runs in the eighth inning to defeat the Senators 11–5 at League Park. Hal Trosky hit a grand slam. The highlight of the day, however, was a bizarre play in the first inning. Billy Knickerbocker hit a long fly that stuck in the latticework of the right field wall. A noisy and prolonged argument followed after the umpires ruled the play a ground-rule double. Manager Steve O'Neill claimed that Knickerbocker should be awarded a home run. O'Neill played the game under protest, which became moot when the Indians won.

August 22 Play is halted briefly during a 1–0 loss to the Athletics at League Park as spectators pay silent tribute to beloved humorist Will Rogers, who was buried that day in Glendale, California. Rogers died on August 16 in a plane crash in Alaska.

August 24 Earl Averill hits a two-out, two-run, walk-off homer in the 15th inning to beat the Athletics 2–0 at League Park. Willis Hudlin and A's hurler George Turbeville both pitched complete games. Hudlin pitched an eight-hitter. Turbeville walked 13 and surrendered nine hits but managed to hold the Indians scoreless for 14 innings with the help of six double plays.

August 25 Part of an overflow crowd of 28,000 at League Park causes a commotion during a 5–4 and 8–2 double-header loss to the Red Sox. The crowd protested umpire Brick Owens's decision on a bunt by Boston's Oscar Melillo in the seventh inning of the second game. Owens first called the bunt fair and called Melillo out at first base, but after an objection by Red Sox manager Joe Cronin and a consultation with fellow umpire Lou Kolls, Owens reversed the call and ruled that the bunt was foul. Approximately 200 fans jumped onto the field from the right-center field bleachers while others threw bottles at the umpires. Police were necessary to quell the disturbance, which lasted about ten minutes. Both umpires were escorted from the field under police protection at the conclusion of the twin bill.

August 31 Vern Kennedy of the White Sox pitches a no-hitter against the Indians at Chicago, winning 6–0. The final out was recorded on a strikeout by Joe Vosmik.

September 7 Third baseman Odell Hale starts one of the most unusual triple plays in major league history by using his head to end a 5–3 win over the Red Sox in the first game of a double header at Fenway Park. Boston entered the ninth inning trailing 5–1, then scored two runs and loaded the bases with none out. With Oral Hildebrand on the mound, Joe Cronin hit a vicious line drive that deflected off Hale's glove and then struck his forehead with such force that it bounced high and to his left, where shortstop Billy Knickerbocker caught the ball before it touched the ground. Knickerbocker threw to Roy Hughes at third base to force Billy Werber. Hughes whipped the ball to first baseman Hal Trosky before Mel Almada could return to the bag to complete the triple play. Cleveland also won the second game 5–4.

September 14 Earl Averill collects five hits, including a triple and two doubles, in five at-bats, but receives little help from his teammates as the Indians lose 5–1 to the Senators in Washington.

September 15 The Indians sweep the Senators 16–4 and 6–3 in Washington. In the opener, Eddie Phillips drove in six runs on three doubles and a single.

September 18 The Indians sweep the Athletics 10–0 and 10–5 in a double header in Philadelphia.

September 22 The Indians win their eighth game in a row with a 6–3 decision over the White Sox in the first game of a double header at League Park. The winning streak ended with a 9–2 loss in the nightcap.

September 24 The Indians rout the Tigers 14–7 at League Park.

September 28 Mel Harder records his 22nd win of the season with a 3–0 decision over the Browns in the first game of a double header at League Park. Cleveland completed the sweep with a 7–2 triumph in the nightcap.

Harder was 22–11 with a 3.29 ERA in 287⅓ innings in 1935.

September 29 On the last day of the season, Joe Vosmik loses the batting title to Buddy Myer of the Senators. Vosmik went into the day leading Myer .349 to .345. The Indians were scheduled to play a double header against the Browns at League Park. Vosmik asked manager Steve O'Neill if he could sit out the twin bill to protect his lead over Myer. O'Neill consented, although Vosmik pinch-hit in the ninth inning of a 9–7 loss and made an out that dropped his average to .348. Between games, however, the Indians received word that Myer went 4-for-5 against the Athletics to boost his average to .349. When the second game started, Vosmik went back to left field, knowing he would need a hit in his first at-bat, or two hits in no less than four at-bats, to pass Myer. Vosmik went 1-for-3 during a 7–4 Indians win that was called after six innings by darkness. Myer won the batting title with an average of .3490 compared to .3484 for Vosmik.

Although he lost the batting championship, Vosmik did lead the AL in hits (216), doubles (47), and triples (20) while hitting ten homers and driving in 110 runs.

NOVEMBER 18 Billy Evans resigns as general manager.

Evans was critical of Walter Johnson when the former Indians manager suspended Willie Kamm and released Glenn Myatt in May (see May 23, 1935). Johnson accused Evans of "disloyalty." At the end of the season, the Indians board of directors voted to slash Evans's salary from $12,500 to $7,500. This was on top of a previous cut from $30,000 two years earlier. Evans wasn't out of a job for long. He was hired by the Red Sox as farm director and later served as president of the Southern Association and general manager of the Tigers. Because of his long service to baseball as an umpire and executive, Evans was elected to the Hall of Fame in 1973. He was replaced as general manager of the Indians by Cy Slapnicka, who had previously served as a scout for the club. Among his discoveries were Bob Feller, Lou Boudreau, Earl Averill, Mel Harder, Jeff Heath, Hal Trosky, Ken Keltner, Odell Hale, Bobby Avila, Jim Hegan, and Herb Score. Slapnicka served as Cleveland general manager until 1941.

DECEMBER 11 The Indians trade Monte Pearson and Steve Sundra to the Yankees for Johnny Allen.

The deal worked out well for both clubs. Pearson was 56–22 for the Yankees from 1936 through 1939 and pitched in four World Series for the club. A controversial figure because of his volcanic temper, Allen won 49 and lost only 19 during his first three seasons in Cleveland. Overall, he was 67–34 with the Indians for a winning percentage of .663 that is second best among Indians pitchers with at least 100 decisions with the club.

1936

Season in a Sentence

Teenage pitching sensation Bob Feller excites Indians fans during an otherwise mundane 80–74 season.

Finish • Won • Lost • Pct • GB

Finish	Won	Lost	Pct	GB
Fifth	80	74	.519	22.5

Manager

Steve O'Neill

Stats

	Indians	AL	Rank
Batting Avg:	.304	.289	1
On-Base Pct:	.364	.363	5
Slugging Pct:	.461	.421	2
Home Runs:	123		2
Stolen Bases:	66		4 (tie)
ERA:	4.83	5.04	4
Fielding Avg:	.971	.971	5
Runs Scored:	921		2 (tie)
Runs Allowed:	871		5

Starting Line-up

Billy Sullivan, Jr., c
Hal Trosky, 1b
Roy Hughes, 2b
Odell Hale, 3b
Billy Knickerbocker, ss
Joe Vosmik, lf
Earl Averill, cf
Roy Weatherly, rf
Frankie Pytlak, c
Bruce Campbell, rf

Pitchers

Johnny Allen, sp
Mel Harder, sp
Oral Hildebrand, sp
Lloyd Brown, sp
Thornton Lee, rp
Denny Galehouse, rp-sp
George Blaeholder, rp-sp

Attendance

500,391 (fourth in AL)

Club Leaders

Batting Avg:	Earl Averill	.378
On-Base Pct:	Earl Averill	.438
Slugging Pct:	Hal Trosky	.644
Home Runs:	Hal Trosky	42
RBIs:	Hal Trosky	162
Runs:	Earl Averill	136
Stolen Bases:	Roy Hughes	20
Wins:	Johnny Allen	20
Strikeouts:	Johnny Allen	165
ERA:	Johnny Allen	3.44
Saves:	Oral Hildebrand	4

April 11 — The Indians sell Clint Brown to the White Sox.

April 14 — The Indians lose the season opener 3–0 to the Tigers before 18,000 at League Park. Schoolboy Rowe pitched the shutout.

Indians home and away games were broadcast in 1936 over radio station WHK with Jack Graney handling the announcing chores.

April 15 — Trailing 5–1, the Indians score eight runs in the third inning and win 14–7 over the Tigers at League Park.

April 17 — The Indians score three runs in the tenth inning to defeat the Browns 13–10 in St. Louis.

April 19 — The Indians trounce the Browns 13–6 in St. Louis.

After being shut out on Opening Day, the Indians scored 47 runs in their next four games.

April 26 — The Indians win an 8–7 decision over the Browns in 16 innings at League Park. In the 16th, the Indians loaded the bases with none out with the help of an error by St. Louis catcher Rollie Hemsley. Roy Hughes bounced to pitcher Jim Walkup, who threw home to force Frankie Pytlak. Hemsley threw to first to retire Hughes, and Johnny Allen, who started the play on second, rounded third. First baseman Jack Burns threw to Hemsley, who tagged Allen with what would have been the last out of a triple play, but the force of Allen's slide knocked the ball from Hemsley's grasp. Allen was safe with the winning run. He also pitched 8⅔ innings of relief and allowed only two hits.

In his first season with the Indians, Allen was 20–10 with a 3.44 ERA. He had a record of 4–5 during the first week of June, then went 16–5 the rest of the way.

May 1 Bruce Campbell is stricken with spinal meningitis for the third time in seven months (see August 3, 1935).

After the attack, manager Steve O'Neill declared that Campbell would never play again. "I have no doubt that his exertion this year restored to activity the germ that had laid dormant since last winter," said O'Neill. "If he gets better, I intend to insist that he get into some business where there is less chance of great physical fatigue that follows every hard-fought ball game." Campbell wouldn't quit, however. He returned to playing status six weeks later (see June 16, 1936), remained in the majors until 1942, then served three years in the Air Force during World War II.

May 2 Spectators are kept away from Indians players during a 7–3 win over the Red Sox at Fenway Park. Fans were moved away from the area around the Cleveland dugout. The restrictions were imposed by Boston health authorities because Bruce Campbell was hospitalized with a contagious form of spinal meningitis, and it was feared that Indians players exposed to Campbell might pass on the disease. Joe Vosmik contributed two homers and two singles to gain the victory.

May 10 The Indians win 9–7 in 15 innings over the Tigers in Detroit. Roy Hughes drove in the go-ahead run with a triple and scored on a single by Frankie Pytlak.

May 24 Lloyd Brown pitches a two-hitter for a 7–0 win over the Tigers at League Park. The only Detroit hits were singles by Gee Walker in the first inning and Jack Burns in the seventh.

May 27 Billy Sullivan, Jr. collects five hits, including two doubles, in five at-bats during a 12–2 victory over the Browns at League Park. The Indians collected 21 hits in all.

In his first season with the Indians, Sullivan batted .351. His father, Billy Sullivan, Sr., played in the majors as a catcher from 1899 through 1916.

May 28 With the Indians trailing 4–2, Odell Hale hits a grand slam off Jack Knott in the seventh inning to key a 6–5 win over the Browns at League Park.

Hale batted .316 with 50 doubles, 13 triples, 14 homers, 87 RBIs, and 126 runs scored in 1936.

June 4 Johnny Allen raises a ruckus during a drunken rage at the Brunswick Hotel in Boston. Irked by the size of the stools at the hotel bar, Allen upended most of them.

Then he got into arguments with a hotel porter and a room service waiter. Allen snatched a fire extinguisher, doused the porter, and slugged the waiter with the contents of the apparatus. A hotel maintenance man, perched on a stepladder while changing a light bulb, was sent to the floor when Allen jerked the support out from under him. Next, he picked up the ladder and smashed it through the plaster in the walls of a hallway. Allen was handed a $50 bill for damages and fined $250 by the Indians.

JUNE 7 The Indians go 16 innings without striking out but lose 5–4 to the Yankees at League Park. The Indians set an American League record for the longest game without a batter striking out.

The game ended on a home run by George Selkirk off Oral Hildebrand, who like, Red Ruffing of the Yanks, pitched a complete game.

JUNE 13 The Indians score in each of the first seven innings and wallop the Athletics 19–1 in the second game of a double header at Shibe Park. The game was called after eight innings by darkness. Philadelphia won the opener 7–3.

JUNE 16 In his first game back after an attack of spinal meningitis (see May 1, 1936), Bruce Campbell collects three hits during an 8–4 win over the Yankees at League Park. Before the game, Campbell was presented with a set of golf clubs and a traveling bag.

JUNE 18 The Indians lose a double header 15–4 and 12–2 to the Yankees in New York.

Hal Trosky's 162 RBIs in 1936 remained a team record for more than sixty years.

JUNE 24 The Indians sweep the Athletics 5–3 and 14–2 at League Park. Earl Averill hit two home runs in the first game and two more in the second. The Indians scored seven runs in the second inning of the nightcap.

Averill led the AL in hits (232) and triples (15) in addition to hitting .378 with 26 homers, 126 RBIs, and 136 runs scored in 1936.

JUNE 26 Joe Vosmik hits a walk-off homer in the tenth inning to defeat the Red Sox 8–7 at League Park.

June 27 In his major league debut, 21-year-old right fielder Roy Weatherly collects three hits in five at-bats during a 14–5 win over the Red Sox at League Park.

Standing five-foot-six and weighing 170 pounds, Weatherly looked like a coming star during his first seven weeks in the majors. After 48 games, he had 83 hits in 208 at-bats for an average of .399. He hit only .241 over the rest of the season, however, to finish at .335, and batted just .201 in 1937. Because of his inconsistent play, inability to hit left-handers, and fiery temper, Weatherly had trouble holding a regular position in the line-up during his seven seasons in the majors.

June 28 The Indians score seven runs in the seventh inning of an 11–3 win over the Red Sox at League Park.

The Indians Sign an Icon

Bob Feller tops the Indians pitching lists in almost every category. Despite missing three full seasons and most of a fourth while serving in the Navy during World War II, he is first in wins (266), first in innings pitched (3,827), first in strikeouts (2,581), first in games started (484), first in complete games (279), second in games (570), second in shutouts (44) and sixth in winning percentage (.621). Feller threw three no-hitters and 12 one-hitters while pitching for the club from 1936 until 1956.

Feller was signed for a "bonus" of one dollar and an autographed ball on July 25, 1935, by Indians scout Cy Slapnicka when Feller was only 16-years-old and in between his sophomore and junior years of high school. The youngster was living on a farm in Van Meter, Iowa, and was blessed with an amazing fastball. He made a spectacular major league debut a year later in 1936. During an exhibition game against the Cardinals on July 6, Feller fanned eight batters in six innings. In his first regular season start on August 23 against the Browns, he struck out 15 batters. On September 13, Feller struck out 17 Athletics batters, which matched the modern major league record then in existence for strikeouts in a game, set by Dizzy Dean, and broke the American League mark of 16.

Because of his tremendous speed, Feller drew immediate comparisons to Walter Johnson, who pitched for the Senators from 1907 through 1927 and at the time was baseball's all-time strikeout leader. Overall, Feller pitched in 14 games, eight of them starts, as a 17-year-old rookie and posted a 5–3 record and a 3.34 ERA. He struck out 76 batters (and walked 47) in 62 innings, an average of 11.0 strikeouts per nine innings. Among qualifiers (minimum 154 innings), the major league leader in the category that season was Van Mungo of the Dodgers, who fanned 6.9 batters per nine innings. The major league average in 1936 was 3.3 strikeouts per nine innings (compared to 6.6 per game in 2006).

A problem developed, however, because Slapnicka, either intentionally or inadvertently, violated the major-minor league agreement then in effect. The Indians nearly lost Feller because of it. Slapnicka had signed Feller to a contract with the Fargo-Moorhead of the Class D Northern League. Then he had that club assign Feller to New Orleans of the Class A Southern Association. Both Fargo-Moorhead and New Orleans were farm clubs of the Indians.

Instead of going to Fargo-Moorhead or New Orleans, Feller remained at his home in Van Meter and was placed on the "voluntary retired list." He attended high school until late-May 1936, after which he reported directly to Cleveland. For nearly a month, Feller worked out with the Indians and pitched for a local amateur team.

Thus Feller got to Cleveland without ever wearing a minor league uniform, though he had been listed in the office of commissioner Kenesaw Landis as having been the property of both Fargo-Moorhead and New Orleans. The rule (since changed) prohibited the signing of an amateur to a major league contract.

After Feller made his exhibition game debut against the Cardinals, Lee Keyser, owner of the Des Moines club in the Class A Western League, claimed that he had attempted to sign Feller, but that Slapnicka had beat him to the punch, a violation of the rules. Landis conducted an investigation that continued through the end of the 1936 season. During a hearing early in the case, Feller told Landis, "I don't want to play anywhere else. I want to play for Cleveland." His father was also adamant and threatened to sue baseball if his son was not allowed to remain an Indian, in part because of his relationship with Slapnicka, a fellow Iowan. The elder Feller and Slapnicka became fast friends.

Landis didn't announce his decision in the Feller case until December 10. In similar cases, the commissioner had ruled players free agents. (He once made 91 players in the Cardinals farm system free agents for violating the major-minor league agreement.) If Feller would have become a free agent and sold himself to the highest bidder, it would have been a financial bonanza for the young pitcher and his family. Feller could have signed with another club for far more money than the Indians were paying him. Based on his performance during the 1936 season, his vast potential, and the fact that he was already a national celebrity because of his record-breaking strikeout performances, it's likely that Feller would have drawn as much as $250,000 on the open market from such wealthy clubs as the Yankees, White Sox, or Tigers. He wanted to remain in Cleveland, however.

In the end, Landis allowed the Indians to keep the pitching phenom but ruled that the club had to pay the Des Moines club $7,500 in damages, an amount that proved to be a tremendous bargain.

JULY 1 Hal Trosky collects five hits, including a double, in six at-bats, but the Indians lose 16–12 in the first game of a double header against the Browns in St. Louis. The second game was tied 5–5 when called by darkness after nine innings.

JULY 2 Just two months after an attack of spinal meningitis, Bruce Campbell collects six hits, including a double, in six at-bats and drives in five runs during a 14–6 win over the Browns in the first game of a double header in St. Louis. Roy Hughes scored five runs. Campbell extending his streak of hits in consecutive at-bats to seven by singling in his first plate appearance in the second game, a 4–2 Cleveland victory, then was taken out for a rest.

JULY 6 Bob Feller makes his debut in an Indians uniform by pitching during a 7–6 exhibition game victory against the St. Louis Cardinals at League Park. Only 17-years-old, Feller struck out eight batters in three innings.

JULY 10 The Yankees swamp the Indians 18–0 in New York.

JULY 19 The Indians run their winning streak to nine games by defeating the Senators 11–5 in the first game of a double header in Washington. The winning streak was snapped in the second tilt with a 9–5 loss that was notable because of the regular season debut of Bob Feller. He went into the game as a reliever in the eighth and pitched one inning, allowing no hits and no runs but walking two.

Feller made his debut at the age of 17 years and 243 days. He is the youngest player in Indians history.

July 24 Earl Averill scores five runs during a 16–3 win over the Athletics at League Park. The Indians scored in seven of eight turns at bat and collected 22 hits in all.

July 28 Roy Weatherly runs his hitting streak to 20 games during a 6–3 win over the Senators at League Park.

July 30 The Indians smack five home runs during an 11–8 win over the Senators at League Park. Hal Trosky hit two homers with Bruce Campbell, Odell Hale, and pitcher Lloyd Brown providing the others.

After the victory, the Indians were 7½ games behind the first place Yankees. The Yanks came to Cleveland for a three-game series beginning on July 31, and the New York club won two with the third ending in a tie. By the end of August, the Indians were 16½ games out of first.

August 2 Playing at Municipal Stadium for the first time since 1933, and the only time in 1936, the Indians and Yankees draw 65,342 fans and tie 4–4 in a contest called after 15 innings by darkness. Hal Trosky ran his hitting streak to 28 games. The game was marred by a horrific injury to Frankie Pytlak. The Cleveland catcher lost a Monte Pearson fastball in the white-shirted crowd sitting in the center field bleachers and was struck flush in the face. Pytlak suffered a triple fracture of his jaw.

Before the game, three of the Marx Brothers (Groucho, Harpo, and Chico), then at the height of their fame, entertained the crowd with a comedy routine.

August 7 The Indians end an 8–1 win over the White Sox at League Park with a triple play. With Luke Appling on second base and Jackie Hayes on first, Tony Piet lined to first baseman Hal Trosky, who fired to shortstop Billy Knickerbocker to force Appling. Knickerbocker then whipped the ball to Trosky before Hayes could scramble back to the bag.

August 8 Earl Averill collects five hits in five at-bats, but the Indians lose 9–7 to the White Sox at League Park.

August 14 The Indians outlast the Browns 12–10 at Sportsman's Park. Cleveland led 10–1 in the fifth inning before stemming the St. Louis comeback.

August 18 The Indians collect 21 hits but lose 11–10 in ten innings to the White Sox Chicago. Odell Hale had five hits, including a homer and a double, in five at-bats.

August 23 In his first starting assignment, 17-year-old Bob Feller becomes an instant national celebrity by striking out 15 batters during a 4–1 win over the Browns at League Park. His catcher was fellow rookie Greek George.

August 27 Trailing 9–7, the Indians score two runs in the ninth inning and one in the tenth to defeat the Senators 10–9 in Washington. Earl Averill's single drove in the winning run.

August 29 The Indians pummel the Athletics 13–2 in the first game of a double header at Shibe Park. Philadelphia won the second game, called after five innings by rain, 5–3.

SEPTEMBER 10 The Indians score three runs in the ninth inning, the last two on a walk-off homer by Hal Trosky, to beat the Yankees 5–4 at League Park.

SEPTEMBER 13 Bob Feller ties the existing modern major league record for strikeouts in a nine-inning game and breaks the American League mark by fanning 17 Athletics during a 5–2 Cleveland win in the first game of a double header at League Park. In 1936, the strikeout record was held by Dizzy Dean, who struck out 17 for the Cardinals in 1933. The American League record was 16, set by Rube Waddell of the A's in 1908. Feller allowed only two hits during the afternoon, although he walked nine, hit a batter, and threw a wild pitch. It was his fifth major league start. Cleveland also won the second game 5–4.

Roy Weatherly's father caused a commotion during the afternoon. When Weatherly was called out on a close play at first, his white-haired father hopped out of a field-level box to register his protest with startled umpire Brick Owens. No punches were thrown, as the elder Weatherly was restrained by several players before he could reach Owens. The apple apparently didn't fall far from the tree. The younger Weatherly had so much trouble with umpires early in his career that his 1940 contract with the Indians called for a $500 bonus if he could make it through the season without arguing with the arbiters.

SEPTEMBER 15 Johnny Allen records his 20th win of the season with a 13–2 decision over the Red Sox at League Park. Hal Trosky drove in seven runs on two homers (his 39th and 40th of the season), a double, and a single.

SEPTEMBER 16 The Indians crush the Red Sox 13–3 at League Park. The contest was called after six inning by rain. Hal Trosky collected four hits, including a homer and a double, in four at-bats. Combined with the performance the day before, Trosky collected eight hits and drove in 12 runs in consecutive games.

Trosky led the American League in RBI in 1936 with 162 and also set a club record that stood until Manny Ramirez collected 165 in 1999. Trosky's 405 total bases led the AL and established a club record that has yet to be surpassed. In addition, he clubbed 42 homers to become the first Cleveland batter to pass the 40 mark. Trosky also had a .343 batting average, 216 hits, and 45 doubles in 1936.

SEPTEMBER 23 The Indians explode for 11 runs in the seventh inning and beat the White Sox 17–2 in the first game of a double header at League Park. Chicago won game two, called after six innings by darkness, 8–3.

OCTOBER 13 An explosion rocks Municipal Stadium, shattering windows, cracking grandstand concrete in three sections, and ripping out some 500 seats. Fire squads rushed to the scene, and at first, it was thought that a bomb had gone off. The subsequent investigation, however, revealed that the blast resulted when a frayed electrical wire in a workroom sparked gas from a leaking line. Fortunately, there were no injuries, as the explosion occurred when there was no one in the vicinity.

December 10 Five weeks after Franklin Roosevelt defeats Alf Landon in the presidential election, commissioner Kenesaw Landis awards Bob Feller to the Indians in a dispute over the rights to his contract. The Des Moines club of the Western League also claimed they owned Feller. Landis ruled that the Indians had signed Feller illegally and awarded the club to pay Des Moines $7,500.

On the same day, the Indians traded Thornton Lee to the White Sox and received Earl Whitehill from the Senators in a three-team deal. Lee was 30 years old and had a record of 12–17 in four seasons with the Indians while Whitehill was a proven veteran. It seemed like a great deal, but the transaction proved to be one the worst the club made during the 1930s. Lee was a steady, above-average pitcher for the White Sox, winning 74 games in the first five seasons following the trade and 105 over the remainder of his career. Lee was still pitching as late as 1948. Whitehill had 197 big league victories when acquired by the Indians but was only 17–16 with a 6.06 ERA in two seasons in a Cleveland uniform.

1937

Season in a Sentence

The Indians continue to spin their wheels in the middle of the American League standings, leading to another change in managers from Steve O'Neill to Ossie Vitt.

Finish • Won • Lost • Pct • GB

Finish	Won	Lost	Pct	GB
Fourth	83	71	.539	19.0

Manager

Roger Peckinpaugh

Stats

Stats	Indians	AL	Rank
Batting Avg:	.280	.281	5
On-Base Pct:	.352	.355	4
Slugging Pct:	.400	.415	5
Home Runs:	103		3
Stolen Bases:	78		4
ERA:	4.39	4.62	3
Fielding Avg:	.974	.972	2
Runs Scored:	817		4
Runs Allowed:	768		3

Starting Line-up

Frankie Pytlak, c
Hal Trosky, 1b
Odell Hale, 2b-3b
Roy Hughes, 3b-2b
Lyn Lary, ss
Moose Solters, lf
Earl Averill, cf
Bruce Campbell, rf
John Kroner, 2b
Bill Sullivan, Jr., c

Pitchers

Mel Harder, sp
Johnny Allen, sp
Willis Hudlin, sp-rp
Denny Galehouse, sp
Bob Feller, sp
Earl Whitehill, sp-rp
Joe Heving, rp

Attendance

564,849 (fourth in AL)

Club Leaders

Batting Avg:	Moose Solters	.323
On-Base Pct:	Bruce Campbell	.392
Slugging Pct:	Hal Trosky	.547
Home Runs:	Hal Trosky	32
RBIs:	Hal Trosky	128
Runs:	Earl Averill	121
Stolen Bases:	Lyn Lary	18
Wins:	Mel Harder	15
	Johnny Allen	15
Strikeouts:	Bob Feller	150
ERA:	Johnny Allen	2.55
Saves:	Joe Heving	5

JANUARY 17 The Indians trade Joe Vosmik, Oral Hildebrand, and Billy Knickerbocker to the Browns for Lyn Lary, Moose Solters, and Ivy Andrews.

In an effort to shake up the team, the Indians traded a starting outfielder, shortstop, and pitcher for a starting outfielder, shortstop, and pitcher. In the long term, neither the Browns nor the Indians gained or lost much in the three-for-three swap.

APRIL 14 Kenesaw Landis declares Tommy Henrich, a free agent. Henrich was a 24-year-old minor league outfielder in the Indians farm system. He had complained to the commissioner that he had been kept in the minors unfairly. Four days later, Henrich signed with the Yankees. Hailing from nearby Massillon, Ohio, Henrich would have been a natural in Cleveland but instead became a star in New York. With the Yanks, Henrich played on eight AL pennant-winners and was named to five All-Star teams.

APRIL 20 The Indians open the season with a 4–3 loss to the Tigers at Detroit. Roy Hughes collected three hits in four at-bats.

APRIL 23 The Indians win the home opener 9–2 over the Browns before 21,000 at League Park.

In May, the Indians entered into a deal with the city of Cleveland to play 13 games on nine dates, including four double headers, at Municipal Stadium. The club split the schedule between the lakefront stadium and League Park from 1937 through 1946. The contests at Municipal Stadium were usually played on weekends and holidays and against big attractions such as the Yankees. Night games were also played there beginning in 1939. After abandoning League Park at the end of the 1946 season, the Indians played at Municipal Stadium exclusively from 1947 through 1993.

APRIL 25 The Indians score two runs in the ninth inning and one in the 11th to defeat the Browns 5–4 at League Park. Earl Averill's two-run single in the ninth tied the contest 4–4. Moose Solters drove in the winner with a single in the 11th to score Lyn Lary.

In his first season with the Indians, Lary played in every inning of every game, batting .290 with 110 runs scored and 46 doubles.

APRIL 28 Earl Averill hits a grand slam off ex-teammate Thornton Lee in the third inning of a 7–2 win over the White Sox at League Park.

Averill hit .299 with 21 homers, 92 RBIs, and 121 runs scored in 1937.

MAY 20 Two weeks after the German dirigible *Hindenburg* erupts in flames at Lakehurst, New Jersey, killing 56 people, the Indians take first place with a 16–5 win over the Red Sox in Boston.

The Indians started the season winning 12 of their first 20 games. On June 9 the club was 24–17 and one-half game out of first, but were below the .500 mark by the end of June and had a 43–51 record on August 10. From August 11 through the end of the season, the Indians posted a mark of 40–20.

MAY 26 The Indians score four runs in the ninth inning to defeat the Athletics 8–6 in Philadelphia. Cleveland garnered two pinch-hit home runs during the afternoon from

Billy Sullivan, Jr., and Bruce Campbell. Sullivan homered with two out in the sixth and Campbell leading off the ninth.

MAY 29 The Indians trounce the White Sox 15–3 in the second game of a double header at League Park. Moose Solters contributed a grand slam off Bill Dietrich in the third inning, Chicago took the opener 4–1.

Whit Wyatt was 2–3 with a 4.44 ERA in 73 innings as a 29-year-old reliever with the Indians in 1937. Despite the unimpressive performance, the club should have kept him. A classic late-bloomer, Wyatt was 78–39 for the Brooklyn Dodgers from 1939 through 1943.

JUNE 7 The Indians score eight runs in the third inning and bombard the Senators 17–5 at League Park. Earl Averill batted twice during the rally and collected a triple and a homer.

JUNE 8 Ahead 8–2 at League Park with victory over the Red Sox seemingly assured, the Indians allow eight runs in the ninth inning to lose 10–8.

JUNE 20 The Indians score two runs in the ninth inning to defeat the Red Sox 8–7 in the second game of a double header at Fenway Park. Cleveland trailed 5–0 after five innings. A double by Moose Solters broke the 7–7 tie. Boston won the opener 5–2.

In his first season with the Indians, Solters hit .323 with 20 homers and 109 RBIs.

JUNE 21 Johnny Allen goes under the knife for an appendectomy. He had a 4–0 record at the time of the operation and didn't return to action until early August. Previously, Allen missed four weeks in April and May with stomach pains. He made four starts in May and June before his problem was diagnosed as appendicitis.

JULY 5 The Indians sweep the Browns 14–4 and 15–4 in St. Louis. Hal Trosky clubbed three homers and drove in seven runs in the opener. He struck a three-run homer off ex-teammate Oral Hildebrand in the fifth inning, a solo shot against Hildebrand in the seventh, and a blast with two men on base facing Sheriff Blake in the ninth.

Trosky hit .298 with 32 homers and 128 RBIs in 1937.

JULY 7 Mel Harder closes out the All-Star Game, played at Griffith Stadium in Washington, with three shutout innings to earn a save in an 8–3 American League win.
Earl Averill contributed to one of the most famous injuries in All-Star Game history. A line drive off the bat off Averill struck and broke the big toe of Cardinals hurler Dizzy Dean with two out in the third inning. Dean tried to come back too soon following the injury and was never again a consistently effective pitcher.

JULY 11 Bob Feller pitches a two-hitter but walks six and loses 3–2 to the Tigers in Detroit.

JULY 14 An altercation between Steve O'Neill and Washington pitcher Carl Fischer highlights an 11–3 win over the Senators at League Park.

The Indians released Fischer in May after a verbal clash with O'Neill. Before the July 14 game, Fischer taunted the Cleveland manager over the club's losing record. O'Neill followed Fischer into the Senators clubhouse and challenged him to a fight. The 31-year-old Fischer refused to spar with the 56-year-old Indians skipper, who was pushed to the exit by the Washington players.

JULY 21 Three days after Amelia Earhart disappears over the Pacific, the Indians sweep the Athletics 9–8 and 8–7 at League Park, with a pair of ninth-inning rallies, both with the help of two-baggers by Bruce Campbell. In the opener, the score was 8–8 when Bruce Campbell doubled and Odell Hale singled for the win. In the second tilt, Cleveland trailed 8–7 when entering the final inning before Hal Trosky hit a triple, Moose Solters walked, and Campbell struck a two-run double.

AUGUST 6 Bob Feller strikes out 12 in nine innings but walks ten, and the Indians lose 7–6 in ten innings to the Yankees in New York. The Yanks tied the score 5–5 with three runs in the ninth off Feller, the last two on a two-out homer by Joe DiMaggio. Cleveland scored in the top of the tenth, but New York rallied for two in their half against reliever Joe Heving for the win. The Indians outfield had no putouts during the game.

AUGUST 19 Bruce Campbell collects a homer, triple, and double during a 9–1 victory over the Browns in St. Louis.

AUGUST 25 Bob Feller strikes out 15 batters during an 8–1 win over the Red Sox at League Park.

SEPTEMBER 2 Bob Feller fans 12 during a 4–2 win over the Yankees at League Park.

SEPTEMBER 3 A nine-run rally in the eighth inning caps a 15–3 win over the Browns at League Park.

SEPTEMBER 18 Trailing 6–1, the Indians score six runs in the eighth inning to beat the Red Sox 7–6 in Boston. Odell Hale drove in the tying and winning tallies with a double.

SEPTEMBER 21 With the Indians down 3–1 in the fifth inning, Hal Trosky hits an inside-the-park grand slam off Wes Ferrell leading to a 6–3 win over the Senators in Washington. Center fielder Mel Alamda tried for a shoestring catch of Trosky's drive and missed, and the ball rolled toward the wall with Hal circling the bases. Johnny Allen won his 13th straight game of 1937, running his record to 13–0. Combined with two wins at the end of the 1936 season, Allen had collected 15 wins in a row.

SEPTEMBER 28 Moose Solters homers in the tenth inning to defeat the White Sox 7–6 in Chicago.

SEPTEMBER 30 Johnny Allen defeats the White Sox 6–0 in the first game of a double header in Chicago giving him a record of 15–0 in 1937. His total winning streak, over two seasons, was 17.

With the victory, Allen was one shy of the single season American League record for consecutive wins in a season. Walter Johnson of the Senators and Joe Wood of the Red Sox both won 16 in a row in 1912. Lefty Grove matched the record streak in 1931 while pitching for the Athletics, and Schoolboy Rowe also won 16 in succession with the Tigers in 1934. He also had a chance at the record for most wins in a season without a loss. The previous mark was a 12–0 campaign by Tom Zachary of the Yankees in 1929. Manager Steve O'Neill announced that Allen would start the season finale on October 3 on two day's rest.

October 3 Johnny Allen loses his chance for an American League record-tying 16th consecutive with a 1–0 loss to the Tigers in Detroit. Jake Wade pitched a one-hitter for the Tigers. The lone Cleveland hit was a single by Hal Trosky in the seventh. The run scored in the first inning on a double by Pete Fox and a sharply hit single by Hank Greenberg that sizzled past third baseman Odell Hale. Allen's final record in 1937 was 15–1 with a 2.55 ERA in 173 innings. He did set an AL record for most consecutive wins over two seasons with 17 over 1936–37. The mark was tied by Dave McNally of the Orioles in 1968 and 1969 and broken when Roger Clemens won 20 straight for the Blue Jays and Yankees in 1998 and 1999.

Allen was irate in the clubhouse after the game. He accused Hale of sloppy fielding, insisting that Greenberg's grounder should have been the third out in the first inning instead of a run-scoring single. Hale didn't appreciate Allen's criticism and heated words were exchanged, before the intervention of Steve O'Neill stopped a fight. Returning to Cleveland on the train that night, Allen continued his abuse of Hale in the dining car. Again, O'Neill stepped in and prevented bloodshed.

Jake Wade had a career record of 10–15 a 5.56 ERA and one shutout entering the October 3, 1937, contest, compared to Allen's lifetime mark of 84–29 and an earned run average of 3.52. Wade didn't pitch another shutout in the majors until 1943 and finished his career in 1946 with a record of 27–40.

October 20 Ossie Vitt replaces Steve O'Neill as manager.

O'Neill was often criticized by the front office, the press, and the fans for being too easygoing and too lenient. Cleveland management believed that the club would play better if O'Neill was tougher on the players, but it just wasn't part of his personality. Ossie Vitt was hired by Alva Bradley to instill a fighting and combative spirit on the ball club. Vitt was 47 years old had been a light-hitting but fine-fielding infielder with the Tigers and Red Sox from 1912 through 1921. He gained fame as a smart and feisty minor league manager with Salt Lake City, Hollywood, and Oakland in the Pacific Coast League and Newark, a Yankee farm club, in the International League. His 1937 Newark club was 109–43 and won the pennant by 25½ games. Vitt presided over three of the most turbulent seasons in Indians history. He had constant problems getting along with players, often by levying petty fines following verbal brow beatings. Vitt liked to air his team's problems to reporters and was not bashful about taking verbal shots at his players in print. He changed the line-up at the slightest provocation. Under Vitt, the Indians continued to spin their wheels as a good, but not great, club posting records of 86–68 in 1938 and 87–67 in 1939. The 1940 campaign was different. Cleveland finished second, only one game behind the pennant-winning Tigers. Nonetheless, many players appealed to Bradley in June seeking to have Vitt fired because of his abrasiveness. Ossie remained through the end of the season but was fired on October 28. He never managed another big league club despite an impressive 262–198 record in three seasons in Cleveland. O'Neill later managed the Tigers from 1943 through 1948, winning the World Series in 1945. He was also the skipper of the Red Sox in 1950 and 1951, and the Phillies from 1952 through 1954.

1938

Season in a Sentence

Under new manager Ossie Vitt, the Indians hold first place for 72 days from the start of the season through July 12 but are out of the pennant race by Labor Day.

Finish • Won • Lost • Pct • GB

Finish	Won	Lost	Pct	GB
Third	86	68	.566	13.0

Manager

Ossie Vitt

Stats

Stats	Indians	AL	Rank
Batting Avg:	.281	.281	3
On-Base Pct:	.350	.358	6
Slugging Pct:	.434	.415	3
Home Runs:	113		3
Stolen Bases:	83		2
ERA:	4.60	4.78	4
Fielding Avg:	.974	.971	3
Runs Scored:	847		4
Runs Allowed:	782		4

Starting Line-up

Frankie Pytlak, c
Hal Trosky, 1b
Odell Hale, 2b
Ken Keltner, 3b
Lyn Lary, ss
Jeff Heath, lf
Earl Averill, cf
Bruce Campbell, rf
Roy Weatherly, cf
Rollie Hemsley, c
Moose Solters, lf

Pitchers

Bob Feller, sp
Mel Harder, sp
Johnny Allen, sp
Earl Whitehill, sp
Willis Hudlin, sp-rp
Johnny Humphries, rp
Denny Galehouse, rp-sp

Attendance

652,006 (third in AL)

Club Leaders

Batting Avg:	Jeff Heath	.343
On-Base Pct:	Earl Averill	.429
Slugging Pct:	Jeff Heath	.602
Home Runs:	Ken Keltner	26
RBIs:	Ken Keltner	113
Runs:	Hal Trosky	106
Stolen Bases:	Lyn Lary	23
Wins:	Bob Feller	17
	Mel Harder	17
Strikeouts:	Bob Feller	240
ERA:	Mel Harder	3.83
Saves:	Johnny Humphries	6

FEBRUARY 10 The Indians trade Billy Sullivan, Jr., Roy Hughes, and Ed Cole to the Browns for Rollie Hemsley.

Nicknamed "Rollicking Rollie," Hemsley was 31 when acquired by the Indians, his fourth club in the majors. The first three teams got rid of him in large part because of his frequent drunken behavior, which he continued in Cleveland (see April 24, 1938). Hemsley was the Indians starting catcher from 1938 through 1941, a period in which he whipped alcoholism by joining Alcoholics Anonymous. He joined the organization in 1939 after being suspended by the Indians for fighting with a New York Times *reporter and throwing lit matches on the bunk of the Indians traveling secretary during a train trip.*

APRIL 19 The Indians lose 6–2 to the Browns on Opening Day before 31,600 at Municipal Stadium. Johnny Allen, who had a 15–1 record in 1937, took the loss.

After the Opening Day defeat, the Indians won six in a row. Allen won his next 12 decisions (see July 3, 1938).

APRIL 20 In his first start of the season, Bob Feller pitches a one-hitter for a 9–0 win over the Browns at League Park. The only St. Louis hit occurred in the sixth inning when

Billy Sullivan, Jr., who played for the Indians in 1936 and 1937, beat out a tap to Feller on a close decision.

At the age of 19, Feller was 17–11 with a 4.08 earned run average in 277⅔ innings in 1938. He led the AL in strikeouts (240), walks (208), most strikeouts per nine innings (7.8), fewest hits per nine innings (7.3), and lowest opponents batting average (.220).

APRIL 24 Rollie Hemsley is suspended for three days and fined $250 by Ossie Vitt. Hemsley was roaring drunk when he bumped into Vitt at the team hotel in Detroit. Hemsley was also suspended during spring training for getting into a bar fight in New Orleans.

MAY 2 The Indians score ten runs in the fifth inning of an 11–3 win over the Tigers at League Park.

MAY 3 Ken Keltner hits two homers and drives in six runs during a 10–9 win over the Senators in Washington.

Keltner was a 21-year-old rookie third baseman in 1938 and hit .279 with 26 homers and 113 RBIs. He remained with the club until 1949 and played in seven All-Star Games. Keltner ranks fifth among Indians in total bases (2,494), sixth in games played (1,513), sixth in at-bats (5,655), sixth in doubles (306), seventh in runs-batted-in (850), eighth in hits (1,561), and tenth in homers (163).

MAY 4 The Indians lose a 13-inning, 1–0 heartbreaker to the Senators in Washington. Bob Feller pitched the first ten innings and allowed only three hits.

MAY 19 The Indians take first place with a 15–3 thrashing of the Senators at League Park. Jeff Heath hit a grand slam during the afternoon.

As a 23-year-old outfielder in his first full season in the majors, Heath hit .343 with 21 homers, 112 RBIs, and a league-leading 18 triples. A native of Fort William, Ontario, Canada, Heath played in 1,383 games for the Indians from 1936 through 1945. His slugging percentage of .506 with the club still ranks eighth among players with at 2,000 plate appearances in a Cleveland uniform. Heath was plagued by injuries and inconsistency, however, and often rankled Indians management with his volatile temper and lack of hustle.

JUNE 3 Down 5–0, the Indians score three runs in the sixth inning, six in the eighth, and one in the ninth to defeat the Athletics 10–5 in Philadelphia.

JUNE 4 The Indians score eight runs in the fourth inning of an 11–4 win over the Senators in Washington.

JUNE 5 A double by relief pitcher Willis Hudlin in the tenth inning drives in the winning run during a 5–4 win over the Senators in Washington.

JUNE 7 In the second inning of a 7–5 win over the Red Sox at Fenway Park, umpire Bill McGowan directs Johnny Allen to cut the tattered sleeves off his undershirt. McGowan responded to complaints from Boston hitters that the shirt was a distraction. Allen was sent to the clubhouse to change. After a five-minute delay, manager Ossie Vitt went to investigate Allen's tardiness. When the pitcher refused to obey McGowan's order to change his shirt and return to the field, Vitt replaced Allen with Bill Zuber. Zuber gave up three runs, and was relieved by Johnny Humphries, who pitched 6⅔ hitless innings retiring 20 of the 21 batters to face him.

Allen was fined $250 by Vitt. In response, Allen threatened never to pitch for the Indians again. He relented when team president Alva Bradley bought the undershirt from Allen, along with the rest of the uniform he wore that day, for the same $250 that the hurler was fined. The Higbee department store, where Alva's brother Chuck was president, exhibited the garments on a mannequin in the front window facing Public Square as a publicity stunt. People flocked to the store to see the display, no doubt spending much more inside the store than the $250 it cost the Bradley brothers to purchase the shirt.

JUNE 22 The Indians sweep the Yankees 3–1 and 7–1 before 67,459 at Municipal Stadium. The two wins gave Cleveland a record of 36–20.

JUNE 24 The Indians defeat the Red Sox 7–6 at League Park to take a 4½-game lead in the AL pennant race.

JUNE 30 Johnny Allen wins his 11th game in a row by hitting a two-out, walk-off single in the ninth inning to beat the Tigers 10–9 at League Park. Frankie Pytlak's triple set the stage for Allen's blow. Allen came into the contest as a reliever in the eighth inning replacing Bob Feller.

JULY 3 Johnny Allen wins his 12th straight game with a 2–1 decision over the White Sox in the first game of a double header at Comiskey Park. Chicago won the second tilt 3–0. On the same day, the 1920 Indians played the 1908 Indians in a game at League Park. Nearly 7,000 turned out for the event. Tris Speaker's 1920 club defeated Nap Lajoie's 1908 outfit 8–0. Earl Smith hit a home run. Cy Young pitched one inning at the age of 71.

The July 3 win gave Allen a record of 12–1 in 1938. He also had records of 29–2 since September 1936, and 43–7 since June 1936. As of July 3, 1938, Allen had a career record of 96–32 and was 32-years-old. He was not nearly as effective afterward, however. Allen began complaining of a sore arm and was shelved for the 1938 season in September after losing seven of his last nine decisions. In January 1939, he underwent surgery to repair his shoulder and was 18–15 for the Indians over two seasons before being sold to the Browns after the 1940 season. Allen finished his career in 1944 with 142 wins and 75 losses.

JULY 12 Odell Hale hits for the cycle but the Indians lose 9–8 to the Senators at Griffith Stadium. His homer in the ninth inning completed the cycle and tied the score 8–8 before Washington broke the deadlock in the bottom half.

JULY 13 A 4–3 loss to the Senators at Griffith Stadium knocks the Indians out of first place. Washington scored three times in the ninth inning off Bob Feller for the win.

The Indians held first place continuously from May 19 through July 12. The club failed to regain the top spot for the remainder of he 1938 season.

Boston slugger Jimmy Foxx presents Earl Averill with a questionable-looking bat at a pre-game ceremony.

July 27 The Indians win a 12–11 slugging match against the Athletics at League Park. Cleveland broke a 9–9 tie with three runs in the eighth inning.

August 3 Earl Averill is presented with a luxury Cadillac Sixty Special prior to a double header against the Red Sox at Municipal Stadium. The car, valued at $2,400, was purchased with donations from Indians fans. Averill was driven around the playing field while perched on the fender. Red Sox slugger Jimmie Foxx, who was one of Averill's rivals for the batting title, was presented with an over-sized bat full of holes as a gag gift. Foxx good-naturedly posed for photographers holding the bat. Boston won the first game 4–3, while Cleveland took the nightcap 8–6.

Averill hit .330 with 14 homers in 1938.

August 5 Bob Feller walks 11 batters during a 6–1 loss to the Yankees at Municipal Stadium.

The Indians went into the August 5, 6, and 7 series against the Yankees 2½ games out of first place. The Yanks swept the three-game set to take a 5½-game lead in the race. By August 20, the Indians were ten games out, curing the case of pennant fever hovering over Cleveland for most of the season.

August 10 The Indians score five runs in the ninth inning to beat the Browns 9–6 in St. Louis. Hal Trosky broke the 6–6 tie with a three-run homer.

Trosky hit .334 with 19 homers and 110 runs-batted-in during the 1938 season.

August 13 The Indians score nine runs in the first inning and wallop the White Sox 13–4 in the first game of a double header at Comiskey Park. Chicago won the nightcap 2–1.

August 20 Hank Helf, the Indians third-string catcher, snares a ball dropped 708 feet from a position near the top of the Terminal Tower in downtown Cleveland. The Terminal Tower was built in 1930, and in 1938 it was the tallest building in the U.S. outside of New York City. Helf made his catch one-handed. The ball popped straight up out of his mitt, and he secured it before it hit the ground. Later, Frankie Pytlak grabbed another ball tossed from the building. Rollie Hemsley and coaches Johnny Bassler and Wally Schang, both former catchers, also made attempts to latch on to some of the 12 balls dropped by Ken Keltner, but missed, as the missiles bounced off the concrete or landed in nearby shrubbery. Helf and Pytlak set "altitude" records for catching balls. The previous mark was set by several players who caught balls dropped from the 550-foot-tall Washington Monument, among them Pop Shriver (1894), Gabby Street (1908) and Billy Sullivan, Sr. (1910). Mathematicians calculated that the balls were traveling 138 miles per hour when they struck the gloves of Helf and Pytlak. Some 25,000 gathered to watch the stunt, which was sponsored by the Come to Cleveland Committee. According to the Associated Press report, the organization was formed principally to "let the world know that Cleveland does other things besides having relief crises and torso murders."

Helf played two seasons for the Indians and had a single in 14 at-bats for a batting average of .077.

August 23 The Indians lose 13–3 and 14–12 to the Red Sox in a double header in Boston. The second game ended on a grand slam by Jimmie Foxx off Willis Hudlin.

August 26 Bob Feller allows 15 runs in seven innings in a 15–9 loss to the Yankees in the first game of a double header in New York. In the second tilt, Frankie Pytlak hit an inside-the-park homer, a two-run triple, and a two-run single to lead Cleveland to an 8–5 victory.

August 27 Monty Pearson of the Yankees no-hits the Indians for a 12–0 win in the second game of a double header in New York. Bruce Campbell flied out to end the game. Pearson played for the Indians from 1932 through 1935. The Yanks also won the opener 8–7.

Due to early-season postponements, the Indians played 38 games in August 1938, including ten double headers. From August 21 through August 27, the club played 12 games in seven days.

September 7 Mel Harder pitches a two-hitter to defeat the Tigers 1–0 in Detroit. Bruce Campbell's single in the eighth inning drove in the lone run of the game. The only hits off Harder were singles by Dixie Walker and Chet Morgan.

Harder was 17–10 with a 3.83 ERA in 1938.

September 9 Lou Boudreau makes his major league debut during an 11–5 loss to the Tigers at League Park. Boudreau went into the game as a substitute for Ken Keltner at third base in the seventh inning. In two plate appearances, Boudreau walked and grounded out.

Boudreau would become one of the most famous figures in Cleveland baseball history, although he didn't play in another big league game for nearly a year. Lou returned to the minors to hone his skills with Buffalo in the International League in 1939 before earning a late-season recall to the majors (see August 7, 1939).

September 29 Roy Weatherly hoists a pitch over the wall in the tenth inning to lift the Indians to a 9–8 win over the White Sox at League Park.

October 2 On the final day of the season, Bob Feller fans 18 batters to set the existing modern major league record for strikeouts in a nine-inning game but loses 4–1 to the Tigers in the first game of a double header before 27,000 on a cold and drizzly day at Municipal Stadium. Feller allowed seven hits and walked seven. Harry Eisenstat was the winning pitcher. Feller toppled the previous record of 17, set by Dizzy Dean of the Cardinals in 1933 and Feller himself in 1936. The 18th strikeout victim was Chet Laabs in the ninth inning. Laabs fanned five times during the contest. Feller, then 19-years-old, admitted he was tiring at the end. "Wait 'til I get to be 22 or 23," he said. "I won't tire then." Detroit also won the second tilt, called after seven innings by darkness, 10–8. The crowd came to the ballpark that afternoon to see if Tiger slugger Hank Greenberg could tie or break another record. Greenberg entered the day with 58 home runs, two shy of Babe Ruth's single season mark of 60 set in 1927. Greenberg collected four hits in seven at-bats but failed to hit a homer.

Feller held the strikeout record for a nine-inning game alone until Sandy Koufax fanned 18 in 1959. That mark was broken in 1969 when Steve Carlton struck out 19 (also in a loss) while pitching for the Cardinals. The current record is 20 by Roger Clemens, twice with the Red Sox in 1986 and 1996, and Cubs pitcher Kerry Wood in 1998. Randy Johnson also fanned 20 in the first nine innings of an 11-inning contest with Arizona in 2001. Tom Cheney of the Senators struck out 21 while hurling a 16-inning complete game in 1962.

DECEMBER 15 Six weeks after Orson Welles fools many Americans into believing that Martians are invading New Jersey during his Mercury Theater radio program on Halloween Eve, the Indians trade Denny Galehouse and Tommy Irwin to the Red Sox for Ben Chapman.

1939

Season in a Sentence

Amid growing discord between the players and manager Ossie Vitt, the Indians finish a distant third with a strong September.

Finish • Won • Lost • Pct • GB

Finish	Won	Lost	Pct	GB
Third	87	67	.565	20.5

Manager

Ossie Vitt

Stats

Stats	Indians	AL	Rank
Batting Avg:	.280	.279	3
On-Base Pct:	.350	.352	4
Slugging Pct:	.413	.407	4
Home Runs:	85		6
Stolen Bases:	72		4 (tie)
ERA:	4.08	4.62	2
Fielding Avg:	.970	.969	4
Runs Scored:	797		4
Runs Allowed:	700		2

Starting Line-up

Rollie Hemsley, c
Hal Trosky, 1b
Oscar Grimes, 2b-1b-ss
Ken Keltner, 3b
Skeeter Webb, ss
Jeff Heath, lf
Ben Chapman, cf
Bruce Campbell, rf
Roy Weatherly, lf-cf-rf
Odell Hale, 2b
Lou Boudreau, ss
Frankie Pytlak, c

Pitchers

Bob Feller, sp
Mel Harder, sp
Al Milnar, sp
Johnny Allen, sp
Willis Hudlin, sp
Harry Eisenstat, rp
Joe Dobson, rp

Attendance

563,926 (fifth in AL)

Club Leaders

Batting Avg:	Hal Trosky	.335
On-Base Pct:	Hal Trosky	.405
Slugging Pct:	Hal Trosky	.589
Home Runs:	Hal Trosky	25
RBIs:	Hal Trosky	104
Runs:	Ben Chapman	101
Stolen Bases:	Ben Chapman	18
Wins:	Bob Feller	24
Strikeouts:	Bob Feller	246
ERA:	Bob Feller	2.85
Saves:	Al Milnar	3
	Willis Hudlin	3

APRIL 18 The scheduled season opener against the Browns in St. Louis is rained out. The contests of April 19 and 20 were also postponed.

APRIL 21 The Indians finally get the 1939 season underway by defeating the Tigers 5–1 before 20,000 at Municipal Stadium. Bob Feller pitched a complete game. Skeeter Webb collected three hits. Playing in his major league debut, Indians second baseman Jim Shilling was taken out of the game when hit on the head with a throw while sliding into third base on a triple.

Before the game, manager Ossie Vitt was made a member of the Oneida tribe. A Native American band paraded on the field and presented Vitt with a huge floral piece and a tomahawk. Judy Garland, then 16-years-old, sang the National Anthem. Miss Garland had just finished filming The Wizard of Oz, *which was released to theaters on August 15, 1939.*

APRIL 24 Two Indians pitchers combine to walk 15 batters during a 9–3 loss to the White Sox at League Park. Starter Johnny Humphries issued five passes in 1⅓ innings and Tom Drake walked ten in 5⅓ innings before Johnny Allen made it through 2⅓ innings without walking anyone.

The game was Drake's major league debut. He pitched five games and 15 innings with the Indians and walked 19 batters while striking out only one.

APRIL 25 Inserted into the line-up for slumping Earl Averill, Bruce Campbell hits two homers and drive in five runs during a 7–1 win over the White Sox at League Park.

APRIL 29 Bob Feller strikes out 13 batters during a 7–1 win over the Tigers in Detroit.

Feller was 24–9 with a 2.85 ERA in 1939. He led the American League in wins, complete games (24 in 35 starts), innings pitched (296⅔), strikeouts (246), and lowest opponents batting average (.210).

MAY 3 The Indians sell Lyn Lary to the Dodgers.

MAY 5 Al Milnar pitches an 11-inning complete game and scores the winning run for a 2–1 win over the Yankees at League Park. In the 11th, Milnar walked against Lefty Gomez and scored on a double by Hal Trosky.

MAY 7 A two-run, walk-off single by Odell Hale in the tenth inning beats the Senators 8–7 at Municipal Stadium.

The Indians played 30 games at Municipal Stadium in 1939, with the remainder at League Park.

MAY 11 Roy Weatherly collects five hits in five at-bats during a 7–0 win over the Athletics at League Park.

MAY 14 Bob Feller's mother is hit by a batted ball during a 9–4 win over the White Sox at Comiskey Park. Feller's parents traveled to Chicago from Van Meter, Iowa, to see him pitch on Mother's Day. In the third inning, a foul ball off the bat of Marv Owen hit Mrs. Feller, breaking her glasses and causing a cut requiring six stitches. After checking on the condition of his mother, Feller struck out Owen.

MAY 16 At Shibe Park in Philadelphia, the Indians participate in the first night game in American League history. The Indians scored five runs in the tenth inning to defeat the Athletics 8–3.

The Cincinnati Reds were the first club in the majors to play home games at night in 1935. The Reds were followed by the Dodgers in 1938, the Athletics, Phillies, Indians, and White Sox in 1939, the Giants, Browns, Pirates and Cardinals in 1940, the Senators in 1941, the Braves and Yankees in 1946, the Red Sox in 1947, and the Tigers in 1948. Of the 16 pre-expansion clubs, the Cubs were the last holdout, playing night games at Wrigley Field for the first time in 1988 (see June 27, 1939).

May 25 Bob Feller pitches a one-hitter and Ken Keltner hits three consecutive homers during an 11–0 win over the Red Sox in Boston. All three homers by Keltner were struck off Emerson Dickman in the fifth, seventh, and ninth innings. The only hit off Feller was a single in the second inning by Bobby Doerr.

Keltner hit .325 with 13 homers and 97 RBIs in 1939.

May 28 Johnny Allen is at the center of controversy during a 6–0 win over the White Sox at Municipal Stadium. Allen and Chicago manager Jimmie Dykes threatened to trade blows in the third inning, and Gee Walker of the White Sox charged the Indians pitcher after being hit on the head with a pitched ball in the sixth. Players of both teams stepped in before any blows were struck.

May 30 Odell Hale and Jeff Heath hit inside-the-park home runs on consecutive pitches off Johnny Marcum in the seventh inning of a 7–2 win over the Browns in the first game of a double header at Municipal Stadium. Bruce Campbell scored all three runs during a 12-inning, 3–2 Cleveland victory in the nightcap. In the 12th, Campbell tripled and crossed the plate on Ben Chapman's sacrifice fly.

June 6 Down 7–2, the Indians score five runs in the eighth inning and one in the ninth to win 8–7 over the Red Sox at League Park. Doubles by Ben Chapman and Oscar Grimes produced the ninth-inning tally.

June 10 Johnny Allen pitches a two-hitter to defeat the Athletics 6–0 at League Park. The only Philadelphia hits were singles by Earle Brucker in the second inning and Dick Siebert in the fourth.

For much of the 1939 season, the Indians lead-off batter was Rollie Hemsley. Though Ossie Vitt has to be given credit for thinking outside the box by putting a catcher at the top of the batting order, Hemsley had an on base percentage of .309 in 1939, compared to the AL average of .352. In addition, Rollie had only two stolen bases in six attempts.

June 14 The Indians send Earl Averill to the Tigers for Harry Eisenstat and cash.

Indians fans were angry over the trade of Averill for a second-line pitcher, but Earl was 37-years-old and had little left in the tank. He played only 159 more major league games after leaving Cleveland, hitting .261 with 12 homers.

June 23 The Indians score seven runs in the seventh inning and mash the Athletics 13–5 in Philadelphia.

June 25 Ben Chapman, Hal Trosky, and Jeff Heath hit three consecutive homers off Athletics pitcher Buck Ross with two out in the seventh inning of an 8–4 win in the first game of a double header in Philadelphia. The Indians lost the second game 10–2.

Trosky hit .335 with 25 homers and 104 runs-batted-in during the 1939 season.

JUNE 27 The Indians play the first home night game in club history, beating the Tigers 5–0 before 55,305 at Municipal Stadium. Bob Feller was the star, allowing only one hit and striking out 13. The only Detroit hit was a single in the sixth inning by Earl Averill, who had been traded by the Indians 13 days earlier.

Rules in both leagues limited clubs to playing only seven night games a season in 1939. The Indians didn't play a majority of their home games at night until 1961.

JULY 1 After Willis Hudlin puts the Indians in a 5–0 hole, Johnny Broaca pitches 7⅓ innings of shutout relief allowing only one hit in securing an 8–5 win over the Browns at League Park. Cleveland scored one run in the second inning, two in the third, three in the fourth and two in the sixth during the comeback.

JULY 3 Ben Chapman ties an American League record by collecting three triples during a 4–2 win over the Tigers in Detroit.

JULY 9 The Indians sweep the Browns 14–2 and 5–1 during a double header in St. Louis.

JULY 11 At Yankee Stadium, Bob Feller closes out a 3–1 American League win in the All-Star Game with 3⅔ shutout innings. He allowed one hit, one walk, and fanned two.

JULY 13 The Indians score five runs in the ninth inning to tie the score 5–5, only to lose 6–5 in ten innings to the Red Sox at League Park.

JULY 23 The Indians sweep the Senators 11–2 and 4–3 at Municipal Stadium. In the opener, the Indians score seven runs in the eighth inning. Cleveland scored two runs in the ninth for the game two victory. A pinch-hit, walk-off single by Frankie Pytlak drove in the winning run. The rally started on a double by Jeff Heath.

JULY 25 A total of 14 runs are scored in the ninth inning of a 12–8 Indians win over the Athletics in Philadelphia. The score was 3–3 before Cleveland scored nine runs in the top of the ninth. The A's countered with five in their half in a futile rally.

AUGUST 2 The Indians sell Moose Solters to the Browns.

Solters was dealt to the White Sox after the 1939 season. While playing for the Sox in 1941, he was struck in the temple with a ball during fielding practice. Shortly thereafter, he began to lose his eyesight and within a few years was totally blind.

AUGUST 6 The Indians sweep the Yankees 5–4 and 7–1 before 76,753 at Yankee Stadium.

AUGUST 7 Lou Boudreau makes his first major league start, collecting a triple and a single in five at-bats during a 6–5 win over the Browns during a night game at Municipal Stadium.

A slick-fielding shortstop and steady hitter, Boudreau played for the Indians from 1938 through 1950 and managed the club from 1942 through 1950. He was named manager of the Indians despite being only 24 years old *(see November 25, 1941)**. His leadership skills were evident early in his life.*

Boudreau was captain of the basketball and baseball teams at the University of Illinois when he agreed to sign a contract with the Indians in 1938. He played professional basketball for the Hammond Pros of the National Basketball League in 1938–39 and was coach of the team briefly the following season. Boudreau also was the head coach of the freshman basketball team at Illinois before becoming Indians skipper. His peak season was 1948, when he led the Indians to a world championship. Not only did he mange the club, but won the MVP award by batting .355 with 18 homers, 106 RBIs and 116 runs scored. The club retired Boudreau's number 5 in 1970, the same year that he was elected to the Hall of Fame. The street next to Municipal Stadium was named Boudreau Boulevard in his honor.

AUGUST 18 Bob Feller loses an 11-inning, 1–0 decision to the White Sox in the first night game ever played at Comiskey Park. Feller allowed only one hit through the first ten innings. In the 11th, he walked opposing pitcher Eddie Smith, then allowed a double to Jackie Hayes and a single to Mike Kreevich.

AUGUST 24 The Indians sweep the Athletics 10–2 and 17–2 in a double header at League Park. Cleveland scored ten runs in the sixth inning of the second game.

AUGUST 27 The Indians win by scores of 1–0 and 5–3 in a double header against the Red Sox at Municipal Stadium. Bob Feller pitched the shutout. Bruce Campbell drove in the lone run with a triple in the eighth inning.

AUGUST 28 Jeff Heath punches an abusive fan during a 6–5 loss to the Red Sox at League Park. After he fouled out on a 3–0 pitch in the ninth inning with the tying run on third base, Heath was heaped with abuse by the fan. Heath walked over and punched the man on the shoulder. After Heath landed the blow, Cleveland police quickly hustled the fan out of the ballpark.

Four days later, Germany invaded Poland, triggering a declaration of war from England and France and the beginning of World War II. The conflict would embroil the United States militarily on December 7, 1941, with the attack by the Japanese on Pearl Harbor.

SEPTEMBER 8 Bob Feller wins his 20th game of the season with a 12–1 decision over the Browns in St. Louis.

SEPTEMBER 12 Oscar Grimes hits a home run off Lefty Gomez in the tenth inning to defeat the Yankees 4–3 in New York.

SEPTEMBER 17 Roy Weatherly collects five hits in seven at-bats during an 18–5 win in the second game of a double header against the Athletics in Philadelphia. The Indians lost the opener 4–2.

SEPTEMBER 23 Mel Harder is given a new Buick by fans prior to a 6–3 loss to the Tigers at League Park.

THE STATE OF THE INDIANS

The 1940 Indians just missed the pennant, finishing one game behind the Tigers with a record of 89–65. In spite of the success, the players were in open revolt over the Captain Bligh behavior of manager Ossie Vitt, who was fired at the end of the season. In 1941, the club was 75–79 under Roger Peckinpaugh, the worst record of any Cleveland club since 1928. Peckinpaugh was then promoted to general manager and 24-year-old Lou Boudreau was hired to run the club as player-manager. During the first five years under Boudreau's leadership, the Indians had only one winning record. Things began to change in July 1946 when Bill Veeck bought the club. The Indians were 68–86 in 1946, 80–74 in 1947, and 97–58 with a world championship in 1948. Although Veeck sold the Indians in 1949, the club was a pennant-contender yearly through the mid-1950s. Overall, the Indians were 800–731 during the 1940s, a winning percentage of (.523) that was the fourth best in the American League behind the Yankees, Red Sox, and Tigers. AL pennant-winners outside of Cleveland were the Tigers (1940 and 1945), Yankees (1941, 1942, 1943, 1947, and 1949), Browns (1944) and Red Sox (1946).

THE BEST TEAM

The 1948 Indians finished the regular season in a tie for first place with the Boston Red Sox. After winning a one-game playoff at Fenway Park, the Indians won the World Series in six games over the Boston Braves.

THE WORST TEAM

Just two years before the world championship, the Indians were 68–86 and finished in sixth place, 36 games out of first. The winning percentage of .442 was the worst of any Indian team between 1928 and 1969.

THE BEST MOMENT

The Indians won their second, and to date last, world championship by defeating the Braves 4–3 in Boston on October 11, 1948.

THE WORST MOMENT

The Indians lost the 1940 pennant by one game to the Tigers during a season in which the players battled with manager Ossie Vitt nearly as fiercely as it did the opposition.

THE ALL-DECADE TEAM • YEARS W/INDIANS

Jim Hegan, c	1941–42, 1946–57
Les Fleming, 1b	1941–42, 1945–47
Joe Gordon, 2b	1947–50
Ken Keltner, 3b	1937–44, 1946–49
Lou Boudreau, ss	1938–50
Jeff Heath, lf	1936–45
Roy Weatherly, cf	1936–42
Hank Edwards, rf	1941–43, 1946–49
Bob Feller, p	1936–41, 1945–56
Bob Lemon, p	1941–42, 1946–58
Steve Gromek, p	1941–53
Al Smith, p	1940–45

Boudreau, Feller, and Lemon are all in the Hall of Fame. Gordon and Keltner are not in the Hall of Fame, but Gordon was named to nine All-Star teams and Keltner to seven. Both deserve consideration for enshrinement at Cooperstown. Feller was also on the 1930s All-Decade Team. Dale Mitchell (1946–56) was the second best outfielder to play for the Indians during the 1940s, but was a left fielder and ranks behind Heath. The Indians had difficulty finding a capable center fielder from the time Earl Averill was traded in 1939 until Larry Doby moved to the position in 1948. Other top players with the Indians during the 1940s included second baseman Ray Mack (1938–44, 1946) and pitchers Jim Bagby, Jr. (1941–45) and Al Milnar (1936, 1938–43).

THE DECADE LEADERS

Batting Avg:	Lou Boudreau	.300
On Base Pct:	Lou Boudreau	.385
Slugging Pct:	Jeff Heath	.490
Home Runs:	Ken Keltner	124
RBIs:	Lou Boudreau	692
Runs:	Lou Boudreau	758
Stolen Bases:	Lou Boudreau	47
Wins:	Bob Feller	137
Strikeouts:	Bob Feller	1,396
ERA:	Bob Feller	2.90
Saves:	Ed Klieman	30

THE HOME FIELD

At the start of the decade, the Indians continued to play in two different ballparks as they had during the late 1930s. Generally, League Park was used for weekday afternoon games, and Municipal Stadium for all other contests. The Indians abandoned League Park after the 1946 season, and Municipal Stadium was used exclusively from 1947 through 1993.

THE GAME YOU WISH YOU HAD SEEN

On August 8, 1948, in a key game during the pennant race, the Indians win the first game of a double header against the Yankees by overcoming a 6–1, seventh-inning deficit to win 8–6 with Lou Boudreau, out of the game with injuries, coming off the bench to deliver a game-tying single. The Indians also won the second tilt 2–1.

THE WAY THE GAME WAS PLAYED

There were two significant developments during the 1940s. The first was World War II, which involved the United States from 1941 and 1945 and depleted major league rosters as many players donned military uniforms and saw combat. The other was integration with the arrival of Jackie Robinson with the Dodgers in 1947. The Indians became the first American League club, and the second in the majors, to integrate by signing Larry Doby in July 1947. League stats and averages in 1949 looked very similar to those of 1940, although offense dipped during the war years and there was a surge in home runs at the end of the decade.

THE MANAGEMENT

Alva Bradley owned the Indians from November 1927 through July 1946. His clubs were consistent winners but seldom contended for the pennant and never reached the World Series. There was a dramatic change in the fortunes of Cleveland baseball when Bill Veeck purchased the club from Bradley in 1946. He immediately revived a nearly dormant franchise, not only on the field but at the box office. In 1945, the Indians drew 558,182 fans to rank 11th among the 16 big league clubs. In 1948, the club attracted 2,620,627 into Municipal Stadium to set a baseball attendance record that stood until the Dodgers drew 2,755,184 in 1962, the first year that Dodger Stadium opened. No American League club topped the Indians 1948 mark until the Yankees drew 2,627,417 in 1980. The restless Veeck didn't remain in Cleveland for long, however. He sold the Indians to a group headed by Ellis Ryan in November 1949. General managers under Bradley were Cy Slapnicka (1935–41) and Roger Peckinpaugh (1941–46). Veeck did not hire a general manager, taking on the role himself. The two individuals who were second in command under Veeck were Harry Grabiner (1947–48) and Hank Greenberg (1948–49). Greenberg became general manager when Ryan bought the club. Field managers were Ossie Vitt (1938–40), Peckinpaugh (1941), and Lou Boudreau (1942–50).

THE BEST PLAYER MOVE

The Indians purchased Larry Doby from the Newark Eagles of the Negro Leagues in July 1947, which integrated the American League and gave the Indians a future Hall of Famer. The best trade brought Early Wynn and Mickey Vernon from the Senators for Joe Haynes, Eddie Klieman, and Eddie Robinson in December 1948.

THE WORST PLAYER MOVE

During the 1946–47 off-season, the Indians acquired Joe Gordon and Gene Bearden from the Yankees and Al Lopez from the Pirates in three separate deals. Gordon and Bearden helped the Indians win the 1948 world championship, while Lopez would manage the club to the 1954 World Series. However, the Indians gave up talented players Allie Reynolds, Gene Woodling, and Sherm Lollar in those deals.

1940s

1940

Season in a Sentence

The players demand that Alva Bradley fire manager Ossie Vitt in June during a pennant race in which the club finishes one game short of reaching the World Series.

Finish • Won • Lost • Pct • GB

Finish	Won	Lost	Pct	GB
Second	89	65	.578	1.0

Manager

Ossie Vitt

Stats

Stats	Indians	AL	Rank
Batting Avg:	.265	.271	5
On-Base Pct:	.332	.342	7
Slugging Pct:	.398	.407	5
Home Runs:	101		6
Stolen Bases:	53		5
ERA:	3.63	4.38	1
Fielding Avg:	.975	.970	1
Runs Scored:	710		6
Runs Allowed:	637		1

Starting Line-up

Rollie Hemsley, c
Hal Trosky, 1b
Ray Mack, 2b
Ken Keltner, 3b
Lou Boudreau, ss
Ben Chapman, lf-rf
Roy Weatherly, cf
Beau Bell, rf
Jeff Heath, lf
Frankie Pytlak, c

Pitchers

Bob Feller, sp
Al Milnar, sp
Al Smith, sp
Mel Harder, sp
Johnny Allen, sp-rp
Joe Dobson, rp

Attendance

902,576 (third in AL)

Club Leaders

Batting Avg:	Roy Weatherly	.303
On-Base Pct:	Hal Trosky	.392
Slugging Pct:	Hal Trosky	.529
Home Runs:	Hal Trosky	25
RBIs:	Lou Boudreau	101
Runs:	Lou Boudreau	97
Stolen Bases:	Ben Chapman	13
Wins:	Bob Feller	27
Strikeouts:	Bob Feller	261
ERA:	Bob Feller	2.61
Saves:	Johnny Allen	5

January 20 The Indians trade Bruce Campbell to the Browns for Beau Bell.

April 16 On Opening Day, Bob Feller pitches a no-hitter to defeat the White Sox 1–0 on a 47-degree day at Comiskey Park. His parents and sister were among the 14,000 in the stands. Eddie Smith was the hard-luck losing pitcher. Feller walked five and struck out eight. He worked out of a bases-loaded jam in the second inning caused by a two-base error by center fielder Roy Weatherly and two walks. The inning ended on a strikeout of Bob Kennedy. The run scored in the fourth on a single by Jeff Heath and a two-out triple by Rollie Hemsley, who also caught the no-hitter. In the ninth, Mike Kreevich led off by grounding out to second baseman Ray Mack. Moose Solters then popped up to shortstop Lou Boudreau for the second out. Luke Appling followed, worked the count to 3–2, fouled off four pitches, then walked. Taffy Wright pulled a grounder that was earmarked for right field, but Mack darted to his left, knocked down the ball, and while on his knees threw a strike to first baseman Hal Trosky. Wright was out by half a step.

Feller is the only pitcher to hurl a complete game no-hitter on Opening Day in major league history. Red Ames of the Giants held the Dodgers hitless for nine innings in the 1909 opener, but yielded a hit in the tenth and lost the game 3–0 in the 13th. Feller finished the 1940 season with a record of 27–11. He led the league in wins, games pitched (43), games started (37), complete games (31), shutouts (four), innings pitched (320⅓), strikeouts (261), strikeouts per nine innings (7.3), earned run average (2.61), opponents batting average (.210), and opponents on base percentage (.285).

APRIL 19 In the home opener, the Indians defeat the Tigers 4–0 before 26,529 at Municipal Stadium. Johnny Allen pitched a three-hit shutout on a day in which the temperature was in the low 40s. Cleveland scored all four runs in the sixth inning, three of them on a homer by Jeff Heath.

The Indians played 49 games at Municipal Stadium in 1940. The rest of the games were held at League Park.

APRIL 27 Lou Boudreau hits the first two homers of his career during a 4–2 win over the Tigers in Detroit. He led off the first inning with a home run, and clubbed his second in the eighth to break a 2–2 deadlock.

In his first full season in the majors, Boudreau played in every game and hit .295 with 46 doubles, nine homers and 101 RBIs.

APRIL 28 Hal Trosky hits a two-run homer in the tenth inning to defeat the Tigers 11–9 in Detroit. The Tigers scored six runs in the ninth inning to force extra innings.

Trosky hit .295 with 25 homers and 93 RBIs in 1940.

MAY 3 Utility infielder Oscar Grimes shatters a cheekbone when struck in the face by a ball during pre-game practice before a game against the Senators in Washington that was eventually rained out.

MAY 9 Feller pitches a three-hitter to win 4–0 over the Yankees in New York. Feller had a no-hitter in progress until Joe DiMaggio singled in the seventh.

MAY 11 Johnny Allen pitches the Indians to a 1–0 win over the Browns at League Park. Rollie Hemsley drove in the lone run with a walk-off single in the ninth inning.

MAY 17 The Indians score ten runs in the first inning and wallop the Senators 18–1 at League Park. The first inning runs scored on seven walks and five hits.

MAY 24 The Indians are the visiting team in the first night game played at Sportsman's Park in St. Louis, and defeat the Browns 3–2. Bob Feller pitched a complete game and struck his first major league home run.

MAY 26 The Indians trounce the Browns 13–1 in the second game of a double header at Sportsman's Park. St. Louis won the opener 5–3.

JUNE 8 Eleven days after the surrender of Holland and Belgium to Germany, and four days after 350,000 British troops are evacuated at Dunkirk, Al Milnar pitches a two-hitter to defeat the Yankees 3–0 at Yankee Stadium. The only New York hits were singles by Charlie Keller and Buster Mills.

The Case of Indians Players Vs. Ossie Vitt

Things seemed to be going reasonably well for the Indians early in the 1940 season. On the morning of June 13, the club had a record of 28–21 and was in third place, one game out of first. But the club had just lost eight of their last 13 games, all on an Eastern road trip. A vast majority of the players believed that manager Ossie Vitt, who was in his third year with the club, was responsible for many of the defeats. In a mass protest unprecedented in baseball, 12 members of the Indians confronted team president Alva Bradley demanding that Vitt be fired. The spokesman for the players was Mel Harder, who had been with the team since 1928. "We think we have a good chance to win the pennant," said Harder, "but we'll never win it with Vitt as manager. If we can get rid of him, we can win. We all feel sure of that." Others at the meeting included Hal Trosky, Ken Keltner, Jeff Heath, Oscar Grimes, and Rollie Hemsley.

The players told Bradley they could not play the kind of baseball of which they were capable as long as Vitt remained at the helm. According to the protesters, Vitt had ridiculed them in conversations with newspapers writers, fans, and opposing players and managers, had undermined the confidence and morale of the players by sarcastic comments on their failures during the course of games, and held grudges. "Naturally I am going to look into the matter," said Bradley. "But until I have investigated thoroughly I can't say what action will be taken." Bradley also told the players, "If this story gets out, you'll be ridiculed for the rest of your lives." It did, in the *Cleveland Plain Dealer* the very next morning, sharing page one with the news that the Nazis had captured Paris.

Cleveland fans made their feeling known. During the first few home games following the June 13 meeting between Bradley and his players, Ossie Vitt was given a tremendous ovation when he took the line-up card to the umpires at home plate prior. Many of the insurgent players were booed whenever they stepped to the plate.

After the June 16 twin bill, a statement signed by 21 of the 24 players on the team called off the rebellion against Vitt. The statement read: "We, the undersigned, publicly declare to withdraw all statements referring to the resignation of Ossie Vitt. We feel this action is for the betterment of the Cleveland Baseball Club."

The players and Vitt managed to co-exist with a tenuous truce for the rest of the season, though the atmosphere in the clubhouse and the dugout was strained to say the least. The press dubbed the players the "Cry Babies" the "Bawl Team" and "Half Vitts," and they were jeered mercilessly by fans in opposition ballparks, many of whom brought baby bottles and rattles. During a game in Detroit, a baby carriage was wheeled across the top of the Cleveland dugout. Despite the visible dissension on the club between the players and Vitt, the Indians were in the pennant race until the final weekend, and finished one game behind the first-place Detroit Tigers. A month after the final game of the season, Bradley fired Vitt.

A native of Cleveland, Milnar had the best season of his career in 1940 with an 18–10 record, a 3.27 ERA and four shutouts.

June 11 — Bob Feller has a rare bad outing, losing 9–2 to the Red Sox in Boston. "Look at him," hollered Ossie Vitt on the bench. "He's supposed to be my ace. How am I supposed to win a pennant with that kind of pitching?"

June 12 — Mel Harder is the losing pitcher in a 9–5 defeat at the hands of the Red Sox in Boston. At the end of the game, Ossie Vitt confronted Harder and said, "It's about time you win one with the money you're making."

Indians players had chafed under the criticisms of Vitt since he became manager in 1938. The June 12 loss was Cleveland's eighth in the last 13 games to drop their record to 28–21. A promising season seemed to be slipping away, and on the train from Boston to Cleveland, Indians players met and decided to try to oust Vitt as manager.

JUNE 13 A contingent of 12 Indians, speaking on behalf of nearly every player on the roster, meet with team president Alva Bradley and present a petition demanding that manager Ossie Vitt be fired. The players complained about Vitt's "dugout demeanor, criticism and disparaging comments." Bradley promised only that he'd "look into the matter." At the time, the Indians had a record of 29–21 and were in second place, one-half game behind the Red Sox.

JUNE 14 Johnny Allen pitches a two-hitter in defeating the Athletics 5–0 at League Park. After walking Benny McCoy to lead off the first inning, Allen retired 22 batters in a row. Just five outs from a no-hitter, Allen allowed a single to Sam Chapman. Two batters later, Joe Gantenbein also singled.

JUNE 16 Bob Feller strikes outs 12 batters during a 4–3 win over the Athletics in the first game of a double header at Municipal Stadium. The Indians also won game two by the same 4–3 score.

After the game, 21 Indians withdrew their call for the firing of Ossie Vitt saying the action was in "the best interest of the team."

JUNE 17 Declaring he had "upset nerves" and wasn't feeling well, Frankie Pytlak leaves the Indians to return to his home in Buffalo. He first left the club in Boston a week earlier to seek medical counsel, but physicians could find nothing wrong with him. Pytlak rejoined to the Indians, but hit only .141 in 62 games. He was traded to the Red Sox at the end of the season.

JUNE 20 The Indians move into first place by hammering the Senators 12–1 at League Park.

JUNE 23 The day after France surrenders to Germany, the Indians extend their winning streak to eight games with a 4–1 decision over the Red Sox in the first game of a double header at Municipal Stadium. The streak ended with a 2–0 loss in the nightcap.

JULY 12 Bob Feller strikes out 13 batters and pitches a one-hitter to defeat the Athletics 1–0 in Philadelphia. Feller was six outs from his second no-hitter of 1940 when Dick Siebert singled leading off the eighth inning.

JULY 23 Al Milnar pitches the Indians to a 1–0 win over the Athletics at Municipal Stadium. Roy Weatherly drove in the winning run with a single in the fifth inning.

JULY 26 The Indians bang out 20 hits and thrash the Senators 13–2 at League Park.

JULY 31 The Indians win a thrilling 12–11 come-from-behind decision over the Red Sox at Municipal Stadium. Down 7–0, Cleveland scored five times in the fourth, four of them on a grand slam by Ken Keltner off Denny Galehouse. The Indians still trailed 11–5 before scoring three runs in the seventh inning and four in the eighth.

AUGUST 12 Bob Feller earns his 20th victory with an 8–5 decision over the Tigers at League Park.

August 14 Al Smith pitches a one-hitter for a 4–0 win over the White Sox before 59,063 at Municipal Stadium. The only Chicago hit was a single by Skeeter Webb in the third inning.

Smith entered the 1940 season as a 32-year-old pitcher who seemed to be completely washed-up after being released by the Phillies the previous season. He was a pleasant surprise in 1940, winning eight of his first nine decisions and posting a 15–7 record. He remained with Cleveland until 1945.

August 19 In his major league debut, Cal Dorsett enters a 16–7 loss to the Red Sox in Boston as a reliever in the eighth inning and allows a homer to Bobby Doerr, the first batter he faces.

The August 19 appearance was the only game that Dorsett pitched in 1940. He played in five contests in 1941 and two more in 1947, closing his career with eight games pitched, 13⅔ innings, and an 11.85 ERA.

August 20 Trailing 5–2, the Indians score seven runs in the eighth inning and win 11–6 over the Red Sox in Boston. Ken Keltner drove in six runs, four of them on a grand slam.

August 21 The Indians defeat the Red Sox 4–2 in Boston to take a 5½-game lead in the American League pennant race.

The Indians had a 71–46 record at the conclusion of the August 21 game. With a golden opportunity to reach the World Series, the club was 15–19 over the remainder of the 1940 season.

August 31 Down 4–0, the Indians score four runs in the ninth inning and one in the tenth to defeat the White Sox 5–4 in Chicago. In the 12th, Ray Mack singled, stole second, and scored on a single by Frankie Pytlak.

September 9 The Indians drop out of first place with a 2–1 loss to the White Sox at Municipal Stadium. It was Cleveland's seventh defeat in a span of eight games. The Indians closed the day one-half game behind the Tigers and one-half game ahead of the third-place Yankees.

September 11 The Indians split a double header against the Yankees before a crowd of 33,471 at Municipal Stadium who spent much of the afternoon throwing lemons and other edibles at the opposition. New York third base coach Art Fletcher was a particular target. The Yanks won the opener 3–1, while Cleveland took the second contest, called after six innings by darkness, 5–3.

Lights had been installed at Municipal Stadium the previous season, but an American League rule prevented lights from being turned on to finish day games. The rule was in effect until 1951.

September 13 The Indians win 1–0 over the Red Sox at Municipal Stadium. There were only five hits in the game, as Al Milnar pitched a three-hitter and Boston's Jim Bagby, Jr. surrendered just two hits. The only two Cleveland base hits occurred in the fourth inning on singles by Roy Weatherly and Jeff Heath. Weatherly scored on a double play ground out by Lou Boudreau.

September 15 The Indians retake first place with a 5–0 and 8–5 sweep of the Athletics at Municipal Stadium. Bob Feller threw a two-hitter in the opener. He retired the first 22 batters to face him before Dick Siebert singled with one out in the eighth. Siebert also broke up a no-hit bid by Feller on July 12. Frankie Hayes added the second Philadelphia hit with a single in the ninth.

September 16 Mel Harder retires the first 20 Athletics batters to face him before Frankie Hayes singles with two out in the seventh inning. Harder allowed five more hits, but won 8–3 in the first game of a double header. The Indians scored seven runs in third inning. Philadelphia won the second game 3–2.

The Indians entered a three-game series in Detroit from September 20 through 22 tied for first place with the Tigers with identical 85–61 records.

September 20 In the first game of a crucial three-game series against the Tigers in Detroit, the Indians take a 4–1 lead, but allow five runs in the eighth inning off Mel Harder and reliever Bob Feller and lose 6–5. Ossie Vitt drew criticism for bringing Feller into the game. Feller had pitched two complete games during the previous five days. He allowed singles to all three batters he faced.

When the Indians arrived at the train station in Detroit the previous evening, they were ambushed by a mob of some 1,000 to 5,000, depending upon the source. When the club walked up the ramp and through the station foyer, they were hit with tomatoes, eggs, lemons, and other forms of produce, much of it in a decided state of decay.

September 21 The Indians fall two games behind the Tigers with a 5–0 loss to the Tigers in Detroit. Schoolboy Rowe pitched the shutout.

September 22 The Indians salvage the third game of the pennant-showdown series against the Tigers in Detroit winning 10–5. Bob Feller pitched a complete game for his 27th victory of the season and struck one of five Cleveland homers on the day. The others were hit by Hal Trosky, Ben Chapman, Roy Weatherly, and Ken Keltner.

The Indians split two games against the Browns in Cleveland on September 24 and 25 and fell two games behind in the pennant race because the Tigers won twice against the White Sox in Detroit in a double header on the 25th. The Yankees were 2½ games back and still had a slim mathematical chance for the pennant. The Indians closed the season with three games against the Tigers on September 27, 28, and 29. Cleveland needed to win all three games to claim their first AL pennant since 1920.

September 27 The Indians are eliminated from the pennant race by losing 2–0 to the Tigers on a cold and gloomy day before a riotous crowd of 45,553 on a Friday afternoon at Municipal Stadium. Little-known pitcher Floyd Giebell beat Bob Feller, who allowed only three hits. Rudy York drove in both runs with a homer in the fourth inning with Charlie Gehringer on base. The game was interrupted frequently by a barrage of fruits and vegetables from partisan Cleveland fans and crews had to come onto the field to clean up the litter. In the first inning, Hank Greenberg was hit with two or three tomatoes as he tried to catch a fly ball. Umpire Bill Summers grabbed the public address microphone and warned the crowd that every Cleveland player who hit a fly ball would be out if Detroit fielders were interfered by the throwing of debris. After Summers threatened to forfeit the contest to the Tigers, Ossie Vitt also pleaded with the fans to desist via the p.a. system. Later, a stadium vendor dropped a basket of green tomatoes and empty beer bottles out of the upper deck of the grandstand and hit Tiger catcher Birdie Tebbetts, who was sitting in the bullpen. Tebbetts was knocked out by the deluge, which landed on his head, but he was not injured seriously. When he regained consciousness, Tebbetts chased after the culprit, who was being escorted from the stadium by a policeman and planted a solid punch to the man's nose. Even in the ninth inning, eggs were thrown at Detroit players while they were in the batter's box.

The choice by Detroit manager Del Baker to pitch 30-year-old Floyd Giebell, a longtime minor leaguer with little big league experience, was a shock. Since the Tigers only had to win one game out of three in the series to clinch the pennant, Baker virtually conceded the first game by using a rookie against Bob Feller and saving his top two starters for the final two games. Entering the contest, Giebell had made only one big league start and had a record of 2–1. Giebell wasn't even eligible to pitch in the 1940 World Series because he was added to the roster after September 1. He spent most of the season at Buffalo in the International League, where he was 15–17 with a 3.73 ERA. The September 27, 1940, win was Giebell's last in the majors and his only shutout. In 1941, his last year in the big leagues, he was 0–0 in 17 games and 34⅓ innings with an earned run average of 6.06.

September 29 On the final day of the season, the Indians clinch second place with a 3–2 win in 14 innings against the Tigers at Municipal Stadium. The game ended when Beau Bell was hit by a pitch with the bases loaded. The Indians finished one game behind Detroit and one game ahead of the Yankees.

The Tigers lost the World Series four games to three to the Cincinnati Reds. There has never been an all-Ohio Fall Classic.

October 28 Ossie Vitt is fired as manager of the Indians.

Alva Bradley ended weeks of speculation by firing Vitt following the rebellion of his players and missing the World Series. Vitt never managed another major league team.

November 12 Seven days after Franklin Roosevelt defeats Wendell Willkie in the presidential election, Roger Peckinpaugh is named manager of the Indians. He had previously managed the club from 1928 through 1933. From 1934 through 1940, he managed Kansas City in the American Association and New Orleans in the Southern Association and worked for the AL promotional bureau.

December 20 The Indians trade Frankie Pytlak, Odell Hale, and Joe Dobson for Jim Bagby, Jr., Gee Walker, and Gene Desaultels.

The son of Jim Bagby, Sr., who won 31 games in 1920 for the world champion Indians, Jim, Jr. was a fine addition. He captured 17 victories for Cleveland in both 1942 and 1943. The Indians would have been much better off keeping Dobson instead of Bagby, however. The youngest of 14 children born to a poor

Texas farming family, Dobson lost his thumb and left forefinger playing with a dynamite cap at the age of nine. Despite the handicap, he was an effective pitcher in the American League into the early 1950s.

DECEMBER 24 The Indians trade Ben Chapman to the Senators for Joe Krakauskas and sell Johnny Allen to the Browns for $20,000.

1941

Season in a Sentence

Roger Peckinpaugh is given a second chance as manager, and the club holds first place for 60 days early in the season before finishing with a losing record for the first time in eight years.

Finish • Won • Lost • Pct • GB

Finish	Won	Lost	Pct	GB
Fourth (tie)	75	79	.487	26.0

Manager

Roger Peckinpaugh

Stats

	Indians	AL	Rank
Batting Avg:	.256	.266	7
On-Base Pct:	.323	.341	7
Slugging Pct:	.393	.389	3
Home Runs:	103		3
Stolen Bases:	63		4
ERA:	3.90		3
Fielding Avg:	.976	.972	1
Runs Scored:	677		7
Runs Allowed:	668		3

Starting Line-up

Rollie Hemsley, c
Hal Trosky, 1b
Ray Mack, 2b
Ken Keltner, 3b
Lou Boudreau, ss
Gee Walker, lf
Roy Weatherly, cf
Jeff Heath, rf
Soup Campbell, cf
Oscar Grimes, 1b
Gene Desaultels, c

Pitchers

Bob Feller, sp
Al Milnar, sp
Al Smith, sp
Jim Bagby, Jr., sp
Clint Brown, rp

Attendance

745,948 (second in AL)

Club Leaders

Batting Avg:	Jeff Heath	.340
On-Base Pct:	Jeff Heath	.396
Slugging Pct:	Jeff Heath	.586
Home Runs:	Jeff Heath	24
RBIs:	Jeff Heath	123
Runs:	Lou Boudreau	95
Stolen Bases:	Lou Boudreau	18
Wins:	Bob Feller	25
Strikeouts:	Bob Feller	260
ERA:	Bob Feller	3.15
Saves:	Clint Brown	5
	Joe Heving	5

FEBRUARY 3 The Indians purchase Joe Heving from the Red Sox.

FEBRUARY 7 The Indians purchase Clint Brown from the White Sox.

APRIL 15 The Indians lose 4–3 to the White Sox on Opening Day before 46,064 at Municipal Stadium. Bob Feller, who pitched a no-hitter against Chicago in the opener in 1940, pitched only six innings and walked seven. Ray Mack homered for the Indians.

APRIL 16 Al Milnar pitches a two-hitter to defeat the White Sox 6–0 at League Park. The only Chicago hits were consecutive fifth-inning singles by Larry Rosenthal and Mike Kreevich.

April 30 The Indians win 6–5 over the Athletics at League Park with a three-run rally in the ninth inning that started with two out and no one on base. Red Howell walked as a pinch-hitter, Roy Weatherly doubled, and Ken Keltner smacked a three-run, walk-off homer into the wooden bleachers in left-center field.

May 1 The Indians win 13–8 over the Athletics at League Park. Bob Feller drove in four runs and recorded his 1,000th career strikeout. Feller was 22 years and 179 days old when he recorded his 1,000th strikeout. He is the youngest pitcher to reach that figure since the 60-foot, six-inch pitching distance was established in 1893. Bert Blyleven, at 23, is the second youngest with 1,000 K's.

May 5 The Indians stretch their winning streak to 11 games with a 2–1 win over the Senators at League Park. Bob Feller struck out 12 batters. Rollie Hemsley drove in the winning run with a walk-off single in the ninth inning.

The win gave Cleveland a 16–4 record and a 4½-game lead in the AL race.

May 13 Lou Boudreau homers in the tenth inning to defeat the Yankees 2–1 in New York.

Boudreau hit .257 with ten homers and a league-leading 45 doubles in 1941.

May 17 The Indians win 12–9 over the Red Sox in Boston. The victory gave Cleveland a 23–9 record and a five-game lead.

May 21 The Indians score four runs in the 11th inning to defeat the Senators 4–0 in Washington. Bob Feller pitched a complete game, allowing only four hits.

May 25 Bob Feller fans 13 batters during a 6–0 victory over the Browns at Municipal Stadium. Jeff Heath became the first player to homer into the upper deck at the stadium.

With the victory, Cleveland was 28–12 and were 4½ games ahead in the pennant race.

May 29 Bob Feller pitches his third consecutive shutout, beating the Tigers 9–0 in Detroit.

Feller pitched 30 consecutive scoreless innings over four starts from May 21 through June 2.

June 6 Bob Feller records his fourth shutout in five starts, beating the Athletics 2–0 at League Park.

June 11 The Indians defeat the Senators 6–4 at League Park. The victory gave Cleveland a 36–20 record and a 4½-game lead in the AL pennant chase.

June 18 The Indians score seven runs in the second inning and defeat the Athletics 14–2 in Philadelphia. There were five Cleveland home runs, all by infielders. Hal Trosky struck two, with Ray Mack, Lou Boudreau, and Ken Keltner each adding one.

June 19 The Indians swamp the Athletics 12–1 in Philadelphia.

June 21 Al Milnar pitches a 13-inning complete game but is the losing pitcher in a 1–0 decision against the Senators in Washington. The lone run crossed the plate on a throwing error by Lou Boudreau.

June 22 On the day that Germany invades the Soviet Union, Bob Feller runs his won-lost record to 15–3 with a 6–0 win over the Senators in Washington. Feller made it halfway to the 30-win circle in just the 65th game played by the Indians in 1941. It was also his fifth shutout in a span of 33 days.

Feller won number 16 on June 26 in Cleveland's 68th game. Number 19 came on July 18 in the club's 86th contest of 1941. From June 27, 1940, through June 26, 1941, Feller won 32 games. The Indians played 158 games during that span.

June 26 The Indians use a device to protect their heads while batting for the first time in history during an 11–8 win over the Red Sox in Boston.

Major league players in 1941 tried out lightweight plastic shields that were inserted into their caps while at the plate. Batting helmets didn't become commonplace until the late-1950s.

June 28 The Indians drop out of first place with a 6–4 loss at Municipal Stadium.

The Indians failed to regain the top spot in the league over the remainder of the 1941 season. The club stayed within sight of first place until mid-July but went 25–47 over the last 72 games to finish the season with a losing record. The win percentage of .487 was the Indians worst since 1928.

July 4 The Indians score five runs in the ninth inning to defeat the Browns 9–8 in the first game of a double header at Municipal Stadium. Ken Keltner hit a two-out, three-run homer to pull Cleveland within one at 8–7. The tying and winning runs scored on a single by Jeff Heath and an error by right fielder Joe Grace. The second tilt was scheduled to end at 5:45 p.m. by prior agreement between the two clubs so that the Festival of Freedom celebration could be staged at the stadium. The Indians trailed 2–1 heading into the bottom of the seventh with the appointed moment fast approaching. After two reached base, Lou Boudreau smacked a double for a 3–2 Indians win.

July 8 In the All-Star Game in Detroit, Bob Feller is the starting pitcher for the American League and throws three shutout innings, allowing one hit and striking out four. The AL won 7–5 with four runs in the ninth inning, the last three on a walk-off homer by Ted Williams.

July 10 On Bob Feller Night at Municipal Stadium, Feller triples in the ninth inning and scores on Lou Boudreau's walk-off single to defeat the Athletics 3–2. It was his 100th career victory. Feller was honored in pre-game ceremonies.

Feller was 22 years and 249 days old when he won his 100th career game. On his 23rd birthday, Feller had 107 career victories. No one since 1900 has recorded that many wins at that age. The next closest pitcher to Feller has been Joe Wood, who won 81 games before turning 23 in 1912. The most wins by a pitcher at 23 since 1940 is Dwight Gooden, who was 73–26 during his major league career when he reached his 23rd birthday in 1987.

JULY 16 Joe DiMaggio extends his record-breaking hitting streak to 56 games during a 10–3 Yankee win over the Indians at Municipal Stadium. DiMaggio was 3-for-4 with two singles off Al Milnar and had a double against Joe Krakauskas.

JULY 17 Due to the pitching of Al Smith and Jim Bagby, Jr. and the fielding brilliance of third baseman Ken Keltner, Joe DiMaggio's record-breaking hitting ends at 56 games. DiMaggio was hitless in three at-bats during a 4–3 Yankee win before 67,468 at Municipal Stadium. In the first and seventh innings with Smith pitching, Keltner made sensational backhanded stops of hot smashes and threw out DiMaggio with equally astonishing throws. Keltner fielded both balls behind the bag. In the fourth, Smith walked the Yankee star on a 3–2 pitch. DiMaggio lost his last chance in the eighth, coming to bat against Bagby with the bases filled and one out. However, he bounded to shortstop Lou Boudreau, who was celebrating his 24th birthday. The ball took a bad hop off Boudreau's chest, but he grabbed it in time to throw to second to start a double play.

DiMaggio collected a hit the following afternoon against the Indians to start a 16-games hitting streak. If he had garnered a hit on July 17, his streak would have reached 73 games. DiMaggio's 56-game streak is still the record.

Flanked by General Manager Cyril Slapnicka (left) and Club President Alva Bradley (right), Bob Feller signs a contract reportedly worth $30,000, making him the highest paid pitcher in the majors.

The second longest hitting streak in major league history is 44 by Willie Keeler 1897 and Pete Rose in 1978. The second longest hitting streak of DiMaggio's major league career was 23 games in 1940. He did have a 61-game hitting in the minors with the San Francisco Seals of the Pacific Coast League in 1933.

AUGUST 3 Bob Feller records his 20th win of 1941 with a 6–3 decision over the Athletics in the first game of a double header in Philadelphia. The A's won the second tilt 4–3.

Feller's 20th victory occurred in Cleveland's 99th game of the season. He was still on a pace to win 30 games but finished the year with a 25–13 record and a 3.15 ERA. He led the league in wins, games pitched (44), shutouts (six), innings pitched (343), and strikeouts (260). Feller completed 28 of his 40 starts and walked 194 batters.

AUGUST 6 The Tigers score all 11 of their runs in the third inning of an 11–2 victory over the Indians at League Park.

AUGUST 7 Bob Feller walks 11 batters during a 13-inning complete game and loses to the Tigers 4–3 at League Park.

AUGUST 17 Gee Walker mixes it up with a fan in Chicago between games of a double header against the White Sox. Walker and George Mack, a pro wrestler, swapped punches. Mack was a friend of Cleveland pitcher Clint Brown and made a remark that Walker didn't care for, leading to a heated exchange before fists were raised. The Indians lost both games 8–3 and 4–3 in ten innings.

AUGUST 27 Jeff Heath drives in seven runs on two homers and a triple during an 11–4 win over the Red Sox at League Park. Soup Campbell collected five hits in five at-bats.

Clarence (Soup) Campbell had 96 career hits and a .246 batting average. Heath rebounded from a terrible season in 1940 in which he batted .219 in 100 games. In 1941, he batted .340 with 24 homers, 123 RBIs, 199 hits, and a league-leading 20 triples.

SEPTEMBER 9 The Indians trounce the Athletics 13–7 in Philadelphia.

SEPTEMBER 11 The Indians score three runs in the ninth inning to edge past the Senators 6–5 in the first game of a double header in Washington. Cleveland also annexed the second tilt 3–2.

SEPTEMBER 14 Held to no runs and one hit by Yankees pitcher Marv Breuer through seven innings, the Indians score five times in the eighth to win 5–2 in the second game of a double header in New York. The game was called by darkness at the end of the inning. The Yanks won the first game 6–3.

SEPTEMBER 21 The Indians collect 18 hits and smash the Browns 14–0 in the first game of a double header at League Park. Cleveland bats went silent in the second tilt, picking up only two hits off Denny Galehouse during a 2–0 loss.

SEPTEMBER 26 Bob Feller pitches a one-hitter to defeat the Browns 3–2 in the second game of a double header at Sportsman's Park. The lone St. Louis hit was a single by

Rick Ferrell in the fifth inning. The Browns collected two runs on two walks, an error, and a sacrifice fly in the first inning. The Indians lost the opener 6–5 in 11 innings.

September 27 Al Smith wins his own game with a homer in the ninth inning to beat the Browns 4–3 in St. Louis. Smith hit only two homers in 535 career at-bats over 12 seasons. The other home run was struck as a member of the Giants in 1935.

On the same day, Cy Slapnicka resigned as general manager of the Indians. Slapnicka cited health problems and said that he desired to get back to scouting, which was his "first love." He scouted for the Browns and the Cubs before returning to the Indians as a scout under Bill Veeck in 1946. Slapnicka retired in 1970 and died in 1979 at the age of 93.

November 25 The Indians hire 24-year-old Lou Boudreau as manager, replacing Roger Peckinpaugh, who is promoted to general manager.

Boudreau is the youngest manager in major league history to start a season since 1900. The only younger manager was Peckinpaugh, who served as interim manager at 23 for the Yankees over the final 20 games of the 1914 season. The hiring of Boudreau was a complete surprise. Not only was he just 24, but he was forced into a dual role as manager and starting shortstop. Lou was dubbed, sometimes derisively, as the "Boy Manager." Two weeks after Boudreau took over the managerial job, World War II intervened and Bob Feller enlisted in the Navy. During his first six seasons with the Indians, Boudreau was 450–464. After Bill Veeck bought the club in June 1946, the situation began to improve. In 1948, Boudreau had a career year as a player, winning the American League Most Valuable Award and leading the Indians to the world championship, the only one the franchise has won between 1920 and the present. In both 1949 and 1950, the Indians finished in fourth place, and Lou was let go as manager at the end of the 1950 season.

December 4 The Indians sell Rollie Hemsley to the Reds.

December 5 The Associated Press reports that Bob Feller plans to enlist for military service before his draft board calls his number. The call appeared to be imminent. According to the news item, Feller "said he would have an announcement next week regarding his intentions toward the armed forces. The very fact that he feels an announcement is necessary is a pretty good indication that he's not going to let himself be drafted, friends believe." If he enlisted, rather than be drafted, Feller would be allowed to choose the branch of service he wished to join. On December 9, two days after Japan's attack on Pearl Harbor, Feller enlisted in the Navy. During the war, he was a chief specialist on the battleship *Alabama* and won five campaign ribbons and eight battle stars.

December 7 The Japanese attack Pearl Harbor in Honolulu with an early morning air raid. The following day, the United States declared war on Japan, signaling the U.S. involvement militarily in World War II. The following day, the U. S. declared war on Germany (see January 15, 1942).

December 11 The Indians purchase Vern Kennedy from the Senators.

1942

Season in a Sentence

Lou Boudreau takes over as manager and the Indians win a club record 13 games in a row in April and May before finishing with the same 75–79 record as the previous season.

Finish • Won • Lost • Pct • GB

Finish	Won	Lost	Pct	GB
Fourth	75	79	.487	28.0

Manager

Lou Boudreau

Stats

Stats	Indians	AL	Rank
Batting Avg:	.253	.257	5
On-Base Pct:	.320	.329	5
Slugging Pct:	.345	.357	4
Home Runs:	50		5
Stolen Bases:	69		2 (tie)
ERA:	3.59	3.66	6
Fielding Avg:	.974	.971	3
Runs Scored:	590		5
Runs Allowed:	659		6

Starting Line-up

Otto Denning, c
Les Fleming, 1b
Ray Mack, 2b
Ken Keltner, 3b
Lou Boudreau, ss
Jeff Heath, lf
Roy Weatherly, cf
Oris Hockett, rf
Buster Mills, cf
Jim Hegan, c
Gene Desaultels, c

Pitchers

Jim Bagby, Jr., sp
Mel Harder, sp
Al Smith, sp
Chubby Dean, sp
Al Milnar, sp
Tom Ferrick, rp
Vern Kennedy, rp-sp

Attendance

459,447 (fourth in AL)

Club Leaders

Batting Avg:	Les Fleming	.292
On-Base Pct:	Les Fleming	.412
Slugging Pct:	Jeff Heath	.442
Home Runs:	Les Fleming	14
RBIs:	Les Fleming	82
Runs:	Oris Hockett	85
Stolen Bases:	Oris Hockett	12
Wins:	Jim Bagby, Jr.	17
Strikeouts:	Mel Harder	74
ERA:	Jim Bagby, Jr.	96
Saves:	Tom Ferrick	3
	Joe Heving	3

JANUARY 15 President Franklin Roosevelt gives baseball commissioner Kenesaw Landis the go-ahead to play ball despite the nation's involvement in World War II. In his statement, Roosevelt said he believed that the continuation of the sport would be beneficial to the country's morale.

Bob Feller was in the service prior to the start of spring training in 1942 (see December 5, 1941) as were pitcher Cal Dorsett, infielder Jack Conway, and outfielder Soup Campbell.

MARCH 26 The Indians sell Gee Walker to the Reds.

APRIL 14 On Opening Day, the Indians win 5–2 over the Tigers in Detroit. Les Fleming contributed a homer, double, and single in four at-bats. Jim Bagby, Jr. was the winning pitcher.

The game was played five days after the fall of Bataan, one of the many shocking military defeats suffered at the hands of Japan early in 1942. Four days after the opener, Major General James Doolittle staged a daring air raid on Tokyo.

APRIL 17 In the home opener, the Indians lose 1–0 to the White Sox before 26,509 at Municipal Stadium.

During the duration of World War II, balls hit into the stands at League Park and Municipal Stadium were returned by fans and donated to the recreation departments of the Armed Forces.

APRIL 18 Behind the pitching of Jim Bagby, Jr., the Indians win 1–0 over the White Sox at Municipal Stadium. Fabian Gaffke drove in the lone run of the game with a single as a pinch-hitter with two out in the ninth inning. Bagby retired 20 batters in a row from the third inning through the ninth.

Bagby had a 17–9 record with a 2.96 ERA in 270⅔ innings in 1942.

APRIL 28 The Indians record their ninth win in a row and take sole possession of first place with a 10–3 record by defeating the Athletics 6–4 in Philadelphia. The victory gave Cleveland a 14–3 record on the season.

MAY 1 The Indians set a club record with their 13th straight victory, defeating the Senators 12–3 in Washington. Jeff Heath contributed a homer, triple, and double.

The streak ended the following day with a 6–4 loss to the Red Sox in Boston. It was the first of six losses in a row, a string that knocked Cleveland out of first place. The 1941 and 1942 seasons were eerily similar. In 1941, the club started the season winning 16 of their first 20 and wound up with a 75–79 record. In 1942, the Indians started with 14 victories in 17 games, and again ended with a 75–79 mark. Both were under new managers, with Roger Peckinpaugh running the team in 1941 and Lou Boudreau in 1942. The Indians were 60–47 on August 5, 1942, before losing 32 of the final 47 games.

MAY 10 Down 5–0, the Indians stun the Tigers with five runs in the ninth inning and one in the tenth to win 6–5 in the second game of a double header at Municipal Stadium. The five ninth-inning tallies were recorded on four hits, a walk, a hit batsman, and two errors. In the tenth, Lou Boudreau tripled and Ken Keltner singled for the winning run. Detroit won the opener 5–1.

MAY 11 The Indians win for the second day in a row after trailing the Tigers 5–0 in the late innings. Cleveland score five times in the eighth and once in the ninth for the 6–5 victory at League Park. Les Fleming broke the 5–5 tie with a walk-off homer.

Fleming took over at first base for Hal Trosky, who retired at the end of the 1941 season because of chronic migraine headaches. Fleming hit .292 with 14 homers and 106 walks. He was expected to be a star for the Indians for years. But after the death of his infant child and the lingering illness of his wife, Fleming chose to remain home in Beaumont, Texas, during the 1943, 1944, and 1945 seasons while working as a pipe fitter in a shipyard, a job that kept him out of military service during World War II. Fleming returned to play for the club again when the war ended in August 1945 but failed to come close to posting his 1942 numbers before his career in the majors ended in 1949.

May 25 All of the gate receipts from an Indians-White Sox game at Municipal Stadium go to the Army-Navy Relief Fund. A total of 7,959 paid their way into the game, earning the fund $9,390.86. The Indians lost 5–1.

May 27 The Indians score two runs in the ninth inning to beat the White Sox 2–1 at Municipal Stadium. Les Fleming drove in both runs with a single that followed a walk to Ken Keltner and a double by Buster Mills.

Night games in Cleveland in 1942 started at 8:45 p.m.

June 4 The Indians score three runs in the ninth inning to beat the Red Sox 4–2 in Boston. Les Fleming drove in the tying and winning runs with a two-out double.

June 8 Two days after America's victory over Japan in the Battle of Midway, Ken Keltner collects five hits, including a triple and a double, but the Indians lose 11–10 in 11 innings to the Yankees in New York.

June 20 Al Smith pitches a one-hitter for a 1–0 win over the Yankees at League Park. Joe DiMaggio provided the only New York hit with a single in the seventh inning. The lone run of the game scored on a single by Buster Mills in the seventh inning.

The Indians experimented with several games played in the morning on week days in 1942. The time was set to attract second-shift workers at the various war plants in Cleveland.

July 1 The first seven Cleveland batters in the first inning reach base and score, and while the Indians are shut down the rest of the way, it's enough to defeat the White Sox 7–2 in Chicago.

July 6 Lou Boudreau leads off the top of the first inning in the All-Star Game with a home run off Mort Cooper. The American League won 3–1 at the Polo Grounds in New York.

By a pre-arranged agreement, the winning team in the 1942 All-Star Game was scheduled to play a team of All-Stars from the various branches of the military the next night at Municipal Stadium in Cleveland.

July 7 The American League All-Star team defeats the Service All-Stars 5–0 before a crowd of 62,094 at Municipal Stadium. Bob Feller was the starting pitcher for the service team but was ineffective, allowing three runs and four hits before being relieved with no one out in the second inning. Besides Feller, the Service team included Pat Mullin, Sam Chapman, Cecil Travis, Morrie Arnovich, and Mickey Harris. Among the AL stars were Lou Boudreau, Ken Keltner, Jim Bagby, Jr. of the Indians, plus future Hall of Famers Joe DiMaggio, Ted Williams, Bobby Doerr, and Phil Rizzuto.

The game raised $120,000 for war charities. In addition, one dollar was added to each ticket for the purchase of War Bonds. Before the game, tanks rumbled all over the field along with jeeps, mobile anti-craft and anti-tank guns, and transport and motorcycle equipment. The Great Lakes Naval Training Station and the Fort Hayes bands played selections, including the National Anthem.

A company of the United States Marine Corps from the Navy Pier in Chicago gave an exhibition of precision drilling. Sailors from the Great Lakes station and from the Coast Guard paraded. By the time the first pitch was thrown, the field was torn up by the festivities and displays of American military might and was hardly in a condition to conduct a game.

JULY 22 The Indians win a thrilling 3–2 decision in 11 innings against the Yankees at Municipal Stadium. Cleveland trailed 2–0 in the ninth with two out and no one on base, Yankee shortstop Phil Rizzuto booted a grounder that should have ended the game. Three straight singles by Chubby Dean, Roy Weatherly, and Lou Boudreau tied the score 2–2. In the 11th, pinch-hitter Otto Denning drove in the winning run with a single.

JULY 24 The Indians play the first twi-night double header at Municipal Stadium, beating the Senators 4–3 and 5–4 in 12 innings.

AUGUST 11 Al Milnar pitches 14 innings of shutout baseball while allowing only two hits without recording a strikeout or receiving a victory for his superb efforts during a strange evening at Municipal Stadium. Two games were scheduled as a twi-night double header against the Tigers. In the opener, Milnar had a no-hitter in progress with two out in the ninth inning when Doc Cramer singled. Tommy Bridges of the Tigers kept the Indians scoreless, and the contest went into extra innings. Milnar went five more innings allowing just one more hit, a 13th-inning single by Rudy York. At the end of the 14th, the score was still 0–0 with Milnar and Bridges still pitching. The contest began under the late afternoon sunlight and was considered a day game, meaning that, according to American League rules then in effect, lights couldn't be turned on to finish a day game. Therefore, the game was called a 0–0 tie on account of darkness, and then the lights were switched on to start the second tilt. The Tigers won that one 3–2.

AUGUST 13 The Indians score three runs in the ninth inning to beat the Tigers 3–2 at League Park. Detroit hurler Virgil Trucks retired the first two batters to face him in the ninth, then walked Lou Boudreau, Chubby Dean, and Al Milnar. The latter two were pitchers, sent to the plate by Boudreau as pinch-hitters. Jack Wilson went into the game to relieve Trucks and gave up a three-run, walk-off double to Oris Hockett.

AUGUST 23 Jim Bagby, Jr. pitches a ten-inning shutout to defeat the White Sox 1–0 in the second game of a double header at Municipal Stadium. Ken Keltner drove in the lone run of the game with a walk-off double. Chicago won the opener 3–1.

SEPTEMBER 2 The Indians score eight runs with two out in the first inning and defeat the Athletics 12–3 in Philadelphia.

SEPTEMBER 8 The Indians trounce the White Sox 10–0 in Chicago.

SEPTEMBER 20 Mel Harder pitches a two-hitter to defeat the Indians 2–0 in the first game of a double header in Detroit. The only hits off Harder were a double by Dutch Meyer and a single by Pinky Higgins. The Tigers won the second contest 6–5.

SEPTEMBER 25 A "crowd" of only 200 attends an 8–1 loss to the White Sox at League Park.

DECEMBER 17 The Indians trade Roy Weatherly and Oscar Grimes to the Yankees for Roy Cullenbine and Buddy Rosar.

1943

Season in a Sentence

With the manpower shortage increasing due to the military draft and enlistments, the Indians post a winning record after two consecutive losing campaigns.

Finish • Won • Lost • Pct • GB

Finish	Won	Lost	Pct	GB
Third	82	71	.536	15.5

Manager

Lou Boudreau

Stats

	Indians	AL	Rank
Batting Avg:	.255	.249	3
On-Base Pct:	.329	.322	3
Slugging Pct:	.350	.341	3
Home Runs:	55		5
Stolen Bases:	47		6
ERA:	3.15	3.30	3
Fielding Avg:	.975	.973	2
Runs Scored:	600		4
Runs Allowed:	577		3

Starting Line-up

Buddy Rosar, c
Mike Rocco, 1b
Ray Mack, 2b
Ken Keltner, 3b
Lou Boudreau, ss
Jeff Heath, lf
Oris Hockett, cf-lf
Roy Cullenbine, rf
Hank Edwards, cf
Rusty Peters, 3b
Gene Desaultels, c

Pitchers

Jim Bagby, Jr., sp
Al Smith, sp
Allie Reynolds, sp
Vern Kennedy, sp
Mel Harder, sp

Attendance

438,894 (fifth in AL)

Club Leaders

Batting Avg:	Roy Cullenbine	.289
On-Base Pct:	Roy Cullenbine	.407
Slugging Pct:	Jeff Heath	.481
Home Runs:	Jeff Heath	18
RBIs:	Jeff Heath	79
Runs:	Oris Hockett	70
Stolen Bases:	Oris Hockett	13
Wins:	Jim Bagby, Jr.	17
	Al Smith	17
Strikeouts:	Allie Reynolds	151
ERA:	Al Smith	2.55
Saves:	Joe Heving	9

MARCH 15 The Indians open spring training camp in West Lafayette, Indiana.

During World War II, teams had to train north of the Ohio River and east of the Mississippi to save on travel expenses. The Indians trained on the campus of Purdue University in West Lafayette in 1943, 1944, and 1945 before returning to Clearwater, Florida in 1946.

APRIL 21 On Opening Day, the Indians defeat the Tigers 1–0 before 13,847 at Municipal Stadium. Jim Bagby, Jr. pitched a three-hit shutout and had a big day at the plate with two singles and a sacrifice fly in the ninth inning that drove in the lone run of the contest. Bagby's game-winning RBI followed a walk to Roy Cullenbine and a double from Buddy Rosar.

Due to a shortage of available materials because of the war, an inferior batch of baseballs with different specifications was used at the start of the 1943 season.

After a series of low-scoring games, a more resilient ball was rushed into use in May.

APRIL 24 The Indians score three runs in the ninth inning to defeat the Tigers 3–2 at League Park. Jeff Heath singled in the first two runs, reached third base on an error, and scored when Detroit catcher Paul Richards threw the ball into left field on a pick-off attempt.

Several Indians players entered military service between the 1942 and 1943 seasons, including Harry Eisenstat, Tom Ferrick, Jim Hegan, Joe Krakauskas, Bob Lemon, Buster Mills, and Eddie Robinson. During the 1943 campaign, Pete Center, Chubby Dean, and Gene Woodling joined the service.

MAY 13 The day after Germany surrenders in the North Africa campaign, Indians radio announcer Jack Graney is notified that his son, First Lieutenant John G. Graney, Jr., died from injuries suffered from a plane crash at Fort Bragg, North Carolina.

MAY 23 The Indians take first place by sweeping a double header 3–1 and 5–2 over the Yankees at Municipal Stadium.

The Indians record on May 23 was 16–11. Cleveland's last day in first in 1943 was on May 27. It was the third year in a row that the Indians were in first place in May and hopelessly out of the pennant race by mid-July.

JUNE 12 Substitutions by Lou Boudreau leaves the Indians short-handed at the end of an 11-inning, 7–6 loss to the Browns at League Park. Boudreau finished the game as the catcher while Jim Bagby, Jr. played shortstop.

Boudreau hit .286 for the Indians in 1943.

JUNE 17 Two late-inning rallies beats the Tigers twice at Municipal Stadium. In the opener, the Indians scored three runs in the ninth inning for a 3–2 victory. In the second tilt, Cleveland tallied once in the ninth and again in the 12th to win 6–5.

The Indians played 46 games at Municipal Stadium in 1943 with the remainder at League Park.

JUNE 19 Jeff Heath homers in the tenth inning to start a four-run rally, and after withstanding two runs by the White Sox in the bottom half, the Indians win 10–8 in the second game of a double header in Chicago. The Indians also won the opener 5–4.

Reliever Pete Center pitched 13⅓ consecutive hitless innings in June.

JULY 2 In one of the strangest games in major league history, the Indians score 12 times in the fourth inning to account for all of the runs in a 12–0 win over the Yankees at Municipal Stadium. The Indians also collected ten of their 11 hits in the big inning and were hitless after the explosion in the fourth. Only one of the hits went for extra bases. It all started when Roy Cullenbine and Jeff Heath singled. Ken Keltner doubled in the first run. Buddy Rosar was intentionally walked and Mike Rocco hit into a force with the out recorded at the plate. Ray Mack singled in two runs and Allie Reynolds followed with a single. Oris Hockett was intentionally walked, loading the bases again. Lou Boudreau beat out an infield single and Cullenbine reached on an error. Heath drove in two and Keltner one with singles to make the score 9–0. Rosar walked to load the bases. Rocco plated one more with an infield single, and Mack contributed his second two-run single of the inning, but was out overrunning first. Reynolds grounded out to end the procession.

In his first season with the Indians, Cullenbine hit .289.

JULY 9 Jim Bagby, Jr. allows only one run in a 13-inning complete game, but loses 1–0 to the Senators at League Park. The lone tally scored on a squeeze play.

Bagby was 17–14 with a 3.10 ERA and led the AL in innings pitched with 273.

JULY 18 The Indians score seven runs in the third inning of a 10–7 win over the Browns in the second game of a double header in St. Louis. The Indians also won the opener 4–3.

After the twinbill, Lou Boudreau and coaches Burt Shotton, George Susce, and Del Baker vowed not to shave until the Indians lost again. The club won seven in a row before the Cleveland brain trust broke out the razors.

JULY 21 Al Smith pitches a two-hitter to defeat the Athletics 7–0 in Philadelphia. Smith also collected three hits with a triple, double and single and drove in two runs. The only Philadelphia hits were a double by Dick Siebert and a single from Pete Suder.

Smith was 17–7 with a 2.55 ERA in 1943.

JULY 23 A home run by Ray Mack in the sixth inning off Don Black accounts for the lone run of a 1–0 victory over the Athletics in Philadelphia. Mel Harder pitched the shutout.

JULY 28 The Indians win 6–2 over the Yankees before a crowd of 27,281 at Yankee Stadium. All of the gate receipts went to wartime charities. Before the game, a combined team of Indians and Yankees, managed by Babe Ruth, played a club from the Great Lakes Naval Training Station and won 11–5. Ruth, then 48 years old and more than eight years removed from his last big league game, went to the plate as a pinch-hitter and walked.

AUGUST 3 The Indians outlast the Red Sox 11–9 in Boston. Cleveland nearly blew an eight-run lead by allowing six runs in the ninth. On the day his second son was born, Ken Keltner hit two homers.

AUGUST 8 The Indians win two games by scores of 6–5 and 5–2 over the Browns at Municipal Stadium. The first game went 14 innings. The winning run was driven in by reliever Chubby Dean, who also pitched five shutout innings.

Alfred (Chubby) Dean reached the majors in 1936 with the Athletics as a first baseman and was later converted into a pitcher. He hit .274 in 1,047 career at-bats and was often used as a pinch-hitter in between pitching assignments.

AUGUST 11 Al Smith pitches a two-hitter in defeating the Athletics 2–1 in the second game of a double header at Municipal Stadium. The only Philadelphia hits were a double by Irv Hall and a single from Jo-Jo White.

Lou Boudreau flips the ball to Ray Mack with a fancy, backhanded move. The duo formed one of the best keystone combos in baseball during the early 1940s.

August 14 The Indians slip past the Athletics 12–9 at League Park.

August 15 The Indians extend their winning streak to eight games with a 6–2 win over the Senators in the first game of a double header at Municipal Stadium. The streak was broken with a 4–0 defeat in the second tilt.

August 18 The Indians win a thrilling 14-inning, 7–5 decision over the Yankees in the second game of a double header at Municipal Stadium. The Indians score three runs in the ninth to tie the score 4–4. After the Yanks took a 5–4 lead in the top of the 13th, Cleveland matched it with the tally in their half. Jeff Heath ended the game with a two-run homer in the 14th. The Indians also won the opener 9–8 after surviving a five-run New York rally in the ninth.

Heath hit eight homers in a span of eight days from August 18 through 25 in which the Indians played 12 games, including four double headers. Over the course of the 1943 season, he batted .274 with 18 homers.

August 25 The Indians sweep the Red Sox 8–3 and 4–1 in a double header at Municipal Stadium.

The Indians played an eight-game series against the Red Sox from August 22 through 26 with three twin bills and two single games. It was originally scheduled as a four-game set. Four contests were added because of postponements earlier in the season.

AUGUST 27 The Indians sell Al Milnar to the Browns.

SEPTEMBER 10 Seven days after the beginning of the Allied invasion of the Italian mainland, a walk-off homer in the ninth inning by Hank Edwards is the lone run of a 1–0 victory over the Tigers in the second game of a double header in Detroit. The pitching victim was Rufe Gentry. Jim Bagby, Jr. hurled the shutout. The Tigers won the opener 2–1.

SEPTEMBER 17 Allie Reynolds strikes out 12 batters but loses 2–1 at League Park when the Tigers score two runs in the ninth inning.

SEPTEMBER 19 The Indians sweep the Tigers 1–0 and 6–2 at Municipal Stadium. Jim Bagby, Jr. pitched a two-hitter in the opener. The only Detroit hits were singles by Dick Wakefield and Doc Cramer.

SEPTEMBER 24 In his major league debut, Ed Klieman pitches nine shutout innings before losing 1–0 by giving up a run in the tenth to the Red Sox at Fenway Park. Ex-Indian Joe Dobson pitched a two-hitter for Boston.

Klieman pitched for the Indians from 1943 through 1948, mostly as one of the club's first relief specialists. He led the American League in games pitched (58) and saves (17) in 1947.

SEPTEMBER 25 Ray Mack hits a three-run homer in the tenth inning to put the Indians ahead of the Red Sox 5–2 in Boston. Each team added another run for a 6–3 final.

NOVEMBER 6 The Indians sell Hal Trosky to the White Sox.

1944

Season in a Sentence

Lou Boudreau finishes first in the AL batting race, but his club finishes in a tie for fifth place in the AL pennant race and last in the AL in attendance.

Finish • Won • Lost • Pct • GB

Finish	Won	Lost	Pct	GB
Fifth (tie)	72	82	.468	17.0

Manager

Lou Boudreau

Stats

Stats	Indians	AL	Rank
Batting Avg:	.266	.260	2
On-Base Pct:	.331	.325	4
Slugging Pct:	.372	.353	3
Home Runs:	70		4
Stolen Bases:	48		6
ERA:	3.65	3.43	7
Fielding Avg:	.974	.971	2
Runs Scored:	643		5
Runs Allowed:	677		7

Starting Line-up

Buddy Rosar, c
Mike Rocco, 1b
Ray Mack, 2b
Ken Keltner, 3b
Lou Boudreau, ss
Pat Seerey, lf
Oris Hockett, cf-lf
Roy Cullenbine, rf
Rusty Peters, 2b
Myril Hoag, cf
Paul O'Dea, lf
Jeff Heath, lf

Pitchers

Mel Harder, sp
Steve Gromek, sp-rp
Allie Reynolds, sp
Al Smith, sp
Jim Bagby, Jr., sp
Ed Klieman, rp-sp
Joe Heving, rp
Ray Poat, rp

Attendance

475,272 (eighth in AL)

Club Leaders

Batting Avg:	Lou Boudreau	.327
On-Base Pct:	Lou Boudreau	.406
Slugging Pct:	Ken Keltner	.466
Home Runs:	Roy Cullenbine	16
RBIs:	Ken Keltner	91
Runs:	Roy Cullenbine	98
Stolen Bases:	Lou Boudreau	11
Wins:	Mel Harder	12
Strikeouts:	Steve Gromek	115
ERA:	Steve Gromek	2.56
Saves:	Joe Heving	10

April 18 The scheduled season opener between the Indians and the White Sox in Chicago is rained out.

April 19 The Indians get the 1944 season underway with a 3–1 loss to the White Sox in Chicago.

Between the 1943 and 1944 seasons, catcher Gene Desaultels, infielder Ted Sepkowski, and outfielder Hank Edwards entered the armed forces. Before the end of the 1944 campaign ended, Buddy Rosar left the club to work in a war plant, and Jim Bagby, Jr. joined the Merchant Marines.

April 21 In the home opener, the Indians defeat the Tigers 7–4 before 13,643 at Municipal Stadium. Pat Seerey blasted a home run into the upper deck.

Nicknamed "Fat Pat" because of his 200 pounds on a five-foot-ten-inch body, Seerey could hit the ball a long way when he connected, but it wasn't often enough to satisfy his employers. He played for the Indians from 1943 through 1948, and the White Sox in 1948 and 1949. Seerey hit 86 homers in 1,815 major league at-bats despite playing in poor hitter's parks. He clubbed 54 of those 86 home runs on the road. In 1945, Seerey struck three homers in a game, and in 1948 with Chicago he hit four in a contest against the Athletics to tie major league record. On the negative side, he led the AL in strikeouts in each of the four seasons in which he played in at least 100 games and had a career batting average of .224.

MAY 1 The Indians score seven runs in the eighth inning to defeat the White Sox 9–3 at League Park.

MAY 10 Mel Harder records his 200th career win with a 5–4 decision over the Red Sox in Boston.

MAY 21 Lou Boudreau homers in the 11th inning to defeat the Athletics 5–4 in the first game of a double header at Shibe Park. Philadelphia won the second contest 3–2.

Boudreau collected 191 hits in 1944 and won the AL batting title with an average of .327. He also topped the circuit in doubles with 45.

JUNE 6 All major league games are postponed in observance of the D-Day landing in France. President Franklin Roosevelt urged Americans to spend a day in prayer at home or in church.

JUNE 11 The Indians hammer the Browns 13–1 in the first game of a double header at Sportsman's Park. St. Louis took the second tilt 4–2.

JULY 2 Ken Keltner collects seven hits, including a homer, in eight at-bats during a double-header sweep of the Senators in Washington. The Indians won by scores of 4–3 in ten innings and 6–3 in the regulation nine. In the second game, Steve Gromek held the Senators hitless for the first seven innings but gave up three runs and five hits before being relieved in the ninth.

JULY 14 Steve Gromek pitches all 14 innings of a 3–2 win over the Browns at League Park and drives in the winning run with a walk-off single.

Gromek played for the Indians from 1941 through 1953, compiling a record of 78–67.

JULY 15 The Indians clobber the Browns 13–2 at League Park.

JULY 25 Ken Keltner hits a grand slam during a 10–0 win over the Yankees at Municipal Stadium.

Keltner hit .295 with 41 doubles, 13 homers and 91 runs-batted-in during the 1944 season.

JULY 28 The Indians sell Vern Kennedy to the Phillies.

JULY 31 Steve Gromek pitches a two-hitter, but loses 1–0 to the Red Sox at Municipal Stadium on an unearned run in the ninth inning. Gromek retired the first 21 batters to face him and had a no-hitter until Roy Partee singled with two out in the eighth. In the ninth, first baseman Mike Rocco committed a two-base error. The lone run scored on a single by Catfish Metkovich. The Indians collected only two hits off Boston pitchers Mike Ryba and Red Barrett.

AUGUST 12 The Indians edge the Senators 1–0 in 12 innings in Washington. Al Smith pitched the complete game shutout, allowing only four hits. Dutch Leonard went all the way for Washington, and also surrendered just four hits. Ken Keltner drove in the lone run with a single.

AUGUST 21 The Indians tie a major league record with three extra-inning home runs during a 7–6 victory over the Red Sox in Boston. Jim Bagby, Jr. and Pat Seerey homered in the 11th inning to give Cleveland a 6–4 lead, but Bagby gave up two runs in the bottom half of the inning to deadlock the contest again at 6–6. Mike Rocco settled the issue with a home run in the 13th.

AUGUST 25 On the day Allied troops liberate Paris, Ken Keltner hits a grand slam off Bill Dietrich in the seventh inning of a 10–2 win over the White Sox at Municipal Stadium.

AUGUST 27 Roy Cullenbine hits a walk-off home run off Johnny Humphries in the ninth inning for the lone run of a 1–0 triumph over the White Sox in the second game of a double header at Municipal Stadium. Steve Gromek pitched the shutout. The Indians also won the opener 4–3.

Cullenbine hit .289 with 16 homers and 98 runs scored in 1944.

AUGUST 30 Down 7–4, the Indians score eight runs in the eighth inning to defeat the Browns 12–7 at League Park.

SEPTEMBER 2 Mike Rocco drives in all five runs of an 11-inning, 5–2 win over the White Sox in Chicago. Rocco hit a two-run homer in the eighth inning to tie the score 2–2, then clubbed a three-run shot in the 11th.

SEPTEMBER 20 The Indians score two runs in the last of the 13th to beat the Red Sox 11–10 before a crowd of only 500 at League Park. Cleveland trailed 7–2 in the third inning, took a 9–7 lead, then fell behind 10–9 when Boston plated two tallies in the ninth and one in the top of the 13th. The Indians won the game on two walks, a double by Lou Boudreau and a sacrifice fly by Ken Keltner.

DECEMBER 12 Two months after 130 die in Cleveland following an explosion of two liquid natural gas storage tanks and a fire that spread over 20 blocks, and five weeks after Franklin Roosevelt defeats Thomas Dewey in the Presidential election, the Indians trade Oris Hockett to the White Sox for Eddie Carnett.

1945

Season in a Sentence

In the last year of World War II, Bob Feller is discharged from the Navy in August, but it's much too late to salvage the season.

Finish • Won • Lost • Pct • GB

Finish	Won	Lost	Pct	GB
Fifth	73	72	.503	11.0

Manager

Lou Boudreau

Stats

Stats	Indians	AL	Rank
Batting Avg:	.255	.255	6
On-Base Pct:	.326	.325	4
Slugging Pct:	.359	.346	3
Home Runs:	65		3
Stolen Bases:	19		8
ERA:	3.31	3.36	4
Fielding Avg:	.977	.973	1
Runs Scored:	557		7
Runs Allowed:	548		1 (tie)

Starting Line-up

Frankie Hayes, c
Mike Rocco, 1b
Dutch Meyer, 2b
Don Ross, 3b
Lou Boudreau, ss
Jeff Heath, lf
Felix Mackiewicz, cf
Pat Seerey, rf-lf
Al Cihocki, ss-3b-2b
Paul O'Dea, rf
Les Fleming, rf

Pitchers

Steve Gromek, sp
Allie Reynolds, sp-rp
Jim Bagby, Jr., sp
Al Smith, sp
Mel Harder, sp
Bob Feller, sp
Red Embree, sp
Ed Klieman, rp-sp
Pete Center, rp

Attendance

558,182 (sixth in AL)

Club Leaders

Batting Avg:	Jeff Heath	.305
On-Base Pct:	Jeff Heath	.398
Slugging Pct:	Jeff Heath	.508
Home Runs:	Jeff Heath	15
RBIs:	Jeff Heath	61
Runs:	Mike Rocco	81
Stolen Bases:	Felix Mackiewicz	5
Wins:	Steve Gromek	19
Strikeouts:	Allie Reynolds	112
ERA:	Steve Gromek	2.55
Saves:	Allie Reynolds	4
	Ed Klieman	4

April 17 Five days after Franklin Roosevelt dies of a cerebral hemorrhage and is succeeded as president by Harry Truman, the Indians open the season by losing 5–2 to the White Sox before 20,588 at Municipal Stadium. Lou Boudreau was the victim of a hidden ball play when he stepped off third base and was tagged by Chicago third baseman Tony Cuccinello, who took the throw from the outfield and kept the ball instead of returning it to the pitcher.

The war in Europe was winding to a close, but the end of the conflict with Japan was nowhere in sight. The country was well into its fourth year of war, and everyone in the Municipal Stadium stands on Opening Day could claim a loved one, friend, or neighbor who had been or currently was involved in the fighting somewhere in the world. The only brother of Indians pitcher Pete Center was killed in action on the Italian mainland in April 1945. While the 1945 opener was taking place, U.S. forces were involved in a deadly struggle to capture Okinawa. Indians players who entered the armed forces between the 1944 and 1945 seasons were Ken Keltner, Ray Mack, and Rusty Peters. Before the season ended, Eddie Carnett, Red Embree, and Hank Ruszkowski joined the service, although Bob Feller returned to baseball following his discharge from the Navy in August (see August 22, 1945), as did Gene Desautels. Les Fleming, who had been working in a war plant in Texas, appeared in 42 games late in the season.

April 27 The Indians trade Roy Cullenbine to the Tigers for Dutch Ross and Dutch Meyer.

Lambert Dalton (Dutch) Meyer was a pleasant surprise in 1945. A 29-year-old second baseman with only 94 games of big league experience, he played in 130 games and hit .292.

May 24 Sixteen days after Germany surrenders, ending the European phase of World War II, Steve Gromek pitches a ten-inning, complete-game shutout to defeat the Senators 1–0 in Washington. The winning run scored on doubles by Pat Seerey and Jim McDonnell.

Gromek was 19–9 with a 2.55 ERA in 1945. Allie Reynolds had a record of 18–12 and an earned run average of 3.21.

May 29 The Indians trade Buddy Rosar to the Athletics for Frankie Hayes.

While playing for the Browns, Athletics, and Indians, Hayes set a major league record for consecutive games played by a catcher with 312 from October 2, 1943, through April 21, 1946.

May 31 Indians right fielder Paul O'Dea is temporarily blinded during a 6–2 loss to the Red Sox in Boston. Occasionally, O'Dea lost vision in his left eye due to the formation of a vitreous crystal. His vision was restored in the dressing room by the application of medication prescribed to dissolve the crystal. O'Dea was already permanently blind in the right eye as a result of being struck by a batted ball during spring training in 1940. Overcoming the handicap, O'Dea began his courageous comeback on the sandlots in 1942, earned another opportunity in the minor leagues in 1943, and won a place on the Indians roster in 1944. After his playing days ended, O'Dea became a scout in the Cleveland organization. He was director of minor league operations when he died of a heart attack in 1978.

June 5 Hurling his last game before induction into the armed forces, Red Embree pitches a complete game to defeat the Tigers 9–0 at Municipal Stadium. It was Embree's only career shutout in 90 starts while playing in the majors from 1941 through 1949.

Radio broadcasts of Indians games were stopped in 1945 because team president Alva Bradley believed they harmed attendance. The broadcasts weren't restored until Bill Veeck bought the club in June 1946.

June 28 Seven days after Japan surrenders Okinawa to U.S. forces and on the day in which the United Nations charter is signed, the Indians clobber the Athletics 11–0 at League Park.

July 4 The Indians record no assists during a 4–2 win over the Yankees in the first game of a double header at Municipal Stadium. Steve Gromek kept the ball in the air all day. He struck out only four. There were 17 putouts by the three outfielders. New York won the second contest 3–2.

Through the 2007 season, only four major league clubs have played nine or more innings in the field without an assist.

JULY 9 — A crowd of 6,066 at Municipal Stadium watches the Indians win 6–0 in an exhibition game against the Reds. All of the proceeds, a total of $7,500, went to war charities.

JULY 13 — On Friday the 13th, Pat Seerey clubs three homers and drives in eight runs during a 16–4 win over the Yankees in New York. Seerey also hit a triple in the first inning that skipped to the 457-foot sign in center field. A faster runner than the slow-footed Seerey might have had an inside-the-park homer on the play. Seerey struck a solo homer off Atley Donald in the third inning, a grand slam against Monk Dubiel in the fourth, and a three-run shot facing Steve Roser in the eighth. Jeff Heath clubbed two homers during the game.

AUGUST 2 — A grand slam by Pat Seerey during an eight-run Cleveland third inning is the highlight of a 13–7 trouncing of the White Sox at League Park.

The Indians played 46 games at Municipal Stadium in 1945, with the remainder at League Park.

AUGUST 5 — Jeff Heath breaks a 3–3 tie with a three-run homer in the ninth inning to defeat the Browns 6–3 in the first game of a double header at Sportsman's Park. St. Louis won the second contest 10–9.

Heath held out for a higher salary until signing a contract in June, then hit .305 with 16 homers.

AUGUST 6 — On the day an atom bomb is dropped on Hiroshima, Frankie Hayes hits a three-run homer in the ninth inning to break a 6–6 tie in a 9–7 win over the Browns at Sportsman's Park. The Indians also won the second tilt 8–4.

AUGUST 8 — The Indians edge the Yankees 1–0 at Municipal Stadium. Al Smith not only pitched the shutout, but drove in the lone run of the game with a double in the fifth inning.

AUGUST 13 — Al Smith pitches his second consecutive shutout, defeating the Red Sox 10–0 at Municipal Stadium. The victory was costly, however, as Lou Boudreau fractured an ankle and was out for the rest of the season. The injury happened as Boudreau covered second base on a double play and was hit hard by Dolph Camilli.

AUGUST 22 — Eight days after Japan surrenders, ending World War II, Bob Feller is given his discharge from the Navy after 44 months in the service. The discharge allowed Feller to join the Indians immediately. Fortunately, he was in playing shape. Feller had been assigned to the Great Lakes Naval Training Station awaiting orders on his next assignment. While there, he had been pitching for the base team.

AUGUST 23 — Bob Feller signs a contract with the Indians for the remainder of the 1945 season.

AUGUST 24 — In his first major league game since 1941, Bob Feller strikes out 12 batters and defeats the Tigers 4–2 before a crowd of 46,477 at Municipal Stadium. He allowed four hits and pitched hitless ball over the last 6⅔ innings.

Earlier in the day, a civic luncheon was held in Feller's honor at Hotel Carter's Rainbow Room. Before the game, he was presented with one of the first Jeeps to come off the assembly line for civilian use. Among the presenters were Tris Speaker and Cy Young.

SEPTEMBER 19 Bob Feller pitches a one-hitter defeating the Tigers 1–0 at League Park. The only Detroit hit was a single by Jimmy Outlaw on a blooper into right field in the fifth inning. The Indians collected only three hits, but one of them was a towering two-run homer by Jeff Heath.

NOVEMBER 11 A section of temporary bleachers at League Park stands collapses during the Cleveland Rams 20–7 victory over the Green Bay Packers before a crowd of 28,686. Some 700 fans fell to the ground, but no one was seriously injured.

The Rams posted a 9-1-0 regular season record and won the 1945 National Football League championship, defeating the Washington Redskins 15–14 in the title game at Municipal Stadium on December 16. It was the franchise's last game in Cleveland. In March 1946, Rams owner Daniel Reeves was given permission to move his club to Los Angeles. By the start of the 1946 football season, Cleveland had a new club called the Browns (see September 6, 1946).

DECEMBER 12 The Indians trade Jim Bagby, Jr. to the Red Sox for Vic Johnson.

DECEMBER 14 The Indians trade Jeff Heath to the Senators for George Case.

1946

Season in a Sentence

Bob Feller wins 26 games and strikes out 348 batters during a season in which Bill Veeck buys the Indians and ushers in a new era in Cleveland baseball history.

Finish • Won • Lost • Pct • GB

Finish	Won	Lost	Pct	GB
Sixth	68	86	.442	36.0

Manager

Lou Boudreau

Stats

Stats	Indians	AL	Rank
Batting Avg:	.245	.256	8
On-Base Pct:	.313	.328	7
Slugging Pct:	.356	.364	6
Home Runs:	79		5
Stolen Bases:	57		3
ERA:	3.62	3.50	5
Fielding Avg:	.975	.973	2
Runs Scored:	537		7
Runs Allowed:	638		5

Starting Line-up

Jim Hegan, c
Les Fleming, 1b
Dutch Meyer, 2b
Ken Keltner, 3b
Lou Boudreau, ss
George Case, lf
Pat Seerey, cf-rf-lf
Hank Edwards, rf
Jack Conway, 2b
Frank Mackiewicz, cf
Ray Mack, 2b
Frankie Hayes, c
Don Ross, 3b
Heinz Becker, 1b

Pitchers

Bob Feller, sp
Allie Reynolds, sp
Red Embree, sp
Steve Gromek, sp
Mel Harder, sp
Bob Lemon, rp

Attendance

1,057,289 (fourth in AL)

Club Leaders

Batting Avg:	Hank Edwards	.301
On-Base Pct:	Hank Edwards	.361
Slugging Pct:	Hank Edwards	.509
Home Runs:	Pat Seerey	26
RBIs:	Pat Seerey	62
	Lou Boudreau	62
Runs:	Hank Edwards	62
Stolen Bases:	George Case	28
Wins:	Bob Feller	26
Strikeouts:	Bob Feller	348
ERA:	Bob Feller	2.18
Saves:	Bob Feller	4
	Steve Gromek	4

FEBRUARY 20 The Indians open training camp in Clearwater, Florida, the first in peacetime in five years.

The 1946 major league training camps were unique as returning war veterans competed with wartime fill-ins for spots on the roster. The Indians spring training roster included 24 players who had spent all or most of the 1945 season in the military. Many of them, such as Ken Keltner, Hank Edwards, and Ray Mack were regulars before the war. Others included top prospects like Bob Lemon, Jim Hegan, and Gene Woodling. Of the 36 players who appeared in at least one game with the Indians in 1945, only 15 returned with the club in 1946.

APRIL 16 On Opening Day, Bob Feller pitches a three-hit shutout and strikes out ten batters to defeat the White Sox 1–0 at Comiskey Park. The lone run scored in the fifth inning when George Case walked, moved to second on a sacrifice, and scored on a single by Hank Edwards. The game ended when center fielder Bob Lemon made a diving catch of a looping fly off the bat of Jake Jones and threw to second base to double Bob Kennedy off the bag.

The full team nickname appeared on a jersey for the first time in 1946. "Indians" was written across the front of the home shirts in red script outlined in navy blue.

April 20 In the home opener, the Indians lose 7–0 to the Tigers before 42,775 at Municipal Stadium. Hal Newhouser pitched a two-hit shutout for Detroit.

April 24 The consecutive game streak of Frankie Hayes comes to an end at 312 games, the all-time major league record for a catcher. Sherm Lollar was the Cleveland catcher during a 5–1 win over the Browns in St. Louis. Hayes caught the final two games of the 1943 season with the Browns, all 155 Athletics games in 1944, and the first 32 contests for the A's in 1945. After a trade to the Indians, Hayes was the catcher in the last 119 games for the Tribe in 1945 and the first four in 1946.

April 28 Red Embree not only pitches a 12-inning complete game, beating the Tigers 3–1 in Detroit, but he also drives in both 12th-inning runs with a double.

April 30 Bob Feller pitches a no-hitter to defeat the Yankees 1–0 at New York. Catcher Frankie Hayes contributed the lone run with a home run with one out in the ninth inning off Bill Bevens. It was the first no-hitter against the Yankees since 1919, and the first ever at Yankee Stadium, which opened in 1923. Feller struck out 11 and walked five. Cleveland's center fielder was Bob Lemon, who was converted to a pitcher a few weeks later (see May 12, 1946) and pitched a no-hitter of his own in 1948. In the Yankee ninth, Snuffy Stirnweiss led off and reached base on an error when his bunt rolled through the legs of first baseman Les Fleming. Stirnweiss reached second base on a bunt by Tommy Henrich and a slow roller hit by Joe DiMaggio to shortstop Lou Boudreau. Feller faced Charlie Keller needing just one out for a no-hitter with the tying run on third base. Keller rolled out to second baseman Ray Mack on an 0–2 pitch to end the game.

May 12 Bob Lemon makes his pitching debut during a 9–3 loss to the Browns in the second game of a double header at Municipal Stadium. Lemon entered the game in the seventh inning and allowed two runs and two hits in three innings. The Indians won the opener 4–3.

Lemon made his major league debut in 1941 as a third baseman. During his three years in the Navy beginning in 1943, he pitched for a service team in Hawaii with and against many major leaguers. When he returned to the Indians in 1946, the club already had Ken Keltner at third and tried out Lemon in center field. Off to a slow start, Lemon was on the verge of being sent to the minors when players who had competed against him in the service, among them Ted Williams, suggested to Lou Boudreau that he try Lemon as a pitcher. Lemon, convinced he was a hitter, fought the position switch every step of the way. He didn't earn a regular role in the starting rotation until late in the 1947 campaign but went on to win 20 or more games in a season seven times. He topped the AL in wins three times, in complete games five times, innings pitched in four, strikeouts once, and shutouts once. Lemon was 207–128 during his career, all of which was spent with the Indians, and earned a plaque in the Hall of Fame. Among Indians pitchers Lemon ranks third in wins, third in shutouts (31), third in strikeouts (1,277), third in innings (2,850), third in games started (350), fourth in games (460), four in complete games (188), and fifth in winning percentage (.618). Naturally for a player who started out as a position player, Lemon was an excellent hitting pitcher. He hit 37 homers in 1,183 at-bats. His number 21 was retired by the Indians in 1998.

MAY 15 The Indians win both ends of a double header against the Athletics at League Park with a pair if shutouts. Mel Harder won the opener 3–0 and Steve Gromek the nightcap 5–0.

MAY 20 Ken Keltner hits a walk-off homer in the ninth inning to defeat the Yankees 4–3 at Municipal Stadium.

MAY 25 Pat Seerey homers in the sixth inning off Sam Zoldak for the lone run of a 1–0 victory over the Browns in St. Louis. Allie Reynolds pitched the shutout.

Hurricane Veeck Blows into Cleveland

Bill Veeck was baseball's most imaginative promoter. At the major league level, he owned the Indians (1946–49), the St. Louis Browns (1951–53), and the White Sox (1959–61 and 1975–80). A maverick who loved being different, Veeck was an admitted publicity hound who frequently upset baseball's more staid and humorless officials with his outrageous stunts, but he was also a sound baseball man. Under his guidance, the Indians won the world championship in 1948 in the first World Series appearance for the franchise since 1920. The year that Veeck bought the White Sox, the club captured the AL pennant in 1959, the only one to fly over Chicago between 1919 and 2006.

Veeck literally grew up in a ballpark. His father, William, Sr., was president of the Cubs from 1918 until his death in 1933. The junior Veeck was 19 at the time of his father's passing, and worked under Cubs owner P. K. Wrigley in a variety of capacities. One of Veeck's ideas was to plant ivy on the outfield wall at Wrigley Field in 1938. He also designed the hand-operated center field scoreboard atop the bleachers that exists to this day.

Veeck was anxious to strike out on his own, and bought the nearly bankrupt Milwaukee Brewers club in the American Association in 1941. Four years later he sold the club for a $275,000 profit after setting minor league attendance records and winning three pennants. During this period, he also served in the Marines during World War II and suffered serious injuries in the South Pacific when the recoil of an artillery weapon crushed his foot. It would eventually required a long series of operations that required the removal of his leg.

Veeck put together a syndicate to purchase the Indians in 1946, a season in which the team had a record of 68–86. A year earlier the club had drawn 558,182 fans, which ranked seventh in the American League and 12th in the majors. Veeck was an instant hit in Cleveland. By 1948, the Indians won the World Series and attracted an astonishing 2,620,627 into Municipal Stadium, the all-time major league record until 1962, the American League record until 1980, and the Indians standard until 1995. The 1948 world title couldn't have been accomplished if Veeck hadn't become the first American League owner and the second in the majors to add African-American players to his roster. Larry Doby and Satchel Paige were keys to the club's success.

Before the arrival of Veeck, big league teams did little to promote their clubs other than to place advertisements in the newspapers announcing the opponent and the starting time of the game. Veeck staged a constant stream of promotions, including fireworks displays, vaudeville acts, band concerts, special nights for various individuals including one for a "typical" fan, funeral and burial services for the 1948 pennant after the Indians were mathematically eliminated in 1949, and appearances by baseball clowns Max Patkin and Jackie Price who were also signed as "coaches." There was one giveaway after another of beer, cases of food, orchids, cigarettes, perfume, nylon stockings, and even live pigs. Many of these promotions weren't announced in advance so that fans came to the ballpark in expectation of the next offbeat idea that Veeck had up his sleeve.

Veeck's stay in Cleveland was brief, however. He sold the Indians in 1949 partly to offset the financial fallout from the end of his first marriage and partly because he was perpetually restless and always looked for a fresh challenge.

June 4 Bob Feller strikes out 14 batters during a 10–2 win over the Senators in Washington.

June 21 A bonehead play by first baseman Les Fleming leads to a 1–0 loss to the Red Sox at Municipal Stadium. Fleming caught Rudy York's pop-up in foul territory in the second inning allowing Bobby Doerr to score from third base. Bob Feller was the hard luck loser.

June 22 Alva Bradley sells the Indians to a group headed by 32-year-old Bill Veeck. Bradley had owned the Cleveland club since 1927. The purchase price was $1.25 million. Veeck's fellow investors included several Chicago businessmen and entertainer Bob Hope, a Cleveland native. Veeck owned 30 per cent of the stock. No other individual held for than a six per cent share.

June 25 Bob Feller strikes out 13 batters during an 8–3 win over the Yankees at Municipal Stadium.

June 29 Gene Woodling hits a pinch-hit triple in the eighth inning to drive in the only two runs of a 2–0 triumph over the White Sox in Chicago. Bob Feller hurled the shutout.

July 9 At Fenway Park, Bob Feller is the starting pitcher in the All-Star Game and pitches three shutout innings during a 12–0 American League win.

July 14 Lou Boudreau inaugurates his famous "Boudreau shift" against Ted Williams during the second game of a double header against the Red Sox at Fenway Park. In the opener, Boudreau had a career day with four doubles and a home run. He tied major league records for most doubles in a game and most extra base hits in a game. Unfortunately, the Indians lost 11–10 in large part because Ted Williams smacked three homers and drove in eight runs. In the second game, a 6–4 Boston victory, the Indians player-manager deployed the "Boudreau shift" by moving his fielders to the right side of the diamond with only the left fielder on the left side. Boudreau positioned first baseman Jimmy Wasdell and right fielder Hank Edwards virtually on the foul line, second baseman Jack Conway close to first base and back on the grass. Boudreau played to the right of second base, third baseman Ken Keltner directly behind second on the edge of the outfield grass, center fielder Pat Seerey in right-center and left fielder George Case about 30 feet closer to the infield than normal, so that he was practically playing a deep shortstop. The maneuver was an attempt to frustrate Williams. The Boudreau shift was soon copied by other AL clubs and used for several years. Williams refused to change his batting style by slicing hits to the opposite field, but the shifts failed to slow him down.

Boudreau is the only player in American League history to collect five extra base hits in a game and one of only five major leaguers in the modern era. During the 1946 season, Boudreau hit .293.

July 15 The Indians sell Frankie Hayes to the White Sox.

July 19 Pat Seerey hits a grand slam off Bob Savage in the fifth inning of a 6–1 win over the Athletics in Philadelphia.

July 24 Hank Edwards homers in the fourth inning off Bob Savage to provide the lone run in a 1–0 victory over the Athletics at League Park. Bob Feller pitched the shutout.

July 25 Relief pitcher Joe Berry drives in the winning run with a walk-off single to defeat the Athletics 9–8 at League Park.

July 31 Bob Feller pitches a one-hitter to defeat the Red Sox 4–1 at Municipal Stadium. The lone Boston hit was a single by Bobby Doerr in the second inning.

The victory was Feller's 20th of the season in the Indians 99th game of 1946. He was on a pace for a 30-win season but finished with a record of 26–15. He led the AL in wins, games pitched (48), games started (42), complete games (36), shutouts (ten), strikeouts (348), and innings pitched (371⅓). The innings pitched, strikeout, complete game, and shutout figures are all Indians single-season records. The 348 strikeouts by Feller are the highest between 1904 and 1965 and the seventh highest since the 60-foot, six-inch pitching distance was established in 1893, trailing only Nolan Ryan (383 in 1973 and 367 in 1974), Sandy Koufax (382 in 1965), Randy Johnson (372 in 2001 and 364 in 1999), and Rube Waddell (349 in 1904).

August 2 Allie Reynolds pitches a two-hitter to defeat the Yankees 3–0 at Municipal Stadium. The only New York hits were a double by Billy Johnson and a single by Snuffy Stirnweiss.

August 4 A crowd of 74,529 at Municipal Stadium watches the Indians lose 2–0 to the Yankees in the first game of a scheduled double header. The second contest was postponed by rain.

Though not as spectacular as the Big Four of the 1950s, the Indians starting rotation in 1946 was impressive. From left to right: Allie Reynolds, Steve Gromek, Red Embree, and Bob Feller.

The Indians drew over one million fans for the first time in 1946 with a total of 1,057,289. The previous record was 912,832 in 1920. Despite the record, the Indians ranked fourth in the American League and ninth in the majors in attendance in 1946. The boost was part of a nationwide trend. The 16 major league teams drew 18,534,444 fans in the first postwar season, shattering the old mark of 10,951,502 set in 1945.

AUGUST 8 Bob Feller hurls a one-hitter to defeat the White Sox 5–0 in the first game of a double header at Comiskey Park. The only hit off Feller fell in the seventh inning when three Indians got mixed up on two pop flies by Frankie Hayes, who started the season with Cleveland and homered for the only run in Feller's no-hitter on April 30. Hayes's foul fly fell between third baseman Ken Keltner and left fielder George Case. Given new life, Hayes lofted another ball into the air that landed among shortstop Lou Boudreau, second baseman Jack Conway, and right fielder Pat Seerey for a single. Chicago took the second tilt 7–6.

AUGUST 13 The Indians lose 1–0 to the Tigers on Max Weisman Night before 65,765 at Municipal Stadium. Weisman was in his 25th year as the Indians trainer. He was brought to the plate in an old fire truck and given over $6,000 in cash and gifts, including a wheelbarrow filled with 5,000 silver dollars. The wheelbarrow was so heavy that Bill Veeck had a tow truck come onto the field to haul it away. Weisman was still the club's trainer when he died in 1949 at the age of 54.

AUGUST 18 The Indians mash the White Sox 13–3 in the second game of a double header at Municipal Stadium. Chicago won the opening tilt 6–4 in 11 innings.

AUGUST 20 Bob Feller's pitches are clocked before a 5–4 loss to the Senators at Griffith Stadium in Washington. Without the use of the radar gun some three decades in the future, it was impossible to accurately determine the speed of pitches. Using a device developed by the United States Army to measure the velocity of shells, Feller threw five pitches from the mound, the fastest of which was 98.6 miles per hour. The Indians star claimed that he threw harder during games and but wasn't completely warmed up at the time of the speed demonstration.

AUGUST 26 A midget "plays" third base for the Indians during a 5–1 loss to the Red Sox at Fenway Park. With Ted Williams preparing to bat against the Boudreau shift, three-foot-tall Mario Songini ran out of the stands and onto the field. Songini occupied the empty third base position before he was ejected from the premises.

SEPTEMBER 6 The Cleveland Browns play their first regular season game, and defeat the Miami Seahawks 44–0 before 60,135 at Municipal Stadium. At the time, it was the largest crowd ever to see a professional football game.

The first edition of the Browns played in the All-American Football Conference from 1946 through 1949, and in the NFL from 1950 through 1995. Municipal Stadium was the club's home all 50 seasons, tying the Chicago Bears for the longest tenure by one pro football club at one venue. The Bears played at Wrigley Field from 1921 through 1970. The Green Bay Packers will break the record in 2007 when they play their 51st season at Lambeau Field.

SEPTEMBER 11 The Indians score seven runs in the fifth inning of an 11–2 win over the Yankees in New York.

SEPTEMBER 13 Ted Williams hits the only inside-the-park homer of his career for the only run in a 1–0 Red Sox win over the Indians at League Park. The victory also clinched the AL pennant for Boston. Williams foiled the Boudreau shift by hitting an opposite field fly ball into the empty left field and circled the bases before left fielder Pat Seerey could retrieve the ball, which rolled into a gutter about 400 feet from home plate. Seerey had been stationed 20 feet behind the skinned portion of the infield. If Seerey had been playing in a conventional defense, he probably would have caught the ball for an out. Williams's homer was one of only two hits off Cleveland pitcher Red Embree.

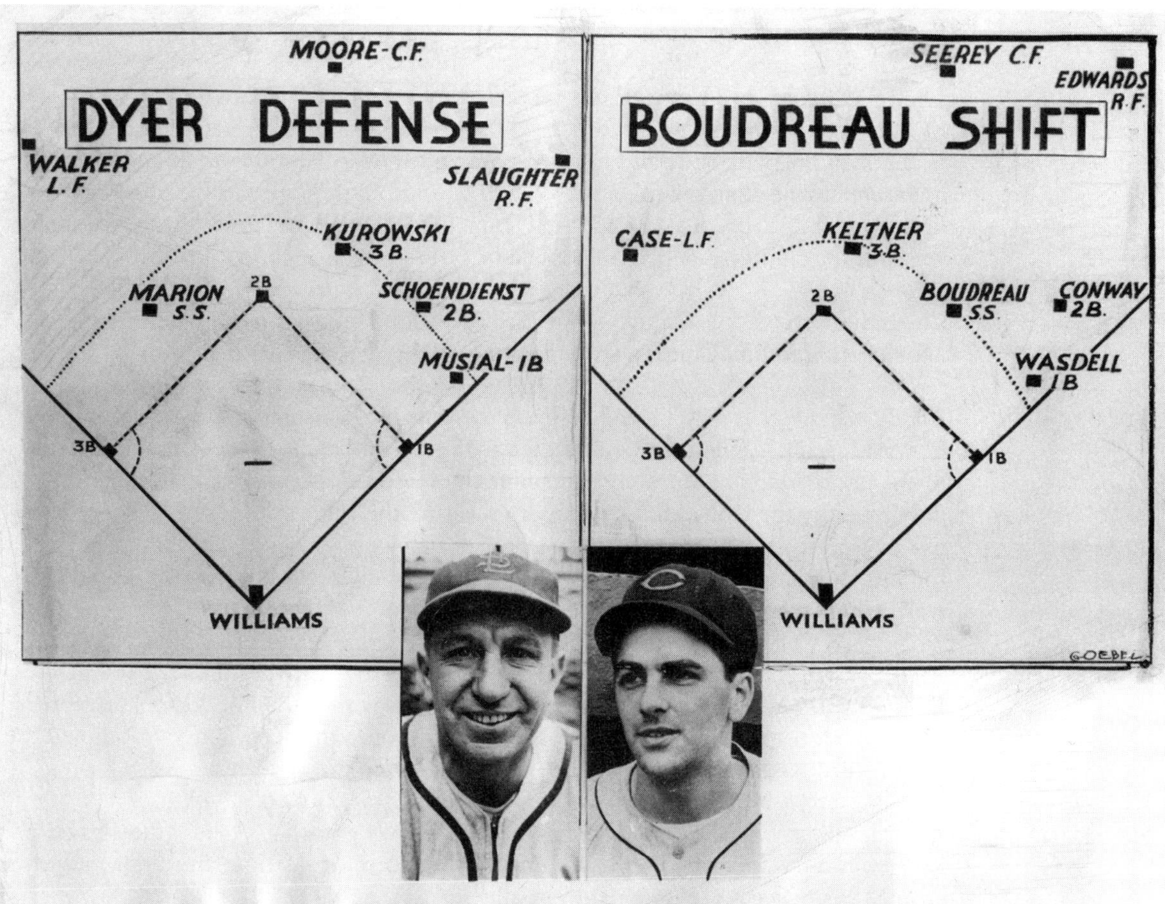

To defend against Red Sox slugger Ted Williams, Indians manager Lou Boudreau devised a strategy that became known as the Boudreau Shift. In the World Series that year, St. Louis Cardinals manager Eddie Dyer adapted the plan to stop Williams, who hit only .200 in the seven-game set.

SEPTEMBER 18 Indians pitcher Ralph McBride allows a homer to the first batter he faces in his first major league game, and is the losing pitcher in an 8–1 defeat at the hands of the Senators at League Park. The batter was Sherry Robertson leading off the first inning.

A native of Canada, McCabe never played in another major league game. He allowed five runs in four innings.

SEPTEMBER 21 The Indians play their last game at League Park and lose 5–3 in 11 innings to the Tigers. Only 2,772 attended the contest.

Beginning in 1947, the Indians played all of their home games at Municipal Stadium. The permanent move to the downtown facility ended the switches back and forth from League Park to Municipal Stadium, a situation that had existed for 15 years. Many believed it was a factor in the Indians failure to win a pennant because the club couldn't tailor the roster to take advantage of one ballpark. League Park, with its short right field foul line and distant left and center field fences, had radically different dimensions that the symmetrical and spacious Municipal Stadium. "It was like we were on the road even when we were at home," explained Lou Boudreau. The city of Cleveland purchased League Park from the Indians in 1951, tore down all but the East 66th Street (first base) side of the facility, and turned it into a playground.

SEPTEMBER 25 Bill Veeck opens the gates at Municipal Stadium and allows fans to attend free of charge. A total of 12,800 took advantage of the opportunity on a Wednesday afternoon and watched the Indians defeat the White Sox 4–1.

OCTOBER 19 The Indians trade Allie Reynolds to the Yankees for Joe Gordon and Eddie Bockman.

Gordon was the American League's Most Valuable Player in 1942 and a six-time All-Star when acquired by the Indians to play second base. He missed the 1944 and 1945 seasons due to military service and batted only .210 in 1946. With Cleveland, he played in three more All-Star Games and the 1948 World Series, hitting .268 with 81 homers and 300 RBIs from 1947 through 1949. The trade was not without cost, however. Born in Oklahoma of Creek Indian descent, Reynolds was merely an average pitcher with the Indians and posted a 51–47 record in five seasons with the club, largely against wartime competition. He was 31-years-old at the time of the trade. (Reynolds and Gordon were born eight days apart.) In New York, Reynolds was named to four All-Star teams and played in six World Series in eight seasons and posted 131 wins and 60 defeats.

DECEMBER 7 The Indians trade Gene Woodling to the Pirates for Al Lopez.

The Indians acquired Lopez as a manager-in-waiting for Lou Boudreau, who Bill Veeck planned to fire at the first opportunity. Fan protests over the impending dismissal of Boudreau and the 1948 world championship put those plans on hold. Lopez played for Cleveland in 1947 as a back-up catcher, then managed the Pittsburgh Pirates farm club in Indianapolis from 1948 through 1950. He did replace Boudreau after the 1950 season. Lopez led the Indians for six seasons, winning a pennant in 1954 and finishing second five times. Woodling didn't look like much of a prospect when he hit .188 in 61 games for the Indians in 1946. However, he lasted in the majors until 1962 with six different clubs, including a second stint with Cleveland from 1955 through 1957.

Like Reynolds, Woodling played on each of the Yankee clubs that won five consecutive World Series from 1949 through 1953.

DECEMBER 20 The Indians trade Sherm Lollar and Ray Mack to the Yankees for Gene Bearden, Hal Peck, and Al Gettel.

Utilizing a knuckleball, Bearden was 20–7 with a league-leading 2.43 ERA with the Indians as a 27-year-old rookie in 1948. His 20th victory was the pennant-clincher and he pitched a shutout in the World Series. Part of the reason for the late start to his career in the majors was his service in the Navy during World War II. Bearden suffered a fractured skull and a severe knee injury when his ship, the USS Helena, *was sunk in the South Pacific near the Solomon Islands on August 9, 1942. He was in the engine room when the ship was struck by a torpedo fired by a Japanese destroyer. Bearden came home with an aluminum plate in his head and a screw in his knee, and the resumption of his professional baseball career was very much in doubt. After his astonishing 1948 campaign, Bearden faded into obscurity almost as quickly as he burst into stardom. He was dealt to the Senators in 1950, and over the course of the remainder of his career, which ended in 1953, he won 25 and lost 31 with a 4.55 earned run average. Sherm Lollar had longtime success in the majors, mostly with the White Sox. He caught 1,571 big league games from 1946 though 1963, was named to seven All-Star teams, and played in the 1959 World Series with Chicago.*

1947

Season in a Sentence

The Indians integrate the American League with the signing of Larry Doby, draw over 1.5 million, and win 80 games for the first time since 1940.

Finish • Won • Lost • Pct • GB

Finish	Won	Lost	Pct	GB
Fourth	80	74	.519	17.0

Manager

Lou Boudreau

Stats

Stats	Indians	AL	Rank
Batting Avg:	.259	.256	3
On-Base Pct:	.324	.333	5
Slugging Pct:	.385	.364	2
Home Runs:	112		2
Stolen Bases:	29		7
ERA:	3.44	3.71	2
Fielding Avg:	.983	.977	1
Runs Scored:	687		4
Runs Allowed:	588		2

Starting Line-up

Jim Hegan, c
Eddie Robinson, 1b
Joe Gordon, 2b
Ken Keltner, 3b
Lou Boudreau, ss
Dale Mitchell, lf-cf
Catfish Metkovich, cf
Hank Edwards, rf-lf
Hal Peck, rf
Les Fleming, 1b
Pat Seerey, lf

Pitchers

Bob Feller, sp
Don Black, sp
Al Gettel, sp-rp
Red Embree, sp
Mel Harder, sp
Ed Klieman, rp
Bob Lemon, rp-sp
Bryan Stephens, rp

Attendance

1,521,978 (second in AL)

Club Leaders

Batting Avg:	Dale Mitchell	.316
On-Base Pct:	Lou Boudreau	.388
Slugging Pct:	Joe Gordon	.496
Home Runs:	Joe Gordon	29
RBIs:	Joe Gordon	93
Runs:	Joe Gordon	89
Stolen Bases:	Joe Gordon	7
Wins:	Bob Feller	20
Strikeouts:	Bob Feller	196
ERA:	Bob Feller	2.68
Saves:	Ed Klieman	17

FEBRUARY 17 The Indians begin training exercises in Tucson, Arizona for the first time. They were joined in Arizona in 1947 by the New York Giants, who trained in Phoenix. The Indians and Giants were the first two clubs to conduct spring training in Arizona on a yearly basis.

Veeck chose Tucson because he owned a ranch outside the city that he used occasionally to recuperate from a chronic asthmatic condition. Although Veeck sold the club in 1949, the Indians continued to train in Tucson until 1992.

MARCH 4 The Indians trade George Case to the Senators for Roger Wolff.

MARCH 29 Indians coach Jackie Price is sent home during a spring training trip for releasing live snakes on a train. Price let loose two five-foot long reptiles on a crowded coach train between San Diego and Los Angeles, two cities in which the Indians played exhibition games. "I hope I can see a joke as well as anyone," said Lou Boudreau, "but this is a big league club, not a traveling circus."

Price and Max Patkin were listed on the Indians roster as coaches in 1946 and 1947, but passed on little knowledge to the players. They were hired by Bill Veeck to entertain the fans. Price was an acrobat who specialized in hitting and catching baseballs while suspended from a horizontal bar, catching fungoes while driving a jeep, and by throwing three baseballs simultaneously to three different catchers. A gangly, double-jointed former minor league pitcher, Patkin delighted fans with a pantomime act in which he would contort his body into seemingly impossible positions. Price and Patkin occasionally coached at first base during games.

APRIL 2 The Indians purchase Catfish Metkovich from the Pirates.

APRIL 15 The Indians open the season with a 2–0 loss to the White Sox in near freezing temperatures before 55,014 at Municipal Stadium. Ed Lopat pitched the shutout, defeating Bob Feller.

Bill Veeck moved in the fences at Municipal Stadium in 1947. A five-foot high wire inner-fence covered with green canvas was installed. The foul lines remained at 320 feet, but the power alleys were reduced from 435 feet to 365 and the distance to center field from 450 feet to 410. Later, Veeck made the fences portable depending upon the opponent. The fences were moved in when a weak-hitting team visited Cleveland, and were pushed back when a power-hitting club invaded the Stadium. The American League soon passed a rule, however, preventing fences from being moved during a season.

APRIL 22 Bob Feller pitches a one-hitter to defeat the Browns 5–0 at Municipal Stadium. Feller retired the first 19 batters to face him before allowing a single to Al Zarilla with one out in the seventh inning.

Radio broadcasts were carried on WGAR in 1947 with Jack Graney and Van Patrick at the mike.

APRIL 24 Pat Seerey's home run in the second inning off Johnny Rigney is the lone run of a 1–0 win over the White Sox at Comiskey Park. Don Black pitched the shutout.

APRIL 26 Bob Feller hurls his second consecutive shutout, defeating the Tigers 6–0 on three hits at Municipal Stadium.

MAY 2 Bob Feller pitches a one-hitter beating the Red Sox 2–0 at Municipal Stadium. It was also Feller's third consecutive shutout in which he pitched two one-hitters and a three-hitter. The lone Boston hit was a single by Johnny Pesky in the first inning.

MAY 3 Joe Gordon hits a grand slam off Al Widmar in the fourth inning of a 9–3 win over the Red Sox at Municipal Stadium.

In his first season with the Indians, Gordon hit .272 with 29 homers and 93 RBIs.

MAY 11 The Indians overwhelm the Browns 16–1 in St. Louis.

MAY 13 Bob Feller walks ten batters during a 7–6 loss to the Athletics in Philadelphia.

JUNE 14 Midget auto racing makes its debut at Municipal Stadium.

Midget auto racing was then gaining in popularity and was booked into the stadium on a trial basis. To make the field suitable for midget races, ten feet of sod on the inner side of the track had to be removed to provide for a 30-foot racing strip. Then a rail fence, 18 inches high, had to be erected along the inner track line. The cinder track surrounding the playing field was replaced with clay. These changes brought an immediate protest from Bill Veeck, who believed that baseball and auto racing were incompatible. Despite the protest, Cleveland mayor Thomas Burke approved the auto races. Only three races were held, however, before Burke canceled the events because of damage done to the field.

JUNE 20 Jim Hegan is honored by citizens from his hometown of Lynn, Massachusetts, in pre-game ceremonies, then drives in all three Cleveland runs in a 3–2 win over the Red Sox at Fenway Park. He hit a two-run homer in the second inning and broke a 2–2 deadlock with a sacrifice fly in the ninth. Hegan was presented with a car, a refrigerator, a portable radio, and a check for $1,000.

Hegan hit just .228 in 1,666 big league games but was a five-time All-Star because of his superb defensive talents as a catcher. He played for the Indians in 1941 and 1942, and following three years in the Coast Guard during World War II, again from 1946 through 1957.

JULY 2 Mel Harder is honored prior to a 6–5 loss to the Tigers at Municipal Stadium. Harder received a new Buick and a check for $2,000.

JULY 3 The Indians purchase 22-year-old Larry Doby from the Newark Eagles of the Negro Leagues for $15,000.

Doby became the first African-American player in the American League and the second in the major leagues following Jackie Robinson, who debuted with the Dodgers on April 15, 1947. As a racial pioneer, Doby had to face more than his share of hostility. On the road, he was often denied entrance to hotels and restaurants frequented by his teammates. On the field, Doby had to endure a steady stream of racial epithets, taunts and insults from opposing players and fans and was even spat upon. He came to the Indians as a second baseman, but the Indians already had one of the best infields in baseball at the time. He sat mostly on the bench in 1947, accumulating only 32 at-bats and hitting just .156. But in 1948, the Indians moved Doby to center field and he went on to a career that led to seven consecutive All-Star appearances, his number 14 being retired by the Indians, and induction into the Hall of Fame. He led the AL in homers (twice), runs, runs-batted-in, on base percentage and slugging percentage. Among Indians players, Doby ranks sixth in home runs (215), sixth in walks (703), ninth in slugging percentage (.500), ninth in RBIs (776), and tenth all-time in runs (808).

JULY 4 The Indians smack five homers to defeat the Tigers 13–6 in the first game of a double header at Municipal Stadium. Eddie Robinson and Joe Gordon each hit two homers and Ken Keltner one. The second contest ended in a 4–4 tie after nine innings. It was called to clear the stadium for the Festival of Freedom fireworks display.

JULY 5 Larry Doby makes his major league debut. Acting as a pinch-hitter for Bryan Stephens in the seventh inning, Doby struck out facing Earl Harrist in a 6–5 loss to the White Sox in Chicago.

Stephens had an 8–16 record with a 5.16 ERA in two seasons with the Indians. He lost the ring finger of his non-pitching hand while in the service during World War II.

JULY 6 Larry Doby makes his first major league start. Batting fifth and playing first base, he had one hit in four at-bats during a 3–1 win in the second game of a double header against the White Sox at Comiskey Park. Chicago won the opener 3–2.

Doby played only three career games at first base. The other two were 12 years later in 1959 with the White Sox.

JULY 10 Don Black pitches a no-hitter to defeat the Athletics 3–0 in the first game of a double header at Municipal Stadium. Black, who played for the A's from 1943 through 1945, struck out five and walked six in the first no-hitter at the stadium. He also collected two singles in two at-bats and drove in a run. In the ninth inning, George Binks popped out, Ferris Fain grounded out to first baseman Eddie Robinson, and Sam Chapman tapped out to Black for the final out. Cleveland won the second game 3–1.

Black was one of the more obscure pitchers to throw a no-hitter. He was 34–55 with a 4.35 ERA over a career from 1943 through 1948 in which he battled a drinking problem before joining Alcoholics Anonymous. Black's playing days ended tragically with a near-fatal brain hemorrhage (see September 13, 1948).

JULY 11 Larry Doby makes his Cleveland debut. He was retired as a pinch-hitter during a 4–2 loss to the Athletics at Municipal Stadium.

The Indians were the second major professional team in Cleveland to integrate. The Browns had several African-American players in both 1946 and 1947, including Marion Motley.

JULY 20 Dale Mitchell delivers a hit in both ends of a double header against the Senators at Municipal Stadium to run his hitting streak to 22 games. The Indians won the first game 1–0 but won the second 6–1.

Mitchell played for the Indians from 1946 through 1956, and hit .312 with 41 home runs in 1,108 games.

JULY 30 The Indians score six runs in the first inning and seven in the sixth to beat the Red Sox 13–7 in Boston.

The Indians bottomed out at 43–50 on August 7 before winning 37 of their last 61 games.

AUGUST 9 African-Americans face each other for the first time in a major league game during a ten-inning, 5–4 Indians win over the Browns in the second game of a double header at Municipal Stadium. Larry Doby pinch-hit for Cleveland while Hank Thompson played second base for St. Louis. The Indians also won the opener 5–2.

AUGUST 12 Al Gettel pitches a one-hitter to defeat the Tigers 11–0 in the second game of a double header against the Tigers at Municipal Stadium. The only Detroit hit was a fluke double by Eddie Mayo in the second inning. Mayo's hit went through the infield when shortstop Jack Conway broke toward second base on a hit-and-run play. Cleveland also won the opener 3–1.

AUGUST 19 The Indians sweep the Senators 13–2 and 9–1 during a double header at Municipal Stadium. Cleveland scored eight runs in the eighth inning of the opener.

AUGUST 27 Solo homers produce all three runs in a 2–1 win over the Athletics at Municipal Stadium. Hank Majeski of the A's struck first in the fifth inning off Bob Feller. For the Indians, Hank Edwards homered in the sixth inning and Ken Keltner in the seventh.

SEPTEMBER 3 The Indians score two runs in the ninth inning to defeat the White Sox 6–5 in the second game of a double header at Municipal Stadium. Hank Edwards tripled in the tying run and scored on a single by Hal Peck. Chicago won the opener 8–3.

SEPTEMBER 4 Lou Boudreau and Bill McKechnie go pigeon-hunting at Municipal Stadium. McKechnie drew a bead on a bird perched on the top tier, blasted away with his 12-gauge shotgun, and missed the pigeon, bringing down two reflectors and glass fragments from a half-dozen light bulbs.

Boudreau led the AL in doubles in 1947 with 45 and batted .307.

SEPTEMBER 11 Joe Gordon drives in six runs with a homer, double, and a single during a 10–8 win over the Red Sox in the first game of a double header at Fenway Park. Boston won the second tilt, shortened to 5½ innings by darkness, 8–3.

SEPTEMBER 22 The Indians score four runs in the ninth inning to defeat the Tigers 7–6 in the second game of a double header in Detroit. Three singles produced the first run, and then Hank Edwards clubbed a three-run homer. Detroit won the opener 6–4.

SEPTEMBER 24 Bob Feller records his 20th win of the season with a 9–1 decision over the Browns in St. Louis.

Feller was 20–11 with a 2.68 earned run average in 1947. He led the AL in wins, strikeouts (196), innings pitched (299), and shutouts (five).

NOVEMBER 20 The Indians send Dick Kokos, Bryan Stephens, Joe Frazier, and $25,000 to the Browns for Walt Judnich and Bob Muncrief.

NOVEMBER 24 The Indians sign Lou Boudreau to a two-year contract as manager.

When the 1947 season ended, Veeck wanted to make a change. He contemplated trading Boudreau to the Browns for Vern Stephens and naming Al Lopez as manager. When the notion became public, the fans reacted violently to the impending deal and interceded on behalf of the popular Boudreau. Petitions were circulated and boycotts of Indians games were threatened. The Cleveland News *printed a "Boudreau Ballot" on page one and asked readers to vote to keep Boudreau or trade him. Of the more than 100,000 respondents, 90 percent wanted to keep Boudreau in Cleveland. After reviewing the results, Veeck announced he was bowing to the will of the people and re-signed Boudreau.*

In 1948, Lou had a career year as a player, winning the American League Most Valuable Player Award and leading the Indians to the world championship.

DECEMBER 4 The Indians trade Les Fleming to the Pirates for Elbie Fletcher.

DECEMBER 9 The Indians purchase Johnny Berardino from the Browns.

While growing up in Los Angeles, Berardino was a child actor, appearing in Our Gang *comedies. During his days as a major leaguer from 1939 through 1952, Berardino worked as an actor in the off-season. Always looking for a publicity angle, Bill Veeck had Berardino's face insured for one million dollars to protect against disfigurement of his handsome features. After his baseball career ended, Berardino began a full-time acting career as John Beradino, dropping the second "r" in his name to make it easier to pronounce. His big break came in 1963 with the role of Dr. Harvey in the afternoon soap opera* General Hospital. *Beradino played the role for over 30 years and earned a star on the Hollywood Walk of Fame.*

1948

Season in a Sentence

With Lou Boudreau managing the club and winning an MVP Award, the Indians set an all-time attendance record, edge the Red Sox and Yankees in a thrilling pennant race, and defeat the Boston Braves in the World Series.

Finish • Won • Lost • Pct • GB

Finish	Won	Lost	Pct	GB
First	97	58	.626	+1.0

World Series

The Indians defeated the Boston Braves four games to two

Manager

Lou Boudreau

Stats

Stats	Indians	AL	Rank
Batting Avg:	.282	.266	1
On-Base Pct:	.360	.349	2
Slugging Pct:	.431	.382	2
Home Runs:	155		1
Stolen bases:	54		3
ERA:	3.22	4.29	1
Fielding Avg:	.982	.977	1
Runs Scored:	840		3
Runs Allowed:	568		1

Starting Line-up

Jim Hegan, c
Eddie Robinson, 1b
Joe Gordon, 2b
Ken Keltner, 3b
Lou Boudreau, ss
Dale Mitchell, lf
Thurman Tucker, cf
Larry Doby, rf-cf
Allie Clark, rf-lf
Wally Judnich, cf
Hank Edwards, rf
Johnny Berardino, 2b-1b-ss

Pitchers

Bob Lemon, sp
Bob Feller, sp
Gene Bearden, sp
Sam Zoldak, sp-rp
Russ Christopher, rp
Ed Klieman, rp
Steve Gromek, rp
Satchel Paige, rp

Attendance

2,620,627 (first in AL)

Club Leaders

Batting Avg:	Lou Boudreau	.355
On-Base Pct:	Lou Boudreau	.453
Slugging Pct:	Lou Boudreau	.534
Home Runs:	Joe Gordon	32
RBIs:	Joe Gordon	124
Runs:	Lou Boudreau	116
Stolen Bases:	Dale Mitchell	13
Wins:	Bob Lemon	20
	Gene Bearden	20
Strikeouts:	Bob Feller	164
ERA:	Gene Bearden	2.43
Saves:	Russ Christopher	17

JANUARY 27 The Indians trade Ralph Weigel to the White Sox for Thermion Tucker.

MARCH 27 Hank Greenberg joins the Indians front office.

Greenberg retired as a player at the end of the 1947 season at the age of 36. During his 13-year career, 12 of them with the Tigers, he hit .313 and clubbed 331 homers despite missing three full seasons and most of two others in the service. When Greenberg let it be known that he was interested in entering the business side of baseball, he received a call from Bill Veeck. Greenberg became what was announced as "the second largest stockholder" in the club and was put in charge of the farm system. When Veeck sold the Indians in November 1949 to a group headed by Ellis Ryan, Greenberg was named general manager, a post he held until 1957. The Indians had a record of 738–493 under Greenberg from 1950 through 1957, the best eight-year period in club history. On the negative side, attendance plummeted from 2,233,771 in 1949 to 722,256 in 1957. Greenberg blamed a negative press in Cleveland for the slide in attendance. During his final season as general manager, Greenberg tried to relocate the Indians from Cleveland to Minneapolis-St. Paul. He also had serious differences with managers Lou Boudreau and Al Lopez, which led to instability at the top of the organization. On October 16, 1957, following a season in which the Indians posted a losing record for the first time in 11 years, the Indians board of directors dismissed Greenberg with a year remaining on his contract.

An aging Satchel Paige finally gets a chance to pitch in the major leagues. Here he tosses while Tribe owner Bill Veeck observes.

April 3 The Indians purchase Russ Christopher from the Athletics.

Christopher played only one season with the Indians but played a role on the 1948 world championship club with a 3–2 record, 17 saves, and a 2.90 ERA.

April 20 On Opening Day, the Indians draw 73,163 into Municipal Stadium and defeat the Browns 4–0. Bob Feller pitched a two-hit shutout. The only St. Louis hits were singles by Whitey Platt in the second inning and Bob Dillinger in the sixth. Jim Hegan hit a homer and two singles and drove in three runs.

Jimmy Dudley joined Jack Graney in the radio booth in 1948, broadcasting over WJW. Dudley remained as the club's radio play-by-play man until 1967. Telecasts also began in 1948 over WEWS with Van Patrick at the mike.

April 25 The day after the start of the Berlin airlift, Larry Doby strikes out five times in five plate appearances during a 7–4 loss to the Tigers in Detroit.

In his first full season in the majors, Doby hit .301 with 14 homers.

April 26 The Indians edge the White Sox 12–11 in 14 innings at Comiskey Park. At the end of the fifth inning, Chicago led 11–9. Cleveland scored twice in the ninth to send the game into extra innings. The two runs scored on a two-base hit by Lou Boudreau, who had a terrific day with five hits, four of them for extra bases, in six at-bats. He collected two triples, two doubles and a single. Eddie Robinson's home run in the 14th accounted for the winning tally. The win gave the Indians a 5–0 record on the season.

Boudreau was at the center of Indians victories all season, both as a manager and a player. Putting together a career year with the bat, he hit .355 with 18 home runs, 106 RBIs, 116 runs and 199 hits.

April 29 The Indians run their season record to 6–0 with a 5–2 victory over the Browns in St. Louis.

May 6 Ken Keltner hits a grand slam off Dick Fowler in the second inning, but the Indians lose 8–5 to the Athletics in Philadelphia.

Keltner batted .297 and hit 31 homers and drove in 119 runs in 1948.

May 20 At Municipal Stadium, Red Sox pitchers Mickey Harris and Mickey McDermott combine to walk 18 Cleveland batters to tie a major league record for a nine-inning game. The Indians won the contest 13–4.

May 23 The Indians draw 78,431 to a double header against the Yankees at Municipal Stadium. In the opener, Joe DiMaggio struck three homers to lift the Yankees to a 6–5 win. The Indians won the second contest 5–1.

May 29 Bob Lemon pitches his second consecutive shutout, beating the White Sox 4–0 in Chicago.

Lemon pitched 28 consecutive scoreless innings from May 21 through June 2.

May 30 Trailing 6–4, the Indians score nine runs in the eighth inning and defeat the White Sox 13–8 in the second game of a double header at Comiskey Park. Chicago won the opener 4–2.

There were several oddities during the nine-run inning in the nightcap. The topper was a pinch-runner who ran for a pinch-hitter for a pinch-runner. With one out, one run in and the bases loaded, Thermion Tucker went into the game as a pinch-runner for Eddie Robinson. Tucker had a splint on his broken finger. As the Indians batted around, it was Tucker's turn to bat, but his injury prevented him from doing so. Joe Tipton was sent to the plate as a pinch-hitter and was hit by a pitch on the left wrist, which sent him to the sidelines. Pat Seerey went into the game as a pinch-runner. Starting catcher Jim Hegan was removed for a pinch-hitter during the inning, and Tipton was the back-up. With both catchers out of action, Boudreau had to don the mask and chest protector and finish the contest as the catcher. In addition, Allie Clark singled as a pinch-hitter, and when his turn to bat came up once more, he singled a second time.

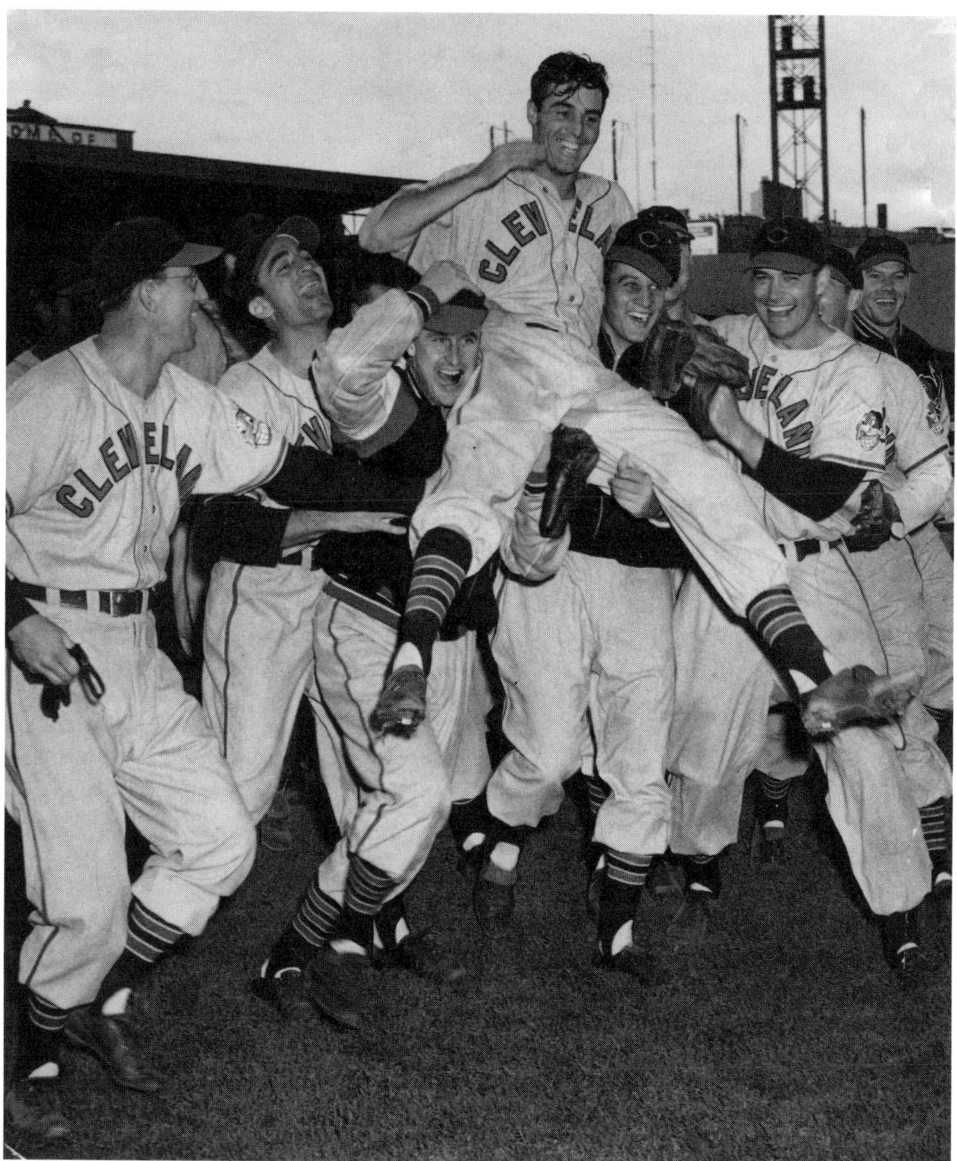

Pitcher Gene Bearden is carried off the field by teammates after winning the playoff game against the Boston Red Sox, bringing a pennant to Cleveland.

May 31 Lou Boudreau hits a grand slam during the sixth inning of an 8–3 win over the Browns in the first game of a double header at Municipal Stadium. Each of the nine Cleveland players in the game collected exactly one hit. St. Louis won the second tilt 6–0.

June 2 The Indians trade Pat Seerey and Al Gettel to the White Sox for Bob Kennedy.

June 4 After 14 scoreless innings, the Indians blast out five runs in the 15th inning to win 5–0 over the Senators in Washington. Bob Feller went 11 innings allowing only four hits. Bob Muncrief followed with four hitless innings of relief.

Bob Feller was 19–15 with a 3.56 ERA in 1948 in addition to striking out a league-leading 164 batters in 280 1/3 innings. It was the seventh consecutive full season in which Feller led the AL in strikeouts. He did so from 1938 through 1941, and after missing all of the 1942, 1943 and 1944 seasons and most of 1945 in the military, Feller continued his streak from 1946 through 1948.

June 6 The Indians sweep the Athletics 5–3 and 11–1 in Philadelphia. In the second game, Joe Tipton collected five hits, including two doubles, in five at-bats.

A back-up rookie catcher who hit .289 in 90 at-bats in 1948, Tipton collected nine hits in nine consecutive at-bats over a 12-day period. He was 3-for-3 in the first game of a double header on May 30. In the second tilt that day, Tipton was hit by a pitch on the wrist and was unable to play for a few days. After his 5-for-5 day on June 6, Tipton sat behind Jim Hegan until playing again on June 10 and picked up a hit in his first at-bat.

June 8 The Indians win 2–0 over the Red Sox at Fenway Park on a disputed homer by Lou Boudreau in the fourth inning. The drive landed about six rows into the stands in the right field corner, and nearly everyone in the park thought it was foul except first base umpire Charlie Berry, who signaled home run. Gene Bearden pitched the shutout.

June 11 The Indians outlast the Yankees 10–8 before 67,924 at Yankee Stadium. The crowd interrupted the contest in the fourth inning after throwing debris at umpire Cal Hubbard after he tossed Yogi Berra out of the game.

June 20 The Indians draw 82,781 into Municipal Stadium for a double header against the Athletics. The Indians swept the twin bill 4–3 in ten innings and 10–0. Among those in the ballpark was Indians stockholder Bob Hope, who joined Jimmy Dudley in the radio booth.

June 30 Bob Lemon pitches a no-hitter to defeat the Tigers 2–0 at Municipal Stadium. He walked three and struck out three. A brilliant defensive play by left fielder Dale Mitchell kept Lemon's bid alive. After a long run, Mitchell made a miraculous leaping stab of George Kell's drive, hit the wall, and crashed into the stands. In the ninth, Lemon personally set the Tigers down in order. He snatched up a grounder by Vic Wertz for the first out, struck out Eddie Mayo, and forced Kell to tap back to the pitcher's box.

Lemon was 20–14 with a 2.62 ERA in 1948 and led the AL in innings pitched (293⅓), complete games (20), and shutouts (ten).

July 7 The Indians sign legendary pitcher Satchel Paige.

Paige's exact birthrate is unknown, but the best estimates place it at July 7, 1906, which meant that he was signed by the Indians on his 42nd birthday. Paige was arguably the greatest pitcher in the history of the Negro Leagues but never received a chance to pitch in the majors until an advanced age because of baseball's color ban. Many believed that his acquisition by the Indians was just another of Bill Veeck's blatant publicity stunts. J. G. Taylor Spink of The Sporting News *was the most vocal. "To bring in a pitching 'rookie' of Paige's age casts a reflection on the entire scheme of operations in the major leagues," wrote Spink in an editorial. "To sign a hurler of Paige's age is to demean the standards of baseball in the big circuits. Further complicating the situation is the suspicion that if Satchel were white he wouldn't have drawn a second thought from Veeck." Spink further accused Veeck of being a "cheap showman" because Paige was a "washed-up old-timer." Paige made Spink eat his words. The Indians couldn't have won the 1948 pennant without Satchel. He posted a 6–1 record and a 2.46 ERA in 21 games, seven of them starts. His starting assignments, both at home and on the road, drew huge crowds. In 1949, Paige had a 4–7 mark and a 3.04 earned run average in 31 games, including five starts. He was released by the Indians during the following off-season shortly after Veeck sold the club. When Veeck bought the Browns in 1951, he signed Paige again. Paige played three seasons in St. Louis and made the All-Star team in both 1952 and 1953.*

July 8 The Indians smother the White Sox 14–1 at Municipal Stadium.

July 9 Satchel Paige makes his big league debut pitching two innings of scoreless relief during a 5–3 loss to the Browns at Municipal Stadium.

There were only four African-American players in the majors in 1948, and all four eventually reached the Hall of Fame. The four were Paige and Larry Doby of the Indians and Jackie Robinson and Roy Campanella of the Dodgers.

July 21 Jim Hegan hits a grand slam off Karl Drews in the eighth inning to climax a 12–8 win in the second game of a double header in New York. Down 8–4, Cleveland scored three runs in the seventh and five in the eighth. Hegan's slam broke an 8–8 tie. The Yanks won the first game 7–3.

July 22 Dale Mitchell runs his hitting streak to 21 games during a 6–5 loss to the Yankees in New York.

Mitchell hit .306 and collected 204 hits in 1948.

July 31 The Indians score two runs in the ninth inning and one in the 11th to defeat the Red Sox 10–9 at Municipal Stadium. Joe Gordon drove in the winning run with a single.

Gordon hit .280 with 32 homers and 124 runs-batted-in during the 1948 season.

August 1 The Indians sweep the Red Sox 12–2 and 6–1 before 70,702 at Municipal Stadium. The wins put the Indians ahead of the Red Sox and into first place in the AL standings. The victories, however, were costly. Hank Edwards dislocated his right shoulder robbing Stan Spence of a home run. Edwards caught the ball, but landed on the railing. The injury put him out for the season.

AUGUST 3 Satchel Paige makes his first big league start and is the winning pitcher in a 5–3 decision over the Senators before 72,434 at Municipal Stadium. Paige allowed three runs in seven innings.

AUGUST 5 First baseman Eddie Robinson takes part in six double plays during a 3–0 win over the Senators at Municipal Stadium. Gene Bearden pitched the shutout.

AUGUST 8 The Indians sweep the Yankees 8–6 and 2–1 before 73,484 at Municipal Stadium. In the opener, the Indians trailed 6–1 before scoring five runs in the seventh inning and two in the eighth. The key blow occurred in the seventh when the Indians were still behind 6–4. Lou Boudreau, who had been sidelined for three days with an ankle injury, put himself into the game as a pinch-hitter and delivered a two-run single to tie the score 6–6. Eddie Robinson's second homer of the game broke a 6–6 tie.

Lou Boudreau waves to the crowd of jubilant fans during the victory parade celebrating the Indians triumph in the World Series. Owner Bill Veeck is perched on Boudreau's right. Others in the car are unidentified.

AUGUST 12 After losing the first game of a double header in St. Louis to the Browns 8–4, the Indians explode for a club record 29 hits in the nightcap and win 26–3. The Indians set the pace with nine runs in the first inning and added four in the third, two in the fourth, four in the fifth, three in the sixth, three in the seventh, and one in the eighth. The 29 hits were four homers, a triple, five doubles, and 19 singles. It was a team effort as 14 different players collected at least one hit, 12 drove in at least one run, and 11 scored. The Indians picked up six hits from their catchers as Jim Hegan and Joe Tipton each went 3-for-4 at the plate batting eighth in the line-up.

Pitcher Gene Bearden had four hits and four RBIs giving Cleveland ten hits from the eight and nine spots in the batting order.

AUGUST 13 Before a sell-out crowd of 51,013 at Comiskey Park, Satchel Paige pitches his first shutout, defeating the White Sox 5–0.

AUGUST 15 The Indians sweep the White Sox 6–2 and 6–0 in Chicago. Bob Lemon pitched the game-two shutout.

AUGUST 17 Gene Bearden blanks the Browns 8–0 at Municipal Stadium.

AUGUST 19 Sam Zoldak records the third consecutive shutout by Cleveland pitchers with a 3–0 triumph over the Browns at Municipal Stadium.

AUGUST 20 The Indians run their streak of consecutive shutouts to four as Satchel Paige defeats the White Sox 1–0 before 78,832 at Municipal Stadium. Larry Doby drove in the lone run of the game with a single in the fourth inning. The victory was Cleveland's eighth in a row.

During a span of seven games from August 13 through August 20, the Indians pitching staff allowed only four runs.

AUGUST 21 The Indians extend their streak of consecutive scoreless innings to 47 before allowing three runs in the ninth inning to lose 3–2 to the White Sox at Municipal Stadium. Bob Lemon pitched the first eight innings before the ninth-inning blow-up.

AUGUST 25 Bob Lemon shuts out the Red Sox 9–0 in Boston.

AUGUST 29 Bob Lemon pitches his second consecutive shutout, defeating the Senators 6–0 in the first game of a double header at Griffith Stadium. Washington won the second tilt 5–2.

SEPTEMBER 3 Bob Lemon pitches his third straight shutout, all on the road, defeating the Browns 7–0 in the first game of a double header at Sportsman's Park. St. Louis won the second contest 4–3.

Lemon pitched 31 consecutive scoreless innings from August 25 through September 8.

SEPTEMBER 9 The Indians win 3–2 in 13 innings on Ken Keltner Night at Municipal Stadium. Before the game, Keltner was given $8,000 in cash and gifts, including a station wagon.

At the end of the day, the Indians were in third place, 4½ games behind the first place Red Sox with 21 games left on the schedule.

SEPTEMBER 11 Bob Lemon wins his 20th game of the season with a 4–1 decision over the Browns in the first game of a double header at Municipal Stadium. St. Louis won the nightcap 1–0.

SEPTEMBER 13 Don Black suffers a near-fatal brain hemorrhage during a 3–2 loss to the Browns at Municipal Stadium. Batting in the second inning, Black swung viciously and fouled off a pitch from Bill Kennedy. Black staggered slightly as he finished his swing, then walked away from the plate and turned in a small circle in back of umpire Bill Summers. The Cleveland pitcher sagged to the ground and lapsed into unconsciousness as blood flooded his brain and spinal cord. He was rushed to the hospital where surgery was considered but dismissed because Black's condition was considered too serious. Doctors gave him a 50–50 chance to live. Black survived but never pitched again. Nine days after he was stricken, while still in critical condition, the Indians held a "night" in his honor and raised $40,000 for him. Black was seriously injured in an auto accident in 1957 and died in 1959 at the age of 42 while watching the Indians on television.

SEPTEMBER 16 Larry Doby hits a grand slam off Sid Hudson in the first inning of a 6–3 win over the Senators at Municipal Stadium.

SEPTEMBER 19 The Indians sweep the Athletics 5–3 and 2–0 at Municipal Stadium. Larry Doby clubbed a two-run walk-off homer in the ninth inning of the opener. In the second contest, Lou Boudreau hits solo homers in the fourth and sixth inning off Dick Fowler to produce the only two tallies of the game. Steve Gromek pitched the shutout.

SEPTEMBER 22 The Indians move into a tie for first place with the Red Sox by defeating the Boston club 5–2 before 76,772 at Municipal Stadium. It was the first time since August 25 that the Indians had been in first place. The Yankees were in third place just one-half game back.

SEPTEMBER 28 The Indians take a two-game lead in the pennant race with an 11–0 victory over the White Sox before 60,405 at Municipal Stadium. The Red Sox and Yankees were tied for second place.

It was "Joe Earley Night" at Municipal Stadium. Earley was a 26-year-old night security guard at an automobile plant who sent a letter to Bill Veeck pointing out that many players have nights in their honor and suggested that he, too, should have a night as a "typical" Cleveland fan. Veeck took him up on the offer and the result was a 30-minute pre-game ceremony in which Earley received a new Ford convertible and a truck loaded with all manner of household appliances, clothes, luggage, and books. Veeck also gave out 20,000 orchids to female fans and presented other ticket holders with "gag gifts" such as poultry, livestock, rabbits, and stepladders.

SEPTEMBER 29 The Indians maintain a two-game lead over both the Red Sox and Yankees with a 5–2 triumph over the White Sox at Municipal Stadium. Bob Feller pitched a complete game on two days' rest. Each of the three contenders had three games left to play.

OCTOBER 1 The Indians lose a chance to clinch at least a tie for the pennant with a 5–3 loss to the Tigers at Municipal Stadium. Detroit scored three runs in the ninth inning for the win. Cleveland closed the day with a one-game lead over both the Red Sox and Yankees with two games left on the schedule.

OCTOBER 2 The Indians clinch a tie for the pennant with an 8–0 win over the Tigers at Municipal Stadium. Gene Bearden pitched the shutout. The Red Sox defeated the Yankees 5–1 in Boston to eliminate the Yankees from the pennant race. Heading into the final day, the Indians needed only a win or a Red Sox loss to clinch the pennant. If the Indians lost and the Red Sox won, a one-game playoff to determine the AL World Series representative would be held in Boston on October 4.

OCTOBER 3 The Indians lose 7–1 to the Tigers at Municipal Stadium with Hal Newhouser defeating Bob Feller, while the Red Sox beat the Yankees 10–5 in Boston to force a playoff for the pennant. Both the Indians and Red Sox had 96–58 records.

OCTOBER 4 The Indians clinch the American League pennant with an 8–3 win over the Red Sox at Fenway Park. Both managers made controversial pitching selections. Lou Boudreau selected rookie Gene Bearden, who pitched nine innings two days earlier. Boston's skipper went with journeyman Denny Galehouse, who was well rested but went into the game with an 8–7 record on the 1948 season. Both teams scored in the first inning, the Indians scoring on a homer by Lou Boudreau over the Green Monster. It was still 1–1 when Cleveland exploded for four runs in the fourth. Boudreau started the rally with a single and Ken Keltner belted a three-run homer. In the fifth, Boudreau homered again for a 6–1 lead. Later, Boudreau added another single and Bearden pitched a complete game for his 20th win of the season.

The Indians met the Boston Braves in the World Series in a match-up of two franchises with long post-season dry spells. The Braves had last appeared in the Fall Classic in 1914, and the Indians in 1920. Managed by Billy Southworth, the Braves were 91–62 in 1948.

OCTOBER 6 In the first game of the 1948 World Series, the Braves edge the Indians 1–0 at Braves Field in Boston. Bob Feller was the losing pitcher in the heartbreaker. Through the first seven innings he pitched a one-hit shutout. In the eighth, Bill Salkeld walked and Phil Masi ran for him. After moving to second on a sacrifice, Masi was apparently picked off by Feller, but umpire Bill Stewart claimed that Masi eluded Lou Boudreau's tag. Nearly everyone in the ballpark believed that Masi was out, but Stewart's opinion was the only one that mattered. Tommy Holmes drove in Masi with the lone run of the game. Johnny Sain pitched a four-hitter for Boston.

OCTOBER 7 The Indians bounce back to defeat the Braves 4–1 in Boston in game two. Cleveland scored their first two runs in the Series in the fourth inning to take a 2–1 lead. Bob Lemon pitched the complete game victory.

OCTOBER 8 The Indians take game three 2–0 with Gene Bearden pitching a five-hit shutout before 70,306 at Municipal Stadium. He faced only 30 batters and threw 84 pitches. Bearden also scored a run and collected a double and a single to account for two of Cleveland's five hits. In a span of seven days, Bearden pitched three complete game victories. The game lasted just 96 minutes.

Fans in Cleveland saw a World Series on television for the first time in 1948 but only those games emanating from Municipal Stadium. The technology to transmit images from Boston to Cleveland was not yet available. The 1947 Series was the first televised but was shown only in New York, Philadelphia, Washington, and Schenectady.

OCTOBER 9 The Indians move within one game of a world championship with a 2–1 win over the Braves before 81,897 at Municipal Stadium. Steve Gromek pitched a complete game. Larry Doby homered in the third inning to give the Indians a 2–0 advantage.

OCTOBER 10 The Braves spoil the Indians chances of clinching the world championship before the home crowd with an 11–5 win in front of 86,288 at Municipal Stadium. The large crowd included an estimated 8,500 standees behind the outfield fence. Boston broke a 5–5 tie with six runs in the seventh inning. Bob Feller took the loss, allowing seven runs in 6⅓ innings. Jim Hegan popped a three-run homer in the fourth to give the Indians a brief 5–4 lead. Satchel Paige became the first African-American pitcher in a World Series with two-thirds of an inning of relief in which he retired both batters he faced.

Feller was the losing pitcher in both Cleveland defeats in the 1948 Series.

OCTOBER 11 The Indians win the world championship with a 4–3 win over the Braves in Boston. With the help of Joe Gordon's sixth-inning homer, the Indians led 4–1 heading into the bottom of the eighth with Bob Lemon on the mound. The Braves scored two runs off Lemon before Gene Bearden was called in to put out the fire with 1⅔ innings of relief. The final out was recorded on a fly ball by Tommy Holmes to Bob Kennedy on left field.

OCTOBER 12 A parade is held in Cleveland in the Indians honor. A crowd estimated at 200,000 lined Euclid Avenue.

NOVEMBER 20 Two weeks after Harry Truman defeats Thomas Dewey in the presidential election, the Indians sell Bob Muncrief to the Pirates.

NOVEMBER 22 The Indians trade Joe Tipton to the White Sox for Joe Haynes.

The Indians acquired Haynes in to trade him to the Senators (see December 14, 1948). Haynes was the son-in-law of Washington owner Clark Griffith.

DECEMBER 14 The Indians trade Eddie Robinson, Joe Haynes, and Eddie Klieman to the Senators for Mickey Vernon and Early Wynn.

The Indians pulled off a brilliant deal in acquiring future Hall of Fame pitcher Early Wynn. He played in Cleveland from 1949 through 1957 and again in 1963. At the time of the trade, Wynn was three weeks shy of his 29th birthday and had a 72–87 lifetime record. He was coming off of a 1948 season in which he was 8–19 with a 5.85 ERA. In a reversal of fortune, Wynn won 20 or more four times with the Indians and overall was 164–102 with the club. He credited Indians pitching coach Mel Harder with making him a consistent winner by improving the grip and delivery of his curveball and teaching him to throw a knuckleball. Wynn currently ranks fifth among Indians hurlers in career wins, third in strikeouts (1,277), sixth in winning percentage (.617), seventh in shutouts (24), seventh in innings (2,296⅔), seventh in games started (296), and eighth in complete games (144). In 1963 with the Indians, Wynn won his 300th career game. An unrelenting competitiveness helped him achieve those totals. Mickey Mantle once said that Wynn was "so mean he'd knock you down in the dugout."

1949

Season in a Sentence

The defending world champions stumble out of the gate with 17 losses in their first 29 games and struggle to score runs all year, burying any hopes for a repeat.

Finish • Won • Lost • Pct • GB

Finish	Won	Lost	Pct	GB
Third	89	65	.578	8.0

Manager

Lou Boudreau

Stats

Stats	Indians	AL	Rank
Batting Avg:	.260	.263	4
On-Base Pct:	.339	.353	5
Slugging Pct:	.384	.379	3
Home Runs:	112		4
Stolen Bases:	44		4
ERA:	3.36	4.20	1
Fielding Avg:	.983	.977	1
Runs Scored:	675		5
Runs Allowed:	574		1

Starting Line-up

Jim Hegan, c
Mickey Vernon, 1b
Joe Gordon, 2b
Ken Keltner, 3b
Lou Boudreau, ss-3b
Dale Mitchell, lf
Larry Doby, cf
Bob Kennedy, rf
Ray Boone, ss
Thermion Tucker, cf

Pitchers

Bob Lemon, sp
Bob Feller, sp
Early Wynn, sp
Gene Bearden, sp-rp
Mike Garcia, rp-sp
Al Benton, rp
Satchel Paige, rp
Steve Gromek, rp-sp

Attendance

2,233,771 (second in AL)

Club Leaders

Batting Avg:	Dale Mitchell	.317
On-Base Pct:	Larry Doby	.389
Slugging Pct:	Larry Doby	.468
Home Runs:	Larry Doby	24
RBIs:	Larry Doby	85
Runs:	Larry Doby	106
Stolen Bases:	Larry Doby	10
	Dale Mitchell	10
Wins:	Bob Lemon	22
Strikeouts:	Bob Lemon	138
ERA:	Bob Lemon	2.89
Saves:	Al Benton	10

JANUARY 12 The Indians purchase Mike Tresh from the White Sox.

FEBRUARY 9 The Indians sell Walt Judnich to the Pirates.

APRIL 19 The Indians lose the opener 5–1 to the Browns in St. Louis. Bob Feller was the starting pitcher and left the game in the second inning with a sore arm. He didn't pitch again for three weeks. Minnie Minoso made his major league debut as a pinch-hitter in the seventh inning. A native of Cuba, Minoso was the first dark-skinned Latin player to play in the major leagues.

APRIL 20 The Indians purchase Al Benton from the Tigers.

APRIL 21 Steve Gromek pitches a two-hitter to defeat the Browns 8–2 at Sportsman's Park. The two St. Louis hits were back-to-back homers by Jack Graham and Dick Kokos in the fifth inning.

APRIL 22 In the home opener, the Indians win 4–3 in ten innings over the Tigers before 63,725 at Municipal Stadium. The winning run scored on a single by Mickey Vernon on his 31st birthday.

April 26 Lou Boudreau homers off Red Embree in the fourth inning to defeat the Browns 1–0 at Municipal Stadium. Bob Lemon pitched the shutout.

May 1 Bob Lemon pitches a two-hitter but loses 3–2 against the Tigers in Detroit. All three runs off Lemon scored in the first inning, two of them on a homer by Dick Wakefield.

Lemon had a 22–10 record with a 2.99 ERA in 1949.

May 15 The Indians lose 10–0 and 2–0 to the White Sox in a double header at Comiskey Park.

After the Indians failed to score in the double header, White Sox vice-president Chuck Comiskey and general manager Frank Lane dug up home plate and sent it to Bill Veeck with a note reading: "We thought you might like to know what this looks like." Going along with the gag, Veeck had the plate installed at Municipal Stadium (see May 27, 1949).

May 25 Larry Doby hits a home run estimated at 500 feet off Sid Hudson during a 6–2 loss to the Senators in Washington. The ball cleared the scoreboard at Griffith Stadium in right-center field and landed on the roof of a house across the street.

May 26 The Indians record drops to 12–17 with a 5–4 loss to the Senators in Washington. The game was called after 7½ innings to allow both teams to catch trains.

May 27 In order to get a fresh start on the 1949 season after 17 losses in their first 29 games, Bill Veeck stages a "re-opener" at Municipal Stadium and the Indians defeat the White Sox 4–0. Al Benton, in his first start with Cleveland, pitched the shutout. In pre-game ceremonies for "Let's Forget the Horrible Past Booster Night," Veeck installed the home plate given to him by White Sox execs Chuck Comiskey and Frank Lane (see August 15, 1949), after which mayor Thomas Burke threw out the first ball.

May 28 Early Wynn pitches an 11-inning complete game and retires the last 21 batters to face him and defeats the White Sox 3–2 at Municipal Stadium. Mickey Vernon drove in the winning run with a bases-loaded single.

May 31 Cleveland druggist Charley Lupica climbs onto a four-foot by six-foot platform built at the top of a 16-foot high flag pole on the roof of his drug store on the east side of the city. Adding the 49-foot height of the building, Lupica was 65 feet above the street. He vowed not to come down until the Indians reached first place. The club was in seventh place and seven games out of first place when Lupica started his lonely vigil. A tent-like canvas protected Lupica from the elements and hid him from curious spectators below. Toilet facilities were installed and meals were sent up by his wife. For entertainment, he had a television and a radio. While Lupica was aloft, his wife gave birth to their fourth child, a son, on August 7. Later, a dentist climbed up to Lupica's roost to treat him. Lupica remained on the flagpole for 117 days (see September 25, 1949).

June 6 Trailing 5–2, the Indians score nine runs in the eighth inning to win 11–5 over the Athletics at Municipal Stadium. Lou Boudreau played third base for the first time in his career, moving Ken Keltner to the bench. Ray Boone took over at shortstop.

The Indians run production dropped from 840 in 1948 to 675 in 1949 in part because Boudreau, Keltner, and Joe Gordon seemed to age almost overnight. Every member of the 1948 World Series infield-Eddie Robinson, Gordon, Boudreau, and Keltner was traded or released by the start of the 1951 season.

June 7 The Indians outlast the Senators 13–11 at Municipal Stadium. Cleveland took a 12–9 lead with four runs in the sixth inning. Play was halted for 15 minutes in the seventh by a brouhaha following a Walt Masterson pitch that nicked Joe Gordon. The second baseman charged the mound and players leaped from both dugouts. Umpires and police broke up the melee before anyone was touched, but later umpire Bill Grieve was almost hit with an empty whiskey bottle thrown by a fan after a line drive by Larry Doby was ruled foul.

June 12 The Indians sweep the Yankees 6–0 and 3–1 before 77,543 at Municipal Stadium. The second game was ended after 7½ innings by rain.

June 14 Joe Gordon hits a grand slam off Joe Dobson during a six-run first inning, leading to a 10–5 win over the Red Sox in Boston. During the first inning, the Red Sox allowed the Indians to use a "courtesy runner." Lou Boudreau was hit on the elbow by a pitch and was taken to the dressing room for treatment. The man who went in to run for Boudreau was Ken Keltner, who was already in the game and scored earlier in the inning. While serving as a runner for Boudreau, Keltner scored again. He was credited with two runs scored in the inning. Boudreau returned to the game in the second inning.

June 15 Ray Boone hits his first two major league homers during an 8–5 win over the Red Sox in Boston. The homers were struck in the eighth and ninth innings.

Boone headed the first three-generation baseball family in major league history. Ray's son Bob played in the big leagues as a catcher from 1972 through 1990. Bob's eldest son Bret played from 1992 to 2005. Bret's younger brother Aaron debuted in 1997 and was still active in the majors in 2007.

June 19 A two-run homer by Mickey Vernon in the 11th inning beats the Yankees 4–2 in New York.

The Indians had an 18–1 record in extra-inning games in 1949, including a streak of 17 wins in a row.

June 29 The Indians score six runs in the ninth inning to stun the Tigers 8–7 in the second game of a double header at Municipal Stadium. Cleveland had narrowed the gap to 7–5 when Bob Lemon stepped to the plate with the bases loaded. Lemon doubled in two runs to tie the score 7–7, then scored the winning run when center fielder Pat Mullin booted the ball. Detroit won the opener 4–0.

July 3 The Indians score two runs in the ninth inning and one in the tenth to defeat the Browns 4–3 in the second game of a double header at Municipal Stadium. Mickey Vernon's two-out, two-run single tied the score 3–3. Jim Hegan's bases-loaded hit drove in the winner. The Indians won the opener by the same 4–3 score.

JULY 12 Lou Boudreau manages the American League to an 11–7 win in the All-Star Game, played at Ebbets Field in Brooklyn. Dale Mitchell drove in a run with a double. It was also the first time that African-Americans participated in the Midsummer Classic. Larry Doby was one of the quartet. The other three were Jackie Robinson, Roy Campanella, and Don Newcombe of the Dodgers.

There were only nine players of African descent in the majors in 1949. Four were members of the Indians, the only four in the American League that season. Besides Doby, the roster included Satchel Paige, Luke Easter, and Minnie Minoso.

JULY 18 Mike Garcia pitches the Indians to a 1–0 win over the Red Sox at Municipal Stadium. The lone run of the game scored in the fifth inning on a double by Jim Hegan.

In 1949, his first full season in the majors, Garcia posted a 14–5 record and his 2.36 ERA led the American League. He pitched for the Indians from 1948 through 1959 and posted a record of 142–96. Among Indians pitchers all-time, he ranks ninth in wins, fifth in shutouts (27), sixth in games (397), seventh in winning percentage (.597), eighth in strikeouts (1,095), ninth in innings pitched (2,138), and ninth in games started (281).

JULY 19 Jim Hegan hits a walk-off homer in the ninth inning to beat the Yankees 5–4 at Municipal Stadium.

JULY 24 Bob Lemon hits two home runs during a 7–5 win over the Senators in the first game of a double header at Municipal Stadium. The Indians completed their sweep with a 5–2 win in the second tilt.

In 108 at-bats in 1949, Lemon hit seven home runs and posted a batting average of .269 and slugging percentage of .556.

AUGUST 4 The Indians sweep the Senators 6–3 and 14–1 in Washington. The opener went 12 innings. In the second contest, Cleveland collected 20 hits.

The wins gave the Indians a 60–40 record on the season and 48 victories in their last 71 games. The club was in second place, only 2½ games out of first, but could draw no closer to the top of the standings.

AUGUST 18 The Indians wallop the Browns 14–4 in St. Louis.

AUGUST 31 Jim Hegan hits a walk-off homer in the 14th inning to defeat the Athletics 7–6 in the first game of a double header at Municipal Stadium. Joe Gordon tied a major league record for second basemen by participating in six Cleveland double plays. Philadelphia won the nightcap 3–1.

SEPTEMBER 3 The film *The Kid from Cleveland* opens in theaters.

The movie centers on the story of a wayward youth, played by Russ Tamblyn, who turned his life around by becoming a batboy for the Indians. Many Indians players, including Bob Feller, Gene Bearden, Satchel Paige, Bob Lemon, Steve Gromek, Joe Gordon, Mickey Vernon, Ken Keltner, Ray Boone, Dale Mitchell, Larry Doby, Bob Kennedy, and Jim Hegan took part in the production. Bill Veeck, Lou Boudreau, Hank Greenberg, and coach Tris Speaker also played themselves. Johnny Berardino, who acted in films during the off-season (see December 9, 1947), played a character named "Mac." The movie roles required the players to be available almost every morning they were home for filming at League Park and proved to be a major distraction. The Kid from Cleveland *was not well received by either the critics or the public and quickly disappeared from theaters. It was so bad that Lou Boudreau said that he would like to burn every copy. Bill Veeck had a standing rule in his house that no one was ever allowed to mention* The Kid from Cleveland. *Despite the lack of rave reviews, it is still shown occasionally on television on some of the classic movie channels, although in the case of* The Kid from Cleveland, *the word "classic" must be applied loosely.*

SEPTEMBER 4 Prior to a 5–0 win over the Tigers at Municipal Stadium, the 1920 world championship Indians lose a two-inning game 6–1 against a team of players who played on other Indian clubs through the years. All of the living 1920 players attended the event except Joe Wood.

SEPTEMBER 23 On the day President Harry Truman announces that the Soviet Union has developed and tested an atomic bomb, Bill Veeck stages an unusual show before a 5–0 loss to the Tigers at Municipal Stadium. With the Indians mathematically eliminated from the 1949 American League title chase, a "funeral" was held for the 1948 world championship pennant. The flag was placed in a casket carried by a horse-drawn hearse to a spot between the outfield fence and the center field bleachers, where it was buried with appropriate ceremony with front office executives wearing top hats and tails. A "tombstone" read: 1948 Champs.

SEPTEMBER 25 Charley Lupica descends from his perch (see May 29, 1949) above his east side drug store. At the invitation of Bill Veeck, Lupica's flagpole and platform were transported by lift truck on a 15-mile journey to Municipal Stadium on September 24. Just before game-time on the 25th, Charley was carted to home plate. While the band blared, "Charley My Boy," Lupica came down to greet his wife and four children and to receive such assorted gifts as a 50-foot flagpole, a four-poster bed, a bathtub filled with suds, bicycles, puppies for the youngsters, a cooking range for Mrs. Lupica, and a new Pontiac.

NOVEMBER 21 Bill Veeck sells the Indians to a group headed by Ellis Ryan for $2.2 million. Veeck purchased the Indians for $1.25 million in June 1946.

After the Indians failed to repeat as AL champions in 1949 and attendance dropped from 2,620,627 to 2,233,771, Veeck decided to look for new challenges. He sold the Indians to a group headed by Cleveland insurance executive Ellis Ryan. Ryan was 45-years-old and was named team president. One of his first acts was to name Hank Greenberg as general manager. Ryan was a polar opposite of the freewheeling Veeck, who had contempt for convention and craved publicity. Ryan preferred remaining behind the scenes and was described by one Cleveland newspaperman as "a perfect candidate for a 'man of distinction' advertisement." A former World War II lieutenant colonel in the U.S. Army Air Corps and the Office of Strategic Services (the forerunner of the CIA), Ryan commanded a unit that trained personnel in espionage and commando tactics against the Japanese in China, Burma, and India. Prior to his involvement with the Indians, Ryan had been a vice-president of both the Cleveland Barons, a minor league hockey team, and the Cleveland Browns. The Indians finished in fourth place in 1950, resulting in the firing of Lou Boudreau. Al Lopez took over as manager, and the club finished a close second in 1951 and 1952. A serious rift developed among the stockholders during the period. Many, including Ryan, wanted to oust Greenberg. A slim majority, however, desired to retain the general manager. In December 1952, Ryan was deposed as president of the Indians. Veeck later owned the St. Louis Browns (1951–53) and Chicago White Sox (1959–61 and 1975–80).

THE STATE OF THE INDIANS

During the 1950s, the Indians posted the best won-lost record of any decade in franchise history. The club had a record of 904–634 for a winning percentage of .588 that was the third best in the majors during the decade behind only the Yankees and Dodgers. But success is relative. The Yankees won eight pennants and six world championships during the 1950s, while the Dodgers claimed five pennants and two World Series titles. The Indians took just one AL championship, in 1954, and were swept in the Fall Classic by the Giants. The Indians finished second in the American League in 1951, 1952, 1953, 1955, 1956 and 1959. In four of those seasons (1951, 1952, 1955 and 1959), the Indians ended the season five games or less from first place. The Yankees won every American League pennant during the 1950s except 1954 and 1959. Cleveland won it in 1954 and the White Sox in 1959. Both of those clubs were managed by Al Lopez.

THE BEST TEAM

The 1954 Indians were 111–43, the highest number of wins by any major league team between 1906 and 1998. The winning percentage of .721 is still the American League record and the best of any big league club since the 1909 Pirates were 110–42 (.724). The great year by the 1954 Indians ended badly, however, when the club was swept the New York Giants in the World Series.

THE WORST TEAM

The only team during the 1950s to post a losing record was in 1957 when the Indians were 76–77 under Kerby Farrell.

THE BEST MOMENT

Rocky Colavito hit four consecutive homers during an 11–8 win over the Orioles in Baltimore on June 10, 1959.

THE WORST MOMENT

Herb Score looked as though he might become one of the greatest pitchers in baseball history, but his career took a tragic turn on May 7, 1957, when he was struck in the face by a line drive off the bat of Gil McDougald of the Yankees at Municipal Stadium.

THE ALL-DECADE TEAM • YEARS W/INDIANS

Jim Hegan, c	1941–42, 1946–57
Vic Wertz, 1b	1954–58
Bobby Avila, 2b	1949–58
Al Rosen, 3b	1947–56
George Strickland, ss	1952–57, 1959–60
Dale Mitchell, lf	1946–56
Larry Doby, cf	1947–55, 1958
Rocky Colavito, rf	1955–59, 1965–67
Bob Lemon, p	1941–42, 1946–58
Early Wynn, p	1949–57, 1963
Mike Garcia, p	1948–59
Bob Feller, p	1936–41, 1945–56

Feller, Lemon, and Hegan were also on the 1940s All-Decade Team. In addition, Feller was on the 1930s team. Feller, Lemon, and Wynn are all in the Hall of Fame. Colavito is one of those players who have been overlooked for induction at Cooperstown. Rosen was well on his way toward building a Hall of Fame resume before injuries ended his career prematurely. Other outstanding Indians players of the 1950s were outfielder-third baseman Al Smith (1953–57, 1964), outfielder Minnie Minoso (1949, 1951, 1958–59), first basemen Luke Easter (1949–54) and Vic Power (1958–61), and pitchers Ray Narleski (1954–58) and Herb Score (1955–59).

THE DECADE LEADERS

Batting Avg:	Al Rosen	.287
On-Base Pct:	Larry Doby	.391
Slugging Pct:	Al Rosen	.500
Home Runs:	Al Rosen	192
RBIs:	Al Rosen	712
Runs:	Bobby Avila	685
Stolen Bases:	Bobby Avila	75
Wins:	Bob Lemon	150
Strikeouts:	Early Wynn	1,186
ERA:	Early Wynn	3.20
Saves:	Ray Narleski	53

THE HOME FIELD

The only significant change at Municipal Stadium was the construction of a new scoreboard in 1953, which replaced the original 1932 board.

THE GAME YOU WISHED YOU HAD SEEN

Bob Feller pitched his third career no-hitter on July 1, 1951, beating the Tigers 2–1 at Municipal Stadium.

THE WAY THE GAME WAS PLAYED

The number of home runs continued to rise during the 1950s, with AL teams averaging 120 homers per season compared with 85 per year during the 1930s. The number of complete games continued to decline from 63 per team in 1950 to 46 in 1959. Relievers were making more appearances, and the relief specialist emerged, including Ray Narleski and Don Mossi of the Indians. The increased use of relievers to close out victories led to a new statistic called the "save," although it wasn't officially recognized by major league baseball until 1969. Games were also taking longer to play. The average length of a game rose from two hours and 23 minutes to two hours and 38 minutes. In addition, the first franchise shifts in 50 years took place. In the NL, the Boston Braves moved to Milwaukee in 1953. In the AL, the St. Louis Browns moved to Baltimore in 1954, where they were renamed the Orioles. A year later, the Athletics transferred from Philadelphia to Kansas City. In 1958, major league baseball was played west of the Rockies for the first time when the Dodgers and Giants moved from New York to California. Integration of the big leagues accelerated during the 1950s. In 1950, there were only nine African-American or dark-skinned Latin players in the major leagues. By 1959, that number increased to 67. Much of the success that Cleveland fans enjoyed during the 1950s can be traced to the Indians employing more minority players than any other American League club. Among them were Larry Doby, Bobby Avila, Luke Easter, Minnie Minoso, Al Smith, and Vic Power.

THE MANAGEMENT

Despite the success on the field, there was instability at the top of the organization, which often placed the franchise's continued future in Cleveland in jeopardy. Team presidents were Ellis Ryan (1949–52), Mike Wilson (1952–56), and William Daley (1956–62). General managers were Hank Greenberg (1950–57) and Frank Lane (1957–61). The field managers included Lou Boudreau (1942–50), Al Lopez (1951–56), Kerby Farrell (1957), Bobby Bragan (1958), and Joe Gordon (1958–60).

THE BEST PLAYER MOVE

The best player move was the signing of Rocky Colavito out of high school in 1951. After four seasons in the minors, he reached the big leagues in 1955. Despite the club's success during the 1950s, Hank Greenberg and Frank Lane had a miserable record when it came to making trades. The best deal with another club brought Tito Francona from the Tigers for Larry Doby in March 1959.

THE WORST PLAYER MOVE

The worst trade was completed on April 30, 1951, as part of a three-team deal involving the White Sox and Athletics in which the Indians gave up Minnie Minoso, Sam Zoldak, and Ray Murray for Lou Brissie. In other less-than-inspired transactions, the Indians dealt away Mickey Vernon, Ray Boone, Sam Jones, Jim Lemon, Early Wynn, Al Smith, Don Mossi, Hank Aguirre, Roger Maris, and Hoyt Wilhelm. Most, if not all, of the close second-place finishes in 1951, 1952, 1955, and 1959 can be attributed to poor trades by Greenberg and Lane.

1950

Season in a Sentence

After another fourth-place finish, general manager Hank Greenberg announces sweeping changes, beginning with the firing of Lou Boudreau and the hiring of Al Lopez.

Finish • Won • Lost • Pct • GB

Finish	Won	Lost	Pct	GB
Fourth	92	62	.597	8.0

Manager

Lou Boudreau

Stats

Stats	Indians	AL	Rank
Batting Avg:	.269	.271	4
On-Base Pct:	.358	.356	4
Slugging Pct:	.422	.402	3
Home Runs:	164		1
Stolen Bases:	40		3
ERA:	3.75	4.48	1
Fielding Avg:	.978	.976	4
Runs Scored:	806		4
Runs Allowed:	654		1

Starting Line-up

Jim Hegan, c
Luke Easter, 1b
Joe Gordon, 2b
Al Rosen, 3b
Ray Boone, ss
Dale Mitchell, lf
Larry Doby, cf
Bob Kennedy, rf
Lou Boudreau, ss
Bobby Avila, 2b
Allie Clark, lf-rf

Pitchers

Bob Lemon, sp
Early Wynn, sp
Bob Feller, sp
Mike Garcia, sp
Steve Gromek, rp-sp

Attendance

1,727,464 (third in AL)

Club Leaders

Batting Avg:	Larry Doby	.326
On-Base Pct:	Larry Doby	.442
Slugging Pct:	Larry Doby	.545
Home Runs:	Al Rosen	37
RBIs:	Al Rosen	116
Runs:	Larry Doby	110
Stolen Bases:	Larry Doby	8
Wins:	Bob Lemon	23
Strikeouts:	Bob Lemon	170
ERA:	Early Wynn	3.20
Saves:	Three tied with	4

JANUARY 10 The Indians fire coach George Susce, Sr. after his son George, Jr., a star high school pitcher, signs a contract with the Red Sox.

George Sr. had been a coach with the Indians since 1941. The Red Sox signed him as a coach a few weeks after he was fired. Altogether, George Sr. was a big league coach for five different franchises before retiring in 1972. George, Jr. had a five-year career in the majors from 1955 through 1959 in which he posted a record of 22–17.

APRIL 18 The Indians lose 7–6 in ten innings to the Tigers before an Opening Day crowd of 65,744. Bob Lemon carried a 4–2 lead into the eighth before allowing four runs. Al Rosen clubbed a two-run homer in the bottom half to tie the score 6–6. Dale Mitchell collected five hits, including a triple and a double, in six at-bats. Larry Doby homered and singled and drove in three runs. Jim Hegan was taken out of the game when a foul ball glanced off his own bat, bounced off the ground, and struck him on the nose.

All Indians home games were televised in 1950 over WXEL with Jimmy Dudley, Jack Graney, and Al Hoegler at the mike.

May 16 Larry Doby hits a grand slam, a triple, and a single to account for six RBIs during a 15–4 win over the Athletics at Municipal Stadium. The Indians collected 20 hits.

Doby's on-base percentage of .442 led the American League in 1950. He also hit 25 homers, drove in 102 runs, and scored 110 times, along with a .326 batting average.

May 21 A crowd of 79,570 turns out at Municipal Stadium for a double header and watches the Indians lose 14–5 and 12–4 to the Yankees. A total of 22 special trains and over 200 buses brought out-of-town fans.

In 1950, the Indians became the first major league club to provide transportation for relief pitchers from the bullpen to the mound, utilizing a red jeep for the journey. Yankees manager Casey Stengel wouldn't allow his pitchers to use the motorized transportation. "The Yankees ride only in Cadillacs," said Stengel. The Indians later provided Cadillac convertibles, but the Yanks still let the vehicles sit idle during pitching changes.

June 6 The Indians unleash a 22-hit bombardment and rout the Yankees 16–2 in New York.

June 8 Al Rosen hits a grand slam off Bob Kuzava in the first inning for a 4–0 lead, but the Indians lose 7–6 to the Senators in Washington.

With the loss, the Indians had a record of 22–22 and were in fourth place 9½ games out of first. The club then won 54 of their next 78 games.

June 11 A solo homer by Al Rosen and a two-run shot from Jim Hegan accounts for three runs in the tenth inning to defeat the Athletics 6–3 in the first game of a double header at Shibe Park. Philadelphia grabbed the nightcap 9–6.

Playing in his first full season in the majors at the age of 26, Rosen led the AL in home runs with 37 and drove in 116 runs along with 100 runs scored and a .287 batting average. It took him awhile to find a place in the Indians line-up because he failed in brief trials in 1947, 1948 and 1949 by hitting .155 in 58 at-bats, had a reputation as a poor fielder, and Ken Keltner was firmly entrenched at third base. Rosen was a four-time All-Star and the AL MVP in 1953 before a back injury that originated in a 1955 auto accident ended his career prematurely in 1956.

June 14 The Indians trade Mickey Vernon to the Senators for Dick Weik.

The Indians had two stellar first baseman in Vernon and Luke Easter and had to trade one of them. While Easter gave Cleveland three great seasons, the Indians would have been better off keeping Vernon, who was a regular in the American League until 1956 and won the batting title in 1953 with an average of .337, which deprived Al Rosen of winning the triple crown (see September 27, 1953). In addition, the Indians received nothing in exchange for Mickey. Weik played only 11 games in Cleveland. To say that he struggled with his control during his career is putting it mildly. In five big league seasons, Weik issued 237 walks in 213⅔ innings, which contributed to a 6–22 record and a 5.90 earned run average.

June 17 Gene Bearden walks ten batters in 5⅔ innings, but the Indians recover to defeat the Athletics 8–7 at Municipal Stadium. Cleveland scored two runs in the ninth inning on two errors by Philadelphia second baseman Kermit Wahl with the bases loaded. The two teams combined for 25 walks and 29 men left on base.

June 18 The Indians clobber the Athletics 7–0 and 21–2 in a double header at Municipal Stadium. In the opener, Bob Feller pitched a two-hitter. The only Philadelphia hits were singles by Wally Moses and Mike Guerra. In the second tilt, the Indians exploded for a club record 14 runs in the first inning. Jim Hegan hit a grand slam in the third for an 18–0 lead. The Indians drew an American League record 23 walks during the double header, 16 of them in game two.

A familiar sight to Cleveland fans in the post-war era: Larry Doby crossing home plate. He scored a career-high 110 runs in 1950 and tallied 954 in his career with the Indians.

The 14 runs in the first inning of the second game were accomplished on only six hits. Seven of the first 11 Cleveland batters drew walks. With Lew Brissie on the mound, Dale Mitchell led off with a double. After Bob Kennedy lined out, Brissie walked Luke Easter, Larry Doby, Al Rosen, Joe Gordon, and Ray Boone in succession to force in three runs. Jim Hegan hit a two-run single and Mike Garcia followed with another single for a 6–0 lead. Mitchell walked, and Carl Scheib replaced Brissie. Kennedy walked with the bases loaded, and Easter hit a two-run single. Doby singled and Rosen reached on an error for an 11–0 advantage before Gordon flied out. Boone's three-run homer boosted the score to 14–0. Hegan ended the inning by popping out.

JUNE 22 The Indians swat five home runs during a 6–2 win over the Yankees in New York. Luke Easter and Jim Hegan each homered twice, and Ray Boone added one.

JUNE 23 Luke Easter hits two home runs for the second day in a row, leading the Indians to a 13–4 win over the Senators at Municipal Stadium. One of Easter's homers landed in the upper deck in right field and was estimated as a drive of 477 feet.

Luscious "Luke" Easter didn't reach the majors until 1949, when he was 34 years old, because of baseball's color barrier. He gave the Indians three solid seasons, with a .271 average, 86 homers and 307 RBIs from 1950 through 1952 until age and a bad knee caught up with him. Although Easter played his last big league game in 1954, he was a minor league legend for another decade. He played in over 100 games as late as 1960 and was a player-coach with Rochester in the International League until 1964 at the age of 50. Easter's life ended tragically. In 1979, he was a union steward at TRW, Inc., in Cleveland. He was in the habit of taking his fellow workers' checks each payday and cashing them at a local bank. On March 29 of that year, two men accosted Easter as he was leaving the bank and demanded the cash, which amounted to some $40,000. He refused to give it up and was struck above the heart with a shotgun blast. A park on Cleveland's east side was later named after him.

JUNE 25 Al Rosen hits a grand slam off Connie Marrero in the eighth inning of a 7–6 win over the Senators in the first game of a double header at Municipal Stadium. Washington won the second contest 5–3.

On the same day, North Korean military forces attacked South Korea. The United States quickly entered the conflict on the side of South Korea. The Korean War lasted until 1953 and affected big league rosters, as many players were drafted or called to duty from their reserve units. Among those were Indians players Al Aber (1951–52), Jim Lemon (1951–52), Dick Weik (1951–52), Bob Kennedy (1952), and Hal Naragon (1952–53). Kennedy had also served as a Marine during World War II. He is one of two players to have their big league careers interrupted by serving in the Armed Forces in both the Second World War and the Korean War. The other was Ted Williams.

JUNE 28 The Indians score 11 runs and 11 hits in the seventh inning of an 18–2 victory over the Browns in St. Louis. Cleveland collected 20 hits in all.

JULY 2 Bob Feller wins his 200th career game with a 5–3 decision over the Tigers in the first game of a twin bill before 78,187 at Municipal Stadium. Detroit won the second tilt 8–5.

Feller was 16–11 with a 3.43 ERA in 1950.

JULY 11 Entering the All-Star Game in the fourth, Bob Lemon pitches three scoreless innings. Larry Doby contributed a double and a single in six at-bats, but the American League lost 4–3 in 14 innings at Comiskey Park.

July 17 Joe Gordon collects five hits, including a homer, in five at-bats during an 11–6 win over the Red Sox at Fenway Park. Boston won game two 7–5.

July 20 Sam Zoldak pitches five innings of shutout relief and drives in the winning run with a single in the 11th inning for a 3–2 win over the Athletics in Philadelphia.

July 22 The Senators score three runs in the ninth inning to tie the score 3–3, but the Indians come right back with five runs in the tenth to win 8–3 in Washington.

July 28 Three consecutive homers by Larry Doby, Al Rosen, and Luke Easter off Dick Littlefield in the eighth inning highlights a 13–1 trouncing of the Red Sox at Municipal Stadium. Al Rosen hit another homer earlier in the contest. Joe Gordon also went deep.

August 2 Larry Doby hits three consecutive homers during a 10–0 win over the Senators at Municipal Stadium. Doby hit his home runs against Connie Marrero in the first, third, and fifth innings. Doby walked and struck out in his last two plate appearances. Bob Lemon pitched the shutout and hit a homer of his own. Joe Gordon also homered for the Indians. On the same day, the Indians sold Gene Bearden to the Senators.

With the August 2 victory, the Indians had a record of 61–38 and were in second place, two games behind the first-place Tigers. Cleveland had won 39 of their last 55 games.

August 17 Acting as a pinch-hitter, Early Wynn hits a walk-off single to beat the Browns 5–4 at Municipal Stadium.

August 19 Luke Easter homers in the eighth inning off Ken Holcombe for a 1–0 win over the White Sox at Municipal Stadium. Early Wynn pitched the shutout.

Wynn had a record of 18–8 and a league-leading 3.20 ERA in 1950.

August 26 Bob Lemon wins his 20th game of the season by pitching 1⅔ innings of relief during a 5–4 win over the Athletics in Philadelphia.

The win gave the Indians a record of 76–46. The club was in third place just 1½ games behind the league-leading Tigers. The Yankees were second, two percentages points back.

August 27 The Indians score seven runs in the third inning to take a 7–0 lead but lose 11–9 to the Red Sox in Boston. Ray Boone hit a grand slam.

August 28 The Indians blow a big lead at Fenway Park for the second day in a row. Cleveland took a 12–1 advantage in the top of the fourth inning with Bob Lemon on the mound, but Boston rallied to win 15–14. The Indians still led 13–11 in the eighth when the Red Sox scored four runs.

After the pair of damaging losses, the Indians went to New York and lost four games in a row to the Yankees to run their losing streak to six.

September 4 The Indians edge the White Sox 1–0 in the second game of a double header at Comiskey Park. Mike Garcia (five innings) and Sam Zoldak (four innings) combined on the shutout. Garcia had to leave the game after being hit by a Nellie Fox line drive. The lone run crossed the plate on a single by Bob Kennedy in the third. Chicago won the opener 7–1.

September 7 The Indians tie the Tigers 13–13 in Detroit in a game that ended by darkness after ten innings. Cleveland had plenty of chances to win. The Indians scored seven runs in the top of the first inning but couldn't hold the lead. The Tribe took a 13–11 advantage in the top of the tenth, but the Tigers tied it their half.

At the conclusion of play on September 7, the Indians were in fourth place with an 80–54 record, four games back of the Tigers. The Yankees were second, two percentage points behind, and the Red Sox were positioned 1½ games back in third. The Indians headed into a three-day, four-game series at Municipal Stadium against the lowly Browns, a club with a 45–88 record, on September 8. The Indians stunningly lost all four, three by one run, to virtually end any hopes for the pennant in 1950. Cleveland scored only six runs in the four games. Following the defeats, general manager Hank Greenberg publicly criticized Lou Boudreau, saying, "We may lose the flag again in 1951, but not with this team." Boudreau was fired on November 10, 1950.

September 12 A two-out, three-run homer by Luke Easter climaxes a four-run ninth inning that defeats the Yankees 8–7 at Municipal Stadium. Easter also homered in the fifth.

The Indians completely remade the infield in 1950, installing Easter at first base, Bobby Avila at second, Al Rosen at third, and Ray Boone at short. Entering the season, the four combined had only 380 big league at-bats, and Boone had 263 of those.

September 15 A two-run walk-off homer in the ninth inning by Luke Easter defeats the Senators 4–2 in the first game of a double header at Municipal Stadium. Washington won the second contest 4–1.

September 17 Playing the Athletics at Municipal Stadium, the Indians lose an excruciating 10–9 decision in 11 innings. After falling behind 9–0, Cleveland rallied with one run in the third inning, one in the fourth, one in the fifth, four in the sixth, and two in the ninth to force extra innings, before allowing the deciding run.

September 22 Joe Gordon hits a walk-off homer in the ninth inning off Hal Newhouser to defeat the Tigers 4–3 at Municipal Stadium. Detroit scored two runs in the top of the ninth to tie the game.

The Tigers came into the game tied for first place with the Yankees. The Indians swept the three-game series with Detroit from September 22 through 24, putting a severe jolt into the World Series plans of the club.

September 23 Larry Doby hits a grand slam off Art Houtteman in the third inning of a 10–2 win over the Tigers at Municipal Stadium.

September 24 The Indians defeat the Tigers for the third day in a row with a ten-inning, 2–1 decision at Municipal Stadium. A mental lapse by Detroit catcher Aaron Robinson was crucial. Because of a heavy smoke pall from Canadian forest fires, it was necessary to switch on the lights at the start of the Sunday afternoon contest. Bob Lemon and Ted Gray hooked up in the duel. With the score tied 1–1, Lemon opened the Tribe's tenth inning with a triple. The next two batters were walked intentionally to load the sacks. After Larry Doby popped up, Luke Easter grounded down the first base line. Don Kolloway, fielded the ball, tagged first base, and threw home. Robinson believed the play was a force and stepped on the plate instead of tagging Lemon, allowing the winning run to score.

Lemon was 23–11 with a 3.84 ERA in 1950. He led the AL in wins, complete games (22), strikeouts (170), and innings pitched (288).

September 29 The Indians clobber the Tigers 12–2 in Detroit.

September 30 To prevent an expected bunt by Hal Newhouser, Lou Boudreau uses a five-man infield in the eighth inning of a 3–1 loss to the Tigers in Detroit. Bob Kennedy came in from right field to play first base, and Luke Easter was stationed at third to handle the throw. Mike Garcia walked Newhouser on four pitches, however. After Cleveland resumed its normal defense, George Kell smacked a two-run double.

October 1 The Browns play a regular season National Football League game at Municipal Stadium for the first time, and lose 6–0 to the New York Giants before 37,647.

The Browns won the title in their first season in the NFL. The championship game was played at Municipal Stadium on December 24, with the Browns taking a 30–28 decision over the Los Angeles Rams before a crowd of 29,751.

November 10 Al Lopez replaces Lou Boudreau as manager.

Boudreau had been a player with the Indians since 1938 and player-manager since 1942 and was arguably the most popular individual in franchise history. Club management was never completely sold on Boudreau's managerial abilities, however. Bill Veeck tried to trade Boudreau following the 1947 season, but the fans intervened, preventing the deal (see November 24, 1947). Leading the Indians to a world championship in 1948 further cemented the idolization of Boudreau in Cleveland, and even after finishing in third place in 1949 and fourth in 1950, his popularity remained strong. Club president Ellis Ryan and general manager Hank Greenberg were willing to face the public's wrath, however, by dismissing Boudreau and hiring Al Lopez. The announcement, made on November 10, 1950, came as a shock as there was little indication that Boudreau was about to be fired. The son of Spanish immigrants who settled in Tampa, Florida, Lopez played in the majors as a catcher from 1928 through 1947. He caught 1,918 big leagues, the all-time record that stood until Bob Boone passed it in 1987. From 1948 through 1950, Lopez managed the Pittsburgh Pirates farm club in Indianapolis. As manager of the Indians from 1951 through 1956, Lopez had a remarkable record of 570–354, a winning percentage of .617, but the club won only one pennant and failed to win a World Series. Cleveland finished in second place to the Yankees in five of those six years, many of them frustratingly close. The Indians finished five games out of first place in 1951, two in 1952, and three in 1955. In 1954, the Indians captured the AL flag with a league record 111 victories, only to be swept by the Giants in the World Series. At the end of the 1956 season, Lopez resigned and took a job as manager of the White Sox. Boudreau was signed by the Red Sox as a player two weeks after being fired by the Indians. He was later a manager again with the Red Sox (1952–54) and Athletics (1955–57). Boudreau then settled into a long broadcasting career, covering the Cubs on radio and television from 1958 through 1990. He also managed the Cubs for 139 games in 1960.

1951

Season in a Sentence

Under new manager Al Lopez, the Indians win 13 games in a row in August and take a three-game lead on August 23 but fumble a chance for the pennant by losing 18 of their last 33 games.

Finish • Won • Lost • Pct • GB

Finish	Won	Lost	Pct	GB
Second	93	61	.604	5.0

Manager

Al Lopez

Stats

Stats	Indians	AL	Rank
Batting Avg:	.256	.262	7
On-Base Pct:	.336	.342	6
Slugging Pct:	.389	.381	3
Home Runs:	140		1 (tie)
Stolen Bases:	52		3
ERA:	3.38		1
Fielding Avg:	.978	.975	1
Runs Scored:	696		5
Runs Allowed:	594		1

Starting Line-up

Jim Hegan, c
Luke Easter, 1b
Bobby Avila, 2b
Al Rosen, 3b
Ray Boone, ss
Dale Mitchell, lf
Larry Doby, cf
Bob Kennedy, rf
Harry Simpson, rf
Sam Chapman, cf-lf

Pitchers

Bob Feller, sp
Early Wynn, sp
Mike Garcia, sp
Bob Lemon, sp
Lou Brissie, rp
Steve Gromek, rp

Attendance

1,704,984 (second in AL)

Club Leaders

Batting Avg:	Bobby Avila	.304
On-Base Pct:	Larry Doby	.428
Slugging Pct:	Larry Doby	.512
Home Runs:	Luke Easter	27
RBIs:	Luke Easter	103
Runs:	Larry Doby	84
Stolen Bases:	Bobby Avila	14
Wins:	Bob Feller	22
Strikeouts:	Bob Lemon	132
ERA:	Early Wynn	3.02
Saves:	Lou Brissie	9

April 1 — The Indians trade Freddie Marsh to the Browns for Snuffy Stirnweiss and Merrill Combs.

April 17 — Six days after President Harry Truman removes General Douglas MacArthur from his command in Korea, the Indians win the season opener 2–1 over the Tigers on a 37-degree day in Detroit. Cleveland broke a 1–1 tie in the ninth on Larry Doby's double off Hal Newhouser, followed by a sacrifice and an error. Bob Lemon pitched a two-hitter. Jerry Priddy collected both Tigers hits, including a third inning double that led to the only Detroit run.

All Indians home games were on television in 1951, along with a few road games for the first time. Road games were a rarity in the infant days of television because of the high costs of transmitting the images from one city to another.

APRIL 20 In the home opener, the Indians win 4–1 over the Browns before 48,316 at Municipal Stadium. Bob Feller pitched the complete game.

APRIL 30 In a three-team deal, the Indians send Minnie Minoso to the White Sox and Sam Zoldak and Ray Murray to the Athletics and receive Lou Brissie from the A's.

The Big Four—one of the most dominating pitching staffs ever assembled in major league history and certainly one of the most consistent over a number of seasons. They are posed here to show the "rotation" in a literal way. Clockwise from the top: Early Wynn, Bob Feller, Bob Lemon, and Mike Garcia.

The trade was a daring gamble that backfired horribly as Minoso, a rookie in 1951, became one of the greatest stars of the 1950s. Brissie was 26 years old when he arrived in Cleveland and had a 37–43 lifetime record. He reached the majors in 1947 after being badly wounded during World War II. Fighting in Italy in December 1944, Brissie was the only member of his squad of 12 to survive a German attack and suffered shrapnel wounds of the feet, legs, hands, and shoulders, which required 23 operations. The Indians had the best starting rotation in baseball with Bob Feller, Bob Lemon, Early Wynn, and Mike Garcia but were badly in need of a lefthander who could relieve and serve as a spot starter. Brissie added depth to the staff but was little more than an average reliever in Cleveland and was out of the majors by 1953. Minoso, on the other hand, was a seven-time All-Star who hit over .300 eight times during his career. He led the AL in stolen bases and triples three times each and once in slugging percentage, hits, and doubles. The trade was made in part because the Indians had no place in the lineup for Minoso, who could play a number of positions but none of them adequately. Cleveland management also believed that Harry Simpson was a much better prospect than Minoso. Simpson and Minoso were teammates on the club's San Diego farm club in the Pacific Coast League in 1950, and Simpson put up slightly better batting numbers, was superior defensively, and was three years younger. In three seasons with the Indians, however, Simpson batted just .246 with 24 homers in 1,120 at-bats.

MAY 1 Lou Boudreau returns to Municipal Stadium as a shortstop for the Red Sox. Stepping to the plate for his first plate appearance, he received a standing ovation. Boudreau was 1-for-4 during a 7–1 Indians victory.

Of the 25 players who played 15 or more games for the 1948 world champions, only seven remained in 1951. The seven were Larry Doby, Bob Feller, Jim Hegan, Steve Gromek, Dale Mitchell, Bob Kennedy, and Bob Lemon.

MAY 8 Bob Feller is burned in an accident in the Indians clubhouse. He was attempting to pour water for his whirlpool bath when the hose slipped out of his hands causing him to be scalded. Feller suffered first and second degree burns.

Feller was back on the mound a few days later, although in severe discomfort, and went on to have a comeback season. He led the AL in wins and winning percentage with a 22–8 record. Feller's earned run average was 3.50. He was no longer the fireballer of his youth, however. A seven-time American League strikeout champion, Feller ranked only fourth in strikeouts on the Indians staff in 1951. He fanned 111 batters in 249⅔ innings and his 4.0 strikeouts per nine innings ratio was only slightly higher than the AL average of 3.7. Feller was part of the Indians "Big Four" starting rotation. Three of them won at least 20 games. Early Wynn was 20–13 with 21 complete games and a 3.02 ERA and 133 strikeouts in 274⅓ innings. Mike Garcia also posted a 20–13 record, six saves, and an earned run average of 3.15 in 254 innings. Bob Lemon had a 17–14 ledger and had an ERA of 3.52 along with 132 strikeouts in 263⅓ innings. In innings pitched, Wynn ranked first in the AL, with Lemon second, Garcia fourth and Feller fifth. Feller, Wynn, Garcia, and Lemon combined for a 79–48 record with nine saves and an earned run average of 3.29. With those four pacing the staff, the Indians led the American League in earned run average for the fourth straight year.

MAY 10 The Indians trade Allie Clark and Lou Klein to the Athletics for Sam Chapman. On the same day, the Indians signed Johnny Vander Meer as a free agent following his release by the Cubs.

MAY 13 Al Rosen hits a grand slam off Bob Mahoney in the sixth inning of an 11–2 win over the White Sox in the first game of a double header in Chicago. The second contest ended after nine innings in a 4–4 tie to allow the Indians time to catch a train to New York.

MAY 19 Al Rosen hits his second grand slam in a week by connecting off Mel Parnell in the fourth inning, but the Indians lose 9–4 to the Red Sox in Boston.

Rosen hit .265 with 24 homers and 102 RBIs in 1951. He was part of a potent center of the batting order. Luke Easter batted .270 with 27 home runs and 103 runs batted in. Larry Doby hit .295 and clubbed 20 homers.

MAY 27 The Indians thrash the Senators 16–0 at Griffith Stadium. Bob Feller pitched a two-hitter. The only Washington hits were singles by Gil Coan in the first inning and Eddie Yost in the sixth.

The Indians stumbled out of the gate in 1951 with a 15–19 record that put them ten games out of first place.

MAY 29 Bob Lemon allows only one batter to reach base in hurling a one-hitter to defeat the Tigers 2–1 in Detroit. Lemon retired the first 21 batters to face him before Vic Wertz homered leading off the eighth inning to ruin the bid for a perfect game. Lemon then set down the last six batters in order. He didn't pitch from the stretch during the entire game.

On the same day, the Indians signed high school pitcher Billy Joe Davidson for $125,000, which was then a record bonus for an amateur player. He signed less than 24 hours after graduating from Oak Ridge Military Institute in Oak Ridge, North Carolina. Davidson proved to be one of the greatest busts of all-time. He reported to the Indians with a twisted knee suffered in an intramural basketball game and was 30 pounds overweight. In 1951 with two Cleveland farm clubs, he had a 4–8 record with 103 walks in 109 innings and a 5.61 ERA. Davidson never rose above the Class B level in the minor leagues.

JUNE 3 A crowd of 75,163 at Municipal Stadium watches the Indians sweep the Yankees 8–3 and 4–1.

JUNE 4 The Indians defeat the Yankees 8–2 on "Beat Ed Lopat Night" at Municipal Stadium. Lopat had defeated the Indians 11 times in a row and had a 30–6 lifetime record against Cleveland. A total of 15,000 rabbit's feet were distributed to fans entering the stadium. Just before game time, a crate was opened at home plate containing four live rabbits, but the frightened bunnies refused to leave the enclosure. As Lopat finished his warm-up pitches, a fan bounced over the railing and ran to the mound carrying a black cat. The fan draped the animal on Lopat's shoulder and then dropped it at his feet. A shaken Lopat allowed five runs in the first inning, setting the stage for the Indians victory.

JUNE 20 Bobby Avila clubs three homers, a double, and a single during a 14–8 win over the Red Sox at Fenway Park. Avila entered the game with two career homers in 377 at-bats. He homered in the first inning off Bill Wight, in the seventh against Ellis Kinder, and in the ninth facing Paul Hinrichs. The first two homers cleared the left field wall. The third was an inside-the-park homer. The ball crashed off of the wall and the flag pole in the deepest part of center field.

Avila took over as the Indians starting second baseman during the second half of the 1950 season and hit .304 with ten home runs in 1951. A native of Mexico, Avila was already 27 when he finally nailed down a regular spot in the line-up. He made three All-Star teams and won the 1954 AL batting title during his ten seasons with the Indians. After his playing career ended, Avila became the president of the Mexican League and the mayor of his hometown of Veracruz.

JUNE 23 Al Rosen hits a grand slam off Stubby Overmire in the third inning, giving the Indians a 5–0 lead over the Yankees at Yankee Stadium, but New York roars back and wins 7–6 after scoring three runs in the ninth.

JUNE 26 A two-run walk-off homer by Luke Easter in the 11th inning beats the Browns 6–4 at Municipal Stadium.

The Indians entered the contest with a 32–30 record in fourth place, 8½ games from first.

JULY 1 Bob Feller pitches his third career no-hitter, defeating the Tigers 2–1 in the first game of a double header at Municipal Stadium. He walked three and struck out five. The Detroit run scored in the fourth inning when Johnny Lipon reached on an error by shortstop Ray Boone, stole second, moved to third when Feller threw the ball into center field on an attempted pick-off, and scored on a sacrifice fly by George Kell. The score was 1–1 in the eighth when Sam Chapman tripled and crossed the plate on a Luke Easter single. In the Detroit ninth, Charlie Keller flied out to right fielder Bob Kennedy. Kell also flied to right. Vic Wertz was the last out, looking at a called third strike. The Indians won the nightcap 2–0 when rookie pitcher Bob Chakales pitched his only career shutout.

JULY 4 The Indians sweep the Browns 6–3 and 4–3 in a double header In St. Louis. The second game went 15 innings. The winning run scored when Harry Simpson singled, stole second, and crossed the plate on Bobby Avila's single. Bill Veeck was among those in attendance. He completed a deal to purchase the Browns the next day.

JULY 12 Allie Reynolds of the Yankees tosses a no-hitter to defeat the Indians 1–0 at Municipal Stadium. Bob Feller pitched for Cleveland only 11 days after recording a no-hitter of his own, and held the Yanks hitless for the first 5⅓ innings. The lone run scored on a seventh-inning home run by Gene Woodling. Feller surrendered four hits in all. Bobby Avila struck out to end the game.

JULY 14 Early Wynn pitches a two-hitter to defeat the Yankees 8–2 at Yankee Stadium. The only New York hits were singles by Gil McDougald in the fourth inning and Jackie Jensen in the ninth.

JULY 19 Daring base running by Bobby Avila helps defeat the Red Sox 5–4 in 11 innings at Municipal Stadium. The Indians trailed 4–3 heading into the bottom of the 11th. Bob Lemon doubled and scored on Avila's single. Running on a pitch on which Sam Chapman hit a bloop single to left, Avila had almost reached third when Ted Williams picked up the ball. Third base coach Ben Flowers signaled for Avila to stop, but he ran through the sign. Williams held the ball momentarily believing that Avila would hold up at third and was stunned to see him heading for home. Avila easily beat Williams's delayed throw.

July 20 Bobby Avila's walk-off double in the tenth inning beats the Athletics 1–0 at Municipal Stadium. Mike Garcia pitched the shutout.

July 21 The Indians purchase Barney McCosky from the Reds.

August 8 The Indians take control of first place with a 2–1 win over the Browns at Municipal Stadium.

August 11 Solo homers account for all three runs in a 2–1 win over the White Sox at Municipal Stadium. Eddie Robinson homered for Chicago and Al Rosen for Cleveland in the second inning. Early Wynn broke the 1–1 tie with a home run in the seventh. Wynn also pitched a complete game. It was the Indians ninth win in a row.

August 13 Bob Feller celebrates a night in his honor by defeating the Tigers 2–1 at Municipal Stadium. He was given the keys to the city among other gifts.

August 15 The Indians extend their winning streak to 13 games with a 9–4 decision over the Browns in St. Louis.

The victory gave the Indians 40 wins in a stretch of 49 games.

August 16 The 13-game winning streak comes to an end with a 4–0 loss to the Browns at Sportsman's Park. St. Louis pitcher Tommy Byrne drove in all four runs.

August 21 Bob Feller wins his 20th game of the season with a 6–0 decision over the Senators at Municipal Stadium.

August 22 Bobby Avila hits a walk-off homer in the 14th inning to beat the Senators 6–5 at Municipal Stadium.

August 23 The Indians defeat the Yankees 2–1 in New York.

The victory gave the Indians a 78–43 record and a three-game lead over the Yanks in the AL pennant race. Cleveland had won 63 of their last 87 games. The club went on to lose 18 of their last 33, however, to blow a chance to reach the World Series. At the end of the season, the Indians were five games back of New York.

August 28 Bob Kennedy smacks a home run off Sam Zoldak to beat the Athletics 1–0 at Municipal Stadium. Early Wynn pitched the shutout.

September 2 Harry Simpson, Al Rosen, and Luke Easter hit consecutive homers off Ned Garver in the third inning of a 5–1 win over the Browns at Municipal Stadium. Simpson's home run was inside-the-park on a drive in which left fielder Ken Wood missed an attempt at a shoestring catch.

The Indians entered a two-game series against the Yankees in New York on September 16 and 17 with a one-game lead in the pennant race.

September 16 The Indians fall into second place three percentage points behind the Yankees following a 5–1 loss to the Yanks before 68,760 at Yankee Stadium.

The loss ended the Tribe's six-day reign at the top of the American League. Allie Reynolds was the winning pitcher and drove in what proved to be the winning run with a single in the second. Bob Feller, who went into the game with 22 victories on the season, was the losing pitcher.

SEPTEMBER 17 The Indians drop one game behind the Yankees with a 2–1 loss in New York. The winning run scored in the ninth inning on a squeeze bunt by Phil Rizzuto off Bob Lemon with one out and the bases loaded. The bunt scored Joe DiMaggio from third base.

Over the remainder of the season, the Yankees won nine of 12 decisions while the Indians lost five of eight. The Indians had a record of 7–15 against the Yankees in 1951 and lost ten of 11 at Yankee Stadium.

SEPTEMBER 18 Mike Garcia earns his 20th win of the season with a 6–4 win over the Red Sox in Boston. The win put the Indians just three percentage points behind the Yankees.

SEPTEMBER 19 Early Wynn earns his 20th win of 1951 with a 15–2 walloping of the Red Sox in Boston. Larry Doby walked five times in five plate appearances.

SEPTEMBER 21 The Indians blow a 5–0 lead and lose 7–6 to the Tigers in Detroit.

Cleveland lost all three games of the series against the Tigers from September 21 through September 23. The defeats dropped the Indians 2½ games behind the Yankees and all but eliminated the Tribe from the pennant chase. Before the three successive defeats, the Indians dominated the Tigers all season, winning 16 of 17. The Yankees defeated the Giants in six games in the World Series.

SEPTEMBER 29 Luke Easter hits two homers, one a grand slam off Bob Cain in the sixth inning, to help the Indians to a 13-inning, 7–6 win over the Tigers at Municipal Stadium. Easter also tripled and singled during the game but didn't figure in the game-winning rally. A pinch-single by Paul Lehner ended the contest.

1952

Season in a Sentence

With a vastly improved offense, the Indians lead the American League in runs scored but a slight decline in pitching performance and an abysmal defense leads to another agonizingly close second-place finish.

Finish • Won • Lost • Pct • GB

Finish	Won	Lost	Pct	GB
Second	93	61	.604	2.0

Manager

Al Lopez

Stats

Stats	Indians	AL	Rank
Batting Avg:	.262	.253	2
On-Base Pct:	.342	.330	2
Slugging Pct:	.404	.365	1
Home Runs:	148		1
Stolen Bases:	46		6
ERA:	3.32	3.67	3
Fielding Pct:	.975	.977	7
Runs Scored:	763		1
Runs Allowed:	606		3

Starting Line-up

Jim Hegan, c
Luke Easter, 1b
Bobby Avila, 2b
Al Rosen, 3b
Ray Boone, ss
Dale Mitchell, lf
Larry Doby, cf
Harry Simpson, rf
Jim Fridley, lf-rf

Pitchers

Early Wynn, sp
Bob Lemon, sp
Mike Garcia, sp
Bob Feller, sp
Lou Brissie, rp
Steve Gromek, rp-sp

Attendance

1,444,607 (second in AL)

Club Leaders

Batting Avg:	Dale Mitchell	.323
On-Base Pct:	Dale Mitchell	.387
	Al Rosen	.387
Slugging Pct:	Larry Doby	.541
Home Runs:	Larry Doby	32
RBIs:	Al Rosen	105
Runs:	Larry Doby	104
Stolen Bases:	Bobby Avila	12
Wins:	Early Wynn	23
Strikeouts:	Early Wynn	153
ERA:	Mike Garcia	2.37
Saves:	Mike Garcia	4
	Bob Lemon	4

April 15 On Opening Day, the Indians win 3–2 over the White Sox in Chicago. Early Wynn was the winning pitcher.

April 16 Playing in his second major league game, Jim Fridley get his first major league hit—a home run that beats the White Sox 1–0 in Chicago. It was struck off Joe Dobson. Bob Lemon hurled the shutout.

April 17 The Indians take the first trip by airplane in club history, flying from Chicago to Cleveland.

The first team to take a trip by air was the Cincinnati Reds in 1934. Air travel wasn't common in baseball until the late-1950s, however.

April 18 In the home opener, the Indians win 5–0 over the Tigers before 56,068 at Municipal Stadium. Bob Feller (8⅔ innings) and Bob Lemon (⅔ of an inning) combined on the shutout.

APRIL 20 The Indians run their season record to 7–0 with a 3–2 and 7–2 sweep of the Tigers in a double header at Municipal Stadium.

APRIL 22 The Indians purchase Mickey Harris from the Senators.

APRIL 23 Bob Cain of the Browns and Bob Feller both pitch one-hitters at Sportsman's Park. Feller and the Indians came out on the short end of a 1–0 score. The lone St. Louis hit was a triple by Bobby Young leading off the first inning. It was a catchable drive, but left fielder Jim Fridley initially broke toward the foul line and couldn't catch up the ball before it hit the ground in left center. Young scored on an error by third baseman Al Rosen. The only Cleveland hit was a single by Luke Easter in the fifth inning.

APRIL 24 The Indians score three runs in the ninth inning to beat the White Sox 5–4 at Municipal Stadium. Luke Easter drove in the winning run with a sacrifice fly.

APRIL 26 Harry Simpson breaks up the no-hit bid of Tigers pitcher Art Houtteman by stroking a single with two out in the ninth. The Tigers won the contest in Detroit by a 13–0 score.

APRIL 29 Al Rosen and Jim Fridley star in a 21–9 rout of the Athletics at Shibe Park. Fridley collected six hits in six at-bats. Al Rosen collected three homers and a single and drove in seven runs. Cleveland opened with six runs in the first inning, took a 14–2 advantage in the fourth, then added seven more in the eighth. There were 43 hits in the contest, 25 of them by the Indians. Bob Feller surrendered all 18 Philadelphia hits in a complete game.

The six-hit outburst came in Fridley's 13th major league game. He was a 27-year-old rookie outfielder in 1952 and had eight career hits in 36 at-bats prior to April 29. Fridley beat out Dale Mitchell for the starting left field job in spring training, but lost it back to Mitchell in May. Mitchell went on to hit .323 and make the All-Star team. Fridley played only 62 games for the Indians and 152 during his career. He had a .248 lifetime batting average and eight homers in 424 at-bats.

MAY 5 The Indians score twice in the tenth inning on a homer by Bobby Avila and back-to-back triples by Al Rosen and Ray Boone to defeat the Red Sox 4–2 in Boston.

Avila hit .300, scored 102 runs, and led the AL in triples with 11 in 1952.

MAY 6 Steve Gromek pitches the Indians to a 1–0 win over the Yankees in New York. Birdie Tebbetts drove in the lone run with a single in the second inning.

MAY 11 The Indians sweep the Browns 1–0 and 3–1 at Municipal Stadium. In the opener, Bob Lemon pitched a two-hitter. The only St. Louis hits were singles by Gordon Goldsberry and Clint Courtney. The lone run scored in the ninth on a two-out, bases loaded single by Dale Mitchell.

Although it opened in 1932, Municipal Stadium was the newest stadium in baseball in 1952. Yankees Stadium, built in 1923, was the second youngest, and Braves Field in Boston, which was constructed in 1915, ranked third.

May 21 Bob Kennedy Night is held at Municipal Stadium just prior to his return to the Marine Air Corps. The Indians won 3–1 over the Red Sox.

Among his many gifts was a down payment on a new home. Kennedy flew dozens of missions over Korea before returning to baseball in 1953.

June 4 Larry Doby hits for the cycle and drives in six runs, but the Indians lose 13–11 to the Red Sox in Boston. Doby homered in the first inning and doubled in the third off Mel Parnell, then tripled in the fifth and singled in the ninth facing Dizzy Trout.

Doby led the AL in home runs (32), slugging percentage (.541), and runs scored (104) in 1952 in addition to collecting 104 RBIs and batting .276.

June 7 Luke Easter hits a grand slam off Alex Kellner in the seventh inning of a 14–0 trouncing of the Athletics in Philadelphia.

The Indians of the 1950s have a reputation of possessing clubs dominated by pitching, but the 1952 outfit led the American League in runs scored with 763 despite playing in a pitcher's park. The club scored only 333 runs in 77 games at Municipal Stadium, but 430 in 78 contests on the road. The team earned run average of 3.67 that season ranked third. While the Indians possessed some of the best pitchers in baseball, depth was a weakness and the club didn't possess a great staff from top to bottom (see September 3, 1952).

June 10 The Indians purchase Hank Majeski from the Athletics.

June 22 The Indians sweep the Red Sox 7–0 and 5–4 in a double header at Municipal Stadium. In the opener, Steve Gromek (eight innings) and Mickey Harris (one inning) combined on a two-hitter. The only Boston hits were a double by Billy Goodman and a single by George Kell. Before the contest, Gromek passed out cigars in the clubhouse to celebrate the birth of his third son.

July 1 The Indians win a 19-inning marathon over the Browns at Municipal Stadium by a count of 4–3. Lou Brissie pitched nine shutout innings of relief before allowing a run in the top of the 19th. Satchel Paige pitched ten shutout innings of relief for St. Louis before surrendering two Cleveland runs in the bottom half. The tying and winning runs scored on a single by Bobby Avila, a double by Al Rosen, and a single by pinch-hitter Hank Majeski. Larry Doby drew five walks in nine plate appearances.

Rosen hit .302 with 101 runs, 28 homers, and a league-leading 105 RBIs in 1952.

July 4 The Indians hammer the Tigers 11–0 and 10–1 in a double header in Detroit. In the opener, Early Wynn pitched a two-hitter. The only Detroit hits were singles by Jerry Priddy and Johnny Groth. In the nightcap, Joe Tipton smacked a grand slam off Virgil Trucks in the sixth inning.

July 7 The Indians and Brooklyn Dodgers announce a world tour to take place following the 1952 World Series. The trip of was arranged with the approval of the U.S. State Department. The two teams were chosen because of the presence of African-American players such as Larry Doby, Luke Easter, Harry Simpson, and Sam Jones of the Indians and Jackie Robinson, Roy Campanella, Don Newcombe, and Joe Black on the Dodgers. In 1952, there were 21 African-Americans in the majors, and 11 of them were on the rosters of the Indians and Dodgers. The government hoped that the trip would "combat communistic propaganda that racial minorities are discriminated against and denied equal opportunity in the United States." The tour was slated to cover Japan, the Philippines, Australia, Singapore, India, Israel, Greece, Italy, Spain, Portugal, Morocco, Bermuda, Puerto Rico, Venezuela, the Dominican Republic, and Cuba. The grandiose plan fell through, however, because of a lack of financing and the reluctance of many players to spend two months of the off-season touring the world. Only seven Indians players were willing to embark on the journey.

JULY 8 In the All-Star Game at Shibe Park in Philadelphia, Bobby Avila drives in a run in the fourth inning to give the American League a 2–1 lead, but the National League wins 3–2. The game was called after five innings by rain.

JULY 13 The Indians eke out 1–0 and 2–1 wins over the Senators in Washington. Mike Garcia pitched a two-hitter in the opener. The only Washington hits were a double by Jackie Jensen and a single from Mickey Vernon. The lone run scored in the second inning on Al Rosen's triple and Harry Simpson's single.

JULY 22 The Indians lose 7–3 and 8–1 in a double header at Municipal Stadium. The defeats dropped the Indians 7½ games behind the Yankees. Cleveland was in fourth place with a 49–42 record. The club was 46–19 the rest of the way in a vain attempt to catch the Yankees.

JULY 29 Early Wynn strikes out 12 batters during a 4–1 win over the Red Sox at Municipal Stadium.

AUGUST 1 Larry Doby hits a walk-off homer in the tenth inning to defeat the Athletics 6–5 at Municipal Stadium. Philadelphia scored five runs in the ninth to tie the score.

AUGUST 7 The Indians purchase Wally Westlake from the Reds.

AUGUST 8 After spotting the Browns an 8–0 lead in the second inning, the Indians rally to win 10–9 in St. Louis. Larry Doby hit a three-run homer in the ninth to tie the game 9–9. Bill Glynn's home run in the 12th inning ended the game.

AUGUST 15 The Indians fall behind the Browns 5–0 in St. Louis before recovering to win 7–6 in 12 innings at Municipal Stadium. The winning run scored on a triple by Harry Simpson.

AUGUST 18 The Indians send Johnny Berardino, Charlie Ripple, and $50,000 to the Pirates for George Strickland and Ted Wilks.

AUGUST 20 Down 3–0, the Indians erupt for ten runs in the third inning and defeat the Red Sox 18–8 in Boston. Luke Easter drove in five runs in the big inning on a single and a grand slam off Willard Nixon.

Easter was a flop during the first half of the season. On June 30, with his batting average at .208, he was sent to the minors. Recalled on July 15, Easter staged a spectacular comeback. In the 64 games following his return, he batted .319 with 20 homers and 64 RBIs.

AUGUST 22 The Indians vault into first place with a 6–4 win over the Yankees in New York. Dale Mitchell collected five hits in five at-bats.

AUGUST 23 The Indians' stay in first place lasts just one day, as the club drops back into second after losing 1–0 to the Yankees in New York.

AUGUST 27 Al Rosen hits a grand slam off Alex Kellner in the first inning, but the Indians lose 6–5 to the Athletics in Philadelphia.

SEPTEMBER 3 Down 6–0, the Indians score eight runs in the fifth inning, but wind up losing 11–8 to the Tigers at Municipal Stadium.

Bob Feller was the starting pitcher in the September 3 game and placed the Indians in the early hole. He struggled all year, with a record of 9–13 and an ERA of 4.74, and the lack of his usual contribution to the big four undermined the team's ability to win the pennant. Early Wynn, Bob Lemon, and Mike Garcia, on the other hand, were brilliant. The three ranked first, second, and third in the AL in innings pitched, and second, third, and fourth in wins. Wynn had a record of 23–12, 153 strikeouts and 2.90 ERA in 285⅔ innings. Garcia was 22–12, with 143 strikeouts and a 2.37 earned run average while pitching 292⅓ innings. He not only tied for the league lead in games started (36), and shutouts (six), but made ten relief appearances and recorded four saves. Lemon was 22–11 with an ERA of 2.50 and topped the American League in innings pitched (309⅔), games started (36), and complete games (28). He hurled five shutouts and saved four games in six relief efforts. The 1952 Indians were the first club since the 1913 New York Giants with three pitchers winning 22 or more games. It hasn't happened since 1952. Combined, Wynn, Garcia, and Lemon were 67–34 with an earned run average of 2.59 in 887⅔ innings. The rest of the staff failed to pick up the slack, however. The other ten Indians to pitch in at least one game in 1952 were 26–27 with an ERA of 4.58. As a result, Al Lopez went to a three-man rotation during the last month of the season. Wynn, Garcia, and Lemon started 18 of the Indians 19 games during a 21-day stretch beginning on September 4. They usually pitched with two days' rest. The only pitcher other than the "Big Three" to start a game during that period was Steve Gromek in the second game of a double header on September 6. Despite pitching on short rest, the trio was almost unbeatable during the stretch pennant run. Garcia was 5–2 with a 1.61 ERA; Wynn 5–0 with a 1.13 earned run average; and Lemon 5–1 with an ERA of 1.81.

SEPTEMBER 5 A three-run homer by Luke Easter off Billy Pierce in the fourth inning defeats the White Sox 3–0 at Municipal Stadium. Early Wynn pitched the shutout.

SEPTEMBER 9 Early Wynn records his 20th win of the season with a 6–1 decision over the Athletics at Municipal Stadium.

SEPTEMBER 11 Mike Garcia wins his 20th game of the season and pitches a two-hitter to defeat the Athletics 1–0 at Municipal Stadium. The only Philadelphia hits were singles by Ferris Fain in the first and fourth innings. Bobby Avila accounted for the lone run of the game with a fourth-inning homer off Harry Byrd.

SEPTEMBER 12 The Indians extend their winning streak to nine with a 5–0 win over the Red Sox at Municipal Stadium. The victory placed the Indians only one-half game back of the Yankees in the pennant race.

SEPTEMBER 14 The Indians suffer a crucial 7–1 loss to the Yankees before 73,609 at Municipal Stadium. Mike Garcia entered the game with 28 consecutive scoreless innings and extended it to 30 before allowing four runs in the third.

SEPTEMBER 17 Bob Lemon wins his 20th game of the season with a 6–1 decision over the Senators at Municipal Stadium.

SEPTEMBER 22 The Indians pull within one game of the Yankees in the pennant race with a 6–3 win over the Tigers at Municipal Stadium.

The Indians were 90–60 at the conclusion of the game, while the Yanks had a record of 90–58. Cleveland won three of their last four games, but the Yankees won five of six to take the pennant. From September 4 through the end of the season, the Indians were 18–3, but the Yankees won 16 of 19 over the same period. The largest difference between the Yankees and the Indians in 1952 was defensively, particularly in the infield. The Indians tied for the AL lead in errors (155) while making the fewest double plays (141).

DECEMBER 18 Six weeks after Dwight Eisenhower defeats Adlai Stevenson in the presidential election, internal differences lead to a change in club presidents from Ellis Ryan to Myron (Mike) Wilson.

A rift that had developed between Ryan and many of the club's other officers broke into the open in early December. A meeting of stockholders was called for December 18. The division among shareholders had strained relations between Ryan, who sought a more active role in the affairs of the club, and general manager Hank Greenberg. Ryan made it known that he wanted to oust Greenberg. In the showdown, Ryan was unable to muster a majority of the nearly 3,000 voting shares, receiving the support of 1,464 compared to 1,526 for the anti-Ryan group. Having failed to gain a vote of confidence, Ryan resigned as president, and he and his friends agreed to sell their stock to the opposition group. Ryan assumed a handsome profit in the transaction. He received $330,000 for his 551 shares, which he purchased for $55,000 three years earlier. Wilson, a 65-year-old insurance man, was elected as president to succeed Ryan. Wilson said that he wished "to restore unity and management" to the club. He knew little about the day-to-day operation of a baseball team, and deferred to Greenberg, whose position was strengthened with the restructuring of the club.

1953

Season in a Sentence

The Indians win more than 90 games for the fourth year in a row, but again they finish second to the Yankees for the third season in succession as attendance figures at Municipal Stadium fall to less than half of what the club drew in 1948.

Finish • Won • Lost • Pct • GB

Finish	Won	Lost	Pct	GB
Second	92	62	.597	8.5

Manager

Al Lopez

Stats

	Indians	AL	Rank
Batting Avg:	.270	.262	2
On-Base Pct:	.349	.337	2
Slugging Pct:	.410	.383	2
Home Runs:	160		1
Stolen Bases:	33		5 (tie)
ERA:	3.64	3.99	4
Fielding Avg:	.979	.978	3
Runs Scored:	770		2
Runs Allowed:	627		4

Starting Line-up

Jim Hegan, c
Bill Glynn, 1b
Bobby Avila, 2b
Al Rosen, 3b
George Strickland, ss
Dale Mitchell, lf
Larry Doby, cf
Harry Simpson, rf
Bob Kennedy, lf-rf
Wally Westlake, lf-rf
Luke Easter, 1b
Al Smith, rf

Attendance

1,069,138 (third in AL)

Club Leaders

Batting Avg:	Al Rosen	.336
On-Base Pct:	Al Rosen	.422
Slugging Pct:	Al Rosen	.613
Home Runs:	Al Rosen	43
RBIs:	Al Rosen	145
Runs:	Al Rosen	145
Stolen Bases:	Bobby Avila	10
Wins:	Bob Lemon	21
Strikeouts:	Early Wynn	138
ERA:	Mike Garcia	3.25
Saves:	Bob Hooper	7

April 1 Ray Boone is called out by a snowball during a 12–11 win over the New York Giants during an exhibition game in Denver. Nine inches of snow had fallen on the city two days earlier. Snow plows had cleared the field, but they left a giant snow bank all around the outfield about 15 feet from the fence. Boone hit a drive over the head of right fielder George Wilson, who tumbled over the snow bank out of sight. Wilson arose with what appeared to be a baseball in his glove, threw it toward, and the umpires called Boone out. But the white stuff in Wilson's glove wasn't a baseball, but a snowball he packed into his glove while lying on the ground.

The game in Denver was part of a 14-day, 12-city tour by the Indians and Giants leading up to Opening Day. After leaving Arizona, the two clubs played in New Mexico, Colorado, Kansas, Texas, Louisiana, Alabama, Tennessee, Virginia, and New York.

April 14 Bob Lemon pitches a one-hitter in the season opener, defeating the White Sox 6–0 before 53,698 at Municipal Stadium. The lone Chicago hit was a single by Minnie Minoso with two out in the first inning. Lemon also homered during the contest, as did Bobby Avila.

Lemon was 21–15 with a 3.36 ERA and a league-leading 286⅔ innings in 1953. Mike Garcia was 18–9 with a 3.25 earned run average in 271⅓ innings. Early Wynn had a 17–12 record and a 3.93 ERA.

APRIL 18 The Indians lose an odd 7–6 decision to the White Sox in Chicago. Seven pitchers on the two clubs combined for 26 walks and two hit batsmen, but surrendered only seven hits. Luke Easter was one of those struck by a pitch. He was hit in the foot by a Lou Kretlow delivery, causing a broken bone that put Easter out of action for two months.

APRIL 26 The Indians sweep the Tigers 2–1 and 12–2 in a double header at Municipal Stadium. Cleveland scored nine runs in the eighth inning of game two. Al Rosen hit a grand slam off Bill Wight.

MAY 8 Trailing 4–3 with two out and no one on base in the ninth inning, the Indians explode for four runs to defeat the Browns 7–4 in St. Louis. Two walks were followed by a two-run double by Barney McCosky and a homer from Dale Mitchell.

MAY 10 Held scoreless for seven innings, the Indians erupt for four runs in the eighth inning and eight in the ninth to wallop the Browns 12–3 in St. Louis. Ray Boone smacked a grand slam off Hal White in the ninth. Cleveland pitcher Dave Hoskins pinch-hit for Bob Feller in the seventh and hit a double, then homered in the ninth in addition to throwing three scoreless innings.

A former outfielder in the Negro Leagues, Hoskins broke the color barrier in two minor leagues. He was the first African-American player in the Central League with Grand Rapids in 1948 and the first in the Texas League in 1952 with Dallas, where he shook off death threats to post a 22–10 record and a 2.12 ERA. Hoskins pitched two seasons in the majors, both with the Indians, and had a 9–4 record, mostly as a reliever.

MAY 12 Early Wynn collects the only Cleveland hit off Whitey Ford during a 7–0 loss to the Yankees in New York. In the sixth inning, Wynn topped a slow roller down the third base line and beat the throw. In the eighth, Bob Lemon, Wally Westlake, and Hank Majeski all struck out as pinch-hitters.

MAY 17 The Indians score eight runs in the tenth inning to stun the Athletics 9–1 in the second game of a double header in Philadelphia. Cleveland also won the opener 7–3.

The Indians had a 19–3 record against the Athletics and were 17–5 against the Browns in 1953.

MAY 24 Ray Boone hits a grand slam off Bob Cain in the fourth inning of a 9–8 win over the Browns in the first game of a double header at Municipal Stadium. Larry Doby was twice prevented from going to the mound to challenge Cain in the third inning. Hit in the side by a delivery from Cain, Doby left the plate and headed toward the mound before the umpires and players from both teams intervened. After the field was cleared and Doby went to first, a verbal exchange started and the Indians outfielder again walked toward the mound before he was halted by umpire Ed Rommel. The Indians also won the opener 5–1.

Boone hit four grand slams in 1953, striking two with the Indians and two with the Tigers.

MAY 26 A walk-off homer by Larry Doby in the ninth inning beats the Tigers 9–8 at Municipal Stadium. Detroit scored five runs in the top of the ninth to tie the score.

It wasn't Bob Feller's night. He allowed the five ninth inning runs and was robbed of a home run and a single as a result of spectacular catches by Tiger fielders. After the game, Feller drove to the train station to board a train to St. Louis when a motorist ran a traffic light and crashed into the pitcher's car. Fortunately, he received only a slight scratch on his arm.

JUNE 4 Larry Doby hits a grand slam off Bill Kennedy in the fifth inning of an 8–1 win over the Red Sox at Municipal Stadium.

Doby hit .263 with 29 homers and 102 runs-batted-in during the 1953 season.

JUNE 5 The Indians celebrate Jim Hegan Night with a 3–2 win over the Athletics in ten innings at Municipal Stadium. In pre-game ceremonies, Hegan received a sky blue Cadillac, a washer and dryer, an autographed silver tray, and a dining room set.

The Cleveland Orchestra played pre-game concerts before about a dozen Indians games in 1953. To accommodate the musicians, a special stage was built in front of the bleachers and a new amplification system was installed.

JUNE 9 Bob Lemon pitches a two-hitter for a 2–1 win over the Senators at Municipal Stadium. The only Washington hits were singles by Ed FitzGerald in the third inning and Mickey Vernon in the fifth.

JUNE 14 The Yankees extend their winning streak to 18 by beating the Indians 6–2 and 3–0 in a double header at Municipal Stadium.

The Indians finished the day with a record of 30–21 in second place, but were 10½ games out of first. Cleveland closed the gap to 5½ games by July 9, but could draw no closer. The Yankees won a record five consecutive American League pennants and five straight world championships from 1949 through 1953.

JUNE 15 The Indians trade Ray Boone, Steve Gromek, Al Aber, and Dick Weik to the Tigers for Art Houtteman, Bill Wight, Joe Ginsberg, and Owen Friend.

Houtteman was a 19-game winner in 1950, but was 8–20 in 1952 and started the 1953 season 2–6. He had also experienced considerable tragedy during his big league career. Houtteman suffered a fractured skull and nearly died as a result of an auto accident in 1949. His infant daughter was killed in another car crash in 1952 in which his pregnant wife suffered injuries that caused a miscarriage. Houtteman was only 26 at the time of the trade, and the Indians hoped to revive his career. He did so with a 15–7 record on the 1954 AL champion Indians club that won 111 games, but Gromek was even better that season, posting an 18–15 and a 2.74 ERA for a Detroit team that was 68–86. In addition, the Indians lost Ray Boone, who gave the Tigers four solid seasons. Boone was a shortstop in Cleveland, and while a good hitter,

In 1953, Al Rosen produced one of the greatest seasons in team history, leading the league in many offensive categories.

struggled defensively. Indians fans booed him often because he was the man who replaced the popular Lou Boudreau at the position. The Tigers moved him to third base and Boone made an easy transition. In hindsight, the Indians would have been much better off passing on this deal, and moving Boone to third themselves while shifting Al Rosen across the diamond to first.

Rosen receives the Most Valuable Player Award.

JUNE 24 The Indians outlast the Red Sox 13–9 in Boston.

JUNE 25 The Indians climax a 15–4 win over the Red Sox in Boston with eight runs in the ninth inning. Larry Doby hit two homers, a double and a single and drove in five runs.

JULY 3 Al Rosen homers in his fifth consecutive game, helping the Indians to an 8–1 win over the Tigers at Municipal Stadium.

JULY 8 The Browns break a major league record 20-game home losing streak by defeating the Indians 6–3 in St. Louis.

July 10 The Indians score three runs in the tenth inning to defeat the White Sox 3–0 in the first game of a double header at Comiskey Park. Bob Feller pitched the complete game shutout. Al Rosen broke the tie with an RBI-single. Later in the inning, Luke Easter drove in two more tallies with a one-base hit. In the second contest, Chicago won 16–5. Dale Mitchell extended his hitting streak to 21 games.

July 16 Al Rosen hits a grand slam off Marion Fricano in the third inning of a 5–3 win over the Athletics at Municipal Stadium.

July 25 A two-run walk-off homer by Al Rosen in the tenth inning beats the Senators 6–4 at Municipal Stadium.

July 26 After falling behind 6–0 to the Senators in the second game of a double header at Municipal Stadium, the Indians score two runs in the second inning, two in the sixth, one in the seventh, and two in the eighth to win 7–6. Washington won the opener 4–3 with two runs in the ninth inning.

July 31 Four days after the signing of the armistice that ends the Korean War, Wally Westlake collects five hits, including a homer, in five at-bats during a 12–6 win over the Athletics in Philadelphia.

August 14 Luke Easter delivers two homers, a single, and five runs-batted-in during an 8–7 win over the Browns in St. Louis.

August 16 The Indians play the Browns in St. Louis for the last time, and lose 7–6 and 7–5 in a double header.

At the end of the 1953 season, the Browns moved to Baltimore, where they were renamed the Orioles.

August 20 The Indians clobber the Tigers 13–7 in Detroit.

August 27 A two-run, walk-off homer by Wally Westlake in the 11th inning beats the Yankees 4–2 at Municipal Stadium.

The Indians were 53–24 at home in 1953, but only 39–38 away from Cleveland.

September 1 The Indians roll to a 13–6 win over the Red Sox at Municipal Stadium.

September 4 The Indians celebrate Jack Graney Night at Municipal Stadium. The event was arranged following Graney's announcement several weeks earlier that he would retire at the close of the 1953 season after 21 years as the broadcaster of Indians games. He also played for the club from 1908 through 1922. Among the gifts presented to the 67-year-old Graney were $10,000 in cash, numerous trophies and cups, and a wrist watch.

Attendance at Municipal Stadium suffered an alarming drop from 1948 through 1953. From the record high of 2,620,627 in 1948, attendance figures dipped to 2,233,771 in 1949, 1,727,464 in 1950, 1,704,984 in 1951, 1,444,607 in 1952 and 1,069,176 in 1953.

September 15 Bob Lemon wins his 20th game of the 1953 season with a 1–0 decision over the Yankees in New York. Al Rosen's single in the first inning drove in the lone run of the game.

September 25 Indians pitcher Dick Tomanek makes his major league debut and defeats the Tigers 12–3 at Municipal Stadium.

When Tomanek signed a professional contract, his father, George, vowed to walk to Municipal Stadium if his son ever reached the majors. Before the September 25 game, his father made good on his vow, walking the 18-mile distance from his home in Avon Lake to downtown Cleveland with a friend. They left at 2:00 p.m. for the night game, but realized they would probably reach the stadium too late for the first pitch and boarded a bus. After the vehicle broke down, they moved to another and made it just in time. Despite the impressive debut, Tomanek struggled and didn't win another big league game for four years. He closed his career in 1959 with a 10–10 record.

September 27 On the last day of the season, Al Rosen just misses winning the American League triple crown during a 7–2 loss to the Tigers at Municipal Stadium.

Rosen was the AL Most Valuable Player in 1953 with one of the best seasons ever by an Indians batter and one of the best by a third baseman in big league history. He led the league in home runs (43), runs-batted-in (145), runs scored (118), and slugging percentage (.613) in addition to collecting 201 hits. He was just one hit shy of winning the triple crown, batting .336, one point behind Mickey Vernon. Over the last three games of the season, Rosen batted in the lead-off spot to accumulate as many at-bats as possible in order to catch Vernon. Rosen responded with eight hits in 15 at-bats, including a 3-for-5 day in the final contest, but couldn't pass Vernon.

1954

Season in a Sentence

After three straight frustrating second-place finishes, the Indians win the American League pennant with an astonishing 111–43 record, only to be swept in the World Series by the New York Giants.

Finish • Won • Lost • Pct • GB

Finish	Won	Lost	Pct	GB
First	111	43	.721	+8.0

Manager

Al Lopez

World Series

The Indians lost four games to none to the New York Giants.

Stats

Stats	Indians	AL	Rank
Batting Avg:	.262	.257	4
On-Base Pct:	.345	.334	4
Slugging Pct:	.403	.373	2
Home Runs:	156		1
Stolen Bases:	30		6 (tie)
ERA:	2.78	3.72	1
Fielding Avg:	.979	.977	3
Runs Scored:	746		1
Runs Allowed:	502		1

Starting Line-up

Jim Hegan, c
Vic Wertz, 1b
Bobby Avila, 2b
Al Rosen, 3b-1b
George Strickland, ss
Al Smith, lf
Larry Doby, cf
Dave Philley, rf
Wally Westlake, lf
Rudy Regalado, 3b
Bill Glynn, 1b
Sam Dente, 3b

Pitchers

Early Wynn, sp
Bob Lemon, sp
Mike Garcia, sp
Art Houtteman, sp
Bob Feller, sp
Ray Narleski, rp
Don Mossi, rp

Attendance

1,335,472 (second in AL)

Club Leaders

Batting Avg:	Bobby Avila	.341
On-Base Pct:	Al Rosen	.404
Slugging Pct:	Al Rosen	.506
Home Runs:	Larry Doby	32
RBIs:	Larry Doby	126
Runs:	Bobby Avila	112
Stolen Bases:	Bobby Avila	9
Wins:	Early Wynn	23
	Bob Lemon	23
Strikeouts:	Early Wynn	155
ERA:	Mike Garcia	2.64
Saves:	Ray Narleski	13

FEBRUARY 19 The Indians trade Bill Upton and Lee Wheat to the Athletics for Dave Philley.

APRIL 12 The Indians sign Hal Newhouser following his release by the Tigers.

Newhouser had 200 career victories when signed by the Indians. He was well past his prime but gave the Indians a lift as a reliever in 1954 with a 7–2 record and a 2.51 ERA in 46⅔ innings.

APRIL 13 The Indians open the season with an 8–2 win over the White Sox in Chicago. Wally Westlake and George Strickland hit back-to-back homers in the fourth inning off Billy Pierce. Strickland also contributed two singles and scored three runs. Bobby Avila collected four hits, including a double, in six at-bats. Early Wynn pitched a complete game.

The Yankees entered the 1954 season with five consecutive world championships and were heavily favored to win a sixth. Most experts believed that the Indians window of opportunity to dethrone the Yanks had closed. In a pre-season poll of sports writers conducted by The Sporting News, *the Indians were picked third behind the Yankees and White Sox. Most of the Indians regulars were past their prime. Bob Feller was 35, Early Wynn and Dave Philley 34, Bob Lemon 33 and Wally Westlake 33, Bobby Avila, Al Rosen, Larry Doby, and Mike Garcia 30, and Vic Wertz 29. The Cleveland press was extremely negative and all but wrote off the Indians pennant chances in 1954, reviling the club as "choke-up" artists after three consecutive second place finishes.*

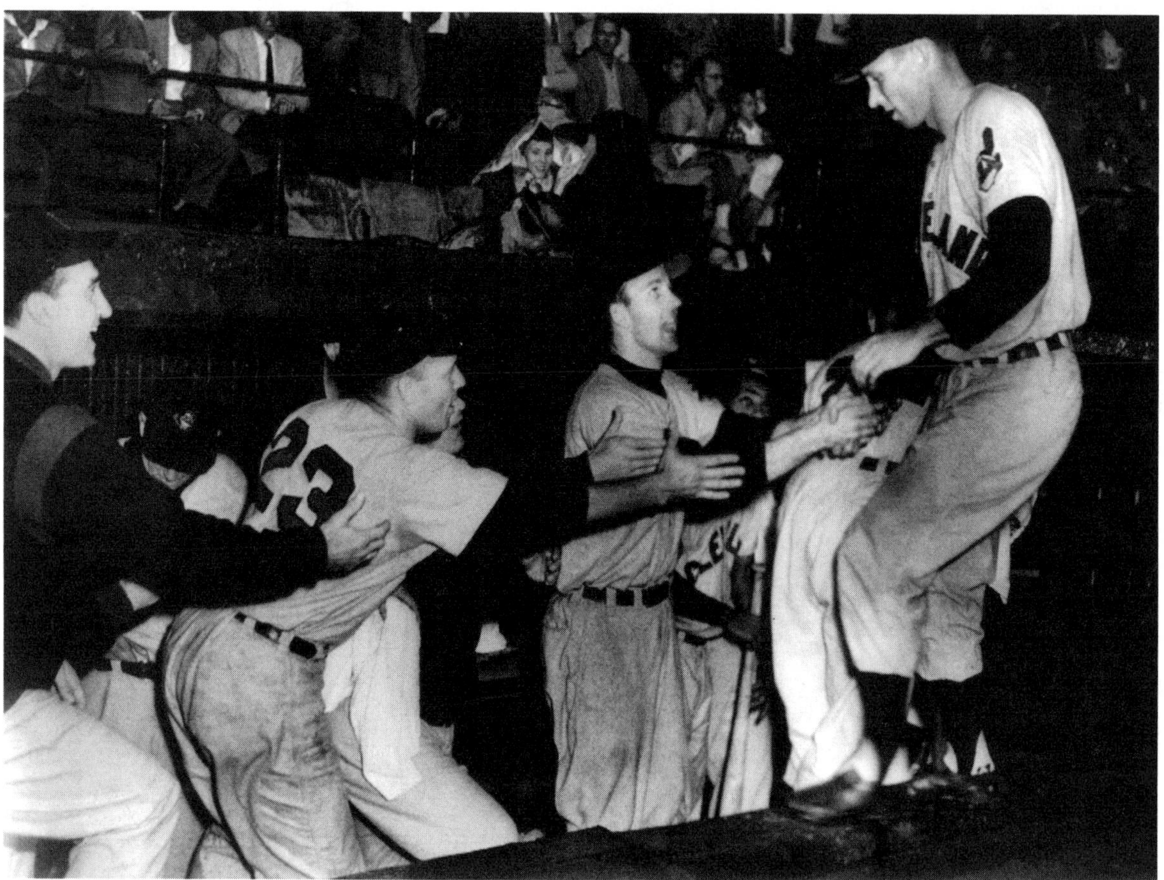

Jim Hegan is congratulated after hitting a game-winning, pennant-clinching homerun in Detroit on September 18. Vic Wertz (23), George Strickland (shaking hands), and the rest of the Indians rush to celebrate.

April 15 — In the home opener, the Indians lose 3–2 to the Tigers before 40,221 at Municipal Stadium.

Ed Edwards joined Jimmy Dudley in the radio booth in 1954. Edwards replaced Jack Graney, who retired. Covering the games on TV were Jim Britt and Ken Coleman, both in their first seasons with the Indians. Britt formerly worked in Boston as the radio man for both the Red Sox and the Braves. In 1953, all of the Indians home games were on television, but due to large drop in attendance at Municipal Stadium, no home games at all were telecast in 1954. Attendance improved from 1,069,716 in 1953 to 1,335,472 in 1954. The figure was far below what Indians management expected with a club that won 111 games and won the American League pennant, however. The 1954 total was lower than the 1952 attendance (1,444,607) and far lower than the record-breaking 1948 season (2,620,627).

APRIL 17 The Indians trade Bob Kennedy to the Orioles for Jim Dyck.

APRIL 21 The Indians win a thrilling 2–1 decision over the Orioles in Baltimore with two runs in the ninth inning. Through the first eight innings, Orioles pitcher Bob Turley held Cleveland without a hit and struck out 14 batters. With one out in the ninth, Al Rosen broke up the no-hit bid with a single. Larry Doby followed with a home run into the right field stands.

The game was the first time since 1902 that the Indians played a regular season game in Baltimore. It was also the first time that the Indians played at Memorial Stadium, the home of the Orioles from 1954 through 1991. The Orioles were formerly the St. Louis Browns. The club moved at the end of the 1953 season, the first franchise shift in the American League since a previous Baltimore team moved to New York City during the 1902–03 off-season and were eventually renamed the Yankees.

APRIL 23 A lack of uniforms and equipment causes an hour delay in a game against the Tigers in Detroit. When the Indians arrived in Detroit on a trip from Baltimore by train, they learned that the baggage car containing their uniforms, bats, baseballs, and medical supplies had been mistakenly detached in Pittsburgh. Eventually, Capital Airlines located a cargo plane in Washington, D.C. and dispatched it to Pittsburgh to pick up the equipment and bring it to Detroit. The plane left Pittsburgh at 12:27 p.m., and at the Detroit airport, the equipment was transferred to a truck, which followed a police escort and arrived at Briggs Stadium at 2:20 p.m., 20 minutes after the scheduled start of the game. The first pitch occurred at 3:00 p.m., and Indians lost 6–1.

APRIL 25 Dave Philley hits a two-run homer in the tenth inning to break an 8–8 tie in a 10–9 win over the Tigers in Detroit. Philley had one hit in 26 at-bats during the 1954 season when he stepped to the plate. He entered the game as a defensive replacement for Dale Mitchell in the eighth inning.

The Indians began the day with a 3–6 record on the 1954 season and six losses in their last seven games. Over the remainder of the regular season campaign, Cleveland won 108 and lost only 37.

APRIL 30 The Indians score five runs in the tenth inning off Whitey Ford to defeat the Yankees 9–4 in New York.

MAY 10 The Indians score eight runs in the first inning to take an 8–3 lead, and hang on to defeat the Yankees 8–7 at Municipal Stadium. Dave Philley hit a grand slam off Bob Kuzava.

MAY 12 The Indians sell Jim Lemon to the Senators.

Lemon was a 26-year-old who had showed little hitting prowess in brief trials with the Indians in 1950 and 1953, sandwiched around two seasons in the service during the Korean War. He continued to struggle for two more years in Washington. Lemon found his home run stroke in 1956 with 27, and clouted 33 in 1959 and 38 in 1960, driving in 100 runs in his two best seasons.

MAY 13 The Indians stun the Senators 8–7 in 11 innings at Municipal Stadium. Cleveland trailed 7–1 heading into the ninth. Through the first eight innings, Washington hurler Mickey McDermott had allowed only one hit, a second inning homer by Rudy Regalado. Al Rosen led off the ninth with a homer, and the Indians added five more to send the contest into extra innings. The key blow was a three-run double by Dave Philley, which tied the score 7–7. The 11th inning run scored on two walks and a double by Rosen.

Rosen's batting numbers fell from the lofty heights of his MVP season of 1953, but he still hit .300 with 24 homers and 102 RBIs. He was hitting well with a .372 average with 13 homers and 48 RBIs on May 25 when he broke a finger. It was the start of a series of injuries that ended Rosen's career in 1956. Bobby Avila picked up much of the slack with the best season of his career. He led the AL in batting with a .341 and scored 112 runs with 189 hits and 15 homers.

MAY 14 George Strickland hits a grand slam off Chuck Stobbs in the first inning of a 5–2 win over the Senators at Municipal Stadium.

MAY 16 Mike Garcia pitches a one-hitter to defeat the Athletics 6–0 in the second game of a double header at Municipal Stadium. The lone Philadelphia hit was a single by Joe DeMaestri in the fourth inning. The Indians also won the opener 12–7.

Garcia had a 19–8 record in 1954. He led the American League in earned run average (2.64) and shutouts (eight).

MAY 23 Six days after the Supreme Court rules that segregation of public schools is illegal in the case of *Brown vs. the Board of Education of Topeka,* Bob Feller records his 250th career win with a 14–3 decision over the Orioles in the first game of a double header at Municipal Stadium. The Indians also won the second game 2–1 in 12 innings. Art Houtteman not only pitched a complete game, but drove in the winning run with a walk-off double. The dual triumphs extended the Indians winning streak to 11 games and gave the club a record of 24–10.

MAY 28 Early Wynn pitches a two-hitter to defeat the Tigers 3–0 at Municipal Stadium. Frank House collected both Detroit hits with a double in the third inning and a single in the eighth.

Wynn had a record of 23–11 with an ERA of 2.73. He led the AL in wins and innings pitched (270⅔) in addition to striking out 155 batters and hurling 20 complete games in 36 starts.

MAY 29 The Indians rout the Tigers 12–0 at Municipal Stadium. The game was enlivened by a near brawl during the seventh inning when Dave Philley, accusing Tiger pitcher Ralph Branca of throwing at him, bunted along the first base line in the hope that Branca would field the ball. First baseman Walt Dropo made the play instead and prevented Philley from charging Branca. Philley and Dropo then squared off, but were restrained before any blows were struck.

MAY 30 The Indians win their 14th straight home game, with a 3–1 decision over the Tigers at Municipal Stadium.

Indians fans urge on their heroes at the start of the 1954 World Series.

JUNE 1 The Indians trade Bob Chakales to the Orioles for Vic Wertz.

This was the best trade completed by Hank Greenberg during his tenure as general manager of the Indians from 1949 through 1957. Wertz was 29 years old when acquired by the Indians and had been an outfielder during his entire career. The Indians had a weakness at first base, and asked Wertz to try his hand at fielding the position. It proved to be a smashing success. Wertz was the club's starting first baseman until 1957, and twice he drove in over 100 runs.

June 2 The Yankees score seven runs in the first inning, but the Indians battle back with three runs in the third, three in the fourth, one in the ninth, and one in the tenth to win 8–7 in New York. Bobby Avila's homer in the ninth inning tied the score. Al Smith's home run in the tenth was the game-winner. Five Cleveland relievers combined to pitch no-hit baseball over the final nine innings. Don Mossi pitched the second, Ray Narleski the third, Bob Hooper the fourth and fifth, Mike Garcia the sixth and seventh, and Hal Newhouser the eighth through the tenth.

June 5 Mike Garcia allows only two hits during an 11-inning complete game to win 4–1 over the Athletics in Philadelphia. Two of the three runs in the 11th scored on a long sacrifice fly by Dave Philley to deep center. Al Smith scored all the way from second base on the play. The only Philadelphia hits were singles by Joe DeMaestri in the fourth inning and Elmer Valo in the 11th.

In his season as a regular, Smith hit .281 and scored 101 wins.

June 9 Mike Garcia pitches the Indians to a 1–0 win over the Senators in Washington. Bob Porterfield held the Indians scoreless until the seventh inning when Cleveland scored on singles by Vic Wertz and Dave Philley and an error.

June 12 The Indians take first place with a 4–3 win over the Red Sox in Boston. Bob Feller recorded his 2,500th career strikeout.

Feller finished his career in 1956 with 2,581 strikeouts. At the time, he trailed only Walter Johnson (3,509) and Cy Young (2,803) on the all-time strikeout list.

June 14 The Indians bang out 22 hits and beat the Red Sox 13–5 in Boston.

June 16 Don Mossi's streak of retiring 27 batters in a row, the equivalent of a perfect game, comes to an end during a 5–1 win over the Senators at Municipal Stadium.

In relief appearances, Mossi retired the last two batters to face him on June 2, followed by two on June 4, one on June 6, three on June 8, three on June 10, and nine on June 12 for 20 in succession. Making his first big league start on June 16, Mossi set down the first seven batters before Joe Tipton broke the string with a home run. Mossi then finished out the contest without allowing another run.

June 18 The Indians extend their winning streak to nine games with a 2–0 decision over the Red Sox at Municipal Stadium.

July 3 The Indians score two runs in the 15th inning to defeat the White Sox 5–4 at Municipal Stadium. Chicago took a 4–3 lead in the top of the 15th, but the Indians rallied to win in their half, loading the bases before Hank Majeski delivered a two-run single.

July 4 Mike Garcia (1⅓ innings), Ray Narleski (5⅔) innings and Early Wynn (two innings) combine on a one-hitter to defeat the White Sox 2–1 at Municipal Stadium. Garcia was forced to retire because of a hemorrhage of the middle finger of his right hand. Narleski followed in relief and was removed with none out in the eighth after walking a batter. Wynn relieved Narleski, and Chicago scored a run on an infield out and an error. Entering the ninth, the Sox still had not collected a hit. Wynn retired the first two batters in the inning, placing the Indians one out away from a three-pitcher no-hitter, when Minnie Minoso singled.

The Indians had a deeper pitching staff in 1954 than they possessed in previous seasons because of the emergence of right-hander Ray Narleski and left-hander Don Mossi, both of whom were 25-year-old rookies. The pair pitched mainly out of the bullpen. Narleski was 3–3 with 13 saves and had an ERA of 2.22 in 89 innings. Mossi had a 6–1 record, seven saves and a 1.94 earned run average in 93 innings on the mound.

JULY 5 Batting in the lead-off spot, first baseman Bill Glynn shows a surprising display of power with three homers and eight RBIs during a 13–6 win over the Tigers in the first game of a double header at Detroit. Glynn entered the game with six homers and 41 homers in 592 career at-bats. He flied out in his first two plate appearances. In the third inning, Glynn hit a grand slam off Ralph Branca and followed with a two-run shot facing Ted Gray in the fifth, and a solo homer against Dick Weik in the seventh. Glynn batted with the bases loaded in the eighth and hit a sacrifice fly to deep center. The Indians lost the second game 1–0 in 11 innings on a walk-off homer by Harvey Kuenn. In a rare start, Don Mossi pitched the complete game to take the tough loss, the only defeat he suffered all year. George Zuvernik pitched all 11 innings for the Tigers, and allowed just three hits.

After his tremendous batting explosion in the opener of the July 5, 1954, double header, Glynn hit only one more major league homer and drove in just seven runs in 86 at-bats. The one home run came the following day (see July 6, 1954). He finished his career with ten homers, 56 RBIs and a .249 average in 684 at-bats over four seasons.

JULY 6 The Indians score 11 runs in the first inning, with eight crossing the plate before the first out, in a game against the Orioles at Municipal Stadium. The first ten batters reached base. The Indians didn't score again, but coasted to an 11–3 win. With Joe Coleman pitching for Baltimore, Bill Glynn led off the first inning with a home run. Bobby Avila and Larry Doby singled, Al Rosen walked, and Wally Westlake tripled in three runs. After Dave Philley walked, George Strickland singled. Mike Blyzka replaced Coleman. Jim Hegan greeted Blyzka with a single and Early Wynn beat out a bunt. Glynn, up for the second time, singled to make the score 8–0 before Bobby Avila flied out. Doby resumed the attack with a single and Rosen walked. Westlake popped up, but Philley drove in the tenth and 11th runs with a single. Strickland ended the inning by grounding out.

JULY 13 The All-Star game is played before 68,751 fans at Municipal Stadium, and the American League wins the free-swinging contest 11–9. Cleveland batters accounted for eight runs-batted-in. Al Rosen led the way, thrilling the hometown crowd by driving in five runs with a pair homers. Larry Doby and ex-Indian Ray Boone also homered for the AL. Rosen's and Boone's homers were hit back-to-back in the third inning off Robin Roberts. Rosen's second round-tripper was struck against Johnny Antonelli in the fifth. Bobby Avila collected three singles in three at-bats and drove in two runs. Doby hit a pinch-homer in the eighth facing Gene Conley, which tied the score 9–9. Later in the inning, Nellie Fox hit a two-run single to break the deadlock. Ted Kluszewski and Gus Bell each homered for the Nationals.

Future Hall of Famers on the rosters of the two clubs were Yogi Berra, Roy Campanella, Larry Doby, Whitey Ford, Nellie Fox, George Kell, Bob Lemon, Mickey Mantle, Willie Mays, Stan Musial, Pee Wee Reese, Robin Roberts, Jackie Robinson, Red Schoendienst, Duke Snider, Warren Spahn, and Ted Williams.

JULY 17 Bob Feller pitches a two-hitter to defeat the Athletics 6–0 in Philadelphia. The only hits off Feller were singles by Don Bollweg in the first and fourth innings.

Feller was a spot pitcher for the Indians in 1954. He was 13–3 with a 3.09 ERA in 140 innings over 19 starts. Feller never achieved his dream of winning a World Series game. He lost both of his starts in 1948 and didn't pitch at all during the 1954 Fall Classic.

JULY 20 The Indians and Red Sox play to a 16-inning, 5–5 tie at Fenway Park. The game was called because of an American League rule stipulating that no inning could start after 12:50 a.m. The game was called at 12:57 a.m. A two-run homer by Bobby Avila tied the score 5–5.

JULY 21 The Indians and Red Sox play a tie game for the second day in a row with the contest ending with the score 7–7 at the end of the eighth inning because of rain.

The Indians played 13 games at Fenway Park in 1954 and won 11 and tied two.

JULY 24 A two-run homer by Larry Doby in the top of the tenth inning breaks a 3–3 tie in a 5–4 victory over the Yankees in New York.

Doby led the American League in home runs (32) and runs-batted-in (126) and batted .272 in 1954.

AUGUST 15 The Indians win for the 27th straight time at Municipal Stadium against the St. Louis Browns/Baltimore Orioles franchise by sweeping a double header 5–2 and 3–1.

The 27 wins in a row against one club at home is a modern major league record. The Browns lost their last five games in Cleveland in 1952 and all 11 in 1953. Transplanted in Baltimore as the Orioles, the team lost all 11 at Municipal Stadium again in 1954.

AUGUST 19 The Indians extend their winning streak to nine games with a 4–3 win over the Tigers in the first game of a double header at Municipal Stadium. The skein stopped with an 8–2 defeat in game two.

AUGUST 22 The Indians crush the Orioles 12–1 with a 20-hit attack in Baltimore.

AUGUST 25 The Indians play the Athletics in Philadelphia for the last time and win 4–3 in ten innings.

The Athletics moved to Kansas City at the end of the 1954 season.

AUGUST 26 Early Wynn pitches a two-hitter for a 2–1 hit over the Senators at Griffith Stadium. The only Washington hits were a double by Roy Sievers in the fourth inning and a single by Jim Busby in the eighth.

AUGUST 29 Bob Lemon records his 20th win of the season with an 8–2 decision over the Red Sox in the first game of a double header in Boston. The Indians completed the sweep with an 8–1 victory in the second tilt.

Lemon was 23–7 in 1954 and compiled an ERA of 2.72 in 258⅓ innings. He led the league in wins and complete games (21 in 33 starts). It was Lemon's sixth season of 20 or more wins.

AUGUST 31 Early Wynn pitches his second consecutive two-hitter, defeating the Yankees 6–1 in New York. Wynn's no-hit bid was broken up by a homer from Irv Noren in the seventh inning. Enos Slaughter added a single in the eighth.

SEPTEMBER 8 Early Wynn records his 20th win of the season with a 5–2 decision over the Athletics at Municipal Stadium.

SEPTEMBER 9 In the 140th game of the season, the Indians post win number 100 with an 11-inning, 5–4 decision over the Athletics at Municipal Stadium.

The Indians were 11–11 against both the Yankees and White Sox in 1954 but were 89–21 against the rest of the field. Cleveland was 20–2 versus the Red Sox, 19–3 playing the Orioles, 18–4 against both the Senators and Athletics and 14–8 facing the Tigers. Counting the World Series, the Indians were 22–26 against teams with a winning record in 1954.

SEPTEMBER 12 The Indians all but wrap up the 1954 pennant by sweeping the Yankees 4–1 and 3–2 before a double header crowd of 84,587 at Municipal Stadium.

The crowd on September 12, 1954 is the largest for a regular season game in major league history.

SEPTEMBER 17 Bobby Avila hits a grand slam off Ned Garver in the seventh inning of a 6–3 win over the Tigers in Detroit. It was the Indians eighth win in a row.

SEPTEMBER 18 The Indians clinch the pennant with a 3–2 win over the Tigers in Detroit. The game was delayed by rain for an hour and 15 minutes at the start and another 53 minutes in the eighth that made the field almost unplayable, but the Indians sloshed to their ninth win in a row.

The Yankees finished the season with a record of 103–51. It was one of only two times that the Yankees failed to win a pennant under the 12-year stewardship of Casey Stengel, which lasted from 1949 through 1960. Oddly, the 1954 Yankee club had a better record than any of Stengel's 11 other clubs. In fact, it was the only one to win 100 or more games. One of the reasons that the Indians were able to overcome the Yankees in 1954 was the depth of the roster. The Indians had role players like Wally Westlake, Dave Pope, Hank Majeski, Dale Mitchell, Sam Dente, Rudy Regalado, and Hal Newhouser to help the club survive injuries to starters. Cleveland had always lacked those players in previous seasons.

SEPTEMBER 20 The Indians win their 11th game in a row with a 7–4 decision over the White Sox at Municipal Stadium.

SEPTEMBER 21 Larry Doby droves in six runs on a homer and a double, but the Indians lose 9–7 to the White Sox at Municipal Stadium, ending the 11-game winning streak.

SEPTEMBER 25 On the second-to-last day of the season, the Indians win their 111th game of the season with an 11–1 decision over the Tigers at Municipal Stadium. Early Wynn pitched a two-hitter. He held Detroit hitless until the ninth inning, when he yielded a single to Fred Hatfield and a triple to Steve Souchock. The victory broke the American League record of 110 set by the 1927 New York Yankees.

The Indians faced the New York Giants in the World Series. Managed by Leo Durocher, the Giants finished 97–57 in 1954 and beat out the Dodgers by five games to win the NL pennant. The 1954 Fall Classic opened at the Polo Grounds, a bathtub-shaped facility that featured some of the strangest outfield dimensions in major league history. It was only 279 feet from home plate to the left field pole and just 257 feet to right field. The deepest part of center field was a distant 483 feet from home plate. The odd shape of the field was a major factor in the 1954 World Series. The Indians entered the post-season as huge favorites to emerge with the world championship. Not only did Cleveland win 111 games, but the American League had won the Fall Classics seven times in a row from 1947 through 1953. The Indians were anything but a mystery to the Giants, however. The two clubs had been spring training partners in Arizona for many years. They met in 21 exhibition games in 1954, with the Giants taking 13 of them.

SEPTEMBER 29 The Indians open the World Series by losing 5–2 in ten innings to the Giants in New York. Cleveland took a 2–0 lead in the first inning. Al Smith led off and was hit by a pitch from Sal Maglie. Bobby Avila followed with a single and Vic Wertz hit a two-run triple. The Giants tied the score 2–2 with a pair of tallies in the third on a walk and three hits off Bob Lemon. The score was still tied 2–2 in the eighth when Willie Mays made one of the most memorable catches in baseball history. Larry Doby walked and Al Rosen singled to start the inning. Leo Durocher responded by replacing Maglie with Don Liddle to face Vic Wertz with none out. Wertz drove the ball on a line to deep center, and Mays raced toward the distant center field wall with his back to the plate and caught the ball over his left shoulder 460 feet from home plate. At any other ballpark in the majors, Wertz's drive would have been a home run. The Indians still had a tremendous opportunity to score after Hank Majeski walked to load the bases with one out, but Dave Pope struck out and Jim Hegan flied out. In the New York tenth, Willie Mays and Hank Thompson walked. Durocher sent Dusty Rhodes to pinch-hit for Monte Irvin, and Rhodes whacked Lemon's first pitch down the right field line. The ball just cleared the wall and settled into the first row only 260 feet from home plate for a three-run homer with Dave Pope standing against the wall. At any other ballpark in the majors, it would have been an out. The Indians left 13 men on base.

Wertz played 17 seasons in the majors but is best remembered for hitting the ball on which Mays made his miraculous catch. Few recall that Wertz had a tremendous Series in 1954. In his other four plate appearances in game one, he hit a triple, a double, and two singles. Overall in the four contests, Wertz collected eight hits, including a homer, a triple, and two doubles, in 16 at-bats for a .500 batting average and a .938 slugging percentage. Unfortunately, the remainder of the Indians hitters were almost helpless at the plate with 18 hits in 121 at-bats for an average of .149.

SEPTEMBER 30 The Giants take a two games to none lead in the World Series with a 3–1 win in New York. On the first pitch of the game, Al Smith homered off Johnny Antonelli. The ball cleared the left field roof only five feet from the foul line. The Indians failed to score again, however. Early Wynn retired the first 12 batters to face him before the Giants struck back with two runs in the fifth. Dusty Rhodes pinch-hit and provided an RBI-single. In the seventh, Rhodes homered. The Indians left 13 men on base for the second game in a row.

Residents of Cuba were able to watch a World Series on television for the first time in 1954. A Cuban television network chartered a DC-3 to fly over the Gulf of Mexico to serve as a relay for the transmission from a station in Miami.

OCTOBER 1 The tide continues to flow against the Indians as the Giants win their third in a row with a 6–2 decision before 71,555 at Municipal Stadium. New York broke the game open with three runs in the third to take a 4–0 lead with the help of a pinch-single by Dusty Rhodes.

In his first four plate appearances in the 1954 Series, three of them as a pinch-hitter, Rhodes collected two homers and two singles.

OCTOBER 2 The Giants complete a four-game sweep of the Indians in one of the greatest upsets in World Series history by winning 7–4 in front of 78,102 at Municipal Stadium. The Giants put the contest away early, taking a 7–0 lead with four runs in the fifth inning. During Cleveland's futile comeback, Hank Majeski hit a three-run, pinch-hit home run.

The Giants were the first National League team to win the Fall Classic since 1946 and the first to sweep one since 1914. It was the first world championship for the Giants franchise since 1933. The club, which moved to San Francisco in 1958, hasn't won a World Series since defeating the Indians in 1954.

NOVEMBER 16 The Indians send Sam Jones, Gale Wade, and $60,000 to the Cubs for Ralph Kiner.

A future Hall of Famer, Kiner led the National League in home runs seven consecutive seasons from 1946 through 1952 while playing for the Pirates. He played in six All-Star Games, drove in over 100 runs six seasons and scored 100 or more six times. Kiner and Greenberg were teammates on the 1947 Pirates and became close friends. By the time he arrived in Cleveland, however, Kiner was nearly finished. Hampered by a bad back he lasted only one more season before retiring, batting .249 with 18 home runs in 321 at-bats. At the time he was traded by the Indians, Jones was nearly 29 and had a major league career record of 2–4 with an ERA of 6.25. He was a huge loss, however. After leaving Cleveland, Jones appeared in two All-Star Games, led the NL in strikeouts three times, pitched a no-hitter, and won 21 games for the Giants in 1959.

DECEMBER 26 Nearly three months after the Indians lose the World Series, the Browns bring a world championship to Cleveland by defeating the Detroit Lions 56–10 in the NFL championship game before 43,827 at Municipal Stadium.

1955

Season in a Sentence

Looking to repeat as pennant winners and vindicate their loss in the 1954 World Series, the Indians are in first place with ten games left in the season but finish second to the Yankees.

Finish • Won • Lost • Pct • GB

Finish	Won	Lost	Pct	GB
Second	93	61	.604	3.0

Manager

Al Lopez

Stats

Stats	Indians	AL	Rank
Batting Avg:	.257	.258	6
On-Base Pct:	.353	.339	2
Slugging Pct:	.394	.381	4
Home Runs:	148		2
Stolen Bases:	28		6
ERA:	3.39	3.96	3
Fielding Avg:	.981	.977	1
Runs Scored:	698		5
Runs Allowed:	601		3

Starting Line-up

Jim Hegan, c
Vic Wertz, 1b
Bobby Avila, 2b
Al Rosen, 3b
George Strickland, ss
Ralph Kiner, lf
Larry Doby, cf
Al Smith, rf
Gene Woodling, lf

Pitchers

Early Wynn, sp
Bob Lemon, sp
Herb Score, sp
Mike Garcia, sp
Ray Narleski, rp
Don Mossi, rp
Art Houtteman, rp-sp
Bob Feller, rp-sp

Attendance

1,221,780 (third in AL)

Club Leaders

Batting Avg:	Al Smith	.306
On-Base Pct:	Al Smith	.407
Slugging Pct:	Al Smith	.505
Home Runs:	Larry Doby	26
RBIs:	Al Rosen	81
Runs:	Al Smith	123
Stolen Bases:	Al Smith	11
Wins:	Bob Lemon	18
Strikeouts:	Herb Score	245
ERA:	Early Wynn	2.82
Saves:	Ray Narleski	19

April 12 The Indians open the season with a 5–1 win over the White Sox before 50,230 at Municipal Stadium. Bob Lemon pitched a complete game and Ralph Kiner homered in his Cleveland debut. Al Smith also homered.

Smith had a career year in 1955. He accumulated a league-leading 123 runs along with 186 hits, 22 homers, 77 RBIs and a .306 batting average.

April 15 Making his major league debut, Herb Score strikes out nine batters and walks nine during a nine-inning complete game, defeating the Tigers 7–3 in Detroit.

Score was a sensation as a rookie in 1955. He posted a 16–10 record and a 2.58 ERA in 227⅓ innings. Score's 245 strikeouts led the American League and his 154 walks ranked second.

April 18 The Indians overcome an 8–0 deficit to defeat the Athletics 11–9 in Kansas City. Cleveland scored five times in the fifth inning, two in the seventh and one in the eighth and entered the ninth trailing 9–8. Larry Doby hit a two-out, three-run homer for the win.

The game was the first that the Indians played in Kansas City since the Athletics moved there in October 1954. The game was played at Municipal Stadium, which was the home of the A's from 1955 through 1967 and the Royals from 1969 through 1972.

April 26 The crowd at Cleveland's Municipal Stadium numbers only 972 in 40-degree weather for a 3–2 win over the Senators.

Over the course of 162 regular season games from April 25, 1954, through May 1, 1955, the Indians posted a record of 119–43. The major league record for wins in a season is 116, set by the 1906 Cubs and tied by the 1998 Yankees and the 2001 Mariners.

April 27 The Indians emerge with a 17-inning, 6–5 win over the Senators at Municipal Stadium. The winning run scored on a bases-loaded sacrifice fly by Bobby Avila. There was no scoring by either team from the bottom of the seventh inning through the top of the 17th.

Avila batted .272 with 13 homers in 1955.

May 1 Great pitching by 36-year-old veteran Bob Feller and 21-year-old rookie Herb Score highlights a double-header sweep of the Red Sox at Municipal Stadium. In the opener, Feller pitched his 12th career one-hitter in a 2–0 win. Feller missed his chance for a fourth career no-hitter when Sammy White singled in the seventh inning. Battery mate Jim Hegan drove in both Cleveland runs with a single in the second inning and a triple in the seventh. In the second tilt, Score struck out 16 batters during a 2–1 victory. He fanned nine through the first three innings and 12 batters in the first five innings. A two-run double by Larry Doby in the first inning plated both Indians runs.

Feller's 12 career one-hitters is a major league record, which he shares with Nolan Ryan. Combined with his three no-hitters, Feller had 15 games in which he surrendered one hit or less, a figure exceeded only by Ryan, who hurled seven no-hitters in addition to his 12 one-hitters. The May 1, 1955, game, however, was the last great pitching performance by Feller. Between that contest and his retirement at the end of the 1956 season, Feller was 3–7 with an ERA of 4.18 in 127 innings.

May 8 Al Rosen hits a walk-off homer in the 11th inning to defeat the Athletics 2–1 in the second game of a double header in Cleveland. All three runs scored on solo homers. Gus Zernial connected for the A's in the fifth inning and Al Smith for the Tribe in the eighth. Smith also homered twice in the opener, which the Indians won 9–6.

May 11 The Indians sell Harry Simpson to the Athletics.

Simpson never panned out with the Indians but had a couple of fine seasons after leaving Cleveland. In Kansas City, he made the All-Star team, drove in 105 runs, and led the league in triples in 1956.

May 18 The Indians explode for 11 runs in the fifth inning and wallop the Red Sox 19–0 in Boston. During the big inning, Vic Wertz drove in five runs with a grand slam off Russ Kemmerer and an RBI single. Herb Score pitched the shutout.

May 22 Early Wynn pitches a one-hitter to defeat the Tigers 4–0 in Detroit. The only hit off Wynn was a single by Fred Hatfield in the fourth inning.

Wynn had a 17–11 record and a 2.82 ERA in 1955.

May 24 Herb Score carries a no-hitter into the seventh inning but loses 4–1 to the White Sox at Municipal Stadium.

May 31 After saving the Indians from defeat with a homer in the ninth inning that ties the score 1–1, Dave Philley scores the winning run in the 13th for a 2–1 victory over the Orioles at Municipal Stadium. Philley walked and crossed the plate on Sam Dente's walk-off double.

June 2 Dave Pope hits a grand slam off Saul Rogovin in the second inning of a 9–3 win over the Orioles at Municipal Stadium.

June 9 Red Sox relief pitcher Ellis Kinder almost meets with disaster before entering the ninth inning of a 4–2 Boston win against the Indians at Municipal Stadium. Called

Al Rosen (left) and Bob Avila (right) congratulate Al Smith after a bases-clearing homerun. At 27 years old, Smith was the youngest starter in an aging lineup that included six players in their thirties.

to the mound to relieve Frank Sullivan, Kinder was riding the red convertible used to transport hurlers from the bullpen to the mound when the vehicle rammed the left field stands. Neither Kinder nor the driver was injured, however, and Kinder snuffed out the Cleveland rally to earn a save.

June 11 The Indians spot the Yankees five runs in the first inning but rally to win 7–6 at Municipal Stadium. The winning run scored on a single by Bobby Avila.

June 14 Herb Score walks 11 batters and hits one but pitches a two-hitter to win 3–1 in the second game of a double header against the Senators at Griffith Stadium. The only Washington hits were singles by Ed FitzGerald in the first inning and Eddie Yost in the second. Cleveland also won the opener 6–4 in 11 innings.

June 15 The Indians trade Wally Westlake and Dave Pope to the Orioles for Gene Woodling and Billy Cox.

Cox retired rather than go to Cleveland, claiming that his legs were gone and that he suffered from a hernia. The Orioles sent cash to the Indians to compensate.

June 19 Gene Woodling sparks a rhubarb with the umpires which holds up play for ten minutes during an 11–7 loss to the Red Sox at Fenway Park. In the seventh inning, umpire Bill Summers called Woodling out on a close play at first base. During the ensuing debate, Summers ejected both Woodling and Vic Wertz. Al Lopez somehow managed to avoid being thumbed despite a physical confrontation with the arbiters. Lopez and Summers, a former boxer, went nose to nose. Umpire Ed Hurley tried to move Lopez out of range, but Summers grabbed Hurley and shoved him aside. Hank Soar, the plate umpire and a former tackle in the National Football League, rushed in and grabbed Lopez, quickly putting distance between the Indians manager and Summers. Soar held back Lopez while Cleveland coach Tony Cuccinello kept Summers at bay. Summers explained to reporters that he didn't eject Lopez because he never became "disrespectful."

June 22 Early Wynn shuts out the Orioles 5–0 at Municipal Stadium.

June 26 Early Wynn pitches his second consecutive shutout, beating the Yankees 5–0 in the first game of a double header at Yankee Stadium. New York won the second contest 3–0.

The Indians had a 13–9 record against the pennant-winning Yankees in 1955 but were 9–13 against the last-place Senators.

June 27 The Indians trade Hank Majeski to the Orioles for Bobby Young.

The Indians ended the month of June with a 42–30 record in third place, seven games out of first.

July 1 Early Wynn pitches his third consecutive shutout for a 1–0 over the White Sox at Municipal Stadium. The lone run scored on a homer by Larry Doby off Billy Pierce in the fifth inning.

Doby hit .291 with 26 homers in 1955.

July 2 The Indians sell Dave Philley to the Orioles.

July 3 The Indians belt the White Sox 14–9 at Municipal Stadium. Cleveland trailed 6–5 before scoring four times in the sixth inning.

July 4 The Indians win a 15-inning marathon by a 6–5 score against the Tigers in the first game of a double header at Municipal Stadium. In the 15th, Ralph Kiner doubled and scored on Larry Doby's single. Cleveland also won the second tilt 8–5.

July 7 Kenny Kuhn, an 18-year-old infielder, has a memorable major league debut during a 9–1 win over the Athletics in Kansas City. He entered the contest as a pinch-runner at first base in the eighth inning. Kuhn rounded second on a single but lost his stride and sprawled into the dirt. He managed to scramble back to second safely, but there was a gaping hole in his pants near the knees. Al Lopez sent Kuhn out to play shortstop, but the game had to be delayed while his trousers were patched up with adhesive tape.

Kuhn was on the team because of a rule passed in 1955 stipulating that any amateur player who signed a contract with a bonus of at least $4,000 would have to remain on the major league roster for two years. A native of Louisville, Kentucky, Kuhn signed with the Indians for $50,000 out of high school. During his required two years in the majors, Kuhn hit .210 in 71 games and 81 at-bats. He appeared in his last big league contest at the age of 20. The bonus rule was rescinded in 1958.

July 8 Bob Lemon shuts out the White Sox 1–0 in Chicago. The lone run scored on a double by Al Rosen in the first inning.

Lemon was 18–10 with a 3.88 ERA in 1955.

July 12 Al Lopez manages the American League to a 12-inning, 6–5 loss in the All-Star Game at County Stadium in Milwaukee. Early Wynn took the mound in the fourth inning and pitched three shutout innings.

Lopez managed the AL All-Stars in five games and lost all of them.

July 13 The Indians trade Jim Wright to the Orioles for Hoot Evers.

July 14 The Indians sign Ferris Fain as a free agent following his release by the Tigers.

July 21 Shut out through eight innings, the Indians score three runs in the ninth inning and one in the tenth to defeat the Senators 4–3 at Municipal Stadium. A three-run pinch double by Vic Wertz tied the score. In the tenth, Al Smith singled and then scored on a Larry Doby single. Smith took advantage of Washington center fielder Carlos Paula, who lobbed the ball back to the infield, allowing Smith to advance three bases on a one-base hit.

July 30 Herb Score pitches a one-hitter to defeat the Orioles 7–0 at Memorial Stadium. The only Baltimore hit was a single by Jim Dyck in the seventh inning.

July 31 The Indians purchase Sal Maglie from the Giants.

Maglie was 38 years old at the time he was acquired by the Indians but was still a successful pitcher. He started game one in the 1954 World Series against Cleveland and had a lifetime record of 95–42. The Indians claimed Maglie on waivers primarily to keep him from joining the Yankees, and he was used rarely by Al Lopez. Maglie was dealt to the Dodgers the following season (see May 15, 1956).

AUGUST 10 Ralph Kiner hits a walk-off grand slam off Al Aber in the ninth inning to defeat the Tigers 6–4 at Municipal Stadium. Kiner entered the game as a pinch-hitter for Gene Woodling in the seventh inning.

AUGUST 12 The Indians sweep the Athletics 17–1 and 6–5 in Kansas City. The Indians scored seven runs in the first inning of the opener. Jim Hegan hit a grand slam off Bill Harrington.

AUGUST 13 The Indians take a two-game lead in the American League pennant race with a 5–3 win over the Athletics in Kansas City.

The Indians record was 70–45. The club had won 28 of their previous 38 games.

AUGUST 18 Herb Score strikes out 13 batters during a 5–3 victory over the Tigers in Detroit.

AUGUST 24 A homer by Bobby Avila leading off the first inning and another home run from Al Smith in the sixth beats the Red Sox 2–0 at Municipal Stadium. Mike Garcia pitched the shutout.

AUGUST 26 Vic Wertz is stricken with polio.

Wertz was done for the season, but fortunately the illness was of the non-paralytic type and he returned in 1956 with a comeback season, batting .264 with 32 homers and 106 RBIs.

SEPTEMBER 7 Early Wynn posts his 200th career win with a 6–0 decision over the Orioles in Baltimore.

SEPTEMBER 8 Larry Doby homers in the tenth inning to defeat the Orioles 5–3 in Baltimore.

Doby hit seven homers in seven games from September 3 through September 8.

SEPTEMBER 10 The Indians take a 1½ game lead in the pennant race with a 10–7 triumph over the Red Sox in Boston. Al Smith collected five hits in five at-bats.

SEPTEMBER 13 The Indians sweep the Senators 3–1 and 8–2 to take a two-game lead in the American League pennant race.

The Indians had a 90–55 record with nine games left on the schedule. The Yankees were 87–56 with 11 contests remaining on the schedule.

SEPTEMBER 16 The Indians are knocked out of first place with a 3–0 loss to the Tigers in Detroit.

The Indians lost all three games in Detroit from September 16 through September 18 to all but doom their chances for a pennant in 1955. Over the last 12 days of the season, the Indians had a record of 3–6 while the Yankees were 9–2.

SEPTEMBER 24 In his first major league start, Hank Aguirre shuts out the Tigers 7–0 in the second game of a double header at Municipal Stadium. He had made three prior relief appearances, allowing two runs in $3^2/_3$ innings. Cleveland also won the first game 8–2.

Al Lopez met with general manager Hank Greenberg after the season ended and said he planned to resign citing "stomach problems." Lopez, like everyone connected with the Indians, was frustrated over finishing second to the Yankees four times in five years, and by losing the World Series in 1954 after winning the AL pennant. Lack of fan support was another contributing factor. The loss in the Fall Classic after second place finishes in 1951, 1952 and 1953 seemed to have a negative psychological impact on Indians followers. The club was booed often at home despite being in pennant contention all year, and Lopez had some pointed comments about the Cleveland fans. "All I can say is their behavior hasn't helped us a bit. There's no question in my mind that their merciless booing hurt the fellows and affected their playing. It don't mind when they boo me, but it galls me to no end when they get on the players." Greenberg talked Lopez into returning in 1956, however.

OCTOBER 25 The Indians trade Larry Doby to the White Sox for Jim Busby and Chico Carrasquel.

Doby was near the end of his career but gave the White Sox two solid seasons. He returned to the Indians in 1958. Carrasquel and Busby were both disappointments in Cleveland.

1956

Season in a Sentence

The Indians finish second to the Yankees for the fifth time in six years, attendance plummets below the one million mark for the first time in 11 years, Bob Feller and Al Rosen retire, and Al Lopez resigns as manager.

Finish • Won • Lost • Pct • GB

Finish	Won	Lost	Pct	GB
Second	88	66	.571	9.0

Manager

Al Lopez

Stats

	Indians	AL	Rank
Batting Avg:	.244	.260	8
On-Base Pct:	.337	.344	6
Slugging Pct:	.381	.394	5
Home Runs:	153		2
Stolen Bases:	40		4 (tie)
ERA:	3.32	4.16	1
Fielding Avg:	.978	.975	2
Runs Scored:	712		5
Runs Allowed:	581		1

Starting Line-up

Jim Hegan, c
Vic Wertz, 1b
Bobby Avila, 2b
Al Rosen, 3b
Chico Carrasquel, ss
Gene Woodling, lf
Jim Busby, cf
Al Smith, rf-lf
Rocky Colavito, rf
George Strickland, 2b-ss-3b
Preston Ward, 1b

Pitchers

Early Wynn, sp
Bob Lemon, sp
Herb Score, sp
Mike Garcia, sp
Don Mossi, rp

Attendance

865,467 (seventh in AL)

Club Leaders

Batting Avg:	Al Smith	.274
On-Base Pct:	Al Smith	.378
Slugging Pct:	Vic Wertz	.509
Home Runs:	Vic Wertz	32
RBIs:	Vic Wertz	106
Runs:	Al Smith	87
Stolen Bases:	Bobby Avila	17
Wins:	Bob Lemon	20
	Herb Score	20
	Early Wynn	20
Strikeouts:	Herb Score	263
ERA:	Herb Score	2.53
Saves:	Don Mossi	11

March 29 Three months after the Browns win the NFL championship with a 38–14 win over the Rams in Los Angeles, a three-man syndicate headed by William Daley purchases the Indians.

Daley was a 63-year-old Cleveland industrialist. He completed arrangements to buy all 2,556 shares at $1,550 per share, representing a total outlay of $3,961,800. The price was believed to be the highest ever paid for a big league franchise up to that time. Daley's partners were Ignatius O'Shaughnessy of St. Paul, Minnesota, and Indians general manager Hank Greenberg. As part of the transaction, the new owners issued a total of 6,000 shares at $100 each. They also permitted the former stockholders to buy one share in the new organization for each one they owned in the old corporation, which was headed by Myron (Mike) Wilson. Daley was named chairman of the board, and Wilson remained as president. Daley headed the Cleveland organization until 1962 during a rough period in which there were frequent rumors that the team was headed out of the city to either Minneapolis or Houston.

April 17 The Indians lose the season opener 2–1 against the White Sox in Chicago. The winning run scored in the seventh inning on a bases loaded walk by Bob Lemon to

Jim Rivera. The lone Cleveland run scored on a home run by Jim Busby in his debut with the Tribe.

APRIL 19 Jack Harshman of the White Sox and Herb Score both pitch two-hitters in a contest won by Chicago 1–0 at Comiskey Park. The lone run scored without a hit in the seventh inning. Minnie Minoso walked and moved up two bases on a wild pitch by Score, then crossed the plate on a sacrifice fly by Larry Doby. The two hits for both teams were back-to-back. Harshman surrendered singles to Bobby Avila and Al Smith in the fourth inning. Score held the Sox hitless until the eighth, when Walt Dropo and Luis Aparicio singled.

APRIL 20 In the home opener, the Indians win 3–1 over the Tigers before 31,689 at Municipal Stadium. Gene Woodling homered.

APRIL 26 Chico Carrasquel drives in seven runs during a 14–2 victory over the Athletics in Kansas City. He struck a grand slam off Lou Kretlow in the third inning and a three-run double in the fifth against Jack Crimian.

APRIL 27 A two-run homer by Bobby Avila in the tenth inning gives the Indians a 4–2 lead in a 4–3 win over the Tigers in Detroit.

APRIL 29 Herb Score strikes out 13 batters and allows only three hits but loses 1–0 in ten innings in the first game of a double header against the Tigers in Detroit. It was Score's second 1–0 loss in a span of eleven days. The lone run scored on a two-out home run in the tenth by Bill Tuttle. Billy Hoeft pitched the shutout for the Tigers. Cleveland won the second game 8–4 behind five home runs. Vic Wertz and Al Smith each homered twice and Hal Naragon once.

MAY 13 The Indians trade Hoot Evers to the Orioles for Dave Pope.

MAY 14 Al Smith hits a walk-off homer in the ninth inning to beat the Yankees 3–2 at Municipal Stadium.

MAY 15 The Indians sell Sal Maglie to the Dodgers.

The Indians had little use for Maglie, who was 39. Without him, the Dodgers wouldn't have won the 1956 NL pennant. Maglie was 13–5 for Brooklyn with a 2.87 ERA in 191 innings over the remainder of the 1956 season and pitched a no-hitter during the heat of the pennant race in late September. He made two starts in the World Series against the Yankees, one of them as the opposing pitcher in Don Larsen's perfect game.

MAY 18 During an 11-inning, 5–4 loss against the Senators in Cleveland, Al Rosen injures his knee. As he writhed on the ground in obvious pain, fans at Municipal Stadium cheered. "It was the nastiest, most bush, meanest thing I ever heard," declared Al Lopez. "Those fans don't deserve a winner. They don't even deserve a major league club."

Rosen also suffered a back injury in January as the result of an auto accident in Florida that adversely affected his play on the field. He was booed by Cleveland fans almost every time he came to bat in 1956 and retired at the end of the season.

May 19 Herb Score strikes out 15 batters and defeats the Senators 5–1 at Municipal Stadium. Four Washington pitchers (Camilo Pascaul, Tex Clevenger, Bob Wiesler, and Dean Stone) combined on a two-hitter, but walked 11 batters.

The Tribe's three 20-game winners have a group hug. From left to right: Bob Lemon, Herb Score, and Early Wynn.

May 30 The Indians score six runs in a futile ninth-inning rally, losing 9–8 to the White Sox in the second game of a double header at Municipal Stadium. Cleveland hammered five home runs during the contest. Gene Woodling homered twice with Al Smith, Rocky Colavito, and Chico Carrasquel each striking one. The Indians also lost the opener 6–3.

June 2 Herb Score strikes out 13 batters during a 15–0 trouncing of the Senators in Washington. Jim Hegan hit a grand slam off Connie Grob in the eighth inning.

From 1946 through 1956, the Indians had 20-win seasons 18 times from six different pitchers. The eight were Bob Lemon (seven seasons), Early Wynn (four), Bob Feller (three), Mike Garcia (two), Gene Bearden (one) and Herb Score (one). Cleveland had three 20-game winners in 1956. Score had a record of 20–9 with an ERA of 2.53 and a league-leading 263 strikeouts in $249\frac{1}{3}$ innings. He also topped the AL in shutouts with five. Early Wynn also posted a 20–9 record and an earned run average of 2.73 in $277\frac{1}{3}$ innings. Bob Lemon was 20–14 with an ERA of 3.03 in $255\frac{1}{3}$ innings and led the league in complete games with 21 in 35 starts. Score, Wynn, and Lemon finished second, third and fourth in the American League in ERA. The Indians led all American League clubs in earned run average, but like much of the 1950s, however, the club lacked depth in *their pitching staff. The rest of the staff outside of the three 20-game winners combined for a 28–34 record and an ERA of 4.05.*

JUNE 4 Mike Garcia strikes out 12 batters during a 7–0 win over the Senators in Washington.

JUNE 9 Trailing 6–0 after three innings, the Indians roar back to defeat the Yankees 15–8 in New York. Cleveland took an 11–8 lead with four runs in the seventh inning.

JUNE 26 Al Smith collects a hit in his eighth consecutive at-bat during a 4–3 win over the Orioles at Municipal Stadium.

Smith collected four hits in four at-bats during a 9–8 win over the Senators at Municipal Stadium on June 23, and three hits in three at-bats in a 7–2 victory over Washington on June 24 in Cleveland. The latter contest was stopped after 5½ innings by rain.

JULY 1 The Indians score three runs in the ninth inning to defeat the White Sox 7–6 in the first game of a double header in Cleveland. A single by Chico Carrasquel ended the contest. Cleveland also won the second tilt 6–1.

JULY 5 Jim Busby hits a grand slam off Frank Lary, but the Indians lose 13–7 to the Tigers in Detroit.

JULY 6 Jim Busby ties a major league record by hitting grand slams in consecutive games. His bases-loaded homer accounted for all four Indians runs during a 4–2 win over the Athletics in Kansas City. The blow was struck in the fourth inning off Troy Herriage.

Busby is the only Indians player to hit grand slams in consecutive games, a feat that has been accomplished only 23 times in major league history.

JULY 8 The Indians score 11 runs in the seventh inning during a 17–3 clobbering of the Athletics in Kansas City. The 11 runs scored on five walks, four singles, and three doubles. Bob Lemon hit a pinch-hit homer in the eighth inning. Al Smith extended his hitting streak to 22 games.

JULY 16 After losing the opener of a double header against the Senators 7–5 in Washington, the Indians rebound to win the nightcap 11–1.

JULY 24 The Indians hammer the Senators 11–0 at Municipal Stadium.

JULY 26 A homer by Gene Woodling off Chuck Stobbs in the sixth inning accounts for the only run of a 1–0 win over the Senators at Municipal Stadium in a contest called by rain after 5½ innings. Bob Lemon pitched the shutout.

JULY 29 The Indians wins both games of a double header against the Orioles at Municipal Stadium with shutouts. In the opener, Herb Score defeated Baltimore 3–0. Hank Aguirre took game two 4–0. Aguirre didn't pitch another shutout as a major leaguer until 1962 when he played for the Tigers.

On the same day, the Indians sold Dale Mitchell to the Dodgers. Like Sal Maglie (see May 15, 1956), Dale Mitchell had a date with destiny. As a pinch-hitter in game five of the 1956 World Series against the Yankees, he struck out for the final out of Don Larsen's perfect game.

August 2 The Indians defeat the Yankees 4–0 at Municipal Stadium with four solo home runs. Tom Sturdivant allowed all four round-trippers. Bobby Avila hit an inside-the-park homer in the third inning when left fielder Elston Howard missed a shoestring catch. Preston Ward and Rocky Colavito hit consecutive homers in the fourth. One inning later, Chico Carrasquel connected for the fourth Cleveland home run. Herb Score pitched the shutout.

August 12 Herb Score strikes out 14 batters during a 6–3 win over the Athletics in Kansas City.

Score started 32 games in 1955 and 33 in 1956. He is the only Indians lefthander to start at least 20 games in consecutive seasons between Al Smith (1940–44) and Jack Kralick (1963–64).

August 13 The Indians play an exhibition game at Metropolitan Stadium in Bloomington, Minnesota, and lose 5–4 to the Minneapolis Millers of the American Association 5–4 before a capacity crowd of 22,000.

Metropolitan Stadium opened in 1956 in the Minneapolis suburb of Bloomington. The facility was built in the hopes that it would attract a big league club to the Minneapolis-St. Paul area. Indians general manager and minority owner Hank Greenberg was an interested spectator at the August 13 contest. He began making plans almost immediately with the idea of moving the Cleveland club to Minnesota. Indians attendance plummeted from 1,221,780 in 1955 to 865,467 in 1956. It was the first time that the club drew fewer than one million since 1945. Attendance had plunged almost 1.8 million from the high of 1948, and Greenberg believed that baseball was dead in Cleveland. He also felt that the negativity of the media in the city had poisoned the atmosphere and kept fans away from Municipal Stadium. Greenberg's beliefs were reinforced in 1957 when attendance figures dropped to 722,256. He pleaded with other members of the Indians board of directors to move the club but was unable to muster a majority that would assent to taking the club out of Cleveland. At the same time, the New York Giants owner Horace Stoneham was also seriously considering moving his club to Minneapolis but instead transferred his franchise to San Francisco in August 1957. Minnesota finally gained a big league club in October 1960 when the Washington Senators moved there and were renamed the Twins.

August 14 Three homers are struck in the 15th inning by both teams during a 6–4 loss to the Tigers at Municipal Stadium. Wayne Belardi and Ray Boone homered for Detroit in the top of the inning off Don Mossi. Gene Woodling struck a home run for Cleveland in the bottom half facing Jim Bunning. Two Indians pitchers retired 28 consecutive batters from the fourth through the 13th. Early Wynn retired the last 11 batters he faced, and Mossi set down the first 17 to face him.

August 16 Rocky Colavito hits a grand slam off Billy Hoeft in the first inning of a 5–2 win over the Tigers at Municipal Stadium.

With his slugging ability, strong right arm, and good looks, Rocco Domenico Colavito was one of the most popular players ever to wear an Indians uniform.

Hundreds of fans, many of them adoring young women, would gather at the stadium gates after each game for an autograph, and Rocky would patiently oblige them all, a process that sometimes took hours. Steadily improving, he hit 21 homers in 1956, 25 in 1957, 41 in 1958 and 42 in 1959, a season in which the Indians finished a close second. Cleveland fans were outraged when he was traded to the Tigers in 1960 for Harvey Kuenn (see April 17, 1960). It would be more than three decades before the Indians had another pennant-contender. After hitting 173 homers from 1960 through 1964 with the Tigers and Athletics, the Indians re-acquired Colavito for a return engagement in order to placate disgruntled Indians followers, but the transaction was costly as the club lost two young stars in Tommy John and Tommie Agee (see January 20, 1965). Rocky's second tour in Cleveland lasted from 1965 through 1967.

August 21 Herb Score pitches a two-hitter, strikes out 11, and clubs the only home run of his major league career during a 3–0 win over the Yankees in New York. Score had a no-hitter in progress until the eighth inning when Elston Howard doubled. Mickey Mantle added a single in the ninth.

September 3 The Indians score two runs in the ninth inning to defeat the Athletics 2–1 in the second game of a double header in Kansas City. Jim Busby started the rally with a single, stole second, and crossed the plate on a double by Gene Woodling. Early Wynn, who pitched a complete game on two days' rest, drove in the winning run with a one-base hit. Kansas City won the opener 5–2.

September 11 Bob Lemon wins the 200th game of his career with a 3–1 decision over the Orioles at Municipal Stadium.

September 14 Bobby Avila hits a grand slam off Mel Parnell in the eighth inning of a 10–2 victory over the Red Sox in the first game of a double header at Municipal Stadium. Boston won the second tilt 4–3.

After hitting .341 in 1954, Avila's batting average slid all the way to .224 in 1956.

September 18 The Indians win twice with shutouts in a double header against the Senators at Municipal Stadium . In the opener, Herb Score fanned 14 batters for a 1–0 victory. The lone run scored on doubles in the eighth inning by Vic Wertz and Jim Hegan. Mike Garcia hurled a complete game in the second tilt in a 6–0 decision.

September 19 Bob Lemon collects his 20th win of the season with a 6–0 decision over the Senators in Cleveland. The game was stopped by rain in the seventh inning. The contest drew a minuscule crowd of only 365 in massive Municipal Stadium.

September 25 Early Wynn records his 20th win of the season with a ten-inning, 4–1 decision over the Athletics in Cleveland. Preston Ward homered with two out in the ninth to tie the game 1–1. Rocky Colavito ended it with a three-run homer.

September 26 Herb Score becomes Cleveland's third 20-game winner in 1956 with an 8–4 triumph over the Athletics in Cleveland. He struck out 12 batters. Vic Wertz tied a major league record with four consecutive doubles. He also singled and drove in five runs.

September 30 Given a start on the last day of the season, Bob Feller pitches the last game of his major league career. He went nine innings and lost 8–4, allowing 14 hits. Feller officially retired on December 28. During his last season, Feller had an 0–4 record and a 4.97 ERA in 58 innings.

After the game, Al Lopez announced he was resigning as manager of the Indians. Lopez told reporters that his nerves were shot after six years of failing to win a world championship. His record with the Indians was 570–354, a winning percentage of .617. Lopez signed a contract to manage the White Sox four weeks later. In nine full seasons in Chicago, the same pattern of second place finishes continued. He won the AL pennant in 1959, but lost the World Series to the Dodgers. Lopez finished second five times, four of them to the Yankees. Over a 15-year period from 1951 through 1965, his clubs won two American League flags, lost the Fall Classic twice, and landed in second place in the standings ten times.

November 28 Three weeks after Dwight Eisenhower wins a second term as president by defeating Adlai Stevenson, the Indians hire 43-year-old Kerby Farrell as manager.

Before offering Farrell the job, Hank Greenberg tried to persuade Leo Durocher to manage the Indians. Durocher was a major league skipper from 1939 through 1955 with the Dodgers and the Giants. In 1956, Leo worked as a television commentator for NBC and decided to remain with the network. Farrell's playing career was limited to two years as a first baseman during World War II, playing for the Braves in 1943 and the White Sox in 1945. He was a successful minor league manager for ten years in the Indians farm system. The last three were at Class AAA with Indianapolis in the American Association, but Farrell wasn't successful at the big league level. He lasted only one season in Cleveland, posting a 76–77 record in 1957, the first losing season by the franchise in 11 years.

1957

Season in a Sentence

A collapse of the Indians vaunted pitching staff leads to the first losing season since 1946 and the dismissal of Hank Greenberg and Kerby Farrell.

Stats

Stats	Indians	AL	Rank
Batting Avg:	.252	.255	5
On-Base Pct:	.332	.329	4
Slugging Pct:	.382	.382	4
Home Runs:	140		4
Stolen Bases:	40		4
ERA:	4.06	3.79	6
Fielding Avg:	.974	.979	8
Runs Scored:	682		4
Runs Allowed:	722		7

Starting Line-up

Jim Hegan, c
Vic Wertz, 1b
Bobby Avila, 2b
Al Smith, 3b-cf
Chico Carrasquel, ss
Gene Woodling, lf
Roger Maris, cf
Rocky Colavito, rf
Larry Raines, 2b-ss
Dick Williams, cf-3b-lf
George Strickland, 2b-3b
Russ Nixon, c

Pitchers

Early Wynn, sp
Mike Garcia, sp
Don Mossi, sp-rp
Bob Lemon, sp
Ray Narleski, rp-sp
Cal McLish, rp
Bud Daley, rp

Attendance

722,256 (seventh in AL)

Club Leaders

Batting Avg:	Gene Woodling	.321
On-Base Pct:	Gene Woodling	.408
Slugging Pct:	Gene Woodling	.521
Home Runs:	Vic Wertz	28
RBIs:	Vic Wertz	105
Runs:	Vic Wertz	84
Stolen Bases:	Al Smith	12
Wins:	Early Wynn	14
Strikeouts:	Early Wynn	184
ERA:	Ray Narleski	3.09
Saves:	Ray Narleski	16

APRIL 16 The Indians open the season with an 11-inning, 3–2 loss to the White Sox before 31,145 at Municipal Stadium. Herb Score went the distance and struck out ten batter, but he also walked 11. The winning run scored on two walks and a double by Larry Doby.

Bob Neal joined Jimmy Dudley in the radio booth in 1957. Between his stints on television and the radio, Neal broadcast Indians games from 1952 until 1972.

APRIL 18 The Indians score five runs in the 11th inning to defeat the Tigers 8–3 in Detroit. Playing in his second major league game, Roger Maris hit a grand slam off Jack Crimian.

Maris was 22 years old when he made his debut with the Indians as the starting left fielder on Opening Day in 1957. He never clicked in Cleveland, batting .228 with 23 homers in 540 at-bats before a trade to the Athletics (see June 15, 1958).

APRIL 30 Bob Lemon (7⅓ innings) and Ray Narleski (1⅔ innings) combine on a two-hitter to defeat the Senators 5–1 at Municipal Stadium. The Washington hits were singles by Lou Berberet in the fifth inning and Pete Runnels in the sixth.

The Tragic Tale of Herb Score

As Herb Score took the mound for a game against the Yankees at Municipal Stadium on May 7, 1957, he seemed destined to become one of the greatest pitchers of all-time. In the first inning, a line drive off the bat of Yankee infielder Gil McDougald smashed into Score's face. He was never again the same pitcher.

Score reached the Indians as a 21-year-old rookie in 1955. That season, he was 16–10, posted a 2.85 ERA, and struck out a big league-high of 245 batters in 227⅓ innings. Score's 9.7 strikeouts per nine innings easily topped the majors. Second in the category was Bob Turley with 7.7. The Baseball Writers' Association of America elected Score of the AL Rookie of the Year.

He was even better in 1956. Score went 20–9 and led the league with five shutouts and 263 strikeouts in 249⅓ innings. His ERA of 2.53 was second-best in the AL. At the start of the 1957 season, Red Sox owner Tom Yawkey offered the Indians $1 million for Score's contract. The Indians turned him down.

In his first four starts of the season, Score was 2–1 and had a 2.00 earned run average with 39 strikeouts in 36 innings. One of the few problems with Score's game was a frequent inability to control his blazing fastball. He walked 309 batters in the first 512⅓ innings of his career. Also, the delivery that allowed Score to throw the ball past hitters left him in an awkward fielding position.

Making his 12th pitch of the May 7 game, Score didn't see the line drive from McDougald until it was a foot or two from his face. The ball crashed squarely against the bone surrounding the right eye and caught the top of the eyebrow, the cheekbone and the nose. The nose was fractured, and Score bled profusely from the nose and mouth. His face was badly cut, and his eye was hemorrhaging. He never lost consciousness.

Score's middle name was Jude after St. Jude, whose intercession Roman Catholics invoke in "desperate cases." Score's situation fit that description as doctors worked around the clock to save his eyesight. He spent eight days in a Cleveland hospital and in total darkness.

Score didn't pitch again in 1957. He returned in 1958 but was never the same. From that season until the end of his career in 1962, he was 17–26 with an earned run average of 4.42. He spent the 1958 and 1959 seasons with Cleveland, and the next three with the White Sox. According to Score, however, the eye injury "had nothing to do with my losing my effectiveness. The following spring I was pitching as well as I ever did. Then I was pitching in Washington. In the third and fourth inning my arm started to bother me. I didn't say anything. I figured it would work out. These are the mistakes you make when you're young." Given the number of innings that Score pitched between the ages of 20 and 23, which included 251 innings in the minors in 1954, an arm injury isn't surprising. He also ran up large pitch counts because of his high number of walks and strikeouts.

After Score retired as a player, he went into broadcasting. He did play-by-play on the Indians telecasts from 1964 through 1967 and on radio from 1968 through 1997.

MAY 1 Herb Score strikes out 12 batters in 6⅓ innings but allows five runs and earns a no decision in a 7–6 Indians win over the Senators at Municipal Stadium.

MAY 7 Herb Score is struck in the face by a liner in the first inning of a 2–1 win over the Yankees at Municipal Stadium. The drive by Gil McDougald hit Score in the right eye. The Indians pitcher was hit so hard that the ball caromed to third baseman Al Smith. Score's eye was severely damaged, causing a hemorrhage, and his nose was broken. He didn't pitch again for the remainder of the 1957 season and was never again a consistently effective pitcher.

May 15 The Indians win a 16-inning marathon by an 11–8 score against the Orioles in Baltimore. Kerby Farrell used 24 players in the contest. Cleveland scored three times in the top of the 14th, but Baltimore tied the game in the bottom half. The Orioles, however, couldn't answer the Indians three-run salvo in the 16th.

May 20 The Indians sell Art Houtteman to the Orioles.

May 21 Chico Carrasquel hits a grand slam off Dave Sisler in the seventh inning of an 8–2 win over the Red Sox in Boston.

The victory gave the Indians an 18–10 record, but a complete meltdown of the pitching staff sent the club reeling to a 76–77 mark by season's end. Cleveland led the AL in earned run average in 1948, 1949, 1950, 1951, 1954, and 1956 but were sixth in 1957. In 1956, Herb Score, Early Wynn, and Bob Lemon combined for a 60–32 record and an ERA of 2.76. In 1957 Score and Lemon were hampered by injuries (see May 7, 1957) and Wynn was healthy but ineffective. That season, the threesome won 22 times, lost 29 and compiled an earned run average of 4.19.

May 22 Indians pitcher Cal McLish allows four home runs during the sixth inning of an 11–0 loss to the Red Sox in Boston. Gene Mauch and Ted Williams hit the first two, and after Jackie Jensen walked, Dick Gernert and Frank Malzone joined the homer parade. The four homers surrendered by McLish tied a major league record.

McLish's given name was Calvin Coolidge Julius Caesar Tuskahoma McLish. When he made his debut with the Indians in 1956, McLish was 30 years old, possessed an 8–21 lifetime record and a 5.36 ERA in the majors, and had spent the previous four seasons in the minors. After two seasons pitching mostly out of the Cleveland bullpen, McLish posted records of 16–8 with a 2.99 ERA in 1958 and was 19–8 along with compiling an earned run average of 3.63 in 1959 before a trade to the Reds.

May 26 The Indians lose a ten-inning, 1–0 heartbreaker to the White Sox in the first game of a double header at Municipal Stadium. Bud Daley pitched a complete game for Cleveland and contributed to his own defeat. In the tenth, Luis Aparicio singled, reached third on a two-base error by Daley on an attempted pick-off play, and then scored on an infield out. Billy Pierce hurled the shutout for Chicago. The Indians won the second tilt 4–3.

During Daley's birth in 1932, an instrument slipped and pinched a nerve in his right shoulder. The incident caused permanent damage. His right shoulder carried forward slightly and his elbow was twisted awkwardly. Despite the injury, Daley fashioned a ten-year major league career. He played for the Indians from 1955 through 1957.

May 28 A two-run pinch-hit homer by Eddie Robinson in the ninth inning beats the Tigers 4–3 in Detroit.

The homer was the only one that Robinson hit in 1957 and was the last of his career. It came eight days after the Indians re-acquired Robinson following his release by the Tigers. The starting first baseman on the 1948 world champions, Robinson was released by the Indians on June 27.

MAY 29 The Indians score two runs in the ninth inning and four in the tenth to beat the White Sox 8–4 at Comiskey Park. The pair of ninth-inning runs scored on a homer by Vic Wertz.

Wertz hit 28 homers, drove in 105 runs, and batted .282 in 1957.

JUNE 13 Ted Williams hits three home runs during a 9–3 Red Sox win over the Indians at Municipal Stadium. Williams hit two homers off Early Wynn and one facing Bob Lemon.

On the same day, the Indians traded Jim Busby to the Orioles for Dick Williams.

JUNE 25 Rocky Colavito hits a grand slam off Al Cicotte in the ninth inning of an 11–2 win over the Yankees in New York.

During the 1957 season, the Indians had a flowerbed and a waterfall installed at Municipal Stadium between the center field wall and the bleachers.

JULY 12 A two-run, walk-off homer by Gene Woodling in the ninth inning beats the Orioles 8–6 at Municipal Stadium. Cleveland trailed 6–0 before rallying with four runs in the fourth inning and two in the fifth.

Woodling hit .321 with 19 home runs in 1957.

JULY 14 The Indians take two games from the Red Sox by scores of 3–2 and 17–4 in a double header at Municipal Stadium. Cleveland scored two in the ninth to win the opener. Gene Woodling and Vic Wertz each doubled to tie the contest. Hal Naragon won it with a sacrifice fly. In the second tilt, the Indians scored nine runs in the eighth.

JULY 24 The Indians score two runs in the ninth inning to defeat the Senators 4–3 in the first game of a double header at Griffith Stadium. Al Smith drove in the winning run with a sacrifice fly. Smith hit two homers in the nightcap, but Cleveland lost 5–4 when Washington scored three times in the ninth.

AUGUST 15 Chico Carrasquel hits a grand slam off Jack Harshman in the sixth inning to lift the Indians to a 5–4 win over the White Sox at Municipal Stadium. The drive struck the glove of left fielder Minnie Minoso and dropped over the fence.

AUGUST 30 A two-run, walk-off double by Al Smith in the tenth inning defeats the Tigers 6–5 at Municipal Stadium.

SEPTEMBER 13 The Indians bang out 21 hits and defeat the Red Sox 16–3 in Boston. Dick Williams collected four singles and a double in five at-bats.

SEPTEMBER 14 Vic Wertz drives in seven runs in consecutive innings, but the Indians lose 13–10 to the Red Sox in Boston. Wertz hit a grand slam in the first inning off Mike Fornieles, giving the Indians a 4–0 lead before a batter was retired. He added a three-run homer in the second. Both teams scored four runs in both the first and second innings.

September 21 The Indians purchase Hoyt Wilhelm from the Cardinals.

A future Hall of Famer, Wilhelm pitched for the Indians until he was sold to the Orioles in August 1958. In Cleveland, he made six starts and 26 relief appearances and had a 2–8 record, but his ERA was only 2.49.

September 29 The Indians fire Kerby Farrell as manager and replace him with 39-year-old Bobby Bragan.

Farrell never again managed a big league club but remained in baseball until his death in 1975 as a minor league manager and major league coach and scout. Bragan reached the majors as a shortstop with the Phillies in 1940 and left as a catcher with the Dodgers in 1948. After an apprenticeship running clubs in the Dodgers farm system, Bragan managed the Pirates in 1956 and 1957 to a 102–155 record. He lasted less than half a season in a Cleveland uniform. After a 31–36 start in 1958, he was fired.

October 16 In a surprise move, the Indians board of directors vote 10–2 to oust Hank Greenberg as general manager. Greenberg was one of the 13 directors but abstained from voting. He had been the general manager for eight seasons and farm director for two years prior to that. Greenberg also owned 19 percent of the Indians shares, which he retained after being dismissed. Asked for the reason that Greenberg was unseated, President Myron (Mike) Wilson said: "Fan reaction. The fans insisted on it." Pressed for elaboration, Chairman of the Board William Daley said that the board's feeling resulted from criticism of Greenberg in the newspapers and bitter complaints against the general manager by fans who blamed him for everything from not being able to get a good seat at the stadium to the failure to televise more games.

Attendance had fallen to 722,256 in 1957, second lowest in the American League and the poorest draw in Cleveland since 1945. Greenberg was also actively seeking to move the Indians to Minneapolis (see August 13, 1956), rankling many members of the board, which consisted mostly of Cleveland residents. Greenberg's eight years as general manager were always controversial. The club had a record of 738–493 during his tenure, a winning percentage of .600 but won only one American League pennant and failed to win a World Series. He made many more poor trades than successful ones. However, he did a great job of building a farm system. The club had plenty of young talent in 1957. Among those in the organization who were 25 or younger on December 31, 1957, included Hank Aguirre, Gary Bell, Dick Brown, Rocky Colavito, Gordy Coleman, Bud Daley, Gary Geiger, Mudcat Grant, Roger Maris, Billy Moran, Russ Nixon, Jim Perry, Herb Score, and Hal Woodeshick. Unfortunately, Greenberg's successors traded most of these players before they had their greatest success in the majors. As a minority investor and member of the board of directors, Greenberg declared that baseball "was dead in Cleveland" during the 1958 season and continued to urge that the club be moved to Minnesota. He and two other dissident board members were bought out in November 1958. After Bill Veeck bought the White Sox in March 1959, Greenberg served as an executive with the Chicago club. It was Veeck who brought Greenberg to Cleveland in 1948.

November 12 The Indians hire Frank Lane as general manager.

During the weeks following the dismissal of Hank Greenberg as general manager, the Indians board of directors met with Bill DeWitt about coming to Cleveland. DeWitt had previously owned the St. Louis Browns and was the president of the Tigers. At the same time, Frank Lane was on his way out as general manager of the Cardinals and applied for the job heading the Indians front office. The club's directors jumped at the chance to hire Lane. Born on December 1, 1896, Lane got into baseball rather late in life. In 1933, Reds president Larry MacPhail hired him as business manager. Lane served in the Navy during World War II, and then followed MacPhail to New York when Larry bought the Yankees. Lane was president of the American Association when hired as general manager of the White Sox at the end of the 1948 season. Through a series of brilliant trades, Lane took over one of the worst franchises in baseball and turned it into a winner. But in 1955, after the Sox finished third for the fourth year in a row Lane resigned after a series of disagreements with club vice-president Chuck Comiskey. Lane was hired immediately by the Cardinals. He again turned a loser into a winner as the Cards rose to second in 1957, but Lane couldn't get along with owner August Busch, Jr., who had no problem letting Lane leave for Cleveland. With the Indians, Lane followed his pattern. After frantically overturning the roster, he brought the Indians from sixth place in 1957 to second in 1959 but couldn't put the club over the top. He inherited a core of young talent from Hank Greenberg (see October 16, 1957), but didn't have the patience for long-term development schemes. Just before the start of the 1960 season, Lane committed the unpardonable sin of trading fan favorite Rocky Colavito (see April 17, 1960). At the end of the 1960 campaign, after a fall to fourth place, Lane's three-year contract was not renewed.

December 4 — The Indians trade Early Wynn and Al Smith to the White Sox for Minnie Minoso and Fred Hatfield.

Frank Lane jump-started the White Sox in 1951 by trading for Minoso (see April 30, 1951). The new general manager hoped to do the same for the Indians by bringing Minoso back to Cleveland. Lane surmised that Wynn was finished after he posted a 14–17 record and a 4.31 ERA in 1957 at the age of 37. His career was far from over, however. Wynn had a 22–10 record for the White Sox in 1959, a year in which Chicago finished in first place five games ahead of Cleveland in the pennant race. The deal may have cost the Indians the pennant that season, but the club received some value in the deal, as Minoso gave the club two excellent seasons.

1958

Season in a Sentence

Frank Lane turns over most of the roster and changes managers, but the club fails to improve as attendance continues to slide amid rumors that the Indians would be moved to Minneapolis.

Finish • Won • Lost • Pct • GB

Finish	Won	Lost	Pct	GB
Fourth	77	76	.503	14.5

Managers

Bobby Bragan (31–36) and Joe Gordon (46–40)

Stats

Stats	Indians	AL	Rank
Batting Avg:	.258	.254	3
On-Base Pct:	.327	.325	5
Slugging Pct:	.403	.383	2
Home Runs:	161		2
Stolen Bases:	50		2
ERA:	3.73		5
Fielding Avg:	.974	.979	8
Runs Scored:	694		3
Runs Allowed:	635		5

Starting Line-up

Russ Nixon, c
Mickey Vernon, 1b
Bobby Avila, 2b
Vic Power, 3b-1b-2b
Billy Harrell, ss-3b
Minnie Minoso, lf
Larry Doby, cf
Rocky Colavito, rf
Billy Moran, 2b-3b
Gary Geiger, cf
Billy Hunter, ss
Roger Maris, cf-rf
Dick Brown, c
Chico Carrasquel, ss
Preston Ward, 3b-1b
Woodie Held, cf

Pitchers

Cal McLish, sp
Ray Narleski, sp-rp
Gary Bell, sp-rp
Mudcat Grant, sp-rp
Don Mossi, rp
Hoyt Wilhelm, rp
Don Ferrarese, rp-sp

Attendance

663,805 (seventh in AL)

Club Leaders

Batting Avg:	Rocky Colavito	.303
On-Base Pct:	Rocky Colavito	.405
Slugging Pct:	Rocky Colavito	.620
Home Runs:	Rocky Colavito	41
RBIs:	Rocky Colavito	113
Runs:	Minnie Minoso	94
Stolen Bases:	Minnie Minoso	14
Wins:	Cal McLish	16
Strikeouts:	Mudcat Grant	111
ERA:	Cal McLish	2.99
Saves:	Hoyt Wilhelm	5

JANUARY 29 A month after the Browns win the NFL championship by trouncing the Lions 59–14 in Detroit, the Indians purchase Mickey Vernon from the Red Sox.

FEBRUARY 18 The Indians trade Hank Aguirre and Jim Hegan to the Tigers for Hal Woodeshick and J. W. Porter.

The trade ended the Indians career of Hegan, who joined the club in 1941. Hegan was near the end of his career and the Indians had better, and much younger, options at catcher in Russ Nixon and Dick Brown, but Aguirre proved to be a big loss. He was still pitching in the majors until 1970 and led the AL in ERA in 1962. Both Woodeshick and Porter lasted only a year in Cleveland.

MARCH 30 Vic Wertz breaks his ankle sliding into second base during a 12–10 loss to the San Francisco Giants in Tucson.

APRIL 1 The Indians trade Bud Daley, Gene Woodling, and Dick Williams to the Orioles for Larry Doby and Don Ferrarese.

April 15 The Indians lose 5–0 to the Athletics before an Opening Day crowd of 35,307 in Cleveland. Herb Score, pitching in his first game since being struck in the face by a batted ball (see May 7, 1957), allowed three runs in three innings.

Bill McColgan joined Ken Coleman in the TV booth in 1958. McColgan replaced Jim Britt.

April 17 Mickey Vernon hits a two-run, pinch-hit, walk-off double with two out in the ninth to defeat the Athletics 3–2 in Cleveland.

In 1958, fans yelled "taxi" whenever an opposing pitcher got himself into trouble because the Indians used taxicabs to transport pitchers from the bullpen to the mound. Previously, the club utilized jeeps and convertibles. The taxis were put back into the garage after one season. In 1959, the Indians used station wagons to carry the relief pitchers. Each Friday night, one of the station wagons was presented to a lucky ticket holder.

April 20 The Indians use solo homers from Roger Maris, Rocky Colavito, Minnie Minoso, and Dick Brown to provide the runs necessary for a 4–2 win over the Tigers in Detroit.

Colavito became a major star in 1958. His .620 slugging percentage led the American League. Rocky also batted .303 with 41 home runs and 113 RBIs.

April 25 The Indians coast to a 12–2 win over the Tigers at Municipal Stadium. Mickey Vernon hit a grand slam off Jim Bunning in the third inning.

There were new uniforms for the Indians in 1958. The name "Indians" was presented in red capital letters outlined in blue and pinstripes were added. The Chief Wahoo symbol inside the letter "C" on the cap was removed, but remained on the left sleeve.

May 14 Trailing 6–4, the Indians score five runs in the top of the ninth inning, then survive a Tigers rally in the bottom half to win 9–8 in Detroit. Ray Boone's failure to note that Cleveland first baseman Mickey Vernon dropped a throw set the stage for a zany wind-up to the game. With two out and runners on second and third base, Boone rifled a shot to the mound, where Mudcat Grant, after being momentarily stunned by the blow, picked up the ball and threw to Vernon. Boone, seeing the ball arrive ahead of him, did not see Vernon drop the ball and fired his helmet toward right field as the two runners crossed the plate. While teammates on the bench yelled at him, Boone went to retrieve the helmet, and after discovering that Vernon had erred on the play, tried to go to second base and was tagged out.

May 16 Acting as a pinch-hitter for Roger Maris, Carroll Hardy hits a three-run, walk-off homer in the 11th inning to defeat the White Sox 7–4 in the first game of a double header at Municipal Stadium. Confusion over an umpire's signal led Hardy to believe the drive was foul, and he returned to the plate before being waved around the bases. Chicago manager Al Lopez angrily argued with the umpires over the call.

The homer was Hardy's first in the majors. Although a .225 batter in 433 big league games, Hardy was a pinch-hitter for the stars. In addition to hitting for

Maris, Hardy pinch-hit for Ted Williams in 1960 and Carl Yastrzemski in 1961 while with the Red Sox. Hardy also played halfback for the San Francisco 49ers in 1955 and scored four touchdowns.

MAY 21 Minnie Minoso hits a walk-off home run in the 12th inning to defeat the Red Sox 3–2 at Municipal Stadium. Dick Tomanek pitched a complete game for the Indians, allowing only five hits.

Minoso hit .303 with 24 homers and 94 runs scored in 1958.

MAY 27 The Indians score two runs in the ninth inning and one in the tenth to win 7–6 over the Orioles at Municipal Stadium. J. W. Porter's homer tied the score. The winning run scored on a bases loaded walk to Mickey Vernon by Billy O'Dell.

JUNE 8 The Indians sweep the Yankees 14–1 and 5–4 in New York.

JUNE 12 The Indians trade Chico Carrasquel to the Athletics for Billy Hunter.

Hunter was a weak-hitting but slick fielding shortstop who hit .195 in 76 games for the Indians. During a six-year career with four franchises, he batted .219 in 1,875 big league at-bats.

JUNE 15 The Indians trade Roger Maris, Preston Ward, and Dick Tomanek to the Athletics for Vic Power and Woodie Held.

Maris spent a season and a half in Kansas City before being dealt to the Yankees, where he was the American League MVP in both 1960 and 1961. He hit 61 home runs in 1961, breaking Babe Ruth's record of 60 set in 1927. Maris held the record until Mark McGwire clubbed 70 in 1998. In addition, Roger played in seven World Series with the Yankees and the Cardinals. Fortunately, the Indians received some value for Maris. Both Power and Held became regulars. Flamboyant and controversial, Power was a starter at first base until he was traded to the Twins in April 1962 and was named to two All-Star teams and won four Gold Gloves with the Indians. In 1960, he attempted to charge into the stands behind the Indians dugout to retaliate against Ohio State football coach Woody Hayes, who was heckling Power for "showboating." Held was a versatile and underrated player who appeared in 853 games for Cleveland over seven seasons.

JUNE 22 The Indians win two from the Senators 4–3 and 1–0 at Municipal Stadium. Minnie Minoso provided the lone run in game two with a home run off Chuck Stobbs. Mudcat Grant pitched the shutout.

James (Mudcat) Grant received his nickname from a minor league teammate who mistakenly believed that the Florida-born Grant hailed from Mississippi, which is sometimes called the "Mudcat State." In seven seasons with the Indians, he had a record of 67–63.

JUNE 26 Joe Gordon replaces Bobby Bragan as manager.

Bragan was hired at the end of the 1957 season before Frank Lane was given a contract as general manager. Bragan and Lane failed to agree on much of anything, leading to Bragan's dismissal with the club holding a record of 31–36. In informing Bragan he was being fired, Lane told the outgoing manager: "I don't know how we're going to get along without you, but starting tomorrow we're going to try." Bragan later managed the Braves from 1963 through 1966. Gordon was a star season baseman in the American League with the Yankees and Indians from 1938 through 1943 and after two year in the Armed Forces, again from 1946 through 1950. He played in five World Series, and on four world champions, including one with the Indians in 1948. Between 1951 and 1957, Gordon managed in the minors and coached for the Tigers. Despite a tempestuous relationship with Lane (see September 18, 1959), Gordon led Cleveland to a second place finish in 1959. He was traded to the Tigers in a bizarre transaction the following season (see August 3, 1960).

JULY 2 Bob Lemon is released by the Indians.

Lemon won 20 games in 1956, but was hampered by bone chips in his elbow, was 6–12 with a 4.73 ERA in 1957 and 1958 combined. During the 1970s and 1980s, he managed the Royals, White Sox, and Yankees, winning a world championship with the New York club in 1978.

JULY 12 Vic Power collects five hits in six at-bats during a 12–2 win over the Yankees in New York. The Indians broke a 1–1 tie with seven runs in the eighth inning, and added four more in the ninth.

JULY 20 Indians catcher J. W. Porter uses a first baseman's glove to try to corral Hoyt Wilhelm's knuckleball during a ten-inning, 3–2 loss to the Orioles in Baltimore.

JULY 27 Rocky Colavito hits a grand slam off Bob Turley in the sixth inning of a 7–2 win over the Yankees in the second game of a double header at Municipal Stadium. Colavito also homered in the opener, won by the Indians by the same 7–2 score.

JULY 28 Rocky Colavito pitches two innings of an exhibition game against the Reds in Cincinnati. Colavito allowed one run and two hits and struck out five during a 4–3 loss (see August 13, 1958).

AUGUST 1 The Indians collect only two hits, but win 3–1 over the Red Sox in the second game of a double header at Municipal Stadium. Rocky Colavito broke a 1–1 tie with a two-run homer off Dave Sisler in the seventh inning. In the opener, all seven runs of a 7–1 win scored in the sixth inning.

AUGUST 4 The Indians purchase Randy Jackson from the Dodgers.

Jackson was a college football star at Texas Christian University and played in the 1945 and 1946 Cotton Bowls. He was one of 13 third basemen tried out by the Indians in 1958. The 13 were Billy Harrell (45 games), Vic Power (42), Bobby Avila (33), Jackson (24), Preston Ward (24), Earl Averill (17), Chico Carrasquel (14), Woodie Held (four), Gary Geiger (two), Fred Hatfield (two), Billy Hunter (two), Minnie Minoso (one) and J. W. Porter (one).

August 13 Rocky Colavito pitches the last three innings of a 3–2 loss to the Tigers in the second game of a double header at Municipal Stadium. Colavito allowed no runs, no hits, and three walks, striking out one.

The Indians were intrigued by the notion of using Colavito's powerful right arm as a late-inning reliever, bringing him in from right field to snuff out a late-inning rally. Risk of injury and the lack of a proper warm-up put an end to the idea. Radar guns didn't come into use until the 1970s, but many scouts believed that Rocky's fastball traveled close to 100 miles per hour. He pitched only one more regular season game after August 13, 1958, while with the Yankees in 1968.

August 14 Vic Power steals home twice during a ten-inning, 10–9 win over the Tigers at Municipal Stadium. Power's first theft of home occurred in the eighth inning with Bill Fischer as the pitcher and Charlie Lau as the catcher. With the score 9–9 in the tenth and Frank Lary on the mound, Power singled with one out and reached third on another single and a walk. Rocky Colavito was at bat when Power, after dancing up and down the base line, suddenly broke for home in a successful steal that provided the winning run.

Power is one of only 11 players in major league history to steal home twice in one game and is the only one to accomplish the feat since 1924. Oddly the steals on August 14 were the only two that Power recorded in 93 games for the Indians in 1958. He had a total of three stolen bases during the season, the other coming as a member of the Athletics.

August 22 Bobby Avila is the victim of a freak accident during a 4–3 loss to the Red Sox at Fenway Park. Batting in the first inning, Avila fouled off a pitch that struck a pole along the facing of the grandstand behind home plate. The ball rebounded and struck Avila on the back of the head. He remained in the game.

August 23 The Indians sell Hoyt Wilhelm to the Orioles.

The Indians dealt Wilhelm when he was 35 years old. At that advanced age, he didn't seem to have a bright future, but a month after leaving Cleveland, he used his knuckleball to hurl a no-hitter for the Orioles. Wilhelm led the American League in earned run average in 1959 and pitched until 1972 when he was 49. Following the sale of his contract by the Indians, Wilhelm pitched 1,497⅓ innings, most of them as a reliever, and had an ERA of 2.28. He was elected to the Hall of Fame in 1985.

August 26 Don Ferrarese suffers a tough 12-inning, 1–0 loss to the Orioles in Baltimore. Through the first 11 innings, he allowed only four hits. In the 12th, two walks and two singles produced the winning run. Hal Brown threw the shutout for the Orioles.

August 30 A two-run homer by Larry Doby in the 14th inning beats the Athletics 8–6 in Kansas City. Doby also homered in the eighth.

August 31 The Indians win on an extra-inning home run for the second day in a row when Minnie Minoso smacks a pitch over the wall for a 3–2 victory over the Athletics in Kansas City.

SEPTEMBER 9 The Indians score eight runs in the fifth inning for a 9–2 lead over the Yankees at Municipal Stadium before the game is called by rain at the end of the fifth.

SEPTEMBER 10 A crowd of 50,021 turns out at Municipal Stadium on a Wednesday for an 8–3 loss to the Yankees on "Back the Indians Night." It was promoted by a civic committee of leading politicians and businessmen in an attempt to keep the Indians in Cleveland.

An Indians fan's favorite sight in the late 1950s—Rocky Colavito taking a big swing. In 1958 he produced his breakout year, leading the majors in slugging percentage.

The Indians drew only 663,805 fans in 1958. It was the lowest figure since 1945, the fourth year in a row that attendance had declined, and it represented precipitous drop from the figures of 2,620,627 in 1948 and 1,335,472 in 1954. Rumors had been swirling since 1956 that the team was headed for Minneapolis. In May 1958, Indians board chairman William Daley declared that it could be the club's last year in Cleveland. He said he had just about reached the conclusion that Clevelanders would not support the team. Later it was revealed that the directors received several attractive offers. One was for nearly $6,000,000 from a group called Houston Sports Association that intended to *move the Indians to the Texas city. This was about two million dollars more than Daley paid for the Indians in 1956 (see February 29, 1956). Bill Veeck came close to buying the Indians again but reasoned that it would be impossible to "recapture the rapture" that the Indians enjoyed a decade earlier. Veeck instead purchased the White Sox in March 1959. On October 15, 1958, Daley ended the conjecture about the club's immediate future by announcing that he had rejected all bids and that the Indians would remain in Cleveland.*

SEPTEMBER 12 Rocky Colavito hits a grand slam off Murray Wall in the seventh inning of a 5–4 win over the Red Sox at Municipal Stadium.

SEPTEMBER 16 Gary Bell pitches a two-hitter to defeat the Senators 5–1 at Municipal Stadium. The only Washington hits were singles by Herb Plews in the first inning and Bob Allison in the ninth.

Bell played under seven different managers with the Indians from 1958 through 1967, compiling a record of 96–92.

SEPTEMBER 23 Down 5–0, the Indians score one run in the fifth inning, two in the seventh, one in the eighth and three in the ninth to win 7–5 over the Athletics in Cleveland. Randy Jackson hit a three-run homer in the ninth.

NOVEMBER 20 The Indians trade Don Mossi, Ray Narleski, and Ossie Alvarez to the Tigers for Billy Martin and Al Cicotte.

"He's the kind of guy you'd like to kill if he's playing for the other team," said Frank Lane upon acquiring Martin, "but you'd like ten of him on your side." Playing second base, Martin was the spark plug on six Yankee teams that reached the World Series. He was traded by the Yanks to the Athletics in May 1957 shortly after getting into a fight with a patron at New York's Copacabana nightclub. The A's swapped Martin to the Tigers during the 1957–58 off-season. Martin played only one injury-marred season with the Indians. In 1959, a shoulder injury in June sidelined him for three weeks, and then on August 5, his jaw and cheekbone were broken when he was hit by a pitch by Washington's Tex Clevenger. Ray Narleski was about finished as an effective pitcher, but Don Mossi still had some good years ahead of him. Mossi was 15–7 for Detroit in 1959, won 17 games in 1961, and lasted in the majors until 1965.

DECEMBER 2 The Indians send Bobby Avila to the Orioles for Russ Heman and $30,000. On the same day, the Indians swapped Vic Wertz and Gary Geiger to the Red Sox for Jimmy Piersall.

Playing for the Red Sox as a rookie in 1952, Piersall suffered a nervous breakdown and landed in a mental hospital. He returned to the playing field in 1953 as Boston's starting right fielder. Piersall's battle with mental illness was chronicled in his book Fear Strikes Out, *which was made into a movie in 1957. He played three controversial seasons with the Indians from 1959 through 1961. Many of the players acquired by Frank Lane since he took over as general manager in November 1957 were brought to Cleveland as much for their box office appeal as their on-field performance as the Indians were trying to boost attendance at Municipal Stadium. The 1959 club included such entertaining players as Rocky Colavito, Mudcat Grant, Billy Martin, Minnie Minoso, Piersall, and Vic Power.*

1959

Season in a Sentence

With a colorful cast of characters, the Indians are surprise pennant contenders and spend 90 days in first place, but finish second to the White Sox.

Finish	Won	Lost	Pct	GB
Second	89	65	.578	5.0

Manager

Joe Gordon

Stats	Indians	AL	Rank
Batting Avg:	.263	.253	1
On-Base Pct:	.323	.326	5
Slugging Pct:	.408	.384	1
Home Runs:	167		1
Stolen Bases:	33		8
ERA:	3.75	3.86	4
Fielding Avg:	.978	.977	3
Runs Scored:	745		1
Runs Allowed:	646		3

Starting Line-up

Russ Nixon, c
Vic Power, 1b
Billy Martin, 2b
George Strickland, 3b-ss
Woodie Held, ss-3b
Minnie Minoso, lf
Tito Francona, cf-1b
Rocky Colavito, rf
Jimmy Piersall, cf
Jim Baxes, 2b-3b

Pitchers

Cal McLish, sp
Gary Bell, sp-rp
Mudcat Grant, sp-rp
Herb Score, sp
Don Ferrarese, sp-rp
Jim Perry, rp-sp
Al Cicotte, rp

Attendance

1,497,976 (second in AL)

Club Leaders

Batting Avg:	Tito Francona	.363
On-Base Pct:	Tito Francona	.414
Slugging Pct:	Tito Francona	.566
Home Runs:	Rocky Colavito	42
RBIs:	Rocky Colavito	111
Runs:	Vic Power	102
Stolen Bases:	Minnie Minoso	8
Wins:	Cal McLish	19
Strikeouts:	Herb Score	147
ERA:	Cal McLish	3.63
Saves:	Gary Bell	5
	Dick Brodowski	5

MARCH 21 Two months after Alaska is admitted as the 49th state, the Indians trade Larry Doby to the Tigers for Tito Francona.

The Indians pulled off a terrific deal. Doby was 35 and played in only 39 more big league games. Francona came to the Indians as a 25-year-old with a .250 career average and 17 homers in 921 at-bats. After sitting on the bench for most of the first two months of the 1959 season, Francona finally got a chance to play and hit .363 with 20 homers and 79 RBIs in 399 at-bats, and played for the club until 1964. Tito's son Terry played for the Indians in 1989.

APRIL 10 In the opener, the Indians defeat the Athletics 6–4 in Kansas City. Gary Bell was the winning pitcher. George Strickland collected three hits in four at-bats.

APRIL 11 The Indians trade Mickey Vernon to the Braves for Humberto Robinson.

April 14 In the home opener, the Indians win 8–1 over the Tigers before 33,098 at Municipal Stadium. Herb Score pitched a complete game. Woodie Held hit two homers, and Minnie Minoso and George Strickland each added one. One of Held's homers was a grand slam off Ray Narleski in the eighth inning.

April 15 Woodie Held hits a two-out, walk-off homer off Ray Narleski in the tenth inning to beat the Tigers 2–1 at Municipal Stadium.

Held hit .251 with 29 homers in 1959. He started the season as the regular third baseman but switched to shortstop in June.

April 18 The Indians run their season record to 6–0 with a 13–4 win over the Athletics at Municipal Stadium.

The Indians lost their next game, and then won four in a row to run their record to 10–1.

April 21 Minnie Minoso collects two homers and three singles in five at-bats and drives in six runs during a 14–1 battering of the Tigers in Detroit.

Minoso hit .302 with 21 homers and 92 RBIs in 1959.

May 1 With the Indians behind 2–1, Tito Francona hits a three-run, pinch-hit walk-off homer to defeat the Yankees 4–2 at Municipal Stadium.

May 2 Herb Score strikes out 13 batters during a 5–2 win over the Yankees at Municipal Stadium.

May 3 Mudcat Grant pitches a two-hitter to defeat the Senators 5–0 in the first game of a double header at Municipal Stadium. The only Washington hits were a double by Julio Becquer in the first inning and a single by Bob Allison in the third. The Senators won the second tilt 3–1.

An action-packed brawl marred the first game. In the seventh inning, Pedro Ramos threw a high inside pitch to Jimmy Piersall, who started for the mound, setting off a general melee as players from both dugouts rushed onto the field. The umpires stepped between the Piersall and Ramos and peace seemed to be restored when Joe Gordon and Ramos had words. The Senators hurler threw a punch at the Indians manager with the ball still in his hand. Piersall rushed in and threw a punch at Ramos that accidentally struck Washington's Julio Becquer. A mob of Senators immediately went after Piersall. The battle spread into individual fights all over the field. Several players on both clubs needed medical attention for spike wounds.

May 5 Don Ferrarese carries a no-hitter into the seventh inning before settling for a four-hit, 9–1 win over the Orioles at Municipal Stadium. The first Baltimore hit was a home run by Bob Nieman.

May 22 The Indians collect only two hits off Paul Foytack, but defeat the Tigers 1–0 at Municipal Stadium. The only Cleveland hits were doubles by in the seventh inning by Minnie Minoso and Vic Power, which produced the lone run of the contest.

Power hit .289 with ten homers and 102 runs scored in 1959.

MAY 26 Don Ferrarese pitches $6^{2}/_{3}$ shutout innings and collects three doubles in three at-bats to lead the Indians to a 3–0 win over the White Sox at Chicago.

JUNE 6 The Indians send Jim Bolger and cash to the Phillies for Willie Jones.

JUNE 10 Rocky Colavito ties a major league record with four consecutive home runs during an 11–8 win over the Orioles in Baltimore. Colavito walked his first trip to the plate and homered in the third, fifth, sixth, and ninth innings. Jerry Walker was the victim of the first blow, Arnie Portocarrero the next two, and Ernie Johnson the last one. Colavito drove in six runs. Minnie Minoso and Billy Martin also homered for Cleveland. Rocky hit the four homers in a tough environment. There were 103 homers struck at Memorial Stadium in 1959, the fewest of any ballpark in the American League.

There have been only 15 players in major league history with four homers in a game, and six of those hit them in consecutive at-bats. Colavito is the only Indians batter with a four-homer game. During the 1959 season, he led the AL in homers with 42. He also drove in 111 runs and batted .257.

JUNE 13 Rocky Colavito hits a grand slam off Tex Clevenger in the sixth inning of an 8–7 win over the Senators in Washington.

JUNE 14 Minnie Minoso drives in nine runs during a 9–5 and 12–6 sweep of the Senators during a double header in Washington. He drove in four in the opener on two singles, a double and a homer. Minoso accounted for five RBIs in the second contest, four of them with a grand slam off Tex Clevenger in the ninth inning. It was the second day in a row that Clevenger allowed a grand slam to a Cleveland hitter.

JUNE 21 The Indians sweep the Yankees 4–2 and 5–4 in New York. The second game went 14 innings with Vic Power providing the winning run with a home run.

JUNE 28 Herb Score pitches a two-hitter to defeat the Red Sox 1–0 in the second game of a double header at Municipal Stadium. Jim Baxes accounted for the lone run with a homer off Ted Wills in the seventh inning. The only Boston hits were a double by Wills in the third inning and a single by Bobby Avila in the fifth. Cleveland also won the first tilt 5–4.

Baxes was a 30-year-old rookie infielder in 1959. He hit .239 with 15 homers in 247 at-bats for Cleveland in what proved to be the only season of his big league career.

JULY 1 The Indians sell Willie Jones to the Reds.

JULY 3 After giving up a grand slam to Bob Cerv in the first inning before a batter is retired, Herb Score settles down and strikes out 14 batters during an 8–4 win over the Athletics in Kansas City.

JULY 4 Home runs by Tito Francona and Jim Baxes in the 11th inning produce three runs for a 12–9 win over the Tigers in the second game of a double header in Detroit. Cleveland also won the opener 6–1.

July 7 At Forbes Field in Pittsburgh, Vic Power drives in a run with a single in the eighth inning, but the American League loses 5–4 in the first of two All-Star Game played in 1959.

There were two All-Star Game played each season from 1959 through 1962.

July 17 Minnie Minoso and Joe Gordon raise a ruckus during an 8–7 win over the Red Sox at Fenway Park. With the Indians leading 8–4 in the eighth inning, umpire Jim Honochick ruled that Vic Power interfered with Boston second baseman Herb Plews while Power ran from first base to second. Gordon bolted out of the dugout and was ejected for arguing the call. After one pitch to Minnie Minoso, Gordon reappeared and resumed his tirade with the arbiters. Minoso stepped out of the batter's box. Umpire Frank Umont ordered Minoso back to the plate, but he refused. Umont then told Red Sox reliever Leo Kiely to deliver the ball to the plate. Kiely threw two pitches that Umont called strikes while Minoso was 15 feet from the plate. Minoso tossed a tantrum and flung his bat, which narrowly missed Umont. Minnie raced right at Umont but was grabbed by Rocky Colavito and Cleveland coaches. Minoso was ejected for the indiscretion.

Gordon and Minoso were both fined $200 and suspended for three days by AL president Joe Cronin.

July 23 Trailing 4–0, the Indians score seven runs in the sixth inning and win 8–5 over the Yankees at Municipal Stadium. The last four runs of the big inning scored on a grand slam by Minnie Minoso off Eli Grba.

July 26 The Indians move into first place with a 9–0 and 5–4 sweep of the Senators at Municipal Stadium. Jim Perry pitched a two-hitter in the opener. The only Washington hits were a single by Gene Green in the fourth inning and a double by Julio Becquer in the ninth. The second game went 12 innings. The winning run scored on a double by Minnie Minoso and a single from Jim Baxes.

Lesser known than his brother Gaylord, Jim Perry had a fine career of his own with a 215–174 record in 17 years. He pitched for the Indians from his rookie year in 1959 through 1963, and again in 1974 and 1975. With Cleveland, Perry was 70–67. During his last two seasons with the Indians, he was a teammate with his younger brother Gaylord, who also won 70 games with the club from 1972 through 1975.

July 28 The Indians drop out of first place with a double header split against the Red Sox at Municipal Stadium. Cleveland won the opener 5–4 but lost the nightcap 8–4.

The Indians failed to regain the top spot in the American League in 1959 but remained in contention for the pennant until mid-September.

July 30 Minnie Minoso drives in all of the Indians runs during a 4–3 win over the Red Sox at Municipal Stadium. Minoso delivered a two-run single in the third inning, a single in the fifth, and a walk-off single in the ninth.

On the same day, the Indians purchased Jack Harshman from the Red Sox.

August 2 A three-run, walk-off homer by Tito Francona defeats the Orioles 6–3 in the second game of a double header at Municipal Stadium. Baltimore won the opener 5–4 in ten innings.

The Indians drew 1,497,978 fans in 1959, more than double the 1958 total of 683,805. The increase was helped by a promotional tie-in with the Fisher Brothers food chain, which operated 85 stores in northern Ohio. Register tapes totaling $50 could be exchanged for a voucher that could be exchanged for a $1.75 reserved seat. Over 350,000 of the vouchers were turned in at the stadium box office. The Indians didn't draw over one million fans again until 1974.

August 3 At Memorial Coliseum in Los Angeles, Rocky Colavito lofts a home run off Roy Face in the eighth inning of the second All-Star Game of 1959, helping the American League to a 5–3 victory.

August 22 The day after Hawaii is admitted as the 50th state in the Union, Woodie Held hits a grand slam off Milt Pappas to account for all of the runs of a 4–2 win over the Orioles at Municipal Stadium.

August 23 A walk-off homer by Tito Francona off Tom Brewer provides the only run of a 1–0 win over the Red Sox at Municipal Stadium. Jim Perry pitched the shutout. Francona also homered in the first inning of the second game, a 6–2 Cleveland win.

The Indians went into a four-game series against the White Sox in Cleveland on August 28 just 1½ games out of first place.

August 28 The Indians lose the opening game of the pennant-showdown against the White Sox 7–3 before 70,398 at Municipal Stadium.

August 30 The White Sox complete a four-game sweep of the Indians by winning 6–3 and 9–4 in a double header at Municipal Stadium before 66,586.

The White Sox left Cleveland with a 5½-game lead. The Indians cut the advantage to two games on September 20 but could draw no closer. During the 1959 season, the Indians were 7–15 against the White Sox.

September 6 A two-run double by Vic Power in the ninth inning defeats the White Sox 2–1 in Chicago.

September 7 The Indians win a thrilling 15–14 decision over the Tigers in the first game of a double header at Municipal Stadium. Trailing 12–4, the Indians scored five runs in the fifth inning and three in the sixth to deadlock the contest 12–12. Detroit plated two in the seventh to lead 14–12, but the Tribe bounced back with three in the ninth for the win. The last two runs scored on a single by Jimmy Piersall. Another three-run rally in the ninth won the second tilt 6–5. Vic Power ended the contest with a sacrifice fly.

September 13 The Indians pennant hopes are dealt a crushing blow with a double header loss to the Yankees in New York. Cleveland lost the opener 2–1 in 11 innings and the second encounter 1–0.

September 18 Joe Gordon resigns as manager of the Indians.

A feud broke out between Gordon and general manager Frank Lane late in the season. Irked by Lane's public criticism of his strategy, Gordon announced on September 18 that he would not be returning in 1960, regardless of whether or not Cleveland won the 1959 pennant. The following day, Lane went to Pittsburgh to sound out Leo Durocher, who earlier had disclosed that he was giving up his position as a television commentator for NBC at the close of the season. At the same time, Lane said that Gordon would be relieved of his duties as manager as soon as the Indians were mathematically eliminated from the pennant race. That took place on September 22. Lane said that Gordon was through "as of now" and that coach Mel Harder would handle the reins for the remainder of the season. However, the next day, Lane apparently disenchanted by Durocher's reported demand for a better financial package to manage the Indians, did an about-face. Calling a press conference on September 23 to announce the new manager for the 1960 season, Lane stunned everyone by introducing Gordon. Smoothing over his differences with Lane, Joe signed a two-year contract through 1961.

SEPTEMBER 19 The Indians clobber the Athletics 13–7 in Kansas City.

SEPTEMBER 25 The Indians score three runs in the ninth inning to defeat the Athletics 8–7 in the second game of a double header in Cleveland. The Indians trailed 7–1 before scoring four times in the sixth to set-up the game-winning rally.

DECEMBER 6 The Indians trade Minnie Minoso, Dick Brown, Don Ferrarese, and Jake Striker to the White Sox for Johnny Romano, Bubba Phillips, and Norm Cash.

This could have been one of the greatest trades in Indians history if the Indians had kept Cash (see April 12, 1960). As it was, it was still a good deal for Cleveland. Minoso gave the White Sox two fine seasons but was near the end of the line. Romano was the club's starting catcher for five seasons and made the All-Star team in 1961 and 1962. During both of those seasons, he topped the 20-home run, 80-RBI mark before a hand injury caused a steep decline in his batting numbers. Phillips was Cleveland's starting third baseman for three years.

DECEMBER 15 The Indians trade Cal McLish, Billy Martin, and Gordy Coleman to the Reds for Johnny Temple.

The Indians hoped that Temple would fill a gaping hole at second base. He made the All-Star team for the third time in 1959, batting .311, but never came close to reaching those numbers for Cleveland. McLish had five more seasons as a back-of-the-rotation pitcher. A first baseman, Coleman hit 26 homers for Cincinnati in 1961 and 28 more in 1962. Martin lasted only two more seasons in the majors as a player. In 1969, he began his tempestuous and volatile managerial career. Before his death in an auto accident on Christmas Day in 1989, Martin managed the Twins, Tigers, Rangers, Athletics, and Yankees.

THE STATE OF THE INDIANS

The Indians failed to field a contending team during the 1960s, a condition that continued throughout the 1970 and 1980s and into the early 1990s. The team would often race to a fast start, only to collapse during the heat of the summer. The Indians held first place in June in 1960, 1961, 1962, 1965 and 1966, but none of the clubs finished a season closer than 15 games from first place. Overall, the Indians posted a record of 783–826 for a winning percentage of .487 that was the sixth best in the American League. AL pennant winners were the Yankees (1960, 1961, 1962, 1963 and 1964), Twins (1965), Orioles (1966 and 1969), Red Sox (1967) and Tigers (1968).

THE BEST TEAM

There were only two Cleveland teams with winning records during the 1960s. In 1965, the Indians were 87–75 and finished fifth. The 1968 outfit was 86–75 and landed in third.

THE WORST TEAM

The Indians saved the worst for last, as the 1969 team won 62 and lost 99, ending the season 46½ games out of first. Despite the presence of two first-year expansion teams, Cleveland had the worst record in the American League.

THE BEST MOMENT

Early Wynn ended his long quest to win his 300th career game with a victory on July 13, 1963.

THE WORST MOMENT

General manager Frank Lane traded Rocky Colavito to the Tigers for Harvey Kuenn on April 17, 1960, in a deal that raised the hackles of Indians fans everywhere.

THE ALL-DECADE TEAM • YEARS W/INDIANS

Johnny Romano, c	1960–64
Tony Horton, 1b	1967–70
Woodie Held, 2b	1958–64
Max Alvis, 3b	1961–69
Larry Brown, ss	1963–71
Tito Francona, lf	1959–64
Vic Davalillo, cf	1963–68
Rocky Colavito, rf	1955–59, 1965–67
Sam McDowell, p	1961–71
Gary Bell, p	1958–64
Luis Tiant, p	1964–69
Sonny Siebert, p	1964–69

Colavito was also on the 1950s All-Decade Team. Held played 508 games at shortstop and 151 at second base as an Indian but is included as the second baseman on the 1960s All-Decade Team because a lack of other viable candidates. No one played 120 games at second in consecutive seasons for Cleveland between Bobby Avila (1951–56) and Duane Kuiper (1976–79). Other outstanding Indians players of the 1960s included left fielder Leon Wagner (1964–68), pitcher Jim Perry (1959–63, 1974–75), first baseman Fred Whitfield (1963–67) and catchers Joe Azcue (1963–69) and Duke Sims (1964–70).

THE DECADE LEADERS

Batting Avg:	Vic Davalillo	.278
On Base Pct:	Rocky Colavito	.344
Slugging Pct:	Johnny Romano	.461
Home Runs:	Leon Wagner	97
RBIs:	Max Alvis	361
Runs:	Max Alvis	405
Stolen Bases:	Jose Cardenal	76
Wins:	Sam McDowell	89
Strikeouts:	Sam McDowell	1,663
ERA:	Luis Tiant	2.84
Saves:	Gary Bell	39

THE HOME FIELD

Efforts to modernize aging Municipal Stadium were undertaken during the 1960s. Improvements included a more modern scoreboard and new box seats. Lack of attendance was a decade-long problem. The Indians drew fewer than one million fans every season from 1960 through 1973. During that period, the Indians attracted a figure higher than the American League average only in 1965, when attendance hit 934,786. Cleveland failed to exceed the average major league attendance figure in any season between 1959 and 1994. Rumors were frequent that the Indians were headed for Atlanta, Oakland, Dallas-Fort Worth, Milwaukee, or Seattle during the sixties.

THE GAME YOU WISHED YOU HAD SEEN

Sonny Siebert pitched a no-hitter at Municipal Stadium against the Senators on June 10, 1966.

THE WAY THE GAME WAS PLAYED

Baseball was played in new cities and ballparks during the 1960s with franchise shifts and expansion from 16 teams to 24. American League baseball was played for the first time in Minnesota, Southern California, Oakland, and Seattle. The expansion of the strike zone in 1963 brought a decline in offense during the 1960s until the owners lowered the mound for the 1969 season. The league ERA dipped to 2.98 in 1968, the only time it has been lower than 3.00 since 1918.

THE MANAGEMENT

A syndicate headed by William Daley purchased the Indians in 1956. Daley served as chairman of the board until August 1966 when Vernon Stouffer bought his stock. General managers were Frank Lane (1957–61), Hoot Evers (1961) and Gabe Paul (1961–73). Changes in field manager were frequent as the club searched for a winning combination. Guiding the club from the dugout were Joe Gordon (1960), Jo-Jo White (1960), Jimmy Dykes (1960–61), Mel Harder (1961), Mel McGaha (1962), Harder again (1962), Birdie Tebbetts (1963–66), George Strickland (1964 while Tebbetts was convalescing from a heart attack and again in 1966), Joe Adcock (1967) and Al Dark (1968–71).

THE BEST PLAYER MOVE

The best player move was the signing of Sam McDowell for $75,000 shortly after his graduation from Central Catholic High School in Pittsburgh. The best trade brought Joe Azcue and Dick Howser to Cleveland from Kansas City in May 1963.

THE WORST PLAYER MOVE

The trade of Rocky Colavito to the Tigers for Harvey Kuenn on April 17, 1960, makes many lists as the worst trade in Indians history. But in terms of talent given up for talent received, there were at least three deals and possibly as many as five during the 1960s alone that were worse than the Colavito transaction. Far worse was the deal on January 20, 1965, in which the Indians re-acquired Colavito, who was near the end of his career, along with Cam Carreon in exchange for Tommy John, Tommie Agee, and Johnny Romano. Another bad deal sent Joe Rudi to the Athletics in October 1965. Swapping Jim Perry in May 1963 and Luis Tiant in December 1969, both to the Twins, also inflicted considerable long-term damage to the franchise, along with the sale of Ted Abernathy to the Cubs in 1965 and losing both Lou Piniella and Tommy Harper in the expansion draft in 1968. The worst transaction of the decade took place on April 12, 1960, when Norm Cash was swapped to the Tigers for Steve Demeter.

1960

Season in a Sentence

Frank Lane angers fans by trading Rocky Colavito two days before the opening game of the season, and the mood doesn't improve when Lane trades managers with the Tigers in August and the club slides to fourth place.

Finish • Won • Lost • Pct • GB

Finish	Won	Lost	Pct	GB
Fourth	76	78	.494	21.0

Managers

Joe Gordon (49–46), Jo-Jo White (1–0) and Jimmy Dykes (26–32)

Stats

	Indians	AL	Rank
Batting Avg:	.267	.255	2
On-Base Pct:	.328	.331	5
Slugging Pct:	.388	.388	4
Home Runs:	127		4
Stolen Bases:	58		3
Fielding Avg:	.978	.978	5
Runs Scored:	667		5
Runs Allowed:	693		5

Starting Line-up

Johnny Romano, c
Vic Power, 1b
Ken Aspromonte, 2b
Bubba Phillips, 3b
Woodie Held, ss
Tito Francona, lf
Jimmy Piersall, cf
Harvey Kuenn, rf
Johnny Temple, 2b
Mike de la Hoz, ss

Pitchers

Jim Perry, sp
Mudcat Grant, sp-rp
Gary Bell, sp
Barry Latman, sp-rp
Johnny Klippstein, rp
Dick Stigman, rp-sp
Bobby Locke, rp-sp

Attendance

950,985 (sixth in AL)

Club Leaders

Batting Avg:	Harvey Kuenn	.308
On-Base Pct:	Harvey Kuenn	.379
Slugging Pct:	Tito Francona	.460
Home Runs:	Woodie Held	21
RBIs:	Vic Power	84
Runs:	Tito Francona	79
Stolen Bases:	Jimmy Piersall	18
Wins:	Jim Perry	18
Strikeouts:	Jim Perry	120
ERA:	Jim Perry	3.62
Saves:	Johnny Klippstein	14

April 11 The Indians purchase Johnny Klippstein from the Dodgers.

April 12 The Indians trade Norm Cash to the Tigers for Steve Demeter.

This was arguably the worst deal in Indians history. A third baseman, Demeter put up terrific minor league numbers and was considered to be a tremendous prospect but played in just four games for Cleveland and was hitless in five at-bats. Cash, on the other hand, was Detroit's starting first baseman for 13 seasons. He was acquired by the Indians in a trade with the White Sox four months earlier (see December 6, 1959). It was apparent early that Frank Lane had been hoodwinked when Cash won the batting title in 1961 by hitting .361 along with 41 homers and 132 RBIs. After leaving the Tribe, he struck 373 homers, drove 1,087 runs and score 1,028. Had Cash posted the same numbers in Cleveland that he did with in Detroit, he would rank first in homers, first in RBIs, first in total bases, first in walks, third in runs, and fifth in hits on the Indians all-time career lists.

April 17 The Indians trade Rocky Colavito to the Tigers for Harvey Kuenn.

This deal still sticks in the craw of Indians fans. It would be more than 30 years before Cleveland had another pennant-contender. Colavito slugged 83 home runs during the 1958 and 1959 seasons, the most in the American League and the second highest figure in the majors behind only Ernie Banks. Rocky was also one of the most popular players in franchise history. But Frank Lane considered Colavito to be "selfish" because of Rocky's determination to hit home runs. The Indians general manager thought that Kuenn, who won the batting title by hitting .353 in 1959 (compared to .257 for Colavito) along with a league-leading 42 doubles, to be the better all-around player. At the start of the 1960 season, Kuenn had a .314 lifetime and had shown himself to be capable of

Indians fans express their feelings about the trade of Rocky Colavito to the Tigers at the season opener against Detroit.

playing shortstop, third base, and all three outfield spots. Fans in Cleveland were outraged. Lane added fuel to the fire when he asked, "What's all the fuss about? All I did was trade hamburger for steak." Lane was hanged in effigy as dummies of his likeness were strung from several telephone poles and lampposts in the city, and from the upper deck at Municipal Stadium on Opening Day. The trade turned out be a disaster, not only on the field but at the box office. Colavito hit 173 homers during the next five seasons and attendance declined rapidly before

Gabe Paul brought him back to Cleveland (see January 20, 1965). Kuenn, who was three years older the Colavito, hit .308 in his lone season with the Indians before being traded to San Francisco.

APRIL 18 The Indians trade Herb Score to the White Sox for Barry Latman.

Frank Lane further demonstrated that there were no sacred cows on the Indians roster by trading another fan favorite in Herb Score. It was hoped that a change of scenery would help him after two ineffective seasons following the horrific blow to his face by a line drive (see May 7, 1957). It didn't help. Score won only six games with the White Sox before calling it quits as a player. He returned to Cleveland in 1964 to begin a broadcasting career that lasted over 30 years. Latman was only 21 when acquired by the Indians and pitched for the club for four seasons, but never fulfilled his considerable promise.

APRIL 19 A dramatic season opener features Rocky Colavito and Harvey Kuenn in new uniforms following the trade two days earlier. The Tigers won the contest 4–2 in 15 innings before 52,756 at Municipal Stadium. Colavito went hitless in six at-bats, striking out four times. Kuenn doubled and singled in seven at-bats. Starting pitchers Gary Bell of the Indians and Frank Lary of the Tigers didn't allow a run for the first ten innings. Both surrendered two tallies in the 11th. Bell left the game with 12 strikeouts in 10⅓ innings. He gave up only four hits. Detroit scored two times in the 15th off Mudcat Grant.

The Indians began the season losing their first four games.

MAY 10 Jimmy Piersall hits a three-run homer during the Indians four-run tenth inning that defeats the Yankees 5–1 in New York.

MAY 12 Russ Nixon homers in the tenth inning to beat the Yankees 3–2 in New York.

MAY 15 A three-run walk-off homer by Harvey Kuenn in the tenth inning downs the White Sox 6–3 in the second game of a double header at Municipal Stadium. It was the third extra-inning home run by a Cleveland batter in six days. Dick Stigman (5⅔ innings), Gary Bell (1⅔ innings) and Johnny Klippstein (three innings) combined on a two-hitter. The only Chicago hitters were singles by Luis Aparicio and Al Smith off Stigman in the sixth inning. Cleveland lost the first game 4–0.

On the same day, the Indians traded Pete Whisenant to the Senators for Ken Aspromonte, who came to Cleveland as a 27-year-old with a .258 lifetime average in 317 games. He was a pleasant surprise in 1960, batting .290 with ten homers while winning the job as the starting second baseman. Aspromonte went to the Angels in the expansion draft at the end of the 1960 season and never again came close to matching those numbers. He later managed the Indians from 1972 through 1974.

MAY 18 Jimmy Piersall and Yankees catcher Elston Howard nearly come to blows during a 4–2 New York win over the Indians at Municipal Stadium. After Yankee pitcher Duke Maas hit Gary Bell with a pitch, Piersall, standing in the on deck circle, shouted to Howard, accusing him of ordering the knockdown pitch. Howard rushed at Piersall but was held back by umpire Al Smith.

May 23 — Vic Power hits a grand slam off Hal Brown in the third inning, but the Indians lose 7–6 to the Orioles at Municipal Stadium in a contest shortened to five innings by rain.

May 25 — Jim Perry pitches an 11-inning shutout to defeat the Senators 1–0 at Municipal Stadium. The winning run scored when Jimmy Piersall singled, was sacrificed to second, and scored on Tito Francona's single.

Perry and Francona both starred during the 1960 season. In an unusual year in which there were no 20-game winners in the American League, Perry tied for the lead in victories with 18, and also led in winning percentage (.643) and shutouts (four). He was 18–10 with a 3.62 ERA. Francona hit .292 with 17 homers and a league-leading 36 doubles. Johnny Romano contributed a .272 average and 16 home runs.

May 29 — During the twin bill against the Tigers in Detroit, bleacher fans at Tiger Stadium shower Jimmy Piersall with paper clips, bolts, fire crackers, and other dangerous objects. An announcement was made asking the fans to cease, but it was not a complete success. The Tigers won the first game 6–5 and were leading the second tilt 4–3 when Piersall gained revenge by blasting a three-run homer in the ninth inning for a 6–4 Indians victory. Piersall hopped, skipped and jumped around the bases during his home run "trot."

May 30 — Jimmy Piersall is again the center of attention during a double header, as the Indians win twice 9–4 and 4–1 against the White Sox in Chicago.

In the first game, Piersall was ejected while a base runner on second base and a strike was called on Harvey Kuenn. Piersall let home plate umpire Larry Napp know how he felt about the call. The Indians outfielder yelled and jumped up and down on the bag, while Cal Drummond, the umpire at second, tried to quiet him. Meanwhile, Napp started out to the center of the diamond and gave Piersall the thumb. When he reached the Indians dugout, Piersall threw out bats, balls, helmets, towels, and anything else that wasn't nailed down. Then he firmly stalked to the runway leading to the dressing room, next to the White Sox bench, and threw a sand bucket onto the field. The game was delayed for ten minutes while batboys cleaned up the mess. In the second game, Piersall stood still in center field on a drive over his head off the bat of Minnie Minoso that went for a double. The scoreboard operator thought it was a home run, and triggered the fireworks display atop the new exploding scoreboard at Comiskey Park, which made its debut a month earlier. Piersall caught a fly ball for the final out and threw the ball at the scoreboard, breaking a couple of light bulbs.

June 5 — Jimmy Piersall puts on another display during a double header against the Tigers at Municipal Stadium. Detroit won the opener, but Piersall sparked a 9–0 Indians victory in the nightcap. He socked a third-inning homer off Pete Burnside into the left field stands, and after hitting the ball, made mocking gestures toward the Tigers third base dugout. Then, he raced full speed around the bases to third, where he stopped, again faced the Detroit bench, doffed his cap and bowed before resuming his journey to the plate. When Piersall batted again in the fifth, he wore an oversized Little League batting helmet and promptly became engaged in an argument with Tigers catcher Red Wilson that nearly erupted into a fight. Burnside responded by throwing three consecutive pitches at Piersall.

June 8 Woodie Held hits a grand slam off Dave Hillman during a 5–2 win over the Red Sox in the second game of a double header in Boston. The Indians also won the opener 8–7.

June 9 The Indians defeat the Red Sox 3–2 at Fenway Park. The win gave the Indians a 1½-game lead in the pennant race and a record of 28–17.

June 13 The Indians trade Russ Nixon and Carroll Hardy to the Red Sox for Marty Keough and Ted Bowsfield.

Nixon was one of only two players to survive Frank Lane's house cleaning of the Cleveland roster long enough to appear in a game for both the 1957 Indians and the 1960 Indians. The other one was George Strickland.

June 17 Playing against the Indians at Municipal Stadium, Ted Williams hits the 500th home run of his career in the third inning of a 3–1 Red Sox victory. The milestone homer came against Wynn Hawkins, a rookie who was three years old when Williams made his major league debut.

June 18 Dick Stigman (seven innings) and Ted Bowsfield (two innings) combine on a one-hitter to beat the Red Sox 2–1 at Municipal Stadium. The lone Boston hit was a single by Ed Sadowski in the second inning.

June 22 Nine days after being acquired by the Indians, Ted Bowsfield throws a shutout to defeat the Senators 1–0 at Municipal Stadium. The run scored in the first inning on a triple by Jimmy Piersall and a single from Harvey Kuenn.

This was Bowsfield's only shutout as a member of the Indians. He had a 3–4 record with the club and a 5.09 ERA in 40⅔ innings.

June 29 On the advice of a psychiatrist, the Indians order Jimmy Piersall to stay away from the ballpark and rest for five days. The enforced vacation was given to Piersall after he was tossed from the premises by the umpires for arguing a call during an 11-inning, 7–6 win over the Yankees at Municipal Stadium. It was Piersall's fourth ejection of the season.

July 2 The Indians hammer the Senators 12–2 in Washington. Mudcat Grant was the winning pitcher.

Grant entered the contest with a 13–0 career record against the Senators. Before the game, the Washington club passed out 2,000 rabbit's feet and 2,000 "Beat Mudcat" lapel pins to fans, while a Boy Scout group staged a snake dance to try to break the hex. At the end of the 1960 season, Grant had a 16–2 record against Washington and a 13–24 mark against the rest of the American League.

July 11 At Municipal Stadium in Kansas City in the first of two All-Star Games played in 1960, Gary Bell retires all six batters he faces, including Willie Mays, Hank Aaron, Ed Mathews, and Ernie Banks. The American League lost 5–3.

July 16 The Indians defeat the Senators 9–4 at Municipal Stadium.

The victory put the Indians $1\frac{1}{2}$ games out of first place with a 45–33 record. The club was 31–45 the rest of the way.

JULY 17 Vic Power fights Senators catcher Earl Battey during the first game of a double header against the Senators at Municipal Stadium. Battey objected to Power's spikes-high slide on a play at the plate. The two had words and began swinging at each other before being separated and ejected by the umpires. The Indians lost both contests, 3–2 and 5–2.

JULY 18 Vic Power argues with controversial Ohio State University football coach Woody Hayes during a 9–2 loss to the Yankees at Municipal Stadium. Hayes didn't like the way that Power played first base. "I told him he should act like a big league ball player and catch the ball with two hands," said Hayes. "I like team men myself. It looked like showboating to me, and I told him so." Power walked over to the box seat and shouted back at Hayes. "He should stick to football," remarked Power.

JULY 23 Jimmy Piersall is ejected by umpire Ed Hurley for dashing back and forth in the outfield while Ted Williams is batting during the sixth and eighth innings of a 4–2 Indians win in Boston. Piersall rushed in to confront Hurley, slamming his glove, hat, and sunglasses to the grass on the way, and argued vehemently with the umpire for ten minutes that he had a right to change his position in the outfield.

JULY 29 The Indians purchase Don Newcombe from the Reds.

AUGUST 3 Frank Lane and Tigers president Bill De Witt complete an unprecedented trade by swapping managers. Joe Gordon went to the Tigers, while Detroit skipper Jimmie Dykes was transferred to Cleveland. It was the first time that managers were traded for each other, and it hasn't happened since. Coach Jo-Jo White managed the Indians for one game while Dykes was en route. White then joined Gordon as a coach in Detroit while Tigers coach Luke Appling came to the Indians with Dykes.

The Indians had lost 13 of the last 17 when the move was made. Dykes was 63-year-old when he joined the Indians. He had a 22-year playing career with the Athletics and White Sox from 1918 through 1939, and managed the Sox from 1934 through 1946. Dykes was later the skipper of the Athletics (1951–53), Orioles (1954), Reds (1958) and Tigers (1959–60). The Indians were 26–32 under Dykes in 1960, and in a surprise move, he was brought back in 1961. Shortly after the beginning of the 1961 season, Gabe Paul was named general manager of the Indians. Paul was previously the general manager of the Reds when he let Dykes go at the end of the 1958 because he considered Jimmie to be "too old." After a losing campaign in 1961, Paul fired Dykes again. Gordon finished the 1960 season in Detroit, and then was hired by the Kansas City Athletics as manager. A few months later, Charlie Finley bought the A's, and hired Frank Lane as general manager after Lane's contract was terminated by the Indians (see January 3, 1961). Working for Lane again was not a happy situation for Gordon, who was dismissed 59 games into the 1961 season.
He later managed the Kansas City Royals in 1969.

AUGUST 9 Red Sox outfielder Lu Clinton kicks Vic Power's fly ball over the fence for a home run leading to a 6–3 Indians win at Municipal Stadium. The game was tied 3–3 in the bottom of the fifth inning with a Cleveland runner on base when Power hit a drive over Clinton's head. The ball hit the top of the wire fence and bounced toward Clinton, who was running with his back to the infield. The carom fell in front of Clinton and hit his foot while he was running at full speed, causing him to accidentally kick it over the fence. Since the ball never touched the ground, umpire Al Smith ruled it a home run.

SEPTEMBER 3 A three-run homer by Woodie Held with two out in the ninth inning caps a four-run rally that beats the Athletics 6–5 in Kansas City.

SEPTEMBER 4 Woodie Held smashes two homers and a double for six runs-batted-in during a 10–2 win over the Athletics in Kansas City.

SEPTEMBER 14 The Indians score seven runs in the third inning to take an 11–1 lead and win 11–7 over the Red Sox at Municipal Stadium.

SEPTEMBER 16 Mudcat Grant is suspended for the remainder of the 1960 season following an argument with bullpen coach Ted Wilks before a 4–2 win over the Athletics in Cleveland. Grant was singing along with the National Anthem, when he improvised the final line. Instead of saying "the land of the free," Grant intoned "It's not the land of the free for me in Mississippi." Grant was referring to the civil rights struggles of his fellow Africans-Americans in Southern states such as Mississippi in an effort to end segregation and attain the right to vote. Wilks, a Texan, took exception to Grant's version of "The Star-Spangled Banner," and an argument ensued. After Wilks made a racial slur, Grant left the bullpen, dressed in the clubhouse, and went home.

SEPTEMBER 18 Bobby Locke (seven innings) and Don Newcombe (two innings) combine on a two-hitter, but the Indians lose 3–2 to the Athletics in the first game of a double header in Cleveland. The Indians won the second tilt 9–2.

SEPTEMBER 24 The Indians score two runs in the ninth inning and one in the 12th to beat the White Sox 6–5 at Municipal Stadium. A two-run single by Ken Aspromonte in the ninth tied the score. A single by Bubba Phillips drove home the winning run.

OCTOBER 1 Down 8–1, the Indians score three runs in the sixth inning, four in the eighth and one in the ninth to win 9–8 in Chicago.

OCTOBER 26 The American League announces plans to expand to ten teams for the 1961 season. The Washington Senators had moved to Minnesota, where they were renamed the Twins, and so a new expansion team would be created in Washington, also named the Senators. A second expansion outfit would be installed in Los Angeles and named the Angels.

DECEMBER 3 A month after John Kennedy wins the Presidential election by defeating Richard Nixon, the Indians trade Harvey Kuenn to the Giants for Willie Kirkland and Johnny Antonelli.

DECEMBER 14 In the expansion draft, the Indians lose Ken Aspromonte, Gene Leek, and Red Wilson to the Angels and Johnny Klippstein, Carl Mathias, Marty Keough, and Jim King to the Senators.

1961

Season in a Sentence

The Indians win 38 of their first 60 games to cause a brief case of pennant fever in Cleveland before slumping to a losing record.

Finish • Won • Lost • Pct • GB

Finish	Won	Lost	Pct	GB
Fifth	78	83	.484	30.5

Managers

Jimmy Dykes (77–83) and Mel Harder (1–0)

Stats

Stats	Indians	AL	Rank
Batting Avg:	.266	.256	2
On-Base Pct:	.328	.332	6
Slugging Pct:	.406	.395	3
Home Runs:	150		5
Stolen Bases:	34		9
ERA:	4.15	4.02	5
Fielding Avg:	.977	.976	4
Runs Scored:	737		5
Runs Allowed:	752		5

Starting Line-up

Johnny Romano, c
Vic Power, 1b
Johnny Temple, 2b
Bubba Phillips, 3b
Woodie Held, ss
Tito Francona, lf
Jimmy Piersall, cf
Willie Kirkland, rf
Mike de la Hoz, 2b-ss-3b
Chuck Essegian, cf-lf-rf

Pitchers

Mudcat Grant, sp
Gary Bell, sp
Jim Perry, sp
Wynn Hawkins, sp
Barry Latman, rp-sp
Frank Funk, rp
Bob Allen, rp

Attendance

725,547 (seventh in AL)

Club Leaders

Batting Avg:	Jimmy Piersall	.322
On-Base Pct:	Jimmy Piersall	.378
Slugging Pct:	Johnny Romano	.483
Home Runs:	Willie Kirkland	27
RBIs:	Willie Kirkland	95
Runs:	Tito Francona	87
Stolen Bases:	Johnny Temple	9
Wins:	Mudcat Grant	15
Strikeouts:	Gary Bell	163
ERA:	Mudcat Grant	3.86
Saves:	Frank Funk	11

JANUARY 3 Frank Lane resigns as general manager of the Indians to take a similar job with the Kansas City Athletics.

Lane's contract with the Indians still had two years left, but Cleveland fans wanted to run him out of town after the club sank to fourth place in 1960 following the trade of Rocky Colavito. When Charlie Finley bought the Athletics in December 1960, he wanted Lane as general manager, and the Indians board of directors were happy to have Finley take the unpopular G.M. off their hands. Finley was a Chicago insurance executive who had become friendly with Lane when he ran the White Sox. The warm regards that Finley had for Lane evaporated quickly, however, when the two had to work together. Finley fired Lane in June 1961. Lane later served in the front offices of the Orioles and Brewers. Indians farm director Hoot Evers was promoted to general manager on an interim basis until a replacement for Lane could be found (see April 27, 1961).

APRIL 11 The Indians open the season in Detroit, and win 9–5 over the Tigers. Jimmy Piersall collected three singles and a double in six at-bats. Vic Power had two doubles and two singles in five at-bats. Bubba Phillips homered and Jim Perry pitched a complete game.

Piersall entered the 1961 season as a 31-year-old with a .272 batting average, but hit a surprising .322 in 121 games.

APRIL 14 The Indians play the expansion Senators for the first time, and lose 3–2 at Griffith Stadium in Washington.

The second version of the Senators moved to Texas after the 1971 season and were renamed the Rangers.

APRIL 16 On the day of the unsuccessful Bay of Pigs invasion of Cuba, the Indians suddenly explode for three runs in the ninth inning for a 3–2 win over the Senators in Washington. Tito Francona's two-run homer tied the score. Three singles the last by Jimmy Piersall, produced the winning run.

Francona hit .301 with 16 homers in 1961.

APRIL 19 In the home opener, the Indians lose 5–2 to the Tigers before 28,216 at Municipal Stadium.

Harry Jones began his long career broadcasting Indians games on both radio and television by joining Ken Coleman in the TV booth in 1961.

APRIL 23 Down 6–1 after four innings, the Indians rally to win 10–8 over the Athletics in Kansas City. Cleveland scored two runs in the ninth to break an 8–8 tie.

A's third baseman Andy Carey challenged the entire Cleveland bench following a rhubarb with Indians infielder Jack Kubiszyn in the eighth inning. Kubiszyn crashed into Carey on a play at third and the pair exchanged heated words. When the Indians heckled Carey during the dispute, he offered to fight anyone in the dugout. Walt Bond took the challenge but was restrained by teammates.

APRIL 24 Bubba Phillips hits a grand slam off Milt Pappas in the sixth inning of a 6–1 win over the Orioles in Baltimore.

APRIL 27 Gabe Paul is named general manager of the Indians.

Paul joined the Cincinnati Reds in 1936 as a publicity director and worked his way up to general manager by 1951. He left the Reds in October 1960 to join the new National League franchise in Houston, which was to begin play in 1962. Paul suddenly left Houston for "personal reasons" to take the position with the Indians. He had been close friends for years with Indians vice-president Nate Dolin. Paul would remain in Cleveland for years, although the club never came close to winning a pennant, fielded only two winning teams, and never drew as many as one million fans during any of those dozen seasons. He was named club president in November 1962 when he became a part owner of the franchise.

MAY 9 Four days after Alan Shepard becomes the first American in space, the Indians tie an unusual record for fewest official at-bats in a nine-inning game with 23 during a 4–2 loss to the White Sox at Comiskey Park. While pitching a complete game two-hitter for Chicago, Herb Score faced 34 Cleveland batters. Six drew walks, three collected sacrifice bunts, and two hit sacrifice flies.

May 10 The Indians score six runs in the 11th inning to win 8–2 over the White Sox in Chicago. Chuck Essegian and Bubba Phillips homered during the outburst.

On the same day, the Indians traded Joe Morgan to the Cardinals for Bob Nieman. The Joe Morgan dealt by the Indians was not the future Hall of Fame second baseman. This Joe Morgan was a utility infielder who hit .193 in 88 big league games with five clubs over four seasons and later managed the Boston Red Sox.

May 14 The Indians win a 15-inning marathon 1–0 over the Orioles in the first game of a double header at Municipal Stadium. Jim Perry (eight innings) and Frank Funk (seven innings) combined on the shutout. The winning run scored on a walk by Johnny Romano, a single from Bubba Phillips and an error. Cleveland also won the second game 6–4. *Romano hit .299 with 21 homers in 1961.*

May 15 The Indians collect 21 hits and trounce the Red Sox 13–2 in Boston.

May 17 The Indians win 1–0 over the Red Sox in Boston. Bobby Locke (6²/₃ innings) and Barry Latman (2¹/₃ innings) combined on the shutout. The run scored in the fifth inning on a disputed call. Power was a base runner on third and held up while the Red Sox started a double play on a grounder by Johnny Romano. Power raced for the plate, and on a close play, beat first baseman Pete Runnels's throw to catcher Jim Pagliaroni.

May 21 The Indians sweep a double header from the Twins in Minnesota, winning both games by shutouts. Wynn Hawkins pitched a two-hitter in the opener for a 9–0 win. The only hits off Hawkins were singles by Billy Gardner in the third inning and Lenny Green in the ninth. Mudcat Grant hurled the game two shutout, winning 2–0.

The games were the first that the Indians played in Minnesota against the Twins.

May 22 The Indians defeat the Twins 7–5 in 15 innings in Minnesota. The two final runs scored on four singles.

May 23 The Indians play a regular season game in California for the first time and lose 9–0 to the Angels. The game was played at Wrigley Field in Los Angeles, which served as the Angels home for one year.

Wrigley Field was used by L.A.'s Pacific Coast League club, also named the Angels, from 1925 through 1957. The ballpark was built by the Wrigley family, which owned the Cubs from 1919 through 1981. The Los Angeles version of Wrigley Field can still be seen on the 1959 TV series Home Run Derby, *which is available on DVD, and as a backdrop for Hollywood movies. It was torn down in 1965. The Angels franchise has been known as the Los Angeles Angels (1961–65), the California Angels (1965–96), the Anaheim Angels (1997–2004) and the Los Angeles Angels of Anaheim (since 2005).*

May 25 The Indians rout the Angels 13–5 in Los Angeles.

May 30 The Twins play in Cleveland for the first time, and lose 4–3 and 7–5 to the Indians in a Memorial Day double header at Municipal Stadium.

June 2 The Angels play in Cleveland for the first time, and lose 6–4 to the Indians at Municipal Stadium.

June 6 The Indians take first place with a 14–3 win over the Senators in Washington. Cleveland scored seven runs in the sixth inning. It was the club's eighth win in a row.

June 7 The Indians extend their winning streak to nine games by crushing the Senators 11–0 in Washington.

June 8 The Indians win 1–0 over the Tigers in the first game of a double header. It was Cleveland's tenth win in a row. Jim Perry (seven innings) and Frank Funk (two innings) combined on the shutout. The lone run scored in the first inning on doubles by Johnny Temple and Vic Power. The winning streak ended with a 2–1 loss in the second game, highlighted by a controversial play. In the eighth inning, Bob Hale of the Indians was called safe on a close play, and the Tigers soon surrounded umpire Larry Napp. While the argument was going on, Hale made a dash for second base and was tagged out. Jimmie Dykes argued for 15 minutes complaining that Hale could not be called out because Tiger manager Bob Scheffing was on the field.

The Indians started the season 12–13, then won 22 of 26 for a 34–17 record. Fans in Cleveland were all steamed up over the fast start, but soon were subject to a cold dose of reality. The club was knocked out of first place on June 17, were out of contention by July 4, and posted a 44–66 record over the final 110 games.

June 11 After entering the contest as a pinch-runner for Jimmy Piersall in the sixth inning, Chuck Essegian remains in the line-up and hits two homers and drives in five runs during a 7–3 win over the Athletics in the first game of a double header in Cleveland. In the second tilt, Essegian delivered a walk-off double that drove in the winning run in a 4–3 victory.

Essegian played linebacker for Stanford in the 1952 Rose Bowl. In 502 at-bats for the Indians over two seasons, he hit 33 home runs.

June 25 Pinch-hitting with the score 3–3 and one out in the ninth inning of the second game of a double header against the Tigers at Municipal Stadium, Chuck Essegian drives in the winning run by sending a drive off the right field wall, scoring Mike de la Hoz. Essegian did not get credit for a hit, however, because of a gaffe by Vic Power, who was the runner on first base. Believing the game was over, Power did not run to second and was out when Al Kaline threw to the base for a force out. Detroit won the first game 6–3.

June 27 Dick Stigman allows consecutive home runs to Gene Green, Willie Tasby, and Dale Long in the first inning of an 8–5 loss to the Senators at Municipal Stadium.

July 2 The Indians score six runs in the tenth inning to defeat the Red Sox 12–6 in Boston.

July 3 The Indians purchase Ken Aspromonte from the Angels.

July 4 The Indians sell Johnny Antonelli to the Braves.

JULY 9 In the final game before the All-Star break, Willie Kirkland hits three homers in his first three plate appearances, but the Indians lose 9–8 to the White Sox in the second game of a double header at Municipal Stadium. Kirkland drove in four runs with home runs in the second, fourth, and sixth inning off Cal McLish, all on two-strike pitches. Kirkland walked in the seventh facing Frank Baumann. In the ninth, he batted with runners on first and second, none out, and Cleveland trailing by a run, and delivered a successful sacrifice bunt. The Indians also lost the opener 7–5 when Chicago scored five runs in the ninth.

JULY 13 In the first game following the All-Star break, Willie Kirkland ties a major league record for most homers in consecutive official at-bats with four. Kirkland hit home runs in his first three plate appearances on July 9 before drawing a walk and collecting a sacrifice. On July 13, Willie homered in his first plate appearance, but the Indians lost 9–6 to the Twins at Municipal Stadium.

The only other Cleveland players with homers in four consecutive at-bats are Rocky Colavito, who did it in one game on June 10, 1959, and Manny Ramirez over two games on September 15 and 16 in 1998.

JULY 14 Willie Kirkland hits his fifth homer over a period of three games helping the Indians to a 7–5 win over the Angels in Municipal Stadium.

JULY 19 Barry Latman runs his season record to 9–0 after winning a 4–1 decision over the Red Sox in the first game of a double header at Municipal Stadium. The Indians also won the second tilt 9–8.

Latman won six of the last seven decisions in 1960, giving him a 15–1 record over two seasons.

JULY 20 The Indians outlast the Red Sox 12–11 at Municipal Stadium. Four runs in the seventh inning gave Cleveland a 12–10 advantage. Jimmy Piersall put the Indians into the lead with a three-run homer, which was followed by a Tito Francona home run.

AUGUST 3 Bubba Phillips hits a grand slam off Frank Baumann in the first inning, but the Indians lose 8–6 to the White Sox at Municipal Stadium.

The Indians debuted a new scoreboard at Municipal Stadium in 1961. Whenever a member of the home team hit a home run, trumpets blared and flame throwers shot huge blasts into the air. Smoke poured out, and finally rockets exploded in the sky.

AUGUST 17 The Indians win 4–3 in 14 innings over the Red Sox at Municipal Stadium. Down 3–0, Woodie Held hit a solo home run in the eighth, followed by Johnny Romano's two-run homer in the ninth. The winning run scored on a bases-loaded walk to Ken Aspromonte by Mike Fornieles.

Held hit .277 with 23 homers in 1961.

SEPTEMBER 3 Gary Bell pitches ten shutout innings but gains only a no decision during an 11-inning, 1–0 loss to the Orioles in Baltimore. The winning run scored in 11th came on two walks and a single given up by Bob Allen and Frank Funk.

SEPTEMBER 10 The Indians lose both ends of a testy double header against the Yankees in New York by scores of 7–6 and 9–3.

During the fifth inning of the first game, Yankee hurler Jim Coates hit Vic Power with a pitch. Once on first base, Power yelled insults at Coates, who threw several times toward first even though Power was planted firmly on the bag. A couple of the throws nearly hit Power again. In the seventh, two young fans dashed into center field and went after Jimmy Piersall, who hit one assailant with a right hook. He shot a right at the second with a punch that hit the teenaged fan on the temple. As the intruder turned and ran in the opposite direction, Piersall pursued him then kicked him in the seat of the pants. Johnny Temple and Walt Bond also took turns throwing punches at the two fans before park police intervened. When play resumed, Piersall made a spectacular catch on a deep fly ball by Johnny Blanchard. In the second game, Clete Boyer hit a controversial drive off Jim Perry in the sixth inning. The ball hit a railing on top of the fence and bounced onto the outfield grass. Home plate umpire Jim Linsalata signaled it a home run. Piersall, who was not in the game and was seated in the left field bullpen, ran toward the infield contending that the ball was in play. Second base ump Charlie Berry and third base arbiter Frank Umont agreed with Piersall. Meanwhile, Boyer was in his home run trot and was tagged out between second and third base. The Yankees vigorously protested, and fans held up the game for 17 minutes by throwing debris onto the field.

SEPTEMBER 15 Six days before his 19th birthday, Sam McDowell makes his major league debut and pitches 6⅓ scoreless innings against the Twins at Municipal Stadium but leaves with a pain in his side that is later diagnosed as two cracked ribs. The Indians lost 3–2 when Minnesota scored three times in the ninth.

The Indians signed McDowell for $75,000 in 1960 shortly after he graduated from Central Catholic High School in Pittsburgh. It wasn't until 1964 before McDowell spent a full season in the majors, but during a stretch from 1965 through 1970, he was as dominating as any pitcher in baseball. During that period, McDowell earned the nickname "Sudden Sam" for a blistering fastball that helped him compile a 92–74 record on some terrible Cleveland clubs. He led the AL in strikeouts five times, lowest opponents' batting average twice, innings pitched once, and ERA once. McDowell had five games of 15 or more strikeouts, and threw four one-hitters including two in back-to-back starts in 1966. He struck out 2,159 batters with the Indians, which is second only to Bob Feller's 2,581. Bob Lemon is a distant third with 1,277. Sam is also eighth in shutouts (22), eighth in games started (295), ninth in ERA (2.99) and tenth innings (2,109⅔) on the all-time Indians lists. McDowell's numbers declined, however, after a salary dispute during spring training in 1971, and he was traded to the Giants for Gaylord Perry in November 1971. Alcoholism also led to his downfall. After his career ended, McDowell said, "There is absolutely no doubt in my mind that I would be in the Hall of Fame if I had not been a drunk." He later became a highly successful alcohol and drug addiction counselor working for several major league teams.

September 28 Woodie Held hits two homers and drives in five runs during a 12–5 win over the Twins in Minnesota.

October 1 On the last game of the season, Walt Bond hits a grand slam off Ryne Duren in the third inning of an 8–5 win over the Angels in Los Angeles.

Coach Mel Harder served as interim manager during the game because Jimmy Dykes was fired earlier in the day. Dykes never managed another team but served as a coach with the Braves in 1962 and the Athletics in 1963 and 1964.

October 2 The Indians name 35-year-old Mel McGaha as manager.

McGaha was a three-sport star at the University of Arkansas and played one season with the New York Knicks in 1948–49. A promising baseball career ended in 1948 during a bus crash while playing for Duluth in the Northern League. Four of his teammates and the driver were killed in the accident. McGaha suffered a dislocated shoulder that never properly healed. He managed for seven seasons in the minors before coaching under Jimmie Dykes in 1961. After McGaha was hired to replace him, Dykes called the job as Indians manager "suicide" because of the preponderance of "clubhouse lawyers and malcontents." Under McGaha, the Indians were in first place in July in 1962, but after the club finished with an 80–82 record he was fired.

October 5 The Indians trade Jimmy Piersall to the Senators for Dick Donovan, Gene Green, and Jim Mahoney.

Donovan was 34-years-old when acquired by the Indians, but he gave the club the only 20-win season of his career. In 1962, Donovan was 20–10 with 3.59 earned run average in 250⅔ innings and posted a league-high five shutouts. He slipped after that, however, compiling a 19–25 record from 1963 until the end of his career in 1965.

November 16 The Indians trade Johnny Temple to the Orioles for Ray Barker, Harry Chiti, and Art Kay.

1962

Season in a Sentence

Despite another fast start (first place on July 7), the Indians finish with another losing record (80–82) and another change in managers (from Mel McGaha to Birdie Tebbetts).

Finish • Won • Lost • Pct • GB

Finish	Won	Lost	Pct	GB
Sixth	80	82	.494	16.0

Managers

Mel McGaha (78–82) and
Mel Harder (2–0)

Stats

	Indians	AL	Rank
Batting Avg:	.245	.255	10
On-Base Pct:	.314	.328	9
Slugging Pct:	.388	.394	5
Home Runs:	180		4
Stolen Bases:	35		9
ERA:	4.14	3.97	8
Fielding Avg:	.977	.978	8
Runs Scored:	682		8
Runs Allowed:	745		8

Starting Line-up

Johnny Romano, c
Tito Francona, 1b
Jerry Kindall, 2b
Bubba Phillips, 3b
Woodie Held, ss
Chuck Essegian, lf
Ty Cline, cf
Willie Kirkland, rf
Al Luplow, lf
Willie Tasby, cf
Don Dillard, lf-cf

Pitchers

Don Donovan, sp
Jim Perry, sp
Pedro Ramos, sp
Mudcat Grant, sp
Sam McDowell, sp-rp
Gary Bell, rp
Frank Funk, rp
Barry Latman, rp-sp

Attendance

716,076 (ninth in AL)

Club Leaders

Batting Avg:	Tito Francona	.272
On-Base Pct:	Johnny Romano	.363
Slugging Pct:	Johnny Romano	.479
Home Runs:	Johnny Romano	25
RBIs:	Johnny Romano	81
Runs:	Tito Francona	82
Stolen Bases:	Willie Kirkland	9
Wins:	Dick Donovan	20
Strikeouts:	Barry Latman	117
ERA:	Dick Donovan	3.59
Saves:	Gary Bell	12

January 23 Bob Feller is elected to the Hall of Fame on his first time on the ballot.

April 2 The Indians trade Vic Power and Dick Stigman to the Twins for Pedro Ramos.

April 10 In his debut with the Indians, Dick Donovan shuts out the Red Sox for a 4–0 Opening Day victory in Boston. Johnny Romano collected three hits.

April 11 In his major league debut, Ron Taylor suffers a heartbreaking 12-inning, 4–0 loss to the Red Sox at Fenway Park. Taylor pitched 11 shutout innings before allowing four runs in the 12th without retiring a batter. Carl Yastrzemski led off with a triple, and following two intentional walks, Carroll Hardy hit a grand slam. Bill Monbouquette pitched 12 shutout innings for Boston.

A native of Toronto, Taylor made 16 more major league starts and never pitched a shutout, although he had an 11-year career, mostly as a reliever. His stay in Cleveland was brief. The Indians sent him to the minors after eight games, a 2–2 record, and a 5.94 ERA in 33⅓ innings. Taylor was traded to St. Louis during the following off-season (see December 15, 1962). He pitched in the World

Series for the Cardinals in 1964 and the Mets in 1969. After his playing career ended, Taylor went to medical school and received his degree. He served as the trainer for the Blue Jays when they won the world championship in both 1992 and 1993. Taylor is the only individual to participate in the World Series as both a player and a trainer.

April 13 — The home opener is stopped by rain and snow in the bottom of the sixth inning with the Senators winning 5–2. The crowd at Municipal Stadium was 17,543.

April 17 — In his second game with the Indians, Dick Donovan pitches his second shutout, beating the Red Sox 5–0 at Municipal Stadium.

April 21 — The Indians lose 3–1 to the Yankees in New York for their 19th consecutive defeat at Yankee Stadium, dating back to May 12, 1960.

April 22 — The Indians break their 19-game losing streak at Yankee Stadium by sweeping New York 7–5 and 9–3 in a double header.

The Indians were 12–6 against the pennant-winning Yankees in 1962 but split 18 games with the last-place Senators.

April 24 — The Indians play at Dodger Stadium, also known as Chavez Ravine, for the first time and win 3–2 over the Angels.

The Angels shared Dodger Stadium with the Dodgers from 1962 through 1965 before moving to Anaheim.

April 29 — The Indians sell Bob Nieman to the Giants.

May 3 — The Indians trade Steve Hamilton and Don Rudolph to the Senators for Willie Tasby.

Rudolph played only one game with the Indians but left an unusual legacy. He was married to an exotic dancer named Patti Waggin and acted as her press agent and manager. The two met in 1954 while Rudolph pitched for a minor league club in Colorado Springs. At the time, she was working her way through college as a stripper billed as "The Co-Ed With the Educated Torso." Hamilton played in just two games with the Indians, but after being traded he appeared in 419 more big league contests as an effective reliever with five clubs before his career ended in 1972. He stood six-foot-seven, and played in the NBA with the Lakers, then based in Minneapolis, from 1958 through 1960.

May 16 — Johnny Romano smacks a two-out, two-run walk-off homer in the ninth inning to beat the Athletics 10–9 in Cleveland.

Romano hit .261 with 25 homers in 1962.

May 18 — Dick Donovan hits two homers during a 9–2 win over the Tigers at Municipal Stadium.

May 20 — To demonstrate the ease with which the new Sabin polio vaccine can be administered, each Indians player takes the serum prior to a double header against the Tigers at Municipal Stadium. The Indians won 7–6 and lost 8–6.

MAY 21 A two-out, three-run, walk-off homer by Johnny Romano in the ninth inning beats the Orioles 10–7 at Municipal Stadium.

The Indians hit a remarkable 28 homers during a nine-game stretch from May 13 through May 21. The 28 homers were struck by Chuck Essegian (seven), Willie Kirkland (four), Romano (four), Jerry Kindall (three), Woodie Held (two), Dick Donovan (two), Gene Green (two), Don Dillard (one), Bubba Phillips (one), Pedro Ramos (one) and Tito Francona (one). Essegian hit nine homers in 12 games from May 13 through May 25.

The Perry brothers, Jim and Gaylord, square off in an exhibition game in March 1962. Jim and the Indians won 5–4. In their careers, both won 70 games for the Tribe.

MAY 23 Back-to-back homers by Chuck Essegian and Al Luplow in the ninth inning beats the White Sox 5–4 at Comiskey Park. Dick Donovan was the winning pitcher, running his record to 8–0.

MAY 25 The Indians play at D. C. Stadium in Washington for the first time, and win 2–1 over the Senators.

The ballpark was reamed Robert F. Kennedy Stadium in 1968. It was the home of the Senators from 1962 through 1971 when the franchise moved to Texas and was renamed the Rangers. The facility was re-introduced to baseball in 2005 with the arrival of the Nationals, who played their last game there in 2007.

MAY 30 Pedro Ramos hits two homers, one a grand slam, and pitches a three-hit shutout for a 7–0 win over the Orioles in the first game of a double header at Memorial Stadium.

The slam was struck in the sixth inning off Chuck Estrada. Baltimore won the second contest by the same 7–0 score.

JUNE 8 The Indians score six runs in the 13th inning to defeat the Red Sox 15–9 in Boston. The highlight of the rally was a two-run homer by Willie Kirkland.

JUNE 9 The Indians outlast the Red Sox 14–10 in Boston. Cleveland led 12–2 in the sixth inning before hanging on for the victory. The club scored 29 runs in consecutive games.

JUNE 11 The Indians clobber the Red Sox 10–0 in Boston.

JUNE 15 In the first meeting of a four-game series against the Yankees at Municipal Stadium, Mudcat Grant pitches the Indians to a 5–0 victory.

JUNE 16 The Indians take first place with a thrilling 10–9 win over the Yankees at Municipal Stadium. The game ended on a two-run homer by Jerry Kindall.

Kindall hit .228 with 20 homers in 789 at-bats over three seasons with the Indians.

JUNE 17 The Indians complete a four-game sweep of the Yankees with 6–1 and 6–3 wins during a double header before 70,918 at Municipal Stadium. In the second inning of the opener, Jerry Kindall, Bubba Phillips, and Jim Mahoney hit consecutive homers off Bill Stafford.

The wins gave the Indians a 36–24 record and a two-game lead in the AL pennant race.

JUNE 24 The Indians trade Ken Aspromonte to the Braves for Bob Hartman.

JUNE 26 A two-run homer by Al Luplow beats the Tigers 3–1 in Detroit. The Indians lost the first game 6–0.

JULY 2 Dick Donovan pitches a two-hitter to defeat the Orioles 2–0 at Municipal Stadium. He faced the minimum 27 batters. The only Baltimore hits were singles by Whitey Herzog in the fourth and seventh innings.

JULY 4 The Indians win two extra inning games 1–0 and 6–2 during a double header against the Tigers at Municipal Stadium. In the opener, Jim Perry pitched a ten-inning complete game to win 1–0. He also scored the lone run of the game. Perry led off the tenth with a single, moved to second on a sacrifice, and scored on a single by Gene Green. In the second contest, the Indians scored a run in the ninth for a 1–1 tie. Both teams plated a run in the tenth, with Cleveland scoring on the first major league home run by catcher Doc Edwards. The game ended in the 13th on a grand slam by Don Dillard off Jerry Casale.

JULY 5 Don Dillard hits a walk-off homer for the second game in a row, breaking a 6–6 tie in the ninth inning for a 7–6 victory over the Tigers at Municipal Stadium. Dillard entered the game in the fifth inning as a replacement for Al Luplow, who left with a pulled leg muscle. Rocky Colavito hit three consecutive home runs for Detroit.

JULY 8 The Indians are knocked out of first place with a 6–3 and 8–4 double-header loss to the White Sox at Municipal Stadium.

JULY 12 Trailing 3–1, the Indians score five runs in the ninth inning and defeat the Orioles 6–4 in Baltimore. All five runs in the ninth were driven in by pinch-hitters. Willie Tasby connected for a two-run single and Chuck Essegian blasted a three-run homer.

The Indians had a 48–36 record on July 12 but then lost nine in a row and 28 of 38 to spiral into the lower half of the American League standings.

JULY 18 The Twins tie a major league record with two grand slams during an 11-run first inning and beat the Indians 14–3 in Minnesota. Bob Allison hit the first off Barry Latman and Harmon Killebrew hit the second one facing Jim Perry.

AUGUST 3 Shortstop Jack Kubiszyn hits a home run off Bill Fischer that accounts for the only run in a 1–0 win over the Athletics at Cleveland. Dick Donovan pitched the shutout.

The home run was the only one of Kubiszyn's career. He played in 50 major league games, all with the Indians, and had a .188 batting average and just two runs-batted-in in 101 at-bats.

AUGUST 6 The Indians win 6–5 at Municipal Stadium despite three homers from Tigers third baseman Steve Boros.

AUGUST 15 Shutout through eight innings, the White Sox suddenly explode for ten runs in the ninth inning to beat the Indians 10–2 in the first game of a double header at Municipal Stadium. The Indians also won the second game 3–2.

AUGUST 20 The Indians trade Ruben Gomez to the Twins for Jackie Collum and Georges Maranda.

AUGUST 26 Dick Donovan pitches a two-hitter to win 4–0 over the Red Sox in the second game of a double header at Municipal Stadium. Frank Malzone collected both Boston hits with a single in the second inning and a double in the eighth. The Indians also won the first game 10–5.

AUGUST 31 Dick Donovan hits two homers during a 9–6 win over the Orioles at Municipal Stadium. It was his second two-home-run game in 1962. The two games accounted for all four of his homers, and four of his five extra base hits, in 89 at-bats in 1962.

SEPTEMBER 7 The Indians score two runs in the ninth inning and Pedro Ramos pitches a two-hitter to defeat the Athletics 2–1 in Cleveland. Bubba Phillips drove in the tying run with a bases loaded single. The winning marker came across when Jerry Kindall walked with the sacks full. The only Kansas City hits were a double by Jerry Lumpe in the fourth inning and a single by Gino Cimoli in the ninth.

SEPTEMBER 20 Walt Bond drives in six runs and Johnny Romano four during a 10–9 win over the Athletics in Kansas City. The pair hit back-to-back homers twice in the first and seventh inning. Each of them also collected two-run doubles. It was Dick Donovan's 20th win of the season.

Bond stood six-foot-seven and weighed 235 pounds. He was traded to Houston during the 1962–63 off-season and died of leukemia in 1967 when he was only 29-years-old.

SEPTEMBER 30 The Indians dismiss Mel McGaha as manager just prior to s season-ending double header against the Angeles at Municipal Stadium. Coach Mel Harder served as interim manager, and Cleveland won both games 4–1 and 6–1.

McGaha later managed the Athletics for 110 games in 1964.

OCTOBER 5 Birdie Tebbetts is named manager of the Indians. Before hiring Tebbetts, the Indians negotiated with Leo Durocher, as the club had done following nearly every managerial opening since 1956, but Durocher wanted too much money and more control over the future of the franchise than ownership was willing to concede.

George (Birdie) Tebbetts had a 14-year career as a catcher in the majors, the last two of which were spent with the Indians in 1951 and 1952. He earned his nickname from his high, squeaky voice. While general manager with the Reds, Gabe Paul hired Tebbetts to guide the Cincinnati franchise. He took a club with 12 consecutive losing seasons to within two games of the NL pennant in 1956, but after the club returned to its losing ways, Tebbetts was fired in 1958. He later managed the Milwaukee Braves in 1961 and 1962 before Paul hired him a second time. Tebbetts would remain with the Indians until August 1966.

NOVEMBER 20 In a $6 million deal, the Indians ownership changes hands.

The old corporation was liquidated and a new one was set up by William Daley, who was chairman of the board of the old group, along with general manager Gabe Paul. The largest stockholder in the new corporation was Paul, owning 20 percent of the 6,000 shares. Paul was elected president, along with continuing his duties as general manager. Daley, who held 18 percent of the stock, remained as chairman of the board.

NOVEMBER 27 A month after America's nerves are frazzled by the Cuban missile crisis, the Indians trade Ty Cline, Frank Funk, and Don Dillard to the Braves for Joe Adcock and Jack Curtis. On the same day, the Indians traded Bubba Phillips and Gordon Seyfried to the Tigers for Ron Nischwitz.

For a club in a rebuilding phase, this deal made little sense as the Indians swapped three young players for Adcock, who was 35 years old. Adcock started the 1963 season as Cleveland's first baseman, but soon lost his job to Fred Whitfield, who was ten years younger and was acquired three weeks later in a trade with the Cardinals.

DECEMBER 15 The Indians trade Ron Taylor and Jack Kubiszyn to the Cardinals for Fred Whitfield.

Whitfield hit 84 homers for the Indians from 1963 through 1966, but was typical of the one-dimensional players on the club during the period. He was nicknamed "Wingy" because of his sidearm throwing motion due to an injured arm and was slow afoot and virtually immobile on defense.

1963

Season in a Sentence

Gabe Paul and Birdie Tebbetts turn over the bulk of the roster, but the result is one fewer win than the previous season and a further decline in attendance, which spurs more relocation rumors.

Finish • Won • Lost • Pct • GB

Finish	Won	Lost	Pct	GB
Fifth (tie)	79	83	.488	25.5

Manager

Birdie Tebbetts

Stats

	Indians	AL	Rank
Batting Avg:	.239	.247	9
On-Base Pct:	.304	.315	9
Slugging Pct:	.381	.380	5
Home Runs:	169		4
Stolen Bases:	59		5
ERA:	3.79	3.63	6
Fielding Avg:	.977	.978	7
Runs Scored:	635		7
Runs Allowed:	702		6

Starting Line-up

Joe Azcue, c
Fred Whitfield, 1b
Woodie Held, 2b
Max Alvis, 3b
Larry Brown, ss
Tito Francona, lf
Vic Davalillo, cf
Willie Kirkland, rf-cf
Al Luplow, rf
Joe Adcock, 1b
Johnny Romano, c
Jerry Kindall, ss-2b
Dick Howser, ss

Pitchers

Mudcat Grant, sp
Jack Kralick, sp
Dick Donovan, sp
Pedro Ramos, sp
Barry Latman, sp-rp
Gary Bell, rp
Ted Abernathy, rp
Bob Allen, rp
Jerry Walker, rp

Attendance

562,507 (ninth in AL)

Club Leaders

Batting Avg:	Max Alvis	.284
On-Base Pct:	Woodie Held	.352
Slugging Pct:	Max Alvis	.460
Home Runs:	Max Alvis	22
RBIs:	Max Alvis	67
Runs:	Max Alvis	81
Stolen Bases:	Max Alvis	9
	Tito Francona	9
Wins:	Mudcat Grant	13
	Jack Kralick	13
Strikeouts:	Pedro Ramos	169
ERA:	Jack Kralick	2.92
Saves:	Ted Abernathy	12

FEBRUARY 27 The Indians trade Chuck Essegian to the Orioles for Jerry Walker.

APRIL 9 The Indians win the opener 5–4 over the Twins in Minnesota behind home runs from Johnny Romano, Fred Whitfield, Max Alvis, and Woodie Held. It was Whitfield's first game with Cleveland, and Alvis's first big league homer. All four of the homers came at the expense of Camilo Pascaul. Mudcat Grant pitched the complete game.

The Indians introduced new sleeveless uniforms in 1963, an idea of Gabe Paul, who also outfitted his Cincinnati Reds club in sleeveless jerseys in 1956. The new Cleveland uniforms also contained more red than any previous edition. The undershirts were solid red. The caps and socks were predominately red with blue and white trim. The numbers on the front were blue, both those too would switch to red in 1965. The "Chief Wahoo" symbol was on the left breast. The uniforms were used with little change until 1969. In addition, there was a new numbering system. Manager Birdie Tebbetts, his coaches and the catchers wore single digit numerals. Infielders were numbered from 10 to 19, outfielders from 20 to 29, and pitchers from 30 to 49. Among those changing numbers from 1962 to 1963 were Jerry Kindall (1 to 14), Woodie Held (3 to 12), Tommie Agee

(4 to 23), Willie Tasby (6 to 28), Mike de la Hoz (7 to 17), Willie Kirkland (8 to 27), Johnny Romano (11 to 9), Gene Green (12 to 23), Tito Francona (14 to 24), Sam McDowell (17 to 34), Barry Latman (18 to 32), Dick Donovan (20 to 30), Bob Allen (24 to 40), Doc Edwards (25 to 6), Pedro Ramos (28 to 35), Al Luplow (32 to 22), and coach Mel Harder (43 to 2).

APRIL 11 In the home opener, the Indians lose 6–1 to the Tigers before 25,812 at Municipal Stadium. Don Mossi pitched a two-hitter for Detroit after retiring the first 19 Cleveland batters.

The lower stands at Municipal Stadium were painted citrus yellow in 1963, which brought a rash of complaints from infielders, who had difficulty following the ball against the light-colored seats. Empty seats were a problem all year at the stadium, as attendance dipped to 562,507, the lowest attendance figure since 1945.

APRIL 16 Sam McDowell pitches a two-hitter and strikes out 13 batters for a 3–0 win over the Senators at Municipal Stadium. The only Washington hits were singles by Dick Phillips in the third inning and Marv Breeding in the fifth.

APRIL 24 A two-run homer by Woodie Held off Earl Wilson in the fifth inning are the only runs in a 2–0 win over the Red Sox at Municipal Stadium. Gary Bell (eight innings) and Mudcat Grant (one inning) combined on the shutout.

MAY 2 Woodie Held hits a grand slam off Diego Segui in the sixth inning of a 15–6 win over the Athletics in Kansas City.

On the same day, the Indians traded Jim Perry to the Twins for Jack Kralick. Perry had 163 career wins in his future, 18 of which came in a return engagement with the Indians in 1974 and 1975. Kralick gave the Indians two serviceable seasons before losing his effectiveness.

MAY 8 After the Indians score twice in the top of the 13th, the Senators rally for five runs in their half, the last four on a grand slam by Don Lock off Ron Nischwitz, to win 6–3.

MAY 15 Mudcat Grant pitches the Indians to a 1–0 win over the Athletics at Municipal Stadium. The lone run of the game scored on a single by Tito Francona in the first inning.

MAY 16 Max Alvis hits a walk-off homer in the ninth inning to defeat the White Sox 5–4 at Municipal Stadium.

Alvis had a fine rookie season in 1963 with a .274 batting average and 22 home runs. He was off to a fine start in 1964, when he was diagnosed with spinal meningitis in June (see June 26, 1964). He would later play in the All-Star games in both 1965 and 1967 but would never again enjoy the success he had as a rookie.

MAY 17 Bob Allison hits three home runs for the Twins during an 11–4 win over the Indians at Municipal Stadium.

MAY 25 The Indians send Doc Edwards and $100,000 to the Athletics for Joe Azcue and Dick Howser.

This was Cleveland's best trade of the 1960s. Azcue was acquired merely to back-up Johnny Romano. He came to the Indians with a .209 career average with two homers in 258 at-bats. The day after Azcue arrived, Romano broke the little finger on his throwing hand tagging out Jackie Brandt of the Orioles on a play at the plate. Azcue was suddenly thrust into the starting role, and over the remainder of the 1963 season, hit .284 with 14 home runs in 320 at-bats. He remained as the Cleveland starting catcher until he was traded to the Red Sox in 1969. Howser gave the Indians one great season, scoring 101 runs in 1964, before injuries reduced his effectiveness.

June 2 — Jack Kralick pitches a two-hitter for a 5–0 win over the Yankees at Municipal Stadium. The only New York hits were singles by Clete Boyer in the third inning and Mickey Mantle in the seventh inning. Cleveland also won game two 7–2.

June 3 — The Indians sign Early Wynn as a free agent.

Wynn recorded his 299th career victory with the White Sox on September 8, 1962. He made three more starts with Chicago before the end of the season, but couldn't come up with his 300th win. Wynn went to spring training with the White Sox in 1963, but was released on April 2. He was unemployed for more than two months before the Indians inked his name on a contract. Early posted a record of 163–100 for Cleveland from 1949 through 1957.

June 8 — The Indians score eight runs in the eighth inning to account for all of the runs in an 8–1 win over the Senators in Washington.

June 14 — The Indians play 28 innings during a twi-night double header against the Senators at Municipal Stadium. Washington won the opener 5–2 in the conventional nine innings. The second tilt was a 19-inning marathon won by Cleveland 3–2. Willie Kirkland was the hero, driving in all three Indians runs, two of them with extra-inning home runs. He started the scoring with an RBI-single in the first inning. After the Senators scored in the top of the 11th, Kirkland tied the contest in the bottom half with a homer. His walk-off home run in the 19th decided the issue.

Kirkland is one of only five players in major league history with two extra inning home runs in a single game.

June 15 — Pedro Ramos (seven innings) and Ted Abernathy (two innings) combine on a one-hitter for a 4–0 win over the Senators at Municipal Stadium. The only Washington hit was a single by Jim King in the seventh inning.

June 16 — A three-run, pinch-hit homer by Fred Whitfield in the ninth inning beats the Senators 6–4 in the second game of a double header at Municipal Stadium. The Indians also won the opener 6–4.

June 17 — The Indians complete a five-game series sweep of the Senators at Municipal Stadium with a 1–0 win. Jack Kralick pitched the shutout.

June 19 — A walk-off homer by Jose "Joe" Azcue defeats the Orioles 5–4 in the first game of a double header at Municipal Stadium. Baltimore won the second tilt 6–2.

On June 20, the Indians had a record of 35–28 and were in fourth place, 3½ games out of first.

JUNE 20 Max Alvis hits a grand slam off Stu Miller in the seventh inning of an 11–8 win over the Orioles at Municipal Stadium.

JUNE 21 In his first appearance with the Indians since 1957, Early Wynn tries for his 300th career win, and loses 2–0. Wynn held the White Sox scoreless until Ron Hansen homered with a man on base in the ninth inning.

JUNE 23 Before a crowd of 46,019 at Municipal Stadium, an Old-Timers Game is held between games of a double header with the 1948 Indians facing a team of American League stars, including Joe DiMaggio, Bobby Doerr, and Hal Newhouser. Playing the White Sox, the 1963 Indians lost the first game 2–1, and won the second 2–0.

JUNE 27 Right fielder Al Luplow makes a spectacular catch to help the Indians defeat the Red Sox 6–4 in the second game of a double header at Fenway Park. With Cleveland leading 6–3 in the eighth inning and two Boston runners on base, Dick Williams hit a drive to right. Running at full speed, Luplow headed toward the five-foot-high barrier that fronted the bullpen. He reached the fence and backhanded the ball with a leaping catch just as his knees hit the wall. Luplow flipped over the fence headfirst and hung on for the out. The Red Sox won the first contest 6–5.

JUNE 28 Early Wynn makes a second start in an attempt to win his 300th career game, and earns a no decision in a 4–3 win over the White Sox in Chicago. Wynn allowed three runs in six innings.

JULY 4 Jerry Kindall hits a walk-off homer in the 14th inning to defeat the Red Sox 4–3 in the first game of a double header at Municipal Stadium. Early Wynn started the game in his attempt to achieve his 300th win. Wynn hurled six shutout innings, but was forced to leave with a sore shoulder. Cleveland also won the second tilt 7–5.

JULY 9 The All-Star Game is played at Municipal Stadium, and the National League wins 5–3 before a crowd of 44,160 that fell well short of a sell out. Willie Mays was the star of the game, driving in two runs and scoring two. He singled, drew a walk, stole two bases, and made a tremendous catch in center field. Mudcat Grant was the only Cleveland player on the AL roster but didn't appear in the game.

Future Hall of Famers on the rosters of the two clubs included Hank Aaron, Luis Aparicio, Jim Bunning, Orlando Cepeda, Roberto Clemente, Don Drysdale, Nellie Fox, Al Kaline, Harmon Killebrew, Sandy Koufax, Mickey Mantle, Juan Marichal, Willie Mays, Bill Mazeroski, Willie McCovey, Stan Musial, Brooks Robinson, Duke Snider, Warren Spahn, and Carl Yastrzemski.

JULY 13 Early Wynn finally records his 300th career win with a 7–4 decision over the Athletics in Kansas City. Wynn allowed four runs in five innings and left the game for a pinch-hitter with the Indians leading 5–4. He contributed a single to a four-run Cleveland rally in the fifth that gave the club a 5–1 lead. Wynn nearly gave it away by surrendering three runs in the bottom of the fifth. Jerry Walker pitched four shutout innings to preserve the victory. Wynn made six starts between his

299th victory, achieved on September 8, 1962, and number 300. Three of the six starts were with the White Sox at the end of the 1962 season.

Wynn made 15 more appearances for the Indians in 1963 but failed to win another game. He finished his career with 300 wins and 244 defeats.

JULY 17 The Indians visit the set of the television series *The Greatest Show on Earth* during a visit to Los Angeles. The invitation was extended by actor Jack Palance, a close friend of Early Wynn. The series debuted on ABC-TV on September 17, 1963, and lasted only one season.

JULY 22 Tito Francona hits a walk-off homer in the 13th inning to defeat the Twins 3–2 at Municipal Stadium. Mudcat Grant pitched all 13 innings.

JULY 28 Trailing 7–3, the Indians score seven runs in the sixth inning and win 12–6 over the Athletics in the second game of a double header in Cleveland. Kansas City won the first game 3–0.

Among those in attendance was Jacqueline Mayer, the 1963 Miss America. She hailed from Sandusky, Ohio.

JULY 31 The Indians win 1–0 and 9–5 during an eventful double header against the Angels at Municipal Stadium. In the opener, Barry Latman pitched the shutout. Fred Whitfield accounted for the lone run of the game with a home run off Fred Newman in the seventh inning. In the second game, Pedro Ramos not only struck out 15 batters in 8⅓ innings but hit two home runs. He connected in the third and the sixth innings. The second homer was part of a sequence in the sixth in which Cleveland hit four home runs in a row off Paul Foytack. The Indians entered the inning leading 5–1. After the first two batters were retired, Woodie Held, Ramos, and Tito Francona rocketed drives over the fence. On an 0–2 count, Larry Brown tagged Foytack with another four-bagger. It was Brown's first homer in the majors. The four home runs were struck by the 8-9-1-2 hitters in the batting order.

The Indians are one of only three clubs in major league history to club four consecutive home runs. The other two are the 1961 Milwaukee Braves and the 1964 Minnesota Twins. Indians pitchers set an American League record for most strikeouts during an 18-inning double header with 25. In addition to the 15 fanned by Ramos in game two, Latman set down ten batters on strikes in the opener.

AUGUST 2 A seven-run rally in the eighth inning falls a run short as the Indians lose 10–9 to the Tigers in Detroit.

AUGUST 4 After being held scoreless for the first inning of a double header, the Indians explode for three runs in the ninth inning of the second tilt to win 3–2 over the Tigers in Detroit. Tito Francona drove in the tying and winning runs with a single. Detroit won the opener 2–0.

AUGUST 8 Joe Azcue scores both runs in a 2–0 win over the Orioles in Baltimore. He stole home in the seventh inning, and doubled and scored on Tito Francona's single in the ninth. Dick Donovan pitched the shutout.

August 14 Willie Kirkland hits a home run off Ray Herbert in the 11th inning to account for the only run in a 1–0 win over the White Sox in Chicago. Dick Donovan hurled his second consecutive shutout.

August 19 Dick Stuart of the Red Sox hits a freak inside-the-park homer during an 8–3 Indians win at Fenway Park. The drive hit a ledge on the scoreboard in left-center field, caromed off the head of center fielder Vic Davalillo and bounced crazily into the left field corner.

August 23 Pedro Ramos strikes out 14 batters during a 13-inning complete game, but loses 3–2 to the Red Sox at Municipal Stadium. Three of the Red Sox five hits were home runs.

August 25 Tito Francona drives in both runs during a 15-inning, 2–1 win over the Red Sox in the second game of a double header at Municipal Stadium. With two out in the tenth inning and Cleveland trailing 1–0, Tito hit a home run. He drove in the winning tally with a single in the 15th. Boston won the opener 8–3. The Indians set a record for strikeouts by batters during a double header that included at least one extra inning game with 27, including 16 in game two.

August 30 Two days after Martin Luther King Jr.'s "I Have a Dream" speech in Washington, Larry Brown hits a walk-off homer in the ninth inning to defeat the Tigers 5–4 at Municipal Stadium.

September 1 Mike de la Hoz hits a grand slam off Don Mossi in the first inning of a 6–3 win over the Tigers in the first game of a double header at Municipal Stadium. The Indians also won the second contest 3–1.

September 3 The Indians win 15–3 over the Senators in the first game of a double header at Municipal Stadium. Washington won the second tilt 8–7.

September 6 In a game calculated as the 100,000th in major league history dating back to 1871, the Indians lose 7–2 to the Senators in Washington.

Herb Score began his long broadcasting career in September 1963, subbing for Ken Coleman, who left the Indians to broadcast Cleveland Browns games. Score replaced Coleman full-time in 1964. Coleman was later the play-by-play man for the Red Sox and the Reds.

September 13 A homer by Joe Adcock in the 12th inning beats the Angels 7–6 in Los Angeles.

September 28 Jack Kralick pitches a shutout and hits a home run for a 7–0 win over the Athletics in Kansas City.

September 30 The Indians purchase Don McMahon from Houston.

November 15 The Indians sign Wally Post as a free agent, following his release by the Twins.

December 2 Ten days following the assassination of President Kennedy, the Indians trade Joe Adcock and Barry Latman to the Angels for Leon Wagner.

Nicknamed "Daddy Wags," Wagner proved to be a tremendous short-term acquisition. In his first season in Cleveland, he hit 31 homers, drove in 100 runs, and scored 94.

DECEMBER 4 The Indians send Willie Kirkland to the Orioles for Al Smith and cash.

1964

Season in a Sentence

During another difficult season, Birdie Tebbetts suffers a heart attack during spring training, another fine start is wiped out by a long losing stretch, and the club nearly leaves Cleveland.

Finish • Won • Lost • Pct • GB

Finish	Won	Lost	Pct	GB
Sixth (tie)	79	83	.488	20.0

Managers

George Strickland (33–39) and Birdie Tebbetts (46–44)

Stats

Stats	Indians	AL	Rank
Batting Avg:	.247	.247	6
On-Base Pct:	.315	.317	7
Slugging Pct:	.380	.382	6
Home Runs:	164		4
Stolen Bases:	79		1
ERA:	3.75	3.63	6
Fielding Avg:	.981	.980	4
Runs Scored:	689		4
Runs Allowed:	693		7

Starting Line-up

Johnny Romano, c
Bob Chance, 1b
Woodie Held, 2b-3b-cf-lf
Max Alvis, 3b
Dick Howser, ss
Leon Wagner, lf
Vic Davalillo, cf
Tito Francona, rf
Larry Brown, 2b
Fred Whitfield, 1b
Chico Salmon, rf-2b
Joe Azcue, c
Billy Moran, 2b

Pitchers

Jack Kralick, sp
Sam McDowell, sp
Luis Tiant, sp
Dick Donovan, sp
Pedro Ramos, sp
Tommy John, sp-rp
Lee Stange, sp-rp
Don McMahon, rp
Gary Bell, rp
Ted Abernathy, rp
Sonny Siebert, rp-sp

Attendance

653,293 (eighth in AL)

Club Leaders

Batting Avg:	Vic Davalillo	.270
On-Base Pct:	Dick Howser	.335
Slugging Pct:	Leon Wagner	.434
Home Runs:	Leon Wagner	31
RBIs:	Leon Wagner	100
Runs:	Dick Howser	101
Stolen Bases:	Vic Davalillo	21
Wins:	Jack Kralick	12
Strikeouts:	Sam McDowell	177
ERA:	Sam McDowell	2.70
Saves:	Don McMahon	16

MARCH 3 The Indians spring training exercises are interrupted by a five-inch snow fall that descends upon Tucson, Arizona. Training moved indoors to a municipal recreation center and at nearby David-Monthan Air Force Base.

APRIL 1 Birdie Tebbetts suffers a heart attack.

The 51-year-old Tebbetts was stricken in his hotel room in Tucson at 10 p.m. The original diagnosis called for a recovery period of six to eight months, which would have put Tebbetts away from the ball club for the remainder of the season. Coach George Strickland was named interim manager. Tebbetts was healthy enough to return to his duties on July 3.

APRIL 14 In the midst of Beatlemania, with the Fab Four holding the top five spots on the Billboard singles chart, the Indians lose the season opener 7–6 to the Twins before 25,617 at Municipal Stadium. The Indians had a 6–3 lead after four innings, but couldn't hold the advantage. In his Cleveland debut, Leon Wagner drove in four runs with a homer and a single. Woodie Held also homered.

A total of 38 mayors from the surrounding areas of Cleveland jointly threw ceremonial first pitches. Bob Hope was the "catcher." The mayors each threw plastic balls at the same time, deluging Hope.

APRIL 23 The Indians score three runs in the 16th inning to outlast the Angels 5–2 in Los Angeles. The 16th-inning runs were driven in by Johnny Romano, Don McMahon and Dick Howser.

MAY 3 Tommy John records the first of his 288 career victories with a 3–0 decision over the Orioles in Baltimore. Robin Roberts, who won 286 games from 1948 through 1966, was the losing pitcher.

MAY 4 Leon Wagner hits a grand slam in the seventh inning off Bill Spanswick during a 7–5 win over the Red Sox in Boston.

MAY 11 Fred Whitfield hits a grand slam off Jack Lamabe in the fifth inning of an 11–7 win over the Red Sox at Municipal Stadium.

On May 16, the Indians had a record of 16–9 record.

MAY 23 The Indians outslug the Tigers 11–9 at Municipal Stadium.

MAY 30 Leon Wagner collects five hits, including two triples, in five at-bats during a 10–2 win over the Senators in Washington.

MAY 31 The Indians sweep the Senators 9–6 and 8–3 in Washington.

Cleveland won the opener with the help of a muffed third strike. The Indians trailed 6–5 with two out in the ninth, Dick Howser on first, and Vic Davalillo at bat. Davalillo swung at and missed a two-strike pitch from Ron Kline for what should have been a game-ending strikeout, but the ball glanced off the glove of catcher Mike Brumley. While Brumley tried frantically to locate the ball, Davalillo dashed safely to first base and Howser went to second. Leon Wagner singled to score Howser, Max Alvis brought Davalillo home with a squeeze bunt, and Johnny Romano capped the uprising with a two-run double.

JUNE 2 Sam McDowell strikes out 14 batters during a 3–2 win over the White Sox at Municipal Stadium.

The game was McDowell's first start since his recall from Portland in the Pacific Coast League, where he was 8–0, including a no-hitter and a one-hitter in back-to-back starts, and 102 strikeouts and a 1.18 ERA in 76 innings.

June 7 The Indians travel 15 innings to defeat the Senators 3–2 in the first game of a double header at Municipal Stadium. A single by Al Smith drove in the winning run. Home runs by Bob Chance in the second and seventh innings accounted for the first two runs. Washington won the second tilt 6–3.

Centerfielder Vic Davalillo is presented with a Gold Glove Award by Rawlings representative Tom Feldhaus. Davalillo provided top-notch defense throughout his years with the team.

June 15 The Indians trade Mudcat Grant to the Twins for Lee Stange and George Banks.

Grant never developed any consistency with the Indians. The Twins were happy to obtain Grant, if for no other reason than he would no longer be pitching against them. Including the time the franchise was based in Washington, Grant was 22–6 lifetime against the Senators/Twins (and 45–55 against the rest of the league) at the time of the trade. It proved to be a terrible trade for the Indians. Mudcat had a 21–7 record and pitched in the World Series for Minnesota in 1965. Later, he was an effective reliever, and saved 24 games while posting a 1.82 ERA for the Athletics in 1970.

June 17 A walk-off homer by in the ninth inning by Max Alvis beats the Senators 3–2 in the first game of a double header at Municipal Stadium. Alvis also homered in the second contest, a 5–0 victory.

June 24 Max Alvis hits a grand slam off Jim Roland in the third inning of a 12–3 win over the Twins in the first game of a double header at Metropolitan Stadium. Minnesota won game two 3–2.

JUNE 26 Max Alvis is stricken with spinal meningitis while the club is in Boston. He missed the next six weeks.

JULY 3 The day after the passage of the Civil Rights Act, prohibiting racial discrimination in employment and places of public accommodation, Tito Francona collects three doubles and a triple in five at-bats hitting out of the lead-off spot during a 2–1 win over the White Sox in Chicago. His triple in the 11th inning scored Dick Donovan with the winning run. Francona had four of Cleveland's six hits in the contest off Fred Talbot. The contest also marked the return of Birdie Tebbetts to the Indians following his April 1 heart attack.

JULY 4 Sam McDowell strikes out 12 batters, but walks 11 and hits a batter in $7^{2}/_{3}$ innings during a 4–0 loss to the White Sox in Chicago.

JULY 9 The Indians celebrate "Welcome Back Birdie Night" at Municipal Stadium. Birdie Tebbetts was honored in between games of a double header. Telegrams were read from President Lyndon Johnson, former President Dwight Eisenhower and Ohio Governor James Rhodes. The Orioles won both games 3–2 and 2–1.

JULY 10 On his 24th birthday, Bob Chance hits two homers and drives in five runs during an 8–0 win over the Orioles at Municipal Stadium.

JULY 16 The Indians blow a seven-run lead but recover to defeat the Athletics 12–9 in ten innings in Kansas City. Cleveland scored seven runs in the first inning, but the A's countered with five in their half, three more in the third and one in the sixth for a 9–7 lead. The Tribe tied the game with two runs in the eighth, and won it with three in the tenth.

JULY 18 The Indians need 15 innings to defeat the Yankees 6–4 in New York. Fred Whitfield smacked a two-run homer in the 12th to give Cleveland a 4–2 lead, but the Yanks tied it in their half. In the 15th, Bob Chance delivered an RBI-triple, then scored on a squeeze bunt by Billy Moran.

Whitfield hit ten of his 26 homers in 1965 against the Yankees.

JULY 19 In his major league debut, Luis Tiant strikes out 11 batters and pitches a shutout to win 3–0 over the Yankees in the second game of a double header in New York. The Yanks won the opener 6–2.

A native of Cuba, Tiant's father, also named Luis, was a star pitcher who played in the Negro Leagues from 1930 through 1947. The younger Tiant was called up by the Indians at the age of 23 after compiling a 15–1 record and a 2.04 ERA at Portland in the Pacific Coast League during the first half of the 1964 season. As a rookie with Cleveland, he was 10–4, pitched two more shutouts, and compiled an earned run average of 2.83. His herky-jerky, pirouette pitching motion in which he stopped momentarily in his delivery was controversial from the beginning and baffled hitters for 19 big league seasons. Tiant was 65–64 on Cleveland teams that were never in contention for a pennant. After he followed a 21–9 season in 1968 with a 9–20 mark, the Indians dealt him to Minnesota. By 1971, Luis found a home in Boston and produced three more seasons of 20 or more wins.

July 31 Gary Bell pitches $6^2/_3$ innings of hitless relief during a 12–3 win over the Tigers in the first game of a double header in Detroit. The Indians also won the second tilt 4–2.

August 8 The Indians rout the Twins 16–8 at Municipal Stadium.

August 22 The Indians sweep the Angels 1–0 and 5–1 at Municipal Stadium. Sonny Siebert pitched the opening game shutout.

Siebert was a 27-year-old rookie for the Indians in 1964. He was a hard-hitting first baseman and basketball player at the University of Missouri and was selected by the St. Louis Hawks in the NBA draft. During his first two seasons in the Indians farm system, Siebert was a first baseman-outfielder and realized he was never going to reach the majors as a hitter. He threatened to quit unless the club let him pitch. The Indians acquiesced in 1960. Siebert had a 61–48 record and pitched a no-hitter for Cleveland before a trade to the Red Sox in April 1969.

August 29 Fred Whitfield hits a home run in the 11th inning to defeat the Athletics 4–3 in Kansas City. It was the Indians eighth win in a row.

August 30 A two-run single by Max Alvis in the ninth inning defeats the Athletics 6–5 in the second game of a double header in Kansas City. The A's won the opener 9–3.

September 2 Lee Stange ($7^2/_3$ innings) and Gary Bell ($1^2/_3$ innings) combined on a two-hitter to defeat the Senators 9–0 in Washington. Stange fanned four batters in the seventh inning. He was credited with a strikeout when Joe Azcue let a ball get past him on a swinging third strike allowing Don Lock to reach first base. Stange later struck out Willie Kirkland, Don Zimmer, and John Kennedy. The only Senators hits were singles by Joe Cunningham in the sixth inning and Mike Brumley in the seventh.

September 5 The Indians send Pedro Ramos to the Yankees for Ralph Terry, Bud Daley, and cash.

With the Cleveland franchise drowning in red ink, Ramos was dealt for two aging pitchers and cash. He was remarkable down the stretch, helping the Yankees win the AL pennant by making 13 relief appearances with a 1.25 ERA, and 21 strikeouts and no walks in $21^2/_3$ innings. The Yanks finished the season one game ahead of the White Sox.

September 12 The Indians outlast the White Sox 11–10 at Municipal Stadium. Cleveland led 9–3 in the fourth inning before hanging on for the win.

September 30 Three days after the release of the Warren Commission, which declared that Lee Harvey Oswald acted alone in the assassination of John Kennedy, the Indians win 5–0 and 3–0 over the Red Sox during a double header in Boston. Luis Tiant and Sam McDowell pitched the shutouts.

October 1 A crowd of only 306, the smallest in the history of Fenway Park, watches the Indians lose 4–2 to the Red Sox.

October 16 The Indians board of directors votes to remain in Cleveland.

The Indians ownership gave serious consideration to moving prior to the vote. In 1963, the Indians drew only 562,507 fans, the second worst figure in the majors, exceeding only the Washington Senators, a franchise that moved to Texas eight years later. In 1964, the Cleveland attendance increased to 653,293, but it was still the third worst in the big leagues ahead of only the Senators and the Kansas City Athletics. The A's would move to Oakland following the 1967 season. Early in September 1964, Indians President Gabe Paul disclosed the Indians deficit for the year would approximate the $1,200,000 loss suffered in 1963. In order to have an operating fund, Paul revealed that each stockholder had been called upon to contribute cash over and above his original investment. In his case, Paul said, this amounted to $60,000. Reports that Seattle was wooing the Indians were conformed on September 17 by Seattle's mayor. At the same time, Paul revealed that an Oakland syndicate had sought to buy the club, reportedly offering $6,500,000 in a deal that would transfer the Indians to the city. Tribe owners turned down that bid, but left open the possibility that the club might leave Cleveland. "The situation cannot remain as at present with the huge annual losses," said Paul. "We just cannot retain a big league status and continue to compete for playing talent with our present income." Sensing the seriousness of the situation, the Greater Cleveland Growth Board, a committee of industrial and business leaders, and the Chamber of Commerce launched a drive in late-September to sell $1,000,000 worth of tickets for 1965. By October 6, when the Indians directors met to consider their position, the ticket drive was almost halfway toward its goal. However, the board members had just about made up their minds to sell to the highest bidder and move the franchise. Paul and William Daley, the Indians chairman of the board, went on a three-day "fact-finding" tour of the three cities that were seeking to lure the Indians. Dallas-Fort Worth was in the mix in addition to Seattle and Oakland. Paul and Daley reported to the directors that, if a satisfactory lease could be worked out with the city of Cleveland, it would be the best for all concerned for the Indians to stay in the city. On October 16, the Indians directors held another meeting, which lasted four hours, and voted to remain in Cleveland, ending weeks of speculation. The club's contract with the city for the use of Municipal Stadium was due to expire at the end of the year, but Paul immediately agreed to a new ten-year lease with a cancellation clause. The pact provided that either party could cancel the deal at the end of any calendar year upon 90 days' notice. Terms of the new lease arranged for a reduction in rental from seven per cent to six per cent of gross receipts. The Indians also paid less for stadium maintenance under the agreement, and the city consented to several improvements. The Cleveland picture brightened during the off-season when the ticket drive closed with more than 4,500 season tickets sold, representing in excess of $900,000. The club further pleased the fans by bringing back Rocky Colavito (see January 20, 1965). Attendance in 1965 increased to 934,786, which would represent the highest total from 1960 through 1973.

December 1 A month after Lyndon Johnson defeats Barry Goldwater in the presidential election, the Indians trade Woodie Held and Bob Chance to the Senators for Chuck Hinton.

The versatile Hinton played for the Indians from 1965 through 1967 and again from 1969 through 1971. He played every position but shortstop and pitcher with Cleveland, appearing in 172 games in left field, 157 in center, 153 in right, 106 at first base, 33 at second, 17 at third and nine as a catcher.

DECEMBER 15 The Indians sell Tito Francona to the Cardinals.

1965

Season in a Sentence

Rocky Colavito returns, attendance increases, and the Indians are in first place on the Fourth of July before another second-half collapse.

Finish • Won • Lost • Pct • GB

Finish	Won	Lost	Pct	GB
Fifth	87	75	.537	15.0

Manager

Birdie Tebbetts

Stats

Stats	Indians	AL	Rank
Batting Avg:	.250	.252	3
On-Base Pct:	.317	.314	4
Slugging Pct:	.379	.369	3
Home Runs:	156		3
Stolen Bases:	109		2
ERA:	3.30	3.46	6
Fielding Avg:	.981	.978	1
Runs Scored:	663		4
Runs Allowed:	613		7

Starting Line-up

Joe Azcue, c
Fred Whitfield, 1b
Pedro Gonzalez, 2b
Max Alvis, 3b
Larry Brown, ss
Leon Wagner, lf
Vic Davalillo, cf
Rocky Colavito, rf
Chuck Hinton, cf-lf-1b
Dick Howser, ss

Pitchers

Sam McDowell, sp
Sonny Siebert, sp-rp
Luis Tiant, sp
Ralph Terry, sp
Jack Kralick, sp-rp
Gary Bell, rp
Don McMahon, rp
Lee Stange, rp

Attendance

934,786 (fifth in AL)

Club Leaders

Batting Avg:	Vic Davalillo	.301
On-Base Pct:	Rocky Colavito	.383
Slugging Pct:	Fred Whitfield	.513
Home Runs:	Leon Wagner	28
RBIs:	Rocky Colavito	108
Runs:	Rocky Colavito	92
Stolen Bases:	Vic Davalillo	26
Wins:	Sam McDowell	17
Strikeouts:	Sam McDowell	325
ERA:	Sam McDowell	2.18
Saves:	Gary Bell	17

JANUARY 20 Three weeks after the Browns win the NFL championship by defeating the Colts 27–0 at Municipal Stadium, the Indians participate in a three-team deal to re-acquire Rocky Colavito. The White Sox traded Jim Landis, Mike Hershberger, and Fred Talbot to the Athletics for Colavito, then swapped Rocky and Cam Carreon to Cleveland for Johnny Romano, Tommy John, and Tommie Agee.

The trade was cause for civic celebration. The trade of Colavito to the Tigers in April 1960 coincided with a decline in both overall team success and attendance at Indians games at Municipal Stadium. Gabe Paul believed that bringing back Rocky was necessary to bring back fans to the ballpark. For a season, the trade was beneficial. In 1965, Rocky led the AL in RBIs (108) and walks (93) and added 26 homers, 92 runs, and a .287 batting average. The team posted a winning record for the first time since 1959, and attendance increased by 43 percent. But Colavito's stats dropped off dramatically after 1965, and by

1967 he was spending more time on the bench than on the field. In the long-term, the trade was a disaster, as John and Agee developed into All-Stars. John pitched as a rookie for the Indians in 1963 and 1964 and posted a 2–11 record and a 3.61 ERA. The Indians brass was unimpressed, but John was only 21 years old when sent to Chicago. Over the remainder of his career, which lasted until 1989, John won 286 games, lost 220, was named to four All-Star teams and pitched in four World Series. Agee was considered one of the top prospects in the Indians farm system and was given brief trials as an outfielder in 1962, 1963, and 1964. He hit only .170 in 31 games, however, and many in the organization believed that he would never reach his potential. It was obvious he was merely rushed too soon, as Agee was only 22 when traded by the Indians. In 1966, he was the Rookie-of-the-Year and made the All-Star team, and in 1969 he was a key component of the Mets team that won the world championship.

MARCH 8 The Indians play an exhibition game against the Monterey club of the Mexican League in Monterey. The Tribe won the game 5–1.

The Indians played three games in Mexico City on March 9, 10, and 11, and in Nogales on March 26. The club also played spring exhibitions in Mexico in 1966 and 1967.

MARCH 22 An angry swarm of bees interrupts a spring training game against the Giants in Tucson as the players dash for cover. The game was halted after 13 innings with the score 3–3 because the sun was in the eyes of the batters.

MARCH 30 The Indians purchase Stan Williams from the Yankees.

APRIL 13 The Indians win the season opener 7–1 against the Angels in Los Angeles. Ralph Terry threw a complete game four-hitter. Leon Wagner hit a home run.

APRIL 14 The Indians sell Ted Abernathy to the Cubs.

With his submarine style of pitching, Abernathy was considered to be little more than a novelty by the Indians brass, who couldn't find a place for him on their 1965 staff. With the Cubs that season, he led the National League in saves, and did so a second time with the Reds in 1967. Abernathy was an effective major league reliever into the early 1970s.

APRIL 21 In the home opener before a crowd of 44,335, Leon Wagner hits a walk-off homer in the tenth inning to defeat the Angels 6–5. It was Wagner's second home run of the game. The Angels scored three runs in the ninth to surge ahead 5–4, but Cleveland tied the game in their half of the inning.

Wagner had a brief fling with an acting career while with the Indians. He appeared in an episode of the TV series The Man From U.N.C.L.E. *as a "tough good guy." In 1965, Wagner batted .294 with 28 home runs.*

MAY 9 Fred Whitfield collects seven hits, including two doubles and a homer, in nine at-bats and drives in six runs during a double header against the Red Sox in Boston. The Indians won 9–4 and 10–7.

May 15 Chuck Hinton hits a grand slam off Ron Kline in the seventh inning, but the Indians lose 9–7 to the Senators in Washington.

May 16 Fred Whitfield hits a pinch-hit grand slam off Steve Ridzik in the sixth inning of a 7–3 win in the second game of a double header in Washington. The Indians lost the opener 8–7 in 11 innings.

May 18 The Indians edge the Orioles 1–0 at Municipal Stadium. Jack Kralick (seven innings) and Don McMahon (two innings) combined on the shutout. Fred Whitfield drove in the lone run of the game with a single in the sixth inning.

Whitfield hit .293 with 26 homers and 90 RBIs in 1965.

May 21 Vic Davalillo drives in six runs with a homer, double, and single during an 11–6 win over the Red Sox at Municipal Stadium.

May 28 The Indians lose 1–0 to the Tigers on Detroit.

May 29 The Indians lose 1–0 to the Tigers in Detroit for the second day in a row, this time in ten innings. Jack Kralick shut out the Tigers for nine innings and then allowed doubles to George Thomas and Dick McAuliffe in the tenth.

June 5 Sam McDowell strikes out 15 batters in ten innings and defeats the Tigers 2–1 at Municipal Stadium. The winning run scored on a walk-off double by Vic Davalillo.

In a season in which he didn't turn 23 until September, McDowell was 17–11 in 1965 while leading the American League in earned run average (2.18) and strikeouts (325 in 273 innings).

June 7 Luis Tiant pitches a two-hitter to defeat the Twins 2–1 at Metropolitan Stadium. The only Minnesota hits were doubles by Tony Oliva and Don Mincher in the fourth inning. The only Cleveland runs scored in the top of the fourth on back-to-back homers by Leon Wagner and Rocky Colavito.

June 8 In the first amateur free agent draft in major league history, the Indians select catcher Ray Fosse from Marion High School in Marion, Illinois.

Prior to the draft, the Indians brass went to great lengths to tell fans how well the scouting staff prepared for the draft. While the club picked up a gem in Fosse, the only other future major leaguer chosen was fourth rounder Vic Albury, whose entire four-year career was spent with the Twins from 1973 through 1976.

June 16 Luis Tiant pitches a one-hitter to beat the Senators 5–0 at Municipal Stadium. The lone Washington hit was a single by Woodie Held in the seventh inning.

June 17 Sonny Siebert strikes out 15 batters and pitches a three-hit shutout to defeat the Senators 5–0 at Municipal Stadium.

With the help of pitchers like Siebert, Sam McDowell, Luis Tiant, and Gary Bell, the Indians pitching staff led the American League in strikeouts six consecutive seasons from 1963 through 1968.

June 19 Ralph Terry pitches the Indians to a 1–0 win over the Angels at Municipal Stadium. Fred Whitfield drove in the lone run with a walk-off single with the bases loaded in the ninth inning.

June 20 Sam McDowell pitches a two-hitter to defeat the Angels 2–0 in the first game of a double header at Municipal Stadium. The only hits off McDowell were a double by opposing pitcher Marcelino Lopez and a single by Jim Fregosi, both in the sixth inning.

Spirits were high in 1965 as the Indians put together their best record of the decade. In this photo, taken during spring training, manager Birdie Tebbetts, in headdress, is flanked by (left to right) Ralph Terry, Max Alvis, Chuck Hinton, Dick Howser, and Leon Wagner.

June 21 Chuck Hinton hits a walk-off homer in the tenth inning to defeat the Twins 5–4 at Municipal Stadium.

The win was the tenth in a row for the Indians and gave the club a record of 37–24.

June 25 Sam McDowell strikes out 13 batters in 8⅔ innings for a 2–0 win over the Athletics in Cleveland. McDowell received relief help from Gary Bell, who fanned the only batter he faced. Solo homers by Rocky Colavito in the second inning and Chuck Hinton in the fourth off Catfish Hunter produced the only two runs of the contest.

JUNE 27 Chuck Hinton hits a three-run, walk-off homer in the tenth inning for a 10–7 win over the Athletics in the first game of a double header in Cleveland. The Indians also won the second tilt 11–7.

JUNE 29 The Indians take sole possession of first place with an 8–5 win over the Red Sox in Boston.

The Indians stay in first place for six days. The club peaked on July 3 with a record of 46–28. Over the last 88 games, Cleveland was 41–47 to finish at 87–75. The modest winning percentage of .537 was the best of any Indians team from 1959 through 1994.

JULY 16 Larry Brown hits a home run in the tenth inning to beat the Orioles 4–3 at Municipal Stadium.

AUGUST 15 Pinch-hit home runs key a 15-inning, 6–4 win over the Twins in the second game of a double header at Municipal Stadium. Batting for Joe Azcue with the Indians trailing 3–1, Max Alvis hit a two-run homer in the ninth to tie the score. Both teams scored in the 11th. In the 15th, Leon Wagner batted for Duke Sims and stroked a two-run walk-off homer for the victory. Minnesota won the opener 4–3.

AUGUST 22 Vic Davalillo collects five hits, including three doubles, during a ten-inning, 8–5 win over the Senators in Washington.

AUGUST 31 Sam McDowell pitches a one-hitter for an 8–1 win over the Athletics in the first game of a double header in Kansas City. The A's won the second game 3–2 in 11 innings.

SEPTEMBER 2 The Indians waste brilliant pitching by Sam McDowell and lose 1–0 to the Orioles in 11 innings at Memorial Stadium. McDowell pitched ten innings, allowed only two hits, and struck out 16 batters. The only Baltimore hits were singles by Luis Aparicio and Sam Bowens.

SEPTEMBER 7 Chico Salmon hits a grand slam off Tommy John during the sixth inning of a 9–5 win over the White Sox at Comiskey Park.

A native of Panama, Salmon was renowned throughout baseball for his belief in ghosts, and because of it, he always slept with the lights on in his bedroom. In five seasons with the Indians, Salmon was a "super sub," playing all over the field. He appeared in 134 games at second base, 100 at first, 90 at shortstop, 33 at third base, 74 in right field, 55 in left and five in center.

SEPTEMBER 10 In his debut with the Indians, left fielder Lu Clinton drops one fly ball and misplays another, leading to a 2–0 loss to the Tigers at Municipal Stadium.

SEPTEMBER 16 Dave Morehead, a 23-year-old pitcher with the Red Sox, no-hits the Indians for a 2–0 win at Fenway Park. The only Cleveland base runner was Rocky Colavito, who walked leading off the second on a 3–2 pitch that was 12 inches outside the plate.

The final out was recorded when Vic Davalillo hit a hopper toward the mound. Morehead tried to field the ball over his head, but it got away and landed about four feet behind him. He retrieved the ball, took a couple of steps toward first, stumbled momentarily, and then threw to first baseman Lee Thomas. The throw was aimed and too soft, but Thomas scooped it out of the dirt in time to retire Davalillo by a step.

September 20 The Indians win 5–4 over the Tigers in 14 innings at Municipal Stadium in a game highlighted by a vicious brawl. Chico Salmon drove in the winning run with a single.

Detroit pitcher Larry Sherry threw two tight pitches to Pedro Gonzalez on successive deliveries in the fifth inning. Both hit Gonzalez's bat and were called fouls by umpire Bill McKinley. After the second pitch, Gonzalez backed away from the plate and charged toward the mound waving his bat. Sherry at first backed off, then rushed into the Tribe second baseman. There was some dispute over what happened next. Most press box observers claimed that Gonzalez swung twice at Sherry with his bat but missed. The umpires reported to AL president Joe Cronin that Gonzalez landed one blow, and Sherry displayed a welt on his arm to prove it. Indians third base coach Solly Hemus was the first to reach the combatants and wrestled the bat out of Pedro's grasp. By then, both dugouts had emptied and three or four Tigers were holding Gonzalez before Al Luplow fought his way into the mob and pulled Gonzalez away from the scene of the action. Cronin suspended Gonzalez for the final 13 games of the season and fined him $500.

September 26 Tom Kelley pitches a two-hitter to win 7–1 over the Tigers in the second game of a double header in Detroit. The only Detroit hits were a single by Jerry Lumpe in the second inning and a homer by Norm Cash in the seventh. The Indians lost the opener 2–0.

The two-hitter came in Kelley's third major league start. He was 21-years-old. A promising career was hampered by arm trouble, however. In four seasons with the Indians he had a 6–9 record, and was 20–22 overall during his big league career.

October 1 The Indians trade Joe Rudi and Phil Roof to the Athletics for Jim Landis.

The Indians traded a 19-year-old outfielder with a bright future for a washed-up 31-year-old outfielder. Rudi reached the majors in 1967 and hit below .200 in each of his first three seasons, but the A's showed patience with young players at a time when the Indians management gave up on promising athletes much too quickly. Rudi was Oakland's starting left fielder on the world championship teams of 1972, 1973, and 1974, played on three All-Star teams, and during his career led the AL in hits, doubles, and triples. He played 16 seasons in the big leagues.

November 30 The Indians sign Del Crandall as a free agent following his release by the Pirates.

1966

Season in a Sentence

The Indians win their first ten games and are in first place on June 12, but once again early season excitement turns to severe disappointment as the club struggles to score runs and drifts back to the .500 mark.

Finish • Won • Lost • Pct • GB

Finish	Won	Lost	Pct	GB
Fifth	81	81	.500	17.0

Managers

Birdie Tebbetts (66–57) and George Strickland (15–24)

Stats

Stats	Indians	AL	Rank
Batting Avg:	.237	.240	5
On-Base Pct:	.299	.308	8
Slugging Pct:	.360	.369	6
Home Runs:	155		4
Stolen Bases:	53		6 (tie)
ERA:	3.23	3.44	3
Fielding Avg:	.977	.978	4
Runs Scored:	574		7 (tie)
Runs Allowed:	586		3

Starting Line-up

Joe Azcue, c
Fred Whitfield, 1b
Pedro Gonzalez, 2b
Max Alvis, 3b
Larry Brown, ss
Leon Wagner, lf
Vic Davalillo, cf
Rocky Colavito, rf
Chico Salmon, ss-2b
Chuck Hinton, cf-lf
Jim Landis, cf-lf-rf

Pitchers

Sonny Siebert, sp
Gary Bell, sp
Steve Hargan, sp
Luis Tiant, sp
Sam McDowell, sp
John O'Donoghue, rp-sp
Tom Kelley, rp

Attendance

903,359 (seventh in AL)

Club Leaders

Batting Avg:	Leon Wagner	.279
On-Base Pct:	Rocky Colavito	.336
Slugging Pct:	Leon Wagner	.441
Home Runs:	Rocky Colavito	30
RBIs:	Fred Whitfield	78
Runs:	Leon Wagner	70
Stolen Bases:	Chico Salmon	10
	Chuck Hinton	10
Wins:	Sonny Siebert	16
Strikeouts:	Sam McDowell	225
ERA:	Steve Hargan	2.48
Saves:	Dick Radatz	10

March 5 The Major League Players Association hires Marvin Miller to be the new executive director of the organization. Miller formally took office on July 1. Under Miller's leadership, the association would take actions that led to a revolution in player-owner relations, including free agency by 1976.

April 6 The Indians trade Ralph Terry to the Athletics for John O'Donoghue.

April 11 With Vice-President Hubert Humphrey on hand to throw out the first pitch, the Indians defeat the Senators in the season opener in Washington by a 5–2 score with four runs in the ninth inning. Vic Davalillo and Max Alvis each hit two-run singles during the rally. Sam McDowell was the winning pitcher. It was the first of ten straight season opening victories for the Indians.

April 15 In the home opener, the Indians win 8–7 over the Red Sox in 12 innings before 33,198 at Municipal Stadium. Cleveland trailed 4–0 before scoring six runs in the sixth inning, then fell behind again 7–6 when Boston tallied three runs in the seventh. The Tribe tied the score 7–7 in the eighth, then won the contest in the 12th. Max Alvis drove in the winning run on a two-out single.

April 17 In his first start of the season, Luis Tiant shuts out the Red Sox 6–0 at Municipal Stadium.

April 19 Sam McDowell strikes out 12 batters during a 3–1 victory over the Yankees at Municipal Stadium. A homer with two men on base by Fred Whitfield in the fourth inning provided all of the Cleveland runs.

> *McDowell led the AL in strikeouts in 1966 with 225 in 194⅓ innings but struggled with arm problems and had a won-lost record of 9–8.*

April 25 Sam McDowell pitches a one-hitter to beat the Athletics 2–0 at Cleveland. The victory gave the Indians an 8–0 record on the season. The only Kansas City hit was a single by Jose Tartabull in the sixth inning. Larry Brown drove in both runs with a single in the sixth.

April 26 In his second start of the season, Luis Tiant pitches his second shutout, defeating the Athletics 4–0 in Cleveland. Tiant struck out 12 batters. The win gave the Indians a 9–0 record on the season.

April 28 The Indians run their season record to 10–0 with a 2–1 win over the Angels at Municipal Stadium.

> *The season-opening ten-game winning streak has been bettered by only four clubs in major league history and matched by two others. The 1982 Braves and 1987 Brewers each won their first 13 games, the 1884 New York Giants the first 12, and the 1981 Athletics the first 11. The 1955 Dodgers and 1962 Pirates also started 10–0. Cleveland 10–0 start in 1966 actually took 18 days to complete. There were three scheduled days off and five games were postponed.*

April 29 The Indians ten-game winning streak is stopped by a 4–1 loss to the White Sox at Municipal Stadium.

May 1 Following up on his gem of April 25, Sam McDowell pitches his second consecutive one-hitter and defeats the White Sox 1–0 at Municipal Stadium. The lone Chicago hit was a bloop double in the third inning by Don Buford. Cleveland scored their lone run in the second inning off Tommy John on a double by Pedro Gonzalez and a single by Larry Brown.

May 3 In his third start of the season, Luis Tiant pitches his third shutout, defeating the Yankees 1–0 in New York.

May 4 Shortstop Larry Brown and left fielder Leon Wagner are both hurt in a severe collision during a 2–1 win over the Yankees in New York.

> *The two collided while chasing a short fly by Roger Maris that fell for a double. Wagner escaped with a concussion and broken nose and was able to play two days later. Brown wasn't so lucky. He incurred multiple fractures of the skull, above and below the eye sockets, and a broken nose. After being rushed to the hospital Brown lapsed into a coma for three days and remained in intensive care for a week. He was unable to play for six weeks.*

MAY 5 The Indians run their season record to 14–1 with a 4–0 win over the Yankees in New York.

The Indians allowed only 24 runs during the first 15 games of the season, while scoring 55.

MAY 7 The Indians score six runs in the ninth inning to defeat the Orioles 6–3 in Baltimore. Leon Wagner tied the score with a single and Duke Sims drilled a three-run homer to cap the rally.

Wagner hit .279 with 23 homers in 1966.

MAY 13 The Indians lose 1–0 to the Orioles in 13 innings in the first game of a double header at Municipal Stadium. Gary Bell pitched the first 11 innings. Frank Robinson drove in the lone run with a single. Cleveland won the second tilt 2–1.

MAY 25 The Indians wallop the Tigers 13–2 in Detroit.

MAY 28 The Indians defeat the Twins 2–1 at Municipal Stadium.

The victory gave Cleveland a 27–10 record and a 4½ game lead in the AL pennant race.

MAY 30 The Indians play the Angels in Anaheim for the first time, and lose a double header 4–3 and 5–1.

MAY 31 The Indians win a 17-inning marathon by a 7–5 score over the Angels in Anaheim. Cleveland took a 4–0 lead in the third, then didn't score again until the 17th, when they took a 7–4 advantage. Pedro Gonzalez broke the 4–4 tie with a bases loaded single. There were 19 strikeouts by Indians pitchers. Sonny Siebert fanned ten batters in 6⅔ innings and Steve Hargan struck out nine during ten innings of relief. In the 17th, Luis Tiant retired the only batter he faced to choke off a one-run California rally.

JUNE 2 The Indians trade Don McMahon and Lee Stange to the Red Sox for Dick Radatz.

Radatz was the top reliever in baseball from 1962 through 1964, but then took a quick downward turn. The Indians hoped to reverse the trend but failed. Radatz pitched in 42 games for the Indians and posted an 0–3 record and a 4.68 ERA.

JUNE 3 Fred Whitfield collects four hits, including a homer, in five at-bats and drives in five runs during a 6–5 triumph over the Twins in Minnesota.

JUNE 7 In the first round of the amateur draft, the Indians select pitcher John Curtis of Central High School in Smithtown, New York.

Curtis didn't sign with the Indians and chose instead to play at Clemson University. He was drafted by the Red Sox in 1968 and went on to have a 15-year major league career. The only Indians chosen in the regular phase of the June 1966 draft to reach the majors was Russ Nagelson (14th round) and Billy Harris (27th round). In the secondary phase of previously drafted players,

Cleveland picked Ted Ford, Phil Hennigan, and Bert Gramly. None of them had careers that lasted longer than five years.

JUNE 10 Sonny Siebert pitches a no-hitter and defeats the Senators 2–0 before a crowd of 10,469 at Municipal Stadium. The only two Washington batters to reach base were Dick Nen, who walked in the fifth inning, and Paul Casanova, who reached on an error by shortstop Chico Salmon in the eighth. Siebert threw 116 pitches and struck out seven. Fred Valentine batted for Senators pitcher Phil Ortega to start the ninth and grounded out to second baseman Dick Howser. Don Blasingame followed with a grounder to first baseman Fred Whitfield, who threw to Siebert covering the bag. Bob Saverine was the next hitter. On a 1–2 pitch, Siebert fired a chest-high fast ball. Saverine started to swing, then held back. The Indians thought the pitch was a strike and began congratulating the pitcher. Umpire Jim Honochick, however, called the pitch ball two. Saverine hit the next pitch to left fielder Chuck Hinton for the final out.

Siebert had a record of 16–8 with a 2.80 ERA in 1966.

JUNE 12 The Indians hold on to first place with a 6–3 win over the Senators at Municipal Stadium.

The Indians were knocked off their first-place perch the following day. On June 15, the club had a 36–19 record, then went 45–62 the rest of the way.

JUNE 14 Rocky Colavito hits a grand slam off Don McMahon in the eighth inning to tie the Red Sox 7–7, but the Indians lose 8–7 in the second game of a double header at Municipal Stadium. Cleveland won the opener 8–7.

JUNE 24 Rocky Colavito drives in all five Cleveland runs with two homers and a single, but the Indians lose 7–5 to the Athletics in Cleveland.

JUNE 26 The Indians score seven runs in the sixth inning and beat the Athletics 14–3 in the second game of a double header in Cleveland. Kansas City won the opener 4–2.

JUNE 29 Gary Bell pitches a two-hitter and defeats the Twins 4–1 at Metropolitan Stadium. The only Minnesota hits were singles by Jerry Zimmerman and Zoilo Versalles in the fifth inning.

JULY 1 Sam McDowell strikes out 13 batters and pitches a two-hitter to defeat the Angels 5–0 at Municipal Stadium. The only California hits were singles by Jose Cardenal in the first inning and Rick Reichardt in the fifth.

JULY 12 In the All-Star Game at Busch Memorial Stadium in St. Louis, Sonny Siebert pitches the eighth and ninth innings and retires all six batters he faces, including Willie Mays, Roberto Clemente, Hank Aaron, and Willie McCovey. The National League won 2–1 in ten innings.

JULY 17 The Indians slam seven home runs during a 15–2 win over the Tigers in the second game of a double header in Detroit. Rocky Colavito and Chuck Hinton each struck two homers, with Buddy Booker, Max Alvis, and Leon Wagner adding one each. Colavito and Hinton struck for back-to-back homers in both the third and seventh innings. Hinton and Joe Azcue homered in the opener, a 7–3 Cleveland victory.

The homer by Booker was the second of just two that he hit during his big league career. He had only 33 at-bats in the majors, 28 of them with the Indians.

JULY 19 The Indians trade Tony Curry to the Astros for Jim Gentile.

AUGUST 13 Vernon Stouffer purchases a controlling interest in the Indians. It marked the fifth major change in ownership since 1946, when Bill Veeck bought the club.

Stouffer, a 65-year-old Cleveland restaurant and frozen food magnate, purchased the stock held by William Daley and his associates for a reported $8 million. Stouffer immediately took over as chairman of the board and announced plans to revamp the board of directors to include only Clevelanders "to make sure the club stays here." The transaction squelched rumors that the Indians were headed for Oakland in 1967. Stouffer said that the club would not move out of Cleveland "in the near future." He had been a minority stockholder and member of the board of directors since 1962. Prior to gaining control, he owned only 150 of the 9,000 shares outstanding. Stouffer announced plans to buy out all of the shareholders, paying each nearly $300 per share. The shares originally cost $100. In addition, he intended to purchase all of the stockholders' debentures at a cost of $2.5 million. All told, it was estimated that Stouffer was putting up about $5.5 million of his own money and was also picking up a bank loan of more than $2.5 million. In all, he owned 73 percent of the stock. A contingency in the purchase, Stouffer disclosed, was acceptance by Gabe Paul of a new ten-year contract as president and general manager. Paul, the largest individual shareholder from November 1962 through August 1966, was permitted to buy 100 shares of stock in the Cleveland club and was given a stock-option plan. Stouffer appeared to have the financial resources to bring a winning team back to Cleveland. Under his ownership, however, the club only got worse, bottoming out with a 62–99 record in 1969. Attendance at Municipal Stadium continued to lag, and the downturn in the stock market in 1970 put a large dent in Stouffer's bankroll, leading to an austerity program. After turning down an offer from George Steinbrenner to buy the Indians, Stouffer sold the franchise to Nick Mileti in March 1972.

AUGUST 14 The Indians commit six errors during the fourth inning of a 6–4 loss to the Yankees in the second game of a double header in New York. Shortstop Dick Howser and first baseman Fred Whitfield started the error-fest by bobbling grounders. Three errors occurred on one play. When Steve Hamilton singled to score Roger Maris, the throw to the plate got away from Joe Azcue. Pitcher Tom Kelley, backing up the play, fired the ball into center field in an attempt to nab Hamilton at second. As Hamilton headed for third, center fielder Vic Davalillo made a wild throw in return. Later, in the inning Whitfield dropped a throw. The Yankees won the opener 7–3.

On the same day, the Beatles made an appearance at Municipal Stadium before a crowd of 24,646. In 1990, Paul McCartney returned for a solo concert. Other rock concerts at the stadium featured the Beach Boys, Rolling Stones, Fleetwood Mac, Aerosmith, Michael Jackson, Bruce Springsteen, Pink Floyd, U2, the Who, and Crosby, Stills, Nash & Young.

August 18 Chuck Hinton drives in both Cleveland runs for a 2–0 win over the White Sox at Municipal Stadium. Hinton drove in a run with a double in the fifth inning and clubbed a homer in the seventh. Sam McDowell pitched the shutout.

August 19 Home runs produce all three Cleveland runs of a ten-inning, 3–2 win over the White Sox at Municipal Stadium. Fred Whitfield homered in the fourth inning, Rocky Colavito in the sixth, and Leon Wagner a walk-off blast in the tenth.

On the same day, Birdie Tebbetts resigned as manager. The club had a record of 66–57. Overall, Tebbetts was 278–259 as the Cleveland manager. He is the only individual to win at least 275 games in Cleveland between Al Lopez (570 from 1951 through 1956) and Mike Hargrove (721 from 1991 through 1999). Tebbetts never managed another club. Coach George Strickland served as interim manager for the remainder of the 1966 season.

September 4 Sam McDowell strikes out 12 batters during a 12-inning complete game, but the Indians lose 4–3 to the Tigers at Municipal Stadium.

September 9 Appearing as a pinch-hitter with the Indians trailing 7–6 and two out in the tenth inning, Bill Davis smacks a two-run walk-off homer for an 8–7 win over the Angels at Municipal Stadium.

The homer was the only one of Davis's career in 105 at-bats as a major leaguer. A first baseman, he had a lifetime batting average of .181.

September 15 The Athletics use seven pitchers in beating the Indians 1–0 in 11 innings at Municipal Stadium. Sonny Siebert pitched a complete game for Cleveland.

September 18 Cleveland pitchers strike out 21 batters during a ten-inning, 6–5 win over the Tigers in Detroit. Sam McDowell fanned 14 in six innings before leaving with shoulder stiffness. John O'Donoghue recorded two strikeouts in 1⅔ innings, and Luis Tiant five in 2⅓ innings.

October 3 The Indians hire 38-year-old Joe Adcock as manager.

Adcock played for the Angels in 1966, completing a 17-year career as a first baseman in which he hit 336 homers. He appeared in an All-Star Game and in two World Series and was a member of the Indians in 1963. The Indians hoped that Adcock would bring discipline to the club. He was given a two-year contract, but was fired after the 1967 season after the club posted a record of 75–87.

December 20 The Indians trade Dick Howser to the Yankees for Gil Downs.

1967

Season in a Sentence

In Joe Adcock's only year as manager, the Indians post their worst winning percentage since 1946 while drawing only 662,980 fans, the lowest figure in the major leagues.

Finish • Won • Lost • Pct • GB

Finish	Won	Lost	Pct	GB
Eighth	75	87	.463	17.0

Manager

Joe Adcock

Stats

Stats	Indians	AL	Rank
Batting Avg:	.235	.236	6
On-Base Pct:	.295	.305	8
Slugging Pct:	.359	.351	5
Home Runs:	131		4 (tie)
Stolen Bases:	53		7 (tie)
ERA:	3.25	3.23	5
Fielding Avg:	.981	.979	2
Runs Scored:	559		6
Runs Allowed:	613		6

Starting Line-up

Joe Azcue, c
Tony Horton, 1b
Vern Fuller, 2b
Max Alvis, 3b
Larry Brown, ss
Leon Wagner, lf
Vic Davalillo, cf
Chuck Hinton, rf-cf
Lee Maye, rf
Duke Sims, c
Fred Whitfield, 1b
Chico Salmon, lf-1b-2b-ss
Rocky Colavito, rf
Pedro Gonzalez, 2b

Pitchers

Steve Hargan, sp
Sam McDowell, sp
Luis Tiant, sp
Sonny Siebert, sp
John O'Donoghue, sp-rp
George Culver, rp
Orlando Pena, rp
Bob Allen, rp

Attendance

662,980 (tenth in AL)

Club Leaders

Batting Avg:	Max Alvis	.256
On-Base Pct:	Larry Brown	.308
Slugging Pct:	Max Alvis	.403
Home Runs:	Max Alvis	21
RBIs:	Max Alvis	70
Runs:	Max Alvis	66
Stolen Bases:	Chico Salmon	10
Wins:	Steve Hargan	14
Strikeouts:	Sam McDowell	236
ERA:	Sonny Siebert	2.38
Saves:	Orlando Pena	8

JANUARY 4 Eleven days before the Green Bay Packers defeat the Kansas City Chiefs in the first Super Bowl, the Indians trade Jim Landis, Doc Edwards, and Jim Weaver to the Astros for Lee Maye and Ken Retzer.

Maye was an accomplished singer who recorded two albums and more than two dozen singles. He starred in the group Arthur Lee Maye and the Crowns and occasionally sang with the Platters.

APRIL 11 The Indians open the season with a 4–3 loss to the Athletics at Kansas City. The score was 3–3 in the seventh inning when first baseman Fred Whitfield dropped the throw with two-out and the bases loaded, allowing the run to score.

Indians games were telecast in color for the first time in 1967.

APRIL 13 The game against the Angels in Anaheim is postponed by a power failure.

APRIL 14 A three-run homer by Fred Whitfield in the tenth inning defeats the Angels 4–1 at Anaheim.

April 19 In the home opener, the Indians win 4–1 over the Athletics before 26,133 at Municipal Stadium. Max Alvis, Duke Sims, and Chuck Hinton each homered.

New field boxes were built at Municipal Stadium in 1967, bringing fans 20 feet closer to the field. The boxes weren't altogether successful, however, as they were built too low to provide a clear view of the diamond. The problem was solved in 1975 when the entire field was lowered.

April 25 Steve Hargan pitches a two-hitter and scores the lone run in a 1–0 win over the Twins at Municipal Stadium. Hargan singled in the sixth inning, went to third on a double by Vic Davalillo, and scored on a sacrifice fly from Max Alvis. The only Minnesota hits were singles by Zoilo Versalles in the second inning and Tony Oliva in the fourth.

On the same day, the Indians traded Dick Radatz to the Cubs for Bob Raudman and cash.

April 27 Sam McDowell strikes out 12 batters in eight innings and defeats the Twins 5–4 at Municipal Stadium.

May 1 The Indians sell Jack Kralick to the Yankees.

May 6 The Indians purchase Orlando Pena from the Tigers.

May 17 Leon Wagner hits a grand slam off Fred Talbot in the second inning of an 8–7 win over the Yankees in New York.

May 20 Chuck Hinton's two-run homer in the tenth inning beats the Red Sox 5–3 in Boston.

May 23 Rocky Colavito hits a three-run walk-off homer in the tenth inning to defeat the Senators 4–1 at Municipal Stadium.

May 24 Luis Tiant strikes out 12 batters during a 9–1 victory over the Senators at Municipal Stadium.

May 31 Luis Tiant fans 13 hitters during a 9–0 win over the Tigers at Detroit.

June 1 Indians pitcher John O'Donoghue hits a grand slam off Denny McLain in the sixth inning and is the winning pitcher in an 8–2 win over the Tigers in Detroit.

June 4 The Indians trade Gary Bell to the Red Sox for Tony Horton and Don Demeter.

Horton almost immediately became the Indians starting first baseman. It appeared as though he would hold the position for a long time when he batted .278 with 27 homers and 93 RBIs at the age of 24 in 1969. But Tony was intensely driven to succeed and it adversely affected his mental state. He suffered a nervous breakdown a year later (see August 28, 1970), was hospitalized after attempting suicide, and never played again.

June 6 Fred Whitfield hits a two-run pinch-homer in the tenth inning to lift the Indians to a 6–4 win over the Twins in the first game of a double header in Minnesota. The Indians lost game two 7–1.

June 7 In the first round of the amateur draft, the Indians select shortstop Jack Heidemann from Brenham High School in Brenham, Texas.

Heidemann reached the majors in 1969 as a 19-year-old, but batted only .211 in 426 major league games. The best amateur selection made by the Indians in 1967 was Dick Tidrow, who was picked in the secondary phase of the January draft. Future major leaguers besides Heidemann who were picked in June were Mark Ballinger (second round), Ed Farmer (fifth round), Vic Correll (ninth round), Mike Paul (20th round), and Jack Brohamer (34th round) in the regular phase and Eddie Leon (second round) and Lou Camilli (third round) in the secondary phase.

June 8 The Indians score four runs in the ninth inning to defeat the Twins 7–5 in Minnesota. Max Alvis broke the 5–5 tie with a two-run homer.

June 9 The Indians lose 2–0 and 6–0 to the Athletics in a double header in Kansas City. Steve Hargan lost the opener despite allowing only two hits. The runs crossed the plate on a two-run homer by Jim Gosger.

June 11 The Indians sweep the Athletics 12–1 and 3–2 in Kansas City. The first game was won with six two-run rallies in the first, second, third, fourth, eighth and ninth innings.

June 19 Steve Hargan wins his own game with a two-run, two-out, walk-off homer in the ninth inning to beat the Athletics 4–2 in the first game of a double header in Cleveland. The Indians also won the second tilt 2–1.

The homer was the only one for Hargan in 325 major league at-bats.

June 30 The Indians win 6–5 in 14 innings over the Orioles in the first game of a double header in Baltimore. Vic Davalillo drove in the winning run with a sacrifice fly. Cleveland lost the second contest 8–1.

July 13 The Indians win 4–3 over the Yankees in 14 innings at New York. The winning run scored on a double by Max Alvis, a sacrifice bunt, and an infield grounder from Joe Azcue, which brought Alvis in from third base.

July 28 Steve Hargan pitches a 12-inning complete game to beat the Orioles 1–0 at Municipal Stadium. The lone run scored on a walk-off homer by Tony Horton off Moe Drabowsky.

Hargan led the American League in shutouts in 1967 with six. He posted a 14–13 record and a 2.62 ERA. Hargan was an American League All-Star that season at the age of 24, but began to struggle with arm trouble beginning in 1968. From then until the end of his career in 1977, Hargan had a record of 56–81.

July 29 The Indians trade Rocky Colavito to the White Sox for Jim King and Marv Staehle.

Fans openly revolted when Colavito was traded in 1960. At the time of the 1967 deal, he was a platoon outfielder with a .241 average and five homers in 191 at-bats. After leaving Cleveland, he played for the Sox, Dodgers, and Yankees over two seasons and hit only .216 along with just 11 home runs in 394 at-bats.

August 5 Indians pitcher Stan Williams records his first major league win since July 28, 1964 with a 5–3 defeat of the Tigers in Cleveland.

Williams was a strapping six-foot-five right-hander who struck out 205 batters as a 24-year-old for the Dodgers in 1961. Arm trouble developed three years later, however, and Williams struggled for another three seasons before regaining his form. In a remarkable comeback, he was 19–15 with a 2.54 ERA in 273⅓ innings for the Indians in 1967 and 1968.

August 8 Indians pitcher Ed Connolly records his first major league win since 1964 with a 5–3 win over the Orioles in Baltimore.

Unlike Williams, a comeback wasn't in the cards for Connolly. He won only one more big league game and closed his career with a 6–12 record and a 5.88 ERA.

August 10 Stan Williams strikes out 14 batters in 13 innings for a 2–1 win over the Orioles at Municipal Stadium. Chuck Hinton drove in both Cleveland runs with a homer in the second inning and a walk-off double in the 13th.

August 13 Steve Hargan pitches the Indians to a 1–0 win over the Senators in Washington. Tony Horton drove in the lone run of the game with a double in the ninth inning.

August 17 The Indians explode for five runs in the 16th inning to defeat the Senators 8–3 in Washington. The big blow was a bases loaded triple by Vic Davalillo.

August 19 John O'Donoghue pitches a one-hitter to defeat the Tigers 5–0 in Detroit. The only hit off O'Donoghue was a single in the third inning off Bill Freehan in the second inning.

August 22 Luis Tiant strikes out 16 batters during a 3–2 win over the Angels at Municipal Stadium. Joe Azcue won the game with a walk-off homer in the ninth inning.

August 23 On the first day of rioting in Detroit that left 43 dead, the Angels collect 25 hits off five Cleveland pitchers and win 16–5 at Municipal Stadium.

August 25 Dean Chance of the Twins pitches a no-hitter to defeat Indians 2–1 in the second game of a double header at Municipal Stadium. Among the 10,519 in the crowd were Chance's parents from Wooster, Ohio. The Tribe scored their run in the first inning on two walks, an error, and a wild pitch. The Twins countered with runs in the second and sixth facing Sonny Siebert. The final out was recorded when Chuck Hinton grounded to third baseman Cesar Tovar. Minnesota also won the opener 6–5 in ten innings.

AUGUST 28 A pair of two-run extra inning home runs powers the Indians to an 8–7 win in 11 innings over the Athletics in Kansas City. Chuck Hinton hit a two-run homer in the top of the tenth inning, but the A's tied it 6–6 in their half. Max Alvis homered with a man on base in the 11th. Kansas City plated one run in their half before the Indians closed out the victory.

SEPTEMBER 2 The Indians lose 1–0 to the Angels in 12 innings in Anaheim.

SEPTEMBER 8 Tony Horton hits a grand slam off Blue Moon Odom in the first inning of a 6–3 win over the Athletics in Cleveland.

SEPTEMBER 10 The Indians win 1–0 over the Athletics in the first game of a double header in Cleveland with John O'Donoghue pitching the shutout. The lone run crossed the plate on a single by Vern Fuller in the fourth inning. The A's won the second game 5–2.

SEPTEMBER 13 The Indians lose 1–0 to the White Sox in a 17-inning affair at Comiskey Park. Sonny Siebert and Gary Peters were the starting pitchers and each went 11 innings. Siebert allowed just four hits. Peters walked ten and hit a batter, but surrendered only one Cleveland hit, a triple by Joe Azcue in the third inning. The lone run scored on a single by Rocky Colavito.

SEPTEMBER 14 The Indians lose an extra-inning shutout for the second game in a row, dropping a 4–0 decision to the White Sox in Chicago. A walk-off grand slam by Don Buford off Orlando Pena accounted for all four runs.

SEPTEMBER 22 Tony Horton hits a walk-off homer on the first pitch of the 13th inning to defeat the White Sox 2–1 at Municipal Stadium.

OCTOBER 2 Al Dark replaces Joe Adcock as manager of the Indians.

The 81–81 finish in 1966 was blamed on a lack of discipline and fundamentals. Adcock was hired at the end of that season to bring a hard-nosed approach to the Indians. Adcock's strict rules failed to work, as the club slipped to 75–87 in 1967. A lack of attendance was also a factor in the change of managers. Only 667,623 fans came through the Municipal Stadium turnstiles, a drop of more than 235,000 from 1966. It was the lowest figure in the majors. The dismissal ended Adcock's career in baseball. He returned to his farm in Louisiana to raise thoroughbred horses. Gabe Paul turned to 45-year-old Al Dark for 1968. Dark was a college football star at L.S.U. as a halfback, and was drafted by the Philadelphia Eagles in the third round as the 25th player taken in the 1945 N.F.L. draft. He rejected the pro football offer and played shortstop in the National League from 1946 through 1960. Dark was named to three All-Star teams and played in the World Series for the Boston Braves in 1948 and the New York Giants in 1951 and 1954. He managed the San Francisco Giants from 1961 through 1964 and won the NL pennant in 1962 before losing the Fall Classic in seven games against the Yankees. The Giants were pennant contenders all season in 1964, but Dark was fired by the club after telling reporters that the African-American and Latin players were "just not able to perform up to the white player when it comes to mental alertness." Dark later was the skipper of the Kansas City Athletics in 1966 and 1967, and was let go by Charlie Finley largely because the A's owner believed his club lacked discipline after a rowdy airplane flight in August of Dark's second season at the helm. Although the Indians improved to 86–75 in Dark's first season, Paul soon regretted hiring him. Dark thought that Paul moved too slowly, and believed that the Indians should be more aggressive in making trades. Dark made his opinions known to owner Vernon Stouffer, and a power struggle developed. Stouffer gave Dark more authority, and the manager soon made deals on his own, including one with the Red Sox that brought Ken Harrelson to Cleveland (see April 19, 1969). Though an official announcement was never issued by the Indians, Stouffer acknowledged in a newspaper story on July 8, 1969, that he had placed Dark in charge of all player personnel matters, as well as calling the shots on the field. Paul retained the title of president and general manager but was responsible only for financial, marketing and promotional affairs of the franchise. Few of Dark's players moves worked out, however, and the club declined to an abysmal 62–99 record in 1969. After a 76–86 mark in 1970, Paul was again restored to power in the front office, leaving Dark in charge on the field only. It was an awkward situation for everyone connected with the organization, and Paul and Dark were cool to each other. Trust was almost non-existent. After a 42–61 start in 1971, Dark was dismissed as manager.

NOVEMBER 21 The Indians trade George Culver and Fred Whitfield to the Reds for Tommy Harper.

NOVEMBER 28 The Indians trade John O'Donoghue and Gordon Lund to the Orioles for Eddie Fisher, George Scott, and John Scruggs.

NOVEMBER 29 The Indians trade Chuck Hinton to the Angels for Jose Cardenal.

1968

Season in a Sentence

The Indians lead the AL in earned run average, but outscore only two teams in the league and finish in third place.

Finish • Won • Lost • Pct • GB

Finish	Won	Lost	Pct	GB
Third	86	75	.534	16.5

Manager

Al Dark

Stats

Stats	Indians	AL	Rank
Batting Avg:	.234	.230	5
On-Base Pct:	.294	.300	6
Slugging Pct:	.327	.339	7
Home Runs:	75		9
Stolen Bases:	115		2
ERA:	2.66	2.98	1
Fielding Avg:	.979	.978	4
Runs Scored:	516		8
Runs Allowed:	504		3

Starting Line-up

Duke Sims, c
Tony Horton, 1b
Vern Fuller, 2b
Max Alvis, 3b
Larry Brown, ss
Lee Maye, lf
Jose Cardenal, cf
Tommy Harper, rf-lf
Joe Azcue, c
Chico Salmon, 2b
Russ Snyder, rf
Lou Johnson, lf-rf
Dave Nelson, 2b
Vic Davalillo, rf

Pitchers

Luis Tiant, sp
Sam McDowell, sp
Stan Williams, sp
Sonny Siebert, sp
Steve Hargan, sp
Vicente Romo, rp
Eddie Fisher, rp
Mike Paul, rp

Attendance

857,994 (seventh in AL)

Club Leaders

Batting Avg:	Jose Cardenal	.257
On-Base Pct:	Jose Cardenal	.305
Slugging Pct:	Tony Horton	.411
Home Runs:	Tony Horton	14
RBIs:	Tony Horton	59
Runs:	Jose Cardenal	78
Stolen Bases:	Jose Cardenal	40
Wins:	Luis Tiant	21
Strikeouts:	Sam McDowell	283
ERA:	Luis Tiant	1.60
Saves:	Vicente Romo	12

April 8 While staying at the Biltmore Hotel in Los Angeles, the Indians are shaken by an earthquake. The club was in Southern California to play a series of spring training exhibition games against the Dodgers in both San Diego and Los Angeles.

April 9 The season opener against the White Sox in Chicago is postponed to avoid conflict with the funeral of Dr. Martin Luther King, Jr., who was murdered in Memphis on April 4.

April 10 The 1968 season gets underway with a 9–0 win over the White Sox at Comiskey Park. Sonny Siebert pitched a two-hitter. The only Chicago hits were singles by Duane Josephson in the fifth inning and Ken Boyer in the seventh. Siebert also added three sacrifice bunts. Duke Sims hit two home runs and Max Alvis added one. In his Indians debut, Jose Cardenal collected three hits, including a triple and a double, in five at-bats. Cardenal hit one of three Cleveland triples in the fifth inning, joining Vern Fuller and Tony Horton.

Legendary broadcaster Mel Allen was a Cleveland television announcer for one season, joining Harvey Jones in the booth in 1968.

April 11 In the home opener, the Indians lose 7–5 to the Angels before 29,241 at Municipal Stadium.

The Indians moved back the fences in the power alleys at Municipal Stadium from 380 feet to 395 feet. Home runs by the opposition dropped from 69 in 1967 to 56 in 1968, but it was the Indians who were harmed the most. Cleveland hitters clubbed 76 homers at Municipal Stadium in 1967, but only 36 in 1968. In 1970, the club moved the power alleys in to 385 feet and brought the center field barrier forward from 410 feet to 400.

April 24 Steve Hargan pitches a one-hitter to defeat the Tigers 2–0 at Municipal Stadium on a night in which the temperature hovers in the 30s. The only Detroit hit was a single by Jim Northrup.

April 28 Luis Tiant pitches a two-hitter and defeats the Senators 2–0 in the second game of a double header in Washington. The only hits off Tiant were singles by Del Unser in the first inning and Ken McMullen in the fifth. Tony Horton singled, doubled, and homered in four at-bats and scored both Cleveland runs.

May 1 Sam McDowell strikes out 16 batters and walks no one in beating the Athletics 3–1 at Municipal Stadium. It was the first time that McDowell pitched at least nine innings in a game without issuing a walk. He allowed just three hits and retired the last 20 batters in succession.

McDowell led the AL in strikeouts in 1968 with 283 in 269 innings. He also had a 1.81 ERA but only a 15–14 record to show for his efforts.

May 3 Luis Tiant pitches his second consecutive shutout, beating the Twins 4–0 at Municipal Stadium with a three-hitter.

May 5 Sonny Siebert (seven innings) and Stan Williams (two innings) combine on a two-hitter for a 2–1 win over the Twins at Municipal Stadium. Siebert also figured in both Cleveland runs with an RBI-single in the fifth inning and a single and a run scored in the seventh. A single by Ron Clark off Siebert in the seventh was the first Minnesota hit. Tony Oliva added a double in the eighth.

May 7 Luis Tiant registers his third consecutive shutout, beating the Yankees 8–0 in New York with a five-hitter.

During a 37-game stretch from April 21 through May 30, the Indians pitching staff gave up only 67 runs, an average of only 1.8 per contest, and 195 hits, an average of 5.3 per game. Over the course of the season, Indians pitchers compiled a league-leading 2.66 earned run average and recorded more strikeouts (1,157) than hits allowed (1,087). The team ERA was the lowest of any Indians team since 1918.

May 8 Tony Horton faces off against Yankees shortstop Gene Michael during a 2–1 win over the Yankees in New York. The rumble began when Horton slapped an attempted pick-off throw on Michael. Michael thought that Horton had tried to push him off the bag and responded with a swipe to the face of the Cleveland first baseman. Horton threw a right hook and caught Michael on the left side of his

Luis Tiant shows the formidable form that produced a dominating performance in 1968, when he led the league in ERA.

face before Yankee first base coach Whitey Ford and Indians catcher Duke Sims intervened. Both dugouts and bullpens emptied in a hurry, but no further blows were struck and peace was restored in about ten minutes.

MAY 10 The Indians trounce the Orioles 12–0 in Baltimore.

MAY 12 Luis Tiant pitches his fourth consecutive shutout with a 2–0 decision over the Orioles in the first game of a double header in Baltimore. Tiant surrendered four hits. The Indians also won the second contest 4–1.

Tiant allowed 14 hits in 36 innings during his streak of four straight shutouts. He pitched 41 consecutive scoreless innings over six starts from April 21 through May 17. Tiant was brilliant all season as he posted a 21–9 record and his 1.60 ERA led the American League. The only lower earned run averages by an Indians pitcher throughout the club's long history were compiled by Addie Joss, who had a 1.59 mark in 1904 and 1.16 in 1908. Luis also led the league in 1968 in shutouts (nine), fewest hits allowed per nine innings (5.3), lowest opponent's batting average (.168) and lowest opponent's on base percentage (.233). He fanned 264 batters in 258 innings.

MAY 18 Stan Williams pitches a ten-inning, two-hitter and strikes out 12 batters to defeat the Orioles 1–0 at Municipal Stadium. Williams not only pitched superbly but drove in the lone run of the game with a single that followed a pinch-hit double by Willie Smith. The only Baltimore hits were singles by Brooks Robinson in the fifth inning and Boog Powell in the seventh.

MAY 19 Sonny Siebert hurls a one-hitter to down the Orioles 2–0 in the second game of a double header at Municipal Stadium. The lone Baltimore hit was a single by Curt Blefary with one out in the seventh inning. The Indians also won the first game 11–6.

MAY 21 The Indians play the Athletics in Oakland for the first time, and win 1–0 and lose 2–0 during a double header. The first game victory went 11 innings. Sam McDowell pitched a complete game four-hitter and fanned 12 batters. Jose Cardenal accounted for the lone run with a home run off Pat Dobson, who also pitched a complete game and surrendered just four hits.

MAY 28 In conjunction with expansion to 12 teams, the American League owners vote to split the league into two divisions along with a postseason playoff to determine the champion beginning with the 1969 season. The two new teams were the Kansas City Royals and Seattle Pilots. The Indians were placed in the Eastern Division with the Yankees, Red Sox, Tigers, Orioles and Senators.

JUNE 2 Joe Azcue collects five hits in five at-bats during a 10–5 win over the Senators in the first game of a double header at Municipal Stadium. Washington won the second tilt 11–3.

JUNE 3 A walk-off homer by Jose Vidal in the 14th inning defeats the White Sox at Municipal Stadium. He entered the game in the tenth inning as a defensive replacement in left field. Alvin Dark used all 15 of his healthy position players, and at the end of the game, back-up catcher Ken Suarez played in the infield.

Suarez played third base against left-handed batters and second base versus right-handed hitters, alternating with Chico Salmon.

Vidal hit only three homers while batting just .164 in 146 big league at-bats.

JUNE 5 On the day that Robert Kennedy is shot while campaigning for the Democratic Party nomination for the presidency, the Indians defeat the White Sox 1–0 at Municipal Stadium. The lone run scored on a double by Duke Sims and a single from Jose Cardenal in the second inning. Stan Williams (8⅓ innings), Mike Paul (⅓ of an inning), and Hal Kurtz (⅓ of an inning) combined on the shutout.

JUNE 6 On the day that Robert Kennedy dies from bullet wounds inflicted the previous day, the Indians select shortstop Robert Weaver from Paxon High School in Jacksonville, Florida, in the first round of the amateur draft.

Weaver was a bust, never advancing past Class AA. Future major leaguers drafted by the Indians in the regular phase of the June draft were Bob Kaiser (third round), Larry Doby Johnson (ninth round), Vince Colbert (11th round), Charles Machemehl (12th round), and John Lowenstein (18th round). In the second phase, the club picked Rick Sawyer and Rick Austin.

JUNE 8 Jose Cardenal pulls off an unassisted double play during a 3–1 loss to the Tigers in Detroit. Cardenal caught a shallow fly ball and kept running to double the runner off second base.

The Indians were the third of nine teams that employed Cardenal during his 18-year major league playing career. He played with Cleveland in 1968 and 1969 and led the club in stolen bases both seasons.

JUNE 9 Duke Sims homers and doubles and scores the only two runs of a 2–0 win over the Tigers in Detroit. Luis Tiant pitched the shutout.

JUNE 13 Sam McDowell strikes out 14 batters during an 11-inning complete game, but loses 1–0 to the Athletics at Municipal Stadium.

On the same day, the Indians traded Leon Wagner to the White Sox for Russ Snyder.

JUNE 14 Ken Harrelson hits three homers and drives in all seven Red Sox runs during a 7–2 win over the Indians at Municipal Stadium.

JUNE 15 The Indians trade Vic Davalillo to the Angels for Jimmie Hall.

JUNE 17 The Indians lose 2–1 to the White Sox at County Stadium in Milwaukee. The White Sox played nine "home" games in Milwaukee in 1968 and eleven more in 1969.

On the same day, Los Angeles architect Charles Luckman unveiled a model of a proposed domed stadium he hoped to build in Cleveland. Luckman displayed the model before a group that included Ohio Governor James Rhodes, Cleveland Mayor Carl Stokes, City Council President James Stanton, and officials of the Indians and Browns. Luckman's triple-decked stadium featured movable seats and a retractable opaque dome. It would seat 65,000 for baseball and football and 17,000 for basketball and hockey. The dome would drop to near ground level for basketball and hockey creating a stadium within a stadium. The site for the proposed facility was to be determined in the future. The project was highly praised by Gabe Paul and Browns owner Art Modell, but it never got off the ground.

June 21 After the Tigers score in the top of the 13th inning, Tony Horton hits a two-run walk-off blast in the bottom half for a 4–3 Indians win at Municipal Stadium.

June 24 Jim Northrup of the Tigers ties a major league record by hitting two grand slams in consecutive at-bats against the Indians during a 14–3 Detroit win over the Municipal Stadium. Northrup hit a home run with the bases loaded off Eddie Fisher in the fifth inning and against Billy Rohr in the sixth.

June 29 Luis Tiant strikes out 13 batters during an 8–1 win over the Red Sox in the first game of a double header in Boston. The Indians also won the second game 4–1.

June 30 The Indians score four runs in the tenth inning, three on a home run by Duke Sims, then hold off the Red Sox for a 7–5 win in Boston.

July 3 Luis Tiant strikes out 19 batters and walks no one during a ten-inning complete game to defeat the Twins 1–0 at Municipal Stadium. A single by Joe Azcue drove in the winning run.

The 19-strikeout game is an Indians record. Bob Feller still holds the mark for a nine-inning contest with 18 on October 2, 1938. Tiant also set an American League record (since tied) for most strikeouts in consecutive games with 32. He fanned 13 on June 29.

July 6 Sam McDowell strikes out 14 batters but loses 2–0 to the Angels at Municipal Stadium.

July 9 Sam McDowell and Luis Tiant both pitch during a 1–0 American League loss in the All-Star Game at the Astrodome in Houston. Tiant was the starting pitcher and allowed an unearned run in two innings of work. McDowell pitched the seventh inning and struck out three, including Willie Mays and Willie McCovey, while allowing no runs and a base hit.

July 12 Sam McDowell strikes out the first five batters he faces and 15 in all over 8⅔ innings, and defeats the Athletics 6–3 in Oakland.

July 16 Jose Cardenal ties a major league record for outfielders with his second unassisted double play of the 1968 season. With Chuck Hinton batting during a ten-inning, 2–1 victory over the Angels in Anaheim, Cardenal caught a fly ball off his shoetops and ran into second base to double off the runner.

On July 22, the Indians were 55–42 and five games out of first place behind the Tigers.

July 30 Senators shortstop Ron Hansen pulls of an unassisted triple play during a 10–1 Indians win over Washington at Municipal Stadium. The feat was accomplished in the first inning with Joe Azcue batting, Russ Snyder on first base, and Dave Nelson on second. On a 3–2 pitch, Nelson broke for third and Hansen caught Azcue's liner, stepped on second to double Nelson and tagged Snyder going into second base.

The unassisted triple play was the only one in the major leagues during a 65-year period between 1927 and 1992. Oddly, Hansen was traded by the Senators to the White Sox three days later.

August 6 The Indians lose 2–1 in 17 innings against the Tigers in Detroit.

The Indians entered the four-game series trailing the first-place Tigers by 8½ games and harbored hopes of jumping into the thick of the pennant race. The Indians lost all four games, however, and dreams of a World Series in Cleveland went up in smoke as they had so often during the summers of the 1960s.

August 13 Sonny Siebert pitches the Indians to a 1–0 win over the Tigers at Municipal Stadium. The lone run scored in the second inning on a single by Larry Brown.

August 24 Two days before the start of the Democratic National Convention in Chicago, an event marred by violent confrontations between anti-war demonstrators and police, the Indians win 2–1 in a 16-inning marathon over the Senators in Washington. The winning run followed a double steal in which Jose Cardenal swiped third base and Jimmie Hall took second. Senators catcher Jim French threw the ball into center field trying to nab Hall on the play, allowing Cardenal to cross the plate.

September 9 Luis Tiant strikes out 16 batters and wins his 20th game of the season with a 6–1 decision over the Twins at Minnesota.

September 10 Tony Horton clubs a home run and hits into a triple play during a 6–2 win over the Twins in Minnesota.

September 11 The Indians outlast the Twins 1–0 in 12 innings in Minnesota. Lou Johnson drove in the lone run with a pinch-single in the 12th. Sam McDowell (nine innings), Vicente Romo (two innings) and Horacio Pina (one inning) combined on the shutout.

September 25 Luis Tiant records his 21st win of the season with a one-hitter and a 3–0 decision over the Yankees in New York. The only hit off Tiant was a single by Mickey Mantle in the first inning.

September 27 Entering the game as a pinch-runner, Tommy Harper steals second and third base and scores on a throwing error by Orioles catcher Elrod Hendricks to cap a 2–0 win in Baltimore.

October 8 The Indians trade Eddie Fisher to the Angels for Jack Hamilton.

October 15 In the expansion draft, the Indians lose Lou Piniella, Tommy Harper, and Chico Salmon to the Seattle Pilots and Fran Healy, Mike Hedlund, and Billy Harris to the Kansas City Royals.

The Indians made two huge mistakes in failing to protect Piniella and Harper. Piniella was a 26-year-old outfielder who had failed to collect a base hit in six big league at-bats when drafted by the Pilots. Traded by the Pilots to the Royals just prior to the 1969 season, Piniella played for Kansas City and the Yankees in a big league playing career that lasted until 1984. He batted .291 during his 1,747 games in the majors, and played in four World Series and an All-Star Game. Piniella later managed the Yankees, Reds, Mariners, Devil Rays, and Cubs. Harper batted only .217 in his lone season in Cleveland, but after being drafted by Seattle, played in 880 more major league games. He was an All-Star with the Milwaukee Brewers in 1970, hitting .296 with 31 homers and 38 stolen bases.

OCTOBER 21 Two weeks before Richard Nixon defeats Hubert Humphrey in the Presidential election, the Indians trade Bill Davis to the Padres for Zoilo Versalles.

1969

Season in a Sentence

The third-place finish of 1968 brings hope of better times in Cleveland, but that illusion is shattered when the Indians lose 15 of their first 16 games and finish with the worst record in the AL.

Finish • Won • Lost • Pct • GB

Finish	Won	Lost	Pct	GB
Sixth	62	99	.385	46.5

Manager

Al Dark

Stats

Stats	Indians	AL	Rank
Batting Avg:	.237	.246	9
On-Base Pct:	.309	.324	11
Slugging Pct:	.345	.369	9
Home Runs:	119		8
Stolen Bases:	85		6
ERA:	3.94	3.62	10
Fielding Avg:	.976	.978	10
Runs Scored:	573		10
Runs Allowed:	717		9

Starting Line-up

Duke Sims, c
Tony Horton, 1b
Vern Fuller, 2b
Max Alvis, 3b
Larry Brown, ss
Russ Snyder, lf-cf-rf
Jose Cardenal, cf
Ken Harrelson, rf
Lou Klimchock, 3b
Zoilo Versalles, 2b-3b
Eddie Leon, ss
Richie Scheinblum, lf-rf
Frank Baker, lf

Pitchers

Sam McDowell, sp
Luis Tiant, sp
Dick Ellsworth, sp-rp
Steve Hargan, sp
Stan Williams, rp
Juan Pizarro, rp
Mike Paul, rp

Attendance

619,970 (11th in AL)

Club Leaders

Batting Avg:	Tony Horton	.278
On-Base Pct:	Ken Harrelson	.341
Slugging Pct:	Tony Horton	.461
Home Runs:	Tony Horton	27
	Ken Harrelson	27
RBIs:	Tony Horton	93
Runs:	Ken Harrelson	83
Stolen Bases:	Jose Cardenal	36
Wins:	Sam McDowell	18
Strikeouts:	Sam McDowell	279
ERA:	Sam McDowell	2.94
Saves:	Stan Williams	12

APRIL 4 The Indians trade Lou Johnson to the Angels for Chuck Hinton.

APRIL 8 The Indians open the season in Detroit and lose 6–2 to the Tigers. Larry Brown hit a home run.

Dave Martin joined Harry Jones in the TV booth in 1969. Martin was a Cleveland telecaster for three seasons.

APRIL 11 In the home opener, the Indians play 16 innings and lose 2–1 to the Red Sox before 25,596 at Municipal Stadium.

APRIL 14 The Indians sell Jimmie Hall to the Yankees.

APRIL 15 After losing the first five games of the season, the Indians finally win 3–2 in ten innings over the Tigers at Municipal Stadium. Jose Cardenal drove in the winning run with a sacrifice fly.

APRIL 19 The Indians trade Sonny Siebert, Joe Azcue and Vicente Romo to the Red Sox for Ken Harrelson, Juan Pizarro, and Dick Ellsworth.

Harrelson played for Al Dark in Kansas City and was a favorite of the Indians manager. He was coming off of a season with the Red Sox in which he drove in 109 runs to lead the American League. Harrelson played for the Sox for only 20 months, but became a cult hero in Boston with his eccentric personality, Southern charm, long hair (one of the first athletes to do so), and wildly colored "mod" outfits that included love beads and Nehru jackets. He was a particular favorite of young fans in a city full of college students at the height of anti-establishment rebellion against authority. Fitting right in with the changing times of the "psychedelic sixties," Harrelson drove to the ballpark in a lavender dune buddy with flowers on the roof. He even had his own television program. The Indians traded for him largely in an attempt to boost attendance. Harrelson, however, had no desire to come to Cleveland. He immediately announced his retirement in an attempt to nullify the trade. Harrelson explained that he couldn't leave Boston because of outside business interests that earned him considerably more than his $50,000 annual salary. According to his agent, Bob Wolff, the move from New England would cost Harrelson $750,000. The trade was held up for three days before Harrelson was placated when the Indians convinced him that business opportunities in Cleveland were equal to those in Boston and agreed to double his salary. When he finally arrived in Cleveland, Harrelson made an entrance befitting a movie star. He was greeted at the airport by a throng of teenagers and led them through the terminal to his waiting limousine. Ken quickly got his own TV show called The Hawk's Nest, *a talk-variety show that aired over WJW on Saturday afternoons. The acquisition of Harrelson proved to be a complete waste of money, however. Although he was only 27 at the time of the trade, Harrelson played in just 218 more big league games and hit only .220 with 33 homers in 719 at-bats, in part because of a fractured ankle suffered during spring training in 1970. After his career ended, Harrelson became a broadcaster, first with the Red Sox, then with the White Sox. Pizarro and Ellsworth also flopped in Cleveland. Siebert, on the other hand, had a 45–28 record during his first three years in Boston.*

April 27 The Indians lose their tenth game in a row with a 6–5 decision to the Senators at Municipal Stadium. The club's record sank to an abysmal 1–15.

April 30 Sam McDowell strikes out 12 batters and beats the Yankees 3–0 in New York. The victory ended the Indians ten-game losing streak.

May 6 Sam McDowell pitches the Indians to a 1–0 win over the Twins at Municipal Stadium. Tony Horton drove in the lone run of the game with a homer off Dave Boswell in the seventh inning.

McDowell led the league in strikeouts in 1969 with 279 in 285 innings. On a club that won 62 and lost 99, he had an 18–14 record and a 2.94 ERA.

Everyone was smiling after a series of meetings in April of 1969, during which Ken Harrelson agreed to play ball with Cleveland after refusing a trade from Boston. Indians General Manager Gabe Paul (left) and MLB Commissioner Bowie Kuhn (right) flank the "mod" and unpredictable Harrelson.

May 13 The Indians play the Royals in Kansas City for the first time and win 8–6.

May 14 Jose Cardenal uses his speed to score the winning run in the 11th inning of a 3–2 victory over the Royals in Kansas City. Cardenal singled, then stole second and third. When Tony Horton grounded to shortstop Jackie Hernandez, Cardenal broke for the plate on the throw to first baseman Chuck Harrison. Harrison's relay to the plate arrived in time to nip Cardenal, but catcher Ellie Rodriguez dropped the throw.

May 20 The Royals play in Cleveland for the first time and lose 4–1 to the Indians. Sam McDowell threw a two-hitter. The only Kansas City hits were a single by Ed Kirkpatrick in the third inning and a home run by Lou Piniella in the seventh.

May 23 The Seattle Pilots play in Cleveland for the first time and lose 7–1 to the Indians.

May 30 Jose Cardenal hits a grand slam off Ed Sprague during an eight-run first inning and the Indians coast to a 9–2 win over the Athletics in the first game of a double header in Oakland. It was Luis Tiant's first win after an 0–7 start. The A's won game two 5–1.

May 31 Sam McDowell holds the Athletics hitless until Sal Bando singles with two out in the seventh inning and wins 5–2 in Oakland. McDowell allowed a total of four hits before needing ninth inning relief help to close out the win.

June 3 The Indians play a regular season game in Seattle for the first time, and win 3–1 over the Pilots.

The Pilots lasted only one season in Seattle. The club moved to Milwaukee in 1970 and were renamed the Brewers. Seattle received another major league club in 1977 when the Mariners began play as an expansion team.

June 5 In the first round of the amateur draft, the Indians select outfielder Alvin McGrew from Parker High School in Fairfield, Alabama.

McGrew never reached the majors. The Indians did pick two longtime major leaguers, however, in Alan Ashby (third round) and Buddy Bell (16th round). Others chosen in 1969 who reached the big leagues were Rob Belloir (eighth round of the regular phase) and Rich Hand (first round of the secondary phase).

June 7 Luis Tiant pitches a two-hitter and defeats the Angels 7–0 at Municipal Stadium. The only California hits were a double by Jim Fregosi in the first inning and a single from Bill Voss in the seventh.

June 8 The Indians allow three hits during a double header against the Angels at Municipal Stadium, but gain only a split. Sam McDowell tossed a two-hitter in the opener to win 3–0. The California hits were singles by Jim Spencer in the sixth inning and Tom Egan in the seventh. Ken Harrelson drove in all three Cleveland runs with a homer and a double. In game two, Mike Paul (five innings), Gary Kroll (one inning), Jack Hamilton (two-thirds of an inning), and Stan Williams (1⅓ innings) combined on a one-hitter, but the Indians lost 3–2. The three Angels runs scored in the fifth inning off Paul on two walks, a double by Aurelio Rodriguez, an intentional walk, a sacrifice fly, and a double steal in which Rodriguez swiped home.

Along with the June 7 contest, Indians pitchers allowed only five hits in three consecutive games.

June 14 The Indians rout the Twins 12–0 in Minnesota.

June 20 The Indians sell Lee Maye to the Senators.

July 9 — President Richard Nixon attends a 3–0 Indians loss to the Senators in Washington.

July 11 — Ken Harrelson drills a grand slam off Daryl Patterson in the third inning of an 8–1 win over the Tigers in Detroit.

July 23 — During the All-Star Game at Robert F. Kennedy Memorial Stadium in Washington, Sam McDowell enters the fray in the seventh inning and retires all six batters he faces, four of them on strikeouts, although the American League loses 9–3.

In four All-Star appearances, McDowell pitched eight innings and allowed one run and five hits while striking out 12 batters.

July 26 — The Indians sell Zoilo Versalles to the Senators.

July 29 — The Indians score two runs in the ninth inning to tie 3–3 and Duke Sims whacks a walk-off homer in the 11th for a 4–3 win over the White Sox in the first game of a double header at Municipal Stadium. Cleveland also won the nightcap 9–5.

August 4 — Solo homers by Frank Baker (his first as a major leaguer) in the fourth inning and Ken Harrelson in the seventh beats the Orioles 2–0 at Municipal Stadium. Steve Hargan pitched the shutout.

August 10 — Sam McDowell strikes out 14 batters and allows three hits in beating the Royals 8–1 at Municipal Stadium.

August 15 — Jose Cardenal homers in the 12th inning for the winning tally in a 2–1 victory over the Angels in Anaheim.

August 19 — Sam McDowell pitches a one-hitter and defeats the Athletics 3–0 in Oakland. The lone hit off McDowell was a single by Bert Campaneris in the fifth inning.

September 14 — Sam McDowell is ejected for objecting to the calls of home plate umpire Larry Barnett in the sixth inning of a 7–3 loss to the Orioles in Baltimore. On his way to the dugout, McDowell fired the ball into the upper deck about ten rows from the top of the stands.

September 21 — The Indians sell Juan Pizarro to the Athletics.

October 2 — Rain on the final day of the season saves the Indians from a possible 100th defeat by canceling a game against the Yankees in New York.

Despite the presence of two first-year expansion teams, the Indians posted the worst record in the American League in 1969.

November 21 — The Indians trade Jose Cardenal to the Cardinals for Vada Pinson.

During the 1960s, the Indians often traded and acquired players at the wrong ends of their careers. Pinson and Cardenal were examples. Pinson had been a star in the National League, mostly with the Reds, for more than a decade, but had little left by the time he arrived in Cleveland. Cardenal had seven seasons ahead of him as a big league regular.

DECEMBER 10 The Indians trade Luis Tiant and Stan Williams to the Twins for Graig Nettles, Dean Chance, Bob Miller, and Ted Uhlaender.

The Indians believed that Tiant was finished after he posted a 9–20 record in 1969. The Twins concurred and released him in 1971. Tiant was picked-up by the Red Sox and revived his career, putting together a streak of 96 wins and 58 losses from 1972 through 1976. Williams gave the Twins one great season with a 10–1 record and a 1.99 earned run average in 1970. Chance was the key to the deal for the Indians. A native of Wooster, Ohio, Chance won 20 games for the Angels in 1964 and another 20 with the Twins in 1967. By the time he arrived in Cleveland, however, Chance was suffering from arm problems and won just nine games with the Tribe. Miller had been an effective veteran reliever for many years but was a disappointment as an Indian. Still, the Indians might have broken even on the deal if they had hung on to Nettles instead of trading him to the Yankees in 1972.

Indians by the Numbers

Uniform numbers have long been part of baseball. The following are a list of numbers and the key Indians players, managers, and coaches who have worn them since the club began sporting permanent numerals on the jerseys in 1929. In parenthesis are the years the individuals wore those particular numbers. Uniform numbers are retired in honor of Earl Averill (3), Lou Boudreau (5), Larry Doby (14), Mel Harder (18), Bob Feller (19), Bob Lemon (21) and Jackie Robinson (42)

00—Paul Dade (1977–79)

1 Dick Porter (1930), Johnny Burnett (1931–34), Lyn Lary (1937–38), Oscar Grimes (1939–42), Roy Cullenbine (1943–45), Don Ross (1945–46), Bobby Avila (1949–58), Jerry Kindall (1962), Birdie Tebbetts (1963–66), Jose Cardenal (1968–69), Al Dark (1970–71), Johnny Grubb (1977–78), John McNamara (1990–91), Tony Fernandez (1997), Casey Blake (2003–07)

2 Joe Sewell (1930), Dick Porter (1931–33), Boze Berger (1935–36), Gee Walker (1941), Buddy Rosar (1943–44), George Strickland (1952–56), Kerby Farrell (1957), Bobby Bragan (1958), Ken Aspromonte (1960–62, 1972–74), Mike Ferraro (1983), Brett Butler (1984–87), Alex Cole (1990–92), Einar Diaz (1996–2002), Jhonny Peralta (2005–07)

3 Earl Averill (1930–39), Eddie Robinson (1947–48), Mickey Vernon (1949–50), Woodie Held (1958–62). Retired in honor of Averill in 1975.

4 Joe Sewell (1929), Johnny Hodapp (1931), Bill Cissell (1932–33), Bill Knickerbocker (1934–36), Odell Hale (1937–40), Joe Gordon (1947–50), Jim Hegan (1951–57), George Strickland (1959–60), Tony Bernazard (1984–87)

5 Earl Averill (1929), Willie Kamm (1931–35), Roy Hughes (1936–37), Lou Boudreau (1939–50), Bubba Phillips (1960–62), Al Dark (1968–70). Retired in honor of Boudreau in 1970.

6 Lew Fonseca (1929), Eddie Morgan (1930), Joe Vosmik (1931–36), Moose Solters (1937–39), Ray Mack (1939–43), Ken Keltner (1947–50), Dale Mitchell (1951–56), Rocky Colavito (1958–59), Joe Azcue (1963–66, 1968–69), Joe Adcock (1967), Jorge Orta (1980–81), Andy Allanson (1986–91)

7 Hal Trosky (1934–41), Al Rosen (1948–56), Harvey Kuenn (1960), Johnny Romano (1964), Joe Azcue (1967), Jack Brohamer (1972), John Ellis (1973–75), Alan Bannister (1980–83), Pat Corrales (1985–87), Kenny Lofton (1992–96, 1998–2001, 2007)

8 Luke Sewell (1931–32), Frankie Pytlak (1937–40), Ken Keltner (1942–44), Les Fleming (1945–47), Ray Boone (1949–53), Mickey

Vernon (1958), Willie Kirkland (1961–62), Ray Fosse (1967–72), Von Hayes (1982), Albert Belle (1990–96), Jason Michaels (2006–07)

9 Rollie Hemsley (1938–41), Mickey Rocco (1943–44), Ken Keltner (1946), Luke Easter (1949–54), Ralph Kiner (1955), Minnie Minoso (1958–59), Johnny Romano (1963), Duke Sims (1965–70), Buddy Bell (1972), Rico Carty (1975–77), Rich Hassey (1978–84), Pete O'Brien (1989), Carlos Baerga (1990–96, 1999), Matt Williams (1997), Jody Gerut (2003–05)

10 Roger Peckinpaugh (1931–33), Walter Johnson (1933–35), Harry Eisenstat (1939–42), Mickey Rocco (1945–46), Jim Hegan (1947–50), Al Lopez (1951–56), Vic Power (1958–61), Jack Brohamer (1973–75), Ray Fosse (1976–77), Jeff Torborg (1977–79), Pat Tabler (1983–87), Coco Crisp (2002–05)

11 Frankie Pytlak (1932–36), Ben Chapman (1939–40), Joe Heving (1941–45), Frankie Hayes (1945–46), Art Houtteman (1953–56), Johnny Romano (1960–62), Tony Horton (1967–70), Ted Uhlaender (1971), Dave Duncan (1973–74), Toby Harrah (1979–83), Doug Jones (1988–91), Paul Sorrento (1992–95), Matt Lawton (2002–04)

12 Joe Shaute (1929), Willis Hudlin (1930–40), Vern Kennedy (1942–44), Lou Brissie(1951–53), Don Mossi (1954–58), Woodie Held (1963–64), Graig Nettles (1970–72), Roberto Alomar (1999–2001)

13 Walt Williams (1973), Ernie Camacho (1984–87), Omar Vizquel (1994–2004)

14 Jake Miller (1929), Wes Ferrell (1930–33), Billy Sullivan (1936), Bob Feller (1937–38), Larry Doby (1947–55, 1958), Gene Woodling (1956–57), Tito Francona (1959–62), Chris Chambliss (1971–74), Larvell Blanks (1976–78), Julio Franco (1983–88), Jerry Browne (1987–91). Retired in honor of Doby in 1994.

15 Willis Hudlin (1929), Sarge Connally (1932–34), Johnny Allen (1936–40), Russ Nixon (1957–60), Fred Whitfield (1963–67), Frank Duffy (1972–77), Tom Veryzer (1979–81), Sandy Alomar, Jr. (1990–2000)

16 Clint Brown (1930–35), Denny Galehouse (1937–38), Chubby Dean (1941–43), Eddie Klieman (1947–48), Al Smith (1955–57), Johnny Temple (1960–61), Larry Brown (1963–71), Bo Diaz (1978–81), Jerry Willard (1984–85), Felix Fermin (1989–93), Dwight Gooden (1998–99)

17 Ken Holloway (1929), Jim Bagby, Jr. (1941–43), Dave Philley (1954–55), Chico Carrasquel (1956–58), Johnny Klippstein (1960), Chico Salmon (1964–68), Dave LaRoche (1975–77), Wayne Garland (1977–81), Marquis Grissom (1997), Travis Fryman (1998–2002), Aaron Boone (2005–06)

18 Mel Harder (1930–47), Barry Latman (1960–62), Dick Howser (1963–68), Duane Kuiper (1975–81), Pat Corrales (1983–84), Ken Schrom (1986–87), Chris James (1990). Retired in honor of Harder in 1990.

19 Oral Hildebrand (1932–36), Bob Feller (1939–41, 1945–56). Retired in honor of Feller in 1957.

20 Al Milnar (1938–43), Ray Narleski (1954–58), Dick Donovan (1962), George Hendrick (1973–74), Frank Robinson (1975–77), Rick Manning (1981–83), Gorman Thomas (1983), Willie Upshaw (1988), Candy Maldonado (1990, 1993–94), Steve Karsay (1998–2001), Ronnie Belliard (2004–06)

21 Lloyd Brown (1934–37), Allie Reynolds (1943–46), Bob Lemon (1947–60), Bob Chance (1963–64), Rocky Colavito (1965–67), George Hendrick (1975–76), Mike Hargrove (1979–85, 1992–98), Greg Swindell (1987–91). Retired in honor of Lemon in 2000.

22 Wes Ferrell (1929), Thornton Lee (1934–36), Roy Weatherly (1938–42), Al Benton (1949–50), Cal McLish (1956–59), Tommy McCraw (1972), Jim Bibby (1975–77), Brian Giles (1996–98), Juan Gonzalez (2001), Eric Wedge (2003–07)

23 Pete Appleton (1930–31), Roy Weatherly (1936), Bruce Campbell (1937–39), Beau Bell (1940–41), Les Fleming (1942), Pat Seerey (1943–46), Vic Wertz (1954–58), Chuck Hinton (1965–67, 1969–71), Oscar Gamble (1973–75), Stan Thomas (1976), Bruce Bochte (1977), Victor Cruz (1979–80), Chris Bando (1982–87), Mitch Webster (1990–91), Mark Whiten (1991–92), Julio Franco (1995–96), Dave Justice (1997–2000), Ellis Burks (2001–03), Ben Broussard (2004–06)

24 Jeff Heath (1937–44), Dutch Meyer (1945), Al Gettel (1947–48), Early Wynn (1949–57), Tito Francona (1963–64), Pedro Gonzalez (1965–67), Eddie Leon (1968–71), Charlie Spikes (1973–77), George Vuckovich (1983–85), Manny Ramirez (1993–2000), Milton Bradley (2002), Grady Sizemore (2004–07)

25 Odell Hale (1933), Denny Galehouse (1936), Ken Keltner (1938–41), Steve Gromek

(1943–46), Mike Garcia (1949–59), Vic Davalillo (1963–68), Buddy Bell (1973–78), Bobby Bonds (1979), Jim Thome (1992–2002), Ryan Garko (2005–07)

26 Steve O'Neill (1937), Ossie Vitt (1938–40), Lee Maye (1967–69), Ted Uhlaender (1970), Boog Powell (1975–76), Brook Jacoby (1984–92), Bob Wickman (2000–06)

27 Roger Peckinpaugh (1941), Steve Gromek (1948–53), Herb Score (1955–59), Willie Kirkland (1963), Leon Wagner (1964–68), Russ Snyder (1968–69), Roy Foster (1970–72), Jim Norris (1977–79), Miguel Dilone (1980–83), Mel Hall (1984–88), Jaret Wright (1997–2002)

28 Pedro Ramos (1962), Vada Pinson (1970–71), Rick Manning (1975–80), Bert Blyleven (1981–85), Cory Snyder (1986–90), Derek Liliquist (1992–94), Ben Broussard (2002–03)

29 Lou Klimchock (1969–70), John Lowenstein (1971–76), Andre Thornton (1977–87), Jack McDowell (1996–97)

30 Steve O'Neill (1936), Gene Bearden (1948–50), Chuck Essegian (1961–62), Ray Lamb (1971–73), Joe Carter (1984–89)

31 Catfish Metkovich (1947), Wally Westlake (1952–55), Jim Busby (1956–57), Jim Perry (1959–63, 1974–75), Jack Kralick (1963–67), Steve Mingori (1970–73), Steve Olin (1990–92), Chuck Finley (2000–02), Brian Anderson (2003), Cliff Lee (2005–07)

32 Al Smith (1940–45), Hank Edwards (1946–49), Al Smith (1953–54), Roger Maris (1957), Dean Chance (1970), Ed Whitson (1982), Doc Edwards (1987–89), Dennis Martinez (1994–96), Charlie Manuel (2000–02)

33 Eddie Morgan (1931–32), Monte Pearson (1933–35), Hank Edwards (1941–43), Dale Mitchell (1947), Bob Kennedy (1949–54), Mudcat Grant (1958–64), Luis Tiant (1964–69), Eddie Murray (1994–96), Russell Branyan (1999–2001)

34 Odell Hale (1934–36), Oris Hockett (1942–44), Hal Peck (1947), Dale Mitchell (1948–50), Steve Hargan (1965–72), Jim Kern (1975–78), Joe Charboneau (1980–82), Dave Burba (1998–2001)

35 Bruce Campbell (1935–36), Harry Simpson (1951–53), Joe Gordon (1958–60), Jimmy Dykes (1960–61), Pedro Ramos (1963–64), Stan Williams (1967–69), Tom Buskey (1974–77), Gary Alexander (1978–80), Phil Niekro (1986–87), Wayne Kirby (1992–96), Joel Skinner (2002)

36 Gaylord Perry (1972–75), Rick Waits (1975–83)

37 Jimmy Piersall (1959–61), Dennis Eckersley (1975–77), Dan Spillner (1978–84), Chad Ogea (1994–98), Jake Westbrook (2001–07)

38 Tom Ferrick (1942), Rocky Colavito (1955–57), Frank Funk (1960–62), Lary Sorensen (1982–83), Eric Plunk (1992–98)

39 Eddie Klieman (1943–45), Gary Bell (1958–67), Len Barker (1979–83)

40 Ken Harrelson (1969–71), Tom Hilgendorf (1972–74), Rick Wise (1978–79), John Denny (1980–82), Bud Black (1988–90, 1993), Bartolo Colon (1997–2002)

41 Frankie Mackiewicz (1945), Dick Tidrow (1972–74), Joe Dobson (1976–77), Charles Nagy (1990–2002), Victor Martinez (2004–07)

42 Mel McGaha (1962), Sonny Siebert (1964–69), Mike Jackson (1997–99). Retired in honor of Jackie Robinson in 1997.

43 Lee Stange (1964–66), Vicente Romo (1967–69), Sid Monge (1977–81), Rick Sutcliffe (1982–84)

44 Don McMahon (1964–66), Cliff Johnson (1979–80), Neal Heaton (1982–86), Richie Sexson (1997–2000)

45 Rich Hand (1970–71), Brad Komminsk (1989)

46 Steve Dunning (1970–73), Doug Jones (1987), Marty Cordova (2001)

47 Jesse Orosco (1989–91)

48 Sam McDowell (1964–71), Mike Paxton (1978–79), Ted Power (1992–93), Travis Hafner (2004–07)

49 Tom Candiotti (1986–91), Jose Mesa (1992–98)

50 Julian Tavarez (1993–96)

51 Bibb Falk (1929), Eddie Morgan (1930)

52 John Farrell (1987–91), C. C. Sabathia (2001–07)

53 Paul Shuey (1994–2002)

54 Tom Waddell (1984–87), Mark Clark (1993–95), David Riske (1999–2005)

55 Orel Hershiser (1995–97), Fausto Carmona (2006–07)

61 Eddie Morgan (1929)

71 Johnny Hodapp (1929)

THE STATE OF THE INDIANS

Cleveland baseball fans endured a succession of teams that ranged from bad to mediocre. The only Indians teams during the 1970s that posted a winning record were in 1976 (81–78) and 1979 (81–80). None finished higher than fourth in the AL East. Overall, the Indians had a 737–866 record for a .460 winning percentage. Of the 12 AL teams in existence in 1970, the only one with a worse record was the Milwaukee Brewers, who finished 738–873 and had a winning percentage of .458. AL pennant-winners during the decade were the Orioles (1970, 1971, and 1979), Athletics (1972, 1973, 1974), Red Sox (1975), and Yankees (1976, 1977, and 1978). Eastern Division champions were the Orioles (1970, 1971, 1973, 1974, and 1979), Tigers (1972), Red Sox (1975) and Yankees (1976, 1977, and 1978).

THE BEST TEAM

The 1976 outfit posted a record of 81–78 and finished in fourth place, 16 games out of first.

THE WORST TEAM

The 1971 Indians were 60–102 for the worst winning percentage (.370) of any Cleveland club between 1914 and 1985.

THE BEST MOMENT

With the help of Gaylord Perry's 15-game winning streak, the Indians were in first place as late as July 12 in 1974.

THE WORST MOMENT

On June 4, 1974, the Indians sold beer at ten cents a cup, leading to a rowdy crowd and a forfeit to the Rangers.

THE ALL-DECADE TEAM • YEARS W/INDIANS

Player	Years
Ray Fosse, c	1967–72, 1975–76
Andre Thornton, 1b	1977–79, 1981–87
Duane Kuiper, 2b	1974–81
Frank Duffy, ss	1972–77
Buddy Bell, 3b	1972–78
George Hendrick, lf	1973–76
Rick Manning, cf	1975–83
Charlie Spikes, rf	1973–77
Rico Carty, dh	1974–77
Gaylord Perry, p	1972–75
Dennis Eckersley, p	1975–77
Sam McDowell, p	1961–71
Rick Waits, p	1975–83

Perry and Eckersley are in the Hall of Fame. McDowell was also on the 1960s All-Decade Team. Third baseman Graig Nettles (1972–77) was another prominent player during the 1970s. Hendrick was primarily a center fielder with the Indians but is listed here in left because of a lack of viable alternatives. No one played 100 or more games in left field in consecutive seasons for Cleveland between Leon Wagner (1964–67) and Mel Hall (1986–88).

THE DECADE LEADERS

Batting Avg:	Rico Carty	.303
On-Base Pct:	Andre Thornton	.367
Slugging Pct:	Andre Thornton	.495
Home Runs:	George Hendrick	89
RBIs:	Buddy Bell	386
Runs:	Buddy Bell	462
Stolen Bases:	Rick Manning	86
Wins:	Gaylord Perry	70
Strikeouts:	Gaylord Perry	790
ERA:	Gaylord Perry	2.71
Saves:	Jim Kern	46

THE HOME FIELD

Municipal Stadium resembled a morgue for much of the 1960s and 1970s. The attendance figure of 1,011,644 in 1979 was the first above one million since 1959. The most significant change was the erection of an electronic scoreboard in 1978.

THE GAME YOU WISHED YOU HAD SEEN

On April 8, 1975, Frank Robinson became the first African-American to manage a major league club in a regular season game. Before a cheering throng of 56,715 at Municipal Stadium, Robinson homered in his first trip to the plate and the Indians defeated the Yankees 5–3.

THE WAY THE GAME WAS PLAYED

Speed and defense were more prominent during the 1970s than in any decade since the lively ball was introduced in 1920. Stolen bases per team in the American League rose from 72 in 1970 to 107 in 1979, while home runs per team declined from 146 in 1970 to 94 in 1976 before surging upward at the end of the decade. The designated hitter rule was introduced in the AL in 1973.

THE MANAGEMENT

A lack of leadership contributed to the malaise of the organization during the 1970s. The Indians were headed by Vernon Stouffer (chairman of the board from 1966 through 1972), Nick Mileti (president in 1972 through 1975), Ted Bonda (president from 1975 through 1978), and Gabe Paul (president and chief executive officer from 1978 through 1985). General managers were Paul (1961–73) and Phil Seghi (1973–85). Field manager included Al Dark (1968–71), Johnny Lipon (1971), Ken Aspromonte (1972–74), Frank Robinson (1975–77), Jeff Torborg (1977–79), and Dave Garcia (1979–82).

THE BEST PLAYER MOVE

The best short-term trade brought Gaylord Perry and Frank Duffy from the Giants in November 1971 for Sam McDowell. In the long-term, the best deal was made in December 1976 in which Andre Thornton came to Cleveland for Jackie Brown.

THE WORST PLAYER MOVE

In a trade of minor leaguers buried in the small type of the Cleveland papers on April 3, 1974, the Indians swapped 17-year-old Pedro Guerrero to the Dodgers for Bruce Ellingsen. It didn't seem like a big deal at the time, but Guerrero reached the majors in 1978 and became a four-time All-Star. The deal which sent Dennis Eckersley to the Red Sox in March 1978 also had long-lasting negative repercussions. Eckersley, Rick Manning, and Duane Kuiper were all rookies together in 1975. That the Tribe traded Eckersley and kept Manning and Kuiper speaks volumes as to why the Indians failed to field a pennant contender during the Gabe Paul regime.

1970

Season in a Sentence

With an almost entirely new roster, the Indians win 14 more games than the previous season, but it's not enough to prevent a losing season.

Finish • Won • Lost • Pct • GB

Finish	Won	Lost	Pct	GB
Fifth	76	86	.469	32.0

Manager

Al Dark

Stats

	Indians	AL	Rank
Batting Avg:	.249	.250	8
On-Base Pct:	.316	.325	10
Slugging Pct:	.394	.379	4
Home Runs:	183		2
Stolen Bases:	25		12
ERA:	3.91	3.71	9
Fielding Avg:	.979	.978	6
Runs Scored:	649		7
Runs Allowed:	675		5

Starting Line-up

Ray Fosse, c
Tony Horton, 1b
Eddie Leon, 2b
Graig Nettles, 3b
Jack Heidemann, ss
Roy Foster, lf
Ted Uhlaender, cf
Vada Pinson, rf
Duke Sims, c-lf-1b
Chuck Hinton, 1b-rf-lf
Buddy Bradford, cf
Larry Brown, ss-3b-2b

Pitchers

Sam McDowell, sp
Steve Hargan, sp
Rich Hand, sp
Steve Dunning, sp
Mike Paul, sp-rp
Dennis Higgins, rp
Dean Chance, rp-sp
Fred Lasher, rp
Phil Hennigan, rp

Attendance

729,752 (11th in AL)

Club Leaders

Batting Avg:	Ray Fosse	.307
On-Base Pct:	Ray Fosse	.361
Slugging Pct:	Vada Pinson	.481
Home Runs:	Graig Nettles	26
RBIs:	Vada Pinson	82
Runs:	Graig Nettles	81
Stolen Bases:	Vada Pinson	7
Wins:	Sam McDowell	20
Strikeouts:	Sam McDowell	304
ERA:	Sam McDowell	2.92
Saves:	Dennis Higgins	11

MARCH 19 Ken Harrelson breaks his leg, tears ligaments and tendons, and dislocates his ankle while sliding into second base during a 9–0 exhibition game loss to the Athletics in Mesa, Arizona. Harrelson was injured when his spikes caught in the dirt. He didn't play again until September 6. Harrelson boldly predicted that would hit at least 40 home runs in 1971, but the leg never properly healed and he retired in mid-season (see June 21, 1971).

APRIL 4 The Indians trade Max Alvis and Russ Snyder to the Brewers for Roy Foster and Frank Coggins.

The Indians turned over most of the roster between the 1969 and 1970 seasons. Of the 26 players on the Opening Day roster (including injured Ken Harrelson), only ten were with the club in 1969. The ten were Larry Brown, Ray Fosse, Vern Fuller, Steve Hargan, Harrelson, Tony Horton, Chuck Hinton, Sam McDowell, Mike Paul, and Duke Sims. Of those ten, none would still be with the club by 1973.

APRIL 7 The Indians lose the opener 8–2 to the Orioles before 38,180 at Municipal Stadium. Playing in his first major league game, Roy Foster drove in both Cleveland runs with a single in the first inning and a homer in the fourth. Sam McDowell struck out 11 while allowing three runs and three hits in 6⅔ innings. Dave McNally fanned 13 Indians batters.

The fences were brought in about 15 feet at Municipal Stadium in 1970, causing a wide disparity between the club's home and road home run statistics. The Indians hit 133 homers at home in 1970 but only 50 on the road. The team ranked first in the AL in homers in their home park but had the second fewest at visiting venues. The pitching staff gave up 103 home runs at home (the most in the AL) and 60 on the road (the fewest in the league).

April 11 A diving catch by center fielder Ted Uhlaender with two out in the ninth inning and the bases loaded saves a 3–0 win over the Yankees in New York. Roy White was the batter. Dean Chance (seven innings), Mike Paul (1⅓ innings) and Dennis Higgins (two-thirds of an inning) combined on the shutout.

The Indians abandoned the sleeveless uniforms of the late-1960s for more conventional jerseys with sleeves in 1970. The predominate color also changed from red to navy blue. The club's uniforms changed almost yearly throughout the 1970s. The most significant change was the fabric, as the Indians joined the trend in switching from button-front flannels with belted trousers to pullover double knits and beltless waistbands in 1972. The most memorable uniform of the 1970s was the one in use as an alternative home and road outfit from 1975 through 1977, which featured a red shirt accompanied by red pants. In 1978, Gabe Paul became president of the club and returned the jersey style to the traditional white at home and gray on the road.

May 2 The Indians lose 4–3 in 17 innings to the Royals in Kansas City. Sam McDowell started the contest and walked ten and struck out ten in 8⅓ innings.

May 3 The Indians turn five double plays during a 6–3 win over the Royals in Kansas City.

May 5 The day after Ohio National Guardsmen shoot and kill four students at Kent State University, the Indians turn five more double plays during a 2–1 loss to the White Sox at Comiskey Park. There were nine double plays total in the contest, with Chicago contributing four.

May 6 Sam McDowell strikes out 15 batters, but the Indians lose 2–1 to the White Sox in Chicago.

McDowell won 20 games and lost 12 in 1970 while posting a 2.92 ERA. He led the AL in strikeouts for the fifth time in six years with 304 in 305 innings.

May 13 The Indians lose 1–0 in 12 innings to the Royals at Municipal Stadium.

May 21 Ray Fosse hits a grand slam during an eight-run fifth inning as the Indians win 10–7 over the Red Sox at Municipal Stadium. Fosse's blast was struck off Vicente Romo.

As a rookie catcher, Fosse hit .307 with 18 homers in 1970. He was on the way to posting even better numbers before he was run over by Pete Rose during the All-Star Game (see July 14, 1970).

May 23 Duke Sims figures in all of the scoring during a 13-inning, 4–3 win over the Yankees at Municipal Stadium. Sims hit a two-run homer in the fourth inning and a solo shot in the eighth. In the 13th, Duke was hit by a pitch and scored on a double by Larry Brown and a single from Jack Heidemann.

May 24 Tony Horton hits three homers in a game, but the Indians are swept by the Yankees 6–5 and 8–7 in 11 innings at Municipal Stadium. Horton hit his three homers in the second game, one of the six struck by the Indians in the losing cause. Ray Fosse added two homers and Jack Heidemann one. Horton hit home runs off John Cumberland in the second and fourth innings and Fritz Peterson in the eighth.

Throughout his career, Sam McDowell sparked fear and fury in batters who faced him. In this photo Minnesota's Bob Allison takes exception to a close pitch. Indians Duke Sims (in front of Allison) and Joe Azcue (in catcher's gear) fend off the attack while manager Alvin Dark stands in front of McDowell (far right).

May 29 Sam McDowell strikes out 13 batters and pitches a two-hitter to defeat the Athletics 2–1 in Oakland. The only hits off McDowell were a homer by Joe Rudi in the fourth inning and a single by Felipe Alou in the seventh.

Among Indians pitchers since 1960, McDowell ranks first in shutouts (22), first in innings pitched ($2{,}109\frac{2}{3}$), first in strikeouts (2,159), first in games *started (295), first in complete games (97), second in wins (122), and third in ERA (2.99).*

MAY 30 The Indians sign Rich Rollins as a free agent following his release by the Brewers.

JUNE 2 The Indians play the Brewers in Milwaukee for the first time and win 4–1 and 9–5 at County Stadium. Sam McDowell pitched a two-hitter in the opener. He had a no-hitter in progress until Danny Walton doubled and Roberto Pena singled in the eighth. Cleveland struck five homers in the nightcap. Graig Nettles and Duke Sims each hit two and Ray Fosse one.

JUNE 3 Duke Sims hits two home runs for the second game in a row, leading the Indians to a 7–6 victory over the Brewers in Milwaukee.

JUNE 4 In the first round of the amateur draft, the Indians select pitcher Steve Dunning from Stanford University.

The second overall pick, Dunning made his major league debut ten days later (see June 14, 1970) but was only 23–41 with a 4.56 ERA during his seven-year career. After leaving baseball, Dunning enrolled in law school and became an attorney in Irvine, California. Other future major leaguers chosen in the June draft were Tommy Smith (fifth round), Dennis Kinney (tenth round) and Jeff Newman (26th round). None of them made much of an impact in Cleveland. The Indians did make a great selection in the secondary draft in January 1970 in Chris Chambliss.

JUNE 11 The Indians win a thrilling ten-inning 6–5 decision over the Athletics at Municipal Stadium. Pinch-hitter Chuck Hinton struck a two-run homer in the ninth to tie the score 4–4. The A's scored in the top of the tenth, but the Indians came back to win on a double by Vada Pinson and a homer by Roy Foster.

Foster looked like a star when hit 23 homers and batted .268 as a 24-year-old rookie outfielder in 1970. He proved to be a one-year wonder, however, and was out of the majors after the 1972 season.

JUNE 12 The Milwaukee Brewers play in Cleveland for the first time and beat the Indians 4–1 at Municipal Stadium.

JUNE 13 The Indians score seven runs in the second inning and defeat the Brewers 10–6 at Municipal Stadium.

JUNE 14 Without spending a single day in the minors, Steve Dunning makes his major league debut and is the winning pitcher, allowing two runs and five hits in five innings as the Indians take a 9–2 decision over the Brewers at Municipal Stadium.

JUNE 15 The Indians trade Barry Moore and Bob Miller to the White Sox for Buddy Bradford.

JUNE 20 Roy Foster hits two solo home runs off Earl Wilson for the only two runs in a 2–1 win over the Tigers at Municipal Stadium. Foster homered in the third and eighth innings.

June 21 Tigers shortstop Cesar Gutierrez collects seven hits in seven at-bats during a 12-inning, 9–8 win over the Indians in the second game of a double header at Municipal Stadium. Tony Horton hit a grand slam in the first inning off Mike Kilkenny and later added two doubles. Detroit won the opener 7–2.

A .235 lifetime hitter in four seasons in the majors, Gutierrez is one of the only three players in major league history to go seven-for-seven in a single game. The other two are Wilbert Robinson with Baltimore in 1892 and Rennie Stennett of the Pirates in 1977.

June 24 The Indians win 7–2 and lose 5–4 during an event-filled double header against the Yankees in New York. Tony Horton provided some humor in the ninth inning of the opener. Six-foot-seven-inch Yankee pitcher Steve Hamilton twice threw the Indians first baseman his "folly floater," a stop-action, high-arcing pitch. After fouling out, Horton walked toward the dugout, and angrily threw his cap and bat into the air. Then he got down on his hands and knees and crawled into the dugout. In the fifth inning of the second tilt, Vada Pinson and Yankee hurler Stan Bahnsen squared off after a play at the plate. Bahnsen tagged out Pinson, and the Cleveland outfielder responded by decking him. Pinson was ejected. Shortly after play resumed, a cherry bomb thrown by a fan exploded at home plate and burned Ray Fosse on the instep. After receiving first aid, he stayed in the game. Bobby Murcer hit four homers during the afternoon, three of them in game two.

A Rose Runs Over a Mule

The 1970 All-Star Game in Cincinnati, played on July 14, was one of the most exciting in the history of the series. It ended with Pete Rose ramming into Ray Fosse to score the winning run in the 12th inning to lift the National League to a 5–4 victory. In the book *The Midsummer Classic: The Complete History of Baseball's All-Star Game,* published in 2001, authors David Vincent, Lyle Spatz, and David W. Smith wrote: "Of all of the plays in all the All-Star Games in all the sports, the one that is almost certainly the best remembered is the collision at home plate between Pete Rose and Ray Fosse that ended the 1970 game."

Until the bottom of the ninth inning, the game was routine. The American League held a 4–1 lead. With Catfish Hunter of the Athletics on the mound, Giants catcher Dick Dietz led off the NL ninth with a home run. Bud Harrelson singled, and after Cito Gaston popped out, Joe Morgan singled Harrelson to second. After Fritz Peterson relieved Hunter, Willie McCovey singled to score Harrelson and move Morgan to third. Mel Stottlemyre was brought in to pitch to Roberto Clemente, who tied the game with a sacrifice fly. Rose had a chance to win the game in front of his hometown crowd, but he struck out.

The score was still tied 4–4 when Rose batted again in the 12th inning with one on base and two out against Clyde Wright of the Angels. He hit a single to center field. Billy Grabarkewitz followed with another single, with Rose stopping at second. Jim Hickman lined the third straight single off Wright, which was fielded by Amos Otis. Rose rounded third, drawing a throw. About two-thirds of the way down the third base line, Rose leaned over to begin a headfirst slide but saw that Fosse was blocking the plate. Fosse was firmly planted about five feet up the line from the plate with one foot on each side of the foul line. Rose had a split second to make one of three choices. He could slide head first and risk injury by banging into Fosse's shinguards, and had he done so, still would have been well short of touching home plate. He could try to run through Fosse, also an injury risk. Or he could try to evade Fosse and swipe home plate with his hand, in which he would almost assuredly have been out unless Otis made a terrible throw. Fosse was so far up the line, that if Rose had tried to run around the catcher, he would have missed the plate by five to ten feet and would had to backtrack to score. Complicating the situation, Rose was off-balance. Running full-speed, he had bent low to slide and found it difficult to straighten up.

Rose knew of only one way to play baseball, and that was full bore to win, even in an All-Star Game. Fosse played with the same mindset and stood like a rock in Rose's path. The collision sent Fosse tumbling backward and Rose falling to Fosse's left. The ball sailed past home plate and the National League won 5–4. Rose was criticized for slamming into Fosse, but it was typical of the way Rose played throughout his 24-year big league career. In a nearly identical situation a little over three months before the Fosse play, Rose lowered his shoulder into Indianapolis catcher Jim Hibbs in a meaningless exhibition game.

At first it appeared that Pete came out of the collision in worse shape than Fosse. The Reds moved on to Pittsburgh immediately after the break and played a four-game series against the Pirates. Rose's only appearance in the series was as a pinch-hitter in the fourth game, sitting out with a bruise just above his left knee. The first three games of the Pittsburgh series were the only three that Rose failed to play all year. He didn't make his first start after the 1970 All-Star Game until July 20.

Fosse, on the other hand, played in the Indians first nine games after the All-Star Game, including both ends of a double header on July 24 and collected 11 hits in his first 31 at-bats after colliding with Rose. Fosse didn't play on July 25 and 26, not because of injury, but to attend his grandmother's funeral. He hit .312 before the All-Star break in 1970 and .297 afterward, but his power numbers fell precipitously, as the pain in his shoulder wouldn't allow him to drive the ball for distance. Fosse had 16 homers and 30 extra base hits in 292 at-bats at the break. After his encounter with Rose, Fosse had only six extra base hits, two of them homers, in 158 at-bats over the remainder of the 1970 season. He finished the year with a .307 batting average and 18 homers. Fosse never reached those figures again as the shoulder became progressively worse. He was 23-years-old in 1970 and looked like an All-Star for years to come, but never appeared in the Midsummer Classic again. His playing career ended in 1979 with a .256 batting average and 61 homers.

Ironically, Rose and Fosse met for the first time the evening prior to their fateful meeting at home plate in the All-Star Game. Pete invited both Fosse and his Indians teammate Sam McDowell to dinner at his home in Cincinnati. In another incredible coincidence, Rose served a five-month prison sentence for tax evasion in a federal prison in Fosse's hometown of Marion, Illinois.

June 28 — Jack Heidemann collects five hits in five at-bats during an 8–2 win over the Tigers in the first game of a double header in Detroit. The Indians lost the second tilt 5–1.

July 2 — Tony Horton hits for the cycle during a 10–9 win over the Orioles in Baltimore. Facing Jim Hardin, Horton singled in the first inning and tripled in the fourth, then added a single against Moe Drabowsky in the seventh and a home run off Pete Richert in the ninth. In the same game, Ray Fosse extended his hitting streak to 23 games.

July 5 — Sam McDowell strikes out 15 batters and plays second base during a 6–4 win over the Senators at Municipal Stadium. In the eighth inning with two on and two out, Al Dark brought in Dean Chance from the bullpen to face Frank Howard. Dark moved McDowell, a left-hander, to second. Chance walked Howard intentionally, then retired Rick Reichardt on a grounder to third baseman Eddie Leon, who threw to McDowell at second with the massive Howard bearing down on him. McDowell returned to the mound in the ninth and struck out all three batters he faced.

JULY 8 Trailing 5–1, the Indians score five runs in the eighth inning and defeat the Senators 6–5 at Municipal Stadium. The rally was capped by a grand slam from Buddy Bradford off Darold Knowles.

JULY 12 A fight erupts during an 8–2 loss to the Red Sox in the second game of a double header at Municipal Stadium. Tony Conigliaro charged the mound after being hit by a pitch from Indians pitcher Fred Lasher. Conigliaro punched and kicked Lasher, setting off a full-scale brawl that lasted 20 minutes. The Red Sox also won the opener 6–2.

JULY 14 At Riverfront Stadium in Cincinnati, Indians catcher Ray Fosse is involved in one of the most famous plays in All-Star Game history, as the National League wins 5–4. With the score 4–4 in the 12th inning and Pete Rose as the base runner on second base, Jim Hickman hit a single to center, which was fielded by Amos Otis. Otis's throw arrived at the same time as Rose, causing a violent collision between the Rose and Fosse. Rose was safe on the play to score the game's winning run.

JULY 17 Steve Dunning (eight innings) and Phil Hennigan (one inning) combine on a two-hitter for a 6–0 win over the Royals in Kansas City. The only Royals hits were singles by Jim Campanis in the sixth inning and Lou Piniella in the seventh.

JULY 18 Stave Hargan pitches a two-hitter and defeats the Royals 4–1 in Kansas City. It was the second day in a row that the Indians held the Royals to two base hits. The only hits off Hargan were a single by Pat Kelly in the first inning and a homer by Bill Sorrell in the fifth.

JULY 24 Tony Horton hits a pinch-hit homer in the sixth inning, stays in the game, and smacks a three-run homer in the seventh to lead the Indians to a 9–6 win over the Royals in the second game of a double header at Municipal Stadium. Kansas City won the opener 5–2.

JULY 29 The Indians take a 9–1 lead on the Twins with the help of a third-inning grand slam by Vada Pinson off Pete Hamm, then hang on to win 9–8 at Municipal Stadium.

AUGUST 7 Trailing 4–1, the Indians score seven runs in the seventh inning and beat the Orioles 10–4 at Municipal Stadium.

On the same day, the Indians sold Dick Ellsworth to the Brewers.

AUGUST 22 Three consecutive homers in the sixth inning highlights a ten-inning, 6–5 win over the Athletics at Municipal Stadium. Duke Sims, Graig Nettles, and Eddie Leon each connected off Pat Dobson. Chuck Hinton, who entered the game in the ninth inning as a defensive replacement for Sims at first base, drove in the winning run with a single in the tenth.

AUGUST 28 Rich Hand pitches a one-hitter to defeat the Angels 5–1 in the second game of a double header at Municipal Stadium. The only California hit was a home run by Roger Repoz with one out in the first inning. The Indians lost the opener 3–2.

During the second game of the double header, Tony Horton suffered a nervous breakdown. After popping out in the first and third innings, Horton went into the clubhouse and refused to come back to the field. Horton appeared to be headed for stardom after an excellent season in 1969 but was a holdout during spring training in a salary squabble and reported three weeks late. Al Dark was handling contract negotiations as well as managing the team on the field, and publicly criticized Horton. The media also aligned against the first baseman and portrayed Horton as selfish and greedy. After a slow start, Horton was booed almost every time he stepped to the plate. Tightly wound under the best of circumstances and driven by an insatiable desire to succeed and a fear of failure, the circumstances unsettled Horton's mental stability. Following the breakdown, he was hospitalized in Cleveland after attempting suicide. Only 25-years-old, Horton returned to his home in Santa Monica, California, and went to work for a bank. He never played another game of organized baseball.

AUGUST 29 The Indians hit five home runs during a 14–1 thrashing of the Angels at Municipal Stadium. Roy Foster and Buddy Bradford each contributed two homers, and Eddie Leon one.

AUGUST 30 Nine different players hit home runs during a 10–9 loss to the Angels at Municipal Stadium. Alex Johnson, Jay Johnstone, Bill Voss, Sandy Alomar, and Ken McMullen went deep for California, and Chuck Hinton, Graig Nettles, Vada Pinson, and Ray Fosse homered for Cleveland.

SEPTEMBER 10 The Indians pummel the Senators 13–4 at Municipal Stadium.

SEPTEMBER 12 Duke Sims hits a walk-off homer in the 11th inning, his second of the game, to beat the Yankees 4–3 at Municipal Stadium. Sims also homered in the second inning.

SEPTEMBER 13 Steve Hargan pitches a two-hitter and wins 3–1 over the Yankees at Municipal Stadium. The only New York hits were singles by Roy White in the fourth inning and Danny Cater in the sixth.

After posting a 5–14 record and a 5.70 ERA in 1969, Hargan was off to a slow start in 1970 and spent five weeks in the minors. He came back strong, winning ten games after the All-Star break and finishing with an 11–3 mark and an earned run average of 2.90. Unfortunately, Hargan regressed again in 1971, and was 1–13 while his ERA ballooned to 6.19.

SEPTEMBER 17 Sam McDowell records his 20th win of the season with a 6–2 decision over the Tigers at Municipal Stadium.

SEPTEMBER 18 The Indians sell Dean Chance to the Mets.

SEPTEMBER 26 Fred Lasher is suspended by Al Dark for the remainder of the season after a display of temper during a 7–4 loss to the Orioles at Municipal Stadium. When Dark came to the mound to relieve Lasher, the pitcher threw the ball down in disgust and fired his glove into the stands.

DECEMBER 11 Two months after the Cavaliers play their first NBA game, the Indians trade Duke Sims to the Dodgers for Alan Foster and Ray Lamb.

1971

Season in a Sentence

Hopes are high with a roster of rising young players, but the Indians lose 100 games for the first time since 1914 and change managers twice.

Finish • Won • Lost • Pct • GB

Finish	Won	Lost	Pct	GB
Sixth	60	102	.370	43.0

Managers

Al Dark (42–61) and Johnny Lipon (18–41)

Stats

Stats	Indians	AL	Rank
Batting Avg:	.238	.247	9
On-Base Pct:	.302	.320	11
Slugging Pct:	.342	.364	9
Home Runs:	109		7
Stolen Bases:	57		10
ERA:	4.28	3.46	12
Fielding Avg:	.981	.980	3
Runs Scored:	543		9
Runs Allowed:	747		12

Starting Line-up

Ray Fosse, c
Chris Chambliss, 1b
Eddie Leon, 2b
Graig Nettles, 3b
Jack Heidemann, ss
Ted Uhlaender, lf
Vada Pinson, cf
Roy Foster, rf-lf
Ted Ford, rf-cf
Frank Baker, rf-lf
Ken Harrelson, 1b

Pitchers

Sam McDowell, sp
Steve Dunning, sp
Alan Foster, sp
Phil Hennigan, rp
Steve Mingori, sp
Vince Colbert, sp
Ray Lamb, rp-sp
Ed Farmer, rp
Steve Hargan, sp-rp

Attendance

591,361 (12th in AL)

Club Leaders

Batting Avg:	Ted Uhlaender	.288
On-Base Pct:	Graig Nettles	.350
Slugging Pct:	Graig Nettles	.435
Home Runs:	Graig Nettles	28
RBIs:	Graig Nettles	86
Runs:	Graig Nettles	78
Stolen Bases:	Vada Pinson	25
Wins:	Sam McDowell	13
Strikeouts:	Sam McDowell	192
ERA:	Sam McDowell	3.42
Saves:	Phil Hennigan	14

APRIL 5 The Indians sign Camilo Pascaul as a free agent following his release by the Dodgers.

APRIL 6 On Opening Day, the Indians lose 8–2 to the Tigers in Detroit.

APRIL 8 In the home opener, the Indians rally with one run in the eighth inning and two in the ninth to defeat the Red Sox 3–2 before 40,462 at Municipal Stadium. In just his second major league game, Gomer Hodge keyed the victory. In the eighth inning, he hit a pinch-hit double and scored on a single. Hodge remained in the game and drove in both ninth-inning runs with a single.

A 27-year-old rookie infielder in 1971, Harold (Gomer) Hodge became a cult hero in Cleveland, with hits in his first four major league at-bats. He earned his nickname from a North Carolina drawl, and an appearance and demeanor similar that of the popular television character Gomer Pyle created by Jim Nabors. After the hot start, it soon became apparent why Hodge spent so many seasons in the minors. He finished the 1971 campaign with a .205 batting average and one home run in 80 games and 83 at-bats.

April 10 The Indians outlast the Red Sox 11–10 at Municipal Stadium. Cleveland broke a 5–5 tie with three runs in the fourth inning.

April 13 Four American League umpires escape a fire at Cleveland's Pick-Carter Hotel that causes the deaths of seven people. The umpires were Jim Odom, Jim Honochick, Marty Springstead, and Larry McCoy. Odom was forced to climb down a fire department ladder from the fourth floor to escape the blaze.

April 18 Steve Dunning pitches a one-hitter to beat the Senators 1–0 in the second game of a double header at Municipal Stadium. The only Washington hit was a single by Tommy McCraw in the second inning. Ted Uhlaender drove in the lone run with a single in the sixth inning. Washington won the first game 4–0.

April 19 Roy Foster hits a two-run homer in the top of the 13th inning and the Indians fight off a Red Sox rally in the bottom half to win 5–4 in Boston.

May 9 On Mother's Day, the Indians give each female fan a can of deodorant and a pair of panty hose and draw only 4,288 for a 4–1 win over the Angels at Municipal Stadium.

May 11 Steve Dunning stakes himself to a 5–0 lead with a grand slam off Diego Segui in the second inning but lets the Athletics back in the game by allowing five runs in four innings. Phil Hennigan added five innings of shutout relief for a 7–5 win.

The grand slam was the last struck by an American League pitcher before the designated hitter rule was passed in 1973.

May 17 Left fielder John Lowenstein, center fielder Vada Pinson, and shortstop Jack Heidemann collide in the fourth inning of a 6–3 win over the Senators at Municipal Stadium. The three were chasing a pop fly by Tommy McCraw in shallow left. As the trio lay stunned, McCraw circled the bases for an inside-the-park home run. Lowenstein, Pinson, and Heidemann all had to leave the game. Lowenstein spent a month on the disabled list with a bruised right leg and left foot.

May 18 Sam McDowell walks ten batters and allows only one hit in six innings of work during a 7–3 win over the Senators in Washington.

May 23 The Yankees and Indians engage in a free-for-all during a 2–1 Cleveland win in the second game of a double header at Municipal Stadium. It began when Sam McDowell slid hard into Yankee shortstop Gene Michael trying to break up a double play. McDowell claimed he was kicked by Michael and wrestled him to the ground. Both dugouts and bullpens emptied and New York first baseman John Ellis threw haymakers at a few Indians players before order was restored. No one was ejected. The Indians lost the first game 6–3.

May 28 Sam McDowell walks nine, strikes out 11, pitches a two-hitter, and defeats the White Sox 4–0 at Comiskey Park. The only White Sox hits were singles by Rick Reichardt in the first inning and Rich McKinney in the third.

June 4 In the first round of the amateur draft, the Indians select pitcher David Sloan from Santa Clara High School in Santa Clara, California.

Sloan never reached the majors, peaking at Class AA. The only future major leaguers chosen by the Indians in June 1971 were Wayne Cage (third round) and Larry Andersen (17th round). Jim Norris was picked in the fifth round of the secondary phase in January.

June 13 Sam McDowell two-hits the Brewers for an 11–0 win at Municipal Stadium. The only Milwaukee hits were a double by Rick Auerbach in the sixth inning and a single from Dave May in the seventh.

June 16 Batting lead off, Graig Nettles collects five hits, including a double, in five at-bats, but the Indians lose 3–2 to the Twins at Municipal Stadium.

June 18 A 7–0 win over the Tigers at Municipal Stadium is featured by an eighth-inning melee in which five players are ejected. After Ray Fosse was hit in the back by a pitched ball from Bill Denehy, the Cleveland catcher rushed the mound. Both benches cleared, and fights broke out all over the field. Detroit's Willie Horton dropped Ray Lamb with a right to the jaw. Tossed out were Fosse and Gomer Hodge of the Indians and Denehy, Horton, and Ike Brown of the Tigers.

Fosse hit 12 homers and batted .276 in 1971.

June 19 Graig Nettles and Vada Pinson start the first inning with back-to-back homers off Dean Chance, but the Indians lose 5–3 to the Tigers at Municipal Stadium.

Nettles batted .261 and clubbed 28 homers in 1971. He also set major league records for most assists (412) and double plays (54) by a third baseman in a season.

June 20 Chuck Hinton smacks a home run in the 11th inning to beat the Tigers 7–6 in the first game of a double header at Municipal Stadium. The second tilt was suspended in the top of the eighth with Cleveland leading 7–6 because a bank of lights failed. The contest was completed on September 28 with the Indians winning 8–7.

June 21 Ken Harrelson retires as an active player at the age of 29.

The broken leg suffered by Harrelson a year earlier (see March 19, 1970) never properly healed. He hit only .199 with five homers in 161 at-bats in 1971. By 1975, Harrelson became a broadcaster of Red Sox games at the start of a career behind the mike that has lasted over 30 years. He shifted to the White Sox in 1982.

June 22 The Indians score seven runs in the sixth inning and win 9–3 over the Red Sox in the first game of a double header at Fenway Park. Cleveland lost the second contest 2–0 despite Rich Hand (six innings) and Ed Farmer (two innings) combining on a two-hitter. Both runs scored on a home run by George Scott in the fourth inning.

From June 22 through the end of the season, the Indians had a record of 28–68.

June 28 The Indians break a scoreless tie with three runs in the ninth inning to defeat the Yankees 3–0 in the first game of a double header in New York. Ray Lamb (eight innings) and Steve Mingori (one inning) combined on the shutout. Cleveland also won the second contest 5–2.

Ted Uhlaender left the club on the same day because he was upset over his lack of playing time. He returned three days later.

JULY 15 Sam McDowell (seven innings) and Phil Hennigan (one inning) combine on a two-hitter but lose 1–0 to the Royals in Kansas City. Lou Piniella drove in the lone run with a single in the sixth inning.

Hennigan served during the Vietnam War and won a medal for valor. Indians outfielder Ted Ford was also a Vietnam veteran.

Ray Fosse puts a tag on Chicago's Tom Egan in a rundown between third and home. Fosse produced a solid year in 1971 but never regained the form he showed the year before.

JULY 17 Sam McDowell is fined $1,000 for "rowdyism" on the team bus traveling from the Los Angeles International Airport to the Grand Hotel in Anaheim. Alcohol was banned on all future team flights.

JULY 30 Johnny Lipon replaces Al Dark as manager of the Indians.

The change was made with the club holding a 42–61 record after 27 losses in their last 37 games. The season began with high hopes because the Indians had what seemed to be a strong corps of young players, including Graig Nettles, Ray Fosse, Roy Foster, Eddie Leon, Rich Hand, Phil Hennigan,

Jack Heidemann, Chris Chambliss, Alan Foster, Steve Dunning, Ray Lamb, Fred Stanley, Vince Colbert, Ed Farmer, Ted Ford, and John Lowenstein. The infusion of youth failed to help. In addition to his field duties, Dark had been handling many of the general manager's duties, such as negotiating with and signing players to contracts, and initiating and approving all player trades. He had been granted that privilege in 1969 when the duties were taken away from Gabe Paul, who was relegated to heading only the marketing and promotional aspects of the franchise. Team unity was destroyed, however, when Dark signed contracts with Sam McDowell, Vada Pinson, Ken Harrelson, and Graig Nettles that contained performance bonuses that were ruled illegal by commissioner Bowie Kuhn. McDowell was angry enough over the situation to jump the club for nine days beginning on July 31 while his contract was re-negotiated. In the wake of Dark's departure, Paul's authority over player personnel matters was restored. Dark later managed the Athletics (1974–75) and Padres (1977). The A's won the World Series in Dark's first season with the club. Lipon broke into the majors as a shortstop in 1942 with the Tigers, and after three years in the Navy, remained in the big leagues until 1954. He had been a Cleveland coach since 1968. As manager, Lipon was 18–41 with the Indians, and his contract wasn't renewed.

AUGUST 11 A home run by Ray Fosse in the 12th inning beats the White Sox 3–2 at Comiskey Park.

AUGUST 21 Roy Foster hits a grand slam off Tommy John in the first inning of a 9–4 win over the White Sox in Chicago.

AUGUST 28 Ray Fosse slugs a grand slam off Steve Luebber in the third inning of a 9–8 win over the Twins at Municipal Stadium.

SEPTEMBER 3 Indians pitcher Bob Kaiser allows a home run to the first batter he faces as a major league leaguer during the eighth inning of a 9–2 loss to the Red Sox in Boston. The blow was struck by George Scott.

Kaiser was only 21 when he made his debut, but his career lasted only five games.

SEPTEMBER 4 Held to one hit through the first five innings, the Indians erupt for four runs in the sixth inning and seven in the seventh to defeat the Red Sox 11–9 in Boston.

SEPTEMBER 6 The Indians win 1–0 over the Orioles in the second game of a double header at Memorial Stadium. Fred Stanley drove in the lone run with a single in the fourth inning. Vince Colbert (eight innings) and Steve Dunning (one inning) combined on the shutout. Baltimore won the opener 10–5.

SEPTEMBER 14 After winning the first game of a double header 3–1 against the Senators at Municipal Stadium, the second contest is suspended after 16 innings with the score 5–5 because of the American League's 1:00 a.m. curfew. Washington scored three times in the ninth to send the contest into extra innings. It was completed on September 20 in Washington.

SEPTEMBER 20 The Indians and Senators complete their suspended game of September 14 in Washington, and the Senators win 8–6 in 20 innings. Since the game began in

Cleveland, the Senators batted first and scored three times in the top of the 20th. The Indians came back with one in their half. The two clubs set a major league record (since tied) for most pitchers used in a game with 18. Each team sent nine hurlers to the mound. The 18 pitchers issued 30 walks, which tied another big league mark. Washington pitchers accounted for 19 of the 30. The Senators won the regularly scheduled game 3–2.

SEPTEMBER 21 Dave Dixon, executive director of the Louisiana Superdome Commission, appears before an American League meeting in Boston. Dixon was asked to come to Boston by Vernon Stouffer and Gabe Paul. Stouffer and Paul had hoped to convince AL owners to allow the Indians to play about 30 "home" games in New Orleans when the Superdome was scheduled for completion in 1974. Paul continued to push for the plan for several more years, but Stouffer sold the Indians to Nick Mileti in March 1972 and Mileti refused to sign off on the deal.

SEPTEMBER 22 The Indians play the Senators in Washington for the last time, and lose 3–2.

The previous day, the Senators were given permission by the American League to move to Dallas-Fort Worth beginning with the 1972 season. The club was renamed the Texas Rangers.

SEPTEMEBR 25 The Indians drop their 100th game of the season with a 6–4 loss in 11 innings to the Orioles at Municipal Stadium.

OCTOBER 5 The Indians trade Vada Pinson, Frank Baker, and Alan Foster to the Angels for Alex Johnson and Gerry Mason.

Johnson won the AL batting title in 1970 with the Angels by hitting .329, but unstable behavior led to his trade to Cleveland. During the 1971 season, Johnson was benched four times and suspended on 29 occasions. His transgressions included brawling with teammate Chico Ruiz and dumping coffee grounds into the typewriter of a reporter. Ruiz claimed that Johnson pulled a gun on him. The Indians were the fifth of eight teams that employed Johnson during his 13-year career in the hopes of harnessing his tremendous talent. It didn't work in Cleveland. Johnson was dealt to the Rangers after batting .239 with eight home runs in 108 games in 1972.

OCTOBER 13 Johnny Lipon is released as manager of the Indians. Dave Bristol was offered the job, but turned it down.

NOVEMBER 9 The Indians hire Ken Aspromonte as manager.

Aspromonte had been an infielder in the majors from 1957 through 1963 with six different clubs. He played for the Indians from 1960 through 1962. Aspromonte guided the Indians through three losing seasons to an overall record of 220–260.

NOVEMBER 29 The Indians trade Sam McDowell to the Giants for Gaylord Perry and Frank Duffy.

The trade with San Francisco turned out to be one of the best trades in club history. McDowell was only 19–25 with three different teams over the remainder of his career. Perry became the ace of the Cleveland staff. Playing three full seasons and part of a fourth with the Tribe, he had a record of 70–57 on some dismal teams. Duffy was the Indians starting shortstop for six seasons.

DECEMBER 2 The Indians trade Roy Foster, Ken Suarez, Mike Paul, and Rich Hand to the Rangers for Del Unser, Denny Riddleberger, Gary Jones, and Terry Lee.

DECEMBER 6 The Indians trade Ted Uhlaender to the Reds for Milt Wilcox.

1972

Season in a Sentence

With a new owner (Nick Mileti), new manager (Ken Aspromonte) and pitching ace (Gaylord Perry), the Indians win 18 of their first 28 games and a spot atop the AL East, but fade again to a losing record.

Finish • Won • Lost • Pct • GB

Finish	Won	Lost	Pct	GB
Fifth	72	84	.462	14.0

Manager

Ken Aspromonte

Stats

Stats	Indians	AL	Rank
Batting Avg:	.234	.239	9
On-Base Pct:	.295	.308	10
Slugging Pct:	.330	.343	10
Home Runs:	91		8
Stolen Bases:	49		11
ERA:	2.92	3.06	4
Fielding Avg:	.981	.979	3
Runs Scored:	472		10
Runs Allowed:	519		4

Starting Line-up

Ray Fosse, c
Chris Chambliss, 1b
Jack Brohamer, 2b
Graig Nettles, 3b
Frank Duffy, ss
Tommy McCraw, lf-rf-cf-1b
Del Unser, cf
Buddy Bell, rf-cf
Alex Johnson, lf
Eddie Leon, 2b-3b
John Lowenstein, rf-lf
Roy Foster, rf-lf

Pitchers

Gaylord Perry, sp
Dick Tidrow, sp
Milt Wilcox, sp
Steve Dunning, sp
Steve Mingori, rp
Ed Farmer, rp
Ray Lamb, rp

Attendance

626,354 (11th in AL)

Club Leaders

Batting Avg:	Chris Chambliss	.292
On-Base Pct:	Chris Chambliss	.327
Slugging Pct:	Chris Chambliss	.397
Home Runs:	Graig Nettles	17
RBIs:	Graig Nettles	70
Runs:	Graig Nettles	65
Stolen Bases:	Tommy McCraw	12
Wins:	Gaylord Perry	24
Strikeouts:	Gaylord Perry	234
ERA:	Gaylord Perry	1.92
Saves:	Steve Mingori	10

January 15 Russell Means, director of the Cleveland American Indian center, says the Chief Wahoo symbol used by the Indians is "racist, degrading and demeaning" to the American Indians and that he would file a lawsuit to halt use of the symbol. "How long do you think the stadium would stand if the team were called the Cleveland Negroes with a caricature of Aunt Jemina or Little Black Sambo and every time a ball was hit some guy would come out and do the soft shoe?" asked Means. "The whole viewpoint America takes of the Indian is that we don't count. Why don't they use a picture of an Indian that shows respect instead of a pointed-headed, big-toothed clown?"

Many colleges and high schools have responded to concerns over Native American nicknames and symbols and have eliminated them. Despite the objections of many Native American individuals and groups, Chief Wahoo and the Indians nickname have remained in use.

March 22 The Indians change hands with the sale of the club from Vernon Stouffer to 41-year-old Nick Mileti for about $9 million.

Mileti was a law school graduate of Ohio State University and a self-made millionaire. He headed an eight-man group to buy the franchise. The group included future U. S. Senator Howard Metzenbaum and banker Ted Bonda. To get the club, Mileti outbid another local group headed by former Indians player Al Rosen and Cleveland industrialist George Steinbrenner. Mileti already owned the Cleveland Cavaliers of the NBA and the Cleveland Barons of the American Hockey League. In addition, Mileti was in the process of building The Coliseum in suburban Richfield, the home of the Cavaliers from 1974 through 1994. Mileti made his fortune in construction and broadcasting. Like Stouffer, Mileti ran into financing problems hampered by a limited cash flow due to the diminished attendance figures at Municipal Stadium and a losing club. Due to mounting financial losses, the Indians board of directors removed Mileti from heading the day-to-day operation of the club in August 1973, and replaced him with Bonda. Stouffer's rejection of the efforts by well-heeled George Steinbrenner to purchase the Indians remains one of the great "what-ifs" in Cleveland baseball history. Steinbrenner had an agreement in place to buy the Indians in December 1971, but at the last minute Stouffer pulled out of the deal. Steinbrenner bought the Yankees in January 1973, and within a week named Gabe Paul as the number two man in his organization (see January 10, 1973).

April 3 The Indians trade Ted Ford to the Rangers for Roy Foster and Tommy McCraw.

The Indians dealt Foster to Texas the previous December, then re-acquired him in another deal. He never played in another big league game, however.

April 7 The Indians scheduled season opener against the Brewers in Milwaukee is canceled by baseball's first players' strike. Cleveland's first six games were eliminated by the labor action, which began on April 1 and ended on April 13.

April 15 With the strike settled, the Indians open the season with a 5–1 win over the Brewers before 22,831 at Municipal Stadium. Gaylord Perry, in his Cleveland debut, was the losing pitcher.

Rocky Colavito joined Harry Jones in the TV booth in 1972. Colavito was a coach with the Indians in 1973, and then coached once more from 1976 through 1978. In 1977, he was both a coach on the field and an announcer on TV. On days in which Indians games were televised, Colavito worked with the hitters before the game, then changed into street clothes and ascended to the broadcast booth.

APRIL 17 In his debut with the Indians, Milt Wilcox pitches a two-hitter to defeat the Red Sox 4–0 at Fenway Park. Duane Josephson collected both Boston hits with a double in the fifth inning and a single in the eighth.

APRIL 22 Buddy Bell doubles in the fourth inning for his first major league RBI, then hits a grand slam off Eddie Watt in the seventh for his first homer to lead the Indians to a 9–2 win over the Orioles at Municipal Stadium.

Twenty-year-old rookie Buddy Bell tags Minnesota's Rod Carew sliding into third base. Bell was a fixture at the hot corner in Cleveland for seven seasons.

Bell was in the middle of a three-generation baseball family. His father Gus was an outfielder in the majors from 1950 through 1964, primarily with the Reds. Buddy's son David debuted in the majors in 1995 and was still active in 2007. David played for the Indians in 1995 and 1997. Mike Bell, another of Buddy's sons, played briefly for the Reds in 2000. Buddy was drafted in the 16th round in 1969 and became the best late-round bargain in club history. He started his professional career at second base, shifted to third a year later, and played in right and center fields as a 20-year-old rookie in 1972 because Graig Nettles was firmly planted on third base in the Cleveland line-up. With the trade of Nettles in November 1972, Bell moved back to third and was the Indians starter at the position until he was traded to the Rangers in December 1978.

APRIL 30 The Indians take 16 innings to beat the Royals 5–3 in Kansas City. A sacrifice fly by Jack Brohamer broke the 3–3 tie.

MAY 2 The Indians play the Rangers in Texas for the first time, and win 4–2 at Arlington Stadium. Gaylord Perry struck out 12 batters in 7⅔ innings.

MAY 6 The Indians overwhelm the White Sox 12–0 in Chicago.

MAY 14 Chris Chambliss hits a walk-off homer in the tenth inning to beat the Rangers 4–3 at Municipal Stadium. Chambliss entered the game as a defensive replacement at first base for Jerry Moses.

MAY 23 The Indians defeat the Yankees 3–0 in New York.

The win gave the Indians an 18–10 record and a 2½-game lead in the AL East. The club lost 41 of the next 58 games, however, to fall to 35–51 and erase any delusions that the franchise would dramatically improve on the dismal record of 1971.

JUNE 1 Gaylord Perry pitches the Indians to a 1–0 win over the Tigers at Municipal Stadium. Tommy McCraw's single in the third inning drove in the lone run of the game.

JUNE 6 With the second overall pick in the first round of the amateur draft, the Indians select shortstop Rick Manning from LaSalle High School in Niagara Falls, New York.

Manning reached the majors as a 20-year-old outfielder in 1975, and was touted as the next great superstar. He had a 13-year big league career, nine of them in Cleveland, that was always long on promise and short on results. Manning hit .289 in 1,032 at-bats during his first two seasons and won a Gold Glove. Thereafter, he batted just .249 with 47 homers in 4,216 at-bats. Manning had a greater impact on the ball club as a long-time broadcaster of Indians games, a job he has held since 1990. The Indians did much better in the third round with the selection of Dennis Eckersley. The Tribe also picked Duane Kuiper in the secondary phase in January along with Eric Raich.

JUNE 9 Jack Brohamer hits the first two home runs of his major league career during a 7–1 win over the Twins at Municipal Stadium. Gaylord Perry picked up his tenth win in only the Indians 43rd game of the season.

JUNE 15 Vince Colbert shuts out the Angels 1–0 in Anaheim. A double by Graig Nettles in the fourth inning drove in the lone run of the game.

The shutout was the only one of his career, and the victory was the only one Colbert collected in 1972. He never won another big league game. He finished the 1972 campaign with a 1–7 record. During the following off-season, the Indians traded him to the Rangers in November, and then re-acquired him during another transaction in March, but he failed to make the team in spring training.

July 4 Two days weeks after the break-in of Democratic Party National Committee headquarters at the Watergate complex in Washington, John Lowenstein hits a two-run homer off Rich Hand in the fifth inning for the only runs of a 2–0 win over the Rangers at Municipal Stadium. Mike Kilkenny ($2^2/_3$ innings) and Dick Tidrow ($6^2/_3$ innings) combined on the shutout. Kilkenny had to leave the game after being hit by a batted ball, fracturing a finger.

Kilkenny played on four teams in 1972. He appeared in one game with the Tigers, one with the Athletics, five with the Padres, and 22 with the Indians.

July 14 After the game is scoreless for 13 innings, the Indians plate two runs in the 14th inning for a 2–0 win over the Rangers in Arlington. The runs were driven in on singles by Buddy Bell and Jack Brohamer. Gaylord Perry pitched 13 innings for his 15th win of the season in the Indians 78th game of 1972. Dick Tidrow hurled an inning for the save.

July 19 The Indians play the Royals at Municipal Stadium in Kansas City for the last time and win 6–1.

The Royals moved into Royals Stadium in 1973.

July 23 Chicago manager Chuck Tanner asks plate umpire Mark Anthony three times to inspect Gaylord Perry in search of a foreign substance. The inspections revealed nothing, but Perry seemed unnerved. Tanner twice asked for the searches with Richie Allen at bat in the seventh and ninth innings. Allen delivered a homer in the seventh and a single in the ninth that led to the winning run.

Perry had to endure similar circumstances several times during the season. Despite the intrusions, Perry had a 24–16 record in 1972, leading the AL in wins and complete games (29 in 40 starts). He had a 1.92 ERA in $342^2/_3$ innings. The wins, innings, and complete games figures are the best of any Indians pitcher since Bob Feller in 1946.

July 31 The Indians win twice in their final at-bat while sweeping the Brewers 3–2 and 1–0 at Municipal Stadium. In the first game, Jack Brohamer smacked a walk-off homer in the tenth inning. In the nightcap, the lone run scored in the ninth on two singles, a walk, and an error. Dick Tidrow pitched the shutout.

August 1 Buddy Bell hits a two-run homer off Dave McNally in the second inning for the only runs in a 2–0 win over the Orioles at Municipal Stadium. Gaylord Perry pitched a two-hitter. The only Baltimore hits were singles by Boog Powell in the second inning and Merv Rettenmund in the sixth.

August 4 — Dick Tidrow pitches his second consecutive shutout, beating the Tigers 1–0 at Municipal Stadium. Frank Duffy accounted for the lone run by slugging a home run off Mickey Lolich in the seventh inning.

August 11 — Buddy Bell collects four singles in five at-bats to spark the Indians to a 5–1 victory over the Tigers in Detroit.

August 12 — Buddy Bell has four singles in five at-bats for the second game in a row to lead the Indians to a 6–1 win over the Tigers in Detroit.

August 13 — Tigers manager Billy Martin chooses his batting order by drawing names out of a hat and defeats the Indians 3–2 in the first game of a double header in Detroit. Martin used a conventional batting order in game two, and lost 9–2 to the Tribe.

August 27 — The Indians lose 1–0 to the Angels in 12 innings in Anaheim.

September 9 — Gaylord Perry picks up his 20th win of the season by pitching a ten-inning complete game and defeating the Red Sox 2–1 at Municipal Stadium.

October 4 — Larry Doby Johnson makes his major league debut during a 4–3 loss to the Orioles in Baltimore in the final game of the season. Subbing for Ray Fosse, Johnson caught four innings and collected a single in two at-bats.

Johnson was born in 1950 in Cleveland and was named after the Indians star center fielder Larry Doby. Johnson had a curious career. He played two games with the Indians with one in 1972 and one in 1974. During the latter season, Doby was a coach with the Indians. Johnson played in five different seasons over a seven-year period that included appearances in just 12 games. He closed his stay in the majors with three games with the White Sox in 1978 when Doby was the manager in Chicago.

October 19 — The Indians trade Eddie Leon to the White Sox for Walt Williams.

Williams was nicknamed "No Neck" because of his stocky, fire hydrant-shaped body. He carried 185 pounds on a five-foot-six-inch frame. Williams hit .289 in 104 games in 1973, his lone season in a Cleveland uniform.

November 27 — Three weeks after Richard Nixon defeats George McGovern in the Presidential election, the Indians trade Graig Nettles and Gerry Moses to the Yankees for John Ellis, Jerry Kenney, Charlie Spikes, and Rusty Torres.

The Indians were faced with a dilemma. The club had holes at almost every position but possessed two of the best young third baseman in baseball in Graig Nettles and Buddy Bell. To get both of them into the line-up, Bell was tried in the outfield in 1972, but it was apparent his best position was at third. Nettles was the one that the Indians decided to trade, in part because he feuded with manager Ken Aspromonte for much of the season. The Indians dealt Nettles to the Yankees along with a back-up catcher for four players they hoped would become regulars. Ellis and Spikes did crack the starting line-up but were barely adequate. Kenney and Torres were dismal failures. An outfielder, Torres was given 462 at-bats by the Indians and hit only .199.

Nettles played 16 more big league seasons in which he played in six All-Star Games and five World Series.

NOVEMBER 29 The Indians trade Phil Hennigan to the Mets for Brent Strom and Bob Rauch.

NOVEMBER 30 The Indians trade Del Unser and Terry Wedgewood to the Phillies for Oscar Gamble and Roger Freed.

During his three seasons in Cleveland, Gamble is remembered for his giant Afro sticking out from beneath his cap. He hit .274 with 54 homers in 1,192 at-bats in an Indians uniform.

DECEMBER 10 The American League votes to adopt the designated hitter rule on a three-year experimental basis. Under the new rule, the designated hitter replaced the pitcher in the batting order unless otherwise noted before the game. The rule was adopted permanently by the AL in 1975, but to this day the NL has declined to go along with the change.

1973

Season in a Sentence

The Indians draw over 74,000 on Opening Day, but a 30–58 start ends any optimism over the immediate future, and the club finishes last in the AL East with the worst attendance figure in the league.

Finish • Won • Lost • Pct • GB

Finish	Won	Lost	Pct	GB
Sixth	71	91	.438	26.0

Manager

Ken Aspromonte

Stats

Stats	Indians	AL	Rank
Batting Avg:	.256	.259	8
On-Base Pct:	.317	.331	12
Slugging Pct:	.387	.381	7
Home Runs:	158		1
Stolen Bases:	60		9
ERA:	4.58	3.82	11
Fielding Avg:	.978	.977	4
Runs Scored:	680		7
Runs Allowed:	826		11

Starting Line-up

John Ellis, c-dh
Chris Chambliss, 1b
Jack Brohamer, 2b
Buddy Bell, 3b
Frank Duffy, ss
Charlie Spikes, lf
George Hendrick, cf
Rusty Torres, rf
Oscar Gamble, dh-rf
Dave Duncan, c
Walt Williams, lf
John Lowenstein, rf-2b-dh
Leo Cardenas, ss
Tom Ragland, 2b

Pitchers

Gaylord Perry, sp
Dick Tidrow, sp
Milt Wilcox, sp
Brent Strom, sp-rp
Dick Bosman, sp
Tom Timmerman, sp-rp
Tom Hilgendorf, rp
Ray Lamb, rp

Attendance

615,107 (12th in AL)

Club Leaders

Batting Avg:	Buddy Bell	.268
	George Hendrick	.268
On-Base Pct:	Chris Chambliss	.342
Slugging Pct:	George Hendrick	.452
Home Runs:	Charlie Spikes	23
RBIs:	Charlie Spikes	73
Runs	Buddy Bell	86
Stolen Bases:	Walt Williams	9
Wins:	Gaylord Perry	19
Strikeouts:	Gaylord Perry	238
ERA:	Gaylord Perry	3.38

JANUARY 10 Gabe Paul leaves the Indians to become one of George Steinbrenner's investment partners with the Yankees. Steinbrenner purchased the Yanks a week earlier. Paul became president of the Yankees as the number two person on the organizational chart under Steinbrenner, who was listed as general partner. Phil Seghi replaced Paul as general manager of the Indians.

Seghi first joined the Indians in November 1971 as vice-president and director of player personnel. He had previous worked in the front offices of the Reds and Athletics. Seghi remained as general manager until 1985. Paul would return to the Indians as an investor in a group headed by Steve O'Neill in February 1978, and again became president and chief executive officer.

MARCH 8 The Indians trade Alex Johnson to the Rangers for Rich Hinton and Vince Colbert.

MARCH 24 The Indians trade Ray Fosse and Jack Heidemann to the Athletics for George Hendrick and Dave Duncan.

Nicknamed "Silent George" because of his reluctance to talk to reporters, Hendrick was a productive player during his four seasons in Cleveland but frustrated managers Ken Aspromonte and Frank Robinson with his aloofness and apathy. Hendrick was fined often for lack of hustle on the field.

APRIL 2 The Indians trade Tommy McCraw and Bob Marcano to the Angels for Leo Cardenas.

APRIL 7 The Indians win 2–1 over the Tigers in the season opener before 74,420 at Municipal Stadium. It was the largest Opening Day crowd in American League history. Chris Chambliss accounted for the Cleveland runs with a two-run homer in the first inning. Gaylord Perry pitched the complete game. John Ellis was in the starting line-up as the first designated hitter in Indians history.

Despite the big crowd, the Indians drew only 615,107 fans in 1973, the lowest figure in the American League.

APRIL 15 Gaylord Perry pitches a two-hitter to defeat the Tigers 7–0 in Detroit. The only hits off Perry were singles by Dick McAuliffe in the third inning and Mickey Stanley in the eighth.

Joe Tait began broadcasting Indians games on radio in 1973. He covered the club on radio and TV until 1987. Former Indians player Mudcat Grant joined Harry Jones in the TV booth.

APRIL 22 The Indians stun the Red Sox 8–7 in the first game of a double header at Municipal Stadium by wiping out a three-run deficit with a walk-off grand slam by Ron Lolich with two out in the ninth inning. Boston scored three runs in the top of the ninth to take a 7–4 lead. In the bottom half, Cleveland loaded the bases on an error, a single, and a walk before the blast by Lolich off Sonny Siebert. The Red Sox won game two 5–2.

Lolich hit .211 with four homers in 228 career at-bats.

April 25 Dick Tidrow pitches the Indians to a 1–0 win over the Athletics in Oakland with a two-hitter. The only hits by the A's were singles by Bert Campaneris in the first inning and Ray Fosse in the fifth.

With the changing times, many Indians began growing mustaches and beards in 1973, the first Cleveland players to do so since early the 20th century. Among those sporting facial hair were Chris Chambliss, Tom Ragland, Dave Duncan, Leo Cardenas, and Steve Mingori.

May 10 The Indians trade Steve Dunning to the Rangers for Dick Bosman and Ted Ford.

May 26 The White Sox and Indians battle 16 innings at Comiskey Park before the game is suspended with the score 2–2 because of the American League's 1:00 a.m. curfew. The contest was scheduled to be completed the following day.

May 27 The completion of the May 26 suspended game is postponed by rain.

May 28 The White Sox and Indians complete their May 26 suspended game at Comiskey Park with the White Sox winning 6–3 in 21 innings. The Indians scored in the top of the 21st, but the White Sox rallied for four in their half, the last three on a walk-off homer by Richie Allen. In the regularly scheduled contest, the White Sox won 4–0. Wilbur Wood was the winning pitcher in both games by pitching the last five innings of the suspended game, then hurling the complete game shutout.

June 1 The Indians play at Royals Stadium in Kansas City for the first time and lose 5–4 to the Royals.

June 5 In the first round of the amateur draft, the Indians select first baseman Glenn Tufts from Raynham High School in Bridgewater, Massachusetts.

Tufts was on a date the night before Thanksgiving in 1973 when the car he was driving skidded on ice and slammed into a pole. He severely damaged his ankle and missed the entire 1974 season. He played a few seasons in the minors but never reached the big leagues as a player. He did coach with the Giants in 1994. The accident set the stage for a terrible 1973 draft. The only future major leaguers picked that year were Tommy McMillian (second round) and Dave Oliver (third round), two players who played a grand total of only nine games at the big league level.

June 10 The Indians lose their tenth game in a row, dropping a 5–3 decision to the White Sox in the first game of a double header at Municipal Stadium. The streak ended with a 6–5 victory in game two. The winning run crossed the plate in the ninth inning on a single by John Ellis.

June 12 The Indians trade Lowell Palmer to the Yankees for Mike Kekich.

Kekich and Yankee teammate Fritz Peterson made headlines during spring training in 1973 by revealing that during the previous off-season they had traded wives. Kekich's children went to live with Peterson and their mother, and vice-versa. The two pitchers even traded the family pets. Peterson married the former Susanne Kekich in 1974, and the two later had a child together. The relationship between Kekich's and Peterson's former wife Marilyn failed to last. Peterson was traded by the Yankees to the Indians in April 1974, but by that time Kekich had already been released by the Cleveland club.

JUNE 19 George Hendrick hits three home runs in his first three plate appearances and contributes a walk-off single to lead the Indians to an 8–7 win over the Tigers at Municipal Stadium. Hendrick homered off Woodie Fryman in the first, fourth, and sixth innings. He walked in the seventh inning before his game-winning single in the ninth.

JUNE 20 A hero for the second game in a row, George Hendrick hits a home run and a walk-off single that beats the Tigers 7–6 at Municipal Stadium.

JUNE 21 Gaylord Perry strikes out 14 batters and George Hendrick clubs his fifth homer in three games as the Indians mash the Brewers 9–1 in Milwaukee.

Hendrick hit ten home runs in 14 games from June 8 through June 21. During that stretch, he had 17 hits in 65 at-bats, a .262 average. He drove in 14 runs and scored 14.

JULY 3 The Perry brothers face each other, as Gaylord starts for the Indians and Jim for the Tigers at Municipal Stadium. Gaylord gave up five runs in 6⅔ innings, and drew a 5–4 loss. Jim had a no decision, surrendering four runs in 5⅔ innings.

JULY 6 George Hendrick is fined $300 for lethargic play following an 11-inning, 8–7 win over the Angels at Municipal Stadium. California tied the score 7–7 with six runs in the ninth inning, during which Hendrick failed to catch a fly ball that fell for a two-run single.

JULY 10 Trailing 5–0, the Indians score three runs in the eighth inning and four in the ninth to beat the Athletics 7–5 at Municipal Stadium. Pinch-hitters drove in all four ninth-inning runs. Ron Lolich accounted for the first with an RBI-single, and Rusty Torres clubbed a three-run homer.

JULY 12 The Indians score five runs in the ninth inning to defeat the Twins 7–4 in the second game of a double header in Minnesota. The Twins won the opener 8–4.

JULY 18 Trailing the Angels 8–3 in Anaheim, the Indians score two runs in the sixth inning, one in the eighth, two in the ninth, and two in the 11th to win 10–8. The pair of 11th-inning runs scored on a homer by John Ellis.

Following the game, 240-pound Indians coach Joe Lutz threw a punch at Cleveland Plain Dealer *reporter Russell Schneider. Ken Aspromonte and his coaches were livid over an article that Schneider wrote, quoting Yankee coach Elston Howard saying that Indians coach Rocky Colavito asked Howard to help motivate George Hendrick. Schneider questioned the fraternization between the coaching staffs of the Indians and Yankees. Lutz started berating Schneider and poked the writer in the chest with his finger. Colavito and Aspromonte joined in the tirade. Schneider was backed into a corner for several minutes before Lutz threw a punch over Aspromonte's shoulder. The Indians manager knocked a glass and a cigar from the writer's hand. Club president Nick Mileti apologized to Schneider over the incident. Lutz was let go as coach at the end of the season and took a job managing in Japan with the Hiroshima Carp. That gig ended when Lutz stood on home plate after losing an argument with an umpire and refused to move. The president of the club had to come down from the stands to persuade Lutz to leave.*

JULY 23 — At Royals Stadium in Kansas City, pinch hitter Buddy Bell hits a triple in the All-Star Game, but the American League loses 7–1.

AUGUST 4 — Brewers outfielder Johnny Briggs collects six hits in six at-bats during a 9–4 Milwaukee win over the Indians at Municipal Stadium. Briggs had four singles and two doubles.

AUGUST 8 — The Indians score nine runs in the first inning and beat the White Sox 13–1 with a 22-hit attack in Chicago. Chris Chambliss had five of the hits in six at-bats.

Chambliss put together a 19-game hitting streak in early August in which he collected 37 hits in 80 at-bats, an average of .462.

AUGUST 21 — Stan Bahnsen of the White Sox is only one out away from a no-hitter against the Indians at Municipal Stadium when Walt Williams singles with two out in the ninth. Bahnsen had to settle for a one-hitter and a 4–0 win.

AUGUST 22 — The Indians win 1–0 over the White Sox in 12 innings at Chicago. Gaylord Perry pitched the complete game. After drawing a walk in the 12th, Buddy Bell scored from first base on a bunt and a throwing error.

Perry was 19–19 in with a 3.38 ERA in 344 innings in 1973 and threw seven shutouts. His 29 complete games (in 41 starts) led the AL.

AUGUST 24 — The Indians grant John Adams the right to bring his bass drum into the Municipal Stadium bleachers for a game against the Rangers. The Indians won 11–5.

Adams has continued pounding away at his drum at Indians games for more than 30 years and over 2,000 games. He was 22 when he started the practice in 1973. After the club moved to Jacobs Field in 1994, he took up residence in section 183 at the highest bleacher seat in left-center field. Adams bought his own season tickets, including one for the drum. In 2006, the Indians gave away a bobblehead doll depicting Adams. Recipients could bobble the arms up and down and bang on the little instrument. In 2007, Adams threw out the ceremonial pitch prior to game one of the playoff series against the Yankees.

AUGUST 25 — Buddy Bell hits two home runs, the second a walk-off blast in the ninth, to beat the Rangers 6–5 at Municipal Stadium.

AUGUST 29 — Ted Bonda becomes executive vice-president "in charge of all operations." Bonda, a longtime Cleveland businessman and civic leader, was one of the eight original investors in the group headed by Nick Mileti that bought control of the Indians in

March 1972. Bonda was thrust into the position because of disenchantment with Mileti's leadership and mounting financial losses that left the club on the brink of insolvency. Mileti retained the title of president, but it was Bonda who ran the show. Bonda replaced Mileti as president in March 1975 and held the position until Steve O'Neill and Gabe Paul bought the franchise in February 1978. In many ways, Bonda was born to be president of the Indians. His full name was Alva Teddy Bonda. He was named after Alva Bradley, the owner of the building where Bonda's father worked. In 1927, a decade after Bonda's birth, Bradley bought the Indians.

SEPTEMBER 4 The Indians score three runs in the ninth inning on two homers to beat the Brewers 5–4 in Milwaukee. John Lowenstein struck a solo homer and Frank Duffy hit a two-run blast.

SEPTEMBER 6 Chris Chambliss drives in six runs on a two-run homer and a grand slam during a 10–4 win over the Tigers at Municipal Stadium. The slam came off Mike Strahler in the fourth inning.

SEPTEMBER 15 John Ellis drives in six runs on a bases-loaded double and a three-run homer to lead the Indians to a 9–8 win over the Red Sox in Boston.

SEPTEMBER 18 The Indians score three runs in the ninth inning, the last two on a pinch-hit, walk-off homer by John Ellis, to defeat the Brewers 6–5 at Municipal Stadium.

SEPTEMBER 26 Gaylord Perry pitches the Indians to a 1–0 win over the Red Sox at Municipal Stadium. John Ellis accounted for the lone run with a homer off Bill Lee in the second inning.

OCTOBER 10 On the day that vice-president Spiro Agnew resigns due to financial improprieties, the City of Cleveland turns the operation of Municipal Stadium to a newly formed entity called the Cleveland Stadium Corporation. The corporation was headed by Art Modell, who also owned the Cleveland Browns. The agreement was made because of the financial difficulties of the city and its inability to adequately operate and maintain the stadium. Modell agreed to undertake $10 million worth of improvements to the facility, which was then 41-years-old. The Indians became tenants of the Cleveland Stadium Corporation.

1974

Season in a Sentence

The Indians draw over one million fans for the first time since 1959 with a club that is in first place in July and stays in the pennant race into August, before wilting and finishing with another losing record.

Finish • Won • Lost • Pct • GB

Finish	Won	Lost	Pct	GB
Fourth	77	85	.475	14.0

Manager

Ken Aspromonte

Stats

Stats	Indians	AL	Rank
Batting Avg:	.255	.258	8
On-Base Pct:	.312	.326	10
Slugging Pct:	.370	.371	6
Home Runs:	131		3 (tie)
Stolen Bases:	79		8
ERA:	3.80	3.62	9
Fielding Avg:	.977	.977	5
Runs Scored:	662		8
Runs Allowed:	694		9

Starting Line-up

Dave Duncan, c
John Ellis, 1b-c
Jack Brohamer, 2b
Buddy Bell, 3b
Frank Duffy, ss
John Lowenstein, lf
George Hendrick, cf
Charlie Spikes, rf
Oscar Gamble, dh
Leron Lee, lf

Pitchers

Gaylord Perry, sp
Jim Perry, sp
Fritz Peterson, sp
Dick Bosman, sp
Tom Buskey, rp
Milt Wilcox, rp

Attendance

1,114,262 (seventh in AL)

Club Leaders

Batting Avg:	Oscar Gamble	.292
On-Base Pct:	Oscar Gamble	.363
Slugging Pct:	Oscar Gamble	.469
Home Runs:	Charlie Spikes	22
RBIs:	Charlie Spikes	80
Runs:	Oscar Gamble	74
Stolen Bases:	John Lowenstein	36
Wins:	Gaylord Perry	21
Strikeouts:	Gaylord Perry	216
ERA:	Gaylord Perry	2.51
Saves:	Tom Buskey	17

FEBRUARY 4 The Indians trade Leo Cardenas to the Rangers for Ken Suarez.

MARCH 19 Six weeks after the kidnapping of Patty Hearst, the Indians trade Rick Sawyer and Walt Williams to the Tigers for Jim Perry.

Jim had been in the majors since 1959 and his brother Gaylord since 1962, but the two were teammates for the first time in 1974. Coming back to Cleveland was a homecoming for Jim in another way because he played for the Indians from 1959 through 1963. Although he was 38-years-old in 1974, he gave the Indians an excellent season with a 17–12 record and a 2.96 ERA. The Perry brothers were 38–25 for the Indians in 1974. The rest of the staff was 39–60.

MARCH 23 The Indians trade Steve Hargan to the Rangers for Bill Gogolewski.

APRIL 3 The Indians trade Pedro Guerrero to the Dodgers for Bruce Ellingsen.

The transaction seemed insignificant at the time, but it proved to be one of the worst in franchise history. The Indians signed Guerrero in 1973 as a

16-year-old out of the Dominican Republic. He played 44 games for Cleveland's Sarasota farm club in the Gulf Coast League, that season, batting .255 with just two homers. The Dodgers offered Ellingsen, a 24-year-old pitcher, for the raw Guerrero and the Indians took the bait. Ellingsen's big league career lasted only 16 games. Guerrero reached the majors in 1978, and during a 15-year career, batted .300 with 215 home runs in 1,536 games and appeared in four All-Star Games.

APRIL 6 The Indians open the season with a 6–1 loss to the Yankees at Shea Stadium. Gaylord Perry was the starting and losing pitcher.

The Yankees played at Shea Stadium during the 1974 and 1975 seasons while Yankee Stadium was being remodeled.

APRIL 9 The scheduled home opener against the Brewers is postponed by snow.

APRIL 10 The Indians get the home portion of the schedule underway with a 6–4 loss to the Brewers before 22,036 at Municipal Stadium. Don Money provided the winning blow with a grand slam off Cecil Upshaw in the ninth inning.

Oscar Gamble's wife Juanita sang the National Anthem.

APRIL 12 After opening the season with five straight losses, the Indians finally win 9–1 against the Yankees at Municipal Stadium.

APRIL 14 Graig Nettles hits four home runs for the Yankees in a double header against the Indians at Municipal Stadium. The Yanks won the opener 9–5, while the Indians captured the victory in game two 9–6.

APRIL 18 The Indians lose 5–4 in 16 innings to the Brewers in Milwaukee. Gaylord Perry pitched the first 15 innings and struck out 14 batters. He seemed to have the game well in hand but allowed two runs in the eighth and two more in the ninth. Ken Sanders came into the game in the 16th and gave up a home run to Bob Coluccio, the first batter he faced.

APRIL 21 The Red Sox score four runs in the ninth inning and one in the tenth to defeat the Indians 6–5 in Boston. Milt Wilcox was the final Cleveland pitcher but didn't face a batter. He entered the game with runners on first and second and Cecil Cooper at the plate. Before delivering a pitch to Cooper, Wilcox tried to pick Dick McAuliffe off second, but threw the ball into center field, allowing McAuliffe to score the winning run.

APRIL 27 The Indians trade Chris Chambliss, Dick Tidrow, and Cecil Upshaw to the Yankees for Fritz Peterson, Steve Kline, Fred Beene, and Tom Buskey.

The Indians were desperate for pitching and received four hurlers from the Yankees. Buskey saved 17 games for the Indians in 1974 and Peterson was 14–8 in 1975, but neither distinguished themselves afterward. Kline and Beene were failures in Cleveland. Both Chambliss and Tidrow were key figures during the Yankees run of three consecutive AL pennants beginning in 1976 and back-to-back world championships in 1977 and 1978. Chambliss will always be a hero in New York for his walk-off home run in the ninth inning of the fifth and deciding game of the 1976 American League Championship Series that beat the Royals 7–6. His career in the majors lasted until 1988.

APRIL 28 George Hendrick hits two homers, one a grand slam, during a 10–2 win over the Angels at Municipal Stadium. The slam came off Dick Selma in the eighth, an inning in which the Indians scored eight runs in break a 2–2 tie.

MAY 8 Trailing 2–0, the Indians score runs in the seventh, ninth, and 11th innings to win 3–2 over the Angels in Anaheim. George Hendrick scored all three runs following a double and two singles.

MAY 19 Gaylord Perry pitches a two-hitter to defeat the Tigers 2–1 in the first game of a double header at Municipal Stadium. The two runs scored in the fifth inning on a homer by Jack Brohamer. The Indians also won the second contest 9–4.

MAY 22 The Indians lose 1–0 in 12 innings to the Orioles in Baltimore.

MAY 29 The Indians and Rangers brawl during a 3–0 loss in Arlington. In the eighth inning, Milt Wilcox buzzed Lenny Randle with a pitch in apparent retaliation for Randle taking out Jack Brohamer with a hard slide in attempting to break up a double play earlier in the game. After getting out of the way of the Wilcox pitch, Randle laid down a drag bunt on the next one and collided with Wilcox on the way to first base. Both teams streamed onto the field. After order was restored, fans behind the visiting team dugout showered the Indians with beer, and several players had to be restrained from going into the stands after their antagonists.

Ten-Cent Beer Night

It seemed like a good idea at the time. In order to attract a crowd on June 4, 1974, Indians management decided to sell beer at ten cents a cup. It had been tried by the Milwaukee Brewers in 1972. Although security personnel were kept busy with unruly fans, the stands were nearly full, and the Milwaukee club scheduled the promotion again in 1973 and 1974.

The Indians "Ten-Cent Beer Night" was held on a Tuesday night against the Rangers and attracted 25,135. During that period, the Indians were lucky to draw 5,000 on a weekend against a losing club like Texas. The team expected 12,000 to 15,000 for the game and planned security for a crowd of that size.

On various occasions, a few dozen fans pranced across the field, delaying the start of almost every inning. One of them was a woman who tried to kiss umpire Larry McCoy. A male fan undressed in right field and streaked back and forth around the outfield and leaped over the fence, where he was immediately arrested. As the game progressed, fans became increasingly bold and hostile. The Rangers bullpen crew had to be moved into the dugout in the seventh inning after being subjected to firecrackers, smoke bombs, and beer cups.

The Indians entered the bottom of the ninth trailing 5–3, but tied the score and had runners on first and third. As Jack Brohamer stepped to the plate, two individuals jumped out of the stands and raced toward Texas right fielder Jeff Burroughs. When Burroughs tried to elude them, then fought them off, others raced onto the field and players from both teams went to rescue Burroughs. With the players fighting about 50 spectators, a metal folding chair was hurled onto the field, landing on the head and shoulders of Cleveland pitcher

Tom Hilgendorf. Umpire Nestor Chylak was cut on the right wrist, Burroughs jammed a thumb, and Rangers coach Art Fowler and pitcher Steve Foucault were struck in the eye by blows. Bottles were flying in every direction. As the Rangers walked across the infield, they had to fight another wave of fans, and the umpires declared the game a forfeit.

Indians president Ted Bonda and general manager Phil Seghi were incensed over the forfeit, not at the fans who caused it by running onto the field, but at the umpires. The club filed a formal protest to President Lee MacPhail. Seghi said that the forfeit should be overruled because "no warning was given to fans that continual interruptions could lead to forfeiture." He added that the umpires "should have made a more concerted effort to have our police clear the field." Seghi also said that the Indians would go on with the three additional "Ten-Cent Beer Nights," scheduled for later in the season. MacPhail not only upheld the forfeit but prevented the Indians from selling beer at ten cents a cup in the future.

JUNE 1 Leron Lee drives in all three Cleveland runs during a 5–2 win over the Royals at Municipal Stadium. Lee hit a grand slam in the third inning and a solo swat in the sixth. Both were struck off Bruce Del Canton.

JUNE 4 On Ten-Cent Beer night at Municipal Stadium, unruly fans storm the field with the score 5–5 in the bottom of the ninth inning and cause the contest to be forfeited to the Rangers.

JUNE 5 The Indians hit five homers to defeat the Rangers 9–3 at Municipal Stadium. The home runs were struck by Charlie Spikes, George Hendrick, Frank Duffy, Oscar Gamble, and Dave Duncan.

On the same day, the Indians chose pitcher Tom Brennan from Lewis University in the first round of the amateur draft. The fourth overall pick of the draft, Brennan didn't reach the majors until 1981 and had a 9–10 record with a 4.40 ERA during five years in the big leagues. The only other future major leaguers drafted and signed by the Indians were Orlando Gonzalez (18th round of the regular phase) and Sandy Wihtol (second round of the secondary phase). Neither had a career that lasted longer than three years.

JUNE 12 The Indians score eight runs in the fourth inning and win 10–1 over the White Sox in Chicago. It was Gaylord Perry's 11th win a row and ran his season record to 12–1.

JUNE 15 The Indians trade Brent Strom and Terry Ley to the Padres for Steve Arlin.

Arlin's grandfather, Harold Arlin, was the first person to announce a baseball game over the radio. It happened in 1921 over KDKA in Pittsburgh. Steve was a dentist in the off-season and talked of opening a dental practice in Cleveland, but he didn't last long with the Indians, posting a 2–5 record and a 6.60 ERA.

JUNE 22 The Indians collect 20 hits and defeat the Red Sox 11–0 in the first game of a double header at Fenway Park. Gaylord Perry pitched the shutout for his 13th win in a row. Jim Perry, who entered the game with 199 career victories, started the second game, but Boston won 8–3.

June 24 John Lowenstein hits a grand slam off Mike Wallace during the fourth inning of a 10–3 win over the Yankees in New York.

June 27 Jim Perry records his 200th career win with a 2–1 decision over the Red Sox at Municipal Stadium.

Perry finished his career with a record of 215–174.

June 28 Gaylord Perry wins his 14th game in a row with a 2–1 decision over the Red Sox at Municipal Stadium. The lone run scored on a double by George Hendrick.

July 3 Gaylord Perry wins his 15th game in a row with a 4–2 decision over the Brewers in Milwaukee. John Lowenstein drove in all four Cleveland runs on a three-run homer and a sacrifice fly. Perry pitched a complete game despite waiting out a rain delay in the seventh inning that lasted an hour and 24 minutes. The 15-game winning streak tied the club record set by Johnny Allen in 1937 and gave Perry a 15–1 record in the 76th game of the season.

In addition to his 15–1 record, Perry had an ERA if 1.31 in 165 innings and allowed just 93 hits. He put together his 15-game winning streak despite pitching on a severely sprained ankle he suffered in April. Perry lost his next start (see July 8, 1974) in attempt to tie American League record of 16 wins in a row, which was shared by Walter Johnson (1912 Senators), Joe Wood (1912 Red Sox), Lefty Grove (1931 Athletics), and Schoolboy Rowe (1934 Tigers). It was the start of a six-game losing streak. He finished the season with a record of 21–13 and a 2.51 earned run average in 322⅓ innings.

July 6 The Indians move into first place with a 1–0 win over the Angels in Anaheim. The lone run scored on a single by Buddy Bell. Dick Bosman (6⅓ innings) and Tom Buskey (2⅔ innings) combined on the shutout.

On the same day, Indians pitcher Tom Hilgendorf saved the life of 13-year-old Jerry Zaradte. Hilgendorf dived fully clothed into a motel swimming pool when he saw Zaradte motionless at the bottom.

July 7 The Indians take a 1½-game lead with a 6–2 victory over the Angels in Anaheim.

The win gave the Indians a record of 45–35 on the season. The club was 23–10 since June 1. But beginning with the July 8 defeat, the Indians lost nine of ten and were 32–50 over the remainder of the season. The flirtation with pennant contention dramatically improved attendance. After drawing 615,107 fans in 1973, the Indians attracted 1,114,262 in 1974. It was the club's highest attendance figure between 1959 and 1986.

July 8 Gaylord Perry's 15-game winning streak comes to an end with a 4–3 loss to the Athletics in ten innings at Oakland. Perry was two outs from victory before the A's tied the score 3–3 in the ninth. Claudell Washington drove in the winning run with a single on only his second big league hit. His first hit was a triple off Perry in the eighth.

July 17 The Indians purchase Tommy McCraw from the Angels.

JULY 19 Dick Bosman pitches a no-hitter to defeat the Athletics 4–0 at Municipal Stadium. Among those in the stands were Bosman's parents, who traveled from Kenosha, Wisconsin. There was only one Oakland base runner during the evening. Bosman deprived himself of a perfect game with a throwing error that sailed over the head of Tommy McCraw and allowed Sal Bando to reach base in the fourth inning. Bosman threw only 79 pitches and had four strikeouts. In the ninth, he retired Dick Green on a grounder to third baseman Buddy Bell for the first out. Pinch-hitter Jesus Alou grounded out to second baseman Jack Brohamer. Billy North ended the game by striking out.

Teammates congratulate George Hendrick (center) after a grand slam. From left to right: John Ellis, Buddy Bell, Hendrick, Oscar Gamble, and Charley Spikes.

> *The Indians tried to trade Bosman before the June 15 trade deadline but found no takers because he had a history of arm trouble and compiled a 3–13 record and a 5.64 ERA in 1973. He was put into the starting rotation only three weeks earlier when Steve Kline went on the disabled list. The gem that Bosman pitched on July 19, 1974, wasn't indicative of his career with the Indians. With the club from 1973 through 1975, he had an 8–15 record and 4.91 ERA in 253 innings. The no-hitter was his only shutout with Cleveland and the last of his major league career. Bosman's lifetime record from 1966 through 1976 was 82–85.*

JULY 23 At Three Rivers Stadium in Pittsburgh, Gaylord Perry is the starting pitcher for the American League and allows a run in three innings, but the National League wins 7–2.

JULY 25 The Indians win an entertaining double header over the Orioles by scores of 8–7 and 5–4 at Municipal Stadium. The second tilt went 13 innings. Buddy Bell tied the score 3–3 with a two-run homer in the ninth. After Baltimore scored in the top of the 13th, Cleveland came back with two in their half. Tommy McCraw drove in the deciding tally with a pinch-single.

August 6 John Ellis collects five hits, including a homer, in five at-bats during a 9–7 win over the Tigers in Detroit. He pulled a hamstring on the fifth hit running to first base and had to leave the game.

August 17 Nine days after the resignation of Richard Nixon as President, the Indians purchase Rico Carty from Cordoba in the Mexican League.

Carty's future in major league baseball appeared to be as dead as Nixon's political career when he was acquired by the Indians. Carty had hit .366 to win the National League batting title with the Braves in 1970, but knee injuries caused his average to fall to .229 in 1973, a season in which he played for three teams. His acquisition proved to be a great transaction for the Indians. Carty made an immediate impact in Cleveland with 22 hits in his first 55 at-bats. In four seasons with the Indians, mostly as a designated hitter, he hit .303 with 47 homers in 1,487 at-bats.

August 27 The Indians win 12–8 and lose 13–2 during a double header against the Royals in Kansas City.

September 12 The Indians trade Ken Suarez and Rusty Torres to the Angels for Frank Robinson.

As soon as the trade was announced, it was expected that Robinson would be the Indians next manager. He was 39 years old but still an effective player. Robinson made his 11th All-Star team in 1974, and hit 20 homers for the Angels in 427 at-bats. He came to the Indians with 572 career home runs and two Most Valuable Player Awards (1961 with the Reds and 1966 as an Oriole), and had appeared in five World Series (1961 in Cincinnati and 1966, 1969, 1970, and 1971 in Baltimore).

September 15 Gaylord Perry records his 20th victory of the 1974 season with a 1–0 decision over the Orioles in Baltimore. The run scored on a bases-loaded walk from Ross Grimsley to John Lowenstein.

Through the 2007 season, no Indians pitcher since Perry has won at least 20 games in a season.

September 21 The Indians score seven runs in the third inning to take a 7–2 lead but lose 14–7 to the Yankees in New York.

September 27 The Indians announce that Ken Aspromonte will not return as manager in 1975.

Aspromonte never managed another big league club. After leaving Cleveland, he joined his brother Bob, also a former major leaguer, in a Coors Brewery distributorship in Houston.

September 28 John Ellis hits a grand slam off Larry Gura in the fourth inning, but the Indians lose 9–7 to the Yankees in the second game of a double header in New York. The Yanks also won the opener 9–3.

October 3 The Indians name Frank Robinson as manager, replacing Ken Aspromonte. With the appointment, Robinson became the first African-American manager in major league history. In addition, it was announced that Robinson would continue as an active player and served as one of the club's designated hitters.

For years, the media had speculated on who would become baseball's first black manager. The names included Bill White, Junior Gilliam, Larry Doby, Maury Wills, Gene Baker, Ernie Banks, Willie Mays, and Elston Howard. Robinson was usually at the head of the list because of the leadership skills he exhibited during a playing career that began with the Reds in 1956. In order to make himself a viable candidate as a big league manager, Robinson went to the Puerto Rican Winter League and managed the Santruce club for six seasons, where he won two pennants. The announcement that Robinson would become the manager of the Indians was a major event, and hundreds of writers rushed to Cleveland to report on the press conference. The audience included commissioner Bowie Kuhn and AL president Lee MacPhail. Robinson managed the Indians two full seasons to records of 79–80 in 1975 and 81–78 in 1976. The latter was Cleveland's first winning record since 1968. Robinson became the first African-American manager to be fired on June 19, 1977, with the club holding a 26–31 record.

1975

Season in a Sentence

Frank Robinson hits a home run on Opening Day, but the Indians need a late spurt to finish at 79–80 in his first season as manager.

Finish • Won • Lost • Pct • GB

Finish	Won	Lost	Pct	GB
Fourth	79	80	.497	15.5

Manager

Frank Robinson

Stats

Stats	Indians	AL	Rank
Batting Avg:	.261	.258	4
On-Base Pct:	.337	.333	6
Slugging Pct:	.392	.379	3
Home Runs:	153		1
Stolen Bases:	106		4
ERA:	3.84	3.78	5
Fielding Avg:	.978	.975	2
Runs Scored:	688		6
Runs Allowed:	703		5 (tie)

Starting Line-up

John Ellis, c
Boog Powell, 1b
Duane Kuiper, 2b
Buddy Bell, 3b
Frank Duffy, ss
Oscar Gamble, lf
Rick Manning, cf-rf
George Hendrick, rf-cf
Rico Carty, dh
Charlie Spikes, rf-lf
Alan Ashby, c
John Lowenstein, rf-lf-dh
Jack Brohamer, 2b

Pitchers

Dennis Eckersley, sp
Fritz Peterson, sp
Roric Harrison, sp
Don Hood, sp-rp
Eric Raich, sp
Gaylord Perry, sp
Jim Bibby, sp-rp
Dave LaRoche, rp
Tom Buskey, rp

Attendance

977,039 (ninth in AL)

Club Leaders

Batting Avg:	Boog Powell	.297
On-Base Pct:	Boog Powell	.377
Slugging Pct:	Boog Powell	.524
Home Runs:	Boog Powell	27
RBIs:	Boog Powell	86
	George Hendrick	86
Runs:	George Hendrick	82
Stolen Bases:	Rick Manning	19
	Duane Kuiper	19
Wins:	Fritz Peterson	14
Strikeouts:	Dennis Eckersley	152
ERA:	Dennis Eckersley	2.60
Saves:	Dave LaRoche	17

February 25 The Indians trade Dave Duncan and Al McGrew to the Orioles for Boog Powell and Don Hood. On the same day, the Indians traded Milt Wilcox to the Cubs for Dave LaRoche and Brock Davis.

Powell was a teammate of Robinson's on four World Series teams in Baltimore and gave the Indians one great season with a .297 average and 27 homers in 1975. Boog's numbers declined to .215 and nine home runs the following season, however. The Indians gave up on Wilcox too soon. He was 96–72 for the Tigers from 1977 through 1984.

April 8 In one of the most dramatic openers in Cleveland history, Frank Robinson the manager wins his first game by a 5–3 score over the Yankees with the help of Frank Robinson the player. With Robinson becoming the first African-American to manage a regular season game, Opening Day drew a crowd of 56,204 to Municipal

Stadium and was a huge media event. Rachel Robinson, widow of Jackie, threw out the ceremonial first pitch to link her husband's breaking the players' color barrier with Frank's breaking the managerial one. Commissioner Bowie Kuhn was also in attendance. About 50 out-of-town newspaper and magazine writers were given press credentials, in addition to numerous television, movie, and still photographers. Robinson hit second in the batting order as the designated hitter. Rising to the occasion, Robinson hit a home run off Doc Medich in his first at-bat. It came on a 2–2 count on the eighth pitch of the at-bat after Robinson had fouled off three deliveries. It was home run number 575 of Robinson's career and hit number 2,901. The blast gave the Indians a 1–0 lead. The Yanks scored three times in the top of the second, but the Tribe came back for the victory. Boog Powell contributed a homer, a double, a single, and three runs scored in three at-bats in his Indians debut.

April 13 Gaylord Perry records the 200th win of his career when the Indians erupt for three runs in the ninth inning to defeat the Brewers 3–1 in Milwaukee. John Lowenstein's homer tied the score. John Ellis broke the deadlock with a two-run homer.

April 29 The Indians hit into six double plays but defeat the Yankees 3–1 in New York. Batting lead-off, Frank Duffy drove in all three Cleveland runs.

May 17 Frank Robinson draws a fine and suspension for an altercation with umpire Jerry Neudecker during a 10–1 loss to the White Sox at Municipal Stadium.

Robinson was ejected after an argument with Neudecker in the sixth inning. The two made contact, and Robinson was fined $250 and suspended three days by AL president Lee MacPhail for pushing the arbiter. Robinson had to sit out a three-game series against the Angels in Anaheim on May 26, 27, and 28. The penalty so angered Indians players that they wrote and signed a statement that they, too, would sit out the suspension with Robinson, and therefore, forfeit the three games. Robinson expressed gratitude for the show of support but ordered the players to play the games.

May 20 The Indians trade Dick Bosman and Jim Perry to the Athletics for Blue Moon Odom.

May 25 In his first major league start, 20-year-old Dennis Eckersley pitches a three-hit shutout to defeat the Athletics 6–0 in the first game of a double header at Municipal Stadium. Oakland won the second game 6–3.

Eckersley had made ten previous relief appearances, covering 14 innings, without allowing an earned run. Altogether, he didn't surrender an earned run in his first 28 big league innings. Eckersley closed out his rookie season with a 13–7 record and a 2.60 ERA in 186⅔ innings.

June 4 In his first start with the Indians, Blue Moon Odom pitches a two-hitter to defeat the Royals 4–0 at Municipal Stadium. The only Kansas City hits were singles by Hal McRae and John Mayberry in the sixth inning. All of the Cleveland runs came on home runs off Steve Busby. Boog Powell hit a two-run shot in the first, followed a solo homers from John Lowenstein, also in the first, and Alan Ashby in the fifth. Odom made two prior relief appearances for the Indians.

His June 4 gem was his last game for the club. Odom was traded to the Braves three days later.

On the same day, the Indians selected Rick Cerone from Seton Hall University in the first round of the amateur draft. Cerone played only 14 games for the Indians before being dealt to Toronto to re-acquire an aging Rico Carty. Cerone went on to an 18-year major league career. The only other player drafted and signed by the Indians in 1976 was tenth-rounder Dave Schuler.

JUNE 5 Buddy Bell hammers a walk-off homer in the 11th inning to beat the Royals 8–7 at Municipal Stadium. The Indians scored three runs in the eighth inning and one in the ninth to tie the game 7–7.

A total of 108 heated and air-conditioned bi-level loges which held between six and eight seats were added to Municipal Stadium in 1975. They were suspended from the bottom of the upper deck and ran its entire length, with the exception of the area occupied by the baseball press box. The boxes were an immediate hit with the Cleveland business community and sold out quickly. The rental figures ranged from $10,500 to $15,000 and included season tickets for all Indians and Browns games and reserved parking spaces.

JUNE 6 Frank Robinson drives in six runs on a pair of three-run homers in leading his club to a 7–3 victory over the Rangers at Municipal Stadium.

JUNE 7 The Indians trade Blue Moon Odom and Bob Belloir to the Braves for Roric Harrison.

JUNE 8 The Indians play a 26-inning double header at Municipal Stadium, beating the Rangers 3–2 in the opener before losing the nightcap 7–6 in 17 innings.

JUNE 13 The Indians trade Gaylord Perry to the Rangers for Jim Bibby, Jackie Brown, and Rick Waits.

The day that Frank Robinson joined the Indians the previous September, he became involved in an argument with Perry that nearly came to blows. They had been longtime adversaries from their days in the National League when Robinson played for the Reds and Perry for the Giants. Perry was angry because Robinson was making more money than he was. A few weeks later, Robinson became manager, and the two headstrong athletes continued their feud during spring training and into the regular season in 1975. Gaylord's brother Jim also objected to Robinson's managerial methods. As a result, both Perrys were gone by mid-season. After leaving Cleveland, Perry had a record of 75–51 for the Rangers and Padres from 1975 through 1979.

JUNE 14 With the Indians slumping, Frank Robinson picks his line-up out of a hat and loses 2–1 to the Rangers in Arlington. Boog Powell hit in the lead-off spot and Duane Kuiper batted fourth.

The Indians hit bottom on June 21 with a 24–39 record. The club pulled to .500 at 70–70 on September 10 before finishing at 79–80.

JUNE 22 Rico Carty is hit by a pitch from Eduardo Rodriguez with the bases loaded in the tenth inning to force in the winning run to give the Indians a 3–2 win over the Brewers at Municipal Stadium.

JUNE 24 The Indians score four runs in the ninth inning to win 8–6 over the Red Sox in Boston. A pinch-double by Boog Powell drove in the tying run. A three-run homer by George Hendrick put Cleveland into the lead. It was Hendrick's second homer of the game.

JULY 5 Buddy Bell drives in six runs, four of them on a grand slam off Steve Barr in the second inning, to lead the Indians to a 12–2 win over the Red Sox at Municipal Stadium. Bell also hit a solo homer in the fourth inning and an RBI-double in the eighth.

The Indians rally around player-manager Frank Robinson after he hit a game-winning homerun.

Bell led the voting for starting third basemen in the All-Star Game until the final day of the balloting when he lost the spot to Graig Nettles. Bell was named to the team as a reserve but declined because he believed that he didn't deserve the honor. Buddy was batting only .227 with six homers on July 3. He hit .311 over the remainder of the season to finish at .271.

JULY 6 After trailing 5–0 in the second inning, the Indians claw back to beat the Red Sox 11–10 in the second game of a double header at Comiskey Park. Boston won the first game 5–3.

JULY 13 With an 8–7 decision over the Angels, the Indians win their 13th game in a row in Anaheim over three seasons. Cleveland was 6–0 in Anaheim in both 1974 and 1975.

JULY 18 On Ladies Night at Municipal Stadium, Frank Robinson and John Ellis argue in the dugout during a 7–6 loss to the Athletics. Upon entering the stadium, each woman received "an official Indians halter top."

Ellis, who was batting .217 at the time, was angry over being lifted for a pinch-hitter in the eighth inning and began throwing equipment all over the dugout. Robinson confronted him, and the two engaged in a heated exchange that nearly came to blows. After the game, Robinson announced that Ellis had played his last game with the Indians, but Ellis finished out the season in Cleveland and was dealt to the Rangers during the off-season.

JULY 21 — A walk-off homer by Oscar Gamble leading off the 11th inning beats the Angels 2–1 at Municipal Stadium.

JULY 23 — The Indians lose a tough 9–8 decision to the Rangers in 13 innings at Arlington. Cleveland scored five runs in the ninth inning to tie the contest 7–7 and took an 8–7 lead in the top of the 13, only to have Texas come back with two in their half.

AUGUST 6 — Dave LaRoche strikes out three batters in the ninth inning to close out a 5–3 win over the Yankees at Municipal Stadium. LaRoche fanned Graig Nettles, Chris Chambliss, and Sandy Alomar, Sr.

Finding a consistent closer was a problem for the Indians for years. LaRoche led the club in saves with 17 in 1975 and 21 in 1976. He was the first pitcher to lead the Indians in saves in two consecutive seasons since Ray Narleski did it in 1954 and 1955. In the interim, Cleveland saves leaders included Don Mossi, Hoyt Wilhelm, Dick Brodowski, Johnny Klippstein, Frank Funk, Gary Bell, Ted Abernathy, Don McMahon, Dick Radatz, Orlando Pena, Vicente Romo, Stan Williams, Dennis Higgins, Phil Hennigan, Steve Mingori, Tom Hilgendorf, and Tom Buskey.

AUGUST 17 — The Indians score eight runs in the second inning for an 11–0 lead and wallop the Twins 14–5 in Minnesota.

AUGUST 25 — Dennis Eckersley pitches a three-hitter to beat the White Sox 5–1 at Municipal Stadium. Eckersley had a no-hitter in progress until Bill Melton singled in the seventh inning.

AUGUST 29 — Rick Manning hits a grand slam off Vic Albury in the eighth inning to cap a 9–6 win over the Twins at Municipal Stadium.

SEPTEMBER 19 — Fritz Peterson records his 10th win in a row with a 3–2 decision over the Yankees at Municipal Stadium.

SEPTEMBER 22 — A two-run, pinch-hit, walk-off single by Oscar Gamble in the ninth inning defeats the Brewers 7–6 at Municipal Stadium.

SEPTEMBER 29 — In the last game of the season, Alan Ashby hits a grand slam off Dick Pole in the ninth inning of an 11–4 win over the Red Sox in Boston.

NOVEMBER 22 — The Indians trade Oscar Gamble to the Yankees for Pat Dobson.

DECEMBER 9 — The Indians purchase Ray Fosse from the Athletics and trade John Ellis to the Rangers for Stan Thomas and Ron Pruitt.

The Indians re-acquired Fosse at a time when he was at the lowest ebb of his career. Over the previous two seasons with Oakland, Fosse hit .174 in 340 at-bats. He batted .301, although with only two home runs, in 90 games for Cleveland in 1976.

DECEMBER 12 The Indians trade Jack Brohamer to the White Sox for Larvell Blanks.

1976

Season in a Sentence

Frank Robinson guides the Indians an 81–78 record, the highest winning percentage (.509) of any Cleveland club between 1968 and 1986.

Finish • Won • Lost • Pct • GB

Finish	Won	Lost	Pct	GB
Fourth	81	78	.509	16.0

Manager

Frank Robinson

Stats

Stats	Indians	AL	Rank
Batting Avg:	.263	.256	4
On-Base Pct:	.324	.323	6
Slugging Pct:	.359	.361	7
Home Runs:	85		8
Stolen Bases:	75		11
ERA:	3.47	3.52	7
Fielding Avg:	.980	.977	2
Runs Scored:	615		8
Runs Allowed:	615		5

Starting Line-up

Ray Fosse, c
Boog Powell, 1b
Duane Kuiper, 2b
Buddy Bell, 3b
Frank Duffy, ss
George Hendrick, lf
Rick Manning, cf
Charlie Spikes, rf
Rico Carty, dh
Larvell Blanks, ss-2b
Alan Ashby, c
John Lowenstein, rf-cf-lf
Tommy Smith, rf

Pitchers

Pat Dobson, sp
Dennis Eckersley, sp
Jim Bibby, sp-rp
Jackie Brown, sp
Rick Waits, sp
Dave LaRoche, rp
Jim Kern, rp
Tom Buskey, rp
Stan Thomas, rp

Attendance

948,776 (ninth in AL)

Club Leaders

Batting Avg:	Rico Carty	.310
On-Base Pct:	Rico Carty	.379
Slugging Pct:	George Hendrick	.448
Home Runs:	George Hendrick	25
RBIs:	George Hendrick	81
Runs:	Buddy Bell	75
Stolen Bases:	Rick Manning	16
Wins:	Pat Dobson	16
Strikeouts:	Dennis Eckersley	200
ERA:	Jim Bibby	3.20
Saves:	Dave LaRoche	21

APRIL 10 In the season opener, the Indians lose 3–1 to the Tigers before 58,478 at Municipal Stadium.

APRIL 23 Dennis Eckersley pitches a two-hitter to defeat the Athletics 3–0 at Municipal Stadium. The only Oakland hits were singles by Billy Williams in the second inning and Claudell Washington in the ninth.

APRIL 25 The Indians brawl with the Athletics during a 9–1 loss at Municipal Stadium. In the sixth inning, A's shortstop Bert Campaneris hit Buddy Bell in the face with the ball after forcing the Cleveland third baseman at second base. Bell tackled Campaneris and both benches emptied. Bell was taken to the hospital for precautionary X-rays. Boog Powell sprained his ankle when he was stepped on during the melee.

April 30 — A three-run, walk-off homer by George Hendrick in the ninth inning beats the Angels at Municipal Stadium.

May 12 — The Red Sox end their ten-game losing streak by defeating the Indians 6–4 in 12 innings at Municipal Stadium with the help of a "witch." In an attempt to break the streak, a Boston television station sent Laurie Cabot, an instructor of witchcraft at Salem State College, to Cleveland to cast a favorable spell on the Sox. First baseman John Lowenstein helped the Boston overcome a 4–1 deficit by making three errors. "It wasn't the witch," insisted Lowenstein. "It was simply incompetence."

Rick Manning (stretching) and Dennis Eckersley were the best of friends at this moment, but their later falling out over Manning's involvement with Eckersley's wife provided one of the strangest stories in team history.

May 13 — In response to the Red Sox use of a witch the previous day, the Indians dress a woman in a fairy godmother costume. The "fairy" was former ball girl Debbie Berndt in a white gown and white wig. Her job was to counteract the spell of Laurie Cabot (see May 12, 1976). She sprinkled "magic dust" on Rick Manning, but Manning misplayed one fly ball into a triple and committed a three-base error on another. The Red Sox won 7–5.

May 18 — Duane Kuiper collects five hits in eight at-bats, but the Indians lose 11–6 when the Yankees score five runs in the top of the 16th inning at Municipal Stadium.

May 24 Dennis Eckersley (eight innings) and Stan Thomas (one inning) collaborate on a one-hitter to defeat the Orioles 4–0 at Memorial Stadium. The only Baltimore hit was a single by Al Bumbry leading off the first inning.

May 26 The Indians play at remodeled Yankee Stadium for the first time, and lose 4–3 to the Yankees.

May 28 The Indians trade Fritz Peterson to the Rangers for Stan Perzanowski.

May 29 After nine scoreless innings, the Indians erupt for six runs in the tenth inning to defeat the Brewers 6–0 in Milwaukee. Duane Kuiper hit a two-run single to break the deadlock and Rick Manning slugged a grand slam off Tom Murphy.

June 8 In the first round of the amateur draft, the Indians select catcher Tim Glass from South High School in Springfield, Ohio.

Glass never advanced beyond Class AA ball. The only future major leaguer drafted and signed by the Indians in June 1976 was Ron Hassey in the 18th round.

June 13 With the Indians trailing 4–3 with two out in the 13th inning, Frank Robinson puts himself into the game as a pinch-hitter for Orlando Gonzalez and delivers a two-run, walk-off homer to beat the White Sox 5–4 at Municipal Stadium.

June 30 Frank Robinson is ejected from a 13–1 exhibition game win in Toledo for slugging Mud Hens pitcher Bob Reynolds. Reynolds was cut from the Indians roster in the spring of 1976 and still harbored resentment over the demotion. After Robinson flied out in the fifth inning, he exchanged heated words with Reynolds on the way back to the dugout, and then threw two punches. The second dropped Reynolds to the ground.

July 4 As the nation celebrates the bicentennial, the Yankees beat the Indians 4–3 before 62,504 at Municipal Stadium.

The Indians peaked on July 1 with a 36–33 record and in second place, seven games behind the Yankees. Three losses in a row to the Yanks on July 2, 3, and 4 ended any pennant hopes.

July 6 Facing Sid Monge, Frank Robinson hits the last of his 586 career home runs during a 7–3 win over the Angels in Anaheim.

July 19 Karl Wallenda and his troupe help attract 24,682 to Municipal Stadium. Prior to a double header against the Athletics, the act formed a human pyramid on a 40-foot wire above home plate. The Indians won the first game 3–2 but lost the second 10–3.

July 22 Charlie Spikes hits a grand slam off Frank Tanana in the first inning of a 7–5 win over the Angels at Municipal Stadium.

July 30 Dennis Eckersley strikes out 12 batters in seven innings during a 7–2 win over the Brewers in Milwaukee. The game was stopped in the eighth inning by rain.

AUGUST 3 Dennis Eckersley pitches a three-hit, complete-game win to defeat the Red Sox 1–0 at Municipal Stadium. The winning run scored on a sacrifice fly by Tommy Smith.

AUGUST 28 The Indians win a 17-inning marathon 4–3 against the Twins at Municipal Stadium. Cleveland scored two runs in the ninth to tie 3–3 on an RBI-single by Rico Carty and a sacrifice fly from Boog Powell. The winning run scored on a triple by George Hendrick and a wild pitch by Jim Hughes.

SEPTEMBER 18 Frank Robinson plays the last game of his career, delivering a pinch-single off Rudy May during a 3–2 loss to the Orioles in the first game of a double header at Municipal Stadium. Cleveland won the first game 5–1.

Robinson ended his career with 2,808 games, 10,006 at-bats, 1,829 runs, 2,943 hits, 528 doubles, 586 home runs, 1,812 runs-batted-in, and a .294 batting average.

SEPTEMBER 24 Tommy Smith scores both runs in a 2–0 win over the Brewers at Municipal Stadium. Smith reached base both times on singles. Dennis Eckersley pitched the shutout.

SEPTEMBER 28 Dennis Eckersley strikes out 12 batters during a 6–1 win over the Tigers in the second game of a double header at Municipal Stadium. Detroit won the opener 4–0.

NOVEMBER 5 Three days after Jimmy Carter defeats Gerald Ford in the Presidential election, the Indians lose Stan Thomas, Joe Lis, Tom McMillan, and Tommy Smith to the Mariners and Rico Carty to the Blue Jays in the expansion draft. On the same day, the Indians traded Alan Ashby and Doug Howard to the Blue Jays for Al Fitzmorris.

Ashby proved to be a loss. He played another 13 seasons in the majors, 11 of them with the Astros, as a competent catcher. Carty was re-acquired in another trade a month later.

NOVEMBER 19 The Indians sign Wayne Garland, most recently with the Orioles, as a free agent.

In December 1975, a ruling by arbitrator Peter Seitz struck down the reserve clause, which bound a player to one club in perpetuity. In an agreement between the players and owners completed in 1976, a player had a right to declare himself a free agent after six seasons in the majors. The cash-strapped Indians made a stunning offer to Garland, giving him $2.3 million over ten years. At the time, it was the longest contract for a player in baseball history and one of the highest in monetary value. Garland made the major league minimum of $19,000 in 1976. He had a career record of only 7–11 before breaking loose with a 20–7 mark that season. The Indians hoped that Garland would be the staff ace for years to come, but he suffered a shoulder injury during spring training in 1977, later diagnosed as a torn rotator cuff. To his credit, Garland pitched through the pain and threw 282⅔ inning in 1977 with an ERA of 3.60 that was below the league average of 4.06, but his won-lost record was only 13–19. From 1978 until he was released by the club at the end of the 1981 season, Garland pitched 330⅔ innings with an earned run average of 5.28 and a record of 15–29.

December 3 The Indians trade Stan Perzanowski to the Angels for Bill Melton.

December 6 The Indians trade John Lowenstein and Rick Cerone to the Blue Jays for Rico Carty.

The Indians made a mistake in exposing Carty in the expansion draft and by trading promising catcher Alan Ashby (see November 5, 1976). The club compounded the problem by trading another catching prospect in Cerone to bring Carty back to Cleveland. After the trade, Cerone played 16 more seasons in the majors. Lowenstein came back to the Indians in a trade during spring training in 1977.

December 8 The Indians trade George Hendrick to the Padres for John Grubb, Fred Kendall, and Hector Torres.

Hendrick was a constant headache to Indians managers Ken Aspromonte and Frank Robinson for his aloofness and lackadaisical play. He was traded by the Padres to the Cardinals in 1978 and found a way to co-exist with demanding manager Whitey Herzog in St. Louis. Hendrick was named to two All-Star teams with the Cards and was starting outfielder on the 1982 World Series team. He was still in the majors in 1988. None of the three players acquired for Hendrick provided significant contributions to the Indians.

December 10 The Indians trade Jackie Brown to the Expos for Andre Thornton.

This was a deal that worked to the Indians benefit. For a mediocre pitcher with one season left in the big leagues, Cleveland acquired a player who would start as a first baseman and designated hitter well into the 1980s. On the all-time Indians lists, Thornton ranks seventh in home runs (214) and seventh in walks (685).

1977

Season in a Sentence

The Indians fire Frank Robinson after a slow start, but the slide continues under Jeff Torborg.

Finish • Won • Lost • Pct • GB

Finish	Won	Lost	Pct	GB
Fifth	71	90	.441	28.5

Managers

Frank Robinson (26–31) and Jeff Torborg (45–59)

Stats

Stats	Indians	AL	Rank
Batting Avg:	.269	.266	7
On-Base Pct:	.337	.333	7
Slugging Pct:	.380	.405	11
Home Runs:	100		13 (tie)
Stolen Bases:	87		9
ERA:	4.10	4.06	7
Fielding Avg:	.979	.977	3
Runs Scored:	676		9
Runs Allowed:	739		7

Starting Line-up

Fred Kendall, c
Andre Thornton, 1b
Duane Kuiper, 2b
Buddy Bell, 3b
Frank Duffy, ss
Bruce Bochte, lf
Jim Norris, cf-rf
Paul Dade, rf-lf-cf
Rico Carty, dh
Larvell Blanks, ss
Rick Manning, cf
Ray Fosse, c
Ron Pruitt, rf-lf

Pitchers

Wayne Garland, sp
Dennis Eckersley, sp
Jim Bibby, sp
Al Fitzmorris, sp
Pat Dobson, sp
Jim Kern, rp
Don Hood, rp
Rick Waits, rp-sp

Attendance

900,365 (13th in AL)

Club Leaders

Batting Avg:	Buddy Bell	.292
On-Base Pct:	Andre Thornton	.378
Slugging Pct:	Andre Thornton	.527
Home Runs:	Andre Thornton	28
RBIs:	Rico Carty	80
Runs:	Andre Thornton	77
Stolen Bases:	Jim Norris	26
Wins:	Dennis Eckersley	14
Strikeouts:	Dennis Eckersley	191
ERA:	Dennis Eckersley	3.53
Saves:	Jim Kern	18

MARCH 29 The Indians trade Hector Torres to the Blue Jays for John Lowenstein.

APRIL 7 The Indians open the season at Fenway Park and score two runs in the ninth inning and one in the 11th to defeat the Red Sox 5–4. In the ninth, Buddy Bell smashed a two-run homer to tie the contest. In the 11th, Frank Duffy walked, went to third on a single by Rick Manning, and scored on an infield out from Duane Kuiper.

APRIL 10 The Indians and Red Sox set a major league record by combining to score 19 runs in the eighth inning of a 19–9 Cleveland victory at Fenway Park. The game was routine through seven innings, with score 3–3. In the top of the eighth, the Tribe exploded for 13 runs on ten hits, three walks and an error. Buddy Bell and Duane Kuiper each drove in three runs with two hits during the outburst. In the bottom half, Boston scored six times to account for the 19 runs by the two clubs. The inning took 53 minutes to complete. The Indians plated three runs in the ninth to round out the scoring. There were no home runs hit despite the 28 runs.

APRIL 16 In the home opener, the Indians lose 8–4 to the Red Sox before 51,165 at Municipal Stadium.

April 25 Rico Carty blasts Frank Robinson for a lack of leadership during a luncheon in Cleveland.

Carty received the Indians Man of the Year Award for 1976 at the luncheon, attended by 600 people. Robinson was seated at the head table less than three feet away when Carty criticized the manager for what Carty perceived as "a lack of leadership" and implored Robinson to be more positive in directing the ball club. "You pick up the paper and see the criticism and it destroys us," said Carty. He then turned to Robinson and said: "Frank, you have to help us." A few days later, broadcaster Joe Tait said that Robinson didn't have the "mental and emotional capacity to manage well," and "couldn't communicate with guys of lesser talent." Carty would challenge Robinson again six weeks later (see June 6, 1976).

April 27 The Indians play the Blue Jays for the first time and lose 6–5 in 12 innings at Municipal Stadium.

April 30 The Indians win 1–0 over the Brewers in a 12-inning contest at County Stadium. Dennis Eckersley was brilliant, pitching 11 innings while allowing just three hits. Fred Kendall gave Cleveland the lead with a sacrifice fly in the top of the 12th. Dave LaRoche closed out the victory by retiring Milwaukee in the bottom half.

May 9 Johnny Grubb hits a grand slam off Francisco Barrios in the fifth inning of a 7–5 loss to the White Sox at Municipal Stadium.

May 10 Larvell Blanks hits a walk-off homer off Jim Slaton in the ninth inning for the lone run in a 1–0 win over the Brewers in the first game of a double header at Municipal Stadium. Jim Bibby pitched the shutout. The Indians completed the sweep with a 7–4 victory in the nightcap.

Bibby spent two years in Vietnam and one full season on the disabled list following a spinal fusion operation before finally reaching the majors at the age of 27 in 1972. He spent 12 years in the majors, three of them with the Indians. Bibby's brother Henry played in the NBA, as did Henry's son Mike.

May 11 The Indians trade Dave LaRoche and Dave Schuler to the Angels for Bruce Bochte and Sid Monge.

The Indians also received $250,000 in a deal designed to cut salary costs and help meet the payroll. It turned out the be an excellent short-term transaction, however, as Monge established himself as the closer and made the All-Star team in 1979 in which he was 12–10 with 19 saves and a 2.40 ERA.

May 15 Rick Manning strikes out five times in five plate appearances during a 4–3 win over the White Sox in Chicago.

May 21 The Indians score five runs in the 12th inning to beat the Royals 12–7 in Kansas City. Cleveland led 7–1 before the Royals scored three runs in the eighth and three more in the ninth.

May 24 The Indians play the Mariners for the first time and win 7–5 at Municipal Stadium.

May 25 Dennis Eckersley pitches a 12-inning complete game, allowing just five hits, for a 2–1 win over the Mariners at Municipal Stadium. Eckersley held the Mariners hitless over the last $7\frac{2}{3}$ innings.

May 30 Dennis Eckersley pitches a no-hitter to defeat the Angels 1–0 at Municipal Stadium. He allowed only two base runners. Tony Solaita walked in the second inning. In the eighth, Bobby Bonds reached first after he swung at and missed an 0–2 pitched that sailed past Ray Fosse. The Indians scored in the first inning off Frank Tanana on a triple by Duane Kuiper and a suicide squeeze from Jim Norris. In the ninth, Bobby Grich led off and struck out. Pinch-hitter Willie Aikens flied out to left fielder Paul Dade. Gil Flores looked at a called third strike for the final out. Eckersley fanned 12 and threw 114 pitches. He extended his steak of hitless innings to $16\frac{2}{3}$, counting his previous start on May 25.

Dennis Eckersley rushes toward catcher Ray Fosse after hurling a no-hitter on May 30, 1977, against the California Angels. Known for his cockiness, Eckersley maintained a running argument throughout the game with equally cocky Angels pitcher Frank Tanana.

June 3 In his first start since his no-hitter, Dennis Eckersley pitches hitless ball for the first $5\frac{2}{3}$ innings against the Mariners in Seattle. The first hit was a single by Ruppert Jones with two out in the sixth. Eckersley was taken out of the game at the end of the sixth. Jim Kern pitched the final three innings to close out a 7–1 victory. It was also the Indians first game ever at the Kingdome in Seattle.

With $7\frac{2}{3}$ hitless innings to finish his start on May 25, a nine-inning no-hitter on May 30, and $5\frac{2}{3}$ hitless innings at the beginning of the game on June 3, Eckersley had a streak of $22\frac{1}{3}$ consecutive innings without allowing a hit. It is the second longest streak in major league history. The only longer one was by Cy Young with 23 for the Red Sox in 1904.

JUNE 6 Rico Carty is fined $1,000 and suspended 15 days for "insubordination." Out of action with an injury, Carty openly questioned the moves of Frank Robinson during a 3–1 win over the Athletics in Oakland, leading to a shouting match.

JUNE 7 In the first round of the amateur draft, the Indians select outfielder Bruce Compton from Norman High School in Norman, Oklahoma.

Compton was one of Cleveland's worst first round picks as he never advanced beyond Class A ball. The only future major leaguers drafted and signed by the Indians in 1977 were Eric Wilkins (sixth round), Kevin Rhomberg (14th round), and Jerry Dybzinski (15th round).

JUNE 17 Andre Thornton drives in six runs, three of them on a walk-off homer in the 12th inning to beat the Tigers 8–5 at Municipal Stadium. The Indians trailed 5–1 after five innings. Before the game-winning home run, Thornton contributed a run-scoring single in the sixth and a two-run homer during Cleveland's three-run eighth. The "Beer Night" crowd included Billy Carter, the brother of President Jimmy Carter.

A new computerized scoreboard above the center field bleachers was supposed to be ready by July 1, but it wasn't functional before the end of the season. Line scores were posted on a hand-operated scoreboard in front of the left field stands.

JUNE 19 The Indians fire Frank Robinson and hire Jeff Torborg.

Robinson's tumultuous reign as manager of the Indians ended with the club holding a 26–31 record. Baseball's first African-American manager, Robinson took over a team that was 77–85 in 1974, and guided them to a 79–80 mark in his first year in 1975. Another small improvement occurred in 1976 when Cleveland had a record of 81–78, the best of any Indians club from 1968 through 1986. The two-season record of 160–158 was the best in any two-year period by the Indians between 1965–66 (168–156) and 1993–94 (166–111). Torborg was only 35 years old when appointed as manager of the Indians. He was a catcher with the Dodgers (1964–70) and Angels (1971–73). In California, Torborg was a teammate of Robinson's, and when Frank became manager of the Indians, he hired Torborg as a coach. Under Torborg, a bad situation grew worse, and the Indians were 45–59 over the remainder of 1977 and 69–90 in 1978. After a 43–52 start in 1979, Torborg was fired and replaced by Dave Garcia. Less than a month after being fired by the Indians, Robinson joined the Angels as a coach. He later managed the Giants (1981–84), Orioles (1988–91), Expos (2002–04) and Nationals (2005–06).

June 20 The Indians play a regular season game outside of the United States for the first time and defeat the Blue Jays 8–5 in 11 innings in Toronto. A bases-loaded triple by Ray Fosse drove in the three extra inning runs. It was Fosse's only triple of the season.

June 24 The Indians record their ninth win in a row with a 4–2 decision over the Tigers in Detroit. Andre Thornton drove in all four runs with two homers and a sacrifice fly.

In 1977, his first season with the Indians, Thornton hit .263 with 28 home runs.

July 8 Jim Norris ties a club record with five walks in five plate appearances during an 11–5 win over the Blue Jays at Municipal Stadium.

July 9 A two-out, two-run, walk-off homer by pinch-hitter Andre Thornton beats the Blue Jays 3–2 at Municipal Stadium.

July 19 At Yankee Stadium, Jim Kern and Dennis Eckersley combine for three perfect innings during the American's League 7–5 loss in the All-Star Game. Kern retired all three batters he faced in the third, fanning Dave Parker and George Foster. Eckersley retired all six batters in the fourth and fifth, including Johnny Bench, Joe Morgan, and Steve Garvey.

Standing six-foot-five, Kern was nicknamed "Emu" because teammates thought he resembled an ostrich-like bird. He saved 46 games for the Indians from 1976 through 1978 before a trade to the Rangers.

August 8 Larvell Blanks collects five hits in five at-bats, but the Indians lose 6–3 to the Orioles in Baltimore.

August 12 Dennis Eckersley pitches a one-hitter to defeat the Brewers 2–0 in the first game of a double header at Municipal Stadium. The only Milwaukee hit was a triple by Cecil Cooper with two out in the first inning. After Jimmy Wynn reached on an error by Buddy Bell leading off the second, Eckersley retired 24 batters in a row. Andre Thornton drove in both Cleveland runs with a two-run double in the sixth. The Indians completed the sweep with a 5–4 victory in the nightcap. Rico Carty drove in the winning run with a walk-off single in the ninth.

August 14 The Indians wallop the Brewers 12–4 and 14–5 during a double header at Municipal Stadium. Cleveland scored nine runs in the fifth inning of the first game.

August 20 Andre Thornton homers in the 12th inning to defeat the Athletics 5–4 in Oakland. The A's scored three runs in the ninth to tie the contest.

August 22 Buddy Bell hits a grand slam off Bill Laxton in the sixth inning of a 12–1 win over the Mariners in the first game of a double header at the Kingdome. Jim Bibby pitched a two-hitter, allowing only a single to Dave Collins in the sixth inning and a homer to Dan Meyer in the ninth. Seattle won game two 4–3.

August 27 The Indians trounce the Mariners 10–0 at Municipal Stadium.

AUGUST 28 Rico Carty collects two homers and his first triple since 1975 during a 10–6 win over the Mariners at Municipal Stadium.

AUGUST 29 Duane Kuiper hits the only home run of his major league career during a 9–2 win over the White Sox at Municipal Stadium. The pitching victim was Steve Stone. It was struck in Kuiper's 1,381st at-bat.

Kuiper played with the Indians from 1974 through 1981 and for the Giants from 1982 and 1985, and hit just one home run in 3,379 major league at-bats.

SEPTEMBER 9 The Indians trade Ray Fosse to the Mariners for Bill Laxton.

SEPTEMBER 10 The Indians score four runs in the ninth inning to tie the score 4–4 and one in the 11th for as 5–4 lead, but lose 6–5 to the Orioles in Baltimore, when the opposition scores twice in the bottom of the 11th.

SEPTEMBER 24 Dennis Eckersley strikes out 12 batters in 8⅓ innings but loses 4–1 to the Orioles at Municipal Stadium.

SEPTEMBER 29 Wayne Garland avoids his 20th loss of the season by defeating the Yankees 4–1 in New York. Garland was 13–19 in 1977.

OCTOBER 2 On the last day of the season, Jim Bibby pitches six innings, allowing only one hit, and Don Hood hurls four innings of hitless baseball, but the Indians lose 2–1 in 11 innings to the Blue Jays in the first game of a double header in Toronto. Gary Woods collected both Blue Jays hits. The first was a single in the sixth inning. The second was also a single struck off Larry Andersen, the third Cleveland pitcher, and led to the winning run. The Tribe won the second tilt 5–4.

OCTOBER 17 Andre Thornton's wife and two-year-old daughter are killed in an auto accident on the Pennsylvania Turnpike. Andre and his five-year-son survived the accident. The vehicle skidded and crashed in a snow squall.

DECEMBER 9 The Indians trade Charlie Spikes to the Tigers for Tom Veryzer.

DECEMBER 20 Bruce Bochte signs a contract with the Mariners as a free agent.

1978

Season in a Sentence

A new ownership group that includes some old and familiar faces fails to revive the Indians as the club loses 90 games and attendance declines for the fourth year in a row.

Finish • Won • Lost • Pct • GB

Finish	Won	Lost	Pct	GB
Sixth	69	90	.434	29.0

Manager

Jeff Torborg

Stats

	Indians	AL	Rank
Batting Avg:	.261	.261	8
On-Base Pct:	.326	.329	10
Slugging Pct:	.379	.385	9
Home Runs:	106		9 (tie)
Stolen Bases:	64		13
ERA:	3.97	3.76	11
Fielding Avg:	.980	.978	4
Runs Scored:	639		10
Runs Allowed:	694		11

Starting Line-up

Gary Alexander, c
Andre Thornton, 1b
Duane Kuiper, 2b
Buddy Bell, 3b
Tom Veryzer, ss
Johnny Grubb, lf
Rick Manning, cf
Jim Norris, rf-lf
Bernie Carbo, dh
Paul Dade, rf
Ted Cox, lf-3b
Larvell Blanks, ss
Ron Pruitt, c
Willie Horton, dh

Pitchers

Rick Waits, sp
Mike Paxton, sp
Rick Wise, sp
David Clyde, sp
Don Hood, sp-rp
Jim Kern, rp
Sid Monge, rp
Paul Reuschel, rp

Attendance

800,584 (13th in AL)

Club Leaders

Batting Avg:	Duane Kuiper	.283
On-Base Pct:	Andre Thornton	.377
Slugging Pct:	Andre Thornton	.516
Home Runs:	Andre Thornton	33
RBIs:	Andre Thornton	105
Runs:	Andre Thornton	97
Stolen Bases:	Three tied with	12
Wins:	Rick Waits	13
Strikeouts:	Rick Wise	106
ERA:	Rick Waits	3.20
Saves:	Jim Kern	13

FEBRUARY 3 A new ownership group purchases the Indians.

The group headed by Nick Mileti and later by Ted Bonda, which bought the club in March 1972, sold to a syndicate of seven men, with Francis J. "Steve" O'Neill as the largest of the investors. O'Neill was a 78-year-old trucking executive from Cleveland who had been one of George Steinbrenner limited partners with the Yankees. Bonda reinvested in the O'Neill group. Gabe Paul was another stockholder and returned to the Indians as president and chief executive officer. He was general manager of the Indians from 1961 through 1973, as well as serving as president for a portion of that time. He went to the Yankees in 1973 to help operate the franchise under Steinbrenner. Paul was instrumental in building the Yankee clubs that won AL pennants in 1976 and 1977 and would eventually win two more in 1978 and 1981. But working for Steinbrenner was never easy, and Paul returned to the Indians because he eager to run a club on his own. The Yankees had virtually unlimited funds, while the Indians were nearly bankrupt. Paul simply didn't have the money to operate successfully in Cleveland. O'Neill was not involved in the day-to-day operation of the Indians and avoided publicity at all costs. His only position on the hierarchy was as one of the seven board of directors. O'Neill died on August 29, 1983, and his nephew, Patrick O'Neill, became chairman of the board.

FEBRUARY 28 The Indians trade John Lowenstein and Tom Buskey to the Rangers for David Clyde and Willie Horton.

Clyde was the number one overall pick by the Rangers in the 1973 draft. He pitched in the regular season only days after graduating from high school but was ineffective and soon developed arm trouble. The Indians hoped to revive Clyde's career, but he was 11–15 with a 4.66 ERA in Cleveland. Clyde was only 24 when he pitched his last major league game. Horton was at the other end of the spectrum. He was 35 with four All-Star Games in his career, the last in 1973. The Indians hoped to revive his career as well, but after 50 games he was dealt to the Athletics. Lowenstein landed with the Orioles in 1979 and was a valuable reserve on two World Series teams in Baltimore.

MARCH 6 Jim Bibby is declared a free agent following an arbitration hearing. The Indians defaulted on Bibby's 1977 contract with the late payment of a $10,000 bonus. Bibby received the bonus for starting 30 games that season. He made his 30th start in the final game. The payment was due on November 2, but the Indians didn't pay Bibby until December 23.

MARCH 15 Jim Bibby signs a contract with the Pirates as a free agent.

Bibby was 33 when he inked his deal with Pittsburgh but had enough left for a 12–4 record for the world champions Pirates in 1979 and followed up with a 19–6 mark in 1980.

MARCH 24 The Indians trade Frank Duffy to the Red Sox for Rick Kreuger.

MARCH 30 The Indians trade Dennis Eckersley and Fred Kendall to the Red Sox for Rick Wise, Bo Diaz, Mike Paxton, and Ted Cox.

The Indians made a huge mistake in letting Eckersley out of the organization. He was only 23 when traded. Active in the majors until 1998, and Eckersley was elected to the Hall of Fame on the first ballot in 2004. The Indians believed he would have a short career because his unorthodox delivery would lead to arm trouble. Eckersley also had marital troubles. His wife Denise left him for teammate Rick Manning. Eckersley was brilliant during his first two seasons in Boston, posting records of 20–8 in 1978 and 17–10 in 1979. For the next several years afterward, however, he was a starter who usually posted records around the .500 mark with earned run averages near the league average. He was traded by the Red Sox to the Cubs in 1984 and wound up with the Athletics in 1987. In Oakland, Tony LaRussa converted Eckersley into a reliever. From 1988 through 1992, he was virtually unhittable, with an ERA of 1.90 in 359⅔ innings. Wise was ten years older than Eckersley. In two seasons in Cleveland, Wise had records of 9–19 and 15–10. Diaz made the All-Star team in 1981 before being dealt to the Phillies.

APRIL 8 The Indians open the season with an 8–5 win over the Royals before 52,433 at Municipal Stadium. The Tribe scored four runs in the first inning for a 4–0 lead, and after Kansas City tied with four in the top of the second, Cleveland came back with two in their half. Paul Dade, Andre Thornton, and Ron Pruitt hit home runs.

April 17 Rick Waits pitches a two-hitter to defeat the Rangers 6–0 at Municipal Stadium. All six Cleveland runs scored in the sixth inning. The only Texas hits were singles by Mike Hargrove in the first inning and Toby Harrah in the seventh.

April 22 Andre Thornton hits for the cycle off four different pitchers during a 13–4 win over the Red Sox at Municipal Stadium. Thornton singled in the first inning against Allen Ripley, third in the second facing Bob Stanley, homered in the seventh versus Jim Wright and doubled in the eighth off Tom Burgmeier.

Thornton hit .262 with 33 homers and 105 RBIs in 1978.

April 25 Paul Dade hits a grand slam off Jerry Garvin in the fourth inning of a 6–5 win over the Blue Jays in Toronto.

Dade wore uniform number "00" during his three seasons with the Indians. The only other Cleveland player to wear "00" was Rick White in 2004.

May 3 Willie Horton hits a grand slam off Byron McLaughlin in the first inning of a 10–5 win over the Mariners in Seattle.

June 8 In the first round of the amateur draft, the Indians select shortstop Phil Lansford from Wilcox High School in Santa Clara, California.

The Indians had one of the smallest scouting staffs in baseball throughout most of the 1970s, and it showed on draft day. Lansford was an extreme disappointment, never advancing past Class A. The only future major leaguer drafted and signed by the Indians in 1978 was second rounder Chris Bando.

June 13 The Indians blow a 9–0 lead and lose 10–9 to the White Sox at Comiskey Park. Cleveland scored four runs in the first inning, four in the second, and one in the third. Chicago countered with six in the bottom of the third and four in the fourth. Sid Monge gave up eight runs, four earned, and Alan Fitzmorris surrendered two tallies.

June 14 The Indians trade Dennis Kinney to the Padres for Dan Spillner.

June 15 The Indians purchased Bernie Carbo from the Red Sox.

June 24 Gary Alexander hits a grand slam off Mike Willis in the fourth inning of a 12–3 win over the Blue Jays at Municipal Stadium.

June 25 Rick Waits sings the National Anthem before a double header against the Blue Jays at Municipal Stadium. The Indians lost the first game 2–1, and won the second 3–2.

An operatic tenor, Waits sang on the NBC television program The Today Show.

July 9 Buddy Bell hits a grand slam off Allen Ripley in the sixth inning of a 6–1 win over the Red Sox at Municipal Stadium.

July 14 The Indians roll to an 11–1 win over the Athletics in Oakland.

July 21 Mike Paxton pitches a two-hitter and ties a major league record by striking out four consecutive batters in a single inning as the Indians wallop the Mariners 11–0 at Municipal Stadium. Dan Meyer reached first to lead off the fifth inning when catcher Gary Alexander missed the third strike. Paxton then struck out Bruce Bochte, Tom Paciorek, and Bill Stein in succession. The only Seattle hits were singles by Bob Stinson in the third inning and Julio Cruz in the eighth.

July 27 The Indians go from one extreme to the other, losing 11–0 and winning 17–5 during a double header against the Yankees in New York. In the second tilt, the Indians scored nine runs in the first inning. Duane Kuiper tied a major league record by hitting two bases-loaded triples to account for six runs batted in. The triples were struck in the first and fifth innings and came off pitcher Bob Kammeyer.

Kuiper is one of only six players in major league history to collect two bases-loaded triples in a single game, one of only three to accomplish the feat since 1900, and the only one to do it since 1959.

August 5 The Indians take leads with runs in the eighth, tenth, and 12th innings but allow the Rangers to come from behind each time in the bottom of each time and lose 4–3 in Arlington. The game ended on a two-run walk-off homer off Jim Kern by ex-Indian John Lowenstein.

August 6 The Indians lose on a two-run walk-off homer for the second day in a row when pinch-hitter Gary Gray drives a pitch over the fence for a 3–2 Rangers win in Arlington. Gray's drive was struck in the ninth inning on an 0–2 pitch from Rick Waits and hit the left field foul pole. The Indians had scored twice in the top of the ninth for a 2–1 lead.

August 10 The Red Sox score twice in the 13th inning to defeat the Indians 6–5 at Fenway Park. Cleveland scored in the top of the 13th on Andre Thornton's homer to take a 5–4 lead. The first Boston run in the 13th scored on a horribly botched play by two Cleveland fielders. Butch Hobson led the inning with a high pop-up, which Thornton, playing first base, dropped 90 feet from home plate. The hustling Hobson kept running, and was rounding second when the ball kicked away from Thornton. Catcher Bo Diaz retrieved the ball and threw wildly past third in an attempt to retire Hobson, who crossed the plate on a pop-up and two errors. The winning run scored on a double by George Scott and a single from Rick Burleson.

August 24 Andre Thornton's homer in the 11th inning beats the Twins 9–8 in Minnesota. The Indians trailed 8–3 before tying the game with four runs in the seventh and one in the ninth. Gary Alexander keyed the comeback with five runs-batted-in.

August 31 The Indians trade John Grubb to the Rangers for Bobby Cuellar and Dave Rivera.

September 26 Gary Alexander breaks up the no-hit bid of Mike Flanagan of the Orioles with a home run with two out in the ninth inning. Flanagan gave up singles to Ted Cox and Duane Kuiper before closing out the 3–1 win at Baltimore.

October 1 On the final day of the season, the Indians prevent the Yankees from clinching the pennant with a 9–2 win in New York. Rick Waits was the winning pitcher.

The Yankees and Red Sox were tied for first at the end of the day. On October 2, the Yankees beat the Red Sox 5–4 in Boston with Bucky Dent delivering the key blow with a homer in the seventh inning.

OCTOBER 3 The Indians trade Jim Kern and Larvell Blanks to the Rangers for Bobby Bonds and Len Barker.

Kern had a 13–5 record, 29 saves, and a 1.57 earned run average for Texas in 1979 but was ineffective afterward. Bonds played for eight clubs from 1974 through 1981. He spent one season in Cleveland, hit 25 homers and stole 34 bases. Barker twice led the AL in strikeouts while with the Indians, had a 19–12 record in 1980, and pitched a perfect game in 1981.

DECEMBER 5 The Indians trade Alfredo Griffin and Phil Lansford to the Blue Jays for Victor Cruz.

Griffin played in 1,931 major league games after leaving the Indians and was still active in 1993. He led the AL in triples in 1980 and made the All-Star team in 1984.

DECEMBER 8 The Indians trade Buddy Bell to the Rangers for Toby Harrah.

In a deal involving a pair of starting third baseman, this one has to be rated as an even swap, although Bell played in more All-Star Games (four) after the trade than Harrah (one). Harrah was an underrated performer. During his first four years in Cleveland, he had a .282 batting average and a .385 on base percentage, hit 61 homers, and scored 363 runs in 574 games. Harrah played in 476 consecutive games from 1979 through 1983.

1979

Season in a Sentence

A strong finish after Dave Garcia replaces Jeff Torborg as manager results in a winning season.

Finish	Won	Lost	Pct	GB
Sixth	81	80	.503	22.0

Managers

Jeff Torborg (43–52) and Dave Garcia (38–28)

Stats	Indians	AL	Rank
Batting Avg:	.258	.270	12
On-Base Pct:	.344	.338	6
Slugging Pct:	.384	.408	12
Home Runs:	138		8
Stolen Bases:	143		3
ERA:	4.22	4.57	11
Fielding Avg:	.978	.978	7
Runs Scored:	760		7
Runs Allowed:	805		11

Starting Line-up

Gary Alexander, c
Andre Thornton, 1b
Duane Kuiper, 2b
Toby Harrah, 3b
Tom Veryzer, ss
Mike Hargrove, lf
Rick Manning, cf
Bobby Bonds, rf
Cliff Johnson, dh
Jim Norris, lf-rf-cf
Ron Hassey, c
Ted Cox, 3b
Paul Dade, lf-rf
Ron Pruitt, lf-rf-dh

Pitchers

Rick Waits, sp
Rick Wise, sp
Mike Paxton, sp
Len Barker, sp
Wayne Garland, sp
Sid Monge, rp
Victor Cruz, rp
Dan Spillner, rp

Attendance

1,011,644 (12th in AL)

Club Leaders

Batting Avg:	Toby Harrah	.279
On-Base Pct:	Toby Harrah	.389
Slugging Pct:	Andre Thornton	.449
Home Runs:	Andre Thornton	26
RBIs:	Andre Thornton	93
Runs:	Toby Harrah	99
Stolen Bases:	Bobby Bonds	34
Wins:	Rick Waits	16
Strikeouts:	Rick Wise	108
	Sid Monge	108
ERA:	Rick Wise	3.73
Saves:	Sid Monge	19

April 5 — Five days after the nuclear disaster at Three Mile Island, the Indians lose the opener 7–1 to the Red Sox in Boston.

April 7 — In the first game of the season at Municipal Stadium, Rick Waits pitches a one-hitter to defeat the Red Sox 3–0 before 47,231. The lone Boston hit was a single by Jerry Remy in the sixth inning.

May 6 — In the first of many incredible late-inning rallies in 1979, the Indians score five runs in the ninth inning to defeat the Royals 5–4 in Kansas City. The RBIs were by Duane Kuiper (a two-run single), Ron Pruitt and Tom Veryzer (both with singles), and Rick Manning (on a bases-loaded walk).

May 14 — Rick Waits pitches a two-hitter to beat the Blue Jays 1–0 at Municipal Stadium.

May 20 — A two-run walk-off homer by Gary Alexander in the ninth inning beats the Tigers 9–7 at Municipal Stadium.

In 860 at-bats with the Indians from 1978 though 1980, Alexander hit 37 homers, but his batting average was only .230 and he struck out 252 times. In 1979, he led AL catchers in errors with 18 in 91 games.

MAY 22 Andre Thornton hits a grand slam off Mark Lemongello in the third inning of an 8–6 win over the Blue Jays in Toronto.

JUNE 4 The Indians pull out a 14-inning, 5–4 win over the Athletics in Oakland. A sacrifice fly by Rick Manning drove in the winning run. The A's scored three runs in the ninth to tie the game 4–4.

JUNE 5 In the first round of the amateur draft, the Indians select pitcher Jon Bohnet from Hogan High School in Vallejo, California.

Bohnet's major league career lasted only three games. The only other future major leaguers drafted and signed by the Indians in 1979 were Von Hayes (seventh round) and Larry White (31st round).

JUNE 12 The Indians score a run in the eighth inning and three in the ninth to defeat the Angels 11–10 at Municipal Stadium. All three runs in the ninth scored after

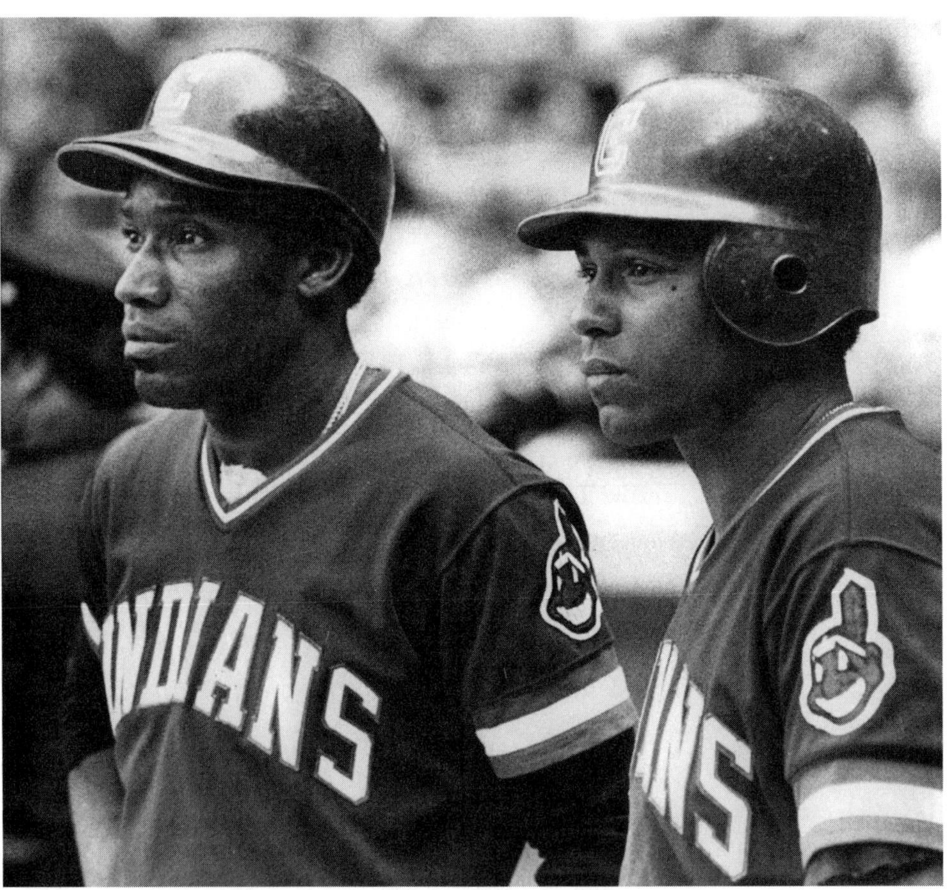

Bobby Bonds (left) and Andre Thornton (right) supplied most of the power for the Tribe in 1979 and developed a close friendship during the year they played together.

two were out. Ted Cox walked and Toby Harrah homered to tie the score. Bobby Bonds followed with a single, stole second, and scored on a one-base hit by Andre Thornton.

In his first season with the Indians, Harrah hit .279 with 20 homers, 20 stolen bases, and 99 runs scored.

JUNE 14 A two-run, walk-off triple by Jim Norris in the ninth inning beats the Athletics 2–1 at Municipal Stadium.

On the same day, the Indians traded Paul Dade to the Padres for Mike Hargrove. The club pulled off a brilliant trade in acquiring Hargrove. He played for the club for seven seasons and later was the team's manager in two World Series. Dade played only one more year, batting .189 in 1980.

JUNE 15 The Indians score seven runs in the third inning and win 13–3 over the Mariners at Municipal Stadium.

On the same day, the Indians traded Don Hood to the Yankees for Cliff Johnson. Johnson was traded to the Indians after breaking the thumb of Yankee teammate Goose Gossage during a locker room scuffle. Johnson set a major league record for pinch-hit homers with 20 during his career. He hit three of them while with the Indians in 1979 and 1980.

JUNE 17 Bobby Bonds hits a grand slam off Glenn Abbott for a 4–3 lead, but the Indians wind up losing 6–5 to the Mariners at Municipal Stadium.

JUNE 27 The Indians extend their losing streak to ten games, dropping a 3–1 decision to the Orioles in Baltimore.

JULY 3 Cliff Johnson hits a grand slam off Ken Kravec in the first inning of a 7–3 win over the White Sox at Municipal Stadium.

JULY 22 Dave Garcia becomes manager of the Indians, replacing Jeff Torborg.

After a 10–2 loss to the Tigers on July 2, Torborg announced that he was resigning, effective at the end of the season. After the Indians lost 10 of 19 to drop to 43–52 on the season, the club decided not to wait until the end of the season and hired Garcia to replace Torborg. Garcia was 58 years old and had never played at the major league level. He was a coach for the Indians in 1975 and 1976, and then took a similar position with the Angels in 1977. Garcia was the manager in Anaheim the second half of that season. Just 46 game into the 1978 campaign, he was fired and returned to Cleveland as coach in 1979. The Indians won their first ten games with Garcia as manager and were 38–28 over the rest of the season. He remained as manager through the end of the 1982 season, and posted a 247–244 record. He is the only Cleveland manager between Birdie Tebbetts (1963–66) and Mike Hargrove (1991–99) to guide the club to a winning record. In between Tebbetts and Hargove, 13 different individuals took a turn at running the club. Just four days after being fired as manager of the Indians, Torborg became a coach with the Yankees, a job he held until 1988.

He later managed the White Sox (1989–91), Mets (1992–93), and Expos (2001). Torborg also did broadcasting work on CBS and FOX.

JULY 25 Rick Waits pitches a two-hitter to defeat the Twins 2–0 at Metropolitan Stadium. The only hits off Waits were singles by Bombo Rivera in the seventh inning and Glenn Borgmann in the ninth.

JULY 28 The Indians score seven runs in the eighth inning and defeat the White Sox 10–5 in Chicago.

JULY 29 The Indians score seven runs in the second inning, capped by a grand slam from Rick Manning off Ken Kravec, and defeat the White Sox 9–6 in Chicago.

JULY 31 The Indians extend their winning streak to ten games, all in Dave Garcia's first ten games as manager, with an 11–10 and 3–0 sweep of a double header against the Red Sox at Municipal Stadium. In a spectacular comeback in the opener, the Tribe scored five runs in the ninth inning to tie the game 10–10 before winning in the 11th. The tying run came home on a two-out wild pitch by Boston's Bill Campbell. In the 11th, Rick Manning singled, went to second on a sacrifice, and scored on a double by Tony Harrah. In the second tilt, Len Barker (7⅓ innings) and Sid Monge (1⅔ innings) combined on a two-hitter. The only Red Sox hits were a double by Carl Yastrzemski in the first inning and a single by Fred Lynn in the eighth, both off Barker.

AUGUST 4 Toby Harrah hits a grand slam off Jerry Johnson in the first inning of a 12–8 win over the Rangers at Municipal Stadium.

AUGUST 22 The Indians rout the Angels 13–3 in Anaheim.

AUGUST 23 Andre Thornton hits a grand slam off Rick Langford in the first inning, but the Indians lose 8–6 to the Athletics at Municipal Stadium.

AUGUST 29 In a fantastic finish, the Indians score five runs in the ninth inning to defeat the Mariners 5–4 in the first game of a double header at Municipal Stadium. A two-run homer by Andre Thornton cut the deficit to two. Mike Hargrove contributed a two-out, two-run double. A single by Rick Manning drove in the winner. Cleveland also won the second tilt 2–1.

SEPTEMBER 1 Andre Thornton hits a grand slam off Jim Barr in the sixth inning to tie the score 4–4, but the Indians lose 7–4 to the Angels at Municipal Stadium. Carney Lansford hit three homers for California.

SEPTEMBER 7 After trailing 8–0, the Indians rally to win 9–8 against the Blue Jays at Municipal Stadium with a run in the sixth inning, two in the seventh, and six in the ninth. Still down 8–3, the Indians had the bases loaded and none out in the eighth inning when Ted Cox grounded into a triple play. But Toronto was unable to stop Cleveland hitters in the ninth. Toby Harrah led off the inning with a home run, and when he came to bat a second time he drove in the winning run with a single.

SEPTEMBER 9 In yet another incredible ninth-inning rally, the Indians score five runs in the ninth inning to defeat the Blue Jays 14–10 at Municipal Stadium. Mike Hargrove drove in the first run with a single and Bobby Bonds capped the rally with a grand slam off Tom Buskey.

SEPTEMBER 18 The Indians score eight runs in the fourth inning and trounce the Yankees 16–3 at Municipal Stadium.

SEPTEMBER 30 On the final day of the season, the Indians defeat the Orioles 6–5 in 11 innings at Municipal Stadium to post a winning a record. Cleveland finished the season with a record of 81–80. Attendance also exceeded 1,000,000 for only the second time since 1959.

NOVEMBER 19 Two weeks after Iranian militants seize the U.S. Embassy in Teheran, taking 52 hostages, Rick Wise signs a contract as a free agent with the Padres.

DECEMBER 7 The Indians trade Bobby Bonds to the Cardinals for Jerry Mumphrey and John Denny.

DECEMBER 19 The Indians sign Jorge Orta, most recently with the White Sox, as a free agent.

DECEMBER 21 The Indians trade Larry Andersen to the Pirates for Larry Littleton and John Burden.

THE STATE OF THE INDIANS

Much like the 1960s and 1970s, the Indians struggled just to achieve respectability during the 1980s. The only clubs to post winning records were in 1981 and 1986. None finished higher than fifth in the seven-team AL East. The Indians were the only AL East club that didn't finish first at least once. Overall, Cleveland was 710–849 during the decade, a winning percentage of .455. Only the Mariners had a worse record in the American League. AL champs in the 1980s were the Royals (1980 and 1985), Yankees (1981), Brewers (1982), Orioles (1983), Tigers (1984), Red Sox (1986), Twins (1987), and Athletics (1988 and 1989). AL East champs were the Yankees (1980 and 1981), Brewers (1982), Orioles (1983), Tigers (1984 and 1987), Blue Jays (1985 and 1989), and Red Sox (1986 and 1988).

THE BEST TEAM

The 1986 Indians had a record of 84–78 under Pat Corrales and finished in fifth place, 11½ games out of first in a tough AL East.

THE WORST TEAM

The 1985 club sank to 60–102 and were buried in the basement of the AL East 39½ games from first place.

THE BEST MOMENT

Indians fans swelled with pride and optimism when the April 6, 1987, issue of *Sports Illustrated* hit the newsstands proclaiming: "Believe It! Cleveland is the Best Team in the American League."

THE WORST MOMENT

The moment that reality set in during the 1987 season as the Indians nose-dived to a 61–101 record.

THE ALL-DECADE TEAM • YEARS W/INDIANS

Ron Hassey, c	1978–84
Mike Hargrove, 1b	1979–85
Tony Bernazard, 2b	1984–87
Brook Jacoby, 3b	1984–92
Julio Franco, ss	1983–88, 1996–97
Joe Carter, lf	1984–89
Brett Butler, cf	1984–87
Cory Snyder, rf	1986–90
Andre Thornton, dh	1977–79, 1981–87
Tom Candiotti, p	1986–91, 1999
Bert Blyleven, p	1981–85
Doug Jones, p	1986–91, 1998
Len Barker, p	1979–83

None of the members of the 1980s All-Decade Team are in the Hall of Fame, but Blyleven and Franco deserve a plaque in Cooperstown. Other outstanding players included third baseman Toby Harrah (1979–83), first baseman Pat Tabler (1983–88), left fielder Mel Hall (1984–88), and pitcher Greg Swindell (1986–91, 1996).

THE DECADE LEADERS

Batting Avg:	Julio Franco	.299
On-Base Pct:	Mike Hargrove	.395
Slugging Pct:	Joe Carter	.472
Home Runs:	Joe Carter	151
RBIs:	Joe Carter	530
Runs:	Julio Franco	501
Stolen Bases:	Brett Butler	164
Wins:	Len Barker	50
	Tom Candiotti	50
Strikeouts:	Len Barker	606
ERA:	Bert Blyleven	3.23
Saves:	Doug Jones	78

THE HOME FIELD

The Indians continued to play at Municipal Stadium, built in 1932, throughout the 1980s while exploring the possibility of building a baseball-only facility in Cleveland.

THE GAME YOU WISHED YOU HAD SEEN

Len Barker pitched a perfect game at Municipal Stadium on May 15, 1981.

THE WAY THE GAME WAS PLAYED

The 1980s had a little something for everybody. Trends that surfaced in the 1970s continued, with teams still emphasizing speed. In 1987, offense spiked in a year that combined the speed of the dead-ball era with the power of the 1950s. AL teams averaged 124 stolen bases and 188 home runs.

THE MANAGEMENT

Underfinanced ownership characterized Indians baseball from the 1950s through the 1980s. A group headed by Francis J. "Steve" O'Neill bought the club in 1978 with Gabe Paul installed as president and chief executive officer. O'Neill died in 1983, and the club was run by his estate for three years. O'Neill's nephew, Patrick O'Neill, became chairman of the board with Paul continuing as president. Paul relinquished the position to Peter Bavasi in 1984. In December 1986, Richard and David Jacobs bought the franchise, and soon hired Hank Peters to run the day-to-day operation as president. General managers were Phil Seghi (1973–85), Joe Klein (1985–87) and Peters (1987–91). Field managers were Dave Garcia (1979–82), Mike Ferraro (1983), Pat Corrales (1983–87), Doc Edwards (1987–89), and Jim Hart (1989).

THE BEST PLAYER MOVE

The best move was the selection of Jim Thome in the 13th round in the June 1989 draft. The best trade brought Brett Butler, Brook Jacoby, and Rick Behenna from the Braves for Len Barker in August 1983.

THE WORST PLAYER MOVE

The worst trade sent Jay Bell to the Pirates for Felix Fermin in March 1989. A close second was the deal in which Julio Franco went to the Rangers for Pete O'Brien, Jerry Browne, and Oddibe McDowell in December 1988.

1980

Season in a Sentence

Rookie sensation Joe Charboneau distracts Indians fans from another losing season.

Finish • Won • Lost • Pct • GB

Finish	Won	Lost	Pct	GB
Sixth	79	81	.494	23.0

Manager

Dave Garcia

Stats

Stats	Indians	AL	Rank
Batting Avg:	.277	.269	4
On-Base Pct:	.355	.335	1
Slugging Pct:	.381	.399	11
Home Runs:	89		14
Stolen Bases:	118		4
ERA:	4.68	4.03	14
Fielding Avg:	.983	.978	2
Runs Scored:	738		8
Runs Allowed:	807		14

Starting Line-up

Ron Hassey, c
Mike Hargrove, 1b
Alan Bannister, 2b-rf
Toby Harrah, 3b
Tom Veryzer, ss
Miguel Dilone, lf
Rick Manning, cf
Jorge Orta, rf
Joe Charboneau, dh-lf
Jerry Dybzinski, ss
Bo Diaz, c
Gary Alexander, dh
Cliff Johnson, dh

Pitchers

Len Barker, sp
Dan Spillner, sp
Rick Waits, sp
Wayne Garland, sp
John Denny, sp
Sid Monge, rp
Victor Cruz, rp
Mike Stanton, rp
Bob Owchinko, rp-sp

Attendance

1,033,827 (11th in AL)

Club Leaders

Batting Avg:	Miguel Dilone	.341
On-Base Pct:	Mike Hargrove	.415
Slugging Pct:	Joe Charboneau	.488
Home Runs:	Joe Charboneau	23
RBIs:	Joe Charboneau	87
Runs:	Toby Harrah	100
Stolen Bases:	Miguel Dilone	61
Wins:	Len Barker	19
Strikeouts:	Len Barker	187
ERA:	Len Barker	4.17
Saves:	Sid Monge	14

FEBRUARY 15 The Indians trade Jerry Mumphrey to the Padres for Bob Owchinko and Jim Wilhelm.

Acquired in a trade two months earlier with the Cardinals, Mumphrey never put on an Indians uniform. The club should have kept him. Over the remainder of his career, which ended in 1988, Mumphrey hit .295 in 3,422 at-bats.

MARCH 8 Rookie outfielder Joe Charboneau is stabbed in Mexico City, where the Indians were playing a series of exhibition games.

Charboneau was stabbed by a ballpoint pen wielded by Mexican radical Oscar Martinez who simply said he didn't like Americans. The incident occurred while Charboneau was waiting for a bus outside the hotel. The pen penetrated one inch on his left side and struck a rib. Martinez was wrestled to the ground while he attempted to stab Charboneau in the eyes. It took almost an hour for police to arrive. Martinez spent only two hours in jail and was fined 50 pesos ($2.27 American). During the games played in Mexico City against teams from the Mexican League, security was inadequate and the players and club had *thousands of dollars worth of equipment stolen, and hordes of fans often ran across the field. At the hotel, players and club officials were billed for phantom purchases.*

The stabbing incident was the first time that many fans had heard of Charboneau, who had yet to appear in a major league game. He was 25 years old and had been obtained from the Phillies organization in a minor league deal on December 6, 1978. Joe recovered from his wound and returned to the field in four days. The Indians had him tagged for another season in the minors, but Charboneau tore through exhibition pitching to earn a starting spot as an outfielder and designated hitter. Sportswriters dubbed him "Super Joe" and reports of his exploits during training camp in Tucson were a daily feature in the Cleveland newspapers. By Opening Day, he was already a popular figure among Indians fans, who were desperate for a hero, with his play on the field and idiosyncratic and offbeat personality. He cemented his place in the hearts of Indians fans with a home run in the season opener (see April 10, 1980) and home opener (see April 19, 1980). Charboneau stories included opening beer bottles with his eye socket; drinking beer through a straw in his nose; streaking his hair with red dye in the punk rock style of the era, then shaving his head a decade before it became fashionable; cutting off a tattoo with a razor blade; sewing up a cut with a needle and fishing line; pulling out his own tooth and fixing a broken nose, both with a pair pliers; eating cigarettes and raw eggs; and fighting in boxcars for $25 a match. To relax after games, Charboneau hooked rugs. He reveled in the attention. By mid-summer, a rock song called "Go, Go Charboneau" was being played several times a day on Cleveland radio stations. By the end of the season, he was the AL Rookie-of-the-Year Award with a .289 average, 23 homers and 87 RBIs. But Charboneau injured his back during spring training in 1981 and lost his batting stroke. He played only two seasons after 1980, combining to hit .211 with six home runs in 194 at-bats. He was released by the Indians organization in 1983 after flashing fans an obscene gesture while playing for the club's minor league affiliate in Buffalo. His three-year big league career is tied for the shortest ever by a Rookie-of-the-Year. The only other Rookie-of-the-Year with a three-year career was Ken Hubbs, who played second base for the Cubs from 1961 through 1963 before dying in a plane crash on February 13, 1964.

APRIL 10 In the season opener, the Indians lose 10–2 to the Angels in Anaheim. In his first major league game and second at-bat, Joe Charboneau hit a home run.

The announcing teams for the Indians games in 1980 were Herb Score and Nev Chandler on radio and Joe Tait and Bruce Drennan on TV.

APRIL 14 Jorge Orta hits a grand slam off Doc Medich in the top of the first inning, but the Rangers score six runs in bottom half and defeat the Indians 7–4 in Arlington.

A native of Mexico, Orta was 29 when he joined the Indians as a free agent after eight seasons with the White Sox. He turned down a basketball scholarship under John Wooden at UCLA to play baseball. Orta's father Pedro was known as the Babe Ruth of Cuban baseball but never got a chance to play in the majors because of the pre-1947 color barrier.

April 19 In the home opener, the Indians win 8–1 over the Blue Jays before 61,753 at Municipal Stadium. Joe Charboneau collected three hits in three at-bats and received a two-minute standing ovation after hitting a home run.

The Indians foisted one of the worst mascots in baseball history on Municipal Stadium patrons in 1980. Looking to follow the success of the San Diego Chicken and the Phillie Phanatic, the Indians introduced an insect of indeterminate origin called "The Baseball Bug." The costume consisted of a red globe-shaped body, with a blue vest and antennae of springs with baseballs on the ends. Fans understandably failed to embrace the idea, and "The Baseball Bug" was sidelined after the 1981 season.

April 26 Down 5–0 in the fifth inning, the Indians rally to beat the Rangers 8–7 at Municipal Stadium. Toby Harrah tripled to tie the score 6–6 in the seventh and scored the go-ahead run on a single by Mike Hargrove. Rookie infielder Jerry Dybzinski, a native of Cleveland, connected on a home run for his first major league hit.

Dybzinski didn't hit another home run until 1983. He hit three homers in 909 career at-bats.

April 29 The Brewers hit seven home runs off Cleveland pitchers to defeat the Indians 14–1 at Municipal Stadium. Ben Oglivie and Sal Bando each hit two homers, with Sixto Lezcano, Larry Hisle, and Paul Molitor adding the rest.

May 2 Len Barker (seven innings) and Mike Stanton (two innings) combine on a two-hitter for a 6–1 win over the Blue Jays at Exhibition Stadium. Damaso Garcia collected both Toronto hits with doubles in the third and seventh innings.

May 4 During a double header in Toronto, Otto Velez of the Blue Jays hits four home runs and drives in ten runs to lead his club to a sweep of the Indians. Velez hit three homers and drove in seven runs in the opener as the Jays won 9–8 in ten innings. His third blast was the game-winner. There were five Cleveland home runs in the game by Jorge Orta, Toby Harrah, Gary Alexander, Mike Hargrove, and Cliff Johnson. Toronto won the second tilt 7–2.

Hargrove was nicknamed "The Human Rain Delay." Before each plate appearance, he called time, grabbed some dirt, tugged at his shirt and sleeves, hitched up his pants, adjusted his hair, tapped down his batting helmet, squeezed his batting helmet deeper into his batting glove, drained all the moisture from his mouth, and stepped in the batter's box after raking the dirt with his cleats.

May 7 The Indians purchase Miguel Dilone from the Cubs.

Dilone was a huge surprise. He came to the Indians as a 26 year old with a .209 batting average and two home runs in 465 at-bats. During the 1980 season, he batted .341 in 528 at-bats and stole 61 bases. Dilone proved to be a one-year wonder, however, and never came close to those numbers again.

May 15 Mike Hargrove extends his hitting streak to 23 games during a 6–2 loss to the Red Sox at Municipal Stadium.

Coach Joe Nossek congratulates Joe Charbeneau as he rounds third after hitting a home run. "Super Joe" was one of the most popular—and eccentric—players in team history.

The Indians had a team ERA of 4.68 in 1980 that was the worst in the majors.

MAY 28 Ten days after the volcanic eruption of Mt. St. Helens, the Indians explode for eight runs in the fifth inning and defeat the Orioles 10–6 in Boston.

JUNE 1 The Indians hit four sacrifice flies, contributed by Ron Hassey, Dave Rosello, Gary Alexander, and Dell Alston but lose 8–7 to the Mariners at Municipal Stadium.

JUNE 3 A two-run, walk-off homer by Cliff Johnson in the tenth inning beats the Athletics 6–4 at Municipal Stadium.

On the same day, the Indians selected shortstop Kelly Gruber from Westlake High School in Austin, Texas, in the first round of the amateur draft. The club exposed Gruber to the Rule 5 draft at the end of the 1983 season, and he was chosen by the Blue Jays, Gruber had a ten-year big league career as a third baseman that included being named to two All-Star teams. Other future major leaguers drafted and signed by the Indians in 1980 were Rich Thompson (sixth round), Mike Jeffcoat (13th round), Mike Simple (29th round), and Dave Gallagher (first round of the secondary phase).

JUNE 8 The Indians tie a major league record with three consecutive sacrifice bunts in the sixth inning of a 7–2 win over the White Sox in Chicago. The successful bunts were by Bo Diaz, Dave Rosello, and Jerry Dybzinski.

JUNE 15 Jorge Orta collects six hits in six at-bats and Toby Harrah drives in seven runs during a 14–5 win over the Twins at Municipal Stadium. All six of Orta's hits were singles. Harrah hit a three-run homer in the first inning, tripled in a run in the fourth, singled home two in the sixth, and had another RBI-single in the seventh.

Orta had hits in nine consecutive at-bats over three consecutive games. He connected for a hit in his last at-bat on June 14, a 3–2 victory over Minnesota at Municipal Stadium. Orta garnered two more hits in his first two at-bats on June 16, a 5–3 triumph over the White Sox in Cleveland.

JUNE 16 Indians pitcher Mike Stanton has an art show at the Cleveland Stadium Club. Ten of his works sold for $200 each. The proceeds were donated to charity.

JUNE 20 The Indians outlast the Twins 4–3 in Minnesota. Toby Harrah drove in the winning run with a double.

JUNE 23 The Indians trade Cliff Johnson to the Cubs for Karl Pagel.

JUNE 25 Cleveland pitchers combine to walk 14 batters, five of them with the bases loaded, during a 13–3 loss to the Tigers in Detroit. The base on balls were issued by Dan Spillner (six), Don Collins (three), Mike Stanton (four), and Sid Monge (one). Spillner walked five batters in a row.

JULY 1 Down 7–2, the Indians score four runs in the sixth inning and two in the seventh to win 8–7 over the Tigers in Detroit. Bo Diaz hit a grand slam off Roger Weaver in the sixth.

JULY 3 Wayne Garland pitches a two-hitter to beat the Yankees 7–0 before 73,096 at Municipal Stadium. The only New York hits were singles by Reggie Jackson in the fourth inning and Joe Lefebvre in the ninth.

JULY 6 A three-run pinch-homer by Gary Alexander in the sixth inning sparks the Indians to a 5–3 win over the Yankees at Municipal Stadium.

The homer was Alexander's second as a pinch-hitter in consecutive at-bats. The first occurred on the previous day during a 3–2 defeat at the hands of the Yankees in Cleveland.

JULY 11 The Indians trade Dave Oliver to the Expos for Ross Grimsley.

JULY 20 The Indians score five runs in the ninth inning to tie the Athletics 5–5 but lose 6–5 in the 14th in Oakland. The ninth-inning rally was capped by a grand slam from Toby Harrah off Rick Langford.

JULY 23 The Indians score seven runs in the seventh inning, four on a grand slam by Joe Charboneau off Joey McLaughlin, and defeat the Mariners 12–6 in Seattle.

JULY 25 Down 8–3, the Indians score three runs in the eighth inning and three in the ninth to beat the Angels 9–8 in the first game of a double header at Municipal Stadium. The three ninth-inning runs scored after two were out on a walk, a hit batsman, an error, and a single by Bo Diaz. Cleveland also won the second contest 10–2.

JULY 26 The Indians trounce the Angels 14–4 at Municipal Stadium.

JULY 30 The Indians record their eighth win in a row with a 5–2 decision over the Mariners at Municipal Stadium.

The Indians won 17 of 22 between July 21 and August 14.

AUGUST 13 The Indians clobber the Rangers 14–3 in Arlington.

AUGUST 18 Len Barker strikes out 12 batters during a 4–2 victory over the White Sox in the first game of a double header at Comiskey Park. Chicago won the second game 7–2.

AUGUST 20 At Comiskey Park, Dan Spillner takes a no-hitter into the ninth inning before Leo Sutherland of the White Sox singles with one out. Spillner had to settle for a one-hitter and a 3–0 win.

The Indians had a record of 72–66 on September 9 but blew a chance at a winning season by losing 15 of their final 22 games.

SEPTEMBER 14 Gary Gray stars in a 13-inning, 5–4 win over the Tigers in the first game of a double header at Municipal Stadium. Gray hit a two-run, pinch-hit homer in the ninth inning to tie the score 4–4. Remaining in the contest in left field, Gray delivered a walk-off single in the 13th. The Indians completed the sweep with a 3–0 triumph in the nightcap.

The game was Gray's only moment of glory in a Cleveland uniform. He played in 28 games for the Indians and hit just .148 with two homers in 54 at-bats.

SEPTEMBER 30 The Indians win a strange 12–9 decision over the Yankees at Municipal Stadium. The Tribe scored eight runs in the second inning to take an 8–2 lead but allowed the Yanks to surge back ahead 9–8. Cleveland regained the advantage with four tallies in the eighth. Ron Hassey batted twice during the second-inning explosion and hit a home run and a double.

Hassey hit .318 with eight home runs in 1980.

October 1 Len Barker tries for his 20th win of the season but allows six runs in 1⅔ innings, and the Indians lose 18–7 to the Yankees at Municipal Stadium.

Entering the season with a lifetime record of 12–12, Barker was 19–12 in 1980 with a league-leading 187 strikeouts and a 4.17 ERA.

October 30 Indians shareholders agree to sell the franchise to Broadway producer James Nederlander and Los Angeles attorney Neil Papiano. The sale was called off on January 6, 1981, however, for reasons that were never made clear to the public.

December 9 A month after Ronald Reagan defeats Jimmy Carter in the presidential election, the Indians trade Gary Alexander, Bob Owchinko, Victor Cruz, and Rafael Vasquez to the Pirates for Bert Blyleven and Manny Sanguillen.

Blyleven battled elbow miseries during much of his five seasons in Cleveland, but the trade was well worth the loss of four players. He gave the Indians moments of excellence, posting an 11–7 record and a 2.88 ERA in the strike-interrupted season of 1981, and was 19–7 with an earned run average of 2.87 in 1984. Sanguillen retired rather than play for the Indians.

December 29 Three weeks before the U.S. Embassy hostages are released from captivity in Iran, the Indians sign Pat Kelly, most recently with the Orioles, as a free agent.

1981

Season in a Sentence

Len Barker pitches a perfect game, the Indians host the All-Star Game, finish last in the AL in home runs, first in stolen bases, and post a winning record in a season stopped for 50 days by a players' strike.

Finish • Won • Lost • Pct • GB

Finish	Won	Lost	Pct	GB
*	52	51	.505	*

* Because of the players' strike, the season was split in two. The Indians finished in sixth place with a record of 26–24, five games behind, in the first half, and fifth place with a record of 26–27, five games behind, in the second half.

Manager

Dave Garcia

Stats

Stats	Indians	AL	Rank
Batting Avg:	.263	.256	6
On-Base Pct:	.331	.324	5
Slugging Pct:	.351	.373	12
Home Runs:	39		14
Stolen Bases:	119		1
ERA:	3.88	3.66	11
Fielding Avg:	.978	.980	11
Runs Scored:	431		7
Runs Allowed:	442		8

Starting Line-up

Ron Hassey, c
Mike Hargrove, 1b
Duane Kuiper, 2b
Toby Harrah, 3b
Tom Veryzer, ss
Miguel Dilone, lf
Rick Manning, cf
Jorge Orta, rf
Andre Thornton, dh
Alan Bannister, lf-rf-2b
Bo Diaz, c
Joe Charboneau, lf
Von Hayes, dh-lf

Pitchers

Bert Blyleven, sp
John Denny, sp
Len Barker, sp
Rick Waits, sp
Wayne Garland, sp
Dan Spillner, rp
Sid Monge, rp

Attendance

661,395 (12th in AL)

Club Leaders

Batting Avg:	Mike Hargrove	.317
On-Base Pct:	Mike Hargrove	.424
Slugging Pct:	Mike Hargrove	.401
Home Runs:	Bo Diaz	7
RBIs:	Mike Hargrove	49
Runs:	Toby Harrah	64
Stolen Bases:	Miguel Dilone	29
Wins:	Bert Blyleven	11
Strikeouts:	Len Barker	127
ERA:	Bert Blyleven	2.88
Saves:	Dan Spillner	7

April 11 Two weeks after Ronald Reagan is wounded by John Hinckley in an assassination attempt, the Indians open the season with a 5–3 loss to the Brewers before a huge throng of 71,067 at Municipal Stadium. Milwaukee broke a 1–1 tie with three runs in the eighth inning off Bert Blyleven.

April 16 Four days after the launch of the Columbia, the first space shuttle, the Indians edge the Brewers 1–0 in Milwaukee. Wayne Garland pitched the shutout. A double by Bo Diaz in the second inning scored the lone run of the game.

April 26 The Indians score three runs in the ninth inning to defeat the Rangers 4–3 in Arlington. Mike Hargrove drove in the tie-breaking run with a two-out single.

Hargrove hit .317 and his .432 on base percentage led the American League. Tony Harrah batted .291 and led the Indians in runs (64) and hits (105).

The 27 Outs of Len Barker's Perfect Game

First Inning
Alfredo Griffin grounded out to shortstop Tom Veryzer on a 1-and-2 count. Lloyd Moseby grounded out to Veryzer on a 1–0 count. George Bell grounded out to first baseman Mike Hargrove on the first pitch.

Second Inning
John Mayberry flied out to center fielder Rick Manning on a 2–2 count. Willie Upshaw grounded out to second baseman Duane Kuiper on a 1–2 count. Damaso Garcia flied out to Manning on an 0–1 count.

Third Inning
Rick Bosetti grounded out to Veryzer on a 2–0 count. Danny Ainge grounded out to Kuiper on a 2–0 count. Buck Martinez flied out to Manning on a 1–1 count.

Fourth Inning
Griffin flied out to right fielder Jorge Orta on a 2–2 count. Moseby struck out swinging on a 1–2 count. Bell struck out swinging on a 2–2 count.

Fifth Inning
Mayberry struck out swinging on a 1–2 count. Upshaw fouled out to third baseman Toby Harrah on a 1–1 count. Garcia struck out swinging on a 2–2 count.

Sixth Inning
Bosetti grounded out to Kuiper on an 0–1 count. Ainge struck out swinging on a 2–2 count. Martinez struck out swinging on a 2–2 count.

Seventh Inning
Griffin grounded out to Kuiper on the first pitch. Moseby struck out swinging on a 2–2 count. Bell struck out swinging on a 2–2 count.

Eighth Inning
Mayberry struck out swinging on a 1–2 count. Upshaw grounded out to Kuiper on an 0–2 count. Garcia struck out swinging on a 2–2 count.

Ninth Inning
Bosetti popped out to Harrah on a 1–1 count. Al Woods, batting for Ainge, struck out swinging on an 0–2 count. Ernie Whitt, batting for Martinez, flied out to Manning on a 1–2 count.

The Long Drought

The best single season won-lost percentage compiled by the Indians from 1960 though 1993 was .537 in 1965, a club that won 87 and lost 75. It is the longest stretch in major league history in which a franchise failed to field a team with a winning percentage of .540 or better.

Team	Years Without a Winning Pct. of .540 or Better	
Cleveland Indians	34	1960–93
Philadelphia Phillies	32	1918–49
Boston Braves	30	1917–46
St. Louis Browns	21	1923–43
Chicago Cubs	21	1946–66
Philadelphia/Kansas City/Oakland Athletics	20	1949–68
Washington Senators/ Texas Rangers	20	1961–80
St. Louis Cardinals	19	1902–20
Boston Red Sox	19	1919–37
Los Angeles/ California Angels	18	1961–78
Seattle Mariners	18	1977–94

MAY 6 Bert Blyleven carries a no-hitter into the ninth inning before settling for a two-hit, 4–1 victory over the Blue Jays in Toronto. On the first pitch of the ninth inning, Lloyd Moseby hit a twisting liner that left fielder Larry Littleton overran for a double. George Bell followed with a single to score the run.

MAY 9 Jorge Orta eludes a rundown to score the winning run that beats the Twins 2–1 in Minnesota. Orta tried to score from second base on an infield single by Miguel Dilone, but pulled up ten feet short of home plate when he saw catcher Sal Butera with the ball. During the ensuing rundown, shortstop Chuck Baker flipped the ball to the plate, but nobody was there to handle it and Orta crossed the plate.

MAY 10 The Indians play at Metropolitan Stadium in Bloomington, Minnesota, for the last time, and defeat the Twins 5–1.

The Twins moved into the Metrodome in downtown Minneapolis in 1982.

MAY 11 Indians players help break up a mugging near Comiskey Park following a 3–1 win over the White Sox. On the bus ride back to the hotel, the players witnessed a car pulling up alongside two men and a woman, and three men jumped out and began beating them, one wielding a baseball bat. Pitching coach Dave Duncan and several players told the bus driver to pull over to the curb. The players interrupted the brawl and held the three assailants until police arrived. The three attackers were charged with simple battery, but later sued some of the players accusing them of assault. The case was thrown out of court a few months later.

MAY 13 The Indians outlast the White Sox 4–3 when Jorge Orta hits a home run in the 16th inning in Chicago.

MAY 15 Len Barker pitches a perfect game in defeating the Blue Jays 3–0 before 7,290 at Municipal Stadium. As Barker took the mound in the tension-filled ninth inning, a misty rain blew in off Lake Erie. The temperature was 47 degrees. Rick Bosetti popped out to third baseman Toby Harrah on a 1–0 pitch. Al Woods, pinch-hitting for Danny Ainge, struck out on three pitches. Ernie Whitt, batting for Buck Martinez, sailed a short fly to Rick Manning in center field for the final out. Barker fanned eleven batters, all swinging. The 11 strikeouts were recorded while facing the final 17 batters of the perfect game. Barker threw 103 pitches, 75 of them for strikes. Just five balls reached the outfield, and he never went to a three-ball count. The catcher was Ron Hassey. Barker was the second Indian with a perfect game. The other was Addie Joss in 1908.

There have been 17 pitchers credited with pitching a perfect game in major league history, including Don Larsen in the 1956 World Series. There are two other pitchers who retired the first 27 batters to face them before allowing a base runner in extra innings. Barker's perfect game is among the unlikeliest. Among the 19 hurlers to set down either all 27 or the first 27 batters in a game, Barker's 74 wins are the second fewest. Only Charlie Robertson, who pitched a perfecto with the White Sox in 1922 during a career in which he won 49 times, compiled fewer victories than Barker. Barker's career winning percentage of .493 is the third worst of the perfect game pitchers, ahead of only Robertson (.380) and Larsen (.471). Barker's career ERA of 4.34 was exceeded only by Robertson's 4.44.

Ron Hassey is the only catcher in major league history to catch two perfect games. The other one was thrown by Dennis Martinez with the Expos in 1991.

May 17 — The Indians sweep the Blue Jays 1–0 and 2–1 in ten innings during a double header at Municipal Stadium. Rick Waits (eight innings) and Sid Monge (one inning) combined on the shutout in game one. A single by Miguel Dilone drove in the lone run. The winning run of the second contest scored on a triple by Rick Manning and a single from Jorge Orta.

The wins gave the Indians a record of 18–9 on the 1981 season. Cleveland spent 22 days in first place during the month of May.

June 8 — In the first round of the amateur draft, the Indians select outfielder George Alpert from Livingston High School in Livingston, New Jersey.

Alpert was a bust, never advancing beyond the Class A level. The only future major leaguers drafted and signed by the Indians in 1982 were Neal Heaton (second round) and Dwight Taylor (seventh round).

June 10 — In the last game before the players' strike, the Indians lose 4–3 to the Angels in Anaheim.

June 12 — Major League baseball players begin a strike that lasts 50 days and wipes out nearly two months of the 1981 season. The strike reduced the Indians schedule to 103 games. The labor action also postponed the All-Star Game, scheduled for Cleveland (see July 14, 1981).

July 14 — Although the strike is still on with no end in sight, there is action at Municipal Stadium on the night of the scheduled All-Star Game. A couple of television producers from WKYC-TV played a Strat-O-Matic Game at home plate. One wore a Philadelphia Phillies jersey and the other wore a shirt of the Kansas City Royals, representing All-Star managers Dallas Green and Jim Frey. The Baseball Bug, the Indians mascot, was on hand to perform. Rocco Scotti, who was to sing before the real game, belted out the Canadian and American national anthems. The National League won the "game" 15–2. It took 61 minutes to complete (see August 9, 1981).

July 31 — Two days after Prince Charles marries Lady Diana Spencer in London, the players and owners hammer out an agreement to end the strike.

August 6 — The owners vote to split the 1981 pennant race with the winners of the two halves of the season to compete in an extra round of playoffs for the division title.

August 9 — The All-Star Game is played before 72,086 at Municipal Stadium on the night prior to the resumption of the second half of the season. Vice-President George Bush threw out the ceremonial first pitch. The National League won 5–4. The AL took a 1–0 lead in the second inning on a home run by Ken Singleton off Tom Seaver. The NL came back with homers by Gary Carter in the fifth and Dave Parker in the sixth for a 2–1 advantage. The American Leaguers surged ahead with three runs in the bottom of the sixth, but the Nationals win with a tally in the seventh, on Carter's second homer, and two in the eighth on Mike Schmidt's home run with a man on base. Len Barker thrilled the home crowd by pitching scoreless ball in the third and fourth innings. Notorious stripper Morganna Roberts, also known as "The Kissing Bandit," provided a diversion by running onto the field to kiss AL starting pitcher Jack Morris. Future Hall of Famers on the rosters of the two clubs were George Brett, Rod Carew, Steve Carlton, Gary Carter, Rollie Fingers, Carlton Fisk, Reggie Jackson, Eddie Murray, Nolan Ryan, Tom Seaver, Ozzie Smith, Bruce Sutter, and Dave Winfield. Other prominent players included Pete Rose, Andre Dawson, Goose Gossage, Dave Parker, Tim Raines, Jack Morris, Steve Garvey, Dave Concepcion, Dwight Evans, Ted Simmons, and Fernando Valenzuela.

Municipal Stadium is the only facility to host four All-Star Games. The previous games at the stadium were in 1935, 1954, and 1963. The ballparks in which three All-Star Games have been played include the first Comiskey Park in Chicago (1933, 1950, and 1983), Yankee Stadium in New York (1939, 1960, and 1977), the first Busch Stadium in St. Louis (1940, 1948, and 1957), Tiger Stadium in Detroit (1941, 1951, and 1971), Fenway Park in Boston (1946, 1961, and 1999) and Wrigley Field in Chicago (1947, 1962, and 1990).

AUGUST 20 Down 5–1 against the Mariners in Seattle, the Indians rally with a run in the seventh inning, three in the ninth, and one in the 14th to win 6–5. Dan Spillner (seven innings) and Mike Stanton (5⅔ innings) combined for 12⅔ innings of shutout relief. Alan Bannister drove in the winning run with a single.

AUGUST 23 A 6–3 win over the Angels in Anaheim is interrupted by an 11-minute brawl. John Denny hit Dan Ford with a pitch in the third inning. Ford started toward the mound and was restrained by the umpires, but Rod Carew raced out of the California dugout toward Denny and players from both benches ran onto the field. A shoving match followed in which Don Baylor grabbed Denny and was ejected. After order was restored, Ford and Denny resumed yelling at each other, and both benches and bullpens rushed onto the field again. Andre Thornton sprained his wrist trying to act as peacemaker during the melee and didn't play again for two weeks.

AUGUST 25 Len Barker pitches a shutout and Duane Kuiper drives in both runs for a 2–0 win over the Athletics in Oakland. Kuiper had RBI-singles in the seventh and ninth innings.

AUGUST 26 The Indians score seven runs in the third inning to build a 12–0 lead, and thrash the Mariners 12–2 at Municipal Stadium.

AUGUST 28 John Denny pitches the Indians to a 1–0 win over the Mariners at Municipal Stadium. Rick Manning drove in the lone run with a walk-off single in the ninth inning.

AUGUST 30 Trailing 11–7, the Indians erupt for ten runs in the eighth inning and whip the Mariners 17–11 at Municipal Stadium. The eighth inning rally was accomplished with four doubles, three singles and three walks. Chris Bando, who had four RBIs during the game, drove in the go-ahead tally with a ground out.

SEPTEMBER 2 The Indians sweep the Athletics 2–0 and 10–4 during a double header at Municipal Stadium. In the opener, Jerry Dybzinski drove in both runs with a single in the second inning. John Denny pitched his second consecutive shutout. Cleveland scored seven runs in the seventh inning of the second tilt.

September 6 John Denny pitches his third straight shutout, beating the Angels 2–0 in Anaheim.

Denny pitched 34 consecutive scoreless innings over four starts. He was 10–6 with a 3.15 ERA in 1981. It took him four seasons to collect his next three shutouts. Denny pitched one for the Phillies in 1983 and two in 1985.

November 14 The Indians trade Duane Kuiper to the Giants for Ed Whitson.

November 20 In a three-team deal, the Indians trade Bo Diaz to the Phillies for Lonnie Smith and Scott Munninghoff, and then swap Smith to the Cardinals for Lary Sorensen and Silvio Martinez.

December 9 The Indians trade Jorge Orta, Larry White, and Jack Fimple for Rick Sutcliffe and Jack Perconte.

The Indians made a good short-term transaction, as Sutcliffe led the AL in ERA in 1982, winning 14 games that season, and then won 17 games in 1983. Perconte was a throw in and added little to the team. Orta's best years were behind him, White pitched a total of 19 innings in the majors, and Fimple complied a lifetime batting average of .228 in less than 200 at-bats.

1982

Season in a Sentence

During spring training, Gabe Paul assures fans that the Indians are "not just another .500 team," but after compiling a 78–84 record, Dave Garcia is fired as manager.

Finish • Won • Lost • Pct • GB

Finish	Won	Lost	Pct	GB
Sixth (tie)	78	84	.481	17.0

Manager

Dave Garcia

Stats

	Indians	AL	Rank
Batting Avg:	.262	.264	8
On-Base Pct:	.343	.331	3
Slugging Pct:	.373	.402	12
Home Runs:	109		13
Stolen Bases:	151		2
ERA:	4.12	4.07	11
Fielding Avg:	.980	.980	7
Runs Scored:	683		10
Runs Allowed:	748		11

Starting Line-up

Ron Hassey, c
Mike Hargrove, 1b
Alan Bannister, lf-2b
Toby Harrah, 3b
Mike Fischlin, ss
Miguel Dilone, lf
Rick Manning, cf
Von Hayes, rf
Andre Thornton, dh
Larry Milbourne, 2b
Jack Perconte, 2b
Jerry Dybzinski, ss
Chris Bando, c

Pitchers

Len Barker, sp
Rick Sutcliffe, sp
Lary Sorensen, sp
John Denny, sp
Rick Waits, sp
Dan Spillner, rp
Ed Glynn, rp
Ed Whitson, rp
Tom Brennan, rp
Bud Anderson, rp

Attendance

1,044,021 (13th in AL)

Club Leaders

Batting Avg:	Toby Harrah	.304
On-Base Pct:	Toby Harrah	.398
Slugging Pct:	Toby Harrah	.490
Home Runs:	Andre Thornton	32
RBIs:	Andre Thornton	116
Runs:	Toby Harrah	100
Stolen Bases:	Miguel Dilone	33
Wins:	Len Barker	15
Strikeouts:	Len Barker	187
ERA:	Rick Sutcliffe	2.96
Saves:	Dan Spillner	21

FEBRUARY 16 The Indians trade Sid Monge to the Phillies for Bake McBride.

The acquisition of McBride was a gamble because of a history of knee problems. After 27 games in 1982, he had batting average of .365 but missed the rest of the year with a serious eye infection. He developed conjunctivitis, and then contracted a staph infection on top of the original ailment.

APRIL 6 Snow postpones the season opener against the Brewers in Milwaukee. Snow also postponed games against the Brewers on April 7 and 8.

APRIL 10 The Indians finally get the 1982 season underway and lose 8–3 to the Rangers before 62,443 at Municipal Stadium on a day in which the temperature is 35 degrees. Toby Harrah homered for the Indians. Bake McBride, in his Cleveland debut, collected three hits in four at-bats. Buddy Bell clubbed two home runs for Texas.

Indians games were broadcast on pay television for the first time in 1982 over Ten TV. The play-by-play and commentary were provided by Joe Castiglione and Bob Feller. Ten TV telecast the Indians games for only a season. In 1983, Feller, Denny Schreiner, and Jack Corrigan announced the games over Sports Extra, another venture that lasted only one year.

APRIL 11 The Indians pound the Rangers 13–1 at Municipal Stadium.

APRIL 27 Toby Harrah's 14-game hitting streak comes to an end when he is ejected for using an illegal bat during an 11-inning, 7–4 loss to the Mariners at Municipal Stadium. Harrah's bats were delivered with a length of 35 inches. He had specified 34½-inch bats, and instead of re-ordering, sawed a half-inch off the handle in violation of the rules.

Harrah had an average of .387 on June 18 and finished the year with a .304 average along with 25 homers, 78 RBIs, and 100 runs scored in 1982. He played in every game for the third straight year.

MAY 7 The Indians weather a five-run first inning by the Athletics and win 15–6 in Oakland. Cleveland took a 7–5 lead with seven runs in the fourth inning. Ed Whitson pitched $4^{2}/_{3}$ innings of scoreless relief with six strikeouts.

MAY 9 The Indians score eight runs in the ninth inning to cap a 14–2 win over the Athletics in Oakland.

MAY 11 The Indians outlast the Mariners 5–4 in 14 innings at the Kingdome. The Indians had a seemingly safe lead until Seattle scored two runs in the eighth inning and two more in the ninth. The winning run scored on a walk and stolen base by Alan Bannister and a single from Von Hayes.

MAY 18 A walk-off homer by Toby Harrah beats the Blue Jays 6–5 at Municipal Stadium.

MAY 23 The Indians win 6–4 in a 14-inning struggle against the White Sox at Comiskey Park. Ron Hassey broke the 4–4 tie with an RBI-double, then scored on a single by Rick Manning.

MAY 24 The Indians play at the Metrodome in Minneapolis for the first time, and win 9–2 over the Twins. It was also the Indians first game ever in a domed stadium.

JUNE 3 In the first round of the amateur draft, the Indians select pitcher Mark Snyder from Beardon High School in Knoxville, Tennessee.

The 1982 draft was one of the worst in club history. Snyder never advanced past the Class A level. The only future major leaguers drafted and signed by the Indians were Jim Wilson (second round) and Jeff Barkley (13th round). The two combined played in only 33 major league games.

JUNE 4 The Indians run their winning streak to 11 games with a 6–3 decision over the Blue Jays in Toronto.

The 11-game winning streak in 1982 was the longest by the Indians since 1951 and hasn't been matched or exceeded since. The streak gave Cleveland a 26–23 record, but the club was just 52–61 the rest of the way.

Len Barker made team—and major league—history in 1981 when he threw a perfect game. In 1982 he notched 15 wins. In this photo he is congratulated by teammate Jack Perconte after one of those victories.

JUNE 9 After a 2–1 loss to the Tigers in the first game of a double header in Detroit, the second contest is suspended after 14 innings because of the American League's 1:00 a.m. curfew with the score tied at 3–3. The tilt was completed on September 24 (see September 24, 1982).

JUNE 20 Ron Hassey's walk-off single in the 14th inning beats the Red Sox 5–4 at Municipal Stadium. Dan Spillner pitched four innings of scoreless relief.

Spillner had a streak of 28⅔ consecutive scoreless innings in May and June.

JULY 16 The Angels score ten runs in the fifth inning off John Denny and Ed Whitson and beat the Indians 15–0 at Municipal Stadium.

JULY 18 A two-run, pinch-double by Bill Nahorodny beats the Angels 5–4 at Municipal Stadium. The rally started with two out and no one on base. Ron Hassey and Karl Pagel walked before Nahorodny's double.

JULY 29 Andre Thornton breaks a 1–1 tie in the 12th inning with a grand slam off Jim Slaton for a 5–1 win over the Brewers in Milwaukee.

Thornton batted .273 with 32 homers and 116 RBIs in 1982.

AUGUST 24 The Indians score 13 runs in the first four innings and beat the White Sox 14–7 at Municipal Stadium.

SEPTEMBER 2 A three-run homer by Von Hayes off Don Sutton in the ninth inning beats the Brewers 4–2 in the second game of a double header at County Stadium. Milwaukee won the opener 2–1.

SEPTEMBER 12 The Indians trade John Denny to the Phillies for Wil Culmer, Jerry Reed, and Roy Smith.

Denny was swapped for three minor leaguers. In 1983, he won the National League Most Valuable Player Award with a 19–6 record and a 2.37 ERA. The trio all saw action with the Tribe but none had much success. In 19 at-bats, Culmer hit .105, Reed went 4–6 with 8 saves over three seasons, and Smith compiled a 6–9 record in two seasons with the team.

SEPTEMBER 13 Ron Hassey hits a home run in the 11th inning to beat the Red Sox 4–3 in the second game of a double header in Boston. The Indians also won the opener 3–1.

SEPTEMBER 19 The Indians score four runs in the ninth inning to defeat the Yankees 9–8 in the first game of a double header in New York. Mike Hargrove hit a two-run single and scored on a double by Larry Milbourne, who crossed the plate with the winning run on an error. The Tribe lost the opener 6–2.

SEPTEMBER 24 The Indians and Tigers finish the game of June 9, which was suspended at the end of the 14th inning with the score 3–3. Play was resumed in the top of the 15th, and after four more innings the Tigers won 4–3 in the 18th on a wild pitch from Ed Glynn with the bases loaded. Cleveland won the regularly scheduled contest 6–2.

OCTOBER 1 Carmen Castillo hits a walk-off homer in the ninth inning to beat the Tigers 3–2 in the first game of a double header at Municipal Stadium. Len Barker struck out 13 batters. Detroit won the second contest 4–2.

The 78–84 finish led to the resignation of Dave Garcia as manager. Gabe Paul had predicted in spring training that the Indians would win 90 games and compete for the AL pennant, but the lofty expectations went out the window with a 15–23 start. Garcia never managed another major league team.

NOVEMBER 18 The Indians hire Mike Ferraro as manager and trade Ed Whitson to the Padres for Juan Eichelberger and Broderick Perkins.

Ferraro was only 38-years-old. After a brief big league career as a third baseman that lasted 162 games over four seasons, Ferraro was a manager in the Yankees minor league system from 1974 through 1978. He was a coach with the Yanks from 1979 through 1982. Ferraro didn't last long as the Cleveland manager. Battling health problems (see February 9, 1983) and another slow start by the Indians, he was fired 100 games into the 1983 season (see July 31, 1983).

DECEMBER 9 The Indians trade Von Hayes to the Phillies for Manny Trillo, Julio Franco, George Vuckovich, Jerry Willard, and Jay Baller.

Despite receiving five players for one, the Indians just about broke even on the deal. Hayes had a solid career with the Phillies that included appearances in a World Series and an All-Star Game. Franco hit .295 over six seasons with the Indians as a starting shortstop and second baseman. Trillo represented the Indians in the 1983 All-Star Game but was a free agent at the end of the 1983 season and said he had no intention of returning to Cleveland. The Indians traded him to the Expos in August 1983. None of the other three players acquired in the deal made any significant long-term contributions to the success of the Indians.

1983

Season in a Sentence

New manager Mike Ferraro undergoes surgery for a cancerous kidney in February and is fired in July as the Indians finish last in the AL East and draw fewer fans than any club in the majors.

Finish • Won • Lost • Pct • GB

Finish	Won	Lost	Pct	GB
Seventh	70	92	.432	28.0

Managers

Mike Ferraro (40–60) and Pat Corrales (30–32)

Stats

Stats	Indians	AL	Rank
Batting Avg:	.265	.266	8
On-Base Pct:	.341	.331	2
Slugging Pct:	.369	.401	12
Home Runs:	86		14
Stolen Bases:	109		7
ERA:	4.43	4.06	13
Fielding Avg:	.981	.979	6
Runs Scored:	704		11
Runs Allowed:	785		13

Starting Line-up

Ron Hassey, c
Mike Hargrove, 1b
Manny Trillo, 2b
Toby Harrah, 3b
Julio Franco, ss
Pat Tabler, lf
Gorman Thomas, cf
George Vuckovich, rf
Andre Thornton, dh
Alan Bannister, lf-rf
Bake McBride, rf
Mike Fischlin, 2b
Rick Manning, cf
Broderick Perkins, 1b-rf-dh

Pitchers

Rick Sutcliffe, sp
Lary Sorensen, sp
Len Barker, sp
Bert Blyleven, sp
Juan Eichelberger, sp-rp
Dan Spillner, rp
Jamie Easterly, rp
Neal Heaton, rp-sp

Attendance

768,941 (14th in AL)

Club Leaders

Batting Avg:	Pat Tabler	.291
On-Base Pct:	Mike Hargrove	.388
Slugging Pct:	Andre Thornton	.439
Home Runs:	Gorman Thomas	17
	Andre Thornton	17
RBIs:	Julio Franco	80
Runs:	Toby Harrah	81
Stolen Bases:	Julio Franco	32
Wins:	Rick Sutcliffe	17
Strikeouts:	Rick Sutcliffe	160
ERA:	Bert Blyleven	3.91
Saves:	Dan Spillner	8

February 9 Manager Mike Ferraro undergoes surgery for the removal of a cancerous kidney. He was released from the hospital five days later and reported for the start of spring training in Tucson barely two weeks after the operation. Ferraro moved around the complex on a golf cart to minimize his fatigue.

February 20 The father of Toby Harrah dies in an auto accident near his home in Marion, Ohio. The tragedy occurred only a day after a fire caused $100,000 in damage to Toby's home in Fort Worth, Texas.

April 1 The Indians trade Jerry Dybzinski to the White Sox for Pat Tabler.

The Indians made an excellent deal, as Tabler was a regular at first base in Cleveland until he was traded to the Royals in June 1988. He made the AL All-Star team in 1986. Tabler was especially strong as a clutch hitter. While with the Indians, he collected 29 hits in 55 at-bats with the bases loaded, an average of .527.

April 4 In the season opener, the Indians defeat the Athletics 8–5 in Oakland. A home run by Andre Thornton in the first inning triggered the victory. Rick Sutcliffe was the winning pitcher. Toby Harrah collected four hits, including a double, in six at-bats. Rick Manning and Ron Hassey each had three hits.

In the first four games of the season, Thornton had nine hits in 13 at-bats.

April 8 In the home opener, the Indians break a 2–2 tie with six runs in the eighth inning and beat the Orioles 8–4 before 52,150 at Municipal Stadium. The eighth-inning rally was highlighted by a grand slam from George Vuckovich off Tippy Martinez.

Reggie Rucker was an announcer for Indians games over WUAB in 1983 and 1984. Rucker played wide receiver for the Browns from 1975 through 1981.

April 17 Toby Harrah misses a 6–1 loss to the Orioles in Baltimore due to a broken hand. The injury ended his streak of consecutive games played at 476.

April 19 Dan Spillner allows a pair of two-out, two-run homers in the ninth inning to Cliff Johnson and Lloyd Moseby resulting in a 9–7 loss to the Blue Jays in Toronto. The temperature was 32 degrees with a wind chill of 13 degrees above zero.

April 22 Bert Blyleven pitches a two-hitter to defeat the White Sox 5–1 at Municipal Stadium. Scott Fletcher collected both Chicago hits with a double in the third inning and a single in the sixth.

April 26 The Indians sue the Cleveland Stadium Corporation, which operates Municipal Stadium, for $1.25 million contending they are owed additional money from concessions. Paul was also angry over the increase in concessions prices, particularly the cost of a beer to $2 a cup. In addition, the Indians were upset about the poor condition of the playing field. Art Modell, president of both the stadium corporation and the Cleveland Browns, was not only livid about what he termed a “frivolous” legal action but that the Indians announced the suit on the day of the NFL draft.

May 8 The Indians score six runs in the sixth inning to take an 11–0 lead, and defeat the White Sox 13–6 in Chicago.

May 11 Rick Sutcliffe pitches a two-hitter to defeat the Royals 2–0 at Municipal Stadium. The only Kansas City hits were singles by Hal McRae in the second inning and Joe Simpson in the ninth.

May 24 The Indians score four runs in the ninth inning to beat the Mariners 6–4 in Seattle. Toby Harrah walked to force in the first run, and then Mike Hargrove hit a two-run single to put Cleveland into the lead.

May 31 During a 5–2 win over the Mariners, Andre Thornton hits the first home run by a Cleveland player at Municipal Stadium since April 9. The Indians went homerless in 17 straight games at the stadium.

June 6 In the first round of the amateur draft, the Indians select outfielder Dave Clark from Jackson State University.

Clark played his first four seasons with the Indians and played in a total of 905 big league games over 13 years, batting .264 with 62 homers. The only other future major leaguer drafted and signed by the Indians in 1983 was second rounder Andy Allanson.

On the same day, the Indians traded Rick Manning and Rick Waits to the Brewers for Gorman Thomas, Jamie Easterly, and Ernie Camacho. Neither Manning nor Waits had achieved the level of success the Indians had anticipated and both continued to have mediocre careers after leaving. Thomas smacked 17 homers in his partial season with the Tribe, while Camacho managed two 20-save seasons during five years with the club.

JUNE 18 The Indians outlast the Tigers 12–8 at Municipal Stadium.

JULY 14 A walk-off homer by Alan Bannister in the tenth inning beats the Royals 4–3 at Municipal Stadium.

JULY 16 The Indians score seven runs in the seventh inning to cap a 17–3 thrashing of the Royals at Municipal Stadium.

JULY 25 The season reaches a low point when the Indians trot off the field in the sixth, believing the inning is over after recording only the second out, and lose 6–1 to the Royals in Kansas City.

JULY 31 In their first game under new manager Pat Corrales, the Indians defeat the Rangers 16–11 in Arlington. The Tribe broke a 7–7 tie in the fifth inning on a three-run double by Toby Harrah, who collected five hits in five at-bats. Mike Hargrove scored five runs in five plate appearances.

Corrales replaced Mike Ferraro as manager with the club holding a 40–60 record. In 1984, Ferraro became a coach with the Royals under Dick Howser. When Howser was forced to step down in 1986 because of a brain tumor that eventually took his life, Ferraro served as interim manager, leading Kansas City to a 36–38 record. Ferraro returned to the Yankees as a coach from 1987 through 1991. Corrales was 42 years old when hired by the Indians. As a player, he was a back-up catcher with four National League clubs from 1964 through 1973. Corrales managed the Rangers in 1979 and 1980 to a 159–164 record before being fired. Hired by the Phillies, he led his new club to an 89–73 record in 1982. The Phils were 43–42 and in first place in 1983 when Corrales was dismissed on July 18 after bruising the egos of the club's superstars. General manager Paul Owens took over as manager and led the Phils to a 47–30 record the rest of the way and a spot in the World Series before losing to the Orioles. Corrales was hired by the Indians only 13 days after being canned by the Phillies. In three full seasons under Corrales, the Indians were 75–87 in 1984, plummeted to 60–102 in 1985, then rose to 84–78 in 1986. Sports Illustrated *predicted that the Indians would reach the World Series in 1987, but the club lost 10 of their first 11 games and Corrales was let go in July with a 31–56 record.*

AUGUST 17 The Indians send Manny Trillo to the Expos for Don Carter and cash.

AUGUST 24 The day after the Soviets shoot down a South Korean passenger plane, resulting in the deaths of 269 people, the Indians sweep the Athletics 1–0 and 4–2 at Municipal Stadium. Neal Heaton pitched the shutout in the opener.

AUGUST 25 The Indians trade Miguel Dilone to the White Sox for Rich Barnes.

AUGUST 28 The Indians trade Len Barker to the Braves for Brook Jacoby, Rick Behenna, cash, and a player to be named later. Brett Butler was transferred by the Braves to the Indians on October 21 to complete the deal.

The Indians pulled off a superb trade. Barker had a record of 12–21 over the remainder of his career. Butler was Cleveland's regular center fielder for four seasons before leaving the club as a free agent. Jacoby was the starting third baseman from 1984 through July 1991, when he was traded to the Athletics.

Mike Hargrove may have been practicing for his role as manager of the Indians when he argued with umpire Dallas Parks about the "safe" call on a pickoff play involving Seattle's Manny Castillo.

AUGUST 29 Indians chairman of the board Francis J. "Steve" O'Neill dies at the age of 83. A nephew, Patrick O'Neill, succeeded him as chairman.

The death of Steve O'Neill cast the future of the Indians in doubt. On September 15, Patrick revealed that the club was for sale. He said that a "sincere effort" would be made to keep the club in Cleveland, but hedged by stating: "In my judgment, anything can happen. The franchise may be lost."

SEPTEMBER 3 Trailing 5–3, the Indians explode for ten runs in the ninth inning and defeat the Athletics 13–6 in Oakland. A's manager Steve Boros set a major league record by using six pitchers in the inning. The ten runs scored on an RBI-double by Gorman Thomas, run-producing pinch-singles from Chris Bando and Andre Thornton, a three-run double by Toby Harrah, a two-run double by Pat Tabler, and a two-run homer from Thomas in his second turn at-bat in the rally.

SEPTEMBER 20 Mike Fischlin's grand slam in the second inning off Mike Caldwell gives the Indians a 6–0 lead, but the Brewers rally to win 11–7 at Municipal Stadium.

Fischlin hit only three homers in 941 at-bats during a ten-year major league career.

SEPTEMBER 21 Alan Bannister hits a pinch-hit grand slam off Rick Waits in the eighth inning, but the Indians lose 10–7 to the Brewers at Municipal Stadium.

The Indians drew only 768,911 fans in 1983, the lowest figure in the major leagues.

NOVEMBER 11 Donald Trump denies he will purchase the Indians.

The Indians board of directors entered into negotiations with Trump, but backed out over concerns that Trump would move the club out of Cleveland and because of his casino interests in Atlantic City. Edward DeBartolo, Sr. also expressed an interest in purchasing the Indians. DeBartolo was a 72-year-old shopping center magnate from Youngstown, Ohio, with an estimated worth of $500 million. He also owned the Pittsburgh Penguins of the National Hockey League. His son, Edward, Jr., owned the San Francisco 49ers. DeBartolo previously tried to purchase the Mariners, Athletics, and White Sox, but was blocked by Commissioner Bowie Kuhn and AL owners. His opponents expressed concern that DeBartolo would be an out-of-town owner, and that he owned race tracks and was therefore connected to gambling interests. It was a hypocritical stance, because other owners, including George Steinbrenner of the Yankees and John Galbreath of the Pirates both operated their clubs from a city other than where their ball club was located, and both had racing interests. There were also unfounded rumors that DeBartolo was connected to organized crime. After Kuhn was voted out of office in 1983, DeBartolo resumed his dream of owning a big league club by bidding for the Indians. As a native of nearby Youngstown, he believed the objections to his owning the team from outside of the city would be lifted, and he put his race tracks in the name of relatives. DeBartolo backed out, however, when it was made clear that American League owners would never approve of his owning the Indians. Meantime, the DeBartolo family built the 49ers into one of the National Football League's most enduring dynasties.

The family still owns the club. In Cleveland, the estate of Steve O'Neill, who died on August 29, 1983, continued to own the Indians until 1986.

DECEMBER 5 The Blue Jays select Kelly Gruber from the Indians in the Rule 5 draft.

The failure to protect Gruber on the 40-man roster was a huge mistake. He had a ten-year career as a third baseman and was named to two All-Star teams.

DECEMBER 7 The Indians trade Gorman Thomas and Jack Perconte to the Mariners for Tony Bernazard.

1984

Season in a Sentence

With yet another youth movement causing a massive roster upheaval, the Indians lose 33 of their first 50 games and finish the year with a 75–87 record.

Finish • Won • Lost • Pct • GB

Finish	Won	Lost	Pct	GB
Sixth	75	87	.463	29.0

Manager

Pat Corrales

Stats

Stats	Indians	AL	Rank
Batting Avg:	.265	.264	6
On-Base Pct:	.339	.329	4
Slugging Pct:	.384	.398	10
Home Runs:	123		10
Stolen Bases:	126		3
ERA:	4.26	3.99	12
Fielding Avg:	.977	.979	13
Runs Scored:	761		3
Runs Allowed:	766		12

Starting Line-up

Jerry Willard, c
Mike Hargrove, 1b
Tony Bernazard, 2b
Brook Jacoby, 3b
Julio Franco, ss
Pat Tabler, lf-1b-3b
Brett Butler, cf
George Vuckovich, rf
Andre Thornton, dh
Mel Hall, lf
Joe Carter, lf
Chris Bando, c
Carmen Castillo, rf

Pitchers

Bert Blyleven, sp
Neal Heaton, sp
Steve Comer, sp
Steve Farr, sp
Rick Sutcliffe, sp
Roy Smith, sp-rp
Don Schulze, sp
Ernie Camacho, rp
Mike Jeffcoat, rp
Tom Waddell, rp

Attendance

734,079 (14th in AL)

Club Leaders

Batting Avg:	Pat Tabler	.290
On-Base Pct:	Andre Thornton	.366
Slugging Pct:	Andre Thornton	.484
Home Runs:	Andre Thornton	33
RBIs:	Andre Thornton	99
Runs:	Brett Butler	108
Stolen Bases:	Brett Butler	52
Wins:	Bert Blyleven	19
Strikeouts:	Bert Blyleven	170
ERA:	Bert Blyleven	2.87
Saves:	Ernie Camacho	23

FEBRUARY 5 The Indians trade Toby Harrah and Rick Browne to the Yankees for George Frazier, Otis Nixon, and Guy Elston.

Harrah was 35, wanted to play on a pennant contender, and didn't fit into the Indians latest youth movement. His career continued a downward spiral, and he played only three more seasons, mostly as a reserve. Nixon was near the start of a 17-year big league career. He played four seasons with the Indians, and hit .214 in 365 at-bats with only three home runs, but swiped 57 bases in limited playing time.

APRIL 3 The Indians open the season with a 9–1 victory over the Rangers in Arlington. Cleveland scored six runs in the second inning. The big blow was a three-run double by Julio Franco. Pat Tabler collected four hits in four at-bats. Rick Sutcliffe pitched a complete game.

APRIL 14 In the home opener, the Indians win 8–2 over the Orioles before 57,114 at Municipal Stadium.

Pitcher Jamie Easterly started the season on the disabled list because of an injured back suffered when he was running backward on his property in Texas. Easterly was hurt after stepping in a hole and falling to the ground.

APRIL 28 The Indians play 19 innings and defeat the Tigers 8–4 in Detroit. The game was tied 3–3 in the second inning and there was no more scoring until both teams crossed the plate once in the tenth. In the 19th, the Indians loaded the bases on a single and errors by Detroit pitcher Glenn Abbott on two successive bunt attempts. Tony Bernazard broke the tie with a sacrifice fly. Mike Hargrove later cleared the sacks with a three-run double. The contest lasted five hours and 44 minutes. Relievers Mike Jeffcoat (two-thirds of an inning), George Frazier (2⅓ innings), Tom Waddell (five innings), and Luis Aponte (two innings) allowed only one hit over the last ten innings.

Waddell was born in Dundee, Scotland. He was one of two European-born players on the Indians roster in 1984. The other was Bert Blyleven, who was born in the Netherlands in the town of Zeist.

MAY 2 The Indians win their second marathon in less than a week with a 16-inning, 9–7 decision over the Orioles in Baltimore. Cleveland trailed 6–2 after five innings before rallying to send the contest into extra innings. A three-run homer by Brook Jacoby in the eighth tied the score 6–6, only to see the Orioles take the lead in their half of the inning. The Tribe tied the score in the ninth on a Tony Bernazard suicide squeeze. In the 16th, Jacoby's sacrifice fly was followed by an RBI-single from Ron Hassey. Andre Thornton tied a major league record by drawing six walks in eight plate appearances.

MAY 8 A $150 million property tax levy that would allow Cuyahoga County to build a domed stadium for both the Indians and Browns is soundly defeated by the voters, 277,845 to 147,211.

MAY 15 Pitching for the Red Sox against the Indians at Municipal Stadium, Roger Clemens makes his major league debut at the age of 21. He allowed five runs, four of them earned, and 11 hits in 5⅔ innings of a 7–5 Cleveland victory.

MAY 18 Andre Thornton hits a grand slam off Pete Ladd in the seventh inning of an 8–4 win over the Brewers in Milwaukee.

June 4 In the first round of the amateur draft, the Indians select shortstop Cory Snyder from Brigham Young University.

Converted into an outfielder, Snyder looked like a coming star when he arrived in Cleveland in 1986. He was an instant hit with his movie star good looks framed by long, shaggy blond hair. During his first three seasons, Snyder hit 73 homers in 1,504 at-bats, but in the remaining six years of his career he never matched that level of production. The only other future major leaguers drafted and signed by the Indians in 1984 were John Farrell (second round of the regular phase) and Mark Higgins (first round of the secondary phase).

June 12 In what proves to be his last game as an Indian, Rick Sutcliffe sparks a brawl during a 11–5 win over the Athletics in Oakland. Sutcliffe drilled Mike Heath with a fastball. Heath raced to the mound and dove at Sutcliffe's feet. Others piled on and peripheral skirmishes broke out all over the field. Carmen Castillo and Dave Kingman squared off near third base. Castillo took a classic boxer's pose and stung Kingman with three jabs to the face.

June 13 The Indians trade Rick Sutcliffe, Ron Hassey, and George Frazier to the Cubs for Joe Carter, Mel Hall, Don Schulze, and Darryl Banks. The trade was held up until June 19, however, because Cubs general manager Dallas Green neglected to place Carter and Hall on waivers, which at the time was required for inter-league deals in mid-season.

Sutcliffe was 16–1 with a 2.69 ERA with the Cubs in 1984 and helped the club reach the post-season for the first time since 1945. In the long run, the Indians came out ahead in the transaction, however, although they did so in spite of themselves. Gabe Paul actually preferred two other outfielders playing for the Cubs Iowa farm club, but the Cubs insisted he take Carter and Hall. Carter blossomed into a star and hit 151 home runs and stole 126 bases for the Indians over six seasons. In a four-season span from 1986 through 1989, he drove in 430 runs. Hall gave Cleveland several productive seasons.

June 20 The Indians trade Dan Spillner to the White Sox for Jim Siwy.

June 21 After months of speculation and fears that the Indians might leave for another city, David LeFevre announces he has arranged to buy the 53 percent of the stock held by the estate of Steve O'Neill for $16.5 million.

The ownership of the Indians had been in a state of flux since Steve O'Neill died in August 1983. The following January, Gabe Paul revealed that the financial firm of E. F. Hutton had made inquiries about purchasing the team. Several weeks later, LeFevre, a New York attorney, sold his ten percent holdings in the Houston Astros and began serious negotiations to buy the Indians. He was a native of Cleveland and the grandson of the late millionaire Cyrus Eaton, a Cleveland industrialist. The entire transaction was contingent upon LeFevre's ability to negotiate a lease with the Cleveland Stadium Corporation, operated by Browns owner Art Modell. Several minority owners filed suit, claiming they weren't being treated fairly. LeFevre also raised eyebrows in August when he announced he had a deal in place with Fidel Castro that would allow the Indians exclusive use of Cuban players, but Commissioner Bowie Kuhn blocked the idea.

Ensuing legal entanglements led LeFevre to withdraw his bid on November 14, and Steve O'Neill's heirs continued to operate the Indians until 1986.

JUNE 22 The Indians clobber the Mariners 13–3 in Seattle.

JUNE 23 Mike Hargrove belts a grand slam off Edwin Nunez in the fourth inning of an 11–4 victory over the Mariners in Seattle. The Indians scored six runs in the first inning as the first seven batters reached base.

JUNE 24 Bert Blyleven pitches a two-hitter to defeat the Mariners 5–0 at the Kingdome. The only Seattle hits were a double by Jim Presley in the fifth inning and a single by Jack Perconte in the eighth.

JUNE 27 After the Twins score in the top of the tenth inning, the Indians rebound with three in their half on a two-out, walk-off homer by Mel Hall to win 6–4 at Municipal Stadium.

JUNE 29 The Indians win a 13–12 slugfest in 13 innings over the Rangers at Municipal Stadium. Texas led 8–2 before Cleveland scored five times in the fifth. The Rangers took a 10–7 advantage in the sixth, before the Tribe surged ahead 11–10 with four tallies in the eighth, only to have the Rangers tie the game 11–11 in the ninth. Both teams scored in the 12th. Brook Jacoby drove in the winning run with a walk-off single in the 13th. The two clubs tied a major league record for most home runs in an inning with five in the fifth. Buddy Bell and Pete O'Brien homered for the Rangers. In the bottom of the inning, Mike Hargrove, Andre Thornton, and Mel Hall hit consecutive home runs.

JULY 1 Carmelo Castillo hits a grand slam off Joey McLaughlin in the fourth inning of a 13–5 win over the Rangers at Municipal Stadium.

JULY 3 Using a 23-hit barrage, the Indians rout the Royals 15–3 at Municipal Stadium.

JULY 13 Bert Blyleven pitches a one-hitter and beats the Rangers 5–0 at Arlington. The only Texas hit was a single by Larry Parrish in the fourth inning.

Blyleven was brilliant in 1984 with a 19–7 record, a 2.87 ERA, four shutouts, and 170 strikeouts in 245 innings.

JULY 15 A homer by Chris Bando in the 11th inning defeats the Rangers 5–4 in Arlington.

Throughout the 1960s, 1970s, and 1980s, the Indians lacked the money to properly build a farm system. By 1984, it was in tatters. The only four members of the club that season who were drafted and developed by the club were Bando, Neal Heaton, Mike Jeffcoat, and Carmen Castillo. Bando was one of those who looked like a coming star, only to prove to be mirage. A catcher, Bando hit .291 with 12 homers and 41 RBIs in 220 at-bats in 1984. A year later, he batted only .139 in 173 at-bats without hitting a single home run.

AUGUST 12 Joe Carter drives in all six runs of a 6–0 win over the Yankees at Municipal Stadium. Carter hit a two-run homer in the fifth inning and a grand slam in the sixth, both off Ron Guidry. Bert Blyleven pitched the shutout.

AUGUST 15 The Indians sweep the Blue Jays 16–1 and 4–3 at Municipal Stadium. The second game went 13 innings. Joe Carter drove in the winning run with a walk-off single.

AUGUST 16 The Indians score a run in the eighth inning and four in the ninth to stun the Blue Jays 6–5 at Municipal Stadium. A two-out, two-run, walk-off double by Andre Thornton provided the winning tallies.

AUGUST 19 The Indians sweep the Brewers 8–6 and 2–1 in a double header at Municipal Stadium with a pair of ninth-inning rallies. In the opener, a two-run walk-off homer by Mel Hall broke a 6–6 deadlock. In the second tilt, Hall singled and scored on a game-ending triple by Pat Tabler.

AUGUST 22 A seven-run first inning propels the Indians to a 13–3 win over the Blue Jays in Toronto. The triumph was Cleveland's eighth in a row.

SEPTEMBER 2 The Indians break a 3–3 tie with five runs in the eighth inning to beat the Red Sox 8–3 at Municipal Stadium. A grand slam by Julio Franco off John Henry Johnson climaxed the rally.

SEPTEMBER 7 The Indians erupt for nine runs in the fifth inning and rout the Athletics 13–2 at Municipal Stadium.

SEPTEMBER 8 Andre Thornton collects five hits in five at-bats during a 9–5 loss to the Athletics in Oakland.

SEPTEMBER 9 Down 5–0, the Indians score a run in the third inning, four in the sixth, and one in the seventh to defeat the Athletics 7–5 at Municipal Stadium.

SEPTEMBER 12 Bert Blyleven pitches a two-hitter and strikes out 12 to defeat the Angels 9–1 in Anaheim. The only California hits were a single by Rod Carew in the sixth inning and a homer from Brian Downing in the eighth.

Blyleven's given name was Rik Aalbert Blyleven.

SEPTEMBER 14 Brett Butler hits a grand slam off Chris Codiroli in the second inning of a 6–1 win over the Athletics in Oakland.

SEPTEMBER 25 Pat Tabler drives in six runs during a 13–5 victory over the Mariners at Municipal Stadium. Tabler collected a two-run double off Mark Langston in the second inning and a grand slam against Dave Beard in the fifth after Andre Thornton was intentionally walked to load the bases.

SEPTEMBER 26 Bert Blyleven pitches the Indians to a 1–0 win over the Mariners at Municipal Stadium. The lone run scored on a sacrifice fly by Jerry Willard in the fifth inning.

SEPTEMBER 27 A walk-off homer by Jamie Quirk in the ninth inning beats the Twins 4–3 at Municipal Stadium. Quirk entered the game as a catcher in the top of the ninth after starting backstop Jerry Willard was lifted for a pinch-hitter during Cleveland's three-run eighth, which tied the score.

The home run came during Quirk's only plate appearance in his only game as an Indian. He was sold to the Indians by the White Sox on September 24, and then was released on October 15. After leaving Cleveland, Quirk played eight more seasons in the majors as a reserve. Catching was his primary position, but Quirk played seven positions during his career.

SEPTEMBER 28 The Indians rally from a 10–0 deficit to defeat the Twins 11–10 at Municipal Stadium. The comeback started with two runs in the third inning on a home run by Joe Carter. Seven more tallies were added in the sixth, then one in the eighth, on another Carter homer, and one in the ninth. The winning run scored on walks to Pat Tabler and Jerry Willard and singles from Brett Butler and Mel Hall. The stunning losses inflicted on the Twins by the Indians on September 27 and 28 eliminated Minnesota from the AL West pennant race. The Twins entered the contest two games behind the Royals with three games to play.

NOVEMBER 29 Three weeks after Ronald Reagan wins a second term as president in an election race against Walter Mondale, Peter Bavasi is named president and CEO of the Indians.

Peter's father Buzzie Bavasi was general manager of the Dodgers from 1951 through 1968 and part-owner of the Padres from 1968 through 1977. Peter was an executive in San Diego under his father and was president of the Blue Jays from 1977 through 1981. At the time he was hired by the Indians, Bavasi was 42 years old and was a paid consultant for Tampa-St. Petersburg and Indianapolis interests in the efforts of those cities to obtain major league franchises. There were fears in Cleveland that Bavasi would move the Indians out of Cleveland, which led to an immediate distrust. He did nothing to quell those fears, alienating most of what was left of the Indians fan base after the club finished last in the majors in attendance the previous two seasons. With the hiring of Bavasi, Gabe Paul, the previous president and CEO, retired. In addition, general manager Phil Seghi was reassigned as a scout and Bob Quinn, the head of player development and scouting, was fired. Joe Klein became the new general manager on March 8, 1985. Klein had previously been general manager of the Rangers from 1982 to 1984. Bavasi headed the Indians organization during a tumultuous 26 months. He raised ticket prices and banned what he believed were derogatory banners at the stadium. Bavasi cited an American League rule that banned such signs, but the league denied such a rule existed. He closed the popular and modestly priced bleacher section for night games as an economy move and consistently blamed the negative comments in the media for the club's attendance problems. Bavasi also cut the number of available general admission seats, which were priced at $3.50, by 50 percent. Seats that were previously in the general admission sections were re-classified as reserved seats and box seats and were priced at $6.00 and $8.00. Almost all discounts and promotions were eliminated, including some that had been part of the schedule for more than 50 years such as Ladies' Days, Senior Citizens' Days, and Sandlot Little League Days. Many concession stands at Municipal Stadium were closed, leading to long lines at the few that were open. Bavasi also tried to break the unions of the club's employees, such as the ticket takers and ushers, an ill-advised move in a city in which industry was heavily unionized. On the field, the club lost 102 games in 1985, and then improved to 84–78 in 1986. Bavasi resigned on January 23, 1987, shortly after the Jacobs brothers purchased the club. Klein exited as general manager the following November.

December 22 The Indians sign Vern Ruhle, formerly with the Astros, as a free agent.

Ruhle came to the Indians following a season in which he posted a 1–9 record for Houston. He was 2–10 with Cleveland in 1985, his only year with the club.

1985

Season in a Sentence

The youth movement that was started the previous season fails to produce results as the Indians crash to 102 losses and draw the fewest number of fans in the majors for the third year in a row.

Finish • Won • Lost • Pct • GB

Finish	Won	Lost	Pct	GB
Seventh	60	102	.370	39.5

Manager

Pat Corrales

Stats

Stats	Indians	AL	Rank
Batting Avg:	.265	.261	4
On-Base Pct:	.327	.330	8
Slugging Pct:	.385	.406	12
Home Runs:	116		13
Stolen Bases:	132		3
ERA:	4.91	4.15	14
Fielding Avg:	.977	.979	12
Runs Scored:	729		8 (tie)
Runs Allowed:	861		14

Starting Line-up

Jerry Willard, c
Pat Tabler, 1b
Tony Bernazard, 2b
Brook Jacoby, 3b
Julio Franco, ss
Joe Carter, lf
Brett Butler, cf
George Vuckovich, rf
Andre Thornton, dh
Mike Hargrove, 1b
Carmen Castillo, rf
Chris Bando, c
Otis Nixon, lf-cf

Pitchers

Neal Heaton, sp
Bert Blyleven, sp
Don Schulze, sp
Rich Thompson, rp
Jamie Easterly, rp
Tom Waddell, rp
Vern Ruhle, rp-sp

Attendance

655,181 (14th in AL)

Club Leaders

Batting Avg:	Brett Butler	.311
On-Base Pct:	Brett Butler	.377
Slugging Pct:	Brett Butler	.431
Home Runs:	Andre Thornton	22
RBIs:	Julio Franco	90
Runs:	Brett Butler	106
Stolen Bases:	Brett Butler	47
Wins:	Bert Blyleven	9
	Neal Heaton	9
Strikeouts:	Bert Blyleven	129
ERA:	Bert Blyleven	3.26
Saves:	Tom Waddell	9

April 3 The Indians sign Doug Jones as a free agent following his release by the Brewers.

April 8 The Indians lose the season opener 5–4 to the Tigers at Tiger Stadium. Detroit scored two runs in the eighth inning to take the lead.

The announcing teams in 1985 were Herb Score and Steve Lamar on radio and Joe Tait and Jack Corrigan on TV.

April 13 In the home opener, the Indians lose 6–3 to the Yankees before 61,978 at Municipal Stadium.

The opener accounted for nearly ten percent of the Indians attendance in 1985. The club drew only 655,181, the lowest by the Indians franchise between 1973 and the present day.

APRIL 20 Julio Franco misses a game against the Yankees in New York. He said he was ill because he overslept at a friend's house in the Bronx and that the friend didn't have a phone. The Indians lost 5–2.

APRIL 27 Held to one hit through seven innings by Scott McGregor, the Indians explode for eight runs in the eighth inning and defeat the Orioles 10–4 in Baltimore.

MAY 7 Brook Jacoby hits a grand slam off Floyd Bannister in the first inning for a 4–0 lead, but the Indians lose 7–4 to the White Sox at Municipal Stadium.

On the same day, the Indians traded Mike Jeffcoat and Luis Quinones to the Giants for Johnnie LeMaster. The trade speaks volumes about what was wrong with the Cleveland franchise during this period. At the time he was acquired by the Indians, LeMaster was a 31-year-old shortstop who had played in 986 games, compiling a batting average of .225. He was hitless in 16 at-bats in 1985. To make room for LeMaster, the Indians moved Julio Franco from shortstop to second base, a position he had never played before. Second baseman Tony Bernazard, who was two years younger than LeMaster and was batting .318 in the young 1985 season, was benched. Eight games later, Franco was moved back to short and Bernazard was freed from the bench. The Indians then traded LeMaster to the Pirates on May 30 for Scott Bailes. During the 1985 season, LeMaster played 12 games for San Francisco, 11 for Cleveland, and 22 with Pittsburgh. All three clubs finished the season in last place and all three lost 100 or more games.

MAY 10 Mel Hall suffers a broken collarbone and a fractured pelvis in an auto accident in front of the Indians hotel in Arlington, Texas. Hall was out of action for the rest of the year.

JUNE 3 In the first round of the amateur draft, the Indians select pitcher Mike Poehl from the University of Texas.

Poehl never advanced beyond the Class AA level. The only future major leaguers drafted and signed by the Indians in 1985 were Scott Jordan (fourth round), Rod Nichols (fifth inning), and Luis Medina (ninth round).

JUNE 6 The Indians score seven runs in the eighth inning and win 9–1 over the Mariners at Municipal Stadium.

JUNE 8 Pat Tabler belts a grand slam off Jim Beattie in the first inning and later adds two run-scoring singles for a total of six RBIs to lead the Indians to a 12–8 triumph over the Mariners at Municipal Stadium. The home team scored six runs in the first for a 6–3 lead, but Seattle went ahead 8–7 before the Tribe erupted for five tallies in the eighth.

From the start of his career in 1981 through the 1988 season, Tabler collected 37 hits in 64 at-bats with the bases loaded for an astonishing batting average of .578.

JUNE 14 Bert Blyleven earns his 200th career victory with a 6–1 decision over the Athletics at Municipal Stadium.

June 25 Ruppert Jones of the Angels belts a walk-off grand slam off Neal Heaton in the 13th inning, resulting in a 7–3 Indians defeat at Anaheim.

July 7 The Indians break a 2–2 tie with eight runs in the seventh inning and defeat the White Sox 10–3 at Municipal Stadium.

July 21 A home run by Tony Bernazard in the tenth inning defeats the White Sox 4–3 in Chicago.

July 23 George Vuckovich hits a grand slam off Charlie Hough in the second inning to give the Indians a 4–1 lead, but the Rangers rally to win 8–4 in Arlington.

August 1 The Indians trade Bert Blyleven to the Twins for Jay Bell, Jim Weaver, Curt Wardle, and Rich Yett.

Blyleven's desire to pitch for a contending team led to the trade. He returned to Minnesota where he began his major league career in 1970, and made two starts for the Twins in the 1987 World Series, helping the franchise claim its first world championship with a victory over the Cardinals. After leaving Cleveland, Blyleven had a record of 83–72 before his career ended in 1992. In a strange coincidence, Jay Bell homered in his first big league at-bat while facing Blyleven (see September 29, 1986). Bell hit only .223 in three seasons with the Indians before being traded to Pittsburgh, where he blossomed into an All-Star (see March 25, 1989). None of the other three players acquired for Blyleven had significant big league careers.

August 6 The Indians game against the Yankees in New York is postponed by a strike called by the players. The August 7 contest between the same two clubs was also called off. The strike ended on August 8, and the two missed games were made up later with double headers.

August 15 Down 6–2, the Indians score a run in the eighth inning and four in the ninth to win 7–6 over the Tigers in Detroit. A three-run homer by Andre Thornton put Cleveland into the lead.

August 25 A two-run homer by George Vuckovich off Danny Darwin in the fifth inning provides the only two runs of a 2–0 win over the Brewers in the second game of a double header at Municipal Stadium. Ramon Romero (five innings) and Bryan Clark (four innings) combined on the shutout. The Indians also won the opener 6–2.

The win was only the second of two that Romero earned during his big league career, in which he posted a 2–3 record and a 6.29 ERA.

August 28 Julio Franco hits a grand slam off Mark Clear in the seventh inning of a 7–4 win over the Red Sox at Municipal Stadium.

Franco hit .288 with six homers and 90 RBIs in 1985.

August 29 The Red Sox pummel the Indians 17–2 at Municipal Stadium. Relief pitcher Rich Thompson allowed 11 runs in 3⅓ innings.

In July, the Indians had the bright idea to turn Thompson into a submarine pitcher like Dan Quisenberry. He had never used the motion previously, and trying to drastically alter his pitching mechanics at the age of 26 in the middle of a season led to ineffectiveness, and then to pain in his knees, back, and neck. In 1985, Thompson pitched in 80 innings over 57 games and had a 3–8 record and a 6.30 ERA.

SEPTEMBER 14 The Indians win 11–9 and lose 5–3 during a double header against the Twins at Municipal Stadium.

SEPTEMBER 16 The Indians score six runs in the ninth inning and defeat the Yankees 9–5 in New York. A two-run triple by Julio Franco put the Indians into the lead.

SEPTEMBER 17 The Indians rout the Athletics 15–8 at Municipal Stadium.

SEPTEMBER 28 Down 5–0, the Indians score five runs in the eighth inning and two in the ninth to beat the Angels 7–5 at Municipal Stadium. Jerry Willard ended the game with a two-run homer.

SEPTEMBER 29 The Indians lose their 100th game of 1985 by dropping a 9–3 decision to the Angels at Municipal Stadium.

OCTOBER 2 The Indians clobber the Mariners 12–2 at Municipal Stadium.

The Indians pitching staff finished the 1985 season with an earned run average of 4.91, the highest in the major leagues between 1962 and 1987.

DECEMBER 10 The Indians sell George Vuckovich to the Seibu Lions of the Japanese League.

DECEMBER 12 The Indians sign Tom Candiotti, most recently with the Brewers, as a free agent.

When signed by the Indians, Candiotti was a 28-years-old knuckleball pitcher with a 6–6 lifetime record and a 3.99 ERA. He found new life in Cleveland, posting a 16–12 record and a 3.57 ERA in 1986 while completing a league-high 17 games. Overall, Candiotti had a 72–65 record on some terrible Indians teams between 1986 and 1991.

1986

Season in a Sentence

After losing 102 games in 1985, the Indians more than double their attendance, win 84 games, and both score the most runs and allow the most runs in the American League.

Finish • Won • Lost • Pct • GB

Finish	Won	Lost	Pct	GB
Fifth	84	78	.519	11.5

Manager

Pat Corrales

Stats

Stats	Indians	AL	Rank
Batting Avg:	.284	.262	1
On-Base Pct:	.337	.330	5
Slugging Pct:	.430	.408	2
Home Runs:	157		10
Stolen Bases:	141		1
ERA:	4.58	4.18	12
Fielding Avg:	.975	.979	14
Runs Scored:	831		1
Runs Allowed:	841		14

Starting Line-up

Andy Allanson, c
Pat Tabler, 1b
Tony Bernazard, 2b
Brook Jacoby, 3b
Julio Franco, ss
Mel Hall, lf
Brett Butler, cf
Joe Carter, rf-lf-1b
Andre Thornton, dh
Cory Snyder, rf-ss
Chris Bando, c

Pitchers

Tom Candiotti, sp
Ken Schrom, sp
Phil Niekro, sp
Don Schulze, sp
Ernie Camacho, rp
Scott Bailes, rp

Attendance

1,471,805 (ninth in AL)

Club Leaders

Batting Avg:	Pat Tabler	.326
On-Base Pct:	Pat Tabler	.368
Slugging Pct:	Joe Carter	.514
Home Runs:	Joe Carter	29
RBIs:	Joe Carter	121
Runs:	Joe Carter	108
Stolen Bases:	Brett Butler	32
Wins:	Tom Candiotti	16
Strikeouts:	Tom Candiotti	167
ERA:	Tom Candiotti	3.57
Saves:	Ernie Camacho	20

January 7 — The Indians trade Roy Smith and Ramon Romero to the Twins for Ken Schrom.

February 25 — The Indians sign Jim Kern, most recently with the Brewers, as a free agent.

April 3 — The Indians acquire Phil Niekro from the Yankees on waivers.

A native of northeastern Ohio, Niekro came to the Indians at the age of 47 with a career record of 300–250. He was 16–8 in 1984 and 16–12 in 1985 for the Yanks. Niekro compiled an 18–22 in Cleveland before a trade to the Blue Jays on August 9, 1987.

April 7 — The Indians open the season with a 6–4 win over the Orioles in Baltimore. President Ronald Reagan threw out the ceremonial first pitch. The Indians led 5–0 after four innings. Ken Schrom was the starting and winning pitcher. In his major league debut, Andy Allanson collected three hits in four at-bats.

Allanson had 15 hits in his first 33 at-bats, but finished the year with a .225 batting average and only one home run in 101 games.

April 11 — In the home opener, the Indians lose 7–2 to the Tigers before 32,441 at Municipal Stadium.

May 2 — Two weeks after the United States bombs Libya in response to terrorist attacks, the Indians rally to win 7–5 in ten innings against the White Sox in Chicago. The Indians trailed 4–2 heading into the ninth before Joe Carter helped the club to a 5–4 advantage with a two-run double before scoring on an error. The Sox tied the contest in their half of the ninth. During the tenth, the Tribe scored twice on RBI-singles by Tony Bernazard and Chris Bando.

Carter led the American League in runs-batted-in in 1986 with 121. He also scored 108 runs, collected 200 hits, batted .302 ,and clubbed 29 homers.

May 7 — The Indians win their tenth game in a row with a 2–1 decision over the Royals at Municipal Stadium.

The ten-game winning streak gave the Indians a 17–8 record and put the club in first place. The Tribe lost nine of their next ten games, however, and never again returned to the top spot. By May 30, the Indians were 22–24. Cleveland reversed the slide and had a record of 51–41 on July 23, just five games behind the first-place Red Sox, but were unable to keep the pace and finished at 84–78, 11½ games behind Boston. Nonetheless, it was the closest the Indians had been to first place at the end of a season (excluding the 1981 strike-shortened campaign) since 1959. The 84 wins were the most since 1968. The 24-game turnaround from the 60–102 record posted in 1985 marked the best improvement in consecutive seasons in club history. The progress in the fortunes of the club stirred the Indians long-slumbering fan base. After drawing 655,181 in 1985, the team attracted 1,471,805 in 1986, the highest figure since 1959 and the second highest since 1951.

May 12 — The Rangers rout the Indians 19–2 at Municipal Stadium. Texas scored 18 of their runs over the last four innings. One fan threw a glass bottle at Jim Kern after he allowed eight runs in 1⅓ innings of relief.

May 13 — Pat Tabler hits a 3–2 pitch in the tenth inning for a walk-off homer, lifting the Indians to a 3–2 victory over the Rangers at Municipal Stadium.

Tabler hit .326 with six homers in 1986.

May 20 — The Indians score eight runs in the top of the first inning but lose 12–9 to the Brewers in Milwaukee.

May 23 — Don Schulze downs the Blue Jays 3–1 with a two-hitter before a crowd of 61,340 at Municipal Stadium. The only Toronto hits were a home run by George Bell and a single by Ernie Whitt, both in the second inning.

May 27 — The Red Sox beat the Indians 2–0 in a game at Municipal Stadium that is stopped by fog in the bottom of the sixth inning. The fog started filling the stadium in the third inning and became noticeably denser in the bottom of the fifth. The umpires halted play for 15 minutes after Cleveland coach Bobby Bonds hit a couple of test fly balls to right field to determine whether or not it was safe to continue the game.

Play resumed after the fog momentarily lifted, but visibility became limited again. Boston center fielder Tony Armas made a remarkable catch to save the game. With Cleveland runners on base, Mel Hall hit a shot into the fog. Armas saw it off the bat, guessed where it was going to land, ran back to the fence, and caught it out of sight of almost everyone in the ballpark, perhaps even the umpires. The game was stopped at 9:44 p.m. After a wait of 94 minutes, the contest was called. "That's what you get when you build a ballpark by the ocean," noted Red Sox pitcher Oil Can Boyd.

June 3 With the second overall pick in the amateur draft, the Indians select pitcher Greg Swindell from the University of Texas.

Swindell made his major league debut two months later (see August 24, 1986). He showed flashes of being a number one starter with an 18–14 record in 1988 and a 13–2 mark just after the All-Star break in 1989, but arm problems prevented him from realizing his great potential. Overall, he was 60–55 in six seasons in Cleveland and 123–122 during a 17-year big league career. Other future major leaguers drafted and signed by the Indians in 1986 included Jeff Shaw, Kevin Wickander, Joe Skalski, Rudy Seanez, Tommy Hinzo, Mike Walker, Jim Bruske, and Tom Lampkin. A sophomore at Cuyahoga Community College in Cleveland, Shaw was the first player chosen in the regular phase of the January draft. He played for the Indians from 1990 through 1992 and had a 4.90 ERA in 128⅔ innings. Shaw continued to struggle for several more years, but from 1997 through 2001 he saved 194 games and played in two All-Star Games for the Reds and Dodgers.

June 6 Ken Schrom pitches a two-hitter to defeat the Angels 3–0 at Municipal Stadium. The only California hits were singles by Gary Pettis in the first inning and Jack Howell in the second.

Schrom made the All-Star team and had a record of 11–2 on July 23. He won only nine more games over the remainder of his big league career, however, finishing the 1986 season with a record of 14–7, then compiling a 6–13 mark with a 6.50 ERA in 1987, his last year in the majors.

June 8 Julio Franco leaves the club prior to an 11–4 win over the Angels at Municipal Stadium. Franco left without telling anyone less than an hour before the first pitch. He returned the following day, saying he was upset because he had a fight with his wife, and he was suspended for two days without pay by the club.

Franco hit .306 with ten homers in 1986.

June 9 Joe Carter's 21-game hitting streak is stopped during a 6–5 win over the Athletics at Municipal Stadium.

June 10 The day after his 21-game hitting streak came to a halt, Joe Carter collects five hits during an 8–7 win over the Athletics at Municipal Stadium. In five at-bats, Carter hit three singles and two doubles. The Indians scored two runs in the ninth on an RBI-double by Carter and a walk-off single from Mel Hall.

June 16 Ernie Camacho, Don Schulze, Otis Nixon, and Bobby Bonds endure a scary boat trip on Lake Erie. The four were on a 23-foot inboard craft along with four other individuals, including the owner of the boat. After a full day of fishing, a sudden storm caused the lake to turn violent, and the boat stalled off the shore of Kelley's Island, about 50 miles west of Cleveland. The ordeal finally ended when the Coast Guard towed the boat to shore.

June 20 Joe Carter hits a grand slam in the sixth inning, but the Indians lose 9–8 to the Twins in Minneapolis.

On the same day, the Indians traded Neal Heaton to the Twins for John Butcher.

June 22 Phil Niekro holds the Twins hitless over the final eight innings for a two-hitter and a 4–1 Indians victory at the Metrodome. The only Minnesota hits were singles by Kirby Puckett and Kent Hrbek, both in the first inning.

At the age of 47, Niekro was 11–11 in 1986. He is the oldest pitcher in major league history to win at least ten games in a season.

July 1 The Indians hit five homers during a 9–0 win over the Athletics in Oakland. Mel Hall and Tony Bernazard both homered twice, and Brook Jacoby hit one. Bernazard's homers came from both sides of the plate. He went deep on lefty Rick Honeycutt and right-hander Dave Stewart.

A brawl erupted in the seventh inning. After Bernazard homered, Stewart's next pitch to Julio Franco was a high and tight fastball. Pat Corrales went to home plate umpire Derryl Cousins and demanded that the Oakland pitcher be ejected. Corrales yelled at Stewart, who motioned for the Indians manager to come out to the mound. Corrales, who was 45 years of age and had a brown belt in karate, obliged. Corrales, kicked at the 28-year-old Oakland hurler, who also was a practitioner of the martial arts. Stewart sent Corrales sprawling to the ground with a punch to the face. By that time, both benches had emptied and a ten-minute brawl ensued with altercations developing all over the diamond. A's slugger Dave Kingman unleashed several fierce punches before being knocked down by a blind-side, powerhouse punch from Joe Carter. Cleveland pitchers Ernie Camacho and Tom Candiotti were both treated in the clubhouse with injured hands.

July 2 Batting clean-up, Andre Thornton hits a grand slam off Bill Mooneyham with none out in the first inning, igniting the Indians to a 7–3 win over the Athletics in Oakland.

On the same day, it was announced that Cleveland businessmen Richard and David Jacobs had signed an agreement to purchase the Indians for $35.5 million, including the assumption of approximately $12 million in debts. The agreement was finalized on November 13, 1986, and approved by the AL owners on December 11. The franchise had been for sale since the death of Steve O'Neill three years earlier. The primary business of the Jacobs brothers was a real estate partnership that ranked as one of the largest shopping mall developers in the country. Representatives from Indianapolis, Denver, Tampa, and Orlando had submitted bids for the team, but club chairman of the board Patrick O'Neill, who was Steve's nephew, had insisted on selling to local owners. On the *organizational chart Richard Jacobs became the new chairman of the board and chief executive officer and older brother David was named vice chairman of the board (see January 23, 1987). After decades of frequent ownership changes among individuals without the finances to compete with other AL clubs, the Jacobs brothers, with strong loyalties to the city, gave the franchise renewed spirit and stability. It took several years for their plan to come to fruition, however. During the first seven years under the ownership of the Jacobs brothers, the Indians posted losing records. But by 1995, the Indians reached the World Series for the first time since 1954, and returned to the Fall Classic in 1997. The Jacobs brothers' greatest legacy is the ballpark that bears the family name. At a time when most politicians and city planners envisioned a multi-purpose stadium that would house both the Indians and Browns to replace aging Municipal Stadium, Richard and David Jacobs insisted on a smaller baseball-only facility. It became a reality in 1994 when the Tribe began playing at Jacobs Field.*

JULY 4 The Indians win 10–3 over the Royals before a holiday crowd of 73,303 at Municipal Stadium.

JULY 9 Julio Franco collects five singles in five at-bats during a 6–3 triumph over the White Sox in Chicago.

JULY 23 The Indians pull to within five games of the first-place Red Sox with a 7–2 win over the White Sox at Municipal Stadium.

The Indians hopes for the post-season were dashed with 27 losses in 43 games from July 24 through September 3. The club won 15 of their last 22 contests to achieve a winning season.

JULY 31 Trailing 7–1, the Indians rally to win 8–7 over the Tigers at Municipal Stadium with three runs in the fifth inning and four in the eighth.

AUGUST 3 The Indians and Yankees combine for 16 runs in the fifth inning of a 12–8 Cleveland defeat at Municipal Stadium. The Yanks scored ten runs in the top of the fifth for a 12–1 lead. and the Tribe countered with six in their half.

AUGUST 21 The Red Sox collect 24 hits and rout the Indians 23–5 at Municipal Stadium. The 24 runs was the most ever allowed by Cleveland in a single game. Boston shortstop Spike Owen tied a major league record by scoring six runs. Greg Swindell was the starting pitcher. It was his major league debut after making just three minor league appearances following his selection as the second overall pick in the 1986 amateur draft (see June 3, 1986). Swindell pitched two scoreless innings before surrendering six runs in the third and fourth innings. The Sox exploded for 12 runs in the sixth off Dickie Noles, Jose Roman, and Bryan Oelkers.

AUGUST 29 Joe Carter hits three homers and two singles in five at-bats to lead the Indians to a 7–3 win over the Red Sox in Boston. Carter homered off Tom Seaver in the third inning, Sammy Stewart in the seventh, and Bob Stanley in the ninth.

SEPTEMBER 4 The Indians clobber the Brewers 15–4 in Milwaukee. Cory Snyder drove in six runs with a pair of three-run homers in the first and eighth innings. Joe Carter hit a grand slam in the fourth off John Henry Johnson. It was the beginning of a three-game series at County Stadium in which the Indians would score 45 runs.

SEPTEMBER 5 The Indians score in seven of nine innings in beating the Brewers 13–5 in Milwaukee.

SEPTEMBER 6 The Indians reach double digits in runs for the third consecutive game with a 17–9 defeat of the Brewers in Milwaukee. Cleveland scored seven runs in the first inning. Joe Carter was the star of the game by scoring five runs, which tied an Indians record, along with five hits, four of them for extra bases. In six at-bats, Carter collected two homers, two doubles and a single. It was his third five-hit game of 1986. The first two were on June 10 and August 29.

The Indians led the American League in runs scored in 1986 with 831. On the other hand, the club allowed 841 runs, more than any other AL club. Municipal Stadium was not a factor in the run spree. In fact, the ballpark favored the pitchers. In 82 home games, there were 818 runs scored, 403 of them by the Indians. In the Indians 81 road games, there were 854 runs scored, with the Tribe accounting for 426.

SEPTEMBER 27 The Indians score in seven of nine innings and defeat the Mariners 12–4 in Seattle.

SEPTEMBER 28 Indians batters strike out 21 times against four Mariners pitchers, but win 5–4 in 12 innings in Seattle. Mark Langston fanned 14 batters in seven innings. Cory Snyder drove in the winning run with a single.

As a rookie in 1986, Snyder hit .272 with 24 homers in 103 games. On the negative side, he struck out 123 times while drawing only 16 walks.

SEPTEMBER 29 Jay Bell hits a home run on the first pitch thrown to him in his major league debut during a 6–5 loss to the Twins in Minneapolis. Bell's homer came in the third inning off Bert Blyleven. Oddly, Bell was one of three players traded by the Twins to the Indians in exchange for Blyleven on August 1, 1985. In addition, it was the 47th home run allowed by Blyleven in 1986, breaking the major league record of 46 set by Robin Roberts of the Phillies in 1956.

Bell is one of three Indians to homer in his first big league at-bat. The other two were Earl Averill in 1929 and Kevin Kouzmanoff in 2006. Bell is the only Cleveland batter to homer on the first pitch.

OCTOBER 3 Down 5–0, the Indians score five runs in the seventh inning and one in the ninth to win 6–5 over the Mariners at Municipal Stadium. A single by Chris Bando drove in the winning run.

There were seven AL East clubs during the 1970s. In a six-year span from 1981 through 1986, each of the six residing outside of Cleveland won division titles. The Yankees captured the division championship in 1981, the Brewers in 1982, the Orioles in 1983, the Tigers in 1984, the Blue Jays in 1985, and the Red Sox in 1986.

OCTOBER 4 Phil Niekro "steals" second base during a 6–5 win over the Mariners at Municipal Stadium. One of the few things that Niekro failed to accomplish during his 24-year big league career was to steal a base. The Indians led 5–2 in the eighth inning with Brook Jacoby on first when Jay Bell stepped out of the batter's box. Suddenly the 47-year-old Niekro burst out of the Indians dugout wearing a red bandanna over his face. He ran toward second and dove headfirst into the bag. Umpire Vic Voltaggio, who was in on the gag, signaled "safe." Niekro then pulled the base out of the ground and sprinted back to the dugout.

The improvement of the Indians from a 60–102 club in 1985 to an 84–78 record in 1986 brought a wave of optimism in Cleveland. The core of the club was still young and on the upside of their careers. At the end of the season, Joe Carter was 26, Brook Jacoby 26, Mel Hall 26, Julio Franco 25, and Cory Snyder 23.

1987

Season in a Sentence

After being called "the best team in the American League" by *Sports Illustrated* during spring training, the Indians lose 101 games.

Finish • Won • Lost • Pct • GB

Finish	Won	Lost	Pct	GB
Seventh	61	101	.377	37.0

Managers

Pat Corrales (31–56) and Doc Edwards (30–45)

Stats

	Indians	AL	Rank
Batting Avg:	.263	.265	7
On-Base Pct:	.324	.333	12
Slugging Pct:	.422	.425	9
Home Runs:	187		8
Stolen Bases:	140		3 (tie)
ERA:	5.28	4.46	14
Fielding Avg:	.975	.980	14
Runs Scored:	742		12
Runs Allowed:	957		14

Starting Line-up

Chris Bando, c
Joe Carter, 1b-lf
Tony Bernazard, 2b
Brook Jacoby, 3b
Julio Franco, ss
Mel Hall, lf
Brett Butler, cf
Cory Snyder, rf
Pat Tabler, dh-1b
Tommy Hinzo, 2b
Carmen Castillo, dh-rf

Pitchers

Tom Candiotti, sp
Ken Schrom, sp
Phil Niekro, sp
Greg Swindell, sp
Steve Carlton, sp
Doug Jones, rp
Scott Bailes, rp-sp
Rich Yett, sp-rp

Attendance

1,208,660 (12th in AL)

Club Leaders

Batting Avg:	Julio Franco	.319
On-Base Pct:	Brett Butler	.399
Slugging Pct:	Brook Jacoby	.541
Home Runs:	Cory Snyder	33
RBIs:	Joe Carter	106
Runs:	Brett Butler	91
Stolen Bases:	Brett Butler	33
Wins:	Three tied with	7
Strikeouts:	Tom Candiotti	111
ERA:	Tom Candiotti	4.78
Saves:	Doug Jones	8

January 23 Peter Bavasi resigns as president of the Indians. He had held the position since November 1984. The presidency was not filled for over nine months (see November 2, 1987).

February 9 The Indians sign 37-year-old Rick Dempsey, most recently with the Orioles, as a free agent.

Expected to stabilized the catching position and provide veteran leadership for the young pitching staff, Dempsey cost the Indians a first round draft choice and hit only .177 with one home run in 60 games.

April 4 The Indians sign Steve Carlton, most recently with the White Sox, as a free agent.

Carlton was 42 years old and had a lifetime record of 323–229 when signed by the Indians. He gave the club two 300-game winners in 1987 along with Phil Niekro. With the Indians, Carlton was 5–9 with a 5.37 ERA. The Indians traded both Carlton and Niekro during a ten-day span in July and August.

April 6 The Indians lose the opener 7–3 to the Blue Jays in Toronto. Pat Tabler and Cory Snyder hit home runs.

April 9 During a 14–3 win over the Blue Jays in Toronto, Phil Niekro and Steve Carlton become the first, and to date only, 300-game winners to pitch for the same team in the same game. Niekro, age 48, allowed three runs and seven hits in five innings. Carlton, age 42, hurled four shutout innings, surrendering four hits. Niekro won the 312th game of his career. Carlton entered the day with 323 victories. Cory Snyder was the batting star with a grand slam off Joe Johnson in the first inning.

After the victory, the Indians lost eight in a row to fall to 1–10 on the season. The club not only failed to reach the .500 mark in 1987, it never even reached a .400 winning percentage. The high point was a 9–14 record on May 1. A precipitous slide in offense was a key. The Indians led the AL in runs in 1986 with 831, but ranked 12th in runs in 1987 with 742.

April 10 In the home opener, the Indians lose 12–11 to the Orioles in ten innings before 64,540 at Municipal Stadium. Pat Tabler hit a home run.

The game was delayed for a few minutes in the first inning when a hot air balloon in the shape of Mickey Mouse's head floated over the field.

April 28 Ken Schrom pitches the Indians to a 1–0 win over the White Sox at Municipal Stadium. Mel Hall drove in the lone run of the game with a walk-off single in the ninth inning.

While a collegian, Schrom played quarterback at the University of Idaho.

April 29 Doug Frobel hits a pinch-hit, walk-off homer in the ninth inning to give the Indians a 6–5 win over the White Sox at Municipal Stadium. The home run was hit in Frobel's second at-bat as a member of the Indians.

Frobel had only four hits, two of them homers, in 40 at-bats with the Indians for a batting average of .100.

MAY 1 Mel Hall hits a two-run homer in the seventh inning off Mark Gubicza for the only runs of a 2–0 win over the Royals in Kansas City. Phil Niekro (7⅓ innings) and Rich Yett (1⅓ innings) combined on the shutout.

At the age of 48, Niekro completed two of his 22 starts with the Indians in 1987. He is the oldest pitcher in major league history with a complete game. In the 1987 season Niekro also became the oldest to both start at least 20 games in a season and to pitch at least 100 innings.

MAY 5 After the Indians score three runs in the top of the ninth inning for a 5–1 lead, the Rangers score four times in the bottom half and one in the tenth to win 6–5 at Arlington.

MAY 10 Greg Swindell strikes out 15 batters, including three in the ninth, and beats the Royals 4–2 at Municipal Stadium.

MAY 19 A two-run walk-off homer by Cory Snyder in the ninth inning defeats the Twins 4–3 at Municipal Stadium. He stepped to the plate with only six hits in his previous 68 at-bats. Snyder entered the game as a pinch-hitter in the sixth inning.

MAY 21 Cory Snyder hits three solo homers during a 6–3 win over the Twins at Municipal Stadium. He homered in the second and fourth innings off Bert Blyleven and in the eighth facing Mark Portugal.

MAY 28 Joe Carter hits three home runs, but the Indians lose 12–8 to the Red Sox in Boston. He smacked a three-run homer in the first off John Leister, and solo shots in the fifth against Tom Bolton and in the ninth facing Wes Gardner. Carter also singled during the contest.

Carter became the first player ever with two three-homer games at Fenway Park. He first accomplished the feat on August 29, 1986. The second player to hit three home runs in a game twice at Fenway was Mo Vaughn in 1996 and 1997.

JUNE 1 Phil and Joe Niekro become the record holders for most major league wins by brothers when Phil beats the Tigers 9–6 in Detroit. It was Phil's 314th victory. Joe, then pitching for the Twins, had 216 wins. The previous record holders were Gaylord and Jim Perry. Gaylord won 314 career games and Jim had 215, figures that were almost identical to those compiled by the Niekros.

The Niekro brothers would win nine more games between them. Phil finished his career with a record of 318–274. Joe was 221–204.

JUNE 2 The Indians have no first round choice in the amateur draft, but in the second round select outfielder Albert Belle from LSU. Other future major leaguers drafted and signed by the Indians in 1987 were Tom Kramer (fifth round), Steve Olin (16th round), and Beau Allred (25th round).

Many scouts believed Belle was among the most talented players in the draft, but he fell to the second round because of discipline problems at LSU. He was suspended by the school for the 1986 College World Series following a confrontation with a fan, and again near the end of the 1987 season. Belle's volatile behavior would continue after becoming a professional. In the minors, Belle was suspended twice during the 1988 season, and then during the following off-season, was kicked out of the Mexican Winter League. In 1990, he spent ten weeks in an alcoholism rehabilitation center. In separate incidents, he threw a baseball at a photographer and a fan at close range and tried to chase down a trick-or-treater with his car. Overall, Belle was suspended either by the league or the team five times in his eight major league seasons with the Indians. But, his batting numbers were outstanding. As an Indian, Belle hit .295 with a slugging percentage of .580 that ranks second all-time to Manny Ramirez. On the all-time club lists, Belle also stands second in home runs (242), ninth in extra base hits (481), and tenth in RBIs (751).

JUNE 4 The Indians sign Sammy Stewart, most recently with the Red Sox, as a free agent.

JUNE 5 Tom Candiotti walks ten batters in seven innings, but allows only three hits and is the winning pitcher in a 4–3 decision over the Athletics in Oakland.

JUNE 7 The Indians collect only eight hits but win 12–2 in Oakland with the help of seven errors by the Athletics.

JUNE 8 Solo homers by Cory Snyder in the fifth inning and Brook Jacoby in the eighth beat the Angels 2–0 in Anaheim. Both home runs were struck off Don Sutton in a match-up of 300-game winners. Phil Niekro (7⅓ innings) and Scott Bailes (1⅔ innings) combined on the shutout. It was Niekro's 315th career win. Sutton entered the contest with 312 victories.

JUNE 10 Tony Bernazard hits a grand slam off John Candelaria in the fifth inning, but the Indians lose 16–7 to the Angels in Anaheim.

JUNE 27 Mark McGwire hits three homers for the Athletics during a 13–3 victory over the Indians at Municipal Stadium.

JUNE 28 Mark McGwire hits two more home runs during a 10–0 Athletics win over the Indians at Municipal Stadium. The five homers in consecutive games tied a major league record.

JULY 3 Brook Jacoby hits three homers during a 14–9 loss to the White Sox at Municipal Stadium. Jacoby had solo homers off Bill Long in the first and third innings and another against Jim Winn in the eighth. Joe Carter and Cory Snyder also homered for Cleveland. The Tribe scored six runs in the eighth inning for a 9–8 lead, but the White Sox scored six times in the ninth.

Jacoby was one of three Indians with three homers in a game in 1987. The others were Snyder on May 21 and Carter on May 28. All three hit over 30 home runs during the season. Carter had 32 along with 106 RBIs. He also stole 31 bases to become the only player in club history with at least 30 homers and

30 steals in a season. Like Carter, Jacoby hit 32 homers in addition to batting .300. Snyder topped the club by hitting 33 home runs, but hit only .236 with an on base percentage of .273 and struck out 166 times. Julio Franco batted .319 to become the Indians batting average leader for the season.

JULY 5 The White Sox wallop the Indians 17–0 at Municipal Stadium.

JULY 6 Cory Snyder hits a grand slam off Steve Farr in the eighth inning to give the Indians a 9–7 win over the Royals at Municipal Stadium.

JULY 7 Both benches empty during a 6–4 win over the Royals at Municipal Stadium. In the third inning, Willie Wilson was decked by a Ken Schrom pitch. After flying out, Wilson rounded first base, raced to the mound, and tackled Schrom. After order was restored, Wilson was ejected. The game ended on a two-run, walk-off homer in the ninth inning by Joe Carter.

JULY 8 The bad blood between the Indians and Royals continues during a 9–8 Cleveland victory at Municipal Stadium. Brett Butler led off the Indians first inning, and the first two pitches from Kansas City starter Danny Jackson nearly struck the Cleveland hitter. Butler rushed the mound and landed punches to Jackson's face and neck before the two fell to the ground. Butler and Jackson were both ejected. The game ended on a two-run, walk-off double by Cory Snyder in the ninth inning.

Butler and Jackson were both suspended for three games because of the incident.

JULY 15 The Indians trade Tony Bernazard to the Athletics for Brian Dorsett and Darrel Akerfelds.

JULY 16 The Indians fire Pat Corrales as manager and hire Doc Edwards. The club had a 31–56 record at the time of the switch.

On October 1, 1986, Corrales was given a "perpetual contract" by the Indians, but the deal failed to last a full year. Overall, he had a record of 280–355 managing the Indians between 1983 and 1987. Corrales is the only individual to manage the Indians for 600 or more games between the terms of Al Lopez (1951–56) and Mike Hargrove (1991–99). Corrales became a coach for the Braves in 1990 and held the job until retiring at the end of the 2006 season. Edwards was a back-up catcher with four clubs from 1962 through 1970. He played for the Indians in 1962 and 1963 and managed in the minors for 13 seasons, including four in the Cleveland chain. He was a coach for the Indians from 1985 until hired as manager in 1987. He lasted as the skipper of the club until 1989.

JULY 21 In a bone-jarring collision more commonly seen in an NFL game, Royals outfielder Bo Jackson barrels into Indians catcher Rick Dempsey during a 3–2 Cleveland loss to the Indians in Kansas City. Jackson tried to score from third base on a grounder back to the pitcher. Dempsey went reeling backward several feet with his glove and mask flying in opposite directions. He managed to get the out by holding the ball in his right hand but didn't play again until September.

July 30 Cory Snyder breaks out of an 0-for-20 slump with a two-run, walk-off homer in the tenth inning to enable the Indians to defeat the Orioles 6–4 at Municipal Stadium.

July 31 The Indians trade Steve Carlton to the Twins for Jeff Perry.

August 3 Tom Candiotti pitches a one-hitter to beat the Yankees 2–0 at Municipal Stadium. Candiotti carried a no-hitter into the eighth inning before Mike Easler hit a bloop single with none out.

August 5 The Indians mash the Yankees 15–3 at Municipal Stadium.

August 6 Pinch-hitter Casey Parsons hits a grand slam off Mark Eichhorn in the sixth inning of a 14–5 win over the Blue Jays at Municipal Stadium.

The homer was the second of only two that Parsons hit in 53 at-bats during his brief career. The other home run was struck with the Mariners in 1981. Four days after his August 6, 1987, grand slam, Parsons was sent to the minors and never played in the major leagues again.

August 9 The Indians trade Phil Niekro to the Blue Jays for Darryl Landrum and Don Gordon.

Niekro wanted to pitch in a World Series, something he failed to do during his 24 seasons in the majors. The Blue Jays ended the 1987 campaign with a 96–66 record but finished second to the Tigers in the AL East. On the final day of the season, Niekro started for the Braves in Atlanta, where he pitched from 1964 through 1983. He allowed five runs in three innings in what was the final game of his career.

August 16 The Indians blank the Yankees 1–0 in New York. Rich Yett (7⅔ innings) and Doug Jones (1⅓ innings) combined on the shutout. The game's lone tally came in the eighth inning on a double by Cory Snyder.

August 18 Pat Tabler's bases loaded, walk-off single in the 12th inning beats the Brewers 9–8 at Municipal Stadium. Trailing 7–1, the Indians scored seven runs in the sixth inning before Milwaukee tied it with a tally in the eighth.

August 26 Paul Molitor's 39-game winning streak is stopped during a 1–0 Milwaukee win over the Indians in ten innings at Municipal Stadium. John Farrell held Molitor hitless in four at-bats. Farrell made his major league debut only eight days earlier.

Farrell had a 5–1 record as a rookie in 1987 and finished 14–10 in 1988, but was only 17–35 over the remainder of his career, which ended in 1996.

August 29 A walk-off homer by Cory Snyder in the ninth inning beats the Red Sox 2–1 in the second game of a double header at Municipal Stadium. Snyder had only six hits in his previous 55 at-bats. Tommy Hinzo's homer in the eighth tied the score 1–1. Rich Yett pitched a two-hitter, allowing only singles to Mike Greenwell in the second and seventh innings. Cleveland also won the opener 7–2.

September 2 Tom Candiotti holds the Tigers to one hit in Detroit, but walks seven and loses 2–1. The only Tiger hit was a single by Matt Nokes in the eighth inning.

September 5 The Indians score eight runs in the fourth inning of a 15–2 win over the Red Sox in Boston. Cleveland collected 22 hits in the contest. Tommy Hinzo had five of them on four singles and a double in six at-bats.

September 12 The Indians score two runs in the ninth inning to beat the Twins 5–4 at Municipal Stadium. Brook Jacoby tied the score with an RBI-triple, and then scored on a sacrifice fly by Cory Snyder.

September 26 The Indians outlast the Angels 11–10 in ten innings at Municipal Stadium.

October 2 The Indians lose their 100th game of 1987 by dropping a 10–4 decision to the Angels in Anaheim.

October 3 Wally Joyner hits three homers for the Angels during a 12–5 win over the Indians in Anaheim.

The pitching staff was awful all season, compiling an ERA of 5.28. It was the worst of any major league team since the 1956 Washington Senators had an earned run average of 5.33. No pitcher on the 1987 Indians won more than seven games. The team leaders in the category were Tom Candiotti (7–18), Phil Niekro (7–11) and Scott Bailes (7–8).

November 2 Hank Peters becomes president of the Indians in addition to serving as the club's general manager.

Peters was a veteran of more than 40 years in professional baseball. Working in the front offices of the Browns, Orioles, Athletics, and Indians. He had previously been the vice-president and director of player personnel for the Indians from 1966 through 1971. As general manager of the Orioles from 1975 through 1987, Peters led the club to American League pennants in 1979 and 1983 and the World Series title in 1983. He failed to bring any such success to Cleveland, however. The Indians didn't post a winning record before Peters retired in 1991. Some ill-advised trades, primarily the ones that sent Julio Franco to the Rangers and Jay Bell to the Pirates, set back the club's rebuilding efforts. Under Peters's watch, the Indians did a great job in the draft, however, selecting Manny Ramirez, Jim Thome, Brian Giles, David Bell, and Paul Byrd. Peters also picked up Sandy Alomar, Jr. and Carlos Baerga in trades.

December 1 Two weeks after the end of the six-month Congressional hearings investigating the Iran-Contra scandal, Brett Butler signs a contract as a free agent with the Giants.

After four seasons in Cleveland, Butler had enough of losing and sought greener pastures. He played another ten years in the majors, and during that period he led the NL three times in triples, twice in runs scored, once in hits, and once in walks. He played in a World Series and an All-Star Game. On the bright side, the Indians received an extra first round draft choice as a result of losing Butler, and used it to select Charles Nagy (see June 2, 1988).

1988

Season in a Sentence

A 36–22 start gives Indians fans false hope once again before reality bites back with another losing season.

Finish • Won • Lost • Pct • GB

Finish	Won	Lost	Pct	GB
Sixth	78	84	.481	11.0

Manager

Doc Edwards

Stats

Stats	Indians	AL	Rank
Batting Avg:	.261	.259	8
On-Base Pct:	.314	.324	12
Slugging Pct:	.387	.391	8
Home Runs:	134		8
Stolen Bases:	97		9
ERA:	4.16	3.97	11
Fielding Avg:	.980	.981	9
Runs Scored:	666		10
Runs Allowed:	731		8

Starting Line-up

Andy Allanson, c
Willie Upshaw, 1b
Julio Franco, 2b
Brook Jacoby, 3b
Jay Bell, ss
Mel Hall, lf
Joe Carter, cf
Cory Snyder, rf
Ron Kittle, dh
Ron Washington, ss

Pitchers

Greg Swindell, sp
Tom Candiotti, sp
John Farrell, sp
Scott Bailes, rp
Rich Yett, sp
Doug Jones, rp

Attendance

1,411,610 (12th in AL)

Club Leaders

Batting Avg:	Julio Franco	.303
On-Base Pct:	Julio Franco	.361
Slugging Pct:	Cory Snyder	.483
Home Runs:	Joe Carter	27
RBIs:	Joe Carter	98
Runs:	Julio Franco	88
Stolen Bases:	Joe Carter	27
Wins:	Greg Swindell	18
Strikeouts:	Greg Swindell	180
ERA:	Greg Swindell	3.20
Saves:	Doug Jones	37

February 9 The Indians sign Ron Kittle, most recently with the Yankees, and Dan Schatzeder, most recently with the Twins, as free agents.

February 14 Rick Dempsey signs a contract as a free agent with the Dodgers.

March 25 The Indians purchase Willie Upshaw from the Blue Jays.

April 4 The Indians lose the season opener 4–3 to the Rangers in Arlington. Julio Franco started the Cleveland baseball season by hitting a home run leading off the first inning. The Tribe had a 3–1 lead but allowed Texas to score two runs in the seventh inning and one in the eighth. Pete O'Brien hit two home runs for the Rangers.

After losing on Opening Day, the Indians won their next six games. By April 27, the club had a record of 16–4.

April 8 The Indians win 3–0 in the home opener against the Orioles before 53,738 at Municipal Stadium. All three runs scored in the seventh inning. Scott Bailes pitched a three-hit shutout.

April 9 The Indians collect 20 hits and rout the Orioles 12–1 at Municipal Stadium.

APRIL 16 A run-scoring single by Willie Upshaw in the 11th inning accounts for the lone run in a 1–0 victory over the Orioles in Baltimore. Greg Swindell (ten innings) and Doug Jones (one inning) combined on the shutout.

APRIL 22 Cory Snyder and Joe Carter both hit grand slams during an 11–0 win over the Twins in Minneapolis. Snyder hit his slam off Bert Blyleven in the first inning. Carter homered with the bases loaded in the eighth facing Keith Atherton.

After compiling an ERA of 5.28 in 1987, the Indians allowed only 30 runs in the first 15 games of the 1988 season. By the end of the season, the club's ERA was 4.16, an improvement by more than a run a game over the previous season, but Cleveland still ranked 11th in a 14-team league.

APRIL 26 Joe Carter hits two homers and drives in five runs during a 12–6 win over the Mariners at Municipal Stadium. Carter hit a two-run homer in the first inning and a three-run blast in the fourth.

MAY 2 Greg Swindell pitches a two-hitter and beats the Angels 3–0 at Municipal Stadium. The only California hits were a double by Johnny Ray and a single from Dick Schofield.

MAY 19 Cory Snyder hits a walk-off homer off Bobby Thigpen in the ninth inning for the lone tally of a 1–0 victory over the White Sox at Municipal Stadium. Greg Swindell pitched his second two-hitter of the young season. Kenny Williams collected both Chicago hits with a single in the seventh inning and a double in the ninth.

MAY 22 The Indians win a thrilling ten-inning, 8–7 decision over the Royals in Kansas City. A three-run homer by Julio Franco in the ninth tied the score 7–7. The winning run scored on a single by Ron Washington.

After moving from shortstop to second base, Franco hit .303 with ten home runs in 1988 along with putting together hitting streaks of 21 and 22 games.

MAY 28 At Municipal Stadium, Brewers pitcher Odell Jones holds the Indians hitless until Ron Washington singles with one out in the ninth. It was Jones's first major league start since 1981. Dan Plesac relieved Jones and allowed another single to Julio Franco before closing out a 2–0 Milwaukee victory.

MAY 30 During a 4–1 win over the Royals at Municipal Stadium, Greg Swindell pitches no-hit ball through six innings before allowing a run and three hits in seventh.

Swindell had a 10–1 record at the end of May in 1988. He failed to earn victory number 11 until July 24, however, losing eight decisions in between. Swindell finished the season with an 18–14 record, four shutouts, and a 3.20 ERA.

JUNE 2 In the first round of the amateur draft, the Indians select shortstop Mark Lewis from Hamilton High School in Hamilton, Ohio, and pitcher Charles Nagy from the University of Connecticut. Greg McMichael was picked in the seventh round.

Lewis was the second overall pick, while Nagy was drafted 17th. Though by no means a bust, Lewis failed to live up to the expectations of a number two pick in the draft. He lasted 11 seasons in the majors, four of them with the Indians, and hit .263 with 48 home runs. A member of the U.S. Olympic baseball team which won a gold medal in Seoul, Nagy reached the majors in 1990 and played 13 seasons for the Indians, in which he compiled a record of 129–103, had six seasons of 15 or more wins, and made three All-Star teams. From 1995 through 1999, Nagy was 80–53, including a stretch of 33 wins in 44 decisions. On the all-time Indians lists, he ranks tenth in wins, fifth in strikeouts (1,235), and sixth in games started (297). Among Cleveland pitchers since 1960, Nagy is first in victories, first in games started, second in innings, and second in strikeouts.

Greg Swindell proved to be a potent power pitcher in 1988, leading the Tribe's staff in a number of categories and producing the best season of his career.

JUNE 3 Julio Franco runs his hitting streak to 21 games during a 6–3 win over the Tigers in Detroit.

On the same day, the Indians traded Pat Tabler to the Royals for Bud Black.

JUNE 7 A two-run, walk-off homer by Cory Snyder lifts the Indians to a 5–3 win over the Blue Jays at Municipal Stadium.

JUNE 8 The Indians run their season record to 36–22 with a 4–2 triumph over the Blue Jays at Municipal Stadium.

The victory put the Indians in second place, one game behind the Yankees. Over the remainder of the season, the Cleveland club was 42–62.

June 19 Andy Allanson hits a grand slam off Tim Stoddard in the seventh inning of an 11–3 win over the Yankees at Municipal Stadium.

July 8 Bud Black ties a major league record by hitting three batters in the fourth inning of a 10–6 loss to the Angels at Municipal Stadium. Trailing 3–0 with a runner on base, Black struck Jack Howell above the right ear. Howell walked off the field under his own power and was taken to the hospital for precautionary X-rays. One out later, Black hit Devon White on the upper left arm, loading the bases. White started toward Black but was tackled by home plate umpire Larry Young as both benches cleared and some players wrestled near the mound. No one was ejected. Johnny Ray was next up, and a Black pitch grazed Ray's left leg. Black was then relieved by Jon Perlman.

July 15 Brook Jacoby hits a grand slam off Mike Jackson in the sixth inning for a 5–2 lead, but the Indians lose 8–5 to the Mariners in Seattle.

July 27 Julio Franco extends his hitting streak to 22 games with three doubles and five RBIs during a 12–2 thrashing of the Orioles at Municipal Stadium.

August 3 Indians catcher Ron Tingley hits a homer in his first at-bat with the Indians during an 8–3 loss to the Orioles in Baltimore.

The homer also came in Tingley's first major league at-bat since 1982 when he was a member of the Padres. It was also his only home run in 24 at-bats with the Indians. Tingley didn't homer again in the majors until 1991 when he played for the Angels.

August 28 A pinch-hit home run by Ron Kittle in the 11th inning beats the White Sox 5–4 in Chicago.

September 2 Julio Franco collects five hits in seven at-bats during a 13-inning, 4–3 win over the White Sox at Municipal Stadium. Franco's fifth hit set up the winning run. He singled with two out in the 13th, went to second on a balk, and scored on Andy Allanson's single.

September 4 Dave Clark hits a walk-off homer in the ninth inning to beat the White Sox 3–2 in the first game of a double header at Municipal Stadium. Chicago won the second tilt 5–2.

September 6 Greg Swindell pitches the Indians to a 1–0 win over the Yankees in New York. Ron Kittle accounted for the lone run with a homer off Al Leiter in the fourth inning.

September 7 Luis Medina hits his first two major league home runs during a 5–4 win over the Yankees in New York. Medina struck in the third and fourth innings off Tommy John.

Medina played three years in the majors, all with the Indians, and hit ten home runs in 150 at-bats, but struck out 60 times and batted only .207.

September 17 The Indians score eight runs in the fifth inning of a 12–3 win over the Blue Jays in Toronto. Jay Bell hit a pair of run-scoring singles in the big inning.

SEPTEMBER 24 A bad-hop single that should have been a routine ground out off the bat off Julio Franco with two out in the bottom of the ninth inning spoils the no-hit bid of Blue Jays pitcher Dave Stieb. It proved to be Cleveland's only hit of a 1–0 Toronto victory at Municipal Stadium.

In his next start against the Orioles in Toronto on September 30, Stieb incredibly was one out from a no-hitter again, only to allow a bloop single to Jim Traber. Stieb had to settle for his second straight one-hitter and a 4–0 win. Stieb finally got his no-hitter two years later while pitching for the Blue Jays against the Indians (see September 2, 1990).

OCTOBER 1 A homer by Luis Medina with one out in the eighth inning breaks up a no-hitter by Jeff Sellers of the Red Sox and provides the only run of a 1–0 Cleveland win at Municipal Stadium. The Indians finished the contest with two hits. John Farrell (eight innings) and Doug Jones (one inning) combined on the shutout.

Jones finished the season with 37 saves, shattering the club's previous record of 23 saves by Ernie Camacho in 1984. Entering the 1988 season, Jones was 30 years old and had yet to pitch a full season in the majors. He was a non-roster invitee to spring training but earned a job as the club's closer. Over a three-year stretch in Cleveland from 1988 through 1990, Jones made the All-Star team each season and compiled 112 saves with an ERA of 2.39. After a bad year in 1991, he was released by the Indians, but the decision proved to be premature. In a career that lasted until 2000, Jones appeared in two more All-Star games.

NOVEMBER 22 Two weeks after George Bush defeats Michael Dukakis in the presidential election, Ron Kittle signs a contract as a free agent with the White Sox.

DECEMBER 3 The Indians sign Jesse Orosco, most recently with the Dodgers, as a free agent.

Orosco finished his 24-year career in 2003 with a major league record 1,252 games pitched. He pitched in 175 games with the Indians over three seasons with a 3.11 ERA.

DECEMBER 6 The Rangers trade Julio Franco to the Rangers for Pete O'Brien, Jerry Browne, and Oddibe McDowell.

The Indians believed that Franco was too immature and was a bad influence in the clubhouse, but the club made a horrible trade. Franco had resisted the move from shortstop to second base, but he made the All-Star team as a second baseman in each of his first three seasons in Texas. In 1991, Franco won the AL batting title by hitting .341 with 201 hits. None of the three players received in exchange for Franco made a lasting impact in Cleveland. Franco returned to Cleveland to play for the Indians in 1996 and 1997.

1989

Season in a Sentence

Fielding the worst offense in the league, the Indians finish in one of the last two spots in the seven-team AL East for the 11th time in 12 years, leading to another change in managers.

Finish • Won • Lost • Pct • GB

Finish	Won	Lost	Pct	GB
Sixth	73	89	.451	16.0

Managers

Doc Edwards (65–78) and John Hart (8–11)

Stats

Stats	Indians	AL	Rank
Batting Avg:	.245	.261	13
On-Base Pct:	.310	.326	14
Slugging Pct:	.365	.384	13
Home Runs:	127		6 (tie)
Stolen Bases:	74		13
ERA:	3.65	3.88	5
Fielding Avg:	.981	.980	5
Runs Scored:	604		14
Runs Allowed:	654		5

Starting Line-up

Andy Allanson, c
Pete O'Brien, 1b
Jerry Browne, 2b
Brook Jacoby, 3b
Felix Fermin, ss
Dion James, lf
Joe Carter, cf-lf
Cory Snyder, rf
Dave Clark, dh
Oddibe McDowell, lf
Albert Belle, rf-lf
Brad Komminsk, cf

Pitchers

Tom Candiotti, sp
Bud Black, sp
Greg Swindell, sp
John Farrell, sp
Doug Jones, rp
Jesse Orosco, rp
Scott Bailes, rp-sp
Rich Yett, sp-rp

Attendance

1,285,542 (13th in AL)

Club Leaders

Batting Avg:	Jerry Browne	.299
On-Base Pct:	Jerry Browne	.370
Slugging Pct:	Joe Carter	.465
Home Runs:	Joe Carter	35
RBIs:	Joe Carter	106
Runs:	Joe Carter	84
Stolen Bases:	Jerry Browne	14
Wins:	Tom Candiotti	13
	Greg Swindell	13
Strikeouts:	John Farrell	132
ERA:	Tom Candiotti	3.10
Saves:	Doug Jones	32

MARCH 19 The Indians trade Mel Hall to the Yankees for Joel Skinner and Turner Ward.

MARCH 25 In one of the worst trades in franchise history, the Indians trade Jay Bell for Felix Fermin.

The Indians had grave doubts about Bell's abilities to play at the major league level, both offensively and defensively. In 350 at-bats, he had hit only .223 and made 19 errors in 110 games at shortstop. But Bell was only 23 and had plenty of room to grow. By the time his career ended in 2003, he had collected 1,963 hits with 195 home runs, developed into one of the best defensive shortstop in the game, and played in two All-Star games and a World Series. Fermin was the Indians starting shortstop for five years but never came close to posting Bell's numbers. Fermin was acquired largely for his defensive capabilities, but he twice led American League shortstops in errors. With the bat, he brought new meaning to the term "banjo hitter." In 2,107 at-bats with the Indians, Fermin had only 70 extra base hits and a slugging percentage of .298.

APRIL 3 Ten days after the Exxon Valdez spills oil into Alaska's Prince William Sound, the Indians win 2–1 over the Brewers in the season opener before 40,618 at

Municipal Stadium. Both Cleveland runs scored in the third inning on a double by Oddibe McDowell, who was making his Indians debut. Greg Swindell retired the first 12 batters to face him and went 8⅓ innings for the win.

In 1989, the uniform was modified to feature red, white, and blue shoulder stripes from the neck to sleeve ends and piping down the length of the uniform on both sides from the armpit to the bottom of the pants.

April 7 — A fluke three-run homer by Joe Carter in the first inning sparks a 4–2 win over the Yankees in New York. The ball popped out of the glove of Yankee center fielder Roberto Kelly and went over the fence at the 399-foot sign.

On the same day, the movie Major League *premiered in theaters. Starring Charlie Sheen as pitcher Ricky (Wild Thing) Vaughn, and written and directed by longtime Indians fan David Ward, the comedy centered on a fictional Indians owner played by Margaret Whitton. Her character was an ex-showgirl who inherited the team from her late husband and sought to get out of her franchise by organizing a team that was guaranteed to lose, then relocate it to Miami. The baseball scenes were filmed at the Indians training camp in Tucson, Arizona, and at County Stadium in Milwaukee, which doubled for Cleveland's Municipal Stadium. Brewers announcer Bob Uecker played Indians play-by-play man Harry Doyle and provided many of the laughs with his commentary. In the end, the ragtag team succeeded in winning the AL East, something the real Indians failed to accomplish during any of their 25 seasons in the division.* Major League *was followed by sequels released in 1994 and 1998.*

April 8 — The Indians thrash the Yankees 11–1 in New York.

The 1989 season was the first for Mike Hegan as an Indians broadcaster, teaming with Jack Corrigan on WUAB-TV. Prior to providing analysis for Tribe games on television, he spent 12 seasons as a television announcer for the Brewers. Hegan played in the majors from 1964 through 1977.

April 12 — Cory Snyder drives in six runs with a pair of two-run homers in the second and fourth innings and RBI singles in the eighth and ninth during a 10–6 win over the Red Sox in Boston.

May 1 — The Indians rout the Rangers 11–1 in Arlington.

May 4 — John Farrell carries a no-hitter into the ninth inning of a 3–1 win over the Royals at Municipal Stadium. Farrell started the ninth by walking Willie Wilson, then gave up a single to Kevin Seitzer that dropped inside the right field line. Doug Jones relieved Farrell and retired all three batters to face him, although Wilson scored on a ground out.

May 7 — After the Twins score three runs in the top of the ninth inning to tie the score 4–4, Dave Clark smacks a walk-off homer in the bottom half for a 5–4 Cleveland victory in the first game of a double header at Municipal Stadium. The Indians won the second tilt 12–1. Both benches cleared when Juan Berenguer sailed a pitch over the head of Indians catcher Joel Skinner.

May 17 The Indians play at Exhibition Stadium in Toronto for the last time and parlay a six-run third inning into a 6–3 victory.

The Indians were in first place at the end of the day, although with a record of only 18–19. The club stayed around the .500 mark for the first two-thirds of the season, which was good enough to stay in pennant contention in the weak AL East until early August. On August 4, Cleveland had a record of 54–54 and were only 1½ games behind the first place Orioles. In the end, the Tribe finished at 73–89 after losing 35 of their last 54 games. The club finished fifth in the AL in ERA, the highest finish by a Cleveland staff since 1975. On the other hand, the Indians scored the fewest runs in the league in 1989, just three seasons after leading the circuit in 1986.

May 28 Joe Carter's walk-off, squeeze bunt in the ninth inning scores Felix Fermin from third base for the lone run of a 1–0 victory over the Orioles at Municipal Stadium. Greg Swindell pitched the shutout.

June 4 Dave Stewart and Andy Allanson exchange blows during a bench-clearing brawl in the seventh inning of a 4–0 loss to the Athletics in Oakland. Allanson was hit by a Stewart pitch with two out and a man on in the seventh. The two exchanged words before being restrained by the umpires and teammates. At the conclusion of the inning, Stewart and Allanson fought between the mound and second base. Both were ejected.

June 5 In the first round of the amateur draft, the Indians select third baseman Calvin Murray from White High School in Dallas, Texas.

Murray chose not to sign with the Indians and attended the University of Texas instead. He was drafted in the first round by the Giants in 1992 and had a five-year career in the majors as an outfielder in which he batted .231 with eight homers. Although Murray was a wasted pick, the 1989 draft was one of the best in club history. Future major leaguers drafted and signed by the Indians that season were Jerry DiPoto (third round), Jesse Levis (fourth round), Alan Embree (fifth round), Curtis Leskanic (eighth round), Kelly Stinnett (eleventh round), Jim Thome (13th round), Brian Giles (17th round), Robert Person (25th round) and Bill Wertz (31st round). Thome and Giles were two of the best players ever taken in the draft by the Indians, although Giles became a star after being traded by the club. Thome played 13 seasons in Cleveland.

June 7 Greg Swindell pitches a two-hitter to beat the Angels 1–0 in Anaheim. Luis Medina provided the lone run of the game with a homer off Chuck Finley in the seventh inning. The only California hits were singles by Devon White in the fourth inning and Wally Joyner in the fifth.

June 16 Bud Black pitches the Indians to a 1–0 win over the Royals at Municipal Stadium. It was Black's first shutout since 1985. The game ended on a bases-loaded walk from Tom Gordon to Pete O'Brien with two out in the ninth.

June 24 In a bizarre 7–6 win over the Rangers in Arlington, the Indians fail to collect a single, double, or triple, but each of the club's six hits are home runs. Charlie Hough was the victim of five of Cleveland's six home runs. Joe Carter hit three homers off Hough, connecting in the fourth, sixth, and eighth innings. A two-run round-tripper by Andy Allanson broke a 3–3 tie in the seventh. The other Indians homers came from Pete O'Brien and Cory Snyder.

JULY 2 The Indians trade Oddibe McDowell to the Braves for Dion James.

JULY 18 Joe Carter hits two homers, but the Indians lose 5–5 in 11 innings to the Twins In Minneapolis.

JULY 19 Joe Carter hits three home runs during a 10–1 win over the Twins at Minneapolis. In the process, he tied a major league record for most homers in consecutive games with five. The five home runs came over a span of six official at-bats. It was also his second three-homer game in a span of 26 days. During the July 19 contest, Carter hit two-run homers against Allan Anderson in the first and third innings. After walking in the fifth, Carter smacked a solo homer off German Gonzalez in the eighth. Carter added a sacrifice fly in the ninth to give him six runs-batted-in on the day.

Carter had five career games in which he hit three home runs, four of which were with the Indians. Previously, he homered three times on August 29, 1986, May 28, 1987, and June 24, 1989. He also launched a three-home-run salvo while playing for the Blue Jays on August 23, 1993, which ironically came against the Indians. The major league record for most three-home run games in a career is six, set by Johnny Mize and tied by Sammy Sosa. The only other Indians with multiple three-home runs games are Hal Trosky (1934 and 1937), Albert Belle (1992 and 1995), Jim Thome (1994 and 2001), and Manny Ramirez (1998 and 1999).

JULY 20 Greg Swindell (seven innings), Jesse Orosco (one inning), and Doug Jones (one inning) combine on a two-hitter to defeat the Royals 4–0 in Kansas City. The only hits off Indians pitchers were a single by Bo Jackson in the second inning and a double by Danny Tartabull in the fifth.

JULY 22 The Indians clobber the Royals 17–5 in Kansas City. Dion James contributed four hits, including a homer and a double, and drove in five runs.

JULY 23 Brook Jacoby's RBI-double with two out in the ninth inning provides the lone run of a 1–0 victory over the Royals in Kansas City. Tom Candiotti (eight innings) and Doug Jones (one inning) combined on the shutout.

JULY 24 Albert Belle snaps a 3–3 tie with a grand slam off Eric Plunk in the seventh inning of a 7–3 win over the Yankees at Municipal Stadium.

AUGUST 2 Jerry Browne's homer off Chris Bosio in the third inning is the lone run of a 1–0 win over the Brewers in Milwaukee. Tom Candiotti (eight innings) and Jesse Orosco (one inning) combined on the shutout.

Coming from the Rangers in the Julio Franco trade, Browne hit .299 in his first season with the Indians.

AUGUST 22 Brad Komminsk hits a walk-off homer in the tenth inning for a 3–2 win over the Mariners at Municipal Stadium. Felix Fermin tied a major league record with four sacrifice hits during the game.

Fermin is one of only seven players in major league history with four sacrifice hits in a game, and the only one to accomplish the feat between 1919 and 2004.

AUGUST 29 Brad Komminsk hits a two-run walk-off homer in the ninth inning to defeat the Orioles 3–1 at Municipal Stadium. It was Komminsk's second walk-off homer in a span of eight days.

AUGUST 31 The Indians rout the Orioles 11–0 at Municipal Stadium. John Farrell pitched the shutout.

SEPTEMBER 6 The Indians trade Ron Tingley to the Angels for a player to be named later. Cleveland received Mark McLemore in exchange on August 17, 1990.

SEPTEMBER 12 Bud Black pitches the Indians to a 1–0 win over the Tigers at Municipal Stadium. Jerry Browne drove in the lone run of the game with a single in the eighth inning.

On the same day, the Indians fired Doc Edwards as manager and replaced him, on an interim basis, with John Hart. The club had a 65–78 record and had lost 24 of their previous 35 games. At the time of the switch in managers, Hart was serving as Cleveland's special assignment scout. Edwards never managed another big league club (see November 3, 1989).

SEPTEMBER 15 The Indians play at SkyDome in Toronto for the first time and lose 5–2 to the Blue Jays.

SEPTEMBER 21 The Indians win a 17-inning struggle 5–4 over the Angels at Municipal Stadium. Cleveland scored four runs in the eighth inning for a 4–1 lead, but the Angels countered with three tallies in the ninth. Brook Jacoby ended the long night with a sacrifice fly to drive in the winning run.

SEPTEMBER 24 The Indians score two runs in the ninth inning to beat the Angels 5–4 at Municipal Stadium. Albert Belle drove in the tying run and scored on a walk-off single by Brook Jacoby.

OCTOBER 1 In the final game of the season, the Indians win 1–0 over the White Sox in Chicago. A single by Dion James in the eighth inning broke up a scoreless tie. Greg Swindell (six innings), Jesse Orosco (one inning), and Doug Jones (two innings) combined on the shutout.

NOVEMBER 3 Two weeks after an earthquake strikes San Francisco during the World Series, the Indians hire 67-year-old John McNamara as manager.

The Cleveland job was McNamara's sixth managerial assignment. He had previously managed the Athletics (1969–70), Padres (1974–77), Reds (1979–81), Angels (1982–83,) and Red Sox (1984–88). In Cincinnati, McNamara won a division title. In Boston, he led the Red Sox to the World Series in 1986. The Sox were one out from beating the Met in game six of the series before losing on the infamous ground ball that rolled through the legs of first baseman Bill Buckner. Overall, McNamara was 1,048–1,078 as a big league skipper when he joined the Indians. He wasn't a good fit for a team rebuilding with youth. The Tribe was 77–85 in 1990 and 25–52 in 1991 when he was fired on July 6.

November 20 The Indians trade Dave Clark to the Cubs for Mitch Webster.

November 28 The Indians sign Candy Maldonado, most recently with the Giants, as a free agent.

Maldonado spent only a year in Cleveland, but it was a productive one as he hit 22 homers and drove in 95 runs.

December 6 The Indians trade Joe Carter to the Padres for Sandy Alomar, Jr., Carlos Baerga, and Chris James.

Carter was a year away from free agency and made it clear he had no intention of signing with the Indians. After leaving Cleveland, he drove in over 100 runs seven times, made five All-Star teams, and hit one of the most famous home runs in baseball history with a walk-off blast that clinched the world championship for the Blue Jays in game six in 1993 against the Phillies. Nonetheless, the Indians made a great trade. Alomar and Baerga both played key roles in the Indians resurgence during the 1990s. Alomar won the Rookie-of-the Year Award in 1990 and played in six All-Star Games over his 11 seasons with the Indians, although he missed considerable time with an assortment of injuries. He spent parts of seven seasons on the disabled list while in Cleveland. In 1997, he was the MVP of the Midsummer Classic at Jacobs Field. Baerga was Cleveland's starting second baseman for seven seasons. He hit .314 with 71 homers over a four-year period from 1991 through 1994, and he played in four All-Star Games.

December 7 The Indians sign Keith Hernandez, most recently with the Mets, as a free agent.

Hernandez was signed to a two-year contract with a guaranteed $3.4 million, which at the time the highest salary ever paid to a member of the Indians. Then 36, Hernandez had played in five All-Star Games and two World Series and had won an MVP award during his career. But he had an awful season with the Mets in 1989, and nearly everyone but the Indians front office believed he was finished as a productive player. The club thought his career would rebound and that he would provide veteran leadership in the clubhouse. Hernandez proved to be a monumental waste of money. He played only 46 games in a Cleveland uniform and batted an abysmal .200 with one home run.

December 8 The Indians sign Tom Brookens, most recently with the Yankees, as a free agent.

THE STATE OF THE INDIANS

When the 1994 season started, the Indians were a symbol of futility and fans hadn't experienced a pennant contender since 1959. No one under the age of 40 had a vivid memory of the Indians playing a meaningful game in September. With the exception of the 1981 strike season, the club didn't finish within ten games of first place from 1960 through 1993. It is the second longest such streak in major league history and the longest by a club in one city. The Athletics failed to finish within ten games of first between 1932 and 1968, but resided in Philadelphia, Kansas City, and Oakland during that period. Cleveland fans suffered through seven consecutive losing seasons from 1987 through 1993. The long-awaited revival of the franchise finally occurred in 1994 when the club posted a 66–47 record in a season that ended on August 12 when the players went on strike. The 1995 campaign was shortened by 18 games due to a work stoppage, but the Indians had enough time to win 100 games and reach the World Series for the first time since 1954. The club won five straight AL Central titles from 1995 through 1999 and made the Fall Classic again in 1997. Overall, the Indians were 823–728, a winning percentage of .531 that was the second best in the AL behind the Yankees. AL champions other than the Indians were the Athletics (1990), Twins (1991), Blue Jays (1992 and 1993) and Yankees (1996, 1998, and 1999).

THE BEST TEAM

The Indians had a record of 100–44 during the 1995 regular season before losing the World Series to the Braves in six games. The .694 winning percentage is the second best in club history behind the .721 mark posted by the 1954 outfit, which went 111–43.

THE WORST TEAM

The Indians hit rock bottom in 1991 with a 57–105 record. The .352 winning percentage was the worst of any Cleveland club since 1914, and the 105 defeats is a franchise record.

THE BEST MOMENT

In Seattle on October 17, 1995, the Indians advanced to the World Series for the first time in 41 years by beating the Mariners 4–0 in game six of the American League Championship Series.

THE WORST MOMENT

Cleveland players Steve Olin and Tom Crews were killed and Bob Ojeda was seriously injured in a spring training boating accident near Orlando, Florida, on March 22, 1993.

THE ALL-DECADE TEAM • YEARS W/INDIANS

Sandy Alomar, Jr., c	1990–2000
Paul Sorrento, 1b	1992–95
Carlos Baerga, 2b	1990–96, 1999
Jim Thome, 3b	1991–2002
Omar Vizquel, ss	1994–2004
Albert Belle, lf	1989–96
Kenny Lofton, cf	1992–96, 1998–2001, 2007
Manny Ramirez, rf	1993–2000
Dave Justice, dh	1997–2000
Charles Nagy, p	1990–2002
Jose Mesa, p	1992–98
Eric Plunk, p	1992–98
Dave Burba, p	1998–2002

Alomar made six All-Star teams while playing for the Indians, followed by Lofton (five), Belle (four), Ramirez (four), Baerga (three), Nagy (three), Thome (three), Vizquel (three), Mesa (two), and Justice (one). Among those on the 1990s All-Decade Team, only Sorrento, Plunk, and Burba failed to play in the Midsummer Classic. Despite the success of the team, the pitching staff was in an almost constant state of flux throughout the 1990s. During the decade, Nagy and Mesa were the only pitchers to hurl 600 or more innings with the club.

THE DECADE LEADERS

Batting Avg:	Kenny Lofton	.309
On-Base Pct:	Jim Thome	.413
Slugging Pct:	Albert Belle	.592
Home Runs:	Albert Belle	235
RBIs:	Albert Belle	714
Runs:	Jim Thome	609
Stolen Bases:	Kenny Lofton	404
Wins:	Charles Nagy	121
Strikeouts:	Charles Nagy	1,143
ERA:	Jose Mesa	3.45
Saves:	Jose Mesa	104

THE HOME FIELD

Municipal Stadium hosted its last baseball game on October 3, 1993, and closed for good when the Browns left for Baltimore after the 1995 NFL season. The Indians quest for a baseball-only facility finally came on April 4, 1994, when Jacobs Field opened in downtown Cleveland, which coincided with an abrupt change in the fortunes of the franchise from habitual losers to consistent winners. Unlike the yawning expanse of empty seats that usually accompanied Indians games at Municipal Stadium, capacity crowds were the norm at Jacobs Field during the 1990s. The Indians sold out 455 consecutive games from 1995 through 2001. The 1948 club attendance record of 2,620,627 stood for 47 years, but the Indians exceeded that figure seven consecutive seasons beginning in 1995. The money spent on tickets also allowed the Indians to compete for free agents and sign young players to long-term contracts, which the club had been unable to accomplish while at Municipal Stadium.

THE GAME YOU WISHED YOU HAD SEEN

On October 3, 1995, Tony Pena's game-winning homer in the 13th inning of game one of the Division Series against the Red Sox gave the Indians a 5–4 victory, the first for the franchise in the post-season since 1948.

THE WAY THE GAME WAS PLAYED

Baseball experienced one of its pivotal transitions during the 1990s, as offensive numbers soared to new heights. Fueled by the expansion to 30 teams, newer ball parks with fences closer to home plate, and the rumored use of performance-enhancing substances, the average number of home runs in the AL increased from 123 per team in 1989 to 188 per team in 1999, with a peak of 196 in 1996. The average number of runs per game leaped from 8.6 per game in 1989 to 104 in 1999, with a high of 10.8 in 1996. The trend of the 1970s and 1980s toward artificial turf ended as every new ballpark that opened or was on the drawing board featured a grass field. Most of the new ballparks, beginning with Camden Yards in Baltimore in 1992, had "retro" features that tried to emulate the older, classic venues. Four new teams were added in Miami, Denver, St. Petersburg, and Phoenix. Beginning in 1994, there were three divisions in each league, adding a new tier of playoffs. Inter-league play started in 1997, giving the Indians a chance to settle their intra-state rivalry with the Reds on the field.

THE MANAGEMENT

Richard and David Jacobs bought the Indians in 1986. Richard was chairman of the board and CEO, while David had the title of vice chairman of the board. David died in 1992. In November 1999, Richard Jacobs sold the Indians to a group headed by Lawrence Dolan. General mangers were Hank Peters (1987–91) and John Hart (1991–2001). Field managers were John McNamara (1990–91) and Mike Hargrove (1991–99).

THE BEST PLAYER MOVE

The best player move was the drafting of Manny Ramirez in the first round in 1991. The best trade brought Kenny Lofton from the Astros in December 1991 for Willie Blair and Eddie Taubensee.

THE WORST PLAYER MOVE

The worst move sent Jeff Kent, Julian Tavarez, and two others to the Giants for Matt Williams in December 1996. During the second half of the decade, the Indians often traded youngsters for veterans, which cost the club Sean Casey, Brian Giles, Danny Graves, Jeromy Burnitz, David Bell, Paul Byrd, and Steve Kline in addition to Kent.

1990

Season in a Sentence

The first season of the 1990s looks like most of those during the 1960s, 1970s, and 1980s as the Indians post a 77–85 record.

Finish • Won • Lost • Pct • GB

Finish	Won	Lost	Pct	GB
Fourth	73	89	.475	11.0

Manager

John McNamara

Stats

Stats	Indians	AL	Rank
Batting Avg:	.267	.259	2
On-Base Pct:	.324	.327	10
Slugging Pct:	.391	.388	7
Home Runs:	110		8 (tie)
Stolen Bases:	107		7 (tie)
ERA:	4.26	3.91	13
Fielding Avg:	.981	.981	5
Runs Scored:	732		4 (tie)
Runs Allowed:	737		12

Starting Line-up

Sandy Alomar, c
Brook Jacoby, 1b-3b
Jerry Browne, 2b
Carlos Baerga, 3b-ss
Felix Fermin, ss
Candy Maldonado, lf
Mitch Webster, cf
Cory Snyder, rf
Chris James, dh
Dion James, 1b-lf
Alex Cole, cf

Pitchers

Tom Candiotti, sp
Greg Swindell, sp
Bud Black, sp
Sergio Valdez, sp-rp
John Farrell, sp
Doug Jones, rp
Jesse Orosco, rp
Steve Olin, rp

Attendance

1,225,240 (14th in AL)

Club Leaders

Batting Avg:	Chris James	.299
On-Base Pct:	Brook Jacoby	.365
Slugging Pct:	Candy Maldonado	.446
Home Runs:	Candy Maldonado	22
RBIs:	Candy Maldonado	95
Runs:	Jerry Browne	92
Stolen Bases:	Alex Cole	40
Wins:	Tom Candiotti	15
Strikeouts:	Greg Swindell	135
ERA:	Bud Black	3.53
Saves:	Doug Jones	43

FEBRUARY 15 The owners lock the players out of spring training because of a lack of progress during negotiations for a new basic agreement.

MARCH 18 The labor dispute between the players and owners is resolved.

Spring training camps opened on March 20. The season, scheduled to start on April 2, was delayed a week, with missed games made up on open dates, with double headers, and by extending the close of the campaign by three days.

APRIL 10 The Indians season opener against the Yankees at Municipal Stadium is postponed by rain. The game the following day was also postponed, this time by snow.

APRIL 12 The Indians finally get the 1990 season underway and lose 6–4 to the Yankees in New York. Cory Snyder hit a home run.

The Indians began televising games on SportsChannel cable in 1990. The announcers were Rick Manning and Dan Coughlin. It was Manning's first season in the booth after playing for the club from 1975 through 1983. Tom Hamilton began his long association with the Indians on radio, teaming with Herb Score on WWWE.

April 19 The Indians play their first game of the season at Municipal Stadium and win 1–0 over the Yankees. Tom Brookens tripled in the sixth inning and scored on a passed ball for the lone run of the contest. Greg Swindell (6⅓ innings) Cecilio Guante (1⅔ innings) and Doug Jones (one inning) combined on the shutout. The losing pitcher was Pascaul Perez. The contest drew a crowd of only 6,000. It was played on what was originally an open date on the schedule because of the postponements of April 10 and 11. The Indians had promoted the April 20 game against the White Sox as the official home opener, but that contest was also rained out.

April 21 The Indians beat a Perez brother for the second game in a row, downing Melido Perez and the White Sox 8–4 at Municipal Stadium.

April 26 Tom Candiotti pitches no-hit ball through six innings and has a 4–0 lead over the Blue Jays in Toronto before allowing three runs in the seventh. The Indians hung on to win 4–3.

April 28 Mitch Webster drives in all three runs of a 3–0 win over the Twins at Municipal Stadium with a bases-loaded triple in the fifth inning off Allan Anderson. John Farrell (8⅓ innings) and Jesse Orosco (⅔ innings) combined on the shutout.

The Indians were last in the American League in attendance in 1990, drawing 1,225,240. The only major league team with a lower attendance figure was the Braves with 980,129.

May 8 Voters in Cuyahoga County approved a measure to help pay for a new downtown ballpark for the Indians and an arena to house the Cavaliers, hockey games, and other indoor events. The Cavaliers were playing home games in suburban Richfield, nearly 20 miles from downtown Cleveland. The ballot initiative was approved by a slim margin of 197,044 to 185,209.

Total cost of the project was pegged at $375 million to be funded with a tax on alcohol and cigarettes. The tax would pay for about half of the sports complex. The rest of the money would come from team owners, sales of luxury boxes, club seating and other private sources. During the campaign, Baseball Commissioner Fay Vincent and American League President Bobby Brown had indicated that unless a new ballpark was built, Cleveland could lose the Indians to another city. Owners of the Indians did not deny suggestions that the team could be moved or sold to out-of-town interests unless a stadium more suitable than outmoded Municipal Stadium was built. Despite the tremendous capacity of the stadium, the owners believed the Indians couldn't be economically successful there. The size of the facility worked against the Indians because fans could wait until the day of the game to buy tickets instead of purchasing them well in advance. A losing streak had a disastrous effect on attendance. The franchise had trouble attracting and keeping free agents in part because of the dreary and cavernous edifice. The playing surface was also a problem for the players. The turf took a severe beating from at least ten Browns exhibition and regular season games a year and usually didn't fully recover until well into spring because of the cold Cleveland winters. The new baseball stadium and arena were to be built on a 28-acre site a few blocks from the Public Square in the Gateway section on the southern edge of downtown on a 12-acre site bounded by Ontario Street, Carnegie Avenue, and East Ninth Street. The location was selected in *the hopes of revitalizing the declining area, encourage downtown development, increase the city's attractiveness as a convention center, and extend the urban center south to the main highway exits. Jacobs Field, seating 43,068, opened in April 1994. Adjoining Gund Arena (now called The Quicken Loans Arena), holds 20,562, and opened later the same year.*

MAY 16 The Indians blow a 4–0 lead and lose 7–6 to the A's in Oakland. Jeff Shaw gave up consecutive homers to Jose Canseco, Mark McGwire, and Ron Hassey in the fourth inning. McGwire hit a two-out, two-run, walk-off homer in the ninth off Doug Jones.

MAY 28 The Indians score three runs in the tenth inning to defeat the Angels 3–0 in Anaheim. Brook Jacoby's one-out single broke the scoreless tie, and Cory Snyder followed with a two-run homer. Bud Black (eight innings), Cecilio Guante (one inning), and Doug Jones (one inning) combined on the shutout.

Jones saved 43 games with an ERA of 2.56 in 66 games and 84⅓ innings in 1990.

MAY 30 Indians pitcher Kevin Wickander slips and falls on a concrete runway at Anaheim Stadium and breaks his left (pitching) elbow. He was out for the rest of the year.

JUNE 3 Roger Clemens sparks a first-inning fight at Municipal Stadium by hitting Indians leadoff hitter Stan Jefferson on the right elbow with his second pitch. It was in retaliation for a brushback by Doug Jones of Tony Pena in the ninth inning the night before. During the brawl prompted by Clemens's pitch, Pena and Chris James of the Indians were ejected.

JUNE 4 In the first round of the amateur draft, the Indians select shortstop Tim Costo from the University of Iowa.

Costo was traded to the Reds before appearing in his first big league game in 1992. Converted to an outfielder-first baseman, Costo played in only 43 games in the majors and hit just .224. Other future major leaguers drafted and signed by the Indians in 1990 were Darrell Whitmore (second round), Jason Hardtke (third round), David Bell (seventh round), Dave Mlicki (17th round), Steve Gajkowski (18th round) and Carlos Crawford (51st round). Bell was the son of Buddy Bell, who played for the Indians from 1972 through 1979 at the start of an 18-year playing career. David made his debut in 1995 with the Indians and was still active in the majors in 2007. The Bells were part of a three-generation baseball family. Buddy's father Gus played in the big leagues from 1950 through 1964. David's brother Mike had a brief 19-game stay in the majors.

JUNE 6 Cecil Fielder hits three homers for the Tigers in a 6–4 win over the Indians at Municipal Stadium.

JUNE 16 The Indians take a thrilling 10–9 decision from the Brewers at Municipal Stadium. Trailing 7–2, Cleveland took a 9–7 lead with seven runs in the eighth inning. After Milwaukee scored twice in the top of the ninth, the Tribe countered with a tally in their half for the win. Jerry Browne scored the winning run from second base when the Brewers failed to complete an inning-ending double play. With Browne on second and Maldonado on first, Brook Jacoby hit a ground ball to pitcher Bob Sebra, who threw to Bill Spiers at second to start an apparent double play. But Spiers's throw to first pulled first baseman Greg Brock off the bag. When Brock turned to argue the safe call, Browne rounded third and crossed the plate.

June 17 The Indians club five home runs, including three in a row, during a 12–4 victory over the Brewers at Municipal Stadium. In the seventh inning, Candy Maldonado, Brook Jacoby, and Cory Snyder hit back-to-back-to-back homers. Snyder hit another homer earlier in the contest, as did Carlos Baerga.

June 25 Brook Jacoby collects four hits, including a homer, and drives in five runs in five at-bats during a 10–5 win over the Brewers in Milwaukee.

July 6 The Athletics hit seven homers during a 12–1 thrashing of the Indians in the second game of a double header at Municipal Stadium. Rickey Henderson and Mark McGwire each hit two homers, with Carney Lankford, Jose Canseco, and Jamie Quirk adding the rest. The Indians won the opener 6–1.

July 7 Bud Black pitches the Indians to a 1–0 win over the Athletics at Municipal Stadium. Chris James drove in the lone run of the game with a single in the fourth inning.

July 8 The Indians lose 8–3 to the Athletics in the first regularly scheduled Sunday night game at Municipal Stadium. The contest was part of ESPN's Sunday night television package.

July 10 Sandy Alomar, Jr. collects two singles in three-at bats during the American League's 2–0 win in the All-Star Game at Wrigley Field in Chicago.

Alomar won the American League Rookie of the Year Award in 1990 by hitting .290 with nine home runs.

July 11 The Indians trade Tom Lampkin to the Padres for Alex Cole.

July 12 Down to their last out, the Indians rally for two runs in the ninth inning to defeat the Mariners 5–4 in Seattle. With two out and no one on base, Carlos Baerga and Jerry Browne walked, and after both advanced on a wild pitch, Mitch Webster smacked a two-run double.

July 13 The Indians break a 1–1 tie with eight runs in the seventh inning and beat the Mariners 13–7 at the Kingdome. Cleveland took a 13–1 lead with four tallies in the eight before Seattle countered with six runs in their half.

July 25 The Indians play at old Comiskey Park for the last time and beat the White Sox 6–1.

July 29 The Indians unveil their new mascot "Slider" during a double header against the Yankees at Municipal Stadium. The Tribe lost 8–5 and 4–3.

A purple-colored hairy giant with yellow spots and eyebrows, Slider became a popular addition at Indians games at both Municipal Stadium and Jacobs Field as well as at personal, family, and business gatherings. The mascot was in its 18th season in 2007.

AUGUST 1 Just five days after making his major league debut, Alex Cole sets an Indians record by stealing five bases during a 4–1 win over the Royals at Municipal Stadium.

Cole was acquired by the Indians in a trade with the Padres on July 11 and made his big league debut on July 27. Over the remainder of the 1990 season, he hit .300 and swiped 40 bases in 63 games. He looked like a coming star, but a lack of power kept Cole from keeping a job as a regular. He stole 76 bases but failed to hit a single home run in 711 at-bats with the Indians before a trade to the Pirates in 1992.

AUGUST 3 Tom Candiotti carries a no-hitter into the eighth inning, but the Indians lose 6–4 to the Yankees in New York. The Yanks scored two unearned runs in the first inning and kept the 2–0 advantage until the Indians scored four times. The Yankees rallied for four runs in the bottom of the eighth. Candiotti retired the first two batters before two walks and an error loaded the bases. The Indians hurler was still four outs from a no-hitter when Oscar Azocar singled in a run. Doug Jones relieved Candiotti and gave up a three-run homer to Mel Hall.

AUGUST 4 The Indians smash the Yankees 17–3 in New York. Cory Snyder's grand slam off Tim Leary in the sixth inning broke a 3–3 tie, which sparked a rally in which Cleveland scored 14 unanswered runs over the final four innings.

AUGUST 10 Mitch Webster hits a grand slam off Steve Searcy in the fourth inning of a 5–2 win over the Tigers at Municipal Stadium.

AUGUST 11 The Indians rout the Tigers 13–4 at Municipal Stadium.

SEPTEMBER 2 Dave Steib of the Blue Jays pitches a no-hitter to defeat the Indians 3–0 at Municipal Stadium. Previously, Steib had taken four no-hitters into the ninth inning, only to fail to complete one, including a contest against Cleveland (see September 24, 1988). Jerry Browne ended the game by lining out to Junior Felix in right field. It was the first no-hitter against the Indians since 1967.

SEPTEMBER 9 Trailing 5–1, the Indians score seven runs in the seventh inning and beat the Twins 12–9 in Minneapolis.

SEPTEMBER 12 The Indians pound out a 12–2 win over the White Sox at Municipal Stadium.

SEPTEMBER 15 Right fielder Turner Ward drives in six runs during a 14–6 victory over the Royals in Kansas City. Ward drove in three with his first major league homer in the first inning, and with the bases loaded in the eighth, hit the first triple of his career.

Ward made his debut in the majors only six days earlier. The homer and triple on September 16 were the only ones he accumulated in 146 at-bats with the Indians in 1990 and 1991. Ward didn't hit another big league homer until 1992 or a triple until 1993, both while playing for the Blue Jays.

SEPTEMBER 16 The Indians trade Bud Black to the Blue Jays for Steve Cummings, Mauro Gozzo, and Alex Sanchez.

Black was eligible for free agency at the end of the season, and the Indians dealt him as a cost-cutting move. Black continued to be an effective starter with the Blue Jays and Giants for a couple more seasons. None of the three players acquired for Black ever played a game for Cleveland.

SEPTEMBER 21 Sandy Alomar, Jr. leads off the 13th inning with a home run to beat the Blue Jays 2–1 in Toronto.

OCTOBER 2 The Indians score nine runs in the first inning and beat the Royals 12–3 at Municipal Stadium. Chris James drove in three runs in the big inning with a pair of singles.

DECEMBER 4 The Indians trade Cory Snyder and Lindsay Foster to the White Sox for Shawn Hillegas and Eric King.

The Indians gave up on Snyder after five seasons with the club. He hit 115 homers in 2,431 at-bats in Cleveland, but those round-trippers came with 642 strikeouts and an abysmal on base percentage of only .283 as Snyder never mastered the strike zone. He played for four more clubs between 1991 and 1994, and the same problems continued to plague him.

1991

Season in a Sentence

The Indians reach triple digits in the loss column for the third time in eight years with a club record 105 defeats.

Finish • Won • Lost • Pct • GB

Finish	Won	Lost	Pct	GB
Seventh	57	105	.352	34.0

Managers

John McNamara (25–52) and Mike Hargrove (32–53)

Stats

Stats	Indians	AL	Rank
Batting Avg:	.254	.260	13
On-Base Pct:	.313	.329	14
Slugging Pct:	.350	.395	14
Home Runs:	79		14
Stolen Bases:	84		12
ERA:	4.23	4.10	9
Fielding Avg:	.976	.981	14
Runs Scored:	576		14
Runs Allowed:	759		9

Starting Line-up

Joel Skinner, c
Brook Jacoby, 1b
Mark Lewis, 2b
Carlos Baerga, 3b-2b
Felix Fermin, ss
Albert Belle, lf
Alex Cole, cf
Mark Whiten, rf
Chris James, dh-lf-rf
Jerry Browne, 2b
Carlos Martinez, dh-1b

Pitchers

Greg Swindell, sp
Charles Nagy, sp
Eric King, sp
Tom Candiotti, sp
Rod Nichols, sp-rp
Dave Otto, sp
Steve Olin, rp
Shawn Hillegas, rp
Jesse Orosco, rp

Attendance

1,051,863 (14th in AL)

Club Leaders

Batting Avg:	Alex Cole	.295
On-Base Pct:	Alex Cole	.386
Slugging Pct:	Albert Belle	.540
Home Runs:	Albert Belle	28
RBIs:	Albert Belle	95
Runs:	Carlos Baerga	80
Stolen Bases:	Alex Cole	27
Wins:	Charles Nagy	10
Strikeouts:	Greg Swindell	169
ERA:	Greg Swindell	3.48
Saves:	Steve Olin	17

April 2 Three months after the U.S. and its allies attack Iraq to start the Persian Gulf War, and five weeks after President George Bush orders a cease fire to end the war, Candy Maldonado signs a contract as a free agent with the Brewers.

April 4 The Indians purchase Eddie Taubensee from the Athletics.

April 8 In the season opener, the Indians lose 4–2 to the Royals in Kansas City. Albert Belle hit a home run.

The 1991 season was the first for John Sanders in the television booth. He teamed with Rick Manning on SportsChannel. Sanders came to Cleveland after spending nine seasons as the play-by-play announcer with the Pirates.

April 15 Brook Jacoby breaks open a scoreless tie in the 13th inning with a home run off Dennis Lamp to lift the Indians to a 1–0 win over the Red Sox in Boston. Charles Nagy (8⅓ innings), Steve Olin (3⅔ innings) and Doug Jones (one inning) combined on the shutout.

April 16 The Indians lose the home opener 3–1 to the Rangers before 46,606 at Municipal Stadium.

With a speedy team that had a lack of home run power, the Indians moved the fences at Municipal Stadium in 1991. The center field wall was moved back from 400 feet to 415 feet with the power alleys also extended about 15 feet. The change caused a dramatic decrease in home runs at the stadium. In 1990, the Indians hit 52 homers at home and 58 on the road. In 1991, the club struck only 22 home runs in Cleveland and 57 in away games. In 1992, the fences were moved back in to 404 feet in center with the power alleys about 25 feet shorter than those of the previous season. As a result, the Indians had 62 home runs at home and 65 on the road in 1992.

April 22 Charles Nagy pitches six perfect innings before faltering in the seventh by allowing four runs, but the Indians win 10–4 over the Royals at Municipal Stadium.

The Indians drew only 1,051,863 fans in 1991, to rank last in the American League for the second year in a row. Among major league teams, Cleveland outdrew only the Montreal Expos.

May 4 Chris James sets an Indians record by driving in nine runs during a 20–6 win over the Athletics in Oakland. James broke the record of eight, set by Earl Averill in 1930 and tied by Pat Seerey in 1945 and Bill Glynn in 1954. James hit three-run homers in both the first and second innings and an RBI-single in the fourth, all off Kirk Dressendorfer. After grounding out in the sixth, James added a two-run single against John Briscoe. Playing first base, James left the game in the bottom of the eighth and was replaced by Jeff Manto. The Indians collected 21 hits in the contest.

The nine RBIs represented 22 percent of James's 1991 season total of 41. Chris's brother Craig was a running back with the Patriots from 1984 through 1988 and later served as an analyst on ABC and ESPN college football telecasts.

May 5 The Indians collect 19 hits and clobber the Athletics 15–6 in Oakland. The outburst gave the Indians 35 runs in consecutive games after scoring just 54 times in the first

19 games of the season. It was the most runs scored by the Indians in back-to-back contests since 1923.

The two-day explosion in Oakland was an aberration. The Indians scored only 576 runs, the fewest of any team in the majors. It was the only time in history that the club finished last in the majors in runs.

MAY 11 Albert Belle throws a ball at a heckler during a 2–1 loss to the Angels at Municipal Stadium. Jeff Pillar, a 30-year-old fan in the left field stands, jokingly invited Belle to a keg party. Belle, who spent ten weeks in an alcoholism rehabilitation center the previous season, took exception to the remarks. Belle picked up a foul ball and heaved it hard at Pillar from a distance of about 15 feet hitting Pillar in the chest. Pillar went to the first-aid station but was not seriously hurt. AL president Bobby Brown suspended Belle for seven days because of the incident.

MAY 16 The Indians trade Mitch Webster to the Pirates for Mike York.

MAY 31 The Indians take an 8–2 lead after two innings and hang on to defeat the Tigers 11–9 at Municipal Stadium.

JUNE 3 In the first round of the amateur draft, the Indians select third baseman-outfielder Manny Ramirez from George Washington High School in New York City. Other future major leaguers drafted and signed by the Indians in 1991 were Herbert Perry (second round), Chad Ogea (third round), Paul Byrd (fourth round), Pep Harris (seventh round), Albie Lopez (20th round), and Damian Jackson (44th round).

Ramirez was born in the Dominican Republic and grew up in New York City. He reached the majors with the Indians in 1993 at the age of 21 and made his first All-Star team in 1995. It would be an almost annual trip for Ramirez, who was named to ten All-Star teams through 2007, four of them with the Indians before moving to Boston in 2001. In Cleveland, Ramirez, set the all-time single-season record for RBI's with 165 in 1999. He also led the AL in slugging percentage twice. On the all-time club lists, Ramirez ranks first in slugging percentage (.592), third in home runs (236), and eighth in runs-batted-in (804).

JUNE 6 Albert Belle is sent to the minors for failing to hustle during a 2–1 loss to the White Sox at Municipal Stadium. At the time, Belle led the Indians with nine homers and 27 RBIs.

Belle spent 19 days in the minor leagues at the Indians Triple A affiliate in Colorado Springs. He finished the season with a .282 average, 28 homers, and 95 runs-batted-in.

JUNE 18 The Indians play at new Comiskey Park for the first time and lose 6–3 to the White Sox.

From May 7 through September 9, the Indians had a record of 34–82 on the way to a club record 105 losses. The club used 24 rookies in 1991. Most Indians fans believed that the club was in the process of another fruitless rebuilding program, but this one took hold. Among the 1991 Indians who were on the 1995 World Series team included Sandy Alomar, Jr., Carlos Baerga, Albert Belle, Wayne Kirby, Charles Nagy, and Jim Thome.

June 26 The Indians score nine runs in the first inning and defeat the Orioles 10–4 at Municipal Stadium. Albert Belle, in his first game back from the minors (see June 5, 1991) hit a two-run double and an RBI-single in the big inning.

June 27 The Indians trade Tom Candiotti and Turner Ward to the Blue Jays for Mark Whiten, Glenallen Hill, and Denis Boucher. A 15-game winner the season before, Candiotti continued his major league career through the 1999 season with middling success. Ward, too, remained in the majors for years, though never found a starting role. The trio the Tribe received in return made no impact on the team.

July 6 The Indians fire John McNamara as manager and hire 41-year-old Mike Hargrove.

At the time of the switch, the Indians were 25–52 and had lost 25 of their last 30 games. The club believed that Hargrove was a better choice to lead the Indians youth movement. Hargrove played 12 seasons in the majors, including seven with the Indians from 1979 through 1985. He had been the club's first base coach since 1990 after managing three years in the minors. It took awhile for Hargrove to become successful as a big league manager. The club was 32–53 over the remainder of the 1991 season before back-to-back 76–86 campaigns in 1992 and 1993. The Indians were on the verge of their first post-season appearance in 40 years in 1994, but the players's strike put a stop to the season with Cleveland holding a 66–47 record. In 1995, the Tribe was 100–44 and reached the World Series before losing in six games to the Braves. It was the first of five straight AL Central crowns for Hargrove and the Indians. In 1997, the team was three outs from a world championship in the ninth inning of game seven against the Marlins, but lost the game in the 11th.

July 12 Rod Nichols is the losing pitcher when the Mariners defeat the Indians 7–0 in Seattle. It was Nichols 13th consecutive defeat, a streak that lasted over three seasons. He lost his last two decisions in 1989, all three in 1990 and the first eight in 1991. The 13 losses in a row tied the club record set by Guy Morton in 1914.

Nichols was 11-30 with the Indians over five seasons from 1988 through 1992.

July 23 Carlos Baerga collects five hits, including a double, but the Indians lose 10–7 to the Athletics at Municipal Stadium.

There were seven different players who led the Indians in hits from 1985 through 1991. They were Brett Butler (184 in 1985), Joe Carter (200 in 1986), Pat Tabler (170 in 1987), Julio Franco (198 in 1988), Jerry Browne (179 in 1989), Brook Jacoby (162 in 1990), and Baerga (171 in 1991).

July 26 The Indians trade Brook Jacoby to the Athletics for Apolinar Garcia and Lee Tinsley.

August 2 Royals pitcher Kevin Appier hits Carlos Martinez with a pitch in the eighth inning sparking a bench-clearing brawl during a 6–4 Indians loss at Municipal Stadium. Martinez charged the mound after Appier hit him with a high pitch. Martinez was restrained by home plate umpire Jim Evans and Kansas City catcher Brent Mayne and never got to Appier, but was ejected.

August 3 The Indians survive a gaffe by Alex Cole to beat the Royals 3–1 at Municipal Stadium. With one out in the first inning, Cole caught George Brett's fly ball at the warning track in left field and ran off the field, believing the inning was over. Brian McRae, meanwhile, tagged up and scored from second base.

AUGUST 5 Eric King pitches a two-hitter for a 9–0 win over the Rangers in Arlington. The only Texas hits were singles by Ruben Sierra in the second inning and Jeff Huson in the fifth.

AUGUST 10 The Indians edge the Royals 1-0 in Kansas City. Dave Otto (eight innings) and Steve Olin (one inning) combined on the shutout. Albert Belle drove in the lone run with a single in the seventh inning.

AUGUST 16 The Indians win 13–9 over the Rangers in the second game of a double header at Municipal Stadium. Four runs in the seventh inning broke an 8–8 tie. Texas won the opener 5–3.

AUGUST 20 The Indians sign a contract to conduct spring training in Homestead, Florida, beginning in 1993. The club had been training in Tucson, Arizona, since 1947. The new complex in Homestead included a 6,500-seat stadium and five practice fields. The town was 25 miles south of Miami. Many questioned the Indians judgment in selecting such a remote location. At the time, the only other big league club training within 75 miles of Homestead was the Yankees, who were 50 miles away in Fort Lauderdale (see August 24, 1992).

AUGUST 25 Swarms of flying insects repeatedly interrupt a 3–0 win over the White Sox at Municipal Stadium. Batters continually stepped out of the box and pitchers walked off the mound to clear the tiny bugs from their eyes.

SEPTEMBER 4 Jim Thome makes his major league debut during an 8–4 win over the Twins in Minneapolis. Playing third base and batting seventh, Thome collected two singles in four at-bats.

SEPTEMBER 5 Architectural plans for the Indians new downtown ballpark are unveiled.

The new ballpark, eventually named Jacobs Field, was designed by the Kansas City firm of Hellmuth, Obata and Kassabaum, which also designed Camden Yards in Baltimore. Camden Yards, which opened in April 1992, was the first of the "retro" ballparks that evoked baseball's past. Jacobs Field was built along the same lines and brought fans much closer to the action than cavernous Municipal Stadium. Like Camden Yards, Cleveland's ballpark had a view of the downtown skyline, giving it the feel of an urban ball park. Jacobs Field opened in 1994 with the largest free-standing scoreboard in the United States. It stands 220-feet wide and 120-feet high. The first row of the bleachers was built atop the 19-foot-high wall in left field. The lighting system is unique with vertical towers resembling giant toothbrushes. The towers, which topped out 200 feet above street level, were modeled after the factories in Cleveland's industrial zone. The brick, stone, and granite exterior with a white-steel rim was designed to blend in with the landscape of the city's downtown renaissance. The playing field is 18 feet below street level.

SEPTEMBER 9 The Indians draw only 1,695 fans for a 4–3 loss to the Red Sox at Municipal Stadium.

September 10 Reggie Jefferson hits a grand slam off Bill Wegman in the fifth inning of a 5–2 win over the Brewers in Milwaukee. Doug Jones was the winning pitcher on in the first start of his career.

September 15 The Indians play at Memorial Stadium in Baltimore for the last time, and lose 4–3 to the Orioles.

September 17 Doug Jones strikes out 13 batters in eight innings of a 3–1 win over the Tigers at Municipal Stadium.

The 13-strikeout performance came during an attempt to convert Jones from a reliever into a starter. Jones was 34 years old and made 272 prior relief appearances before winning three of four starts with the Indians in 1991. After three years as an All-Star closer, Jones had a 5.54 ERA in 1991 and spent some time in the minors. The four 1991 starts were the only ones of Jones's 16-year career in which he pitched in 846 games.

September 18 The Indians name Rick Bay as club president and chief operating officer. Bay had previously worked as an athletic director at Ohio State University and the University of Minnesota. On the same day, the Indians promoted John Hart to general manager, replacing Hank Peters, who announced his retirement.

Bay didn't last long, leaving the team in November 1992 to "pursue other interests." Hart would have a lasting impact, however, guiding the Indians through a highly successful period during the second half of the 1990s. Before Hart arrived, the Indians were the poster child for mismanagement and front office ineptitude. Within a few short years, Cleveland was suddenly baseball's model organization. Hart showed unusual foresight in anticipating and successfully dealt with the changing economics of the sport by signing key players to long-term contracts beginning over the winter of 1991–92. This plan was designed to avoid arbitration hearings and to protect the franchise against the loss of the Indians stable of promising young players. Among them were Sandy Alomar, Jr., Carlos Baerga, Albert Belle, Charles Nagy, and Kenny Lofton. In one of the most remarkable improvements in baseball history, a team that had a 57–105 record in 1991 was 100–44 in 1995 and went to the World Series. The 1995 campaign marked the first of five straight AL Central championships. During the five-year run of division titles, Hart showed a willingness to make dramatic changes to a winning roster with bold trades and by letting free agents such as Albert Belle walk away. The only players to play in each post-season from 1995 through 1999 were Manny Ramirez, Jim Thome, Omar Vizquel, and Charles Nagy.

September 22 The Indians score two runs in the ninth inning to defeat the Orioles 2–1 at Municipal Stadium. A suicide squeeze by Mark Lewis tied the score. Carlos Baerga drove in the winning tally with a double.

October 2 The Indians lose a team record 103rd game with an 11–4 loss to the Brewers at Municipal Stadium. The club previously lost 102 games in 1914, 1971 and 1985.

The Indians lost 105 games in 1991, and the winning percentage of .352 was the second worst in club history. The only worse club was in 1914, when the Indians were 51–102 (.333).

October 4 Jim Thome hits a two-run, walk-off homer with two out in the ninth inning to beat the Yankees 3–2 in New York. It was Thome's first homer in the majors and came in his 89th career at-bat.

A 13th round draft choice in 1989, Thome had just turned 21 when he hit his first homer. It took him several more years to establish a permanent place in the Indians line-up. Thome didn't spend a full season in the majors until 1994. In the minors from 1989 through 1992, Thome hit .307 in 914 at-bats and hit only 25 home runs. He was often compared favorably to George Brett, a perennial .300-hitter with moderate power. In his first 215 big league at-bats, Thome had only three homers and batted .228. The Indians questioned that Thome possessed the power stroke to hold down a corner infield spot, but he proved them wrong. When he left Cleveland at the end of the 2002 season via free agency, Thome was the club's all-time leading home run hitter with 334. He also ranks first in walks (997), second in runs-batted-in (927), third in extra bases hits (613), third in slugging percentage (.567), fourth in total bases (2,633), fifth in runs (917), and tenth in doubles (259).

November 15 The Indians trade Greg Swindell to the Reds for Jack Armstrong, Scott Scudder, and Joe Turek.

Swindell was a year away from free agency, and the Indians had no intention of getting into a bidding war for his services. After leaving Cleveland, he was a capable pitcher for another decade, both as a starter and a reliever. The Indians received next to nothing in exchange for Swindell. Armstrong was the National League's starter in the All-Star Game in 1990 before going into a rapid decline. With the Indians, he posted a 6–15 record after losing 13 of his first 15 decisions in 1992, his only season with the club.

November 20 The Indians purchase Derek Liliquist from the Padres.

December 6 The Indians sell Jesse Orosco to the Brewers.

December 10 The Indians trade Eddie Taubensee and Willie Blair to the Astros for Kenny Lofton and Dave Rohde.

The Indians pulled off a brilliant deal in acquiring Lofton, who stands as the club's all-time stolen base leader. Lofton was a point guard on a University of Arizona team that made it to the Final Four in 1988 and was the top-ranked team in the nation for much of the 1988–89 season. He turned to baseball as a career, however, making Arizona's baseball team as a walk-on as a junior. At the time Lofton was acquired by the Indians, he was 24 and had played in only 20 big league games. He made an impact immediately, leading the American League in steals five straight seasons from 1992 though 1996, in addition to topping the circuit in hits in 1994 and triples in 1995. As an Indian, Lofton scored over 100 runs six times, batted over .300 five times, won four Gold Gloves and played in five All-Star Games. On the all-time club lists, he ranks first in stolen bases (452), third in runs (975), ninth in hits (1,512) and tenth in at-bats (5,045).

1992

Season in a Sentence

With Jacobs Field under construction, the Indians sign a bevy of promising young players to multi-year contracts, launching another rebuilding program.

Finish • Won • Lost • Pct • GB

Finish	Won	Lost	Pct	GB
Fourth (tie)	76	86	.469	20.0

Manager

Mike Hargrove

Stats

	Indians	AL	Rank
Batting Avg:	.266	.259	3
On-Base Pct:	.323	.328	9
Slugging Pct:	.383	.385	9
Home Runs:	127		8
Stolen bases:	144		3
ERA:	4.11	3.95	11
Fielding Avg:	.978	.981	13
Runs Scored:	674		11
Runs Allowed:	746		10 (tie)

Starting Line-up

Sandy Alomar, Jr., c
Paul Sorrento, 1b
Carlos Baerga, 2b
Brook Jacoby, 3b
Mark Lewis, ss
Glenallen Hill, lf-dh
Kenny Lofton, cf
Mark Whiten, rf
Albert Belle, dh-lf
Thomas Howard, lf
Junior Ortiz, c
Carlos Martinez, 1b-3b
Felix Fermin, ss

Pitchers

Charles Nagy, sp
Jack Armstrong, sp
Dennis Cook, sp
Scott Scudder, sp
Jose Mesa, sp
Steve Olin, rp
Derek Liliquist, rp
Ted Power, rp
Eric Plunk, rp
Kevin Wickander, rp

Attendance

1,224,274 (14th in AL)

Club Leaders

Batting Avg:	Carlos Baerga	.312
On-Base Pct:	Kenny Lofton	.362
Slugging Pct:	Albert Belle	.477
Home Runs:	Albert Belle	34
RBIs:	Albert Belle	112
Runs:	Kenny Lofton	96
Stolen Bases:	Kenny Lofton	66
Wins:	Charles Nagy	17
Strikeouts:	Charles Nagy	169
ERA:	Charles Nagy	2.96
Saves:	Steve Olin	29

JANUARY 13 Excavation of the Jacobs Field construction site begins. On the previous day, the implosion of the Cold Storage Building marked the final major building remaining on the site.

JANUARY 15 Chris James signs a contract as a free agent with the Giants.

JANUARY 24 Doug Jones signs a contract as a free agent with the Astros.

The Indians believed that Jones was finished after he compiled an ERA of 5.54 in 63⅓ innings in 1991. He rebounded, however, and recorded 175 more saves before his career ended in 2000, and he appeared in the All-Star Game in both 1992 and 1994.

MARCH 28 The Indians trade Curt Leskanic and Oscar Munoz to the Twins for Paul Sorrento.

The Indians made an excellent transaction in the short run, as Sorrento was the club's starting first baseman for four seasons. Leskanic had yet to play in the majors when the trade was made, but he had a successful 12-year big league career as a reliever beginning in 1993.

April 3 The Indians purchase Jose Hernandez from the Rangers.

April 5 The Indians sign Ted Power, most recently with the Reds, as a free agent.

April 6 In the season opener, the Indians play the first game ever at Camden Yards in Baltimore and lose 2–0 to the Orioles. President George Bush threw out the ceremonial first pitch. Rick Sutcliffe pitched the shutout in his Orioles debut. Kenny Lofton was the first batter at the new facility. Indians first baseman Paul Sorrento collected the first hit. Charles Nagy took the complete-game loss.

April 8 Paul Sorrento becomes the first player to hit a home run at Camden Yards in Baltimore during a 4–0 win over the Orioles. Steve Olin ($6\frac{1}{3}$ innings) and Rod Nichols ($2\frac{2}{3}$ innings) combined on the shutout.

April 9 The Indians sign Eric Plunk as a free agent following his release by the Blue Jays.

Charles Nagy emerged in 1992 to give the Tribe a reliable hurler for the rest of the 1990s.

Plunk proved to be a reliable reliever for the Indians for several seasons. He posted ERAs under 3.00 in four consecutive seasons from 1993 through 1996 while pitching in 223 games during that stretch. He was traded to the Brewers in 1998 with 373 appearances with the Indians, all in relief. Plunk holds the all-time club record for games pitched as a reliever.

April 11 The first game of the season at Municipal Stadium goes 19 innings before the Indians lose 7–5 to the Red Sox. A two-run homer by Tim Naehring off Eric Bell in the 19th drove in the winning runs. It was Bell's first game with the Indians. The crowd was 65,130, but fewer than half remained at the finish of the six hour and 30 minute marathon, which ended at 8:13 p.m. Carlos Baerga collected six of the Tribe's 20 hits in nine at-bats. Each of Baerga's hits were singles.

Just before the first pitch, an exotic dancer named Lulu Divine raced toward the mound and planted a kiss on the cheek of Indians starter Dennis Cook. She was arrested and escorted from the park. After playing 19 innings on a Saturday afternoon, and early evening, the Indians and Red Sox were scheduled to play a double header the following day.

April 12 The day after collecting 20 hits in a loss, the Indians win 2–1 over the Red Sox in the first game of a double header at Municipal Stadium without a single base hit off Boston hurler Matt Young. Young walked seven and struck out six in eight innings in the no-hitter. He didn't pitch the ninth since the Indians had the one-run lead. The Indians squeezed out their runs in the first and third innings. In the first inning, Kenny Lofton walked, stole second and third, and scored on an error by Boston shortstop Luis Rivera. In the third, Mark Lewis and Lofton walked, Glenallen Hill hit into a force play, and Lewis scored on a fielder's choice. The Sox plated their run in the fourth. Lofton stole four bases in the game. Charles Nagy (seven innings), Brad Arnsberg (one inning), and Derek Liliquist (one innings) pitched for Cleveland. In the second contest, Roger Clemens hurled a two-hitter to defeat the Indians 3–0. The two hits by the Tribe set a record for the fewest ever by a major league team in a double header.

Lofton stole a league-leading 66 bases and batted .285 in 1992. The 66 steals broke the American League record for rookies and the Indians single-season record.

April 17 The Indians clobber the Yankees 11–1 in New York.

April 18 The Yankees score ten runs in the fourth inning off Dave Otto and Ted Power and beat the Indians 14–0 in New York. The first eleven Yankee batters reached base in the fourth, eight of them off Otto.

The Indians had a record of 54–108 from May 7, 1991, through April 28, 1992.

May 3 Four days after riots begin in the South Central section of Los Angeles, resulting in the deaths of 52 people, Alex Cole collects four hits and ties his own club record with five stolen bases, including third base twice, but the Indians lose 6–3 to the Angels at Municipal Stadium.

The Indians finished last in the American League in attendance for the third consecutive season, drawing 1,224,274. The only major league club with a lower figure in 1992 was the Houston Astros.

MAY 4 A brawl erupts during an 11–6 loss to the Royals at Municipal Stadium. Kansas City pitcher Neal Heaton was ejected after consecutive inside pitches to Albert Belle in the eighth inning. Belle was also ejected after charging the mound. Belle and Heaton were both suspended for three games.

MAY 7 The Indians survive errors by each of their four infielders to beat the Rangers 8–7 in Arlington. The offending fielders were first baseman Paul Sorrento, second baseman Carlos Baerga, shortstop Mark Lewis, and third baseman Brook Jacoby.

MAY 19 At Municipal Stadium, a grand slam by Mark Whiten off Jeff Robinson in the seventh inning gives the Indians a 7–3 lead, but the Rangers rally to win 8–7 with two runs in the eighth and three in the ninth.

MAY 24 The Mariners score three runs in the ninth inning to beat the Indians 5–4 in Seattle.

The game represented the low point of the Cleveland season. The Indians had a 14–30 record on May 24, but were 62–56 the rest of the way.

MAY 26 A homer by Mark Lewis off Bob Welch in the fifth inning is the only run in a 1–0 victory over the Athletics in Oakland. Dave Otto (six innings), Eric Plunk (2⅓ innings), Kevin Wickander (one-third of an inning), and Steve Olin (one-third of an inning) combined on the shutout.

MAY 29 The Indians hammer the Angels 14–2 in Anaheim. Albert Belle hit two home runs.

Belle struck seven homers in a six-game span from May 23 to May 29. He finished the season with 34 homers, 112 RBIs, and a .260 batting average.

JUNE 1 In the first round of the amateur draft, with the second overall pick, the Indians select pitcher Paul Shuey from the University of North Carolina.

Shuey's career wasn't worthy of being a second overall pick, but he was an effective reliever during his nine seasons with the Indians. While in Cleveland, Shuey had a record of 34–21 and an ERA of 3.60. His 361 games pitched with the Indians ranks eighth all-time. Other future major leaguers drafted and signed by the Indians in 1992 were Jon Nunnally (third round) and Mitch Meluskey (12th round).

JUNE 3 The Indians break a scoreless tie with seven runs in the fourth inning and beat the Mariners 8–3 at Municipal Stadium. Sandy Alomar, Jr. hit a grand slam off Jim Acker.

JUNE 9 Glenallen Hill hits two homers during a 6–1 win over the Tigers in Detroit.

JUNE 10 Glenallen Hill and Brook Jacoby hit back-to-back homers in the 11th inning for a 4–2 win over the Tigers in Detroit. Hill also homered earlier in the contest, giving him four home runs in consecutive games.

JUNE 25 At the Jacobs Field construction site, with the infield dirt laid out and temporary bleachers installed, current Indians pitcher Charles Nagy and former Cleveland hurler Mel Harder throw ceremonial pitches over where home plate would eventually be installed. Nagy and Harder both wore uniforms from their respective eras.

JULY 3 The Indians trade Alex Cole to the Pirates for John Carter and Tony Mitchell.

JULY 8 Albert Belle's grand slam off Joe Grahe in the seventh inning breaks a 4–4 tie and leads the Indians to an 8–4 win over the Angels at Municipal Stadium.

JULY 14 In the All-Star Game at Jack Murphy Stadium in San Diego, Carlos Baerga doubles in a run and scores in the sixth inning to help the American League to a 13–6 victory.

On the same day, the Indians traded Kyle Washington to the Orioles for Jose Mesa. When acquired by the Indians, Mesa was 26-years-old and a below average starting pitcher. In 1994, the club converted Mesa into a reliever with brilliant results. He made the All-Star team in both 1995 and 1996.

JULY 23 The Indians outlast the Royals 1–0 in a 14-inning marathon at Municipal Stadium. The game ended on a one-out, bases-loaded sacrifice fly by Carlos Baerga, which was barely deep enough to let Sandy Alomar, Jr. beat Brian McRae's throw. Rod Nichols (eight innings), Derek Liliquist (one inning), Eric Plunk (four innings), and Kevin Wickander (one inning) combined on a six-hit shutout.

JULY 25 Carlos Baerga beats the Royals in extra innings again by striking a walk-off homer with two out in the 13th inning for a 2–1 win at Municipal Stadium.

Baerga hit .312 with 205 hits, 20 homers, and 105 RBIs in 1992. He was the first second baseman with an average of at least .300, 20 homers, 100 RBIs, and 200 hits in a season since Rogers Hornsby in 1929.

AUGUST 3 Kenny Lofton hits a home run and a triple before adding a tie-breaking double in the 12th inning to lead the Indians to an 8–6 win over the Yankees in New York.

AUGUST 8 Charles Nagy pitches a one-hitter and beats the Orioles 6–0 at Camden Yards. The lone Baltimore hit was an infield single by Glenn Davis in the seventh inning.

Nagy had a 17–10 record and a 2.96 ERA in 252 innings in 1992.

AUGUST 10 Down 5–0, the Indians score three runs in the third inning, one in the fourth, and four in the eighth for an 8–5 win over the Indians in Boston. Carlos Baerga broke the 5–5 tie with a three-run homer.

AUGUST 24 Hurricane Andrew damages the Homestead, Florida, training camp of the Indians, which was under construction. The club was scheduled to begin training there in 1993. The Indians front office made hasty plans to train at Winter Haven, Florida, that season. The Winter Haven site was used by the Red Sox from 1966 through 1992 before the club moved to Fort Myers (see March 6, 1993).

SEPTEMBER 4 Carlos Martinez hits a homer, triple, and a double during a 7–0 win over the Mariners at Municipal Stadium.

September 6 Albert Belle hits three homers and Carlos Martinez smacks a walk-off grand slam during a 12–9 win over the Mariners at Municipal Stadium. Belle hit homers in his first three official at-bats and drove in five runs. He struck a three-run shot off Brian Fisher in the first, and solo homers off Fisher in the third and Rich DeLucia in the fifth. Belle was taken out of the game in the ninth for defensive purposes with Cleveland holding a 7–6 lead, but Seattle tied it 7–7 forcing extra innings. The Mariners scored two in the top of the 12th on a homer by Jay Buhner. In the bottom of the inning, Carlos Baerga drove in the first run with a single. An intentional walk to Thomas Howard loaded the bases, and Martinez ended the contest with a home run off Mike Schooler.

September 9 Robin Yount collects his 3,000th career hit before the Indians rally for two runs in the ninth to beat the Brewers 5–4 in Milwaukee. Yount collected the milestone base hit with a single off Jose Mesa in the fourth inning. The Indians held Yount hitless in seven consecutive at-bats after he picked up hit number 2,999 off Jack Armstrong the previous night in a 7–3 Milwaukee win.

September 17 Indians vice-chairman of the board David Jacobs dies at the age of 71 from pneumonia and sepsis.

September 28 Reggie Jefferson collects four hits in four at-bats during a 6–4 win over the Yankees at Municipal Stadium.

After being recalled from the minors on September 18, Jefferson put together a streak of 16 hits in 25 at-bats from September 22 through 28.

November 17 Two weeks after Bill Clinton defeats George Bush in the presidential election, the Indians lose Darrell Whitmore and Jack Armstrong to the Marlins and Denis Boucher to the Rockies in the expansion draft.

December 8 The Indians sign Bobby Ojeda, most recently with the Dodgers, as a free agent (see March 22, 1993).

1993

Season in a Sentence

The deaths of Steve Olin and Tim Crews in a spring training boating accident casts a pall over the Indians seventh consecutive losing season, and the last one at Municipal Stadium.

Finish • Won • Lost • Pct • GB

Finish	Won	Lost	Pct	GB
Sixth	76	86	.469	19.0

Manager

Mike Hargrove

Stats

Stats	Indians	AL	Rank
Batting Avg:	.275	.267	3
On-Base Pct:	.335	.337	7
Slugging Pct:	.409	.408	7
Home Runs:	141		9
Stolen Bases:	159		3
ERA:	4.58	4.32	11
Fielding Avg:	.976	.981	14
Runs Scored:	790		5
Runs Allowed:	813		11

Starting Line-up

Junior Ortiz, c
Paul Sorrento, 1b
Carlos Baerga, 2b
Alvaro Espinosa, 3b
Felix Fermin, ss
Albert Belle, lf
Kenny Lofton, cf
Wayne Kirby, rf
Reggie Jefferson, dh
Carlos Martinez, 3b-1b-dh
Jeff Treadway, 3b-2b
Sandy Alomar, Jr., c

Pitchers

Jose Mesa, sp
Mark Clark, sp
Jeff Mutis, sp
Eric Plunk, rp
Derek Liliquist, rp
Jerry DiPoto, rp
Jeremy Hernandez, rp
Tom Kramer, rp-sp

Attendance

2,177,908 (7th in AL)

Club Leaders

Batting Avg:	Carlos Baerga	.321
On-Base Pct:	Kenny Lofton	.408
Slugging Pct:	Albert Belle	.552
Home Runs:	Albert Belle	38
RBIs:	Albert Belle	129
Runs:	Kenny Lofton	116
Stolen Bases:	Kenny Lofton	70
Wins:	Jose Mesa	10
Strikeouts:	Jose Mesa	118
ERA:	Jose Mesa	4.92
Saves:	Eric Plunk	15

March 6 Eight days after a terrorist bomb explodes in the parking garage of the World Trade Center, killing six people, the Indians play the first of two exhibition games against the Florida Marlins at Homestead, Florida. The proceeds of the games went to hurricane relief efforts. The Indians were scheduled to conduct spring training in Homestead in 1993, but Hurricane Andrew devastated the city in August 1992, forcing the club to alter its plans and move to Winter Haven, Florida (see August 24, 1992). In March 1993, the Indians said they were committed to returning to Homestead in 1994, but in April 1993 the club abandoned those plans because of concerns that the area may never fully recover from the damage caused by the storm.

March 22 Indians pitchers Steve Olin and Tim Crews are killed and Bob Ojeda is seriously injured in a boating accident on Little Lake Nellie in Clermont, Florida, near Orlando. It is the only multiple fatality in baseball history. On an off day in the Indians spring training schedule, the families of the three players were picnicking at a house Crews owned. Just after dark, Olin, Crews, and Ojeda, riding in an aluminum 18-foot open-air bass fishing boat piloted by Crews, slammed into the side of a long L-shaped pier at high speed. The dock stretched about 185 feet into the lake. Crews apparently didn't see the obstruction. An investigation later showed that Crews's blood alcohol level was 0.14 per cent, over the state's legal limit of 0.10 per cent.

Olin, age 27, was killed instantly by multiple head fractures. Crews, age 31, died the next morning of a damaged lung and massive head injuries at the Orlando Regional Medical Center. Ojeda, age 35, underwent surgery for severe damage to his scalp, which had to be surgically re-attached, and was released from the hospital three days later. He underwent several months of therapy and didn't pitch again for the Indians until August. Olin left a wife and three children. The previous season he led the Indians in saves with 29. Crews had pitched for the Dodgers from 1987 through 1992 and was in the Indians camp as a non-roster player. He also left a wife and three children. Ojeda was signed by the club as a free agent the previous December.

MARCH 31 The Indians trade Mark Whiten to the Cardinals for Mark Clark and Juan Andujar.

APRIL 5 In the season opener, the Indians lose 9–1 in front of a crowd of 73,290 on the last Opening Day at Municipal Stadium. Before the game, there was an hour-long tribute to Steve Olin and Tim Crews, who died in the boating accident two weeks earlier (see March 22, 1993). The wives of Olin and Crews were presented with uniforms of their late husbands.

APRIL 8 Carlos Baerga becomes the first player in major league history to hit homers from both sides of the plate in the same inning during a 15–5 win over the Yankees at Municipal Stadium. It happened during a nine-run seventh inning. Baerga homered off right-hander Steve Howe on a 3–2 pitch with a runner on base and a solo shot against lefty Steve Farr on a 2–0 offering.

Baerga hit .321 with 105 runs, 200 hits, 21 homers, and 114 RBIs in 1993.

APRIL 16 The Indians clobber the Blue Jays 13–1 at Municipal Stadium. Kenny Lofton scored four runs and collected four hits, including a triple and a double.

Lofton hit .325, scored 118 runs, and stole a league-leading 70 bases in 1993.

MAY 1 Two weeks after the raid on the Branch Davidian compound in Waco, Texas, the Indians edge the Athletics 1–0 at Municipal Stadium. A double by Albert Belle in the first inning scored the lone run of the game. Jose Mesa (8⅓ innings) and Eric Plunk (⅔ inning) combined on the shutout.

The loss of Steve Olin, Tim Crews, and Bob Ojeda in the spring training boating accident hurt the pitching staff. Mesa was the only pitcher with more than 125 innings pitched or more than 15 starts. The Indians used 26 pitchers during the season, 18 of them in a starting role.

MAY 7 The Indians sign Lance Parrish, most recently with the Mariners, as a free agent.

MAY 17 Albert Belle hits a two-run homer off Ben McDonald in the first inning for the only two runs of a 2–0 victory over the Orioles in Baltimore. Jose Mesa (eight innings), Derek Liliquist (⅔ inning), and Eric Plunk (⅓ inning) combined on the shutout.

Belle hit 38 homers, drove in 129 runs, and batted .290 in 1993.

MAY 24 Indians pitcher Tom Kramer pitches a one-hitter in beating the Rangers 4–1 at Municipal Stadium. The only Texas base runner was Julio Franco, who homered in the fourth inning. Kramer retired the first ten batters he faced, as well as the last 17, and didn't pitch out of the stretch all night. It was only Kramer's third big league start.

The one-hitter was Kramer's only complete game in the majors. He pitched in just two big league seasons and had a 7–3 record and a 4.51 earned run average.

MAY 26 Rangers right fielder Jose Canseco uses his head during a 7–6 Indians win at Municipal Stadium. A drive by Carlos Martinez in the fourth inning hit Canseco on the top of his head and went over the wall. Canseco had a chance to catch the ball, but as he reached the warning track, he momentarily took his eye off the ball to look for the wall.

JUNE 1 Carlos Baerga collects a homer, a triple, and a double during a 15–6 pounding of the Yankees in New York.

On the same day, the Indians traded Jose Hernandez to the Cubs for Heathcliff Slocumb.

JUNE 3 In the first round of the amateur draft, the Indians select pitcher Daron Kirkreit from the University of California at Riverside.

Kirkreit never reached the majors. Future big leaguers drafted and signed by the Indians in 1993 included Steve Kline (eighth round), Roland Delamaza (15th round), and Richie Sexson (24th round).

JUNE 18 Carlos Baerga hits three homers and drives in five runs, but receives little help from his teammates and the Indians lose 9–5 to the Tigers in Detroit. All three of Baerga's homers came off Mike Moore. The Cleveland second baseman hit a three-run shot in the first inning and solo home runs in the third and the eighth.

JUNE 24 Paul Sorrento hits a grand slam off Tom Gordon in the eighth inning of a 6–1 win over the Royals at Municipal Stadium. Sorrento was the first batter Gordon faced after relieving Mark Gubicza.

JUNE 26 A walk-off homer by Reggie Jefferson in the ninth inning beats the Royals 3–2 at Municipal Stadium.

JUNE 29 Kenny Lofton hits a grand slam off Rod Bolton in the fourth inning of an 8–2 victory over the White Sox at Municipal Stadium. It was the only home run that Lofton hit all year in 569 at-bats.

The Indians drew 2,177,908 fans in 1993, the last one at Municipal Stadium, an increase over the figure of 1,224,274 of 1992. It was the first time since 1949 that the club attracted over 2,000,000 in a season. Season ticket sales increased from about 3,000 to approximately 10,000 as fans sought preferred seating at Jacobs Field.

JULY 1 The Indians announce they will keep the Chief Wahoo symbol when the club moves into Jacobs Field in 1994.

Native American groups had lobbied for years to drop the beet-red, wide-eyed logo, stating it is a racially insensitive caricature. The symbol was featured prominently on a large sign above the Lake Shore Drive entrance to Municipal Stadium. A grinning Chief Wahoo held a bat in stride ready to whack a ball out of the park. It was erected in 1962. On July 5, 1993, a bill was introduced in the Ohio legislature to block public money for the new stadium if the club continued to use Chief Wahoo, but the measure failed to pass. However, Native Americans continued to protest the use of the symbol.

JULY 3 The Indians extend their winning streak to eight games with a 5–3 decision over the Angels in Anaheim.

JULY 6 Pinch-hitter Carlos Martinez hits a three-run homer in the ninth inning to beat the Athletics 11–8 in Oakland.

JULY 13 In the All-Star Game at Camden Yards in Baltimore, Albert Belle hits a run-scoring single and later scores in the fifth inning to help the American League to a 9–3 victory.

JULY 20 Carlos Baerga hits a grand slam off Joe Boever in the second inning of a 9–5 win over the Athletics at Municipal Stadium. The blow came on Boever's second pitch after relieving Mike Mohler.

JULY 25 The Indians outlast the Mariners 11–9 at Municipal Stadium. Cleveland scored five runs in the first inning for a 5–0 lead, fell behind 9–8, then scored a run in the seventh inning and two in the eighth.

AUGUST 1 The Indians score eight runs in the second inning and beat the Royals 9–5 in Kansas City.

AUGUST 7 Bob Ojeda makes his first appearance since being injured in the March 22 boating accident that killed two teammates. During an 8–6 loss to the Orioles in Baltimore, Ojeda allowed two runs, one earned, in two innings. He received a standing ovation from the Camden Yards crowd when he entered the game in the fourth inning.

AUGUST 11 Trailing 5–0, the Indians score a run in the sixth inning, another in the seventh, two in the eighth, and three in the ninth to win 7–6 over the Brewers in Milwaukee.

AUGUST 12 Carlos Baerga hits a three-run homer in the 11th inning to break a 5–5 tie and help the Indians beat the Brewers 8–6 in Milwaukee.

AUGUST 17 The Indians trade Thomas Howard to the Reds for Randy Milligan.

AUGUST 19 The Indians trade Glenallen Hill to the Cubs for Candy Maldonado.

AUGUST 23 Joe Carter hits three homers for the Blue Jays during a 9–8 Indians win in Toronto. It was Carter's fifth career three-home run game. The first four came while playing for the Indians (see July 19, 1989).

AUGUST 31 The Indians lose 5–4 to the Twins in 22 innings in Minneapolis. It is the longest game in Indians history. The contest ended on a home run by Pedro Munoz off Jason Grimsley. It took six hours and 22 minutes to complete. The Tribe broke a 1–1 tie with three runs in the eighth, but Minnesota tied the score with two runs in the bottom of the eighth and one in the ninth. There were 12 consecutive scoreless innings from the tenth through the 21st.

SEPTEMBER 1 The Indians collect 22 hits and beat the Twins 12–7 in Minneapolis.

SEPTEMBER 2 Manny Ramirez makes his major league debut during a 4–3 loss to the Twins in Minneapolis. Batting sixth as the designated hitter, he was hitless in four at-bats.

SEPTEMBER 3 In his second big league game, Manny Ramirez hits the first two homers of his career and a double during a 7–3 victory over the Yankees in New York. Ramirez played high school ball in New York after his family came to the United States from the Dominican Republic when he was 13. Bob Ojeda was the winning pitcher, his first victory since the March 22 boating accident.

SEPTEMBER 8 Light-hitting Felix Fermin drives in six runs with a triple, a double, and a single during a 15–8 win over the Twins at Municipal Stadium. The Indians scored 12 runs over the first four innings.

SEPTEMBER 14 Major League Baseball announces its three-division alignment and extra round of playoffs, to be put into effect during the 1994 season. The Indians were placed in the Central Division with the White Sox, Royals, Brewers, and Twins. In 1998, the Brewers were transferred to the National League and the Tigers moved from the AL East to the AL Central.

SEPTEMBER 15 The Indians play at Arlington Stadium for the last time and lose 7–4 to the Rangers.

SEPTEMBER 19 The Indians rout the Tigers 12–2 in Detroit. Mark Clark took a no-hitter into the seventh inning before allowing two runs and seven hits. Sam Horn, in his second game with the Indians, hit two homers.

Horn played in just 12 games with the Indians, all in 1993, the seventh season of an eight-year career. In a Cleveland uniform, Horn hit .455 with four homers in 33 at-bats.

SEPTEMBER 27 The Royals score two runs in the ninth inning to defeat the Indians 6–5 in Kansas City. Pitcher Jerry DiPoto made one of three Cleveland errors in the inning and walked Gary Gaetti with the bases loaded to let in the winning run.

OCTOBER 1 The Indians start the final weekend at Municipal Stadium with a 4–2 loss to the White Sox before a Friday night crowd of 72,454.

OCTOBER 2 In the next-to-last game at Municipal Stadium, the Indians lose 4–2 in ten innings against the White Sox before 72,060.

OCTOBER 3 In the final baseball game at Municipal Stadium, the Indians lose 4–0 to the White Sox before a crowd of 72,390. Jose DeLeon fanned Mark Lewis for the final out.

Mel Harder, at the age of 83, threw out the ceremonial first pitch. He wore a replica 1932 Indians jersey for the occasion. Harder was the Cleveland pitcher in the first game at Municipal Stadium on July 31, 1932. Bob Hope, age 90, a Cleveland native and former part-owner of the Indians, also participated in pre-game ceremonies by singing his trademark song "Thanks for the Memories." The grounds crew wore tuxedos as they swept the field.

NOVEMBER 4 Tragedy strikes the Indians again, as pitcher Cliff Young dies in an auto accident in his hometown of Willis, Texas. Young was 29. He was the third Indians player to die in 1993, following Steve Olin and Tim Crews (see March 22, 1993). Young was on his way to pick up a young cousin from a dance class when his car went off the road and hit a tree, killing him instantly. Two passengers survived the accident.

DECEMBER 2 The Indians sign Dennis Martinez, most recently with the Expos, and Eddie Murray, most recently with the Mets, as free agents.

Both Martinez and Murray were near the ends of their careers but proved to be tremendous short-term acquisitions. Nicknamed "El Presidente," Martinez was in Cleveland's starting rotation for three years and posted a record of 32–17. Murray was the club's first option at designated hitter for three seasons. Both played key roles in the 1995 American League championship season.

DECEMBER 13 The Indians trade Randy Milligan to the Expos for Brian Barnes.

DECEMBER 20 The Indians trade Felix Fermin and Reggie Jefferson to the Mariners for Omar Vizquel.

The Indians pulled off one of the best deals in club history in this trade. Jefferson had a solid career but never became the power hitter people had anticipated, while Fermin remained a light-hitting shortstop with adequate defensive skills. Vizquel is considered to be one of the greatest fielding shortstops to ever play the game. He was the club's starting shortstop for eleven seasons, played in three All-Star Games and two World Series, and won nine consecutive Gold Gloves from 1993 through 2001. Among Indians, Vizquel ranks tenth in games played (1,478), second in stolen bases (279), fifth in at-bats (5,708), sixth in runs (906), seventh in hits (1,616), eighth in doubles (288), and tenth in total bases (2,162).

1994

Season in a Sentence

Jacobs Field opens and the Indians finish the strike-shortened season 19 games over .500, the highest figure since 1959.

Finish • Won • Lost • Pct • GB

Finish	Won	Lost	Pct	GB
Second	66	47	.584	1.0

Manager

Mike Hargrove

Stats

Stats	Indians	AL	Rank
Batting Avg:	.290	.273	2
On-Base Pct:	.351	.345	5
Slugging Pct:	.484	.434	1
Home Runs:	167		1
Stolen Bases:	131		2
ERA:	4.36	4.80	5
Fielding Avg:	.980	.981	11
Runs Scored:	679		1
Runs Allowed:	562		5

Starting Line-up

Sandy Alomar, jr.
Paul Sorrento, 1b
Carlos Baerga, 2b
Jim Thome, 3b
Omar Vizquel, ss
Albert Belle, lf
Kenny Lofton, cf
Manny Ramirez, rf
Eddie Murray, dh
Alvaro Espinoza, 3b-ss-2b
Wayne Kirby, rf

Pitchers

Dennis Martinez, sp
Charles Nagy, sp
Mark Clark, sp
Jack Morris, sp
Jason Grimsley, sp
Jose Mesa, rp
Eric Plunk, rp
Derek Liliquist, rp

Attendance

1,995,174 (4th in AL)

Club Leaders

Batting Avg:	Albert Belle	.357
On-Base Pct:	Albert Belle	.438
Slugging Pct:	Albert Belle	.714
Home Runs:	Albert Belle	36
RBIs:	Albert Belle	101
Runs:	Kenny Lofton	105
Stolen Bases:	Kenny Lofton	60
Wins:	Dennis Martinez	11
	Mark Clark	11
Strikeouts:	Charles Nagy	108
ERA:	Charles Nagy	3.45
Saves:	Paul Shuey	5
	Jeff Russell	5

JANUARY 28 Three weeks after Nancy Kerrigan is attacked by assailants connected to rival skater Tonya Harding, Bob Ojeda signs with the Yankees as a free agent.

FEBRUARY 7 The Indians sign Tony Pena, most recently with the Red Sox, as a free agent.

FEBRUARY 10 The Indians sign Jack Morris, most recently with the Blue Jays, as a free agent.

Morris had a 244–182 lifetime record when signed by the Indians at the age of 38. He was 10–6 with Cleveland in 1994, his last season in the majors, but his ERA was 5.60. The Indians released Morris on August 9, in part because he was spending time between starts on his farm in Great Falls, Montana, helping with the wheat harvest, putting into question his dedication to the team.

MARCH 22 Jerry DiPoto has surgery to remove a cancerous thyroid gland. He didn't pitch again until July. DiPoto was one of two Cleveland pitchers with cancer in 1994. Matt Turner was diagnosed with lymphatic cancer, underwent chemotherapy, and never pitched in the majors again.

MARCH 23 The Indians new ballpark finally gets a name when it is announced that it will be known as Jacobs Field. Club owner Richard Jacobs put his name on the facility by agreeing to pay the project board $13.9 million over 20 years.

APRIL 2 The Indians open Jacobs Field with a 6–4 exhibition game loss to the Pirates before 40,523.

Home plate at Jacobs Field was moved from Municipal Stadium.

APRIL 4 The Indians play their first regular season game at Jacobs Field and beat the Mariners 4–3 in 11 innings before a sellout crowd of 41,459. The contest, played on a sunny day with the temperature at 48 degrees, was exciting from start to finish. Randy Johnson no-hit the Tribe until Sandy Alomar, Jr. singled in the eighth. Later in the inning, Manny Ramirez smacked a two-run double that tied the score 2–2. Seattle scored in the tenth and the home team countered with a tally in their half. In the 11th, Eddie Murray doubled and scored on Wayne Kirby's single for the winning run. The winning pitcher was Eric Plunk. Eddie Murray, in his Indians debut, broke the major league record for most career games played at first base. It was Murray 2,269th game at the position, passing Jake Beckley, who played from 1888 through 1907. Dennis Martinez threw the first pitch, a strike, to Rich Amaral. Other firsts were achieved by Eric Anthony of the Mariners (hit and home run) and Edgar Martinez of Seattle (run scored)

Among the dignitaries at the opening were President Bill Clinton, Ohio Governor George Voinovich and Cleveland Mayor Mike White. Clinton threw out the ceremonial first pitch. He wore an old-style Indians hat with the letter "C" instead of the one the club used in 1994 that featured Chief Wahoo, a symbol many Native Americans found offensive. Clinton watched the Indians victory from the owner's luxury box. After the game, the president boarded Air Force One for Charlotte, North Carolina, where he watched Arkansas defeat Duke in the NCAA basketball championship game. On the same day, Hillary Clinton threw out the first pitch at Wrigley Field.

APRIL 7 In the first night game at Jacobs Field, the Indians beat the Mariners 6–2. The game was played in near-freezing temperatures. Eddie Murray hit the first home run by an Indian at the new ballpark.

The Indians donned new uniforms during the 1994 campaign. The home jersey was solid white with red piping one-half inch from the bottom of the sleeve, buttons down the front outlined by red piping, and featured red INDIANS script lettering outlined in navy on the front, and the Indians logo on the left sleeve. The pants had red, white, and navy piping down both sides. The road uniform duplicated the home but was solid gray with navy piping outlining the buttons and featured script CLEVELAND in red and outlined in blue on the front. The Indians also had an alternative navy blue jersey with script INDIANS in red. It was worn only during home games. A blue road jersey, with CLEVELAND in script, was added in 1998.

APRIL 11 Manny Ramirez hits two homers and drives in five runs during a 9–6 win over the Angels in Anaheim.

APRIL 13 Kenny Lofton homers in the tenth inning to beat the Angels 6–5 in Anaheim. Bo Jackson tied the game with a three-run homer for California in the bottom of the ninth off Jose Mesa.

Lofton played in 112 of the Indians 113 games in 1994 and hit .349. He scored 105 runs and led the AL in hits (160) and stolen bases (60).

APRIL 21 Eddie Murray homers from both sides of the plate during a 10–6 win over the Twins in Minnesota. Murray homered off right-hander Pat Mahomes and lefty Larry Casian. It was the 11th time that Murray hit home runs from both sides of the plate in the same game, breaking the record of ten set by Mickey Mantle.

Murray's record of switch-hit homers in 11 games was later tied by Chili Davis.

APRIL 22 The Indians play at the Ballpark at Arlington for the first time and lose 7–3 to the Rangers.

APRIL 27 After the White Sox score twice in the top of the 12th inning, the Indians counter with three runs in their half to win 8–7 at Jacobs Field. Manny Ramirez tied the game 7–7. Mark Lewis drove in the winning run with a walk-off double.

APRIL 29 A walk-off homer by Kenny Lofton in the 12th inning beats the Rangers 5–4 at Jacobs Field.

MAY 6 Dennis Martinez allows only three hits in a ten-inning complete game to beat the Orioles 4–2 in Baltimore. Carlos Baerga drove in both tenth-inning runs with a double.

Baerga hit .314 with 19 homers in 1994.

MAY 14 Pitching in the ninth inning of a 9–3 win over the Tigers at Jacobs Field, Paul Shuey faces six batters and records four strikeouts and two walks. He fanned Chad Kreuter, Chris Gomez, Travis Fryman, and Cecil Fielder. Fryman reached base by swinging for strike three on a ball that Shuey sailed past the catcher for a wild pitch.

MAY 19 Albert Belle hits a two-run, walk-off homer in the 13th inning to defeat the Brewers 4–2 at Jacobs Field.

Belle reached base 25 times in 36 plate appearances over eight games from May through May 23. He had 15 hits and ten walks. The hot streak included a stretch of reaching base 16 times on eight hits and eight walks in 17 consecutive trips to the plate. Overall, Belle hit .357 with 35 doubles, 36 homers, 101 RBIs, and a league-leading 294 total bases in 106 games in 1994. His .714 slugging percentage is an Indians single season record. The only seven games he missed were while serving a suspension (see July 15, 1994).

MAY 27 Paul Sorrento hits a walk-off homer in the ninth inning to beat the Athletics 3–2 in Oakland. The other two Cleveland runs scored on back-to-back homers by Jim Thome and Sandy Alomar, Jr. in the third inning.

Alomar hit .288 with 14 homers in 1994.

JUNE 2 In the first round of the amateur draft, the Indians select pitcher Jaret Wright from Katella High School in Anaheim, California.

The son of former major league pitcher Clyde Wright, Jaret reached the majors in 1997 at the age of 21. He was 8–3 during the regular season in his rookie year and 3–0 in the post-season. Wright was a starter in two World Series games that fall, including game seven. He was one of the most promising pitchers in the game, but persistent arm troubles wrecked his career. Wright had a 35–32 in six seasons with the Indians. Other future major leaguers drafted and signed by Cleveland in 1994 were Danny Graves (fourth round), Russell Branyan (seventh round), Bruce Aven (30th round), and Chan Perry (44th round).

June 5 The Indians extend their winning streak to eight games with an 8–1 decision over the Athletics in Oakland.

June 12 The Indians score eight runs in the second inning and win 12–6 over the Brewers in Milwaukee. Albert Belle hit a grand slam in the second inning off Jaime Navarro.

June 15 Jim Thome hits a walk-off homer in the 13th inning to beat the Blue Jays 4–3 at Jacobs Field.

June 19 Two days after 95 million Americans tune in to the eight-hour police chase of O. J. Simpson and his Ford Bronco, the Indians extend their winning streak at home to a club record 18 games and their overall winning streak to nine contests with a 6–5 decision over the Red Sox at Jacobs Field. It was Jack Morris's 250th career victory. The previous club record for consecutive home wins was 16 in 1951 at Municipal Stadium.

June 20 The Indians win their tenth game in a row with a 7–1 decision over the Tigers in Detroit.

The Indians had a 14–17 record on May 21, then won 27 of their next 35 games.

June 21 The Indians ten-game winning streak comes to an end when the Tigers score six runs in the ninth inning to win 7–5 in Detroit. The contest ended on a grand slam by Lou Whitaker off Derek Liliquist.

June 22 The Indians increase their lead in the AL Central to five games with a 9–6 victory over the Tigers in Detroit.

June 25 The Indians 18-game home winning streak comes to a halt in a game that takes two days to complete. The contest started on June 24 and was suspended after seven innings by rain with the Yankees leading 9–5. The final two innings were completed on June 25 with the Indians losing 11–6.

June 26 Down 12–4, the Indians score seven runs in the eighth inning, but the rally falls short and results in a 12–11 loss to the Yankees at Jacobs Field.

June 28 The Indians blow an 8–3 lead when the Orioles score six runs in the ninth inning at Jacobs Field. Cleveland added a run in the ninth and lost 9–6.

July 1 The Indians trade Steve Farr and Chris Nabholtz to the Red Sox for Jeff Russell.

July 3 Larry Doby's uniform number 14 is retired in ceremonies before an 11-inning, 10–9 win over the Twins at Jacobs Field.

At that time the club had retired the numbers of Bob Feller (19), Lou Boudreau (5), Earl Averill (3), and Mel Harder (18). Since then they have retired the numbers for Bob Lemon (21), Jackie Robinson (42-along with all MLB teams), and 455, to honor their fans and to commemorate selling out 455 consecutive games between 1995 and 2001, which is currently an MLB record.

July 6 The Indians score six runs in the first inning and four in the second and rout the Rangers 13–4 in Arlington.

July 12 In the All-Star Game at Three Rivers Stadium in Pittsburgh, Kenny Lofton hits a two-run single in the seventh, but the American League loses 8–7 in ten innings.

July 15 Albert Belle has his bat confiscated in the first inning of a 3–2 win over the White Sox in Chicago. Sox manager Gene Lamont alleged that Belle's bat was corked.

The incident became known as "Batgate" and over the next few days contained as many twists and turns as a crime novel. The bat in question was removed to the umpire's locker room, but before the game was over, someone broke into that supposedly secure area and replaced Belle's bat with one belonging to Paul Sorrento. The culprit who switched the bats entered the umpire's room through ceiling tiles, and then departed by the same route. Indians general manager John Hart admitted that the individual who switched the bats was a non-uniformed member of the club's traveling squad but wouldn't reveal his name. A bat thought to be the original was returned to the umpires on July 17 and sent to the league office in New York. There it was sawed in half and found to be corked. AL President Bobby Brown suspended Belle for ten days, but Belle appealed and continued to play until a hearing with Brown on July 29. At that time, the suspension was reduced to six days and seven games, which Belle began serving on August 1. In 1999, Jason Grimsley, who was a pitcher for the Indians in 1994, admitted that he was the one who switched the bats. Grimsley's career came to a dramatic end in 2006 when he was found with a supply of human growth hormone while playing for the Arizona Diamondbacks.

July 19 The Indians club five homers during a 12–3 win over the Rangers at Jacobs Field. Paul Sorrento struck a pair of home runs with Wayne Kirby, Albert Belle, and Jim Thome adding the rest.

July 20 The Indians hit five homers for the second game in a row, but lose 13–11 in 11 innings against the Rangers at Jacobs Field. The home runs were struck by Paul Sorrento, Jim Thome, Albert Belle, Eddie Murray, and Wayne Kirby.

Sorrento hit five homers in five games from July 19 through July 23.

July 22 Jim Thome hits three of the Indians six home runs and Albert Belle homers for the fourth consecutive game during a 9–8 victory over the White Sox at Jacobs Field. Thome homered in his first three at-bats, hitting one off Jason Bere and two facing Scott Sanderson. The other Cleveland homers were collected by Paul Sorrento and Kenny Lofton.

While appealing his suspension for allegedly using a corked bat (see July 15, 1994), Belle hit nine homers in a span of 12 games from July 19 through July 30.

JULY 30 The Indians drop out of first place with a 6–5 loss to the Yankees in New York.

The Tribe was 0–9 against the Yankees in 1994.

AUGUST 4 In the last home game before the players's strike, the Indians defeat the Tigers 5–0 at Jacobs Field.

The contest was the 28th consecutive sellout for the Indians in 1994. The club drew 1,995,174 fans in 51 home games and were on a pace to draw well over three million, which would have broken the Cleveland attendance record of 2,620,627 set in 1948.

AUGUST 6 In the first of two consecutive double headers against the Red Sox at Fenway Park, Dennis Martinez pitches a two-hitter in game two for a 7–0 win. The only Boston hits were singles by Otis Nixon in the first inning and Tim Naehring in the second. The Red Sox won the opener 8–4.

In his first season with the Indians, Martinez had a record of 11–6 and an ERA of 3,52. Charles Nagy was 10–8 and compiled an earned run average of 3.45.

AUGUST 7 The Indians score five runs in the 12th inning to beat the Red Sox 15–10 in the second game of a double header at Fenway Park. Both teams scored once in the 11th. Boston won the opener 4–1.

AUGUST 10 In the last game before the strike, the Indians defeat the Blue Jays 5–3 in Toronto.

When the strike was called, Cleveland was one game behind the White Sox in the AL Central and held a 2½-game advantage over the Orioles in the wild card race.

AUGUST 12 With about 70 percent of the season completed, the major league baseball players go on strike.

The strike, baseball's eighth interruption since 1972, had been anticipated all season. The owners wanted to put a lid on escalating payrolls by capping salaries and revising if not eliminating salary arbitration procedures. The players who were obviously not interested in these reforms had only one weapon once talks broke down: a strike.

AUGUST 31 The Indians obtain 42-year-old Dave Winfield from the Twins for a player to be named later.

Winfield was acquired for a stretch pennant run that was canceled due to the strike (see September 14, 1994). He played 46 games for the Indians in 1995, the last of his Hall of Fame career, and batted only .191. Winfield was not placed on Cleveland's 1995 post-season roster.

SEPTEMBER 14 The owners of the 28 major league clubs vote 26–2 to cancel the remainder of the season, including the playoffs and the World Series.

NOVEMBER 9 The Indians sell Derek Liliquist to the Braves.

NOVEMBER 18 The Indians trade Paul Byrd, Jerry DiPoto, Dave Mlicki, and Jesse Azauje to the Mets for Jeromy Burnitz and Joe Roa.

1995

Season in a Sentence

The season is shortened by 18 games due to the strike, but the Indians have enough time to win 100 regular season games and reach the World Series for the first time since 1954.

Finish • Won • Lost • Pct • GB

Finish	Won	Lost	Pct	GB
First	100	44	.694	+30.0

Manager

Mike Hargrove

American League Division Series

The Indians defeated the Boston Red Sox three games to none.

American League Championship Series

The Indians defeated the Seattle Mariners four games to two.

World Series

The Indians lost four games to two to the Atlanta Braves.

Stats

Stats	Indians	AL	Rank
Batting Avg:	.291	.344	1
On-Base Pct:	.361	.344	1
Slugging Pct:	.479	.427	1
Home Runs:	207		1
Stolen Bases:	132		1
ERA:	3.83	4.71	1
Fielding Avg:	.982	.982	6
Runs Scored:	840		1
Runs Allowed:	607		1

Starting Line-up

Tony Pena, c
Paul Sorrento, 1b
Carlos Baerga, 2b
Jim Thome, 3b
Omar Vizquel, ss
Albert Belle, lf
Kenny Lofton, cf
Manny Ramirez, rf
Eddie Murray, dh
Sandy Alomar, Jr., c
Wayne Kirby, rf-cf

Pitchers

Charles Nagy, sp
Orel Hershiser, sp
Dennis Martinez, sp
Mark Clark, sp
Chad Ogea, sp
Ken Hill, sp
Jose Mesa, rp
Julian Tavarez, rp
Eric Plunk, rp
Paul Assenmacher, rp
Jim Poole, rp

Attendance

2,842,745 (2nd in AL)

Club Leaders

Batting Avg:	Eddie Murray	.323
On-Base Pct:	Manny Ramirez	.402
Slugging Pct:	Albert Belle	.690
Home Runs:	Albert Belle	50
RBIs:	Albert Belle	126
Runs:	Albert Belle	212
Stolen Bases:	Kenny Lofton	54
Wins:	Charles Nagy	16
	Orel Hershiser	16
Strikeouts:	Charles Nagy	139
ERA:	Dennis Martinez	3.08
Saves:	Jose Mesa	46

January 13 Major league owners vote to use replacement players during the 1995 season if the strike is not settled.

April 2 The 234-day major league strike of major league players comes to an end.

The opening of the season, originally scheduled to begin on April 3, was pushed back to April 26 with each team playing 144 games. The replacement players were either released or sent to minor league teams.

April 7 The Indians sign Bud Black, most recently with the Giants, as a free agent.

The 1995 Indians packed a punch throughout the lineup, but Albert Belle clearly was the offensive leader, powering the Tribe to 100 wins.

April 8 The Indians sign Orel Hershiser, most recently with the Dodgers, as a free agent.

Hershiser came to the Indians with a 134–102 career record and World Series experience. In three seasons with Cleveland, Hershiser was 45–21 and pitched in two more Fall Classics.

April 10 The Indians sign Paul Assenmacher, most recently with the Cubs, as a free agent.

April 27 In the opening game of the strike-delayed season, the Indians hit five home runs and roll to an 11–6 win over the Rangers in Arlington. The Tribe scored three runs in the second inning and six in the third. The home runs were struck by Paul Sorrento, Albert Belle, Eddie Murray, Manny Ramirez, and Carlos Baerga. Ramirez had four hits in all, scored three runs and drove in three. Dennis Martinez was the winning pitcher.

Ramirez hit .308 with 31 homers and 107 RBIs in 1995.

May 1 In Detroit's home opener, the Indians win 11–1 before an unruly crowd at Tiger Stadium as fans expressed their displeasure over the strike and the lopsided score by throwing objects and repeatedly running onto the field. At least 20 fans were taken off the field by security. Before the game began, fans threw magnetized schedules onto the field. Later, they delayed the action on several occasions with a barrage of bottles, cans, batteries, beach balls, and toilet paper. Kenny Lofton had a scary moment in the fifth inning after he was nearly struck by a napkin holder someone pilfered from a concession stand.

Lofton led the AL in triples (13) and stolen bases (54) in 1995.

May 3 Paul Sorrento drives in six runs, three on a homer run, to lead the Indians to a 14–7 win over the Tigers in Detroit.

May 5 In the home opener, the Indians win 5–1 over the Twins before 41,434 at Jacobs Field. Charles Nagy was the winning pitcher on his 28th birthday.

May 7 The Indians win 10–9 over the Twins at Jacobs Field in a contest that lasts 17 innings and six hours and 36 minutes. There was no scoring between the ninth and 16th innings and the two teams combined utilized 17 pitchers. Kenny Lofton drove in the winning run with a walk-off single. Eddie Murray drove in five runs with two homers and two singles. Cleveland certainly had its chances to put the game away much earlier. Nine Minnesota hurlers allowed 26 hits and eight walks. The Indians left 23 men on base.

In his 19th big league season, Murray batted .323 with 21 home runs.

May 9 The Indians hit three home runs and score eight runs before a batter is retired in a 10–0 win over the Royals at Jacobs Field. Facing Kansas City pitcher Doug Linton, Kenny Lofton led off with a home run. He was followed by Omar Vizquel (walk), Carlos Baerga (two-run home run), Albert Belle (single), Eddie Murray (single), Jim Thome (walk), Manny Ramirez (bases-loaded walk) and Paul Sorrento (grand slam home run). Tony Pena ended the streak by grounding out.

Sorrento's grand slam was the first in Jacobs Field history.

MAY 21 The Indians score three runs in the eighth inning and three more in the ninth to defeat the Red Sox 12–10 in Boston. Paul Sorrento's home run in the eighth tied the score 9–9. Carlos Baerga and Jim Thome broke the deadlock with doubles in the ninth.

Baerga batted .314 with 175 hits and 15 homers in 1995.

MAY 29 Down 6–0, the Indians score four runs in the sixth inning, two in the seventh, and one in the eighth to beat the White Sox 7–6 at Jacobs Field. Tony Pena drove in the winning run with a double.

In 162 games from May 6, 1995, through April 26, 1996, the Indians had a record of 110–52.

JUNE 1 In the first round of the amateur draft, the Indians select first baseman David Miller from Clemson University.

Miller never played in the majors. Future big leaguers drafted and signed by the Indians in 1995 were Sean Casey (second round), Scott Winchester (14th round), and Jason Rakers (25th round).

JUNE 4 Trailing 8–0, the Indians rally for a 9–8 win over the Blue Jays at Jacobs Field. Toronto scored seven runs in the first inning and one in the third. Cleveland countered with one in the bottom of the third, two in the fourth, two in the fifth, one in the sixth, and three in a thrilling ninth-inning rally. The game ended on a two-run homer by Paul Sorrento.

JUNE 8 Down 6–4 to the Brewers in Milwaukee, the Indians erupt for four runs in the ninth inning and win 8–7. The final-inning runs scored on a two-run double by Albert Belle and a two-run homer from Jim Thome.

Thome batted .314 with an on base percentage of .438 and 25 home runs in 1995.

JUNE 12 The Indians achieve the first of what would become 455 consecutive sellouts and beat the Orioles 4–3 at Jacobs Field.

The Indians sold out every home game from June 12, 1995, through Opening Day in 2001. In 1995, the club drew 2,842,745, breaking the 1948 record of 2,620,627. The 1995 figure compared to 2,177,908 in 1993 and 1,224,274 in 1992. The Indians were the only one of the 28 major league teams to draw more fans in 1995 than they had in 1993, the last full-season before the 1994–95 strike by the players.

JUNE 13 The Indians hammer the Orioles 11–0 at Jacobs Field.

JUNE 17 Herbert Perry hits the first two home runs of his career during a 7–4 win over the Yankees at Jacobs Field. Perry hit both of them off Andy Pettitte.

Perry hit three home runs as an Indian over 63 games and 183 at-bats from 1994 through 1996. He missed the 1997 and 1998 seasons with injured knees before returning to the majors with Tampa Bay in 1999. At the University of Florida, Perry played quarterback.

June 29 Eddie Murray collects two hits to run his career total to 2,999 during a 10–5 win over the Twins in Minneapolis.

June 30 Eddie Murray collects his 3,000th career base hit during a 4–1 win over the Twins in Minneapolis. The milestone hit was a single in the sixth inning off Mike Twombley.

Murray finished his career in 1997 with 3,255 hits. He had 339 of them with the Indians from 1994 through 1996.

July 5 Dennis Martinez (six innings), Jim Poole (two innings), and Jose Mesa (one inning) combined on a two-hitter to beat the Rangers 2–0 in a contest twice delayed by rain at Jacobs Field. Martinez allowed only an infield single to Rusty Greer in the first inning. Otis Nixon collected the second Texas hit with a single in the ninth.

A 40-year-old grandfather in 1995, Martinez started the season with a 9–0 record. He finished with a 12–5 record and a 3.08 ERA.

July 11 In the All-Star Game at The Ballpark in Arlington, Carlos Baerga collects a double and two singles in three at-bats and scores a run, although the American league loses 3–2.

July 14 The Indians sweep the Royals 1–0 and 7–6 at Jacobs Field. Carlos Baerga drove in the lone run of the first game with a single in the sixth inning. Alan Embree (six innings), Julian Tavarez (two innings) and Jose Mesa (one inning) combined on the shutout.

On the same day, the Indians released Bud Black.

July 16 After the Athletics score in the top of the 12th, Manny Ramirez hits a two-out, two-run homer on a 2–2 pitch from Dennis Eckersley in the bottom half of the inning to lift the Indians to a 5–4 victory at Jacobs Field. Carlos Baerga collected five hits, including a double, in six at-bats.

July 18 Albert Belle hits a walk-off grand slam off Lee Smith with one out in the ninth inning to beat the Angels 7–5 at Jacobs Field.

Belle had an incredible year in 1995. Playing in 143 of the Indians 144 games, he became the only player in major league history to collect at least 50 doubles and 50 homers in a season. Belle had 52 doubles and 50 homers in addition to a .317 batting average, 121 runs and 126 RBIs. His .690 slugging percentage led the American league. Belle hit 31 of his homers over the final two months with 14 in August and 17 in September. He also set a single-season Indians record for extra base hits (103). The 52 doubles are the most of any Indians player since 1926. His 377 total bases in 1995 are the most of any Indian since 1936. The 50 home runs set a team mark that stood until Jim Thome had 52 in 2002. Belle's unpopularity with the media led to a second place finish to Mo Vaughn of the Red Sox in the 1995 MVP voting, however, even though Vaughn had inferior batting statistics.

JULY 19 The Indians rout the Rangers 14–5 in Arlington.

JULY 22 The Indians score three runs in the ninth inning off Dennis Eckersley to beat the Athletics 6–4 in Oakland. Jim Thome drove in the tying and go-ahead runs with a double.

JULY 23 Paul Sorrento hits a two-run single in the fourth inning for the only runs of a 2–0 win over the Athletics in Oakland. Mark Clark (6²/₃ innings), Eric Plunk (1¹/₃ innings) and Jose Mesa (1¹/₃ innings) combined on the shutout.

Mesa was almost unhitable in 1995. In 62 games and 64 innings, he had a 3–0 record, 46 saves and a 1.13 ERA.

JULY 27 The Indians trade David Bell, Rick Heiserman, and Pepe McNeal to the Cardinals for Ken Hill.

AUGUST 2 Paul Sorrento hits a grand slam off Eddie Guardado in the fifth inning of a 12–6 win over the Twins at Jacobs Field.

AUGUST 4 The Indians overpower the White Sox 13–3 at Jacobs Field. Manny Ramirez hits a grand slam off Jason Bere in the third inning.

AUGUST 5 The Indians hit six homers and collect 21 hits during an 11–7 win over the White Sox at Jacobs Field. Albert Belle smacked two home runs, with Kenny Lofton, Carlos Baerga, Eddie Murray, and Paul Sorrento adding the rest.

AUGUST 10 The Indians score five runs in the ninth inning to stun the Yankees 10–9 in New York. Mike Stanley hit three homers to help New York build a 9–5 lead. The first run in the ninth scored on a Sandy Alomar, Jr. double. That was followed by a two-run triple from Kenny Lofton, an RBI-single by Carlos Baerga, and a walk-off sacrifice fly delivered by Jim Thome.

AUGUST 19 Eddie Murray hits a walk-off homer in the ninth to beat the Brewers 4–3 at Jacobs Field.

AUGUST 25 A walk-off homer by Sandy Alomar, Jr. in the 11th inning beats the Tigers 6–5 at Jacobs Field.

AUGUST 26 Charles Nagy strikes out 12 batters in 6²/₃ innings during a 6–2 win over the Tigers at Jacobs Field.

Nagy had a 16–6 record in 1995.

AUGUST 28 The Indians score seven runs in the second inning and defeat the Blue Jays 9–1 at Jacobs Field.

The Indians were 54–18 at home in 1995. From the ballpark's opening in 1994 through the end of the 1996 season, the club was 140–63, a winning percentage of 690.

AUGUST 30 The Indians score two runs in the 14th inning to beat the 4–3 at Jacobs Field. Kenny Lofton doubled, went to third on a bunt, and scored on a sacrifice fly by Carlos Baerga. Albert Belle ended the contest with a home run.

AUGUST 31 Albert Belle hits an extra-inning, walk-off homer for the second straight night with a two-run shot in the tenth inning that beats the Blue Jays 6–4 at Jacobs Field. It was the Indians eight win in a row.

The Indians were 13–0 in extra innings games during the regular season and 2–1 in the post-season in 1995.

SEPTEMBER 1 On the day the Rock and Roll Hall of Fame Museum opens, the Indians run their winning streak to nine games with a 14–4 decision over the Tigers in Detroit. The Indians trailed 4–0 after three innings before scoring 14 unanswered runs. Albert Belle hit a grand slam off Mike Myers in the eighth inning.

SEPTEMBER 6 The Indians score seven runs in the second inning and beat the Brewers 12–2 in Milwaukee.

SEPTEMBER 8 The Indians clinch the AL Central with a 3–2 win over the Orioles at Jacobs Field.

The club won its last five games to finish the season with a record of 100–44 (see October 1, 1995) and won the AL Central by an astonishing 30 games. The next best record in the American League in 1995 was 86–58 by the Red Sox. The Indians 1995 winning percentage .694 was the second best in club history, exceeded only by the .721 percentage of the 1954 team, which went 111–43.

SEPTEMBER 9 Chad Ogea (seven innings), Alan Embree (one inning), and Jose Mesa (one inning) combine on a two-hitter to defeat the Orioles 2–1 at Jacobs Field. The only Baltimore hits were a double by Brady Anderson in the first inning and a single from Rafael Palmeiro in the third.

SEPTEMBER 18 Albert Belle hits two home runs during an 11–1 rout of the White Sox in Chicago.

SEPTEMBER 19 Albert Belle hits three home runs during an 8–2 win over the White Sox in Chicago. In the process, Belle tied a major league record for most home runs in consecutive games with five. He homered in consecutive at-bats off Luis Andujar in the sixth inning, Scott Radinsky in the eighth, and Rod Bolton in the ninth. Each were solo shots.

SEPTEMBER 27 The Indians hit five home runs during a 9–6 win over the Twins in Minneapolis. Albert Belle and Jim Thome each hit two homers, with Jim Thome adding the other one.

SEPTEMBER 30 Albert Belle hits his 50th home run of 1995 during a 3–2 win over the Royals at Jacobs Field.

OCTOBER 1 On the final day of the regular season, the Indians win their 100th game with a 17–7 decision over the Royals at Jacobs Field. Cleveland scored six runs in the first inning, five in the second, and six in the fifth. Eleven different players scored a run and ten collected an RBI.

The Indians played the Red Sox in the American League Division Series. Managed by Kevin Kennedy, the Sox were 86–58 in 1995 in winning the AL East.

OCTOBER 3 On the day O. J. Simpson is found not guilty of the double murder of his ex-wife and her companion, Tony Pena hits a walk-off homer in the 13th inning to lift the Indians to a 5–4 win over the Red Sox in the first game of the American League Division Series before 44,218 at Jacobs Field. It was Cleveland's first post-season win since 1948. The Indians took a 3–2 lead with three runs in the sixth inning off Roger Clemens, two of them on a double by Albert Belle, but the Sox tied the contest 3–3 in the eighth on Luis Alicea's home run. Boston gained a 4–3 advantage in the 11th on a home run by Tim Naehring. Belle forged another deadlock with a home run in the Indians half. Pena, who had hit only five homers in 1995, ended the five hour and one minute game with a two-out homer off Zane Smith. With two rain delays adding to the night's proceedings, the game ended at 2:10 a.m.

OCTOBER 4 In game two of the ALDS, the Indians beat the Red Sox 4–0 before 44,264 at Jacobs Field. Orel Hershiser (7 1/3 innings), Julian Tavarez (one-third of an inning), Paul Assenmacher (one-third of an inning) and Jose Mesa (one inning) combined on the three-hit shutout. The game didn't start well. After four pitches, the Indians had committed two errors and Hershiser threw a wild pitch. Eddie Murray tripled and homered.

OCTOBER 6 The Indians complete the sweep of the Red Sox in the ALDS with an 8–2 win at Fenway Park. The Indians seized the lead with a two-run homer by Jim Thome in the second inning.

The Indians played the Mariners in the American League Championship Series. Managed by Lou Piniella, Seattle trailed the Angels by 11 1/2 games on August 24 before putting together an unbelievable rally to win the AL West. The Mariners lost the first two games of the ALDS to the Yankees, then won three in a row to advance.

OCTOBER 10 The Indians lose the first game of the American League Championship Series 3–2 to the Mariners at the Kingdome in Seattle. Rookie Bob Wolcott, making only his eighth big league appearance, was the winning pitcher after going seven innings. He walked the first three batters he faced on only 13 pitches, but pitched out of the jam without allowing a run. Albert Belle tied the score 2–2 with a homer in the seventh, but Seattle countered with a tally in their half. Cleveland left 12 runners on base. In five plate appearances, Kenny Lofton had a triple, two singles, two walks, and a stolen base, but failed to score or drive in a run.

OCTOBER 11 The Indians even the ALCS with a 5–2 win in Seattle. Orel Hershiser pitched eight winnings for the win. Manny Ramirez hit two homers and two singles in four at-bats.

OCTOBER 13 The Mariners take a 2–1 lead in the ALCS with a 5–2 decision over the Indians in 11 innings before 43,643 at Jacobs Field. Jay Buhner drove in the three 11th inning runs with a homer off Eric Plunk. It was Buhner's second home run of the game.

OCTOBER 14 The Indians even the series again with a 7–0 win over the Mariners before 43,686 at Jacobs Field. Ken Hill (seven innings), Jim Poole (one inning), Chad Ogea (two-thirds of an inning), and Alan Embree (one-third of an inning) combined on the six-hit shutout. The Tribe built a 6–0 lead by the third inning. Jim Thome and Eddie Murray homered.

Albert Belle missed the contest because of an ankle he injured in game three. The Indians mascot Slider suffered torn ligaments in his knee when he fell off the eight-foot right field fence in the fifth inning.

OCTOBER 15 The Indians move one game from the World Series with a 3–2 triumph over the Mariners before 43,607 at Jacobs Field. With Cleveland trailing 2–1, Jim Thome hit a two-run homer in the sixth inning to provide the winning margin. Winds gusting up to 30 miles per hour played havoc on just about every ball hit into the air. Orel Hershiser pitched six innings for the win.

OCTOBER 17 The Indians reach the World Series for the first time since 1954 with a 4–0 win over the Mariners in Seattle. Dennis Martinez (seven innings), Julian Tavarez (one inning), and Jose Mesa (one inning) combined on the shutout. The Indians broke open a close game with three runs in the eighth, capped by a homer from Carlos Baerga off Randy Johnson.

The Indians played the Atlanta Braves in the World Series. Managed by Bobby Cox, the Braves were 90–54 in the regular season in 1995 and were 7–1 in the post-season prior to the Fall Classic in beating the Rockies and the Reds. Atlanta reached the World Series in 1991 and 1992 and lost both times.

OCTOBER 21 In the opening game of the World Series, the Indians lose 3–2 to the Braves at Atlanta-Fulton County Stadium as Greg Maddux outduels Orel Hershiser. Entering the contest, Hershiser was 7–0 in post-season play with the Dodgers and Indians.

The Series was the focus of bitter protests by Native American groups because of the nicknames of the two teams. The primary complaint was the Tomahawk Chop performed by Atlanta fans and the Indians symbol of Chief Wahoo. Protests were held outside the ballparks in both Atlanta and Cleveland. "We're not mascots, we're human beings," said protester Richard Morales. "People make fun of Native Americans at the games, war-whooping, dancing, getting painted up. It is a total insult."

OCTOBER 22 The Indians lose the second game of the 1995 World Series 4–3 to the Braves in Atlanta. Eddie Murray hit a two-run homer in the second inning for a 2–0 Cleveland lead, but the club couldn't hold the advantage.

Kenny Lofton is one of two players to appear in both a Final Four and a World Series. He played for Arizona in the Final Four in 1988. The only other individual to accomplish the feat is Tim Stoddard, who played for the 1974 NCAA champion North Carolina State squad and in the Fall Classic with the Orioles in 1979. Oddly, both Lofton and Stoddard were born in East Chicago, Illinois, and attended Washington High School in that city.

OCTOBER 24 In the first World Series game in Cleveland in 41 years, the Indians beat the Braves 7–6 in 11 innings before 43,584 at Jacobs Field. Eddie Murray drove in the winning run with a walk-off single. Prior to the at-bat, he was 0-for-5 with three strikeouts.

Murray drove in Carlos Baerga, who led off the inning with a double. Baerga also singled twice and drove in three runs. Kenny Lofton reached base in all six plate appearances on two singles, a double, three walks, two of them intentional. He also stole a base. Jose Mesa pitched three shutout innings. The temperature was 49 degrees with gusts of 15 to 22 miles per hour.

The game was marred by an incident involving Albert Belle, who launched into a profanity-laced tirade against NBC television personality Hannah Storm before the game. He felt her presence in the Indians dugout disrupted his preparations for the game. The following February, Commissioner Bud Selig fined Belle $55,000 and forced him to undergo psychiatric counseling during the off-season.

OCTOBER 25 The Braves move one game from the world championship with a 5–2 win over the Indians before 43,578 at Jacobs Field. Atlanta broke a 1–1 tie with three runs in the seventh inning.

OCTOBER 26 The Indians stay alive with a 5–4 win over the Braves in game five before 43,595 at Jacobs Field. Albert Belle hit a two-run homer in the first inning for a 2–0 lead. Eddie Murray followed Belle to the plate and took exception to an up-and-in delivery from Greg Maddux. After starting toward the mound, Murray was intercepted by plate umpire Frank Pulli. After both benches emptied, order was quickly restored. The Tribe broke a 2–2 tie with two runs in the sixth on RBI-singles by Jim Thome and Manny Ramirez. Thome added a homer in the eighth for a 5–2 lead. The Braves scored twice in the ninth.

OCTOBER 27 The Braves win the 1995 World Series with a 1–0 win over the Indians in Atlanta. The lone run scored on a homer by David Justice in the sixth inning off Jim Poole. Tom Glavine (eight innings) and Mark Wohlers (one inning) combined on a one-hitter. The only Cleveland hit was a soft single by Tony Pena in the sixth inning.

On the travel day between the fifth and sixth games, Justice had ripped Atlanta fans for being frontrunners and too nonchalant.

OCTOBER 31 Albert Belle strikes a teenager with his vehicle following a Halloween prank in which five teenagers threw eggs at Belle's condominium in suburban Cleveland. Belle hopped into his Ford Explorer and chased a 16-year-old into a muddy field and bumped into him. Belle was charged with reckless operation of a vehicle and fined $100. He was later sued for $850,000 by the parent's of the teenager struck by Belle. The case was settled out of court in 1997.

NOVEMBER 6 Cleveland Browns owner Art Modell announces he is moving the club to Baltimore, a decision that causes a firestorm of controversy around the country because of the rich legacy of the team. The Browns had been founded in Cleveland by Paul Brown in 1946. Modell was angry over the lack of progress in negotiations with city officials over acquiring a new stadium for his team.

The controversy continued to rage for another three months before the NFL made a deal with Cleveland to give the city a new team by 1999 in a new stadium to be built with the help of a loan up to $48 million from the league. The new team, an expansion outfit, would be called the Browns and retain the

Browns colors, records, and heritage. Modell's team in Baltimore was named the Ravens (see December 17, 1995).

DECEMBER 5 Julio Franco returns to the Indians after signing a free agent contract. Franco played with Chibe Lotte in Japan in 1995.

Franco was the club's starting first baseman in 1996.

DECEMBER 14 The Indians sign Jack McDowell, most recently with the Yankees, as a free agent.

McDowell was the Cy Young Award winner with the White Sox in 1993. He was expected to provide a boost to the Indians starting rotation, but was a disappointment with a 16–12 record and an ERA of 5.10 over two seasons.

DECEMBER 17 The last sporting event at Municipal Stadium is held with a 26–10 Browns win over the Cincinnati Bengals before 55,875. Municipal Stadium was the home of the Indians from 1932 through 1993 and the Browns from 1946 through 1995.

DECEMBER 23 Ken Hill signs as a free agent with the Rangers.

1996

Season in a Sentence

The Indians easily win the AL Central and post the best record in the major leagues for the second year in a row but lose to the Orioles in the first round of the playoffs.

Finish • Won • Lost • Pct • GB

Finish	Won	Lost	Pct	GB
First	99	62	.615	+14.5

Manager

Mike Hargrove

American League Division Series

The Indians lost to the Baltimore Orioles three games to one.

Stats

Stats	Indians	AL	Rank
Batting Avg:	293	.277	1
On-Base Pct:	.369	.350	1
Slugging Pct:	.475	.445	2
Home Runs:	218		5
Stolen Bases:	160		2
ERA:	4.34	4.99	1
Fielding Avg:	.980	.982	10
Runs Scored:	952		2
Runs Allowed:	769		1

Starting Line-up

Sandy Alomar, Jr., c
Julio Franco, 1b
Carlos Baerga, 2b
Jim Thome, 3b
Omar Vizquel, ss
Albert Belle, lf
Kenny Lofton, cf
Manny Ramirez, rf
Eddie Murray, dh

Pitchers

Charles Nagy, sp
Orel Hershiser, sp
Jack McDowell, sp
Chad Ogea, sp
Dennis Martinez, sp
Jose Mesa, rp
Paul Assenmacher, rp
Eric Plunk, rp
Julian Tavarez, rp
Paul Shuey, rp

Attendance

3,318,174 (second in AL)

Club Leaders

Batting Avg:	Kenny Lofton	.317
On-Base Pct:	Jim Thome	.450
Slugging Pct:	Albert Belle	.623
Home Runs:	Albert Belle	48
RBIs:	Albert Belle	148
Runs:	Kenny Lofton	132
Stolen Bases:	Kenny Lofton	75
Wins:	Charles Nagy	17
Strikeouts:	Charles Nagy	167
ERA:	Charles Nagy	3.41
Saves:	Jose Mesa	39

JANUARY 3 Paul Sorrento signs with the Mariners as a free agent.

MARCH 31 The Indians trade Mark Clark to the Mets for Ryan Thompson and Reid Cornelius.

APRIL 2 The Indians open the season with a 7–1 loss to the Yankees before 42,289 at Jacobs Field.

The Indians started the season with three losses at Jacobs Field while being outscored 19–3.

APRIL 6 Two days after "Unabomber" Theodore Kaczynski is arrested, Albert Belle hits a photographer with a ball before a 5–3 win over the Blue Jays at Jacobs Field. Belle threw the ball from the outfield and hit Tony Tomsic, whose left hand was cut by the impact. Tomsic, working for *Sports Illustrated*, was standing near the Cleveland dugout. Belle was angry because Tomsic took his picture while he was stretching.

There were few problems with Belle's performance on the field. He hit .311 with 38 doubles, 375 total bases, 48 homers, 148 RBIs, and scored 124 runs in 1996.

April 13 The Indians rout the Red Sox 14–2 in Boston. Cleveland scored in seven of nine innings, capped by a five-run ninth.

April 14 Julio Franco hits a homer in the 11th inning that lifts the Indians to a 7–6 win over the Red Sox in Boston.

April 28 The Indians pound out 20 hits and thrash the Blue Jays 17–3 in Toronto.

April 30 A computer glitch turns out the lights at Jacobs Field and causes a 14-minute delay during a 5–3 win over the White Sox.

May 1 The game between the Indians and the Mariners at the Kingdome in Seattle is stopped by an earthquake registering 5.4 on the Richter scale. The earthquake hit at 9:04 p.m. Pacific time with the Indians leading 6–3 in the bottom of the seventh inning. Seattle was rallying, and Mike Hargrove was on the mound to remove Orel Hershiser. The shaking continued for 30 seconds. The umpires suspended the contest, and it was completed the following day after an inspection by a team of engineers revealed that the Kingdome suffered no damage.

May 2 The Indians complete the suspended game of May 1 against the Mariners in Seattle and win 6–4. Cleveland also took the regularly scheduled contest 5–2.

May 12 Three solo homers by Albert Belle, Sandy Alomar, Jr., and Jim Thome in the ninth inning beats the Anaheim Angels 4–1 in Anaheim.

Thome batted .311 with a .450 on base percentage, 122 runs scored, 38 homers, and 116 RBIs in 1996.

May 16 Albert Belle hits two homers and drives in five runs during an 8–3 win over the Tigers at Jacobs Field.

May 17 A grand slam by Manny Ramirez caps a six-run seventh inning as the Indians overcome a seven-run deficit to beat the Rangers 12–10 at Jacobs Field. Manny's slam came off Gil Heredia. Texas led 9–2 in the fifth inning and 10–5 before Cleveland's outburst in the seventh.

Ramirez hit .309 and collected 33 home runs and 112 RBIs in 1996.

May 21 A walk-off homer by Julio Franco with two out in the ninth inning beats the Twins 6–5 at Jacobs Field. Albert Belle extended his hitting streak to 21 games.

May 31 Albert Belle decks Brewers second baseman Fernando Vina with a high forearm in the eighth inning of a 10–4 Cleveland win at County Stadium. The trouble started after Belle was hit by a 3–2 pitch. Belle wasted no time trying to get even, flattening Vina as he was about to be tagged out on a grounder in the base path near second base.

The five-foot-nine Vina got up and jawed at the six-foot-two Belle but did not retaliate. Vina suffered a broken nose. The crowd booed the Indians outfielder as he walked off and several sheriff's deputies converged behind the Cleveland dugout where fans were yelling. In the ninth, Brewers pitcher Terry Burrows threw three inside pitches to Belle before hitting him in the left shoulder. In the Milwaukee half of the ninth, the first pitch from Julian Tavarez sailed behind the back of Mike Matheny, who charged the mound. During the ensuing melee, Tavarez picked up umpire Joe Brinkman, who bear-hugged the pitcher from behind. Tavarez threw Brinkman to the ground. Belle, joining the fracas, knocked down Brewers pitcher Steve Sparks.

June 2 The Indians and Brewers stage round two at County Stadium. Kenny Lofton led off the game with a double, then gave Milwaukee second baseman Fernando Vina a shove after pitcher Angel Miranda tried to pick him off. Lofton claimed Vina tried to push him off the base. Lofton and Vina exchanged harsh words, but there were no further incidents. The Brewers won 2–1.

June 3 Albert Belle and Julian Tavarez are both suspended five games by American League President Gene Budig for the June 1 brawl. It was Belle's fifth suspension in six years. Belle appealed, and after a hearing on June 18, the suspension was reduced to two games.

June 4 In the first round of the amateur draft, the Indians select first baseman Danny Peoples from the University of Texas.

Peoples suffered shoulder, back, and knee injuries while in the minors and never reached the big leagues. Future major leaguers drafted and signed by the Indians in 1996 were Paul Rigdon (sixth round), Sean DePaula (ninth round), Joe Horgan (11th round), John McDonald (12th round), Mike Bacsik (18th round), and David Riske (56th round).

June 5 The Indians break a 3–3 tie with seven runs in the seventh inning and beat the Mariners 13–5 at Jacobs Field.

The Indians sold out every home game in 1996 and set a club record with an attendance figure of 3,318,074.

June 14 A 4–3 loss to the Yankees in New York is interrupted when fans throw objects in the direction of Albert Belle. A souvenir bat was thrown at the controversial Cleveland outfielder in the sixth inning, causing a three-minute delay. The Indians left the field in the seventh after more objects, including baseballs, were thrown on the field. That delay lasted four minutes. The conduct of the Yankee crowd prompted an announcement on the public address system that the game could be forfeited unless the barrage ceased.

June 15 The Indians sign Greg Swindell as a free agent following his release by the Astros.

June 18 Omar Vizquel drives in six runs, four on a grand slam off Aaron Sele in the second inning, leading the Indians to a 9–7 win over the Red Sox at Jacobs Field.

June 25 The Indians sell Wayne Kirby to the Dodgers.

JULY 7 With first place on the line, the Indians beat the White Sox 6–1 at Jacobs Field.

The July 7 win gave the Indians a two-game lead over Chicago in the AL Central heading into the All-Star break. Cleveland led by seven games by the end of July and took a ten-game advantage on August 27. The Indians won the division crown by 14½ games.

JULY 9 In the All-Star Game at Veterans Stadium in Philadelphia, Mike Hargrove manages the American League to a 6–0 loss. Charles Nagy was the starting pitcher and allowed three runs and four hits in two innings. Kenny Lofton collected two singles in three at-bats.

Nagy had a record of 11–1 after his first 14 starts, and finished the regular season with a 17–5 record and a 3.41 ERA. In 1995 and 1996 combined, Nagy was 31–11.

JULY 11 Manny Ramirez hits a grand slam off Brad Radke in the second inning of an 11–7 win over the Twins in Minneapolis.

JULY 12 The Indians score four runs in the ninth inning to beat the Twins 7–5 in Minneapolis. The game was tied on a two-out, two-run, pinch-hit homer by Brian Giles. Jim Thome broke the 5–5 deadlock with a two-run single.

The homer by Giles came in his first at-bat after being recalled from Triple-A Buffalo. During the 1995 and 1996 season, Giles batted .369 with six homers in 130 at-bats, but he couldn't crack the line-up on a regular basis because the Indians possessed an All-Star outfield consisting of Albert Belle, Kenny Lofton, and Manny Ramirez.

JULY 13 The Indians tie an American League record with 12 doubles during a 19–11 slugfest against the Twins in Minneapolis. The two teams combined for 18 doubles to break the AL record. The Cleveland doubles were by Kenny Lofton (three), Mark Carreon (two), Omar Vizquel (one), Scott Leius (one), Carlos Baerga (one), Tony Pena (one), Albert Belle (one), Jeromy Burnitz (one), and Manny Ramirez (one). The six Minnesota two-baggers were from Marty Cordova, Rich Becker, Scott Stahoviak, Pat Meares, Matt Walbeck, and Ron Coomer.

JULY 18 Manny Ramirez and Eddie Murray lead off the ninth inning with successive home runs to beat the Twins 5–4 at Jacobs Field. Murray hit his walk-off homer as a pinch-hitter for Jeromy Burnitz.

JULY 20 Alvaro Espinoza hits a walk-off homer in the 11th inning that beats the Twins 6–5 at Jacobs Field. Kenny Lofton collected five hits, including a double, in six at-bats.

Lofton hit .317 with 132 runs, 210 hits, and 75 stolen bases in 1996. The 210 hits are the most of any Indians player since 1936. The stolen base figure not only led the American League for the fifth consecutive season but broke the single-season Indians record. Lofton holds six of the top seven single season stolen base totals in Indians history. In addition to his 75 steals in 1996, he had 70 in 1993, 66 in 1992, 60 in 1994, and 54 in both 1993 and 1998. The only other Cleveland player with more than 54 steals in a season is Miguel Dilone, who had 61 in 1980.

JULY 21 The Indians trade Eddie Murray to the Orioles for Kent Mercker.

Murray played for the Orioles from 1977 through 1988.

JULY 24 The Indians shut out the Blue Jays 10–0 in Toronto.

JULY 25 The Indians outlast the Blue Jays 10–7 in Toronto. Albert Belle hit two homers to break the club record for most home runs in a career. Earl Averill, the previous record-holder, had 226 home runs from 1929 through 1939. Averill held the Cleveland career home run record from 1932 until 1996.

JULY 26 The Indians collect 20 hits and win 14–9 over the Orioles in Baltimore. It was Cleveland's third straight game with ten or more runs.

JULY 28 A three-run homer by Jim Thome in the 13th inning beats the Orioles 6–3 in Baltimore.

JULY 29 The Indians trade Carlos Baerga and Alvaro Espinoza to the Mets for Jeff Kent and Jose Vizcaino.

Indians fans were outraged by the trade when it was announced. Baerga made the All-Star team in 1992, 1993, and 1995 but got off to a slow start in 1996 while battling weight issues. He failed to reverse the slide and never came close to reaching All-Star level play again. This would have been one of the best trades in Indians history had the club held on to Kent (see November 13, 1996).

JULY 31 Albert Belle hits a walk-off grand slam with two out in the ninth inning to beat the Blue Jays 4–2 at Jacobs Field. Trailing 2–0, the Tribe loaded the bases on a double by pinch-hitter Jeromy Burnitz and walks to Kenny Lofton and Omar Vizquel. The game was delayed for two hours by rain in the second inning.

AUGUST 2 Orel Hershiser (seven innings) and Danny Graves (two innings) combine on a two-hitter in an 11–1 rout of the Orioles at Jacobs Field. The only Baltimore hits were singles by Greg Zaun in the third inning and Bobby Bonilla in the fifth.

AUGUST 4 The Indians turn a close game into a blow out with an 11-run explosion in the eighth inning to defeat the Orioles 14–2 at Jacobs Field. In the top of the eighth, Kenny Lofton made a spectacular catch by scaling the center field wall to rob B. J. Surhoff of a home run. The Indians scored all 11 runs in the bottom half after two were out on eight hits and four walks. Jim Thome and Brian Giles both hit three-run homers.

AUGUST 7 The Indians score three runs in the ninth inning to defeat the Mariners 5–4 in Seattle. Omar Vizquel led off the inning with a homer. Jose Vizcaino doubled in the tying run and scored the winning tally on an error.

AUGUST 8 Chad Ogea allows only an infield single in eight shutout innings of a 2–1 win over the Mariners in Seattle.

AUGUST 16 A two-run walk-off homer by Sandy Alomar, Jr. in the 12th inning gives the Indians a 3–1 win over the Tigers at Jacobs Field.

AUGUST 18 Jim Thome hits two homers, including a grand slam, and drives in six runs during an 11–3 win over the Tigers at Jacobs Field. The slam was hit off Gregg Olson in the eighth inning.

The Indians were 23–3 against the Tigers at Jacobs Field from the opening of the ballpark in 1994 through May 26, 1997. During the 1996 season, the Indians had a 12–0 record against the Tigers, with six wins in Cleveland and six in Detroit.

AUGUST 20 Manny Ramirez hits a grand slam off Jeff Russell in the sixth inning of a 10–4 win over the Rangers at Jacobs Field. It was Manny's third grand slam of the season.

AUGUST 27 The Indians rout the Tigers 12–2 in Detroit.

AUGUST 28 Albert Belle hits a grand slam off A. J. Sager in the sixth inning of a 9–3 win over the Tigers in Detroit.

On the same day, the Indians released Greg Swindell.

AUGUST 31 The Indians trade Jeromy Burnitz to the Brewers for Kevin Seitzer.

Seitzer gave the Indians great production for a month. In September 1996, he batted .386 in 83 at-bats. He played only one more year. Burnitz went on to have a fine career with six seasons of at least 30 homers and four years with over 100 RBIs.

SEPTEMBER 1 In his first game with the Indians, Kevin Seitzer collects four hits, including two doubles, in five at-bats during an 8–2 win over the Rangers in Texas. Julio Franco hit a grand slam off John Burkett in the fifth inning.

SEPTEMBER 10 The Indians score four runs in the ninth inning, the last three on a two-out, walk-off homer by Manny Ramirez to beat the Angeles 7–5 at Jacobs Field. Kenny Lofton started the rally with a walk, stole second and third, and scored on a single by Jim Thome.

SEPTEMBER 12 The Indians hit five home runs during an 11–2 win over the Angels at Jacobs Field. Jim Thome and Julio Franco each homered twice and Albert Belle once. In the seventh inning, Thome, Belle, and Franco hit consecutive homers off Greg Gohr.

SEPTEMBER 17 The Indians clinch the AL Central pennant with a 9–4 win over the White Sox in Chicago. Kevin Seitzer hit a grand slam off Alex Fernandez in the second inning. It was Seitzer's first homer as a member of the Indians.

SEPTEMBER 21 The Indians crush the Royals 13–4 at Jacobs Field.

The Indians went into the final three-game series against the Royals in Kansas City on September 27 with a 99–59 record, but blew a shot at 100 wins on the season by losing all three games. The Indians played the Orioles in the American

League Division Series. Managed by Davey Johnson, the Orioles earned a wild card bid with a record of 88–74.

OCTOBER 1 The Indians open the American League Division Series with a 10–4 loss to the Orioles at Camden Yards in Baltimore. Brady Anderson started the first inning with a homer off Charles Nagy. The Orioles broke open a close game with five runs in the sixth inning, four on a grand slam by Bobby Bonilla off Paul Shuey, to take a 9–3 lead. Manny Ramirez hit a homer and two singles in four at-bats.

Orioles second baseman Robert Alomar spit in the face of umpire John Hirschbeck during an argument on September 27. Alomar was suspended for five games by the American League, but immediately appealed the suspension, allowing him to play in the post-season. The October 1 game between the Indians and Orioles was delayed 30 minutes because the umpires, believing that Alomar deserved a longer suspension, threatened to boycott the contest. The brother of Indians catcher Sandy Alomar, Jr., Roberto dropped his appeal on October 3 but was allowed to play in the 1996 post-season and serve the five-game suspension at the start of the 1997 regular season. The umpires threatened to strike over the decision and Major League Baseball successfully sought an injunction in U.S. District Court to prevent the strike.

OCTOBER 2 The Indians lose game two of the Division Series 7–2 against the Orioles in Baltimore. The Indians tied the game 4–4 with a run in the top of the eighth, but the Orioles scored three times in their half. Albert Belle hit a home run.

OCTOBER 4 The Indians keep their post-season hopes alive with a 9–4 win over the Orioles before 44,250 at Jacobs Field. Cleveland tied the game 4–4 with a run in the fourth, and broke the deadlock with four tallies in the seventh on a grand slam by Albert Belle off Arthur Rhodes. Manny Ramirez also homered. Kevin Seitzer drove in three runs and Omar Vizquel scored three runs and collected three hits.

OCTOBER 5 The Orioles win the Division Series three games to one with a 12-inning, 4–3 win over the Indians before 44,280 at Jacobs Field. Roberto Alomar, who many thought shouldn't be playing after spitting in the face of umpire John Hirschbeck (see October 1, 1996) was the star of the game. Alomar tied the game with a single in the ninth inning, and then hit a game-winning homer in the 12th, both hits coming off Jose Mesa. Alomar was booed continually throughout the two games in Cleveland. The Indians lost despite striking out 23 Baltimore batters. The strikeout pitchers were Charles Nagy (12 in six innings), Alan Embree (one in one-third of an inning), Paul Assenmacher (two in two-thirds of an inning), Eric Plunk (two in an inning) and Jose Mesa (six in 3⅔ innings).

NOVEMBER 13 A week after Bill Clinton defeats Bob Dole in the presidential election, the Indians trade Jeff Kent, Julian Tavarez, and Jose Vizcaino to the Giants for Matt Williams.

Williams was acquired to play third base and allow Jim Thome to move across the diamond to first. It proved to be a terrible deal. Williams played only one year in Cleveland before being traded to the Diamondbacks. Kent went on to have a brilliant career, playing in five All-Star Games and setting an all-time major league record for most career homers by a second baseman. In addition, he drove in over 100 runs eight times. Tavarez was also a loss, serving several clubs out of the bullpen for over a decade after leaving the Indians.

NOVEMBER 19 Albert Belle signs a contract as a free agent with the White Sox.

Belle signed a deal worth $55 million over five years, which made him the highest paid player ever up to that time, both in average annual salary and in total compensation. White Sox owner Jerry Reinsdorf inked the contract after urging his fellow owners to undergo an austerity program to put a cap on escalating salaries. Belle had an off-year by his standards in 1997, but he hit 49 homers and drove in 152 runs for the Sox in 1998. After that season, he went to the Orioles and played three more years before a degenerative hip condition ended his career.

DECEMBER 10 Kent Mercker signs a contract as a free agent with the Reds.

DECEMBER 12 Mike Jackson, most recently with the Mariners, signs as a free agent.

DECEMBER 13 The Indians sign Pat Borders, most recently with the White Sox, and Kevin Mitchell, most recently with the Reds, as free agents.

Mitchell hit four homers in his first nine games with the Indians but became a source of ridicule because of his poor physical condition. He hit just .153 in 59 at-bats and was released in June after getting into a fight with teammate Chad Curtis.

DECEMBER 18 Chad Curtis, most recently with the Dodgers, signs as a free agent.

DECEMBER 26 Tony Fernandez, most recently with the Yankees, signs as a free agent.

Fernandez missed the entire 1996 season with a broken elbow but made it back as the Indians starting second baseman in 1997. He played only one season in Cleveland but will be long remembered for his 10th-inning home run that beat the Orioles 1–0 in the pennant-clinching sixth game of the ALCS.

DECEMBER 28 Jose Mesa and another man are arrested on felony charges of carrying a concealed weapon and fondling two women. Two 26-year-old women told police that Mesa and a friend fondled them in a Lakewood, Ohio, motel room on December 22.

Mesa was indicted on one count of rape, two counts of gross sexual imposition, one count of theft, and a charge of carrying a concealed weapon. He was acquitted of all but the weapon charge on April 8, 1997, following a jury trial. He was cleared of the weapon charge a day later because a judge ruled that the police seized the loaded nine-millimeter revolver during an improper search.

1997

Season in a Sentence

After struggling for much of the regular season, the Indians reach the World Series and are two outs away from their first world championship since 1948 before losing game seven to the Marlins.

Finish • Won • Lost • Pct • GB

Finish	Won	Lost	Pct	GB
First	86	75	.534	+6.0

Manager

Mike Hargrove

American League Division Series

The Indians beat the New York Yankees three games to two.

American League Championship Series

The Indians beat the Baltimore Orioles four games to two.

World Series

The Indians lost to the Florida Marlins four games to three.

Stats

Stats	Indians	AL	Rank
Batting Avg:	.286	.271	3
On-Base Pct:	.358	.340	2
Slugging Pct:	.467	.428	2
Home Runs:	220		2
Stolen Bases:	118		5
ERA:	4.73	4.57	9
Fielding Avg:	.983	.982	7
Runs Scored:	868		3
Runs Allowed:	815		7

Starting Line-up

Sandy Alomar, Jr., c
Jim Thome, 1b
Tony Fernandez, 2b
Matt Williams, 3b
Omar Vizquel, ss
Brian Giles, lf
Marquis Grissom, cf
Manny Ramirez, rf
David Justice, dh-lf
Julio Franco, dh

Pitchers

Charles Nagy, sp
Orel Hershiser, sp
Chad Ogea, sp
Bartolo Colon, sp
Jaret Wright, sp
Jose Mesa, rp
Mike Jackson, rp
Paul Assenmacher, rp
Eric Plunk, rp

Attendance

3,404,750 (2nd in AL)

Club Leaders

Batting Avg:	David Justice	.329
On-Base Pct:	Jim Thome	.423
Slugging Pct:	Jim Thome	.579
Home Runs:	Jim Thome	40
RBIs:	Matt Williams	105
Runs:	Jim Thome	104
Stolen Bases:	Omar Vizquel	43
Wins:	Charles Nagy	15
Strikeouts:	Charles Nagy	149
ERA:	Charles Nagy	4.28
Saves:	Jose Mesa	16

JANUARY 11 Tony Pena signs a contract as a free agent with the White Sox.

MARCH 25 The Indians trade Kenny Lofton and Alan Embree to the Braves for Marquis Grissom and David Justice.

Justice gave the Indians four excellent seasons as a designated hitter and outfielder. Lofton returned to the Indians as a free agent after the 1997 season ended.

APRIL 2 The Indians win 9–7 over the Athletics in Oakland in the first game of the season. The Tribe scored four runs in the first inning but allowed the A's back in the game.

In his Indians debut, David Justice broke a 6–6 tie with a two-run homer in the eighth. He also tripled and singled. In addition to Justice, Kevin Mitchell and Jim Thome homered for Cleveland. It was also Mitchell's first game as an Indian.

In his first season with the Indians, Justice batted .329 with 33 homers and 101 RBIs.

APRIL 4 The Indians score two runs in the 11th inning but lose 8–6 to the Angels in Anaheim when Tim Salmon hits a walk-off grand slam off Paul Shuey.

APRIL 6 The Indians score seven runs in the fourth inning but need solo homers from Sandy Alomar, Jr. and Brian Giles in the ninth inning to beat the Angels 10–8 in Anaheim.

APRIL 11 In the home opener, the Indians collect 20 hits and wallop the Angels 15–3 before 42,643 at Jacobs Field. Cleveland scored six runs in the second inning and six more in the fifth. Manny Ramirez and Kevin Mitchell both homered. Sandy Alomar, Jr. scored four runs and had four hits.

Ramirez hit .328 with 26 homers in 1997.

APRIL 13 Amid snow flurries at Jacobs Field, the Indians lose 8–3 to the Angels.

The 1997 season marked the second in a row in which the Indians sold out every home game.

APRIL 23 Trailing 5–0, the Indians score two runs in the fourth inning, two in the sixth, five in the seventh, and two in the eighth and win 11–7 over the Red Sox at Jacobs Field.

Uniform number 42 was retired throughout baseball in 1997 in honor of Jackie Robinson. Those already wearing the number could use it until the end of their career. Mike Jackson, from 1997 through 1999, was the last Indian to wear number 42.

APRIL 25 Matt Williams hits three of the Indians club-record eight home runs during an 11–4 win over the Brewers at County Stadium. The two teams combined for 11 home runs, one shy of the major league record. Williams hit solo homers off Scott Karl in the fourth inning and Ron Villone in the seventh and a two-run shot against Jose Mercedes in the eighth. David Justice homered twice. The others were collected by Sandy Alomar, Jr., Chad Curtis, and Manny Ramirez. Milwaukee round-trippers came from Dave Nilsson, John Jaha, and Jeromy Burnitz.

APRIL 26 Matt Williams hits two more home runs during a 9–8 loss to the Brewers at County Stadium. His five homers in consecutive games tied a major league record. A two-run shot by Williams in the eighth inning gave Cleveland an 8–6 lead, but Milwaukee tallied three times in the ninth for the win.

The 1997 season was the Brewers last one in the American League. The club moved to the NL in 1998.

April 30 Mark McGwire hits a couple of long home runs during the Athletics 11–9 win in ten innings over the Indians at Jacobs Field. He launched a 485-foot shot in the third inning that made a dent between the "e" and "i" in the large Budweiser sign on the scoreboard. In the tenth, McGwire hit a ball that traveled an estimated 459 feet.

May 17 Jim Thome hits a grand slam off Woody Williams in the third inning of an 8–1 win over the Blue Jays in Toronto.

May 21 Jim Thome steals home on the back end of a double steal with two out in the fourth inning that accounts for the only run of a 1–0 win over the Royals at Jacobs Field. Orel Hershiser (7⅓ innings), Alvin Morman (one-third of an inning), Paul Shuey (one-third of an inning), and Mike Jackson (one inning) combined on the shutout.

Thome hit .286 with an on base percentage of .423 in 1997 along with 40 home runs and 102 RBIs.

May 22 The Indians score eight runs in the fifth inning of a 9–1 win over the Royals at Jacobs Field.

May 23 Chad Ogea pitches a two-hitter for a 6–1 victory over the Orioles at Jacobs Field. The only Baltimore hits were a double by Brady Anderson in the first inning and a single from B. J. Surhoff in the second.

May 28 The Indians break a 3–3 tie with seven runs in the eighth inning and defeat the Royals 10–3 in Kansas City.

May 30 Sandy Alomar, Jr. breaks up the perfect game bid of Orioles pitcher Mike Mussina at Camden Yards. After Mussina retired the first 25 Cleveland batters, Alomar lined a 1–1 pitch into left field for a single. Mussina retired the final two hitters to close out a one-hit, 3–0 victory.

June 2 In the first round of the amateur draft, the Indians select pitcher Tim Drew from Lowndes County High School in Hahira, Georgia.

Tim was one of three Drew brothers to play in the majors, joining J. D. and Stephen. J. D. was also drafted by the Phillies in 1997 in the first round as the second overall pick. Tim was the 28th overall selection. It was the first time that two brothers were chosen in the first round of the same draft. Tim reached the majors in 2000 at the age of 21, but the Indians quickly gave up on him. In two seasons in Cleveland, Tim pitched in 11 games and 44 innings and had an ERA of 8.39. Stephen Drew was a first round choice (15th overall) of the Diamondbacks in 2004.

June 3 Playing at Jacobs Field for the first time since signing a free agent contract with the White Sox, Albert Belle makes a tumultuous return to Cleveland in a game won by Chicago 9–5. Belle overcame a crowd that jeered him incessantly to collect three hits including a three-run homer and two doubles. The game was briefly delayed twice because fans were throwing things at Belle, including dollar bills. Belle kicked the debris and motioned to the fans to bring it on. When Belle fouled off a pitch behind the plate in the ninth, a fan threw it back toward the field, missing the outfielder by about 30 feet. After the last out, Belle turned to the fans and flipped an obscene gesture while running off the field.

Belle was fined by the American League for the gesture.

JUNE 4 The White Sox and Indians play another contentious game at Jacobs Field with the Sox winning 9–4. Albert Belle was hit by a pitch from Jose Mesa with the bases loaded in the eighth inning, setting off a series of hit batsmen and close calls that resulted in a bench-clearing situation. Chicago reliever Bill Simas threw inside to Marquis Grissom in the ninth, prompting Grissom to walk toward the mound pointing his bat. Both benches and bullpens emptied, but no punches were thrown.

JUNE 6 Sandy Alomar, Jr. ties a major league record with four consecutive doubles during a 7–3 win over the Red Sox in Boston. All four two-baggers were hit to left field.

The only other Indians players with four doubles in a game are Lou Boudreau (1946) and Vic Wertz (1956).

JUNE 9 The Indians trade Chad Curtis to the Yankees for David Weathers.

JUNE 11 A walk-off squeeze bunt by Omar Vizquel scores Pat Borders from third base with the winning run in the 11th inning of a 4–3 win over the Brewers at Jacobs Field.

JUNE 13 The Indians are scheduled to play their first regular season inter-league game, but the contest against the Cardinals in St. Louis is rained out.

JUNE 14 The Indians play their first two inter-league games with a double header against the Cardinals in St. Louis. Cleveland won the opener 8–3 and lost the second tilt 5–2.

JUNE 16 The Indians play their first regular season game against a National League club in Cleveland and their first against their Ohio rivals from Cincinnati, and they lose 4–1 to the Reds at Jacobs Field.

JUNE 17 Omar Vizquel drives in all five runs of a 5–1 win over the Reds at Jacobs Field. Vizquel had a two-run single in the fourth inning and a three-run homer in the sixth.

JUNE 21 Manny Ramirez drives in six runs, including a grand slam, during a 13–4 win over the Yankees at Jacobs Field. The slam was struck off Graeme Lloyd in the eighth inning. Ramirez also contributed two doubles and a single.

JUNE 27 The Indians become the first American League team to lose 1,000 games to another opponent by dropping a 3–2 decision to the Yankees in New York. At that point, the Tribe was 804–1,000 against the Yanks.

JUNE 28 Matt Williams collects two homers and two singles and drives in six runs during a 12–8 victory over the Indians in New York.

JUNE 30 The Indians play the Astros for the first time and win 6–4 at the Astrodome in Houston. Kevin Seitzer broke a 4–4 tie with a two-run, pinch-hit home run in the ninth.

JULY 5 Larry Doby is honored in ceremonies prior to an 8–4 win over the Royals at Jacobs Field. The date marked the 50th anniversary of Doby's major league debut in which he became the first African-American in the American League.

The celebration may have had an effect on Doby reaching the Hall of Fame. He was elected by the Committee on Veterans in February 1998.

JULY 6 Sandy Alomar, Jr. extends his hitting streak to 30 games during an 8–7 win over the Royals at Jacobs Field.

Omar Vizquel turns a double play against the Orioles despite the slide of Jay Gibbons. Vizquel's outstanding talent with a glove was a key factor in the Tribe's success during this era.

JULY 8 The All-Star Game is played at Jacobs Field, and the American League wins 3–1. Sandy Alomar, Jr. won the MVP award. The AL took a 1–0 lead in the second inning on a home run by Edgar Martinez off Greg Maddux. The NL tied the contest in the seventh with a homer from Javy Lopez. Alomar batted in the seventh after replacing starting catcher Ivan Rodriguez. Entering the game with a 30-game hitting streak, Alomar hit a two-run homer off Scott Estes of the Giants, scoring Bernie Williams, who had walked. Eight AL pitchers held the NL to three hits.

Sandy Alomar's brother Roberto, then with the Orioles, also played in the game. The Alomar siblings wore black armbands to honor their 96-year-old grandmother, who died two days earlier. Comic relief was provided in the second inning when Randy Johnson threw a pitch that sailed about six feet over Larry Walker's head. Walker, a left-handed hitter, smiled broadly, turned his batting helmet backward, and switched to the right side of the plate. Walker reverted to his natural hitting side and drew a walk. Albert Belle was on the AL squad but did not play. He was booed mercilessly during pre-game introductions and asked AL manager Joe Torre not to play him unless absolutely needed because of rough treatment from the Cleveland fans, including the incidents that occurred a month earlier (see June 3 and 4, 1997).

JULY 10 The 30-game hitting streak of Sandy Alomar, Jr. comes to an end during an 8–2 loss to the Twins in Minneapolis. Alomar was hitless in four at-bats.

The hitting streak, which began on May 25, is the second longest in Indians history. Nap Lajoie hit in 31 games in succession in 1906. It is also the second longest by a catcher in major league history. Benito Santiago had a 34-game hitting streak with the Padres in 1987. Alomar finished the season with a .324 average and 21 homers.

JULY 14 Marquis Grissom homers in the tenth inning on an 0–2 pitch from Mariano Rivera with one out to give the Indians a 3–2 win over the Yankees in New York.

JULY 17 The Indians play the Brewers for the last time as American League rivals, and win 3–2 in Milwaukee. The Brewers moved to the National League in 1998.

JULY 31 Mark Whiten pitches the eighth inning of a 12–2 loss to the Athletics in Oakland. Whiten struck out three but walked two, hit a batter, and allowed a hit and a run.

On the same day, the Indians traded Danny Graves, Jim Crowell, Scott Winchester, and Damian Jackson to the Reds for John Smiley and Jeff Branson, then swapped Steve Kline to the Expos for Jeff Juden. The Indians made two terrible trades in one day. Graves was named to two All-Star teams and saved 182 games in Cincinnati. Smiley pitched in only six games for the Indians before suffering a career-ending broken arm (see September 20, 1997). Kline had nearly a decade ahead of him as a successful reliever.

AUGUST 1 Matt Williams hits two of the Indians five home runs during an 8–5 win over the Rangers at Arlington. The other three home runs were collected by Manny Ramirez, Jim Thome, and Tony Fernandez.

On the same day, the Indians released Julio Franco, who had one of the strangest careers in history. A native of the Dominican Republic, Franco played in Japan in 1998, Mexico in 1999, Korea in 2000, and Mexico again in 2001. He returned to the States to play for the Braves from 2001 through 2005 and the Mets in 2006 and 2007. During the 2007 season, Franco was 48-years-old.

AUGUST 10 A blunder by Manny Ramirez leads to a 7–6 loss to the Rangers at Jacobs Field. Ramirez lost a fly ball in the sun while his sunglasses remained in his back pocket.

AUGUST 13 The Indians split a double header with the Tigers at Jacobs Field, losing 13–11 and winning 9–3. Manny Ramirez made a ridiculous base-running gaffe in the first game by running back to first base and getting tagged out after advancing on defensive interference.

After the loss in the first game, the Indians had a 59–56 record, and had lost 18 of their previous 27 games. The club had a lead of just 2½ games in the AL Central and Mike Hargrove's job appeared to be in jeopardy.

AUGUST 14 The Indians drub the Tigers 12–1 at Jacobs Field.

AUGUST 19 David Justice hits a grand slam off Ken Cloude in the fifth inning of a 7–5 win over the Rangers in Arlington.

AUGUST 27 In a bizarre game against the Angels in Anaheim, the Indians score all ten of their runs in the fourth inning of a 10–4 victory. Only two players accounted for the ten runs-batted-in. Matt Williams hit a three-run homer with one out off Allen Watson. After three singles and a force out, Marquis Grissom clubbed a grand slam facing Watson. Four batters later, Williams smacked a bases-loaded double against Shigetoshi Hasegawa.

AUGUST 29 The Indians play the Chicago Cubs for the first time, and win 8–7 at Jacobs Field.

AUGUST 31 On the day that Princess Diana dies following a car accident in Paris, the Indians trade Roland de la Maza to the Royals for Bip Roberts.

SEPTEMBER 1 The Indians play the Pittsburgh Pirates during the regular season for the first time and win 7–5 at Three Rivers Stadium in Pittsburgh. The two teams had co-existed 130 miles apart since 1901 but had never played a game that counted.

SEPTEMBER 5 The Indians wallop the White Sox 11–1 at Jacobs Field.

SEPTEMBER 8 Matt Williams runs his hitting streak to 24 games during a 2–1 win over the Orioles at Jacobs Field. The win was the fifth in a row for the Indians and gave the club a 5½-game lead with 23 contests left to play.

SEPTEMBER 9 The Indians lose 9–3 to the Orioles on a rainy night at Jacobs Field. In a sequence of events straight out of the movie *Major League*, the soggy tarp got stuck just before it reached home plate as fans chanted "Pull! Pull!" The field was finally covered about 15 minutes into the 41-minute delay.

SEPTEMBER 14 Trailing 2–0, the Indians score seven runs in the eighth inning and win 8–3 in Chicago. The Sox used nine pitchers in the contest.

SEPTEMBER 16 Television history is made as the Indians split a double header with the Orioles, winning 4–2 and losing 7–2. It was the first live broadcast of a major league contest in digital, high-definition television. The game was projected on a 16 ft. × 9 ft. screen before 300 invited guests at the National Press Club in Washington. The event was sponsored by the Harris Corporation.

SEPTEMBER 20 Indians pitcher John Smiley suffers a spiral fracture of the bone above his left elbow while warming up before a 5–2 loss to the Royals in Kansas City. Near the end of the warm-ups, he threw a curveball and bystanders heard a crack, followed by a terrifying scream. Smiley never pitched again.

The 1997 season was the last in the Indians broadcast booth for Herb Score, who retired. He began announcing Indians games in 1964.

SEPTEMBER 23 The Indians clinch the AL Central pennant with a 10–9 win over the Yankees at Jacobs Field. Cleveland trailed 9–2 before scoring four runs in the sixth inning, two in the eighth, and two in the ninth for the thrilling victory. David Justice homered with a man on base in the eighth. Sandy Alomar, Jr. drove in the game-winner with a single.

The Indians played the defending world champion New York Yankees in the American League Division Series. Managed by Joe Torre, the Yanks were 96–66 in 1997 and earned the wild card berth with the second best record in the AL. The Indians at 86–75, had the fourth best record in the league and the worst of the AL playoff qualifiers.

SEPTEMBER 30 In the opening game of the Division Series, the Indians score five runs in the first inning but lose 8–6 to the Yankees at Yankee Stadium. The five-run first was highlighted by a three-run homer from Sandy Alomar, Jr. Cleveland still led 6–3 before the Yankees scored five times in the sixth. The last four of the New York runs in the inning scored on consecutive home runs by Tim Raines, Derek Jeter, and Paul O'Neill off Eric Plunk.

The only players to appear in a post-season game for the Indians in both 1995 and 1997 were Sandy Alomar, Jr., Orel Hershiser, Jose Mesa, Charles Nagy, Chad Ogea, Eric Plunk, Manny Ramirez, Jim Thome, and Omar Vizquel.

OCTOBER 2 The Indians rebound by beating the Yankees 7–5 in New York. Rookie Jaret Wright walked the bases loaded in the first inning and allowed three runs, but he settled down and pitched five shutout innings from the second through the sixth. The Indians came back with five runs in the fourth and two in the fifth off Andy Pettitte. Matt Williams hit a two-run homer in the fourth. Omar Vizquel collected three hits.

OCTOBER 4 The Yankees take game three and move within one win of advancing to the Championship Series by defeating the Indians 6–1 before 45,274 at Jacobs Field. In the fourth, Charles Nagy walked the bases loaded before Paul O'Neill hit a grand slam off Chad Ogea.

OCTOBER 5 Trailing 2–1, the Indians score a run in the eighth and another to the ninth to win 3–2 and keep their post-season hopes alive. The contest at Jacobs Field drew 45,274. The eighth-inning run came on a home run by Sandy Alomar Jr. off Mariano Rivera. Marquis Grissom led off the ninth with a bloop single to right and Bip Roberts sacrificed him to second. Omar Vizquel's grounder hit the glove of Yankee pitcher Ramiro Mendoza and deflected past shortstop Derek Jeter into left field, scoring Grissom and triggering a wild celebration.

OCTOBER 6 The Indians win the Division Series by beating the Yankees 4–3 in the fifth and deciding game before 45,203 at Jacobs Field. The Indians scored three times in the third inning and once in the fourth for a 4–0 lead, and they hung on for the win.

The Indians played the Baltimore Orioles in the American League Championship Series. Managed by Davey Johnson, the Orioles were 98–64 in 1997, the best record in the AL.

OCTOBER 8 The Indians lose 3–0 to the Orioles at Camden Yards in the first game of the ALCS. In the first inning, Brady Anderson robbed Manny Ramirez of a home run. Leading off the bottom half of the inning, Anderson hit Chad Ogea's first pitch for a homer.

OCTOBER 9 With the Indians trailing 4–2 in Baltimore, Marquis Grissom hits a three-run homer in the eighth inning to spark a 5–4 victory in game two of the ALCS. Manny Ramirez hit a two-run homer in the first inning before the Orioles scored two in the second and two more in the sixth.

The last two Indians victories against the Yankees and all four wins over the Orioles in the ALCS were by one run.

OCTOBER 11 In game three, the Indians outlast the Orioles 2–1 in 12 innings before 45,047 at Jacobs Field. Mike Mussina struck out 15 Cleveland batters in seven innings but left the game trailing 1–0 because Orel Hershiser held the Orioles scoreless over the same span. Baltimore scored a run in the ninth to send the contest into extra innings. The Indians claimed the victory on a bizarre and controversial play in the 12th inning. With Marquis Grissom stationed at third and Tony Fernandez on first with one out, Omar Vizquel tried to lay down a squeeze bunt. Vizquel missed the bunt, Baltimore catcher Lenny Webster missed the ball, and Grissom, running with the pitch, scored the winning run. The Orioles argued vehemently that Vizquel had fouled the ball, but home plate umpire John Hirschbeck ruled otherwise and television replays seemed to confirm his call. The game took four hours and 51 minutes to complete.

OCTOBER 12 The Indians move within one game of the World Series with an 8–7 win over the Orioles before 45,801 at Jacobs Field. Baltimore led 5–2 before Cleveland took a 7–5 advantage with a run in the fourth and four in the fifth. The Orioles tied the score 7–7 with tallies in the seventh and ninth. The game ended on an RBI-single by Sandy Alomar, Jr., who had four runs-batted-in during the game, including a two-run homer.

Sandy Alomar, Jr. and Roberto Alomar are one of only two sets of brothers to both homer in the same post-season series. The other siblings were Ken Boyer of the Cardianals and Clete Boyer of the Yankees in the 1964 World Series.

OCTOBER 13 A two-run rally in the ninth-inning comes up short, and the Indians lose 4–2 to the Orioles before 45,081 at Jacobs Field.

OCTOBER 14 The Indians reach the World Series with a dramatic 11-inning, 1–0 win over the Orioles in Baltimore. The lone run scored on a home run by Tony Fernandez off Armando Benitez. Fernandez was a last-minute replacement at second base for Bip Roberts, who was injured in batting practice when Fernandez lined a shot off his thumb. It was the first left-handed home run for the switch-hitting Fernandez all season. Charles Nagy (7⅓ innings), Paul Assenmacher (one-third of an inning), Mike Jackson (1⅓ innings), Brian Anderson (one inning) and Jose Mesa (one inning) combined on the shutout. The five hurlers allowed ten hits and walked five. The Orioles stranded 14 base runners.

The Indians played the Florida Marlins in the World Series. Managed by Jim Leyland, the Marlins won the wild card berth with a record of 92–70, and then stunned the Giants and Cubs in the playoffs.

OCTOBER 18 The Indians open the World Series by losing 7–4 to the Marlins at Miami. Florida broke a 1–1 tie with four runs in the fourth inning, highlighted back-to-back homers by Moises Alou and Charles Johnson off Orel Hershiser.

OCTOBER 19 The Indians even the World Series with a 6–1, game-two victory over the Marlins in Miami. Cleveland broke a 1–1 tie with three runs in the fifth inning and added two more in the sixth on a home run by Sandy Alomar, Jr. Marquis Grissom collected three hits including an RBI-single that put the Tribe ahead 2–1. Chad Ogea was the winning pitcher, allowing a run in $6^2/_3$ innings.

OCTOBER 21 In game three, the Marlins outlast the Indians 14–11 before 44,880 at Jacobs Field. The temperature was in the 40s with wind chill readings in the 20s. The game lasted four hours and 12 minutes. Cleveland led 7–3 in the fifth inning before unraveling. Florida scored two runs in the sixth and two in the seventh to tie the game before erupting with seven tallies in the ninth off Eric Plunk, Alvin Morman, and Jose Mesa for a 14–7 advantage. The Tribe made things interesting with four runs in the bottom of the ninth. Jim Thome was the batting star with a home run, a single, two RBIs, and three runs scored. Garry Sheffield drove in five runs and made a sensational catch in right field for the Marlins.

The only game in World Series history that produced more runs was game four in 1993, when the Blue Jays beat the Phillies 15–14.

OCTOBER 22 The Indians even the Series at two wins apiece with a 10–3 victory over the Marlins before 44,877 at Jacobs Field. Cleveland scored three runs in the first inning, two on a Manny Ramirez home run. Matt Williams was 3-for-3, including a two-run homer in the eighth, and scored three runs. Sandy Alomar, Jr. drove in three runs. Rookie Jaret Wright was the winning pitcher, allowing three runs in six innings.

The game-time temperature was 38 degrees with a wind chill of 18. Snow fell during the contest. Befitting the situation, "Jingle Bells" and "Let It Snow" were played over the Jacobs Field speaker system.

OCTOBER 23 The Marlins take a three-to-two lead in the World Series with an 8–7 win over the Indians at Jacobs Field. Cleveland had a 4–2 lead before the Marlins scored four runs in the sixth inning, one in the eighth, and one in the ninth. The Tribe plated three runs in the bottom of the ninth in a rally that fell short. Sandy Alomar, Jr. continued his hot hitting with a home run, a single, and four RBIs.

During the 1997 Series, Alomar had 11 hits in 30 at-bats for a .367 batting average along with two homers and ten runs-batted-in.

OCTOBER 25 The Indians stay alive in the World Series with a 4–1 victory over the Marlins in Miami. Chad Ogea was the star both on the mound and at the plate. He went five innings and allowed only one run. Batting because the designated hitter wasn't used in a National League park, Ogea collected two singles in two at-bats and drove in two runs. He entered the game with only two big league at-bats and said he had not had a base hit since his high school days nine years earlier.

October 26 Just two outs from a world championship, the Indians lose game seven 3–2 in 11 innings to the Marlins in Miami. In a surprise move, Mike Hargrove picked 21-year-old-rookie Jaret Wright as the starting pitcher over the more rested veteran Charles Nagy. Wright started game four just four days earlier. Wright was outstanding, surrendering only a hit over the first six innings. The Indians built a 2–0 lead in the third inning. Jim Thome walked, Marquis Grissom singled and Wright advanced both to second and third with a sacrifice. Tony Fernandez brought Thome and Grissom across the plate with a single. Florida scored in the seventh on a home run by Bobby Bonilla off Wright. The Indians still led 2–1 heading into the ninth with Jose Mesa on the mound. Moises Alou singled, and after Bonilla struck out, Charles Johnson moved Alou to third with another single. Craig Counsell tied the score 2–2 with a sacrifice fly. Charles Nagy succeeded Mesa on the mound in the tenth. It was Nagy's first relief appearance since 1990 and only the second of his big league career. In the 11th, Bonilla led off with a single. With one out, Counsell reached on an error by Fernandez at second base, Bonilla advancing to third. Jim Eisenreich was walked intentionally to load the bases. Devon White bounced to Fernandez, who threw home to force Bonilla for the second out. The bases were still loaded. Edgar Renteria won the game with a single to center, scoring Counsell.

The Indians outscored the Marlins 44–37 in the Series.

November 18 In the expansion draft, the Indians lose Brian Anderson to the Diamondbacks and Albie Lopez to the Devil Rays.

December 1 The Indians trade Matt Williams to the Diamondbacks for Travis Fryman and Tom Martin.

Williams wanted to play in Phoenix so much he agreed to reduce his $7 million salary for 1998 to $4.5 million. Williams divorced his wife the previous June and had joint custody of their three children, who lived in a Phoenix suburb.

December 7 The Indians trade Mike Fetters to the Athletics for Steve Karsay.

December 8 The Indians sign two free agents and lose one. Tony Fernandez signed as a free agent with the Blue Jays. On the same day, Kenny Lofton returned to the Indians as a free agent after a season in Atlanta. Dwight Gooden, who played for the Yankees in 1997, was added to the Cleveland roster. A teenaged sensation when he entered the majors with the Mets in 1984, Gooden was near the end of his career when he arrived in Cleveland. In two seasons with the Indians, he was 11–10 with a 4.91 ERA.

December 9 Orel Hershiser signs as a free agent with the Giants.

December 12 Bip Roberts signs as a free agent with the Tigers.

December 19 David Weathers signs as a free agent with the Reds.

1998

Season in a Sentence

The Indians spend the entire season in first place and win the AL Central for the fourth consecutive year before losing to the Yankees in the ALCS.

Finish • Won • Lost • Pct • GB

Finish	Won	Lost	Pct	GB
First	89	73	.549	+9.0

American League Division Series

The Indians beat the Boston Red Sox three games to one.

American League Championship Series

The Indians lost four games to two to the New York Yankees.

Manager

Mike Hargrove

Stats

Stats	Indians	AL	Rank
Batting Avg:	.272	.271	6
On-Base Pct:	.347	.340	3
Slugging Pct:	.448	.432	6
Home Runs:	198		7 (tie)
Stolen Bases:	143		3
ERA:	4.44	4.65	6
Fielding Avg:	.982	.981	6
Runs Scored:	850		5
Runs Allowed:	783		6

Starting Line-up

Sandy Alomar, Jr., c
Jim Thome, 1b
David Bell, 2b
Travis Fryman, 3b
Omar Vizquel, ss
Brian Giles, lf
Kenny Lofton, cf
Manny Ramirez, lf
David Justice, dh
Mark Whiten, lf-cf

Pitchers

Charles Nagy, sp
Dave Burba, sp
Bartolo Colon, sp
Jaret Wright, sp
Dwight Gooden, sp
Mike Jackson, rp
Paul Assenmacher, rp
Jose Mesa, rp
Eric Plunk, rp

Attendance

3,467,299 (second in AL)

Club Leaders

Batting Avg:	Manny Ramirez	.294
On-Base Pct:	Jim Thome	.413
Slugging Pct:	Jim Thome	.584
Home Runs:	Manny Ramirez	45
RBIs:	Manny Ramirez	145
Runs:	Manny Ramirez	108
Stolen Bases:	Kenny Lofton	54
Wins:	Charles Nagy	15
	Dave Burba	15
Strikeouts:	Bartolo Colon	158
ERA:	Bartolo Colon	3.71
Saves:	Mike Jackson	40

FEBRUARY 16 A month after the Bill Clinton-Monica Lewinsky sex scandal is exposed, Shawon Dunston, most recently with the Pirates, signs as a free agent.

FEBRUARY 26 Jack McDowell signs with the Angels as a free agent.

On the same day, an Indians fan from North Ridgeville, Ohio, was jailed for trying to attack Albert Belle at the White Sox training complex in Sarasota, Florida. David Henry, age 38, was angry that Belle left Cleveland for Chicago. Henry told police he "was on a mission from God."

March 17 Manny Ramirez slaps clubhouse assistant Tom Foster in the face after the two exchange words about two hours after the Indians 8–4 loss to the Devil Rays at Winter Haven. Ramirez had taken two bats out of the equipment room where players are forbidden to go. Foster had berated Ramirez for ignoring the rules.

March 30 The Indians trade Sean Casey to the Reds for Dave Burba.

Burba was traded the day before he was scheduled to be the Cincinnati starter on Opening Day. He gave the Indians three solid seasons as a starter while Casey's path to becoming Cleveland's first baseman was blocked by Jim Thome. Casey was named to three All-Star teams with the Reds and was still a starter with the Tigers in 2007. Burba had a record of 46–25 from 1998 through 2000.

March 31 Playing a regular season game in March for the first time, the Indians win 10–9 in a thrilling Opening Day victory over the Mariners at the Kingdome. All nine Seattle runs were scored off Charles Nagy in 4²⁄₃ innings. Cleveland trailed 9–3 when Nagy departed. The Indians rallied with three runs in the sixth inning and four in the eighth for the victory. The four eighth-inning runs came with the help of five walks. Sandy Alomar, Jr. contributed a homer, a double, and a single. Omar Vizquel had three hits. Relievers Paul Shuey (1⅓ innings), Jose Mesa (2⅓ innings), Paul Assenmacher (one-third of an inning), and Mike Jackson (one-third of an inning) combined to retire all 13 batters they faced.

April 4 The Indians rout the Angels 11–0 in Anaheim.

The Indians started the season 6–0 and were 10–2 by April 14. The club was in first place every day of the 1998 season.

April 10 In the first game of the season at Jacobs Field, Jim Thome hits a three-run, walk-off homer in the tenth inning to beat the Angels 8–5 before a crowd of 42,707.

The Indians sold out every home game for the third year in a row.

April 14 The Indians purchase David Bell from the Cardinals.

April 15 The Indians and the Mariners brawl during a 5–3 Seattle win at Jacobs Field. In the third inning, Randy Johnson threw two pitches that barely missed Kenny Lofton, who charged the mound. Lofton was held back by Mariners catcher Dan Wilson. Sandy Alomar, Jr. tore out of the dugout toward Johnson and had to be restrained by the umpires, while Seattle manager Lou Piniella bolted in the direction of Lofton. After the dust settled, Johnson, Lofton and Alomar were all ejected.

April 21 The Indians beat the White Sox 14–6 at Jacobs Field. The Tribe broke open a close game with two runs in the seventh inning and five in the eighth.

May 1 The Indians play the Tampa Bay Devil Rays for the first time and win 7–5 at Jacobs Field.

May 3 Sandy Alomar, Jr. hits a two-out, two-strike, walk-off grand slam off Roberto Hernandez to cap a five-run ninth-inning Indians that results in a 10–8 against the Devil Rays at Jacobs Field. Tampa Bay led 6–0 after three innings. Cleveland scored two in the fourth, one in the fifth, and two in the seventh to close within a run, but the Devil Rays plated two in the top of the ninth before the Indians stunning comeback.

MAY 6 The Indians rout the Orioles 14–5 at Jacobs Field. Jim Thome chipped in with two doubles, a homer, and five runs-batted-in.

On the same day, the Indians signed Mark Whiten as a free agent. At the time, Whiten was playing for Chetumal in the Mexican League. He previously played for the Indians in 1991 and 1992.

MAY 11 The Indians play a regular season game in St. Petersburg for the first time and lose 4–2 to the Devil Rays.

MAY 15 Brian Giles leads off the 14th inning with a home run to lift the Indians to a 3–2 victory over the Rangers in Arlington.

MAY 19 The Indians score seven runs in the fifth inning and power past the Royals 16–3 in Kansas City. Cleveland collected 20 hits during the contest.

MAY 25 David Bell, facing his father Buddy's team for the first time, hits a tie-breaking two-run double in the sixth inning as the Indians defeat the Tigers 7–4 at Jacobs Field. Buddy Bell managed the Tigers from 1996 through 1998.

MAY 29 Bartolo Colon strikes out 14 batters in a complete-game 7–3 win over the Blue Jays in Toronto.

JUNE 1 Manny Ramirez scores both runs and drives in one as the Indians win 2–0 over the Tigers in Detroit. Jaret Wright pitched the shutout.

The Indians had a record of 45–13 against the Tigers from 1994 through 1998.

JUNE 2 In the first round of the amateur draft, the Indians select pitcher C. C. Sabathia from Vallejo High School in Vallejo, California.

The Indians made one of the best first-round selections in club history in Sabathia, who became the club's number one starting pitcher. Through the 2007 season, Sabathia had a record of 100–65, and his 1,142 strikeouts ranks seventh in franchise history. Other future major leaguers drafted and signed by the Indians in 1998 include Zach Sorensen (second round), Ryan Drese (fifth round), and Matt White (14th round).

JUNE 5 The Indians play a regular season game in Cincinnati for the first time, and lose 2–1 to the Reds at Cinergy Field.

JUNE 7 Dave Burba hits a two-run homer during a 6–1 win over the Reds in Cincinnati. Batting because the designated hitter isn't used in NL ballparks, Burba became the first Cleveland pitcher to homer in a game since Steve Dunning in 1972.

JUNE 8 The Pirates play a regular season game in Cleveland for the first time and beat the Indians 8–0 at Jacobs Field.

June 16 Manny Ramirez drives in six runs on two doubles and a home run during a 9–1 triumph over the Royals at Jacobs Field.

Ramirez clubbed 45 home runs and drove in 145 runs in 1998. He also scored 108 times and had a batting average of .294. Jim Thome hit .293 and clubbed 30 home runs.

June 20 Bob Lemon's uniform number 21 is retired in ceremonies at Jacobs Field prior to a 5–3 loss to the Yankees.

Mike Hargrove wore number 21 as a player from 1979 through 1985, as a coach in 1990 and 1991, and as a manager from 1991 through 1998. He switched to number 30 after the club retired the numeral in honor of Lemon.

June 21 Manny Ramirez hits two of the Indians five homers during an 11–0 victory over the Yankees at Jacobs Field. The others were struck by Shawon Dunston, Travis Fryman, and Mark Whiten.

June 22 The Indians play at Wrigley Field for the first time and beat the Cubs 3–1.

June 24 The Indians play the Cardinals in Cleveland for the first time, and win 14–3 at Jacobs Field. The Tribe scored seven times in the first inning, which included a grand slam by Manny Ramirez off Mark Petkovsek.

On the same day, the Indians traded Geronimo Berroa to the Tigers for Dave Roberts and Tim Worrell.

June 25 Mark McGwire nearly smacks a ball out of Jacobs Field during the Indians 8–2 win over the Cardinals. McGwire's shot off Dave Burba in the first inning hit a steel support beam attached to the scoreboard. The drive was estimated to have traveled 461 feet.

June 26 The Indians play the Astros in Cleveland for the first time and win 4–2 at Jacobs Field.

July 5 Manny Ramirez hits two homers, including a grand slam off Glendon Rusch in the sixth inning, to lead the Indians to a 12–3 win over the Royals in Kansas City.

July 7 Mike Hargrove manages the American League to a 13–8 win in the All-Star Game at Coors Field in Denver. Sandy Alomar, Jr. drove in a run with an eighth-inning single.

July 11 The Indians wallop the Twins 12–2 at Jacobs Field.

July 12 The Indians trade Tim Worrell for Aaron Robinson.

July 18 Brian Giles hits a grand slam off John Snyder in the first inning of a 15–9 win over the White Sox in Chicago. Cleveland led 8–0 before Chicago scored eight times in the fourth off Jaret Wright. The Tribe broke a 9–9 tie with three runs in the eighth.

Giles had to sit out four games in August because of an infection from a spider bite on his left leg.

JULY 23 The Indians trade Jose Mesa, Shawon Dunston, and Al Morman to the Giants for Steve Reed and Jacob Cruz. On the same day, the Indians trade Eric Plunk to the Brewers for Doug Jones.

Indians fans never forgave Mesa for failing to close out the seventh game of the 1997 World Series (see October 26, 1997) in a season that began with Mesa on trial for rape and weapons charges (see December 28, 1996). He had lost the job as Indians closer to Mike Jackson early in the 1998 season. Mesa was still pitching in the majors in 2007, at an indeterminate age. Mesa claimed to have been born in 1966, but in 2007, a Philadelphia sportscaster claimed he had uncovered documents stating that Mesa was actually born in 1960, which meant he was pitching for the Phils at the age of 47. Jackson had 40 saves and a 1.55 ERA in 69 games and 64 innings that season. Jones was previously the Indians closer from 1986 through 1991 and played in the All-Star Game in 1988, 1989, and 1990.

JULY 24 Travis Fryman hits a walk-off homer in the 11th inning to beat the Tigers 2–1 in Detroit.

JULY 30 The Indians outlast the Mariners 9–8 in 17 innings at the Kingdome. Manny Ramirez put the Indians ahead 9–6 with a three-run homer in the top of the 17th. Seattle rallied with two runs in their half. Both teams scored once in the 12th. The contest was the last one that the Indians played at the Kingdome.

AUGUST 5 Manny Ramirez hits a two-run homer in the ninth inning that beats the Angels 6–5 in Anaheim.

AUGUST 13 The Indians sign Cecil Fielder following his release by the Angels.

AUGUST 14 Chris Hoiles hits two grand slams for the Orioles during a 15–3 Baltimore win at Jacobs Field. Hoiles hit his first slam off Charles Nagy in the third inning and the second against Ron Villone in the eighth. Hoiles received a standing ovation from the Cleveland crowd after the second grand slam.

Hoiles is one of only 12 major leaguers with two grand slams in a single game.

AUGUST 25 Manny Ramirez hits two homers, a double, and a single and drives in five runs during a 10–4 win over the Mariners at Jacobs Field. Travis Fryman broke his nose after falling over a tarp while chasing a foul fly in the eighth inning.

AUGUST 28 The Athletics explode for eight runs in the tenth inning and beat the Indians 14–6 at Jacobs Field. All eight runs were surrendered by reliever Steve Reed.

AUGUST 30 Richie Sexson hits a grand slam off Tim Worrell in the seventh inning of a 9–4 win over the Athletics at Jacobs Field.

AUGUST 31 The Indians score ten runs in the first inning and drub the Athletics 15–6 at Jacobs Field. The first eight Cleveland batters reached base on four hits, three walks, and an error.

On the same day, the Indians traded David Bell to the Mariners for Joey Cora.

SEPTEMBER 9 Travis Fryman hits a three-run homer in the 13th inning to defeat the Blue Jays 6–3 in Toronto.

SEPTEMBER 13 The Indians beat the White Sox 6–3 at Jacobs Field in a contest marred by a ten-minute bench-clearing fracas in the third inning after Chicago's Jim Parque threw a pitch over Omar Vizquel's head.

SEPTEMBER 15 Manny Ramirez hits three homers in consecutive at-bats and drives in five runs during a 7–5 win over the Blue Jays at Jacobs Field. Manny connected off Dave Steib in the third and fifth innings and Paul Quantrill in the seventh.

SEPTEMBER 16 Manny Ramirez hits two homers during the Indians division-clinching victory over the Twins at Jacobs Field. It was Cleveland fourth consecutive AL Central title. Ramirez tied two major league records. By homering off Bob Tewksbury in the first inning, Ramirez tied a mark by homering in his fourth consecutive at-bat. He hit home runs in his last three at-bats the previous game (see September 15, 1998). By hitting another homer off Tewksbury in the fifth, Manny tied another record for most home runs in consecutive games with five.

SEPTEMBER 17 Manny Ramirez ties yet another major league record with six homers in three consecutive games after hitting a two-run shot off Eric Milton in the fourth inning of a 9–1 victory over the Twins at Jacobs Field. Ramirez hit three home runs on September 15 and two on September 16.

SEPTEMBER 18 The Indians release Cecil Fielder.

SEPTEMBER 19 Manny Ramirez hits two more homers during a 7–6 loss to the Royals at Jacobs Field. The outburst gave Ramirez eight home runs in five games.

SEPTEMBER 21 A grand slam by Enrique Wilson off Andy Pettitte in the fifth inning accounts for all four runs in a 4–1 win over the Yankees in New York.

The Indians closed out the regular season with six losses in seven games and finished at 89–73. The Tribe had the third-best record in the AL. In the Division Series, Cleveland met the Red Sox, managed by Jimy Williams. The Sox were 92–70 in 1998 and earned the wild card berth.

SEPTEMBER 29 In the opening game of the Division Series, the Indians are pummeled 11–3 by the Red Sox before 45,185 at Jacobs Field. Boston scored three runs in the first inning on a home run by Mo Vaughn off Jaret Wright and led 8–0 in the sixth. Vaughn finished the game with seven RBIs. Kenny Lofton and Jim Thome both homered.

SEPTEMBER 30 The Indians even the ALDS with a 9–5 triumph over the Red Sox before 45,229 at Jacobs Field. Cleveland took a 6–2 lead with five runs in the second inning. Mike Hargrove and starting pitcher Dwight Gooden were both ejected in the first inning for arguing the calls of home plate umpire Joe Brinkman. David Justice drove in four runs, three on a second-inning homer. John Valentin of the Red Sox took exception to an inside pitch from Mike Jackson in the ninth inning. Valentin gestured at Jackson, causing both benches and bullpens to empty, but no punches were thrown.

OCTOBER 2 In game three, the Indians defeat the Red Sox 4–3 at Fenway Park. Cleveland scored single runs in the fifth, sixth, seventh, and ninth innings and survived a scare when Boston tallied twice in the bottom of the ninth. The four Indians runs came on solo homers. Manny Ramirez went deep twice and Jim Thome and Kenny Lofton once. Charles Nagy allowed only one run in eight innings of work.

OCTOBER 3 The Indians win the Division Series with a 2–1 victory over the Red Sox in Boston. Trailing 1–0, Cleveland scored twice in the eighth for the win. David Justice drove in both runs with a double following broken bat singles by Kenny Lofton and Omar Vizquel.

The Indians met the Yankees in the Championship Series. Managed by Joe Torre, the Yankees had one of the best clubs in major league history, with a record of 114–48. They had 22 more regular season wins than any other American League club. The Yanks swept the Rangers in the ALDS.

OCTOBER 6 The Yankees score five runs in the first inning off Jaret Wright and beat the Indians 7–2 in New York in the opening game of the ALCS. Manny Ramirez drove in both Cleveland runs with a ninth inning home run.

OCTOBER 7 The Indians score three runs in the 12th inning and beat the Yankees 4–1 at Yankee Stadium. The 12th-inning rally was keyed by a controversial play. With the score tied 1–1 and pinch-runner Enrique Wilson on first base and no one out, Travis Fryman laid down a bunt that first baseman Tino Martinez fielded inside the line. Martinez fired the ball to second baseman Chuck Knoblauch covering the bag, but it hit Fryman in the back and caromed 20 feet away. Fryman appeared to be running illegally inside the baseline, but umpire Tim Hendry did not call interference. Knoblauch, instead of chasing the ball, argued the non-call with Hendry, allowing Wilson to score all the way from first. Charles Nagy allowed a run in 6⅔ innings and six relievers combined to throw shutout ball the rest of the way.

OCTOBER 8 Former pitcher and retired broadcaster Herb Score is seriously injured in an auto accident. While on his way to Florida with his wife, Score pulled his car in front of a tractor-trailer near New Philadelphia, Ohio, about 80 miles south of Cleveland. He nearly died from head, hip, and pelvic injuries and spent two months in the hospital.

OCTOBER 9 The Indians take a surprising two-to-one lead in the ALCS with a 6–1 win over the Yankees before 44,904 at Jacobs Field. With the Indians ahead 2–1 in the fifth, Andy Pettitte allowed three homers and four runs. The home runs were by Jim Thome, his second of the game, Manny Ramirez, and Mark Whiten. Omar Vizquel contributed three hits. Bartolo Colon pitched a four-hit complete game.

OCTOBER 10 The Yankees even the Championship Series with a 4–0 win over the Indians before 44,981 at Jacobs Field. Yankee starter Orlando Hernandez went seven innings. Omar Vizquel collected three of Cleveland's four hits.

OCTOBER 11 The Indians are one loss from elimination following a 5–3 defeat against the Yankees before 44,966 at Jacobs Field. The Yanks score three runs in the first inning and never trailed. David Wells struck out 11 batters in 7⅓ innings.

October 13 The Yankees take the ALCS four games to two with a 9–5 decision over the Indians in New York. Trailing 6–0, the Indians scored all five of their runs in the fifth inning, but the Yanks countered with three in the sixth. Jim Thome collected a homer and a single and drove in four runs.

The Yankees went on to sweep the World Series against the Padres.

November 13 The Indians trade Chad Ogea to the Phillies for Jerry Spradlin.

November 18 The Indians trade Brian Giles to the Pirates for Ricardo Rinson.

Cleveland made a miserable trade. Rincon was nothing more than a situational lefty for the Indians. Giles blossomed as a power-hitting center fielder and went on the play in the All-Star Game with the Pirates in both 2000 and 2001. He was still a regular in the Padres outfield in 2007.

November 24 The Indians sign Roberto Alomar, most recently with the Orioles, as a free agent.

Roberto was reunited with his brother Sandy for the first time since both were Padres in 1989. Sandy, Jr. was born 20 months before Roberto. Before signing with the Indians, Roberto had been an anathema to Cleveland fans for his role in the 1996 Division Series (see October 1, 1996 and October 5, 1996). Roberto gave the Indians three tremendous seasons at second base, batting .323 with 63 homers and 362 runs scored in 471 games and won three Gold Gloves. He made the All-Star team all three years.

1999

Season in a Sentence

The Indians win the AL Central for the fifth year in a row and become the first major league team since 1950 to score over 1,000 runs, but suffer a shocking loss to the Red Sox in the Division Series.

Finish • Won • Lost • Pct • GB

Finish	Won	Lost	Pct	GB
First	97	65	.599	+21.5

American League Division Series

The Indians lost to the Boston Red Sox three games to two.

Manager

Mike Hargrove

Stats

Stats	Indians	AL	Rank
Batting Avg:	.289	.275	2
On-Base Pct:	.347	.340	3
Slugging Pct:	.467	.439	2
Home Runs:	209		5
Stolen Bases:	147		1
ERA:	4.89	4.86	6
Fielding Avg:	.983	.981	3
Runs Scored:	1,009		1
Runs Allowed:	860		7

Starting Line-up

Einar Diaz, c
Richie Sexson, 1b-lf
Roberto Alomar, 2b
Travis Fryman, 3b
Omar Vizquel, ss
David Justice, lf
Kenny Lofton, cf
Manny Ramirez, rf
Jim Thome, dh-1b
Enrique Wilson, 3b-ss

Pitchers

Bartolo Colon, sp
Charles Nagy, sp
Dave Burba, sp
Jaret Wright, sp
Dwight Gooden, sp
Mike Jackson, rp
Paul Shuey, rp
Steve Karsay, rp
Paul Assenmacher, rp
Ricardo Rincon, rp

Attendance

3,468,456 (first in AL)

Club Leaders

Batting Avg:	Manny Ramirez	.333
	Omar Vizquel	.333
On-Base Pct:	Manny Ramirez	.442
Home Runs:	Manny Ramirez	44
RBIs:	Manny Ramirez	165
Runs:	Roberto Alomar	138
Stolen Bases:	Omar Vizquel	42
Wins:	Bartolo Colon	18
Strikeouts:	Dave Burba	174
ERA:	Bartolo Colon	3.95
Saves:	Mike Jackson	39

JANUARY 11 Doug Jones signs as a free agent with the Athletics.

JANUARY 18 Joey Cora signs as a free agent with the Blue Jays.

FEBRUARY 3 The Indians sign Wil Cordero, most recently with the White Sox, as a free agent.

APRIL 4 Two months after Bill Clinton is acquitted following his impeachment trial in the House of Representatives, the Indians sign Mark Langston, most recently with the Astros, as a free agent.

APRIL 6 The Indians open the season with a 6–5 loss to the Angels in Anaheim. The Tribe led 5–3 before allowing two runs in the seventh inning and one in the eighth.

After the Opening Day loss, the Indians won eight in a row and were 11–2 on April 21, 29–12 on May 22, and 50–25 on June 29. Cleveland's advantage in the AL Central was never less than ten games after June 15.

APRIL 9 The Indians collect 20 hits and rout the Twins 14–5 in Minneapolis.

APRIL 12 In the home opener, Travis Fryman hits a three-run walk-off homer in the 13th inning to defeat the Royals 5–2 before 42,798 at Jacobs Field. Enrique Wilson tied the game 2–2 with a two-run homer in the eighth. It was the second straight year that the Indians won the home opener with an extra-inning, three-run homer (see April 10, 1998).

APRIL 14 Trailing 3–2, the Indians explode for nine runs in the sixth inning and beat the Royals 11–4 at Jacobs Field.

APRIL 17 In the day game of a day-night double header at Jacobs Field, the Indians extend their winning streak to eight games with a 5–2 decision over the Twins. Minnesota won the second contest 13–8 with five runs in the 11th inning.

APRIL 21 The day after 15 die in a shooting at Columbine High School in Littleton, Colorado, the Indians score two runs in the eighth inning and three in the ninth to beat the Athletics 5–4 at Jacobs Field. The two tallies in the eighth scored on back-to-back homers by Roberto Alomar and Manny Ramirez. In the ninth, Cleveland tied the contest on a two-run, pinch-hit homer from Richie Sexson. The winning run scored on a single by Sandy Alomar, Jr. and a three-base throwing error by catcher A. J. Hinch on a bunt by Kenny Lofton.

Ramirez had an outstanding season in 1999. He batted .333 with 44 homers, 165 RBIs, and 131 runs scored. The runs-batted-in total broke the Indians single-season record of 162 by Hal Trosky in 1936. It was also the highest RBI figure of any major league leaguer since Jimmie Foxx had 175 with the Red Sox in 1938.

APRIL 23 The Indians beat the Red Sox 7–6 in Boston in a game that is interrupted by two brawls. In the fifth inning, Jaret Wright set off the first altercation by hitting Darren Lewis, who stood at home plate and shouted at Wright. Both benches and bullpens emptied and Wright and Lewis were ejected after punches were thrown. Wright had hit Lewis in the head in game one of the 1998 Division Series. The Indians trailed 6–5 in the sixth inning when Red Sox reliever Rheal Cormier struck Jim Thome in the ribs, setting off the second brawl. Benches and bullpens cleared again and a wild melee ensued with Boston catcher Jason Varitek tackling David Justice. Thome and Cormier were ejected.

MAY 7 In a strange game against the Devil Rays at Jacobs Field, the Indians trail 10–2 in the sixth inning but rally to win 20–11 with 18 runs in three consecutive innings. Cleveland scored four runs in the sixth inning, seven in the seventh, and seven more in the eighth. David Justice had two homers, two singles, scored four runs, and drove in five. To add to the weirdness, there was a moment of concern when smoke filtered into the ballpark from a burning car nearby.

The Indians scored 1,009 runs in 1999. They are the only major league club since 1950 to score over 1,000 runs in a season. The 1950 Red Sox scored 1,027.

MAY 15 David Justice hits a grand slam off Dave Mlicki in the third inning of a 12–7 win over the Tigers in Detroit.

Justice was married to actress Halle Berry from 1993 through 1996.

MAY 17 Omar Vizquel steals four bases in a 13–9 win over the White Sox in Chicago. Most of the scoring was done early in the game. In the first inning, the Indians scored five runs and the White Sox countered with six. At the end of the third inning, the score was 12–9 in favor of the Indians.

MAY 18 Manny Ramirez hits a grand slam off James Baldwin in the second inning of a 13–0 rout of the White Sox at Comiskey Park. Dwight Gooden (seven innings), Ricardo Rincon (one inning), and Paul Assenmacher (one inning) combined on a two-hit shutout. The only Chicago hits were singles by Chris Singleton in the third inning and Mike Caruso in the ninth.

MAY 19 The Indians score 13 runs against the White Sox in Chicago for the third game in a row, winning 13–7. Richie Sexson hit a grand slam off Bryan Ward in the fifth inning.

In 1999 Manny Ramirez produced one of the greatest offensive seasons in Tribe history. His 165 RBIs remain the most in a season by any player since the 1930s.

Five members of the 1999 Indians scored over 100 runs in 1999. They were Roberto Alomar (138), Manny Ramirez (131), Omar Vizquel (112), Kenny Lofton (110), and Jim Thome (101). Those who drove in at least 100 runs were Ramirez (165), Alomar (120), Richie Sexson (116), and Thome (108).

May 22 A 6–2 loss to the Tigers at Jacobs Field is marred by a brawl. It was sparked by beanings of Tony Clark by Jaret Wright in the top of the sixth inning and Manny Ramirez in the bottom half. Both dugouts emptied, and in the ensuring altercation, Tiger manager Larry Parrish wrestled Wright to the ground.

Ramirez was suspended for three days for his role in the brawl. Wright was called before American League President Gene Budig to discuss Wright's "deportment on the mound." Wright, just 23 and in his third season in the majors, had been involved in several previous incidents in which he was accused of deliberating throwing at hitters.

May 23 Down 4–0, the Indians score two runs in the eighth inning and five in the ninth to stun the Tigers 7–4 at Jacobs Field. In the ninth, singles by Travis Fryman, David Justice and Richie Sexson loaded the bases. Jim Thome walked to force in a run, followed by a one-out, walk-off grand slam by Omar Vizquel off Todd Jones.

The Indians sold out every home game for the fourth year in a row and led the AL in attendance with 3,468,456. It was the first time that Cleveland led the league in attendance since 1949. The 1999 figure still stands as the club record.

May 31 Jim Thome hits a grand slam off Orlando Hernandez in the second inning of a 7–1 win over the Yankees in New York.

Thome hit .277 with 33 homers and 108 RBIs in 1999. He led the AL in both walks (127) and strikeouts (171). The walks figure is the all-time Indians single season record.

June 2 In the second round of the amateur draft, the Indians select catcher Will Hartley from Bradford High School in Stark, Florida.

The Indians had no first round choice due to free agent compensation. Hartley was a complete bust. He never advanced beyond rookie ball. As of 2007, none of the first nine choices reached the big leagues. Future major leaguers drafted and signed by the Indians in 1999 include Fernando Cabrera (tenth round), Jason Davis (21st round), Kyle Denney (26th round), and Mike Bishop (44th round).

June 5 The Indians score two runs in the ninth inning and one in the 11th to defeat the Cubs 8–7 at Jacobs Field. On a strange play in the 11th, Roberto Alomar went from home to third without hitting the ball out of the infield, and he scored on Wil Cordero's one-out single. Alomar hit a hard grounder off Cubs pitcher Scott Sanders. First baseman Mark Grace scrambled to get the ball and made a quick throw to Sanders, who dropped it while covering the bag. As the ball rolled away, Alomar broke for second. Sanders threw the ball into left field attempting to get Alomar, who easily dashed to third base.

Alomar was a sensation in his first season with the Indians. He led the league in runs with 138, and he hit .323, with 40 doubles, 24 homers, and 120 RBI.

JUNE 9 Jacob Cruz, recalled earlier in the day from Triple-A Buffalo, singles home the winning run in the tenth inning to defeat the Brewers 6–5 at Jacobs Field.

On the same day, Charles Nagy attended a dinner at the White House as an invited guest of President Bill Clinton. The dinner was in honor of Hungarian President Arpad Goncz. Nagy, whose family was from Hungary, and his wife, Jackie, were invited after a local woman who works in foreign affairs submitted his name to the White House.

JUNE 11 Dwight Gooden homers during an 8–6 win over the Reds in Cincinnati. It was Gooden's eighth major league home run but his first since 1993.

JUNE 16 The Indians score four runs in the eighth inning and two in the ninth to beat the Athletics 9–8 at Jacobs Field. In the ninth, Kenny Lofton hit a game-tying single, stole second, and scored on Omar Vizquel's single.

Vizquel had the best season of his career at the plate in 1999, batting .333.

JUNE 20 The Indians mash the Mariners 13–5 at Jacobs Field.

JUNE 26 Up 7–0, the Indians give up a run in the seventh inning and ten in the eighth to lose 11–7 to the Royals in Kansas City. The eighth-inning eruption came at the expense of Bartolo Colon, Paul Shuey, Ricardo Rincon, and Steve Karsay.

JUNE 29 The Indians sign Tom Candiotti following his release by the Athletics.

JULY 3 In the day game of a day-night double header, the Indians overcome an 8–0 deficit to defeat the Royals 9–8. Kansas City scored twice in the first inning and six times in the second. Cleveland countered with three tallies in the second inning, six in the sixth and one in the seventh. In his first appearance with the Indians since 1991, Tom Candiotti pitched 5⅔ innings of shutout relief. In the night game, Jim Thome hit a home run that traveled an estimated 511 feet to start an eight-run second inning. Thome's drive bounced through a gate and out of the ballpark, sending fans scurrying down Eagle Avenue for the souvenir.

Candiotti won 72 games for the Indians from 1986 through 1991. Despite the outstanding outing on July 3, his return wasn't successful. Candiotti was released on August 2 with an ERA of 11.05 in seven games and 14⅔ innings.

JULY 7 The Indians participate in another beanball war during a 4–3 loss to the Twins in Minneapolis. Bartolo Colon was ejected in the sixth inning for hitting Corey Koskie. Colon had previously struck Torii Hunter with a pitch in the fourth. Minnesota hurler Joe Mays twice threw over Manny Ramirez's head, the second time in the sixth. Both benches and bullpens emptied after the second errant pitch to Ramirez and again after Koskie was hit, but no punches were thrown.

JULY 10 Omar Vizquel hits a two-out, two-run, walk-off homer in the ninth inning to beat the Reds 11–10 at Jacobs Field. The drive barely cleared the wall. The Indians trailed

9–4 in the fifth inning before mounting the comeback with a run in the fifth, three in the seventh and one in the eighth to tie the game 9–9. Cincinnati plated a run in the top of the ninth to take a 10–9 lead and set the stage for Vizquel's heroics.

JULY 13 With four Indians in the starting line-up, the American League wins the All-Star Game 4–1 at Fenway Park in Boston. The starters were Kenny Lofton (left field), Manny Ramirez (right field), Jim Thome (first base), and Roberto Alomar (second base). Thome singled in Lofton in the first inning off Curt Schilling of the Phillies.

JULY 15 Roberto Alomar drives in both runs with a two-run double in the third inning of a 2–0 win over the Pirates in Pittsburgh. Bartolo Colon (eight innings) and Mike Jackson (one inning) combined on the shutout.

Colon was 18–5 with a 3.95 earned run average in 1999.

JULY 22 A batting mix-up costs the Indians the use of the designated hitter and helps the Blue Jays win 4–3 at Jacobs Field. Charles Nagy had to bat seventh because of a mistake by Mike Hargrove. The Cleveland manager originally listed Manny Ramirez as the designated hitter and Alex Ramirez in right field. But Manny took the field in the top of the first. The rule states that if a designated hitter takes the field, the DH can't be used for the remainder of the game, forcing Nagy into the batting order.

JULY 23 Roberto Alomar hits a grand slam off David Cone in the fourth inning, but the Indians lose 9–8 in ten innings to the Yankees in New York.

JULY 24 The Yankees crush the Indians 21–1 in New York. New York led 18–0 by the end of the sixth inning. After the Indians tallied in the top of the seventh, the Yanks piled on with three more in their half. The 21 runs scored off Mark Langston, Paul Assenmacher, and Tom Candiotti. It was the second worst loss in Indians history, exceeded only by the 21–0 defeat at the hands of the Tigers on September 15, 1901. Later, the Tribe lost 23–2 to the Twins on June 4, 2002.

JULY 27 The Indians score eight runs in the second inning and win 14–5 over the Tigers at Jacobs Field.

JULY 31 Roberto Alomar hits two homers and drives in five runs during a 13–10 win over the White Sox at Jacobs Field. The Indians blew an 8–3 lead allowing Chicago to tie the game 8–8 in the seventh before recovering for the victory.

AUGUST 7 Wade Boggs collects his 3,000th career hit with a sixth-inning homer off Indians pitcher Chris Haney during a 15–10 Cleveland win in St. Petersburg. Manny Ramirez collected three hits in three at-bats, drove in five runs and scored four.

AUGUST 14 Jim Thome hits a grand slam off Jason Johnson in the first inning of a 7–1 win over the Orioles in Baltimore.

AUGUST 16 The Indians purchase Carlos Baerga from the Padres.

John Hart brought back another former Indians All-Star in acquiring Baerga. He played in the All-Star Game in 1992, 1993, and 1995, but by 1999 he was overweight and his skills were declining.

August 19 Making a rare start, Steve Karsay earns his tenth consecutive victory by hurling five shutout innings in an 8–0 decision over the Rangers at Jacobs Field.

Karsay pitched in 50 games in 1999, making three starts and 47 relief appearances. He finished the season with a 10–2 record and a 2.97 ERA.

August 20 The Indians play at Safeco Field in Seattle for the first time and win 7–4.

August 24 Jim Thome hits a grand slam off Tim Hudson in the first inning, but the Indians lose 11–10 to the Athletics in Oakland.

The Indians hit a club record 12 grand slams in 1999. They were hit by Jim Thome (three), Roberto Alomar (two), David Justice (two), Manny Ramirez (two), Dave Roberts (one), Richie Sexson (one), and Omar Vizquel (one).

August 25 Manny Ramirez hits three homers during a 12–4 victory over the Athletics in Oakland. Ramirez drove in four runs, connecting off Mike Oquist in the first inning, Jason Isringhausen in the seventh, and Jimmy Haynes in the eighth. Jim Thome and Omar Vizquel also homered.

August 27 The Indians trade Juan Aracena and Jimmy Hamilton to the Orioles for Harold Baines.

August 28 The Indians and Browns play in Cleveland on the same day for the first time in history. At Jacobs Field, the Indians defeated the Devil Rays 3–0. At Cleveland Browns Stadium, the Browns beat the Bears 35–24 in an exhibition game.

August 31 The Indians take a thrilling 14–12 decision from the Angels at Jacobs Field by overcoming an eight-run deficit with ten runs in the eighth inning. Anaheim scored five runs in the top of the eighth for a 12–4 advantage. The first two runs of the Cleveland half of the eighth scored on a single by Richie Sexson. The Tribe still trailed 12–6 with two out and the bases loaded. The final eight runs came across the plate on singles by Omar Vizquel, Roberto Alomar, and Harold Baines, a walk to Jim Thome, a wild pitch and a three-run homer by Sexson, giving him five RBIs in the inning. After Sexson's home run, Troy Percival hit David Justice with a pitch. Justice charged the mound and hurled his helmet at Percival, sparking a brawl in which the Angels pitcher sustained a cut and a bruise under his right eye.

The 1999 Indians became the first team in history to overcome three deficits of eight runs or more in a season. The other two were on May 7 and August 7.

September 7 The Indians score seven runs in the fifth inning and defeat the Orioles 15–7 in Baltimore.

September 8 The Indians lose 3–0 to the Rangers in Arlington but clinch the AL Central title when the White Sox also lose 6–5 in ten innings to the Angels in Anaheim.

The 1999 division title was the fifth in a row for the Indians. The only Indians to appear in the post-season all five years were Charles Nagy, Manny Ramirez, Jim Thome, and Omar Vizquel.

September 10 The Indians erupt for 12 runs in the fourth inning of a 14–6 win over the White Sox in Chicago. Roberto Alomar began the 12-run outburst with a single. Manny Ramirez followed with a walk and Carlos Baerga hit a two-run double. Baines reached third on an error, David Justice walked, and Sandy Alomar, Jr. and Bip Roberts both singled. Omar Vizquel doubled, followed by walks to Roberto Alomar, Manny Ramirez, Jim Thome, and Harold Baines. David Justice capped the inning with a grand slam off Carlos Castillo.

September 12 The expansion edition of the Cleveland Browns play their first regular season game and lose 43–0 to the Steelers at Cleveland Browns Stadium.

September 22 Roberto Alomar collects his 2,000th career hit during a 9–1 win over the Tigers in Detroit. Jaret Wright (seven innings), Steve Karsay (one inning), and Ricardo Rincon (one inning) combined on the shutout. The only Detroit hits were singles by Dean Palmer in the second inning and Karim Garcia in the fifth.

September 23 The Indians play at Tiger Stadium for the last time, and lose 7–5. Manny Ramirez was pulled from the game by Mike Hargrove for loafing on a fly ball.

September 24 Manny Ramirez and Dave Roberts both hit grand slams during an 8–4 win over the Blue Jays in Toronto. Ramirez drove in a total of eight runs. He hit a three-run homer off Peter Munro off the SkyDome restaurant window in the fourth inning, the grand slam against Mike Romano in the fifth, and an RBI-single. Roberts hit his slam in the eighth facing John Hudek.

The Indians came into the final weekend with the best record in the American League at 97–62, but blew home field advantage throughout the playoffs by losing three in a row to the Blue Jays at Jacobs Field while the Yankees won two of three from the Devil Rays. The Indians faced the Red Sox in the Division Series. Managed by Jimy Williams, the Sox were 94–68 in 1999. The Indians also played Boston in the first round in 1995 and 1998.

October 6 The Indians score the winning run in the ninth inning to open the Division Series with a 3–2 win over the Red Sox before 45,182 at Jacobs Field. Boston led 2–0 after four innings when Pedro Martinez had to leave the game because of a sore back. Jim Thome hit a two-run homer in the sixth to tie the contest. In the ninth, Cleveland loaded the bases before Travis Fryman's walk-off single with one out.

October 7 The Indians go up two games to none in the Division Series with a 11–1 pounding of the Red Sox before 45,184 at Jacobs Field. The Tribe scored six runs in the third inning and four in the fourth. The big blow in the third was a three-run homer from Harold Baines facing Bret Saberhagen. In the fourth, Jim Thome clubbed a grand slam off John Wasdin. Roberto Alomar contributed two doubles and a single.

The defeat was Boston's 18th in a span of 19 post-season games beginning with Bill Buckner's infamous error in the sixth game of the 1986 World Series against the Mets. During that span, the Sox were 1–8 against the Indians.

October 9 In game three, the Red Sox break a 3–3 tie with six runs in the seventh inning and defeat the Indians 9–3 at Fenway Park. Starter Dave Burba pitched four shutout innings but had to leave the game with numbness in his pitching arm.

October 10 The Red Sox even the Division Series with a 23–7 pummeling of the Indians in Boston. The 23 runs marked the most ever scored by a team in the post-season. Boston's 24 hits were also a record. The Sox broke a 2–2 tie with five runs in the second inning off Bartolo Colon. Five relievers fared little better, surrendering 16 runs. The Sox scored in every turn at bat except the sixth. Wil Cordero collected a homer and two singles in the losing cause.

October 11 The Indians stunning collapse against the Red Sox continues with a 12–8 loss that eliminates Cleveland from the post-season before 45,114 at Jacobs Field. The Indians led 5–2 at the end of the second inning and 8–7 at the end of the third. Jim Thome hit two homers and drove in four runs. Travis Fryman also homered. But Boston scored one in the fourth, three in the seventh to break the 8–8 tie, and an insurance tally in the ninth. Pedro Martinez prevented an Indians comeback with a spectacular relief performance by pitching the last six innings without allowing a hit.

The Indians scored 32 runs in the five games but allowed 47. After winning the first two games by a combined score of 14–3, Cleveland was outscored 44–18 over the last three. The pitching staff had an earned run average of 9.64 during the series.

October 15 The Indians fire manager Mike Hargrove. He had directed the Indians to five consecutive division titles from 1995 through 1999 but received much of the blame for the club's failure to win a World Series during that span. The Indians had the best regular season record in the majors in 1995 and 1996 and reached the Fall Classic in 1995 and 1997 but failed to claim a world championship. Hargrove had 721 wins as the Indians manager, second all-time to the 728 victories accumulated by Lou Boudreau. "There is a need for a new energy and a new voice coming from the clubhouse," said general manager John Hart in announcing the move. "This change will create a different atmosphere." Hargrove later managed the Orioles from 2000 through 2003 and the Mariners from 2005 through July 2007. None of the six clubs he managed over a full season in either Baltimore or Seattle posted a winning record. Hargrove finally had a club over the .500 mark in 2007 in Seattle, but he resigned without warning just prior to the All-Star break.

November 1 The Indians hire 55-year-old Charlie Manuel as manager. Manuel had been the club's hitting coach in 1988 and 1989 and again from 1994 through 1999. With the help of his batting tips, the Indians in 1999 became the first team in nearly a half-century to score over 1,000 runs in a season. In between his two stints as a coach, Manuel managed the Indians Triple-A teams in Colorado Springs and Charlotte for four years. He played in 242 games as an outfielder with the Twins and Dodgers from 1969 through 1975. With Manuel as manager, the Indians finished second in 2000 and first in 2001 before exiting in the first round of the playoffs. He was fired midway through a losing season in 2002.

November 5 Larry Dolan purchases the Indians for $323 million from Richard Jacobs. At the time, it was the most ever paid for a baseball franchise. Jacobs and his brother David paid $35 million for the club in 1986. Dolan, age 68, was a Cleveland-area lawyer who was a longtime Indians fan. He had been part of a group that earlier in 1999 tried to buy the Cincinnati Reds. He also put in a bid to buy the Cleveland Browns after the NFL revived the franchise as an expansion club.

November 6 The Indians sign Cuban defector Danys Baez to a contract. Baez defected from Cuba during the 1999 Pan American Games in Winnipeg, Canada.

December 1 Mike Jackson signs with the Phillies as a free agent.

December 9 Harold Baines signs with the Orioles as a free agent.

December 14 Wil Cordero signs with the Pirates as a free agent.

December 16 The Indians sign Chuck Finley, most recently with the Angels, as a free agent.

Finley signed with the Indians at the age of 37 in order to have a chance to pitch in the post-season. He won 165 games with the Angels over 14 seasons. Finley was a 16-game winner in 2000, but Cleveland failed to reach the playoffs. He made two starts against the Mariners in the 2001 Division Series and lost both of them. Unfortunately, Finley's three-season stay in Cleveland is best remembered for an altercation with his wife (see April 3, 2002).

THE STATE OF THE INDIANS

The Indians came into the new millennium having won five consecutive AL Central titles from 1995 through 1999. After narrowly missing the playoffs in 2000, Cleveland won the division pennant again in 2001. The winning team was largely dismantled, however, and the Indians rebuilt with a much younger roster. After years of growing pains, Cleveland reached the ALCS in 2007. From 2000 through 2007, the Indians had a record of 670–626, a winning percentage of .517, to rank eighth among the 14 AL clubs. American League champions during the 2000s have been the Yankees (2000, 2001, and 2003), Angels (2002), Red Sox (2004 and 2007), White Sox (2005) and Tigers (2006). AL Central champs have been the White Sox (2000 and 2005), Indians (2001 and 2007), Twins (2002, 2003, and 2004) and Tigers (2006).

THE BEST TEAM

The 2007 Indians posted a record of 96–66, which tied for the best in the AL with the Red Sox. The Tribe lost to the Red Sox in the ALCS in seven games.

THE WORST TEAM

With a young roster in Eric Wedge's first season as manager, the Indians were 68–94 in 2003.

THE BEST MOMENT

The Indians won game four of the 2007 ALCS to take a three-games-to-one lead over the Red Sox.

THE WORST MOMENT

The Indians lost the last three games of the ALCS by a combined score of 30–5.

THE ALL-DECADE TEAM • YEARS W/INDIANS

Victor Martinez, c	2002–07
Jim Thome, 1b	1991–2002
Roberto Alomar, 2b	1999–2001
Travis Fryman, 3b	1998–2002
Omar Vizquel, ss	1994–2004
Matt Lawton, lf	2002–04
Grady Sizemore, cf	2004–07
Casey Blake, rf	2003–07
Travis Hafner, dh	2003–07
C. C. Sabathia, p	2001–07
Bartolo Colon, p	1997–2002
Jake Westbrook, p	2001–07
Cliff Lee, p	2002–07

Thome and Vizquel were on the 1990s All-Decade Team. Blake has played more games with the Indians at third base than in right field but makes the All-Decade Team as a right fielder because of a lack of viable candidates. The Indians have struggled to find consistent production from their corner outfielders since the dawn of the new millennium.

THE DECADE LEADERS

Batting Avg:	Victor Martinez	.301
On-Base Pct:	Travis Hafner	.400
Slugging Pct:	Travis Hafner	.556
Home Runs:	Travis Hafner	142
RBIs:	Travis Hafner	480
Runs:	Travis Hafner	411
Stolen Bases:	Grady Sizemore	79
Wins:	C. C. Sabathia	100
Strikeouts:	C. C. Sabathia	1,142
ERA:	C. C. Sabathia	3.83
Saves:	Bob Wickman	139

THE HOME FIELD

The Indians sold out 455 consecutive games at Jacobs Field from June 1995 through Opening Day in 2001. Cleveland led the AL in attendance in both 1999 and 2000 and the major leagues in 2000. Since 2003, however, the club has finished in the bottom half of the American League in attendance, even during the 2007 pennant-winning season. In 2004, the Indians debuted a new entertainment system with LED technology throughout Jacobs Field. The upgrade included the largest video screen in North America utilized for sports.

THE GAME YOU WISHED YOU HAD SEEN

On August 5, 2001, the Indians erased leads of 12–0 in the fourth inning and 14–2 in the seventh against the Mariners and rallied to win 15–14 in the 11th.

THE WAY THE GAME WAS PLAYED

The offensive explosion experienced during the last half of the 1990s continued into the 2000s, as did the trend toward new baseball-only ballparks with grass fields. About mid-decade, allegations of the use of performance-enhancing drugs became a hot topic, and Major League Baseball instituted much harsher penalties for players caught using the substances.

THE MANAGEMENT

A group headed by Larry Dolan purchased the Indians from Richard Jacobs in November 1999. General managers have been John Hart (1991–2001) and Mark Shapiro (2001–present). Field managers have been Charlie Manuel (2000–02), Joel Skinner (2002), and Eric Wedge (2003–present).

THE BEST PLAYER MOVE

The jury is still out on most of the player moves of the 2000s, but thus far the acquisition of Travis Hafner from the Rangers in December 2002 shapes up as the best of the bunch.

THE WORST PLAYER MOVE

The Indians let Manny Ramirez escape to the Red Sox via the free agency route following the 2000 season and lost Jim Thome to the Phillies by the same manner in 2002. It would have been extremely expensive to keep both of them, but Ramirez and Thome have justified their exorbitant salaries since leaving Cleveland. It's too early to evaluate the worst trade of the 2000s, but so far, swapping Brandon Phillips to the Reds in April 2006 ranks as the number one blunder.

2000

Season in a Sentence

The run of five consecutive division titles and post-season appearances comes to an end with second place finishes in both the AL Central and the wild card race.

Finish • Won • Lost • Pct • GB

Finish	Won	Lost	Pct	GB
Second	90	72	.556	5.0

In the wild card race, the Indians finished in second place, one game behind.

Manager

Charlie Manuel

Stats

Stats	Indians	AL	Rank
Batting Avg:	.288	.276	1
On-Base Pct:	.367	.349	1
Slugging Pct:	.470	.443	1
Home Runs:	221		4
Stolen Bases:	113		5
ERA:	4.84	4.91	7
Fielding Avg:	.988	.982	1
Runs Scored:	950		2
Runs Allowed:	816		5

Starting Line-up

Sandy Alomar, Jr., c
Jim Thome, 1b-dh
Roberto Alomar, 2b
Travis Fryman, 3b
Omar Vizquel, ss
Richie Sexson, lf-1b
Kenny Lofton, cf
Manny Ramirez, rf
David Justice, dh
Einar Diaz, c
David Segui, 1b-dh
Jolbert Cabrera, rf-cf-lf

Pitchers

Chuck Finley, sp
Dave Burba, sp
Bartolo Colon, sp
Steve Karsay, rp
Paul Shuey, rp
Steve Reed, rp
Justin Speier, sp

Attendance

3,456,278 (first in AL)

Club Leaders

Batting Avg:	Manny Ramirez	.351
On-Base Pct:	Manny Ramirez	.457
Slugging Pct:	Manny Ramirez	.697
Home Runs:	Manny Ramirez	38
RBIs:	Manny Ramirez	122
Runs:	Roberto Alomar	111
Stolen Bases:	Roberto Alomar	39
Wins:	Dave Burba	16
	Chuck Finley	16
Strikeouts:	Bartolo Colon	212
ERA:	Bartolo Colon	3.88
Saves:	Steve Karsay	20

JANUARY 6 Five days after the dawn of the new millennium and the end of worries over the Y2K problem, Dwight Gooden signs as a free agent with the Astros.

JANUARY 19 The Indians sign Bobby Witt, most recently with the Devil Rays, as a free agent.

FEBRUARY 28 Charlie Manuel undergoes emergency colon surgery at Winter Haven Hospital. The new Indians manager had eight inches removed from his colon after being treated for diverticulitis. Doctors found that his colon had ruptured. Manuel was back in the dugout eight days later. He missed two weeks in July with more surgery to reattach his colon. Bench coach Grady Little guided the Indians in Manuel's absence.

APRIL 3 The Indians win the season opener 4–1 in Baltimore over an Orioles team managed by Mike Hargrove. Travis Fryman and Kenny Lofton hit home runs. Bartolo Colon was the winning pitcher.

April 7 The Indians score nine runs in the second inning and beat the Devil Rays 14–5 in St. Petersburg. Omar Vizquel hit a grand slam off Juan Guzman in the big inning. Jim Thome hit a drive that struck a catwalk about 100 feet above center field at Tropicana Field.

Thome hit .269 with 37 homers, 106 RBIs, and 106 runs scored in 2000.

April 9 The Indians pummel the Devil Rays 17–4 in St. Petersburg. The top two hitters in the line-up contributed nine runs-batted-in with four from Kenny Lofton and five by Omar Vizquel. Jim Thome tied a major league record for most strikeouts in a nine-inning game by fanning five times in five plate appearances.

The Indians began the season with a long road trip from Baltimore to St. Petersburg to Oakland. Two weeks later, the Tribe had to travel from Boston to Seattle.

April 14 In the home opener, the Indians lose 7–2 to the Rangers before 42,727 at Jacobs Field.

The Indians sold out every home game for the fifth consecutive year, drawing a total of 3,456,278 to lead the major leagues in attendance. It was the first time that the club led baseball in attendance since 1949. The 2000 season was the second in a row in which Cleveland led the AL in attendance, the first time that had occurred since 1948 and 1949.

April 16 Back-to-back homers by Manny Ramirez and Jim Thome with one out in the ninth inning beats the Rangers 2–1 at Jacobs Field. In his first game as an Indian in Cleveland, Chuck Finley fanned 13 batters, including four in the third inning with the help of a passed ball by Einar Diaz on a third strike.

Matt Underwood began announcing Indians games on WUAB television in 2000. He had previously hosted the pre-game show on the Indians radio network since 1994. Underwood joined the radio team of Tom Hamilton and Mike Hegan over WTAM in 2001.

April 23 The Indians are rained out in Boston for the third day in a row.

April 24 Chuck Finley (eight innings) and Steve Karsay (one inning) combine on a two-hitter to beat the Mariners 6–0 at Safeco Field. Finley walked four batters in the first inning but escaped without allowing a run because Mike Cameron was caught stealing. The only two Seattle hits were singles by Dan Wilson in the fifth inning and Charles Gipson in the eighth.

April 26 Jaret Wright takes a no-hitter into the seventh inning, but the Indians need to go to the tenth to beat the Mariners 5–3 in Seattle. Wright's no-hit bid was broken up by a single from Stan Javier. Wright exited the game at the end of the seventh after allowing two runs and two hits.

May 3 Mark Whiten makes his first start in center field in nearly a year and drops a fly ball in the ninth inning, leading to a 6–5 loss to the Yankees at Jacobs Field. Whiten ran down Ricky Ledee's drive to the warning track but couldn't hold it. Whiten was playing because of injuries to Kenny Lofton and Jacob Cruz.

MAY 5 The Indians collect 20 hits but lose 11–10 to the Blue Jays in Toronto. Cleveland left 15 runners on base. Einar Diaz collected five hits, including three doubles, in five at-bats.

During his five-plus years with the Indians, Bartolo Colon provided the team with a fierce mound presence and consistently strong innings.

The Indians pitching staff was a mess all season. The team used a major league record 32 pitchers. The only hurlers with more than 11 starts were Dave Burba, Chuck Finley, and Bartolo Colon. They were also the only three pitchers with more than 70 innings pitched.

May 7 Down 8–3, the Indians score three runs in the seventh inning, two in the ninth, and two in the 12th to win 10–8 over the Blue Jays in Toronto. Travis Fryman broke the 8–8 tie with a single. David Justice drove in five runs with two doubles and a homer.

Fryman had the best season of his career in 2000 with a .321 batting average, 22 homers, and 106 runs-batted-in.

May 11 A grand slam by Manny Ramirez off Chad Durbin in the first inning gets the Indians rolling to a 16–0 trouncing of the Royals at Jacobs Field. Ramirez later smacked a two-run homer, giving him six runs-batted-in on the night.

Ramirez was limited to 118 games by injuries in 2000, but he batted .351 with 38 homers and 122 RBIs.

May 16 The Indians outlast the Tigers 11–9 at Jacobs Field.

May 17 Bartolo Colon strikes out 12 batters in seven innings as the Indians beat the Tigers 7–2 at Jacobs Field.

Colon was 15–8 and struck out 212 batters in 188 innings in 2000.

May 20 The Indians beat the Yankees 3–2 at Jacobs Field when Jeff Nelson walks four batters in the ninth inning, the last one to Roberto Alomar.

Alomar batted .310 with 40 doubles, 19 homers, and 111 runs scored in 2000.

May 21 In his major league debut, Indians pitcher Paul Rigdon pitches seven shutout innings while allowing only two hits and is the winning pitcher in a 6–1 decision over the Yankees at Jacobs Field.

Rigdon pitched only four more games for the Indians, allowing 15 runs in $10^2/_3$ innings before being traded to the Brewers in July.

May 23 The Indians play at Comerica Park for the first time and lose 10–4 to the Tigers.

June 3 Bartolo Colon carries a no-hit bid into the seventh inning, before allowing two runs and three hits, and strikes out 12 batters in eight innings to defeat the Cardinals 4–2 in St. Louis.

June 5 The Indians strike out 16 times off three pitchers but beat the Cardinals 3–2 at Busch Stadium. St. Louis starter Rick Ankiel fanned 11 in five innings.

On the same day, the Indians selected shortstop Corey Smith from Piscataway High School in Piscataway, New Jersey. By 2007, Smith had yet to reach the majors. Future big leaguers drafted and signed by the Indians in 2000 include Derek Thompson (supplemental pick in the first round), Brian Tallet (second round), Joe Inglett (eighth round) Ryan Church (14th round), and Eric Crozier (41st).

June 15 The Indians sign Jaime Navarro as a free agent following his release by the White Sox.

June 17 Russell Branyan hits a grand slam off Hideo Nomo in the fourth inning of an 8–6 win over the Tigers in Detroit.

June 24 Bobby Higginson hits three homers for the Tigers in leading his club to a 14–8 victory over the Indians in the second game of a double header at Jacobs Field. The Indians led 7–0 after three innings before blowing the advantage. Cleveland won the opener 8–1.

June 27 The Indians clobber the Royals 12–1 in Kansas City. Jim Thome led the way with two homers and two singles.

June 29 The day after six-year-old Elian Gonzalez returns to Cuba following a bitter legal battle in Miami, Bartolo Colon walks the first four batters he faces in the first inning of a 6–1 loss to the Royals in Kansas City. Colon issued passes to Johnny Damon, Jeff Reboulet, Mike Sweeney, and Jermaine Dye.

On the same day, the Indians traded David Justice to the Yankees for Ricky Ledee, Zach Day, and Jake Westbrook. This was one of a succession of deals that helped cost the Indians a spot in the post-season in 2000. Justice had 21 homers at the time of the trade and hit 20 more during the regular season for the Yankees. In the long run, it may turn out to be a good deal, however, as Westbrook had a record of 44–34 from 2004 through 2006 and continues to contribute to the team.

July 1 The Indians lose 4–3 in ten innings to the Twins at Jacobs Field.

The game represented the low point of the season. The Indians had lost 15 of their last 21 games, possessed a 40–39 record, and were 10½ games behind the White Sox in the AL Central race. Charlie Manuel ordered that two leather couches and a Ping-Pong table be removed from the clubhouse, a move he hoped would get his team more focused. Over the remainder of the season, the Indians were 50–33. Although the Indians failed to threaten the White Sox for the top spot in the division during the second half, Cleveland was in the wild card race until the final day of the season.

July 5 After trailing 5–0 in the fourth inning, the Indians rally to win 15–7 over the Blue Jays at Jacobs Field. A six-run, fifth inning put the Tribe ahead 10–7.

July 18 Manny Ramirez hits two homers and drives in five runs during an 8–2 win over the Astros at Jacobs Field.

July 22 Richie Sexson hits a grand slam off Mike Lincoln in the fourth inning for a 6–5 lead, but the Indians lose 10–6 to the Twins in Minneapolis.

July 26 Bartolo Colon strikes out ten batters, including six in a row, during a 5⅓-inning stint, but he is otherwise ineffective, giving up seven runs in an 8–1 loss to the Blue Jays in Toronto.

July 28 The Indians trade Richie Sexson, Paul Rigdon, Kane Davis, and Marco Scutaro to the Brewers for Bob Wickman, Jason Bere, and Steve Woodard. Wickman was traded one day before Bob Wickman Night at County Stadium. On the same day, the Indians swapped Alex Ramirez and Enrique Wilson to the Pirates for Wil Cordero. In a third deal, Ricky Ledee went to the Rangers for David Segui.

> *The trade with the Brewers was completed to help prop up a sinking pitching staff, but it proved to be a disastrous deal for the Indians because of the loss of Sexson, who hit 45 homers for Milwaukee in both 2001 and 2003. On the positive side, Wickman did provide fine moments as a closer. In 248²/₃ innings over 255 games from 2000 through 2006, Wickman had a 3.23 ERA and holds the club career record in saves with 139.*

JULY 29 Manny Ramirez hits two homers and drives in six runs to lead the Indians to a 14–3 victory over the Orioles in the first game of a double header in Baltimore. One of the home runs was a grand slam off Pat Rapp in the second inning. Cleveland collected 20 hits. In the second contest, Steve Woodard gave up a home run to Brady Anderson on his first pitch as an Indian and was the losing pitcher in a 4–0 decision.

JULY 30 In his second game with the Indians, David Segui hits a grand slam off David Parrish in the sixth inning of a 10–7 triumph over the Orioles in Baltimore.

AUGUST 4 A two-run, walk-off homer by Jim Thome in the ninth inning beats the Angels 11–10 at Jacobs Field. The Indians blew a third-inning 9–5 lead by allowing five unanswered runs.

AUGUST 19 Manny Ramirez hits a grand slam off Jamie Moyer in the sixth inning of a 10–4 win over the Mariners at Jacobs Field.

AUGUST 20 Kenny Lofton hits two homers, including a grand slam off Aaron Sele in the second inning, and drives in six runs during a 12–4 victory over the Mariners at Jacobs Field.

AUGUST 21 The Indians take over first place in the wild card race with a 14–6 triumph over the Athletics at Jacobs Field. It was the Indians third straight game scoring ten or more runs.

AUGUST 29 The Indians coast to a 12–1 win over the Rangers in Arlington.

SEPTEMBER 1 On a day in which the temperature reaches a sweltering 108 degrees in the Dallas–Fort Worth area, the Indians play a nine-inning game that lasts four hours and 21 minutes, only to lose 14–7 to the Rangers in Arlington.

SEPTEMBER 2 Mike Hargrove comes to Jacobs Field for the first time since being fired as manager of the Indians, and the home team beats Hargrove's Orioles 5–2. Baltimore turned a strange triple play in the second inning. Cleveland had Travis Fryman on first and Wil Cordero on second with none out when Sandy Alomar, Jr. hit a pop fly into short left about 15 feet behind the infield dirt. Shortstop Melvin Mora went back on the ball, but instead of catching it, purposely let the ball drop. Fryman and Cordero never left their bases, believing the infield fly rule would be called, but none of the umpires made the ruling. Alomar, believing he was out, went back to the dugout and Fryman and Cordero were retired on force plays. Charlie Manuel was ejected in the ensuing argument over the play.

September 3 Kenny Lofton caps a huge day by scoring four runs, stealing five bases, and hitting a walk-off homer in the 13th inning to beat the Orioles 12–11 at Jacobs Field. The five stolen bases tied an Indians single-game record. The Indians led the game 11–7 before Baltimore scored four times in the seventh inning.

Lofton scored in 18 consecutive games from August 15 through September 3 to tie an American League, and modern era major league, record. He scored 26 runs during the streak. The mark was set by Red Rolfe with the Yankees in 1939.

September 4 Manny Ramirez runs his hitting streak to 20 games during a 7–4 win over the Devil Rays at Jacobs Field.

September 6 The Indians lead the wild card race by three games after beating the Devil Rays 6–2 at Jacobs Field. The Tribe had a record of 75–61.

September 15 David Segui hits a grand slam off Jason Grimsley in the sixth inning of an 11–1 victory over the Yankees in New York.

September 17 The Indians take a 15–0 lead at the end of the fifth inning and romp past the Yankees 15–4 in New York.

September 18 Bartolo Colon strikes out 13 batters and pitches a one-hitter to defeat the Yankees 2–0 in New York. Colon had a no-hitter until Luis Polonia singled on a sharp grounder up the middle with one out in the eighth inning.

Due to postponements because of inclement weather, the Indians had to play nine games in six days from September 20 through September 25 against four clubs in three different cities, including back-to-back double headers in Boston on the 20th and 21st and an unusual three-team twin bill (see September 25, 2000). The schedule put added pressure on the club's beleaguered pitching staff. The Indians won five of the nine games.

September 21 Playing a double header in Boston for the second day in a row, the Indians score seven runs in the first inning of game one but lose 9–8 to the Red Sox. Cleveland took game two 8–5.

At the end of the day, the Indians were tied for first place with the Athletics in the wild card race with a record of 83–68.

September 22 The Indians fall out of first place in the wild card chase with a 3–2 loss to the Royals in Kansas City.

September 23 The Indians clobber the Royals 11–1 in Kansas City.

September 25 The Indians play a double header involving three teams at Jacobs Field. On the original schedule, Cleveland was slated to play a night game against the Twins. However, the Indians were rained out against the White Sox in Cleveland on September 10, and because of the pennant implications of the teams involved, the American League decreed that the contest be made up as part of a day game preceding the Indians-Twins nighttime affair on September 25. It was the first time that a club played two different teams in one day since September 13, 1951, when the Cardinals squared off against the Boston Braves and New York Giants in St. Louis. It was also only the second three-team match-up in the majors since 1899, and the first in the American League. With history being made, the Indians sent a ball from each game signed by the starting pitchers, along with tickets and the line-up cards, to the Hall of Fame in Cooperstown. The historic twin bill caused a logistical nightmare with four team buses, two equipment trucks, three TV and radio crews, nearly 100 players, 80,000 fans, and eight umpires. The Indians defeated the White Sox 9–2. In the sixth inning, Roberto Alomar took exception to a hard slide from Chicago's Tony Graffanino on a force out. Both teams streamed onto the field, although no punches were thrown. Minnesota took the nightcap 4–3.

SEPTEMBER 30 On the second-to-last day of the season, the Indians beat the Blue Jays 6–5 at Jacobs Field. In the wild card race, the Indians were one game behind the Mariners. Seattle was one-half game back of the Athletics in the AL West.

OCTOBER 1 On the final day of the regular season, the Indians need to win to stay alive in the wild card race, and do so with an 11–4 win over the Blue Jays at Jacobs Field. In what would prove to be his final plate appearance with the Indians, Manny Ramirez smacked a 452-foot home run. But later in the afternoon, the Indians were eliminated from the post-season when the Athletics defeated the Rangers 3–0 in Oakland and the Mariners downed the Angels 5–2 at Anaheim.

NOVEMBER 16 With the result of the November 7 presidential election between George Bush and Al Gore still in doubt, the Indians trade Jim Brower and Robert Pugmire to the Reds for Eddie Taubensee.

Taubensee was expected to be the Indians starting catcher but wound up as the back-up to Einar Diaz and spent six weeks on the disabled list in June and July with a viral infection that lodged in his liver. In 2002, Taubensee suffered a career-ending back injury.

NOVEMBER 20 The Indians sign Ellis Burks, most recently with the Giants, as a free agent.

DECEMBER 13 On the day after the Supreme Court declares George Bush the winner in the presidential election, Manny Ramirez signs as a free agent with the Red Sox.

The Indians wanted Ramirez back and offered him $119 million over seven years. He elected to go to Boston for a staggering $160 million over eight years. In his first seven seasons with the Sox, Ramirez hit .313 with 254 homers and 800 RBIs.

DECEMBER 18 Sandy Alomar, Jr. signs as a free agent with the White Sox.

DECEMBER 20 The Indians sign Marty Cordova, most recently with the Twins, as a free agent.

DECEMBER 21 David Segui signs as a free agent with the Orioles.

2001

Season in a Sentence

The Indians win their sixth AL Central title in seven years but lose in the first round of the playoffs.

Finish • Won • Lost • Pct • GB

Finish	Won	Lost	Pct	GB
First	91	71	.562	6.0

American League Division Series

The Indians lost three games to two to the Seattle Mariners.

Manager

Charlie Manuel

Stats

Stats	Indians	AL	Rank
Batting Avg:	.278	.267	2
On-Base Pct:	.350	.334	2
Slugging Pct:	.458	.428	2
Home Runs:	212		3
Stolen Bases:	79		12
ERA:	4.64	4.47	9
Fielding Avg:	.982	.981	5
Runs Scored:	897		2
Runs Allowed:	821		9

Starting Line-up

Einar Diaz, c
Jim Thome, 1b
Roberto Alomar, 2b
Travis Fryman, 3b
Omar Vizquel, ss
Marty Cordova, lf
Kenny Lofton, cf
Juan Gonzalez, rf
Ellis Burks, dh
Jolbert Cabrera, lf-cf-rf
Russell Branyan, 3b-lf
Wil Cordero, lf-1b

Pitchers

C. C. Sabathia, sp
Bartolo Colon, sp
Dave Burba, sp
Chuck Finley, sp
Bob Wickman, rp
Ricardo Rincon, rp
Rich Rodriguez, rp
Paul Shuey, rp
Danys Baez, rp
Steve Woodard, rp-sp

Attendance

3,175,523 (second in AL)

Club Leaders

Batting Avg:	Roberto Alomar	.338
On-Base Pct:	Jim Thome	.416
Slugging Pct:	Jim Thome	.624
Home Runs:	Jim Thome	49
RBIs:	Juan Gonzalez	140
Runs:	Roberto Alomar	113
Stolen Bases:	Roberto Alomar	30
Wins:	C. C. Sabathia	17
Strikeouts:	Bartolo Colon	201
ERA:	Bartolo Colon	4.09
Saves:	Bob Wickman	32

January 9 The Indians sign Juan Gonzalez, most recently with the Tigers, as a free agent.

Inked to a one-year deal, Gonzalez gave the Indians a terrific season with a .325 batting average, 35 homers, and 140 RBIs before leaving at the end of the 2001 campaign as a free agent.

April 2 The Indians lose the season opener 7–4 to the White Sox before 42,606 at Jacobs Field. In his first game with the Indians, Juan Gonzalez homered in each of his first two at-bats.

April 4 The Indians defeat the White Sox 8–4 in the first game at Jacobs Field that fails to sell out since June 7, 1995. Attendance was 32,763, about 10,000 shy of capacity.

The game ended a streak of 455 consecutive sellouts. The Indians drew 3,175,523 fans in 2001, some 300,000 tickets short of the 3,456,278 in 2000.

April 6 The Indians beat the Orioles in a fog-shrouded game at Jacobs Field. A dense, fast-moving fog swirled in off Lake Erie in the fifth inning and stopped play for eight minutes. At one point, the fog was so thick that Oriole center fielder Melvin Mora was barely visible from the press box.

On the same day, the Indians signed Rich Rodriguez following his release by the Mets.

April 8 Making his major league debut at the age of 20, C. C. Sabathia is the starting pitcher in a 4–3 win over the Orioles in Baltimore. Sabathia allowed three runs in 5⅓ innings.

C. C. (Carsten Charles) Sabathia was 17–5 with a 4.39 earned run average as a rookie in 2001. The 17 victories were the most of any Indians rookie since Gene Bearden won 20 in 1948.

April 17 Russell Branyan hits a grand slam off B. J. Ryan in the sixth inning of an 8–1 win over the Orioles in Baltimore.

April 21 After the Tigers score in the top of the 11th, Jim Thome clubs a two-run, walk-off homer in the bottom half to give the Indians a 5–4 victory at Jacobs Field.

May 1 The Indians hit five home runs during a 13–2 win over the Royals in Kansas City. Those clearing the fence with drives were Juan Gonzalez, Eddie Taubensee, Marty Cordova, Ellis Burks, and Russell Branyan. All five homers were struck with two out.

May 9 The Indians extend their winning streak to ten games with a 5–1 decision over the Royals at Jacobs Field.

The streak gave the Indians a 22–9 record after a 3–5 start to the 2001 season. By May 25, the Tribe was 31–14 and had a one-game lead over the Twins in the AL Central pennant race. Cleveland barely played above .500 over the remainder of the season, going 60–57, but managed to finish six games in front of Minnesota.

May 11 Ellis Burks drives in six runs during a 10–6 win over the Devil Rays at Jacobs Field. Burks had a three-run homer, a two-run single and a sacrifice fly.

May 16 The Indians score three runs in the ninth inning to win 4–3 over the Rangers in Arlington. Wil Cordero hit a two-run homer to tie the contest 3–3, and Jolbert Cabrera drove in the game-winner with a single. It was Cleveland's 11th straight win on the road.

Cabrera played at least ten games at six different positions in 2001. He appeared in 36 contests in left field, 35 in center, 18 in right, 28 at second base, 27 at third and 14 as a shortstop.

May 17 The Rangers score ten runs in the second inning off Chuck Finley and Justin Speier and defeat the Indians 12–7 in Arlington. Texas collected nine consecutive hits in the big inning. The defeat ended Cleveland's streak of 11 consecutive wins on the road.

May 18 Marty Cordova extends his hitting streak to 22 games during a 7–2 win over the Angels in Anaheim.

May 23 Juan Gonzalez hits a walk-off homer in the tenth inning to defeat the Tigers 4–3 at Jacobs Field.

May 29 Jim Thome becomes the Indians all-time career home run leader during a 6–4 win over the Tigers in Detroit. It was Thome's 243rd homer, allowing him to pass Albert Belle.

June 2 The Indians trade Jacob Cruz to the Rockies for Jody Gerut and Josh Bard.

June 4 The Indians out-homer the Twins 5–0 but lose 11–10 in Minneapolis. Cleveland trailed 8–2 and battled back to tie the contest 10–10, only to allow a run in the ninth for the defeat. Juan Gonzalez hit two of the Indians homers, with Ellis Burks, Jim Thome, and Roberto Alomar adding the rest.

June 5 With their first pick in the amateur draft, the Indians select pitcher Dan Denham from Deer Valley High School in Antioch, California.

Through the 2007 season, the only player drafted and selected by the Indians in 2001 to reach the majors was ninth rounder Luke Scott, who was traded to the Astros in 2004 before making his big league debut a year later.

June 6 Roberto Alomar breaks a 2–2 tie with a bases-loaded triple in the ninth inning to allow the Indians to slip past the Twins 5–2 in Minneapolis.

Alomar batted .336 with 34 doubles, 12 triples, 20 homers, 100 RBIs, and 113 runs scored in 2001 in addition to winning his tenth career Gold Glove.

June 13 A three-run homer by Jim Thome in the tenth inning defeats the Brewers 5–2 at Jacobs Field.

Thome finished the season with 49 homers, 124 runs-batted-in, 101 runs scored, and a .291 batting average. He had a streak of 13 home runs in 18 games in May and June and another of ten homers in 17 contests in July.

June 15 The Indians play at PNC Park in Pittsburgh for the first time and lose 6–3 to the Pirates.

June 19 Ellis Burks hits three homers, but the Indians lose 10–9 to the Twins in 12 innings at Jacobs Field. Minnesota led 6–0 after five innings, but Cleveland battled back to send the game into extra innings before losing. Burks homered in the sixth and eighth innings off Eric Milton and again in the 12th facing Bob Wells after the Twins scored twice in the top half of the inning.

June 21 The Indians beat the Twins 9–6 in a game at Jacobs Field halted twice by heavy rain. The contest was delayed for 41 minutes in the second, and was called by the umpires after a 61-minute stoppage in the top of the seventh when the grounds crew couldn't cover the infield because the water-logged tarp was too heavy to drag.

June 22 The Indians trade Steve Karsay and Steve Reed to the Braves for Troy Cameron and controversial pitcher John Rocker.

With a habit of sprinting to the mound to pitch, Rocker had long drawn attention to himself. He saved 38 games for the Braves in 1999. But he took on Mets fans with derogatory comments during both a September series in New York and the National League Championship Series. Following the season in an article in Sports Illustrated, *Rocker denigrated different groups including homosexuals, AIDS patients, single mothers, African-Americans, Japanese, Koreans, Vietnamese, Indians, Russians, Spanish speakers and riders of the number 7 subway line, which runs to Shea Stadium in Queens from Manhattan. He also called a teammate Russell Simon a "fat monkey." The commentary infuriated people across the country and earned Rocker a 28-day suspension by Commissioner Bud Selig at the start of the 2000 season, although an appeal reduced the suspension to 14 games. The Indians were willing to take a chance on Rocker, hoping he would solidify a weak pitching staff. He was immediately given the closer's job ahead of Bob Wickman. Rocker proved to be a bad investment, with a 5.45 ERA for the Indians in 38 games and 34²/₃ innings. He was traded to the Rangers during the following off-season. The Indians would have been much better off keeping Karsay and Reed. Both helped the Braves reach the playoffs in 2001 and pitched effectively for several years after the trade.*

June 25 Trailing 6–0, the Indians score seven runs in the sixth inning for a 7–6 lead but wind up losing 8–7 to the Yankees in New York.

June 29 Dave Burba ties a major league record by giving up four homers in an inning during a 5–3 loss to the Royals at Jacobs Field. In the fourth, Burba allowed a two-run home run to Jermaine Dye, followed by solo shots from Mike Sweeney, Raul Ibanez, and Carlos Beltran.

July 3 Roberto Alomar collects five hits, including a double, in five at-bats during a 9–1 win over the Red Sox at Jacobs Field.

July 6 Jim Thome hits three homers during a 14–2 clubbing of the Cardinals at Jacobs Field. Each home run was struck with a man on base giving him six runs-batted-in. Thome connected off Matt Morris in the first and third innings and again in the seventh facing Mike James.

July 7 Jim Thome is again the hero with a walk-off homer on the first pitch of the tenth inning to defeat the Cardinals 7–6 at Jacobs Field. The ball traveled an estimated 462 feet. Thome walked in each of his four previous plate appearances.

July 15 The Indians play at Minute Maid Park in Houston for the first time and lose 5–3 to the Astros.

July 17 Bartolo Colon throws over the head of Scott Servais during a 10–4 win over the Astros in Houston. Colon was suspended for seven games by the commissioner's office for the incident.

JULY 21 The Indians defeat the Tigers 8–4 at Jacobs Field in a game celebrating the 100th anniversary of the birth of the franchise. Before the contest, the team honored the 100 best Indians players of all-time.

JULY 23 Juan Gonzalez drives in both runs of a 2–0 win over the White Sox at Jacobs Field. Gonzalez homered in the second inning and added an RBI-single in the eighth.

JULY 31 The Indians trade Zach Day to the Expos for Milton Bradley.

AUGUST 5 The Indians complete the greatest comeback in club history by erasing a 12-run deficit to beat the Mariners 15–14 in 11 innings in a game televised nationally on a Sunday night on ESPN. The Indians were down to their last strike three times before pulling out the victory, and the comeback came against seven different Mariners pitchers. Seattle came into the game with a record of 80–30. The Indians tied a major league record for "biggest run deficit overcome to win a game." The Mariners scored four runs in the second inning and eight in the third to lead the Indians 12–0. The Tribe scored twice in the fourth, but Seattle matched it in the fifth to move ahead 14–2. The comeback started in the seventh with three runs on a home run by Russell Branyan and a two-run single from Jolbert Cabrera. Cleveland scored four more in the eighth on two-run homers by Jim Thome and Marty Cordova to make the score 14–9. Still, the Indians were down by five runs and had a runner on with two outs in the ninth when Cordova doubled. Wil Cordero walked to load the bases and Einar Diaz went to a full count before hitting a two-run single to close the gap to 14–11. A single by Kenny Lofton loaded the bases again. Omar Vizquel worked the count full, then ripped a triple inside the first base line scoring all three runners to tie the score 14–14. John Rocker struck out the three batters he faced in the 11th. With one out in the bottom half, Lofton and Vizquel singled. Cabrera's single into left field brought home Lofton, who slid across the plate head first with the winning run. The hit by Cabrera was the 23rd of the night by the Indians. After Lofton scored the winning run, the crowd refused to leave as the stadium speakers first blasted "Rock and Roll All Night" by Kiss, followed by "Cleveland Rocks."

Two other major league teams have overcome 12-run deficits to win a game. In 1911, the Tigers trailed the White Sox 13–1 in the fifth inning in Detroit and rallied to win 16–15. In 1925, the Indians were ahead of the Athletics 15–3 in the seventh inning in Philadelphia, and lost 17–15 (see June 15, 1925).

AUGUST 8 The Indians break loose with six runs in the tenth inning to defeat the Twins 8–2 in Minneapolis.

AUGUST 12 The Indians pass the Twins take sole possession of first place in the AL Central with a 13–2 win over the Rangers in Arlington.

The Indians remained in first place for the rest of the season.

AUGUST 14 After the Twins score four runs in the top of the ninth inning for a 7–4 lead, the Indians rally with three runs in the bottom of the ninth and one in the 11th to win 8–7 at Jacobs Field. The winning run scored on a triple by Kenny Lofton and a single from Juan Gonzalez.

August 22 Jim Thome's homer in the 11th inning beats the Athletics 5–4 in Oakland. In the bottom half of the inning, David Riske pitched out of a bases-loaded jam with no one out to preserve the victory and earn his first career save.

August 25 A dispute over an earring causes a bench-clearing incident during an 11-inning, 3–2 loss to the Mariners at Safeco Field. In the ninth, Seattle pitcher Arthur Rhodes was ejected by third base umpire Tim McClelland. Rhodes, who had not yet thrown a pitch after relieving Freddy Garcia, yelled at Omar Vizquel, who complained that the bright sunlight was reflecting off the pitcher's right earring. Both benches emptied, and Rhodes had to be restrained by manager Lou Piniella from going after Vizquel.

August 26 Kenny Lofton caps a big afternoon by hitting a two-out, two-run single off Arthur Rhodes that beats the Mariners 4–3 in Seattle. The big blow came less than 24 hours after Rhodes was ejected in a dispute over his earring (see August 25, 2001). Lofton drove in all four Cleveland runs. He hit a lead-off homer in the first inning and collected an RBI-single in the fifth.

August 29 Consecutive homers by Juan Gonzalez and Ellis Burks off Casey Fossum in the sixth inning account for the only Cleveland runs of a 2–1 win over the Red Sox at Jacobs Field. The victory gave the Indians a 6½-game lead in the AL Central.

Charlie Manuel's health problems continued into the 2001 season. He missed five games in late August and early September for surgery to remove scar tissue from his colon (see February 28, 2000). The Indians manager missed more time near the end of September because of an infection near his gall bladder. Manuel had his gall bladder removed during an operation on December 5.

September 3 The Indians score six runs in the top of the second inning, but the White Sox counter with eight in the bottom half and five more in the third and win 19–10 in Chicago.

September 8 Juan Gonzalez hits two homers, including a grand slam off Gary Glover in the first inning, but the Indians need two runs in the eighth inning and one in the ninth to defeat the White Sox 8–7 at Jacobs Field. Kenny Lofton broke the 7–7 tie with an RBI-double.

September 9 Omar Vizquel hits a walk-off homer to defeat the White Sox 9–8 at Jacobs Field. It was the second of only two homers that Vizquel struck in 2001.

September 11 Two hijacked commercial airliners strike and destroy the twin towers of the World Trade Center in New York in the worst terrorist attack ever perpetrated on American soil. A third hijacked plane destroyed a portion of the Pentagon, and a fourth crashed in rural Pennsylvania. Some 3,000 were killed, including about 2,800 at the World Trade center.

Almost immediately, Commissioner Bud Selig canceled the slate of games scheduled for that day, including the Indians-Royals match-up in Kansas City. Later in the week, Selig announced that all games through Sunday, September 16, would be postponed. The contests were made up by extending the regular season by a week. When play resumed, an air of heightened security and patriotism imbued every game. Fans endured close scrutiny by stadium personnel. "God Bless America" replaced "Take Me Out To The Ballgame" as the song of choice during the seventh-inning stretch.

SEPTEMBER 18 In the first game played following the September 11 terrorist attacks, the Indians score seven runs in the fifth inning of an 11–2 win over the Royals at Jacobs Field. Travis Fryman hit a grand slam off Jeff Austin.

In a videotaped message before the game, Fryman thanked Cleveland fans for their support and asked them to pray for the victims of the terrorist attacks.

SEPTEMBER 29 Travis Fryman hits a two-out, two-run walk-off single in the ninth inning to beat the Twins 9–8 at Jacobs Field. The single accounted for Fryman's second and third RBIs of the night. Russell Branyan drove in the other six Cleveland runs with two home runs and a single.

SEPTEMBER 30 The Indians clinch their sixth AL Central title in seven years with a 9–1 victory over the Twins at Jacobs Field.

The Indians played the Seattle Mariners in the American League Division Series. Managed by Lou Piniella, the Mariners compiled a 116–46 record in 2001 to tie a major league record for most wins in a season.

OCTOBER 9 Two days after the United States launches a sustained air campaign in Afghanistan against al-Qaeda, the Indians open the Division Series with a 5–0 victory over the Mariners at Safeco Field in Seattle. Cleveland broke a scoreless tie with three runs in the fourth inning. Bartolo Colon (eight innings) and Bob Wickman (one inning) combined on the shutout. Colon fanned ten batters. Ellis Burks collected a homer, a double, and a single.

OCTOBER 11 The Mariners even the Division Series by beating the Indians 5–1 at Safeco Field. Seattle scored four times in the first inning off Chuck Finley on a pair of two-run homers by Mike Cameron and Edgar Martinez. It was Finley's first post-season game since 1986.

OCTOBER 13 In game three, the Indians pull within one victory of a stunning upset by collecting 19 hits and hammering the Mariners 17–2 before 45,069 at Jacobs Field. The Tribe scored two runs in both the first and second innings, four in the third, one in the fifth, three in the sixth, and five in the eighth. Omar Vizquel led the rout with two singles, a double, a triple, and six runs-batted-in. Juan Gonzalez had a home run, two doubles, and a single and drove in three runs. Robert Alomar had two doubles, a single, and three RBIs. Jim Thome contributed a homer.

OCTOBER 14 The Mariners keep their post-season hopes alive by defeating the Indians 6–2 before 45,025 at Jacobs Field. Bartolo Colon pitched six shutout innings and held a 1–0 lead before allowing three runs in the seventh. Juan Gonzalez hit a home run in the losing cause.

OCTOBER 15 The Mariners eliminate the Indians with a 3–1 victory at Safeco Field. Seattle took a 2–0 lead in the second inning, and Chuck Finley suffered his second loss of the series.

NOVEMBER 1 Mark Shapiro replaces John Hart as general manager of the Indians.

Hart announced before the start of the 2001 season that it would be his last with the Indians. Shapiro was only 34-years-old when promoted to general manager and had worked in the Cleveland organization since 1992 as an assistant in baseball operations, director of minor league operations, and as assistant general manager. He also came from a sports family. Mark's father Ron is a Baltimore-based sports agent whose clients included Cal Ripken, Jr, Jim Palmer, Brooks Robinson, Kirby Puckett, and Eddie Murray. Mark's sister Julie is married to Eric Mangini, head coach of the New York Jets. Shapiro was elevated to the position of general manager at a critical juncture in the history of the Cleveland franchise. The 2001 club won the AL Central, but the roster was made up largely of high-priced veterans near the end of their careers. There was little in the way of top-notch prospects in the minors, because John Hart had traded many of them away. Former Indians farm hands starring on other clubs in 2001 included Sean Casey, Danny Graves, Richie Sexson, Brian Giles, Jeromy Burnitz, Steve Kline, Paul Byrd, and David Bell. At the end of the 2001 campaign, the Indians decided to reduce salary, rebuild through the farm system and trade veterans for prospects. Among the veterans who did not return in 2002 were Roberto Alomar, Kenny Lofton, and Juan Gonzalez. This strategy followed the team's losing Manny Ramirez to free agency prior to the 2001 season. Bartolo Colon was traded during the 2002 season, and Jim Thome left via free agency at the end of the campaign. The Indians had losing records in 2002, 2003, and 2004 before contending for a pennant in 2005 and winning the AL Central in 2007. The fans didn't completely buy into the new plan. The Indians sold out every game from June 1995 through Opening Day in 2001, but the attendance figure dropped to 1,730,001 by 2003, about half of capacity. Even in 2007, when the Indians reached the post-season, sellouts were rare. After leaving Cleveland, Hart served as the general manager of the Rangers from 2002 through 2005 and was a senior advisor with the Texas club in 2007.

DECEMBER 4 Marty Cordova signs with the Orioles as a free agent. On the same day, the Indians signed Brady Anderson, most recently with the Orioles, as a free agent.

DECEMBER 10 Dave Burba signs with the Rangers as a free agent.

DECEMBER 11 The Indians trade Roberto Alomar, Mike Bacsik, and Danny Peoples to the Mets for Matt Lawton, Alex Escobar, Jerrod Riggan, Billy Traber, and a player to be named later.

Alomar was one of the many veterans drawing high salaries who were jettisoned by the Indians during the 2001–2002 off-season. He went into a steep decline after leaving Cleveland and retired after the end of the 2004 season. Lawton was a starting outfielder for the Indians for three seasons. None of the other three players acquired in exchange for Alomar had a significant impact on Indians history.

DECEMBER 17 The Indians sign Ricky Gutierrez, most recently with the Cubs, as a free agent.

Gutierrez was signed to a three-year deal to start at second base following the trade of Roberto Alomar but proved to be an extreme disappointment, partly because of an injury he kept under wraps. In August 2002, Gutierrez told the

Indians about a neck injury he'd had since early April that caused him numbness in his arms. Gutierrez needed a bone graft and two vertebrae in his neck fused, which ended his days as a productive player.

DECEMBER 18 The Indians trade John Rocker to the Rangers for Dave Elder.

DECEMBER 21 The Indians trade Dave Roberts to the Dodgers for Christian Bridenbaugh and Nial Hughes.

2002

Season in a Sentence

After an off-season re-tooling of the roster, the Indians win 11 of their first 12 games but wind up with their first losing season since 1993.

Finish • Won • Lost • Pct • GB

Finish	Won	Lost	Pct	GB
Third	74	88	.457	20.5

In the wild card race, the Indians finished in sixth place, 25 games out of first.

Managers

Charlie Manuel (39–48) and Joel Skinner (35–40)

Stats

Stats	Indians	AL	Rank
Batting Avg:	.249	.264	12
On-Base Pct:	.321	.331	11
Slugging Pct:	.412	.424	10
Home Runs:	192		5
Stolen Bases:	52		13
ERA:	4.91	4.46	10
Fielding Avg:	.981	.982	10
Runs Scored:	739		10
Runs Allowed:	837		10

Starting Line-up

Einar Diaz, c
Jim Thome, 1b
Ricky Gutierrez, 2b
Travis Fryman, 3b
Omar Vizquel, ss
Chris Magruder, lf
Milton Bradley, cf
Matt Lawton, rf
Ellis Burks, dh
John McDonald, 2b

Pitchers

C. C. Sabathia, sp
Danys Baez, sp
Ryan Drese, sp
Bartolo Colon, sp
Chuck Finley, sp
Mark Wohlers, rp
David Riske, rp
Ricardo Rincon, rp

Attendance

2,616,940 (fifth in AL)

Club Leaders

Batting Avg:	Jim Thome	.304
On-Base Pct:	Jim Thome	.445
Slugging Pct:	Jim Thome	.677
Home Runs:	Jim Thome	52
RBIs:	Jim Thome	118
Runs:	Jim Thome	101
Stolen Bases:	Omar Vizquel	18
Wins:	C. C. Sabathia	13
Strikeouts:	C. C. Sabathia	149
ERA:	C. C. Sabathia	4.37
Saves:	Bob Wickman	20

January 9 Juan Gonzalez signs with the Rangers as a free agent. On the same day, the Indians signed Mark Wohlers, most recently with the Yankees, as a free agent.

February 1 Kenny Lofton signs with the White Sox as a free agent.

March 31 The Indians open the season in a nationally televised Sunday night game on ESPN, and win 6–0 over the Angels in Anaheim. Travis Fryman homered during a four-run first inning. Bartolo Colon pitched a five-hit complete game shutout.

Jim Thome won the Roberto Clemente Award in 2002 for his play on the field and his work in the community. He also led the American League in slugging, OPS, walks, runs created, and at bats per home run.

April 3 Chuck Finley is unable to make his scheduled start against the Angels in Anaheim because of a domestic dispute with the wife. Ryan Drese made the emergency start, and the Indians won 6–5.

Finley married actress Tawny Kitaen in 1997 and the couple had two children. Tawny is best known for appearing in many videos of the band Whitesnake during the 1980s. She was then married to Whitesnake lead singer Dave Coverdale. Finley's altercation with Kitaen occurred on April 1. While Finley was driving his vehicle, she allegedly kicked him repeatedly with her high-heeled boots while his foot was on the gas pedal, and severely twisted his ear, leaving visible scrapes and abrasions. Finley was able to gain control of the car and get home safely. He filed for divorce on April 4. Tawny was ordered to undergo a substance abuse program, anger management counseling, and to make a donation to a battered woman's shelter.

APRIL 5 On a blustery, snowy day in Detroit, Matt Lawton homers on the first pitch of the game, sparking the Indians to a 10–1 victory over the Tigers.

APRIL 7 C. C. Sabathia pitches no-hit ball for seven innings during a 5–1 win over the Tigers in Detroit. Russell Simon ended the no-hit bid with a single leading off the eighth. Sabathia left the game at the end of the inning after allowing a run and three hits.

Sabathia dated tennis star Serena Williams early in his career with the Indians.

APRIL 8 In the home opener, Travis Fryman hits a grand slam off Eric Milton in the third inning of a 9–5 win over the Twins before 42,441 at Jacobs Field. Matt Lawton and Ellis Burks also homered.

The Indians introduced new uniforms in 2002, highlighted by silver trim on the home whites and road grays. A sleeveless vest was also worn for the first time that season during Opening Day, holidays, and weekend home games. The solid white vest over a navy shirt featured Chief Wahoo on the left chest. The Indians also wore a solid navy blue hat with a script "I" worn with the vest uniform. The scheme has continued through the 2007 season.

APRIL 10 Jim Thome hits a grand slam off Rick Reed in the fifth inning of a 9–3 win over the Twins at Jacobs Field.

APRIL 13 The Indians win their tenth game in a row with an 8–7 comeback victory over the Royals at Jacobs Field. Trailing 7–2, Cleveland scored five runs in the eighth inning and one in the ninth. Matt Lawton smacked a three-run homer in the eighth. The winning run scored Einar Diaz from third base on a wild pitch by Jason Grimsley.

The Indians started the 2002 season with an 11–1 record. Any illusions that the club would contend for the pennant were shattered when they lost 15 of their next 17 games. By July, Charlie Manuel was relieved of his duties as manager.

APRIL 29 The Indians release Wil Cordero.

APRIL 30 The Angels rout the Indians 21–2 at Jacobs Field. Anaheim scored ten times in the eighth inning off Mark Wohlers and Chad Paronto.

The Indians took a big hit in offensive production following the roster turnover the previous off-season. The club scored 1,009 runs in 1999, 950 in 2000, and 897 in 2001, and then dipped dramatically to 739 runs in 2002.

May 5 Omar Vizquel collects five hits in five at-bats during a 9–2 win over the Rangers at Jacobs Field. Vizquel singled in his first two plate appearances and doubled in the last three.

May 14 The Indians score four runs in the ninth inning to stun the Orioles 6–5 at Jacobs Field. The last two runs scored on a two-out, walk-off homer by Matt Lawton.

May 17 C. C. Sabathia is robbed at gunpoint early in the morning at a downtown Cleveland hotel by a gang of men, who stole his necklace, earrings, and wallet. The cash and jewelry taken from Sabathia was estimated at $44,102. Sabathia and a cousin had gone back to the Marriott Hotel with a group of people they had just met at a nightclub.

May 19 Travis Fryman hits a grand slam off Jeff Suppan in the sixth inning for a 4–2 lead, but the Royals rally for three runs in the ninth to beat the Indians 5–4.

May 21 The Indians release Brady Anderson.

May 22 Jeff Weaver of the Tigers pitches a one-hitter to defeat the Indians 2–0 in Detroit. The lone Cleveland hit was a single by Chris Magruder in the eighth inning in Magruder's first game with the Indians.

May 25 A three-run homer by Travis Fryman off Esteban Loaiza in the eighth inning accounts for the only three runs of a 3–0 victory over the Blue Jays in Toronto. C. C. Sabathia (seven innings), Paul Shuey (one inning) and Bob Wickman (one inning) combined on the shutout.

May 28 Chuck Finley strikes out 11 batters in seven innings, including six in a row, leading the Indians to a 4–2 win over the Tigers at Jacobs Field.

May 29 Jim Thome and Ellis Burks each homer twice during an 11–7 triumph over the Tigers at Jacobs Field. Chris Magruder also homered for Cleveland. It was Magruder's first career home run.

Burks batted .301 with 32 home runs in 2002.

June 1 Trailing 3–0, the Indians score eight runs in the eighth inning and beat the White Sox 8–4 at Jacobs Field.

June 4 The Twins collect 25 hits and tag the Indians with a 23–2 loss at Minneapolis. Minnesota scored ten times in the eighth inning against Charles Nagy and Mark Wohlers. It was the second time in five weeks that the Indians allowed at least 20 runs in a game (see April 30, 2002). The 21-run deficit tied for the most-lopsided loss in Indians history. The club also lost 21–0 the Tigers on September 15, 1901. It was also the second most runs ever surrendered by a Cleveland club. The Red Sox defeated the Indians 24–5 on August 21, 1986.

On the same day, the Indians selected pitcher Jeremy Guthrie from Stanford University with their first pick in the amateur draft. Guthrie reached the majors in 2004 but pitched sparingly for the Tribe, compiling less than 40 innings over three years with little success. The Orioles picked him up off waivers, and in 2007 he started 26 games, compiling a 7–5 record with a 3.70 ERA. Others drafted and signed by the Indians in 2002 who have played in the big leagues include second rounder Brian Slocum and fifth round pick Ben Francisco.

JUNE 5 Jim Thome hits his 300th career homer during a 6–4 victory over the Twins in Minneapolis. The milestone was struck off Eric Milton.

JUNE 7 The Indians play the Mets for the first time during the regular seaso, and lose 4–3 at Jacobs Field.

On the same day, the Indians traded Russell Branyan to the Reds for Ben Broussard.

JUNE 10 The Indians play the Phillies for the first time during the regular season and lose 3–1 at Jacobs Field.

JUNE 12 Tempers flare briefly in the ninth inning of a 7–3 loss to the Phillies at Jacobs Field. Jose Mesa drilled former teammate Omar Vizquel in the back with a pitch. Mesa was unhappy with Vizquel, who in his autobiography suggested that Mesa choked in the seventh game of the 1997 World Series (see October 26, 1997).

JUNE 14 The Indians play the Rockies for the first time during the regular season and lose 5–3 at Coors Field in Denver.

JUNE 18 The Indians play the Marlins for the first time during the regular season and lose 4–0 in Miami.

JUNE 21 The Indians play the Expos for the first time during the regular season and lose 3–1 at Olympic Stadium in Montreal.

JUNE 27 The Indians trade Bartolo Colon and Tim Drew to the Expos for Grady Sizemore, Cliff Lee, Brandon Phillips, and Lee Stevens.

The trade of Colon, the Indians number one starting pitcher, in exchange for four minor leaguers, surprised and angered Indians fans. Signs directed at general manager Mark Shapiro were evident at Jacobs Field the next evening. One read: "Shapiro Bobblehead Night. June 27. No spring needed." When traded, Colon had a record of 75–45 with the Indians since joining the club in 1997. His winning percentage of .625 is the third best in club history (minimum 100 decisions). Colon won 20 games in 2002, posting 10–4 records for both the Indians and Expos. He continued to be an excellent pitcher for a few more years. Colon was 54–33 with the White Sox and Angels from 2003 through 2005, when he posted a 21–8 record, but since then his effectiveness has been limited. Still, Shapiro may have gotten the better end of the trade with the continued development of Sizemore, Lee, and Phillips. Sizemore has become a legitimate star and leader for the team and a fan favorite. Lee compiled a 46–24 record from 2004 through 2006.

JUNE 28 The Indians play the Arizona Diamondbacks for the first time and win 8–2 at Jacobs Field.

JULY 2 During a 10–5 loss to the Yankees in New York, Jim Thome sets a club record by homering in his sixth consecutive game.

JULY 3 Jim Thome hits a home run in his seventh consecutive game, one shy of the major league record, during an 11–8 loss to the Yankees in New York.

JULY 4 Jim Thome is hitless in three at-bats during a 7–1 loss to the Yankees in New York, ending his streak of consecutive games in which he hit a home run at seven.

Thome's home run streak is tied for the fourth longest in major league history. Those with home runs in eight straight games are Dale Long of the Pirates in 1956, Don Mattingly with the Yankees in 1987, and Ken Griffey, Jr. while playing for the Mariners in 1993. Kevin Mench of the Rangers also hit homers in seven contests in a row in 2006.

JULY 7 The Indians score eight runs in the third inning and win 9–3 over the White Sox in Chicago. Milton Bradley hit a grand slam off Todd Ritchie.

JULY 9 In the All-Star Game at Miller Park in Milwaukee, Omar Vizquel drives in a run with a triple in the eighth inning. The game ended in a 7–7 tie after 11 innings.

Vizquel played the final seven innings of the game at second base. The only time he had ever played the position during the regular season was one contest in 1991 while with the Mariners.

JULY 11 The Indians fire Charlie Manuel as manager with the club holding a record of 39–48. Manuel was in the final year of his contract and demanded a longer deal, but club officials had other plans. Third base coach Joel Skinner was named interim manager.

JULY 14 A two-out, walk-off grand slam by Bill Selby off Mariano Rivera caps a six-run ninth inning that stuns the Yankees 10–7 at Jacobs Field. The Indians trailed 7–0 before scoring three runs in the six and one in the seventh. Still, the Tribe trailed 7–4 heading into the ninth with Rivera on the mound. A run-scoring ground out by Chris Magruder and an RBI-double from Ellis Burks made the score 7–6. Rivera walked Jim Thome to load the bases with one out, and then fanned Travis Fryman. Selby's slam cleared the right field fence. It was Selby's first homer as a member of the Indians.

JULY 16 Jim Warfield, the Indians trainer for more than 30 years, dies of a massive brain hemorrhage only a few hours before a 5–4 loss to the White Sox at Jacobs Field. He was 60-years-old. Cleveland players wrote "JW" on their caps in tribute to Warfield. As he took his position in the field in the first inning, Jim Thome dropped to a knee in prayer using his fingers to write Warfield's initials in the dirt.

JULY 17 Torii Hunter of the Twins fires a ball back at Indians pitcher Danys Baez during an 8–5 Minnesota victory at Jacobs Field. Hunter was angry at being hit in the left side in the fifth inning and retaliated by picking up the ball and hitting Baez, who was about 40 feet away, in the upper leg.

JULY 19 Milton Bradley hits a grand slam off Juan Rincon in the third inning to give the Indians a 6–2 lead, but the Twins rally to beat the Indians 8–6 at Jacobs Field.

JULY 20 Ellis Burks drives in all five Indians runs during a 5–3 win over the Royals in the second game of a double header in Kansas City. Burks hit a two-run homer in the first inning and a three-run shot in the tenth to break a 2–2 tie. The Royals won the opener 7–5.

On the same day, the Indians trade Chuck Finley to the Cardinals for Coco Crisp and Luis Garcia. The Indians continued to shed salary by trading Finley but came out ahead on the deal. Finley was very near the end of his career, while Crisp became a starting center field for both the Indians and Red Sox.

JULY 21 The Indians collect 20 hits, but lose 13–12 in ten innings to the Royals in Kansas City. Cleveland pitcher Heath Murray hit Raul Ibanez with a pitch with the bases loaded to score the winning run. Milton Bradley collected five hits, four of them for extra bases, in six at-bats with a homer, three doubles and a single. Chris Magruder and Omar Vizquel led off the first inning with back-to-back home runs.

JULY 23 Milton Bradley hits two Yankees catchers with his bat from opposite sides of the plate during a 9–3 victory over the Yankees at Jacobs Field. Jorge Posada was cut above the left ear when struck by Bradley's backswing in the fifth inning while Bradley was batting from the right side. Posada was taken to the hospital for stitches. Hitting from the left side in the seventh, Bradley also struck substitute catcher Chris Widger on the helmet with his bat. Fortunately, Widger was not injured.

Bradley was on the disabled list for 19 days in August following an emergency appendectomy.

JULY 28 A walk-off grand slam by Jim Thome off Juan Acevedo in the ninth inning caps a 9–6 comeback win over the Tigers at Jacobs Field. Trailing 6–0, the Indians scored two runs in the sixth inning, two in the eighth and five in the ninth.

On the same day, the Indians traded Paul Shuey to the Dodgers for Terry Mulholland, Ricardo Rodriguez, and Francisco Cruceta.

AUGUST 7 The Indians sign Dave Burba following his release by the Rangers.

The Indians used a club record 59 players in 2002, including 31 pitchers.

AUGUST 13 The Indians score seven runs in the fifth inning and beat the Devil Rays 9–5 in St. Petersburg. Karim Garcia hit a grand slam off Tanyon Sturtze.

Garcia was promoted to the Indians from Triple-A Buffalo on August 6 and hit 16 homers with 52 RBIs and a .297 batting average in 53 games over the remainder of the season.

AUGUST 14 Ellis Burks collects his 2,000th career hit during a 6–4 win over the Devil Rays in St. Petersburg. The milestone was a single off Paul Wilson in the first inning.

AUGUST 23 In his major league debut, catcher Josh Bard hits a two-run, walk-off homer in the ninth inning to defeat the Mariners 4–2 at Jacobs Field. Bard was recalled earlier in the day from Triple-A Buffalo after Einar Diaz went on the disabled list. The contest was interrupted by rain for two hours and ten minutes in the sixth inning.

Bard hit .222 in 90 at-bats for the Tribe in 2002.

AUGUST 24 The Indians win on a walk-off home run for the second day in a row, as Karim Garcia clears the wall with a two-run blast to defeat the Mariners 5–3 at Jacobs Field. Josh Bard, who hit a walk-off home run the previous night in his major league debut, homered again in the third inning after Jamie Moyer retired the first seven Cleveland batters.

AUGUST 28 Jim Thome hits two homers for the only runs of a 2–1 victory over the Tigers at Jacobs Field. Thome homered in the second and sixth inning off Brian Powell.

SEPTEMBER 2 Karim Garcia hits two homers and drives in six runs during an 11–1 win over the Tigers in Detroit.

SEPTEMBER 5 Karim Garcia hits a grand slam off Mike Porzio in the sixth inning of an 11–6 win over the White Sox in Chicago. Garcia was the first batter Porzio faced after relieving Gary Glover.

SEPTEMBER 6 Lee Stevens hits two homers and drives in six runs during a 9–7 win over the White Sox in Chicago.

SEPTEMBER 27 Jim Thome hits his 51st home run of the season, breaking the club record, during an 8–3 victory over the Royals at Jacobs Field.

Thome broke the mark of Albert Belle, who hit 50 in 1995 in a season shortened to 144 games by the strike. Thome hit 52 home runs in 2002, in addition to 118 RBIs, 101 runs, 122 walks, and a .304 batting average. His .677 slugging percentage led the AL *(see December 3, 2002)*.

OCTOBER 16 Angels pitching coach Bud Black turns down an offer to manage the Indians.

OCTOBER 29 The Indians hire 34-year-old Eric Wedge as manager. Interim manager Joel Skinner was retained by the club as a third base coach.

Wedge became the youngest manager in the major leagues. He had been a manager in the Indians farm system for five seasons, the last two at Triple-A Buffalo. Wedge's major league playing career lasted 39 games as a catcher over four seasons (1991–94) with the Red Sox and Rockies. Prior to reaching the majors, he played on the 1989 NCAA championship club at Wichita State University.

DECEMBER 3 Jim Thome signs with the Phillies as a free agent.

Thome didn't want to leave Cleveland, but the Indians were in a rebuilding mode and offered him a contract well below market value. The Tribe's proposal to Thome was slightly more than $60 million, but the Phillies won his services with a six-year $85 million deal. Thome would have been worth the investment.

After playing in Philadelphia for three seasons, he was dealt to the White Sox and has continued in a starring role through the 2007 season, when he struck his 500th career home run. Meanwhile, the Indians have struggled to find an adequate first baseman to replace Thome. In 2003, Thome was named the most popular athlete in Cleveland sports history in a poll conducted by the Cleveland Plain Dealer. *Still, he has been booed frequently in appearances at Jacobs Field since then because many Indians fans haven't forgiven him for leaving.*

DECEMBER 6 The Indians trade Einar Diaz and Ryan Drese to the Rangers for Travis Hafner and Aaron Myette.

Mark Shapiro pulled off a heist of the Rangers and his former boss John Hart in dealing for Hafner. The trade already ranks as one of the ten best in Indians history.

DECEMBER 18 The Indians sign Casey Blake, most recently with the Twins, as a free agent.

Mark Shapiro continued to show an eye for talent by acquiring Blake. He came to the Indians at the age of 28 without playing a full season in the majors and had a .232 batting average and two home runs in 112 at-bats with three teams. Nonetheless, Blake cracked the Indians starting line-up in 2003 and has held the position through 2007. In addition to Blake, Shapiro dealt for Travis Hafner, Grady Sizemore, Cliff Lee, Brandon Phillips, and Coco Crisp during the 2002 season.

DECEMBER 23 The Indians sign Brian Anderson, most recently with the Diamondbacks, as a free agent.

2003

Season in a Sentence

New manager Eric Wedge uses 25 rookies during the season and the young roster suffers through growing pains while losing 94 games.

Finish • Won • Lost • Pct • GB

Finish	Won	Lost	Pct	GB
Fourth	68	94	.420	22.0

In the wild card race, the Indians finished in ninth place, 27 games out of first place.

Manager

Eric Wedge

Stats

Stats	Indians	AL	Rank
Batting Avg:	.254	.267	13
On-Base Pct:	.316	.333	13
Slugging Pct:	.401	.428	13
Home Runs:	158		8
Stolen Bases:	86		10
ERA:	4.21	4.52	5
Fielding Avg:	.980	.983	13
Runs Scored:	699		13
Runs Allowed:	778		7

Starting Line-up

Josh Bard, c
Ben Broussard, 1b
Brandon Phillips, 2b
Casey Blake, 3b
Omar Vizquel, ss
Matt Lawton, lf
Coco Crisp, cf-lf
Jody Gerut, rf-lf
Ellis Burks, dh
Milton Bradley, cf
Travis Hafner, dh
Jhonny Peralta, ss
John McDonald, 2b-ss-3b
Shane Spencer, rf-lf

Pitchers

C. C. Sabathia, sp
Brian Anderson, sp
Jason Davis, sp
Jake Westbrook, sp
Billy Traber, sp
Danys Baez, rp
David Riske, rp
Terry Mulholland, rp
Jason Boyd, rp

Attendance

1,730,001 (12th in AL)

Club Leaders

Batting Avg:	Milton Bradley	.321
On-Base Pct:	Milton Bradley	.401
Slugging Pct:	Milton Bradley	.521
Home Runs:	Jody Gerut	22
RBIs:	Jody Gerut	75
Runs:	Casey Blake	80
Stolen Bases:	Milton Bradley	17
Wins:	C. C. Sabathia	13
Strikeouts:	C. C. Sabathia	141
ERA:	C. C. Sabathia	3.60
Saves:	Danys Baez	25

March 28 Nine days after U. S. forces invade Iraq, the Indians participate in the first game ever played at Great American Ball Park in Cincinnati. The Tribe won the exhibition contest 3–0.

March 31 In a snowy opener in Baltimore, the Indians lose 6–5 to the Orioles in 13 innings. Cleveland scored three runs in the third inning with the aid of a routine fly ball that Oriole right fielder Jay Gibbons lost amid the large snowflakes that swirled around Camden Yards. The umpires then halted play, but not soon enough for Baltimore manager Mike Hargrove, who argued in vain that the stoppage should have come before the ball vanished in the falling snow. Karim Garcia homered in the sixth for a 4–1 lead, but the Indians were unable to hold the advantage.

Four years later, Hargrove would become involved in another controversial game involving the Indians and a snowfall (see April 6, 2007).

April 3 Matt Lawton hits a three-run homer in the sixth inning off Rick Helling for the only runs of a 3–0 victory over the Orioles in Baltimore. Brian Anderson (eight innings) and Danys Baez (one inning) combined on the shutout.

April 7 — The Indians scheduled home opener against the White Sox is postponed by rain.

April 8 — The White Sox spoil Cleveland's home opener by beating the Indians 5–3 in ten innings before 42,301 at Jacobs Field.

April 9 — Playing before 14,841, the smallest crowd at Jacobs Field up to that point, the Indians beat the White Sox 5–2. The gametime temperature was 35 degrees.

The Indians drew 1,730,001 in 2003, to rank 12th in the American League ahead of only the Tigers, a club that lost 119 games that season, and the Devil Rays. The 2003 Cleveland attendance figure was barely half of what the team attracted in 2000 when 3,456,278 tickets were sold but exceeded the number of fans the club drew every season played at League Park or Municipal Stadium except for those of 1948, 1949, 1950, 1951, and 1993.

April 21 — Ellis Burks and Karim Garcia each hit two home runs during a 9–2 win over the White Sox in Chicago.

April 22 — Mike Cameron of the Mariners hits a walk-off grand slam that caps a five-run Seattle ninth inning off Danys Baez and beats the Indians 8–5 in Seattle. The Indians scored three runs in the top of the ninth to take a 5–3 lead over the Mariners.

May 8 — Garrett Anderson drives in all seven Angels runs during a 7–1 win over the Indians in Anaheim.

May 11 — Rafael Palmeiro hits his 500th career homer during a 17–10 Rangers win over the Indians in Arlington. Palmeiro struck the milestone off Dave Elder.

May 13 — The Indians lose 8–3 to the Mariners at Jacobs Field. The defeat dropped Cleveland's record to 11–26.

May 19 — The Indians overcome three homers and seven runs-batted-in by Carlos Pena to defeat the Tigers 10–9 at Jacobs Field. Cleveland trailed 9–7 before scoring three times in the seventh inning, two of them crossing the plate on Casey Blake's home run.

June 3 — With their first pick in the amateur draft, the Indians select first baseman Michael Aubrey from Tulane University.

The first three players from the 2003 draft to reach the majors were third rounder Ryan Garko, sixth-round choice Kevin Kouzmanoff, and 16th-round selection Aaron Laffey.

June 6 — The Indians play in Phoenix for the first time during the regular season and beat the Diamondbacks 6–3 at Bank One Ballpark.

June 10 — The Indians play the Padres for the first time during the regular season and win 8–5 at Jacobs Field. The Indians scored six runs in the first inning after San Diego tallied four times in the top of the inning.

June 13 — The Indians play the Dodgers for the first time during the regular season and lose 4–3 in ten innings at Jacobs Field.

June 14 A 5–2 loss to the Dodgers at Jacobs Field features some trash talk between Milton Bradley and Paul LoDuca, who were wired with microphones for TV. After connecting for a home run in the fourth inning, Bradley loosened the straps on his batting gloves as he ran toward first base, an act of showboating that rankled the Dodgers. An inning later, Bradley struck out and argued with umpire Mark Carlson about the call. LoDuca, normally the Dodgers catcher but playing first base on this day, yelled "Take your gloves off for that one," toward Bradley. On his way out to the field, Bradley ripped off the microphone he had been wearing. In the seventh, Bradley threw out LoDuca, who was trying to advance from second to third on a fly ball. Bradley waved toward LoDuca, and the two continued their running argument.

June 20 The Indians play at PNC Park in Pittsburgh for the first time and lose 5–4 in 15 innings to the Pirates. Russell Simon ended the game with a walk-off homer off Danys Baez.

June 21 The Indians lose a 15-inning game for the second night in a row, dropping a 7–6 decision to the Pirates in Pittsburgh. The game ended on a wild pitch by Dan Miceli. Cleveland squandered a 5–1, fifth-inning lead.

June 27 The day after being selected as the NBA's number one draft choice by the Cavs, LeBron James throws out the ceremonial first pitch prior to a 3–0 win over the Reds at Jacobs Field. Earlier, James took batting practice from Cincinnati coach Tom Hume and missed nine pitches before hitting a few lazy fly balls.

June 30 Casey Blake hits homers in both ends of a double header as the Indians sweep the Royals 10–5 and 8–5 in Kansas City. In the opener, Blake hit a grand slam off Kris Wilson in the eighth inning.

July 5 Casey Blake collects five hits in five at-bats and drives in seven runs during a 13–2 crushing of the Twins in Minneapolis. Four of Blake's four hits were for extra bases with two homers and two doubles.

July 6 A two-out, two-run homer by Shane Spencer in the tenth inning beats the Twins 5–3 in Minneapolis.

July 8 Billy Traber retires 27 of the 28 batters to face him while pitching a one-hitter to beat the Yankees 4–0 at Jacobs Field. The only New York base runner was John Flaherty leading off the third inning. Traber retired the first six batters to face him, and the last 21.

Despite the one-hitter, Traber finished the 2003 season with a 6–9 record and a 5.24 ERA. The July 8 game was not only Traber's first career shutout, it was his first complete game. After the 2003 campaign, Traber underwent Tommy John surgery and didn't pitch in the big leagues again until 2006, when he landed with the Washington Nationals. Through the 2007 season, he has yet to pitch another complete game.

July 11 Ben Broussard hits two homers and drives in five runs during a 12–5 win over the White Sox at Jacobs Field.

The Indians scored exactly four runs in seven consecutive games from July 12 through July 20. The Tribe lost 7–4 in ten innings and won 4–2 in a double header against the White Sox in Chicago on July 12. The following day, Cleveland dropped a 7–4 decision to the Sox. Following the All-Star break, the Indians played a four-game series against the Yankees in New York from the 17th through the 20th and lost all four by scores of 5–4, 10–4, 7–4, and 7–4 again.

JULY 26 A grand slam by Jody Gerut off Kyle Lohse highlights an eight-run second inning as the Indians defeat the Twins 9–2 at Jacobs Field.

JULY 27 The Indians outlast the Twins 3–2 in 14 innings in Minneapolis. Tim Laker drove in the winning run with a two-out single. The Indians collected a club record five sacrifices in the game. Laker had two of them, with Casey Blake, Ben Broussard, and Ryan Ludwick adding the rest.

AUGUST 1 The Rangers hit seven homers off Indians pitching during a 10–3 win at Arlington. Todd Greene and Mark Teixeira each had two homers, with Rafeal Palmeiro, Alex Rodriguez, and Matt Young accounting for the remainder. Terry Mulholland allowed four of the Texas home runs and Billy Traber three.

AUGUST 13 The Indians erupt for five runs in the 14th inning to defeat the Twins 5–0 in Minneapolis. A single by Ryan Ludwick broke the scoreless tie before the Indians added four more runs. Jason Davis (six innings), Jack Cressend (one inning), Rafael Betancourt (two innings), Terry Mulholland (four innings), and David Riske (one inning) combined on the shutout.

AUGUST 14 Travis Hafner hits for the cycle during an 8–3 victory over the Twins in Minneapolis. He was the first Indian to hit for the cycle since Andre Thornton in 1978. Hafner homered in the first inning, doubled in the fourth, and singled in the seventh against Brad Radke. Facing James Baldwin in the eighth, Hafner collected a triple.

AUGUST 15 A walk-off single by Josh Bard in the ninth inning drives in the only run of a 1–0 win over the Devil Rays at Jacobs Field. C. C. Sabathia pitched the shutout, the first of his career.

Sabathia has become known for his cap, which he wears slightly sideways and slanted, and his tremendous girth. He stands six-foot-seven, and mlb.com listed his weight in 2007 at 290 pounds. In addition, Sabathia has a tattoo with his name in large letters printed uniform-style across his back.

AUGUST 23 Trailing 5–0, the Indians score six runs in the seventh inning and one in the eighth to defeat the Devil Rays 7–5 at St. Petersburg. Casey Blake put the Indians into the lead with a two-run single.

Blake was one of nine players who suffered through at least part of the 94-loss, 2003 season to remain with the Indians long enough to play in the post-season for in 2007. The others were Rafael Betancourt, Travis Hafner, Cliff Lee, Victor Martinez, Jhonny Peralta, C. C. Sabathia, and Jake Westbrook.

AUGUST 25 The Indians trade Brian Anderson to the Royals for Trey Dyson and Kieran Mattison.

AUGUST 27 Coco Crisp collects four hits and scores four runs during a 9–7 win over the Tigers at Jacobs Field.

AUGUST 28 Jody Gerut hits two homers and drives in five runs during an 8–3 triumph over the Tigers at Jacobs Field.

SEPTEMBER 20 The Indians score 12 runs in their last two at-bats with seven runs in the seventh inning and five in the eighth to beat the Red Sox 13–4 at Jacobs Field before a crowd of 11,751, the smallest of the year.

DECEMBER 26 The Indians sign Ron Belliard, most recently with the Rockies, as a free agent.

Belliard proved to a pleasant surprise, making the All-Star team in his first season with the Indians. He batted .282 and hit 48 doubles.

2004

Season in a Sentence

With a vastly improved offense, the Indians win 12 more games than the previous season but still fall shy of the .500 mark.

Finish • Won • Lost • Pct • GB

Finish	Won	Lost	Pct	GB
Third	80	82	.494	12.0

In the wild card race, the Indians finished in fifth place, 18 games behind.

Manager

Eric Wedge

Stats

	Indians	AL	Rank
Batting Avg:	.276	.270	4
On-Base Pct:	.351	.338	2
Slugging Pct:	.444	.433	6
Home Runs:	184		8
Stolen Bases:	94		6
ERA:	4.81	4.63	10
Fielding Avg:	.983	.982	7
Runs Scored:	858		5
Runs Allowed:	857		13

Staring Line-up

Victor Martinez, c
Ben Broussard, 1b
Ron Belliard, 2b
Casey Blake, 3b
Omar Vizquel, ss
Matt Lawton, lf
Coco Crisp, cf
Jody Gerut, rf
Travis Hafner, dh

Pitchers

Jake Westbrook, sp
Cliff Lee, sp
C. C. Sabathia, sp
Scott Elarton, sp
Jason Davis, sp
David Riske, rp
Rafael Betancourt, rp
Rick White, rp
Matt Miller, rp

Attendance

1,814,401 (12th in AL)

Club Leaders

Batting Avg:	Travis Hafner	.311
On-Base Pct:	Travis Hafner	.410
Slugging Pct:	Travis Hafner	.583
Home Runs:	Travis Hafner	28
	Casey Blake	28
RBIs:	Travis Hafner	109
Runs:	Matt Lawton	109
Stolen Bases:	Matt Lawton	23
Wins:	Cliff Lee	14
	Jake Westbrook	14
Strikeouts:	Cliff Lee	161
ERA:	Jake Westbrook	3.38
Saves:	Bob Wickman	13

February 5 Four days after Janet Jackson's "wardrobe malfunction" during the Super Bowl halftime show, Ellis Burks signs with the Red Sox as a free agent.

February 10 Terry Mulholland signs with the Mariners as a free agent.

April 4 The Indians trade Milton Bradley to the Dodgers for Franklin Gutierrez and Andrew Brown.

Bradley had a breakout year in 2003 with a .321 batting average and ten home runs at the age of 25 but missed the final 61 games because of a bone bruise in his lower back. During the following off-season, he had two confrontations with police. The second one occurred in February 2004 and resulted in a three-day jail term after the Ohio State Highway Patrol stopped Bradley for speeding. Bradley drove away and refused to pull over as ordered. Four days before the trade to the Dodgers, Bradley failed to run out a popup and subsequently argued with Eric Wedge. The Indians were so anxious to be rid of the talented but troubled Bradley, he was dealt for two minor leaguers. How the trade works out remains to be seen, but Gutierrez became the Indians starting right fielder in 2007. Bradley's volatile behavior has continued through stops in Los Angeles, Oakland, and San Diego. In 2004, he was suspended for throwing a water bottle at a fan. In 2007, Bradley tore his ACL while being restrained by Padres manager Bud Black during an argument with umpire Mark Winters.

April 5 In the season opener, the Indians blow a 4–0 lead in the eighth inning and lose 7–4 in 11 innings to the Twins in Minneapolis. The contest ended on a three-run homer by Shannon Stewart off Chad Durbin. C. C. Sabathia was the starting pitcher and allowed just two hits during seven shutout innings. Travis Hafner hit two homers and a double and Jody Gerut also homered. Ben Broussard collected four hits in four at-bats.

Durbin gave up three walk-off homers during the first 28 games of the season.

April 12 The Indians win the home opener 6–3 over the Twins before 42,424 at Jacobs Field. Travis Hafner hit a grand slam in the third inning off Kyle Lohse.

The Indians debuted a new entertainment system with LED technology throughout Jacobs Field in 2004. The new system featured a video screen, which at the time it was erected, was the largest in baseball and the largest in North America for sports.

April 16 Jody Gerut collects five hits, four for extra bases, in five at-bats in leading the Indians to a 10–3 victory over the Tigers at Jacobs Field. Gerut had a homer, three doubles, and a single.

April 18 Matt Lawton smacks two homers, scores four runs, and drives in four to lead the Indians to a 9–7 win over the Tigers at Jacobs Field.

April 19 In a strange game against the Tigers at Jacobs Field, Jake Westbrook pitches seven innings of perfect relief, but the Indians lose 10–4. Westbrook came on to pitch with the Indians trailing 4–0 in the first inning after a 65-minute weather delay. Before the rain shower and hailstorm, Cleveland starter Jeff D'Amico gave up four runs. After Westbrook retired all 21 batters to face him, Rafael Betancourt and Scott Stewart combined to surrender six runs in the eighth.

April 22 Omar Vizquel collects his 2,000th career hit during a 5–4 victory over the Royals at Jacobs Field. The milestone was a single off Jason Grimsley as part of a three-run rally in the eighth inning that gave Cleveland the lead.

April 23 The Tigers score 11 runs in the sixth inning during a 17–3 win over the Indians in Detroit. The 11 runs scored off Jason Davis, Cliff Lee, and Jason Anderson. It was Anderson's only appearance as a member of the Indians.

April 25 In his first start of the season, Jake Westbrook pitches a two-hitter to defeat the Tigers 3–2 in Detroit. Westbrook had retired 27 batters in a row over three appearances before Carlos Pena homered with two out in the second inning. The other Detroit hit was a single by Bobby Higginson in the seventh.

April 28 The White Sox score five runs in the ninth inning to beat the Indians 9–8 in Chicago. Ex-Indian standout Sandy Alomar, Jr. drove in the winning run with a sacrifice fly.

May 14 Casey Blake hits a walk-off home run in the tenth inning to defeat the Devil Rays 8–7 at Jacobs Field. Tampa Bay scored two runs in the ninth to tie the contest 7–7.

May 16 The Indians clobber the Devil Rays 10–0 at Jacobs Field. Cleveland scored six runs in the fifth inning to snap a scoreless tie. C. C. Sabathia (seven innings) and Matt Miller (two innings) combined on the shutout.

May 28 A walk-off homer by Casey Blake leading off the ninth inning accounts for the lone run of a 1–0 triumph over the Athletics at Jacobs Field. The blast came off the third pitch from reliever Jim Mecir. Cliff Lee (6⅓ innings), Rafael Betancourt (1⅓ innings), Matt Miller (one-third of an inning), and Jose Jiminez (one inning) combined on the shutout.

Betancourt had an esoteric journey to the big leagues. He played in his first game in the majors in 2003 at the age of 28 as a converted shortstop with a titanium plate and six screws in his right pitching elbow. The metal was implanted during surgery in 2002. Betancourt pitched in Japan during the 2000 season.

June 7 With their first pick in the amateur draft, the Indians select pitcher Jeremy Sowers from Vanderbilt University.

Sowers was drafted in the first round out of high school by the Reds in 2001 but elected to attend college. He reached the majors in 2006.

June 8 The Indians play the Marlins at Jacobs Field for the first time during the regular season and lose 7–5 when Florida scores two runs on a pair of home runs by Miguel Cabrera and Damion Easley in the ninth inning off Jose Jiminez. Both home runs struck the left field foul pole.

June 13 The Indians trail 7–1 in the fourth inning before storming back with a run in the fourth inning, five in the sixth, and three in the seventh to defeat the Reds 10–8 at

Jacobs Field. Matt Lawton's two-run homer broke the 8–8 tie. Facing Cliff Lee in the third inning, Ken Griffey, Jr. hit his 499th career home run. In the fourth, Lee was ejected after nearly hitting Griffey in the head with a pitch.

Travis Hafner posted a breakout season in 2004, producing the first of four straight 100-RBI seasons.

JUNE 14 The Indians score seven runs in the third inning and rout the Orioles 14–0 at Jacobs Field. Jake Westbrook pitched the shutout, the first of his career. It was a one-game trip to Cleveland for the Orioles to make up a May 2 rain out.

JUNE 15 The Indians play at Shea Stadium for the first time and lose 7–2 to the Mets.

JUNE 18 The Indians play the Braves for the first time during the regular season and win 4–2 at Turner Field in Atlanta.

June 20 Jason Davis is the winning pitcher and collects his first major league hit with a home run during a 5–2 decision over the Braves in Atlanta.

June 22 After trailing 8–0 to the White Sox in Chicago, the Indians score six runs in the fifth inning, two in the sixth, and one in the eighth for a 9–8 lead but wind up losing 11–9 in ten innings. The game ended on a home run by Jose Valentin off Jose Jiminez.

June 23 Ben Broussard hits a pinch-hit grand slam off Mike Jackson in the eighth inning of a 9–5 victory over the White Sox in Chicago.

June 25 The Rockies play at Jacobs Field for the first time and defeat the Indians 10–8 in ten innings.

June 26 Indians rookie Kazuhito Tadano strikes out nine batters in six innings of relief during a 12-inning, 4–3 win over the Rockies at Jacobs Field. Tadano succeeded starter C. C. Sabathia, who left after the first inning with a sore shoulder. Ben Broussard ended the game with an RBI-double.

On the same day, the Indians signed Aaron Boone as a free agent following his release by the Yankees. Boone hit an 11th-inning walk-off homer for the Yankees in game seven of the 2003 American League Championship Series that beat the Red Sox 7–6. The Yankees cut Boone during the following off-season, however, after he injured his knee while playing in a pick-up basketball game. The injury, which required two surgeries, put Boone out of action for the entire 2004 season. He recovered well enough to win the Indians starting third base job in 2005.

July 1 Jody Gerut hits a home run in tenth inning to give the Indians a 7–6 win over the Tigers in Detroit.

July 2 The Indians play at Great American Ball Park in Cincinnati for the first time during the regular season and crush the Reds 15–2. Cleveland scored six runs in both the fifth and eighth innings. Kazuhito Tadano struck out ten batters in seven innings in his first major league start.

July 9 The Indians score three runs in the ninth inning to defeat the Athletics 5–4 at Jacobs Field. Matt Lawton started the rally with a walk. Omar Vizquel followed with a single and Travis Hafner doubled in a run. Stepping to the plate as a pinch-hitter, Lou Merloni drove in both Vizquel and Hafner with a two-out single.

Hafner hit .311 with 28 homers and 109 RBIs in 2004.

July 16 Victor Martinez hits three homers and drives in seven runs to lead the Indians to an 18–6 pasting of the Mariners at Safeco Field. The Indians tied a club record with eight home runs in all and broke a club mark with 50 total bases. The 50 total bases came on 21 hits. In addition to the eight home runs, Cleveland batters accounted for five doubles and eight singles. The switch-hitting Martinez went five-for-five. He hit a three-run homer and a solo shot from the right side and another solo blast from the left. The home runs came off lefties Ron Villone and Travis Blackley and right-hander Julio Mateo. Martinez also collected two singles, one of which drove in two runs. Matt Lawton, Martinez, and Casey Blake connected for consecutive homers in the third inning off Blackley. Martinez, Travis Hafner, Ben Broussard, and Jody Gerut all homered in the ninth to tie another club record for most homers in an inning. After Hafner's homer, Mateo hit Lou Merloni in the back with a pitch and was ejected by umpire Tim Tschida. Both benches emptied but no punches were thrown.

Martinez hit .283 with 23 home runs and 108 runs-batted-in during his first full season in the majors.

July 19 After the Indians score twice in the ninth inning to tie the Angels 5–5, a three-run homer by Travis Hafner in the tenth lifts the Indians to an 8–5 victory in Anaheim. It was Hafner's second homer of the game and gave him five RBIs on the night.

July 20 Travis Hafner connects for three home runs during a 14–5 win over the Angels in Anaheim. Combined with his two homers the previous night, Hafner tied a major league record for most home runs in consecutive games with five. He also drove in six runs, giving him 11 runs-batted-in over back-to-back games, which tied a club record set by Earl Averill in 1930. The three homers by Hafner were in the third and fifth innings off Jarrod Washburn and in the ninth against Francisco Rodriguez.

The Indians were a vastly improved offensive team in 2004, scoring 858 runs compared to 699 in 2003.

July 23 Ben Broussard hits a walk-off homer on a 3–0 pitch with one out in the 11th to defeat the Royals 3–2 at Jacobs Field.

July 27 Coco Crisp hits a grand slam off Gary Knotts in the second inning of a 10–6 win over the Tigers at Jacobs Field. Crisp was a last-minute replacement in left field when Travis Hafner was scratched with a sprained neck and Matt Lawton moved to the designated hitter spot.

Coco's given name is Covelli Loyce Crisp.

How to Beat the Yankees in 22 Easy Steps

The 22–0 pasting of the Yankees at Yankee Stadium on August 31, 2004 was an unexpected treat. The Indians entered the contest having lost 11 of the previous 14 games. The Yanks had a record of 81–49 on the way to a season in which they would win 101 times.

The Line Score	1	2	3	4	5	6	7	8	9	R	H	E
Cleveland	3	3	3	0	6	1	0	0	6	22	22	1
New York	0	0	0	0	0	0	0	0	0	0	5	0

First Inning
With Javier Vasquez pitching for the Yankees, Omar Vizquel singled with one out. Matt Lawton reached on a fielder's choice, and Victor Martinez walked to load the bases. Travis Hafner tripled to deep center to score Vizquel, Lawton, and Martinez. Cleveland 3, New York 0.

Second Inning
Ron Belliard led off with a double, and Jody Gerut followed by drawing a walk. Omar Vizquel and Matt Lawton both drove in runs with one out singles. After Tanyon Sturtze replaced Vasquez as the Yankee hurler, Martinez hit a sacrifice fly. Cleveland 6, New York 0.

Third Inning
Casey Blake and Ben Broussard started the inning with back-to-back walks. Sturtze retired the next two batters before Coco Crisp singled in Broussard

and Vizquel doubled in two runs. Cleveland 9, New York 0.

Fourth Inning
Sturtze retired the Indians in order. Cleveland 9, New York 0.

Fifth Inning
Broussard and Belliard began the inning with consecutive doubles, and both scored on Crisp's one-out home run. Omar Vizquel followed with a single and C. J. Nitkowski replaced Sturtze. With two out, the Indians loaded the bases on a walk to Martinez and an infield single by Hafner. Blake drew a walk to force in Vizquel, and Broussard smacked a two-run single. Cleveland 15, New York 0.

Sixth Inning
Gerut led off with a walk and scored on Vizquel's one-out double. Cleveland 16, New York 0.

Seventh Inning
With Esteban Loaiza pitching for New York, Hafner led off with a walk and Josh Phelps hit a one-out single, but the Indians failed to score. Cleveland 16, New York 0.

Eighth Inning
Vizquel and Martinez both singled, but the Indians failed to score. Cleveland 16, New York 0.

Ninth Inning
With one out, and Loaiza still on the mound, Phelps and Belliard both singled and Gerut hit a three-run homer. Crisp walked, and Vizquel stepped to the plate with a chance to collect his seventh hit in seven at-bats. Only three players in major league history have had seven-for-seven games, but Vizquel missed a chance at joining that select group by flying to right field. Ryan Ludwick advanced Crisp to third with a single, and Martinez homered. Hafner struck out to end the Cleveland scoring spree. In the bottom half of the inning, Jake Westbrook retired the Yankees in order to complete his first big league shutout. Cleveland 22, New York 0.

AUGUST 4 The Indians collect 21 hits and rout the Blue Jays 14–5 in Toronto. Travis Hafner hit two homers and drove in six runs. Casey Blake had five hits, including a double and a triple, in six at-bats.

AUGUST 7 Matt Lawton hits a three-run homer in the ninth inning to defeat the White Sox 6–5 in Chicago.

AUGUST 9 Ben Broussard hits a grand slam off Felix Diaz in the third inning of a 13–11 slugfest against the White Sox in Chicago. The Indians hung on for the victory after leading 8–0 in the sixth inning.

AUGUST 10 Ron Belliard's two-run double in the second inning drives in the only runs of a 2–0 triumph over the Blue Jays at Jacobs Field. Chad Durbin (seven innings), Bobby Howry (one inning), and Bob Wickman (one inning) combined on the shutout.

AUGUST 12 Ben Broussard hits a pinch-hit grand slam off Vinnie Chulk in the seventh inning of a 6–2 win over the Blue Jays at Jacobs Field. The slam broke a 2–2 tie. It was Broussard's second bases-loaded home run in four days and his third of the season. Two of the three grand slams were as a pinch-hitter, which tied a major league record.

AUGUST 14 The Indians move within one game of the first-place Twins with a 7–1 win against the Minnesota club at Jacobs Field.

August 15 With a chance to move within percentage points of first place, the Indians lose 4–2 to the Twins in ten innings in Minneapolis. The game ended on a two-run homer by Corey Koskie off Rick White.

The August 14 win gave the Indians a 63–55 record. Any illusions of reaching the post-season were shattered when the Tribe dropped each of their next nine games, beginning with the August 15 defeat, by a combined score of 61–23.

August 29 Scott Elarton pitches a two-hitter to defeat the White Sox 9–0 at Jacobs Field. It was Elarton's first career shutout. The only Chicago hits were an infield single by Willie Harris in the fourth inning and a one-out single from Joe Crede in the ninth.

Elarton was otherwise ineffective in 2004, with a record of 3–11 and an ERA of 5.90 with the Rockies and Indians.

August 31 In one of the most remarkable games in franchise history, the Indians erupt for a 22–0 win over the Yankees in New York. Omar Vizquel led the way with six hits in seven at-bats. He had four singles and two doubles. Travis Hafner started the scoring with a three-run triple to deep center in the first inning. The Indians added three more runs in the second inning, three in the third, six in the fifth, one in the sixth, and six in the ninth. The Tribe collected 22 hits on three homers, a triple, five doubles, and 13 singles and were beneficiaries of nine walks from four Yankee pitchers. The Indians left ten runners on base. Cleveland batters driving in runs were Vizquel (four), Martinez (four), Crisp (three), Hafner (three), Gerut (three), Ben Broussard (two), Matt Lawton (one), Casey Blake (one), and Ron Belliard (one). Scoring runs were Crisp (four), Vizquel (three), Martinez (three), Belliard (three), Broussard (two), Gerut (two), Lawton (one), Ryan Ludwick (one), Hafner (one), Blake (one), and Josh Phelps (one). Jake Westbrook (seven innings) and Jeremy Guthrie (two innings) combined on the shutout. Along with the 9–0 win two days earlier and an off day on August 30, the Indians won back-to-back games by a 31–0 score.

The game tied the record for the most lop-sided shutout in major league history. The Pirates beat the Cubs 22–0 at Wrigley Field on September 16, 1975. The previous Indians record for a shutout win was 19–0 over the Red Sox on May 18, 1955. It was the largest margin of defeat ever for the Yankees, who had lost by 18 runs in 1925 to the Tigers and in 1928 against the Indians (see July 29, 1928). The 22–0 win came during a stretch of particularly bad baseball for the Indians. It was one of only four victories over a period of 20 games from August 15 through September 5. Heading into the game, the club had lost 11 of their previous 14 games. Following the 22-run victory, the Indians lost their next five games by a combined score of 30–11. Cleveland didn't score more than nine runs in any other contest between August 8 and the end the season.

September 4 A swarm of gnats drives box seat patrons from their seats and harasses the players all night during a 6–1 loss to the Angels at Jacobs Field.

September 10 Casey Blake hits a home run in the tenth inning to defeat the Athletics 4–3 in Oakland.

September 21 Down 7–2 to the Tigers in Detroit, the Indians score three runs in the sixth inning, two in the eighth, and one in the ninth to win 8–7. Casey Blake's RBI-single broke the 7–7 tie.

September 29 Rookie pitcher Kyle Denney is shot while wearing a cheerleader's outfit on the team bus in a bizarre incident in Kansas City. Denney wore a University of Southern California cheerleader's uniform, complete with the white boots, as part of a rookie hazing tradition. Denney chose the outfit because he went to the University of Oklahoma and his Sooners were second to USC in the college football polls. While the bus was sitting on the ramp between Interstates 435 and 70 on the way from the ballpark to the airport, a bullet pierced the side of the vehicle and entered Denney's calf and hitting one of the cheerleader boots. Team trainers removed the bullet and the pitcher was treated and released from the hospital. Doctors speculated that the boots saved Denney from further injury. Ryan Ludwick was also slightly injured when hit by debris. Police had no leads on the shooter.

Denney was a veteran of just four big league games when shot. As of 2007, he had yet to pitch in another game in the majors as a dark cloud continued to surround him. In 2005, Denney was put out of action during spring training when a thrown bat struck him in the knee before a 33-day stint on the disabled list because of an injured elbow. The worst was yet to come. In June of that season, Denney suffered a fractured skull and a ruptured eardrum while playing for Triple-A Buffalo when a batted ball slammed into his head just behind the right ear.

October 2 The Indians game with the Twins in Minneapolis is suspended by a college football game. The two teams were tied 5–5 after 11 innings when the game was halted because the Metrodome's field needed to be changed for a later Minnesota-Penn State football game. The Indians and Twins started their game at 11:10 a.m. local time. Because of the gridiron match-up, no inning could start later than 2:30 p.m. and the 11th inning ended at 2:33. Minnesota and Penn State were set to kick-off at 7:00 p.m. The Indians-Twins game was completed the next day.

October 3 On the final day of the 2004 season, the Indians finish their suspended game of the previous afternoon against the Twins in Minneapolis and lose 6–5 in 12 innings. Cleveland won the regularly scheduled contest, 5–2.

November 14 Two weeks after George Bush defeats John Kerry in the presidential election, Omar Vizquel signs as a free agent with the Giants. Vizquel played for the Indians from 1994 through 2004.

December 11 The Indians trade Matt Lawton to the Pirates for Arthur Rhodes.

December 14 The Indians sign Jose Hernandez, most recently with the Dodgers, as a free agent.

2005

Season in a Sentence

After falling six games under the .500 mark in May, the Indians surge into the lead in the wild card race in late September before losing six of their last seven games to lose a spot in the playoffs.

Finish • Won • Lost • Pct • GB

Finish	Won	Lost	Pct	GB
Second	93	69	.574	6.0

In the wild card race, the Indians finished in second place, two games behind.

Manager

Eric Wedge

Stats

	Indians	AL	Rank
Batting Avg:	.271	.268	5
On-Base Pct:	.334	.330	3
Slugging Pct:	.453	.424	2
Home Runs:	207		3
Stolen Bases:	62		11
ERA:	3.61	4.35	1
Fielding Avg:	.983	.983	8
Runs Scored:	790		4
Runs Allowed:	642		1

Starting Line-up

Victor Martinez, c
Ben Broussard, 1b
Ron Belliard, 2b
Aaron Boone, 3b
Jhonny Peralta, ss
Coco Crisp, lf
Grady Sizemore, cf
Casey Blake, rf
Travis Hafner, dh
Jose Hernandez, 1b-3b

Pitchers

Cliff Lee, sp
Jake Westbrook, sp
C. C. Sabathia, sp
Scott Elarton, sp
Kevin Millwood, sp
Bob Wickman, rp
Bob Howry, rp
David Riske, rp
Rafael Betancourt, rp
Arthur Rhodes, rp

Attendance

2,013,763 (12th in AL)

Club Leaders

Batting Avg:	Victor Martinez	.305
	Travis Hafner	.305
On-Base Pct:	Travis Hafner	.408
Slugging Pct:	Travis Hafner	.595
Home Runs:	Travis Hafner	33
RBIs:	Travis Hafner	108
Runs:	Grady Sizemore	111
Stolen Bases:	Grady Sizemore	22
Wins:	Cliff Lee	18
Strikeouts:	C. C. Sabathia	161
ERA:	Cliff Lee	3.79
Saves:	Bob Wickman	45

JANUARY 8 The Indians sign Kevin Millwood, most recently with the Phillies, as a free agent.

JANUARY 11 The Indians sign Juan Gonzalez, most recently with the Royals, as a free agent.

Gonzalez gave the Indians a terrific season on a one-year contract in 2001 by batting .325 with 35 homers and 140 RBIs in helping the club win a division title. He was not brought back to Cleveland in 2002, however, as a cost-cutting move. Gonzalez wouldn't have been worth the money anyway, as he had three underwhelming seasons with the Rangers and Royals from 2002 through 2004. The Indians decided to take a flyer on Gonzalez in 2005 with a minor league contract loaded with incentives. He didn't meet any of the incentives because he had just one plate appearance during the 2005 season. Gonzalez appeared to have won the starting right field job in spring training, but a week prior to Opening Day he strained his right hamstring. Inserted into the line-up on May 31, Gonzalez aggravated the injury in his first at-bat and never played another big league game.

APRIL 4 The Indians open the 2005 season with a 1–0 loss to the White Sox in Chicago. Mark Buehrle (eight innings) and Shingo Takatsu (one inning) combined to hold Cleveland to two hits. Jake Westbrook pitched a four-hit complete game. The lone run of the game scored on an error by Jhonny Peralta.

Westbrook started the season with an 0–5 record in April and dipped to 2–9 on June 9 before finishing the season at 15–15. Cliff Lee was the Indians top starter in 2005 with a record of 18–5 and a 3.79 ERA.

APRIL 6 Kevin Millwood pitches six shutout innings in his debut with the Indians, but Cleveland loses 4–3 to the White Sox in Chicago when Bob Wickman allows four runs in the ninth inning.

The April 6 game was a rare bad outing for Wickman, who saved 45 games and had a 2.47 ERA in 64 games and 62 innings in 2005.

APRIL 7 With late-inning heroics, the Indians score three runs in the ninth inning and six in the 11th to defeat the White Sox 11–5 in Chicago. Down 5–0, Cleveland scored single runs in the fifth and seventh innings. In the ninth, Casey Blake, Coco Crisp and Ron Belliard each hit solo home runs to tie the contest 5–5. Victor Martinez broke the deadlock with a two-run single in the 11th.

Martinez batted .305 with 20 homers and 80 runs-batted-in during the 2005 season.

APRIL 11 The Indians lose the home opener 2–1 to the White Sox before 42,461 at Jacobs Field.

Reliever Rafael Betancourt started the 2005 season with nine consecutive hitless and scoreless innings while retiring 27 of the first 28 batters to face him.

MAY 5 Jason Davis jaws with Twins outfielder Shannon Stewart during a 9–0 Indians loss in Minneapolis. Both benches emptied when Davis and Stewart engaged in a confrontation near the plate after Stewart scored in the seventh. Davis had hit Stewart with a pitch, but no punches were thrown.

MAY 6 The Indians score seven runs in the first inning and defeat the Rangers 8–6 in Arlington. Cleveland batters collected six hits in a row, including homers by Travis Hafner and Jhonny Peralta.

The unusual spelling of Peralta's first name is attributed to a clerical error on his birth certificate in his native Dominican Republic. The letter combinations "Jh" or "Gh" are sometimes used in the Spanish language to represent the English "J" sound, as the letter "J" in Spanish is pronounced as an English "H."

MAY 9 Kevin Millwood allows only one hit in eight innings of a 3–0 win over the Los Angeles Angels of Anaheim in Anaheim. Millwood retired 18 batters in a row after Jose Molina's double in the third inning. Bob Wickman surrendered a single to Chone Figgins in the ninth.

MAY 17 The first four Indians batters combine to hit for the cycle off Angels pitcher Erwin Santana to spark a 13–5 win at Jacobs Field. It was Santana's major league debut.

Grady Sizemore led off with a triple, followed by Coco Crisp's double, a single by Travis Hafner, and a home run from Ben Broussard. The Indians collected only three runs from the outburst because Crisp was out at third when he missed the base while trying to stretch his double into a triple.

MAY 20 The Indians won-lost record falls to 17–23 with a 2–1 loss to the Reds in Cincinnati. The defeat put the Tribe 12 games behind the White Sox.

MAY 21 C. C. Sabathia hits his first career homer and is the winning pitcher in a 5–3 decision over the Reds in Cincinnati.

One of the reasons for the success of the Indians in 2005 was the health of the pitching staff as five hurlers combined to start 158 of the club's 162 games. The five were Jake Westbrook (34 starts), Cliff Lee (32), C. C. Sabathia (31), Scott Elarton (31), and Kevin Millwood (30). The other four starting assignments were taken by Jason Davis in May and June while Millwood spent 21 days on the disabled list with an elbow injury.

MAY 23 The Indians defeat the Twins 2–1 at Jacobs Field in a game that passes without incident following a letter of admonishment sent by the Commissioner's office. Because the two clubs had engaged in several bench-clearing incidents over the previous seasons, Bud Selig warned the managers and players to behave or there would be serious consequences.

JUNE 3 Orlando Hernandez of the White Sox hits a major league record four batters with pitches but manages to defeat the Indians 6–4 in Chicago. Hernandez struck Travis Hafner twice and Alex Cora and Ben Broussard once each.

JUNE 7 The Indians play the Padres in San Diego for the first time, and win 2–0 in 11 innings. The runs scored on an error by shortstop Khalil Greene and an RBI-single from Victor Martinez. Cliff Lee (seven innings), Arthur Rhodes (1⅓ innings), Bobby Howry (one-third of an inning), Rafael Betancourt (one inning), and Bob Wickman (one inning) combined on the shutout.

On the same day, the Indians selected outfielder Trevor Crowe from the University of Arizona with their first pick in the amateur draft. The first 2005 draftee to reach the majors was third rounder Jensen Lewis.

JUNE 10 The Indians play the Giants for the first time during the regular season and win 10–2 in San Francisco.

JUNE 15 Aaron Boone hits a walk-off homer in the 11th inning to defeat the Rockies 7–6 at Jacobs Field.

JUNE 17 Trailing 3–0, the Indians explode for ten runs in the third inning and defeat the Diamondbacks 13–6 at Jacobs Field. Jhonny Peralta and Grady Sizemore hit consecutive homers during the big inning, and Casey Blake drove in three runs with a pair of hits.

JUNE 19 The Indians run their winning streak to nine games with a 3–2 decision over the Diamondbacks at Jacobs Field.

The winning streak vaulted the Indians into post-season contention. On June 19, the club had a 37–30 record. The Tribe was still 8½ games behind the White Sox in the AL Central but just a game back of the Twins in the wild card race.

JUNE 25 Ben Broussard hits two of the Indians five home runs during a 12–7 win over the Reds at Jacobs Field. The other three homers were struck by Victor Martinez, Travis Hafner, and Grady Sizemore.

The Indians were 15–3 against National League teams in 2005.

JUNE 28 The Indians score five runs in the ninth inning to beat the Red Sox 12–8 in Boston. Jhonny Peralta singled in the first run in the ninth on a 3–2 pitch to tie the score 8–8. Grady Sizemore and Casey Blake walked to load the bases. Travis Hafner followed with a grand slam off Kevin Foulke on an 0-and-2 change-up that reached the seats just inside the right field foul pole. The slam gave Hafner six RBIs during the game.

JULY 4 Travis Hafner hits two homers and drives in five runs during a 9–6 victory over the Tigers in the day game of a day-night double header at Jacobs Field. Hafner homered again in the second tilt, won by Cleveland 3–0.

Hafner hit .305 with 33 home runs and 108 RBIs in 2005.

JULY 8 Grady Sizemore hits the first pitch of the game from Chien-Ming Wang for a home run, but the Indians lose 5–4 to the Yankees in New York. On the same day, Rafael Betancourt was suspended by Major League Baseball for ten days after testing positive for a banned performance-enhancing substance.

In his first full season in the majors, Sizemore batted .289, hit 22 homers, and scored 111 runs. Sizemore was optioned to Triple-A Buffalo on March 28 and was slated to begin the season in the minors but was brought back three days later when Juan Gonzalez went on the disabled list.

JULY 9 Jose Hernandez hits two homers and drives in five runs during an 8–7 triumph over the Yankees in New York.

JULY 18 The Indians trade Jody Gerut to the Cubs for Jason Dubois.

JULY 21 The Indians score seven runs in the seventh inning and defeat the Royals 10–1 at Jacobs Field.

The Indians headed into the game with a 48–47 record and were 15 games behind the White Sox. In the wild card race, Cleveland stood in sixth place, 3½ games out.

AUGUST 5 All nine runs of a 9–6 win over the Tigers in Detroit are scored in the sixth inning. The Indians collected ten hits in the big inning, including home runs and three RBIs from both Casey Blake and Coco Crisp.

AUGUST 9 Trailing 7–2, the Indians erupt for 11 runs in the ninth inning to defeat the Royals 13–7 at Kauffman Stadium. Jhonny Peralta's three-run homer capped the inning. The Indians scored eight unearned runs with the help of three Kansas City errors.

August 10 Grady Sizemore hits a grand slam and an RBI-single to account for five runs-batted-in during the Indians 6–1 win over the Royals in Kansas City. The slam was struck off Zack Greinke in the second inning.

August 11 Jeff Leifer hits a grand slam off D. J. Carrasco in the seventh inning for the only four Indians runs in a 4–2 win over the Royals in Kansas City.

The grand slam was the only homer hit by Liefer in 19 games and 56 at-bats as a member of the Indians.

August 19 Ben Broussard hits a walk-off homer leading off the tenth inning to defeat the Orioles 5–4 at Jacobs Field.

August 22 The Indians break a 4–4 tie with seven runs in the seventh inning to beat the Devil Rays 11–4 in St. Petersburg.

August 25 The Indians score seven runs in the third inning to take a 10–1 lead and defeat the Devil Rays 12–4 in St. Petersburg. Ron Belliard hit a grand slam off Travis Harper. Victor Martinez collected four hits in five at-bats.

August 26 Victor Martinez has a four-hit game for the second day in a row, leading the Indians to a 9–3 win over the Blue Jays in Toronto. Martinez collected a home run, a double, and two singles in five at-bats and also scored four runs.

August 29 On the day that Hurricane Katrina strikes the Gulf Coast of Alabama, Mississippi, and Louisiana and a day before New Orleans is flooded by the storm, the Tigers score five runs in the top of the first inning before the Indians respond with six in their half and win 10–9 at Jacobs Field.

September 7 C. C. Sabathia retires the last 21 batters to face him while pitching a four-hit complete game to defeat the Tigers 4–1 in Detroit.

September 8 The Indians take the lead in the wild card race with a 4–2 win over the Tigers at Jacobs Field.

September 11 The first four Indians batters combine to hit for the cycle, sparking a 12–4 win over the Twins at Jacobs Field. The feat was accomplished on the first nine pitches thrown by Carlos Silva of the Twins. Grady Sizemore led off with a triple, followed by a double from Coco Crisp, Jhonny Peralta's single, and a home run from Victor Martinez. The Indians scored four runs in the first inning and added six more in the second.

The September 11 game was the second time in 2005 that the Indians pulled off the unusual achievement of hitting for the cycle by the first four batters of the first inning. The first was on May 17.

September 13 A 5–2 win over the Athletics at Jacobs Field is delayed 21 minutes in the sixth inning when a computer shuts down and causes several of the toothbrush-shaped light towers to go dark.

September 18 The Indians hammer the Royals 11–0 at Jacobs Field.

SEPTEMBER 21 Travis Hafner homers for the fourth game in a row to lead the Indians to an 8–0 win over the White Sox in Chicago.

The victory completed a series at U. S. Cellular Field in which the Indians won two of three to cut the White Sox margin in the AL Central to 2½ games. The Sox had led the Indians by 15 games on August 1.

SEPTEMBER 22 The Indians trim the White Sox lead in the AL Central to 1½ games with an 11–6 win over the Royals in Kansas City. A two-run homer by Coco Crisp in the seventh inning put Cleveland ahead 7–6. Travis Hafner homered for the fifth game in a row. Grady Sizemore collected five hits, including two doubles, in five at-bats.

SEPTEMBER 23 Travis Hafner homers in his sixth straight game, one shy of Jim Thome's club record, to lead the Indians to a 7–6 triumph over the Royals in Kansas City.

SEPTEMBER 24 The Indians clobber the Royals 11–4 in Kansas City.

The win was Cleveland 17th in their last 19 games. The club had a record of 44–15 since July 21 and 92–63 overall in the 2005 season. The September 24 victory kept the Tribe 1½ games behind the White Sox in the AL Central and maintained a 1½-game advantage in the wild card race ahead of the Yankees and Red Sox, who were tied for first in the Eastern Division. The Indians had seven games left on the schedule, with one against the lowly Royals in Kansas City, three versus the woeful Devil Rays in Cleveland, and three more at Jacobs Field in what appeared to be a pennant showdown with the White Sox.

SEPTEMBER 25 The Indians blow a 3–0 sixth-inning lead and suffer a crucial 5–4 loss to the Royals in Kansas City. The winning run scored in the ninth inning when Grady Sizemore lost a fly ball hit by Paul Phillips in the sun.

The loss started a three-game losing streak, each a one-run decision. The Indians fell to the Devil Rays 5–4 on September 27 and 1–0 on September 28 at Jacobs Field. It was part of an unfortunate trend. The Indians were 22–36 (.379) in one-run games in 2005 and 71–33 (.683) in contests decided by two runs or more. The 304-percentage point differential between the Indians one-run record and in games decided by more than one run is the fourth largest in major league history and the largest since 1963. The 1948 world champion Indians had the second largest differential in the category with a 10–20 (.333) record in one-run contests and a 87–38 (.696) won-lost ledger in those with a margin of two runs one more.

SEPTEMBER 29 The Indians snap their three-game losing streak by beating the Devil Rays 6–0 at Jacobs Field. On the same day, the White Sox clinched the AL Central with a 4–2 victory over the Tigers in Detroit. Heading into the final three games of the season, the Indians were tied with the Red Sox for first place in the wild card race.

SEPTEMBER 30 The Indians lose 3–2 in 13 innings to the White Sox at Jacobs Field. The defeat dropped Cleveland one game behind the Red Sox in the wild card chase with two contests left on the schedule.

The Indians were 5–14 against the White Sox in 2005.

October 1 The Indians lose yet another one-run decision with a 4–3 defeat at the hands of the White Sox at Jacobs Field. It was the Tribe's fifth defeat by one run in a span of six games. Cleveland stayed alive in the wild card race, however, because the Red Sox lost 8–4 to the Yankees in Boston.

October 2 The Indians close out the 2005 season with a 3–1 loss to the White Sox at Jacobs Field. The Red Sox clinched the wild card berth with a 10–1 triumph over the Yankees at Fenway Park. The Indians ended the season two games behind Boston in the wild card race, and six back of the White Sox in the Central Division.

December 5 The Indians sign Paul Byrd, most recently with the Angels, as a free agent.

December 19 The Indians sign Danny Graves, most recently with the Mets, as a free agent.

December 29 Kevin Millwood signs with the Rangers as a free agent.

2006

Season in a Sentence

Expected to contend for the AL Central pennant, the Indians disappoint their fans with a 78–84 season.

Finish • Won • Lost • Pct • GB

Finish	Won	Lost	Pct	GB
Fourth	78	84	.481	18.0

Manager

Eric Wedge

Stats

Stats	Indians	AL	Rank
Batting Avg:	.280	.275	4
On-Base Pct:	.349	.339	3
Slugging Pct:	.457	.437	3
Home Runs:	196		5
Stolen Bases:	55		12
ERA:	4.41	4.56	7
Fielding Avg:	.981	.984	13
Runs Scored:	870		2
Runs Allowed:	782		7

Starting Line-up

Victor Martinez, c
Ben Broussard, 1b
Ron Belliard, 2b
Aaron Boone, 3b
Jhonny Peralta, ss
Jason Michaels, lf
Grady Sizemore, cf
Casey Blake, rf
Travis Hafner, dh
Joe Inglett, 2b

Pitchers

Jake Westbrook, sp
Cliff Lee, sp
C. C. Sabathia, sp
Paul Byrd, sp
Fernando Cabrera, rp
Rafael Betancourt, rp

Attendance

1,997,995 (11th in AL)

Club Leaders

Batting Avg:	Victor Martinez	.316
On-Base Pct:	Travis Hafner	.439
Slugging Pct:	Travis Hafner	.659
Home Runs:	Travis Hafner	42
RBIs:	Travis Hafner	117
Runs:	Grady Sizemore	134
Stolen Bases:	Grady Sizemore	22
Wins:	Jake Westbrook	22
Strikeouts:	C. C. Sabathia	172
ERA:	C. C. Sabathia	3.22
Saves:	Bob Wickman	15

JANUARY 6 The Indians sign Todd Hollandsworth, most recently with the Braves, as a free agent.

JANUARY 27 The Indians trade Arthur Rhodes to the Phillies for Jason Michaels, then deal Coco Crisp, David Riske, and Josh Bard to the Red Sox for Andy Marte, Kelly Shoppach, and a player to be named later. On the same day, Jose Hernandez signed with the Pirates as a free agent.

Grady Sizemore has captured the hearts of Indians fans with his hustle and winning attitude. A dirty uniform is not unusual, given his scrappy style of play.

APRIL 2 The Indians open the season with a 10–4 loss to the White Sox before a crowd in Chicago and a Sunday night national television audience on ESPN2. The score was 3–3 in the fourth inning when rain stopped play for two hours and 57 minutes. The game ended at 2:10 a.m. Cleveland time. Eduardo Perez hit a home run in his Indians debut.

Following the Opening Day loss, the Indians won six games in a row. It marked the high point of the season, as the club was 41–63 over the next 104 games.

April 7 In the home opener, Casey Blake hits a grand slam off Kyle Lohse in the fifth inning of an 11–7 win over the Twins before 42,445 at Jacobs Field. Travis Hafner contributed two homers and two singles and scored four runs.

On the same day, the Indians traded Brandon Phillips to the Reds for Jeff Stevens. The deal may turn out to be one of the worst in Indians history. Phillips never fulfilled his promise with the Indians, batting .206 with six homers in 135 games and 432 at-bats over four seasons. He was 24 at the time of the trade. Phillips immediately blossomed in Cincinnati. In his first two seasons with the Reds, he hit .282 and struck 47 homers. In 2007, Phillips became only the second second baseman in major league history to collect at least 30 homers and steal at least 30 bases in a season.

April 17 The Indians bang out 20 hits and crush the Orioles 15–1 in Baltimore.

April 27 Ben Broussard erupts for eight runs-batted-in during a 15–3 pounding of the Red Sox at Jacobs Field. Broussard collected two homers and two singles in five at-bats. He hit a grand slam in the first inning off Josh Beckett.

May 1 Travis Hafner hits a grand slam off Brandon McCarthy in the seventh inning, but the Indians lose 8–6 to the White Sox at Jacobs Field.

Hafner's nickname is "Pronk." It was coined by a scout during Hafner's younger days. The scout described Hafner as "half-project, half-donkey" after watching him run the bases. In April 2006, O'Malley's Chocolates of Cleveland unveiled the "Pronk Bar," named in honor of Hafner.

May 3 The Indians explode for nine runs in the seventh inning of a 14–3 trouncing of the Athletics in Oakland.

Hafner hit seven home runs in the first 11 games of the 2006 season, and then homered in four consecutive games from May 1 through May 4. He finished the season with 42 homers, 117 RBIs, 100 runs scored, a .308 batting average, and a league-leading slugging percentage of .659.

May 16 The Indians score three runs in the ninth inning with the help of two home runs to down the Royals 6–4 at Jacobs Field. Grady Sizemore homered to tie the game 4–4, and Travis Hafner provided a two-run, walk-off homer for the victory. The victory ended a six-game losing streak.

Sizemore finished the season with league-leading figures in runs (134) and doubles (53). He also hit .290 and collected 11 triples and 28 home runs.

May 17 Travis Hafner hits a grand slam off Jeremy Affeldt in the third inning of a 5–0 win over the Royals at Jacobs Field.

May 28 Jason Michaels hits a grand slam off Bobby Seay in the eighth inning of a 9–0 win over the Tigers in Detroit.

May 30 Indians pitcher Scott Sauerbeck is arrested along with a female companion named Lily Miller. Sauerbeck's 1966 Lincoln convertible, driven by Miller, was observed weaving at 3:45 a.m. in the Cleveland suburb of Avon Lake. Police alleged that Miller and Sauerbeck attempted to avoid arrest by parking the car and hiding in some bushes in a residential backyard. Miller was charged with drunk driving. Sauerbeck pleaded not guilty to obstructing official business and permitting someone intoxicated to drive his car. On July 11, 2006, he changed his plea to guilty and was fined $1,750, sentenced to a 30-day jail sentence, which was suspended provided he had no similar offenses for a year, and to perform community service in the form of speeches to students in three local high schools about alcohol abuse. The Indians released Sauerbeck shortly after his arrest, and he was signed by the Athletics.

June 1 The Indians outlast the White Sox 12–8 at Jacobs Field. Ronnie Belliard's three-run homer in the seventh inning gave Cleveland a 10–8 lead. Belliard fouled off five 1–2 pitches before connecting for the home run.

June 3 On his 29th birthday, Travis Hafner hits a grand slam, a double, and a single to drive in six runs, leading the Indians to a 14–2 thrashing of the Angels at Jacobs Field. The Indians scored eight unearned runs in the sixth inning. With two out and runners on second and third, Angels right fielder Vladimir Guerrero misplayed Ron Belliard's line drive. After a double, two walks, and another error, Hafner hit his grand slam off Brendan Donnelly.

June 6 In the first round of the amateur draft, the Indians select UCLA pitcher David Huff.

June 14 A Johnson vs. Johnson match-up results the clearing of both benches during a 6–1 Yankees win over the Indians in New York. In the sixth inning, Jason Johnson hit Jorge Posada in the elbow with a pitch and angry words were exchanged between the two. An inning later, Randy Johnson threw inside to Eduardo Perez, who pointed his bat at the pitcher and took a few steps toward the mound. Posada stepped in front as Perez as both dugouts emptied. No punches were thrown. Randy Johnson was suspended for five days for the incident.

June 16 The Indians play at Miller Park in Milwaukee for the first time and lose 5–4 to the Brewers.

June 30 Adam Dunn hits a two-out, walk-off grand slam off Bob Wickman in the ninth inning to give the Reds a 9–8 win over the Indians in Cincinnati. Cleveland led 7–0 in the eighth before the Reds mounted their comeback.

July 1 Travis Hafner hits a pinch-hit grand slam off Joe Mays in the fifth inning of a 12–7 win over the Reds in Cincinnati.

Hafner tied an Indians record for most grand slams in a season with four. It was set by Al Rosen in 1951.

July 4 The Indians collect 21 hits and clobber the Yankees 19–1 at Jacobs Field, ruining the 76th birthday of Yankees owner and Cleveland native George Steinbrenner. Cleveland scored nine times in the fifth inning to take a 16–1 lead. Victor Martinez collected five hits, including a double and a home run, in six at-bats. The Indians hit six homers in all. Jhonny Peralta and Travis Hafner each hit two home runs and Ron Belliard one.

JULY 7 Travis Hafner sets an Indians record for most grand slams in a season and becomes the first player in major league history to hit five slams before the All-Star break. Hafner cleared the bases with a shot off Kris Benson in the second inning of a 9–0 win over the Orioles at Jacobs Field.

JULY 16 Both lead-off batters start the first inning with home runs during a 5–2 loss to the Twins in Minneapolis. In the top of the first, Grady Sizemore homered off Carlos Silva. In the bottom half, Luis Castillo went deep on Jeremy Sowers.

JULY 20 The Indians trade Bob Wickman to the Braves for Max Ramirez.

JULY 22 The Indians trounce the Twins 11–0 at Jacobs Field.

JULY 23 A total of 17 Indians batters strike out against five Twins pitchers during a 3–1 loss to the Twins at Jacobs Field. Minnesota starter Francisco Liriano led the way by fanning ten in five innings.

JULY 25 The Indians score seven runs in the first inning off Kenny Rogers and defeat the Tigers 12–7 in Detroit.

JULY 26 The Indians trade Ben Broussard to the Mariners for Shin-Soo Choo.

JULY 28 Jeremy Sowers pitches his second consecutive shutout and Shin-Soo Choo hits his first career homer in his Cleveland debut for the lone run of a 1–0 win over the Mariners at Jacobs Field. Choo's homer was struck in the sixth inning off Felix Hernandez on a 3–0 pitch with two out.

JULY 30 Entering the game with the score tied 3–3, rookie pitcher Fausto Carmona gives up four runs in the ninth inning and the Indians lose 7–3 to the Mariners at Jacobs Field.

On the same day, the Indians traded Ronnie Belliard to the Cardinals for Hector Luna.

JULY 31 Fausto Carmona is victimized in the ninth inning for the second game in a row when David Ortiz hits a three-run, walk-off homer to life the Red Sox to a 9–8 win over the Indians at Jacobs Field.

AUGUST 2 Fausto Carmona is stunned again with a walk-off hit in the ninth inning as Mark Loretta's bases-loaded, two-run double gives the Red Sox a 5–4 victory over the Indians at Fenway Park. Carmona struck out the first two batters in the ninth before hitting Doug Mirabelli and Alex Gonzalez with consecutive pitches and walking Kevin Youkilis.

AUGUST 3 Trailing 3–1, the Indians score six runs in the sixth inning and go on to defeat the Red Sox 7–6 in Boston. The big blow was a grand slam by Shin-Soo Chin off Josh Beckett. Jake Westbrook was the winning pitcher despite allowing 15 hits in eight innings.

August 4 Fausto Carmona becomes the losing pitcher for the fourth time in less than a week by allowing a two-out, two-run homer to Craig Monroe of the Tigers, leading to a 7–6 Indians loss in Detroit.

August 8 The Indians won-loss record in the 2006 season drops to 47–64 with a 5–4 loss to the Angels at Jacobs Field.

The Indians were 18–26 in one-run games in 2006. In 2005 and 2006 combined, the club was 40–62 in contests decided by a single run.

August 9 The Indians trade Todd Hollandsworth to the Reds for a player to be named later.

August 11 The Indians score three runs in the ninth inning on Grady Sizemore's bases loaded walk-off triple to defeat the Royals 4–3 at Jacobs Field.

August 13 The Indians score 11 runs in the first inning and wallop the Royals 13–0 at Jacobs Field. The first ten Indians reached base and scored off Kansas City starter Luke Hudson, who gave up all eleven runs, ten of them earned, in one-third of an inning. The ten to reach base were Grady Sizemore (walk), Jason Michaels (single), Travis Hafner (walk), Victor Martinez (single), Shin-Soo Choo (double), Ryan Garko (single), Jhonny Peralta (error), Joel Inglett (single), Andy Marte (walk), and Sizemore (single). Hafner hit a grand slam during his second plate appearance of the big inning. It was his sixth slam of the year, which tied a major league record set by Don Mattingly in 1987.

Victor Martinez hit .316 with 16 home runs in 2006.

August 20 Jhonny Peralta hits a grand slam off Brian Meadows in the sixth inning of a 9–4 win over the Devil Rays in St. Petersburg.

August 23 The Indians overcome a nine-run deficit to defeat the Royals 15–13 in ten innings in Kansas City. The Royals scored ten runs in the first inning to take a 10–1 lead. Paul Byrd gave up nine of the ten tallies, three of them earned, along with eight hits in one-third of an inning. Cleveland fought back with two in the third, three in the fourth, one in the fifth, and two in the sixth to close to within a run at 10–9, but Kansas City scored three times in their half of the sixth. It was still 13–9 when the Tribe scored four runs in the ninth to send the contest into extra innings. In the tenth, Grady Sizemore was hit by a pitch, moved to second on a sacrifice, and scored on Ryan Garko's two-out single. Hector Luna added a run-scoring single and finished with four RBIs.

August 30 Jhonny Peralta hits a walk-off homer with two out in the tenth inning to beat the Royals 3–2 at Jacobs Field.

The Indians posted a losing record in 2006 despite outscoring the opposition 870–782. The 870 runs in offense represented an increase from 790 runs accumulated in 2005. The club's ERA went from a league-leading 3.61 in 2005 to 4.41 in 2006, however.

September 2 Indians left fielder Kevin Kouzmanoff hits a grand slam on the first pitch thrown to him as a major leaguer, sparking the Indians to a 6–5 win over the Rangers in

Arlington. The blast was struck off Edison Volquez. Kouzmanoff hit his homer only a few hours after being called up from Triple-A Buffalo. He subbed as the designated hitter for Travis Hafner, who was scratched from the line-up with a bruised hand.

Kouzmanoff became only the third player with a grand slam in his first big league at-bat. The first was Bill Duggleby of the Phillies in 1898 and the second was Jeremy Hermida of the Marlins 107 years later in 2005. Kouzmanoff was the only one to accomplish the feat on the first pitch of his first at-bat. He was also just the fourth player with a grand slam in his first game in the majors. Bobby Bonds of the Giants cleared the bases with a homer in the third at-bat of his debut in 1968.

SEPTEMBER 5 A grand slam by Andy Marte off Jeremy Accardo in the eighth inning snaps a 2–2 tie and leads the Indians to a 7–2 win over the Blue Jays in Toronto.

SEPTEMBER 24 During an eight-run sixth inning, Casey Blake hits a grand slam off Boone Logan as the Indians thrash the White Sox 14–1 at Jacobs Field.

The grand slam was the 14th by the Indians during the 2006 season to tie the major league record set by the 2000 Oakland Athletics. Travis Hafner hit six of the 14 slams, and Blake contributed two. The rest were struck by Shin-Soo Chin, Ben Broussard, Andy Marte, Kevin Kouzmanoff, Jhonny Peralta, and Jason Michaels.

DECEMBER 8 The Indians sign Roberto Hernandez, most recently with the Mets, as a free agent.

DECEMBER 12 The Indians sign Joe Borowski, most recently with the Marlins, as a free agent.

Borowski saved 45 games in 2007, which led the American League and was one shy of the club record of 46, set by Jose Mesa in 1995. Proving that the number of saves can often be an overrated statistic, Borowski had an ERA of 5.07. Borowski's earned run average is the highest ever by a league-leader in saves.

DECEMBER 29 Aaron Boone signs as a free agent with the Marlins.

2007

Season in a Sentence

After a snowstorm wipes out the opening home stand, the Indians win the AL Central before blowing a chance at reaching the World Series by squandering a three games to one lead over the Red Sox in the ALCS.

Finish • Won • Lost • Pct • GB

Finish	Won	Lost	Pct	GB
First	96	66	.593	+8.0

American League Division Series

The Indians defeated the New York Yankees three games to one.

American League Championship Series

The Indians lost four games to three to the Boston Red Sox.

Manager

Eric Wedge

Stats

Stats	Indians	AL	Rank
Batting Avg:	.268	.271	7
On-Base Pct:	.343	.338	5
Slugging Pct:	.428	.423	5
Home Runs:	187		3
Stolen Bases:	72		12
ERA:	4.05	4.52	3
Fielding Avg:	.985	.983	6
Runs Scored:	811		6
Runs Allowed:	704		3

Starting Line-up

Victor Martinez, c
Ryan Garko, 1b
Josh Barfield, 2b
Casey Blake, 3b
Jhonny Peralta, ss
Jason Michaels, lf
Grady Sizemore, cf
Trot Nixon, rf
Travis Hafner, dh
Franklin Gutierrez, rf
Chris Gomez, 1b

Pitchers

C. C. Sabathia, sp
Fausto Carmona, sp
Paul Byrd, sp
Jake Westbrook, sp
Cliff Lee, sp
Joe Borowski, rp
Rafael Betancourt, rp
Tom Mastny, rp
Aaron Fultz, rp
Rafael Perez, rp

Attendance

2,275,911 (ninth in AL)

Club Leaders

Batting Avg:	Victor Martinez	.301
On-Base Pct:	Grady Sizemore	.390
Slugging Pct:	Victor Martinez	.505
Home Runs:	Victor Martinez	25
RBIs:	Victor Martinez	114
Runs:	Grady Sizemore	118
Stolen Bases:	Grady Sizemore	33
Wins:	C. C. Sabathia	19
	Fausto Carmona	19
Strikeouts:	C. C. Sabathia	209
ERA:	Fausto Carmona	3.06
Saves:	Joe Borowski	45

JANUARY 19 The Indians sign Trot Nixon, most recently with the Red Sox, as a free agent.

APRIL 2 In the first game of the season, Grady Sizemore homers on the first pitch from Jose Contreras to spark a 12–5 rout of the White Sox in Chicago. The Indians scored five runs in the first inning, four in the second and two in the third for an 11–3 lead. C. C. Sabathia was the winning pitcher. In his Indians debut, Trot Nixon collected three hits, including a double, and scored three runs. Victor Martinez and Jhonny Peralta each drove in three runs.

APRIL 4 In the second game of the season, left fielder Jason Michaels saves an 8–7 victory over the White Sox in Chicago by making a game-ending catch on Joe Crede's drive with two out in the ninth inning while falling down backward on the warning track. Grady Sizemore hit a two-run, two-out homer in the seventh with the Indians trailing 7–6.

Michaels's grandfather, John Michaels, played for the 1932 Boston Red Sox.

APRIL 6 In the home opener, the Indians are one strike from a 4–0 victory over the Mariners when the contest is stopped by snow. There was a 57-minute delay at the start, and after the first pitch, and two more stoppages of 22 minutes and 17 minutes because of the wintry conditions. The Indians led 4–0 heading into the fifth, and Paul Byrd had a no-hitter in progress. Byrd walked the bases full and had a 1–2 count on Seattle's Jose Lopez with two out. The Indians pitcher was just one strike from the contest being declared official when Mariners manager Mike Hargrove, who was known as the "Human Rain Delay" during his playing days (see May 2, 1980), came out of the dugout to insist that the umpires stop the game again because of the limited visibility caused by the falling snow. An animated argument followed, and during the dispute, the snow intensified and the umpires halted play. That brought out Eric Wedge, who became involved in a heated discussion with Hargrove. As he left the field, Hargrove verbally sparred with fans. After another wait of an hour and 17 minutes, the game was called and a day-night double header was planned for the following day.

APRIL 7 A forecast of more snow causes the postponement of the day-night double header against the Mariners at Jacobs Field. Another day-night twin bill was re-scheduled for April 8.

APRIL 8 For the second day in a row, snow and cold weather causes the postponement of a double header between the Indians and Mariners at Jacobs Field. Yet another double header was slated for April 9 to try to salvage two games of the four-game series.

APRIL 9 The Indians and Mariners are unable to play again because of the winter-like conditions that lingered in the Cleveland area. None of the four games of the series were played to a conclusion. The Angels were scheduled to come to Cleveland for three games from April 10 through April 12 with the prospect of more cold weather. In addition, the turf at Jacobs Field was in an unplayable condition because of the snow. It was decided to move the games to Miller Park in Milwaukee. Tickets were sold for $10. Three of the four postponed games against the Mariners were made up on what had been off days on May 21, June 11, and August 30 at Jacobs Field, with another played in Seattle as part of a double header on September 25.

APRIL 10 The Indians play their "home" opener before 19,031 at Miller Park in Milwaukee and beat the Angels 7–6.

The Indians won two of the three games in Milwaukee.

APRIL 13 The Indians finally play an official game at Jacobs Field and lose 6–4 to the White Sox before a crowd of 16,789.

APRIL 14 Paul Byrd pitches six strong innings in his first start of the season and is the winning pitcher in a 4–0 decision over the White Sox at Jacobs Field. He had come within one strike of an abbreviated no-hitter in the Cleveland opener before it was snowed out (see April 6, 2007). Byrd's first pitch against the White Sox was a called strike, which was exactly what he needed eight days earlier to make it an official game.

Byrd is known for being a celebrity look-alike and for his "old-fashioned" delivery to the plate. He bears a striking resemblance to actor Kelsey Grammer, which has earned Byrd the nickname "Frasier." Like many pitchers of past generations, he swings his arms back prior to going into the full wind-up.

APRIL 15 The Indians only hit is a double by Grady Sizemore off Jose Contreras leading off the first inning, but the club defeats the White Sox 2–1 at Jacobs Field. After the double, Sizemore scored on a passed ball and a ground out. In the fourth, Cleveland scored another run on three walks and an error. C. C. Sabathia was the winning pitcher.

The date marked the 60th anniversary of Jackie Robinson's major league debut, and many players around the major leagues honored Robinson by wearing number 42. Indians players wearing number 42 were Sabathia, Sizemore and Ron Belliard.

APRIL 19 Three days after 32 die in a shooting on the campus of Virginia Tech, Joe Borowski gives up six runs in the ninth inning to lose 8–6 in New York. Borowski retired the first two batters to face him before the roof caved in. Josh Phelps homered to make the score 6–3. Three singles and a walk scored two more runs. Alex Rodriguez ended to contest with a three-run homer to center field. Borowski was one strike from a victory three times in the inning.

Matt Underwood moved from radio to television in 2007. He had been part of the radio crew from 1994 through 2006. Underwood joined Jim Donovan and Rick Manning in the TV booth. Tom Hamilton and Mike Hegan continued their duties on radio,

APRIL 22 The Indians score four runs in the ninth inning, the last three on a homer by Ryan Garko, to defeat the Devil Rays 6–4 in St. Petersburg.

APRIL 24 Fausto Carmona ends his 11-game losing streak, dating back to 2006, by defeating the Twins 5–3 in Minneapolis.

Carmona was a 22-year-old rookie in 2006 and compiled a 1–10 record and an ERA of 5.42 while making seven starts and 31 relief appearances. Pitching exclusively as a starter in 2007, he recovered from the debacle by posting a 19–8 record and a 3.06 earned run average.

APRIL 25 Cleveland pitchers combine to strike out 19 batters during an 11-inning, 8–7 win over the Rangers at Jacobs Field. The strikeouts were recorded by C. C. Sabathia (eight), Tom Mastny (three), Rafael Betancourt (one), Joe Borowski (two), and Fernando Cabrera (five).

Sabathia was 19–7 with a 3.21 ERA in 2007. He struck out 209 batters while walking only 37 in 241 innings. His numbers earned him the Cy Young award.

April 28 The umpires retroactively add a run during a 7–4 loss to the Orioles at Jacobs Field. Baltimore led 2–1 in the top of the third with Nick Markakis the runner on third base and Miguel Tejada on first and one out. Ramon Hernandez's line drive to center field was caught, and Markakis tagged up and headed for home. Tejada was around second when the ball was caught and was thrown out tying to get back to first. It appeared that Markakis crossed the plate before Tejada was called out at first, but home plate umpire Marvin Hudson waved off the run. After the Indians scored in the fifth to tie the score 2–2, it was announced in the bottom of the sixth that the umpires had changed their mind about the play and that the Orioles run in the third counted, giving Baltimore a 3–2 lead. The Indians played under protest, but after a review by the Commissioner's office, the protest was denied.

May 6 Trot Nixon collects five hits, including a double, in five at-bats during a 9–6 win over the Orioles in Baltimore.

May 15 The Indians rout the Twins 15–7 at Jacobs Field. Cleveland scored six runs in the first inning, three in the second, and six in the sixth.

May 17 Back-to-back homers by Victor Martinez and Ryan Garko off Johan Santana in the seventh inning accounts for the only runs of a 2–0 victory over the Twins at Jacobs Field. Fausto Carmona pitched his first career shutout.

June 1 The Indians score five runs in the ninth inning to stun the Tigers 12–11 at Jacobs Field. The five runs scored on five hits and two walks. Victor Martinez hit a three-run homer to pull Cleveland within a run. Josh Barfield and David Delucci drove in the tying and winning runs with two-out singles.

Martinez hit .301 with 25 homers and 114 RBIs in 2007.

June 5 Franklin Gutierrez hits a home run off Jorge De La Rosa in the third inning to account for the lone run of a 1–0 victory over the Royals at Jacobs Field. C. C. Sabathia pitched the shutout.

June 7 In the first round of the amateur draft, the Indians select third baseman Beau Mills from Lewis-Clark State College of Idaho.

June 15 The Indians play the Braves at Jacobs Field for the first time during the regular season and win 5–4.

June 17 Casey Blake runs his hitting streak to 26 games during a 5–2 win over the Braves at Jacobs Field.

June 20 Trailing 4–2, the Indians break loose with eight runs in the sixth inning and beat the Phillies 10–6 at Jacobs Field. Casey Blake put the Indians into the lead with a two-run single.

June 22 The Indians play in the city of Washington for the first time since 1971 and lose 4–1 to the Nationals at RFK Stadium.

June 23 Victor Martinez hits a three-run homer in the ninth inning to defeat the Nationals 4–3 in Washington.

June 26 The Indians explode for five runs in the ninth inning for an 8–5 triumph over the Athletics at Jacobs Field. Travis Hafner drove in two runs with a double to tie the score 5–5. Kelly Shoppach broke the deadlock with a three-run, pinch-hit home run.

June 29 Making the first start of his big league career, left fielder Ben Francisco hits a walk-off homer in the ninth inning to defeat the Devil Rays 2–1 at Jacobs Field. It was his first homer and second hit, and the blast came in his sixth at-bat in the majors.

July 2 The Indians score seven runs in the eighth inning of a 10–2 win over the Devil Rays in St. Petersburg. Grady Sizemore capped the scoring with a grand slam off Al Reyes.

Sizemore hit .277 with 118 runs scored and 24 homers in 2007.

July 3 Casey Blake hits a homer in the 11th inning to give the Indians a 5–4 win over the Tigers in Detroit.

The victory gave the Indians a 51–32 record and a two-game lead over the Tigers.

July 10 Victor Martinez hits a two-run pinch-hit homer off Billy Wagner in the eighth inning of a 5–4 American League victory in the All-Star Game, played at SBC Park in San Francisco. The home run by Martinez put the AL ahead 5–2.

July 17 Ryan Garko hits a game-tying, two-run homer in the ninth inning and singles home Jason Michaels for the winning run in the 11th to beat the White Sox 6–5 at Jacobs Field.

July 21 Cliff Lee hits Sammy Sosa in the head with a pitch in the third inning of an 8–5 loss to the Rangers in Arlington. The incident came on a night in which Sosa was honored for hitting his 600th career home run. The beaning sparked an altercation in the dugout between Lee and Victor Martinez.

Lee was sent to the minors six days later. He returned to the Indians on September 1 but was left off of the post-season roster.

July 25 Franklin Gutierrez hits a homer off Josh Beckett in the third inning to account for the lone run in a 1–0 victory over the Red Sox at Jacobs Field. It was the second time in 2007 that Gutierrez won a 1–0 game with a home run. Fausto Carmona (eight innings) and Joe Borowski (one inning) combined on the shutout.

July 27 The Indians trade Max Ramirez to the Rangers for Kenny Lofton. Lofton previously played for the Indians from 1992 through 1996 and from 1998 through 2001.

August 7 Jake Westbrook (eight innings) and Joe Borowski (one inning) combine on a two-hitter to defeat the White Sox 2–1 in Chicago. The only Sox hits were singles by Jerry Owens, leading off the first inning, and Scott Podsednik in the fifth. Westbrook retired 23 of the last 24 batters to face him. Grady Sizemore drove in both Cleveland runs with a fifth-inning single.

August 10 To honor Larry Doby and his role as the first African-American in the American League, all of the Indians wear Doby's number 14 during a 6–1 loss to the Yankees at Jacobs Field.

AUGUST 14 The Indians lose 6–2 to the Tigers in 11 innings at Jacobs Field.

The defeat dropped the Indians one game behind the Tigers in the AL Central. Cleveland had lost 22 of the last 36 games. Eric Wedge openly questioned his club's toughness, and the Indians responded by winning 27 of their the next 36 games.

Since 2001, his first year with the Tribe, C.C. Sabathia has posted a 100-63 record for a .613 winning percentage.

AUGUST 17 The Indians take over first place with a 2–1 win over the Devil Rays in St. Petersburg.

AUGUST 23 The Indians break open a scoreless tie with three runs in the tenth inning and beat the Tigers 3–1 in Detroit. Pinch-hitter Kenny Lofton broke the 0–0 deadlock by driving in a run with a two-out infield single.

AUGUST 31 Down 5–0 to the White Sox at Jacobs Field, the Indians score two runs in the sixth inning and six in the eighth to win 8–5. All six runs in the eighth scored with two out. Casey Blake broke the 5–5 tie with a three-run double.

SEPTEMBER 1 The Indians extend their winning streak to eight games with a 7–0 decision over the White Sox at Jacobs Field.

SEPTEMBER 4 Travis Hafner stars in an 11-inning, 7–5 win over the Twins in Minneapolis. Hafner smacked a two-run homer in the ninth to tie the score 5–5. It was his second home run of the game. In the 11th, Hafner broke the 5–5 tie with a sacrifice fly.

Hafner's 142 career homers through 2007 rank first among players born in North Dakota. His hometown is Jamestown.

SEPTEMBER 14 Casey Blake hits the first pitch of the ninth inning for a walk-off homer that gives the Indians a 5–4 victory over the Royals at Jacobs Field.

SEPTEMBER 17 Casey Blake strikes again with a walk-off homer in the 11th inning to defeat the Tigers 6–5 at Jacobs Field. Jhonny Peralta hit two homers, including one that capped a three-run eighth inning that tied the score 5–5.

SEPTEMBER 19 The Indians complete a three-game sweep of the Tigers with a 4–2 win at Jacobs Field. The victory gave Cleveland a 7½-game lead over Detroit in the AL Central.

The Indians had a streak of 21 wins in 26 games in August and September.

SEPTEMBER 23 The Indians clinch their first AL Central crown since 2001 by defeating the Athletics 6–2 at Jacobs Field.

After every one of Cleveland's home wins, the star player got smacked in the face during their TV interview by a whipped-cream pie, a tradition started by Trot Nixon. After the pennant-clinching victory, Nixon continued the custom by smashing pies in the faces of Eric Wedge and Mark Shapiro.

SEPTEMBER 26 In the first game of a double header at Safeco Field, the Indians score eight runs in the third inning and beat the Mariners 12–4. Luis Rivas tripled and homered during the big inning. The Indians collected five straight hits with two out. Cleveland was the "home" team and batted last in the opener. It was the first time in major league history that the original home team batted last in a contest transferred to another city. The game was one of those made up because of the snowstorm the opening weekend of the season. Seattle won the second tilt 3–2.

The Indians met the Yankees in the American League Division Series. Managed by Joe Torre, the Yankees had a record of 94–68 to make the playoffs for the 13th consecutive year. The 2007 Yanks reached the post-season as a wild card after winning the AL East nine straight seasons from 1998 through 2006. During the 2007 regular season, the Yankees were 6–0 against the Indians while compiling a 42–17 scoring margin.

OCTOBER 4 The Indians open the Division Series with a 12–3 win over the Yankees before 44,608 at Jacobs Field. Johnny Damon opened the first inning with a home run off C. C. Sabathia, but the Indians came back with three runs in the bottom half. Holding a slim 4–3 advantage, Cleveland erupted for five runs in the fifth inning. Asdrubal Cabrera, Travis Hafner, Victor Martinez, and Ryan Garko homered during the contest. Kenny Lofton collected two singles and a double and drove in four runs.

Lofton played in the post-season 11 times in 13 seasons with six different teams from 1995 through 2007. He appeared in the playoffs for the Indians in 1995, 1996, 1998, 1999, and 2007, the Braves in 1997, the Giants in 2002, the Cubs in 2003, the Yankees in 2004, and the Dodgers in 2006. Lofton moved around so often that a DHL television commercial was made about him depicting his equipment being moved from city to city.

October 5 With the help of some pesky bugs, the Indians beat the Yankees 2–1 in 11 innings in game two before a crowd of 44,732 at Jacobs Field. Fausto Carmona pitched nine innings and allowed only a run and three hits in a spectacular start. Rafael Perez followed with two innings of perfect relief. Cleveland trailed 1–0 heading into the eighth, however, because of a home run in the third inning by Melky Cabrera. In the eighth, a swarm of bugs invaded the field, forcing players to lather on bug spray and attempt to swat them away with minimal effect. With bugs sticking to his sweaty neck, Yankee reliever Joba Chamberlain walked two and threw a wild pitch, which led to a run that tied the score 1–1. By the 11th, the bugs had largely dissipated. After a walk, a single, a bunt, and an intentional walk loaded the bases with two out, Travis Hafner stroked a single on a 3–2 pitch, which scored the winning run.

The insects were midges, a gnat-like bug common to Cleveland. The bugs had invaded Jacobs Field on several previous occasions, but veteran observers said the flying nuisances were never as numerous as they were during the Yankees game and that it never happened at such an important moment.

October 7 The Indians lose game three by an 8–4 score to the Yankees in New York. Cleveland scored single runs in the first, second, and third innings off Roger Clemens for a 3–0 lead. Trot Nixon homered in the second, but the Yanks rallied, taking a 5–3 lead with four runs in the fifth.

October 8 The Indians advance to the American League Championship Series for the first time since 1998 with a 6–4 victory over the Yankees in New York. Grady Sizemore led off the first inning with a home run off Chien-Ming Wang, and the Indians added another run later in the inning on an RBI-single from Jhonny Peralta. Cleveland added two more tallies in the second and two in the fourth for a 6–1 lead, and the Tribe hung on for the win. Paul Byrd was the winning pitcher.

The Indians met the Boston Red Sox in the American League Championship Series. Managed by Terry Francona, the Sox were 96–66 in 2007 and won the AL East.

October 12 The Indians open the ALCS with a 10–3 loss to the Red Sox in Boston. The Sox broke a 1–1 tie with four runs in the third inning, and then added three more in the fifth. Travis Hafner homered in the losing cause.

October 13 The Indians erupt for seven runs in the 11th inning to defeat the Red Sox 13–6 at Fenway Park. Jhonny Peralta hit a three-run homer in the fourth inning for a 4–3 lead.

Grady Sizemore added a solo shot in the fifth for a two-run lead. In the bottom half of the inning, back-to-back homers by Manny Ramirez and Mike Lowell produced three runs, putting Cleveland behind 6–5. The Indians tied the contest in the sixth and there was no more scoring until the 11th. Trot Nixon broke the 6–6 tie with a single. Franklin Gutierrez capped the seven-run rally with a three-run homer.

OCTOBER 15 The Indians win game three with a 4–2 decision over the Red Sox before 44,402 at Jacobs Field. Kenny Lofton started the scoring with a two-run homer in the second inning that barely cleared the right field wall. Cleveland added two more runs in the fifth. Jake Westbrook pitched six shutout innings before allowing two runs in the seventh.

OCTOBER 16 The Indians move within one victory of a berth in the World Series by beating the Red Sox 7–3 before 44,008 at Jacobs Field. The Indians scored all seven of their runs in the fifth inning, while the Sox accounted for their tallies with three consecutive homers in the sixth. Casey Blake led off the fifth with a home run. Later, Jhonny Peralta lifted Cleveland to a 6–0 lead with a three-run homer. Blake drove in another run in his second at-bat in the inning with a single. Paul Byrd pitched five shutouts innings before allowing back-to-back homers to Kevin Youkilis and David Ortiz to open the sixth. Byrd was relieved by Jensen Lewis, who immediately gave up a home run to Manny Ramirez.

OCTOBER 18 The Red Sox remain alive in the ALCS by beating the Indians 7–1 before 44,558 at Jacobs Field. Their was a brief dust-up in the fifth inning with the Sox leading 2–1 when Kenny Lofton engaged in a shouting match with Boston pitcher Josh Beckett and both benches emptied. Boston broke open a close game with two runs in the seventh and three in the eighth.

OCTOBER 20 The Red Sox force a seventh game by pummeling the Indians 12–2 in Boston. J. D. Drew started the scoring with a grand slam off Fausto Carmona in the first inning. After Victor Martinez homered in the second, the Red Sox scored six times in the third.

OCTOBER 21 The dream of reaching the World Series evaporates with an 11–2 game seven loss to the Red Sox by an 11–2 score lose game seven at Fenway Park. The turning point came in the top of the sixth inning with Boston leading 3–2. Franklin Gutierrez ripped a ball over the third base bag that caromed off the curving wall in front of the box seats into short left field. Kenny Lofton rounded third only to be stopped by coach Joel Skinner. Lofton screeched to a halt, although it is likely he would have scored easily on the play. The Indians failed to score another run. The Sox blew open the game with two runs in the seventh and six in the eighth. After taking a three-games-to-one lead in the series, the Indians were outscored 30–5 over the last three contests.

Before the game, it was revealed that pitcher Paul Byrd used human growth hormone from 2002 through 2005. Byrd acknowledged use of the banned substance, but maintained it prescribed by a physician after he underwent Tommy John surgery. Byrd joined the Indians in 2006.

By the
Numbers

Indians All-Time Roster

Player Name	Position	Years Played
Paul Abbott	Pitcher	1993
Fred Abbott	Catcher	1903–1904
Al Aber	Pitcher	1950–1953
Bill Abernathie	Pitcher	1952
Ted Abernathy	Pitcher	1963–1964
Harry Ables	Pitcher	1909
Bert Adams	Catcher	1910–1912
Joe Adcock	First Base	1963
Tommie Agee	Outfielder	1962–1964
Luis Aguayo	Shortstop	1989
Hank Aguirre	Pitcher	1955–1957
Darrel Akerfelds	Pitcher	1987
Mike Aldrete	Outfielder	1991
Bob Alexander	Pitcher	1957
Gary Alexander	Catcher	1978–1980
Hugh Alexander	Outfielder	1937
Andy Allanson	Catcher	1986–1989
Johnny Allen	Pitcher	1936–1940
Bob Allen	Pitcher	1961–1967
Neil Allen	Pitcher	1989
Rod Allen	Designated Hitter	1988
Chad Allen	Outfielder	2002
Milo Allison	Outfielder	1916–1917
Beau Allred	Outfielder	1989–1991
Sandy Alomar	Catcher	1990–2000
Roberto Alomar	Second Base	1999–2001
Dell Alston	Outfielder	1979–1980
Dave Altizer	Shortstop	1908
Joe Altobelli	First Base	1955–1957
Luis Alvarado	Shortstop	1974
Max Alvis	Third Base	1962–1969
Ruben Amaro	Outfielder	1994–1995
Larry Andersen	Pitcher	1975–1979
Bud Anderson	Pitcher	1982–1983
Brian Anderson	Pitcher	1996–1997, 2003
Jason Anderson	Pitcher	2004
Dwain Anderson	Shortstop	1974
Brady Anderson	Outfielder	2001–2002
Ivy Andrews	Pitcher	1937
Nate Andrews	Pitcher	1940–1941
Johnny Antonelli	Pitcher	1961

Player Name	Position	Years Played
Luis Aponte	Pitcher	1984
Pete Appleton	Pitcher	1930–1932
Steve Arlin	Pitcher	1974
Mike Armstrong	Pitcher	1987
Jack Armstrong	Pitcher	1992
Brad Arnsberg	Pitcher	1992
Alan Ashby	Catcher	1973–1976
Ken Aspromonte	Second Base	1960–1962
Paul Assenmacher	Pitcher	1995–2000
Keith Atherton	Pitcher	1989
Michael Aubrey	First Base	2006–2008
Rick Austin	Pitcher	1970–1971
Chick Autry	Catcher	1926–1928
Bruce Aven	Outfielder	1997, 2002
Earl Averill	Catcher	1956–1958
Earl Averill	Outfielder	1929–1939
Bobby Avila	Second Base	1949–1958
Benny Ayala	Outfielder	1985
Dick Aylward	Catcher	1953
Joe Azcue	Catcher	1963–1969
Mike Bacsik	Pitcher	2001
Carlos Baerga	Second Base	1990–1996, 1999
Danys Baez	Pitcher	2001–2003
Jim Bagby	Pitcher	1916–1922
Jim Bagby	Pitcher	1941–1945
Scott Bailes	Pitcher	1986–1989
Steve Bailey	Pitcher	1967–1968
Harold Baines	Designated Hitter	1999
Bock Baker	Pitcher	1901
Howard Baker	Third Base	1912
Frank Baker	Outfielder	1969–1971
Neal Ball	Shortstop	1909–1912
Mark Ballinger	Pitcher	1971
Chris Bando	Catcher	1981–1988
George Banks	Third Base	1964–1966
Alan Bannister	Outfielder	1980–1983
Walter Barbare	Third Base	1914–1916
Jap Barbeau	Third Base	1905–1906
Brian Barber	Pitcher	1999–2000
Josh Bard	Catcher	2003–2005
Josh Barfield	Second Base	2006–2008 (Present)
Len Barker	Pitcher	1979–1983
Ray Barker	First Base	1965
Jeff Barkley	Pitcher	1984–1985

Player Name	Position	Years Played
Rich Barnes	Pitcher	1983
Brian Barnes	Pitcher	1994
Les Barnhart	Pitcher	1928–1930
Brian Barton	Left Field	2006
Cliff Bartosh	Pitcher	2004
Jim Baskette	Pitcher	1911–1913
Johnny Bassler	Catcher	1913–1914
Ray Bates	Third Base	1913
Rick Bauer	Pitcher	2007–2008 (Present)
Jim Baxes	Second Base	1959
Harry Bay	Outfielder	1902–1908
Bill Bayne	Pitcher	1928
Johnny Beall	Outfielder	1913
Belve Bean	Pitcher	1930–1935
Gene Bearden	Pitcher	1947–1950
Kevin Bearse	Pitcher	1990
George Beck	Pitcher	1914
Erve Beck	Second Base	1901
Joe Becker	Catcher	1936–1937
Heinz Becker	First Base	1946–1947
Gene Bedford	Second Base	1925
Phil Bedgood	Pitcher	1922–1923
Fred Beebe	Pitcher	1916
Fred Beene	Pitcher	1974–1975
Rick Behenna	Pitcher	1983–1985
Gary Bell	Pitcher	1958–1967
Eric Bell	Pitcher	1991–1992
Rob Bell	Pitcher	2006
Buddy Bell	Third Base	1972–1978
David Bell	Third Base	1995, 1998
Jay Bell	Shortstop	1986–1988
Beau Bell	Outfielder	1940–1941
Albert Belle	Outfielder	1989–1996
Ronnie Belliard	Second Base	2004–2006
Harry Bemis	Catcher	1902–1910
Ray Benge	Pitcher	1925–1926
Stan Benjamin	Outfielder	1945
Henry Benn	Pitcher	1914
Al Benton	Pitcher	1949–1950
Butch Benton	Catcher	1985
Johnny Berardino	Second Base	1948–1950, 1952
Jason Bere	Pitcher	2000, 2003
Moe Berg	Catcher	1931, 1934
Heinie Berger	Pitcher	1907–1910

Player Name	Position	Years Played
Boze Berger	Second Base	1932–1936
Al Bergman	Second Base	1916
Tony Bernazard	Second Base	1984–1987
Bill Bernhard	Pitcher	1902–1907
Geronimo Berroa	Designated Hitter	1998
Joe Berry	Pitcher	1946
Ken Berry	Outfielder	1975
Bob Bescher	Outfielder	1918
Rafael Betancourt	Pitcher	2003–2008 (Present)
Kurt Bevacqua	Third Base	1971–1972
Jason Beverlin	Pitcher	2002
Jim Bibby	Pitcher	1975–1977
Mike Bielecki	Pitcher	1993
Nick Bierbrodt	Pitcher	2003
Josh Billings	Catcher	1913–1918
Steve Biras	Second Base	1944
Joe Birmingham	Outfielder	1906–1914
Lloyd Bishop	Pitcher	1914
Rivington Bisland	Shortstop	1914
Don Black	Pitcher	1946–1948
Bud Black	Pitcher	1988–1990, 1995
George Blaeholder	Pitcher	1936
Willie Blair	Pitcher	1990–1991
Casey Blake	Third Base	2003–2008 (Present)
Ossie Blanco	First Base	1974
Fred Blanding	Pitcher	1910–1914
Larvell Blanks	Shortstop	1976–1978
Bert Blyleven	Pitcher	1981–1985
Bruce Bochte	First Base	1977
Eddie Bockman	Third Base	1947
Joe Boehling	Pitcher	1916–1920
John Bohnet	Pitcher	1982
Joe Boley	Shortstop	1932
Jim Bolger	Outfielder	1959
Cecil Bolton	First Base	1928
Walt Bond	Outfielder	1960–1962
Bobby Bonds	Outfielder	1979
Frank Bonner	Second Base	1902
Bill Bonness	Pitcher	1944
Buddy Booker	Catcher	1966
Red Booles	Pitcher	1909
Dan Boone	Pitcher	1922–1923
Ray Boone	Third Base	1948–1953
Aaron Boone	Third Base	2005–2006

Player Name	Position	Years Played
Pat Borders	Catcher	1997–1999
Joe Borowski	Pitcher	2006–2008 (Present)
Dick Bosman	Pitcher	1973–1975
Harley Boss	First Base	1933
Denis Boucher	Pitcher	1991–1992
Lou Boudreau	Shortstop	1938–1950
Abe Bowman	Pitcher	1914–1915
Ted Bowsfield	Pitcher	1960
Gary Boyd	Pitcher	1969
Jason Boyd	Pitcher	2003
Jack Bracken	Pitcher	1901
Buddy Bradford	Outfielder	1970–1971
Jack Bradley	Catcher	1916
Bill Bradley	Third Base	1901–1910
Milton Bradley	Outfielder	2001–2003
Dick Braggins	Pitcher	1901
Jeff Branson	Third Base	1997–1998
Russell Branyan	Third Base	1998–2002
Ad Brennan	Pitcher	1918
Tom Brennan	Pitcher	1981–1983
Bert Brenner	Pitcher	1912
Lynn Brenton	Pitcher	1913–1915
Bill Brenzel	Catcher	1934–1935
Jamie Brewington	Pitcher	1999–2000
Charlie Brewster	Shortstop	1946
Christian Bridenbaugh	–	2001
Rocky Bridges	Shortstop	1960
John Briggs	Pitcher	1959–1960
Dan Briggs	First Base	1978
Lou Brissie	Pitcher	1951–1953
Johnny Broaca	Pitcher	1939
Dick Brodowski	Pitcher	1958–1959
Jack Brohamer	Second Base	1972–1975, 1980
Herman Bronke	Third Base	1910–1912
Tom Brookens	Third Base	1990
Ben Broussard	First Base	2002–2006
Jim Brower	Pitcher	1999–2000
Frank Brower	Outfielder	1923–1924
Jumbo Brown	Pitcher	1927–1928
Clint Brown	Pitcher	1928–1935, 1941–1942
Lloyd Brown	Pitcher	1934–1937
Jackie Brown	Pitcher	1975–1976
Andrew Brown	Pitcher	2005–2006
Dick Brown	Catcher	1957–1959

Player Name	Position	Years Played
Larry Brown	Shortstop	1963–1971
Jordan Brown	Right Field	2006, 2008
Jordan Brown	Right Field	2006, 2008 (Present)
Jerry Browne	Second Base	1989–1991
Garland Buckeye	Pitcher	1925–1928
Fritz Buelow	Catcher	1904–1906
Dave Burba	Pitcher	1998–2002
Larry Burchart	Pitcher	1969
John Burke	Pitcher	1998–1999
Ellis Burks	Outfielder	2001–2003
Johnny Burnett	Shortstop	1927–1934
Jeromy Burnitz	Outfielder	1995–1996
George Burns	First Base	1920–1921, 1924–1928
T.J. Burton	Pitcher	2007
Ellis Burton	Outfielder	1963
Jim Busby	Outfielder	1956–1957
Tom Buskey	Pitcher	1974–1977
John Butcher	Pitcher	1986
Hank Butcher	Outfielder	1911–1912
Bill Butler	Pitcher	1972
Brett Butler	Outfielder	1984–1987
Bubbie Buzachero	Pitcher	2006–2007
Paul Byrd	Pitcher	2006–2008 (Present)
Fernando Cabrera	Pitcher	2004–2007
Asdrubal Cabrera	Second Base	2007–2008 (Present)
Jolbert Cabrera	Outfielder	1998–2002
Joe Caffie	Outfielder	1956–1957
Ben Caffyn	Outfielder	1906
Wayne Cage	Designated Hitter	1978–1979
Cameron Cairncross	Pitcher	1999–2001
Ray Caldwell	Pitcher	1919–1921
Bruce Caldwell	Outfielder	1928
Dave Callahan	Outfielder	1910–1911
Paul Calvert	Pitcher	1942–1945
Armando Camacaro	Catcher	2006–2008
Armando Camacaro	Catcher	2006–2008 (Present)
Ernie Camacho	Pitcher	1983–1987
Lou Camilli	Shortstop	1969–1972
Bruce Campbell	Outfielder	1935–1939
Soup Campbell	Outfielder	1940–1941
Cardell Camper	Pitcher	1977
Casey Candaele	Second Base	1996–1997
Tom Candiotti	Pitcher	1986–1991, 1999
Bernie Carbo	Outfielder	1978

Player Name	Position	Years Played
Jose Cardenal	Outfielder	1968–1969
Leo Cardenas	Shortstop	1973
Fred Carisch	Catcher	1912–1914
Steve Carlton	Pitcher	1987
Fausto Carmona	Pitcher	2006–2008 (Present)
Eddie Carnett	Outfielder	1945
Charlie Carr	First Base	1904–1905
Chico Carrasquel	Shortstop	1956–1958
Cam Carreon	Catcher	1965
Mark Carreon	Outfielder	1996
Jamey Carroll	Second Base	2007–2008 (Present)
Kit Carson	Outfielder	1934–1935
Paul Carter	Pitcher	1914–1915
Joe Carter	Outfielder	1984–1989
Rico Carty	Outfielder	1974–1977
George Case	Outfielder	1946
Sean Casey	First Base	1997–1998
Larry Casian	Pitcher	1994
Carmen Castillo	Outfielder	1982–1988
Pete Center	Pitcher	1942–1946
Ed Cermak	Outfielder	1901
Rick Cerone	Catcher	1975–1976
Bob Chakales	Pitcher	1951–1954
Chris Chambliss	First Base	1971–1974
Dean Chance	Pitcher	1970
Bob Chance	First Base	1963–1964
Ray Chapman	Shortstop	1912–1920
Ben Chapman	Outfielder	1939–1940
Sam Chapman	Outfielder	1951
Larry Chappell	Outfielder	1916
Joe Charboneau	Outfielder	1980–1982
Charlie Chech	Pitcher	1908
Virgil Cheeves	Pitcher	1924
Shin-Soo Choo	Outfielder	2006–2008 (Present)
Russ Christopher	Pitcher	1948
Mike Christopher	Pitcher	1992–1993
Chuck Churn	Pitcher	1958
Al Cicotte	Pitcher	1959
Al Cihocki	Shortstop	1945
Bill Cissell	Second Base	1932–1933
Uke Clanton	First Base	1922
Ginger Clark	Pitcher	1902
Bob Clark	Pitcher	1920–1921
Watty Clark	Pitcher	1924

Player Name	Position	Years Played
Bryan Clark	Pitcher	1985
Mark Clark	Pitcher	1993–1995
Terry Clark	Pitcher	1997
Allie Clark	Outfielder	1948–1951
Jim Clark	Outfielder	1971
Dave Clark	Outfielder	1986–1989
Nig Clarke	Catcher	1905–1910
Josh Clarke	Outfielder	1908–1909
Sumpter Clarke	Outfielder	1923–1924
Walter Clarkson	Pitcher	1907–1908
Ty Cline	Outfielder	1960–1962
Billy Clingman	Third Base	1903
Lou Clinton	Outfielder	1965
David Clyde	Pitcher	1978–1979
Chris Codiroli	Pitcher	1988
Rocky Colavito	Outfielder	1955–1959, 1965–1967
Vince Colbert	Pitcher	1970–1972
Bert Cole	Pitcher	1925
Alex Cole	Outfielder	1990–1992
Bob Coleman	Catcher	1916
Gordy Coleman	First Base	1959
Allan Collamore	Pitcher	1914–1915
Hap Collard	Pitcher	1927–1928
Don Collins	Pitcher	1980
Kyle Collins	Pitcher	2007
Jackie Collum	Pitcher	1962
Bartolo Colon	Pitcher	1997–2002
Merl Combs	Shortstop	1951–1952
Steve Comer	Pitcher	1984
Bunk Congalton	Outfielder	1905–1907
Sarge Connally	Pitcher	1931–1934
Bruce Connatser	First Base	1931–1932
Ed Connolly	Pitcher	1967
Joe Connolly	Outfielder	1922–1923
Joe Connor	Catcher	1901
Mike Conroy	Left Field	2006
Jim Constable	Pitcher	1958
Jose Constanza	Center Field	2007
Jack Conway	Second Base	1941–1947
Herb Conyers	First Base	1950
Dennis Cook	Pitcher	1991–1995
Jason Cooper	Outfielder	2006–2007
Joey Cora	Second Base	1998–1999
Alex Cora	Shortstop	2005

Player Name	Position	Years Played
Wil Cordero	Outfielder	1999–2002
Marty Cordova	Outfielder	2001
David Cortes	Pitcher	2003
Marlan Coughtry	Second Base	1962
Fritz Coumbe	Pitcher	1914–1919
Stan Coveleski	Pitcher	1916–1924
Ted Cox	Third Base	1978–1979
Howard Craghead	Pitcher	1931–1933
Rod Craig	Outfielder	1982
Del Crandall	Catcher	1966
Keith Creel	Pitcher	1985
Jack Cressend	Pitcher	2003–2004
Coco Crisp	Outfielder	2002–2005
Bill Cristall	Pitcher	1901
Ed Crosby	Shortstop	1974–1976
Frank Cross	Outfielder	1901
Trevor Crowe	Outfielder	2006–2008 (Present)
Francisco Cruceta	Pitcher	2004
Victor Cruz	Pitcher	1979–1980
Jacob Cruz	Outfielder	1998–2001
Roy Cullenbine	Outfielder	1943–1945
Nick Cullop	Pitcher	1913–1914
Nick Cullop	Outfielder	1927
Wil Culmer	Outfielder	1983
George Culver	Pitcher	1966–1967
Tony Curry	Outfielder	1966
Jack Curtis	Pitcher	1963
Chad Curtis	Outfielder	1996–1997
Al Cypert	Third Base	1914
Jeff D'Amico	Pitcher	2001–2002
Jeff D'Amico	Pitcher	2004
Paul Dade	Outfielder	1977–1979
Bill Dailey	Pitcher	1961–1962
Pete Dalena	Designated Hitter	1989
Bud Daley	Pitcher	1955–1957
Tom Daly	Catcher	1916
Lee Dashner	Pitcher	1913
Vic Davalillo	Outfielder	1963–1968
Homer Davidson	Catcher	1908
Steve Davis	Pitcher	1989
Kane Davis	Pitcher	2000
Jason Davis	Pitcher	2002–2007
Harry Davis	First Base	1912
Bill Davis	First Base	1965–1966

Player Name	Position	Years Played
Joe Dawley	Pitcher	2004
Joe Dawson	Pitcher	1924
Chris De La Cruz	Second Base	2006
Keoni De Renne	Second Base	2007
Sean DePaula	Pitcher	1999–2000, 2002
Chubby Dean	Pitcher	1941–1943
Hank Deberry	Catcher	1916–1917
Jeff Dedmon	Pitcher	1988
Mike Dela Hoz	Third Base	1960–1963
Frank Delahanty	Outfielder	1907
David Dellucci	Outfielder	2006–2008 (Present)
Rich Delucia	Pitcher	1999–2000
Steve Demeter	Third Base	1960
Don Demeter	Outfielder	1967
Ben Demott	Pitcher	1910–1911
Rick Dempsey	Catcher	1987
Kyle Denney	Pitcher	2004
Otto Denning	Catcher	1942–1943
John Denny	Pitcher	1980–1982
Sam Dente	Shortstop	1954–1955
Gene Desautels	Catcher	1941–1945
Shorty Desjardien	Pitcher	1916
George Detore	Third Base	1930–1931
Jim Devlin	Catcher	1944
Bo Diaz	Catcher	1978–1981
Einar Diaz	Catcher	1996–2002, 2005–2006
Paul Dicken	–	1964–1966
George Dickerson	Pitcher	1917
Don Dillard	Outfielder	1959–1962
Harley Dillinger	Pitcher	1914
Miguel Dilone	Outfielder	1980–1983
Jerry Dipoto	Pitcher	1993–1994
Walt Doane	Pitcher	1909–1910
Joe Dobson	Pitcher	1939–1940
Pat Dobson	Pitcher	1976–1977
Larry Doby	Outfielder	1947–1955, 1958
Frank Doljack	Outfielder	1943
Red Donahue	Pitcher	1903–1905
Pat Donahue	Catcher	1910
Pete Donohue	Pitcher	1931
Dick Donovan	Pitcher	1962–1965
Mike Donovan	Third Base	1904
Tom Donovan	Outfielder	1901
Todd Donovan	Outfielder	2006

Player Name	Position	Years Played
Bill Doran	Third Base	1922
Red Dorman	Outfielder	1928
Gus Dorner	Pitcher	1902–1903
Cal Dorsett	Pitcher	1940–1947
Brian Dorsett	Catcher	1987
Pete Dowling	Pitcher	1901
Logan Drake	Pitcher	1922–1924
Tom Drake	Pitcher	1939
John Drennen	Outfielder	2006–2007
Ryan Drese	Pitcher	2001–2002
Tim Drew	Pitcher	2000–2001
Jason Dubois	Outfielder	2005
Frank Duffy	Shortstop	1972–1977
Dave Duncan	Catcher	1973–1974
George Dunlop	Shortstop	1913–1914
Steve Dunning	Pitcher	1970–1973
Shawon Dunston	Shortstop	1998
Todd Dunwoody	Outfielder	2001–2002
Chad Durbin	Pitcher	2003–2004
Jerry Dybzinski	Shortstop	1980–1982
Jim Dyck	Outfielder	1954
Truck Eagan	Second Base	1901
Luke Easter	First Base	1949–1954
Jamie Easterly	Pitcher	1983–1987
Ted Easterly	Catcher	1909–1912
Dennis Eckersley	Pitcher	1975–1977
George Edmondson	Pitcher	1922–1924
Eddie Edmonson	First Base	1913
Jim Joe Edwards	Pitcher	1922–1925
Doc Edwards	Catcher	1962–1963
Hank Edwards	Outfielder	1941–1949
Harry Eells	Pitcher	1906
Ben Egan	Catcher	1914–1915
Bruce Egloff	Pitcher	1991
Hack Eibel	Outfielder	1912
Juan Eichelberger	Pitcher	1983
Ike Eichrodt	Outfielder	1925–1927
Harry Eisenstat	Pitcher	1939–1942
Scott Elarton	Pitcher	2004–2005
David Elder	Pitcher	2002–2003
Frank Ellerbe	Third Base	1924
Bruce Ellingsen	Pitcher	1974
John Ellis	First Base	1973–1975
George Ellison	Pitcher	1920

Player Name	Position	Years Played
Dick Ellsworth	Pitcher	1969–1970
Red Embree	Pitcher	1941–1947
Alan Embree	Pitcher	1992, 1995–1996
Joe Engel	Pitcher	1919
Clyde Engle	Outfielder	1916
Johnny Enzmann	Pitcher	1918–1919
Jim Eschen	Outfielder	1915
Jose Escobar	Shortstop	1991
Alex Escobar	Outfielder	2003–2004
Alvaro Espinoza	Shortstop	1993–1996
Chuck Essegian	Outfielder	1961–1962
Jim Essian	Catcher	1983
Fred Eunick	Third Base	1917
Joe Evans	Outfielder	1915–1922
Hoot Evers	Outfielder	1955–1956
Tony Faeth	Pitcher	1919–1920
Jerry Fahr	Pitcher	1951
Ferris Fain	First Base	1955
Bibb Falk	Outfielder	1929–1931
Cy Falkenberg	Pitcher	1908–1913
Steve Falteisek	Pitcher	2000
Harry Fanwell	Pitcher	1910
Ed Farmer	Pitcher	1971–1973
Jack Farmer	Second Base	1918
Steve Farr	Pitcher	1984, 1994
John Farrell	Pitcher	1987–1990, 1995
Bob Feller	Pitcher	1936–1956
Felix Fermin	Shortstop	1989–1993
Tony Fernandez	Shortstop	1996–1997
Don Ferrarese	Pitcher	1958–1959
Wes Ferrell	Pitcher	1927–1933
Tom Ferrick	Pitcher	1942–1946
Cy Ferry	Pitcher	1905
Chick Fewster	Second Base	1924–1925
Cecil Fielder	First Base	1998–1999
Brian Finegan	Second Base	2006–2007
Chuck Finley	Pitcher	1999–2002
Dan Firova	Catcher	1988
Carl Fischer	Pitcher	1937
Mike Fischlin	Shortstop	1981–1985
Eddie Fisher	Pitcher	1968
Gus Fisher	Catcher	1911
Ed Fitz Gerald	Catcher	1959
Paul Fitzke	Pitcher	1924

Player Name	Position	Years Played
Al Fitzmorris	Pitcher	1977–1978
Ray Flanigan	Pitcher	1946
Les Fleming	First Base	1941–1947
Elmer Flick	Outfielder	1902–1910
Jesse Flores	Pitcher	1950
Jose Flores	Second Base	2005–2006
Hank Foiles	Catcher	1953–1956, 1960
Lew Fonseca	First Base	1927–1931
Ted Ford	Outfielder	1970–1971, 1973
Ray Fosse	Catcher	1967–1972, 1976–1977
Ed Foster	Pitcher	1908
Alan Foster	Pitcher	1971
Roy Foster	Outfielder	1970–1972
Keith Foulke	Pitcher	2007
Ben Francisco	Outfielder	2005–2008 (Present)
Julio Franco	Shortstop	1983–1988, 1996–1997
Terry Francona	First Base	1988
Tito Francona	Outfielder	1959–1964
George Frazier	Pitcher	1984
Joe Frazier	Outfielder	1947
Vern Freiburger	First Base	1941
Dave Freisleben	Pitcher	1978
Jim Fridley	Outfielder	1952
Owen Friend	Second Base	1953
Buck Frierson	Outfielder	1941
Doug Frobel	Outfielder	1987
Johnson Fry	Pitcher	1923
Travis Fryman	Third Base	1997–2002
Vern Fuller	Second Base	1964–1970
Aaron Fultz	Pitcher	2006–2008 (Present)
Frank Funk	Pitcher	1960–1962
Fabian Gaffke	Outfielder	1941–1942
Ralph Gagliano	–	1965
Milt Galatzer	Outfielder	1933–1936
Denny Galehouse	Pitcher	1934–1938
Shorty Gallagher	Outfielder	1901
Jackie Gallagher	Outfielder	1923
Dave Gallagher	Outfielder	1987
Oscar Gamble	Outfielder	1973–1975
Chick Gandil	First Base	1916
Bob Garbark	Catcher	1934–1935
Mike Garcia	Pitcher	1948–1959
Karim Garcia	Outfielder	2001–2003
Rob Gardner	Pitcher	1968

Player Name	Position	Years Played
Larry Gardner	Third Base	1919–1924
Ray Gardner	Shortstop	1929–1930
Ryan Garko	First Base	2005–2008 (Present)
Wayne Garland	Pitcher	1977–1981
Clarence Garrett	Pitcher	1915
Charlie Gassaway	Pitcher	1946
Jake Gautreau	Third Base	2005–2006
Gary Geiger	Outfielder	1958
Frank Genins	Outfielder	1901
Jim Gentile	First Base	1966
Lefty George	Pitcher	1912
Greek George	Catcher	1935–1936
George Gerken	Outfielder	1927–1928
Jody Gerut	Outfielder	2003–2005
Al Gettel	Pitcher	1947–1948
Gus Getz	Third Base	1918
Gus Gil	Second Base	1967
Brian Giles	Outfielder	1995–1998
Johnny Gill	Outfielder	1927–1928
Tinsley Ginn	Outfielder	1914
Joe Ginsberg	Catcher	1953–1954
Matt Ginter	Pitcher	2007–2008 (Present)
Keith Ginter	Second Base	2007
Luke Glavenich	Pitcher	1913
Jim Gleeson	Outfielder	1936
Martin Glendon	Pitcher	1903
Sal Gliatto	Pitcher	1930
Ed Glynn	Pitcher	1981–1983
Bill Glynn	First Base	1952–1954
John Gochnauer	Shortstop	1902–1903
Bill Gogolewski	Pitcher	1974
Jonah Goldman	Shortstop	1928–1931
Ryan Goleski	Outfielder	2006–2007
Ruben Gomez	Pitcher	1962
Mariano Gomez	Pitcher	2007
Chris Gomez	Shortstop	2007
Rene Gonzales	Third Base	1994
Orlando Gonzalez	First Base	1976
Pedro Gonzalez	Second Base	1965–1967
Denny Gonzalez	Third Base	1989
Andy Gonzalez	Third Base	2007–2008 (Present)
Jose Gonzalez	Outfielder	1991
Juan Gonzalez	Outfielder	2001, 2005
Raul Gonzalez	Outfielder	2004

Player Name	Position	Years Played
Lee Gooch	Outfielder	1915
Wilbur Good	Outfielder	1908–1909
Dwight Gooden	Pitcher	1997–1999
Don Gordon	Pitcher	1987–1988
Joe Gordon	Second Base	1947–1950
Al Gould	Pitcher	1916–1917
Mauro Gozzo	Pitcher	1990–1991
Rod Graber	Outfielder	1958
Peaches Graham	Catcher	1902
Tommy Gramly	Pitcher	1968
Jack Graney	Outfielder	1908–1922
George Grant	Pitcher	1927–1929
Mudcat Grant	Pitcher	1958–1964
Eddie Grant	Third Base	1905
Jimmy Grant	Third Base	1943–1944
Mickey Grasso	Catcher	1954
Danny Graves	Pitcher	1996–1997, 2006
Ted Gray	Pitcher	1955
Johnny Gray	Pitcher	1957
Gary Gray	First Base	1980
Tyler Green	Pitcher	2000
Gene Green	Outfielder	1962–1963
Vean Gregg	Pitcher	1911–1914
Dave Gregg	Pitcher	1913
Alfredo Griffin	Shortstop	1976–1978
Art Griggs	First Base	1911–1912
Bob Grim	Pitcher	1960
Oscar Grimes	Third Base	1938–1942
Ross Grimsley	Pitcher	1980
Jason Grimsley	Pitcher	1993–1995
Marquis Grissom	Outfielder	1997
Steve Gromek	Pitcher	1941–1953
Bob Groom	Pitcher	1918
Ernest Groth	Pitcher	1947–1948
Harvey Grubb	Third Base	1912
Johnny Grubb	Outfielder	1977–1978
Cecilio Guante	Pitcher	1990
Lou Guisto	First Base	1916–1923
Tom Gulley	Outfielder	1923–1924
Eric Gunderson	Pitcher	2000–2001
Red Gunkel	Pitcher	1916
Jeremy Guthrie	Pitcher	2004–2007
Ricky Gutierrez	Shortstop	2002–2003
Franklin Gutierrez	Outfielder	2005–2008 (Present)

Player Name	Position	Years Played
Yamid Haad	Catcher	2007–2008 (Present)
Travis Hafner	Designated Hitter	2003–2008 (Present)
Rip Hagerman	Pitcher	1914–1916
Bob Hale	First Base	1960–1961
Odell Hale	Second Base	1931–1940
Russ Hall	Shortstop	1901
Jimmie Hall	Outfielder	1968–1969
Mel Hall	Outfielder	1984–1988
John Halla	Pitcher	1905
Bill Hallman	Second Base	1901
Al Halt	Third Base	1918
Doc Hamann	Pitcher	1922
Steve Hamilton	Pitcher	1961
Jack Hamilton	Pitcher	1969
Jack Hammond	Second Base	1915–1922
Granny Hamner	Shortstop	1959
Rich Hand	Pitcher	1970–1971
Chris Haney	Pitcher	1999–2000
Doug Hansen	–	1951
Mel Harder	Pitcher	1928–1947
Jack Hardy	Catcher	1903
Carroll Hardy	Outfielder	1958–1960
Steve Hargan	Pitcher	1965–1972
Mike Hargrove	First Base	1979–1985
Spec Harkness	Pitcher	1910–1911
Tommy Harper	Outfielder	1968
Toby Harrah	Third Base	1979–1983
Billy Harrell	Shortstop	1955–1958
Ken Harrelson	First Base	1969–1971
Bubba Harris	Pitcher	1951
Mickey Harris	Pitcher	1952
Jeff Harris	Pitcher	2006–2008
Jeff Harris	Pitcher	2006–2008 (Present)
Joe Harris	First Base	1917–1919
Billy Harris	Second Base	1968
Roric Harrison	Pitcher	1975
Jack Harshman	Pitcher	1959–1960
Oscar Harstad	Pitcher	1915
Bill Hart	Pitcher	1901
Bruce Hartford	Shortstop	1914
Grover Hartley	Catcher	1929–1930
Bob Hartman	Pitcher	1962
Luther Harvel	Outfielder	1928
Zaza Harvey	Outfielder	1901–1902

Player Name	Position	Years Played
Ron Hassey	Catcher	1978–1984
Fred Hatfield	Third Base	1958
Arthur Hauger	Outfielder	1912
Joe Hauser	First Base	1929
Brad Havens	Pitcher	1988–1989
Wynn Hawkins	Pitcher	1960–1962
Howie Haworth	Catcher	1915
Frankie Hayes	Catcher	1945–1946
Von Hayes	Outfielder	1981–1982
Stephen Head	First Base	2006–2007
Jeff Heath	Outfielder	1936–1945
Neal Heaton	Pitcher	1982–1986
Mike Hedlund	Pitcher	1965–1968
Bob Heffner	Pitcher	1966
Jim Hegan	Catcher	1941–1957
Jack Heidemann	Shortstop	1969–1974
Woodie Held	Shortstop	1958–1964
Hank Helf	Catcher	1938–1940
Russ Heman	Pitcher	1961
Charlie Hemphill	Outfielder	1902
Rollie Hemsley	Catcher	1938–1941
Bernie Henderson	Pitcher	1921
Harvey Hendrick	First Base	1925
George Hendrick	Outfielder	1973–1976
Tim Hendryx	Outfielder	1911–1912
Dave Hengel	Outfielder	1989
Phil Hennigan	Pitcher	1969–1972
Earl Henry	Pitcher	1944–1945
Remy Hermoso	Second Base	1974
Jeremy Hernandez	Pitcher	1993
Roberto Hernandez	Pitcher	2006–2007
Keith Hernandez	First Base	1990
Jose Hernandez	Shortstop	1992, 2005
Aaron Herr	Second Base	2007–2008 (Present)
Alex Herrera	Pitcher	2002–2003
Javi Herrera	Catcher	2005–2007
Orel Hershiser	Pitcher	1995–1997
Otto Hess	Pitcher	1902–1908
Joe Heving	Pitcher	1937–1938, 1941–1944
Jack Hickey	Pitcher	1904
Charlie Hickman	First Base	1902–1904, 1908
Dennis Higgins	Pitcher	1970
Bob Higgins	Catcher	1909
Mark Higgins	First Base	1989

Player Name	Position	Years Played
Oral Hildebrand	Pitcher	1931–1936
Tom Hilgendorf	Pitcher	1972–1974
Herbert Hill	Pitcher	1915
Ken Hill	Pitcher	1995
Hugh Hill	Outfielder	1903
Glenallen Hill	Outfielder	1991–1993
Shawn Hillegas	Pitcher	1991
Harry Hinchman	Second Base	1907
Bill Hinchman	Outfielder	1907–1909
Chuck Hinton	Outfielder	1965–1967, 1969–1971
Tommy Hinzo	Second Base	1987–1989
Myril Hoag	Outfielder	1944–1945
Oris Hockett	Outfielder	1941–1944
Johnny Hodapp	Second Base	1925–1932
Gomer Hodge	First Base	1971
Wes Hodges	Third Base	2007
Bill Hoffer	Pitcher	1901
Tex Hoffman	Third Base	1915
Harry Hogan	Outfielder	1901
Kenny Hogan	Outfielder	1923–1924
Eddie Hohnhorst	First Base	1910–1912
Dutch Holland	Outfielder	1934
Todd Hollandsworth	Outfielder	2006
Dave Hollins	Third Base	2000–2001
Ken Holloway	Pitcher	1929–1930
Don Hood	Pitcher	1975–1979
Bob Hooper	Pitcher	1953–1954
Sam Horn	Designated Hitter	1993
Tony Horton	First Base	1967–1970
Willie Horton	Outfielder	1978
Dave Hoskins	Pitcher	1953–1954
Tyler Houston	Third Base	1999
Art Houtteman	Pitcher	1953–1957
Ben Howard	Pitcher	2006
Ivan Howard	First Base	1916–1917
Doug Howard	First Base	1976
Thomas Howard	Outfielder	1992–1993
Dixie Howell	Pitcher	1940
Red Howell	–	1941
Bob Howry	Pitcher	2004–2005
Dick Howser	Shortstop	1963–1966
Trenidad Hubbard	Outfielder	1997
Willis Hudlin	Pitcher	1926–1940
Mike Huff	Outfielder	1991

Player Name	Position	Years Played
Bobby Hughes	Catcher	2000
Roy Hughes	Second Base	1935–1937
Mark Huismann	Pitcher	1987
Johnny Humphries	Pitcher	1938–1940
Bill Hunnefield	Shortstop	1931
Billy Hunter	Shortstop	1958
Bill Hunter	Outfielder	1912
Butch Huskey	Outfielder	2001
Joe Inglett	Second Base	2006–2007
Happy Iott	Outfielder	1903
Tommy Irwin	Shortstop	1938
Mike Jackson	Pitcher	1973
Mike Jackson	Pitcher	1996–1999
Damian Jackson	Second Base	1996–1997
Randy Jackson	Third Base	1958–1959
Jim Jackson	Outfielder	1905–1906
Joe Jackson	Outfielder	1910–1915
Baby Doll Jacobson	Outfielder	1927
Brook Jacoby	Third Base	1984–1992
Jason Jacome	Pitcher	1997–1998
Bill James	Pitcher	1911–1912
Lefty James	Pitcher	1912–1914
Dion James	Outfielder	1989–1990
Chris James	Outfielder	1990–1991
Charlie Jamieson	Outfielder	1919–1932
Hi Jasper	Pitcher	1919
Tex Jeanes	Outfielder	1921–1922
Mike Jeffcoat	Pitcher	1983–1985
Reggie Jefferson	Designated Hitter	1991–1993
Stan Jefferson	Outfielder	1990
Dan Jessee	–	1929
Johnny Jeter	Outfielder	1974
Jose Jimenez	Pitcher	2004
Houston Jimenez	Shortstop	1988
Tommy John	Pitcher	1963–1964
Vic Johnson	Pitcher	1946
Jerry Johnson	Pitcher	1973
Bob Johnson	Pitcher	1974
Jason Johnson	Pitcher	2006
Larry Johnson	Catcher	1972–1974
Cliff Johnson	Designated Hitter	1979–1980
Lou Johnson	Outfielder	1968
Alex Johnson	Outfielder	1972
Lance Johnson	Outfielder	2000

Player Name	Position	Years Played
Doc Johnston	First Base	1912–1914, 1918–1921
Sam Jones	Pitcher	1914–1915
Sam Jones	Pitcher	1951–1952
Doug Jones	Pitcher	1986–1991, 1998
Hal Jones	First Base	1961–1962
Willie Jones	Third Base	1959
Tom Jordan	Catcher	1946
Scott Jordan	Outfielder	1988
Addie Joss	Pitcher	1902–1910
Jeff Juden	Pitcher	1997
Wally Judnich	Outfielder	1948
Ken Jungels	Pitcher	1937–1941
David Justice	Outfielder	1997–2000
Ike Kahdot	Third Base	1922
Nick Kahl	Second Base	1905
George Kahler	Pitcher	1910–1914
Bob Kaiser	Pitcher	1971
Jeff Kaiser	Pitcher	1987–1990
Scott Kamieniecki	Pitcher	1999–2000
Willie Kamm	Third Base	1931–1935
Paul Kardow	Pitcher	1936
Benn Karr	Pitcher	1925–1927
Steve Karsay	Pitcher	1998–2001, 2006
Marty Kavanagh	Second Base	1916–1918
Pat Keedy	Third Base	1989
Dave Keefe	Pitcher	1922
Mike Kekich	Pitcher	1973
Tom Kelley	Pitcher	1964–1967
Bob Kelly	Pitcher	1958
Pat Kelly	Outfielder	1981
Ken Keltner	Third Base	1937–1949
Fred Kendall	Catcher	1977
Vern Kennedy	Pitcher	1942–1944
Bill Kennedy	Pitcher	1948
Bob Kennedy	Outfielder	1948–1954
Jerry Kenney	Third Base	1973
Jeff Kent	Second Base	1996
Marty Keough	Outfielder	1960
Jim Kern	Pitcher	1974–1978, 1986
Jack Kibble	Third Base	1912
Mike Kilkenny	Pitcher	1972–1973
Ed Killian	Pitcher	1903
Jerry Kindall	Second Base	1962–1964
Ralph Kiner	Outfielder	1955

Player Name	Position	Years Played
Eric King	Pitcher	1991
Curtis King	Pitcher	2000
Jim King	Outfielder	1967
Dennis Kinney	Pitcher	1978
Wayne Kirby	Outfielder	1991–1996
Jay Kirke	Outfielder	1914–1915
Willie Kirkland	Outfielder	1961–1963
Harry Kirsch	Pitcher	1910
Garland Kiser	Pitcher	1991
Ron Kittle	Outfielder	1988
Malachi Kittridge	Catcher	1906
Lou Klein	Second Base	1951
Hal Kleine	Pitcher	1944–1945
Ed Klepfer	Pitcher	1915–1919
Ed Klieman	Pitcher	1943–1948
Lou Klimchock	Third Base	1968–1970
Steve Kline	Pitcher	1974
Steve Kline	Pitcher	1997
Scott Klingenbeck	Pitcher	1998–1999
Johnny Klippstein	Pitcher	1960
Joe Klugmann	Second Base	1925
Cotton Knaupp	Shortstop	1910–1911
Bill Knickerbocker	Shortstop	1933–1936
Ray Knode	First Base	1923–1926
Masahide Kobayashi	Pitcher	2007–2008 (Present)
Elmer Koestner	Pitcher	1910
Brad Komminsk	Outfielder	1989
Larry Kopf	Shortstop	1913
Mike Koplove	Pitcher	2007
Kevin Kouzmanoff	Third Base	2006
Joe Krakauskas	Pitcher	1941–1946
Jack Kralick	Pitcher	1963–1967
Tom Kramer	Pitcher	1991–1993
Gene Krapp	Pitcher	1911–1912
Harry Krause	Pitcher	1912
Rick Kreuger	Pitcher	1978
Rick Krivda	Pitcher	1998
Gary Kroll	Pitcher	1969
John Kroner	Second Base	1937–1938
Ernie Krueger	Catcher	1913
Art Kruger	Outfielder	1910
Jack Kubiszyn	Shortstop	1961–1962
Harvey Kuenn	Outfielder	1960
Bub Kuhn	Pitcher	1924

Player Name	Position	Years Played
Kenny Kuhn	Shortstop	1955–1957
Duane Kuiper	Second Base	1974–1981
Hal Kurtz	Pitcher	1968
Bob Kuzava	Pitcher	1946–1947
Greg LaRocca	Third Base	2002–2003
Dave LaRoche	Pitcher	1975–1977
Bob Lacey	Pitcher	1981
Candy Lachance	First Base	1901
Guy Lacy	Second Base	1926
Aaron Laffey	Pitcher	2007–2008 (Present)
Nap Lajoie	Second Base	1902–1914
Tim Laker	Catcher	2001, 2003–2004, 2006
Ray Lamb	Pitcher	1971–1973
Otis Lambeth	Pitcher	1916–1918
Tom Lampkin	Catcher	1988
Grover Land	Catcher	1908–1913
Jim Landis	Outfielder	1966
Sam Langford	Outfielder	1927–1928
Mark Langston	Pitcher	1999–2000
Mike Lansing	Second Base	2002
Juan Lara	Pitcher	2006–2008 (Present)
Lyn Lary	Shortstop	1937–1939
Fred Lasher	Pitcher	1970
Bill Laskey	Pitcher	1988
Barry Latman	Pitcher	1960–1963
Bill Lattimore	Pitcher	1908
Ron Law	Pitcher	1969
Jim Lawrence	Catcher	1963
Roxie Lawson	Pitcher	1930–1931
Matt Lawton	Outfielder	2002–2004
Bill Laxton	Pitcher	1977
Emil Leber	Third Base	1905
Ricky Ledee	Outfielder	2000
Thornton Lee	Pitcher	1933–1936
Mike Lee	Pitcher	1960
Cliff Lee	Pitcher	2002–2008
David Lee	Pitcher	2003–2004
Cliff Lee	Pitcher	2002–2008 (Present)
Cliff Lee	Outfielder	1925–1926
Leron Lee	Outfielder	1974–1975
Gene Leek	Third Base	1959
Paul Lehner	Outfielder	1951
Norm Lehr	Pitcher	1926
Nemo Leibold	Outfielder	1913–1915

Player Name	Position	Years Played
Dummy Leitner	Pitcher	1902
Scott Leius	Third Base	1996
Jack Lelivelt	Outfielder	1913–1914
Johnnie Lemaster	Shortstop	1985
Bob Lemon	Pitcher	1941–1958
Jim Lemon	Outfielder	1950–1953
Eddie Leon	Shortstop	1968–1972
Joe Leonard	Third Base	1916
Jesse Levis	Catcher	1992–1996, 1999
Dutch Levsen	Pitcher	1923–1928
Dennis Lewallyn	Pitcher	1981–1982
Jensen Lewis	Pitcher	2007–2008 (Present)
Scott Lewis	Pitcher	2007–2008 (Present)
Mark Lewis	Second Base	1991–1994, 2001
Glenn Liebhardt	Pitcher	1906–1909
Jeff Liefer	Outfielder	2005
Derek Lilliquist	Pitcher	1992–1994
Carl Lind	Second Base	1927–1930
Lyman Linde	Pitcher	1947–1948
Bill Lindsay	Third Base	1911
Jim Lindsey	Pitcher	1922–1924
Fred Link	Pitcher	1910
Larry Lintz	Second Base	1978
Bob Lipski	Catcher	1963
Joe Lis	First Base	1974–1976
Pete Lister	First Base	1907
Mark Little	Outfielder	2003–2004
Larry Littleton	Outfielder	1981
Paddy Livingston	Catcher	1901, 1912
Bobby Locke	Pitcher	1959–1961
Stu Locklin	Outfielder	1955–1956
Chuck Lofgren	Pitcher	2007–2008 (Present)
Kenny Lofton	Outfielder	1992–1996, 1998–2001, 2007
Howard Lohr	Outfielder	1916
Ron Lolich	Outfielder	1972–1973
Sherm Lollar	Catcher	1946
Brian Looney	Pitcher	2000
Marcelino Lopez	Pitcher	1972
Albie Lopez	Pitcher	1993–1997
Al Lopez	Catcher	1947
Luis Lopez	Catcher	1991
Bris Lord	Outfielder	1909–1910
Andrew Lorraine	Pitcher	2000

Player Name	Position	Years Played
Grover Lowdermilk	Pitcher	1916
John Lowenstein	Outfielder	1970–1977
Terrell Lowery	Outfielder	2001
Ryan Ludwick	Outfielder	2003–2005
Matt Luke	Outfielder	1998
Hector Luna	Second Base	2006–2007
Gordy Lund	Shortstop	1967
Jack Lundbom	Pitcher	1902
Harry Lunte	Shortstop	1919–1920
Al Luplow	Outfielder	1961–1965
Billy Lush	Outfielder	1904
Rube Lutzke	Third Base	1923–1927
Russ Lyon	Catcher	1944
Chuck Machemehl	Pitcher	1971
Ray Mack	Second Base	1938–1946
Felix Mackiewicz	Outfielder	1945–1947
Clarence Maddern	Outfielder	1951
Ever Magallanes	Shortstop	1991
Sal Maglie	Pitcher	1955–1956
Tom Magrann	Catcher	1989
Chris Magruder	Outfielder	2002–2003
Jim Mahoney	Shortstop	1962
Duster Mails	Pitcher	1920–1922
Hank Majeski	Third Base	1952–1955
Candy Maldonado	Outfielder	1990, 1993–1994
Rick Manning	Outfielder	1975–1983
Jeff Manto	Third Base	1990–1991, 1997–1999
Roger Maris	Outfielder	1957–1958
Fred Marsh	Third Base	1949
Andy Marte	Third Base	2006–2008 (Present)
Morrie Martin	Pitcher	1958
Tom Martin	Pitcher	1997–2001
J.D. Martin	Pitcher	2006–2008 (Present)
Billy Martin	Second Base	1959
Dennis Martinez	Pitcher	1994–1996
Willie Martinez	Pitcher	1999–2000
Victor Martinez	Catcher	2002–2008 (Present)
Sandy Martinez	Catcher	2004
Carlos Martinez	First Base	1991–1993
Tony Martinez	Shortstop	1963–1966
Tom Mastny	Pitcher	2006–2008 (Present)
Carl Mathias	Pitcher	1960
Dave Maurer	Pitcher	2002
Lee Maye	Outfielder	1967–1969

Player Name	Position	Years Played
Jimmy McAleer	Outfielder	1901
Bake McBride	Outfielder	1982–1983
Ralph McCabe	Pitcher	1946
Jack McCarthy	Outfielder	1901–1903
Barney McCosky	Outfielder	1951–1953
Tom McCraw	First Base	1972, 1974–1975
Frank McCrea	Catcher	1925
John McDonald	Shortstop	1999–2004
Darnell McDonald	Outfielder	2005
Jim McDonnell	Catcher	1943–1945
Sam McDowell	Pitcher	1961–1971
Jack McDowell	Pitcher	1996–1997
Oddibe McDowell	Outfielder	1989
Deacon McGuire	Catcher	1908–1910
Jim McGuire	Shortstop	1901
Marty McHale	Pitcher	1916
Stuffy McInnis	First Base	1922
Hal McKain	Pitcher	1927
Mark McLemore	Second Base	1990
Cal McLish	Pitcher	1956–1959
Don McMahon	Pitcher	1964–1966
Harry McNeal	Pitcher	1901
Pat McNulty	Outfielder	1922–1927
George McQuillan	Pitcher	1918
Luis Medina	Designated Hitter	1988–1991
Moxie Meixell	Outfielder	1912
Sam Mele	Outfielder	1956
Bill Melton	Third Base	1977
Paul Menhart	Pitcher	1999
Kent Mercker	Pitcher	1996
Lou Merloni	Second Base	2004, 2006
Matt Merullo	Catcher	1994
Jose Mesa	Pitcher	1992–1998
Bud Messenger	Pitcher	1924
Dewey Metivier	Pitcher	1922–1924
Catfish Metkovich	Outfielder	1947
Dutch Meyer	Second Base	1945–1946
Dan Miceli	Pitcher	2003
Jason Michaels	Outfielder	2006–2008 (Present)
John Middleton	Pitcher	1922
Bob Milacki	Pitcher	1993
Larry Milbourne	Second Base	1982
Johnny Miljus	Pitcher	1928–1929
Jake Miller	Pitcher	1924–1931

Player Name	Position	Years Played
Bob Miller	Pitcher	1970
Matt Miller	Pitcher	2004–2007
Adam Miller	Pitcher	2007–2008 (Present)
Ray Miller	First Base	1917
Ed Miller	First Base	1918
Orlando Miller	Shortstop	1998–1999
Ralph Milliard	Second Base	2001
Randy Milligan	First Base	1993
Frank Mills	Catcher	1914
Jack Mills	Third Base	1911
Buster Mills	Outfielder	1942–1946
Kevin Millwood	Pitcher	2005
Al Milnar	Pitcher	1936–1943
Steve Mingori	Pitcher	1970–1973
Minnie Minoso	Outfielder	1949, 1951, 1958–1959
Willie Mitchell	Pitcher	1909–1916
Dale Mitchell	Outfielder	1946–1956
Kevin Mitchell	Outfielder	1997
Dave Mlicki	Pitcher	1992–1993
Danny Moeller	Outfielder	1916
Mike Mohler	Pitcher	2000
Blas Monaco	Second Base	1937–1946
Sid Monge	Pitcher	1977–1981
Ed Montague	Shortstop	1928–1932
Leo Moon	Pitcher	1932
Earl Moore	Pitcher	1901–1907
Jim Moore	Pitcher	1928–1929
Barry Moore	Pitcher	1970
Eddie Moore	Second Base	1934
Andres Mora	Outfielder	1980
Billy Moran	Second Base	1958–1959, 1964–1965
Ed Morgan	First Base	1928–1933
Joe Morgan	Third Base	1960–1961
Alvin Morman	Pitcher	1997–1998
Jeff Moronko	Third Base	1984
Jack Morris	Pitcher	1994
Warren Morris	Second Base	2005
Guy Morton	Pitcher	1914–1924
Jerry Moses	Catcher	1972
Howie Moss	Outfielder	1946
Don Mossi	Pitcher	1954–1958
Guillermo Mota	Pitcher	2006
Lyle Mouton	Outfielder	2003
Edward Mujica	Pitcher	2006–2008 (Present)

Player Name	Position	Years Played
Ryan Mulhern	Left Field	2005–2006
Terry Mulholland	Pitcher	2002–2003
Fran Mullins	Third Base	1986
Bob Muncrief	Pitcher	1948
Tim Murchison	Pitcher	1920
Heath Murray	Pitcher	2002
Ray Murray	Catcher	1948–1951
Eddie Murray	First Base	1994–1996
Jeff Mutis	Pitcher	1991–1993
Glenn Myatt	Catcher	1923–1935
Elmer Myers	Pitcher	1919–1920
Aaron Myette	Pitcher	2003
Chris Nabholz	Pitcher	1994
Lou Nagelsen	Catcher	1912
Russ Nagelson	Outfielder	1968–1970
Charles Nagy	Pitcher	1990–2002
Bill Nahorodny	Catcher	1982
Hal Naragon	Catcher	1951–1959
Ray Narleski	Pitcher	1954–1958
Ken Nash	Shortstop	1912
Jaime Navarro	Pitcher	2000
Mike Naymick	Pitcher	1939–1944
Cal Neeman	Catcher	1963
Jim Neher	Pitcher	1912
Bernie Neis	Outfielder	1927
Rocky Nelson	First Base	1954
Dave Nelson	Second Base	1968–1969
Graig Nettles	Third Base	1970–1972
Milo Netzel	Third Base	1909
Don Newcombe	Pitcher	1960
Hal Newhouser	Pitcher	1954–1955
Alan Newman	Pitcher	2000
Simon Nicholls	Shortstop	1910
Rod Nichols	Pitcher	1988–1992
Chris Nichting	Pitcher	2000
Dick Niehaus	Pitcher	1920
Phil Niekro	Pitcher	1986–1987
Milt Nielsen	Outfielder	1949–1951
Bob Nieman	Outfielder	1961–1962
Harry Niles	Outfielder	1910
Rabbit Nill	Second Base	1907–1908
Al Nipper	Pitcher	1990
Ron Nischwitz	Pitcher	1963
Russ Nixon	Catcher	1957–1960

Player Name	Position	Years Played
Otis Nixon	Outfielder	1984–1987
Trot Nixon	Outfielder	2007
Junior Noboa	Second Base	1984–1987
Dickie Noles	Pitcher	1986
Jim Norris	Outfielder	1977–1979
Les Nunamaker	Catcher	1919–1922
Pete O'Brien	First Base	1989
Pete O'Brien	Second Base	1907
Jack O'Brien	Outfielder	1901
Paul O'Dea	Outfielder	1944–1945
John O'Donoghue	Pitcher	1966–1967
Hal O'Hagen	First Base	1902
Steve O'Neill	Catcher	1911–1923
Ivan Ochoa	Shortstop	2006
Ted Odenwald	Pitcher	1921–1922
Blue Moon Odom	Pitcher	1975
Bryan Oelkers	Pitcher	1986
Chad Ogea	Pitcher	1994–1998, 2000
Bob Ojeda	Pitcher	1993
Steve Olin	Pitcher	1989–1992
Omar Olivares	Pitcher	2002
Dave Oliver	Second Base	1977
Gregg Olson	Pitcher	1995
Ivy Olson	Shortstop	1911–1914
Eddie Onslow	First Base	1918
Jesse Orosco	Pitcher	1988–1991
Jorge Orta	Second Base	1980–1981
Junior Ortiz	Catcher	1992–1993
Pat Osborn	Third Base	2006–2007
Harry Ostdiek	Catcher	1904
Harry Otis	Pitcher	1909
Dave Otto	Pitcher	1991–1992
Johnny Oulliber	Outfielder	1933
Bob Owchinko	Pitcher	1980
Ernie Padgett	Third Base	1926–1927
Karl Pagel	First Base	1981–1983
Pat Paige	Pitcher	1911
Satchel Paige	Pitcher	1948–1949
Lowell Palmer	Pitcher	1972
Nathan Panther	Right Field	2006
Frank Papish	Pitcher	1949
Harry Parker	Pitcher	1976
Chad Paronto	Pitcher	2001–2003
Lance Parrish	Catcher	1993

Player Name	Position	Years Played
Casey Parsons	Outfielder	1987
Ben Paschal	Outfielder	1915
Camilo Pascual	Pitcher	1971
Mike Paul	Pitcher	1968–1971
Stan Pawloski	Second Base	1955
Mike Paxton	Pitcher	1978–1980
Alex Pearson	Pitcher	1903
Monte Pearson	Pitcher	1932–1935
Hal Peck	Outfielder	1947–1949
Roger Peckinpaugh	Shortstop	1910–1913
Orlando Pena	Pitcher	1967
Tony Pena	Catcher	1994–1996
Geronimo Pena	Second Base	1996
Ken Penner	Pitcher	1916
Jhonny Peralta	Shortstop	2003–2008 (Present)
Jack Perconte	Second Base	1982–1983
Rafael Perez	Pitcher	2006–2008 (Present)
Eddie Perez	Catcher	2002
Eduardo Perez	First Base	2006
Tony Perezchica	Shortstop	1991–1992
Broderick Perkins	First Base	1983–1984
Jon Perlman	Pitcher	1988
Bill Perrin	Pitcher	1934
George Perring	Third Base	1908–1910
Jim Perry	Pitcher	1959–1963, 1974–1975
Gaylord Perry	Pitcher	1972–1975
Herbert Perry	Third Base	1994–1996
Chan Perry	Outfielder	2000
John Peters	Catcher	1918
Rusty Peters	Second Base	1940–1946
Fritz Peterson	Pitcher	1974–1976
Cap Peterson	Outfielder	1969
Jesse Petty	Pitcher	1921
Larry Pezold	Third Base	1914
Ken Phelps	Designated Hitter	1990
Josh Phelps	Designated Hitter	2004
Dave Philley	Outfielder	1954–1955
Tom Phillips	Pitcher	1919
Jason Phillips	Pitcher	2002–2003
Eddie Phillips	Catcher	1935
Brandon Phillips	Second Base	2002–2006
Bubba Phillips	Third Base	1960–1962
Adolfo Phillips	Outfielder	1972
Ollie Pickering	Outfielder	1901–1902

Player Name	Position	Years Played
Marino Pieretti	Pitcher	1950
Jim Piersall	Outfielder	1959–1961
Horacio Pina	Pitcher	1968–1969
Brandon Pinckney	Second Base	2007
Lou Piniella	Outfielder	1968
Vada Pinson	Outfielder	1970–1971
Stan Pitula	Pitcher	1957
Juan Pizarro	Pitcher	1969
Eric Plunk	Pitcher	1992–1998
Ray Poat	Pitcher	1942–1944
Bud Podbielan	Pitcher	1959
Johnny Podgajny	Pitcher	1946
Lou Polchow	Pitcher	1902
Cliff Politte	Pitcher	2007
Jim Poole	Pitcher	1995–1996, 1998–2000
Dave Pope	Outfielder	1952–1956
Jay Porter	Catcher	1958
Dick Porter	Outfielder	1929–1934
Mike Porzio	Pitcher	2003–2004
Wally Post	Outfielder	1964
Lou Pote	Pitcher	2004
Nellie Pott	Pitcher	1922
Bill Pounds	Pitcher	1903
Boog Powell	First Base	1975–1976
Ted Power	Pitcher	1992–1993
Vic Power	First Base	1958–1961
Mike Powers	Outfielder	1932–1933
John Powers	Outfielder	1960
Jackie Price	Shortstop	1946
Ron Pruitt	Outfielder	1976–1981
Frankie Pytlak	Catcher	1932–1940
Jamie Quirk	Catcher	1984
Joe Rabbitt	Outfielder	1922
Dick Radatz	Pitcher	1966–1967
Scott Radinsky	Pitcher	2001–2002
Tom Raftery	Outfielder	1909
Tom Ragland	Second Base	1973
Eric Raich	Pitcher	1975–1976
Larry Raines	Third Base	1957–1958
Jason Rakers	Pitcher	1998–1999
Max Ramirez	Catcher	2007
Manny Ramirez	Outfielder	1993–2000
Alex Ramirez	Outfielder	1998–2000
Pedro Ramos	Pitcher	1962–1964

Player Name	Position	Years Played
Domingo Ramos	Shortstop	1988
Morrie Rath	Second Base	1910
Jerry Reed	Pitcher	1982–1985
Steve Reed	Pitcher	1998–2001
Rudy Regalado	Third Base	1954–1956
Herman Reich	First Base	1949
Duke Reilley	Outfielder	1909
Tom Reilly	Shortstop	1914
Art Reinholz	Third Base	1928
Pete Reiser	Outfielder	1952
Bugs Reisigl	Pitcher	1911
Paul Reuschel	Pitcher	1978–1979
Allie Reynolds	Pitcher	1942–1946
Bob Reynolds	Pitcher	1975
Bob Rhoads	Pitcher	1903–1909
Arthur Rhodes	Pitcher	2005
Kevin Rhomberg	Outfielder	1982–1984
Sam Rice	Outfielder	1934
Denny Riddleberger	Pitcher	1972
Steve Ridzik	Pitcher	1958
Paul Rigdon	Pitcher	2000
Jerrod Riggan	Pitcher	2001–2003
Ricardo Rincon	Pitcher	1999–2002
Billy Ripken	Second Base	1995
David Riske	Pitcher	1999, 2001–2005
Reggie Ritter	Pitcher	1986–1987
Jim Rittwage	Pitcher	1970
Luis Rivas	Second Base	2007
Joe Roa	Pitcher	1995–1996
Jake Robbins	Pitcher	2004
Bip Roberts	Second Base	1997
Dave Roberts	Outfielder	1999–2001
Jeriome Robertson	Pitcher	2004
Humberto Robinson	Pitcher	1959
Eddie Robinson	First Base	1942–1948, 1957
Frank Robinson	Outfielder	1974–1976
Mickey Rocco	First Base	1943–1946
John Rocker	Pitcher	2001
Bill Rodgers	Second Base	1915
Rick Rodriguez	Pitcher	1988
Rich Rodriguez	Pitcher	2001
Nerio Rodriguez	Pitcher	2001–2002
Ricardo Rodriguez	Pitcher	2002–2003
Dave Rohde	Second Base	1992

Player Name	Position	Years Played
Dan Rohn	Second Base	1986
Billy Rohr	Pitcher	1968
Rich Rollins	Third Base	1970
Jose Roman	Pitcher	1984–1986
Johnny Romano	Catcher	1960–1964
Ramon Romero	Pitcher	1984–1985
Niuman Romero	Second Base	2006
Vicente Romo	Pitcher	1968–1969
Phil Roof	Catcher	1965
Buddy Rosar	Catcher	1943–1944
Mike Rose	Catcher	2006–2007
Dave Rosello	Second Base	1979–1981
Al Rosen	Third Base	1947–1956
Larry Rosenthal	Outfielder	1941
Don Ross	Third Base	1945–1946
Claude Rossman	First Base	1904–1906
Braggo Roth	Outfielder	1915–1918
Bob Rothel	Third Base	1945
Mike Rouse	Shortstop	2006–2007
Luther Roy	Pitcher	1924–1925
Dick Rozek	Pitcher	1950–1952
Don Rudolph	Pitcher	1962
Vern Ruhle	Pitcher	1985
Rich Rundles	Pitcher	2008 (Present)
Jack Russell	Pitcher	1932
Jeff Russell	Pitcher	1994
Lloyd Russell	–	1938
Hank Ruszkowski	Catcher	1944–1947
Jim Rutherford	Outfielder	1910
Jack Ryan	Pitcher	1908
Buddy Ryan	Outfielder	1912–1913
C.C. Sabathia	Pitcher	1998–2008 (Present)
Carl Sadler	Pitcher	2002–2003
Mark Salas	Catcher	1989
Chico Salmon	Second Base	1964–1968
Jack Salveson	Pitcher	1943–1945
Ken Sanders	Pitcher	1973–1974
Danny Sandoval	Shortstop	2007–2008 (Present)
Rafael Santana	Shortstop	1990
Jose Santiago	Pitcher	1954–1955
Jose Santiago	Pitcher	2003
Angel Santos	Second Base	2003
Scott Sauerbeck	Pitcher	2005–2006
Germany Schaefer	Second Base	1918

Player Name	Position	Years Played
Joe Schaffernoth	Pitcher	1961
Dan Schatzeder	Pitcher	1988
Frank Scheibeck	Shortstop	1901
Richie Scheinblum	Outfielder	1965–1969
Norm Schlueter	Catcher	1944
Ossee Schreckengost	Catcher	1902
Ken Schrom	Pitcher	1986–1987
Don Schulze	Pitcher	1984–1986
Bill Schwartz	First Base	1904
Herb Score	Pitcher	1955–1959
Ed Scott	Pitcher	1901
Scott Scudder	Pitcher	1992–1993
Rudy Seanez	Pitcher	1989–1991
Bob Seeds	Outfielder	1930–1932, 1934
Pat Seerey	Outfielder	1943–1948
David Segui	First Base	2000
Kevin Seitzer	Third Base	1996–1997
Bill Selby	Third Base	1999–2003
Ted Sepkowski	Second Base	1942–1947
Luke Sewell	Catcher	1921–1932, 1939
Joe Sewell	Shortstop	1920–1930
Richie Sexson	First Base	1997–2000
Gordon Seyfried	Pitcher	1963–1964
Wally Shaner	Outfielder	1923
Joe Shaute	Pitcher	1922–1930
Jeff Shaw	Pitcher	1990–1992
Danny Shay	Shortstop	1901
Danny Sheaffer	Catcher	1989
Pete Shields	First Base	1915
Jim Shilling	Second Base	1939
Ginger Shinault	Catcher	1921–1922
Bill Shipke	Third Base	1906
Milt Shoffner	Pitcher	1929–1931
Kelly Shoppach	Catcher	2006–2008 (Present)
Paul Shuey	Pitcher	1994–2002
Sonny Siebert	Pitcher	1964–1969
Brian Sikorski	Pitcher	2006–2007
Harry Simpson	Outfielder	1951–1955
Duke Sims	Catcher	1964–1970
Tony Sipp	Pitcher	2005–2008 (Present)
Carl Sitton	Pitcher	1909
Grady Sizemore	Center Field	2004–2008 (Present)
Joe Skalski	Pitcher	1989
Joel Skinner	Catcher	1989–1991

Player Name	Position	Years Played
Jack Slattery	Catcher	1903
Brian Slocum	Pitcher	2006–2008 (Present)
Heathcliff Slocumb	Pitcher	1993
John Smiley	Pitcher	1997
Charlie Smith	Pitcher	1902
Pop-Boy Smith	Pitcher	1916–1917
Sherry Smith	Pitcher	1922–1927
Clay Smith	Pitcher	1938
Al Smith	Pitcher	1940–1945
Bob Smith	Pitcher	1959
Roy Smith	Pitcher	1984–1985
Dan Smith	Pitcher	2001
Roy Smith	Pitcher	2001–2002, 2004
Sean Smith	Pitcher	2007
Syd Smith	Catcher	1910–1911
Elmer Smith	Outfielder	1914–1917, 1919–1921
Al Smith	Outfielder	1953–1957, 1964
Willie Smith	Outfielder	1967–1968
Tommy Smith	Outfielder	1973–1976
Earl Snyder	Third Base	2002
Russ Snyder	Outfielder	1968–1969
Cory Snyder	Outfielder	1986–1990
Brad Snyder	Outfielder	2006–2008 (Present)
Bill Sodd	–	1937
Moose Solters	Outfielder	1937–1939
Lary Sorensen	Pitcher	1982–1983
Zach Sorensen	Second Base	2003
Chick Sorrells	Shortstop	1922
Paul Sorrento	First Base	1992–1995
Allen Sothoron	Pitcher	1921–1922
Billy Southworth	Outfielder	1913–1915
Jeremy Sowers	Pitcher	2006–2008 (Present)
Tris Speaker	Outfielder	1916–1926
By Speece	Pitcher	1925–1926
Horace Speed	Outfielder	1978–1979
Justin Speier	Pitcher	1999–2001
Roy Spencer	Catcher	1933–1934
Shane Spencer	Outfielder	2003
Charlie Spikes	Outfielder	1973–1977
Dan Spillner	Pitcher	1978–1984
Jerry Spradlin	Pitcher	1998–1999
Jack Spring	Pitcher	1965
Steve Springer	Third Base	1990
Joe Sprinz	Catcher	1930–1931

Player Name	Position	Years Played
Freddy Spurgeon	Second Base	1924–1927
Jason Stanford	Pitcher	2003–2004, 2007
Lee Stange	Pitcher	1964–1966
Fred Stanley	Shortstop	1971–1972
Mike Stanton	Pitcher	1980–1981
Dolly Stark	Shortstop	1909
George Starnagle	Catcher	1902
Bill Steen	Pitcher	1912–1915
Red Steiner	Catcher	1945
Bryan Stephens	Pitcher	1947
Riggs Stephenson	Outfielder	1921–1925
Dave Stevens	Pitcher	1999
Lee Stevens	First Base	2002
Lefty Stewart	Pitcher	1935
Sammy Stewart	Pitcher	1987
Scott Stewart	Pitcher	2004
Dick Stigman	Pitcher	1960–1961
Snuffy Stirnweiss	Second Base	1951–1952
Tim Stoddard	Pitcher	1989
Jesse Stovall	Pitcher	1903
George Stovall	First Base	1904–1911
Oscar Streit	Pitcher	1902
Jim Strickland	Pitcher	1975
George Strickland	Shortstop	1952–1960
Jake Striker	Pitcher	1959
Brent Strom	Pitcher	1973
Floyd Stromme	Pitcher	1939
Ken Suarez	Catcher	1968–1971
Charley Suche	Pitcher	1938
Bill Sudakis	Third Base	1975
Jim Sullivan	Pitcher	1923
Lefty Sullivan	Pitcher	1939
Billy Sullivan	Catcher	1936–1937
Denny Sullivan	Outfielder	1908–1909
Homer Summa	Outfielder	1922–1928
George Susce	Catcher	1941–1944
Rick Sutcliffe	Pitcher	1982–1984
Darrell Sutherland	Pitcher	1968
Russ Swan	Pitcher	1994
Josh Swindell	Pitcher	1911–1913
Greg Swindell	Pitcher	1986–1991, 1996
Pat Tabler	First Base	1983–1988
Kazuhito Tadano	Pitcher	2004–2006
Brian Tallet	Pitcher	2002–2005

Player Name	Position	Years Played
Jeff Tam	Pitcher	1999
Chuck Tanner	Outfielder	1959–1960
Willie Tasby	Outfielder	1962–1963
Eddie Taubensee	Catcher	1991, 2000–2001
Julian Tavarez	Pitcher	1993–1996
Jackie Tavener	Shortstop	1929
Dummy Taylor	Pitcher	1902
Ron Taylor	Pitcher	1962
Sammy Taylor	Catcher	1963
Birdie Tebbetts	Catcher	1951–1952
Al Tedrow	Pitcher	1914
Dave Telgheder	Pitcher	1998–1999
Johnny Temple	Second Base	1960–1961
Ralph Terry	Pitcher	1965
Jake Thielman	Pitcher	1907–1908
Fay Thomas	Pitcher	1931
Carl Thomas	Pitcher	1960
Stan Thomas	Pitcher	1976
Pinch Thomas	Catcher	1918–1921
Valmy Thomas	Catcher	1961
Gorman Thomas	Outfielder	1983
Art Thomason	Outfielder	1910
Jim Thome	First Base	1991–2002
Rich Thompson	Pitcher	1985
Ryan Thompson	Outfielder	1996
Jack Thoney	Outfielder	1902–1903
Andre Thornton	Designated Hitter	1977–1987
Luis Tiant	Pitcher	1964–1969
Dick Tidrow	Pitcher	1972–1974
Bobby Tiefenauer	Pitcher	1960, 1965, 1967
Tom Timmermann	Pitcher	1973–1974
Ron Tingley	Catcher	1988
Joe Tipton	Catcher	1948, 1952–1953
Chick Tolson	First Base	1925
Dick Tomanek	Pitcher	1953–1958
Wyatt Toregas	Catcher	2006–2008
Wyatt Toregas	Catcher	2006–2008 (Present)
Red Torkelson	Pitcher	1917
Eider Torres	Second Base	2006
Rusty Torres	Outfielder	1973–1974
Happy Townsend	Pitcher	1906
Billy Traber	Pitcher	2003
Jeff Treadway	Second Base	1993
Mike Tresh	Catcher	1949

Player Name	Position	Years Played
Manny Trillo	Second Base	1983
Hal Trosky	First Base	1933–1941
Quincy Trouppe	Catcher	1952
Eddie Tucker	Catcher	1995
Ollie Tucker	Outfielder	1928
Thurman Tucker	Outfielder	1948–1951
Eddie Turchin	Third Base	1943
Matt Turner	Pitcher	1994
Chris Turner	Catcher	1999
Terry Turner	Shortstop	1904–1918
Dave Tyriver	Pitcher	1962
Ted Uhlaender	Outfielder	1970–1971
George Uhle	Pitcher	1919–1928, 1936
Jerry Ujdur	Pitcher	1984
Willie Underhill	Pitcher	1927–1928
Del Unser	Outfielder	1972
Jerry Upp	Pitcher	1909
Cecil Upshaw	Pitcher	1974
Willie Upshaw	First Base	1988
Bob Usher	Outfielder	1957
Dutch Ussat	Third Base	1925–1927
Mike Vail	Outfielder	1978
Juan Valdes	Center Field	2006
Sergio Valdez	Pitcher	1990–1991
Efrain Valdez	Pitcher	1990–1991
Vito Valentinetti	Pitcher	1957
Elmer Valo	Outfielder	1959
Jonathan Van Every	Outfielder	2006–2007
Al Vancamp	Outfielder	1928
Ed Vande Berg	Pitcher	1987
Johnny Vander Meer	Pitcher	1951
Dike Varney	Pitcher	1902
Cal Vasbinder	Pitcher	1902
Ramon Vazquez	Shortstop	2005–2006
Otto Velez	Outfielder	1983
Mickey Vernon	First Base	1949–1950, 1958
Zoilo Versalles	Shortstop	1969
Tom Veryzer	Shortstop	1978–1981
Jose Vidal	Outfielder	1966–1968
Ron Villone	Pitcher	1998
Rube Vinson	Outfielder	1904–1905
Jose Vizcaino	Shortstop	1996
Omar Vizquel	Shortstop	1994–2004
Dave Vonohlen	Pitcher	1985

Player Name	Position	Years Played
Joe Vosmik	Outfielder	1930–1936
George Vukovich	Outfielder	1983–1985
Tom Waddell	Pitcher	1984–1987
Paul Wagner	Pitcher	1998–2000
Leon Wagner	Outfielder	1964–1968
Rick Waits	Pitcher	1975–1983
Howard Wakefield	Catcher	1905, 1907
Ed Walker	Pitcher	1902–1903
Roy Walker	Pitcher	1912–1915
Mysterious Walker	Pitcher	1912
Jerry Walker	Pitcher	1963–1964
Mike Walker	Pitcher	1988–1991, 1998–1999
Gee Walker	Outfielder	1941
David Wallace	Catcher	2006–2008
David Wallace	Catcher	2006–2008 (Present)
Roxy Walters	Catcher	1924–1925
Bill Wambsganss	Second Base	1914–1923
Colby Ward	Pitcher	1990
Preston Ward	First Base	1956–1958
Aaron Ward	Second Base	1928
Turner Ward	Outfielder	1990–1991
Jim Ed Warden	Pitcher	2006–2007
Curt Wardle	Pitcher	1985
Jimmy Wasdell	Outfielder	1946–1947
Ron Washington	Shortstop	1988
Mark Watson	Pitcher	2000
Frank Wayenberg	Pitcher	1924
Roy Weatherly	Outfielder	1936–1942
David Weathers	Pitcher	1997
Floyd Weaver	Pitcher	1962–1965
Skeeter Webb	Shortstop	1938–1939
Les Webber	Pitcher	1946–1948
Ray Webster	Second Base	1959
Mitch Webster	Outfielder	1990–1991
Ralph Weigel	Catcher	1946
Dick Weik	Pitcher	1950, 1953
Bob Weiland	Pitcher	1934
Elmer Weingartner	Shortstop	1945
Ollie Welf	–	1916
Butch Wensloff	Pitcher	1948
Bill Wertz	Pitcher	1993–1994
Vic Wertz	Outfielder	1954–1958
Hi West	Pitcher	1905–1911
Jake Westbrook	Pitcher	2001–2008

Player Name	Position	Years Played
Jake Westbrook	Pitcher	2001–2008 (Present)
Wally Westlake	Outfielder	1952–1955
Gus Weyhing	Pitcher	1901
Ed Wheeler	Third Base	1945
Pete Whisenant	Outfielder	1960
Rick White	Pitcher	2004
Earl Whitehill	Pitcher	1937–1938
Mark Whiten	Outfielder	1991–1993, 1998–2000
Fred Whitfield	First Base	1963–1967
Ed Whitson	Pitcher	1982
Kevin Wickander	Pitcher	1989–1993
Bob Wickman	Pitcher	2000–2006
Bill Wight	Pitcher	1953, 1955
Sandy Wihtol	Pitcher	1979–1982
Milt Wilcox	Pitcher	1972–1974
Hoyt Wilhelm	Pitcher	1957–1958
Denney Wilie	Outfielder	1915
Eric Wilkins	Pitcher	1979
Roy Wilkinson	Pitcher	1918
Ted Wilks	Pitcher	1952–1953
Jerry Willard	Catcher	1984–1985
Stan Williams	Pitcher	1965–1969
Brian Williams	Pitcher	2000
Rip Williams	Catcher	1918
Papa Williams	First Base	1945
Eddie Williams	First Base	1986–1988
Matt Williams	Third Base	1996–1997
Dick Williams	Outfielder	1957
Walt Williams	Outfielder	1973
Reggie Williams	Outfielder	1988
Les Willis	Pitcher	1947
Frank Wills	Pitcher	1986–1987
Art Wilson	Catcher	1921
Red Wilson	Catcher	1960
Enrique Wilson	Second Base	1997–2000
Jim Wilson	Designated Hitter	1985
Frank Wilson	Outfielder	1928
Nigel Wilson	Outfielder	1996
Fred Winchell	Pitcher	1909
Ralph Winegarner	Pitcher	1930–1936
Dave Winfield	Outfielder	1995
George Winn	Pitcher	1922–1923
Rick Wise	Pitcher	1978–1979
Bobby Witt	Pitcher	2000

Player Name	Position	Years Played
Mark Wohlers	Pitcher	2002
Ed Wojna	Pitcher	1989
Ernie Wolf	Pitcher	1912
Roger Wolff	Pitcher	1947
Bob Wood	Catcher	1901–1902
Roy Wood	Outfielder	1914–1915
Joe Wood	Outfielder	1917–1922
Steve Woodard	Pitcher	2000–2001
Hal Woodeshick	Pitcher	1958
Gene Woodling	Outfielder	1943–1946, 1955–1957
Chuck Workman	Outfielder	1938–1941
Tim Worrell	Pitcher	1998
Craig Worthington	Third Base	1992
Gene Wright	Pitcher	1902–1903
Lucky Wright	Pitcher	1909
Jaret Wright	Pitcher	1997–2002
Ab Wright	Outfielder	1935
Whit Wyatt	Pitcher	1937
Joe Wyatt	Outfielder	1924
Early Wynn	Pitcher	1949–1957, 1963
George Yeager	Catcher	1901
Rich Yett	Pitcher	1986–1989
Earl Yingling	Pitcher	1911
Mike York	Pitcher	1991
Elmer Yoter	Third Base	1924
Cy Young	Pitcher	1909–1911
Matt Young	Pitcher	1993
Cliff Young	Pitcher	1993
Jason Young	Pitcher	2005
Bobby Young	Second Base	1955–1956
Mike Young	Outfielder	1989
Ernie Young	Outfielder	2004
George Young	–	1913
Carl Yowell	Pitcher	1924–1925
Chad Zerbe	Pitcher	2004–2005
Jimmy Zinn	Pitcher	1929
Alan Zinter	First Base	2007
Sam Zoldak	Pitcher	1948–1950
Bill Zuber	Pitcher	1936–1940
Paul Zuvella	Shortstop	1988–1989
George Zuverink	Pitcher	1951–1952